UNITED STATES ARMY IN WORLD WAR II

The Technical Services

THE QUARTERMASTER CORPS: OPERATIONS IN THE WAR AGAINST GERMANY

by

William F. Ross

and

Charles F. Romanus

MILITARY INSTRVCTION

OFFICE OF THE CHIEF OF MILITARY HISTORY
DEPARTMENT OF THE ARMY
WASHINGTON, D.C., 1965

This volume, one of the series UNITED STATES ARMY IN
WORLD WAR II, is the fourth to be published in the group of
four Quartermaster Corps volumes in the subseries THE TECH-
NICAL SERVICES. The volumes in the over-all series will be
closely related and will present a comprehensive account of the
activities of the Military Establishment during World War II. A
list of subseries is appended at the end of this volume.

Library of Congress Catalog Card Number: 64–60003

Reprinted 1968

UNITED STATES ARMY IN WORLD WAR II

Stetson Conn, General Editor

Advisory Committee
(As of 15 June 1963)

Office of the Chief of Military History
Brig. Gen. Hal C. Pattison, Chief of Military History

History of

THE QUARTERMASTER CORPS

Organization, Supply, and Services, Volume I
Organization, Supply, and Services, Volume II
Operations in the War Against Japan
Operations in the War Against Germany

. . . to Those Who Served

Foreword

Publication of this volume completes the subseries dealing with Quartermaster operations during World War II. Two companion volumes of this group have described the Quartermaster organization and achievements in the United States, and a third has told about operations in the Pacific in the war against Japan. The principal Quartermaster function in World War II was to supply items needed by all Army troops, most notably, food and clothing. But the Quartermaster Corps was more than a supply force; it provided many services, such as bath and laundry facilities, necessary to the health and comfort of the troops. The prompt collection and careful identification and burial of the dead and the respectful and suitable disposition of their possessions were essential services that contributed much to the morale of the front-line soldier. While established to serve the Army itself, before the war was over in Europe the Quartermaster organization found it had also to provide minimum support for millions of war prisoners and destitute civilians.

However prosaic a history of providing goods and services may seem at first glance, this was an activity of vital concern to the American soldier, and in the Mediterranean and European theaters it was an enormous and highly complicated operation. By the spring of 1945 the Quartermaster organization in the European theater was feeding and clothing and otherwise providing necessities and comforts to more than seven and one-half million people, the largest human support operation by a single organization in all history to that time. Inevitably Quartermaster officers and troops could not satisfy everybody, and made some mistakes; it is to the credit of the authors of this volume that they have tackled fairly and squarely—if not laid to rest—a number of controversial issues. Since so much of the Quartermaster effort was essentially civilian in its character, the general as well as the military reader should find this work instructive.

Washington, D.C.
15 June 1963

HAL C. PATTISON
Brigadier General, USA
Chief of Military History

The Authors

William F. Ross, a graduate of Hamilton College (Clinton, N.Y.), has done graduate work in Germanics at the University of Berlin and at Harvard. Commissioned in the Field Artillery, AUS, in 1942, he then received training as a prisoner of war interrogator at Camp Ritchie, Md., and served in the G–2 Division in the Pentagon. He was an assistant military attaché in Turkey from 1943 to 1946, and was then employed in the National Archives for a year, surveying the federal records created during the war. He is one of the coauthors of *Federal Records of World War II: The Military Agencies* (Washington, 1950). Returning to active military duty late in 1947, he was assigned to OCMH in various capacities for nearly four years. During that time he was the last Army-sponsored editor of *Military Affairs,* and later was senior member of the team that translated and edited the *German Reports Series* of Department of the Army pamphlets. He was transferred to the Historical Division, U.S. Army, Europe, in 1951, and while there edited and brought to press the *Guide to Foreign Military Studies, 1945-54: Catalog and Index* (Darmstadt, 1955). During the years 1957–61, when Mr. Ross was engaged in writing *The Quartermaster Corps: Operations in the War Against Germany,* he was a civilian employee in the Historical Branch, Office of The Quartermaster General. He is now Assistant Historian, Defense Supply Agency.

Charles F. Romanus is coauthor of three volumes on the China–Burma–India Theater already published in the series UNITED STATES ARMY IN WORLD WAR II: *Stilwell's Mission to China* (1953); *Stilwell's Command Problems* (1956); and *Time Runs Out in CBI* (1959). He received the degree of Master of Arts in history from the University of Illinois and pursued his work for a doctorate at Louisiana State University, where he was a teaching fellow in history. Entering the Army in 1943, he was commissioned in March 1945 and became a historian in Headquarters, China Theater. Except for the 3-year period (1953-56) during which he worked on the present volume as a member of the Historical Section, Office of The Quartermaster General, he has been on the staff of the Office of the Chief of Military History since 1946, serving presently as Chief, General Reference Branch. He holds a commission as major in the U.S. Army Reserve.

Preface

This volume completes a series of four on the history of the Quartermaster Corps in World War II, which has been in preparation for some sixteen years. Two earlier volumes dealt with QM organization and activities in the zone of interior, and another was devoted to the Quartermaster role in the war against Japan. The present volume deals with two major overseas theaters of operations—the Mediterranean and the European—and specifically with Quartermaster operations in those theaters. The term "Quartermaster operations" has deliberately been used in a somewhat restrictive sense, as referring to the highest level of active QM participation in military operations. The role of staff adviser on quartermaster matters in a senior headquarters has received only minor emphasis. Rather, the primary focus of attention has been upon varying levels within the military structure at different periods of the narrative. In particular, the reader will note that the European theater has been delineated from the point of view of the Theater Chief Quartermaster, whereas in the Mediterranean theater the roles of corps, army, and base section quartermasters receive far more emphasis. This difference in approach stems from inherent differences in the two theaters. The Mediterranean theater evolved slowly, and always under strong British influence, so that theater-level logistical developments to a great extent bore a British stamp. Moreover, there was a tendency for junior logistical commanders and staff officers in that area to exert an influence upon operations that had no counterpart in the more elaborate and tightly knit theater organization to the north.

The positive and energetic control over QM operations in the European theater exercised by Maj. Gen. Robert M. Littlejohn should be regarded, not as stifling the initiative of his juniors, but as assuring an effective hearing for the Quartermaster point of view within the somewhat monolithic structure of the ETO Communications Zone. Thus, much of the history of QM operations in Europe is to a considerable degree a narrative centering about one man, his actions and reactions, his frustrations, mistakes, and triumphs in maintaining a strong position with respect to G–4 and to the other technical services, some of which were also commanded by strong and colorful personalities. While such a situation is seldom beneficial to a headquarters, it represents good fortune to the logistical historian, who is thereby rescued from a drab recital of routine compliance with policy directions from higher levels of command.

This history had its origins in 1948 when Dr. Alvin P. Stauffer, visiting the AGO Records Administration Center in St. Louis to collect material for his own volume—*The Quartermaster Corps: Operations in the War Against Japan*—also assembled a large amount of data on Quartermaster activities in the ETO. During the following year, Dr. William H. Chaikin collected more material, and wrote a brief portion of a first narrative. Thereafter Dr. Irving Cheslaw completed a preliminary draft that was judged to need rather extensive revision and some expansion. When Dr. Cheslaw left the employ of the OQMG, the task of revision was entrusted to Mr. Charles F. Romanus, who had already collaborated in the writing of three official Army histories of the China–Burma–India Theater. Mr. Romanus worked on the manuscript for about eighteen months, during which time he revised and extended the chapters dealing with Mediterranean operations. He also collected all known wartime histories of Quartermaster troop units, a useful contribution to subsequent research. In March 1957 the undersigned inherited the task of completing the volume, which involved a further revision and extension of the opening chapters and rewriting the larger portion of the manuscript, covering operations in the European theater, to conform to the revised Mediterranean chapters.

The authors are grateful to many people, both military and civilians, whose co-operation and assistance made possible the production of this volume. Only a few can be mentioned by name. For example, it would be impracticable to list the more than forty participating officers, regular and reserve, who read reproductions of the preliminary draft by Dr. Cheslaw and made extensive comments. The comments of Dr. Kent R. Greenfield, the former Chief Historian, who read the entire draft for both form and content, were particularly helpful. All of the authors have profited from the supervision and friendly interest of Dr. Stauffer, and I myself have benefited from the similarly helpful advice afforded by Dr. Erna Risch, who succeeded Dr. Stauffer as Chief, Historical Branch, OQMG. My thanks are due to Dr. Stetson Conn, the present Chief Historian, whose constructive criticism had much influence upon the final form of this volume, and whose counsel and critical judgment added much to its content. General Littlejohn not only made available all of his relevant personal papers but also contributed freely of his time both for interviews and to read and annotate draft manuscripts. Maj. Gen. William H. Middleswart, Brig. Gen. Joseph P. Sullivan, and Mr. William F. Pounder assisted the authors by making available their personal papers. Lt. Gen. Andrew T. McNamara and Brig. Gen. Georges Doriot (Ret.) each read entire chapters and made detailed comments.

The editor was David Jaffé, Chief of the Editorial Branch, whose concrete suggestions and recommendations were always appreciated, and especially during the task of abridgment. Mr. Jaffe' was assisted by Mrs. Loretto Stevens, who demonstrated unusual patience in disentangling various problems occasioned by the varied working methods of successive authors. Mrs. Norma B. Sherris selected the photographs. Maps, with one exception, were prepared by the Cartographic Branch, OCMH. The climatic map showing temperature zones in Europe was prepared by the former QM Research and Engineering Command at Natick, Mass. Over a period of many years, the volume has had the benefit of neat and conscientious typing of repeated drafts by Mrs. Hadasel Hill and Miss Helene Bell.

Washington, D.C.   WILLIAM F. ROSS
15 June 1963

Contents

Tables

Charts

Maps

Illustrations

Illustrations are from Department of Defense files.

CHAPTER I

The Heritage and Mission of Field Quartermasters

By V-E Day, 8 May 1945, the Quartermaster Corps in the Mediterranean and European theaters was feeding, clothing, and equipping more than 3,500,000 Americans on the most elaborate scale ever attempted by any army. It was acting as supply custodian and wholesaler to the far-flung civil affairs organization, and in addition, was providing direct support, largely from military stocks, to at least 5,000,000 Allies, civilians, and prisoners of war. An operation of this magnitude, supported from a base over 3,000 miles away, inevitably developed temporary shortages and local crises, but Quartermaster operations as a whole were outstandingly successful. Paying tribute to the supply effort in which the Quartermaster Corps played a major role, a Congressional report in the immediate postwar period stated: "The supply of our armed forces in Europe has been a remarkable achievement, involving the delivery across the ocean and over beaches and through demolished ports, and then over a war-torn countryside into France and Germany of tonnages far in excess of anything previously within the conception of man." [1]

The overseas Quartermaster organization of World War II was not wholly new; that of the European theater, especially, bore a striking resemblance to the organization in France during World War I. [2] The earlier conflict provided a fairly complete preview, on a more modest scale, of the Quartermaster Corps mission, responsibilities, and problems in the second war against Germany. Before examining in detail the experience of World War II, it might be well therefore to note the heritage, the mission, and the tools of the Corps in the earlier war.

In August 1912, after a decade of legislative debate and delay, a rider to an Army appropriation bill provided for the establishment of the Quartermaster Corps. Military planners thought that

[1] Senate Report 110, 79th Cong., 1st sess., 6 July 1945, Additional Report of the Special Committee to Investigate the National Defense Program [Kil-

gore Committee]: *Investigation Overseas*, pt. 2, Conclusions.

[2] This section on the background of the Quartermaster Corps in the field is based on the following volumes: Erna Risch, *The Quartermaster Corps: Organization, Supply, and Services,* Volume I, UNITED STATES ARMY IN WORLD WAR II (Washington, 1953); Erna Risch, *Quartermaster Support of the Army: A History of the Corps, 1775–1939* (Washington, 1962); Johnson Hagood, *The Services of Supply: A Memoir of the Great War* (Boston: Houghton Mifflin Company, 1927); Maj. Gen. Robert M. Littlejohn, editor and compiler, *Passing in Review* (Fort Lee, Va., 1955). (See Bibliographical Note.)

faulty administrative practices, evident in the Spanish-American War, would be corrected by combining three century-old supply bureaus of the War Department—the Quartermaster's Department, the Subsistence Department, and the Paymaster General's Department—into one corps. This new Quartermaster Corps would provide not only supply but services as well.

The newly organized Corps had in command a Quartermaster General with the rank of major general. The legislation of 1912 gave the new Corps a highly diversified mission. The old Quartermaster's Department had furnished transportation, clothing, and equipment for the U.S. Army and had constructed and repaired quarters and transportation facilities along lines of communication. Under the reorganization plan the QMC kept these traditional functions and added the duties of feeding the Army in garrison and in the field, paying troops, and handling fiscal matters. Moreover, the Corps would continue to administer the national cemeteries in the United States, and would be the agency called upon to develop new policies for graves registration service and overseas cemeteries in time of war.

Probably the most significant aspect of the reorganization of 1912 was in the field of military personnel. The three supply bureaus had been essentially civilian agencies directed by a few high-ranking officers. From the Revolution through the war with Spain, Quartermaster field operations had been supervised by professional and volunteer Quartermaster officers and carried out either by civilian employees or by detachments of combat troops when civilians were not available. The creation of a Quartermaster Corps

meant that such functions would gradually be transferred to Quartermaster officers and enlisted personnel, permanently organized into separate Quartermaster units.

Organization of the QMC was but one of many steps in the process of evolving a modern military establishment, capable of waging a major war. For Army-wide exposition, the Field Service regulations of May 1913 introduced new concepts of the organization and support of a modern field army. The regulations contemplated a theater of operations subdivided into administrative and tactical commands, each with Quartermaster staff officers and assigned or attached Quartermaster service units. Specifically, the regulations foresaw the evolution of two types of field Quartermaster officers: a communication zone, or "pipeline," quartermaster to supervise the filling of a system of base depots with supplies, and a tactical, or "spigot," quartermaster to draw supplies for his unit at a depot or railhead and issue them for consumption in battle. In their respective areas both officers would be concerned with providing services as well as supplies.

The Quartermaster Corps had had little opportunity to test the efficiency of these doctrines in the clash along the Mexican border in 1916. Until the United States entered World War I, the QMC functioned more as a procuring agency than as a field supply service. When war came, there were only four types of Quartermaster field units: bakery, truck, pack, and wagon companies. Now untried officers armed with sets of untested precepts had to adapt the Quartermaster mission to a war that was continental in scope, sluggish in movement, and shallow in front. In the summer of

1917 the Corps sent Col. Harry L. Rogers to France, where he soon became a brigadier general and Chief Quartermaster, American Expeditionary Forces. Once in the field his staff was initiated into the new dimensions in warfare brought about by such technical innovations as the internal combustion engine, track-laying vehicles, military aircraft, chemicals, and barbed wire entanglements.

World War I made several distinct contributions to the future mission and organization of the Quartermaster Corps. First, General John J. Pershing, commander of the American Expeditionary Forces (AEF), used a separate administrative command, called the Services of Supply (SOS), to support his field armies. Under this command and staff arrangement, the Chief Quartermaster, SOS AEF, worked along a lengthy line of communications with chiefs of other overseas technical services such as the Engineers, Ordnance, and the new Transportation Corps. Pershing's General Headquarters and SOS Headquarters each had a staff section headed by an assistant chief of staff, G–4, an officer who planned, co-ordinated, and supervised functions pertaining to supply, services, evacuation, hospitalization, and transportation. Before the organization of the U.S. Army General Staff in 1903, the Quartermaster General had been in effect a G–4 staff officer, handling logistical planning and providing transportation for troops and supplies. Now for the first time in the field a chief quartermaster, as both planner and executive, came under this type of general staff supervision. Thus World War I introduced the Quartermaster Corps to an entirely new command and staff framework.

Another contribution to Quarter-master Corps organization during World War I was a system of echeloning territorial SOS commands along Pershing's lines of communications. Base, intermediate, and advance sections of SOS, each controlled a number of rear area installations, including one or more Quartermaster depots. These provided reserves from which supplies consumed by the troops in battle could readily be replaced. Theoretically, the new system of administration gave SOS section commanders control over all activities within their respective areas and gave chiefs of technical services supervisory functions over branch depots, their own personnel and units, and training activities. In reality, so pronounced was the overlapping of command versus staff responsibilities, and functional versus geographical chains of command, that many problems of co-ordination developed, and these very problems were to vex quartermasters in World War II.

In the field of local procurement, the lessons of World War I seemed particularly valuable, and supply authorities followed precedents then established very closely during the succeeding conflict. A General Purchasing Board (GPB) was established under the chairmanship of Brig. Gen. Charles G. Dawes, a wartime volunteer officer with extensive purchasing experience. All the technical services were represented on this board, which existed primarily to eliminate competition for materials and supplies, both among services and among the various Allied nations. The GPB was a co-ordinating agency which located supplies, assisted the technical services in making purchases, and handled financial arrangements. It did not attempt to control either quantities or quality of supplies purchased. The GPB became a very large organization, with offices in all Allied and neutral countries, and its purchases contributed more than half of the supplies consumed by the AEF, or some ten million ship tons out of a total of eighteen million. More than half of these locally purchased goods were Quartermaster supplies. In both conflicts, the original impetus for local procurement was a severe shipping shortage, aggravated by enemy submarine warfare. In both cases procurement continued unabated after shipping shortages had been overcome, because the needs of combat could not wait for the elimination of production bottlenecks in the United States.

The appearance of twenty-six types of Quartermaster service units in France was another significant development of World War I. As trench and tank warfare increased the scope of combat support, Quartermaster units were organized, many of them locally in the theater, to perform additional supply and service functions for the fighting troops. Some of these innovations were inspired by the example of similar Allied units, while others were prompted by a desire to provide troops in the field, so far as possible, with some of the comforts and amenities of American life. Compiling formal tables of organization for these units and obtaining official sanction for their inclusion in the troop list were long-drawn-out administrative processes, carried on piecemeal and still incomplete at the end of hostilities. Nevertheless, the Army in the zone of interior displayed considerable flexibility and speed in activating and training these new units, and in deploying them overseas. Of 706 Quartermaster units in France on 15 December

1918, 444 or 63 percent had been organized in the United States. Among the more important new units were depot, supply, refrigeration, laundry, sterilization and bath, gasoline supply, graves registration, salvage, remount, and various types of repair units, each supplied with specialized types of equipment. On Armistice Day, 11 November 1918, Quartermaster Service, AEF, had 100,731 troops within an over-all total of 1,925,-000, or 5.2 percent.[3]

Between the two world wars, Quartermaster Corps field doctrine remained relatively static. The whole Army shrank in size and did not institute any tactical innovations that required new types of support. Existing regulations provided for an adequate, combat-tested Quartermaster field organization, to operate in accordance with proved doctrine. A wide variety of QMC service units, also combat-tested, could be activated whenever they were needed and funds became available. Although it was generally agreed that Quartermaster organization and doctrine were sound, planners also recognized that they were neither simple nor easily understood. The Corps therefore devoted its major effort in those years to an intensive indoctrination of its young officers. Academic instruction and peacetime maneuvers are no satisfactory substitutes for war experience, but all the possibilities of such training methods were systematically exploited at QM schools. Classroom instructors taught over and over again the maxims that sup-

---

[3] (1) Risch, *Quartermaster Support of the Army,* ch. XV. (2) Memo, Littlejohn for CG SOS ETOUSA, 15 Feb 44, sub: Detailed Pers Situation and Reqmts of SOS. Littlejohn Collection, sec. III, folder, Sundry Important Documents. (See Bibliographical Note.)

ply is a function of command and that the impetus of supply is from rear to front; the implications of those maxims were illustrated in a wide variety of tactical situations. Fledgling quartermasters practiced requisitioning supplies and providing supplies and services. Property accountability, inventory procedures, and business management were stressed. Lectures emphasized that services and supply are only the broad foundation of logistical organization and administration in time of war and that detailed Quartermaster doctrine and procedures would have to evolve under actual battle conditions.

This schooling proved to be enormously valuable, largely because of a broad, rather than excessively specialized, approach to the whole field of logistics. The small group of graduates had a surprising influence upon the whole American logistical effort in World War II, especially during the emergency period, when the first classes of young Reserve officers were receiving their technical training. In addition to the QMC officers lost by transfer to the Transportation Corps, to Ordnance, and to the Engineers, there was a tremendous demand for these trained, experienced officers by logistical staffs at all levels, and especially by the G–4 staffs of senior headquarters. The result was that too few of these officers were retained by the Quartermaster Corps. It was severely handicapped in its operations in the early phases of World War II and, for want of instructors, never achieved a completely satisfactory standard of wartime officer training.

In general, the policy and concepts which Pershing brought home from France provided the foundation for the staff principles and procedures to guide a future theater level quartermaster in the field. It was clear from AEF experience that this officer would be both a planner and an administrator, and the staff duties required of a theater chief quartermaster determined the structure of his personal office, the Office of the Chief Quartermaster (OCQM). Basically, the staff functions of OCQM were subdivided into three major elements—a planning and training section, a section to deal with both expendable and nonexpendable classes of supply, and a section to supervise a variety of required services.

By 1942 QMC doctrine provided that, as a special staff officer, a chief quartermaster performed six basic missions for his commander. First, he advised the theater commander and his general and special staffs on the Quartermaster mission. He determined requirements for and procured, stored, issued, and "documented," or accounted for, QMC supplies. He recommended the procurement and the employment of Quartermaster units and their allocation to commands. He supervised the operations of all Quartermaster units not assigned or attached to commands. Throughout the theater he also supervised Quartermaster troop training. Lastly, the chief quartermaster planned for and supervised service to the line, providing troops with such services as bakeries, shoe repair, graves registration, gasoline supply, and baths.[4]

By the end of 1942 the Quartermaster Corps had lost several important functions to other technical services. Construction activities and administration of Army-controlled real estate had been transferred to the Engineers, automotive procurement and maintenance to

---

[4] FM 101–5, Staff Officer's Field Manual, 1942.

the Ordnance Department, and transportation service to the newly revived Transportation Corps. A movement to create a general depot service to handle all Army storage gained some momentum but finally failed. OCQM, which had lost some of its storage functions, regained this Army-wide responsibility, but what was more important, recovered the experienced, Quartermaster-trained personnel who operated the warehouses. In general, the loss of functions to other services caused the QMC far less concern than the accompanying losses of personnel; there was still plenty to be done, and all too few trained officers to do it.

During World War II the Quartermaster Corps was one of seven technical services, each of which designed, procured, and issued various items of supplies and equipment.[5] Thus a complete general depot would have seven technical branches or sections, besides an administrative or operating section. In time of war, other technical services performed certain functions for, or in close co-operation with, the QMC. Briefly, the Chemical Warfare Service provided chemicals in which clothing was dipped to give protection against vesicant gases. Chemical Warfare field units, organized to decontaminate clothing and personnel in the event of gas warfare, actually supplemented the laundry and bath services of the Quartermaster Corps. Gasoline pipelines and bulk storage plants were built and operated by the Engineers, as were cold storage facilities and ice plants. Fire fighting and fire safety, of vital importance at Quartermaster gasoline dumps, were Engineer responsibilities at all Army installations. The Medical Department advised the QMC on the adequacy of clothing, footgear, and rations. Its veterinary officers inspected all food, especially meat. The QMC provided hospitals with special laundry facilities and a special hospital ration. Beginning in August 1943, the Transportation Corps assumed technical supervision over all motor transport units, although for more than a year many of them continued to bear the Quartermaster designation. These functions are merely those of particular significance to the QMC.

In addition to the technical services, some of the administrative services also performed functions vital to Quartermaster operations. The Provost Marshal administered all prisoner of war (POW) camps, and reported requirements for POW rations to the QMC. The QMC provided a special ration for POW's, and furnished them with clothing and equipment. Beginning in December 1944, the Provost Marshal in the ETO organized the Military Labor Service, which thereafter administered and disciplined POW labor units employed by all the technical services.

The Adjutant General's Department supplied publications to the entire Army.[6] All requisitioning and issue of all types of supplies were based upon authorizations of various types that were

---

[5] The seven services were Chemical Warfare, Engineer, Medical, Ordnance, Quartermaster, Signal, and Transportation.

[6] In retrospect, it must be said that The Adjutant General's Office was conspicuously inefficient in this function. General Somervell's famous critique of the Communications Zone of the European theater contained a rueful admission that his own AGO "has fallen down badly in filling requisitions for publications. . . ." Memo, Somervell for Lee, 24 Jan 45, p. 21. SHAEF G-4 319.1, Rpts, Gen Somervell, 1945, I.

contained in "publications"—a catchall designation for Army regulations, tables, orders, circulars, and other authoritative papers of the Army. The Adjutant General issued, printed, and distributed such publications to all units and offices that required the information. Thus he was the agent who transmitted vital information from the zone of interior to theater level chiefs of technical services. An additional function of The Adjutant General was maintenance of a command-wide personnel statistics reporting system, completely independent of the strength-for-rations reports received by the Quartermaster Service and therefore immensely valuable for comparison and confirmation purposes.

The Army's logistical system was considered basic in the Mediterranean and European theaters; it supplied all common items to the Army Air Forces and the Navy. Both these services maintained their own requisitioning channels and depot systems, but requisitioned their supplies of common items from Army sources within the theater. The only major exceptions were vehicle fuels and lubricants, common items procured in accordance with joint specifications, but administered on the combined (Allied) level along with characteristic Air Forces and Navy types of petroleum products.

Army supplies were classified under an elaborate system of categories, and subcategories. All items were segregated, first of all, according to the technical service responsible for their procurement. By 1942 War Department manuals listed over 70,000 separate Quartermaster items. In one respect this statistic may be somewhat misleading; the list included each separate spare part for each major piece of equipment, and each

size of each type of clothing was also a separate item. Such an elaborate system of nomenclature was essential for accurate stock control, and gives an idea of the scope of the documentation problem.

A second system of supply categories, designated by five Roman numerals, was also Army-wide. In this system, all Class I items were Quartermaster, and there were no QM Class V items. The intermediate numbers were common to all the technical services. A short discussion of this system will reveal many of the problems and procedures of field quartermasters.

Class I supplies were articles supplied automatically without requisition at the troop level, since in theory they were consumed daily and universally at a steady rate. They were known collectively as subsistence, which embraced food and forage, and the unit of measurement was the ration, defined as the allowance of food for one day for one man or one animal. The two main categories were field and operational rations. Field rations were prepared in unit kitchens; they consisted of the A ration, including perishable foods, and the B ration, comprising nonperishable foods only. Under favorable conditions, kitchen-prepared food could be brought forward to troops actually in combat, so that such troops often received the B ration and sometimes the A ration. Troops heavily engaged in combat, on remote posts, or moving rapidly, as in a beach assault or in pursuit, normally ate operational rations. All of these could be eaten cold in an emergency. [7] In addition the QMC

---

[7] For a detailed account of the development and content of the various operational rations, see Risch, *The Quartermaster Corps: Organization, Supply, and Services,* I, 178–89.

provided hospital, convalescent, and various types of travel rations.

Class I supply also involved some purely administrative problems. Soap and cigarettes sold in post exchanges were PX items, but the same items packed with operational rations and issued gratis to the troops were regarded as Class I, and so was anything else issued on the same basis. Decisions as to what units would receive gratis issues were usually made on the army group level and fluctuated according to the intensity of combat.

Class II Quartermaster items consisted of clothing and individual equipment, organizational equipment, expendable materials for cleaning and preserving, office equipment and supplies, special purpose vehicles, and spare and maintenance parts. British "accommodation stores," such as cots, furniture, and barracks items provided by the British for American troops arriving in the United Kingdom, saved shipping space and replaced the Class II post, camp, and station allowances familiar to U.S. troops. War Department tables, known as Tables of Equipment (T/E's), established the authorized quantities of Class II supplies. These tables, listing thousands of separate items, changed periodically, but the circulars announcing the modifications rarely reached the field in time to affect the Chief Quartermaster's supply situation. It should be borne in mind that Class II included most items of Army supply. The trucks driven by the soldiers of a QM truck company were Class II Ordnance items, and the gas mask each man carried was a Class II Chemical Warfare item. Likewise, the field ranges in the mess of any unit were Class II QMC items. In a somewhat different category were mobile bakeries, mobile laundries, and heavy sewing machines used to repair tents—each a Class II QMC item issued only to a special Quartermaster unit.

Class III items included solid and liquid fuels, the latter commonly referred to during World War II as POL (petrol, oil, and lubricants—a British designation). Strategic reserves of both solid and liquid fuels were controlled during World War II by combined committees representing the British and American Armies, Navies, Air services, and civilian agencies, and American administration was through an Area Petroleum Board. This applied to both Mediterranean and European theaters. The Quartermaster Corps controlled solid fuel destined for the U.S. Army. Aviation gasoline and aircraft lubricants (designated Class IIIA) were controlled by the Army Air Forces, but normally were stored in Quartermaster POL depots. Since the transportation, storage, and distribution of vehicle gasoline involved several technical services, requirements and allocations were controlled by G–4's at lower levels, culminating in the POL Division of Supreme Headquarters. The Transportation Corps was responsible for the Army aspects of POL movement by ocean tankers, and controlled the barges, railroad tank cars, and tanker trucks which moved bulk gasoline in overseas theaters. The Engineers were responsible for bulk storage and movement by pipeline, and gasoline normally came under Quartermaster Corps control at decanting points, where it was poured into drums or jerricans or released in bulk to gasoline supply companies and stored in POL depots. The QMC was charged with computing Army requirements for Class III supplies (except Class IIIA). Beginning late in 1942 Area Petroleum Offices extended their control over many of these activities, ultimately organizing an Area Petroleum Service in each theater—in effect an eighth technical service. But the QMC continued to compute Army Class III requirements and to deliver packaged POL to the troop units.

Class IV items were, in general, those for which no fixed quantity of issue was established. Thus, Class II items of clothing and equipment were reclassified Class IV when sold for cash to officers, Red Cross workers, or others entitled to buy them. Warehouse equipment, medals and decorations, and certain combat items, such as waterproof weapon covers, issued for a specific operation, were also in this category. Post exchange supplies were originally placed in Class IV, but events soon demonstrated the need for a separate category, although this was not sanctioned by Army regulations.[8] The distinction between Class II and Class IV Quartermaster items was never completely clarified, and they were normally grouped together and handled by one subsection of the Quartermaster organization.

Class V, munitions and chemicals, did not include any Quartermaster items. Nevertheless, Quartermaster officers had to keep requirements for these items constantly in mind. In combat, they normally had overriding priorities. For example, a ship with a mixed cargo including ammunition would normally be routed to the point where the ammunition was needed and other cargo would also be unloaded at that point, whether or not this was convenient for the responsible technical service. Delivery of ammunition to units in combat presented a somewhat similar problem: the unit's organic vehicles were available to deliver Quartermaster supplies only after the daily ammunition requirement had been met.

The basic unit for all supply planning was the day of supply, normally subdivided by technical service and class of supplies. One day of QM Class I supply for a given unit would be one ration for each man of that unit. The reserves of various categories maintained for a unit in the depots, expressed in days of supply, were commonly referred to as the *level of supply*. This was a simple and convenient method of referring to the large and complicated assortments of supplies and equipment required to support and maintain a major command. Levels of supply for overseas theaters were established by the War Department. The day-of-supply concept emphasized that reserves of various items should be assembled in the correct proportions, or at least in proportions believed to be correct in the light of all available information. Since this was a form of forecasting—a process always subject to error—rates of consumption and maintenance requirements for supplies and equipment always differed somewhat from anticipated figures. Stocks were then considered "out of balance," a condition to be corrected by changing the proportions in subsequent requisitions.

Theater level requirements based on actual experience, especially combat experience, were always of great interest to zone of interior planning agencies, which were attempting to forecast long-range national requirements for the entire war effort. From the zone of interior point

---

[8] Before World War II, post exchange articles, luxury goods, and alcoholic beverages were assigned to no supply category. In the European theater, supply planning demanded specific levels of supply for post exchange items, so they were treated as a separate, additional category in continental QM depots.

of view, everything shipped to a theater, including cargoes lost at sea, was a factor in that theater's rate of consumption. Planners normally authorized a large basic reserve for a new theater, 90 days of supply or more, to offset the unknown supply factors. For a mature theater, in which rates of consumption had become known, they sometimes reduced basic reserves to 30 days or less. An operating reserve, which might be compared to a revolving fund, was authorized in addition to the basic reserve. It was provided to compensate for fluctuations in the actual arrival of requisitions. In the European theater a normal requisition covered a 30-day period, and the operating reserve was also 30 days of supply. Therefore the basic reserve would remain intact even if the requisitioned items arrived on the last day of the requisition period. The basic reserve plus the operating reserve constituted the maximum level of supply. Officials in the zone of interior carefully examined theater requisitions to ensure that they did not exceed the maximum authorized levels. One important variable deserves special mention: fluctuations in the manpower of a theater changed the rate of consumption, and therefore the levels of supply, even though the tonnage of supplies on hand remained constant. Thus a rapidly expanding theater might exhibit the apparent paradox of more and more supplies constituting a lower and lower level of supply.

The level of supply was a convenient planning concept, but could not be used directly in actual Quartermaster operations. Storage and distribution activities required definite data on each specific item, as did requisitions at all levels. Tables for converting days of supply into tons or cubic feet of various items were officially designated as Quartermaster Supply Reference Data, and unofficially known as the "bible" of the Quartermaster Corps. They were widely distributed and constantly revised, and qualified QMC officers were expected to understand them.[9]

To get his days of supply into the hands of the troops in the right amount at the proper place and time, the Chief Quartermaster had to do far more than simply fill out an order blank. Only by careful planning could he foresee varying requirements for each of 70,000 items. He had to check his inventories against tactical requirements and expected strength fluctuations, and he had to take into account anticipated rather than actual deliveries. For smooth functioning of storage and distribution no detail of weights or cubages could be overlooked. Storage and distribution techniques demanded a mass of detailed information which he had to refine continuously and disseminate throughout the command. He had to know what local products were available, and how local goods compared with those purchased at home. How salvage could increase his inventories was another factor in determining his requisitions. Above all, a sound education in business management was an essential.

The reference data tables already mentioned were indispensable tools for breaking down the Chief Quartermaster's theater-wide mission into accurate portions of manageable size, so that each

---

[9] Office of the Theater Chief Quartermaster, Theater Service Forces, European Theater, Operational Study 2, Quartermaster Supply Reference Data, 1 November 1945 (hereafter cited as OTCQM TSFET Operational Study 2.) (See Bibliographical Note.)

could be delegated to a Quartermaster unit capable of accomplishing it. For example, it might seem logical to charge a major depot with the support of a specific field army and of the air force and service troops in the area immediately behind it. Actually, the strength of an army fluctuated and the military population of a rear area was even more variable, so that a mission stated in such terms would be very vague and success in accomplishing it correspondingly difficult. By contrast, a mission of 15 days' wholesale support for 350,000 men, plus 30 days' retail support for 40,000 men, would also be only an approximation of the support actually required for the same troops, but it represented a definite and achievable objective. Using the reference data, the Chief Quartermaster's inspectors could tell very quickly whether such an objective was being met, and if not what remedial action was necessary. Meanwhile the Chief Quartermaster was personally responsible that the sum of all the depot missions was adequate to meet the variable support requirements of the theater as a whole.

A major element, causing variations in the strength of the theater or of the field armies, was the movement of divisions. Since each division required both tactical and logistical support, such a movement usually involved considerably more personnel than the Table of Organization (T/O) strength of the division itself. The term *division slice* expresses the relationship between the total theater strength (minus air forces) and the number of divisions supported, and represents the total number of men involved in maintaining a division in the field. The normal European theater division slice of 40,000 men was made up

as follows: 15,000 men in the division itself, 15,000 corps and army troops, and 10,000 communications zone troops. Quartermaster supply planning was usually based upon the requirements for a division slice, rather than merely on requirements for the division itself.[10]

Possibly this discussion of the requirements, duties, and procedures of overseas quartermasters has overemphasized administrative detail. Familiarity with administration was by no means enough for a quartermaster to bring to his job. A knowledge of combat organization and tactics, and particularly the logistical implications of changes in tactics, was also required, especially at higher levels. This was something that could hardly be inculcated by Quartermaster schooling alone. A good quartermaster was also a soldier, for no one else could have the insight necessary to provide satisfactory support for soldiers in combat. The operations he was called upon to support were military operations, and despite some resemblances to procedures employed in the world of business, their nature and purpose were quite different.

A trained Quartermaster officer, contemplating the growing trend toward mechanizaton in warfare between 1932 and 1942, as exemplified in Japanese successes against China, Italy's adventures in Africa, and Germany's domination of Europe, could see that the new mobile

---

[10] (1) Roland G. Ruppenthal, *Logistical Support of the Armies*, Volume I, UNITED STATES ARMY IN WORLD WAR II (Washington, 1953), pp. 299–300. (2) Col. Creswell G. Blakeney, ed., *Logistical History of NATOUSA–MTOUSA, 11 August 1942 to 30 November 1945* (Naples, Italy: G. Montanino, 1945), pp. 476–78. The latter source indicates that in the Mediterranean area a division slice was computed as 45,000 men and 6,000 vehicles.

warfare brought with it a whole new category of support problems. Moreover, it appeared that thus far the new weapons had won victories principally against opponents of inferior strength, technology, or organization. All the evidence indicated that the basic problems of support for mobile forces in protracted operations had been evaded rather than solved. Nevertheless, the U.S. Army joined the parade, shifting from a horse-drawn square division to a motorized triangular one, developing its own version of armored and mechanized cavalry units, and organizing new support units capable, at least in theory, of keeping up with the new tempo of warfare. Even before the United States was plunged into the war, the new organization was designed to conquer the German Army—or at least a force of strikingly similar strength, mobility, and fire power. There was every indication that the contest would be a long one, and the American commanders plainly stated their intention of waging it unrelentingly, without those protracted pauses that had marked earlier wars, and had also occurred repeatedly since 1939. The quartermasters who were called upon to support campaigns of this type realized that they were entering largely uncharted territory.

Basically, mechanization for continental warfare resulted in increased depth of deployment, accompanied by much greater mobility within the zone of deployment. For quartermasters, mechanization meant that depots must be kept full on longer lines of communication, while the need for POL would increase until it became more than half of all QM supply. These conditions demanded greater flexibility in command and staff arrangements, particularly within administrative commands, than had those which had applied to the shallow fronts of World War I. Larger tactical groupings for mechanized warfare complicated the command lines and technical channels between pipeline and spigot quartermasters. With time a precious commodity, resources often could not be used as planned.

Mechanization also placed unprecedented demands on the wise use of skilled manpower, and to meet these demands merchants and tradesmen were mustered for Quartermaster duty, in addition to the traditional truck drivers and stevedores, as were young executives of large business corporations, who were rightly considered promising officer material. Because the new conditions of modern warfare had to be experienced before they could be fully met, a common theme developed for Quartermaster planners and administrators in their formative period in the United Kingdom and in North Africa: orientation and improvisation.

CHAPTER II

Early Activities in the United Kingdom and North Africa

First Plans for the United Kingdom

The Quartermaster effort against the Rome-Berlin Axis had a modest beginning in the critical late spring of 1941, when American staff planners assumed that, in the event of a declaration of war, small ground and air forces would be established in the United Kingdom as soon as possible.[1] On 19 May 1941 the War Department created a Special Army Observer Group (SPOBS), under Maj. Gen. James E. Chaney, in London. Chaney included a Quartermaster Section in his group consisting of one officer, Lt. Col. William H. Middleswart.

Born in West Virginia on 19 October 1894, Middleswart was one year over the age limit which the Chief of Staff, United States Army, had set for an overseas observer, but he was nonetheless well qualified for his staff position. His Regular Army commission in the Quartermaster Corps dated back to 1 July 1920. For the next four years he was in the Office of The Quartermaster General and thereafter served five years in field assignments, including one tour of duty in the Philippines. After two years of schooling at the Army Industrial College and Army War College between 1936 and 1938, and a year of staff work in the Panama Canal Zone, Middleswart in July 1940 became the officer in charge of the Procurement Division of the Philadelphia Quartermaster Depot. His call for duty with Chaney came in May 1941, and he immediately left for England.

In the absence of any formal alliance Middleswart's work at first was exploratory and confined to the field of planning. He exchanged points of view with his British colleagues, becoming more and more familiar with the problems of coalition warfare. Making arrangements for the provision of solid fuels to the U.S. troops arriving in Iceland, as British forces there were withdrawn for duty elsewhere, was Middleswart's first practical assignment in SPOBS.[2]

After numerous conferences Middleswart also made plans to provide Quar-

---

[1] Accounts of strategic and logistical planning for the invasion of the European continent are to be found in the following volumes of the series UNITED STATES ARMY IN WORLD WAR II: Mark Skinner Watson, *Chief of Staff: Prewar Plans and Preparations* (Washington, 1950); Maurice Matloff and Edwin M. Snell, *Strategic Planning for Coalition Warfare, 1941–1942* (Washington, 1953); Richard M. Leighton and Robert W. Coakley, *Global Logistics and Strategy, 1940–1943* (Washington, 1955); Ruppenthal, *Logistical Support*, I.

[2] Ltr, Middleswart to Capt James C. Bagg, Hist Br OCQM ETOUSA, 13 Jan 44. Middleswart Papers. (See Bibliographical Note.)

termaster support for U.S. troops in the United Kingdom. In mid-September 1941 he submitted his initial recommendations. Current plans contemplated a force of 107,000 men, including 87,000 ground and air troops and 20,000 service troops, to be distributed under a theater commander within four tactical subcommands, plus a base area. Though no date had been set for their arrival, the combat troops were to be located as follows: in Northern Ireland, 30,000 ground troops; in eastern England, a bomber force of 15,000 air troops and 21,000 ground troops; in Scotland, 13,500 combat troops; and in a small area, thirty-five miles southeast of London, a reinforced regiment of 7,500 men.

Within the Midlands base area, the British were prepared to let Americans select Quartermaster sites and to provide them with all the necessary facilities in full operating condition. Middleswart's major objective was to set up an establishment requiring little assistance from the British. But it was impossible for the Americans to ignore local conditions. The common interest demanded that the independence of American facilities in base and troop concentration areas should not be attained through wasteful duplication of facilities. Supplies had to enter British ports and move over British railways and highways. Depots were to be located in existing British buildings as far as practicable. Services which had to be performed close to the troops, such as laundry and bread baking, were to be handled by the British insofar as their resources permitted.

Middleswart's storage plan provided that half of the contemplated supply stockage would be located in areas contiguous to each of the four troop concentrations, with the remaining portion deposited in two general base areas. He suggested to Chaney that two general depots be operated at first, one in Northern Ireland, the other in the Midlands. These depots were designed to maintain 100,000 men on the full scale of clothing and equipage. Standard American rations were to be furnished automatically from the United States. To support the regiment near London the plan recommended activation of a provisional battalion to provide all Quartermaster services. For area defense against parachute attack, a very real threat in 1941, Quartermaster troops should be armed with rifles instead of pistols, and they should have trucks equipped for driving during blackout conditions.

Middleswart further submitted estimates for Quartermaster troops on a scale commensurate with a 100,000-man force. He recommended that all QMC units and half of the 30-day supply level for depots leave the United States at least a fortnight before the departure of the combat troops. He wanted to have accommodations and depots set up and in operation when they debarked. The advantage of such arrangements was emphasized over and over in subsequent planning of troop priorities and shipping schedules, usually with only limited success.[3]

With the entry of the United States into the war, time became the most important element in Quartermaster plans, which for the moment contemplated support to one army corps, deployed in

---

[3] (1) Min, Mtgs, SPOBS–QMG [British] War Office Subcom, QMB House, London, 3d Mtg, 10 Jul 41, 4th Mtg, 31 Jul 41. USFET AG 337. (2) Rpt, Proposals on Base Area, U.S. Force in England, an. 7 (QM), Mtg, War Office, 18 Sep 41. USFET AG 381.

defensive positions. Without a staff, Middleswart could not handle the administrative details for supporting a corps. Organizationally, SPOBS was enlarged and redesignated Headquarters, United States Army Forces, British Isles (USAFBI), on 8 January 1942, with Chaney retaining command. Until 24 May 1942, Chaney had no separate administrative command, and Middleswart continued as a staff planner. Between 8 January and late May 1942, a Quartermaster staff was gradually assembled. Maj. Thomas J. Wells, an infantry officer borrowed from the office of the London Military Attaché, Maj. Frazier E. Mackintosh, a Regular U.S. Army officer recalled from retirement in London, Capt. John L. Horner, quartermaster of the American Embassy, and 1st Lt. Louis G. Zinnecker comprised the new Quartermaster Section. On 1 May, Lt. Col. Robert F. Carter, Maj. James E. Poore, Jr., Capt. Leo H. McKinnon, Capt. Burton Koffler, Capt. Gordon P. Weber, and a score of enlisted men arrived from the United States.

Early in January 1942, Middleswart received word that V Corps headquarters was to be activated in Northern Ireland and would assume command of MAGNET Force, consisting of an armored division and three infantry divisions, plus appropriate service troops, and totaling approximately 105,000 men. On 7 January Chaney informed the War Department of his quartermaster needs for the first convoy: POL and solid fuels were not to be sent; tentage, gasoline cans, and 35,000 C rations were needed, but not cotton clothing. Chaney also asked that the troops wear old-type steel helmets. The QMC's new type somewhat resembled the German helmet, and training British

troops to recognize it would require time.[4]

Actually, MAGNET Force was scaled down by the War Department before V Corps headquarters assembled. Middleswart meanwhile had arranged with the British for debarking the four divisions, for billeting and feeding V Corps, and for furnishing the divisions with motor vehicles, British accommodation stores, and other essentials pending the unloading and movement of supplies which supposedly were to be shipped with the troops or were to follow them soon. Wells and Zinnecker had gone to Northern Ireland to receive the first arrivals. On 26 January Chaney and Middleswart were at Belfast to greet about 4,000 men of the 34th Infantry Division. Disappointment over the decrease in MAGNET Force soon faded as War Department plans for deploying U.S. air power in the United Kingdom began to unfold. On 20 February Brig. Gen. Ira C. Eaker arranged with the Royal Air Force to provide quartermaster support for units of the U.S. Eighth Air Force. On 11 May, the first airmen arrived in England.

The War Department had announced as early as January 1942 that a 60-day level of supply, except ammunition, would be sent to the United Kingdom for U.S. troops stationed there. Local procurement was definitely encouraged. Except for Middleswart's exploratory planning before 7 December 1941, little or nothing had been accomplished for the reception and storage of the 60-day levels. In fact, the prevailing concept continued that the Americans would decentralize their operations out of two base areas some-

---

[4] Rad, Chaney to AGWAR, 7 Jan 42. USFET AG 400.

where in the Midlands and Northern Ireland. Every day of delay in granting Chaney a definite logistical plan hobbled Quartermaster operations, which after February were almost solely confined to Northern Ireland Base Command, a provisional organization.

To assist V Corps and its new base command Middleswart, with an expanding staff after 1 May, made definite assignments among his personnel. Poore headed plans and procedures; Carter worked on subsistence; Mackintosh handled administration; and Weber, Koffler, and McKinnon attended to matters of supply. In their early planning the staff attempted to draw upon the experience of British quartermasters supporting the Eighth Army in Libya and Egypt.

The first arrivals in V Corps had to use overtaxed British resources. Though Middleswart had continuously requested the inclusion of Quartermaster troops in V Corps and its provisional base command, none came, and the USAFBI Quartermaster Section could provide only a series of "how to do it yourself" circulars to show tactical units how to arrange for their own retail services. For these circulars, Middleswart gathered information from many British war agencies including the War Office, the Air Ministry, and the Ministries of Aircraft Production, Supply, Food, Petroleum, Wool Control, and also the Navy Army Air Force Institute (NAAFI), a service organization corresponding to the U.S. Army Exchange Service.

For two months after its arrival, V Corps subsisted on the regular British ration. The troops found this ration rather scanty, and disliked it because of its high proportion of starches, cabbage, and mutton. On 16 February 1942, Mid-

dleswart had prescribed the American field ration, type A, for V Corps, but this could not be issued until sufficient stocks had arrived, a depot system had been established, and balanced stocks were assured. Supplies did not arrive on schedule, and to fill the gap a modified British-American ration was developed. All items in it were of British origin, but it was a somewhat more generous ration, and better suited to American tastes. Slowly it came into use, and meanwhile V Corps kept one B ration and two C rations in reserve, rotating their use on occasions.[5]

In Class II and III supply planning Middleswart had to improvise at every step. Clothing and individual equipment on the current Table of Allowances (T/BA 21)—a revision appeared in June 1942—included items that had been designed to meet the needs of either trench warfare or peacetime garrison duty. Under the old T/BA initial issues supposedly were to eliminate many of Middleswart's clothing problems. Monthly requisitions were designed to bring clothing levels to the sixty-day mark quickly and planners believed that this would see V Corps through its formative period. But the level was unrealistic. Also, requisitions stayed on file in The Quartermaster General's Office as German submarines, now operating off the coastal shelf of the United States instead of in European waters, forced the Allies to husband their precious shipping. Discussing his clothing problems with the British, Middleswart proposed that ship-

---

[5] (1) Ltr, CG NIBC to CG ETOUSA, 15 Jun 42. USFET AG 430. (2) Cir 28, Hq USAFBI, 29 May 42. (3) Memo, Maj Charles G. Herman for Carter, 28 Aug 42, sub: British-American Rations. Hist Br OQMG. (4) Rations are discussed in detail in Chapter XV, below.

ping space could be conserved through a system of exchange. In brief, Americans would release items manufactured in the United States to British troops in the Pacific; British-made goods would replace items for Americans in the United Kingdom. For many weeks the exchange could not be arranged and direct local procurement remained the only potential source for Class II supplies.

Gasoline, kerosene, diesel oil, and lubricants, all in cans, were to be dispensed to American users when they landed. Vehicles would be serviced at British Army gasoline pumps. This remained the Class III pattern until mid-June 1942 when wholesale issue of POL was arranged for V Corps. Americans found Ireland's winter unexpectedly severe and Middleswart arranged to increase the daily allotment of coal, charged to reverse lendlease. As spring wore on, Middleswart developed more and more standing operating procedures for V Corps use in completing arrangements for local services such as laundry, shoe repair, and dry cleaning. But, as troop strength increased and American thoughts turned from Northern Ireland to England itself as a billeting place, it was evident that tactical commanders would soon require a regularly constituted SOS.[6]

From January until late May 1942, Middleswart's planning for V Corps reflected Allied concern with Britain's immediate defense, even though his American superiors soon learned that Quartermaster requirements for the United Kingdom would have to be recast in a new mold. By the end of April, President Franklin D. Roosevelt and his military advisers, working with comparable British officers, had decided that the most effective move against the Axis Powers was an invasion of northwest Europe, using the United Kingdom as a base of operations. The two governments ordered the new strategy, dubbed BOLERO, executed at the earliest practicable moment. Anglo-American planners projected BOLERO in three phases: concentration of resources in the United Kingdom, a cross-Channel attack, and preparations at beachheads prior to a continental advance. An intensified air attack on the Continent would accompany all three phases. To avoid confusion planners subsequently narrowed the meaning of BOLERO to a purely logistical concept, and applied the code name ROUNDUP to the tactical phase of the operation.[7]

As BOLERO planning progressed, a theater level command to administer its American aspects, calling for a new commander with a redefined and specific mission, became a definite necessity. It was generally anticipated that, following the War Department's lead, the new commander would subdivide his command into three operational commands, consisting of a ground force, an air force, and a service of supply. On 3 May 1942 the Commanding General, Army Service Forces (then SOS), Lt. Gen. Brehon B. Somervell, discussed his SOS concept for

---

[6] (1) Ltr cited n. 2, above. (2) Cir 8, Hq USAFBI, 16 Feb 42, reprinted in Eudora R. Richardson and Sherman Allen, *Quartermaster Supply in the European Theater of Operations in World War II*, vol. II, *Subsistence*, app. XI (QM School, Camp Lee, Va., 1948). (Hereafter cited as *QM Supply in ETO*.) (3) Memo 6, Hq NIBC, Quartermaster Standard Operating Procedure, 8 June 1942. Poore Papers. (See Bibliographical Note.) (4) Cir 29, Hq USAFBI, 29 May 42.

[7] (1) Matloff and Snell, *Strategic Planning, 1941–1942*, chs. V, VIII, X. (2) Ruppenthal, *Logistical Support*, vol. I, chs. I, II.

the new theater with Maj. Gen. John C. H. Lee, the War Department's candidate to command all supply services in the new theater. Four days later The Quartermaster General had been briefed on Lee's SOS plans, and Lee, in turn, received the name of Brig. Gen. Robert M. Littlejohn as Chief, Quartermaster Service.

By 14 May Lee had talked with Littlejohn, described his draft SOS directive, and suggested the assembly of a staff for overseas duty at the earliest practicable date. As May faded into June, Littlejohn estimated his personnel requirements, closely following what he had been able to learn of Lee's tentative plan. He hoped to keep Middleswart as a key planner. Carefully selecting his staff, Littlejohn submitted modest personnel requests. In terms of numbers they reflected his understanding that he would initially play a planner's role, that he would be responsible for a staff to handle his portion of a general depot service, to be operated under G–4, that the depot system would expand in an orderly fashion out of a general base area, and that a transportation service, also under G–4, was not to be a Quartermaster function. War Department manpower agencies had the same impression.

Meanwhile, under USAFBI, on 24 May Chaney established an SOS with Lee commanding. Before the end of May, armed with instructions from the War Department, Lee met with the BOLERO Combined Committee in London, submitting his requirements for U.S. troops either in or about to arrive in the United Kingdom. Using Lee's estimates, the British planners published their first edition of BOLERO Key Plans. It was a bulletin of instructions, not a directive, to British agencies enabling them to co-operate with Americans in receiving, accommodating, and maintaining U.S. troops. Unfortunately, until mid-June, most SOS special staff officers did not see the first Key Plan. This all-important document pinned down previous rough estimates and stated that 1,049,000 troops and their supplies would arrive, before D-day, tentatively set for 1 April 1943. It gave Lee a manpower ceiling of 277,000 SOS troops, including a Quartermaster quota of 53,226 men. Of this quota, 1,386 officers and 11,822 enlisted men, as casuals or non-Table-of-Organization personnel, were scheduled for headquarters and depot duty. Quartermaster personnel would be 19 percent of the SOS troop strength, or 5.1 percent of BOLERO's total troop basis, a proportion reminiscent of World War I experience.

On 5 June 1942 there were 36,178 troops in the United Kingdom, of whom 4,305 were in England, the remainder in Northern Ireland. Three days later the European Theater of Operations, U.S. Army (ETOUSA), was formally established, and the same day, 8 June 1942, atop a "cracker box" in Number 1, Great Cumberland Place, London, in the presence of one other Quartermaster officer, Lt. Col. Michael H. Zwicker, Littlejohn activated the Office of the Chief Quartermaster, ETOUSA. Within five days, while retaining his planning role in Headquarters, ETO, Littlejohn also became Chief, Quartermaster Service, a planning as well as an operating post within General Lee's SOS ETOUSA. Thus, when Maj. Gen. Dwight D. Eisenhower succeeded Chaney as theater commander on 24 June both a Chief Quartermaster, ETO, and a Chief, Quartermaster Service, SOS, were in existence. Both positions were in the hands of one general officer.[8] The history of the Quartermaster support mission in the United Kingdom and later in northwest Europe is largely bound to the fortunes of SOS ETOUSA and its successive commands. Likewise, the Quartermaster story is linked to the officer, who, in June 1942, was named to head it.

Organizing for BOLERO

In the formative period of the ETO staff it would be an error to regard the Chief Quartermaster (CQM) solely in terms of his official position and duties. The personality of a particular incumbent, QMC field doctrine and tradition or lack of them, and the logistical environment of a major military operation constantly interact to make the functioning staff officer different from the legal one. Born in October 1890, a South Carolinian, General Littlejohn, although more than fifty years of age, was notably self-reliant, active, and robust. Graduating from West Point in 1912, he served two years in the Cavalry before being detailed to the Quartermaster Corps. In France, duty with Brig. Gen. Harry L. Rogers gave him quartermaster experience at the highest field level. Over the next two decades his assignments at depots, service schools, on the War Depart-

ment General Staff, in the Philippines, and in the OQMG provided further rich experience. His interests and tastes were logistical in the broadest sense and were not narrowly confined to quartermaster detail. His last assignment before going overseas was as Chief, Clothing and Equipage Division, OQMG.

In the interwar period Littlejohn had spent considerable time in analyzing records and compiling dry-as-dust details about "pounds per man per day" and "square feet per man per day," weight and cube factors—all of which lay at the very basis of any logistical system. Though Quartermaster Corps archives provided little information, he gathered valuable data concerning World War I through correspondence and interviews with Lt. Gen. John L. DeWitt, former G–4, First Army, AEF, and later The Quartermaster General, and with Col. Martin C. Shallenberger, aide to General Pershing.[9] When he arrived in London on 4 June 1942, Littlejohn's first task, apart from drafting BOLERO Quartermaster plans, was to set up the Office of the Chief Quartermaster and prepare to deploy QMC personnel throughout an island base with particular attention to southwestern England.

In beginning work, Littlejohn took note of Lee's early dictum that SOS should figure computations broadly and boldly, always bearing in mind the big picture of ultimate objectives. Fortunately, to get a focus on any size of picture Lee might have had in mind, Littlejohn frequently consulted one of the rare copies, which he later discovered was the only one around the London headquarters, of Pershing's SOS record. Since few

---

[8] (1) Memo, Littlejohn for Lee, 19 May 42, sub: Pers; Memos, Littlejohn for TAG, 20 and 23 May 42, sub: Pers OCQM SOS; Memo, Littlejohn for Col James C. Longino, Rear Ech OCQM, 30 May 42, sub: Pers; Ltr, Littlejohn to Longino, 5 Jun 42. All in Littlejohn Collection, sec. II. (2) Ruppenthal, *Logistical Support*, vol. I, ch. I. (3) Even before Littlejohn's appointment was officially announced he had urged Eisenhower to approve this dual arrangement and the latter had agreed. Interv with Littlejohn, 5 Nov 59.

[9] (1) Littlejohn, ed., *Passing in Review*, ch. 25. (2) Interv with Littlejohn, 10 Aug 55.

SOS officers had had war experience, the volume became a valuable reference tool. As Littlejohn reflected on his organization, his gaze was fixed on the troop basis for Quartermaster Service, including recommendations for the procurement and the use of authorized T/O units and their immediate allotment to projected SOS subcommands. His estimate of manpower needed for such units, known as T/O personnel, like the one for casual or non-T/O personnel who would man SOS agencies and staffs, was at best an educated guess. It was still not clear just how the support command was to operate.

Before leaving the United States Littlejohn had examined Lee's staff chart. It reassigned two important functions traditionally performed by the Quartermaster. A general depot service and a motor transport service would operate under G–4, SOS, direction. On 23 May, The Adjutant General, War Department, had approved Littlejohn's request for 21 officers as non-T/O personnel to staff the Quartermaster Section of a general depot. As casuals, 9 senior officers were earmarked as division chiefs in OCQM. But Littlejohn persuaded Lee to allot him 25 more officers with the understanding that a total of 58 officers would be present in OCQM by the end of 1942. Littlejohn also asked The Quartermaster General, Maj. Gen. Edmund B. Gregory, to allot OCQM 50 junior officers for future service. Such a reserve would remain in training in the United States, becoming conversant with salvage problems, protective clothing, and storage and distribution procedures of Class I and II supply. Consistent with his idea of working directly with Gregory's office during this formative period,

Littlejohn left Col. James C. Longino in charge of OCQM's rear echelon in the United States in order to expedite personnel and supply. Though 44 officers were to have sailed with Littlejohn on 28 May, only one QMC officer actually accompanied him.[10]

Believing that his hand-picked staff would soon arrive, Littlejohn, who never hesitated to get his concepts down on paper, drafted his first organizational chart for OCQM on 8 June. Colonel Middleswart, designated as Deputy Chief Quartermaster, joined the special staff of Headquarters, ETOUSA, where strategic planning for ROUNDUP was centralized. The OCQM itself was to comprise ten divisions, organized mainly on the commodity lines recently discarded by the OQMG in Washington.[11] There was considerable justification for such conservatism in an overseas headquarters, where quartermasters attempting to operate in an unfamiliar environment obtained helpful guidance from familiar organizational concepts. The overseas organization was well suited to its original mission, and included one purely functional subagency, the Procurement Division, which reflected the actualities of operating in a friendly foreign country. Under those circumstances, local procurement was largely a matter of intergovernmental liaison, and not a function that could be handled conveniently on a commodity basis.

---

[10] Ltr, Littlejohn to Longino, 5 Jun 42. Littlejohn Collection, sec. II.

[11] (1) OCQM office Order 1, 8 Jun 42. Littlejohn Reading File, vol. I, item 5. (See Bibliographical Note.) (2) The ten divisions were: Executive, Accounts, Plans and Control, Subsistence, Supply, Fuel, Salvage, Procurement, Personnel, and Graves Registration. (3) Risch, *The Quartermaster Corps: Organization, Supply, and Services*, vol. I, ch. 1.

After 5 June as he talked more and more with General Lee, Littlejohn found that the depot plan which had been conceived in Washington in mid-May was outmoded. To avoid unnecessary construction, a large number of small depots already in existence in England would have to be operated in support of scattered troop stations, each of which would also require a post quartermaster system. Littlejohn had envisaged large quartermaster installations at major ports, but these were already too crowded. In addition, Lee stressed the point that the British would soon release depot facilities throughout southern England, not in the Midlands, in accordance with an elaborate plan worked out by Maj. Gen. Richard M. Wooten, the British Deputy Quartermaster General (Liaison). This news nullified Littlejohn's current personnel requests in the Office of The Quartermaster General. The speed with which Lee wanted his American staff to accept the British offers, plus the fact that SOS had only a vague notion as to where BOLERO's troops were to be concentrated, suggested that Littlejohn's manpower estimates were obsolete before he placed them on paper.

Working under these adverse conditions, Littlejohn instructed his future staff to initiate a series of studies on sundry quartermaster topics and to contact British ministries on retail matters. On 12 June he personally drafted BOLERO's detailed supply requirements. This was a difficult assignment. He had few QMC manuals at hand to work out basic logistical data and he therefore started to develop his own body of BOLERO manuals. Other staff studies estimated the local scene, noting all the prospective changes which OCQM would have to make in taking over quartermaster responsibilities from the British. Another study concerned the depot system or lack of it.

Confronted with a need for more and more studies and with no one to make them, Littlejohn looked to the whereabouts of his missing staff. With Lee's approval, he rushed off a message to Gregory for 400 officers, all of whom were expected before the end of 1942. This request was in addition to the fifty-eight officers whom Lee had already approved.[12] Summarizing his reactions to the local scene after a fortnight in England, Littlejohn wrote to the Deputy Quartermaster General:

. . . If one were given the job of organizing, from the Quartermaster angle, one half of the continental United States and at the same time creating a central office paralleling to a large extent the Office of the Quartermaster General a picture of the problem here would become apparent. . . . In a way I was rather unfortunate in not having moved into the European problem at the time the other individuals did. As a matter of fact, I believe I was the last to come on the scene. This forced me to depart from the United States without a thorough study of the personnel and supply problems and without having set up the necessary plans to make this end operate. . . . The minute I arrived various echelons expected me to start going full blast on every class of supplies in every direction. Actually, for a period of a week Zwicker and I had one desk between us, no typewriters and no clerks. . . . Within a few days I hope to dig into and straighten out the flow of supplies. Theoretically the troops are expected to

----

[12] (1) Interv with Littlejohn, 10 Aug 55. (2) Memo, Littlejohn for Lee, 9 Jun 42; Msg, Littlejohn for Lee to AGWAR, 9 Jun 42. Littlejohn Reading File, vol. 1, items 6, 8.

come into this area with sixty or ninety days supply. From this end the claim is that these supplies are not arriving.[13]

On 17 June Littlejohn submitted the first of a series of BOLERO Quartermaster plans to G–4, SOS.[14] In brief, its features of necessity appeared to be three-fourths British, one-quarter American, but the plan's tone suggested Quartermaster Service would become more American after the inauguration of a sound depot system. As he pondered over his supply plan, talked repeatedly to British colleagues, made trips to the field, and read the initial offerings of his arriving staff officers, Littlejohn's views on what he needed began to change and jell. His desire to apply his talents to the new and unorganized SOS, and the need to move sharply away from dependence on the British in an area where the Americans had not anticipated any large-scale troop concentrations, were powerful incentives in moving him to repeat his argument to General Gregory on the urgent need for 400 more QMC officers. The situation was aggravated by the fact that the Motor Transport Service and the General Depot Service in the ETO, neither of which was any longer connected with the Quartermaster Corps, had arranged to have considerable numbers of QMC officers assigned to them. Feeling that his previous requests for personnel had been evaded, Littlejohn on 26 June wrote to The Quartermaster General with some indignation:

I have been on the receiving end of the most definite "run-around" that I have ever known. . . . In discussing personnel matters with the other services I find an eagerness on the part of the Home Office to solve the problems in the field. Take the Ordnance Department for example. The Chief Ordnance Officer here was furnished with every man he asked for by name. He arrives with his staff consisting of all regular Colonels and all graduates of the Military Academy. I arrive with one Lieut. Colonel of the Regular Army and two Colonels of the Regular Army assigned but not arrived . . . All I ask for is my fair share of the good personnel—no more, no less. . . .[15]

At the end of June there were fifty casual QMC officers in the United Kingdom but only seventeen were in OCQM; the remainder had been attached to expanding SOS staffs. During the same period the arrival of T/O personnel in Quartermaster units was so slow that arranging for their reception was a very minor burden on the OCQM. At the end of June there were only seven such units in the British Isles, comprising less than 500 officers and men, mostly occupied in supporting the Eighth Air Force. The Personnel Division of the OCQM was preoccupied with plans for the somewhat distant future. It had computed the Quartermaster quota of 53,266 men for BOLERO already mentioned, basing this requirement upon the following detailed breakdown: [16]

Type of Unit	Number of Units	Total Strength
Total	163	53,226
Service Battalion	14	13,188
Bakery Company	16	2,608
Graves Registration Company	7	945
Shoe and Textile Repair Company (M)	19	3,838

---

[13] Ltr, Littlejohn to Brig Gen Henry D. Munnickhuysen, OQMG, 12 Jun 42. Littlejohn Reading File, vol. I, item 14.

[14] Memo, Littlejohn for ACofS G–4 SOS, 17 Jun 42. Littlejohn Reading File, vol. I, item 21.

[15] Ltr, Littlejohn to Gregory, 26 Jun 42. Littlejohn Reading File, vol. I, item 33.

[16] QM Supply in ETO, VIII, 2.

Type of Unit	Number of Units	Total Strength
Salvage Depot, Headquarters	2	414
Laundry Company	24	7,224
Sterilization and Bath Company	8	1,352
Salvage Collecting Company	6	1,230
Railhead Company	35	4,060
Depot Supply Company ..	24	3,648
Sales Commissary Company	3	615
Refrigeration Company ..	2	476
Refrigeration Company (M)	3	420
QM Service, Headquarters and Depot Overhead		13,208

In the summer of 1942 Littlejohn appeared to be planning and operating in a vacuum, at times working unwittingly at cross-purposes with the shifting designs of logisticians and authors of grand strategy. He told his officers that his sins would be sins of commission, not omission. He wrote frequent, brief memorandums to his staff, giving them one distinct impression—that OCQM could expect, by running hard, just barely to stay in place. Without warning, G–4, SOS, on 14 July 1942 emphasized his point with the announcement that the Quartermaster BOLERO quota was being cut to 39,000 men. No explanations were given. Immediately, OCQM drafted tables for Lee, indicating how BOLERO and ROUNDUP might suffer if the 14,000-man reduction took place. At the time Lee was sympathetic, but only President Roosevelt and his service advisers could explain all cuts in BOLERO. Throughout July the slowing down of troop arrivals discouraged OCQM. Early in August 2,438 Quartermaster troops in sixteen T/O units were present for a force of

82,000 men,[17] a ratio which Littlejohn considered far from ideal.

One aspect of the personnel problem showed a slight improvement. Competition for high-caliber supply personnel, as casuals, had intensified during the early summer of 1942 as Lee pushed his G–4 operation of the General Depot Service and the Motor Transport Service. A portion of this manpower was returned to the Quartermaster Service after Lee, following the lead of the War Department, abolished the General Depot Service in mid-August.[18] In the process Col. Turner R. Sharp, former Chief, General Depot Service, became a division chief within OCQM. But another need for additional personnel arose when Headquarters, SOS ETOUSA, moved to Cheltenham, a spa about ninety miles west of London. Two Quartermaster staffs came into existence, forcing Littlejohn to keep his deputy, Colonel Middleswart, on the staff of ETOUSA, and to separate the efforts of his BOLERO and ROUNDUP planners.[19]

By mid-July the organizational changes within SOS once again upset the OCQM's manpower estimates. Now its plans had to cover support of from fifteen to eighteen divisional areas and four corps areas as well as provide for items of common use for the expanding Eighth Air Force.

---

[17] (1) Memo, G-4 SOS for OCQM, 14 Jul 42; QM Station List, 7 Aug 42. Both in Hist Br OQMG. (2) Matloff and Snell, *Strategic Planning, 1941–1942*, ch. XIV.

[18] SOS ETOUSA Circular 13, 19 August 1942, failed to mention a General Depot Service, although other subagencies of SOS were listed. Circular 38, 27 October 1942, formally abolished the General Depot Service and assigned the CQM as supervisor of general depots.

[19] (1) GO 19, Hq ETOUSA, 20 Jul 42. (2) Ltr, Littlejohn to Middleswart, 28 Jul 42. Littlejohn Reading File, vol. II, item 65.

A minimum of fifteen general depots each with a Quartermaster Section had to be manned. Each divisional area, post, camp, and station required a post quartermaster system. Behind each corps area a base section was needed, calling for additional Quartermaster staffs and operational units. Four projected base sections would contain a total of fifty quartermaster branch depots and within each base section, districts would be marked off, requiring still more quartermasters in each SOS subdivision. At station hospitals a full Quartermaster complement was needed.[20]

The dimensions of this projected organization moved Littlejohn to revise upward every troop basis. Still preferring to solve his problems through the informal and unofficial QMC channel rather than effect solutions along command lines, Littlejohn addressed several more messages to Gregory. Gregory's reply of 10 July said in part ". . . I hope you will consider in your requirements for officers the whole Quartermaster picture. We have to supply Quartermasters to units all over the world. . . . I hope you will not ask for more officers than you need or faster than you need them. As I understand, we have sent you about 151 and are about to send you 150 more at once. This is a much higher proportion than is present in any other theater. . . ." This sort of answer was quite unsatisfactory to Littlejohn, and he tried to get Gregory to visit the European theater.[21] Failing in this, the Chief Quar-

termaster then redefined his manpower requirements as an official demand, and forwarded it to Somervell through Lee, who approved it without change on 31 July 1942. Quartermaster needs for casual personnel as of 1 April 1943 were summarized as 875 officers, 30 warrant officers, and 2,178 enlisted men, or a total of 3,083. OCQM itself required a strength of 315, including 100 officers.[22]

When OCQM moved to Cheltenham between 9 and 13 July 1942, it consisted of 13 officers, 21 enlisted men, and 16 British civilians, the latter performing clerical work. Operating OCQM on a 12- to 18-hour schedule after 22 July, Littlejohn, who had held Sunday morning conferences in London, now initiated a series of daily seminars among his key officers, opened a map room, and posted the quartermaster situation daily. As officers joined OCQM, they assembled essential planning data in notebooks. An initial assignment called for a geographic survey of their island base. Fledgling quartermasters, many fresh from the world of trade, studied standard logistical works dating back to World War I. Lists of British supply nomenclature and glossaries were compiled so that ignorance would not result in an uneconomical use of shipping space. For example, garbage cans were "dust bins" in Great Britain, and requirements and requisitions had to be so labeled. It was weeks before War Department circulars and technical

[20] Memo, Littlejohn for Longino, 15 Jul 42; Ltr, Littlejohn to Gregory through Lee, 31 Jul 42. Littlejohn Reading File, vol. II, items 52, 71.

[21] Ltr, Littlejohn to Lee for Somervell, 31 Jul 42; Ltr, Littlejohn to Gregory, 26 Jul 42; Ltr, Gregory to Littlejohn, 10 Jul 42; Ltr, Littlejohn to Gregory,

14 Jul 42. Littlejohn Reading File, vol. II, items 36, 40, 59, 70.

[22] (1) Ltr, Littlejohn to Gregory through Lee, 31 Jun 42. Littlejohn Reading File, vol. II, item 71. (2) The planning basis was 20 QMC officers per divisional area, 12 per general depot, and 5 per branch depot, plus an overhead for administration. Memo, Littlejohn for Longino, 15 Jul 42. Littlejohn Reading File, vol. II, item 52.

literature reached Cheltenham or London, and OCQM was therefore forced to formulate its own supply procedures and circulate them throughout the command.

Despite his practice of keeping in close touch with his subordinates' progress, Littlejohn continued to have difficulty getting the right man for the right job. Initially, many so-called experts reached Cheltenham, but not enough with the proper qualifications. Several requested reassignment after struggling with their unfamiliar duties. On the other hand career quartermasters grasped the scope of their responsibilities. As Executive Officer, OCQM, Col. Beny Rosaler, who was in his element in straightening out administrative confusion, supervised the work of briefing the command on Quartermaster procedure. In supply matters, Col. Turner R. Sharp (Depot Division, OCQM), Col. Oliver E. Cound (Stock Control Division, OCQM) and Lt. Col. Robert F. Carter (Subsistence Division, OCQM) indoctrinated reservists. Col. Aloysius M. Brumbaugh, chief of the Supply Division, himself a Reserve officer but one with much experience, also contributed to on-the-job training. The Germans unwittingly made their contribution. Many a young Quartermaster lieutenant fresh from Camp Lee, working late at night on requisitions or other essential staff actions, was rudely interrupted by the urgent need to take shelter. This type of realism accelerated training and produced capable officers just when they were required. Inasmuch as senior quartermasters were needed for depot commands, Littlejohn demanded that junior grade officers assume more of the staff load.[23]

By 8 August, 68 officers and 86 enlisted men were in OCQM and Littlejohn felt better about his staff situation. Now OCQM comprised 14 divisions broken down into 59 branches. The Executive Division administered the OCQM; the others developed policy and procedure, planned projects, and supervised or co-ordinated operations throughout an expanding SOS. The need to supervise and control increasingly decentralized field operations accounted for most of the organizational changes in the OCQM made since June 1942. To tie OCQM closer together, Littlejohn required each officer and branch to make a continuous study of Quartermaster reference data. Early in September eight studies on this subject were prepared and distributed.[24]

An early study grew out of Quartermaster troop planning for a "type" force of 600,000 men.[25] In mid-August ETOUSA asked OCQM to estimate the support for a type force containing a GHQ, 2 armies of 6 corps, and 16 divi-

44, 46. (2) Ltr, Littlejohn to Gregory, 8 Jul 42. Littlejohn Reading File, vol. II, item 21. (3) Critical comments by Maj Gen A. T. McNamara, TQMG, dated 12 Feb 60. Hist Br OQMG.

[24] (1) Ltr, Littlejohn to Gregory, 26 Jul 42; Min, OCQM Mtg of All Div Chiefs OCQM and Depot Comdrs and All QMSO's, 31 Jul 42. Littlejohn Reading File, vol. II, items 59, 72. (2) QM Supply in ETO, I, app. VIII. (3) QM Service Reference Data, vols. I–VIII, September–October 1942 (repeatedly revised and republished; see Bibliographical Note). Hist Br OQMG.

[25] "Type" forces were a mobilization planning concept developed by Army Ground Forces (AGF) to ensure that various types of ground combat troops were activated in the proper proportions. Typical armies and corps would have fixed amounts of organic army and corps troops. The concept was never intended for operational planning, and was abandoned by AGF in the 1943 Troop Basis. See Kent Roberts Greenfield, Robert R. Palmer, and Bell I. Wiley, The Organization of Ground Combat Troops, UNITED STATES ARMY IN WORLD WAR II (Washington, 1947), pp. 279–80.

[23] (1) Littlejohn, ed., Passing in Review, chs. 23,

sions, of which 7 would be triangular infantry divisions, 2 mechanized, 5 armored, and 2 airborne. In retrospect, such planning was academic during this period of watchful waiting. But in response to a G–4 request of 30 August, OCQM related its troop planning and supply support to a new concept. To meet the G–4 request calling for support to a type army of 300,000 men, OCQM hit upon the idea of tabulating troop units by Tables of Organization and Equipment and aggregate strength in proper balance to give maximum support to a type corps.[26] Known later as the 100,000-man plan, this was an important study in percentages and proportions. Continuously refined and revised to meet foreseeable conditions within a typical force under conditions consistent with current plans, this tabulation gave staffs at all echelons a simple arithmetical device for fitting a Quartermaster troop basis into any multiple of 100,000 men. As a reference tool, often used together with supply data, the 100,000-man plan was immediately accepted and applied by commanders to future operations.[27]

The OCQM structure at the beginning of August reflected its growing activities within an expanding SOS. On 20 July 1942 Lee had announced SOS regional subcommands wherein Quartermaster operations were to be decentralized. The projected four corps build-up was approaching reality as Headquarters, II Corps, now arriving in England, joined

Headquarters, V Corps, late in July. With boundaries that closely corresponded to those of British administrative commands, four SOS base sections with respective headquarters were constituted as follows: Northern Ireland Base Command (Belfast); Western Base Section (Chester); Eastern Base Section (Watford); and Southern Base Section (Wilton).[28] *(Map 1)* On 7 August, five general depots, Burton-on-Trent, Thatcham, Ashchurch, Bristol, and Taunton, and three Quartermaster branch depots, Wellingborough, Kettering, and London, were in operation.[29]

As Chief Quartermaster, Littlejohn had authority to supervise and control technical matters at all echelons. Within the base sections and their respective depots, he recommended the selection and placement of Quartermaster supply officers. On the other hand each base section commander controlled operations within his own area. Thus, as in World War I, the overlapping of command and staff responsibilities produced a host of nagging conflicts as depot commanders, usually colonels of the Quartermaster Corps, were caught between OCQM's instructions and the base section commander's orders. One early conflict was of a serious nature, involving the primary mission of the Quartermaster Corps. The case in point developed in Southern Base Section where the commander, Col. Charles O. Thrasher, set arbitrary levels of supply. To OCQM, this action made the retail aspect of supply of greater importance than the wholesale, and threatened the whole carefully organized

---

[26] (1) Memo, Middleswart for Col Stadtman, War Plans Sec ETO, 16 Aug 42. Poore Papers. (2) Ltrs, OCQM to G–4 SOS, 17 Jul 42 and 30 Aug 42. Hist Br OQMG.

[27] After World War II similar data were incorporated in staff officers' basic field manuals and service school courses. See FM 101–10, August 1949.

[28] Ruppenthal, *Logistical Support*, I, 84–87.

[29] For a complete list of United Kingdom depots, see below, Chapter IX, Table 6.

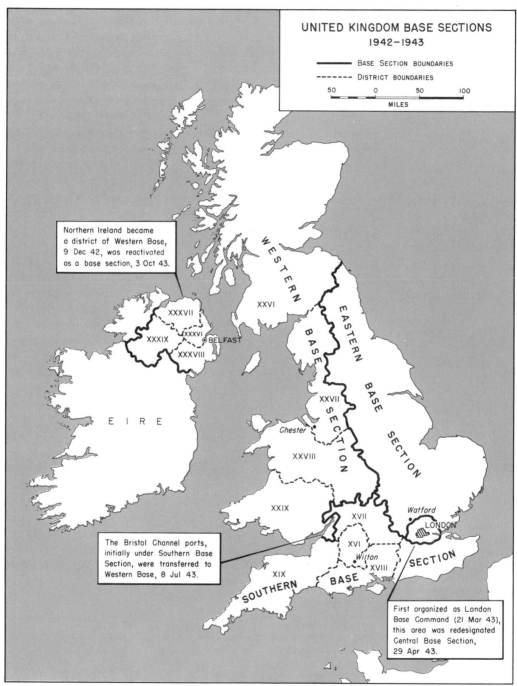

UNITED KINGDOM BASE SECTIONS
1942–1943

——————— BASE SECTION BOUNDARIES
- - - - - - - DISTRICT BOUNDARIES

50   0   50   100

MILES

Northern Ireland became
a district of Western Base,
9 Dec 42, was reactivated
as a base section, 3 Oct 43.

XXXVII

XXXIX   XXXVI

XXXVIII

BELFAST

WESTERN BASE SECTION

EASTERN BASE SECTION

XXVI

XXVII

Chester

XXVIII

XXIX

E I R E

The Bristol Channel ports,
initially under Southern Base
Section, were transferred to
Western Base, 8 Jul 43.

XVII

XVI

Wilton

XVIII

Watford

LONDON

SECTION

XIX

SOUTHERN   BASE

First organized as London
Base Command (21 Mar 43),
this area was redesignated
Central Base Section,
29 Apr 43.

U. Brooks

MAP 1

stock control system with anarchy. If continued, the policy would mean the depletion of stocks being stored for combat at a future date, and deprive the OCQM of control over theater supply levels. Littlejohn had the policy set aside through Lee's personal intervention, and, working through the base section Quartermaster staff, retained the authority to set supply levels.[30]

An early depot problem concerned British civilian workers. For BOLERO, Littlejohn estimated he would need 12,-000 local citizens to fill clerical, supervisory, and laboring jobs. Because British laws were complex and little understood by Americans, civilians were paid and administered by the British War Office. Yet problems over wages, hours, quarters, and conditions of employment soon developed and Littlejohn himself often attended to them. In July 1942 the Chief Quartermaster personally satisfied the charwomen of Cheltenham with a tea and milk ration, and they stayed on his payroll. On occasion, he was able to attract and hold competent civilians by the simple device of giving them the substantial U.S. ration.[31]

Quartermaster depot and service troops created additional problems. The first to arrive were only partially trained in their specialties. Moreover, when they should have been at their regular duties they had to spend precious time mastering their weapons and the manual of arms, since this type of training was also incomplete. Littlejohn deplored the personnel policy which assigned to the QMC enlisted men who were predominantly of inferior intelligence or deficient education, or both. Many of the depot companies and practically all of the service battalions were composed of Negro troops with low Army General Classification Test (AGCT) grades. These units were not representative of Negroes in the Army. Irrespective of color, the number of men who were suitable candidates for commissions, or even for promotion to noncommissioned officers was far too low. Under hastily trained and completely inexperienced young white officers, these troops did not perform very well. The British attitude of friendly tolerance toward all foreigners, regardless of color, surprised both officers and men, and probably aggravated the disciplinary problems in these units. Littlejohn was inclined to lay most of the blame on the officers. He was alarmed to find that even many of the service battalion commanders were lacking in field experience, and he had to devote considerable time to finding competent commanders for these units—something which, he believed, should have been accomplished before they were allowed to leave the zone of interior.[32]

[30] Ltr. Littlejohn to Lee, 11 Feb 43, sub: Relationship Between Base Sec Comds and Supply Installations. Littlejohn Reading File, vol. X, item 13.

[31] (1) QM Supply in ETO, VIII, 55–57. (2) Interv with Littlejohn, 22 Mar 56. (3) Memo, Hq Comdt SOS for Post QM SOS Hq, 27 Jan 43. USFET AG 403. (4) In August 1942, Lt. Col. Samuel M. MacGuire was added to the OCQM staff as British Liaison Officer (Labor). He remained with the U.S. headquarters in the British Isles until May 1945, and was invaluable in solving problems involving procurement, retention, and payment of British civilians. Ltr, CQM to CG ETO, 16 Jun 45, sub: Recommendation for Award of Legion of Merit, Littlejohn Reading File, vol. XXXVII, item 49.

[32] (1) Rpt, OCQM to OQMG for ASF, 12 May 43, sub: Answer to Questions Submitted to CQM. Hist Br OQMG. (2) Risch, The Quartermaster Corps: Organization, Supply, and Services, II, 168ff. (3) Dwight D. Eisenhower, Crusade in Europe (New York: Doubleday & Company, Inc., 1948), p. 58.

In addition to coping constantly with problems of decentralization, by mid-July 1942 Littlejohn found himself coordinating more and more jobs with adjacent and higher headquarters. In London, he kept in touch with Middleswart's planning on ROUNDUP. At Cheltenham he worked with SOS boards of officers, committees, schools, and other chiefs of services. After its creation in late June, Littlejohn became the Quartermaster member on the SOS General Purchasing Board, which set policy for matters of local procurement. The board operated under a General Purchasing Agent, Col. Douglas B. Mackeachie. Littlejohn designated Col. Wayne R. Allen, who had had rich administrative experience as an executive of Los Angeles County, California, as his procurement specialist, and later appointed him to the board. Allen's job called for the highest type of co-ordination, and upon Mackeachie's return to the United States for an important assignment at the end of 1942, Allen became the General Purchasing Agent, a promotion which suggests the high quality of his quartermaster activities.[33]

Centralization of control touched other Quartermaster fields. Littlejohn's Class III responsibilities made him a member of the Area Petroleum Board, headed by an area POL officer, whose job it was to co-ordinate requirements among the Army, Navy, and Air Forces within the theater. To train all sorts of technical specialists, SOS opened the American School Center at Shrivenham, England. Littlejohn added a school course for cooks and bakers on 8 September. Lack of instructors kept OCQM's initial contribution from extending to mess management and food service. These classes were begun later in the year, and Littlejohn also started field courses for bakery platoons at Tidworth.[34]

Having taken over the General Depot Service from G–4, SOS, OCQM acquired additional duties, when, on 19 August 1942, it assumed control of the Army Exchange Service, first of its planning activities, and later of its operations. In the summer of 1942 this was a logical arrangement because OCQM was far advanced in procuring local Army Exchange Service items, had depot facilities, and understood issue problems. Lacking issue clerks, OCQM initially proposed to operate a canteen service, combining the operational features of a sales commissary and a post exchange. On 30 August Littlejohn brought Col. Edmund N. Barnum and his former Army Exchange Service staff to Cheltenham, incorporated them as a division in OCQM, and planned to send mobile sales stores to troop stations.[35]

Mid-September found the Chief Quartermaster hoping that he could devote more and more time to developing Lee's plans, turning details over to his division chiefs and leaving operations to base and depot quartermasters. Much of the organizational confusion of the past summer was subsiding. With emphasis on

---

[33] (1) Memo, DCofS WD for CG USAFBI, 16 May 42, sub: Establishment of a Gen Purch Bd in the British Isles for the European Area. USFET AG 334. (2) Ruppenthal, *Logistical Support*, I, 76–87. (3) First Report of the General Purchasing Board, Covering Operations to 1 September 1942. Hist Br OQMG.

[34] (1) Littlejohn, ed., Passing in Review, ch. 18, pp. 1–5; ch. 32, pp. 7–11.
[35] Ltr, Littlejohn to Barnum, 23 Aug 42; Memo Littlejohn for Barnum, 4 Sep 42. Littlejohn Reading File, vol. III, item 32; vol. V, item 6.

BOLERO instead of ROUNDUP, SOS was expanding rapidly and Littlejohn's colleagues greatly respected the leading role he had played in its development. Momentarily it appeared that his own days of orientation and improvisation were over. He had tried to eliminate defects in his organization, to create a body of Quartermaster literature to fit BOLERO, and to keep his supply planning up to date.[36]

Supply Planning for BOLERO

The authors of BOLERO in spring 1942 had made only a tentative and hurried investigation of the complex supply situation which faced OCQM. In the summer of 1942 the major problems of OCQM arose from a shortage of storage space and from the promise of a surplus of shipping which never materialized. To overcome these obstacles, considerable spadework had to be done. Quartermaster supply planning after 8 June 1942 was closely meshed with that of other staffs at all levels, and influence did not always flow down from the upper staff levels to OCQM. Concurrence, often accompanied by correction of detail and by clarification of missions, came from Littlejohn's staff. With only a few of his division chiefs available, he presented his first supply plan to G–4, SOS, on 17 June 1942. The plan suggests that he had carefully reviewed the BOLERO Key Plans and had attempted to keep abreast of Lee's planning.[37]

OCQM's plan conformed to four estimates which BOLERO planners had outlined late in May.[38] These included estimates of the troop basis for BOLERO, the composition of the force including the priority in which the units were to arrive, the tentative shipping schedule, and the preparations which the British and Americans were making for the reception and accommodation of BOLERO troops and cargo. As bulletins of information, the Key Plans of summer, 1942—a second edition would be published on 25 July to reflect the situation at the end of June 1942—had anticipated remarkably well what OCQM's requirements and problems of procurement, storage, and distribution would be.

BOLERO operated on certain assumptions which conditioned Littlejohn's first draft plan. As strategists had studied invasion plans for ROUNDUP, they agreed that U.S. troops should take the right of the line, the British the left. Logically, this placed the Quartermaster build-up in southwestern England, or on the right of the line as BOLERO troops faced the Continent. Although cargo and a few troops had begun to arrive in the ports on the Clyde and the Mersey, the earliest depots had been located inland from the Bristol Channel. It was logical to continue and expand this deployment of men and their resources. Another assumption was based on the steady growth of the Quartermaster Service. The British were gradually to relinquish their responsibilities toward the Americans as the latter demonstrated that they could handle their own services of supply. While he recognized that the build-up phase would be governed by tactical requirements, Littlejohn planned to concentrate on BOLERO first, and then on

---

[36] Memo, OCQM for G–4 SOS, 1 Aug 42. Littlejohn Reading File, vol. II, item 1.

[37] Memo, Littlejohn for ACofS G–4 SOS, 17 Jun 42. Littlejohn Reading File, vol. I, item 21.

[38] Ruppenthal, *Logistical Support,* I, 59–87.

ROUNDUP. This meant that during the summer of 1942, the Chief Quartermaster might have some time, at least, in which to develop first his organization, next his levels of supply, and then his services.[39]

In terms of his daily wholesale and retail mission, Littlejohn entered a vast unplanned area in summer 1942. His task was to reduce his requirements to a simple expression, namely, pounds of quartermaster supply per man per day. This was difficult to compute because the basic Tables of Organization and Equipment were often not available, were obsolete, were constantly being modified, or were little understood by his freshmen planners. Ultimately, after hundreds of man-hours of tedious work, the estimated gross weight factor appeared to stand steady at 27 pounds per man per day, broken down by class of supply as follows: food, 6 pounds; clothing and equipment, soap, and other expendables, 1½ pounds; petroleum products, 15 pounds; solid fuels, 3½ pounds; and miscellaneous items such as post exchange and sales store items, 1 pound. By multiplying these factors by the number of men involved, Littlejohn could estimate his requirements for a day of supply for the entire ROUNDUP force.

Concurrently OCQM worked out its space requirements as the basis of a storage and distribution system. These factors expressed supply in terms of square feet per man per day. Then both space and weight factors were neatly arranged in tables, ready for the day when supplies rolled in. Late in June OCQM began to requisition its Class II

and IV supply from the United States, to explore what could be procured locally, and to locate storage.[40]

The scene of Quartermaster BOLERO activities, the United Kingdom, was 3,200 nautical miles from Littlejohn's port of embarkation, New York City. The round trip to Bristol Channel ports took forty days for troop ships and sixty days for cargo vessels. Class I and III supplies, automatically issued, and Class II and IV supplies, periodically requisitioned, would come from the New York Port of Embarkation (NYPE). The plan complied with earlier directives that everything possible would be procured locally, and it was in line with the War Department's announced objective of January 1942 to set a 60-day level for Quartermaster supply in the United Kingdom. This objective was revised on 6 July to give zone of interior port commanders more authority in the logistical system, and to set up an additional 15-day cushion of supply. Littlejohn had anticipated this action, and his first Class II and IV requisitions, submitted early in July, recommended the higher levels. Littlejohn's memorandum expressed the hope that the 75-day levels could be reached before the end of September. Thereafter, he proposed to maintain BOLERO stocks by securing shipments for both maintenance and reserve in accordance with troop arrivals within a given month.[41]

To bring Quartermaster supply to the prescribed levels, the War Department had delegated to the Army Service Forces authority to approve overseas allowances,

---

[39] Ltr, Littlejohn to Lee, 14 Jul 42, sub: QM Storage Reqmts. Littlejohn Reading File, vol. II, item 43.

[40] (1) Interv with Littlejohn, 22 Mar 56. (2) Ltr, OCQM to CG SOS ETOUSA, 14 Jul 42, sub: QMC Warehousing Plan. Littlejohn Reading File, vol. II, item 43.

[41] Memo cited n. 37, above.

name the ports of embarkation, place representatives of ASF and of each technical service at the New York Port of Embarkation, provide shipping, and announce policy for port commanders.[42] The New York port commander, with clearer authority after 6 July, controlled the flow of Quartermaster supply, effected automatic issue, filled requisitions, and recommended through ASF to OQMG the minimum reserves to be held at the port and amounts to be stocked in inland depots. The NYPE commander also controlled scarce shipping, edited requisitions, and served as a link between Littlejohn's staff and Gregory's office.

In the United Kingdom OCQM effected distribution by co-ordination with SOS transportation agencies. Early in its history, OCQM insisted that manifests reach its officers in advance so that, where practicable, storage and distribution could be planned ahead. Quartermaster requisitions were submitted through G–4, SOS, to NYPE by class of supply. Special needs, supply shortages, and other difficulties were reported in the same way. Notwithstanding the absence of a depot system in the summer of 1942, Littlejohn prepared a plan requiring his mythical depot supply officers to report weekly stock levels. To receive rations, organizations had to present strength returns, preferably consolidated at divisional level, and at the time of its writing, Littlejohn's plan envisaged the receipt of eighteen divisional reports. He had devised a new requisition form for use as a voucher, and desired each division to consolidate all requisitions to facilitate supply.

Local commanders and Quartermaster supply officers in general depots were to be authorized to sign certificates of expenditure for property to the value of $100.00. Chiefs of technical services would be authorized to approve certificates when the value did not exceed $5,000.00. In regard to local procurement procedure, Littlejohn suggested that he would furnish an estimate of Quartermaster requirements every six months in advance to the general purchasing agent, and report actual needs on a quarterly basis. Whenever practicable, he proposed to decentralize Quartermaster purchasing to depots, camps, posts, and stations.

The first ration plan for BOLERO, which had to conform to the 75-day levels set by the War Department, provided for a field ration at a 55-day level and an operational ration at a 20-day level.[43] The British-American ration, announced on 29 May, was to remain in effect and was to be supplemented by each combat division and air unit through the local procurement of foodstuffs. OCQM had no choice in this planning step, and always considered it tentative as subsistence experts at Cheltenham went about placing all U.S. troops on a type A field ration. Early in July 1942, OCQM championed the cause of outdoor manual workers, increasing their ration by 15 percent. They required more nourishment than the 4,070 calories of the British-American ration.

The 17 June plan announced, meanwhile, that the 20-day level for operational rations was to be broken down into a 17-day stockage of type C or K, and a 3-day level for the D ration. The distribution plan called for the troops to keep

---

[42] Leighton and Coakley, *Global Logistics, 1940–1943*, ch. XIII.

[43] Ltr, Littlejohn to Lee, 2 Jul 42, sub: Ration Reserves. Littlejohn Reading File, vol. II, item 4.

with them a day's D ration, a week's C or K type, and two days of the B ration. In forward areas there was to be a month's supply, of which 10 days, as noted above, was in the troops' hands. It is interesting to note that this distribution plan for operational rations was to influence greatly what the soldiers soon carried ashore in their first amphibious operation, that against North Africa. In reserve depots, a 45-day level was to be held. Aware that the British controlled all cold storage space, Littlejohn estimated that his requirement for refrigerated reserve foods would be a minimum of 30 days. With his subsistence needs on paper, and the first shipments on order at NYPE, Littlejohn's next task was to find storage space for rations.

In the concluding paragraph of his plan Littlejohn asked G–4, SOS, for an early decision on the line of demarcation between the post exchange service and the Quartermaster operation of sales stores. He was not suggesting Quartermaster operation of the post exchange but anticipated confusion if lines of responsibility were not set immediately. OCQM understood that on a wholesale basis it was to procure and store post exchange items, and that the job would be accomplished in line with the retailer's wishes. Littlejohn had no evidence of what the Army Exchange Service needed, and the troops would demand such services immediately upon arrival. Unfortunately, G–4, SOS, was unable to arrive at any immediate decision. Two months later, OCQM incorporated the Army Exchange Service as a staff section on its roster, as already described.[44]

On the same day that he submitted his first detailed supply plan, 17 June 1942, Littlejohn set out with General Lee and other SOS officers on a tour of England, including depot sites at Bristol, Exeter, Taunton, Westminster, Thatcham, and Salisbury, all of which later became key Quartermaster installations. During this trip he strengthened his conviction that all field quartermasters must have a "look-see" for themselves on important depot sites instead of accepting observer reports or the British paper offer. Many depots were converted civilian buildings not built for military use and located far from projected troop cantonments. He also saw that quartermaster resources in the United Kingdom were not fully at his disposal. They were controlled in the interests of a global imperial strategy by the British War Office, whose attention as June came to an end was riveted on recent German successes in Libya that endangered British sea power in the eastern Mediterranean.

In attempting to co-ordinate his own arrangements with the first BOLERO Key Plan, Littlejohn recognized that the British had been as generous as possible in making their resources available. Yet the Key Plan allowed only a glimpse of the real conditions in the United Kingdom. Littlejohn saw that it was not an ideal Quartermaster base.[45] The British Isles had supported 48,000,000 people during more than two years of war, including the supreme crisis which Churchill had eloquently proclaimed as "their finest hour," but the requirements of the U.S. Army weighed down an economy that was already severely and increasingly regimented by a stringent ra-

---

[44] GO 31, SOS ETOUSA, 24 Aug 42.

[45] Entries in Littlejohn Reading File, vol. II, items 1–72, support his views.

tioning system. Military service and war industries had claimed most of the available labor supply. The Axis Powers, concentrating on winning the current Battle of the Atlantic, had made Allied shipping a primary target.

As he traveled Littlejohn perceived many of the problems his future planners would have to consider. First, they must acknowledge the position of the British in supporting their own portion of BOLERO and ROUNDUP as well as playing host to American troops. Second, all scales of accommodation would be upset if procurement quartermasters ignored British standards and wastefully prescribed greater comforts for the Americans. Third, quartermasters had to be patient with centralized British administration, conducted through a complex of ministries. And fourth, in deference to British methods and means, American quartermasters had to unlearn or lay aside their training in such things as mass production and thinking in expansive terms. For example, storage experts could not enjoy the advantages of laying large areas of concrete in a minimum amount of time because this technique was not understood in England.

Littlejohn foresaw that in managing depots American officers might be frustrated by a host of little things. One embarrassment might result from voltage variations as quartermasters tried to operate electric power tools and lights. Tools of American design simply refused to fit local plumbing and electrical systems. Lack of time and resources restricted any alterations in British buildings. Along with colleagues in the engineer and transport services, quartermasters had to share all the griefs which British hard subsoil and insular weather

heaped upon their construction activities. In looking over the sites which he might eventually inherit from the British, Littlejohn foresaw that his staff could easily misunderstand why the British had divorced their depots from access to water, to transportation sidings, to sewage systems, and, above all, to any logistical blueprint that contemplated an offensive against Hitler's Europe. Of course, British depots had been dispersed for defensive warfare long before Americans had entered the war.[46]

Though quartermasters no longer operated a transportation system, they remained an integral part of BOLERO's distribution system. Littlejohn noted in June 1942 that the Irish Sea ports were open, but had obsolescent facilities that were not very well prepared to handle the influx of BOLERO's 1,000,000 men and their supplies in the short space of ten months. He doubted that the rail transport system for clearing the ports could handle the estimated additional monthly burden of 100,000 men and 120 ship cargoes.

As for storage estimates, Littlejohn's field trip confirmed his belief that his own 9 June figures were much more accurate than the estimates he had received from BOLERO planners upon his arrival in London. They had estimated that SOS would require 15,000,000 square feet of covered storage, including 1,230,000 square feet of shop space. This space, beginning 1 July, was needed at the rate of 1,333,000 square feet a month. Of the total space the Quartermaster share approximated 4,000,000 (gross) square feet,

───────────
[46] (1) Littlejohn, ed., Passing in Review, ch. 44. (2) Ltr, Littlejohn to Scowden, 9 Aug 42. Littlejohn Reading File, vol. III, item 13.

a figure which Littlejohn's own slide rule practically tripled.

After his June trip and those of early July the space problem appeared insignificant as compared to the problem of depot location and the condition of the sites. Of necessity, SOS had accepted space for the projected eighteen divisional areas, "in penny postage-stamp size, on a where is, as is" basis. To reach its storage goals many new construction projects were unavoidable unless OCQM was resourceful and uncomplaining. Since there was a critical shortage of construction materials (all lumber would have to be imported) a maximum of ingenuity was clearly indicated. To turn British depots to full account, Littlejohn saw that adroit administration had to be exercised by his depot quartermasters from the beginning.[47]

A field quartermaster could foresee most of the physical limitations which the BOLERO Key Plans imposed on the formative period of his wholesale support mission, but it was more difficult, and just as important, for him to understand the challenge a million Americans away from home invited to his retail support mission—housekeeping. He had to find ways and means to impress his problems on those at home who had the job of supporting him. Equally important, he had to impress upon the combat troops and their commanders the need for supply discipline and a certain amount of self-denial during the period of waiting in the British Isles.

The characteristic traits of the American soldier, while an asset to the combat commander, constitute a grave problem for the quartermaster. The qualities of individual initiative and ready adaptability that make him a formidable opponent in battle also make him demanding and individualistic in his relations with the supply services. American armies have always been composed of citizen soldiers, very conscious of their status as citizens. With combat experience such veterans develop the competence, but never the point of view of professional soldiers. They will endure the privations, the fatigue, and the serious injuries of war—not silently, but with that minimum of grumbling characteristic of good troops. But they protest vociferously against even minor hardships when not actually engaged in combat. Partly trained and untried soldiers vocalize even more loudly regarding the exposure, hunger, and fatigue that inevitably accompany advanced combat training. It should be remembered that the United Kingdom was a training ground as well as a staging area for U.S. troops.

American soldiers expected to find a large part of their accustomed civilian environment in Great Britain. Quartermasters were expected to supply cigarettes requisitioned by brand name, nickel candy bars, two-piece metal razors, comic books, the latest magazines, and all the peacetime gadgetry of a modern industrial nation. The applied psychology of combat commanders convinced the men that they were the best soldiers in the world and tended to carry with it the conviction that they deserved the best the world had to offer in supplies and services. Many officers appeared to share this conviction. The situation inevitably thrust the role of King Solomon upon the theater quartermaster, who had

---

[47] Ltr, OCQM to CG SOS ETOUSA, 14 Jul 42, sub: QMC Warehousing Plan. Littlejohn Reading File, vol. II, item 43.

to approve some demands, deny others, and then attempt to secure the concurrence and co-operation of all concerned. The Americans shared some, but not all, of Britain's wartime hardships in 1942, and possibly their presence speeded up an improvement in the local standard of living in the summer of 1943, when the shipping crisis was overcome.[48]

Normally, Quartermaster operations follow the steps of planning, organization, and logistical preparations. When Littlejohn returned to London at the end of June, all BOLERO phases were abreast. His 17 June plan, his trip, and staff studies by OCQM's division chiefs began to bear fruit in early July. Ably assisted by Colonel Allen, Littlejohn turned his attention to local procurement in order to save shipping space and money. It was a promising vineyard. Deals ranged from beer to undertaker's supplies. But each Quartermaster class of supply involved different acceptable standards and OCQM itself had to decide how far it could go in deviating from those standards in order to co-operate with the British. For instance with rations compromises might possibly be reached as long as the substitute food-stuffs complied with U.S. food laws and provided the American soldier with enough calories, minerals, and vitamins to keep him physically fit. English farmers had large surpluses of potatoes and cabbage but a steady diet of these would be monotonous, and, in the long run, injurious.

With Class II supplies there was more latitude in accepting products which could be procured locally. On the other hand clothing specifications and general supplies and organizational equipment were too highly specialized to permit local procurement by a British or British-American committee not familiar with the items' intended use in the U.S. Army. Once the British had determined there was a capacity to produce U.S. Army requirements (to save transatlantic shipping) and then agreed to produce an item, OCQM was determined to hold the British to the agreement. A companion to his local procurement activities, Littlejohn foresaw, would necessarily be an OCQM research and development program. With it, OCQM could be in a much better position to exploit local facilities, to perfect its own standards, or to entrust OQMG with furthering its field projects.[49]

Littlejohn's proposals regarding local procurement were accepted. Colonel Mackeachie would procure and inspect all local supplies, perfect arrangements with designated agents of British ministries or other allied or neutral governments, make arrangements for services and labor, issue regulations, and consolidate SOS purchases. Colonel Allen, as agent for OCQM, was to present Quartermaster estimates to Mackeachie and Lee six months in advance, and detailed requirements quarterly.

On 1 July 1942 Allen submitted his first estimates outlined in eleven broad listings to Littlejohn. The report gave British light industry sources of supply, suggested products of Ireland, Spain, and Portugal for investigation, noted items definitely available, and listed those of doubtful availability which needed

---

[48] (1) Interv with Littlejohn, 10 Aug 55. (2) Littlejohn, ed., Passing in Review, ch. 25.

[49] Ltr, Littlejohn to Brig Gen Frank F. Scowden, 1 Aug 42. Littlejohn Reading File, vol. II, item 2.

further study by both the British and OCQM. In forwarding Allen's report to Lee, the CQM remarked that some decisions might be reached immediately, others could drag on for months. Specifically, Littlejohn understood that BOLERO's camp equipment could be procured from British sources, initially for 250,000 men, and by D-day for the full troop basis. He also reported that locally produced equipment for laundry, shoe repair, and bakery companies was under discussion and test. Shoe repair equipment, he believed, would have to be imported, while trailer-mounted laundry and bakery machinery, if available, might be delivered locally, in limited quantities.[50]

With many details still to be clarified, the British agreed to furnish from a common pool requirements of frozen pork, lamb, and mutton, and also beans, cereals, National Wheatmeal Flour, potatoes, bread, lard, sugar, sirup, tea, fresh vegetables, and several other foods. Regarding Class II and IV supplies, Allen continued to make considerable progress, having presented orders to British firms for office equipment, furniture, soap, cleaning materials, most camp stores (including a cot and two British blankets per man), all mess gear, and tent poles. Littlejohn told Lee that OCQM intended to recover the issue of the all-wool U.S. blankets, storing them for continental operations.[51] In anticipation of assuming responsibility for the supply of common-use

items to the Eighth Air Force on 1 August, Littlejohn advised Lt. Col. Lois C. Dill, air force quartermaster, of what he might expect from local sources. Dill drew rations from Kettering and clothing from Wellingborough.[52]

As summer advanced and shipping space grew scarcer, Littlejohn's time was almost completely monopolized by local procurement matters. Administrative hitches developed, and procedures had to be established, of which many were not clarified until early 1943. With various economies in mind, meanwhile, on 4 July 1942 OCQM proposed and the British agreed to exchange certain Class I and II items—at first, blankets, wool drawers, and undershirts—before 1 January 1943. On 26 July 1942 the War Department approved the "swap idea," but within a week reversed the policy, holding that items would only be procured on a reverse lend-lease basis. Littlejohn asked Lee to have Somervell reinstate the exchange agreements, especially on food. The British previously had given assurances that components of the recently announced type A field ration (July 1942) could be furnished locally with the possible exception of pork, cheese, evaporated milk, and dried beans. At three-month intervals, both parties would consider issues from the British reserve of foodstuffs.

On 17 September Somervell reaffirmed his original instructions, namely, that local resources were to be exploited to the maximum extent, with reverse lend-lease still to be the basis for the program. Such supplies had to conform with standard American equipment or

[50] (1) Memo, Littlejohn for Lee, 1 Jul 42. Littlejohn Reading File, vol. II, item 2. (2) First Rpt of Gen Purch Bd. . . . Hist Br OQMG. (3) Littlejohn, ed., Passing in Review, ch. 41. (4) Memo, Lt Col O. C. Mood for Chief Proc Div SOS, 2 Jul 42. USFET AG 421, GPA.

[51] Littlejohn, ed., Passing in Review, ch. 44.

[52] Memo, Littlejohn for Dill, 3 Jul 42, sub: Supplies.

comply with U.S. food laws. Foodstuffs and Class II and IV items had to be handled in a simple, direct fashion, remaining under the complete control of Eisenhower. Somervell granted Littlejohn authority to procure (1) food for which no replacement to British stocks was necessary; (2) food whose packaging or processing would appreciably increase cargo tonnage; (3) emergency food, even though replacement was necessary; and (4) perishable food, requiring replacement, which would spoil if unused. Somervell also wanted clearly defined procedures to be established between the British Ministry of Food and OCQM. He said that food, to be replaced by the War Department, would be requisitioned. OCQM continued to procure locally from the NAAFI a wide variety of vegetables, fruits, and condiments.[53] The 17 September directive now cleared the way for Littlejohn to continue negotiations with the British but in the autumn months of 1942 the OCQM found itself confronted with many administrative bottlenecks, involving conditions of purchase, communication channels, and British standards.

Local procurement appeared particularly promising in POL supply. When Littlejohn began to analyze ROUNDUP in detail, he noted on 17 July that the initial invasion plans called for 5-gallon gasoline cans. The assault phase required 6,000,000 cans, of which 400,000 were for water. On 29 July, Mackeachie ordered 50,000 cans from NYPE and enough prefabricated parts to assemble 500,000 more each month prior to D-day in the United

Kingdom. The War Department replied that it would ship one million complete units as a reserve, and also the machinery for assembling the prefabricated cans. As part of his July 1942 procurement program Littlejohn sought a British plant to house the American machinery, which was scheduled to arrive in two months. In November 1942, the War Department for strategic reasons decided to defer this shipment and continued to ship a modest number of cans from the United States. The can assembly project was not revived until early 1943.[54]

Deliveries from OCQM's local procurement activities in 1942 totaled 184,-822 dead-weight long tons and represented a saving in shipping space of 259,334 measurement tons (40 cubic feet per measurement ton), broken down by class of supply as follows: [55]

Class of Supply	Long Tons	Measurement Tons
Total	184,822	259,334
I	57,707	93,579
II	2,825	15,930
III	113,863	128,905
IV	10,427	20,920

TORCH Interrupts BOLERO's Quartermasters

Events far from the British Isles compromised Littlejohn's first Quartermaster plan of 17 June, as well as his later ones of July and August which had grown out of its details. But to its authors, the framing of a detailed Quartermaster plan for BOLERO was an experi-

---

[53] (1) QM Supply in ETO, I, 29–35. (2) Littlejohn, ed., Passing in Review, ch. 41. (3) Ltr, Lee to Eisenhower, 14 Oct 42, sub: Proc and Supply Level of Class I Supplies. USFET AG 400.145.

[54] (1) QM Supply in ETO, IV, 29–31. (2) Ltr, Littlejohn to Lee, 6 Nov 42. Littlejohn Reading File, vol. VI, item 35. (3) See below, ch. VI.
[55] Littlejohn, ed., Passing in Review, ch. 41, p. 31.

ence as valuable to Littlejohn's new Quartermaster staff as a maneuver is to a tactician. Before June had expired, planners were fashioning a Mediterranean strategy, presenting BOLERO quartermasters with a serious rival for resources. In fact, the attack in the western Mediterranean could have meant the end of BOLERO preparations but as a result of a series of compromises the basic plan of BOLERO was preserved, although momentarily suspended. By 25 July 1942 Operation TORCH had been tentatively outlined. Early in August, Allied Force Headquarters (AFHQ) was constituted and General Eisenhower was formally designated Commander in Chief, Allied Expeditionary Force. His Allied staff, meeting at Norfolk House, London, had selected the TORCH objectives before the end of August. By 5 September the tactical phases of planning end 1, the mounting phases commenced. nd D-day, early in November, had been set.[56]

The TORCH strategic plan, on which the logistical plan necessarily had to be based, consisted of a three-pronged assault against French North Africa. In the center of the 800-mile coastal front, landings e to be made against Oran, on the Mediterranean coast of Algeria. (Map 2) On the extreme east flank, after rejecting Tunis or Bône because of the fear of overextending themselves, TORCH planners selected the port of Algiers. A third landing was to be made in the west, near Casablanca on the At-

lantic coast in French Morocco. Since Generalissimo Francisco Franco's attitude was uncertain, this western landing would place a force along the borders of Spanish Morocco to ensure control of the Strait of Gibralter and the railroad from Casablanca to Oran, and to improve the security of the whole North African coast. By effecting a speedy junction of the three forces, AFHQ might create a favorable opportunity for an early capture of distant Tunisia.[57]

Lucid though it was, the TORCH plan became increasingly difficult to carry out. By mid-September a Center and an Eastern Task Force, bound for Oran and Algiers respectively, entered their mounting stage in the United Kingdom. Simultaneously, the Western Task Force, with Maj. Gen. George S. Patton, Jr., commanding, was being readied in the United States and moved to the Moroccan beaches.[58] From the United Kingdom, AFHQ estimated that between 102,000 and 122,000 Allied troops would leave over a two months' span. Of this number, 40,000 men comprised the assault force, broken down into regimental combat teams and an armored combat command, plus supporting troops. The D plus 3 convoy was to follow with 21,000 troops. Drawing from the 1st and 34th Infantry Divisions of II Corps already in England, plus the 1st Armored

---

[56] (1) George F. Howe, *Northwest Africa: Seizing the Initiative in the West*, UNITED STATES ARMY IN WORLD WAR II (Washington, 1957), ch. II. (2) Matloff and Snell, *Strategic Planning, 1941–1942*, pp. 282–93. (3) Leighton and Coakley, *Global Logistics, 1940–1943*, ch. XVI.

[57] Outline Plan, AFHQ, Opn TORCH, 8 Oct 42. PI 492, TORCH.

[58] Patton flew to London, received a hasty briefing on TORCH, and returned to Washington where he established his headquarters in the Operations Division, War Department General Staff. The latter co-ordinated AFHQ's efforts with those of Patton after 2 October when it was definitely decided to carry out the Casablanca operation. Outline Plan cited n. 57.

Division, yet to arrive, Eisenhower organized Center Task Force, Maj. Gen. Lloyd R. Fredendall commanding, and Eastern Task Force. Maj. Gen. Charles W. Ryder commanded the assault force of the Algiers operation.[59]

Apart from the assault phase, AFHQ looked ahead to the time when the task forces would regroup into conventional units, coupled with air and service support. Accordingly, planners assumed that there would be an American field army of seven U.S. divisions (later the Fifth Army), a new air force, the Twelfth, and two base sections to be known as Atlantic and Mediterranean Base Sections. It was hoped that this team could be built in ninety days and that the Americans could be supplied entirely from the United States by that time. Each task force was, meanwhile, to be supplied by the base from which it was mounted. Gradually ETOUSA was to relinquish its supply responsibilities until TORCH and BOLERO, possibly within the framework of a single theater command, developed separate supply channels.[60] But this was in the future and at the level of

high policy. At their own level, pipeline and spigot quartermasters had to be content with a few paragraphs extracted from highly classified TORCH administrative orders.

The supply requirements of TORCH divided the work of quartermasters in the United Kingdom into two phases. The first was a short-range task calling for preparations through D plus 12. The second was a long-range task of phasing 60,000 men into North Africa and bringing reserve supplies to an acceptable level preparatory to basing all TORCH resupply for the Americans on the United States. The first TORCH assignment for ETO quartermasters came on 14 September when II Corps presented its list of requirements for the first twelve days of the operation. For maximum security control, G–4, AFHQ, established a regulating station in London to handle all TORCH administration. Within the station two representatives from the OCQM personally received extracts of requisitions and special calls from II Corps. These embraced initial equipment for individuals and organizations fighting in winter in a temperate zone, exact location not specified. The requisitions were based on a few modifications of Tables of Equipment. Such modifications were to meet situations peculiar to amphibious or desert warfare. At this time depot stocks were frozen to all units except those on alert in II Corps, and, as requests were handed to them, the two officers set about filling the orders around the clock.

Requisitions were given priority numbers in relation to the embarkation dates of the alerted units. Each requisition had a "blue" control number on the master sheets. Littlejohn's representatives ex-

---

[59] Predominately a British affair, Eastern Task Force was to be spearheaded by Ryder's 168th Regimental Combat Team in order to retain the façade of an all-American character for TORCH.

[60] (1) Eisenhower wanted TORCH to have Quartermaster supply reserves in the United Kingdom because his forces might be cut off either from U.S. or U.S. to U.K. supply sources. A firm TORCH supply plan was agreed upon on 4 December 1942. He accepted a 45-day level for D plus 90 providing a 30-day level of supply was stocked in the United Kingdom where it had a shorter distance to travel to Oran and from which convoys departed almost twice as frequently as from the United States. Msg 4132, CG ETOUSA to AGWAR, 26 Oct 42, sub: TORCH Supply Plan; Msg 4404, 2 Nov 42, AFHQ to AGWAR, sub: TORCH Supply Plan 3. Hist Br OQMG. (2) Msg R2576, AGWAR to USSOS, 31 Oct 42. TORCH, AG 495.

tracted data and, through the base sections, forwarded each specific request to a general or branch depot for action. Unit supply officers of II Corps were then notified to pick up certain portions of Blue Number —— at Depot Number ——. This system was fine for security; for depot quartermasters, it hobbled operations. They had no time to notify units just what to pick up or where. In numerous cases three or four trucks arrived to load items which one jeep could haul. At other times, a convoy of 2½-ton trucks was needed when a single ¾-ton weapons carrier drove up.[61]

Under this system OCQM began to fill II Corps' assault needs for 40,000 men and their vehicles. For subsistence, each individual was to carry one C and two D rations. Each kitchen carried a unit's C ration. Seven days of cased rations, plus a 10 percent loss factor for the whole force, were loaded as ship cargo. This food reserve included three C and four British composite rations; the latter were designed for fourteen men for one day. A day's supply of coffee accompanied each British composite ration. Based on approximately 11 percent of the convoy strength, over 4,000 special hospital rations were provided. In addition, 2,000,-000 salt tablets, 42,000 heat units, and 5,000 can openers were packaged.[62]

Gasoline, oil, and greases were loaded on a 12-day basis for each vehicle in the force. Based on current Tables of Equipment, 5-gallon cans, of the returnable type, if available, were placed on each vehicle of an organization. Fifty gallons per day per tracked vehicle and 5 gallons per day per wheeled vehicle were the planning factors. Leaded gasoline for the motor trucks was to serve also as fuel in field ranges. Whether on vehicles or shipped as cargo, each 5-gallon can had identification strands of wire around its 3-bar handle. A single strand over one bar identified 80-octane gasoline for wheeled vehicles; a strand spanning 2 bars, 87-octane for tracked vehicles; and a wire around 3 bars, 100-octane airplane fuel. Cans free of wire contained kerosene. Diesel fuel was shipped only in British "flimsies," thin, nonreturnable cans containing 4 Imperial gallons. The letter "W" painted on any can identified water. Initially, 22,700 long tons of POL were sent to Africa, representing approximately 65 percent of the total SOS tonnage to leave the United Kingdom.

For Class II supplies a modified T/E 21 of June 1942 provided that several khaki cotton garments were to be left behind. Each enlisted man was to be issued (for security purposes while at sea) such articles as eyeshields, a neckcloth, salt tablets, a mattress cover, a mosquito head cover, and a tube of insect repellent. As part of their equipment, organizations were given one barber set per company and a 30-day supply of flypaper and swatters, and each depot company was issued a 5-pound package of rat poison. As for baggage, each man carried a drawstring barracks bag containing a minimum of items of outer and under clothing, plus a pair of shoes. His second bag was to remain in the unit's train. This bag contained a complete set of clothing resupply. Officers

---

[61] Rpt, Maj Hugh A. Allen, Jr., QM Activities of the ETOUSA as of 15 Jan 43 (hereafter cited as Allen Rpt). Hist Br OQMG.

[62] Andrew T. McNamara, Brig. Gen., and Col. Raymond F. McNally, *Quartermaster Activities of II Corps Thru Algeria, Tunisia, and Sicily and First Army Thru Europe* (Fort Lee, Va., 1953), ch. I. (Hereafter cited as McNamara *Memoir*. See Bibliographical Note.)

were allowed a bedding roll and a piece of hand luggage, and in addition to these, general officers could bring a trunk locker.

Lt. Col. Andrew T. McNamara, II Corps quartermaster, converted his calls for man-days of supply into specific quantities of Class II and IV items. Thanks to Littlejohn's pioneer reference data of August, McNamara's work was aided considerably. For M1937 field ranges Littlejohn doubled the normal maintenance parts along with the 90-day combat maintenance of parts to be shipped in the future. Likewise, the allowance on 5-gallon gasoline cans was doubled and the revised factors subsequently proved to be more than off-the-cuff estimates.

Follow-up convoys were to bring a 14-day level of Quartermaster items ashore by D plus 30; by D plus 60, a 30-day level; and by D plus 90, a 45-day level. The D plus 4 convoy would bring the total strength up to 60,000 men, the D plus 13 convoy, a total of 80,000 men, and by D plus 42, a 100,000-man force would be present. Thereafter, in cycles of six or seven days, administrative convoys to Oran were to provide resupply.[63]

Until September 1942 Norfolk House planners had protected their TORCH secrets well. Upon examining II Corps' initial requisition and inquiring about the quartermaster organization for the operation, Littlejohn could for the first time understand the reasons behind the

mysterious blows which had been dealt to his BOLERO activities. In London, Middleswart got his first hint that ROUNDUP planning was being suspended when Maj. Gen. Mark Clark, II Corps commander, called him aside after a briefing and said that another operation had just succeeded ROUNDUP. Since 25 July, BOLERO and ROUNDUP had been superseded by TORCH. This meant that after 5 September, Littlejohn suddenly had to prepare for the imminent mounting out of 40,000 U.S. troops. Sound staff work logically called for co-ordinated efforts by TORCH and BOLERO quartermasters. Yet it did not work out this way. At least until TORCH was assured of a separate supply channel, Littlejohn had to count his costs in personnel losses and lower supply levels.[64] Few quartermasters in OCQM could estimate their contribution to TORCH supply. After 15 September, OCQM was responsible for implementing a supply plan and contributing to an organization which had been worked out by AFHQ, II Corps, and Center Task Force.

Organizationally, OCQM discovered that a sister staff at the Allied level as well as the SOS cadres for two task forces and the Twelfth Air Force had emerged out of Norfolk House planning. AFHQ logistics had been the responsibility of a British officer, Maj. Gen. Humfrey M. Gale, Chief Administrative Officer, with Col. Everett S. Hughes as his American deputy. At AFHQ level Col. Thomas H.

---

[63] (1) The table showing TORCH's unit POL factors for each type of vehicle as prepared and distributed by the Petroleum Division, OCQM, ETOUSA, 19 September 1942 is in the Allen Report. (2) McNamara *Memoir*, p. 10. (3) Ltrs, CG Hq II Corps to All Units Concerned, 14 Sep, 4 Oct 42, sub: Admin Instrs. Hist Br OQMG.

[64] On 3 September Littlejohn wrote Lee that he had 95 days of B rations on hand, a week's supply of C's, 3 days of D's, and no K's. "The stock of clothing is relatively low." He estimated a month's reserve. Except for a few items, regular supplies were sufficient to maintain "the current garrisons for 60 days." Memo, Littlejohn for Lee, 3 Sep 42. Littlejohn Reading File, vol. IV, item 5.

Ramsey, who had been II Corps quartermaster and the former Chief, War Plans Branch, Planning and Control Division, OQMG, was named as the American planner on 14 September. McNamara had succeeded Ramsey at II Corps and continued to work on requirements for Center Task Force. Meanwhile, on 24 August, after taking a final look at British quartermaster problems in Africa, Colonel Middleswart, followed by Poore, McKinnon, and a British volunteer sergeant, left London for the United States, where he was destined to become Chief Quartermaster, SOS, Western Task Force. Colonel Longino then became Deputy Chief Quartermaster, Headquarters, ETO. Before leaving, Poore conscientiously assembled a set of the current series of OCQM circulars and planning papers, including notes on the 100,000-man plan.[65] Subsequently, this collection played a part in Western Task Force planning.

On 13 September when II Corps' requisitions first reached SOS and the supply situation suddenly became confused, Littlejohn himself was appointed Deputy Commander, SOS ETOUSA, and moved into Lee's Cheltenham office when Lee went to London. Throughout the TORCH mounting phase, Littlejohn also continued as Chief Quartermaster, SOS ETOUSA, but administered OCQM through Colonel Sharp, acting Chief Quartermaster. Lee returned to Cheltenham in late October, and Littlejohn succeeded Brig. Gen. Thomas B. Larkin as Chief of Staff, SOS, when Larkin left as G–4, Center Task Force. Within the Chief Quartermaster's office, meanwhile, reservists rose rapidly to positions of responsibility, and as career quartermasters either took over depot assignments or were alerted to fill vacancies in TORCH. Colonel Sharp was destined to become quartermaster of the Mediterranean Base Section (MBS) and Colonel Rosaler was named quartermaster of Twelfth Air Force Service Command. Eventually, Littlejohn furnished eighty-one officers to TORCH. Also, by February 1943 he had released three depot supply companies, two gasoline supply companies, a truck regiment (minus two companies), a bakery battalion plus two platoons, a service battalion plus a service company, a railhead company, a bath company, a salvage collecting company, a mobile refrigeration company, and a mobile laundry section.[66] Even with BOLERO in limbo this loss was a blow, much of it coming at a time when Center Task Force had to be mounted.

Between 15 September and 26 October, the date on which the assault convoys left Glasgow and Liverpool, AFHQ G–4, although ably assisted by OCQM, SOS ETOUSA, found itself ill prepared, variously handicapped, and running short of time in meeting Center Task Force's needs. Difficulties developed on both sides of the Atlantic. Many of the supplies, first requisitioned in June for BOLERO, were in the pipeline from NYPE, along which most logisticians were still learning to operate under ASF's supply directive of 6 July. In the

---

[65] (1) Interv with Middleswart, October 1955. (2) *Hist of AFHQ*, pt. I (Aug–Dec 42), p. 77; pt. II (Dec 42–Dec 43), sec. 3, p. 391. OCMH. (3) Poore Papers.

[66] (1) McNamara *Memoir*, pp. 11, 23, 29, 45. (2) Memo, Littlejohn for Col C. E. Saltzman, 13 Sep 42. Littlejohn Reading File, vol. IVa, item 1. (3) Volumes IVa and V of the Littlejohn Reading File contain valuable information on SOS ETOUSA activities in mounting TORCH. (4) Allen Rpt.

United Kingdom, 101,600 long tons of poorly packaged Quartermaster items had to be moved into several Irish Sea ports, transported across the country, and sorted, preparatory to outloading them at TORCH's two ports of embarkation, Glasgow and Liverpool. Movement was a responsibility of the British, prodded by American expediters.

To mount TORCH, AFHQ's quartermaster machinery rolled over much of the same ground which OCQM had explored for BOLERO. At the ports on the Clyde, the Mersey, and in the Bristol Channel, where German night air raids were now becoming severe, new traffic saturated the facilities. Clearance became a tremendous task. Poor markings, frail commercial packaging, paper labels, inadequate handling, belated transmission of manifests, and reckless transshipment inland from the ports had resulted in the misplacement of rations and packaged POL. Although it had recently taken over supervision of five general depots, the OCQM had to lay aside a logical depot system which had been developed for BOLERO.

On 4 September G–4, SOS, directed OCQM to "open QM branch depots at Hilsea and Cardiff on 7 September and Stowmarket on the 14th." Depot quartermasters continued to improvise. With no time to build new installations, general depots occupied warehouses, open fields, and hastily evacuated British military depots. Liverpool, Barry, and Hilsea depots, located near port complexes which the OCQM would normally have avoided in an orderly situation, became general depots overnight. The Quartermaster branch depots, opened at Stowmarket, Exeter, Lydney, and Glasgow, were far removed from the sites which

OCQM wanted in southwestern England. Hastily, POL depots at Masbury (23 September) and Highbridge (26 October) were activated. Deployed over this network, undermanned staffs had no alternative but to rely on British civilians to operate the inadequately equipped depots. Initially, British civilian employees had great difficulty in understanding American procedures. Necessarily drawn from untested reservists, base and depot quartermasters eagerly sought the few technicians who could assist them in management. After 29 September teams appointed by the various chiefs of technical services and G–4, SOS, visited depots and followed the progress made in filling II Corps requisitions. Armed with OCQM's reference data, quartermasters industriously tackled their assignments. In the absence of service units, quartermasters welcomed the loan of combat and support troops from the 29th Infantry Division and the Eighth Air Force.[67]

Out of the avalanche of supply it was no easy task to separate twelve to fourteen days of specific Quartermaster items. Momentarily, the OCQM ignored the long-range aspects of maintenance supply for TORCH. Twenty-five years of experience had gone into most Quartermaster Tables of Organization and Equipment, but the troops attempted to bring along all manner of extras and Littlejohn and McNamara had to cull out many luxury and excess items. Supplies had been dumped into warehouses or open spaces

---

[67] Memo, Littlejohn for Sharp, 8 Sep 42; Memo, Littlejohn for Hughes, 27 Sep 42, sub: Transmission to SOS of Matters Relating to Supply of Task Forces, etc.; Ltr, Littlejohn to Goodman, 22 Oct 42. Littlejohn Reading File, vol. IV, item 12; vol. IVa, item 41; vol. V, item 79.

without being inventoried, and many items could not be located. Ships had been unloaded for a quick turnaround passage and it took time to rewed II Corps units with their missing organizational equipment. In the confusion no one attempted to fix blame. If boxes at point of origin were marked with paper labels or lead pencils, and bills of lading bore only a vague statement as to the gross tonnage or branch of supply, it is easy to understand the disorder that followed when they were deposited on a British pier that was damaged, overloaded, or manned by untrained civilians. A serious challenge to OCQM developed from the anguished II Corps calls for Class II and IV initial equipment, and AFHQ and the War Department had to make last-minute arrangements to replace a large number of mislaid items by forwarding whole shiploads from the United States.[68]

On 26 October 1942, the day that McNamara left Glasgow with the assault convoy, he and Littlejohn had the satisfaction of knowing that they had done everything in their power for the D-day and D plus 3 convoys. At the last moment McNamara suddenly remembered that there was not a medal in the convoy. He sent a blinker message to shore requesting that a case of decorations be included on the D plus 13 convoy. Meanwhile, the support phase had not been overlooked. Littlejohn and McNamara had done the best they could in setting up supplies for convoys through D plus 72, by which time fifteen convoys were to have left the United Kingdom, sailing on an average of six days apart.

One of OCQM's major concerns for these convoys had been the provision of B rations in order that the troops could dispense with their emergency rations as quickly as possible.[69]

After the logistical nightmare with Torch, Littlejohn proposed to visit Styer, Goodman, and Col. Ira K. Evans, QM port representative at NYPE, to straighten out shipping and supply problems which had developed. Before changes could be announced in SOS ETOUSA, Littlejohn had to know the reasons behind the War Department's policies. For example, the 5-gallon gasoline can was a multilateral item of supply that involved the Ordnance Department, the Quartermaster and Engineer Corps, and the local Area Petroleum Office. The Motor Transport Service was an orphan disowned by several chiefs of services and the G–4, SOS. As yet the War Department had no set policy on impregnated clothing. Logistical literature from the chiefs of services in the United States was conspicuous by its absence. The War Department during the Torch preparations had never given SOS ETOUSA a firm troop basis either for its headquarters or for its operating troops. As for Quartermaster problems, OCQM had had no word on a cased B ration (the proposed 10-in-1), on boneless meat, on a combat service shoe with synthetic sole, on cloth for officers' uniforms, on a suitable combat uniform for nurses, on the disposal

---

[68] Leighton and Coakley, *Global Logistics, 1940–1943*, pp. 429–32.

[69] (1) In June 1943 General Littlejohn was awarded the Distinguished Service Medal for unusual services "in rapidly establishing a QM service throughout the theater which met and solved the many unexpected and seemingly insurmountable problems . . . in the organization and supply of the African task force." (2) McNamara *Memoir*, ch. I.

of surplus baggage, on an effects depot, on a sturdy, manageable, barracks bag, on spare parts for field ranges, on a plan to combine bakery and coffee-roasting units, and on policy regarding local procurement. Lacking answers to specific queries on all these subjects, Littlejohn left for the United States on 6 November 1942.[70]

In the United States, too, the decision to launch TORCH diverted the main stream of resources away from the United Kingdom to the speedy mounting of Patton's Western Task Force and thereafter to the direct support of all TORCH operations. Patton's command was directly responsible to the Operations Division, War Department General Staff (OPD WDGS), which processed Quartermaster requisitions and passed them on to ASF, which in turn gave them to OQMG to fill. OQMG alerted its depots and informed the ports of the availability of items. At Indiantown Gap, Pennsylvania, an SOS, Western Task Force, was assembled, with Brig. Gen. Arthur R. Wilson commanding. Colonel Middleswart was named chief quartermaster, but his staff's planning was confined to the postlodgment period.[71]

Twenty Quartermaster support units were alerted to move with Patton's assault force, but it was later decided that not a single one would land on D-day. Actually, the decision to strip down the assault force almost to its tactical units did not reflect a cold indifference on Patton's part toward service troops. A month before his departure, he alerted Clark and OPD to his need for such troops, saying OPD's allotment was inadequate. Apparently, the shipping shortage motivated Clark's decision to cut out service troops. Yet Center Task Force at the same moment was mounting several Quartermaster support units in addition to the 1st Engineer Special Brigade, a new type of unit for organizing and handling beach operations.[72]

In the haste of assembling Patton's task force, staging area demands could not be met by the Quartermaster depot at Richmond, Virginia. Other depots filled emergency orders. Despite a 50 percent reduction in the D-day tonnage, supplies poured into the ports. Until the last minute commanders deferred decisions on what to take with the result that units retained their full allowances of Quartermaster equipment until the last available cargo space was filled. Patton's last days in the zone of interior witnessed increased authorizations for drawing boards, folding desks, and typewriters, and last-minute requests for paulins, medals, bicycles, and special Christmas rations, while teletype messages spelled out rush orders for flags, staffs, brassards, and even a light launch. Once the port commander called on a depot for Quartermaster items, presumably assembled by an earlier alert order, the operational responsibility of OQMG was fulfilled.

To be reasonably assured of supplies between the time the beachhead was secured and the ports were opened, all transports were combat loaded. Each ves-

---

[70] Littlejohn Reading File, vols. IV, IVa, V, VI.

[71] (1) Ray S. Cline, *Washington Command Post: The Operations Division,* UNITED STATES ARMY IN WORLD WAR II (Washington, 1951), pp. 180–87. (2) Memo, ACofS OPD for CG AGF and SOS, 2 Sep 42, sub: Preparation of Units for Overseas Sv. Atlantic Base Sec, 320.2.

[72] Memo, CG Task Force A for Chief OPD WDGS, 24 Sep 42. Atlantic Base Sec, 320.2.

sel carried a full allotment of each class of supply for its own passengers or for troops landing in a particular area. Though combat loading represented an uneconomical use of space, it reduced the risk of serious losses in any one class of supply at a time when German sea and air raiders threatened every transatlantic convoy.

To facilitate combat loading, the Richmond Quartermaster Depot set up one and one-half million type B field and combat rations in twenty-eight separate lots, or one per transport. Within each set the ration was strapped for rough handling and packed in 70-pound loads to be handled by one man. Patton's ration plan provided for three separate allocations: an individual and initial reserve, a beach reserve, and a B landing ration. It was on a 15-day supply level, backed up by a 60-day floating reserve, and it included tobacco, candy, and toilet articles for gratuitous issue to the troops. In addition, a total of about 50 long tons of tea, sugar, and rice, and some 20,000 yards of cotton cloth were brought along to be bartered for assistance by North Africans.[73]

The vessels of the Western Task Force began to leave Hampton Roads Port of

Embarkation on 23 October, a date better known as marking the opening phases of the Battle of El 'Alamein. H-hour for the TORCH operation was set for 0100, 8 November 1942.[74]

Until a separate theater was created in North Africa, BOLERO quartermasters had the dual job of supporting TORCH and at the same time of sustaining the growing air bombardment of Europe. By February 1943, the demands of TORCH had reduced the American garrison in the United Kingdom to approximately 100,000 men, including 20,000 troops of V Corps, 50,000 men in the Eighth Air Force, 30,000 service troops, and a small headquarters contingent. With such a small number in the British Isles, it appeared that BOLERO quartermasters would have nothing much to do except the routine of housekeeping. On the contrary, the period between November 1942 and August 1943 was one of intense activity for OCQM and Quartermaster Service. The depot system was built on a solid foundation. The field of local procurement continued to be exploited. Above all, a careful planning program was reborn. After September 1943, the bold counterstrokes in secondary theaters gave way to the meticulous calculations that brought together all the components of a great striking force in the United Kingdom. By that time Quartermaster basic plans and organization were ready to support Operation OVERLORD, the new code name for the invasion of northwest Europe. (Map I)

[73] (1) Ltr, Maj R. B. Carhart to Richmond QM Depot, 20 Sep 42, sub: Shipment of Class I for a Task Force. OQMG 400, Move A. (2) Ltr, AGWAR to CG NYPE et al., 25 Sep 42, sub: Shipment of Class II and IV for Task Force. OPD 115. (3) Annex 1 to AdminO 1, Hq Task Force A, 9 Oct 42, sub: QM Supplies; Annex 1, Final Rpt on Opn TORCH. Both in AFHQ G–3. (4) Ltr, AGWAR to CG Task Force A, 4 Oct 42. Middleswart Papers.

[74] Howe, Northwest Africa, p. 67.

CHAPTER III

Mediterranean Quartermasters Improvise During 1943

When the TORCH forces landed in French North Africa in November 1942, the Mediterranean area had already seen more than two years of war. Fighting had begun in June 1940, when Italy hastily declared war on a defeated France and an undaunted Britain. In the months that followed, Metropolitan France, with both American and Canadian missions accredited at Vichy, could be considered a neutral nation, but the French colonial empire was in fact, if not officially, at war with Britain. British attacks on Oran and Dakar in July 1940, and the occupation of Syria a year later, aroused deep French resentment, and made it urgently necessary that TORCH have the appearance of a predominantly American expedition. Hoping to nourish French resentment into a full alliance against the British, the Axis Powers were tactful in their official relations with the colonies. Apart from a small German-Italian observer organization, to enforce the armistice terms, the area was not under direct Axis control as the TORCH operation began.[1]

The British were constrained to action against their recent ally by the need to maintain their position in the Middle East. That Britain's life line ran via Malta to Suez, and thence to India, was one of the truisms of recent history, but by mid-1942, as Japan extended its conquests, the Mediterranean became an American life line as well. The long alternative route around Africa slowed down convoys not only to British bases in Egypt, Iraq, and India, but to U.S. bases already established in Iran, Burma, and Australia. By mid-1942 the Middle East had become a center of American as well as British strategic interest, and succeeding months saw a slow build-up of U.S. Army Air Forces (USAAF) units in the area, largely dependent upon the Royal Air Force (RAF) for logistical support. On 8 November 1942, the same day that far more dramatic events were occurring 2,000 miles to the west, Lt. Gen. Frank M. Andrews formally activated the U.S. Army Forces in the Middle East (USA-FIME), a separate theater headquarters with roughly the same boundaries as its British counterpart.[2] Thus many characteristics of warfare in the Mediterranean, and of American participation in operations there, had emerged before the

---

[1] Howe, *Northwest Africa*, pp. 4–14.

[2] USAFIME later became a very active area of QMC operations, but since it had ceased to be an active theater in the war against Germany, its history will not be covered in this volume.

TORCH expedition. The first objective of Mediterranean combat was control of the sea lanes, a prize to be gained by land and air as well as naval operations. TORCH itself was decided upon primarily because German air power in Sicily and Crete had reduced the utility of Malta as a convoy station, and not solely because of the German Army's threat to Egypt and the Suez Canal. Once maritime supremacy was restored, all further objectives would be more easily attained. The geography of the area assured that every major land campaign could be supported from its own major port, without excessively long lines of rail or highway communication. It was no accident that every major logistical headquarters was named a base section.[3]

The Middle East remained a predominantly British theater, and Americans there learned tactical and logistical concepts from veterans of the Eighth Army, and from the RAF's Western Desert Air Force. The Desert Training Center in California had been selected because the arid climate and terrain resembled that of Libya, but conditions in both areas were widely different from the wet scrubby landscape actually encountered in parts of French Northwest Africa. As Lt. Gen. Sir Bernard L. Montgomery's forces converged with General Eisenhower's, the faded khaki uniforms and pale yellow camouflaged vehicles from the desert country contrasted sharply with the wool olive drab uniforms and dark green vehicles of the units newly arrived from Britain and the United States.

The Anglo-American landings on 8 November 1942 were followed by three days of combat against French troops—a tragedy, but not a futile one. The fighting served to convince the French that TORCH was a major operation, not a series of pinprick raids, and that the outcome should be defined as a French revolt, rather than as an American victory. It can be argued that a more widely heralded operation, with less emphasis on surprise, would have saved American, French, and British lives; but that view underrates the alertness of German intelligence, and the strength and mobility of the opposing forces. The defection of Vichy French forces in Morocco and Algeria only strengthened Axis determination to win the race for securing Tunisia. On 9 November German planes were at Tunis. Two days later, using all-weather fields, hundreds of aircraft had arrived and five Axis cruisers were offshore. German tanks patrolled the streets of Tunis and Bizerte, and the outlying defenses at Mateur were bolstered. By the end of November 1942, the western Mediterranean was alive with the German effort to offset TORCH.[4]

Securing North African Beaches and Bases

In the predawn hours of 8 November 1942, TORCH convoys dropped anchor in Atlantic and Mediterranean waters and began simultaneously discharging assault troops into landing craft that would carry them onto nine North African

---

[3] USAAF operations from Middle East bases are discussed in Wesley Frank Craven and James Lea Cate, eds., "The Army Air Forces in World War II," vol. II, *Europe: TORCH to POINTBLANK, August 1942 to December 1943* (Chicago: The University of Chicago Press, 1949), Chapter 1.

[4] Howe, *Northwest Africa*, Appendix B, gives monthly tonnage figures for German supply shipments to North Africa.

beaches.[5] Against Morocco the operation involved three landings along a 200-mile coastal strip. General Patton's forces landed at Fedala and Safi, primarily to move overland and capture Casablanca without damaging that larger and more modern port. To the north of Casablanca, those striking at Port-Lyautey were to seize the only all-weather airfield in Morocco, secure the rail junctions on the main line from Casablanca to Algiers via Fès, and effect a junction with forces from Oran.

In the Oran area, two columns enveloped the city from the west, and a third column headed south from Arzew, a village some thirty miles northeast of the well-equipped berths at Oran itself. Inasmuch as these columns neglected the mole and piers in Oran's harbor, two companies of the 6th Armored Infantry Regiment were floated in directly toward the docks of Oran at three hours past midnight. Far to the east of Oran, the same envelopment tactics were used against Algiers.

At all points opposition had been expected, and at Oran the French provided no disappointments. Even before the troops touched land, one phase of Quartermaster work began to unfold. From defenses in Oran's harbor, French machine gunners, after a two-hour alert from the three enveloping columns, butchered the advancing infantrymen as they stood below deck in their two unarmored cut-

ters. Those recovered were later buried by Quartermaster troops in Oran's first military cemetery. Landings at other points proceeded without major incident.[6]

Only a few Quartermaster detachments were present during the period of 8–11 November, and the handling of QM classes of supply cannot be separated from the over-all support story. At all points, troops and unit trains went ashore with five days of supply, while another week's supply was offshore as cargo. This meant that a total of twelve days' supply for 107,000 men began moving over nine beaches. Dumps at each landing were the responsibility of each assault group. By merely observing the landings, task force G–4 sections missed an opportunity to carry out their mission of centralizing coordination.

The word "disorganization" summarizes the over-all picture of supply during the first three days. That the operation proved a success can be attributed less to the efficiency of the assault landing than to the essential accuracy of the estimate, largely ignored by tactical commanders, that the French would offer brief, if any, resistance. Much of the difficulty resulted from the inexperience of the participants, the speed with which they had been assembled, and their inability to rehearse the supply phase of the operation. On these points Western Task Force offers a valuable case study.[7]

In Morocco, thanks to what has been described as the calmest surf in sixty-eight years, small amounts of ammunition, rations, drinking water, and gasoline were

---

[5] During World War II, units which participated in an amphibious or airborne assault landing received the bronze service arrowhead to be worn on a theater ribbon. This award was made by the theater commander. In North Africa the following QM units received the arrowhead under War Department General Order 70, 20 August 1945: the 9th QM Company, the 85th QM Depot Supply Company, and the 184th QM Depot Company.

[6] (1) Howe, *Northwest Africa*, chs. VI–VIII. (2) McNamara *Memoir*, pp. 15–16.

[7] (1) Final Rpt of Opns WTF, G–4 an., 8–11 Nov 42. Opns Rpt, WTF. (2) McNamara *Memoir*, p. 20.

ashore by the afternoon of D-day. Because of an acute shortage of motor transportation, the forward movement of supplies from the beach groups to combat units, as well as the relocation of supplies misplaced by confused coxswains of landing craft, was virtually impossible. French resistance at Safi and Fedala terminated on D-day, and combat troops were free to move in the direction of Casablanca. On the first afternoon the surf rose so rapidly and ominously that operations over the beaches were threatened. High ground swells capsized some landing craft and dashed others against rocks with losses of troops, vehicles, and supplies. In the Port-Lyautey sector only tracked vehicles moved inland and shore parties had to scramble to move trucks and stores above the high-water mark.

Final computations on the destruction of landing craft varied, but most estimates agreed that losses for Western Task Force approximated 35 percent, a figure that was too high for efficiency. It was not even creditable by comparison with the higher losses at Algiers. Summarizing his command's experience at Port-Lyautey, Maj. Gen. Lucian K. Truscott, Jr., reported to Patton that "the combination of inexperienced landing craft crews, poor navigation, and desperate hurry resulting from lateness of hour, finally turned the debarkation into a hit-or-miss affair that would have spelled disaster against a well-armed enemy intent upon resistance." [8]

The loss of landing craft and their contents, as well as the lack of service troops on the beaches, quickly demonstrated the dependence of tactical maneuver upon logistical support. Because of insufficient supporting weapons, transportation, and communications equipment, the southward advance from Fedala by elements of the 3d Division stalled as completely as if the French defenders of Casablanca had come out in force. In the hope of exploiting the advantage produced by a show of strength, the 3d Division resumed its march by midnight of 9 November. Marching troops now endured the fatiguing test of hand-carrying supplies which should have been transported in organic vehicles. [9]

Transport quartermasters complained of their lack of authority to control unloading. Compounding the difficulty was the absence of other officers and noncommissioned officers capable of maintaining control on the beaches, piers, or quays. The beach supply-handling parties loafed at their jobs; some wandered away. Drivers of vehicles insisted that they were not obliged to assist with the unloading. Because beach parties consisted largely of combat engineers, there was a tendency to give them other duties. At Fedala, by the evening of D-day, more sailors than soldiers were handling cargo on shore. So haphazard was the unloading at dockside that the search for various items resembled a foraging operation. Even the arrival of thirty-three 2½-ton trucks belonging to the 3d Division's Quarter-

---

[8] (1) Quoted in Rpt, Brig Gen Arthur R. Wilson, G-4 WTF, to CofS WD, 12 Dec 42 (hereafter cited as Wilson Rpt). Opns Rpt, WTF. (2) Samuel Eliot Morison, "History of United States Naval Operation in World War II," vol. II, *Operations in North African Waters, October 1942–June 1943* (Boston: Little, Brown and Company, 1947), p. 123.

[9] (1) Donald G. Taggard, ed., *History of the Third Infantry Division in World War II* (Washington: Infantry Journal Press, 1947), pp. 28–29. (2) Rpt, Sub-Task Force BRUSHWOOD, 7–11 Nov 42. Opns Rpt, WTF.

master company, could not bring quick order to the supply tangle at Fedala.

At Safi, speedy efforts were made to recruit local inhabitants, together with their trucks and wagons, to assist in the unloading and sorting of supplies. Quartermasters made payment in cigarettes, cloth, or canned rations but it shortly became apparent that workers were more interested in the golden opportunity to pilfer. Many native drivers, after being given a loaded truck and directions for delivery, disappeared. Two days after the landing, tons of ammunition and rations were discovered on native fishing boats.[10]

Slowly logistical order prevailed in Morocco. On 19 November 1942 the first administrative convoy docked at Casablanca, carrying thirty days' supply of Quartermaster items and 32,000 service troops, including Headquarters, 6th Port, and its two organic port battalions. In addition, a Quartermaster truck regiment and a service battalion arrived, together with the advance echelon, Quartermaster Section, SOS, Western Task Force, consisting of Lt. Col. James E. Poore, Jr., and Col. Humphrey S. Evans, a supply officer. They made an immediate reconnaissance of Casablanca to determine available storage facilities, to survey the availability of local foodstuffs, coal, and liquid fuels, to determine local labor sources and wages, and to locate bakeries, shoe repair facilities, and other services.

Within the month Evans and Poore were working for Col. Ralph H. Tate, G–4, SOS, Western Task Force, and made the first survey of the Rabat-Meknès-Fès area along the rail line stretching toward Oujda, and thence to Oran. At mid-December, the Chief Quartermaster, SOS, Western Task Force, Colonel Middleswart, accompanied by his executive officer, Col. Neal H. McKay, arrived in Casablanca. With the activation of Fifth Army late in December 1942, Atlantic Base Section was organized and Middleswart became its chief quartermaster. By March 1943, Casablanca's port capacity was not being fully used because, with the shift of operations toward Tunisia, Oran was receiving an increasing proportion of incoming tonnage.[11]

In the Arzew-Oran landings, Fredendall's Center Task Force likewise experienced a shortage of service troops. Its G–4 staff failed to co-ordinate beach operations, and discipline at the beach dumps was lacking. Fredendall had one advantage over Patton. He had provided for the services of 350 men of the 1st Infantry Division's quartermaster battalion as well as men of the 1st Engineer Special Brigade to support the 1st Infantry Division and Combat Command B, 1st Armored Division. Also, II Corps brought along its quartermaster to Arzew on D-day. With seven years of experience as an infantry officer, Colonel McNamara was able to observe the operation with a trained eye. He was on hand to make an early reconnaissance of sites. His presence would become even more important when II Corps assumed responsibility for supply functions for Mediterranean Base Section. By being in the area for D-day,

---

[10] (1) Study, Maj William C. Frierson, Preparations for TORCH, II, p. 134. OCMH. (2) Howe, Northwest Africa, pp. 109, 137–41. (3) Taggard, ed., History of the Third Infantry Division, p. 27.

[11] (1) Joseph Bykofsky and Harold Larson, The Transportation Corps: Operations Overseas, UNITED STATES ARMY IN WORLD WAR II (Washington, 1957), chs. IV, V. (2) Ltr, Poore to Middleswart, 27 Nov 42; Poore Journal, Nov–Dec 43. Both in Poore Papers. (3) History of Quartermaster Section, Atlantic Base Section. Poore Papers. (Hereafter cited as Hist of QM ABS.)

McNamara was able to make this supply transition smoothly.[12]

Resistance at Arzew, the primary D-day objective, was so brief that a detachment of 11 officers and 173 men of the 1st Division's Quartermaster battalion was able to land at Grand Quay by 0930. Simultaneously, a smaller detachment came over Zebra Beach on the south side of the harbor. That afternoon two ships in the assault convoy berthed at Arzew's two piers, and with the help of the Quartermaster detachment that had landed earlier, unloading of the assault cargo began. The detachment commandeered a locomotive and five cars, and, using a native crew, shuttled stores around the docks and from the beaches to the railway station which served as the divisional distribution point.

Inasmuch as three-fourths of the task force strength was being discharged at Arzew, three-fourths of its assault supply was also landing there. Along with the supplies of other services Quartermaster items moved from ship to shore under the supervision of 1st Engineer Special Brigade. For his Class I dump, McNamara selected a little park a few blocks away from the piers at Arzew, and his ration point was operated by 51 men of the 85th QM Depot Supply Company. Northwest of Arzew, 112 men from Company B, 205th QM Gasoline Supply Battalion, found the local gas and oil refinery in good condition and opened a Class III depot, exploiting both the pipeline and a narrow-gauge railroad to Arzew's dock area.

Before landing, McNamara had been

assured that trucks of the brigade would carry supplies, regardless of service, to the dumps for which they were intended. But there was a lack of G–4 supervision, and the engineers merely dumped cargo at spots convenient to them, always at the water line. Moreover, the engineers had no control over the landing area itself, and the Arzew docks and beaches were open to a host of visitors. Unit supply officers had a field day laying in reserves. Fortunately, the Class III dump slowly acquired stock because Company B, 205th QM Battalion, had a few trucks. The Class I officer, despite his resourcefulness in getting one truck to haul his own reserves, barely managed to maintain a balance of supply. Unquestionably, twelve days' rations for 40,000 men should have been adequate until the D plus 4 convoy arrived. But they were exhausted in the course of four days, not as a result of bad planning, but by the overdrawing of rations inspired by the philosophy of getting while the getting was good.

On D plus 2, operations at Arzew harbor were left in the hands of the amphibian engineers, while the 1st Division's Quartermaster battalion devoted itself to operating a divisional dump, distributing supplies, and providing trucks for the deployment of combat units. On 11 November the French commander at Oran surrendered, and McNamara immediately moved into the city. He had to make haste in selecting depot sites to house the shipments scheduled to arrive from the United Kingdom. Fourteen days of supply for a total of 80,000 men, according to the TORCH plan, would be on hand by D plus 30.

Surprised and chagrined to note the unfortunate contrast between representations on maps and photographs and

---

[12] (1) Opns Rpt, 1st QM Bn (Divisional), 22 Nov 42. Hist Br OQMG. (2) This unit was reorganized as a company on 5 January 1943. GO 2, Hq 1st Inf Div, 5 Jan 43.

reality on the ground, McNamara was able, "after much jabbering in French and the use of my active hands," to arrange for the occupancy of usable sites. His first call was on the manager of Oran's large gasoline refinery. The tanks were in excellent condition and by 12 November had absorbed the contents of one tanker. Armed with premarked maps and aerial photos of Oran, McNamara sped to what appeared to be a promising Class I site, the city's bull ring. But under the stadium seats where he had planned to store rations, McNamara found holiday litter which could not be tidied up in a matter of days. Nor was the ring desirable for open storage: it smelled of bulls. What he had thought were good avenues of access to the arena, well paved and broad, turned out to be nothing more than donkey paths. For a ration point he finally settled on a vacant lot at a good street intersection. His next stop was at the city hall where he was able to requisition a Class II and IV warehouse at 66 Rue du Tétre. Availability was the location's only asset. On the southeast side of Oran, he opened a Class III distribution point.

After placing II Corps in the depot business, McNamara drove to Mers el Kébir and met the Quartermaster troops on the first follow-up convoy. The convoy brought the remainder of the 85th Quartermaster Depot Supply Company, the 93d Quartermaster Railhead Company, and elements of the 28th Quartermaster Truck Regiment, a unit destined to operate directly under the II Corps G–4 Section.[13]

On 6 December the Mediterranean Base Section (MBS) was activated, and two days later it assumed supply responsibility for II Corps. Quartermaster installations in operation at that time included five Class I points, the Class II warehouse at 66 Rue du Tétre, eleven Class III points, a salvage dump, a sterilization and bath point, and a laundry service, attached to a medical depot. McNamara had been responsible for the interment of 256 dead in a cemetery at Sidi Chami outside Oran. Years later he wrote with a degree of humility: "Virtually no co-ordination or advanced thinking had preceded or accompanied the Oran operation. Our Quartermaster units had no concepts of their mission until we met them at the pier and told them where to go, what to do, and often, how to do it." [14]

Eastern Task Force repeated the confusion of the other landings. The mishandling of landing craft at Algiers proved as characteristic of British as of American crews. Vessel losses on the first trip were estimated at an appalling 94 percent—by far the highest in the TORCH operation—with serious effects on landing schedules. Some boats became disabled while still in deep water, and the heavily equipped troops had no alternative but to abandon ship and swim ashore. In the Sidi Ferruch sector the Commanding Officer, 168th Regimental Combat Team, beached his vessels seven miles from their destination, and one of his companies landed fifteen miles away. At all beaches, Army shore parties dumped cargo helter-skelter. They called

---

[13] (1) Ltr, McNamara to Ramsey, 19 Nov 42. OQMG MED 319.25. (2) McNamara *Memoir*, ch. III. (3) Opns Rpt, 1st QM Bn, 22 Nov 42; Unit Hist, 85th QM Depot Co. Both in Hist Br OQMG. (4) G–4 Jnl CTF, 8–10 Nov 42. Opns Rpt, CTF.

[14] McNamara *Memoir*, pp. 39–40.

for assistance from the naval crews. One lesson learned at Algiers influenced all subsequent Allied amphibious operations. For political reasons already described, the landings there were spearheaded by the U.S. 168th Regimental Combat Team, although the rest of the Eastern Task Force was British. As supplies for U.S. and British units came ashore, it proved impossible to keep them separated. There was a clearly indicated need for separate beachhead service areas manned by U.S. and British service troops, even when the Allied forces to be supported were small and landing sites were immediately adjacent.[15]

Among the most widely echoed criticisms of TORCH supply and one of immediate interest to the Quartermaster Corps was the charge that assault troops were overloaded with clothing and equipment. An overburdened soldier who became exhausted as he waded or swam through deep water in his effort to get ashore was in serious danger of drowning. Some did. As McNamara remarked:

The enlisted men were physically overburdened with food, ammunition, and accoutrements. The two C rations that he carried on his person as he went into Oran alone weighed 10 pounds. The bandoliers of ammunition, the clothing, gas masks, weapons, and other incidentals that the combat troops carried on their persons weighed an additional 122 pounds, making an aggregate of 132 pounds per man. This simply represented 110 pounds too many for a combat soldier to carry and enough to make anyone utterly useless. Moreover, each man had (either carried by him, or

for him) two barracks bags each full of more equipment and clothing.[16]

TORCH landings also provided the opportunity to observe the adequacy of individual items of Quartermaster Corps equipment. The 1941 field jacket proved neither waterproof nor sufficiently warm, while in contrast the armored force jacket quickly won the popularity that it enjoyed throughout both the Mediterranean and European campaigns. Field shoes turned out to be too light, nondurable, and nonwaterproof, and the leather sole was declared unsatisfactory under field conditions. The field range, M1937, quickly demonstrated its tendency to clog when operated with leaded gasoline. Subsistence, ammunition, medical, and other supplies had been packed in commercial-type cardboard and corrugated paper cartons which were neither waterproof nor resistant to breakage when dropped. Markings in English meant nothing to native handlers. Since rough handling was an inevitable part of an amphibious operation, the remedial measures called for were improved metal strappings, the utilization of sturdier lumber, smaller and lighter packages, and universally recognized markings.[17]

Supply staffs being assembled in North Africa and Army Service Forces in Washington had little time to analyze and correct the deficiencies of the TORCH landings. Planning for further amphibious operations against islands of the western

---

[15] (1) Rpt, Hq SOS, 12 Feb 43, sub: Lessons From Amph Opns in North Africa, an. G, OQMG MED 319.25. (2) Lessons From Opn TORCH, 16 Dec 42. OVERLORD Preinvasion File, 465.

[16] McNamara *Memoir*, pp. 39–40. See also, ch. VII, below.

[17] (1) Wilson Rpt, p. 27. (2) 1st Incl, Rpt, Patton to Eisenhower, 30 Dec 43, sub: Lessons TORCH. Opns Rpt, WTF. (3) Ltr, CG 1st Inf Div to AFHQ, 25 Dec 42, sub: Lessons from Opn TORCH. Opns Rpt, TORCH. (4) Ltr, Littlejohn to Scowden, 8 Apr 43. OQMG ETO 457.

HEAVILY BURDENED SOLDIERS *debarking at Phosphate Pier, Casablanca, 1943.*

Mediterranean got under way almost immediately, and planners in London drew on their own TORCH support experience for lessons useful in planning the cross-Channel attack. Meanwhile the next phase of the Mediterranean war was marked by the first protracted engagement in World War II of a U.S. army corps over wide stretches of a continental land mass. It was the first campaign in which quartermasters would support an independent corps—a miniature army formation—of four divisions for any sustained period.

Supporting II Corps in Tunisia

Allied successes in Oran and Algiers gave rise to hopes for the early conquest of Tunisia. Recklessly outrunning their supply support, elements of Eastern Task Force crossed the Tunisian border on 17 November and drove deep into the province. But the enemy quickly braced himself to defend the vital ports of Tunis and Bizerte. On 1 December the Germans began their counterattack which led to an Allied withdrawal to eastern Algeria and the postponement of the Allied offensive until after the New Year. From General Eisenhower's point of view, this delay would make possible the correction of an operational and logistical situation that markedly conflicted with the doctrines advocated in War College textbooks.[18]

Toward the end of 1942, Fredendall assembled his staff in Algiers and outlined their next mission. Constituted as a task force of some 40,000 men, II Corps was to advance through Sbeïtla toward the port of Sfax. D-day was tentatively set for

---

[18] Howe, *Northwest Africa*, p. 330.

22 January 1943. SATIN Task Force was built around the 1st Armored Division and the 20th Combat Engineer Regiment, plus tank destroyer, antiaircraft, and service troops. A small infantry and paratrooper force under Col. Edson D. Raff was already operating in the Gafsa area. Capture of Sfax would frustrate the enemy's intention to keep open a coastal corridor for joining Rommel's *German Africa Corps (Deutsches Afrika Korps)* with the Tunisian defenders. Fredendall selected the communication center of Tébessa, an old Roman walled city 125 miles east and south of Constantine, as his forward supply base. A highway and a single-track, narrow-gauge railroad parallel to it joined Tébessa and Constantine. To its north, eighty miles away, Tébessa was also linked by a road and meter-gauge rail line with Souk Ahras. At the time, British First Army had administrative control of the lines of communication in and around Tébessa.[19]

Early in January 1943, the II Corps staff moved to Constantine and put the last-minute touches on its supply plan. Planners estimated that a maximum of 250 long tons a day could be moved into Tébessa by rail. At the moment no trucks were available to increase the estimate. To stage supply forward from Oran or Algiers, both towns enjoying standard-gauge rail nets to the east, it would be necessary to transship supplies onto the narrow-gauge freight cars at Ouled Rahmoun, a rail hub a few miles southeast of Constantine. Ouled Rahmoun was also connected by a standard-gauge line with the minor Mediterranean port

of Philippeville, via Constantine. As a communications center, Ouled Rahmoun was destined to become the site of a new base section, later called Eastern Base Section, in support of II corps. From the minor port of Bône, Eastern Base Section could use a second standard-gauge line to Souk Ahras, and thence into Tébessa a narrow-gauge line. *(See Map 2.)*

The II Corps accepted these communication restrictions because it initially anticipated a short campaign. Two command decisions based on that premise affected McNamara's Quartermaster plans and operations. First, SATIN Task Force was to receive only Class I and III supplies, excluding Class II and IV items. Second, SATIN Force would move toward Tébessa after II Corps had finished its supply build-up. In other words the classic concept of supply would be reversed: troops would move toward a stocked base and not supplies toward them. McNamara's first task was to organize a ten-day reserve of food and engine fuels in Tébessa before 17 January. To provide services he was allotted a company each of railhead, depot supply, gasoline supply, service, and salvage troops, and a platoon each of bakery, laundry, fumigation and bath, and graves registration troops, plus a truck battalion less two companies. At authorized strength these units comprised about 1,100 men to give support along a corps front of 110 miles.

Headquarters II Corps became operational on 8 January 1943 with a detachment under the assistant corps G–4, Lt. Col. Samuel L. Myers, consisting of one officer and two enlisted men each from the Quartermaster, Ordnance, Engineer, and Artillery Sections. Moving to

---

[19] (1) McNamara *Memoir*, ch. IV. (2) Final Operational Rpt, SATIN Task Force. Opns Rpt, II Corps.

QM Ration Dump *at Tébessa, February 1943.*

Tébessa, Myers placed his command post in the grandstand office of the greyhound race track. Two companies of the 224th Quartermaster Service Battalion arrived on 9 January. Operated by the 85th Quartermaster Depot Supply Company, the ration dump at Tébessa, previously opened by the British, remained in a good-sized, empty, movie house. Seven miles to the east, in the only wooded ravine in the area, McNamara located his POL dump, operated by Company B, 205th Gasoline Supply Battalion. Arriving at the same time, Companies B and C, 28th Quartermaster Truck Regiment, organized a corps motor pool.

By simply reconsigning freight cars of cased rations and gasoline containers as they arrived in Tébessa, McNamara's daily train moved to Sbeïtla over the 100-mile rail line, traveling first northeast through Haïdra, thence south to Kasserine, then northeast to Sbeïtla. On 9 January a detachment opened a Class I and III railhead at Sbeïtla in support of Combat Command B, 1st Armored Division, and other troops along the corps front. So far forward was the Sbeïtla railhead, in fact, that Capt. James H. Perry, commander of Company D, 244th Quartermaster Service Battalion, reported that daylight patrols "were the only thing between us and the Germans." [20]

Although careful attention was given to the inventories on hand at the Tébessa depot—and McNamara or his assistant met nightly with representatives of the corps G–4 and other technical services to consolidate such information—the emphasis was on providing the fighting troops with their food, ammunition, and gasoline "when they wanted it and where they wanted it, with the least amount of paper work possible." While the daily telegram was maintained, it was used primarily as a reflection of the previous day's expenditures. If the troops asked for a certain number of rations, they were given the quantity without question, notwithstanding the prospect that they might subsequently abandon supplies in their bivouac areas and force quartermaster salvage service to expend extra effort in their recovery. [21]

Build-up of supplies continued. Reserves of POL increased daily while rations mounted in tonnage rather than in balanced items. Still, McNamara never doubted that somewhere between Oran and Sbeïtla his ration shipments were "balanced according to a master menu." Because he failed to receive menus or any

other shipping documents, was unable to keep the ration cars of a train intact, and lacked troops to guard trains properly against pilferage, McNamara curtailed the issue of the B ration. Though clerks of the 85th Depot Supply Company attempted to balance issues, the troops closest to Tébessa were the only ones to enjoy the B ration with any regularity. [22]

With Rommel approaching rapidly from Tripoli and with Fredendall's lines overstretched to prevent a junction of the two enemy forces, it became more and more apparent that the enemy was strong enough to make a dangerous thrust against II Corps. By the time that the French front was disrupted to the north of SATIN Force, the attack on Sfax had already been canceled. On 17 January II Corps headquarters moved from Constantine to an olive grove one mile away from McNamara's gasoline dump near Tébessa. By now enemy pressure along the II Corps front had brought the 1st Infantry Division and the 168th Regiment of the 34th Infantry Division to Tébessa as reinforcements. Some 60,000 men of SATIN Force had to be supplied at the end of two single-track, narrow-gauge rail lines.

To support this augmented force, Eastern Base Section under command of Col. Arthur W. Pence was constituted on 13 February, and became operational at Constantine two weeks later. Col. Vere Painter was quartermaster of the new headquarters.

The command situation meanwhile deviated more and more from orthodox lines as II Corps, under British First Army's operational control, was broken down into various task forces of regi-

[20] (1) Ltr, McNamara to Brig Gen James L. Frink, OQMG Obsv, sub: Tunisian Campaign, 11 Jun 43. OQMG MED 333.1. (2) Quoted in 1st Incl, Memo, OQM Fifth Army for TQMG, 21 May 43, sub: Talk to OQMG by Capt Perry. Sullivan Papers. (See Bibliographical Note.)

[21] (1) Quoted in talk cited n. 20(2). (2) Rpt, Lt Col Norman P. Williams, 15 Mar 43, sub: Obsv at Forward Areas. Hist Br OQMG. (Hereafter cited as Williams Rpt.) (3) Rpt, Supply Status RED VAULT, II Corps. G-4 Jnl II Corps, Mar–May 43.

[22] McNamara *Memoir*, p. 15.

mental and battalion size. To support these formations, McNamara stretched his Quartermaster units very thinly to operate railheads at Gafsa, Maktar, and at Tébessa itself. On 14 February Gafsa was evacuated at night, and Fériana became the railhead, forty-five miles below Tébessa. The next day, the 2d Battalion, 168th Infantry, walked into an ambush near Gafsa, suffering heavily and losing most of its equipment. About 150 men managed to escape and McNamara received orders from the corps chief of staff to re-equip the battalion not later than the 16th.[23] His reaction is of some interest:

> This order in itself was a reflection on the staff work that had been done in the preparation for the operation. . . . the entire campaign was based on the assumption that there would be no maintenance for loss replacements of any Class II and IV equipment . . . it was impossible to meet this request, without spending at least three or four days. The request was met, but it took just about this long in which to gather the supplies by truck from the rear and deliver them to this battalion. With the slightest degree of advance planning this situation would not have prevailed. . . . it would have been simple to re-equip one battalion.[24]

The Commanding General, British First Army, on 15 February directed forces holding the high ground west of Faïd to withdraw and begin preparing a defense of Kasserine gap. Having issued their supplies, Quartermaster troops at Maktar and Sbeïtla pulled back immediately into Tébessa. At Fériana the railhead detachment had no time to evacuate 50,000 gallons of gasoline, and the cache

was ignited. Of all the times when McNamara did *not* want to be in a favorable supply position, the Kasserine pass crisis between 16 and 22 February 1943 headed his list. Tébessa then contained a million rations, a large number of unbalanced B ration components, and 500,000 gallons of gasoline. Ignoring rations and concentrating on the rail evacuation of packaged fuel, McNamara reduced his reserve at Tébessa to 100,000 gallons. Simultaneously, he pulled his support units back to Aïn Beïda, thirty miles west of Tébessa.[25]

By the end of February 1943, the enemy was slowly withdrawing to his original positions beyond Faïd pass and at Gafsa, and the crisis had ended. Its aftermath marked the beginning of a new phase in Quartermaster operations. Throughout March, II Corps counterattacked over rough terrain toward the flank and rear of the Mareth Line. After 1 March 1943 II Corps, with General Patton commanding, operated directly under 18 Army Group. With three infantry divisions and an armored division present along the front, each with its organic Quartermaster staff and supply company, Quartermaster support at corps level functioned more and more in normal staff commands. Yet, in adjusting their activities to the new situation of this enlarged II Corps, staffs of corps and divisions alike encountered some trying problems of supply and salvage.

All four divisions attacked simultaneously along the front during the last week of March. The enemy had prepared his defensive positions well; some had been blasted out of solid rock. Terrain was a formidable obstacle. In climbing jagged

---

[23] (1) Rpt cited n. 19 (2). (2) McNamara *Memoir*, p. 53.
[24] McNamara *Memoir*, p. 54.

[25] *Ibid.*, pp. 54–57.

and barren volcanic rock, the troops literally tore service shoes and clothing to shreds. Patton noticed this. McNamara received an order to have 80 percent of the troops in new shoes within twenty-four hours. Thanks to Colonel Painter, 80,000 pairs of shoes came forward even though QM Class II and IV allocations for II Corps did not officially exist during the southern Tunisia Campaign.

For two days, 23–24 March, the Germans launched a heavy counterattack against 1st Division positions southeast of El Guettar and the corps after action report stated: "The performance of the 1st Division on this day [23d] was in keeping with the finest traditions of the United States Army." But supply shortages existed and Lt. Col. Clarence M. Eymer, 1st Division's G–4, emerged from the battle with a file of unfilled requisitions. He invited the attention of Col. Robert W. Wilson, Corps G–4, to the Quartermaster portion of his list. Wilson confronted McNamara with Eymer's requisitions, repeating that 1st Division now considered itself unable to return to combat unless the items were received. For his part McNamara believed that this division was "probably better equipped with Quartermaster items than any other unit within Corps command." He further believed that Eymer's listings on QMC Requisition Form 400 had been copied directly from War Department Tables of Equipment. As sent to him, the forms were unnumbered, undated, and marked "special." Eymer refused to entertain McNamara's suggested substitutions for many items, including one under the heading of "Trumpet, Slide, 'F' to 'G,'" for a "Trumpet, 'E' to 'F.'" Sensitive to implied criticism in McNamara's proposals, Eymer accompanied

Wilson into the chief of staff's office where misunderstandings on the requisitions were ironed out.

The final battle around El Guettar involved large-scale artillery concentrations resulting in heavy ammunition expenditures. To meet resupply needs McNamara's truck units, which he controlled but did not command, were expanded from the two companies he had in January 1943 to twenty-two companies near the end of March. Drivers of the units had been organized from the surplus boat regiment of the 1st Engineer Special Brigade. A study of the communication net from Tébessa to the railheads at Fériana, Sbeïtla, Gafsa, and El Guettar showed that the highways and railroad forward were limited in capacity. Eight locomotives required repair, and only three were operable. In the evacuation of the Gafsa-Kasserine area, five railroad bridges had been destroyed, and the demolished high-arched bridge near Fériana—the construction of a bypass was out of the question—required months for restoration.[26]

Because the distances between II Corps and its divisions were as great as those between corps and Eastern Base Section, the one armored and three infantry divisions strained their own personnel and transportation resources to move considerable amounts of supplies. When the fighting began at El Guettar, the 1st Armored Division moved from Tébessa to Gafsa and Maknassy, but

---

[26] (1) Rpt, Opn RED VAULT, II Corps Opns Rpt, 15 Mar–10 Apr 43. (2) Quoted in McNamara Memoir, p. 63. (3) Williams Rpt. (4) Brig Gen James L. Frink, QMC, Report of Inspection: South America, North Africa, Europe, 21 May–29 June 1943. AG (QM) 333.1. (Hereafter cited as Frink Rpt.)

corps was only able to locate forward dumps at Bou Chebka, 70 miles from the center of the division's supply area. Because of poor roads, heavy rain, and congested traffic, the 140-mile round trip to the division supply point took twenty-four hours. Since corps could not provide closer support or attach additional transport, the quartermaster of the armored division formed two provisional truck companies from unit baggage trucks and assigned incoming replacements to the task of moving rations, gasoline, and ammunition closer to the combat units.

The 1st Infantry Division fared no better. Since the Class I supply point at Gafsa was initially stocked only with C rations, divisional trucks went as far back as Tébessa when B rations were available. Shortages of clothing and equipment continued to mount, for although requisitions were now authorized for Class II and IV supply, tonnage allocations from Eastern Base Section proved inadequate for the maintenance of the four divisions plus special troops. The absence of certain Quartermaster services was an additional handicap for the forward elements. A shoe repair section had not moved east of Algiers until the southern Tunisia Campaign was well under way. Located far from Tébessa, the 1st Infantry Division, shifting for itself, contracted for the services of a French cobbler in Le Kef. In late February the division obtained the services of a sterilization and bath unit, but laundry facilities were unavailable before March.[27]

Nevertheless, additional service units were joining II Corps at Tébessa. As early as 8 February, the 2d Platoon, Company B, 95th Quartermaster Battalion (Bakery), had begun baking for II Corps, producing a daily average of 24,192 pounds of fresh bread during the remainder of the southern Tunisia Campaign. At the same time, 1st Platoon, Company A, 301st Quartermaster Battalion, opened a fumigation and bath point, using water from a stream in the vicinity of the POL dump. During March approximately 400 men per day enjoyed this service. Additional support was provided by the shoe repair section, 218th Quartermaster Company (Salvage Repair), which processed some 250 pairs of shoes daily, and by the 1st Platoon, Company C, 61st Quartermaster Battalion (Laundry), which handled some 8,000 pieces daily.

As the southern Tunisian fighting drew to a close, McNamara was in the midst of two activities that demanded more and more attention: salvage collection and graves registration. Early in March 1943 the 226th Salvage Collecting Company arrived at Tébessa. The unit policed the roads after the Kasserine crisis, retrieving discarded or abandoned matériel, both friendly and enemy. McNamara believed that his salvage operation had gone beyond his mission, and later commented:

The mere fact that a vehicle becomes worn out or a gas-mask gets a hole in it does not necessarily mean that it automatically becomes salvage. No item of supply becomes salvage until it has been declared useless for any purpose by the *appropriate service in question* [McNamara's italics].

---

[27] (1) Memo, Asst G-4 II Corps for G-4 II Corps, 8 Apr 43, sub: Info Obtained at EBS re QM and Ord Equip. II Corps Opns Rpt, 15 Mar–15 Apr 43. (2) Ltr, CG 1st Armd Div to CG NATOUSA, 26 Jun 43, sub: Adequacy of Pers and Transport for Supply of a Div in Combat. Littlejohn Collection.

Then, when it is relegated to a junk-heap, it becomes salvage and becomes a Quartermaster responsibility. In any case, we did the scavenging for all the services, brought back all types of items of supply to our own salvage dump, and then they sent representatives there to go thru the items. . . .[28]

Far from finished when II Corps came out of the line was the work of its burial parties, consisting of a single platoon of the 47th Quartermaster Graves Registration Company and a salvage collecting company. At Tébessa, a II Corps cemetery had been opened in early January. By the end of March the platoon had supervised the burial of 190 dead, which was about 80 percent of II Corps' reported dead at that time, and in mid-April it was assigned to Eastern Base Section.

Pinched out of its own sector after the juncture of the British First and Eighth Armies, II Corps received a new mission from 18 Army Group on 10 April 1943. With Maj. Gen. Omar N. Bradley commanding, II Corps—100,000 men strong —was given the objective of Bizerte. The movement out of the Tébessa area to the new assembly point northeast of Bédja did not involve extraordinarily long distances, only about 140 miles. But it was, nonetheless, a challenge to II Corps' ability to exploit the capabilities of twenty-two truck companies over an imperfect road net, amidst an atmosphere of secrecy. Necessarily, the move cut across British First Army's supply lines. Of the two main routes selected, both originating at Tébessa, the most direct led just inside the Tunisian border through Le Kef, a main British

transportation center, to Souk el Arba and Tabarka. The other highway ran inside Algeria through Souk Ahras, and eastward to Tabarka. To avoid congestion at Le Kef, most convoys followed the route through Algeria.

Co-ordination of the movement was worked out among officers of the British Movement Control Office, corps G–4, and McNamara's assistant quartermaster, who was in charge of transportation. Because speed and surprise were essential, supply convoys were sandwiched between the convoys carrying troops in order that the infantrymen could go into action immediately upon their arrival without waiting for staged supply. With a minimum of paper work and a constant check on cross traffic, II Corps made the movement—one of the first large marches of the war—in four days. More than 12,000 vehicles and 94,000 troops had arrived in the northern sector of Tunisia by 23 April 1943.

Army Group meanwhile, selected Bédja on the sector line between II Corps and British First Army as Bradley's supply center, with railheads at Sidi Mhimech, a few miles to the northeast, and at Djebel Abiod, thirty-five miles farther north. Behind II Corps, Eastern Base Section planned to establish a ration depot at Bône, a small port eighty miles west of Bédja, and forward Class III dumps at the minor ports of La Calle and Tabarka. Class II and IV supplies would come from Algeria by rail. Having been denied the use of a southerly highway into Bédja from Bône because the British utilized it, the II Corps' road net was restricted to a coastal route from Algiers, Philippeville, Bône, La Calle, and Tabarka, to Bédja, thence pointing northeast toward Ma-

---

[28] (1) II Corps G-4 Jnl, Mar–May 43. (2) McNamara *Memoir*, p. 59.

teur. By rail, II Corps shared with the British the capacity of a line from Bône, via Souk Ahras, to Bédja.

On 15 April Eastern Base Section was notified that the initial Quartermaster requirements amounted to 948 long tons of Class II supplies and 1,256 long tons of Class III supplies. D-day had been set for 23 April and despite the limited capacity of the lines of communication Eastern Base Section exerted every possible effort to meet the requirements. Supplies were not only sent overland by truck from Bône, but they were also transferred onto landing craft which skirted the coast eastward as far as the beach at Tabarka. Here the truck companies backed their vehicles into the shallow water and supplies moved directly from boats to trucks.[29]

The first daily train from Eastern Base Section to Bédja carried 250 tons of supplies. Within this tonnage McNamara had ordered balanced B rations for 50,000 men. When the freight train arrived, it had sixteen carloads of peanut butter, a car full of crackers, a case of grapefruit, and a sack of flour. McNamara used the incident to impress on Eastern Base Section the necessity to balance rations. Because the next supply trains were almost a week late, the troops lacked balanced B rations, even in the comparatively quiet days before the offensive, and gasoline was received only in cumbersome 55-gallon drums. When Tabarka as well as La Calle be-

gan to receive supplies for the support of the new American sector, there was uncertainty as to which of the dumps could supply the units from one day to the next.[30]

By the evening of 22 April, II Corps' supply targets had been met, except for rations and a few types of ammunition. To follow the advance, corps G–4 was soon trying to obtain one hundred additional 2½-ton trucks for each of the forward divisions. As corps was forced to establish new supply points directly behind the divisions, Eastern Base Section took over the Djebel Abiod dumps and pushed daily trains beyond Bédja so that gasoline and rations could be issued from forward railheads. When the Germans surrendered on 8 May, Painter had already taken over the operation of the ration dump and gasoline point at Michaud, a town five miles north of Mateur. He also had inherited the corps' salvage operations, and continued the burying of 421 known dead in the II Corps cemetery at El Aouïna, near the major airfield between Tunis and Bizerte. Painter's graves registration teams still had to locate and identify 877 missing troops. By 8 May McNamara retained control over the corps motor pool only.[31]

The surrender arrangements made new demands on Quartermaster truck companies. By 9 May, II Corps had acquired a total of 41,836 prisoners of war,

[29] (1) Final Rpt RED VAULT, Opns to Capture Bizerte, II Corps Opns Rpt, 16 Apr–13 May 43. (2) General Omar N. Bradley, *A Soldier's Story* (New York: Henry Holt and Company, 1951), pp. 73–74. (3) McNamara *Memoir*, pp. 65–69. (4) March Schedule, 18 Apr 43, G–4 Jnl II Corps, 16 Apr–14 May 43.

[30] (1) Rpt, Asst Div QM 1st Inf Div, 30 May 43. Sullivan Papers. (2) Memo, G–4 II Corps for G–4 1st Armd Div, 21 Apr 43; G–4 II Corps, Notes Mtg at La Calle, 23 Apr 43. Both in II Corps Opns Rpt, 16 Apr–13 May 43.

[31] (1) Final Rpt RED VAULT cited n. 29. (2) Ltr, G–4 II Corps to CofS II Corps, 25 Apr 43, sub: Supply Plan for Future Opns. G–4 Jnl II Corps, 16 Apr–14 May 43.

including 35,934 Germans, 5,861 Italians, and 41 men of other nationalities. Of these, corps hospitals registered 1,128 wounded. Prior to the surrender the evacuation of prisoners to Eastern Base Section's compounds had proceeded in an orderly manner, imposing no undue strain on trucking facilities. But on 11 May 26,000 prisoners had to be moved to the barbed-wire enclosure at Michaud. Fortunately for this mass assembly the docile prisoners co-operated splendidly, moving toward Michaud on foot or riding in automobiles, or on bicycles or motorcycles, and asking only directions to the compounds.

For food, McNamara immediately began hauling captured stocks from the estimated 1,600 tons of subsistence taken at Ferryville. This was sufficient, he believed, to keep a million men fed for one day. Yet he knew the stocks were not balanced. Within their barbed-wire enclosures the prisoners organized their own camps and arranged among themselves for their own messing details. Quartermasters delivered German field kitchens to the compounds and, together with the food, turned them over to the camp commanders or to their designated agents. Water for 40,000 prisoners was a problem that soon overshadowed McNamara's subsistence difficulties. He solved it by moving from Mateur to Michaud a number of wooden winery vats, twenty feet in diameter, which had been cut in the form of half-barrels, open at the center. Once the huge vessels were in place, engineers filled them with water from 750-gallon tank trucks and the prisoners had water for cooking and bathing.[32]

Having turned over support duties to

Eastern Base Section, Headquarters, II Corps, during the next fortnight moved westward by truck to the attractive city of Relizane, located on a good highway about sixty miles southeast of Oran. On 20 May 1943 McNamara learned of his next Quartermaster mission—Sicily. For this operation II Corps for administrative and tactical control was placed under Seventh Army, with Patton commanding, and with headquarters at Mostaganem, about thirty miles from Relizane. Taking elements of his former I Armored Corps, Patton constituted a provisional corps under Maj. Gen. Geoffrey Keyes, which, together with Bradley's II Corps, was to execute the American role in the HUSKY operation. Organizationally, this meant that a new tactical quartermaster and his staff, formerly attached to I Armored Corps, appeared in the field for the first time at army level. Since 12 February 1943 Col. Clyde Massey, the new Seventh Army quartermaster, had been co-ordinating plans with a new team of pipeline quartermasters in Oran.[33]

New Quartermaster Teams Organize in North Africa

Quartermaster service continued to be handled by the staffs and service troops of the three separate task forces for many weeks after the TORCH landings. But as operations shifted toward Tunisia, such a division of effort in a completely decentralized system demanded early revision. With a gravely

---

[32] McNamara *Memoir*, pp. 70–72.

[33] Report of Operations of the United States Seventh Army in the Sicilian Campaign, 10 July–17 August 1943, published September 1943 by the Staff of the Seventh Army. (Hereafter cited as Rpt of Opns SUSA in Sicilian Campaign.)

deficient support organization, II Corps had advanced into southern Tunisia in late January 1943. Adequate support for this advance demanded changes not only in the Allied command structure but also in the American SOS.

The advance echelon of AFHQ moved to Algiers on 25 November 1942, and as the headquarters grew its special staff sections gradually assumed control of operations in the Atlantic Base Section (Casablanca) and Mediterranean Base Section (Oran), the support echelons which had replaced the SOS of Western and Center Task Forces. During the next two months Colonel Ramsey's AFHQ Quartermaster Section, consisting of nineteen officers and enlisted men, American and British, was the only office with authority to co-ordinate Quartermaster operations in North Africa. Ramsey drew supplies from both U.S. and U.K. bases until early February 1943. During this period his enumerated functions ran the gamut of traditional Quartermaster activities, including responsibility for motor transport, construction supplies, and labor procurement. Yet this was intended to be only a short-lived arrangement, pending the organization of an American theater of operations and the inauguration of a separate supply channel.

Constitution of the North African Theater of Operations, United States Army (NATOUSA), was announced on 4 February 1943 and all U.S. resources within its boundaries passed from the control of the Commanding General, ETOUSA, on that date. Eight days later NATOUSA was further developed by the establishment of the Communications Zone, NATOUSA, a purely administrative command without support

functions. For the time being, these organizations were really additional offices within AFHQ, set up to handle General Eisenhower's purely American administrative responsibilities. Eisenhower himself was Commanding General, NATOUSA, and his deputy theater commander, Brig. Gen. Everett S. Hughes, also functioned as Commanding General, COMZ NATOUSA. Similarly, all other important American officers within the AFHQ structure were assigned dual functions with a minimum of extra personnel to assist them.

NATOUSA expanded its administrative structure on 15 February 1943, when Services of Supply (SOS NATOUSA) was constituted and placed under the command of Brig. Gen. Thomas B. Larkin, who immediately began assembling his staff at Oran. All supply activities and service personnel pertaining to, assigned or attached to Mediterranean Base Section, Atlantic Base Section, and Eastern Base Section passed under Larkin's control insofar as their supply functions were concerned. In all other respects the base sections remained under the direct command of General Hughes. In the process of these rapid transitions, Middleswart left Casablanca on 23 February and became Larkin's quartermaster at Oran as II Corps assumed the offensive in southern Tunisia.[34]

When NATOUSA was constituted, following the lead of G–4, AFHQ, Ram-

---

[34] (1) *Logistical History of NATOUSA–MTOUSA*, p. 24. (2) Hist of AFHQ, pt. II (Dec 42–Dec 43), sec. I, pp. 196–99. (3) Remarks to Staff and Command Conference, Fort Leavenworth, Kansas, by The Quartermaster General, Maj. Gen. Thomas B. Larkin, 17 May 1946, *QMR* XXVI (July–August 1946), 35–40. (4) Larkin became a major general on 28 April 1943.

sey divested himself of the responsibility for Quartermaster supply and maintenance operations for U.S. Army forces. Although the NATOUSA activation order had named him Chief, Quartermaster Section, NATOUSA, a title he held throughout the remainder of 1943, he received no extra personnel and was given no major extra duties. His American staff worked within the framework of AFHQ and all organizational charts identified the section by the symbols "AFHQ/NATOUSA (American)."

To interpret his mission and formulate policy, Ramsey found himself handling his staff duties at two separate levels. As Chief, Quartermaster Section, NATOUSA, he defined the Quartermaster mission for the American theater commander through the G–4, NATOUSA, and simultaneously at the AFHQ level he performed the same function for the Allied command through G–4, AFHQ. Specifically in his dual capacity Ramsey made recommendations on the levels of Class I, II, and IV supplies that should be reached in the theater. After the close of the southern Tunisia Campaign, he exercised special staff supervision over the disposition of captured enemy matériel and battlefield clearance. For the U.S. forces in the theater, he recommended the approval of special issues of Quartermaster supplies from American resources to Allied forces. In doing so, he maintained close liaison with Middleswart in order to determine the stocks in American depots. After AFHQ created a Petroleum Section, Ramsey's Class III responsibilities were confined to staff matters concerning coal and coal products. Eventually, problems involving captured matériel and battlefield clear-

ance grew in size and scope and a special Captured Enemy Matériel Technical Committee, AFHQ, took over the function. Meantime, Ramsey himself attended meetings of sundry AFHQ boards and committees, including the Petroleum Section, AFHQ, the North African Economic Board, and the Joint Rearmament Committee, which formulated policy for rebuilding the French Army.[35]

Originally, neither Ramsey nor Middleswart had any direct responsibility for local procurement. Both the Western and Center Task Forces had come to North Africa with officers assigned to local procurement duties but it became quickly apparent that a centralized agency was needed if the Americans and British were to have equal access to available resources. On 30 January 1943, AFHQ set up a General Purchasing Board modeled after the organization established in London six months earlier. During 1943, the board was manned by both American and British officers and was responsible for procurement for both forces. Because certain North African manufactures were very scarce, a separate Local Products Allocation Committee was formed to apportion such items. Locally produced foodstuffs were soon placed on the list of controlled stocks, and both Ramsey and Middleswart became members of this committee.[36]

---

[35] (1) Hist of AFHQ, pt. II. (2) Frink Rpt, exhibit B.

[36] (1) Annual Rpt of ASF for Fiscal Year 1943, pp. 269–70. (2) *Logistical History of NATOUSA–MTOUSA*, chs. XIII, XIV. (3) Leighton and Coakley, *Global Logistics, 1940–1943*, ch XVII. (4) Robert W. Komer, Civil Affairs and Military Government in the Mediterranean Theater, ch. I. OCMH.

Initially, the headquarters designated SOS NATOUSA had supply functions only, without administrative authority, and thus differed markedly from the SOS headquarters recently established in the United Kingdom. It was decided that supply decisions for NATOUSA could be better made at the higher, Allied, level through the G–4 staffs. Thus there was no true communications zone and Eisenhower elected to use his NATOUSA deputy, General Hughes, to co-ordinate the logistical plans at the AFHQ and NATOUSA levels with the supply operations of SOS NATOUSA. This was considered necessary because an additional co-ordination with the British logistical effort was also carried on at the AFHQ level. Effective co-operation between Hughes and Maj. Gen. Humfrey M. Gale, the chief administrative officer (British) of AFHQ, demanded that Hughes be able to speak with the voice of authority regarding U.S. service troops and supplies.[37]

Thus General Larkin was made responsible for supply, but he was not given full authority of command over the base sections and service troops. For example, he was not authorized to transfer personnel between base sections without theater approval or to engage in signal communications, hospitalization, evacuation, and transportation. Similarly, this situation placed base section commanders in the difficult position of reporting to Larkin on matters of supply, distribution, construction, and maintenance, and to the deputy theater commander on all other matters. Nevertheless, SOS

NATOUSA mounted the Sicilian and Italian invasions and established additional base sections in the western Mediterranean to support continuing operations and secondary activities on Corsica and Sardinia. As the various technical service staffs formed in Oran, they constituted an advisory or planning body directly under Larkin, without the benefit of an intermediate general staff and its traditional "G" officers. Larkin permitted his staff full use of his name in communications with AFHQ and NATOUSA and allowed them to deal informally with their opposite numbers at higher or lower headquarters.

When Middleswart's Quartermaster responsibilities were subsequently enumerated within SOS NATOUSA, he had the following staff functions: first, the consolidation of base section stock reports and preparation of the theater-wide requisitions for submission to supporting agencies in the United States, and occasionally to the United Kingdom; second, the maintenance of control over stock levels for the theater and the proper distribution of Class I, II, and IV stocks among the base sections; third, the co-ordination of base section activities pertaining to sales stores, laundries, and other quartermaster services; fourth, the supervision and co-ordination of policies for graves registration, salvage and scrap, and personal effects and baggage throughout the theater; fifth, the maintenance of records of service units, including the status of their equipment, which were assigned or attached to base sections; and sixth, the supervision and co-ordination of subsistence procurement activities. As an SOS supervisory technical staff, the Quartermaster Section issued operating proce-

---

[37] (1) Howe, *Northwest Africa*, p. 496. (2) *Logistical History of NATOUSA–MTOUSA*, p. 24. (3) The ETOUSA solution of this problem is discussed in Chapter IX, below.

dures, technical manuals, ration menus, and special circulars as guides for quartermasters and QM units in base sections, and through frequent inspections checked on the execution of its technical instructions.[38]

On the eve of the HUSKY operation, the Quartermaster Section, SOS NATOUSA, working on its first support mission, consisted of an executive office and six divisions, concerned respectively with administration, planning, Class I, Class II and IV supply, salvage, and graves registration. Middleswart's organization chart showed that his first and foremost mission was to supply clothing and equipment to the ground forces, and additionally to provide such items as rations, kitchen and mess equipment, barracks and office equipment, and stationery common to the ground and air forces. In terms of numbers the supply divisions absorbed most of his personnel. At this time NYPE sent convoys periodically to each of the three base sections, which in turn were in direct support of the combat troops.[39] Because the base section depots were never far from the sea, Quartermaster distribution was no major problem as long as shipping was available. Yet one bad feature of this system hobbled Quartermaster supply. If convoys or individual ships containing ammunition as well as rations and clothing were diverted from their original port of call to another in an emergency, the Quartermaster Section had to locate coastal shipping in order to reroute Quartermaster supplies to their original destination. In a commodity-type organization, each supply division took care of requisitioning, storage, and distribution for its own categories of QMC supplies.

Middleswart's biggest problem during the summer of 1943 was that of personnel, both individuals and service units. He did not control the assignment of Quartermaster officers from base sections to his staff. At the end of the first month he had obtained only 8 officers and 18 enlisted men of an authorized strength of 13 officers and 24 enlisted men. Most quartermasters remained with their organizations when the entire group leapfrogged to another support area. In October 1943, by which time American forces were lodged on the Italian peninsula and his supply responsibilities had grown from 3 to 7 base sections and base commands, he still had only 6 officers more than when his section was created. He intimated to Larkin that only bureaucratic obstacles prevented the assignment of talented officers from the decreasing operations in Atlantic and Eastern Base Sections. Larkin pointed out that manning table increases were out of the question. Plans were afoot to move SOS headquarters to the Italian peninsula, and it was not feasible to enlarge the QM Section. Improvement was slow, and Middleswart complained repeatedly to Littlejohn of the predicament which forced him to adjust his operations to an expanding program with a "pitifully inadequate staff." These difficulties take on added significance when they are related to the growth of tactical formations from two small task forces of 40,000 men each in November 1942 (TORCH), to an

---

[38] (1) *Logistical History of NATOUSA–MTOUSA*, p. 24. (2) Office Memo 4, OQM SOS NATOUSA, 14 Nov 43, sub: Orgn of QM Sec. Sullivan Papers.

[39] In May 1943, 295,338 measurement tons of QM cargo left the United States for North Africa. All except 38,523 tons went to Algerian ports. Monthly Progress Reports (MPR), 1943–45, Statistics Br, Water Div, OCT.

independent corps of 100,000 men (Tunisia), to a miniature army of two corps (Sicily), to an army of three corps (Italy) and to an army group with two armies (southern France), in successive, rapid stages.[40]

Since a larger staff was impossible, a more efficient one was imperative. Unsuitable officers were transferred by various expedients, including reclassification. Energetic company-grade officers were put in charge of personnel, supply, salvage, and administration while Col. Mark V. Brunson, executive officer of the QM Section, gave a good deal of time to their training. Operational planning was a constant source of worry to Middleswart. Though detailed strategic decisions did not reach his level, he knew about the middle of May that the invasion of Sicily was not very far off. This was his second amphibious undertaking and he looked about for quartermasters of Western Task Force days. After repeated calls, Middleswart secured the services of Colonel Poore, who could be spared from his G–4 duty with Atlantic Base Section, to head a new Planning Division. Poore worked closely with officers of the task forces who were sent to Oran to work out the details of the HUSKY operation. Using maintenance allowances based on recent experiences, Middleswart and Poore prepared requisitions for 130,000 troops for the period D-day to D plus 30, and submitted them as advance requisitions on the North African base sections.[41]

Once the plans were on paper, Middleswart placed members of his staff on temporary duty with the base sections. As liaison officers, Poore and his assistants moved around the ports and depots to check on Seventh Army's requisitions. After the assault convoy had gone to sea, the liaison officers dropped their expediter roles and prepared to go to Sicily as observers. Once the HUSKY forces were securely lodged on the island, the Planning Division transferred support of the operation to the regular supply branches and shifted its attention to the next amphibious operation, Italy.[42]

As an alternative to HUSKY, the Planning Branch also computed requirements for an invasion of Sardinia (Operation BRIMSTONE), but this project was discarded in favor of an assault on the Italian mainland (Operation AVALANCHE) in the vicinity of Salerno. Again NATOUSA staffs worked with a Fifth Army panel, which temporarily moved to Algiers. Consisting of several Quartermaster officers and enlisted men, this group prepared requisitions for the first sixty days of supply in Italy, and prepared explicit instructions as to packaging and marking, ports of loading, dates, strength, and designations. If time permitted, requisitions were submitted to NYPE for direct shipment to Italy, thereby eliminating double handling and outloading at North African ports. Poore's

[40] (1) Hist of COMZ NATOUSA, pts. I, IV. OCMH. (Quotation is from Part I.) (2) Cirs 22 and 79, Hq SOS NATOUSA, 13 Jul 43, 29 Dec 43. (3) Ltrs, Middleswart to Littlejohn, 31 Oct 43, 26 Nov 43. Hist Br OQMG. (4) Staff Memo 54, Hq SOS NATOUSA, 11 Sep 43.

[41] (1) Poore Journal, Mar, Aug 43. Poore Papers. (2) Rpt of Opns SUSA in Sicilian Campaign.

[42] (1) Littlejohn sent Middleswart copies of the revised 100,000-man plan and it was used in HUSKY as well as subsequent plans. Ltr, Middleswart to Littlejohn, 21 Jul 43. Littlejohn Reading File, vol. XIV, item 55. (2) Rpt Opns SUSA in Sicilian Campaign.

planning work involved something more than supply. His section drafted Quartermaster Tables of Organization and Equipment for Italian prisoner of war units. Hapless prisoners of the Tunisia Campaign were a definite liability in policed compounds, but an asset in Quartermaster support units under the supervision of U.S. cadres. Once approved by the War Department and constituted with Italian laborers, the tables provided manpower to fill gaps in the ranks of 3,800 Quartermaster troops that were earmarked for Naples.[43]

The widening scope of military activity was reflected in the second reorganization of Quartermaster Section, SOS NATOUSA, on 18 September 1943. Increased record keeping for support units necessitated the creation of a separate Personnel Branch. As a result of Tunisian evacuation and burial experience, graves registration policies and organization were reviewed and changes made. Col. Thomas R. Howard became chief of the Graves Registration Branch and also served as the theater graves registration officer.

With the introduction of special services in the theater, a separate supply branch was set up to meet the needs of the entertainment, recreation, and education programs. With more than 3,000 nurses present by this time, and with the first members of the Women's Army Corps reaching North Africa in summer 1943, Middleswart designated a clothing supply subunit to handle their special needs. A new Baggage Group within the Salvage Branch supervised the disposition of effects, located owners, and stored property belonging to interned or captured personnel. Because the Quartermaster Section had experienced supply shortages and service inadequacies in the Sicilian campaign, Middleswart reorganized his General Supplies Group, subdividing it into four new units.

No matter how well his section was organized, Middleswart could always expect some higher or adjacent command to demand an explanation of why something did not proceed according to plan. Near the end of the Sicilian campaign, he anticipated a formal reprimand because of failure to co-ordinate. His planners had set up an air shipment consisting of 31,000 bottles of halezone tablets, a disinfectant for water. Colonel Poore estimated the shipment at three-quarters of a ton. The planners turned the shipping details over to supply quartermasters, who refigured weights and cubes as given in a new manual. In the process, someone selected a wrong set of figures, and the new estimate reached four tons. To lift 31,000 bottles, the air transport commander ordered out two cargo planes. When the Quartermaster depot truck arrived at planeside, the load weighed in at 1,600 pounds, and a single plane departed for Sicily. The incident was written up in detail in a circular letter, and it became a stern warning for all sections to perfect their staff co-ordination.[44]

After the invasion of Italy a third reorganization of Quartermaster Section, SOS NATOUSA, was announced on 12 No-

---

[43] (1) Col Joseph P. Sullivan, Fifth Army Quartermaster History, pp. 7–18. (Hereafter cited as Sullivan MS.) Hist Br OQMG. (2) Poore Journal, 12, 23 Aug 43.

[44] Ltr, Poore to Lt Col Frederick W. Dennis, Jr., QM ABS, 14 Aug 43. Poore Papers.

vember 1943. Middleswart abolished his Planning Branch, placing important aspects of this function with each of his supply branches in order to have no break in their planning and supervisory responsibilities. Other aspects of planning were centered in a Control Branch, headed by Maj. Ramon Wyer. This new branch exercised staff supervision over transportation, storage, and distribution, which had previously been controlled along commodity lines. The new Control Branch reflected Middleswart's growing concern with statistical control over base section quartermaster supply. Outside his own office, Middleswart at the end of 1943 had to step in and set up a central depot in Oran where he could control theater-wide storage and distribution of critical maintenance and repair parts for quartermaster equipment.[45]

Poore, the former head of the Planning Branch, was meanwhile sent to the Peninsular Base Section at Naples, where pioneer planning activities in support of the Fifth Army were urgently needed. Colonel Brunson, although remaining the executive officer, became the new trouble shooter in Quartermaster liaison and observation work throughout the theater. Eventually, he became Deputy Quartermaster, SOS. It can be argued that the three reorganizations of 1943 exerted an unfavorable influence on Quartermaster support and that personnel were shifted around too often to become proficient in their duties. Middleswart, bearing in mind the intermittent type of warfare in the western Mediterranean, kept his staff small—thirty-

four officers and eighty-one enlisted men —and by eliminating paper work was always ready to shuffle functions and officers from one branch to another as required.

As for intertheater liaison, the unofficial technical channel among Middleswart, Ramsey, Gregory, and Littlejohn throughout 1943 was largely a matter of exchanging personal letters. Few visits occurred. General Gregory toured Casablanca and Oran early in February 1943, but neither Ramsey nor Middleswart had the opportunity to return to Washington. Their knowledge of Quartermaster developments in the United States was sketchy. Not until after Anzio do official papers suggest that the situation had improved. Similarly, OQMG planners do not mention effective liaison with the Mediterranean quartermasters until the early spring of 1944. Formal Quartermaster reports from NATOUSA were not compiled until after the Tunisia Campaign. One of the first OQMC observers was 1st Lt. William F. Pounder, but the results of his tour did not reach the theater until the test of experimental clothing items at Anzio in March 1944. The first OQMG field team to be detailed to Middleswart's section did not arrive in Oran until August 1943. The team's survey of the depot system and replacement rates began to play a part in supply by May 1944. Support to the air forces was not officially reported on until November 1943. The first OQMG observers to join Fifth Army arrived in March 1944. On the other hand, liaison with Allied quartermasters was established early in 1943. At the operating level Middleswart established working relationships with Lt. Col. Paul C. R. St. Aubyn of the British Army, with Maj.

---

[45] (1) Staff Memo 72, Hq SOS NATOUSA, 15 Nov 43. (2) Cir 60, SOS NATOUSA, 31 Dec 43.

Roger Jung of the French Army, and later in 1944 with Col. Sebastiano A. de Carvalho of the Brazilian Expeditionary Force.[46]

Quartermaster Organization in the Base Sections

If Middleswart's staff formed the brain of Quartermaster support at the SOS level, the Quartermaster staffs in the base sections and their depots were the bone and muscle of the supply system. Here were the troops, hired civilians, and later Italian cobelligerent service units which stacked and loaded bales and crates, inventoried and repaired thousands upon thousands of items of equipment, drove the supply trucks, and walked guard around acres and mountains of undramatic but invaluable materials of war. Rarely did they win heroes' awards or the attention of the press, and often they suffered the wrath of the combat man when supplies were lost, stolen, or strayed. But for all of this, it takes little reflection to realize that in modern war everyone could not be on the firing line, that there could be no combat zone without a communications zone, and that—even by comparison with those of the Allies—the American rear areas were not lush vineyards.

Because it quickly became more extensive than the combat zone, the communications zone of a victorious theater

was subdivided in the interests of administrative convenience. Base sections appeared along the coast of North Africa, in Sicily, Corsica, Italy, and southern France, their primary purpose being to accumulate supplies for the ground force elements to draw on and from which the Army Air Forces and Navy could secure items common to all forces. Unlike the fighting organizations, a base section was a comparatively static establishment, populated for the most part by administrative and service troops. Although Field Service regulations distinguished between the base sections and the mobile more temporary advance sections, there was no such explicit distinction in NATOUSA until troops reached southern France in 1944. Base sections bore geographical rather than functional names—Atlantic Base (Morocco), Mediterranean Base (Algeria), Eastern Base (Tunisia), Island Base (Sicily), Peninsular Base (Italy), Northern Base (Corsica), and Continental Base (southern France). Mediterranean geography insured that each section would have direct access to water transportation, and thus to NYPE, and all of them, irrespective of their role in operations, were called base sections.

The base section quartermaster had something more than the job of transmitting or initiating Quartermaster policy or plans. He was also responsible for supervising the operations of the support units in his base section. At Casablanca, Oran, and Constantine, the base section quartermasters found their staffs involved more and more in operations. As early as March 1943, Colonel Evans, Quartermaster, Atlantic Base Section, and Colonel Sharp, Quartermaster, Mediterranean Base Section, almost simul-

[46] (1) Pounder Rpt. Hist Br OQMG. (2) Interv with Middleswart, October 1955. Both Jung and de Carvalho were accredited to Quartermaster Section, SOS. In the fall of 1944 Middleswart recommended Major Jung's services to General Littlejohn, and Jung continued his liaison work with OCQM on the Continent. Middleswart stated that de Carvalho had become an astute student of U.S. Quartermaster staff work.

taneously hit upon the idea of creating a separate command organization to handle operational matters.[47] Because he momentarily had a surplus of officers, Evans proposed that the organization be of the provisional type. Sharp's plan called for a regularly constituted unit, one that would be commanded directly by the base section quartermaster. At the time neither concept was adopted, but these suggestions anticipated a T/O unit known later as the headquarters and headquarters company, quartermaster base depot. In the days ahead such a company would play a significant role in Quartermaster operations at the great base section in Naples.

Officers qualified to handle local purchases had accompanied the original TORCH task forces, and thus antedated the base sections. The daily progress of Quartermaster local procurement depended on the activities of Quartermaster purchasing and contracting officers and on the purchasing agent in each base section. The responsibilities of the purchasing agent within Mediterranean Base Section, for example, involved the standardization of prices for all commodities and services, the approval of all purchases and contracts involving more than $500.00, the allocation among the technical services of scarce supplies, the procurement of identical items needed by several of the services, and the negotiation of arrangements for raw materials that had to be imported from the United States for the manufacture of end items. The procurement officers for the various technical services were meanwhile expected to "make the maximum use of every available source or facility in this area."[48] To enable them to do this readily, they were permitted to sign contracts and make purchases involving amounts less than $500.00 without prior approval of the purchasing agent. In September 1943 the General Purchasing Board developed a reciprocal aid agreement with the French which had the effect of still further decentralizing local procurement activities. Under this system, direct payments of American funds to French businessmen or vendors were discontinued, and a franc account was credited to the U.S. Army through which French authorities settled the claims of French suppliers.[49]

The base section quartermaster had his share of personnel problems. Officers were transferred in and out of a section, moving either to a supply installation within the base section or to another base section. The rank of an officer did not affect his degree of mobility, and the brevity of his tenure in a given position was as much a reflection of greater need elsewhere as a commentary on his competence. In Atlantic Base Section's formative period, January to March 1943, it was not unusual for an officer to hold as many as four successive positions or to remain on any single assignment for as little as one week. In February 1943, six key Quartermaster officers—including the quartermaster, his deputy, and the executive officer—were transferred to the newly formed Quartermaster Sections at SOS NATOUSA and Eastern Base. The following summer Atlantic Base Section suffered a similar

---

[47] Memo, Evans for CG ABS, 15 Mar 43. Poore Papers.

[48] Proc Dir 1, Hq MBS, 21 Dec 43. AG 400.12, NASC.

[49] Hist of AFHQ, pt. II, sec. 3, pp. 412–23.

fate when about fifteen of its Quartermaster officers left Casablanca for a thirty-five-day Mediterranean cruise which ultimately brought them to Naples where they formed the nucleus of the Quartermaster Section, Peninsular Base Section.[50] Meantime, none of the North African base sections provided quartermasters for Island Base Section (Sicily) until two weeks after the close of operations. Since 10 July 1943 all Sicily had been considered a combat zone and no communications zone headquarters was organized there until late August 1943. The area remained a quiet backwater, for subsequent operations were staged from the larger base sections in North Africa.

First Operations on Axis Territory

By 9 May 1943 German forces had been swept from Tunisia, and Allied strength was such that AFHQ was ready to conduct two major operations in quick succession on the enemy's soil. For the tactical role Seventh and Fifth Armies had been constituted early in 1943. By spring the immediate objective of Seventh Army was Sicily, and landings in Italy by Fifth Army were in logical sequence to the occupation of that island.[51]

In working toward their final plans of action, Col. Clyde Massey, quartermaster of Seventh Army, and Col. Joseph P. Sullivan of Fifth Army had studied the shortcomings of TORCH and assembled reports of Tunisian experience. They gave careful attention to British First and Eighth Army reports. Each man listened to Quartermaster observers and inspectors who passed through Mostaganem, Algeria (Massey's headquarters), and Oujda, Morocco (Sullivan's headquarters), and spent much time in the field inspecting base sections or conferring with Ramsey and Middleswart on the status of Quartermaster supply.[52] From these sources, each officer had been impressed with the necessity of perfecting the methods of moving supply over the assault beaches, of decreasing the soldier's load, of weighing and balancing Quartermaster troop lists, and of using new Quartermaster packaging, crating, loading, and marking techniques. Yet at the time no American Quartermaster staff had operated in the field at Army level, so that the recently used Engineer support brigades were not fully understood.

In the thirteen months between July 1943 and August 1944, four landings on Mediterranean beaches—Sicily, Salerno, Anzio, and southern France—offered opportunities for improving Quartermaster supply procedures in amphibious operations. These operations were all beset with troublesome problems, but Sicily left behind the most instructive record. From a Quartermaster point of view, the most conspicuous deficiency in the TORCH landings had been the absence of an efficient beach organization. Center Task Force was unique in employing a specialized amphibian Engi-

---

[50] (1) Hist QMABS, Addenda. Hist Br OQMG. (2) Lt. Col. J. P. Littlejohn, ed., History of Quartermaster Peninsular Base Section, October 1943–May 1945. (Hereafter cited as Hist QM PBS.) Middleswart Papers. (3) Ltr, Middleswart to Littlejohn, 26 Nov 43. Hist Br OQMG.

[51] See Lt. Col. Albert N. Garland and Howard McGaw Smyth, *Sicily and the Surrender of Italy,* UNITED STATES ARMY IN WORLD WAR II (Washington, 1965).

[52] (1) Sullivan Diary. Hist Br OQMG. (2) Poore Journal.

neer brigade, and its techniques served as a model for ship-to-shore and shore-to-shore movements and for beachhead development. Because a beachhead operation at the outset labored under the handicap of shortage of transportation, problems of organization and scheduling required scrupulous attention. If, notwithstanding this handicap, the assault forces could not depend on a steady influx of supplies amidst the confusion of the landings, they were likely to be pushed into the sea and plans for the follow-up rendered worthless.

The details of the tactical plan necessarily determined the basic organization for beachhead supply. As the Sicilian and Salerno assaults were conceived in phases, Massey first, and Sullivan later, had to calculate the needs for each phase of his respective operations and the manner in which deliveries were to be made. For Quartermaster support these phases were separated into three chronological periods: assault, consolidation, and final. In the assault phase scales of equipment and supplies had to be reduced to the minimum necessary to sustain the early combat action. These were in turn divided into those carried by the individual soldier and organizational supply that would be immediately available from dumps along the beach. The consolidation phase witnessed the gradual build-up to whatever levels were considered practicable for the forwardmost army, corps, or division depots once space permitted their establishment. The supplies for the final phase of the amphibious operation were those that became part of the permanent inventory of the new communications zone. Normally, such supply went first into the army depots, but was later turned back

to the quartermaster of the base section that appeared with the opening of the new communications zone. So important was the proper calculation of requirements for each of these phases that Middleswart urged higher echelons to let experienced supply officers accompany all amphibious operations with the sole responsibility of noting what individual and organizational supplies were discarded without use or were issued for the assault phase but not used until later.[53]

The HUSKY plan called for the British Eighth Army to land near Syracuse while the U.S. Seventh Army, consisting of two corps broken down into four separate task forces, made simultaneous landings along a fifty-mile front on Sicily's southern shore. *(Map II)* SHARK Task Force (II Corps) consisted of three subtask forces: CENT (45th Infantry Division) for landings near Scoglitti; DIME (1st Infantry Division) to move ashore east of Gela; and JOSS (3d Infantry Division, reinforced by Combat Command A, 2d Armored Division) to make landings in the vicinity of Licata and Agrigento. Using moonlight to their advantage, elements of the 82d Airborne Division (WOLF Force) were to drop behind the invasion beach on Ponte Olivo airport, seven miles northeast of Gela. At sea in reserve was Task Force KOOL composed of the remainder of two divisions, the 2d Armored and the 82d Airborne.

Because beachheads were not expected to be consolidated quickly, planners agreed that each subtask force was to be self-sustaining for approximately thirty

---

[53] Ltr, QM SOS NATOUSA to Plng Sec SOS NATOUSA, 14 Sep 43, sub: Scales of QM Equip and Supply–Amph Opns; Ltr, Middleswart to Massey, 13 Nov 43. Both in Middleswart Papers.

days. This meant that CENT, DIME, and Joss each had to have a suitable quota of service troops, and that each craft carrying troops to their objective should also carry enough food, water, and gasoline to sustain its passengers during their first several days ashore. Each subtask force, supported by an Engineer shore regiment with attached Quartermaster supply troops, was thereby responsible for supplying its own ships and other landing craft as well as for the operation of all beachheads until that mission reverted back to the task force and the 1st Engineer Special Brigade. In this support concept quartermasters adopted one lesson of TORCH—graves registration platoons were attached to assault divisions. Laundry, bakery, and salvage personnel were not to enter the combat zone until army took over supply responsibilities. For the overland fighting in Tunisia, II Corps had had operational control of staging its own supply support; for the landings and advance inland in Sicily, the 1st Engineer Special Brigade, under Seventh Army, was to control resupply and Quartermaster services, thus eliminating both the army and corps quartermasters from any operational responsibilities. This was a new concept, of dubious validity in the eyes of many technical services officers.[54]

Regarding supply, Massey's ration plan called for all units to land with 4 days' rations, including a day's individual ration of the C or K type and the remainder of a type drawn at the unit commander's option. As cargo the assault convoy was to carry 7 days' supply of cased rations. On D plus 4 another 7

days' rations for all troops ashore were to move onto the beaches, and on D plus 8, a third follow-up convoy was to land another 7 days' rations for all the troops ashore. As to engine fuels in 5-gallon cans, Massey's plan contemplated landing a 7 days' supply for all vehicles ashore on D-day, a second shipment containing a week's supply for all troops ashore was to land on D plus 4, and a third convoy was to bring another 7 days' supply for all vehicles ashore by D plus 8. Thereafter, Mediterranean Base Section released Class III supply as requested by Massey through Headquarters, Army Group. Class II and IV supply would arrive on the D plus 4 follow-up convoy in modified balanced loads for beachhead distribution.

Before the operation Colonel Massey explained to McNamara that in 8 days' time II Corps would have received 21 days' supply of Class I and III items into its Sicilian dumps. McNamara suggested that according to *his* arithmetic, 7 days' supply for those troops ashore on D-day, plus another 7 days' for those ashore on D plus 4, plus a third 7 days' supply for those ashore on D plus 8 did not equal 21 days of supply at any time. He recalled his experience at Arzew where the assault units had exhausted 12 days' supply of rations in 4 days. He recommended larger requisitions if shipping permitted. After the war, he wrote, "my comment, offered simply as a suggestion, was ignored. . . . My own responsibility would be to disseminate the logistical data from a Quartermaster view point thru normal channels and to report on our situation thru Quartermaster channels to Seventh Army."[55]

[54] (1) McNamara *Memoir*, pp. 78–80. (2) Rpt of Opns SUSA in Sicilian Campaign, A–8, P–1.

[55] McNamara *Memoir*, pp. 79–80.

An illuminating insight into supply over a Sicilian beach can be derived from the experiences on 10 July 1943 of the 1st Infantry Division, part of whose Quartermaster troops landed near the fishing village of Gela four hours behind the initial assault waves, and the 3d Infantry Division, which led the Joss Task Force in its attack on the beach of Licata.[56]

Because 1st Division was DIME's key combat unit which also fielded two Ranger battalions and a battalion of combat engineers, the division quartermaster doubled as force quartermaster and divided his company into two staff organizations. One group handled divisional Quartermaster supply while the other concerned itself with supply for the whole task force. Because of limitations on seagoing transportation, certain DIME Quartermaster units and services were eliminated until after D plus 30, and some of the officers remained in North Africa to assure proper loading of organizational supplies and transportation aboard the D plus 4, D plus 8, and D plus 12 convoys.

Once on the beaches of Gela, the Engineer shore battalion handled the receipt of supplies at the water's edge, while the 1st Division's Quartermaster detachments established dumps a half mile inland. These units enjoyed good

weather, no tides, and air and naval superiority. Supplies came ashore faster than the companies could handle them, and by H plus 7 adequate but badly mixed quantities of ammunition, gasoline, water, and rations were on the beach. A traffic jam occurred on the morning of D-day because of the speedy deposit of supplies at the water's edge—including such superfluous items as barracks bags, athletic equipment, and administrative records. Scrambling of items made it impossible to keep satisfactory records of receipts. Somewhat reminiscent of TORCH was the misplacing of supplies by landing craft skippers who were diverted from their course when a landing site was in use or obstructed by another vessel.

The 1st Division met stubborn enemy resistance from the air as well as from tanks and artillery in the hills of Ponte Olivo. The first two days in the Gela sector were fairly hectic, and there were moments during D plus 1 when ration dumps were within point-blank range of German tanks. On 12 July, in the face of American aircraft, of naval gunnery, and of the timely arrival of heavier artillery, the enemy withdrew. Beach operations proceeded more normally, and the movement of stocks inland began.[57]

Joss Force (3d Division) divided its service units among three separate formations, a Force Depot, a Near Shore Control Group, and a Beach Group.

---

[56] For their part in the Sicilian assault landings the following Quartermaster units were entitled to the arrowhead award (GO 70, 20 Aug 45, as amended):

1st QM Co	93d QM Rhd Co
3d QM Co	100th QM Rhd Co
45th QM Co	205th QM GS Bn
46th QM GR Co	361st QM Bn
52d QM Truck Bn	528th QM Sv Bn
53d QM Truck Bn	540th QM Sv Bn
86th QM Rhd Co	1127th QM Co AS Gp

[57] (1)"Hairline Planning by QM's Marks Invasion in Sicily," *Quartermaster Training Service Journal (QMTSJ)*, VI, No. 4 (22 December 1944), 20–22. (2) Taggard, ed., *History of the Third Infantry Division*, pp. 44ff. (3) Unit Hist, 86th QM Rhd Co. Hist Br OQMG. (4) Maj Clement Burnhome, Notes on HUSKY Landings, 23 Jul 43. OQMG MED 319.25.

While the Near Shore Control Group supervised the embarkation of all organizations and the loading of vessels carrying divisional supplies, the Force Depot, consisting of Quartermaster, Ordnance, Chemical, Medical, and Signal supply personnel remained in North Africa until the combat forces advanced beyond the limits of beach supply. With the establishment of the beachhead and the seizure of the port of Licata by D plus 3, the division quartermaster started moving supplies through the harbor.[58]

In addition to the improved organization on the beaches, the landings in Sicily were better than those in North Africa because of several new developments, the outstanding one being the debut of the Dukw, a 6-wheel, 2½-ton amphibian truck. Carried to the assault area aboard LST's and capable of transporting supplies directly from a vessel offshore to an inland dump, this vehicle eliminated the double handling of supplies at the water's edge. In the landings, Dukws demonstrated that their uses could be many and varied. Besides hauling supplies, the amphibian trucks evacuated wounded soldiers to hospital ships, hauled beached landing craft out into deeper water, and rescued immobilized tracked and wheeled vehicles from sand dunes.

Unless the roads were good, it generally proved inefficient to dispatch a Dukw far inland, for this unduly lengthened its turnaround time, retarded its rate of discharge, increased wear and tear, added to the consumption of fuel, and increased the strain on drivers. Except for such evidence of improper use of the Dukw, or a comparatively rare report of over-

loading—somewhat overburdened with ten tons of artillery shells, one Dukw sank immediately upon leaving the ramp of a landing craft—this amphibian truck met most expectations.[59]

Closely related to the success of the Dukw was the experiment in palletized loading at ports. A palletized load—also known as a unit load—was a quantity of supplies fastened, usually by metal straps, to a single or double layered wooden platform, which could be readily lifted, moved, or stacked by a fork-lift truck and ship's gear. The chief advantage lay in the speed and simplification of shipping, in the reduction in the number of handlers, and in lessened damage and pilferage. Widespread employment of palletized loads was discouraged, on the other hand, by the shortage of materials-handling equipment at ports, by the scarcity of personnel trained in dealing with such shipments, and by the fact that such units were wasteful of shipping space. Although numerous exploratory tests were conducted in the United States in late 1942 and early 1943, the desirability of palletized loads remained the subject of considerable debate throughout the war.[60] Considering the distressing amount of breakage and pilferage in the North African landings, the opportunity to experiment with palletized loading at the next amphibious landing was understandably attractive.

---

[58] Rpt, CO 3d QM Co to CG 3d Inf Div, 29 Jul 43, sub: D to D-Day Plus 8. Hist Br OQMG.

[59] (1) Burnhome notes cited n. 57 (4). (2) Obsv Rpt HUSKY–Joss Task Force. Littlejohn Collection, sec I. (3) Notes, Working of Sicilian Beaches. Sullivan Papers. (4) Rpt, CO Co A, 43d QM Truck Bn, sub: War Record, 21 July 43. Hist Br OQMG.

[60] Alvin P. Stauffer, *Quartermaster Depot Storage and Distribution Operations*, QMC Historical Studies, 18 (Washington, 1948), pp. 121ff. This monograph gives the advantages and disadvantages of palletized loading. See also, ch. XI, below.

At the Hampton Roads Port of Embarkation, where the 45th Infantry Division staged for the Sicilian invasion, more than 1,500 palletized units, varying in weight from two to three thousand pounds, had been packed and loaded. On D-day and D plus 1 these units were lowered into landing craft and delivered to the beach, where a bulldozer pulled them out of the landing craft and across the beach into the dump area. Water and gasoline were packaged in 5-gallon cans, with 56 cans on each pallet; oil, in boxes of 24 quart cans, 30 boxes per pallet; and 5-in-1 rations in boxes, 60 fiber boxes per pallet. Those pallets transported directly to the dump in Dukws were lifted out of the vehicle and lowered to the ground by means of an A-frame attached to the rear of another Dukw improvised to serve as a mobile crane. The final phase in the life of the pallet consisted of its unloading, after which the platform was returned to the beach where it proved useful as a sled for the transport of nonpalletized supplies.

Landing on D-day with the 45th Division and remaining around Scoglitti for nine days solely to observe, Capt. Charles J. DaCosta of the OQMG agreed with others that "the palletization of water, oil, gasoline and 5-in-1 rations expedited the delivery to the dump area by 50 percent." [61] So impressed was he by the combined use of the palletized load and the Dukw that he did not echo the general warning against employing the amphibian trucks to transport supplies to inland dumps. He argued, rather, that

the existence of a hard-surfaced road from Scoglitti to Vittoria permitted direct deliveries to a dump five miles inland without any significant loss of time.

Less publicized than the Dukw, but invoking less debate than the palletized load was the initial use of the assault pack. Whereas the palletized load was capable of handling all classes of supplies, and in substantial quantities, the assault pack was primarily designed for the delivery of clothing and equipment in small 50-pound loads. Clothing and equipment were manifestly less vital to the success of an amphibious operation than such rapidly consumed materials as food, gasoline, and ammunition, but inevitably a certain amount was lost or damaged in the confusion and fighting of the assault, and replacements had to be speedily provided. The assault pack worked out in detail by Middleswart's staff and packed by Quartermaster depots was well suited to meet the minimum requirements, while eliminating the need to establish separate collections of individual items until the battle had moved inland.

The assault pack was simple: nothing more than a well-stocked barracks bag, containing the full complement of individual clothing and equipment for one man. A haversack at the bottom held a towel, salt and water-purification tablets, K rations, field jacket, raincoat, meat can, blanket, head net, and insect repellent. The pack also contained a web belt, canteen and cup, ammunition case, and steel helmet. For the Sicilian landing, in midsummer, when a fatigue suit was included in the pack, its pockets held a pair of wool socks, a box of matches, two packages of cigarettes, two

---

[61] Rpt, DaCosta to Gregory, 16 Aug 43, sub: Obsv QM Activities at Sicily, Hist Br OQMG.

handkerchiefs, and a small roll of toilet paper.[62]

Made up in two sizes, medium and large, these packs were generally shipped on the basis of 5 for every hundred combat soldiers participating in the assault. This 5-per-hundred figure was sometimes considered high, and in his notes on the Sicilian campaign Middleswart considered 2.5 per hundred a better factor. The larger figure nevertheless prevailed on the grounds that it was not unduly excessive and that the contents of the unused packs were easily absorbed in the depot inventories, once larger installations began to appear. A less constant planning figure was that governing the proportion of medium-size to large-size packs, for experience transformed a fifty-fifty ratio into one calling for 80 percent medium-size packs. Shoes were packaged in separate waterproof containers, each holding 12 pairs of shoes on the basis of 1 pair per assault pack and 1 pair for each 50 men landed in the force. Each shoe package contained 1 pair of B-width, 7 of D-width, and 4 pairs of EE-width shoes, while even sizes varied from size 5's to 12's, inclusive.[63]

Once beyond the beaches the amphib-ian engineers faced the problem of following a rapid advance. Six days after the landings about a quarter of Sicily was in Seventh Army's hands. The Italian garrison was shattered and the Germans, although resisting strongly, were retreating toward Messina. On 22 July the port of Palermo fell and from the Quartermaster point of view this was welcome news in light of the difficulty which the 1st Engineer Brigade had had in moving supplies forward from the southern beaches.

All Sicily was a combat zone. This meant that army G–4 and the special staff for supply had simply delegated their operational responsibility to a very small brigade support staff. McNamara admitted that the amphibian brigade concept had worked well on the atolls of the Pacific, but pointed out that Sicily is an island of 30,000 square miles. An army of 150,000 troops moving quickly inland could not be supported by a brigade headquarters and attached service troops which had been drawn together specifically to handle a beachhead operation. Phased attachments of Quartermaster service troops to corps and divisions (except for a graves registration platoon) had not been arranged. McNamara explained his plight to Massey who attached two truck companies to II Corps to haul supplies from army dumps to army railheads. Similarly the Quartermaster company at the divisional level was severely handicapped in fulfilling its many missions and barely performed its role as a truck company.[64]

---

[62] (1) Quartermasters in Fifth Army championed Col. James F. Tweedy, Executive Officer, Quartermaster Section, I Armored Corps, as the originator of the assault pack. Memo, 2d Lt. Ernest E. Ballard, Asst Class II off, for Sullivan, 1 May 43. Sullivan Papers. (2) The Ordnance Corps and Chemical Warfare Service also contributed items to the assault packs.

[63] (1) Rpt Opns SUSA in Sicilian Campaign, E–4, P–1. (2) Plng and Movement Phases, QM–HUSKY, n.d. OQMG MED 319.1. (3) Extracts–Notes on Sicilian Campaign, n.d. Middleswart Papers. (4) QM Supply–Amph Opns, Sullivan Diary, 20 Oct 43; Memo, Class II off, sub: Class II and IV Activities for Invasion SHINGLE, 15 Feb 44; Sullivan MS, pp. 14, 23–24, 37–43. All in Sullivan Papers.

[64] (1) McNamara Memoir, pp. 81–86. (2) Mary H. Williams, comp., Chronology, 1941–1945, UNITED STATES ARMY IN WORLD WAR II (Washington, 1960), pp. 120–22.

Throughout the campaign, Massey and McNamara were liaison officers with no control over their quartermaster situation. McNamara was skeptical of the extreme confidence that the army staff placed in the support brigade's overworked small staff to keep track of the arrival, storage, and issue of Quartermaster supply. Within the first fortnight, two emergency requests reached Oran for additional rations, despite the fact that ample requisitions had been placed before the operation began. Several million rations were ashore, but not available in the forward areas. But for excellent Sicilian crops of tomatoes, grapes, and melons and for the nearness of African ports to those of Sicily, the ration shortage might have been far more serious. This situation was grave until Messina fell on 17 August and the campaign ended. On 12 September 1943, upon leaving for England where he was destined to become a quartermaster at army level, McNamara resolved that henceforth he was going to be something more than a liaison officer during a war of movement.[65]

Only when the progress of Allied arms in Sicily assured a rapid occupation of that island did the Allies seriously entertain an assault on Italy. At their level Quartermaster planners within SOS NATOUSA failed to appreciate the last-minute arrangements that brought the U.S. Fifth Army from its training areas into the North African staging ports. In their view, these troop movements should have been completed immediately after the departure of Patton's force for Sicily. On 27 July 1943 AFHQ issued Lt. Gen. Mark W. Clark a directive for Fifth Army instructing him to proceed with tactical planning for seizing Naples and its nearby airfields. Fifth Army was to consist of eight divisions under the command of British 10 Corps and U.S. VI Corps, only the latter being an American supply responsibility.

Fortunately, Colonel Sullivan during his stay in Morocco had developed supply plans for the projected invasion of Sardinia by 186,000 troops, accompanied by 34,400 vehicles. When, on 4 August, G–4, Fifth Army, called for Sullivan's D-day plans for Operation AVALANCHE, it was a rather easy task to adapt the Sardinia requisitions of July 1943 to the scale of the new operation. On the other hand, as August advanced SOS NATOUSA had a difficult time in determining the location of the supplies in the base sections, what surpluses if any could be made available from Sicily, and what supplies had to be ordered from NYPE. At the end of August, Sullivan had completed his plans for the follow-up convoys through D plus 24, and Middleswart was hopeful that his pipeline system was ready to fulfill its mission.[66]

Item by item, Quartermaster supply plans for AVALANCHE did not differ materially from those laid down in HUSKY. Under rations the notable exception was the last-minute inclusion of a prisoner of war ration of the C type for 15,000 men for seven days. This feature, of course, had not anticipated the premature surrender of Italian troops, who subsequently had to arrange for their own subsistence. In addition to the assault pack and shoe package allowance already de-

---

[65] (1) McNamara *Memoir*, pp. 85–86. (2) Poore Journal, July–August 1943.

[66] Sullivan MS, pp. 1–21.

scribed, Class II and IV plans called for a reserve for each 1,000 men consisting of 10 blankets, 2 shelter halves, 100 pounds of soap, and 10,000 sheets of toilet paper per day. As a beach reserve until replacement needs came on the D plus 12 convoy, organizational equipment included intrenching tools, electric lanterns and batteries, British-type emergency cookers, water bags, galvanized cans, field ranges, and wall tents. Class II and IV combat maintenance figures were based on OQMG tables of March 1943, which did not reflect experience in Tunisia or Sicily. One problem of the past was solved early. All medals and decorations were personally delivered to the Assistant Chief of Staff, G–1, Fifth Army, for distribution to units before embarkation. Class III planning factors were based on the 50-mile operational day with 6.25 gallons of gasoline as the normal requirement per vehicle per day.

At the last minute, Clark arranged for an emergency air transport service and Sullivan encountered a new situation in planning with Eastern Base Section quartermasters for stocking the supplies at a Tunisian air base. Sullivan had to arrange for special packaging of rations and POL for the maintenance of a regimental combat team or a tank battalion in action if air supply was needed. By the time of AVALANCHE Quartermaster supply planning for an amphibious operation was practically standardized procedure.[67]

Sullivan, who had the distinction of being in the war against Germany almost twice as long as any other army quartermaster, as early as January 1943 had begun to organize his office and to develop a balanced Quartermaster troop basis for an army. In this planning area there were no modern precedents to serve as a guide. Field Service regulations, field manuals, and War Department Tables of Organization and Equipment reflected ideals, offered only vague suggestions, or listed personnel for an army by rank and ratings. During his stay at Oujda, Sullivan had time to develop War Department tables of early 1942 and his own concepts into a well-planned Quartermaster organization. His earliest section constituted a planning staff of 12 officers, 1 warrant officer, and 15 enlisted men, a strength that was about half what the authorized table of 7 January 1942 allowed for the office of an army quartermaster.

The first structure of the office of Fifth Army quartermaster emerged out of an intense training program which Sullivan had instituted in Morocco. At "Sullivan's College," classes were held daily in all aspects of Quartermaster services of supply, with additional instruction in the evenings. Map exercises drawn from Tunisian battle situations served as a basis for the study of realistic supply problems, and participating enlisted men often presented solutions as if they were officers responsible for the accomplishment of a particular mission. In June 1943, Sullivan developed his office to the point where definite staff assignments were made among three functional divisions—Administrative, Operations and Training, and Supply—with each of these subdivided into operating sections. He contemplated having certain officers serve in command assignments over non-

---

[67] (1) Sullivan MS, ch. I, apps. (2) Admin Instr 2, Hq Fifth Army, 9 Aug 43; Admin Instr 9, Hq Fifth Army, 1 Sep 43. Hist Br OQMG. (3) Sullivan Diary, 9, 11, 17, 27 Aug 43. (4) Plans, Class II and IV Data for AVALANCHE. Sullivan Papers.

divisional Quartermaster troops when his office became operational. For example, he planned for his Class I officer to serve as the battalion commander for all bakery companies. For Operation AVALANCHE, he divided his office into a forward echelon for the D-day landings and a rear element to land when Headquarters, Fifth Army, reached the area. Together with his operations officer and two noncommissioned officers, Sullivan himself planned to participate in the D-day assault.

The only significant change in the development of the office of the Fifth Army quartermaster during the ensuing campaign was the elevation of graves registration activities to the level of an independent division, an amendment to Sullivan's original plans which was mute testimony to the high rate of casualties in Fifth Army. Upon being questioned in April 1944 by the builders of a new Seventh Army staff, Sullivan explained that a graves registration officer "is of the utmost importance to an Army Commander. More repercussions from a military, political, and moral point of view can be felt from poorly regulated graves registration activity than any other under the jurisdiction of the Army Quartermaster. It is a subject that requires the keeping of accurate records which must be referred to for years after the war is over." When the army quartermaster became operational, the classic function of controlling nondivisional Quartermaster truck units was transferred to a separate transportation staff in Fifth Army.[68]

In planning AVALANCHE Sullivan, who was to command his service and supply units in battle, carefully phased the arrival of Quartermaster troops and timed the length of their projected attachment to divisions and corps. To assist the 36th Division's Quartermaster company, Sullivan attached a gasoline supply company, a railhead company, and two sections of a graves registration company. On D plus 3, Sullivan planned for only a graves registration platoon to remain with each division. Between D plus 2 and D plus 11, attachments to corps consisted of a graves registration platoon, 6 service companies, 2 truck battalions (less 2 companies each), and a detachment of 75 men from a depot supply company. On D plus 12 when army assumed responsibility for supply, all attachments to corps were to cease except for the normal use of a truck company and a service company.[69]

The Sicilian campaign had shaken the Italians severely, and on 3 September a successful British landing on the mainland opposite Messina added to their discouragement. Meanwhile the Germans retreated swiftly from Calabria, began to evacuate Sardinia and Corsica, and prepared to defend Naples. On the evening of 8 September, as the Allied convoys approached Salerno, the troops aboard were heartened by Eisenhower's broadcast announcing an Italian armistice.

To an invader from the sea the pro-

---

[68] Quotation in Ltr, Sullivan to DCofS Fifth Army, 23 Apr 44; Sullivan Diary, 31 Aug 43. Both in Sullivan Papers.

[69] (1) Sullivan MS, ch. I. (2) Eudora R. Richardson and Sherman Allan, *Quartermaster Supply in the Fifth Army in World War II* (Fort Lee, Va., 1950), pp. 1–13. (Hereafter cited as *QM Supply in Fifth Army*.) (3) Ltr, Sullivan to Littlejohn, 1 Nov 43, sub: Questionnaire–QM Supply. Hist Br OQMG. (Sullivan's answers cover the period from D to D plus 30.)

posed battleground of Salerno was a very unfavorable arena. The beach itself is flat. So is the country behind it for several miles. Sweeping inland from this oval seaside amphitheater the land rises rapidly. On 9 September 1943 the Germans in strength had reserved each rising tier of seats, and had paid particular attention to the placement of artillery in the arena's gallery. As for the weather, landing conditions were admittedly good, but the clear day also afforded excellent visibility for enemy gunners and bombardiers. Supported by the 531st Engineer Shore Regiment, VI Corps on the right flank assaulted the beaches of Salerno Bay near the old Roman city of Paestum.[70] Having arrived with the D-day convoy, Colonel Sullivan, his operations and training officer, and two noncommissioned officers from the Quartermaster Section, Fifth Army, circulated among the 36th Division's beachhead dumps and the railheads to give advice and assistance. By 14 September the supply of assault packs and shoe packages had been exhausted and no replacements were due until D plus 12. Sullivan recommended that each man turn in his two extra pairs of shoes and four pairs of socks. The 36th Division quartermaster immediately set about redistributing this surplus and Sullivan accepted a requisition for replacement of the original issue of these items. On D plus 3, VI Corps took over the supply responsibility. As he reconnoitered Quartermaster dumps, cemeteries, and depots, Sullivan recorded in his diary that VI Corps Quartermaster personnel—two officers and two enlisted men—should concern themselves with their tactical mission, not any administrative assignment. On 21 September the remainder of the army Quartermaster Section arrived at Paestum and reported to Sullivan's headquarters tent in an olive grove. That same day he assumed control of Quartermaster supply from VI Corps, and began looking toward the day when he would supply three corps of a field army.[71]

It was nearly a month before Fifth Army broke through the encircling hills, seized Naples, and drove the Germans beyond that great port. By 26 October the Quartermaster Section was settled in the royal palace at Caserta, and Sullivan found time to review the Salerno battle and to plan for the next. After operating under his preinvasion plan for a month, Sullivan recorded his disappointment over having combined a service company and a truck company as a substitute organization for a salvage collection company. He recommended to Clark that in future landings regular salvage collecting troops be provided as vital to Quartermaster operations. Acknowledging this recommendation, Clark was more than pleased with the performance of the 242d Service Battalion, the 263d Service Battalion, the 204th Gasoline

---

[70] Arrowhead awards for Salerno and Anzio assault landings went to the following QM units (GO 37, 30 Oct 1950, as amended):

45th QM Co	242d QM Sv Bn
47th QM GR Co	249th QM Sv Bn
48th QM GR Co	263d QM Sv Bn
52d QM Truck Bn	1983d QM Truck Co, Avn
53d QM Truck Bn	
85th QM Dept Co	2037th QM Truck Co, Avn
90th QM Rhd Co	
94th QM Rhd Co	3853d QM GS Co
Co A, 204th QM GS Bn	6723d QM Truck Gp

[71] (1) Sullivan Diary, 15, 21 Sep 43. (2) Ltr cited n. 69 (3). (3) Memo, Sullivan for Tate, 13 Nov 43, Sullivan Diary.

Supply Battalion, the 90th Railhead Company, and the 47th Graves Registration Company at Salerno and Naples. "This is perhaps one of the first operations," Clark wrote to General Gregory, "wherein service units were provided in sufficient number to perform adequately their mission." [72]

---

[72] Ltr, Clark to Gregory, 26 Dec 43. Hist Br OQMG.

CHAPTER IV

Supporting the Armies in Southern Europe

Quartermasters experienced certain advantages and disadvantages in the closing phases of their Mediterranean war. The last battles unfolded on the more familiar terrain of southern Europe, and two American armies, the Fifth in Italy and the Seventh in southern France, matured quickly in combat that alternated between a war of position and one of maneuver.

After Sicily fell a situation developed in the western Mediterranean permitting the Fifth and Seventh Armies to enjoy the many advantages that came from reasserting naval supremacy and air superiority over a vast inland lake. On the average, every ten days a convoy direct from the United States unloaded a ten-day level of Quartermaster supply at a large terminal port located directly behind the Mediterranean front. First from Naples, then Leghorn, and later Marseille, staged supply moved to the armies.

The formal Italian surrender on 8 September 1943 and the King's declaration of war on Germany a month later were the first steps in the development of "cobelligerency," a concept that ultimately gave Italy most of the duties and privileges of an Allied Power. But meanwhile an Allied Control Commission decided upon the scope and the geographical extent of Italian self-government, and defined Italian military and financial obligations to the Allies. These policy decisions were of enormous significance to the Quartermaster Corps, opening up possibilities of labor recruitment and supply procurement on a scale not previously contemplated.

Yet Quartermaster support was not destined to grow in size. The Allies chose not to add weight to their Mediterranean operations, but instead concentrated on invading northwest Europe from the United Kingdom. By mid-December 1943 bold counterstrokes in all the secondary theaters had given way to the carefully planned cross-Channel operation which was now scheduled to begin in late spring, 1944.

Even with the resources at hand after the SEXTANT Conference, it might be argued that the Allies could have attained greater strategic prizes in Italy than the limited ones represented by long-range bomber fields, and by occupying Rome, their first Axis capital. Separated by a mountain range, the American Fifth and British Eighth Armies fought their battles in a series of unrelated, piecemeal encounters, which limited the use of armor. In late January 1944 it appeared that at Anzio the Allies had failed to appreciate the advantage to be gained by giving a surprise amphibious operation the weight and reserves which such an adventure so desperately needed. For the remainder of 1944 and early 1945, the Germans fought the Allies in Italy in two great battles of position. The first was waged along the Gustav Line that covered the Liri corridor below Rome. The second was along the transpeninsular Gothic Line guarding the approaches to the Po valley. In both battles, and also at Anzio, Quartermaster operations quickly conformed to the trends familiar in wars of attrition.

Early in 1944 the supreme command of Allied Force Headquarters passed from American to British leadership, and the boundaries of the Mediterranean theater were extended to take in part of British commands in the eastern half of the Mediterranean. To this situation the Americans of AFHQ responded with new command arrangements of their own. On 8 January 1944 General Eisenhower handed over to Lt. Gen. Jacob L. Devers the strictly American part of his Mediterranean responsibilities. During the next few weeks Devers further developed his command by rearranging staff functions on the American side of AFHQ and of NATOUSA and by increasing the authority of General Larkin, his administrative commander.

The most successful water-borne invasion of the Mediterranean war took place in August 1944 along the southern coast of France. This operation was planned and executed despite the necessity of making inbound shipments for Fifth Army and two U.S. Army air forces, and of giving overriding priorities to the forces already ashore in Normandy. The task force commander of Operation DRAGOON (southern France), Lt. Gen. Alexander M. Patch, recognized these handicaps and kept his quartermaster requirements to the minimum. During September enemy resistance was negligible and apart from short delays to

disperse rearguard formations, logistical limitations alone impeded Seventh Army's drive from Marseille to the foothills of the Vosges. After the link-up with Bradley's 12th Army Group on 12 September, Seventh Army quartermasters sought additional resources from the European theater. In the winter of 1944–45 the process of consolidating the veteran pipeline quartermasters of the Mediterranean with those of the European theater proceeded by stages. General Devers' 6th Army Group, including Patch's Seventh Army and General Jean de Lattre de Tassigny's 1st French Army, came under Eisenhower's operational control on 15 September. But control over logistical support for this force was vested in a succession of transitional headquarters until 12 February 1945, when all the supply agencies supporting the spring offensive into the German heartland were consolidated into one large SOS organization, COMZ ETOUSA.

Assembly at Naples

The Quartermaster assembly at Naples began modestly enough but soon picked up speed until it was recognized as the largest gathering of QMC staff officers and operating units in one place up to this time. The first arrivals were old hands in support procedures, having learned their trade in Atlantic Base Section. Quartermasters reached Naples as part of the 6665th Base Area Group (Provisional), General Pence commanding. Under Clark, Pence also commanded the Fifth Army Base Section, an organization which Clark had planned for during the formulation of AVALANCHE. It was created because Clark had noted the shortcomings of the SOS base section concept in the early phases of Torch and Husky. With the capture of Naples on 1 October 1943 the 6665th Group entered the port city with Fifth Army and coordinated support activities until 1 November, when the group became the nucleus for a regularly constituted SOS base section. Thus, for a month pipeline quartermasters operated under army, not SOS control. From the divisions of Fifth Army came ample testimony to the adequacy of supply under this system, which was the prototype of the one used in Normandy in the late spring of 1944. The 3d Division quartermaster found this transitional organization "immeasurably superior" to that of Seventh Army in Sicily. The 34th Division, arriving in Italy from North Africa, was gratified by Fifth Army's prompt support in contrast to the "20% supply and long hauling of the African campaign." [1]

On 4 October, two days after a reconnaissance by Colonel Sullivan, the new group quartermasters, headed by Col. Wayne M. Pickels, began to survey the shattered city of Naples. By the next evening they had commandeered a lumber yard, a canning factory, and two bakeries as temporary installations while the more permanent ones were being selected. Quite unexpectedly, on 5 October Pickels acquired a responsibility that was new to his semipipeline function —supply of POL products to Fifth Army. Hurriedly, Pickels called Maj. Charles A. Mount from the 49th Quartermaster Truck Regiment to direct the delivery of 75,000 gallons of gasoline to Fifth Army

dumps within twenty-four hours. Because the petroleum administrator was not familiar with tactical POL practices, quartermasters handled POL supply for the next thirty days. During October Fifth Army Base Section absorbed Quartermaster supplies discharged at Naples and adjacent ports. On the 26th, because of a serious illness Pickels was replaced as quartermaster at Naples by Colonel Painter, who was transferred from his dwindling activities in Eastern Base Section. It was now Painter's job to make the final supply transition from Fifth Army to SOS as smooth as possible. On 1 November Peninsular Base Section (PBS) was activated and Painter was named chief of the Quartermaster Section.

One very early function of the Peninsular Base Section was local Quartermaster procurement—in fact, the disbursement records of the Quartermaster Section date back to October 1943, before PBS was formally activated. Immediately after the Husky and Avalanche landings, Sicily and southern Italy had the status of occupied enemy territories, and quartermasters made direct purchases with invasion currency. After Italy became a cobelligerent, the system of direct purchases was retained in the combat zone, using Allied military lire to be redeemed by the Italian Treasury. In the communications zone and in self-governing "King's Italy," the Allies used requisitioning as the normal method of procurement, but there were repeated emergencies which required quick action. Painter maintained close liaison with the Local Resources Board, an agency of AFHQ, and was permitted to make cash payments whenever they were needed to obtain operationally essential supplies.

---

[1] (1) Cir 87, Hq SOS NATOUSA, 2 Aug 44. (2) History of PENBASE, I, 9 Jul–28 Aug. 43. OCMH. (3) Quoted in Rpt, Sullivan to Tate, 10 Feb 44, sub: QM Hist Data, 9 Sep 43-31 Dec 43. G–4 Hist Rpt File, Sullivan Papers.

Such payments were held to a minimum at the request of the Italian Government, which feared inflation.[2] The mechanics of procurement remained virtually the same as in North Africa. In July 1944, when AFHQ moved to Italy, the procurement functions of the General Purchasing Board and the allocation responsibilities of the Local Products Allocation Committee were merged under the Allied Forces Local Resources Section, which supervised separate regional procurement boards in Sicily, Sardinia, and Italy.[3]

Inasmuch as Quartermaster supply—in early November Fifth Army's daily demands were 400 tons of rations and 550 tons of POL—was in the limelight, Painter quickly made the supply section one of the largest on his staff and obtained Colonel Poore to head it. Already Poore was familiar with the details of AVA-LANCHE and had only recently planned and set up supply for the elements of the French Expeditionary Corps, which was then joining Fifth Army. In Poore's section more and more matters developed which involved operations. One of these was the creation of a remount depot and the purchase of pack animals and forage —activities that could only gradually be decentralized to other Quartermaster organizations. Such support called for operating troops, and Painter struggled to find men at a time when all troop replacement pools were closed to quartermasters. The need for staff officers was equally pressing. By 1 December the new section had a total of twenty-three

separate staff reports to compile, most of which were semimonthly SOS studies covering such details as lend-lease, local procurement, inventories, salvage, civilian wages, vehicular data, back-orders on clothing, and medical statistics. At the end of November 1943 Painter sought relief in the reorganization of his section.[4]

On paper, the War Department's Table of Organization dated 11 August 1943 for a headquarters and headquarters company, quartermaster base depot, presented a solution to Painter's difficulties. The need for this type of company had been manifested in the early days of each North African base section. On 14 May 1943 Middleswart had formally presented his concept of the headquarters detachment to The Quartermaster General. At the same time Littlejohn's staff in London, while working on a revised depot and base section Quartermaster scheme for the United Kingdom, drafted a similar type of headquarters detachment. Specifically, it was the Atlantic Base Section quartermaster who had first attempted to use the new concept. As early as January 1943 Colonel Evans had decided that his own staff was too small to exercise efficient control over operating Quartermaster units and installations which were clustered around depots scattered over five different areas of Morocco. Quartermaster planners preparing for AVALANCHE recognized that this type of headquarters detachment was ideally suited to the projected base section at Naples.[5]

[2] (1) Komer, Civil Affairs, ch. XVI. OCMH. (2) Hist QM PBS, p. 216.
[3] Logistical History of NATOUSA–MTOUSA, chs. XIII, XIV.

[4] (1) Hist QM PBS, pp. 13–18. (2) Poore Personal Letter File, Nov–Dec 43. Poore Papers.
[5] (1) T/O 10–520–1, 11 August 1943. (2) Hist QM PBS, pp. 16–17. (3) See above, p. 74. (4) Ltr, Sharp to Littlejohn, 17 Mar 43. Littlejohn Reading File, vol. X, item 57.

Normally, the regularly constituted company comprised 154 persons, including 34 officers, 2 warrant officers, and 118 enlisted men. While operating a single general depot with a number of subdepots, this detachment supervised all attached Quartermaster support units within the base section. When operating at a branch depot, it supervised all attached Quartermaster troops as well as any station complement units such as a signal service platoon, postal unit, finance section, and station hospital. The new company was the War Department's method of streamlining Quartermaster service units in the interest of greater flexibility and economy in manpower. After coordinating the personnel needs for the new company with SOS NATOUSA, Painter decided initially to assemble half the people necessary to staff it. On 26 November 1943, Peninsular Base Section activated Headquarters and Headquarters Company, 6698th Quartermaster Base Depot (Provisional). On 1 December Lt. Col. Rowland S. Brown assumed command.[6]

As the 6698th demonstrated that it could handle more and more operating units, Painter's section concentrated on staff plans and policy. Because of their Allied nature, Painter initially retained three operational functions: the remount service, solid fuel yards, and operations that involved liaison with a growing number of Allied commissions, such as local procurement and civilian food relief. On 7 January 1944 the 6698th relieved Poore's Supply Division of the job of processing and editing all Fifth Army requisitions, including those preparatory

to mounting the Anzio operation. By the end of the month the lines of demarcation between Quartermaster Section, Peninsular Base Section, and the 6698th Headquarters and Headquarters Company were clearly drawn.[7] When Painter was relieved in April 1944 by Col. George H. Bare, the Quartermaster Section had made considerable progress on plans for the expected drive on Rome and the projected invasion of southern France. In June the 6698th dropped its provisional status, reached full strength in manpower, and acquired the designation of Headquarters and Headquarters Company, 61st Quartermaster Base Depot.[8] Five months before the 61st had reached peak strength, Colonel Painter contemplated operating his Neapolitan base with some 6,000 Quartermaster troops, but he had received only 3,575 military personnel. These troops belonged to four battalions of service troops and eighteen separate Quartermaster companies. All were attached to the 6698th Headquarters and Headquarters Company which also employed a total of 5,500 civilians.[9]

When Bare assumed command in April at Naples, the 6698th was supervising the operations of 41 separate Quartermaster installations, including 5 Class I depots and dumps, 4 separate ration distribution points, 2 cold storage plants, 3 bakeries, 3 garbage collecting points, 3 clothing and general supply warehouses, a coal and wood depot, a salvage dump, a metal scrap yard, a typewriter repair shop, a dry

---

[6] Hist QM PBS, p. 18.

[7] Ltr, Poore to Tate, G–4 Fifth Army, 7 Jan 44; Ltrs, Poore to Middleswart, 20, 21 Jan 44. Both in Poore Papers.

[8] Hist QM PBS, pp. 18–19.

[9] Rpt on Peninsular Base Section, 10 Feb 44, sec. V, QM, prepared by Col. Ewart G. Plank, Hq ETOUSA. USFET AG 319.1.

cleaning plant with 8 service shops, 3 laundries, a personal effects depot, 3 cemeteries, 3 remount stations, and 2 forage yards. In addition, the 6698th and its successor, the 61st, had quartermasters working at 2 Italian Army clothing depots and at French Base Depot 901, the organization which supported the French Expeditionary Corps in Fifth Army. In terms of supply the 61st handled approximately 27 pounds of Quartermaster items per man per day for 320,000 men in Fifth Army, of which troops 45,000 were French, Moslems, or Italian cobelligerents, and common-use items for the Twelfth and Fifteenth Air Forces and the U.S. Navy. It also provided limited amounts of supply for five million civilians.[10]

During the 18 months from December 1943 to May 1945, the 61st and its predecessor, the 6698th, controlled the services of 29 Quartermaster support units attached for more than a year and of 99 units attached for periods varying from 1 to 20 months, with 8 months the length of average assignment. Considered together, these attachments present a picture of units constantly moving in and out of Colonel Brown's command. The 61st Quartermaster Base Depot was noteworthy in that it provided direct support to a field army longer than any other similar unit in the war against Germany.

An important port and commercial city the size of Naples might have been expected to offer as many facilities for storage and other quartermaster services as Colonels Pickels, Painter, Bare, and Brown could have possibly used. Instead, when the first quartermasters entered the city on 3 October 1943 and checked on preinvasion map sites, they were quickly disenchanted. Confronting Pickels was an awesome example of demolition. The Germans had scuttled ships in the port area and spread destruction across the suburbs at key communication centers. Allied bombers had added to the devastation. Property in general was demolished, unsuitable, or earmarked by military government staffs for the rehabilitation of the devastated region. The best of available locations either had been reduced to rubble or lacked water, gas, or electricity. Nowhere had quartermasters before encountered such destruction.

But they had to make the best of the situation, and by the end of October 1943 Quartermaster installations were being established around Naples. On the 13th, the Quartermaster Section opened a cemetery near the 95th Evacuation Hospital; it later became the Allied cemetery. Because water could not be obtained from city mains, mobile bakeries and sterilization units were set up on the Italian Fair Grounds, where water could be drawn from several large ponds, which hitherto had served to beautify the landscape. The Naples City Market housed a subsistence dump, but only briefly as the space had to be vacated for a British works. Accessibility to a good highway and rail net encouraged the selection of a new Class I site in Aversa, on the outskirts of Naples, and rations accumulated here before the engineers completed their improvements. But as if some malevolent spirit was afoot, the rainy season started and the stacks of food at Aversa slowly sank into the mud. Thirty thousand tons of rations disappeared, enough for 10,000,000 men for a day.

---

[10] Hist QM PBS, pp. 18–19 and chart facing p. 33.

The second and third tries for Class I sites were considerably better. One was situated near Garibaldi Station in Naples, and the other in Marcianise, about twenty-five miles to the north. Once engineers had cleared and apportioned the areas, both were comparatively capacious. Equipping the dumps with more than six miles of roller conveyors permitted the mass handling, sorting, and stocking of rations without the use of trucks or other warehousing vehicles. In November 1943 more than a dozen Class I points opened in and around Naples. The Campi Flegri railway yards stored wholesale supplies; an athletic stadium provided an open storage area where sheds were constructed to contain sacked goods and fast-moving items; and existing commercial ovens were repaired and added to military baking equipment to produce as much as 75,000 pounds of bread each day. As the 61st expanded its operations, a baking company was taken over at Bagnoli on the north side of the bay, where a large replacement depot and staging area was located. Two ice plants and a cold storage plant were occupied. A three-story stone building and an adjacent sports field housed a retail distribution point popularly called the "delicatessen." Outside this building, three cold storage boxes, special tents for fresh fruits and vegetables, and a complete bakery permitted truckside delivery for SOS units to draw rations.

Twelve miles north of Naples at Gricignano-Teverola station, the 61st opened its main wholesale clothing and equipage depot. Here all Class II and IV stocks were assembled except sales, salvage, and certain inactive goods. Because existing warehouses lacked space for everything, the construction of sheds and Nissen huts

and the early improvement of open areas were mandatory. Although a compact suburban depot offered such theoretical advantages as the ability to conduct its operations with fewer supervisory personnel, more orderly record keeping, and less competitive traffic, this installation had its share of difficulties. Hardly had the site been taken over from Fifth Army before the rapid influx of supplies, delivered to service troops who were too few and inexperienced, resulted in a mountain of unsorted clothing and equipment. Colonel Painter was unable to remedy this situation for several months, and the depot supply company operating the station was "talked about, fussed at, and skinned by all who saw the situation."[11]

An inspection of the Gricignano-Teverola depot as late as April 1944 by Major Wyer's stock control team from Middleswart's office disclosed the spectacle of disorderly stacks and broken, unmarked containers. Wyer reported that shelter halves were scattered about, that individual items were in mixed sizes, and that his team had no way of knowing what the depot contained. The rapid turnover of stocks, limited storage space, and the arrival of supplies at the depot in broken or poorly crated packages largely explained this discouraging situation. But even so Wyer reported to Middleswart that there was no excuse for the visible evidence of loafing by warehousemen.[12]

In the autumn of 1943 the terrain over

---

[11] *Ibid.*, p. 16.

[12] (1) "QM Functions in the Theater of Operations," *QMR*, XXIII (March–April 1944), 42. (2) General Mark W. Clark, *Calculated Risk* (New York: Harper & Brothers, 1950), pp. 216–17. (3) Rpt, Wyer to Middleswart, 18 Apr 44, sub: Rpt of QM Stock Control Team PENBASE, 6–18 Apr 44. OQMG MED 319.25.

which Fifth Army was advancing presented to Painter another supply problem: the small unit under fire in a position to which it was nearly impossible to move supplies. Infantrymen held positions inaccessible to every form of ground transportation, including pack animals. Delivery by air was the only solution, and an air resupply depot was established at Capocichino Airfield in the outskirts of Naples. The depot stored rations, water, medical supplies, POL, and ammunition for both the British and American troops. U.S. packaged rations were used exclusively because of their smaller bulk and better packing. By attaching an element of the 509th Parachute Infantry Battalion to the base section, experienced personnel were obtained to further the work of airdropping. The basic method taught to quartermasters of the 61st prescribed the use of standard containers from C–47 airplanes. But an improvised method was developed whereby supplies were secured with wire and salvaged blankets in belly tanks and dropped from A–36 aircraft.[13]

As the complex of captured airfields in the Bari-Foggia region and on the island bases of Corsica and Sardinia were put into operation, pipeline quartermasters were attached to them, the first to operate solely under United States Army Air Forces control. By the end of 1943, the Twelfth Tactical and the Fifteenth Strategic Air Forces required major quantities of Quartermaster items common to both ground and air force troops. Heretofore SOS base sections had furnished these items, principally rations and clothing. But now the accident of geography

separated the air bases from established SOS support sections. This applied particularly to the Adriatic area, within the British administrative zone. Tentatively, planners considered activating two new SOS base sections, but soon dropped the idea. Already the movement of air groups from North Africa, the development of a network of Italian airfields, and the establishment of 35,000 troops around the Foggia airfield complex had consumed some 300,000 tons of precious shipping. This build-up came at a time when Fifth Army faced a critical situation, and quartermasters in Naples were momentarily in competition with their AAF colleagues.

SOS NATOUSA had no resources to pour into two new special-type base sections. It was therefore decided that items of common supply would be furnished through a general depot. For Quartermaster troops, SOS NATOUSA again turned to the declining Atlantic Base Section and organized two detachments of the Headquarters and Headquarters Company, 2665th Quartermaster Base Depot (Provisional), each consisting of twelve officers and twenty-six enlisted men. These detachments were attached to the XII Air Force Service Command (AFSC), which in turn grouped all its SOS quartermaster service units under the supervision of the 2665th. One detachment went to the Adriatic Depot with headquarters at Bari, Italy, and the other to Cagliari, Sardinia, to operate the Tyrrhenian Depot.[14]

Adriatic Depot—serving an area reach-

---

[13] History of PENBASE, I, 28 Aug 43–21 Jan 44. OCMH.

[14] (1) Cir 22, Hq SOS NATOUSA, 13 Jul 43. (2) *Logistical History of NATOUSA–MTOUSA*, pp. 28–29. (3) Cir 74, Hq SOS NATOUSA, 20 Dec 43. (4) Craven and Cate, eds., *Europe: TORCH to POINTBLANK*, p. 562.

ing from the Italian heel northward to San Severo and inland along the coast to a depth of forty miles—expanded rapidly after November 1943, and the 2665th Company began to operate under unique conditions as a small SOS within a larger USAAF command. In the interest of speedier delivery of rations, clothing, and general supplies, the 2665th was authorized to deal directly with SOS NATO-USA if it first confirmed all strength reports with the XII AFSC. Requisitions provided that common supply was to be shipped directly from NYPE to Bari or Cagliari along with other AAF cargo. On paper the arrangement appeared simple; in practice it proved complex. The 2665th in effect had one direct master and another hidden away in the form of SOS NATOUSA.[15] Another difficulty was the large number of ship diversions to both Bari and Cagliari, causing ground force supplies to become hopelessly tangled with SOS supplies for the XII AFSC. Later, when the French Army mounted on Corsica for DRAGOON and the small ports of Ajaccio and Bastia were unable to berth Liberty ships with supplies specifically earmarked for French use, the cargoes had to be assigned to Cagliari. The 2665th detachment in Sardinia soon had to cope with colossal stocks awaiting reassignment to the French Army while at the same time receiving and issuing AAF supplies.[16]

At Bari the 2665th arrived on the scene late and found that the cargo of four Liberty ships had arrived long before. Quartermaster supplies had been hauled

to Villa Stepelli, a walled-in compound which had formerly been used as an Italian Army depot. Thousands of tons of mixed AAF and SOS supplies—rations, heavy engineer equipment, valuable signal instruments, and lubricating oils—had been dumped indiscriminately over many acres. The first troops to arrive were, moreover, unskilled in the administration of such a large depot. Their transportation means hardly met minimum needs, and contacts with the railheads which served the growing number of airfields at Foggia were unsatisfactory. On 7 November 1943 the arrival of the 246th Quartermaster Depot Company and the 86th Railhead Company brought welcome reinforcements, and the storage and distribution system slowly began to function. By February 1944 the single depot at Bari could no longer serve the overgrown railhead points at Foggia. This situation led to the redesignation of the railhead as Adriatic Depot 2. Because the Bari depot forwarded the daily train to Foggia and the 2665th continued to maintain the records for the newer depot, Adriatic Depot 2 in effect operated as a subdepot of Bari.

During the summer of 1944 as the Air Forces expanded their shuttle operations among bases in the United Kingdom, Italy, and Russia, and followed the ground advance beyond Rome, a third depot was opened at Ancona, two hundred miles north of Foggia. From Bari, supplies came by water and were trucked from Ancona to Jesi, where they were fanned out to nearby air installations. Along the length of Italy's eastern seaboard air operations ultimately involved some 200,000 troops and the 2665th controlled sixteen separate Quar-

---

[15] History of Adriatic Depot, I, 21 Oct 43–1 Jun 44. OCMH.
[16] Ltr, Brunson to Chief OCMH, 27 Sep 54. OCMH.

termaster support units within the XII Air Force Service Command. The 2665th's support extended beyond the boundaries of Italy. At Athens, Air Transport Command planes visited regularly to deliver post exchange items. Supply of the partisans in Yugoslavia was largely a Royal Air Force responsibility, but several U.S. units, especially the 60th Troop Carrier Group, made important contributions. Most supplies were airdropped, but on occasion the C–47 transports of the 60th landed and delivered all types of supplies, even including mules.[17]

One significant factor was common to the operations of these two depots—neither installation was responsible for the support of any ground combat troops. In the Adriatic area, the British Army provided security for AAF bases, and on Corsica and Sardinia the French and Italian forces, respectively, had the same mission. These troops received little American support, and none through the two AAF depots. Nevertheless, considering their very modest size, Adriatic and Tyrrhenian Depots provided very adequate and satisfactory support to the Twelfth and Fifteenth Air Forces.

The Slow Advance on Rome

From somewhere along the lines of the Garigliano and Sangro Rivers, 75 miles south of Rome, Sullivan dispatched an undated requisition to his colleagues at Naples. Only partly in jest it read: "The Army is starving and freezing to death. We need about 50,-000,000 of everything. In fact send all you have. P.S. Also send what comes in next week." The message implied that spigot and pipeline quartermasters were experiencing their first real war of attrition. Actually, the strain on supply started in mid-November 1943 when Fifth Army's drive, which had been continuous since Salerno Bay, came to a temporary halt along the Volturno. Winter rains, flooded rivers, mud, the expensive daily train by truck instead of rail, and a determined enemy in fixed positions demanded the tightest kind of unity among quartermasters. Nowhere had Fifth Army seriously considered abandoning the offensive. By 24 November Clark had deployed his two American and one British corps in anticipation of a drive into the Liri valley. After nearly two months of desperate resistance on the Winter Line, the Germans retired to their Gustav Line, which started at the Tyrrhenian Sea, followed the Garigliano, Gari, and Rapido Rivers, and ended in the hills beyond Cassino.[18] During this period Sullivan, Painter, Middleswart, and Ramsey more clearly than before saw the intimate relationship between tactics and their wholesale mission of supply.

Before encountering the Gustav Line late in December 1943, Allied planners had been considering an amphibious assault to outflank the German transpeninsular position. Delicately, the plan hinged on the availability of fourteen

---

[17] (1) Opn Functions, Adriatic Depot, 3 Dec 44. MTOUSA, Adriatic BS 370.43. (2) Wesley Frank Craven and James Lea Cate, eds., "The Army Air Forces in World War II," vol. III, *Europe: ARGUMENT to V–E Day, January 1944 to May 1945* (Chicago: The University of Chicago Press, 1951), pp. 507–14.

[18] (1) Quoted in Preface, Hist QM PBS. (2) Ernest F. Fisher, Cassino to the Alps, a volume in preparation for UNITED STATES ARMY IN WORLD WAR II.

LST's. By 31 December a third version of Operation SHINGLE against the Anzio-Nettuno beaches was finally approved and scheduled to take place in late January 1944 regardless of the southern position of Fifth Army. The VI Corps, composed of the 3d Infantry Division and the British 1st Division, was to make the assault on 22 January 1944.

On 8 January radio traffic among Quartermaster sections suddenly increased and the train of events then set in motion indicated the course to be taken. That same day quartermasters at Naples received instructions to begin filling Sullivan's phased QM requisitions for SHINGLE. Concurrently, the Quartermaster Section of VI Corps was informed that it would no longer be part of the requisitioning system. The step acknowledged acceptance of the War Department's doctrine, announced in October 1943, eliminating all corps headquarters from supply responsibilities. Accordingly, VI Corps announced a surplus of Quartermaster officers whose services were sorely needed by the Quartermaster Section, Peninsular Base Section. Optimistically, Painter selected Poore to plan for the establishment of a Quartermaster base at Rome. For resources Poore called on Middleswart. The day of 8 January was an opportune time for this appeal. After sharing divided authority and responsibility with NATOUSA for a year, the Quartermaster Section, SOS NATOUSA, was on the verge of benefiting from a theater reorganization, including a realignment of functions between Middleswart and Ramsey.[19]

Also on 8 January, as already described, NATOUSA came under the command of General Devers, who immediately began furthering the development of a separate Communications Zone, NATOUSA. By 20 February 1944 the process was complete. Thereafter Devers agreed not to engage in any operating functions which the new Communications Zone commander, General Larkin, could reasonably handle himself. Specifically, all base sections now came completely under Larkin's control, rather than partly as before. On paper and physically, Devers transferred several theater staff sections to Larkin's headquarters at Oran. With a clear-cut mission Larkin organized his Headquarters, SOS NATOUSA—he decided to retain this familiar name for his new command—along the familiar lines of an orthodox general and special staff. SOS moved to Italy in July 1944.

In the process of these changes, Middleswart acquired a broader area of responsibility. First, he controlled all Quartermaster units and personnel assignments within the Communications Zone. Second, he issued items in excess of authorized Tables of Organization and Equipment. Third, under NATOUSA policies, Middleswart had charge of supervising Quartermaster training throughout the command. Fourth, he handled allocations and issue of supplies which were needed by the U.S. Navy, the merchant marine, and the War Shipping Administration. And lastly, he controlled supply to be released for Allied or cobelligerent forces as outlined in NATOUSA policies. In all this he still had no authority over POL and solid fuels. With that exception, he was by February 1944 the senior quarter-

---

[19] Colonel Ramsey became a brigadier general on 17 September 1943.

master in the Communications Zone of NATOUSA, and in effect the theater quartermaster.[20]

At AFHQ level, on the other hand, Ramsey became involved more and more in two specific missions as the war spread in Italy. First, his AFHQ Quartermaster Section was the channel of communication for captured enemy matériel. It is significant that the Fifth Army had few items of this nature to report, indicating that the enemy was highly disciplined in a war of attrition. Second, through a deputy at Naples— Ramsey had moved to Caserta with AFHQ in July 1944—he controlled the allocation of imported coal for the Allied stockpile, except requisitions by the Royal Navy and the British Ministry of Transport.[21]

Actually the realignment of Quartermaster functions, which began early in January and ranged from corps level to the highest Allied headquarters, was a return to prewar U.S. doctrines. The organization was tightened and the various staffs, by now veterans of a year's labor, obtained no increase in manpower. Standing operating procedures governed supply, and planning on the scale of SHINGLE and ANVIL was no longer dreaded. Achievement of com-

munications zone status and a strengthening of Quartermaster organization at army level drew pipeline and spigot quartermasters closer together than before. They intensified their efforts in such new fields as development of a remount service, organization of repair and spare parts teams, correction of theater stock inventory procedures, collection of replacement factors, prevention of trench foot, development of services of supply within such groups as the French Expeditionary Corps, Italian cobelligerent units, and prisoners of war, and preparation of supplies for delivery by air.[22]

Sullivan was the first quartermaster to benefit from these developments. Plans had already provided that the second and fourth convoys for SHINGLE were to consist of Liberty ships, to be loaded in North Africa. Consequently they had to sail earlier than the first and third convoys, which comprised LST's and sailed from Naples. By 8 January 1944 Sullivan had submitted his requisitions to Middleswart for all four convoys. They were designated A BULL to D BULL, inclusive, BULL being the shipping code designation for Anzio. They covered the QM requirements of the initial landing force—45,000 men and 4,200 vehicles. Based on newly acquired information of what assault troops actually needed, the BULL requisitions represented a major advance in logistical planning.[23]

For the Anzio landings, an ingenious system of preloaded trucks to be car-

---

[20] (1) Remarks to Staff and Command Conference, Fort Leavenworth, Kansas, by The Quartermaster General, Maj. Gen. Thomas B. Larkin, 17 May 1946, QMR, XXVI (July–August 1946), 35–40. (2) Hist of AFHQ, pt. III (Dec 43–Jul 44), sec. II, pp. 752–77; pt. III, sec. I, pp. 697–739. OCMH. (3) Cir 77, Hq SOS NATOUSA, 6 Jul 44. (4) Colonel Middleswart became a brigadier general on 25 May 1944.

[21] Hist of AFHQ, pt. III (Dec 43–Jul 44), sec. III, pp. 895–98, 904–05, 999–12; pt, II, sec. III, pp. 388–92. OCMH.

[22] For a fuller discussion of these topics see below, Chapters V, VII, and VIII.

[23] (1) QM Supply in Fifth Army, pp. 32–34. (2) Sullivan MS, pp. 35–51.

ried on LST's was set up. At Naples a waterproofed 2½-ton truck was loaded to twice its designated capacity with one class of supply. Along with thirty-four other vehicles, the truck was rolled on to one of the fourteen LST's which were to carry the assault reserve of supplies. The idea of spread-loading each LST with trucks carrying rations, clothing, POL, and ammunition was sound. The loss of one vessel would not seriously reduce the loss in any one class of supply. The roll-on-roll-off truck–LST system had other advantages. A truck stopped at one dump in Naples; it had a single destination at Anzio. For the return trip quartermasters could evacuate salvage. If the beachhead were expanded more rapidly than anticipated, it was possible that the trucks would remain at Anzio as a mobile reserve.[24]

Of the total of 500 trucks bearing the beachhead reserve of 3 days' supply for 45,000 troops, Sullivan was allotted 275 2½-ton trucks. Basically, the proportion was ideal, for it reflected past amphibious experience and indicated future trends. Of the 275 trucks, Sullivan earmarked 102 (about 7 per LST) for rations, both combat and hospital, water, and water-purifying chemicals; 9 for critical clothing items (43,480 pounds) and intrenching tools (10,050 pounds); and the remaining 164 for POL.

In terms of pounds per man per day, Sullivan's food and clothing and general supplies corresponded with HUSKY and TORCH plans. For SHINGLE, he still used factors to allow each type of vehicle to move 25 miles per day. As yet he con-

sidered his new experience table, begun after AVALANCHE and based on pounds of POL per man per day, too sketchy. Immediately after D-day he shifted to his new POL factor largely because he was unable to obtain an accurate census of vehicles by type at Anzio on any definite day. In retrospect, the provision of factors for each class of Quartermaster supply furnished for SHINGLE marks the end of the search for a formula applicable to Quartermaster operations in the Mediterranean theater. Subsequent experience merely justified the use of such factors.[25]

The final version of A BULL Class II requisitions did not reflect Sullivan's efforts to define anew what clothing the individual soldier would wear or carry into combat. He had attempted to convince the Army G–4 that the popular armored force combat suit should be worn in lieu of the regular wool olive drab uniform and Parsons field jacket. Likewise he wanted to reduce the contents of the assault pack as used in AVALANCHE, but shortages of some items again forced the use of this pack. The C BULL requisitions, eliminating all clothing and general supplies, covered the first turnaround delivery of the LST-truck shuttle system. This convoy provided three days of Class I and III supply for all troops ashore. Sullivan's B BULL requisitions called for the greatest amount of resupply—ten days. Because

---

[24] (1) QM Supply Plan (SHINGLE), 5 Jan 44. Sullivan Papers. (2) Sullivan MS, ch. III.

[25] (1) See below, Chapter VI, on POL factors. (2) On the eve of AVALANCHE Sullivan had secured a copy of General Littlejohn's revised 100,000-man factors, reflecting both the theories of OCQM, SOS ETOUSA, and earlier Mediterranean experience. This exchange of vital data continued, and unquestionably had a direct bearing on Quartermaster plans behind the OVERLORD-ANVIL operations in summer 1944.

of the time necessary to prepare shipments and because of the type of ships to be loaded—some in North Africa—the B BULL serials were the first to be presented to Painter and Middleswart. The second convoy of Liberty ships, carrying the D BULL requisitions, brought an additional ten days of supply, including the all-important components of the B ration.[26]

The VI Corps assault on 22 January at Anzio completely surprised the Germans. Their counteroffensive equally surprised Fifth Army. By 1 February the attack out of the beachhead had stalled and Clark ordered VI Corps to prepare for the defense. The attritional advance on Rome now continued on two fronts, and Sullivan's BULL requisitions progressed deeper into the alphabet. The events of late January hastened Sullivan's efforts to consolidate planning and control of operations in his office, a process which had been under way since 21 September 1943.[27] Early in February 1944, when VI Corps relinquished control of supply and a semblance of centralized control of the beachhead had been inaugurated, Fifth Army established an advance command post at Anzio to administer the port and dump area.

Sullivan rapidly moved his office into the picture. Though physically separated, three corps—the II and VI Corps and the French Expeditionary Corps, which took the place of VI Corps along the Gustav Line—now adhered to the McNair doctrine of 16 October 1943, which asserted that a corps functioning as part of a field army had no administrative control over supply.[28] For the first time Sullivan was practicing what had been a cherished dream in the U.S. Army. At field army level the Office of the Quartermaster (OQM), whether on a system of automatic supply or requisition, was obligated to deliver or evacuate all Quartermaster resources to and from railheads located as close as possible to the combat divisions, regiments, separate battalions, or smaller units. While the corps quartermaster was expected to devote his activities to the tactical aspects of supply and to recommend appropriate levels, he was no longer to wield authority over army installations lying within corps boundaries.

In mid-March 1944 the major Allied forces regrouped, splitting the shank of Italy in two. The Fifth Army assumed control of the west side bordering on the Tyrrhenian Sea, and the British Eighth continued in control of the Adriatic side. Regroupment necessitated considerable movement of supplies, troops, and headquarters at a time when the situation at Cassino and Anzio demanded increased Quartermaster planning and reconnaissance, and closer coordination of supply activities. On 23 March 1944 Sullivan moved from Caserta to Sparanise along with Fifth Army headquarters. The office of the army quartermaster was now completely organized along the lines projected by Sullivan in Oujda, Morocco, in 1943. During 1944, Quartermaster troops assigned

---

[26] (1) Sullivan MS, ch. III. (2) Memo, Ballard, Asst Class II Off, for Sullivan, 15 Feb 44, sub: Summary of QM Class II and IV Activities, Opn SHINGLE. Sullivan Papers.

[27] Memo, QM Fifth Army for QM VI Corps, 24 Jun 44; Opn Memo 82, OQM Fifth Army, 7 Aug 44, sub: SOP Rhd Opn. Both in Sullivan Papers.

[28] Rpt 493, AGF Bd MTOUSA, 19 Jun 45, sub: QM Questions. OQMG MED 319.25.

to Sullivan comprised some 30 to 35 companies, assembled under the command of from 5 to 7 separate headquarters and headquarters detachments of Quartermaster battalions.[29] Fifth Army's narrow front made it preferable for the OQM to retain this command system. The only use made of the Headquarters and Headquarters Detachment, Quartermaster Group, was to have it administer the several Italian service battalions attached to Sullivan's office.

The seven Quartermaster battalions assigned to Fifth Army in March 1944 included the 62d, with salvage, laundry, and sterilization companies (controlled by the army salvage officer) ; the 204th, with four gasoline supply companies, two attached truck companies, and a single attached French petrol company (controlled by the OQM Class III officer) ; the 94th, 242d, 259th, and 263d, with service, railhead, bakery, depot supply, truck, and graves registration companies (directly under the control of the OQM Class I, Class II, and Class IV, or graves registration officers) ; and the 249th with a representative selection of 11 Quartermaster companies. The Headquarters and Headquarters Detachment, 249th Quartermaster Battalion, was controlled by Lt. Col. Cornelius C. Holcomb, who headed the office of the advance army quartermaster at Anzio.[30]

Hoping to establish an intermediate system of supervisory, rather than directional, control over his field installations, Sullivan outlined an arrangement whereby each area quartermaster served as his field representative. Such a deputy, who was actually the senior quartermaster in a given area, possessed no independent authority over operations.[31] This officer could neither issue orders conflicting with established procedures or policies nor change production orders or supply levels. His only independent responsibilities pertained to sanitation, supply discipline, and security camouflage. Used at Anzio in the form of an advance headquarters, Sullivan's system did not work as intended because the appointed area quartermaster established his own routine and created a procedure of dual control. Because of this awkward development, Sullivan eliminated the job at Anzio several weeks before the main Fifth Army force absorbed the beachhead, and the system was shelved until it could be adapted to a mobile or rapidly moving tactical situation.

Holcomb's organization at Nettuno was exclusively a branch field office. Staff officers in charge of sections in Holcomb's office were also the commanding officers of units assigned or attached to the Headquarters, 249th Quartermaster Battalion, Lt. Col. John C. Strickland

[29] (1) *Fifth Army History*, V, 235–36. (2) Rpt, Orgn of OQM, Fifth Army, prepared by Hq 15th Army Group. Hist Br OQMG. (3) SOP OQM, Field Opns Fifth Army, 2 Aug 44. OQMG MED 319.25. (4) Colonel Sullivan became a brigadier general on 20 February 1944.

[30] (1) *QM Supply in Fifth Army*, app. P, pp. 114–15. (2) Twenty-nine Quartermaster truck companies were assigned to Transportation Section, Fifth Army, for operation. Sullivan had no responsibility over them, As early as 1 December 1943 Sullivan organized a Field Range Inspection and Repair Group, consisting of an officer and two enlisted technicians. Hist Rpt, QM to Tate, 10 Feb 44. Hist Rpts, Sullivan Papers.

[31] (1) Rpt cited n. 29(2). (2) Opn Memo 75, OQM Fifth Army, 15 Jul 44. Sullivan Papers.

commanding.[32] Subsistence was handled by the 94th Railhead Company, POL by the 3853d Gasoline Supply Company, and Class II and IV supply by a detachment of the 85th Depot Supply Company. Salvage matters were supervised by a lieutenant in Holcomb's office, but the evacuation work was carried out by three Quartermaster service companies, plus an Italian labor battalion. Graves registration remained a VI Corps responsibility; one platoon of the 47th Graves Registration Company and two platoons of the 48th Company handled this mission. Forced to disperse because the entire area was under frequent fire, the 249th scattered its installations within the beachhead. The main ration dump was near Nettuno, where damage was small in spite of recurrent shellings. The largest single loss resulted from an air raid when an antipersonnel bomb ignited a stack of tobacco kits. During another bombardment nineteen artillery shells fell in the dump area, but destroyed only seven cases of K rations. The 3853d operated two POL dumps, one of which was just north of Anzio city and the other three miles east of Nettuno. To isolate fires and explosions, POL was segregated into 5,000-gallon lots with each stack of 1,000 cans partially buried in a pit. Of the nine million gallons of POL shipped to the beachhead, the 3853d held losses to 1 percent.

Holcomb's main clothing and equipage depot was approximately six miles from the enemy. Operating there, the 85th Depot Company occupied a former Italian barracks near Nettuno and handled large quantities of supplies under blackout conditions. A bomb destroyed one of the sheds but for the most part the depot suffered little damage. The 85th received only a few calls it could not fill.[33] Shortages appeared in raincoats, underwear, shoes in wide widths, field jackets, and candles, but never in critical proportions. During the first fifteen days, Class II and IV items were shipped automatically on the basis of replacement factors. Later a requisition basis was used because Sullivan had definite evidence that his replacement factors did not reflect adequately supply needs in this war of attrition. With the arrival of spring weather, stocks at Anzio increased steadily.[34]

Since early March food and packaged POL at Anzio had a priority second only to ammunition. The former had been placed on semiautomatic supply—supply against specially prepared status reports. Conditions at Anzio after mid-February had been comparable to the quiet periods of World War I trench warfare. The troops who had been living on combat rations began to receive one hot meal a day in their foxholes. Three hot meals were served in the rear areas, occasionally supplemented by fresh eggs and meat either procured locally from the few remaining Italian farmers or requisitioned by raiding parties in search of chickens and livestock. These forays were as carefully planned as patrols against a tactical objective.

Finally, in May the Fifth Army started

[32] (1) "QM Under Fire," *QMTSJ*, VII, No. 2 (7 January 1945) 2–7. (2) Sullivan MS, p. 82. (3) Msg, Army Advance CP to Clark, 22 Mar 44. Fifth Army, AG 430. (4) Article, QM Supply at Anzio, by Maj Gen E. B. Gregory, The Quartermaster General. Hist Br OQMG.

[33] *QM Supply in Fifth Army*, pp. 38–39.
[34] Sullivan MS, p. 90.

its spring offensive against the Gustav Line and the troops at Anzio could at last look forward to an end of the monotony that had characterized the recent weeks. But if Anzio was quickly left behind, it could not be quickly forgotten. Logistically—because of more efficient supply procedures and continuous deliveries by preloaded trucks, sustained operations under blackout conditions, and effective use of the Dukw to mention only a few improvements—Anzio was a landmark in Quartermaster operations. But it was memorable for another reason. During the 125 days on the beachhead the falling bombs, artillery shells, and flak failed to distinguish between service and combat troops. Here, along with men on the line, 10 percent of the troops under control of the 249th Quartermaster Battalion were killed or wounded.[35]

For the 1944 spring offensive, Allied regroupment along the Gustav Line had begun in mid-March 1944, and Sullivan relocated his installations on the north side of the Volturno River. While this involved a move of less than fifteen miles, the Quartermaster Section required seven weeks to transfer the large tonnages out of the permanent buildings in the Aversa-Capua-Caserta triangle, into the general area of Sparanise. The Class II and IV depot moved to a site adjacent to the Sparanise rail yards, containing Nissen huts and numerous concrete platforms. The salvage collection dump was less fortunate. Sullican called upon engineers to construct a completely new installation with gravel roads, gravel tent flooring, slit trenches, fences, and an unprecedented number of tents. Shifting ration and gasoline dumps was considerably more difficult than moving clothing stocks and salvage yards, because these dumps were obliged to remain open until all the Fifth Army troops had moved out. Not a single Class III dump suspended operations until ten days after the sixth gasoline dump had opened in the forward area. While attempting to straighten out his trans-Volturno supply lines, Sullivan found that he had left behind one completely unsolved matter. The burial of Moslem troops of the French Expeditionary Corps created an unforeseen problem of cemetery design. Deceased Moslems had to face Mecca. A simple solution appeared to be for all grave markers to face in an eastward direction. But this was not always possible when such matters as adequate drainage and easy access to graves were considered. Sullivan solved the problem by dividing Fifth Army's future layouts into three separate sections. One contained American and Allied dead, another enemy remains, and the third Moslem bodies.[36]

Basic to the orderly flow of Quartermaster supplies from Naples to Fifth Army was the daily telegram, which served as the essential requisitioning document.[37] According to accepted doctrine the daily telegram originated with division and corps reports, which gave the strength of their commands in men and animals.[38] Army then consolidated these figures and dispatched a consolidated telegram to the base section.

---

[35] Ibid.

[36] QM Supply in Fifth Army, pp. 40–41, 69.

[37] WD FM 100–10, Field Service Regulations Administration, 15 November 1943, pp. 35–36.

[38] Corps compiled the document for those units attached to the corps for administration.

Since clothing and equipment were consumed at irregular rates, they were not included in the daily telegram.

Early in the campaign Sullivan had learned that it was almost impossible to follow this basic doctrine. He observed that "the daily telegram is . . . not entirely workable because the tactical situation changes so rapidly."[39] Even along the narrow Volturno front, with daily train service and Naples only some twenty-five miles away,[40] Sullivan had difficulty in receiving front-line reports.

With units moving from one sector to another on less than 24-hour notice, with squads and platoons deployed in isolated places, deliveries of food and gasoline on the basis of the telegram more than a day old were likely not to be made in the right place. For that reason the daily telegram was modified in the direction of automatic supply by Fifth Army. A unit could draw quartermaster supply at a railhead simply by submitting a telegram which only indi-

cated the quantities and types of rations desired without anticipating its requirements several days in advance. At the end of the day so-called consolidated telegrams reporting total issues for that period were prepared by each Fifth Army railhead and forwarded by courier to Sullivan's office. After consolidating this information with the daily requirements of each truckhead and balances on hand Sullivan's Class I officer requested replenishment from Peninsular Base Section three days hence.[41]

A prerequisite to the full success of this procedure was the existence of reserve stocks in an army base dump. Availability of such reserves permitted faster replenishment of railheads and narrowed the time lag between the date of requisition and the date of consumption. While there was never serious doubt as to the need of such reserves, G-4 staffs, the spigot quartermaster, and the pipeline quartermaster disagreed as to their size. Sullivan and Painter crossed swords on this point after 1 January 1944, when the daily train ran regularly to Caserta and when Peninsular Base Section had a much better insight into the condition of its stocks. Alert to the difficulties in allocating transportation means equitably among all the technical services, Tate preferred that Sullivan limit his base dumps to a two-day supply of B rations and fractional days of supply of combat rations. Sullivan contended that such low levels jeopardized both the maintenance of balanced rations and prompt delivery to units. He pressed for a ten-day level at base

---

[39] Sullivan Diary, 8 Oct 43.

[40] Fifth Army's quartermaster dumps received supply from Naples by rail for the first time on 9 December 1943. The railroad daily train arrived in four sections at the hours of 0600, 1200, 1600, and 2400. That same day Sullivan and Painter met with the army and base section transportation officers to discuss the standard daily telegram, the coordination of the transportation system, and the use of common terms. Painter said his Quartermaster Section could deliver supplies forty-eight hours after he received Fifth Army's daily telegram, provided that OQM, Fifth Army, got the document to Naples by eleven o'clock each morning. During the conference, the army transportation officer was sensitive to the term "railhead," a word of World War I origin. Sullivan agreed to designate his forwardmost transfer points as "truckheads." Yet in his diary and in correspondence with the Quartermaster company at such points, he preferred the use of the traditional Quartermaster word "railhead." Sullivan Diary, 9 Dec. 43.

[41] (1) Rpt cited n. 29(2). (2) Memo, 1st Lt James M. Demske for CQM MTOUSA, 21 Feb 45, sub: Obsv Rpt. Sullivan Papers.

dumps, including seven days of B rations. For close support during mountain fighting this was not excessive. But Tate was more optimistic than Sullivan regarding the possibility of a breakthrough, and repeatedly pointed out that Fifth Army reserves were too large to be moved readily. During the accelerated advance late in May, Clark stepped in and settled the debate in favor of Tate.[42]

To improve the handling of Class II and IV supplies, the Fifth Army quartermaster instituted an effective "back-order system" that eliminated much duplication of effort. Any item that could not be furnished upon call was extracted from the requisition and recorded in a special file. As the item was received from the base section—and all back orders were filled first—the Class II and IV Section advised the waiting unit that the item was available. Once the troop units became confident that the army quartermaster was vigilantly trying to make the system work effectively, the depots suffered less harassment from duplication of requisitions and repetition of inquiries.[43]

Early in the Italian campaign, Sullivan introduced several other organizational or procedural innovations designed to maintain the flow of supplies or provide better services. Since rugged mountains and muddy, inadequate roads limited use of tanks, trucks, and tractors, the Class

II and IV Section found "an orphan on its doorstep" in the responsibility for animal pack units.[44] The first phase in carrying out this task was a loose one whereby animals and equipment were purchased locally and issued directly to divisions. Moving toward greater centralization, Fifth Army assumed control of the pack mule companies (largely recruited from Italian personnel), organized several more from elements of the inactivated 2d Cavalry Division, and established remount depots in corps areas. Near the end of hostilities more than 4,500 mules and 150 horses were operating under the Fifth Army delivering supplies to troops in otherwise inaccessible areas. Other special projects included the establishment of mobile bath and clothing exchanges, which enabled combat troops to obtain both a shower and a complete change of clothing at the same location, and the maintenance of emergency stocks of essential clothing at ration railheads. Together, these two projects helped reduce the discomforts of living and fighting for month after month in dirt and mud, rain and snow.

As anticipated, the office of the army quartermaster had to ignore the McNair theory of delivering supplies directly to the regiments. At Salerno, Sullivan believed Quartermaster supply might be better controlled by the use of the consolidated requisition and a divisional distribution point.[45] The 36th Division

---

[42] (1) Admin Dir 34, Hq Fifth Army, 24 May 44. (2) Study, Class I System, Fifth Army, prepared by Lt. Col. Francis A. Troy, Class I Officer OQM, 31 Dec 44. Sullivan Diary.

[43] (1) Opn Memo 42, OQM Fifth Army, 25 Feb 44, sub: Back Order Procedure—Class II and IV. (2) Rpt, MTOUSA Stock Control Team, sub: Inspection of QM Class I, II, and IV Installations, 4–11 Mar 45. Sullivan Papers.

[44] Sullivan MS, pp. 76–77.

[45] (1) ASF G–4 Questionnaire, QM 45th Inf Div, 19 Oct 43; AGF G–4 Questionnaire, QM 36th Inf Div, 11 Oct 43. Both in OQMC MED 319.1. (2) Rpt 493, AGF Bd MTOUSA, 19 Jun 43, sub: QM Questions. OQMG MED 319.25.

quartermaster wanted to set up additional supply points even further forward for the convenience of his regiments, battalions, and companies. Though reported a year later, the typical army railhead and divisional distribution point system adopted in Italy was that of the 91st Infantry Division:

We had checkers along with the trucks so they could count the items drawn at the Army Class I distribution point. These men also break down the supplies drawn when they return to their own Division Class I distribution point in Monghidere. The trucks rolled along without any noticeable delay when drawing rations from the various stacks of rations at the Army distribution point. The Army Class I distribution point on Route 65 and a little north of Traversa is so arranged that trucks move in a counterclockwise manner loading strongly cased items first with bread and meats loaded last. The complete circle required approximately one hour that day, then the convoy of trucks were off for the Division Class I distribution point. The division's DP is nothing more than placing [sic] the loaded rations trucks in a single column along the right side of a road through the town so that trucks of the various regiments and drawing organizations can back their trucks against the Division trucks and load the various items of issue authorized for the day. By noon the distribution was completed with nothing on the road to indicate that a DP existed there.[46]

In June 1944, a procedure had been tested whereby the army delivered rations directly to the 34th Division's distribution point, but the results were generally unsatisfactory and the experiment was short-lived. In one instance the division distribution area became so congested with unit vehicles that schedules were upset and unit trains were late in returning to make their own issues. On several other occasions trucks were lost from the army convoy and rations arrived without bread or canned goods. When the division quartermaster could not assure safe delivery by furnishing guides for the army train and maintaining liaison with the army Class I dump, the preferred system of permitting Quartermaster organic vehicles to haul the division's rations was restored.[47]

Inevitably, this use of organic QM transportation for purposes not contemplated by the AGF planners meant that other Quartermaster functions would suffer. To be sure the divisional QM companies, with their fifty-one $2\frac{1}{2}$-ton trucks, could haul all the supplies normally required by a division. But the transportation function amounted to considerably more than hauling the supplies forward. The trucks had to be loaded and unloaded, and the supplies broken down and distributed to the using units. Although the War Department had restored the service platoon to the divisional Quartermaster company in July 1943, it still proved necessary to call on the combat units of the division for assistance.

With the service platoon restored, Quartermaster companies found that the varied tasks they had to perform still taxed their existing structure. Salvage and captured enemy matériel were evacuated to army ration points by divisional Quartermaster companies. Service personnel often worked long hours with attached graves registration teams. Com-

[46] Ltr, 1st Lt Morris L. Kutcher to QM MTOUSA, 13 Jan 45, sub: Narrative of Temporary Duty with Fifth Army. Sullivan Papers.

[47] Ltr, CQM 34th Div to CG 34th Div, 2 Jul 44, sub: QM Opns. Hist Br OQMG.

plaining that in its first year in Africa, Sicily, and Italy his division had never been afforded bathing or washing facilities of any kind—except such "individually devised ones as tin cans, helmets, and other makeshift installations"—General Truscott, commander of the 3d Infantry Division, called for a mobile shower and laundry unit as a permanent attachment. Concerned with the same problem, the 34th Division, after seventy days in combat, instituted a system of bath and clothing exchange units which made for better supply and maintenance of individual clothing while serving as a booster of morale.[48] The facilities offered by such a unit consisted of shower, clean towel, complete change of under and outer clothing, field jacket, and occasionally shoes and leggings. Permitting the elimination of barracks bags by all except motorized elements, this service relieved the strain on transportation facilities. Such economies took on added importance in the spring of 1944, as the long months of position warfare came to an end, and the troops began to move again.

Pursuit to the Arno

The long-awaited offensive on the Gustav Line got under way on 11–12 May 1944. By 18 May the British had captured Cassino, the objective of more than six months of grueling mountain warfare. A week later the main body of Fifth Army relieved the Anzio force, and on 5 June American troops crossed the

Tiber and moved through Rome. The Eternal City was of more political than logistical importance, and few Quartermaster troops lingered there. The day after Rome fell, Clark ordered Fifth Army to capture Leghorn and Pisa, and Quartermaster operations continued to be caught up in a war of movement.

At no time during the advance was it possible to conduct extensive ground reconnaissance for dump sites, installations, adequate road nets, and protective facilities. The office of the army quartermaster selected sites from maps at night and hoped the morning reconnaissance would justify the selection. Rapidity of movement demanded that support units spread out more thinly than before. One railhead company had to disperse its personnel among six widely located dumps simultaneously, while the sterilization and bath troops more than once advanced to designated points, only to find that the troops they were to serve had departed. To determine supply needs, Sullivan placed his officers on wheels, particularly his Class I and III staffs, and they toured all receiving dumps each day, returning at night to order out issues for the next day. The system worked and in one case supplies moved into a location while the engineers were still clearing the area of mines and before the battlefield had been cleared of the dead.[49]

One activity was centralized during the period of the rapid advance. Late in June all bakery companies were assigned to the Headquarters, 94th Quartermaster

[48] Ltr, Truscott to Clark, 7 Nov 43, sub: Deficiencies in Supply and Equip; Ltr, Asst AG Fifth Army to Units, 8 Oct 44, sub: Lessons Learned in Combat, 34th Inf Div. Both in Sullivan Papers.

[49] (1) Sullivan MS, pp. 94–97. (2) 1st Lt. Francis A. Smith, "Quartermaster in The Rome Drive," *QMTSJ*, VI, No. 4 (22 December 1944), 8–9. (3) Ltr, Sullivan to Tate, 9 Jun 44, sub: Hist Data. Sullivan Papers.

Battalion. The 94th also assumed responsibility for the operation and administration of the Field Range Inspection Group and the Typewriter Repair Unit. One of its officers, a trained refrigeration engineer, made all the necessary reconnaissance and preparations for taking over cold storage facilities. To expedite the delivery of bakery products, the 94th used mattress covers to deliver bread, operating the system on the principle used by milk companies in exchanging bottles through a common clearing house.[50] Each mattress cover was marked with the numerical designation of the bakery company to which it belonged. In strict compliance with the "no container, no bread" principle an empty mattress cover was exchanged for a full one at the various railheads, and each day the soiled covers were delivered to a central exchange. They were then sent to laundries which gave 24-hour cleaning service for both covers and baker's uniforms.

Fortunately, the sea was at Sullivan's side for his administrative march. Six days after advancing troops crossed the Tiber, Civitavecchia, a small port forty miles northwest of the Italian capital, was already secure and a convoy of LST's entered the badly damaged harbor. Once restored, Civitavecchia received daily 3,000 tons of supply. On 17 June Piombino fell and engineers soon restored the city sufficiently to convert it into a base dump. The speedy exploitation of these two anchorages, as well as San Stefano midway between them, made it possible for the office of the army quartermaster

to spot rations and fuel directly behind the Fifth Army's advance, which was never more than twenty-five miles inland. One half of the Piombino dump was allocated to the storage of rations, and by September 1944, when it was transferred to Peninsular Base Section, Piombino contained 25,000 tons of B rations and 12,000 tons of combat rations, or what has been described as one-fifth of all Class I supply in Italy at that time.[51]

Supported by tanker ships and favored by the narrow front, the army quartermaster assumed normal base section POL responsibilities from the time the Civitavecchia port was operative until long after the Arno River was reached. Because railroads and pipelines could not keep pace with the advance, the 204th Quartermaster Gasoline Supply Battalion momentarily controlled all can-filling activities and all distribution of packaged fuel to Fifth Army and to base section troops operating within the army area. Believing this imposed no hardships on the 204th, Sullivan recommended to both Clark and petroleum officers in Naples that the system be continued as Fifth Army advanced into the northern Apennines.[52] Thus, until early November, the 204th handled the dual mission, not turning the job over to Peninsular Base Section until the pipeline was extended within the army's boundary from Leghorn.

Fifth Army reached the Arno in six weeks, and on 19 July Leghorn, Italy's fourth major port, fell to its tired, dwindling troops. Its assigned strength had dropped from 248,989 to 153,233 troops.

---

[50] (1) Sullivan MS, p. 101. (2) Article, Lt Col Eckhardt R. Keller, *Bed Sacks Make Good Bread Sacks.* Hist Br OQMG.

[51] Memo, ExO OQM for Sullivan, 16 Jun 44. Sullivan Diary.

[52] *QM Supply in Fifth Army,* pp. 64–65.

QM DEPOT *at Leghorn, August 1945.*

Over a period of seven weeks seven veteran Allied divisions had been contributed to Seventh Army for ANVIL. Sullivan was fortunate in keeping his quartermaster organization intact. By 23 July, Fifth Army had cleared thirty-five miles of the south shore of the Arno from the Ligurian Sea to the Elsa River. Twenty miles to the east of the Elsa, the British occupied Florence on 4 August. Cultural considerations now contributed to a decision not to cross the Arno immediately above Leghorn. Such a crossing might have made good progress across the open Pisa plain, but would have inevitably involved stubborn street fighting within the city itself, where the Leaning Tower was only the most famous of many historical monuments. Further inland, reconnaissance indicated that the Ger-

mans had organized their defenses along the northern slopes of the Arno valley with their usual thoroughness. Forcing such positions would require deliberate preparations by strong and well-equipped troops. Accordingly, during the remainder of August, Fifth Army confined its activity to aggressive patrolling and artillery exchanges. Troops were in need of rest, equipment required replacement or repair. Salvage problems mounted. Meantime, Sullivan himself was at work on Quartermaster plans for Clark's next objective, and behind the Fifth Army, pipeline quartermasters were advancing by sea to establish a new base in Leghorn.[53]

---

[53] (1) *Ibid.,* ch. IV. (2) Sullivan MS, pp. 92-111.

Within a week after that city's fall, an advance party from the 61st Quartermaster Base Depot reconnoitered the port area and decided that the wholesale depot would remain outside the urban limits. A few fixed installations such as the cold storage and ice plant, bakeries, dry cleaning and laundry plants, and the salvage and solid fuel yards would be located in Leghorn itself. As a depot site the 61st selected a sandy, well-drained, partially wooded area a few miles north of Leghorn and almost in range of enemy artillery. It had ample access to railroads and roads, including the national system of express highways (*autostradi*). Here was a challenge to carry out Quartermaster theories of depot arrangement and management which suburban Naples never offered. Engineers accepted the layout plan and began to transform an open field into a centralized depot extending three and a half linear miles.

Confident that the Germans would be unable to send their few remaining bombers against the depot, the 61st quickly brought its facilities into operation. It was not too soon. Despite its exposed position, the port of Leghorn was in full operation by mid-September, discharging from 8,000 to 10,000 tons daily. As the new depot expanded, pipeline quartermasters of Peninsular Base Section made their final organizational adjustment. During October the policy makers of Quartermaster Section, Peninsular Base Section, were consolidated with the operators of the 61st QM Base Depot. On 1 November 1944 COMZONE NATOUSA (SOS NATOUSA) became COMZONE MTOUSA, when the name of the theater changed. For the next twenty days General Middleswart as Quartermaster, COMZONE MTOUSA,

was supporting both Fifth and Seventh Armies.[54]

Close Support in the Gothic Line

Conditions in Italy were such in early September 1944 that the Allies decided to resume the offensive. Fifth Army's objective was Bologna, but first it had to pierce the Gothic Line, an elaborate transpeninsular defense belt high in the Apennines. Running from Leghorn and Pisa on the Ligurian Sea to Rimini on the Adriatic, a series of defensive lines stood as the German shield against a land advance from the south into the Po valley, Italy's only major industrial area. To breach the lines, Clark's mission was to assault the barrier frontally above Florence on the road to Bologna while the British attacked northwestward from Rimini. A simulated attack was called for in the Pisa sector. During daylight smoke pots, vehicular maneuvers, and camouflaged dummy installations deceived the enemy. By night Fifth Army sideslipped secretly toward Florence and the difficult problem of shifting quartermaster resources laterally from an established axis of advance had to be dealt with. For concealment, most supplies were trucked to the Florence area from Piombino, which remained a Fifth Army base.

From his supply base at Piombino, Sullivan's move toward Florence cut across the grain of rough country.[55] Quar-

---

[54] (1) *QM Supply in Fifth Army*, pp. 62–63. (2) *Logistical History of NATOUSA–MTOUSA*, p. 31. (3) On 20 November 1944 Middleswart was in Dijon, France, with a new headquarters. See below, p. 126.

[55] (1) Sullivan MS, pp. 112–22. (2) Article, 1st Lt Alanson Crandall, CO 3839th GS Co, Camouflage in Operation for Gasoline. Hist Br OQMG.

termaster companies and their equipment followed in the immediate wake of, or even preceded, the combat troops. Deployment of mobile laundries and bakeries required the use of many trucks, and their movements had to be co-ordinated closely with the Highway Transportation Section. Secrecy and cultural considerations denied Sullivan the use of Florence itself as a supply base. South of the city the army Class I dump, built to contain a million rations, opened in an olive grove. The trees afforded natural camouflage. By stringing nets over the food stacks, quartermasters turned the whole dump into a model of concealment. A few miles down the road a typical vineyard of the countryside offered a 100-acre site for the POL dump. Before the attack, a million gallons of gasoline lay in containers concealed among the twisted 12-foot-high grapevines. Back in Castelfiorentino, a subdepot of the Class II and IV depot held clothing reserves. Until the lid of silence on tactical plans was lifted, the bath, salvage, and graves registration support units remained around rest areas. For his first ten days in a rest area, each man received a 10 percent increase in B rations. Refrigeration vans brought fresh meats, butter, and eggs to the rest areas. Clothing was replaced, repaired, or salvaged. In August, laundries handled 2,110,697 pounds of wash. A salvage repair company joined Fifth Army and together with Italian seamstresses, tailors, and dry cleaners, relieved the Quartermaster office of the task of taking clothing to Leghorn for repair.[56]

After veteran French and Moslem troops left Fifth Army for France late in July, the Brazilian Expeditionary Force arrived to take their place. The new allies needed support. Their menu varied only slightly from the American B ration, but additional sugar for the extra coffee the Brazilians drank, plus lard, salt, mustard, and black pepper were immediate requirements. Sullivan predicted that the Brazilians' cotton clothing would afford inadequate protection in Apennine altitudes, and so he included American woolens in his clothing requisitions for the South Americans.[57]

The weather was ideal on 10 September, when the Fifth Army launched its attack. The immediate plan called for the clearing of Highway 65 through Futa Pass whose dominating heights the Germans held. Under pressure of a three-pronged attack the Germans withdrew from the pass on 21 September. Over the next month the front widened and four U.S. infantry divisions, the 85th, the 88th, the 91st, and 92d (Negro), plus a Brazilian combat team and the 6th South African Division engaged in a bitter fight for dishearteningly small gains.[58] Apparently the Gothic Line defenders were under orders to die at their mountain posts rather than yield. Terrain obstacles became extremely difficult to cross. Incessant rains changed the pitifully few roads into seas of mud. In mid-October snow fell impartially on friend and foe, blanketing the front. Quartermaster support suffered. When, on 26 October, Sullivan, to his surprise, learned that two divisions were to be pulled out of the line and "put under canvas," he

---

[56] Sullivan MS, pp. 124–40.

[57] *QM Supply in Fifth Army*, pp. 54, 59, 64, 79.

[58] *Ibid.*, pp. 52–53.

feared the worst.[59] On 2 November, when Fifth Army was within ten miles of Bologna, Clark halted the offensive. Wire was strung, mine fields were laid, and combat troops began rotating out of the line for much needed rest and refitting.

In the autumn battles quartermasters learned the supply implications of fighting conducted largely by individual soldiers from gun emplacements and foxholes. There were no spectacular armored charges, no vast sweeps and wheels by large formations, and no far-reaching military decisions. Quartermasters coped with unusual supply problems by exploiting local resources, by filling a system of base dumps and depots with over a week's supply, and by keeping a two-day level at all railheads. Unprecedented demands for Class II, especially the new M1943 items, came from the front lines. Even though the new wet-cold weather clothing had been ordered as early as May 1944, none reached Sullivans' shelves until mid-October. Late shipment from NYPE, the slow editing of requisitions, and the movement through Leghorn hobbled efforts to clothe the troops. Estimates based on low maintenance factors resulted in a shortage of wool socks. To correct this situation, Sullivan resorted to action through command channels. Shortages in stoves became critical during this period. Hospital priorities for space heaters could be barely met. For relief a Florentine industrialist made 8,000 stoves complete with pipes, spark arrestors, and tent baffle plates.[60]

To deliver supplies directly to gun emplacements, foxholes, and outposts, additional Italian pack companies were rushed into use. Mule casualties ran high. When the fighting stopped, 1,000 mules had been replaced. Demand for Class II and IV pack equipment also far exceeded expectations. Hemp rope became a prime casualty of the battle. To keep the mule and his telltale load from tarrying near outpost positions, soldiers cut the lash ropes. They seem never to have heard of untying knots.

The arrival of fresh German troops, giving the enemy numerical superiority, had been one of the major reasons for calling off Fifth Army's fight.[61] In December, Fifth Army's new commander, Lt. Gen. Lucian K. Truscott, Jr., expressed some fear that the Germans intended to roll up his left flank and crash into Leghorn. At the same time as Generalfeldmarschall Gerd von Rundstedt's Christmas Holiday offensive in the Ardennes, Kesselring's forces also pushed southward out of the Gothic Line. By 1 January 1945 Truscott's front had been restored, but the shift of U.S. strength from Florence to the left of the line had weakened the attack along the Bologna road. The Fifth Army consequently required reinforcements. The 92d Division was brought up to full strength, the Brazilian Expeditionary Force fielded a full division, and the first contingent of a major new unit, the 86th Mountain Infantry Regiment, 10th Mountain Division, arrived at the front. Allied instructions early in January 1945 directed Truscott to regroup Fifth Army in order to resume the offensive in April. Until then limited objectives were

---

[59] Sullivan Diary, 26 Oct 44.

[60] (1) *QM Supply in Fifth Army*, ch. IV. (2) Class II supply is discussed in detail in Chapter VII, below.

[61] *QM Supply in Fifth Army*, ch. V.

selected to confuse the Germans and to obtain favorable positions for the spring attack.

Fearful trials of terrain and temperature threatened to upset Truscott's timetable.[62] Between 2 November 1944 and the advent of spring, snow, ice, rain, mud, and floods tested routine Quartermaster operations to the utmost. Normally, the quartermaster office could have handled the job in a relatively short time with a small number of support troops. But here along the Gothic Line every activity became a major engineering feat. Behind the lines the quartermaster workload increased as a large number of troops rotated in and out of the front lines, and as more and more Italian soldiers and civilians took over support duties. Rest hotels, camps, and rest areas were opened in Florence, in Montecatini, and within each corps area. Also, the older established center in Rome continued to operate. During the period B ration issues increased 7 percent over the normal troop strength. To break the monotony of eating bread, Sullivan in vain asked for more lard, baking powder, and yeast to permit field baking of pastries. In an effort to keep the men clean, bath and clothing exchange units processed almost 1,000 more men a day than had been served previously. Laundries handled over three million pounds of wash each month in addition to their current hospital and salvage mission. Clothing, tentage, and camp stoves were requisitioned in increasing quantities. Solid fuel demands increased as thermometers dropped toward zero on the Fahrenheit scale.

In mid-January 1945 Peninsular Base Section established a rail transfer point at Montecatini and Quartermaster distribution problems were eased considerably. At Florence the ration reserve was reduced from a 15-day to a 10-day level. Each day 280 tons of packaged POL arrived in the army Class III base dump, and there was a surplus to cache away for an armored spearhead in the spring offensive. Back orders of clothing and equipment declined sharply from a high of 1,880 requests in November 1944 to 603 by 31 March 1945. With staged supply working better than ever before through Leghorn and Montecatini, Sullivan completed the initial issue of all standard items of winter clothing and equipment to the units in the line by the end of December. About the same time special wet-cold weather clothing, allocated by the G–4, Colonel Tate, was distributed along the front.

In this period of static warfare remount service expanded greatly and graves registration activities contracted. During the winter five new Italian pack companies joined the ten already at the front. Beginning in January 1945, the first troops of the 10th Mountain Divison began to arrive in Leghorn, bringing with them most of their own pack equipment. Sullivan had understood that the 10th also planned to carry its own pack animals overseas. Some did arrive in Italy, but most did not see service in the high Apeninnes. By 1 April, the Fifth Army quartermaster was responsible for a total of 4,692 mules and 168 horses. But as Fifth Army began the descent into the Po valley, armor and its mechanized trains re-entered the battle, and pack trains became surplus.

During the winter of 1944–45 only one cemetery—Mount Beni—was opened

---

[62] *Ibid.*

along the Gothic Line. The site was far from ideal. Not only was Mount Beni located out of line in relation to the deployment of troops but a rocky subsoil added materially to cemeterial work. Yet in spite of the distances involved in the evacuation work of the graves registration teams most bodies were carried to the cemetery within thirty-six hours. In March 1945 another cemetery at Granagliano was laid out near Highway 64, and at the same time the cemetery at Castelfiorentino far to the rear of the army was turned over to Peninsular Base Section.

At mid-April Fifth Army debouched into the Po valley, and a war of movement began. Modena replaced Florence as Fifth Army's base area on 29 April 1945. In following the advance, Peninsular Base Section closed out the Montecatini rail transfer point and shifted its operations to Florence. With the breakthrough Sullivan's Class I and III staffs fanned out behind the troops. On 2 May Quartermaster railheads were serving an area that embraced 38,000 square miles, a figure based on the 190 miles between Modena and the Brenner Pass and a lateral distance of 200 miles. Near the center of this area, Mirandola became the site of Fifth Army's final cemetery. Now that the better communication system of the Po valley spread below the Fifth Army, the fifteen Italian pack companies rested behind the lines. Yet on the day Germany surrendered, the 10th Mountain Division, after beginning its ascent into the Italian Alps, hurriedly placed a call for two pack companies.

The last two weeks of the Po Valley Campaign introduced spigot quartermasters to new problems of support. The first involved captured and abandoned enemy resources. The speed with which Fifth Army advanced and fanned out left its quartermasters not only with a tremendous salvage problem but a touchy one in the face of fratricidal warfare. Pro-Allied Italians considered their fascist fellow-countrymen simply traitors to be shot or lynched on sight, rather than prisoners of war, so U.S. personnel had to replace ISU's at Italian prisoner of war camps. The army quartermaster was greatly handicapped by the lack of security measures to protect captured food stocks. Feeding and supplying some 300,000 German prisoners of war required immediate attention until the Germans could institute their own system under Allied control. After 8 May 1945 Sullivan turned to redeployment and postwar problems, and having found time to review his work, he wrote in his diary: "At no time was the Army ever held up for the lack of any Quartermaster supplies throughout the entire Italian Campaign." [63]

Supporting Seventh Army's Landing and Push Northward

Fifth's Army's advance from the Tiber to the Arno and in the northern Apennines had been greatly handicapped by lack of sustained comunications zone Quartermaster support. At the ports of Civitavecchia, Piombino, and Leghorn, spigot quartermasters initially controlled much of their own wholesale supply support. Nevertheless, this was not by design of SOS NATOUSA. From 9 June 1944 until mid-November 1944 pipeline quartermasters throughout the Mediter-

---

[63] Sullivan MS, p. 186.

ranean area were extended to the limit in meeting strategic changes. The strategy which had created this situation had been roughly shaped by the great Allied conclaves of 1943. At Cairo the SEXTANT Conference of November–December 1943 finally drew the threads of Operation OVERLORD together, and charted an invasion of southern France (Operation ANVIL) to occur simultaneously with the landings on the beaches of Normandy. Early in January 1944 the outline of ANVIL was brought to the attention of Quartermaster Section, SOS NATOUSA, and within a few weeks Middleswart's planners had joined with a new team of spigot quartermasters of Headquarters, Task Force 163, in hammering out a detailed set of requirements for ANVIL.[64]

If planning steps alone could have assured Quartermaster readiness to support the last large-scale amphibious operation against the Germans, ANVIL (later known as DRAGOON) would have been a logistical triumph. Yet planning is always subject to military developments, and between 8 January and 15 August 1944, Quartermaster Section, SOS NATOUSA, experienced several false starts in its preparations for the forthcoming operation. Over the same period Quartermaster planning machinery benefited greatly from major administrative changes in both SOS NATOUSA and theater organization. After 20 February 1944, Middleswart's position was improved by having a G–4 Section, SOS NATOUSA, on hand through which

Quartermaster plans could be co-ordinated with higher and adjacent staffs. The new G–4 staff soon became a clearing house for logistical information and carefully integrated all the sound Quartermaster data and precepts which had been accumulated and successfully applied to past Mediterranean operations. The Quartermaster Section, SOS NATOUSA, was thus in a much better position to work out the requirements and phased requisitions of the Office of the Quartermaster, Task Force 163 (to be known as Seventh Army after March 1944).

In beginning its work the Planning Branch, Quartermaster Section, was particularly interested in the number of troops involved in ANVIL, their vehicles, and their animal strength. As yet Quartermaster requirements could be figured only in general terms. There was no need to tie supply to a firm tactical plan, but the troop basis of 450,000 men was an essential planning figure. Broken down, this total included 175,000 U.S. troops and 150,000 French and Moslem troops who were then fighting in Italy, and 125,000 French and Moslem troops in North Africa. Middleswart's planners assumed that U.S. troops coming out of the line in Italy would require a 75 percent replacement of all items of clothing, and a 50 percent replacement of all allowances of individual and organizational equipment. Recent replacement factors, applied to the troop basis, would easily round out requirements of subsistence, clothing, and general supplies. At this time calculation of packaged POL needs was not a Quartermaster responsibility. Momentarily, Planning Branch prepared the list of materials-handling equipment to be

---

[64] (1) Ltr, Hq Force 163 to All Concerned, 7 Feb 44, sub: Phasing of Maintenance—Draft Plans. Middleswart Papers. (2) Memo, Maj. Daniel L. Lane, QM Plans Sec, for Middleswart, 17 Oct 44, sub: Rpt of Activities QM Planning Br Covering Opn DRAGOON. Middleswart Papers.

used by each of the other technical services but on 1 May this responsibility was handed over to Ordnance Corps planners.

On 1 March 1944 the skeletonized Headquarters, Seventh Army, with General Patch commanding, moved from Sicily to Mostaganem, Algeria, and the army quartermaster, Colonel Massey, assumed the responsibility for preparing requisitions covering the first sixty days of the operation. Subsequent supply was the responsibility of Quartermaster Section, SOS NATOUSA. Specifically, Massey co-ordinated his job with a small staff under Maj. Daniel L. Lane of the Planning Branch. Once agreement was reached, Lane turned the details of requisitioning over to the various commodity branches in the Quartermaster Section. Here it was determined what items were in the theater and how much supply should be ordered from NYPE. Middleswart issued instructions to freeze immediately items available in the base sections. In requisitions on NYPE, Quartermaster Section requested a 15 percent increase for all items in order to compensate for losses from enemy action or the hazards of shipping. After consulting the War Department, NYPE approved the increase for the period from D-day to D plus 30.

On 12 April, amidst the co-ordination of phased requisitions and the preparation of requirements for the period from D plus 31 to D plus 60, word came from the War Department that special loading of cargo ships for the operation had been suspended, and that all requests for direct quartermaster shipments were canceled. On 31 May SOS NATOUSA notified the base sections that those reserves set aside for a special

operation could be made part of the section's general inventory once again. The development reflected the unsettled circumstances surrounding ANVIL. The operation had originally been planned to take place simultaneously with OVERLORD, but revisions had expanded the latter until it required all available Allied landing craft, even including a number earmarked for Southeast Asia. Once it was clear that ANVIL would have to be postponed until after the OVERLORD landings, Montgomery and Churchill proposed to cancel the whole operation. The Prime Minister, in particular, questioned the usefulness of a landing in the south of France and favored using the Seventh Army in the Balkans. But Eisenhower felt very strongly that an undefended right flank would slow down his advance across France, and in the end his views prevailed. All this was hidden from Mediterranean quartermasters. Suddenly on 9 June they learned that ANVIL—in the meantime rechristened DRAGOON—had been reinstated.[65]

The reconstituted Seventh Army—like the Fifth in Italy—was a polyglot aggregation, including three veteran U.S. divisions, the 3d, 36th, and 45th, Headquarters, VI Corps, an airborne task force, some Polish units, and French Army B. Once the tactical units were nominated, Quartermaster Section, SOS NATOUSA, revitalized its earlier planning and prepared supply requisitions. No serious shortages of Quartermaster items were disclosed except for special

---

[65] The argument over ANVIL was one of the great strategic debates of the war; Eisenhower's *Crusade in Europe*, pages 281–83, gives a one-sided version, but with the merit of brevity. See also, Harrison, *Cross-Channel Attack*, pp. 164–73.

waterproof bags and waterproof covers for small arms. Massey insisted that a divisional reserve of some 36 items, ranging from 1½ rolls of toilet tissue per 100 men in the assault force to 1 handkerchief per individual, be approved. Agreement was reached, but with the understanding that the reserve of Class II and IV items was to be deducted from requisitions subsequent to D plus 30.

Army and theater quartermasters developed a strong ration reserve for Seventh Army.[66] It had two sound features. First, before embarking, each division quartermaster was told to load a 10-day level of balanced B rations onto all available organic transportation. Second, and extremely important, was the floating depot reserve of B rations stowed away on cargo ships in the form of "flatting."[67] Realizing that it would be necessary to use cargo vessels for shuttle service after the original invasion cargoes were discharged, the Transportation Section, SOS NATOUSA, asked the Quartermaster Section to make available quantities of supplies not immediately needed in the invasion. Middleswart set up a 45-day reserve and a 10-day operational level of Class I, II, and IV as flatting, the major item being 21,000 tons of subsistence. Transportation Service allocated 600 tons (dead-weight) in each of the 135 cargo ships that would participate in the D to D plus 30 intratheater

convoys for Quartermaster use as flatting. Thus long before D-day Quartermaster supplies were being flatted on ships at ports in the United States. Most Quartermaster flatting arrived in good condition except for bagged subsistence, which was spoiled by rodents, oil drippings, and penetrating fumes. This reserve of rations was over and above the estimated requirements for the operation.

During the summer of 1944 the assault forces were assembled, mounted, and launched in the face of inbound shipments for Allied forces in Italy and against the overriding priority of the cross-Channel invasion. General Patch kept his Quartermaster supply needs to the absolute minimum. He also attempted to create a support command for Seventh Army, but one serious gap developed in its organization.[68] The French element of Seventh Army insisted that the Americans perform the quartermaster function until French Base Section 901 was operating in southern France. The French wanted to shoot Germans and emphasized combat duty at the expense of logistics. In addition, the French pointed out that they had not specifically trained any spigot quartermasters among the warlike tribesmen from Morocco or Algeria. In this delicate situation, Patch delegated full authority to Larkin to enter Seventh Army and to organize, train, and equip quartermaster service units and further the development of supply procedures along U.S. Army lines. As the weeks wore on, this was a difficult task. In Italy the French troops were moving out of the line toward Naples and had to

---

[66] (1) Memo cited n. 64 (2). (2) *Logistical History of NATOUSA–MTOUSA*, pp. 113–14.

[67] In each ship, hatch Number 2 was loaded to the turn of the bilge, and hatches 4 and 5 to the level of the shaft alley; the flatting was floored over, and the cargo destined for discharge in the theater at an early date, principally wheeled vehicles, was stowed atop the flatting. Thus Quartermaster supply filled up dead space that was normally wasted on the ship.

[68] Larkin remarks cited n. 20 (1).

share the crowded Neapolitan staging area with the Americans. Having received enough rations and maintenance equipment at Naples to see them through the assault phase of DRAGOON, the French divisions assembled at the British-operated ports of Brindisi and Taranto. Here they were far removed from SOS NATOUSA, and efforts to create a French Army SOS were shelved. On Corsica, Larkin had little time left before D-day to create a miniature SOS for the French elements there. His effort to have the French Army help itself by organizing a quartermaster support command before D-day failed. This had to wait until a base section was in operation in France.

Procurement plans for southern France were strikingly similar to current procedures in Italy, despite differences in the tactical situation and in the political status of the two areas. Procurement and allocation responsibilities for DRAGOON were delegated to the G–5 Section, Seventh Army, and since that army included a very large French component the hope was that a really effective civil affairs liaison structure could be organized. That hope was only partially realized, for the senior liaison officers were supplied by the French Committee of National Liberation (CFLN), and they were only made available after a political dispute about the future status of the CFLN in liberated France had been settled, a matter of days before the landing. Since the area would ultimately come under SHAEF command, that headquarters issued all basic policy directives, and also provided nearly half of the necessary civil affairs personnel. For quartermasters, the only significant innovation was that they would be respon-

sible for civil affairs relief supplies, which had previously been handled by civil affairs personnel in the Mediterranean theater. Invasion currency was made available as in previous campaigns, and the fact that its status as legal tender had not yet been clarified was of minor consequence to purchasing and contracting officers. Since French law provided for requisitioning through either local government offices or the national administration, procurement operated without major difficulties. On 23 October 1944 the Allied Powers recognized the CFLN as the provisional government of France, and the same day General Charles de Gaulle signed a decree establishing a French zone of the interior. Thereafter, except in the combat zone, all Allied requisitions were handled through one French office in Paris. On 20 November, SHAEF relieved AFHQ of all remaining responsibilities for procurement or allocation of supplies in southern France.[69]

One of the essentials of sustaining the water-borne invasion was a good port. Patch and Larkin planned to use Toulon and establish there a first-class base section. For personnel, SOS NATOUSA turned once more to the shrinking North African bases as a source of staff officers and operating units.

Originally drawn from the Headquarters and Headquarters Company, 21st Port, at Oran, Coastal Base Section began to assemble in Naples early in July. On the 21st Col. James L. Whelchel arrived in that city from the United States and was named quartermaster of

---

[69] (1) Komer, Civil Affairs, ch. XXI. OCMH. (2) For SHAEF procurement functions, see Chapter XII, below.

the new support group behind Seventh Army.[70] He immediately contacted Massey and learned that Seventh Army itself would handle its Quartermaster mission between D-day and D plus 30. On D plus 31, Coastal Base Section's quartermaster and the Headquarters and Headquarters Company, 70th Quartermaster Base Depot, which was being formed at Civitavecchia and assigned to Whelchel, would assume Massey's supply support. This was normal procedure, but Whelchel noted that phasing plans did not provide for the arrival of the first half of the 70th until D plus 45, with the remainder arriving by D plus 60. Similarly Quartermaster troops attached to the 70th Base Depot had been phased to arrive at a late date in France. Whelchel set about revising the schedule so as to call for the arrival of half the 70th on D plus 20 and the remainder by D plus 30. The arrival of Quartermaster service units was correspondingly speeded up.

Before leaving Naples, Quartermaster Section, Coastal Base Section, attempted to solve two administrative problems. One concerned the work of co-ordinating quartermaster support with French Base 901 for French Army B. The language barrier was far less serious than the lack of understanding of how the French handled their quartermaster services of supply. Under the French system, the army commander directly controlled his pipeline quartermasters. Moreover, four distinct services within the French Army performed the work of the Quartermaster Corps in the U.S. Army. These were as follows: Service d'Intendance (supply), Service d'Es-

sence (POL), Service Veterinaire (remount), and Service de Santé (laundry and bath). Whelchel foresaw that his organization would have difficulty in working with Army B unless French officers were constantly on hand to explain their supply situation. The second problem was the future location of Quartermaster installations in southern France. The trend of thinking in Headquarters, Coastal Base Section, envisaged the creation of major facilities in the Toulon area. Each technical service was allocated area sectors around Toulon within which major depots were to be established. Whelchel felt that the Toulon area had no promise. Accordingly, he selected a number of alternate sites in the vicinity of Marseille, a port of entry which had achieved considerable importance for American quartermasters in World War I.

In mid-August 1944 the assault phase of DRAGOON was successfully carried out along an extensive lodgment area of the Côte d'Azur. Apart from some harassing POL shortages, Massey and the division quartermasters adequately supported the beachhead operations. Supply over the beaches at Saint-Raphaël, Sainte-Maxime, and Saint-Tropez—about halfway between Nice and Marseille—continued for several weeks during which the Beach Control Group was assisted by more than thirty-five officers and men from the Coastal Base Section. Seventh Army paused long enough to seize Marseille before striking up the Rhône valley. On the afternoon of 26 August Whelchel moved into that city and spent the remainder of the month in locating and requisitioning sites he had previously selected from maps in Naples. By mid-September Seventh

---

[70] Littlejohn, ed., Passing in Review, ch. 43.

Army had swept northward, swinging around the Swiss border toward Belfort Gap between the Vosges and Jura Mountains. Other elements pushed toward the Italian frontier and toward Bordeaux, creating additional problems of supply and transportation on both wings. On 11 September Dijon fell. On 12 September contact was made with Allied forces racing across France from Normandy, and Seventh Army now took its place on the southern end of the Allied line, ready for the coming battle of Germany.[71]

On 15 September AFHQ transferred the operational control of DRAGOON to Supreme Headquarters, Allied Expeditionary Force (SHAEF) at Versailles. Four days later French Army B was redesignated 1st French Army and passed to the control of 6th Army Group, General Devers commanding. Momentarily, Seventh Army was reduced to a single corps of three divisions. But it soon received more corps as 1st French Army

shifted from left of Seventh Army to the extreme right of the Allied line. Upon reaching the forest-clad defiles of the high Vosges, the Seventh Army slowed down considerably, and support commands found themselves no longer supporting a war of movement.

By D plus 30 DRAGOON's tactical advance had developed to the stage anticipated by D plus 120. Inevitably, logistical support lagged behind with respect to distances and transportation. At the beaches the Seventh Army quartermaster on 14 September relinquished his support mission to Col. William E. Barrott of the 70th Quartermaster Base Depot.[72] Meantime, subunits of the 70th had moved into Marseille and began operating Quartermaster facilities within Coastal Base Section, shortly renamed Continental Base Section (CONBASE). Initially the 70th had only one service battalion to spread among the various

---

[71] For participation in the southern France amphibious landings on 15 and 16 August 1944, the following Quartermaster units received the arrowhead award (GO 70, 20 August 1945):

3d QM Co	Pathfinder Plat, 334th
36th QM Co	Airborne QM Depot
45th QM Co	Co (Airborne Operation, 15–16 Aug 44)
46th QM GR Co	
Hq and Hq Det, 52d QM Bn	Hq and Hq Det, 528th QM Bn
Hq and Hq Det, 53d QM Bn	Hq and Hq Det, 530th QM Bn
93d QM Rhd Co	549th QM Laundry Co
94th QM Rhd Co	829th QM Truck Co
138th QM Truck Co	830th QM Truck Co
144th QM Truck Co	831st QM Truck Co
Hq and Hq Co, 147th QM Bn	832d QM Truck Co
202d QM Car Co	1110th QM Co, S Gp Avn
Hq and Hq Det, 240th QM Bn	1146th QM Co, S Gp Avn
Hq and Hq Det, 259th QM Bn	

1974th QM Truck Co	3340th QM Truck Co
3250th QM Service Co	3353d QM Truck Co
3251st QM Service Co	3354th QM Truck Co
3252d QM Service Co	3356th QM Truck Co
3253d QM Service Co	3357th QM Truck Co
3277th QM Service Co	3360th QM Truck Co
3286th QM Service Co	3425th QM Truck Co
3287th QM Service Co	3426th QM Truck Co
3288th QM Service Co	3427th QM Truck Co
3289th QM Service Co	3633d QM Truck Co
3299th QM Service Co	3634th QM Truck Co
3300th QM Service Co	3856th QM GS Co
3333d QM Truck Co	3894th QM GS Co
3334th QM Truck Co	4053d QM S Co
3335th QM Truck Co	4133d QM S Co
3336th QM Truck Co	4134th QM S Co
3337th QM Truck Co	4135th QM S Co
3338th QM Truck Co	4136th QM S Co
3339th QM Truck Co	6690th QM GR Co

[72] (1) Hist 70th QM Base Depot. Hist Br OQMG. (2) Lt. Col. Floyd W. Oliphant, "QM–188–B, at Miramas," QMR, XXV (September–October 1945), 18–19, 112–14.

installations on the beaches and at ports. A few French Senegalese troops assisted the Quartermaster battalion, and some civilians were hired as laborers. The arrangements for the local French authorities to pay salaries under lend-lease procedures were unsatisfactory. Delays in payment were frequent, and laborers failed to stay on their jobs. Slowly the great port of Marseille began to recover and Quartermaster supplies arrived. Yet the ever-widening gap between Patch's advance and his base section support had to be filled. To remedy the situation, the stay of Continental Base Section on the coast had to be cut short. By the end of September SOS NATOUSA had transformed CONBASE into an Advance Section (CONAD), and moved it up behind the newly designated 6th Army Group. On 30 September Colonel Whelchel arrived in the CONAD headquarters city of Dijon, 275 miles above Marseille. The next day the newly designated Delta Base Section assumed control of the coastal area.

During operations around Dijon, the Quartermaster Section, CONAD, was confronted with several organizational problems not encountered by the coastal base or the theater quartermasters.[73] Because the First French Army was simultaneously drawing supply from both Delta Base Section and Seventh Army, it was difficult to compute issues and to determine whether the quantities drawn were within the prescribed allowances. To solve the problem, and to impress the French with the need to improve their stock accounting practices, CONAD brought several French officers into the Quartermaster Section. Thus, the Quartermaster, French Base 901, became the deputy to the Quartermaster, CONAD, and similarly, the French Class I officer became the assistant to his opposite number in CONAD. At first many vexing problems arose, and Whelchel, after the war, recalled:[74]

These problems had to be solved diplomatically and as quickly as possible to avoid any interruption of the flow of adequate supplies to the French Army. On the other hand, we soon discovered that the French were not the slightest embarrassed by asking for more supplies than were required. Regardless of all supplies furnished the French at this time, we were unable to satisfy their demand, so it became necessary to investigate the complete supply system of the French Army. It soon developed that where their requisitions indicated no supply of an item on hand, that did not mean that there was actually none of that item available.

The basic peculiarity of the French system was that once supplies were earmarked for a specific unit they were no longer considered depot assets. In fairness to the French supply officers, it must be pointed out that they were being called upon to supply considerably more than the official troop basis of First French Army. The French divisions were greeted with enthusiasm in their homeland, and speedily recruited their units to more than T/O strength. Whole volunteer battalions joined the French forces, although SHAEF refused to include them in the official troop basis, or

---

[73] (1) Memo, ExO OQM for QM CONAD, 14 Nov 44, sub: Notes of Weekly Conf; Memo, Chief Supply Div OQM CAS for QM CAS, sub; Min G-4 Mtg, 22 Nov 44; Narrative History, QM Sec Hq CAS, for Nov 44. All in Hist Br OQMG. (2) Rpt, Class II and IV Supply Br, OQM Hq SOLOC. Middleswart Papers.

[74] Littlejohn, ed., Passing in Review, ch. 43.

to provide them any logistical support. On 30 September CONBASE was authorized to clothe and equip 12,000 locally recruited replacements for the French First Army, but this was less than a quarter of the numbers actually involved. Efforts to equip the others from French civilian sources were not very successful. Under the circumstances, the tendency of French regular units to share supplies and equipment with their volunteer comrades was understandable, even if not authorized.[75]

Another question which arose shortly after CONAD's arrival in Dijon was whether POL supply should be a Quartermaster responsibility.[76] The problem was not entirely new in the Mediterranean area for base section quartermasters. Even at this comparatively late date there was no definite decision as to whether the mission was performed better by a separate POL section on CONAD's special staff or by a POL branch in the Quartermaster Section, CONAD. The original support plan for DRAGOON assembled all QM gasoline supply companies, Engineer pipeline companies, and certain QM service companies under a separate section, composed of experienced Quartermaster Corps and Engineer Corps officers. When SOS came to Marseille, the POL section began operations and placed storage facilities in the port area. Arrangements were made for the receipt and storage of pipeline materials, and

barges were obtained to transport gasoline as far as Lyon. When CONAD was constituted, the POL personnel remained with Delta Base and the CONAD quartermaster assumed the supply responsibility of all Class III products. Whelchel handled POL for two months; by the middle of December 1944 the Engineer-operated pipelines had reached St. Jean de Losne, and as a natural consequence a separate POL Section was organized within CONAD. Supply of solid fuels remained with the Quartermaster Section.[77]

The concept of an advance section was new to Mediterranean quartermasters, and working relationships between CONAD and Delta Base Section had to be developed through trial and error. Quartermaster units in the area were allocated on the logical basis of assigning all mobile repair, sterilization and bath, laundry, and salvage units to CONAD, while units operating fixed installations remained with Delta Base. Agreement on supply operations was more difficult to achieve. CONAD contended that it had very limited facilities for storing and distributing supplies, and operated principally by reconsigning loaded freight cars to specific combat units. One observer from Middleswart's office criticized this arrangement as placing too heavy a burden on Delta Base, but in October 1944 CONAD was too short of supply personnel to operate any other

[75] (1) Marcel Vigneras, Rearming the French, UNITED STATES ARMY IN WORLD WAR II (Washington, 1957), pp. 313–14, 323–26. (2) Official Diary for CG Seventh Army, vol. II, 15 August 1944 to 31 January 1945, entry for 30 September. OCMH.

[76] Memo, Chief Exec Div for QM CAS, 6 Dec 44, sub: Weekly Conf. Hist Br OQMG.

[77] (1) Narrative History QM Sec Hq CAS for November 1944, December 1944, and January–June 1945. Hist Br OQMG. (2) Littlejohn, ed., Passing in Review, ch. 43. (3) Continental Advance Section, Communications Zone, European Theater of Operations, U.S. Army, CONAD History, 3 vols. (Heidelberg, Germany: Aloys Gräf, 1945), I 132. (4) Ruppenthal, Logistical Support, II, 436.

way. When applied to salvage repair, the policy of keeping fixed units in the rear proved impractical, since it involved excessive back-hauling. Once the period of swift pursuit was over, it was possible to solve such problems by shifting units or redefining responsibilities.[78]

The Quartermaster S e c t i o n of CONAD was in the unique position of handling support which emanated from two different parts of France.[79] It received operating units from northwestern French ports as well as Marseille. The 71st Quartermaster Base Depot came to Dijon from England, arriving on 26 November. When the 59th Quartermaster Base Depot was transferred southward to Delta Base Section the 71st established itself at Vesoul, a mid-point between Dijon and Nancy, and served as the only Quartermaster base depot in CONAD until mid-February 1945. By this time SOLOC had been absorbed by ETOUSA, and the consolidation of the continental communications zone was complete.[80]

When Delta Base Section arrived from Corsica on 1 October 1944 to replace CONBASE, the 70th QM Base Depot was already carrying out the full complement of quartermaster activities. By late September the 70th was operating twenty-two separate installations in and around Marseille, a number greater than the combined total of facilities being supervised by all the other technical services. Most of this activity was retail support. But the 70th had made one wholesale shipment of woolen clothing and packaged POL by air direct to Seventh Army dumps beyond Besançon. These supplies were unloaded from shipside at Marseille and flown nearly 400 miles to the north without any opportunity for correct documentation and issue procedures. A number of bales of clothing had been processed by Italian prisoners of war in North Africa and marked as Class X (suitable only for issue to POW's).[81] Upon delivery, Massey reacted quite strongly against the unserviceable items, but closer examination revealed that the bales had not been properly marked.

While Delta Base Section's primary mission was wholesale support, the rapid expansion of its territory from the Swiss and Italian borders to the Bay of Biscay, and to Spain and the Mediterranean on the south, created many internal supply problems. Base Section troops grew in numbers until 190,000 men were scattered over 110,000 square miles. On 19 October Col. John P. Neu was appointed Quartermaster, Delta Base Section, and his first job was to establish three major distribution centers to carry out his primary and secondary missions. The first was at Lyon, where a rail center demolished by the Germans had become a bottleneck in forwarding supplies to CONAD. Neu's second center was established at Nice, where the U.S. Riviera Recreational Area had undertaken one of the biggest projects of its kind for

---

[78] (1) *CONAD History*, I, 80. (2) Memo, Brunson for QM COMZONE MTOUSA, 29 Oct 44, sub: Rpt of Inspection Trip. Littlejohn Collection, box 8.

[79] Hist Hq and Hq Co 71st QMBD; Hist Hq and Hq Co 73d QMBD. Both in Hist Br OQMG.

[80] The final development of the continental depot system, including support for 6th Army Group, is discussed in Chapter XIII, below.

[81] Classification of salvaged articles is discussed in Chapter VIII, below.

American soldiers.[82] By May 1945 this rest area was serving the entire European theater, and had under requisition hotels with accommodations for 16,163 troops. In general, front-line soldiers visiting Nice and Cannes had to be completely reclothed. The normal leave period was ten days, and the project constituted a problem of feeding and outfitting the soldiers, both en route to and while on the Riviera. Swimming trunks, ladies bathing suits, bath towels, soap, and recreational supply constituted a retail mission of the utmost emergency. Neu was expected to fill the order overnight. Biarritz on the southwest coast of France developed into a similar leave center; its capacity was about 5,000 troops.[83]

Marseille and vicinity became the largest of the supply points.[84] Neu inherited the Gare du Prado as a Class I wholesale dump and the Gare Arenc as a ration retail point. For fast moving operations Gare du Prado was unsuitably located. It was in a rail yard in the center of the city, surrounded by narrow, crooked streets which hobbled military traffic. In light of the huge ration reserve shipped as flatting and now coming ashore, Neu abandoned the Gare du Prado and transferred his wholesale operations to a new dump at Rognac, a village with an excellent classification yard for rail lines reaching to all parts of France. Beside a large olive orchard the 240th Quartermaster Service Bat-

talion, with Lt. Col. Edward R. Samuels commanding, quickly organized the Rognac dump. The 619th Depot Supply Company, the 3091st Refrigeration Company, and the 4134th Quartermaster Service Battalion arrived in Rognac and the ration reserve began to grow. Two trains a day arrived from the port and at the same time daily trains outloaded for 6th Army Group. Rognac was also located on the Étang de Berre, a lake directly connected to Marseille by the Rhône Canal. Soon barge traffic relieved the pressure on delivery via rail.

From the start Rognac was a round-the-clock operation. Approximately 2,500 U.S. service troops were employed daily, plus a battalion of French SOS troops who assisted in loading and checking of French Class I supplies. More than 3,000 Italian service troops worked at the Rognac dump until they were replaced by 6,000 German prisoners as the supply problem mounted. Using roller-type conveyors, the prisoners could unload twelve freight cars at one time, routing the cases over the feeder conveyors to a main artery that traversed the center of the dump. Branch conveyors then fed off the main system to the mounting stacks of foodstuffs. Perishables began to arrive in great amounts and the engineers constructed three enormous warehouses. The polyglot 6th Army Group received many different African and Asiatic ration components from Rognac, and also bread from the large bakery operated there by prisoners of war.

With an excellent port complex behind him and with the Rognac works in operation, Neu next organized a Class II and IV depot at Miramas. Located forty miles northwest of Marseille and origi-

---

[82] (1) Ltr, Col James W. Younger, QM 12th Army Group, to Littlejohn, 5 Oct 44. Hist Br, OQMG. (2) After the German surrender, a "G.I. University" here was a still larger project requiring QM support.

[83] *QM Supply in ETO,* I, 77.

[84] Lt. Col. Floyd W. Oliphant, "QM Service in Southern France," *QMR,* XXVI, No. 4 (January–February 1947), 19–23, 76–78.

nally built by the French in World War I as a munitions depot, Miramas (designated as Depot Q–188–B) made an ideal storage site. Its excellence had not been ignored by the German supply corps. Its tile and concrete warehouses required renovation, but its trackage facilities and rolling acres of space captivated a depot manager's imagination. The 622d Railhead Company arrived on 17 November and was joined nine days later by the 240th Depot Supply Company. Though the depot's mission was primarily wholesale support, its retail operations were by no means confined to one class of supply. By rail, truck, and barge, a steady flow of Quartermaster items moved into Miramas. Daily trains left for the north, and frequently on a moment's notice the 240th prepared shipments of clothing for air delivery to Seventh Army. Hard labor was compounded by misery from another quarter. Miramas and Rognac stand in the direct path of the violent mistral—the cold, dry, sixty-mile-an-hour wind that whips down from the Alps and sweeps toward the low pressure areas of the Sahara. The mistral persisted for three-, six-, and even nine-day blows, playing havoc with canvas and cord and penetrating layers of wool and sateen. Idle freight cars, unless thoroughly blocked on the rails, moved as runaways before the wind. With an infrequent snow, the steady mistral's intensity rolled the flakes into pellets of ice that stung like hail against the men's faces. In spring the mistral died down, and the watershed of the Rhône then yielded a bountiful variety of fresh produce for procuring quartermasters.

Purchasing and contracting agents of the 70th QM Base Depot contacted the local markets and merchants for food and end-items. During the last quarter of 1944 local procurement resulted in saving an estimated 9,634 ship tons. As in Naples and Leghorn, Marseille itself fostered quartermaster services to the line. Using commercial facilities, the 167th Bakery Company was producing and distributing its products as early as 2 September. With the help of the engineers, the 814th Sterilization and Bath Company, together with the 7071st and 7171st Laundry Companies brought a large plant covering fourteen buildings into operation by 6 October. Meanwhile the 223d Salvage Collecting Company opened a scrap metal yard at Fréjus, and, with the help of the 3068th Salvage Repair Company, supervised a reclamation program which used prisoner of war labor exclusively. Beyond Marseille, the 70th Base Depot Company through its registrars of graves assumed control of cemeteries as Seventh Army fought to the Moselle River. Cemetery quartermasters relocated two burial grounds, left the one at Montelimar undisturbed, and effected a beautification project at all cemeteries.

With every passing day and each advancing mile Seventh Army moved beyond the range of effective support by the Mediterranean theater and closer to that of the European. Organizationally, spigot and pipeline quartermasters, veterans of Mediterranean warfare, approached the day when they would make their final staff adjustments within a framework of command that embraced two army groups, several field armies, and a theater support command replete with regulating stations, advance sections, intermediate sections, base sections, and depots. In November 1944,

General Devers relinquished command of MTOUSA to devote full time to 6th Army Group. Behind the 6th, Larkin moved his headquarters to Dijon and constituted SOLOC (Southern Line of Communications) to superintend the logistical system of southern France and to arrange for its own subsequent merger with COMZ ETOUSA, the northern theater support command. One immediate effect of activating SOLOC was to narrow the authority of MTOUSA to Italy, the islands, and North African base sections which were being rapidly closed out. AFHQ and Peninsular Base Section divided between themselves the supply mission of the old COMZONE MTOUSA, the successor of SOS NATOUSA. Before leaving Caserta for Dijon, Middleswart and Ramsey, the latter remaining as the new Quartermaster of MTOUSA, discussed the division of their respective staffs and reviewed the nature and the problems of supply action for Fifth Army and Peninsular Base Section. On 20 November 1944 General Middleswart became SOLOC quartermaster, bringing with him his deputy, Colonel Brunson, all of his branch chiefs, and key staff officers.[85] The integrity of the team Middleswart had built in Oran after February 1943 is indicated by the fact that ninety-five Quartermaster members of the SOLOC roster had served in SOS NATOUSA.

Because 6th Army Group and SOLOC had been anticipated long before each headquarters was organized, Middleswart had attached one of his staff officers, Capt. John Lapperre, and two enlisted men to serve in liaison to the SOS advance group at Lyon. Thus Lapperre was present with members of the skeleton staff of 6th Army Group in its formative period. As an observer, Lapperre provided Middleswart with information that smoothed the way for SOLOC's assumption of 6th Army Group's support. In Dijon Middleswart organized his SOLOC staff on the pattern of Quartermaster Section, SOS NATOUSA. There were two exceptions. First, graves registration functions were transferred to COMZ ETOUSA, and secondly, a Local Resources Branch was added to handle local procurement of coal and special merchandise.

Once at work, the new staff encountered a new administrative practice that was contrary to its Mediterranean training.[86] SOLOC quartermasters found themselves without control of supplies for which they were responsible. CONAD—actually a large regulating station directly behind Seventh Army—forwarded Quartermaster requisitions from army direct to Delta Base Section without considering what was expected on the basis of previous requisitions. Middleswart objected to this lack of co-ordination through SOLOC. Reviewing the unbalanced stocks that resulted, the Quartermaster Section, SOLOC, noted that CONAD was proposing to perform a co-ordination mission "for which it had neither the experience nor personnel." This judgment was less a commentary on the competence of the personnel than on CONAD's eagerness

---

[85] Hist QM Sec Hq SOLOC ETOUSA, 20 Nov 44–31 Jan 45. Middleswart Papers.

[86] Ltr of Instrs, Hq SOLOC ETOUSA OQM, 16 Jan 45; Ltr of Instrs, Hq SOLOC ETOUSA OQM, 20 Jan 45, sub: CONAD Requisitions; Ltr of Instrs, Hq SOLOC ETOUSA OQM, 25 Jan 45, sub: Procedure CONAD Monthly QM Requisitions by Delta Base Sec. All in Middleswart Papers.

to make deliveries to Seventh Army dumps regardless of the effect on reserve supplies. On Middleswart's recommendation, Larkin decided that CONAD should continue as the direct support command, but that Quartermaster Section, SOLOC, should control CONAD's stock level and relay CONAD's requisitions to the coastal support section after they had been appropriately reviewed. COMZ ETOUSA was entirely in agreement with this procedure, since that headquarters demanded a similar exact accounting in SOLOC's requisitions on NYPE. Beginning in November 1944, General Littlejohn, the ETO quartermaster, reviewed Middleswart's requisitions before passing them on to the zone of interior. Littlejohn had a serious difference of opinion with Larkin and Middleswart regarding exact statements of amounts "on hand and due in," which by ETO regulations had to be noted on the face of each requisition. SOLOC practice had only required a monthly balance sheet, which Littlejohn judged to be insufficient and also based on inaccurate statistics. Middleswart protested that his office overhead did not provide personnel for such elaborate bookkeeping, but ultimately the ETO view prevailed, and Colonel Rosaler, Littlejohn's specialist in inspecting and indoctrinating field installations, installed the new accounting system.[87]

Difficulty in reaching the desired 60-day stock level as well as in balancing the stocks on hand troubled Quarter-master Section, SOLOC.[88] Reaching that level by 1 December 1944 was virtually impossible because more and more troops were transferred to the right of the Allied line in southern France. This the DRAGOON planners had never envisaged. As October waned, a French armored division and two American infantry divisions, lacking much of their authorized equipment, were shifted from COMZ ETOUSA support to the SOLOC zone. Three more divisions originally destined for OVERLORD were enrolled on the DRAGOON roster in November, and an additional three arrived in December. With nine new divisions present, SOLOC's level of supply fell sharply. Quartermaster service troops strained to support a troop basis three times the size of their capability. To assist in handling the workload, COMZ ETOUSA diverted a substantial number of service units and relief was also accorded when SOLOC authorized a 50 percent personnel increase in Middleswart's office. As a further measure to bolster the lengthening supply line from Marseille, COMZ provided an additional base section staff. On 9 February the former headquarters of the Brittany Base Section activated Burgundy District at Dijon as a subordinate unit of CONAD. This was, in effect, an intermediate section, brought in so that CONAD could move forward to a new location at Nancy.[89] Three days later,

[87] (1) Littlejohn, ed., Passing in Review, ch. 9. (2) Memo, CQM for QM UKB, 14 Dec 44, sub: Preparation of Requisitions in U.K. Littlejohn Reading File, vol. XXI, item 51. (3) Quoted in Memo, Middleswart for Rosaler, 18 Jan 45, sub: SOLOC Requisitions. Littlejohn Collection, sec. III.

[88] Hist QM Sec Hq SOLOC ETOUSA, 20 Nov 44–31 Jan 45; Training Memo 1, Hq SOLOC ETOUSA OQM, 23 Jan 45. Both in Middleswart Papers.

[89] Memos, CQM for Chief Pers Div OCQM and G–4 COMZ, 12 Oct 44, sub: QM Troop Reqmts to Support Southern Group of Armies. Littlejohn Reading File, vol. XXIX, items 54, 55. (2) QM Supply in ETO, I, 75–77. (3) See below, ch. XIII.

SOLOC headquarters, also at Dijon, was dissolved and its responsibilities divided between CONAD and COMZ ETOUSA. On 12 February 1945 Middleswart was named deputy to the Chief Quartermaster, COMZ ETOUSA, returning to a vastly enlarged version of the assignment he had held in the summer of 1942.[90]

---

[90] Ruppenthal, *Logistical Support,* II, pp. 378–83.

CHAPTER V

Rations for Mediterranean Troops

Feeding the combat soldier was no simple task, particularly when he came from a country enjoying a high standard of living and campaigned in foreign countries too devastated or too poor to support their own populations adequately, let alone feed an invading army. The daily deliveries and issues of food to troops in the Mediterranean theater provide a record of planning and experimentation, calculation, and frustration. The normal time lag between order and shipment demanded that requirements—often based on tactical plans which were tentative at best—be estimated far in advance of consumption dates. For transportation, Mediterranean quartermasters were dependent on agencies charged with world-wide responsibilities, which inevitably made decisions incomprehensible to those at the overseas operating level. Packaging, a task which seems simple to the uninitiated, required constant attention if automatic food deliveries were to be made promptly each day. These were only a few of the factors which affected Quartermaster activities in the distribution of Class I supply.

The kind of food consumed by the American soldier depended more on his location at any given moment than on any other factor. As a general rule, if the man was in a position to be fed from the kitchen of his own unit he could at least expect to receive the B ration composed of nonperishable meats and vegetables, and bearing a resemblance to the menu served to garrison troops at home. Moreover, Quartermasters in the Mediterranean area made every effort to exploit whatever refrigerated facilities and local agricultural resources were available in the hope of supplying unit messes with fresh meat, fruits and vegetables, and dairy products. In many combat situations, the quartermaster had no choice but to provide the individual soldier with packaged operational rations.

The Packaged Rations for Combat

The development of packaged rations for combat will probably stand as a landmark in the history of food preparation for military forces as well as remain a favorite subject of conversation among veterans of World War II.[1] The QMC had long been interested in developing emergency rations, but funds for research and development were lacking and progress was desultory. Late in the 1930's, research and development activities were accelerated and by the time of

---

[1] (1) A full account is to be found in Harold W. Thatcher, *Development of Special Rations for the Army,* QMC Historical Studies, 6 (Washington, 1945). (2) See also Risch, *The Quartermaster Corps: Organization, Supply, and Services,* vol. I, ch. V.

TORCH, the Office of The Quartermaster General had standardized three types of packaged combat rations.

The first type was the D ration, consisting of three 4-ounce chocolate bars, artificially flavored and fortified with sucrose, skimmed milk, cacao fat, and raw oatmeal flour. Containing only 1,800 calories, the D ration, reminiscent of the "Iron" ration of World War I, could only be considered for use in extreme emergencies or as a supplement to a more nourishing field ration.

The C ration—originally conceived as a "balanced meal in a can"—was composed of six 12-ounce cans, three of which were meat units and three bread units. It also had such complementary items as sugar, soluble coffee, and candy. The National Research Council considered the ration's 3,000 calories adequate for a moderately active man. Despite efforts to introduce a greater variety, meat and beans, meat and vegetable hash, and meat and vegetable stew constituted the major C ration components throughout World War II.

The need for a ration more nourishing than the D and more compact than the C led to the development of the K ration, which was packaged in three rectangular boxes each small enough to fit into a pocket of the paratrooper's uniform. Each box held the constituents of a separate meal, including biscuits and crackers, dextrose tablets, a can of meat, meat and egg, or processed cheese, plus a stick of chewing gum and four cigarettes. Supplementary items distributed as part of the ration included soluble coffee, concentrated bouillon, a 2-ounce bar of D ration, a fruit bar, lemon juice powder, and sugar tablets. The whole ration contained from 3,100 to 3,400 cal-

ories and, because of its convenient dimensions and efficient protective wrapping, was described as "a triumph of the packager's art." [2]

In addition to the D, C, and K rations, the OQMG made progress by late 1942 toward the development of a ration specially packed for small isolated units, such as might engage in desert or mountain fighting. Designed to feed five men for one day, the so-called 5-in-1 ration permitted the preparation of warm meals by troops with limited cooking experience and even more limited kitchen facilities. For variety, three separate menus were prepared, each containing the breakfast, dinner, and supper meals. Illustrating the 5-in-1's substantial contents, one of the menus provided a breakfast of dehydrated tomato juice cocktail, whole wheat cereal, canned bacon, soluble coffee, sugar, and canned milk; a dinner of dehydrated bean soup, canned roast beef, dehydrated potatoes, canned peas, evaporated pears, hard candy, lemon juice crystals, and sugar; and a supper which included meat and vegetable stew, vanilla pudding powder, soluble coffee, sugar, and canned milk. A supply of salt, biscuits, dehydrated fruit spread, and a processed substitute for butter accompanied all cased rations. The nutritive value ranged from 3,400 to 4,100 calories, and the gross weight of the 5-in-1, packed in a solid fiber carton, was almost thirty pounds. [3]

In varying quantities every one of these combat rations moved across nine TORCH beaches. The soldiers also ate these rations in Tunisia. Logistical difficulties held up the balanced B ration,

---

[2] Thatcher, *Development of Special Rations*, p. 61.
[3] *Ibid.*, pp. 73–81.

so the C ration became the basic unit of subsistence. One of the C's most conspicuous advantages over the other packaged rations was the fact that its meat unit could be heated in and consumed from its own container. This saved mess gear cleaning—a drain on precious water in dry Tunisia, yet otherwise necessary for sanitation. But littering the roadsides with empty, shiny tins guided enemy aircraft along the routes and bivouacs of American convoys.

Out of North Africa came many recommendations for improving the C ration. The meat and vegetable hash menu was not well received. The particles of meat were too small; troops preferred chunks of meat that could be chewed. Others proposed to substitute a fruit bar for one of the biscuits, to design a new top to prevent meat juices from spilling on hands or clothes, and to include accessories like chocolate, soap, cigarettes, and toilet paper. Because the C ration was flavorless when cold, soldiers hoped that canned heat could be issued as in the British and German Armies.[4]

From the health standpoint the North African campaign demonstrated the drawbacks of making the C ration a steady diet. After three days of continuous consumption, it became unpalatable. One commander reported that his men suffered spells of nausea and digestive disturbances after three or four days. Distressed by the extent of these disorders and hoping to obviate their recurrence in the next battle, the 1st Division quartermaster cached away as many B rations as possible in the vehicles and trailers which would otherwise have been shipped to Sicily empty. The wisdom of this move, he believed, was borne out by the disappearance of stomach ailments.[5]

By far the most popular combat ration in North Africa was the 5-in-1, which corresponded to the components of the B ration. It was especially appreciated by the Americans who fought under British command in Tunisia, and at first ate British food. Feeding the troops with the British Compo (Composite Pack) ration—packaged in 65-pound boxes and containing enough food for fourteen men—was technically very easy, since it was a balanced ration. But the absence of coffee from the Compo and the inclusion of such dishes as mutton stew and kidney pie was repulsive to American tastes. The roast beef, meat balls and spaghetti, canned bacon, and corned beef of the 5-in-1 were more to the American soldier's liking. The dehydrated elements of the 5-in-1 aroused a mixed reaction among the troops. White and sweet potatoes, onions, soups, and milk of the dehydrated family were well received, but cabbage flakes and tomato juice cocktail were not. Apricot spread and a nonperishable substitute for butter known as Carter's Spread were not liked. Nevertheless, once this ration arrived at the front, the concept of a small-group balanced ration was vindicated. Indeed, so well received was the 5-in-1—often called the U or unit ration—that numerous recommendations came in from the ETO and

---

[4] Pounder Rpt, p. 14.

[5] (1) Memo, Capt J. T. Quirk for TQMG, 3 Jun 43; Memo, Chief Opns Br, Mil Plng Div OQMG, for Chief S&D OQMG, 28 Jul 43, sub: Extracts, Rpts 3d, 9th, and 34th Inf Divs. Both in OQMG MED 319.1. (2) G–4 Rpt, Husky, 1 Aug 43. 1st Inf Div, 301.4.

NATOUSA for its conversion into a larger unit. Advocates of this change suggested that the five-man feeding unit was too small and that too many separate boxes had to be issued to larger groups.[6] Quartermasters debated for six months over the relative merits of a 10-in-1 versus a 12-in-1, the latter designed to feed the basic infantry squad for one day.[7] The final decision favored the 10-in-1 after Army Ground Forces determined that 40 pounds was the maximum load that one man could conveniently handle when carrying the package across a beach, unloading it from a ship or vehicle, or dropping it from an airplane. As designed in August 1943, the new 10-in-1 was packed into a well-marked, single container, holding a K ration for the noon meal, and two overpacked 5-in-1's for the morning and evening meals. The 10-in-1's nutritive value averaged 3,668 calories.[8]

By December 1943, when the Italian campaign was three months old, the 10-in-1 packed in five menus was issued along with other operational rations. At that time medical officers made a number of significant observations as to the nutritional effect of the various packaged rations on the soldier. They noted that combat rations became unpalatable if consumed for long periods of time and that they were all responsible for minor but uncomfortable stomach disorders. Of still more importance was the increasing evidence that the soldier's caloric intake was not enough to replace the energies expended in fighting. This deficiency was partly attributed to the widespread distaste for the biscuits, malted dextrose tablets, and synthetic lemon crystals found in the C and K rations. But even if all these rations were consumed, surgeons were skeptical of their adequacy as nourishment for troops in combat or for men performing moderate work in cold weather.

One medical officer challenged the generally accepted caloric values of the four main types of field rations. He reported to the Fifth Army surgeon that the daily deficiency of troops subsisting on the C or K ration ranged from 400 to 1,800 calories a day depending on the coldness of the weather and the type of physical exertion. Reports from combat soldiers verified these dietary deficiencies. Men lost weight and surgeons reported an increasing incidence of bodily exhaustion. Medical officers observed a decrease in body fat as well as a paleness of muscle substance among wounded patients requiring surgery. Vitamin deficiencies were manifested in skin lesions, lassitude, and neuritis.

Some quartermasters did not agree with this medical survey. One reply to a questionnaire on the 10-in-1 ration called attention to discrepancies between the mathematical calculations of calories by the National Research Council and the Fifth Army surgeon. Nevertheless, the OQMG Research and Development Branch continued its efforts to improve

---

[6] (1) Ltr, Littlejohn to Maj Gen Carl A. Hardigg, OQMG, 1 May 43, and 12 incls. USFET QM 430. (2) Ltr, Littlejohn to Gregory, 31 Mar 43. Littlejohn Reading File, vol. X, item 88. (3) Pounder Rpt, pp. 8–9.

[7] Memo, AGF for TQMG, 17 Feb 43, sub: Obsv Rpt in Algeria and Tunisia; Ltr, Sullivan to Gregory, 17 Mar 43, and 4 Incls; Memo, Maj Clement M. Burnhome, OQMG Obsv, for Chief Mil Plng Div OQMG, 6 May 43. OQMG MED 319.25.

[8] (1) Frink Rpt. (2) Ltr, Ramsey to Gregory, 27 Mar 43. OQMG MED 319.25. (3) Ltr, Chief S&D Div OQMG to Littlejohn, 6 May 43. OQMG ETO 457. (4) Ltr, Frink to Littlejohn, 24 Jul 43. Littlejohn Collection, sec. I, Subsistence File.

the rations which had been developed by the end of 1943. It altered the C ration, changing the type of stew and biscuits offered, eliminating the hash, and adding five new meat components. Caramels replaced the malted milk and dextrose tablets in the K ration. A few officers favored a return to the 5-in-1, largely because of the unpopularity of the K ration provided as a noon meal in the 10-in-1. While OQMG took remedial action to drop the K ration, to curtail excessive use of cold beverages, and to increase the caloric values to 3,893, the modified 10-in-1 of March 1944 did not appear in the Mediterranean theater in time to eliminate criticism before the end of the war.[9]

If the diet of the fighting man was proving deficient, theater quartermasters could not simply wait for relief from the laboratories in the United States. In January 1944 the 3d Battalion, 135th Infantry, 34th Division, co-operated with Sullivan in a combat feeding experiment. During the month-long test, the veteran 3d Battalion was in action near Cassino. To determine the best possible menu for troops beyond the reach of bulk rations and how to organize the battalion's supply system for its preparation and issue, Sullivan authorized the 3d Battalion to draw a fifteen-day supply of special rations.

Essentially, the project called for the establishment of a battalion bakery by borrowing equipment and men from the company kitchens. Bakers made such pastries as fruit turnovers, doughnuts, cookies, cinnamon rolls, and chocolate cakes. At the same time each company kitchen prepared sandwiches of hamburgers, ham, egg, cheese, and jam, and arranged for packing and delivering sandwiches, pastries, and fruit juices to the unit's fighters. As the experiment continued, these additional servings were sent forward by mule or jeep, depending on the terrain, on the days when C's constituted the basic ration. Because supplies of lard and other baking ingredients were inadequate the experiment could not be put into general practice, but its popularity was reaffirmed the next winter, when a similar program was launched among the regiments of the 10th Mountain Division.

For similar reasons, Sullivan authorized extra issues of supplementary foods to combat troops when they moved out of the line and into rest areas. In a further attempt to make the C and K rations more palatable and to provide more hot beverages in cold weather, commanders demanded and quartermasters provided extra allowances of coffee, canned milk, and sugar during both winters in Italy. When these favorites were unavailable, the fortified chocolate bar—generally an unpopular food—was distributed as a nutritive supplement.[10]

---

[9] (1) Ltr, Col Paul M. Howe to Surgeon, Fifth Army, 4 Dec 43, sub: Rationing and Nutritional Status, Fifth Army; Ltr, Sullivan to Middleswart, 1 May 44; Ltr, Doriot to Sullivan, 16 May 44; Ltr, Feldman to Middleswart, 16 Aug 44; Ltr, CO 477th Ord Evac Co to Sullivan, 19 Apr 45, sub: 10-in-1 Ration Questionnaire. All in Sullivan Papers. (2) Rpt, AFHQ-AGF Bd, 3 Dec 43, sub: Complaints Against 5-in-1 and 10-in-1. OQMG MED 319.25. (3) *Fifth Army History,* II, 69; III, 71.

[10] (1) Rpt, Fifth Army Combat Feeding Experiment, 3d Bn 135th Inf, n.d. Hist Br OQMG. (2) Rad 4283, Tate to CG's II and IV Corps, 30 Sep 44; Ltr, Sullivan to Doriot, 19 Dec 44; Rad 2302, Tate to McNarney, 25 Jan 45. All in Sullivan Papers. (3) Rad L 4726, Larkin to Pence, 24 Dec 43. Poore Papers.

In the south of France, despite an extremely mobile situation, the troops consumed a surprisingly large proportion of B rations. Even in the early phases, operational rations comprised less than 30 percent of all issues. About 10 percent of all rations were 10-in-1's, a proportion based on availability rather than preference. This was by far the most popular of the hard rations. Earlier Mediterranean experience was reversed in that the K ration (with D ration supplement) was preferred to the C, possibly because there was a considerable airborne component among DRAGOON troops. No 5-in-1 rations were issued. Consumption of hard rations dropped below 20 percent in October 1944, as the war of movement came to an end.[11]

Kitchen-Prepared Rations

While packaged combat rations served as the main bill of fare during the first fortnight in Casablanca and Oran, unit kitchens of Western and Center Task Forces began to shift to garrison-type foods shortly before Thanksgiving Day, 26 November 1942. Mountains of B ration components had been accumulating in these two port cities since the arrival of the D plus 3 convoys, but task force quartermasters had had considerable difficulty in organizing their Class I depots. Across North Africa, 100,000 men were waiting for a balanced B ration. At Oran, McNamara's labor situation hobbled depot operations. He was forced to divide his depot area into

two compartments. Flour, dried foodstuffs, and any food which was not in sealed cans or containers were put into a restricted area. Because of U.S. sanitary codes, native food handlers worked only among the cased items. Meanwhile, within the restricted enclosures, Quartermaster service troops failed to appreciate any humor in a job which found them sorting cans devoid of paper labels; such confusion further delayed the balancing of B rations.

In planning TORCH, task force quartermasters had been careful not to ask for perishable or frozen foods that required refrigerated storage at an early date. It was known prior to the landings that cold storage facilities existed, but no one knew their condition or capacity. Fortunately, McNamara had made an early reconnaissance of the Oran plant. At the outset he was almost forced to commandeer the building from its French owners. On D plus 13 an unannounced refrigerator ship arrived with a cargo of frozen beef, pork, legs of lamb, and chilled bacon and hams. A second vessel moved into the harbor with more meat and tons of frozen turkeys, but the refrigerated warehouses could not handle this volume of supplies. Determined not to reconsign the cargoes back to the United States, McNamara issued frozen turkey from shipside.

By Christmas Day 1942, problems of local food procurement and storage were being resolved. Task Force quartermasters were moving toward Tunisia leaving base section colleagues with the task of preparing 10-day menus and issue charts for the B ration, augmented by a host of perishables. By March 1943, through use of menus based on circulars

---

[11] (1) Weekly G–4 Rpts SUSA, Sep–Dec 44. Seventh Army, AG 319.1. (2) William G. Ashmore, "Nook and Cranny Reserve Feeds 7th Army," *QMTSJ*, VI, No. 1 (1 December 1944), 7.

from Middleswart's QM Section, SOS, all troops in North Africa were issued the B ration except those in the most forward areas.[12]

The 10-day menu of B rations—the basic cycle which permitted a variety of meals—consisted of approximately 100 separate foodstuffs, plus a few condiments. When all the components were available in the amounts and proportions required by the 10-day cycle, the B ration was nutritionally balanced. But "balances" were easier to chart than to issue. Capt. William F. Pounder, surveying the ration breakdown system for General Gregory, offered one explanation for the difficulties when he wrote that "this ration is not originally shipped on the convoys as a balanced ration." [13]

Other difficulties could be traced to the hazards of storing rations in the open, to the lack of enough Quartermaster service troops, and to the inefficiency of native labor. In one instance, when civilian workers were ordered to match food items by the biggest letters on each case, it was discovered after three days that all cases labeled "Rations" were stacked together. Because there were not enough men to rearrange the meats, vegetables, fruits and juices quickly and properly, a random assortment of B ration components went forward toward Tébessa. Unfortunately, the upset balance was not solely the result of negligence or haste.

Rear area troops sometimes withheld choice foods in excess of their proper allowances. The frequency of this offence was directly proportional to the number of times the food stocks were handled. Rear area troops, on the other hand, were not the only ones at fault. Ration clerks were quick to point out the difference between actual strength and the daily average strength for rations listed on a unit's certified morning report. The explanation that sudden attachments of extra troops had been the basis for requesting extra rations was not always valid. Tallies showed that combat commanders sometimes countenanced overissues. Yet at times other commanders unwillingly accepted overissues of B rations because the food was packed in containers too large for small groups of men. In many situations an accurate ration breakdown at the railheads was impossible. Repeatedly, Sullivan drew Gregory's attention to the ration breakdown problem caused by overly large containers. Lard came in 37-pound cans whereas a small unit required only a 4-pound can; raisins arrived in Number 10 cans although Sullivan had asked for 15-ounce packages; tea reached the front in a 5-pound carton when the troops only needed a ¾-pound package.[14]

Digging deeper into the causes which affected B ration losses in the theater, Middleswart was able to arrive at some significant statistics. In December 1943,

[12] (1) Poore Journal. (2) McNamara *Memoir*, pp. 30–34. (3) Cir 1, OQM ABS, 20 Jan 43; Menu and Issue Charts, QM MBS, 9 Jan 43; Tech Bull 4, OQM SOS NATOUSA, 15 Mar 44 and Tech Bull 7, OQM SOS NATOUSA, 29 May 44. All in Middleswart Papers.

[13] Pounder Rpt, p. 7.

[14] (1) Pounder Rpt, pp. 12–13. (2) Ltr, Middleswart to Doriot, 21 Aug 43. Poore Papers. (3) Ltr and Incls, CG AGF to TQMG, 10 Oct 43, sub: Overseas Rpt. OQMG MED 319.25. (4) Ltr, Sullivan to Painter, 13 Jan 44, sub: Improvement of Rations; Ltr, Sullivan to Doriot, 25 Jul 44. Both in Sullivan Papers.

he expressed the loss factors in the following percentages:

Cause	Percentage
Total	8.00
Improper packaging	0.50
Rehandling damages	1.50
Pilferage	2.00
Enemy action	0.50
Operational movements	1.00
Extra issues	0.50
Spoilage due to container imperfections	0.50
Spoilage due to climate	1.00
Accounting errors in effecting distribution	0.50

After adding 1.5 percent for rations lost at sea to Middleswart's figure, NYPE did not consider NATOUSA's loss factor of 9.5 percent excessive.[15]

The hope was that a B ration, whenever it could be fed at all in the combat zone, would provide about five pounds of food per man per day, including four vegetables, three different meat components, a dessert pudding, and canned fruit or fruit juice. Significantly, printed menus were ignored, and each division made up a daily menu based on supplies actually in stock. During lulls in the Tunisia fighting, the B ration was sometimes brought into the front lines. Field ranges were installed in a 2½-ton truck, whose sides were boarded up to hide the light. Behind the line at a safe distance, cooks prepared the B ration menu and at night

the rolling kitchen rendezvoused with hungry front-line troops. The cooks then tidied up, broke out the breakfast foods, and prepared another meal. Before daybreak, they had served two hot meals and had returned to the rear for more supplies. When this system was not practical, the 34th Division delivered components of the B ration to small combat groups and permitted them to heat their own meals over cans filled with sand and saturated with gasoline or kerosene.[16]

The ration statistics of II Corps in the Tunisia Campaign show that, by weight, the B ration comprised about 60 percent of the rations issued. A refinement of these figures indicates that the B ration was consumed by the 34th Division only in the lull between the end of the southern campaign and the beginning of the drive for Bizerte. When the 34th was in movement to the northern sector and after it was committed to battle, it reverted to the C and 5-in-1 rations, supplemented by freshly baked bread. Mindful of its Tunisian experience, the 1st Armored Division placed emphasis on keeping the B in balance and at an adequate supply level. For example, this unit found the allowances of sugar, coffee, and baking powder low. Some authorized items, especially condiments, were often unobtainable.[17]

In the short Sicilian operation menu planners made no effort to provide a balanced B ration. Instead they pre-

[15] Pilferage headed the list for the following reasons: open storage provided ready access to those bent on pilferage, opportunities abounded for pilferage when rail shipments were made in open cars for distances up to 1,500 miles requiring five to six days en route, black markets flourished in impoverished, underfed communities, and "stealing" was not considered "a debasing profession by certain elements of the native population." Ltr, Col W. D. Cronkhite, OSD NYPE, to Gregory, 15 Jan 44; 1st Ind, Larkin to OSD NYPE, 24 Dec 43. Both in OQMG MED 430.

[16] (1) Pounder Rpt, p. 13. (2) Ltr, G–4 34th Inf Div to G–2 AGF, 25 Mar 43. OQMG MED 319.25.

[17] (1) Compilation of II Corps Ration Statistics, Frink Rpt, exhibit A. (2) Memos cited n. 7. (3) Incl to Ltr, CG 1st Armd Div to CG NATOUSA, 26 Jun 43, sub: Adequacy of Pers and Transport for Supply of a Div in Combat. Hist Br OQMG.

TABLE 1—FIFTH ARMY RATION ISSUES: SELECTED MONTHS

Type of Ration	October 1943	April 1944	October 1944	April 1945
Total Rations[a]	5,768,685	7,431,771	5,593,826	7,028,492
Daily Average[a]	186,087	247,726	180,446	234,283
B ration	2,473,621	5,262,462	4,412,985	5,245,435
C ration	1,205,941	111,768	110,731	845,472
D ration	18,772	42,533	12,864	12,378
K ration	636,919	147,316	516,566	571,253
5-in-1 and 10-in-1	1,433,432	1,867,692	540,680	353,954
Supplementary				
Fresh meat (issues)	0	27	31	30
Bread (pounds)	730,788	3,494,554	2,498,487	3,046,067

[a] U.S. Troops only.

Source: Fifth Army History, II, 72; III, 73–74; IV, 230–31; V, 220; VII, 228; VIII, 129–30; IX, 182.

pared a combined B and 5-in-1 ration and the engineer amphibian brigade distributed it. In Italy the bulk B ration appeared again, and quickly rose to almost 80 percent of the total issue, a figure which persisted through most of the Fifth Army's career in Italy. (*Table 1*) Nonetheless the complaint of poor balance was heard intermittently. When a corps quartermaster visited the Fifth Army's Class I dump at Maddaloni in November 1943, he observed that supplies were issued on a "first come, first served basis," with no attempt to assure an equitable share of scarce items. Because substitutes for the missing B components could not always be provided, late arrivals departed with short rations. A typical complaint by Sullivan during the same month was that Fifth Army did not receive complete deliveries from Peninsular Base Section. "The shortages of items of the B ration," he wrote to the Army G–4, "are regular, but the condition is becoming more serious. . . ." Hoping to obtain adequate stocks, he enumerated the items needed through the first week of December 1943, but deletions,

shortages, and substitutions continued in deliveries from Naples.[18]

At theater level, quartermasters understood the underlying causes of the difficulty more clearly, but were equally helpless to provide a cure. A major consideration was the extreme shortage of intratheater marine transport, which made it virtually impossible to balance ration shortages in one base section by bringing in surpluses from another location within the theater. Although the requisitioning function had been centralized, the NATOUSA quartermaster submitted separate monthly requisitions to NYPE for each major port or base section, treating its supply position as a separate problem. Under this system, imbalances should have been rectified on arrival of shipments from the United States. But zone of interior depots, reflecting world-wide shortages, made

[18] Memo, Lt Col John R. Curry for Sullivan, 13 Nov 43, sub: Q–5–21 Depot; Ltr, Truscott to Clark, 27 Nov 43, sub: Deficiencies, Type B Ration; quotation in Memo, Sullivan for Tate, 21 Nov 43; Memo, Sullivan for Tate, 20 Dec 43. All in Sullivan Papers.

many substitutions, often shipping items which the theater already had in excess. Diversion of shipping to a port other than the original destination was a still more frequent cause of difficulty. Most ships carried a mixed cargo, including ammunition. Rare indeed was the convoy that arrived without at least some of its ships diverted by the urgent needs of combat.[19]

Giving troops the type of ration they desired was as much a problem of stock levels as of balances. The authorized level for NATOUSA in the spring of 1944 was 60 days, but actual theater stocks were higher. Because of the receipt of stocks for future operations, levels rose from 69 days on 25 February to 85 days on 25 April 1944. Within the individual base sections, levels varied widely:[20]

	Days of Supply		
	25 February	25 March	25 April
Atlantic Base	107	85	108
Mediterranean Base	107	111	145
Eastern Base	87	95	74
Island Base	123	128	124
Peninsular Base ...	59	68	59
Adriatic Depot	38	45	59
Tyrrhenian Depot .	70	109	119
Northern Base	12	29	47

Late in the summer of 1944, when Middleswart was resisting efforts to lower the authorized subsistence levels, he divided the 60-day level into a 30-day operating supply and a 30-day theater reserve. NYPE shipped the 30-day operational supply to NATOUSA by

spreading it over three successive convoys. Every ten days, on the average, a convoy left New York City. Thus requisitions were not complete and all components of the B ration were not available until after the last ship of the third convoy had been unloaded. Each base section then required 20 to 30 days to warehouse, inventory, and make final issue. When water-borne operations were in progress, the normal convoy schedule was disrupted and the delay was even greater.

The reserve stock—as differentiated from the operating stock—constituted the safety factor against a tactical situation which might cause a large number of troops to switch overnight from one type of ration to another. Because of transportation difficulties, pilferage, and the substitution problem, Middleswart insisted that the B ration could only be kept in balance in a dispersed and active base section if a 20-day supply was maintained. Once mature, Peninsular Base Section maintained a 45-day level as a reserve and a 10-day level for operating use.[21]

In the combat zone of Italy the problem of levels took on different proportions. A 10-day level at a Fifth Army Class I dump and a 2-day reserve at an army railhead assured a satisfactory supply of rations in areas where bridges might be destroyed or where the pack mule was the only method of transportation. On the other hand a 10-day level was too large for the army quartermaster to move on short notice. When Fifth

[19] Critical comment upon a preliminary MS version of this history by Brig. Gen. Thomas H. Ramsey, dated 18 November 1954. Hist Br OQMG.

[20] 1st Ind, CofS SOS NATOUSA to CG ASF, 13 May 44, sub: Subs Pipeline and Losses. OQMG MED 430.

[21] (1) Memo, QM SOS NATOUSA for ACofS G-4 SOS NATOUSA, 13 Sep 44. Hist Br OQMG. (2) Bykofsky and Larson, The Transportation Corps: Operations Overseas, p. 192.

Army prepared for its drive on Rome and northern Italy, Sullivan preferred to deplete his reserves to a transportable 2-day level of B rations and a single day of operational rations. As the tactical situation stabilized itself north of Florence, and there was a possibility that the many small advanced units and their transportation might be snowbound, Sullivan permitted each division of IV Corps to maintain a minimum reserve of 2 days of B's and 3 days of C's, a larger stock than Fifth Army had reserved for its own Class I dump some months earlier.[22]

In the south of France the same overall supply levels, imposed by NATO-USA, were in force, but a different method of suballocation reflected the special logistical organization for the DRAGOON operation, which was unique within the Mediterranean theater. On 6 October 1944 General Larkin directed that 5 days of supply be kept in the combat zone, 15 days in CONAD, and the balance in Delta Base Section. It was estimated that the supply level would reach 45 days by 1 December, and the authorized maximum of 60 days by 1 January 1945. Theoretically, the CONAD level would consist of 8 days' reserve and 7 days' operating stock, but the practical effect was to place the reserve level in the base section and the operating level in advance section. For the headlong pursuit up the Rhône valley, this was entirely satisfactory. Subsequent supply directives for this area were issued by the European theater.[23]

Perishable Foods

After the TORCH landings, boneless beef, overseas hams, and poultry occasionally arrived in Oran and Casablanca, where they were consumed locally and appreciated as great delicacies. Illustrating the popularity and rarity of these frozen foods, one observer recounted the need to station a guard at the door of the mess where they were served to see that no unauthorized persons entered, and that no one went through the mess line a second time. Because of insufficient refrigeration vessels (reefers) and inadequate refrigeration facilities, static or mobile, in North Africa, fresh meats could not be sent into Tunisia. Before the advent of summer, 1943, Middleswart had to drop any idea of placing orders for fresh meats on his subsistence requisitions. There were no refrigeration facilities in the North African base sections to handle the necessary quantities of frozen meats during the hot weather.[24]

The troops in Italy were the first to receive perishable foods in large quantities. The distribution of fresh meat in Fifth Army from November 1943 through the end of the war increased steadily until it became a regular, almost daily, item of issue. (See Table 1.) One of the first duties of the base section quartermaster on entering

---

[22] (1) Memo, Lt Col F. A. Troy, Class I Off, for Sullivan, 5 Apr 44, sub: 10-Day Army Reserve; Rpt, prepared by Troy, sub: Class I in Italian Theater. Both in Sullivan Papers. (2) Ltrs, AG Fifth Army to CG IV Corps, 12 Nov 44, 27 Feb 45. IV Corps, AG 430.

[23] (1) *CONAD History*, I, 88. (2) Memo, Mil Plng Div OCQM ETOUSA, 9 Nov 44, sub: Gen Info on QM Activities in Southern France. Littlejohn Collection, box 27. (3) For ETO supply levels, see below, ch. XV.

[24] Pounder Rpt, p. 7.

Naples was to select cold storage facilities in preparation for the arrival of reefers from NYPE. From Naples, a platoon of the 67th QM Refrigeration Company (Mobile) attached to Fifth Army delivered frozen meats and fresh foods three times a week to forward railheads. A notable morale builder was the issue of a special holiday menu on Thanksgiving and Christmas of 1943, and New Year's Day, 1944. Fifth Army as well as base section troops enjoyed turkey and ham, olives, celery, apples, walnuts, oranges, and hard candy.[25]

During the stalemate along the Winter Line in February 1944, Fifth Army and Peninsular Base Section agreed on a procedure for delivery of perishables from Naples. Using two platoons, the 67th Refrigeration Company inaugurated a shuttle-type service whereby one platoon loaded seven vans at Naples and delivered them to the Army Class I dump at Santa Maria. Here the loaded vans were hooked onto the trucks of another platoon which moved the vans to Army railheads. There the vans were emptied, and the refrigeration platoon returned to Santa Maria and transferred them to the first platoon for the trip back to Naples. During the summer of 1944, when the lines of communication were extended, the base section forwarded perishables by refrigerated rail cars, and the shuttle truck-van system operated only beyond the rail transfer point. The fall of Civitavecchia opened a port capable of handling a reefer ship and shortened the trip to army railheads.

But by August 1944 the vans were traveling 225 miles per day to bridge the widening gap between the port and the advancing troops.[26]

For the DRAGOON operation, supply of perishables was entirely a problem of land transportation. On 24 September, 5,000 long tons of cold storage space were available at Marseille, with a prospect of 6,000 tons more in a few weeks. But no refrigerated trailers had been brought ashore, the rail lines were not yet running, and meat deliveries to Seventh Army during the preceding week had consisted of one truckload, rushed through to the army headquarters itself. By early November the picture had changed completely. More than 150 reefer rail cars were operating. A 2,000-ton cold storage plant at Dijon was available and rapidly being filled. Meanwhile 15 million rations of frozen meat and 18 million rations of butter were on hand at Marseille, not counting ship cargo waiting to unload. Nevertheless, in the forward areas the shortages persisted. CONAD still had only one mobile refrigeration company, and issues of perishables to combat units averaged four per week.[27]

[25] (1) Hist QM PBS, pp. 96, 106, 221. (2) Memo, QM PBS for G–4 PBS, 30 Oct 43, sub: Purchases for Hospitals. Sullivan Papers.

[26] (1) Opn Memo 37, OQM Fifth Army, 11 Feb 44, sub: SOP for Loading Perishables. Sullivan Papers. (2) Hist Rpt, 67th QM Refrigeration Co (Mobile), 18 Jun 44. Hist Br OQMG. (3) QMTSJ, VI (29 December 1944), 12–13.

[27] (1) Memo, Brunson to QM SOS NATOUSA, 24 Sep 44, sub: Rpt of Inspection Trip to SOS Advance and CONBASE. Littlejohn Collection, box 8. (2) Memo, Mil Plans Div OCQM ETO for Div Chiefs, 9 Nov 44, sub: Gen Info on QM Activities in Southern France; Memo, Maj Daniel L. Lane for QM COMZONE [NATOUSA], 21 Oct 44, sub: Special Rpt of Activities. Littlejohn Collection, sec. II. (3) Weekly G–4 Rpts SUSA, Sep–Dec 44. Seventh Army, AG 319.1.

Local Procurement of Subsistence

French North Africa had been an exporter of foodstuffs throughout the 1930's, and quartermasters immediately began seeking commodities in Morocco and Algeria to supplement their standard rations and thus reduce the quantities of perishables shipped overseas from NYPE. Less than ninety days after TORCH, the French authorities in Morocco furnished the Atlantic Base Section quartermaster with itemized lists of foodstuffs which could be procured locally without hardship to the civilian population. In the period between February and June 1943, 30 percent of the vegetables consumed by American troops were purchased locally, as follows:[28]

Green beans	131,208 lbs.
Cabbage	494,410 lbs.
Carrots	600,000 lbs.
Cauliflower	500,000 lbs.
Onions	270,000 lbs.
Peas	460,000 lbs.
Potatoes	600,000 lbs.
Spinach	50,000 lbs.
Sweet potatoes	77,000 lbs.
Turnips	225,000 lbs.
Grapefruit	712,000 each
Oranges	4,892,000 each

As the theater's strength increased and operations pointed northward across the Mediterranean, American military and French civilian authorities opened negotiations to expand the procurement program. By contracting for future harvests, the U.S. Army encouraged a greater production of foodstuffs—well in excess of civilian needs. The surpluses were earmarked for military consumption. In

the summer of 1943 American officials took steps to import seed, farm machinery, and equipment from the United States. In contrast to the 3,000 tons obtained in Atlantic Base Section in the first half of 1943, the goal through June 1944 envisioned the receipt of 50,000 to 70,000 tons of fresh fruits and vegetables, 5,000 tons of canned vegetables, and 20,000 to 30,000 tons of vegetables for dehydration. In Algeria, potatoes were abundant, and during April 1944 Mediterranean Base Section acquired 11,000,000 pounds. The 1943 wheat crop was poor, but by the summer of 1944 North Africa could contribute 49,000 long tons for civilian relief in southern France.[29]

Until the end of the Tunisian campaign, AFHQ prohibited the buying of fresh meats, poultry, and fish. In Morocco, stocks of commercial meat had become dangerously low. Since 1939 the growing town population had borne the brunt of the meat shortages. Cattlemen were reluctant to exchange their herds for currency which had no purchasing power because of the scarcity of manufactured goods. The civilian meat ration fell to a scanty seven ounces per week during the winter of 1942–43. Rabat, Casablanca, and Meknès experienced meatless periods of three weeks. In May 1943 lifting of the military restriction on local meat procurement stimulated livestock production. Notwithstanding the apparently improved situation, the quantities obtained

---

[28] Ltr, Col J. P. Ratay, CG ABS, to Gen Hughes, Deputy Theater Comdr, NATOUSA, 24 Jun 43. Hist Br OQMG.

[29] (1) Hist MBS, Sep 42–May 44, p. 17. (2) Ltr cited n. 28. (3) Ltr, Ratay to Pickels, 28 Jun 43, sub: Prod and Proc Local Food; Ltrs, Ratay to Larkin, 7 Jan, 9 Feb, 9 Mar, 6 Apr 44, sub: Local Proc of Fresh Fruits, Produce . . .; Ltr, QM MBS to AG MBS, 8 Jun 44. All in Hist Br OQMG. (4) Komer, Civil Affairs, ch. XXI, p. 33. OCMH.

for military consumption were small. Considering foods other than fruits and vegetables, the best procurement records were made by Mediterranean Base Section where fish and wine were obtained for Italian prisoners of war, and in Atlantic Base Section, where enough fresh eggs were available for all three base sections in North Africa.[30]

The island of Sicily fell in August 1943 and citrus fruits and semitropical vegetables became available almost immediately. In March 1944, a typical month, two-thirds of the Quartermaster orders went to twelve Sicilian vendors who marketed $10,000 worth of tangerines, salt, eggs, wine, lettuce, onions, cabbages, radishes, and spaghetti and macaroni. Sicily's unusual capacity as a source of citrus fruits was demonstrated when an overly zealous subsistence officer in Fifth Army's quartermaster office requested 6,000,000 pounds of lemons in a single month. The Quartermaster purchasing and contracting officer of Peninsular Base Section, eager to satisfy Fifth Army, approved the lemon order and made the desired purchase in Sicily. Soon unprecedented quantities of lemons began to arrive in Italy. By the time half of the contract had been delivered—and this quantity provided almost one bushel for every soldier in Italy—it was decided that more than enough lemons were on hand to meet all likely needs.[31]

Base section purchasing and contracting officers were alert to exploit local food markets wherever an area seemed capable of producing a surplus beyond civilian needs. In October 1943, the first month in Italy, Peninsular Base Section bought 209,000 pounds of vegetables. During the first summer, that of 1944, monthly receipts of produce soared to 8 million pounds, and after the liberation of the Po valley, procurement of perishables rose to 14.6 million pounds. Onions, olives, potatoes, peppers, carrots, celery, and various citrus fruits, came into Class I distribution points.

Quartermaster purchase and contract officers co-operated with American Military Government officials to forestall the procurement of perishables that were scarce in commercial markets, but there were occasional lapses in the enforcement of this program. Toward the end of 1944 complaints about encroachments on civilian needs were numerous. Fifth Army circulated a letter reminding purchasing and contracting officers that they could only place orders against allocations approved by the Local Resources Board, the Allied agency that set policy and regulated food allocations. Another violation of approved practices was reflected in the charge that "troops are using government rations as trading material in the procurement of local products." [32]

Subsistence procurement included not only perishables but also a variety of

[30] (1) Ltr, QM MBS to AG MBS, 8 Jun 44; Rpts, OQM MBS to AG MBS, 8 Apr, 8 Jun, 8 Aug 44, sub: Orgn Hist. All in Hist Br OQMG. (2) Hist Rpt, EBS, Aug 43; EBS Monthly Purch Rpts, Sep–Oct 43. Both in EBS SOS NATOUSA, AG 314.7.
[31] (1) Ltr, AG IBS to CG SOS NATOUSA, 11 Dec 43, sub: Monthly Rpt of Nov 43 Purch; Ltr, QM P&C Off IBS to CG IBS, 4 Feb 44, sub: Proc Re-

sources, Jan 44; Rpt QM P&C Off IBS (Purch Orders), Mar 44. All in QM Jnl IBS, AG 314.7. (2) Hist QM PBS, p. 219.
[32] (1) Hist QM PBS, pp. 221–22. (2) Cir 218, Hq NATOUSA, 9 Nov 43. (3) Quotation in Ltr, AG Fifth Army to All U.S. Troops, 1 Jan 45, sub: Illegal Local Proc of Food. Sullivan Papers.

special foods and services. Within urban areas, facilities were requisitioned for processing foods that could enhance the daily ration. In Naples, Rome, Florence, and Leghorn, more than 2,500,-000 pounds of coffee were roasted, ground, and sacked. In smaller cities, such as Marcianise, Francolise, and Montecatini, as well as in the larger urban areas, macaroni and spaghetti plants produced almost 3,000,000 pounds of food for Italians aiding the Allied forces in civilian and military capacities. Yeast-producing plants at Naples, Arqua, and Rome permitted decreases in shipments from New York and sustained the production of Quartermaster bakeries. During the Italian campaign, Peninsular Base Section calculated that 43,379 long tons of fruits and vegetables had been procured locally. Considering the scarcity of reefers and the higher priority enjoyed by ETOUSA from the summer of 1944, it can reasonably be concluded that local procurement made the difference between Fifth Army's relying on cased and individual rations alone and its enjoyment of fresh foods that would have otherwise been unavailable.[33]

The initial landings in southern France were made in the Marseille-Toulon area, which normally received fresh produce from the Rhône valley. Combat operations and German demolitions had disrupted civilian transportation from the hinterland and there was a serious food shortage; no supplies were available for local purchase. Seventh Army was forced to feed laborers at least

one meal a day, and the first quayside unloading of cargo in southern France was of civil affairs supplies. But rich agricultural areas were quickly liberated and during October, the first month of CONAD operations at Dijon, 320 tons of fruits and vegetables were made available to Seventh Army by the *Révitaillement Général*, the central French food rationing agency. As transportation improved, the local surplus was shipped to other parts of France, and the quantities available for U.S. procurement decreased. For the Christmas and New Year menus, CONAD was able to obtain 355 tons of apples, potatoes, onions, lettuce, and leeks.[34]

Field Bakeries

Less involved but no less important than the delivery of perishables was the baking and issue of fresh two-pound loaves of bread. Bread is practically the only item actually produced in the combat zone, amid the general destructiveness of war. Whether consumed as part of the modified B ration or as a substitute for the unpopular dry crackers of the combat ration, bread was always in demand. In fact, quite apart from nutritional aspects, bread was a major factor in good morale, and tended to make any ration acceptable. Therefore everyone in the theater was interested in whether production was high or low, prompt or delayed, available or absent, and these results depended more on the adequacy of the bakery equipment than on any other single factor.

With the introduction of a mechan-

[33] (1) Hist QM PBS, pp. 106, 116–17, 121. (2) Interv, Cheslaw with Capt Edgar Seward, Terminal Sv Div OCT, 3 Jun 53. OCMH.

[34] *CONAD History*, I, 42, 100; II, 618.

ical dough mixer and redesigned ovens for easier movement, American bakery equipment on the eve of Pearl Harbor had been somewhat improved over the old field baking ovens used by the Army since World War I. Yet the new equipment was not trailer-mounted and the dough mixer was the only mechanical equipment. Forty-five 2½-ton trucks had to be begged or borrowed whenever the American bakery company moved its thirty-two ovens and sixteen dough mixers (M1942). Organizationally, the sole advantage of the American company was flexibility. Its four platoons could be widely separated. Each platoon could produce from 6,000 to 8,000 pounds of bread daily. On the land masses of North Africa and Europe, mobility was more valuable than divisibility and quartermasters who baked the bread for combat units had to follow the forces closely.

In planning for BOLERO and ROUND-UP, American quartermasters in Great Britain had been favorably impressed with British-designed mobile field bakeries and with the organization set up to operate them. The trailer-mounted equipment consisted of three ovens, two diesel-electric generators, one mixer, and one dough divider. The bakery unit was virtually self-sufficient with its ten organic trucks and nine trailers. In July 1942, General Littlejohn had placed an order for British equipment, and had arranged for a Quartermaster company to be schooled in British bakery practices. Company B, 95th Quartermaster Bakery Battalion, was the unit selected for this training. It was reorganized as a two-platoon company with twenty organic trucks, capable of moving all its

equipment.[35] In November 1942, Little-john released B Company to TORCH and its first bakers arrived in Oran early in December. Within a week of its arrival, the unit was producing 21,000 pounds of bread per day, and this amount was doubled when the second platoon began to operate. Six weeks later, Company B divided, with one platoon remaining in Oran while the other joined II Corps in Tébessa.

Meanwhile, several other companies had opened bakeries at Rabat, Casablanca, Oujda, and Constantine, using either commercial bakeries when sanitary sites were obtainable or American M1942 equipment. One such unit was Company B, 99th Quartermaster Bakery Battalion, which arrived in Constantine in March 1943. In Eastern Base Section, the 99th Battalion's B Company had no trouble as to mobility, but a host of mechanical failures led Colonel Painter to recommend to Middleswart that no more units with American equipment be sent to North Africa until the deficiencies were corrected. Many ovens were idle for lack of burners, and all fire units required repairs. Because only leaded gasoline was available, the units had to be taken apart for cleaning every few hours, and gaskets, filters, and fuel tubes quickly wore out under these conditions. The supply of spare parts was completely inadequate. While the quality of bread was not materially affected the company had to acquire two

---

[35] (1) Risch, *The Quartermaster Corps: Organization, Supply, and Services*, I, 151ff. (2) Pounder Rpt, pp. 78–79. (3) Interv, Romanus with Col MacManus, 14 Dec 54. OCMH. (4) For details regarding still further reorganization of mobile bakery companies, see below, Chapter XV.

civilian bakeries to achieve the required production.[36]

After observing companies of both the 95th and the 99th Bakery Battalions in action and after reading the journals of the units, Captain Pounder reported to General Gregory:

The American report deals solely with the trouble experienced with the Field Range. That is its main concern, and production is hardly mentioned. The report of the American company using British bakery equipment is exactly opposite. The main point in every part of the report is the actual production and the efforts made to produce greater quantities. . . .[37]

There was no disputing the preference of American quartermasters for British bakery equipment by the time Fifth Army moved onto the beaches of Salerno Bay. Maj. Eckhardt R. Keller, the experienced commander of the 94th Quartermaster Bakery Battalion, predicated his recommendations for the future deployment of bakeries in Italy on the need for "bake-to-bake" mobility. In addition to the need for mobile bakery units, there was also a demand for bakeries to operate in semipermanent installations or to serve comparatively small and isolated units. In this situation, American equipment with its easy adaptability was used effectively, especially after an improved and safer type of burner was provided. Representative units included the 103d Quartermaster Bakery Company, which baked simultaneously at Aversa, Rome, and Bagnoli; the 108th Company, whose units ranged from Marrakech, Morocco,

to Perrégaux, Algeria; the 124th Company, which successively operated in North Africa, Corsica, and Italy; and the 167th Company, which went to southern France and deployed detachments and platoons to bakery sites in Marseille, Lyon, and Dijon. These small units were attached for administration to the nearest larger QM unit and their scattered deployment did not appear to have an ill effect on administrative or operational efficiency.

In each installation, quartermasters baked bread daily (0600 to 0235, with three hours to clean equipment and adjust machinery). Sullivan set a 3- to 5-day level of reserves for such ingredients as flour, salt, sugar, milk, and lard, and a 30-day level for yeast. In the expansion of their operations, bakeries were established in candy, cracker, and soap factories and in churchyards, tents, and garages. Bakers learned to cope with novel situations but found that their routine was often interrupted by the untimely appearance of shell fragments in the dough, fermentation in the water, and worms and weevils in captured flour. Nevertheless, bread production increased monthly. Though 32,000 pounds of bread per day was considered a satisfactory rate of production, the 103d Quartermaster Bakery Company at Aversa, north of Naples, turned out 63,500 pounds daily for the month of July 1944.[38]

Bakery operations in southern France followed the Mediterranean pattern. The 108th QM Bakery Company came

---

[36] (1) McNamara *Memoir*, p. 54. (2) Ltr, Painter to Middleswart, 21 Apr 43, sub: M1942 Field Bake Oven. Pounder Rpt, p. 77. (3) Ltr, CO Co B, 99th QM Bakery Bn, to CQM EBS, 1 May 43, sub: Bakery Rpt. Pounder Rpt, p. 75.

[37] Quoted in Pounder Rpt, p. 79.

[38] (1) Ltr, CO 94th QM Bakery Bn to Sullivan, 24 Oct 43, sub: Use and Control of Bakery Units, Fifth Army. Sullivan Papers. (2) Hist QM PBS, pp. 56–61. (3) Opnl Memo 28, OQM Fifth Army, 26 Jan 44, sub: SOP Bakery Cos. OQMG MED 319.25.

ashore at St. Tropez on 30 August, but was separated from its equipment and did odds jobs around the beach dumps for two weeks. Two platoons reached Vesoul by rail on 24 September, and the first issue of bread for combat troops was made two days later. Temporarily the 32,000 pounds daily production of this unit was the only bread available for Seventh Army, but on 2 October the 178th Bakery Company began baking at Épinal and assumed support for VI Corps. After 6 October the XV Corps was also based on Épinal, and the 108th shipped 12,000 pounds a day to assist the 178th Company. Between 19 and 23 October the 108th moved by platoon increments to Épinal, where it demonstrated that, under ideal conditions, it could bake 41,000 pounds per day. Meanwhile the 7553d (Italian) QM Bakery Company moved up from Dijon to Vesoul. Contrary to ETOUSA doctrine and practice, when mobile bakery companies from northern France became available in November, they were located in the rear areas. The 4362d, a unit with British mobile equipment and Negro personnel, was stationed at Dijon. The 4358th demonstrated its mobility by moving with organic equipment from L'Hermitage to Marseille, a distance of 800 miles, in six days. The versatility of the 167th Bakery Company has already been mentioned. Arriving from Italy on 2 September, it promptly took over operation of two civilian bakeries at Marseille, and was the only bakery unit in CONBASE for several weeks. When CONAD was formed it borrowed two platoons of the 167th, deploying them in section strength at Dijon, Vittel (6th Army Group headquarters), Langres, and Besançon. This unit contained skilled personnel who operated as supervisors of civilian baking operations and only baked, themselves, in emergencies. Delta Base employed men of this unit in much the same way. For example, at Lyon a detachment of one officer and fifteen enlisted men of the 167th operated the Class I railhead and also supervised a large civilian bakery.[39]

Free Smokes, Soaps, and Sweets

The tobacco, candy, chewing gum, and toilet articles distributed free of charge to combat troops provided the basis of one of the Quartermaster Corps' most important morale-building services. According to War Department Circular 245, dated 25 July 1942, theater commanders had authority to issue convenience items as part of their field ration whenever sales facilities, such as commissaries, post exchanges, or commercial shops, were not available. In TORCH plans, the Ration Accessory Convenience (RAC) pack was designed to bring post exchange items to the front lines. Every day a RAC pack was to accompany the ration issue for 200 men. Quartermaster planners had decided that in 24 hours 200 men would need one new plastic razor, 30 razor blades, 16 tubes of shaving cream, 3 tooth brushes, 7 cans of tooth powder, 28 1-ounce bars of soap, 200 packages of cigarettes, 2 1-ounce blocks of chewing tobacco, 16 ounces of pipe tobacco, 400 books of matches, 400 ounces of hard candy, and 400 sticks of gum. On 22 March 1943 the OQMG

---

[39] (1) *CONAD History*, II, 837–58. (2) Unit Histories 108th, 167th, 178th QM Bakery Cos. Hist Br OQMG.

announced that the Ration Accessory pack would be broken down into three separate kits. Procurement and distribution factors prompted this decision. The toilet kit accompanied a ration issue to 800 men, the smoking sundries constituted a packet for 200 men, and the candy case served for 400 men.

Largely because they were produced in mass lots, the composition of the Ration Accessory kits underwent little change after the summer of 1943. Yet the Corps continued to receive complaints from soldiers dissatisfied with the quality of many of the items. Men preferred shaving soap to brushless cream and tooth paste to powder. The three-piece plastic razor clogged constantly when drawn across the shaving cream. Under streams of hot water, the plastic razor lost any resemblance to a precision instrument, and repeated assembly and disassembly hastened its deterioration. Soldiers preferred the two-piece metal instrument.[40]

Of the three convenience kits, the soldier was more willing to forego the candy and toilet articles than the tobacco allowances. Indeed, it was not infrequently asserted that a man would more readily relinquish a meal than a cigarette, and a field commander was prepared to invoke his rank and influence to rectify tobacco shortages among his troops. AVALANCHE planning was quite explicit as to the amounts of tobacco for each phase of the operation. In the first week at Anzio each man was to receive a package of cigarettes, two and a half sheets of cigarette paper and a half-

ounce of tobacco for rolling his own smokes, plus the usual amounts of pipe and chewing tobacco and two books of safety matches. The D plus 2 convoy was to bring an 8-day supply of free tobacco kits for all troops ashore by that time, and the D plus 7 convoy a 14-day supply of a combined tobacco and candy kit.

The D to D plus 19 tobacco plans of AVALANCHE did not materialize and the only tobacco reaching the troops was the allowance which came in the combat rations, giving each man about twelve cigarettes a day. Off Naples there was an ample supply of tobacco on the ships, but limited harbor facilities prevented rapid discharge. Corps and division commanders showed no willingness to wait patiently for their allowances to be delivered. Special air and coastal shipments were dispatched to Sicily, and twice General Clark sent his personal plane to Palermo for tobacco supplies which were brought to a forward airstrip and speedily distributed to the troops. During this emergency none of these high priority stocks were issued to rear area troops, or even to hospital patients, except when the amounts exceeded the needs of the infantrymen.[41]

Aside from the problem of availability, it was difficult to reach an agreement on the tactical area within which tobacco was to be issued gratuitously. Through the summer of 1944 the policy fluctuated. Some officers contended that everyone in Fifth Army ought to obtain

---

[40] (1) Cir 45, Hq MBS, 23 Mar 43. (2) Annex 2 (QM), Admin Instr 2, Hq Fifth Army, 7 Aug 43. Hist Br OQMG. (3) Ltr, Sullivan to Painter, 13 Jan 44, sub: Ration Improvements. Sullivan Papers.

[41] (1) Memo, Sullivan for Tate, 17 Oct 43. Sullivan Papers. (2) Rad 1069, Clark to Larkin, 10 Oct 43; Rad 2731, Tate to Truscott, 11 Oct 43; Memo, Clark for Truscott, 21 Oct 43, sub: Issue of Tobacco Components. Both in Fifth Army, AG 430. (3) *Fifth Army History*, II, 70.

his tobacco without payment, while others recommended that this privilege should be limited to troops forward of divisional rear boundaries. Because the Army Exchange Service could not follow Fifth Army closely enough to make its sales stores accessible in the army area, and because there was a constant movement of troops that could upset any unit or geographical basis of free distribution, it was felt that a parallel system of sales and free issues would result in some units receiving excess allowances and others having none. Since only a single system would be manageable and no one was prepared to advocate a uniform sales system throughout the combat zone, the Fifth Army quartermaster put equity ahead of economy. Sullivan preferred the free issue of candy, gum, tobacco, and toilet articles throughout the army area, and justified it on the grounds that troop morale was more important than saving money. With minor exceptions all Fifth Army troops, even when resting in rear areas, received gratuitous issues from August 1944 to the end of hostilities.[42]

Seventh Army plans for free issues in southern France were a direct outgrowth of Fifth Army experience and were carried out very successfully in the early stages of the DRAGOON operation. The first G–4 report of Continental Base Section, dated 24 September 1944, listed a comfortable total of sixty-three tons of "Tobacco, etc." on hand. During the period of rapid pursuit, deliveries to combat troops in the forward areas were

very uncertain. CONAD status reports never showed more than a one and a half day reserve during 1944, and usually indicated that whatever was received had been issued to combat units the same day. As in Fifth Army, supplies were normally received in the form of RAC kits.[43]

Rations for Friends and Enemies

A casual observer of Fifth Army might assume that its logistical activities were directed exclusively to the support of American troops, but scrutiny reveals that this was an international army, the first of its kind in the war against Germany. In varying strengths throughout its twenty-month campaign in Italy, the Fifth Army was made up not only of American but also of British Commonwealth, Brazilian, French, French protectorate, Italian, Polish, and Yugoslav troops, all of whom at one time or another obtained American supplies and equipment. To paraphrase Rommel's famous epigram, the Fifth Army was a French chef's dream and a quartermaster's nightmare. Indeed, the largest of these forces, the Frenchmen and Moslem troops, was heavily if not exclusively dependent on American services of supply during a substantial part of its career.[44] Illustrating the scope of the program, non-American forces consumed 25 percent of the 350 million rations issued by Peninsular Base Section between October 1943 and June 1945. And these figures might have been considerably higher had it not been for the policy

---

[42] (1) Rad, Clark to Devers, 15 Jul 44; 1st Ind, DQM Fifth Army to Tate, 28 Aug 44, sub: Gratuitous PX; 5th Ind, Troy to Sullivan, 9 Feb 45, same sub. All in Sullivan Papers. (2) Sullivan Diary, 15 Feb 45.

[43] (1) CBS G–4 Periodic Rpt, 28 Sep 44. (2) CONAD History, II, 517-631.

[44] Cir 7, Hq SOS NATOUSA, 16 Jan 44.

TABLE 2—RATION ISSUES TO NON-U.S. PERSONNEL IN ITALY
1 OCTOBER 1943–31 MAY 1945

	20-Month Total	October 1943	April 1944	October 1944	May 1945
British	1,138,505	7,285	24,750	43,369	16,337
French	13,730,762	0	1,055,700	265,174	98,797
Moslems	12,379,110	0	993,240	577,220	41,664
Italian civilians	3,237,675	0	90,750	121,768	379,347
POW'S	10,927,777	5,797	18,300	507,315	7,010,464
Italian military	a25,000,000	15,097	855,030	(b)	2,433,717
Partisans	313,614	0	0	0	186,000
Italian service units	2,257,650	0	0	0	547,956
Brazilians	5,367,331	0	0	351,354	796,948

a Estimated.
b Not Available.

Source: Hist QM PBS, p. 111.

which moved German prisoners of war by the tens of thousands out of this theater. *(Table 2)*

Of the Allied auxiliaries, the Italians drew the most Quartermaster supplies over the longest period of time in the course of the peninsular campaigns. Following its surrender—word of which greeted the Allied assault convoys as they steamed toward the beaches of Salerno—the Italian Government agreed to turn against Germany and make its manpower available to the United Nations. Officers and enlisted men, theoretically still prisoners of war, were formed into provisional service units and sandwiched into the Allied supply system.

Unlike the French and Brazilian forces, few Italians engaged directly in combat. One motorized group fought in the battle of Mignano Gap, and another was committed in the closing months of the war. The Allies discouraged their use because the Germans regarded captured Italians as deserters rather than as prisoners of war and sub-

jected them to more severe treatment. Consequently, most Italians worked in labor and service units. The number of Italian troops working for Sullivan rose to 6,500—about 50 percent of the number hoped for—and made up 24 service companies, 6 battalions, and 2 quartermaster groups.[45]

In the spring of 1944, AFHQ directed that supplies would only be furnished those Italians who were considered "effective," a definition limited to "bona fide members of the Italian armed forces . . . subject to the laws of war and the Geneva Convention, . . . and actually performing the duties to which assigned." [46] Because their functions were considered essentially civilian in char-

---

[45] (1) Hist QM PBS, p. 111. (2) Hq ASF, *Statistical Review of World War II*, p. 158. (3) *QM Supply in Fifth Army*, pp. 16, 56, 148–49, 162–63. (4) Komer, Civil Affairs, ch. X. OCMH. (5) *Fifth Army History*, IV, 230; V, 220; VI, 114; VII, 228; VIII, 129; IX, 182.

[46] (1) Ltr, AFHQ to All Concerned, 22 Sep 44, sub: Supply of Italian Armed Forces. NASC QM (Italy), AG 400.3295. (2) *Fifth Army History*, III, 73; IV, 230; V, 220; VI, 114.

acter, such groups as security police, *carabinieri*, fire brigades, and guards were not included. But the responsibility was defined even more on the basis of parent organization. Those under British command ("BR–ITI's") were supplied by the British; "US-ITI's" by the Americans. The "ITI–ITI's," serving under the Italian War Ministry, drew their rations from the Americans, their medical supplies and fuel from the British, and their clothing from both. Many U.S. supplies were delivered to these troops through lend-lease.

While the French were operating with the Allies in Tunisia they were fighting in and living off their own protectorates; but when in November 1943 the 2d Moroccan and 3d Algerian Divisions crossed the Mediterranean and deployed on Fifth Army's right flank above the Volturno they were less self-sufficient. From a starting figure of a quarter of a million rations to the French in December 1943 and a third of a million to Moslem troops in January 1944, the number issued to the French Expeditionary Corps rose steadily to a peak of three and a half million rations in June 1944.

In January and February 1944, when the weather was cold and tactical operations around Cassino made stringent physical demands on the troops, the French found that their North African diet was inadequate in Italy. They insisted that more fats and sugar were needed and asked the Americans to relieve the monotony of the canned meat that they had eaten exclusively since their arrival in Italy. The supply of livestock in North Africa was meager, according to General Alphonse Juin, commander of the French Expedition-

ary Corps, and he hoped that his forces could share at least twice weekly in the quantities of freshly killed and frozen meat being distributed to the American troops. In effect, Juin called for a B ration with certain variations to suit the French taste.

Fifth Army agreed that the French ration was not adequate for operational needs, but pointed out that approval for an increase could only come from higher authorities, the same authorities who hoped to dissuade the French in Italy from "buying local resources without proper allocation." AFHQ did not subscribe to the request that the limited quantities of American meat should be shared with the French. Yet positive measures were taken to meet the basic requirements and to change the method of ration procurement and issue. Because it was now evident that the French were unable to obtain sufficient foodstuffs from North Africa, NATOUSA determined that after 1 June 1944, all of the French and Moslem rations would be provided from NYPE. Only French-procured brandy, wine, and vegetable oils would flow from North Africa. To the extent that livestock was available at all, a vessel was to shuttle from five to six thousand head of live sheep from Tunis to Naples, exclusively for the French Expeditionary Corps. Juin's troops assumed full responsibility for their slaughter and issue.[47]

---

[47] (1) Quotation in undated indorsement to Memo, Juin for Clark, 25 Apr 44, sub: Supplies of Fresh Meat. Fifth Army Subsistence, AG 430. (2) Sullivan Diary, 9 Jan 44. (3) Memo, Juin for Clark, 5 Jan 44; Ltr, Clark to CinC AFHQ, 26 Feb 44, sub: Increased Ration Allowance for FEC; Rad L–21939, Larkin to Pence, 24 May 44. All in Fifth Army, AG 430. (4) Sullivan MS, p. 102. (5) Vigneras, *Rearming the French*, pp. 256-58.

Because dietary preferences were respected in feeding Allied auxiliaries, the rationing of Algerian and Moroccan troops, 50 percent of whom were of the Mohammedan faith, presented difficulties. While the French soldier expected his ration to include wine and brandy— as the U.S. soldier expected his bread and meat—the Moslem religion forbade alcoholic beverages and pork. Accordingly, it was necessary to prepare two different menus within the French Expeditionary Corps. It was not enough to recognize the Mohammedan proscription against pork and alcoholic beverages; even authorized meat could not be eaten unless the animals had been slaughtered by Mohammedans in conformance to Mohammedan ritual. Veiled Moslem women were recruited to herd the sheep aboard ship in Tunisia, accompany them to Italy, and drive the animals into the lines. With full regard for Moslem precepts, the women slaughtered and dressed the sheep, and returned to North Africa for another shipload.[48]

Shortly after the new French ration procedure was inaugurated, the French Expeditionary Corps was reassigned to Seventh Army to participate in DRAGOON. Sullivan and Bare then learned that Brazilian troops would join Fifth Army. On 16 July 1944, the first contingent of the Brazilian Expeditionary Force (BEF) arrived in Naples. By the end of 1944 the force had grown from a combat team of five thousand to an infantry division drawing twenty thousand rations daily. The Brazilian menu was less complex than the one for the French troops. Essentially, the Brazilians accepted the standard B ration with only minor modifications. Peanut butter, pickles, beets, mustard, tomato extracts, canned corn, and dried beans were not popular with the BEF; eventually these foods were deleted while national dietary preferences led to an increase in the allowances of black beans, rice, lard, salt, sugar, and coffee.[49]

The menu served to Italian cobelligerents also generally followed the B ration, modified to suit Italian tastes. The quantity of meat was considerably less than that eaten by the Americans, but allowances of flour, cheese, and onions were greater. Because they were in their own country, Italians were freer than the French and Brazilians to supplement the ration from local sources so long as the Italian Government paid the bills. Throughout the countryside Italian units obtained fresh vegetables, fruits, nuts, olive oil, salt, wine, and yeast.

With the approach of winter along the Gothic Line, the Fifth Army sought permission to increase the ration allowances of Italian troops. But AFHQ, complying with a War Department directive that reflected growing food shortages in the United States, considerably reduced the allowances instead. Sullivan protested to both Ramsey and Col. Georges F. Doriot in the OQMG in Washington. He did not contest the

---

[48] (1) Sullivan MS, pp. 28–29. (2) Operational Memo 19, OQM Fifth Army, 27 Dec 43. Sullivan Papers. (3) QM Supply in Fifth Army, p. 59.

[49] (1) Fifth Army History, VI, 117. (2) Ltr, Col Currey to G–3 Fifth Army, 21 Aug 44, sub: Inspection BEF; Admin Dir 51, Hq Fifth Army, 24 Aug 44, sub: Supply, Maintenance, and Evacuation of BEF; Rad 7790, Clark to McNarney, 24 Feb 45. All in Fifth Army, AG 319.1. (3) Cir 88, Hq SOS NATOUSA, 3 Aug 44.

wisdom of the decision but felt it should not apply to the relatively small number of Italians giving direct support to combat troops in the forward areas. Those laboring at railheads and in pack mule companies were exposed to the rigors of the weather, and Italians generally were handicapped by inadequate kitchens and cooking utensils. Insisting that it was time to authorize higher allowances, if not to equalize the ration of Italian and American combat troops in the forward areas, the Fifth Army admitted to AFHQ that it had never rigorously conformed to the lower allowances. In fact, where twenty or fewer Italians worked alongside the Americans, Sullivan found that he had to feed them on U.S. rations.[50] He could not operate any other way. "It must be appreciated," Tate and Sullivan wrote in self-defense, "that Italian military units with the Fifth Army are relieving approximately 12,000 U.S. troops."[51]

AFHQ's reply again illustrated that logical but varying conclusions can be drawn regarding any issue, depending on the position from which it is viewed. No one could quarrel with Fifth Army's solicitude for its personnel, but AFHQ felt obliged to see that all Italians obtained the same ration, whether under American or British command. The British claimed that a smaller ration could be issued without serious effect, and the Italian authorities themselves advised that the existing scale was superior to that which Italian troops had obtained when fighting under the Fascist flag. As in the French situation, AFHQ was prepared to temper a broad policy with a touch of mercy. As an emergency measure, AFHQ and MTOUSA authorized Truscott to supplement the flour and meat ration of those Italian troops "forward of the Army Rear Boundary, when engaged in duties of an arduous nature and in extreme weather conditions only." Early in March 1945 these increases were extended for several more weeks, at first only for 7,500 Italian muleteers but shortly afterward for all Italians in Truscott's command.[52]

From the 1899 Hague Conference to the 1929 Geneva Convention, prisoners of war were protected by international agreements. The safety and sanitation of internment camps, welfare, postal conveniences, and the nutritive value of rations were prescribed by provisions to which forty-seven countries subscribed. Inevitably the agreements affected the scope of Quartermaster planning and supply more as to rations than clothing. The typical prisoner brought with him at least the clothes on his back, but he was immediately dependent on his captors for food. Middleswart designed a POW ration to provide a varied menu of bread, meats, dairy products, dehy-

[50] (1) Sullivan MS, pp. 28, 151. (2) Ltr, Exec Off Ln Sec Fifth Army to QM PBS, 27 Oct 43, sub: Rations for Italian Army Pers. PBS AGO 430. (3) Ltr, CG AFHQ to All Concerned, 8 Oct 44, sub: Supply, Proc, and Accounting for Supply and Equip Issued by Allied Depots to Italian Armed Forces. Sullivan Papers. (4) *QM Supply in Fifth Army*, pp. 45, 60. (5) *Logistical History of NATOUSA–MTOUSA*, pp. 285–86.

[51] Msg 1532, Fifth Army to AFHQ, 23 Oct 44; Ltr, Sullivan to Doriot, 16 Nov 44. Both in Sullivan Papers.

[52] Rad G4–482, AAI to Fifth Army, 24 Oct 44; quotation from Rad FX–52252, AFHQ to Fifth Army, 13 Nov 44; Ltr, McNarney to Truscott, 6 Jan 45, sub: Rations for Italian Mil in Forward Area; Rad FX–38744, McNarney to Truscott, 1 Mar 45. All in Sullivan Papers.

drated fruits, and vegetables. As for other groups, adjustments were made to suit national tastes. Italian prisoners, for example, received a ration containing alimentary pastes, and each man was given a daily allowance of local wine in lieu of orange and lemon crystals, tea, and milk. The prisoner of war menu followed in Atlantic Base Section (Morocco) in April 1944 allowed each man 2.537 pounds of food per day broken down as follows: [53]

Item	Pounds
Bread, fresh	.625
Meat and meat substitutes	.583
Canned vegetables	.274
Spreads	.193
Dairy products	.157
Alimentary pastes	.15
Canned fruits	.1215
Dehydrated vegetables	.105
Cereals	.096
Sugar and syrup	.0625
Flour	.06
Beverages	.035
Wine (.034 liters)	.075

From Salerno through the Winter Line the Allies captured only 5,500 Germans, of whom 3,450 were held by the Fifth Army. These prisoners presented no serious quartermaster problems. The policy of providing prisoners of war with a ration "substantially equal in quantity and quality to that of the U.S. troops" was generally adhered to until the end of hostilities. At that time, some 300,000 Germans surrendered and had to be fed until they could be repatriated. Because of food shortages in the United States, the inadvisability of importing large amounts of food when redeployment was going into effect, and because of the unbalanced state of captured enemy rations, allowances were reduced to 2,000 calories for nonworkers and 2,900 calories for manual laborers.[54]

Seventh Army captured more Germans than Fifth Army, but retained only a modest number in southern France to serve as labor troops. Rationing policy was governed by NATOUSA directives, as in Italy, until Sixth Army Group came under ETOUSA command. At the end of 1944, CONAD was feeding nearly 9,000 German POW's utilized by Seventh Army, 7,500 with 1st French Army, and nearly 11,000 within its own area. Additionally, CONAD was supporting more than 11,000 Italian troops. These included 1 base depot, 1 railhead, 1 salvage collecting, 4 salvage repair, 2 laundry, 2 bakery, and 24 service companies, and 5 QM battalion headquarters.[55]

Feeding the American troops in the Mediterranean theater, their Allies, and various dependent groups, was an exacting and complicated task. In accomplishing it successfully, the QMC had to adopt new and flexible procedures. The experience was valuable, and was applied to subsequent operations. Extensive as it was, this cannot be regarded as one of the major Quartermaster operations of World War II. The scale of Quartermaster activities in other theaters, especially in northern Europe, was far greater, and moreover included certain major responsibilities not encountered by Mediterranean quartermasters. During the North African op-

---

[53] Memo, Asst Chief UNRRA Mission for CO ABS, 19 Apr 44, sub: Comparison of Quantities for 1,000 Rations. Hist Br OQMG.

[54] (1) Admin Instr U.S. POW Inclosures, MTOUSA, 21 Nov 44, ch. VII. Sullivan Papers. (2) Min, Conf, Deputy Theater Comdr MTOUSA, 26 Jun 45, p. 45. Hist Br OQMG.

[55] *CONAD History*, II, 623–24, 859.

erations, the Allies decided that the majority of German prisoners were to be transferred elsewhere. Inertia and the fortunes of war conspired to continue this policy and make it practicable throughout the expanding Mediterranean theater until the end of hostilities. Since Italian prisoners were soon transformed into cobelligerents, feeding this category of personnel never presented a really large problem in Mediterranean supply. A far larger responsibility in all theaters was care for the civilian population, but the staff structure of Allied Force Headquarters provided a special organization for this purpose, and it was not a direct Quartermaster responsibility. In the spring of 1944 the campaigns in the Mediterranean represented both the U.S. Army's largest combat operations and greatest supply effort to date in World War II. But these accomplishments were soon to be overshadowed—in scale, in complexity, and in the scope of logistical difficulties to be overcome—by the tremendous military operations in northern France and Germany.

CHAPTER VI

Liquid and Solid Fuels

A plentiful and reliable supply of petroleum products was probably the single most vital factor in establishing Allied logistical superiority over the German Army. In large measure the Allied armies were carried to victory by the internal combustion engine and the fuels with which it operated. The ebb and flow of warfare across the western desert, as the British retreated from Libya to Egypt, and then advanced from El 'Alamein to Tunisia, could be correlated with the relative availability of gasoline supplies to Rommel and Montgomery.[1] More specifically, as the American staff in London began its detailed BOLERO planning, the British War Office notified it that POL had comprised 67 percent of the daily tonnage for the campaigns in Egypt and Libya, a figure verified early in the Tunisian campaign. An American observer aptly summarized the importance of POL with the comment that "without petroleum products the war in North Africa could not be fought." When these statistics and observations are contrasted with the fact that in World War I the number of trucks operated by the entire U.S. Army was only one-third the number of horses and mules used for riding, draft, and pack purposes, the changing nature of modern warfare becomes apparent.[2]

POL Administration

Because of the vast quantities of petroleum products required in time of war by the Army Air Forces, the Navy, the British, and vital elements of the civilian economy, the Quartermaster role in POL matters differed somewhat from that for other supplies. Procurement, wholesale distribution, and final issue of rations, clothing, and equipage were unbroken chains of Quartermaster responsibility. But by contrast, logistical control of petroleum products was delegated among several high-level U.S. and Allied agencies. The Quartermaster Corps was responsible for the computation of Army requirements. In the Mediterranean theater, operational details were handled by a specially designated petroleum officer in each base section, who performed the Class III duties

---

[1] "Operation of the QM Service, Mediterranean Base Sector: Part 5, Gasoline Supply," *QMTSJ*, IV. No. 12 (24 March 1944), 14.

[2] (1) *Logistics in World War II, Final Report of the Army Service Forces* (Washington, 1947), p. 94. (2) *Operations of the Quartermaster Corps, U.S. Army During the World War*, Monograph 5, Report of the Remount Service, A.E.F. (Schuylkill Arsenal, 1929), p. 1. (3) Quotation from Rpt, Maj Joseph M. Sills and Mr. Errol J. Gay, to Maj Gen L. H. Campbell, Jr., CofOrd, 20 Mar 43, sub: Trip to North African Theater, 20 Jan–27 Feb 43. OCofOrd MED 319.25. (4) Middleswart Planning Folder. WTF. Poore Papers.

normally assigned to the base quarter-master. The Quartermaster Corps actively re-entered the POL distribution system at the next-to-last step where fuels were packaged into 5- and 55-gallon containers and carried to the distributing points for delivery to the ultimate consumers.

An AFHQ Petroleum Section, to handle purely military requirements, was set up on 1 January 1943. Its chief, Col. Gustave H. Vogel, and his deputy, Lt. Col. Webster Anderson, were both Americans and both members of the Quartermaster Corps, but this was not considered to be a Quartermaster function. Their requisitions were placed upon the Army-Navy Petroleum Board in Washington. Early in February control over all aspects of POL in the Mediterranean area was centralized in the AFHQ Petroleum Section and the Military Oil Subcommittee, North African Economic Board. Staffed with American and British officers and civilians these offices, both operating under G–4, AFHQ, collated the estimated requirements of the Allied forces, as well as those of vital civil agencies, and prepared a consolidated monthly estimate which was transmitted to the United Kingdom and the United States. In accordance with earlier American-British agreements, American specifications were standardized for the common supply sent into North Africa. It was also agreed that all products would be shipped from the United States until fuel became available from Middle Eastern sources such as Haifa or the Persian Gulf. This pooling system—intended to avoid duplication of stocks and facilities—opened the way for any truck, ship, or airplane of any Allied power to refuel at any depot in the North African theater.[3]

In the combat zone traditional doctrines prevailed, and the army-level quartermaster supervised the co-ordination of requirements, procurement, storage, and distribution of liquid fuels, oils, and lubricants as well as such solid fuels as coal and wood. To simplify the procedures for the handling of POL products, Sullivan appointed Maj. (later colonel) George L. Darley, the commander of the 204th QM Gasoline Supply Battalion, to serve simultaneously as Fifth Army Class III officer. By thus establishing direct contact between his headquarters and the operating units, the army quartermaster eliminated duplication of effort. Darley eventually controlled 2 tank truck companies and 2 gasoline supply companies, which operated an average of 14 POL supply points throughout the Italian campaign.[4]

For the initial landing in the south of France, CONBASE imitated the organization of Peninsular Base Section, setting up a POL Section separate from the Quartermaster Section. This POL Section remained with Delta Base Section when CONAD moved forward to Dijon, and from 1 October to 20 December 1944 the CONAD Quartermaster Section handled POL matters. By the latter date, the pipeline from Marseille had been brought into the

[3] (1) See rpt cited n. 2 (3). (2) Erna Risch, *Fuels for Global Conflict*, QMC Historical Studies, 9 (rev. ed., Washington, 1952), pp. 50ff. (3) Hist of AFHQ, pt. II, Dec 42–Dec 43, sec. 3, pp. 389, 398–99. (4) *Logistical History of NATOUSA–MTOUSA*, pp. 227–28.

[4] (1) Sullivan MS, p. 55. (2) *QM Supply in Fifth Army*, p. 47.

CONAD area, and POL responsibilities became so heavy that a separate POL Section was organized. Within Seventh Army, POL functions closely paralleled those of Fifth Army already described.[5]

Rates of Consumption

In World War II, in terms of pounds per man per day, petroleum products and solid fuels constituted about 50 percent of the total supplies used in an overseas theater.[6] Because of this, the discrepancies brought about by small errors in planning invariably represented massive tonnages in actual operations. In the beginning Sullivan and Darley could not foresee all the factors that had to be taken into account in estimating POL requirements. British experience was only a rough guide, and U.S. experience tables were nonexistent. In planning for the Sardinia operation in 1943, Sullivan reviewed TORCH experience and compiled statistics from the Tunisian operations. Similar studies were also begun by Maj. Victor H. Moore, QMC, a member of the Petroleum Section of AFHQ and of NATOUSA, who carried his work through the experience of II Corps in Tunisia. Moore's report came to the attention of the OQMG in Washington, which extracted considerable data from it and returned it to the field in the form of POL experience tables.[7]

As with ration consumption, North African operations taught Class III planners that the average rate of gasoline consumption varied with terrain and tactical conditions. As already noted, POL requirements for the TORCH landings had been based on an arbitrary calculation of 5 gallons per wheeled vehicle per day and 50 gallons per track-laying vehicle, and on that basis the assault convoys transported a 7-day supply of POL. Thanks to the short duration of TORCH, this supply was adequate until the D plus 3 convoy arrived. Yet the brevity of the fighting, both Sullivan and Moore knew, made it impossible for them to accept the validity of the 5- and 50-gallon factors. Moore therefore examined more closely all POL factors emerging from Tunisian experience.

Two types of experience tables were developed out of the Tunisian battles. One applied to cross-country marches and active combat, and the other reflected experience in the administrative movement of units.[8] In the southern

---

[5] (1) CONAD History, I, 80. (2) See above, ch. IV.

[6] The remaining 50 percent consisted of rations, 10 percent; Class II, 8 percent; Class IV, 20 percent; and ammunition, 12 percent. Cf OTCQM TSFET Operational Study 2, 1 Nov 45, p. 16.

[7] (1) Logistical History of NATOUSA-MTOUSA, pp. 227–47. (2) Ltr, Moore to Gregory, 6 Jul 43,

sub: Rpt II Corps Gasoline Supply in North African Campaign. OQMG NATOUSA 319.25. (Hereafter cited as Moore Rpt.) (3) Opn Dir, OQM Fifth Army, 2 Aug 44. Hist Br OQMG.

[8] Both tables were compiled in terms of gallons of gasoline per mile. The results in detail were as follows:

Vehicles and Units	Gallons per mile
Vehicles in combat	
Light tank	0.76
Medium tank	1.65
Half-track carrier	0.29
¼-ton truck	0.07
2½-ton truck	0.22
Units on administrative march	
Infantry division	193
Tank destroyer battalion	46
Field artillery battalion	35
Field artillery battery	4
QM truck company	11

Tunisian campaign, where the II Corps had lengthy supply lines, the allowance of 5 gallons per day for wheeled vehicles was insufficient while the 50-gallon factor for track-laying vehicles was confirmed. When the II Corps redeployed into northern Tunisia, fighting there for three weeks on a much narrower front, commanders made greater use of armor and the earlier experience was reversed. Actual consumption per mile in the field did not vary to any significant degree from what had been predicted by the War Department. Fluctuations in the number of miles traveled per day by various types of vehicles accounted for the variations in consumption. Nevertheless, a 50-mile average operational day for all types of vehicles appeared to be valid in most combat situations, and was used in computing requirements. Variations in the length of the supply lines were reflected in the level of supply maintained at the forward POL railheads.

For operations in Sicily and at Salerno, the 50-mile factor continued to serve as a basic planning figure. The AVALANCHE Plan was based on a figure of 6.25 gallons at 8 miles per gallon, plus a 10 percent safety factor, which made 6.875 gallons of gasoline per vehicle per day the specific planning factor. When the number of each type of vehicle ashore was known, the 50-mile operational day allowance would be 5 gallons for wheeled vehicles, 30 gallons for half-track vehicles, and 60 gallons for tanks. The requirements for engine oils were computed on a basis of 5.5 gallons for each 100 gallons of gasoline, and greases on the basis of 2 pounds for each 100 gallons—a figure subsequently subdivided into percentages for the vari-

ous weights of greases to be used. When Sullivan and Darley attempted to apply the 50-mile operational allowances on a basis of gallons per day per type of vehicle, they were never able to secure an accurate figure of the number of each type of vehicle present in the command.[9] On 25 November 1943 Darley established a new system. He set POL levels at 4 days for the army dump, 2 days for railheads, with 1 gallon per man per day as the basis of issue. Beginning in January 1944 the Fifth Army published its monthly POL consumption rates in gallons per man per day.

The continued experiments with different methods of calculating requirements would appear to indicate dissatisfaction with the results, even though there were no serious shortages of petroleum products in the Mediterranean war. The only overdrawn calculation— as revealed by experience—was the factor of 5.5 gallons of lubricating oils to each 100 gallons of gasoline for vehicles, a figure of July 1943 that proved to be almost double the actual consumption rate in January 1944. More significant was the confirmation in Italy of the Tunisian experience that fuel consumption varied with the terrain and tactical situation. In the late spring of 1944, when the Fifth Army jumped off from the Gustav Line, broke out of Anzio beachhead, and pursued the Germans northward toward Rome, consumption of gasoline rose from .8592 gallons per man per day to 1.280 gallons. Before the summer was over, the Germans checked the advance. U.S. armor came out of the line and into reserve where it trained. Fifth Army's POL require-

[9] Sullivan MS, pp. 12, 48ff.

ments fell perceptibly—to a daily figure of 1.097 gallons per man in August 1944 —only to rise again to 1.514 gallons per man per day during the winter of 1944–45, when troops also used gasoline for heating purposes. As the weather grew colder, troops also burned diesel oil to keep warm and vehicles required lightweight lubricating oils. Conversely, the resumption of the offensive toward the Po River saw a declining requirement for greases and lubrications; at the same time per capita gasoline consumption soared to 1.678 gallons as armored movements ate up fuel. For the DRAGOON operation, the planning factor was 1.375 gallons per man per day.[10]

Decanting Operations

Because the Quartermaster Corps' POL mission in North Africa was essentially that of a front-line retailer rather than a rear area wholesaler, the transfer of gasoline from its bulk state—in a railroad tanker, a pipeline, or tank truck—into a semiportable 55-gallon drum or a portable 5-gallon can was a responsibility with many ramifications. First of all, the inflammable nature of petroleum products meant that spacious sites had to be found. But wide dispersion was only the beginning of many perplexities in operations. Containers were often so scarce that the impetus of POL toward the railheads was seriously impeded. Drums were so heavy when filled —weighing about 400 pounds—that handlers, who often became careless through

fatigue, suffered hernias and other injuries. It took a minimum of three men to load or unload a full drum on a 2½-ton truck. At best handling was a slow, dangerous, process. Because brass or bronze wrenches were not always available to loosen the bungs on the drums, wooden mallets had to be improvised to eliminate the hazard of sparks. All these factors and many more made themselves felt at the point where POL was packaged, and could often spell the difference between wasteful or economical procedure and between delayed or timely deliveries.

The widespread use of the 55-gallon drum throughout the Mediterranean theater marked a noteworthy deviation from the procedures for gasoline delivery planned for BOLERO and the TORCH operation.[11] There were seldom enough jerricans in the rear areas to permit a direct bulk-to-can transfer, and demolitions hindered the movement of railroad tank cars or tank trucks into the forward areas. Moreover the attempt to extend a pipeline over semimountainous terrain involved a disproportionate expenditure of labor and materials and was not completed in time to support the operation. Thus a gap appeared between the forwardmost bulk delivery point and the rearmost dump where the 5-gallon can could be efficiently handled.

On the Ouled Rahmoun–Tébessa supply line the delivery system illustrates a solution which was practiced in subsequent operations. The II Corps re-

[10] (1) Ltrs and Attachments, Sullivan to Clark, 8 Nov 43, 4 Sep 44–11 May 45, sub: POL Statisical Chart Studies. Sullivan Papers. (2) Ltr, Darley to OCMH, 10 Oct 54. Hist Br OQMG. (3) *Logistical History of NATOUSA–MTOUSA,* p. 479.

[11] By contrast, the use of drums was standard in the Pacific, where 5-gallon cans were rejected by combat units. See Stauffer, *The Quartermaster Corps: Operations in the War Against Japan,* pp. 218–21.

EMPTYING GASOLINE DRUMS *into "catch basins" in Seventh Army area, January 1945.*

ceived its gasoline in 55-gallon drums from Eastern Base Section, but could not ship these heavy containers to railheads where both service personnel and dispensing equipment were scarce. Furthermore, the direct transfer of gasoline from drums to cans, using small inefficient portable dispensers and shifting this equipment from drum to drum, was a very slow process. Attempts to use heavy-duty trailer-mounted dispensers were unsuccessful, for they quickly overheated when subjected to this type of intermittent operation. II Corps decided, therefore, that the contents of the drums should be returned to a bulk state before canning. Satisfactory bulk containers were improvised from 500-gallon tanks taken from old railroad

engines and sunk into the ground or, cruder still, deep pits were lined with tarpaulins. From these dumping vats, heavy gasoline-driven pumps forced the fuel through a network of hoses into thousands of 5-gallon cans aligned in well-dispersed rows. When rain threatened to contaminate the gasoline, each vat was covered with a tarpaulin.

In addition to wastage by spilling and evaporation, this system represented inefficient use of transportation. Carrying 120,000 gallons—the daily turnover—to II Corps, Eastern Base Section used 120 2½-ton trucks between Ouled Rahmoun and Tébessa. This round trip consumed 8,000 gallons or 6½ percent of the payload, a figure almost double the amount that would have been expended by 2,000-gallon tank trucks on the same route. But the few trucks of that type available were assigned to the Army Air Forces.[12]

The numerous handling operations in the three-step procedure—bulk to drum, drum to bulk, and bulk to can—required an extra labor force and put an additional strain on the dispensing equipment. Because the filled drums were too heavy to be handled manually, A-frames and grappling hooks were improvised and attached to cargo trucks to lift the cumbersome drums out of Dukws or trucks. Meanwhile the inefficiency of the system did not end with the delivery of gasoline. The need to store the bulky drums until decanted and again until evacuated added to the space requirements at a Class III supply point. For example, the dump at Tébessa occupied three square miles. But even more important was the fact that

---

[12] (1) Pounder Rpt, p. 60. (2) Moore Rpt. (3) *QMTSJ,* IV, No. 20 (19 May 1944), 20.

a special allocation of trucks had to be made to return the empty drums to the source of supply if the cycle was not to be interrupted. For all of these disadvantages, the realities of field operations demanded the use of available equipment. In the middle of 1944, the Fifth Army recommended additional personnel and equipment for QM gasoline supply companies. Sullivan called for more collapsible containers (Mareng Cells), hoses, coupling valves, sixteen 2½-ton trucks with winches, one 1½-ton fire truck, and additional gasoline dispensers. The War Department's answer came after V–E Day with the publication of a new Table of Organization and Equipment.[13]

Sentiment against the use of drums in forward areas persisted throughout the Mediterranean war, and quartermasters were never loath to employ other techniques of delivery. Beginning in mid-March, gasoline from Eastern Base Section was delivered to II Corps by a motley fleet of American, British, and French tank trucks, with capacities ranging from 750 to 4,000 gallons. Even some old porcelain-lined wine trucks and trailers were pressed into service. Before II Corps shifted to the northern zone, these vehicles moved approximately 3,000 tons of POL directly from the ports of Philippeville and Bône to the canning point at Tébessa, bypassing the drum-filling station at Ouled Rahmoun.

Enjoying considerable success in Italy was the "tanker" which Darley's battalion and divisional units improvised by equipping a 2½-ton cargo truck with eighteen empty 55-gallon oil drums and a portable dispenser. The drums were filled while on the cargo truck and the truck circulated among motor parks and airstrips, using its own dispenser to pump fuel directly into armored tanks and airplanes without removing a single drum. Although it represented a mild infringement of regulations that prohibited the filling of drums while they were aboard trucks, because of dangers from static electricity, this expedient had the advantage of providing a 990-gallon payload in contrast to the regulation 875-gallon load carried by a truck and trailer moving 5-gallon cans, or the 750-gallon load of the standard tank truck.[14]

Another Fifth Army adaptation, inspired by a desire to increase direct delivery of gasoline, was the American-style service station. Wherever surveys revealed a large number of casual trucks—at busy highway crossings, supply installations, or rest centers—Darley erected field dispensing units on each side of the roadway. Five such stations were located at ten-mile intervals on the highway between Leghorn and Florence. A typical station consisted of a captured German 750-gallon tank, mounted on several 55-gallon drums. A simple two-hose system fed the gasoline by gravity into the customer's tank. Instead of military police roadside signs were posted to attract customers. Each sign was large enough to be read at a distance

---

[13] (1) Field Rpts (NATOUSA) to Comdt QM School, Fort Lee, Va., 1944–45, sub: Observations by Persons Returning From Overseas, vol. II, items 60, 95, 125, 145. OQMG MED 319.25. (2) Ltr, Clark to Devers, Jun 44, sub: Permanent Changes in T/O&E's QM Gasoline Supply Co. OQMG MED 319.25. (3) Sullivan MS, pp. 56–57. (4) T/O&E 10–77, 21 Jun 45.

[14] *QMTSJ*, III, No. 14 (9 October 1943), 13. Fifth Army units received 3.2 percent of their gasoline in this manner in late 1943.

and all instructions were printed in several languages. These stations served traffic moving in both directions, and simultaneously reduced the number of 5-gallon cans that would otherwise have been emptied, washed, filled, issued, and perhaps lost.[15]

The 5-gallon Can and Its Army Class III Home

Whether gasoline moved from a port toward the front lines by tank car, tank truck, pipeline, or drum, the 5-gallon can proved to be the indispensable container for delivery of fuel to the combat forces. Strangely enough, when the can was empty of its expendable contents, it became a nonexpendable Class II or IV item of Quartermaster supply, to be drawn from a Class II or IV warehouse. As originally conceived the 5-gallon can was designed primarily to be carried as a reserve tank, more or less permanently identified with a certain vehicle, and with a certain bracket holder on that vehicle. In theory the can was not to wander, but combat experience changed all this, and the can became a constant roamer. In Tunisia Class III officers also demonstrated that a unit's wartime allowance tables for the 5-gallon can were ridiculous. The policy of "no can, no gas" meant that the daily demand for x gallons of gasoline required a minimum capacity in cans of 2x. If there was any depth at all to the can exchange system, the requirement might easily reach 4x or 5x. The Tunisian campaign

also showed that if the can had any temporary home it would be either in a corps (later in an army) Class III base dump where the container was cleaned and refilled or in the Class III railhead where it was momentarily stored or exchanged for an empty one.[16]

Adapted from a German model captured by the British in 1940, the 5-gallon can, known first to the Americans as a blitz can and later as the jerrican, possessed a number of advantages over the heavy and cumbersome 10-gallon drum used by the U.S. Army in the 1930's. The British can was an exact imitation of the captured German model; the American pattern (called ameri-can by the British) was just a bit smaller and lighter, and had a different closure.[17] Because of their shape (almost identical), both cans stacked easily and did not shift or roll in stowage. Moreover, they were light enough to be handled by one man, yet durable enough for extensive use in the field, and the position of the handles made for easy transportability. The American model had a round opening for its screw-type cap, into which a flexible nozzle could be fitted. This was

---

[15] *QMTSJ*, XIV, No. 20 (19 May 1944), 19–24; VII, No. 12 (23 March 1945), 24. Fifth Army units received 5.1 percent of their gasoline in this manner by late 1943.

[16] Ltr, Capt Phillip I. Laser, Class III Off, 1st Inf Div, to Div QM, 3 Jun 43, sub: Critique on Class III Supplies During Combat. Frink Rpt.

[17] Both models were 13¾ by 6¾ by 18½ inches. Shipping specifications were as follows:

	Weight (lbs.)		Cans per Long Ton
	Empty	Filled (MT 80)	
U.S. model...............	10	40	56
German and British models.	11.5	43.9	51

needed to prevent spilling when gasoline was poured into the flush or countersunk openings of tanks on American vehicles. The true jerrican had a cam-operated locked cap and a short spout. Later in the war, it too was fitted with an adapter and a flexible nozzle. But both types of nozzles were sometimes lacking, and in that case the original model which could be opened manually and poured, after a fashion, without a funnel, was more desirable. Two additional merits should be noted for both cans: when filled with gasoline, they would float, and they were excellent for carrying drinking water.[18]

Utility of the 5-gallon can for amphibious operations was demonstrated when every vehicle participating in the assault landings of Torch supplemented its full tank with from two to ten filled cans. In fact, the entire supply of combat-loaded gasoline for Torch was similarly packaged and the assault forces theoretically had enough reserve fuel in cans to meet their needs until the cans, drums, and bulk fuel on the D plus 3 convoy were ashore, stored, and readied for issue. During the Tunisian campaign, more and more bracket attachments for cans appeared on vehicles. Fenders, bumpers, cab tops, and underbody truck space were used to house the cans, thereby increasing the cruising radius. Through use of these brackets, a disabled truck was often a source of cans to other trucks in the convoy.

The Tunisian campaign also brought the 5-gallon can to its proper place in a QM dump or railhead site. A quartermaster arranged the cans in rows of 1,000 and at a glance he could easily make up his tallies in 5,000-gallon lots. Once the

can found its place in a Class III installation, a whole new method of operations began to develop around its storage and issue requirements. The system soon began to acquire standard procedures and an organization tailored to carry them out. In the Husky operation, the Seventh Army quartermaster observed that "all fuels for unloading across beaches must be in 5-gallon cans and use of this container should continue for a maximum of from 20 to 30 days. The 5-gallon can is the only satisfactory container in actual combat and fuel should be so packed, up to the limit of the availability of cans."[19]

For field operations the 5-gallon can early demonstrated superiority over the 5-gallon disposable containers known as "flimsies." Made of thin metals and poorly constructed, both American and British flimsies failed to withstand corrosion, shock, rough handling, or even pressure from normal stacking. Their only advantage over the jerrican was possible usefulness as sheet metal. Estimates of petroleum losses in the flimsies ranged from 40 to 60 percent. Ships loaded with the throwaway containers frequently steamed into North African ports with up to sixteen inches of gasoline in their cargo holds, and at least one vessel exploded because of this dangerous condition. Eager to discourage the use of the flimsies "at once"—in the midst of the Tunisian campaign—several American observers noted that "there was no excuse for the losses experienced from these cans," and attributed the apparently excessive require-

---

[18] Risch, *Fuels for Global Conflict*, pp. 90–91.

[19] (1) Pounder Rpt. (2) Moore Rpt. (3) Suggested QM Plng SOP for Amph Opns, prepared by QM Sec Seventh Army, n.d. Hist Br OQMG.

ments of the theater to "losses of prod-ucts that never reach the vehicle." [20]

The Fifth Army operated three types of Class III installations: the army base dump, in which all POL products were stored at a ten-day level; the Class III railheads (an average of thirteen of which were in operation at all times in Italy), serving the organic divisional units; and the filling stations operated in army or corps areas to serve their own units or along major highways to supply transient trucks. Elements of the 204th Gasoline Supply Battalion operated the POL in-stallations. Darley found that elaborate camouflage of his railheads was not pos-sible as the stacks of 5-gallon cans were issued and replaced several times a day. He placed reliance on wide dispersion, friendly air superiority, and organic or attached antiaircraft units. As a safe-guard against fire, he also emphasized dispersion of the stacks of cans and drums, directing that they be at least seventy-five yards apart. His men did not ditch the ground around the stacks because the danger was not so much from flowing, burning, gasoline as from the explosion of containers and the spread of fire by flying sparks in the air. They piled dirt up and around the stacks of containers in order to cushion the shock of an explosion and force the energy upward, rather than outward.

In laying out an actual dump site, Darley instructed his gasoline supply companies to stack 5-gallon cans in rows, 2 cans high, 25 cans long, and 20 cans wide, or a total of 5,000 gallons per stack. When it was necessary to store drums

within the range of enemy artillery, they were placed on the ground with their bung ends up, rather than on their sides, as exploding gasoline blew out the end of the drums. If the drums were in a horizontal position, the explosion ignited other piles in the vicinity. For fighting fires among the stacks, foam-type extin-guishers were often unsatisfactory as the foamite tended to remain on the tops of cans and did not smother the fire be-low and between the cans. Darley rec-ommended the use of mud and water to fight fires effectively.

Eighty-eight percent of gasoline went forward from railheads to the average in-fantry division in 5-gallon cans. They were issued and filled only by daylight because working at night increased the accident rate and resulted in many costly mistakes. Darley found that cans filled at night were usually too full, which caused leakage the following day while the cans were in transit or in storage at dumps, thus increasing the fire hazard. In the northern Apennines stacks of gasoline cans sometimes became com-pletely buried under snow. Having pre-viously marked all the 5,000-gallon caches, which were dispersed over a large area, with long poles set in the middle of the stacks, the 3840th Gasoline Supply Company experienced no difficulty in locating its stocks.[21]

Since the supply cycle depended on the availability of empty cans at the can-ning point, units were prohibited from accumulating cans beyond their allow-ances, and the "no can, no gas" doctrine was reiterated by Fifth Army in Italy.

---

[20] (1) Rpt cited n. 2 (3). (2) Moore Rpt. (3) Memo, Col William F. Campbell for Gregory, 3 Mar 43. OQMG MED 350.5.

[21] *QMTSJ*, III, No. 14 (9 October 1943), 13; IV, No. 20 (19 May 1944), 19–24; VII, No. 12 (23 March 1945), 24.

So long as supply lines were short, the quantity of cans presented no serious problems, but in the summer of 1944, when the drive to the Arno was in full momentum, the shortage became acute. By mid-June, Clark announced that the supply of 5-gallon cans in Italy was "extremely critical." In moving from one bivouac area to another, units abandoned the empty containers, which were also used for many other purposes than the intended ones. As part of the drive to make every individual "gas-can conscious," all troops were called on to report or turn in abandoned containers. By 1 August 1944, the situation was no better; rather, it had deteriorated, but not because of carelessness or neglect. The urgent demands of another build-up in Italy—in three weeks, Seventh Army was to land over the beaches in southern France—had cut deep into Fifth Army's inventory. Since April 1944, 250,000 full 5-gallon cans of gasoline and 25,000 cans of diesel oil had been frozen in Naples for the assault phase of ANVIL. The seriousness of the can shortage was implicit in the warning that all units operating in corps and army areas would draw their gasoline in 55-gallon drums. Clark soon issued instructions that a way be devised to make this cumbersome container easier to handle.[22]

In the winter of 1944–45 the shortage continued. One factor was the increased amount of time a can spent in transit from the forwardmost railhead to the using unit and in return to the filling point. Snow on high ground and mud in the valleys were serious obstacles to motor transport operations. Fortunately, the Fifth Army was able to borrow some containers from the British Eighth Army, operating along the Adriatic coast. By the spring of 1945 the situation was somewhat better. Moreover, improved weather and the extension of the POL pipeline to Raticosa Pass, halfway from Florence to Bologna, had reduced requirements. In preparation for the final Allied drive into the Po valley in mid-April, 300,000 5-gallon cans were moved up from Florence to Raticosa, and Darley was able to issue additional cans to the infantry divisions and attached mobile units.[23] In the open terrain north of Bologna, units operating under conditions of mobile warfare consumed more gasoline than during any previous phase of the Italian campaign. The combat forces were supplied by decanting operations at the end of the pipeline, which was extended rapidly across the north Italian plain.[24]

In the south of France, pipelines were extended northward from the Marseille area as fast as technical limitations permitted, but Seventh Army's extremely rapid advance soon left them far behind. Since tank cars were scarce, large amounts of POL were packaged and sent forward in freight cars from the

[22] (1) Ltr, AG Fifth Army to All Units, 3 May 44, sub: Illegal Retention of Containers, Gasoline, 5-Gal. IV Corps, AG 400. (2) Ltr, AG Fifth Army to All Units, 14 Jun 44, sub: Supply of 5-Gal. Containers. Fifth Army, AG 457. (3) Ltr, AG Fifth Army to All Units, 25 Jul 44, sub: Reduction in Use of 5-Gal. Cans. Sullivan Papers.

[23] (1) Memo, QM Class III for Tate, 30 Oct 44, sub: 5-Gal. Cans; Rad 2109, G-4 Fifth Army to AFHQ, 4 Nov 44; Ltr, ExO OQM Fifth Army to CO 204th QM Bn, 6 Feb 45, sub: Rpt of Slate Mtg, AFHQ; Class III Daily Jnl, Fifth Army, 1, 11 Apr 45. All in Sullivan Papers. (2) QM Supply in Fifth Army, p. 81.

[24] (1) QM Supply in Fifth Army, pp. 64–66. (2) Sullivan MS, pp. 180–81.

decanting points to CONAD reconsignment points, and thence to unit railheads. Supplemented by tanker barges on the Rhône and its tributaries, this system carried the southern forces all the way to the Rhine.[25]

Solid Fuels

Solid fuels, like POL, were of vital concern to other nations and to other U.S. agencies as well as to the U.S. Army. A combined British-American fuel section was organized in a matter of days after AFHQ was set up in Algiers. It was charged with computing, requisitioning, and allocating all coal requirements of the theater, both military and civil, except those of the Royal Navy. Moreover, it supervised the operation of coal mines in Morocco, Sardinia, and Italy. The AFHQ quartermaster represented the U.S. Army in dealing with this section, and it should be noted that, unlike POL, solid fuels were a Class III Quartermaster Corps responsibility at all levels as far as the Army was concerned. Purely military uses for coal, charcoal, and wood were largely confined to heating billets, tents, and hospitals, and the operation of military railroads, ships, and blacksmiths' forges. The Army also became deeply interested, although not directly concerned, in measures for the relief and economic rehabilitation of liberated areas. Practical experience demonstrated that unless raw materials could be provided to the contractors, local procurement of goods and services was virtually impossible, and in the Mediterranean area solid fuels were the most essential

of raw materials. Quartermasters therefore found it profitable to co-operate closely with the G–5 sections of various headquarters and with such purely civilian agencies as the United Nations Relief and Rehabilitation Administration.[26]

The Quartermaster contingent as part of the SOS for Operation TORCH was armed with a terse mandate to the effect that "coal and other heating fuel will be procured locally, initially." Writing at Casablanca six months later, the historian for the quartermaster of Atlantic Base Section noted wearily that "this masks a complex problem so hopelessly entangled in political and industrial issues that it is still unsolved."[27] Before the war, Morocco's eastern coal mines at Djerada had produced less than a quarter of its requirements, and the situation was only slightly improved after the country was occupied. Early in 1943 when I Armored Corps anticipated a major build-up in Morocco, a series of conferences took place in Casablanca, and both civilian and military needs were studied. The decision at that time, which was rather typical of Mediterranean experience regarding Class III supply, was that less than 1 percent of local coal production could be made available to the U.S. forces.

The shortages of coal and delays in the delivery of field ranges forced the Quartermaster Section of Atlantic Base Section to search for firewood to be used in cooking and heating. Because local stocks were too meager to meet civilian needs, there was some surprise when the Bureau of Forests in Rabat wel-

---

[25] *CONAD History*, I, 105, 109, 132, 233–39.

[26] (1) Hist of AFHQ, pt. II, sec. 3, pp. 388–91. (2) Komer, Civil Affairs, ch. VII, pp. 12–15. OCMH.

[27] Hist QM ABS, p. 15.

comed the inquiries of Col. James E. Poore, Jr., who reconnoitered the area for G–4, Atlantic Base Section. Wood was available in the forests and native labor could be hired to chop the trees, but French charcoal-burning trucks were no match for the crude paths and hills over which these loads had to be hauled. This proved to be only a temporary complication. One officer, 25 men, and 10 ¾-ton trucks were sent to Koebia, on the plain between Port-Lyautey and Petitjean, where they established a shuttle system across the 6-mile gap between the forest and the railroad. While the operation lasted, 15 carloads of wood were loaded daily on the trains returning from Algiers, westbound for Port-Lyautey, Casablanca, and Rabat. By the time the forest in this area was cleared of its available wood, gasoline ranges came into general use and the need to rely on wood for cooking purposes was practically eliminated.[28] Meanwhile, the British War Office assumed the responsibility for procuring coal in the United Kingdom and delivering it to designated ports in North Africa and Italy for use by American forces. By October 1943, the British had agreed to ship 150,000 long tons of coal a month and charge it to reverse lend-lease.

In planning for the Naples base the Allies agreed to maintain common stockpiles of POL products and coal. The Petroleum Section, AFHQ, had the responsibility for allocating petroleum and there was no serious problem in this field. But with coal, thorny problems had to be solved. As in the North African campaigns, Brig. Gen. Thomas

H. Ramsey had over-all responsibilities for the Allied coal stocks and administered coal allocations from Algiers, except for the Royal Navy and the Ministry of Transport. In Italy, Ramsey's deputy, a British brigadier, was chief of the AFHQ coal section. This officer received requirements from six separate military organizations and the Allied Control Commission's coal section. Next to Canada and France, Italy had been the third largest peacetime importer of coal among the nations of the world. In North Africa a French Government-supervised cartel handled distribution for the Allies. In Italy the coal "Monopoli" was a similar cartel but Ramsey could not use its services because the headquarters and records were in enemy-occupied Rome and most of its operations centered in the Po valley. With little local coal available, Ramsey's initial allocation problems were hard to solve. For the U.S. forces, the Quartermaster, Peninsular Base Section, submitted a monthly bid for coal to Ramsey's deputy. Once the allocation was approved, Painter's Class III officer was free to issue coal. Painter in turn had two major customers, the Fifth Army and the French Expeditionary Corps.

During the first few days at Naples a large coal pile reserve caught fire, but Ramsey's agents nevertheless searched out and requisitioned some 30,000 tons. The first colliers soon arrived, but could not discharge coal at Naples because of widespread demolitions. Moreover, the Liberty ships used as colliers, because of their deep draft, could only be discharged at either Naples or Bari. Ultimately a pier of the Ilva Steel Company at nearby Bagnoli came into use. Actual consumption rates were lower

---

[28] (1) Poore Journal, Nov, Dec 42. (2) Hist QM ABS, pp. 16–18.

than preinvasion estimates, for the destruction of industries and utilities was much greater than had been anticipated. Likewise the amount of bagged coal used by the AVALANCHE amphibious force was small. Because rail lines and rolling stock had been thoroughly destroyed, coal was not needed for train service until the end of 1943. During November and December, the Allied stockpile received 10,000 tons, bringing the total amount handled to approximately 100,-000 tons. As the tactical situation permitted, coal piers opened at Civitavecchia, Piombino, and Leghorn through which moved all the imported coal and coke used for steel, cement, gas, and power plants as well as for heating of military quarters.[29]

In its combat zone, the Fifth Army earmarked solid fuels almost exclusively for space heating. Because British coal was in short supply during the first winter, Sullivan restricted its use to the ward tents of field hospitals, allowing ninety-five pounds per tent stove per day. If a hospital was in a building equipped with furnaces, the coal allotment was five pounds of coal per hour per square foot of grate surface. Meriting a low priority, offices and recreation rooms were heated only by cordwood or scrap lumber.[30]

Through the winter months, General Sullivan sent organic Quartermaster transportation to the rear areas to obtain firewood, making purchases wherever he could and then forwarding receipts to the base section quartermaster

for payment. By the end of January 1944, when troops and equipment had been diverted to Anzio, he called upon Peninsular Base Section to undertake the supply and delivery of all firewood, and asked for increased allotments of coal lest wood stocks prove inadequate. During the summer of 1944, hospitals and units operating at altitudes higher than 2,000 feet were the only approved users of fuel for space heating, but even they were restricted to periods when the temperatures fell below 50° Fahrenheit. To preserve its limited stocks, Fifth Army issued coal only when wood was not available. Under no circumstances was coal to be used for cooking and even in hospitals it was not available for heating the quarters of medical personnel.[31]

Early in the fall of 1944, shortly after Fifth Army headquarters moved into Florence, Sullivan initiated action to assure an adequate supply of coal for the second winter campaign. He estimated that Fifth Army would need 600 tons monthly during October and November and twice that amount in December 1944 and January 1945. Because troops were deployed in the Apennines, General Sullivan requested authorization to issue coal on the basis of five pounds per man per day to units occupying buildings heated by furnaces, and two pounds per man per day to units using stoves or fireplaces. Higher headquarters did not concur in these calculations and replied with an authorization of one-half pound per man per day. This figure provoked such a spirited debate between General Sullivan and General

---

[29] (1) Hist QM PBS, p. 128. (2) Poore Journal, Jan 43. (3) Bykofsky and Larson, *The Transportation Corps: Operations Overseas*, p. 217.
[30] Memo, Class III Off, OQM Fifth Army, for All Class III Installations, 18 Nov 43. Sullivan Papers.

[31] (1) Memo, Sullivan for Painter, 29 Jan 44; Memo, Painter for Sullivan, 1 Feb 44. Both in Sullivan Papers. (2) SOP for Class III Installations, OQM Fifth Army [summer 1944]. Hist Br OQMG.

Ramsey, now quartermaster of MTOUSA, that the latter requested Sullivan to "please write me a nice letter apologizing for all the mean thoughts and words used in the recent conversation." A compromise was reached. By the end of November 1944 Ramsey and Sullivan revised the basis of issue retaining the allowance of five pounds of coal per patient per day for hospitals, while accepting the half-pound per man per day for other types of space heating. Contingent on the absence or unsuitability of other solid fuels, coal allowances were approved for such miscellaneous uses as laundry and bath installations, cooking, water-heating, and blacksmiths' forges.[32]

Because Peninsular Base Section furnished only 800 tons of coal during the latter part of 1944, the Fifth Army continued to make local purchases for the larger part of its requirements. The base section quartermaster encouraged all the technical services to search for solid fuels in isolated storage dumps, at factories, and in the vicinity of any industrial activity, and to relay pertinent information to the quartermaster as to the whereabouts of fuel. In turn, Sullivan requested military government officials to release the amounts of fuel required by Fifth Army. He regulated its distribution to combat zone units whether the stocks were within the jurisdictional boundaries of the army or base section.

Lignite, or brown coal, was obtained in sizable quantities from the Italian owners of a mine south of Florence. Wood, cut originally for the Germans, was found in plentiful quantities in a forest about five miles north of Pisa, and additional cuttings were made as needed. Because the carbon content of lignite and wood was less than that of high-grade coal, and their volatility was considerably higher, they had to be issued in quantities double that of coal. Notwithstanding this disadvantage, by March 1945, lignite and wood constituted more than 90 percent of the solid fuels handled by Fifth Army.[33]

Unlike Italy, France had ample coal resources, but only lignite was available in the original DRAGOON lodgment area. As 6th Army Group pushed rapidly northward, locomotive-grade fuel to keep the railway lines operating became a major problem. A preliminary Transportation Corps survey in mid-September reported 2,500 tons in the Marseille area, 13,000 tons near Lyon, and more than 7,000 tons near Grenoble. Although this meager reserve included fuels not suited for locomotives, it had to suffice until rail lines and coal mines, especially the upper Loire basin southwest of Lyon, could be rehabilitated. Stocks dwindled to an eight-day supply in November, and the British War Office agreed to make 25,000 tons available for import through Marseille. But during the same month the southern mines reached 70 percent of peacetime production, largely through the use of prisoner

[32] (1) Quoted in QM Supply in Fifth Army, p. 67. (2) Rad 2005, CG Fifth Army to CG PBS, 25 Sep 44; Rad 6534, G–4 Fifth Army to CG NATOUSA, 31 Oct 44; Admin Instr 85, II, Hq Fifth Army, 30 Nov 44, sub: Fuel for Heating. All in Sullivan Papers.

[33] (1) Sullivan MS, pp. 133–34, 159–60. (2) Class III Jnl, 11 Oct 44, OQM Fifth Army; Ltr, QM Fifth Army to CG Fifth Army, 2 Mar 45, sub: QM Rpt for Week Ending 2 Mar 45; Ltr, CO 204th QM Bn (M) to QM Fifth Army, 2 Apr 45, sub: Rpt for 15–31 Mar 45. All in Sullivan Papers.

of war labor. By the end of the month the vital Tarascon-Beaucaire bridge over the Rhône had been repaired and a coal supply for the Rhône line of rail communications was assured.

Solid fuels allocated for use of the troops reflected the same conditions. Late in September, local French officials in Dijon grudgingly allotted 750 tons per month to CONAD for Seventh Army and French Army B. CONAD actually received 917 tons of coal in October, 1,900 tons in November, and 12,000 tons in December. Even the last figure only amounted to approximately 1.25 pounds per man per day, a very low figure for winter combat in the Vosges highlands. Beginning in November, all solid fuel allocations were co-ordinated through SHAEF and paid for by the French under the reciprocal aid agreement.[34]

As a school of experience for subsequent operations, POL supply in the Mediterranean theater provided a variety of valuable lessons. Probably the most valuable of all concerned the supreme utility of the jerrican, and the possibility of effecting notable economies in personnel and equipment through its use. The British Eighth Army should be credited with this innovation, which antedated the TORCH landings, but the Americans developed various corollary procedures, notably a system of filling jerricans speedily by the use of powered gasoline dispensers. Mediterranean quartermasters learned a useful lesson regarding the standard 750-gallon tank truck used in the MTO. They judged this to be too small, and recommended that the 2,000-gallon semitrailer of the Army Air Forces be adopted instead. That suggestion was never adopted in their own theater, but large numbers of the bigger tankers were used in the ETO, where they proved very satisfactory. Since the Mediterranean theater was not a highly industrialized area and operations there were on a modest scale, there was little opportunity to requisition and exploit really large civilian POL installations. The few important facilities of that type had been thoroughly demolished by the Germans. Coal mines were of minor importance in the theater, and their operation was not a Quartermaster responsibility. Experience with pipelines was also limited, especially in the forward areas. By the time that Peninsular Base Section began to operate a tactical pipeline for Fifth Army in the Po valley, similar operations on a much larger scale were already under way in the European theater. For logistical planners, the most significant contribution of POL operations in the Mediterranean was the system of reporting gasoline consumption in terms of gallons per man per day.

---

[34] (1) *CONAD History,* I, 99; II, 517–638. (2) Ruppenthal, *Logistical Support,* II, 209–14. (3) Pounds per man per day computed by the author from strength figures in *CONAD History,* II, 623. (4) For further information on solid fuels in France, see Chapter XVIII, below.

CHAPTER VII

Outfitting the Mediterranean Troops

Company commanders found in their basic training manuals the statement that "no man feels that he is in the Army until he puts on a uniform." [1] The requisition, storage, and issue of the uniform was a field quartermaster responsibility no less important than furnishing daily foods and fuels to each man, and in some respects, largely because of the unknown life span of Class II or IV property, the mission was more complicated. While the different items of food numbered something less than 200, the list of Class II and IV Quartermaster articles ran into the tens of thousands. Along the shores of the Mediterranean most Class II and IV items, of simple design, of confirmed utility, and of steady replacement factors, such as web belts, wooden tent pins, pick mattocks, motorcycle helmets, canteen covers, and canvas folding cots, to mention just a few, presented no major supply problems. On the other hand quartermasters in North Africa, often assisted by observers or liaison teams fresh from home with new concepts of supply or salesman's kits full of experimental items, found that much of their time went into studying the inadequacies of clothing articles or other items under varying conditions of battle, or terrain, or weather. Because many items were

assembled to form a standard uniform, simultaneously worn by tens of thousands of soldiers, it was plain that inadequacies of clothing design would be considered far more serious by tacticians or technicians than those of the typewriter or the two-burner stove. Nevertheless, inadequacies are always relative, and quartermasters in the field were primarily concerned with shortages of clothing, rather than with its faults.

In time of war the degree of an inadequacy is always open to question, and many factors, notably those of time and space, play an important role in determining how serious the inadequacy may be. Because he is part of the chain between the national base and the front, the pipeline quartermaster, who detects and reports inadequacies to those at home who are in turn responsible for innovation, correction, and production of an item, can easily project himself into a controversy over this question. Unwittingly, his favorable or unfavorable reporting may complicate his primary mission of filling a depot system and avoiding shortages at a time when the spigot quartermaster must open his end of the supply line. Consequently, field quartermasters can always trace their deepest problems and greatest worries to difficulties associated with shortages, not inadequacies.

---

[1] TM 12–250, Administration, 10 October 1942.

North African Testing Ground

As in the supply of rations, the particular location of the wearer of a uniform was an important factor to the quartermaster who hoped to institute and sustain an efficient and economical system of clothing supply. It did not matter that the soldier in support commands was closer to the scene of fighting than he was to the United States; he dressed more like his service brother at home than he did like the soldier in combat. With peace restored across Morocco and Algeria, officers and enlisted men wore service uniforms during office hours, on pass, or at formal ceremonies. At work in base sections, the out-of-doors uniform consisted of olive drab woolens, leggings, and high, russet service shoes. When, around mid-April, the weather became warm, the soldier dipped into his two well-stocked barracks bags to change into cotton khaki shirt and trousers.

In Tunisia the combat soldier, carefully selecting his favorites from a host of articles, wore only the bare essentials. His basic uniform was either the armored force winter combat suit, a two-piece combination of overall-type trouser and a tight-fitting jacket, both made of waterproof cotton lined with wool, or the olive drab wool trousers and shirt, plus the olive drab 1941 field jacket [2] and the wool overcoat with roll collar. If warm weather persisted, he donned the two-piece herringbone twill (HBT) fatigue suit.

To enable the soldier to dress in his favorite service or combat uniform, quartermasters at Glasgow or Hampton Roads before the TORCH landings had issued each man two drawstring bags each containing approximately forty separate items. The eighty-piece load had been set by the War Department's Tables of Allowances of June 1942. Immediately upon landing in North Africa, the troops divested themselves of such generous allowances, and in the wake of their decision quartermasters acquired many new depot and salvage jobs. First, the soldier turned back his impregnated clothing. Second, he discarded one or two of the three pairs of service shoes which added weight to his hand baggage. Finally, he was tempted to barter some of his superfluous clothing for native souvenirs or services.[3] In the end, the man stripped down to what his backbone could bear and to his favorite and comfortable articles, clinging to each of them even though they might not last through the next battle.

Though aware of this situation, pipeline quartermasters were unable to challenge the policy of issuing ultragenerous amounts of clothing. Yet they recognized that it was a wasteful policy that aggravated depot and salvage problems.

As they saw it, it was a mistake for the ports of embarkation to issue at one time full allowances of clothing, both winter and summer, for combat and noncombat purposes.[4] From the be-

---

[2] Commonly called the Parsons jacket after Maj. Gen. James K. Parsons, Commanding General, Third Corps Area, who recommended such a garment in June 1940. Erna Risch and Thomas M. Pitkin, *Clothing the Soldier of World War II*, QMC Historical Studies, 16 (Washington, 1946), pp. 40–41.

[3] Pounder Rpt, p. 39.

[4] The search for storage space to house excess baggage, lost personal effects, and salvage distracted quartermasters from their wholesale support mission in Oran and Casablanca. Poore Journal, December and January 1943. Poore Papers.

ginning of TORCH, the twin barracks bags constituted the heart of the problem. If the soldier's second bag was not lost, diverted, or delayed en route overseas, quartermasters knew of other threats to the contents. While on the way to or deployed at the front a man was divorced from his heavy denim bag, which might lie in a native shack or dump far to the rear under guard. Frequently, these makeshift depositories afforded no protection against vermin, rain, mud, or wind, and by the time belongings were recovered they had deteriorated beyond reclamation. The shortage of means of transportation complicated hopes of recovery. One observer contended that when units got a hundred miles away the soldier had little hope of ever again seeing his items of initial issue.[5] For these reasons quartermasters favored curtailing the issuance of clothing at ports of embarkation, limiting the soldier to articles he needed for his overseas trip and a short time thereafter. All other stocks, quartermasters believed, should be shipped in their original cartons and distributed in accordance with short-run tactical and climatic requirements.[6]

The quantity of issues was not the only clothing problem. After the II Corps entered Tunisia in January 1943 quartermasters began to receive complaints about the quality of clothing. That a desert was a sandy, dry plain, always punished by hot breezes, proved fictional in North Africa, which had been previously described by a German logistician as a "tactician's paradise and a Quartermaster's hell." As the weather turned cold and the winds rose, each

PARSONS JACKET, *worn by Ordnance officers in France, December 1944.*

day and each night severely tested the soldier's uniform and his equipment, and quartermasters heard repeated calls for improvements.[7] Because of its weight

---

[7] In co-ordinating technical information on clothing and equipment in TORCH and in Tunisia, quartermasters exchanged a series of informal, personal letters with OQMG and OCQM SOS ETOUSA. Seemingly, there was no time to prepare formal staff studies. The Pounder Report of early 1943 consisted mainly of a series of observers' reports, and though Captain Pounder relayed some important recommendations to OQMG, his views were not widely disseminated. The Frink Report of late spring 1943, reflecting Tunisian experience, constituted a more formal co-ordination of technical data. A few papers consisted of completed staff studies. The staff studies and other items—what few there are—that theater and bureau quartermasters prepared in the effort to co-ordinate technical data at this early date are in the Littlejohn Reading File or in OQMG MED 319.25, Cases 23550–23555.

---

[5] Frink Rpt.

[6] Pounder Rpt, p. 40.

693–028 O—65——13

and clumsiness, the overcoat became an early battle casualty. The wool serge coat, essentially a parade ground garment after the development of the Parsons 1941 field jacket, proved unpopular since it gave no freedom of movement. Moreover it required frequent dry cleaning, an impossible service in a primitive area. So stocks of coats grew on depot shelves, or rested at the bottom of a barracks bag, and were quietly forgotten. Soldiers had long second thoughts about the coat's field replacement, the zippered olive drab field jacket. They complained that it was not sufficiently windproof or warm, that the zipper broke, that the jacket's cuffs, pocket seams, and collar frayed and soiled quickly, creating an untidy appearance. When washed, it faded and shrank. For combat purposes, it was too long to be a vest, too short to be a blouse. At the waist the soldier constantly tugged to keep the jacket from riding above and over his web belt, a lifeline to his canteen, first aid pouch, and cartridges. If the belt was held up by suspenders across the chest, the jacket's slash pockets were inaccessible.

Quartermasters noted various faults in the uniform. With their pockets filled, the olive drab trousers tightened in the seat or crotch, impairing a man's mobility. Quartermasters observed the American soldier's preference for the British battle dress as an answer to problems of mobility, protection, and neat appearance. Service shoes encountered extreme conditions of wet and cold weather in North Africa, and the leather sole soon proved unsuitable on the wearing march over abrasive soils. Soldiers universally condemned their canvas, shoe-string leggings, which, when wet, never seemed to dry, and when dry,

were always a size shorter. With metal hooks and eyes, leggings were difficult to lace in an emergency. Frequently laces broke, rendering leggings worthless. Wool socks, soldiers noted, should be heavier.

Finding convenient, comfortable, and sturdy clothing for nurses in the field was another problem.[8] Nurses arrived in North Africa with service uniforms and quickly demanded clothing as functional as the soldier's. They also wanted clothing in quantities that would permit frequent changes. But male planners had prepared the Tables of Allowances of the Army Nurse Corps. They thought of women's dress in terms of skirts and Cuban heels for overseas duty; the nurses wanted slacks or coveralls, service shoes, and wool anklets—clothing designed for work under canvas, in ambulances, on evacuation planes, and in jeeps, not in station hospital wards. Nurses could not buy these things locally, and Quartermaster sales stores were nonexistent until after the Tunisian campaign. Nurses accordingly wore men's clothing taken from stocks of small sizes. In this attire they were often ridiculed. On 17 June 1943 the War Department announced a special T/E 21 for nurses, listing a number of new field items with a size tariff to fit women.

Quartermasters also received recommendations for improvements in per-

---

[8] (1) Nurses considered the combination of steel helmet and liner as satisfactory. The helmet's shape offered increased protection. One nurse found twenty-one other uses for the helmet including service as a basket, seat, washbowl, cookstove, water bucket, and shovel. Pounder Rpt. (2) T/E 21, C–1, 17 Jun 43. (3) After Salerno, NATOUSA authorized the special allowances of field and arctic clothing to nurses. Cir 43, Hq SOS NATOUSA, 21 Sep 43, and Cir 2, Hq SOS NATOUSA, 6 Jan 44.

sonal and organizational equipment.[9] White handkerchiefs, towels, and undergarments violated camouflage security. The dyeing of white materials had been discussed in 1917 and 1939, but nothing had been done about it. Soldiers soaked telltale white items in coffee grounds. Many other items posed difficult problems. Gloves provided no protection against blisters. And there were no wire cutters. Although seldom separated from their intrenching tool, especially if it had a hickory handle, Americans were quick to point out the advantages of a product of German ingenuity, a digging tool designed to serve as a pick as well as a shovel. They considered mess utensils an annoying companion on the march and an alarm bell on patrol. To eliminate rattles and clangs, soldiers sought a more compact meat can in which knife, fork, and spoon could be firmly anchored. They also believed that their mess kits needed a better metallic coating than galvanized zinc, which would not withstand heat over an open flame. A deeper can would allow one man to cook for several others. During nontactical marches soldiers found it practically impossible to shoulder the drawstring barracks bag, which when stuffed resembled a puffy medicine ball, because its rope cut into a man's skin.[10] To eliminate

the necessity of dragging or rolling the bag, soldiers requested an improved carrier, made of sturdy canvas, complete with straps and handles, which they could easily balance on their shoulders.

Throughout North Africa by far the most prized clothing allowance was the wind-resistant, water-repellent armored force winter combat uniform. Lined with wool and providing a smooth exterior facing, particularly appropriate for crawling in and out of turrets of armored vehicles, it could be worn over woolen underwear, wool trousers and shirt, or a herringbone twill outfit as the weather demanded. Indeed, the popularity of this suit was not confined to Americans; the large number of Germans captured wearing this ensemble offered mute testimony that enemy soldiers also considered it a highly desirable piece of equipment. The first Quartermaster observers, who were sent out from Washington between March and May 43, received many demands from II Corps units for wider distribution of the armored force combat uniform.

Far from Tunisia, the Quartermaster Corps had its own plans for meeting the criticism of existing clothing.[11] Since the fall of 1942, the Office of The Quartermaster General had considered the development of a single combat uniform for all combat arms and services. This ensemble would be so designed that it would suit all the varieties of climate and terrain in the several theaters of war. It would be worn over wool underwear and woolen clothing in the winter, or alone in the summer, and was

---

[9] (1) Pounder Rpt, pp. 23ff. (2) Lecture, Maj A. Cushman, 15 Apr 43, QM Items on North African Front; Memos, Burnhome for Cowles, Chief Plng Br OQMG, 29 Mar 43, 6 May 43; Memo, 1st Lt H. E. Sommer for CG Jeffersonville QM Depot, 6 Mar 43, sub: Intervs at Fort Knox. All in OQMG MED 319.25. (3) Ltr, Middleswart to Gregory, 14 May 43. Hist Br OQMG.
[10] OCQM SOS ETOUSA had asked OQMG in November 1942 to redesign the bag along the lines of a U.S. Marine Corps canvas carrier and a sample was sent to Washington. Memo, Littlejohn for Cound, 6 Mar 43. Littlejohn Reading File, vol. X, item 19.

[11] (1) Pounder Rpt. (2) Frink Rpt. (3) Risch and Pitkin, *Clothing the Soldier of World War II*, pp. 48ff. (4) Risch, *The Quartermaster Corps: Organization, Supply, and Services*, I, 88–97.

intended to make the specialized armored force and parachutist uniforms obsolete. But this was more than a simplification program. The principle of "layering," gradually adopted by arctic explorers as a basic improvement upon the fur clothing of the natives, inspired the development of a uniform intended for the entire temperate zone at all seasons of the year. Basically, the layering principle relied upon the use of loosely woven woolens, covered by light but tightly woven windproof cotton garments capable of protecting the enclosed warm air from wind erosion. For the outer shell of field trousers and combat jacket, the material used was water-resistant 9-ounce sateen.[12] On 20 February 1943, the QM Research and Development Division prepared to circulate this newly developed combat uniform and several related items of equipment among various technical boards of the War Department's arms and services. This procedure was preliminary to command acceptance of the project. While awaiting the results of staff reports, the OQMG sent a similar kit of items, designated experimental items, M1943, to North Africa.

When the OQMG observer, Lieutenant Pounder, arrived in Africa in the spring of 1943, he brought with him an exhibit, including a preliminary version of the two-piece green sateen combat suit, a trench coat with removable lining, a high-top combat boot with uppers of reversed, flesh-out leather, a similar combat shoe, a blanket-type sleeping bag with water-repellent cover, a combination poncho and shelter half, collapsible canteens, cushion sole socks, wool gloves with leather palms, and a jungle pack with waterproof liner.[13] Having demonstrated the experimental M1943 items to a group of AFHQ officers in Algiers, Pounder displayed and modeled the items in Tunisia although they were not subjected to anything resembling a field test. Nevertheless, Pounder received favorable reports on most of these articles, and in his numerous letters to the OQMG he encouraged further research and development of all M1943 items.

When fighting ended in Tunisia, several other steps had been taken on paper to improve the inadequacies of the 1942 clothing. A new type of table for QM clothing and individual equipment, T/E 21, appeared on 10 March 1943.[14] Because of the late start in research and development, and because of the time lag in the various phases of standardization, in the acceptance of items under either the discretionary or mandatory columns of T/E's, and in production and delivery of new clothing and equipment, more than a year (July 1943–October 1944) would pass before base quartermasters had enough M1943 items to begin issuing them to unit quartermasters.

On TORCH's first anniversary only a

---

[12] In the technical vocabulary of textile engineering, *water-resistance* is an inherent characteristic of certain closely woven materials, while *water-repellency* is imparted by dipping in chemical compounds. See Risch and Pitkin, *Clothing the Soldier of World War II*, p. 92.

[13] Ltrs, Pounder to Cowles, Mar–Apr 43. OQMG MED 319.25.

[14] In T/E 21, Clothing and Individual Equipment, 10 March 1943, arctic, temperate, and tropical issues were shown for the first time as columns in a single table. Also, for the first time special items for parachutists, mountain units, and engineer amphibian units were gathered together in comprehensive lists. There were separate sections for nurses, WAAC officers, and enlisted Waacs.

few frugal soldiers could boast of having clung to some favorite items of their initial overseas issue. On Sardinia one air force service unit reported that it could fall out for roll call in most of its original clothing, but if the commander insisted that the men should dress similarly, each man had only one common outfit–nature's. In reporting this situation, an OQMG observer found one uncomplaining airman who might be considered a supply sergeant's dream. By November 1943 this soldier was wearing the last suit of the three initial sets of fatigue clothing. It was worn thin and ripped out at the seat. The soldier still had his first overcoat, but no woolen underwear, no woolen socks, and no blouse. He had a pair of olive drab woolen trousers, two wool shirts, and three blankets. He had no cot, no mattress. To point up the man's plight, the observer wrote: "He is the type of soldier who doesn't forage for himself and doesn't have a hard-working sergeant to look after him." [15]

Mediterranean Laboratory on Replacement Factors

At the same time that it shed light on the usefulness of Class II and IV items, the Mediterranean campaign offered quartermasters the opportunity to study the distribution and durability of these supplies under combat conditions. Even in the contrived battlefield situations of the prewar Louisiana, North Carolina, or Tennessee maneuvers, quartermasters had found it impossible to simulate the losses that would be suffered from enemy counterattacks, from bombing by enemy aircraft, or from depletion of stock by pilferage. One of the earliest commissions Middleswart carried overseas was the reminder to start immediately assembling data on replacement factors." [16] This information was essential to the success of a logistical system, for the amount of supplies, especially of nonexpendable items, to be stockpiled in North African bases was governed as much by the estimated rate of consumption and replacement as by the initial requirements before a particular operation got under way.

Middleswart's own struggle with replacement rates began in January 1943 when he was Quartermaster, Atlantic Base Section.[17] By that time what had happened to most of the TORCH surpluses could no longer be traced. In gathering statistics Middleswart was also handicapped by the constant turnover of troops in Morocco. The II Corps was redeploying toward southern Tunisia, and all base sections were supporting the move. The authors of strategy at Casablanca also upset efforts to establish replacement factors since they called for additional troops—a reborn French Army—in the Mediterranean area.

Late in February 1943 Middleswart became Quartermaster, SOS NATOUSA, and with more authority and opportunity in this centralized

---

[15] Quoted in Ltr, Col David B. Dill, OQM Twelfth Air Force, to Doriot, 19 Nov 43. OQMG MED 319.25.

[16] Ltr, Middleswart to Tate, G–4 ABS, 26 Feb 43. Poore Papers.

[17] (1) Poore Papers. (2) The Pounder Report contains the first systematic collection of Class II and IV replacement rates. (3) For the evolution of the method of determining replacement rates, see Risch, *The Quartermaster Corps: Organization, Supply, and Services*, vol. I, ch. VI.

agency, he forwarded a few replacement factors which he considered in line with his actual consumption rates to the War Department, NYPE, and SOS ETOUSA. The first comprehensive reappraisal of factors was based on records of the 1st Infantry Division, the 1st Armored Division, and Eastern Base Section in mid-April 1943. It came none too soon. The Quartermaster Section required the data as a basis for additional requisitions on NYPE. Without such revised factors, the port commander could not properly process Class II and IV requisitions for the two new field armies, the Fifth and Seventh, which had recently been activated in North Africa, nor for a growing number of Allied troops, prisoners of war, and dependent civilian groups. Moreover, without revised factors to compare with its own, the OQMG and its administrative superior, ASF, ran the risk of erroneous calculations for both long-range and short-range procurement plans.

Middleswart and the OQMG used the same formulas to derive a replacement factor, which is merely the measure used to express the life span of an item. For example, let us say that the OQMG had found a field jacket lasted a year. Annual replacement, then, was 100 percent, and the monthly replacement rate was 83.3 jackets per thousand, 8.33 percent, or a factor of .833. The annual percentage of replacement was reached by dividing the total quantity of an item replaced in a year by the number of that item in the initial issue. If a man received two flannel shirts initially and within a year drew three more, his annual replacement rate was 1.5, or 150 percent. But for large numbers of men, varying initial issues were an additional complication. In some units men were issued khaki shirts or herringbone twill jackets instead of flannel shirts, so the actual average initial issue for 1,000 men was about 1,800 flannel shirts. As an illustration of the importance of accuracy in such factors, if Middleswart assumed that the replacement factor of an item was 50 per 1,000 men for 30 days, whereas the actual average rate was 100, production and distribution of that item would meet only half the prevailing demand, and a supply crisis in that item would be reached before many months.

Immediately after the Sicilian campaign, Middleswart and his able pupil, Colonel Poore, assembled data on combat maintenance in Seventh Army.[18] In beginning work, Poore's efforts were hindered by the absence of men experienced in statistical procedures, by the loose depot system, and by a fluid tactical situation that interfered with accurate record keeping. Another complication was that stocks intended originally as replacement supplies were often distributed as initial issues to units arriving in North Africa without their authorized equipment, forming into provisional units, re-forming under Tables of Organization and Equipment recently changed by the War Department, or regrouping and refitting in staging areas. Still another complication, Poore found, was careless record keeping throughout

---

[18] (1) Sidney H. Karasik and Robert Stott, "QM Replacements in the N. A. Theater," *QMR*, XXIV (November–December 1944), 26–27. (2) Ltr, Sharp, QM MBS, to Littlejohn, 23 May 43, sub: Maint Factors Class II and IV Supplies. Hist Br OQMG. (3) Ltr, ODQM 1st Inf Div to DQM, 3 Jun 43, sub: Proc and Issue Class II and IV During Tunisian Campaign. Frink Rpt.

North Africa, caused by the much abused assumption that there was no policy of property accountability in an overseas theater. Middleswart speedily corrected this misconception, which was based on a careless reading of Army regulations that applied only to tactical units during combat.

In reviewing records of the 1st Infantry Division's experience in Tunisia, Middleswart found an illustration of the difficulties in gathering careful supply statistics. In the Maktar sector, the first delivery of maintenance stocks to the 1st Division contained many items that could not be used, and the II Corps ultimately received them back into stock. Records of the transaction, though undoubtedly completed, were not available to the Quartermaster Section, SOS NATOUSA, and statistical computations ended. But 1st Division records did show that field jackets and socks had been too numerous in large sizes, too few in small sizes. Generally speaking, existing stocks of clothing and equipment were too low, particularly in mid-February 1943, when one of the division's combat teams returned from operations with the British, and its requisitions created a sudden demand on the 1st Division quartermaster which he could not meet.[19]

By 29 September 1943, Middleswart had completed a study entitled Seventh Army Rates of Consumption, Quartermaster Items, Sicilian Campaign, D Day (12 July) to D plus 60 (10 September 1943).[20] It was based on the records of

the Seventh Army quartermaster, who reminded Middleswart of the difficulties of keeping such records in the midst of amphibious and flanking operations. Because records of supplies moving over beaches and docks were poorly kept, and maintenance equipment was frequently issued without tallies or receipts, it was almost impossible to estimate inventories at the end of the sixty-day period. Nevertheless, Middleswart assembled data capable of furnishing a sketchy basis for estimating his Sicilian factors from such sources as the shortage reports submitted by each organization, fragmentary tallies of dumps or depot issues, known losses by enemy action, and a variety of consumption records which he considered fairly representative of the experience of combat and service organizations. Armed with this information, he turned to collecting strength figures of Seventh Army, breaking its total strength down into fifteen-day periods and into four major categories of troops. In order to evaluate requirements more accurately, in view of the great difference in the rate of use of Quartermaster supplies by troops on various types of duty, he restricted his study to service troops either in support areas or in the combat zone, and to combat troops either in reserve in rear areas, or fighting at the front. Manifestly, this approach represented a degree of refinement that contrasted markedly with the OQMG's conventional March 1943 factors, which treated a theater of operations as an entity.

Middleswart's report showed that the most pronounced attrition appeared in the combat zone among combat troops. It was no surprise that support troops accompanying the task forces suffered the second greatest supply shortages.

---

[19] (1) Ltr cited n. 18 (3). (2) McNamara's *Memoir* explains clearly that he had no tonnage allocation for Class II or IV Supply. See ch. III, above.

[20] Mimeo Incl to Ltr, Middleswart to Gregory (info copy to CQM ETO), 3 Oct 43. Hist Br OQMG.

Among the specific items which required a higher replacement factor than those of the OQMG 1 March 1943 tables were clothing, intrenching tools, cleaning supplies, field desks, barber kits, field ranges, BAR magazine belts, flatirons, and flags. Under combat conditions clothing losses soared, largely because it was impossible to maintain adequate repair and laundry facilities to check the wear and tear of an item of clothing. Apart from losses through carelessness, waste, and enemy action, there were other causes for higher replacement rates. The constant splitting and regrouping of formations brought calls for additional flags, which were useful for identifying headquarters or assembly points. With filth and dirt encountered at every native house or building used by the troops as billets, headquarters, or warehouses, mops, brooms, brushes, and soap were expended at a tremendous rate. All organizational equipment, since it was necessarily scattered throughout many splinter groupings, had to be handled as many as fifteen different times. In the process field desks and ranges suffered a high rate of breakage and loss.

Middleswart was careful to point out that Seventh Army had been obliged to make substantial initial issues to organizations during combat. To meet campaign conditions, provisional battalions, each with a strength of 1,100 men, staging areas capable of processing 40,000 troops and many air transport headquarters had been activated. In addition organizational equipment had been issued to units which were split up to operate in a manner never intended by War Department tables. For example, bakery companies operated by sections in sev-

eral locations. Quartermaster service companies split up and functioned at separate railheads. Depot companies ran dumps by segregated platoons or sections, and hospital units handled field trains or temporary installations by operating in small detachments. The situation created shortages of organizational items, and initial issues necessarily depleted maintenance stocks. In his report, Middleswart explained that it was impossible to correlate these factors, for he had no data showing the extent to which initial issue had been taken from maintenance stocks.

At the same time that Middleswart and Poore had projected their Sicilian study, the War Department, prompted by the OQMG, was eager to test the validity of its own theories for forecasting production requirements in the United States.[21] As early as 21 June 1943, the War Department had asked SOS NATO-USA to prepare monthly matériel status reports, basically involving depot inventories, as a basis for determining OQMG maintenance factors.[22] Set forth in Technical Manual 10–250, this method of forecasting provided that zone of interior production should equal theater demands minus local depot inventories. To solve this simple equation, the War Department wanted Middleswart to supply statistics on each of the following: initial issues, replacement rates in combat, and distribution data. As Middleswart had already noted in his operational studies, there were many variables among each of these three factors. He

---

[21] Risch, *The Quartermaster Corps: Organization, Supply, and Services*, vol. I, ch. VI.

[22] Ltr, Secy War to CG NATOUSA, 24 Jun 43. Littlejohn Reading File, vol. XVI, item 78.

also knew that before any sound scientific basis could be laid for testing this method of forecasting requirements, considerable staff work would have to be done in the theater to collect, process, and record the proper data. During July and August, at a time when operations had ceased in Tunisia but were still progressing on the islands, and when plans had been made to land on the Italian mainland, Middleswart attempted to cope with the War Department directive.

Meanwhile, a team of Quartermaster officers from the OQMG, consisting of Lt. Col. George H. Cless, Maj. Ramon Wyer, and Capt. Richard T. Bentley, arrived in Oran on 13 August to study warehousing and stock control methods in base section depots and to secure, if possible, combat rates of consumption. Using TM 10–250 as a guide, the team reviewed the nomenclature of 6,500 Quartermaster items in order to obtain a sound basis for theater-wide reporting. To simplify the work of depot quartermasters, the team revised and simplified forms and forwarded them to base sections so the preliminary paper work could begin. With this phase of the survey under way Wyer took over the team from Cless in September and began to revamp Middleswart's report on the Sicilian operation for formal presentation to the OQMG. Realizing that the Seventh Army's experience was sketchy, Wyer made arrangements to attach Capt. Bernard A. Courtney to the Fifth Army to develop replacement factors at the divisional level, beginning with the D-day assault at Salerno on 9 September 1943. Courtney arrived at Fifth Army headquarters on 14 October.

The arrival of Wyer's team coincided with the dispatch of Middleswart's first monthly status report to the War Department at the end of August. This document reviewed NATOUSA experience on 350 Quartermaster items since the end of March 1943. When asked if the report had been limited to replacement factors and initial issues to United States troops, Middleswart was unable to provide the answer because depot stock reports failed to make any distinction among issues to Allied forces, prisoners of war, and dependent civilian groups.[23] To correct this situation SOS NATO-USA asked depots to keep separate reports on U.S. Army issues to Allied troops, the U.S. Navy, and other agencies.[24]

The limited scope of the 31 August report and the need for greater refinements made it imperative that Wyer's team visit all North African depots before the next monthly report was compiled.[25] This became all the more important when ASF announced on 30 September that T/O&E replacement factors were for use only in the initial establishment of theater reserves and maintenance levels and that thereafter NATO-USA would requisition supplies on the basis of actual issue to troops. The teams discovered considerable carelessness, insufficient training, a willingness

---

[23] As for consumption rates on rations, Middleswart asked the OQMG experts to reconsider seriously the need for such reports since actual and projected strength returns, the only true basis for ration consumption, were accurately known at NYPE long before Middleswart knew of them. The topic soon disappeared from his correspondence.

[24] Cir 19, Hq SOS NATOUSA, 10 Jul 43.

[25] (1) Wyer's reports attracted favorable attention from supply experts throughout the Army. (2) Ltr, Larkin to Somervell, 22 Dec 43, sub: Maint Factors (QM); Memo, Wyer for Middleswart, 4 Jan 44. Both in OQMG MED 319.25.

on the part of depot quartermasters to accept unknown, unintelligible, or non-standard nomenclature of items without investigation, and a widespread misunderstanding of stock control principles. All these shortcomings increased the normal difficulties of keeping accurate records under complex conditions. Nevertheless the team's December 1943 compilation was able to justify statistically the QM NATOUSA request to the War Department for higher replacement factors. Middleswart knew that his factors had been based on crude empirical observations. Now in accordance with the ASF policy of 30 September the Quartermaster Section's requisitions would be closely edited by NYPE. On 22 December 1943, through NATOUSA, the Quartermaster Section asked the War Department for increases or decreases of factors involving fifty-three major items. Twelve items of personal equipment called for a 200 to 300 percent increase of replacement allowances over those which ASF had listed in its first tables of September 1943.[26]

The QM NATOUSA monthly matériel reports only reflected base depot shortages, not combat replacement experience. So far only the summer operations of Seventh Army had been recorded and there was no comparable report for a winter campaign. For it, eyes centered on the efforts of Captain Courtney in Italy.[27] From October 1943 until January 1944 that officer attempted to secure combat replacement factors from Fifth

Army for units below corps level, but his first reports beginning in mid-October continued to be sketchy, notably on air force experience, since many units used unauthorized reserves built up through false requisitions and the robbing of dumps. Courtney's tables suggest that several divisions and their trains had entered Italy with large maintenance stocks. He understood that divisions kept their excesses apart from army's normal replacement issues. Courtney also ran into the same difficulty that Middleswart had encountered in the Seventh Army. The Fifth Army constantly resorted to splitting formations and the hasty activation of provisional units, making it extremely difficult to distinguish between initial issues and maintenance stocks. Confronted with a host of statistical problems, Courtney repeatedly called on Middleswart to send enough clerks to put one man at each division. Unable to secure the needed technicians from the United States, Middleswart recalled Courtney to Oran on 10 January 1944.

Meanwhile Major Wyer, who had been assigned to Middleswart's staff as head of a new Control and Reports Branch, decided to retrace all of his staff studies since the preceding summer, revisit all base sections and depots, including the new one at Naples, and make a fresh start in Fifth Army. As a result the January 1944 report on rates of consumption and on-hand stocks of Quartermaster supplies was a monumental document. For the logistician, it reflected the type of warfare being fought in the Mediterranean area.[28] As Middleswart and Wyer

[26] Ltr cited n. 25 (2).

[27] (1) Ltr, Wyer to OQMG, 7 Jan 44. OQMG MED 319.25, Case 2066. (2) Ltr, Wyer to OQM SOS NATOUSA, 5 Nov 43, sub: Fifth Army Maint Data; Ltr, Middleswart to Littlejohn, 13 Nov 43. Both in Hist Br OQMG.

[28] Ltr, with 29 Incls, Middleswart to Gregory, 25 Feb 44. OQMG MED 319.25, Case 14700.

studied Courtney's reports from Italy, covering the first thirty-seven days of the campaign, they concluded his figures were inaccurate, almost beyond calculation.[29] Courtney admitted that his conclusions were broad and sweeping statements, that his figures merely reflected the availability of various items in the combat zone, and that his methods of assembling data, notably the interview method, were not being conducted according to Quartermaster manuals. Nevertheless, Middleswart acquired useful knowledge from these reports. He told NYPE and OQMG that NATO-USA's demands for blankets would be greater than experience in North Africa indicated, that existing army stocks of woolen socks were meeting only 10 percent of Fifth Army's requirements, and that all divisions were demanding armored force combat suits though they were unauthorized as a substitute for the 1941 field jacket. Shelter half maintenance in combat was high because almost every soldier had two—the extra one made an excellent wrapper for blanket rolls as well as a moisture-resistant sheet between the ground and the blankets. Italy's rocky, mountainous terrain caused unusually high maintenance requirements for woolen clothing, intrenching tools, blankets, and tentage. Courtney had predicted that the requirements would greatly exceed Tunisian experience.

Inevitably, base and combat zone quartermasters crossed swords on the validity of their own combat replacement factors. The first crisis developed when Peninsular Base Section arbitrarily reduced quantities on Fifth Army's requisitions for the SHINGLE operation (Anzio beachhead), demanding additional justification. Fifth Army contended that the War Department's over-all factors for an entire theater should not be applied to a specific tactical operation. Moreover, the special-project method by which the base section proposed to supply requirements in excess of prescribed replacement factors "will not assure adequate and timely supply to Fifth Army." [30] The Middleswart-Sullivan exchanges coincided with the development of the same issue in COMZ ETO where it provoked considerable confusion and resulted in a lengthy controversy. Though unknown to Sullivan until mid-July, and only informally to Middleswart at the time, the War Department was using NATOUSA replacement tables as a guide in its debates with other theater quartermasters. This policy was without the consent of NATOUSA quartermasters, who were always careful to preface their reports with the statement that such replacement tables applied only to the Mediterranean theater. This practice was especially unfortunate since NATO-USA, where at one time five base sections acted in support of a single field army, did not represent a typical ratio of combat to service troops. Theater-wide issue statistics tended to minimize the impor-

---

[29] Ltrs cited n. 27.

[30] (1) Ltr, Clark to Pence, CG PBS, 22 Apr 44, sub: Requisition J–8–BULL–QM–II–1. Sullivan Papers. (2) WD Supply Bull 10–12, 11 Feb 44. (3) Tech Bull 10, OQM SOS NATOUSA, 24 Jun 44, sub: QM II and IV Repl Factors. OQMG MED 319.25.

tance of replacement experience within a single army.[31]

In the early summer of 1944 after the battles along the Gustav Line and at Anzio, Middleswart and Sullivan each disagreed and continued to disagree with the statistical evidence compiled by the other. In full candor, both men expressed their points of view. After Wyer's Control Branch had completed its full-dress survey of base section depots between January and May 1944, Middleswart felt his staff had acquired enough evidence to maintain that Sullivan's compilations for a six-month period from November 1943 to April 1944 were neither acceptable nor complete.[32] The heart of the matter was—what constituted completeness?

In Middleswart's opinion, the Sullivan figures included data on initial issues, omitted supply reserves at Anzio, inflated all totals by including back orders on items, and failed to account adequately for returns to stock from salvage. To this criticism, Sullivan protested that he, too, had used Wyer's experts and methods to complete Fifth Army's set of factors. He was disturbed when Middleswart's evidence, published as a theater circular, began to acquire a more official aspect. Sullivan was also alarmed when he compared the 24 June 1944 circular with War Department supply documents

of February 1944. Sullivan's reaction suggests a fear that Wyer's original base depot statistics would return to the Mediterranean area carrying all the authority of the War Department. It was difficult for him to understand why so many people and machines had somehow overlooked Fifth Army's experience. He believed that OQMG and War Department factors based on Wyer's reports had not given sufficient weight to Fifth Army's experience of increased maintenance for several important items. Sullivan wrote to Middleswart: "We feel our combat experience is of sufficient importance to merit study by all concerned, and we know now, if stocks are not received based on our issue experience, in many cases we will be short and the combat efficiency of the troops will necessarily suffer." [33]

By October 1944, the Quartermaster Section, NATOUSA, had assembled more data to present to the War Department. The June 1944 tables were soon revised upward. Still the October revisions did not fully meet Sullivan's needs, and much like his brother quartermasters who at the moment were fighting in France, he continued to seek higher replacement factors for Class II and IV

---

[31] As early as 18 March 1944 Middleswart learned from OQMG "that the limited QM Information which we have developed here without this badly needed personnel 'is being used to a large extent to determine replacement factors for all theaters.'" Memo, Middleswart for Lt Col Edward R. Comm, 18 Mar 44. OQMG MED 319.25.

[32] Hq Fifth Army, Quartermaster Class II and IV Maintenance Data—Fifth Army—Italian Campaign, for the Period November 1943 Through April 1944, Inclusive, 10 May 1944 (mimeographed). Hist Br OQMG.

[33] (1) Ltr, Sullivan to Middleswart, 16 July 44. Sullivan Papers. (2) Hq Fifth Army, QM Class II and IV Maint Data, Italian Campaign, Nov 43–Apr 44, Incl, 10 May 44. Hist Br OQMG. This report covered 235 items, giving increased factors for 70, decreased for 122, and no change for 43 items. But most of the increases were in the more important items, such as winter clothing and intrenching tools. They reflected the severity of Italian winter climate and the dispersed tactics of mountain combat. (3) On 28 July 1944 Middleswart told Sullivan that it was true that SOS NATOUSA extracted factors from War Department Supply Bulletins because those factors had originated from Wyer's excellent surveys. Ltr, Middleswart to Sullivan, 28 Jul 44. Sullivan Papers.

supply. In so doing, Sullivan hoped to avoid repeating the difficulties which the Fifth Army had experienced in its first winter campaign in 1943–44.

Problems of the 1943–44 Winter Campaign

With the advantage of hindsight, one may argue that in the later phases Mediterranean commanders did not grasp all the implications of the stringent budget imposed on them by global planners. When resources are slender, an operation like SHINGLE may prove very risky if it can neither be quickly completed nor abandoned. Once it was clear that Anzio would remain an isolated beachhead, this became evident very quickly to Mediterranean quartermasters who had to handle more and more requisitions based on higher and higher replacement rates. Acutely aware that supply was a function of command, quartermasters were inclined to believe that attrition of Allied supply was the real objective of German strategy, and to wonder whether Allied strategy was in tune with the current situation. The unity of the German command in contrast to the very real barrier represented by the inter-Allied boundary—an arbitrary line drawn down the central spine of Italy— seemed to give the enemy an advantage. Some blamed poor staff liaison between the American and British army headquarters; others believed that placing an administrative boundary along a geographic boundary violated a basic principle of war, and that failures of co-ordination were inevitable.[34] Whatever the

explanation, the Allied advance northward was a costly, inch-by-inch affair, marked by repeated tactical failures and a very high attrition rate for Quartermaster items.

In the winter of 1943–44, the 10 March 1943 version of T/E 21 was in force. It allowed each man approximately twenty-one items of individual clothing and twenty-six items of individual equipment. But of these items, the man's woolen undershirt and drawers, his field jacket and overcoat, wool socks, shoes, blankets, mess gear, and shelter half were the critical items of resupply. During the first winter in Italy, Middleswart and Sullivan suffered many disappointments in supplying regular and special winter clothing. As they scanned requisitions, watched replacement factors race upward, read alarming supply reports, and heard rumors that men were suffering because of the lack of clothing or its poor quality, they tried to remedy the situation with every device at their disposal, but there were many factors in the situation which neither man could influence.

During the first twelve days at Salerno, Class II and IV items were issued automatically, drawn largely from the contents of individual assault packs.[35] On 21 September the requisitioning phase began as Fifth Army assumed its responsibility for supply. Immediately, the calls began to come from divisions

[34] Chester G. Starr, *From Salerno to the Alps* (Washington: Infantry Journal Press, 1948), pages

442–43, describes the very critical attitude of U.S. enlisted men, and many officers, regarding Allied strategy in Italy.

[35] (1) Sullivan Diary, entries of September 1943. (2) Msg 231, Clark to Larkin, 2 Oct 43; Msgs, L–3318, L–4199, Larkin to Clark, 6–7 Oct 43. Fifth Army, AG 420. (3) Memo, Tate for Sullivan, 21 Nov 43, sub: Combat Clothing. Sullivan Papers.

and regiments for resupply of stocks. Without time to consolidate all requisitions or to inventory each unit's stocks, Sullivan on 2 October 1943 presented Middleswart with Fifth Army's first replacement needs for 100,000 men. Meanwhile, for lack of anything better, the Fifth Army wore the same type of clothing which the II Corps had worn in the Torch landings and across Tunisia. The men fought in overcoats, which had been criticized a year earlier as heavy and cumbersome, and in 1941 field jackets that were neither warm nor durable. Fortunately, some soldiers had combat service boots which they had tested for over four months while training in North Africa. But of the original 90,000 pairs tested, only a few remained, so that soldiers laced up their detested canvas leggings or tucked their trouser legs inside the top of their wool socks.[36]

As for quantities of clothing, Sullivan's preinvasion plans failed to materialize. Follow-up convoys were delayed in unloading at Naples because of the extensive damage to port facilities or because of the higher priority which other classes of supply enjoyed for the moment. Consequently, a backlog of regular and special items of clothing and equipment was created at North African ports. But even there Middleswart could not piece together any reasonable explanation of what had happened to the M1943 items which had been displayed during the Tunisian campaign. Nor in writing Sullivan was Middleswart able to elaborate on a remark by

General Somervell, currently in Oran on his way to India, that the Mediterranean area would no longer enjoy its favorable supply position. Somervell told Middleswart that hereafter Quartermaster requisitions from NATOUSA were not to leave the theater unless each one was justified. Even with such justification, Somervell warned that NYPE had already begun to sharpen its editing pencils in light of the decision on Overlord.[37]

Somervell could give Middleswart no information on the status of the M1943 experimental items, which had begun their rounds for concurrence, test, and correction among the many bureaus, training centers, and committees of the War Department as early as February 1943. Neither he nor Middleswart could foresee that on 15 December 1943, a revised T/E 21 would appear, listing many of the M1943 items for the first time, but under special headings that would restrict their use to combat operations in arctic and mountainous areas. With their use limited, it was clear that production of the items would also be limited. It would take considerable salesmanship and a liberal interpretation of the special headings under the new T/E to provide all current or projected combat troops with a complete set of the recently approved M1943 items. But this problem lay in the future and the Mediterranean theater was not concerned with production even though it was the potential customer of both regular and special winter clothing under the new T/E 21. Only one M1943 item, the sateen field jacket, was

---

[36] By March 1944 the new combat boots were being issued in greater numbers. Cir 44, Hq SOS NATOUSA, 25 Mar 44.

[37] Ltr, Middleswart to Sullivan, 2 Nov 43. Sullivan Diary.

placed in the universal and mandatory column of the December 1943 T/E 21 for issue to troops going overseas.[38] In that category, the jacket had been divorced from the layering principle, and thus from the original plan for an all-purpose, universal unit of combat clothing and equipment. However, it had been authorized to replace other field jackets, notably the M1941 Parsons type, when theater stocks of nonstandard jackets had been exhausted. But in October 1943, Middleswart was still unaware of these developments and he had to concentrate on getting the Fifth Army its replacement needs based on a T/E that was over a year and a half old and on replacement factors which Wyer and his team had just begun to assemble and report.

Sullivan's 2 October 1943 requisition indicated that the armored force winter combat suit still enjoyed the popularity it had acquired in Tunisia.[39] He sought by the first available transportation 100,-000 suits for equipping all infantry troops. But Middleswart had received bad news. The OQMG had declared the tanker's uniform limited-standard in midsummer of 1943. It was no longer even being manufactured. Fifty thousand suits, which had been ordered earlier by

Middleswart, were en route to Naples, but they would not fill Sullivan's needs. Through channels, Middleswart recommended that, in addition to those already authorized under the June 1942 Table of Basic Allowances (T/BA) only three suits be issued to every two vehicles. Though this procedure was suggested in the interests of economy, cold weather created demands that could not be resisted. Tate, the Army G–4, thus authorized Sullivan to issue 10,000 armored force suits to each infantry division, with proportional allowances going to those artillery, engineer, signal, and chemical battalions which supported the infantrymen.

Through November 1943, with the average temperature and rainfall well in the wet-cold range, combat units called for mufflers, woolen underwear, and overcoats.[40] Footgear was especially wanted. Studies of weather and terrain in the Fifth Army's forward areas led Clark to fear that without additional clothing, casualties from exposure might soon exceed those caused by Germans. Even piecemeal advances through Italian valleys were impossible unless the heights were secured first. It was on these dominating terrain features that the heaviest snow and severest cold winds were likely to be encountered. To complicate quartermaster supply further, terrain studies showed that Italian mountain strongholds, where supplies would be needed

---

[38] (1) Risch and Pitkin, *Clothing the Soldier of World War II*, pp. 48ff. (2) On 7 September 1943 OQMG informed OCQM SOS ETOUSA that AGF, ASF, and AAF had decided to produce 200,000 M1943 items for testing purposes. When the equipment was ready, it would be tested only in northern U.S. stations. Ltr, Col John P. Baum to Zwicker, 7 Sep 43. Littlejohn Collection, sec. II.

[39] (1) Msgs cited n. 35 (2). (2) While disappointed over the news about the tanker's uniform, Sullivan favored the uniform and urged SHINGLE planners to adopt it for the assault troops going to Anzio. The proposal was not favorably considered. Sullivan MS, ch. I.

[40] (1) Ltr, CG 34th Inf Div to CG Fifth Army, 10 Nov 43, sub: Request for Mufflers, Wool; Ltr, AG Fifth Army to Hq 15th Army Group, 21 Nov 43, sub: Winter Clothing and Equip. Fifth Army, AG 420. (2) Ltr, CO 213th Coast Arty Regt to CG 45th AAA Brig, 18 Nov 43, sub: Lack of Winter Clothing. Sullivan Papers.

in quantities, were the most inaccessible to quartermaster trains.

Sullivan tackled his problem immediately. By special allowances, spelled out through many hours of work under trying conditions, and by emergency shipments to his dumps, he slowly remedied the shortages. Not content to wait for staged supply to come forward, Sullivan sent trucks direct to Naples. At shipside, the vehicles picked up clothing and returned it speedily to the Class II dump at Santa Maria near Capua. Owing to this action, quantities issued to Fifth Army units in November 1943 were triple those of October, and those for December and January were more than double those of the preceding two months. By 20 December the Fifth Army Class II stocks at Santa Maria had, in fact, reached such high levels that Tate directed Sullivan to reduce them lest the depot's mobility be seriously handicapped in a proposed advance. Tate understood that Peninsular Base Section was ready to assume its normal supply responsibility.[41]

The effect of Sullivan's activities may be illustrated by the resupply experience of one infantry division, the 34th.[42] By 15 December it had received its special allowance of tanker's uniforms. Handling his Class II allocations with tact and care, the division G–4 was also able to spread special shipments of combat boots among his regimental supply officers to meet their specific operational needs. In January 1944 the 34th Division received its first shipment of special wet-cold weather equipment in sufficient quantities. Yet the division's resupply of regular woolen items continued to fall short. With stocks so scant, these articles had to be taken from casualties moving rearward to hospitals, then laundered and reissued. The unit quartermaster immediately sought more support from the rear, and in late January 1944 Peninsular Base Section responded.

As stocks grew in Fifth Army dumps, Sullivan, on 7 December 1943, proposed a better method of distribution.[43] A month later the office of the army quartermaster asked divisional quartermasters and supply officers of separate units to submit their Class II and IV requisitions daily to commanding officers of the several ration railheads. That same evening railhead Class I officers forwarded the requisitions to army Class II and IV warehouses. The following morning deliveries were made to ration points. To insure arrival of the items, a representative of the army Class II warehouse accompanied each convoy and supervised railhead distribution.

Streamlining his procedure still further, Sullivan deposited at each railhead stocks of clothing, in lots for 10,000 men, consisting of socks, trousers, shirts, underwear, field jackets, and fatigue suits. Railhead quartermasters issued this clothing in direct exchange for worn garments or upon certification that the desired articles had been lost or destroyed in combat. For a war of attrition the system worked well, providing clothing and equipment within twenty-four hours

[41] (1) *Fifth Army History*, II, 70–72; III, 70–73. (2) Memos, Tate for Sullivan, 21 Nov, 20 Dec 43, sub: Combat Clothing. Sullivan Papers.

[42] Monthly Jnls, OQM 34th Div, Dec 43–Jan 44. Hist Br OQMG.

[43] (1) Sullivan MS, p. 29. (2) Operational Memo 35, OQM Fifth Army, 7 Feb 44. Sullivan Papers.

from the time the combat unit declared its need. In keeping his impetus of supply always forward, Sullivan unquestionably reduced the distances combat trains traveled to obtain their supplies and avoided adding to the confusion on roads in the army's rear area.

The most acutely felt shortage in the early days in Italy had been in wool socks and waterproof footwear.[44] The mud-soaked and mountainous terrain, cut by flooded rivers, shortened the life of shoes and socks. During October 1943 the army Class II officer estimated that only 10 percent of the Fifth Army's requirements of socks was being filled. On one occasion, the 45th Division received only 500 pairs of socks whereas it had called for 16,000 pairs. Seeking to supply light woolen socks automatically on the basis of one pair per combat soldier per week, an allowance that exceeded the currently authorized replacement factor more than five times, the Fifth Army commander predicted that coughs, colds, influenza, and pneumonia would increase unless the extra socks were available and wet socks frequently changed. Sullivan warned that trench foot might appear. Peninsular Base Section endorsed his request for a factor that would provide four pairs of socks to 60 percent of the men in the combat area and two pairs to the remaining 40 percent in the army's administrative area. On 19 November 1943, Colonel Painter drew Middleswart's attention to the contrasting climatic conditions of Sicily and

Italy in winter and recommended that Sullivan's estimates be honored.[45]

Middleswart, recalling Somervell's parting remark to him at Oran, urged the Fifth Army, Peninsular Base, and his own staff to provide him with reasons why a requirement of 5.16 times the generally authorized factor on socks was justified. Wyer's Control Branch pointed to the Seventh Army's factor of 1,260 pairs per 1,000 men per month in Sicily in contrast to the Fifth Army's projected factor of 4,334 pairs per 1,000 men per month in Italy. Messages about socks continued to stream back and forth across the Mediterranean, but finally one from across the Atlantic ended the discussion. On 9 December 1943 Middleswart notified Sullivan that the increased factor was "not favorably considered by the War Department." Sock replacements continued to flow to Italy at the rate of 1,680 pairs per 1,000 men per month for combat troops and as low as 840 per 1,000 men per month for support troops on normal duty.[46]

Arctic overshoes were so scarce that existing supplies had to be carefully allo-

[44] (1) *Fifth Army History*, II, 71. (2) Msg 4180, Clark to Larkin, 27 Oct 43; Msg L–8646, Larkin to Clark, 30 Oct 43; Msg 4469, Clark to Larkin, 9 Nov 43. All in Fifth Army, AG 420. (3) Ltr, Sullivan to Doriot, 1 Dec 43. Hist Br OQMG.

[45] (1) Msg 868, CG PBS to CG SOS NATOUSA, 19 Nov 43. Sullivan Papers. (2) Plans to achieve the objective of one pair of socks per man per week undoubtedly included reissue of used stock, whether repaired or merely laundered. But bath and clothing exchange services were still experimental, and even if completely successful the quantity to be recovered from that source was still unknown.

[46] (1) Msg L–2936, Larkin to Clark, 9 Dec 43. (2) In September 1944, on the eve of moving into the Gothic Line, Sullivan reviewed Fifth Army experience with replacement factors of light wool socks. The factor per 1,000 men per 30 days had varied from a low of 606.140 in August 1944 to a high of 2,582.253 in December 1943 with the average factor at 1,288.072 for the 10-month period from November 1943 through August 1944. Ltr, Clark to Larkin, 8 -Sep 44 sub: Repl Factor–Socks, Wool, Light. Sullivan Papers.

cated.[47]   A priority system, established in November 1943, provided for 100 percent distribution to front-line soldiers, 75 percent to corps and army personnel, and 50 percent to base section troops.   Notwithstanding this frugality, maintenance stocks dropped and replacements were unavailable.   The OQMG had only 1,000 12-inch shoepacs to offer, but Clark replied that he had to have enough to carry him through the middle of January 1944.   The Fifth Army received only 135,000 of the 208,000 pairs of arctic overshoes it had requisitioned; quickly issuing 134,000 of these, the army depot had only 1,000 pairs on hand, and all of these were in small sizes, 6 to 8.

Fighting their first long winter campaign of World War II in army strength —only the small force on Attu had been engaged in winter fighting and then only for twenty days during the spring of 1943—an increasing number of American soldiers were now suffering from trench foot, something which had plagued all armies obliged to fight in cold, wet weather.[48]   In October 1943 Sullivan's forecast of trench foot had been largely speculative; alerted to the sudden appearance of numerous trench foot cases, medical officers by early December were anxiously watching sick lists.   By January 1944 Sullivan noted in his diary that "the Medico is excited about the question of trench feet. . . ."   From November 1943 through February 1944 the monthly incidence rose from 371 to 1,805. One detailed report concluded that trench foot alone accounted for nearly 25 percent of the total casualties among American troops.[49]

Trench foot appeared after soldiers were exposed to cold water, mud, and relative inactivity.   The duration of exposure before affliction varied from four to fifteen days, with an average of six days.   Constant wearing of wet socks and shoes, failure to clean or massage the feet, and constriction due to footwear fitted or laced too tightly added to the risks.   Studies of the earliest cases in November 1943 revealed that none had worn footwear other than the regulation service shoe (the combat boot was not worn universally until March 1944), that only one man had worn heavy woolen socks, and that forty-five men had not changed their shoes or socks during the entire period of exposure.[50] In February 1944, when the epidemic was three months old and at its peak, a

---

[47] Memos, Tate for Sullivan, 25 Nov 43, 14 Jan 44, sub: Issue of Rubber Overshoes; Memo, Supply Off OQM for G–4 Fifth Army, 14 Jan 44. All in Sullivan Papers.

[48] In World War I, the American Expeditionary Forces, with less than 2,000 trench foot casualties, had been spared serious disabling effects largely because it had fought its major battles between March and November 1918. The armistice took troops out of trenches before winter weather struck in force. In marked contrast, the British Army suffered 97,414 trench foot casualties in World War I in western Europe alone, with 3,100 cases in France and Flanders during the week ending 16 December 1916. (Maj. Gen. Sir H. L. Tidy, ed., *Inter-Allied Conferences on War Medicine, 1942–1945* (London: Staples Press Ltd, 1947), p. 140.) But by 1917 the British had largely solved their trench foot problem. See below, ch. XVI.

[49] (1) Memo, Surgeon 2626 AAA Brig for AA Off II Corps, 6 Dec 43. Sullivan Papers. (2) Sullivan Diary, 21 Jan 44. (3) *Fifth Army at the Winter Line* (15 November 1943–15 January 1944), in the series AMERICAN FORCES IN ACTION (Washington, 1945) pp. 87–88. (4) Lt Col Fiorindo A. Simeone, Trench Foot in the Italian Campaign, p. 5. MS in Hist Unit, American Medical Society. (Hereafter cited as Simeone Rpt.) (5) Whayne and DeBakey, *Cold Injury, Ground Type*, p. 103.

[50] (1) Simeone Rpt, pp. 15, 17. (2) Cir 44, Hq SOS NATOUSA, 25 Mar 44.

THE M1943 OUTFIT. *Extreme-cold version (left); outfit as tested at Anzio (right).*

survey of over 100 cases revealed that none of the men understood that trench foot could result merely from inactivity in temperatures that were cold but not freezing, while wearing wet shoes and socks. Replacements for the 3d Infantry Division had little, if any, instruction in the care of the feet. Sick call statistics could be directly related to training, or lack of it. Echoing the army quartermaster's views, the 3d Division surgeon summarized the proper preventative measures: "Trench foot is similar to the venereal problem . . . both of them depend on the education of the individual soldier." [51]

[51] Ltr, Maj Robert H. Bates to Doriot, 25 Apr 45. Sullivan Papers.

Anzio Test of New Special Items

Unaware that in the days ahead their offerings would be the subject of both praise and abuse, OQMG observers brought about thirty different Quartermaster Class II and IV experimental items to the Anzio beachhead at the end of March 1944. Each item had won a place on special headings of T/E 21, 15 December 1943, for issue to troops in cold-temperate, low mountain, or alpine areas, and had received War Department sanction to be combat tested. In light of the difficulties during the first winter in Italy and the prospect that Fifth Army might spend another winter there, the scope of the tests at Anzio took on special significance for NATO-USA quartermasters. But in retrospect the test was the halfway mark of a much broader story. It was the climax of a research and development project the OQMG had been working on since mid-1942, and the turning point of a salesmanship effort to convince many wary customers of the value of the product. As salesmen, OQMG representatives would have many questions to answer. Would the items win places in the mandatory columns of a revised T/E 21? Would theater commanders adopt the items for use in their combat zones? Would higher authorities at home interpret the special headings under T/E 21 liberally or strictly, when vital priorities with regard to raw materials, industrial production, sea transportation, and the conflicting demands of other theaters were at stake?

Quartermaster observers were not prepared to answer such questions, and indeed the final answers were largely dependent upon the size of the requisitions submitted in response to the sample offerings. The significance of Tables of Equipment in arriving at such decisions was not widely understood within the Army. These T/E's were simultaneously catalogues of what was available and written authorizations to requisition what was listed. Until they had been seen and studied by supply officers at the grass roots level, a theater quartermaster could only offer a rough guess at what his requirements for a new item might be. Providing enough copies of a T/E for such a theater-wide scrutiny, by local printing or massive airmail shipments from the United States, was a vital step in the process. This was a responsibility of The Adjutant General's Office, which either failed to understand the need for wide distribution or was unable to obtain priorities for tasks of this magnitude. As late as 3 November 1944, when Fifth Army called off its alpine offensive, an OQMG observer reported:

T/E 21 dated 1 June 1944 has not been distributed in this Theatre as yet with the exception of advance copies. As a result, T/E 21 dated 15 December 1943 is being used except in such instances where special attention to certain items has been drawn by correspondence and radios from the War Department. I checked with the publications depot this morning and found that the first copies of the 1 June 1944 edition were received on 21 September and to date 1,013 copies for general distribution have been received. No general distribution is made until at least fifty percent of the total required amount has been received. Eight thousand copies are required for complete distribution. . . . This situation must necessarily be difficult from the point of view of computing requirements in the office and unless it is corrected, I can not see how any degree of accuracy can be attained. While at Headquarters, Peninsular Base Section where requisitions are edited for the 5th and 7th Armies as well as the 12th AF, I found that they had only one copy of the new T/E 21 and this Headquarters [NATOUSA] has but one.[52]

For the Quartermaster Corps, which has on its roster both salesmen and customers of its products, the moral of this episode, unfortunately not an unusual one, was clear: there was a need to improve liaison and co-ordination between bureau and field organizations through a stronger technical channel. In all tests, it proved wise for both user and supplier to see the results personally rather than merely read a series of disconnected command reports based on the findings of a series of observers. For tactical commanders, whose main interest is always in the quantity of items, the lesson is equally simple—sound and prompt command decisions must speedily be channeled to support commands. Every day's delay in making a decision hobbles production and distribution efforts.

In contrast to the few OQMG footlockers of experimental samples displayed across North Africa by Captain Pounder in March 1943, thirty-one new items of the December 1943 T/E 21 were forwarded in sufficient quantity to permit distribution to an infantry battalion.[53] The OQMG had laid the groundwork for the tests in January 1944. Tacticians had been receptive to the project,

and the OQMG hoped that by establishing better controls more meaningful conclusions could be reached. It was understood that troop commanders and quartermasters would consider the precious commodity of time in weighing the quality and quantity of items at stake.

Sent to Italy to supervise the tests were two officers from the Research and Development Branch, OQMG, who had come via slow convoy to assure that the experimental items were not diverted en route. Each officer had a letter of introduction, dated 28 February 1944, from Col. Georges F. Doriot, chief of the Military Planning Division, and also chief of the Research and Development Branch. Maj. Robert H. Bates, an experienced mountain climber and adviser to OQMG on cold weather clothing, and 1st Lt. Michael Slauta, a qualified parachutist with a knowledge of infantry platoon tactics, proceeded to Anzio on War Department orders. General Clark notified the VI Corps that one battalion of the 30th Infantry Regiment was to receive the shipment and test it under actual battle conditions for a month. He asked for a final report, complete with findings, photographs, and recommendations for changes in items under test. Neither Clark nor senior quartermasters, who were not present for the tests, explained to the VI Corps that the experimental items were to be compared with current T/E listings and limited standard items already in use in the theater.

On 28 March 1944 the items to be tested reached the 3d Infantry Division, Brig. Gen. John W. O'Daniel commanding. O'Daniel ordered Lt. Col. Woodrow W. Stromberg, Commanding Officer, 2d Battalion, 30th Infantry, to distribute

[52] Ltr, Capt Knight Ames, OQMG Obsv Hq COMZ NATOUSA, to Doriot, 3 Nov 44. OQMG MED 319.25.

[53] (1) Msg 2810, Clark to CG VI Corps, 25 Mar 44. Sullivan Papers. (2) Ltr and Incls, CG 3d Inf Div to CG Fifth Army, 9 May 44, sub: Test of QM Items, 30 Mar–30 Apr 44. Fifth Army, AG 420. (Hereafter cited as Anzio C&E Rpt.) (3) Ltr, Sullivan to Doriot, 7 Apr 44. Sullivan Papers.

them among 932 men of his command. He also directed his own divisional reconnaissance platoon and the comparable platoons of his three regiments, the 7th, 15th, and 30th Infantry, together totaling 215 men, to test the equipment. Shoelaces and ski socks were to be tested by a hundred men of the division's military police, and wool comforters by 43 men of the division's quartermaster company. Nine men of the 191st Tank Battalion, attached to 3d Division, were to test the suitability of all the items for armored force use.

The Anzio beachhead, 100 square miles between the German lines and the Tyrrhenian Sea, was the test area. Its terrain was low, wet, and muddy, and it was cut by many small streams. Large sandy areas met the sea. No hilly ground was available, but battle action and barbed wire entanglements, in the opinion of tacticians, provided a better test of the durability of the experimental items than rugged physical features. The weather was not cold, temperatures varying from 37° to 70° Fahrenheit. Winds averaged 5 to 8 miles per hour with occasional gusts up to 20 miles per hour. Showers fell on an average of one every third day, and heavy rains occurred on two days of the testing period. Despite the high average daytime temperature, excessive dampness made for chilly nights.

As for the tactical aspects of the test, it took place during a period of near stalemate. Neither side started any attacks involving many men or much armor. During the first fortnight participating units were five miles behind the front, undergoing rigorous field training. Five-mile, speed-conditioning marches, tactical exercises in scouting and patrolling, attacks against mock enemy positions, weapons training, and movement through barbed wire entanglements, all subjected clothing and equipment to stress and strain which commanders felt were comparable to those on the firing line. The last half of the test brought the 2d Battalion, 30th Infantry, with supporting units, back to the front. During daylight hours, the lines were quiet and troops remained in their foxholes or underground shelters. At night, reconnaissance and combat patrols moved actively between the lines. On one occasion Company F with attached armor raided a German position.

The major items tested at Anzio comprised 1,567 M1943 field jackets plus 1,000 hoods, 1,373 high-necked sweaters, and 3,300 cotton field trousers. These items had been projected as an assembly in the fall of 1942, intended to be worn together over woolen underwear, shirts, and trousers, during winter in the temperate zone. That concept had been disapproved, and in T/E 21, 15 December 1943, the M1943 jacket alone was authorized for all enlisted men at all seasons, except in the tropics. The other new items (except the hood, which had not yet been standardized) were authorized for issue in arctic, Zone 1 (cold-temperate), and mountainous areas at the discretion of the theater commander. They were to be turned in upon permanent change of station or upon movement into an area where climatic conditions did not demand this type of clothing. Since Anzio is situated on a Mediterranean coastal plain, it cannot conceivably be regarded as an arctic, cold-temperate, or mountainous area. Clearly, therefore, this test was intended to prove the practicability of the layered uniform in a normal temperate winter climate—the climate for which it was originally designed. If this could be demonstrated to the satisfaction of Clark and his army quartermaster, and Devers and his SOS NATOUSA quartermaster, amendment or an official reinterpretation of the current T/E 21 was highly probable.[54]

After the test Stromberg's battalion rated the M1943 jacket an improvement over the 1941 Parsons jacket in appearance, camouflage, and utility. Stromberg and O'Daniel both approved of the experimental uniform, writing that "the discovery that men could fight out of their jacket and trouser pockets" was the most important feature of the test.[55] As a special modification of the M1943 jacket, Stromberg designed a rear pocket capable of carrying a day's K or C ration, plus a poncho or blanket sleeping bag.

Several types of footwear were also tested, including a service shoe with rubber-cleated soles, a combat boot which was actually a service shoe with an attached leather cuff designed to replace the canvas legging, and a shoepac. Stromberg's battalion received two kinds of woolen socks, one with a cushion sole and reinforced toe and heel, and the other a heavy ski sock. The combat service boot, already tested in North Africa, met with an enthusiastic reception. So did the shoepac. The latter— a high moccasin with rubber foot and leather top—was regarded as indispensable in combating trench foot in wet terrain. Infantrymen considered both types of woolen socks an improvement over the currently issued light woolen socks. They praised cushion sole socks as a companion of combat service boots and felt that the ski sock had considerable promise for similar use with the shoepac.

In an attempt to increase the comfort of the soldier who had to sleep out of doors during winter weather, several types of sleeping bags were tried at Anzio. The mountain sleeping bag, a specialized item containing down and feathers, was lauded by all who used it, and the wool sleeping bag, actually a blanket sewed in the shape of a bag, was also favorably received. If the wool bag was not available, O'Daniel's testers recommended the heavy and bulky wool comforter for use by service troops or by troops who were completely motorized. The report criticized a washable sheet, intended as a liner for the mountain sleeping bag, on the grounds that it twisted in the bag and caused discomfort. General approval was given to the resin-coated ponchos—rectangular pieces of cloth with a hole in the middle— which had been designed originally to replace the unpopular raincoat. This item also exhibited great versatility as a ground cloth to be wrapped around a sleeping bag, as a cover over a foxhole, or as a shelter half.

Gloves, cotton caps, and suspenders were among other clothing items tested while new types of personal equipment appearing on the beachhead included 100 grenade carriers, 1,258 mountain knives, 1,373 field packs, and 950 waterproof clothing bags. Listed also on discretionary columns of T/E 21, these personal items met with varying responses:

---

[54] (1) Study, Supply of Clothing and Equip to ETO, 1944, prepared for CG ASF by TQMG, 5 Apr 45. ASF OQMG File A45–280, drawer 7. (2) Clothing and Individual Equipment, T/E 21, 15 December 1943, sec. X. (3) See Map 3.
[55] Anzio C&E Rpt.

the 30th Infantry recommended some, others required additional testing, and still others were eliminated as prospective objects of issue. The success of the Anzio test, from the Quartermaster Corps point of view, was implicit in General O'Daniel's recommendation on 9 May 1944 that twenty-four of the thirty-one experimental items should be made authorized articles of issue by the theater commander.

A notable omission from the Anzio tests was the wool field jacket. Inspired by the inadequacy of the wool serge coat, by the recent adoption of a short jacket by the Army Air Forces, and by the attractive and functional features of the British battle jacket, this garment was later known as the ETO or Eisenhower jacket. It was finally standardized by compromise between ETO and OQMG models in April, as the Anzio tests were being made. Nevertheless, some 300,000 jackets of the ETO model had been delivered by British manufacturers by the end of 1943, and the OQMG version had reached an advanced stage of design by February 1944. The absence of the wool jacket (either version) at Anzio tends to confirm an impression that Anzio had been selected deliberately to demonstrate the suitability of the M1943 outfit for mild-temperate as well as cold-temperate climates. The complete M1943 outfit, including either a pile jacket or the wool jacket now under consideration to replace it, was clearly the proper uniform for Fifth Army troops in the more mountainous parts of the combat zone, and the pile jacket was authorized for such terrain by the current T/E 21. Presumably plans were already under way to supply the wool jacket to the Mediterranean theater. In

June Colonel Doriot, one of the major proponents of the layering principle, explained the ETO jacket as a part thereof to Sullivan:

. . . when cold your soldiers would wear the Jacket, Field, M–43, under that, the Jacket, Field, Wool and under that, the sweater, high neck. They would wear the cotton trousers and under them the wool trousers. I think, that should give them good fighting equipment with a lot of flexibility and still the ability to look well if they want to go to the city and wear the jacket, field, wool and the wool trousers as outside garments. That is our proposal, but as you realize, the answers to those cables are made by A. S. F., not by us.[56]

As early as 10 May 1944 Middleswart learned that the wool field jacket would soon replace the serge coat on T/E 21 as a mandatory item. On 31 May 1944 NATOUSA submitted exploratory requisitions for several items, including 700,000 ETO wool jackets. The tentatively favorable reply received ten days later was signed "Marshall." It appeared to be routine, but had actually been co-ordinated between the OQMG, the Requirements Division of ASF, and the Policy Branch of G–4. The conclusion reached was that NATOUSA could be designated as low-mountain or alpine terrain, and as such was entitled to the special combat uniform.[57]

Almost two months (30 April–25 June 1944) elapsed between the completion of the tests and the submission of NATO-

---

[56] (1) Ltr, Doriot to Sullivan, 4 Jun 44. Sullivan Papers. (2) See below, ch. XVI.

[57] (1) Cable WARX 48935, Marshall to Devers, 10 Jun 44. Sullivan Papers. (2) Memo, Reqmts Div ASF (Col Denson) for Policy Br G–4, WDGS, 3 Jun 44, sub: Secret Radio CM–IN–157, Dated 1 Jun 44, with Memo for Record attached. SPRMP 422.3, ASF OQMG File A45–280, drawer 7.

USA's requisitions on NYPE. It had taken three weeks to prepare and submit O'Daniel's final report to Clark and to place an exploratory request on the War Department for a total of twenty-six new items. Considerable paper work still had to be done. Ramsey and Middleswart had to consult the eighty-page pamphlet, entitled Table of Equipment 21, dated 15 December 1943, which gave the authorized allowances for individual clothing and equipment for combat purposes. The job was difficult because, as already noted, by June 1944 NATOUSA was dividing its forces between DRAGOON and Italy. Obviously, there could be no replacement experience rates on any of these new items. Another disturbing and time-consuming factor operating against early deliveries was a revised requisition procedure dated 19 April 1944.[58] In effect, it denied any theater the privilege of requisitioning new items on NYPE until the port authorities received word from the OQMG that stocks existed or would soon be available. When NYPE received this information, the port commander would notify the theater that it was ready to accept formal requisitions. Thus considerable exploration had to be done by many commands before SOS requisitions could even be placed in the proper supply channel.

Apparently NATOUSA's exploratory requests had no effect on the issuance of the revised T/E 21, which was dated 1 June 1944. Contrary to most expectations, the new table did not materially broaden the basis of issue for special winter items. Nevertheless, NATO-USA's demand for items to be used in wet-cold or extreme cold conditions soared from modest requirements for high alpine operations to a whole theater's wants in six months. Meanwhile, the largest customer of all the theaters, ETOUSA, had received copies of the new T/E by the middle of June. In competition with this potential customer, on 25 June 1944 NATOUSA and SOS NATOUSA requisitioned on NYPE twenty-seven articles in quantities ranging from 6,000 pairs of ski goggles and 13,000 parkas to 948,000 M1943 field jackets and 1,687,000 pairs of ski socks. Certain items were requested for every individual in the theater, but in the event that complete deliveries could not be made, a list of priorities was furnished to assure the equitable distribution of warm clothing from the front lines rearward. As the receipt of the new clothing and equipment would result in NATOUSA having on hand, unused, large stocks of limited-standard items, the theater intended that these stocks should be issued to French forces and to Italian cobelligerents.[59]

The job of clothing troops during the summer of 1944 was comparatively simple. In the forward areas they continued to wear the woolen trousers and shirts, changing into herringbone twill fatigue suits when the weather was warm. Khaki cotton garments, traditionally worn in summer, failed to meet

---

[58] WD AGO Ltr, sub: Supply of Newly Standardized Items to Overseas Comds, 19 Apr 44. AG 400 (17 Apr 44) OB–S–SPDDL–M.

[59] (1) Rad F–53022, Devers to AGWAR, 31 May 44 (filed by ASF as Rad CM–In–157, 1 Jun 44). Hist Br OQMG. (2) NATOUSA Requisition J–89, 25 Jun 44. SPRMP 422.3, ASFOQMG File A45–280, drawer 7.

TABLE 3—WINTER UNIFORM AND EQUIPMENT FOR FIFTH ARMY

Item	Quantity
T/E 21 Regular Allowances—All U.S. Troops	
Undershirts and drawers, wool	2 each
Shirt and trousers, wool, OD	2 each
Cap, jacket M1943 with hood and trousers, cotton, OD, M1943[a]	1 each
Sweater, high neck, wool[a]	1 each
Jacket, field, wool, ETO type[a]	1 each
Overcoat, or coat, mackinaw	1 each
Blanket, wool, OD	2 each
Bag, sleeping wool w/case (or 2 extra blankets)[a]	1 each
Shoepacs (for combat elements) with socks, ski and insoles[a]	1 pair
Overshoes, arctic (for service troops)	1 pair
Gloves	Usual T/E allowances
Suits, working, HBT	Usual T/E allowances
Boots or shoes	Usual T/E allowances
Ground Combat and Service Force Combat Troops	
Bags, sleeping, mountain[a]	50,000 (9,000 per division)
Overcoats, parka[a]	75,000 (9,000 per division)
Parka, wet weather[a]	5,921 (5 percent of combat strength)
Trousers, wet weather[a]	5,921 (5 percent of combat strength)
Cap, field pile[a]	11,842 (10 percent of combat strength)
Pads, insulating, sleeping bag[a]	11,842 (10 percent of combat strength)
For Army Stock—Anticipated Mountain Operations	
Tents, mountain, 2-man, complete	9,000 each
Skis, and ski boots	1,150 pairs
Snowshoes, bear paw	1,220 pairs
Axe, ice, mountain	1,150 each

[a]New items of issue.

combat camouflage standards, and appeared only within support commands.[60]

The Second Winter in the Apennines

Determined not to repeat the tribulations of the first winter in Italy, the Fifth Army on the eve of crossing the Tiber looked ahead to the time when the troops would need resupply of their regular winter clothing and additional sets of wet-cold weather clothing. As early as 31 May Ramsey cabled the War Department that the Fifth Army required clothing for 361,500 men by 15 August shipment from NYPE.[61] After 9 June the Fifth Army transferred troops to DRAGOON, and Sullivan reduced his

---

[60] (1) At Anzio, some combat troops wore the herringbone twill suit, but commanders objected to its use because it resembled the green of the German field uniform. Ltr, Ramsey to Littlejohn, 4 Feb 43. Hist Br OQMG. (2) Cir 59, Hq SOS NATOUSA, 25 Apr 44.

[61] Memo cited n. 57 (2).

call for clothing to that required for 175,000 U.S. troops. *(Table 3)* [62]

Throughout the summer as Fifth Army swept north to the Arno, Sullivan made repeated representations to support commands for the early delivery of winter clothing and equipment.[63] Reports from the War Department indicated that the supply of some items would be fraught with difficulties. Sullivan replied to each message, pointing out that time was slipping by. On 4 August Florence fell, and Fifth Army made a secret lateral movement eastward toward the Florence-Bologna line of advance. Behind Fifth Army, Leghorn and the line of communications to Florence still had to be developed. The Italian summer would soon end, and by 1 October troops would change into their winter woolens. With each passing day the language of Sullivan's messages became stronger. The first week of September passed, and, with the deadline of the 15th distinctly in mind, Clark asked Peninsular Base Section about the status of Fifth Army's quartermaster requisitions. ". . . In view of lateness of new type items advise availability in PBS stocks, trousers, combat, jackets, combat, and other cold weather clothing as possible substitutes." [64] At the same time, Sullivan told Tate that Fifth Army's stocks of winter clothing had been depleted except for 7,707 combat

jackets and 2,060 combat trousers. No one knew the exact contents of each division's reserve. With the demands of four infantry divisions and one armored division in mind, Clark asked SOS NATOUSA to keep Sullivan constantly advised as to the receipt of the various clothing items so that arrangements could be made for prompt distribution. On 9 September Middleswart presented Sullivan with a detailed account of the status of each item and when convoys could be expected at Naples. The latter were due before the end of September. Meanwhile, SOS NATOUSA alerted base sections to a critical shortage of blankets in the event that sleeping bags arrived late, and prepared to recall all surplus blankets from service troops, rest camps, staging areas, hospitals, and unit storerooms. Simultaneously, Tate queried Sullivan: "Will the delivery dates sufficiently differ from those requested . . . to indicate a letter of protest through channels?" [65]

Early in October stocks of clothing and equipment at Naples, Leghorn, and Florence rose sharply, thus relieving the anxieties of September. These shipments reached the troops none too soon. While Fifth Army was driving toward Bologna the rains never seemed to stop falling. Roads were impassable and supply areas lay in seas of mud. At the front blankets and woolen underwear were among the first winter items to arrive. By mid-October almost enough M1943 sateen jackets, high-neck sweaters,

[62] 2d Wrapper Ind, Hq Fifth Army to Hq Allied Armies in Italy, 27 Aug 44. AG 475-Q. Sullivan Papers.

[63] (1) Rad F-66784, Devers to AGWAR, 2 Jul 44. Fifth Army, AG 420. (2) Msg. Clark to Devers, 20 Jul 44. Sullivan Papers.

[64] (1) Indorsement cited n. 62. (2) Memo, Sullivan for Middleswart, 5 Aug 44. Sullivan Papers. (3) Quoted from Msg 2922, Clark to CG PBS, 4 Sep 44. Sullivan Papers.

[65] Memo, Sullivan for Tate, 16 Sep 44, sub: Status of Requisitions and Shipments of Winter Clothing; Msg, Clark to Larkin, 16 Sep 44; Msgs, CG Fifth Army to CG PBS, 20 and 27 Sep 44; quotation is from 2d Ind, G-4 Rear to QM Fifth Army, 16 Sep 44, sub: Woolen Clothing for Winter Wear. All in Sullivan Papers.

TABLE 4—FIFTH ARMY ISSUES OF WINTER CLOTHING

Division	October 1944 Strength	Item					
		Field Jackets M1943	Wool Sweaters	Shoe-pacs (pairs)	Sleep-ing Bags w/case	Wool Undershirts	Wool Drawers
Totals.....	74,765	74,496	74,333	55,900	51,842	139,904	127,966
34th Infantry...	15,713	12,423	15,286	10,202	10,400	30,108	30,926
85th Infantry...	15,724	15,920	15,000	11,333	10,000	29,326	19,426
88th Infantry...	16,132	16,211	14,763	12,866	10,000	29,100	29,100
91st Infantry...	15,281	17,542	17,542	11,635	10,004	28,840	26,440
1st Armored....	11,915	12,400	11,742	9,864	11,438	22,530	22,074

and shoepacs arrived to outfit every soldier on the line. *(Table 4)* [66]

Journals maintained by divisional quartermaster companies indicated that the new supplies were issued as fast as they were brought forward by army.[67] Shortages of sleeping bags, small-sized shoepacs, and woolen trousers were eased. As Sullivan watched his stock charts move upward, he suddenly learned that two U.S. divisions would pull out of the line, that they would go into tents, and that no offensive would begin until April 1945. This meant that many of the conditions which had existed along the Gustav Line, such as the retention of combat troops in the line for abnormally long periods of time, would not

occur along the Gothic Line. Yet quartermasters would still have the mission of providing additional protection for troops in a few exposed positions. During November 1944 each committed unit gradually received a special allocation of heavy cold weather clothing which had been requisitioned early in August. This allocation included 280 pairs of goggles, 920 sets of wet weather parkas and trousers, 3,200 pile caps, 3,700 mountain sleeping bags, and 10,000 pairs of shell mittens with inserts for each division. Currently employed as infantry on the western flank of the Allied line, where combat after 2 November 1944 was limited but vigorous, several antiaircraft artillery battalions received proportional quantities of special winter equipment.

Because of scheduling and production difficulties in the United States, the delivery of wool field jackets, 700,000 of which had been requisitioned in June 1944, lagged. Early in November 1944 initial issues began to arrive, but Peninsular Base Section froze all stocks until wider distribution was possible. In the interim, SOS NATOUSA authorized the distribution of such pile jackets as were available to provide troops with another

---

[66] Memo and Incl, Sullivan for Clark, 7 Oct 44; Memo, Sullivan for Tate, 15 Oct 44, sub: Status of Winter Clothing Issues. Both in Sullivan Papers.

[67] (1) Memos, G–4 Rear for G–4 Fifth Army, 27 Sep, 11 Oct 44, sub: Winter and Cold Climate Clothing and Equip; Memo, G–4 Rear for QM Fifth Army, 7 Nov 44, sub: Special Cold Climate Clothing and Equip. Both in Sullivan Papers. (2) Ltr, CG 45th AAA Brig to CG Fifth Army, 17 Nov 44, sub: Special Winter Clothing; Ltr and Ind, CG Task Force 45 to CG Fifth Army, 29 Dec 44, sub: Special Winter Clothing. Both in IV Corps, AG 400. (3) Monthly Journals, 34th Div QM and 88th Div QM Co, Sep–Nov 44. Unit Hist Files, Hist Br OQMG.

layer of clothing between the sweater and the M1943 jacket. By January 1945 the ETO type of wool field jacket, originally recommended in June 1944 as one of the layered items, appeared in the field. A prestige item, suitable for dress as well as combat, it was issued on a priority basis. Approximately 5,000 jackets were given to each division during the winter months as supply permitted.[68]

The Fifth Army had hardly issued the new items of winter clothing before adverse comment was heard about their suitability for the alpine climate. The M1943 jacket, the shoepac, and the sleeping bag bore the brunt of the criticism. On 3 November 1944, the Italian edition of *Stars and Stripes,* which served as a sounding board for troops, carried the headline: "New Army Issue Doesn't Meet Battle Test." In contrast, the news release praised the high-neck sweater, saying that everyone from colonel to private liked his.[69] Most wearers of the M1943 sateen jacket echoed the sentiments heard at the Anzio test. They praised the jacket's large pockets, but there was evidence that the cotton sateen did not adequately resist rain and became heavy when wet. In mid-October 1944, a survey of men being evacuated through divisional clearing stations revealed dissatisfaction with the shoepac. It was too wide, and was especially uncomfortable in muddy

soil, permitting the foot to slip easily inside the rubber shoe until the skin was raw and blistered. The sleeping bag was also criticized; because the front-line soldier could seldom remove his shoes, the bag quickly became mud-soaked in wet weather. An even more serious disadvantage, from the infantryman's point of view, was the temporary helplessness of a heavy or broad-shouldered man who had to wriggle out of the tightly zippered bag if awakened by a night alarm.

Reflecting a marked sensitivity to such censure, inspectors at division and army level inaugurated their own surveys, but these only confirmed the authenticity of the adverse reports. The II Corps commander declared that one sleeping bag plus two blankets did not offer as much protection as four blankets; the latter issue, he added, made it possible for two men sleeping together in a pup tent to share eight blankets. Fifth Army therefore revised the basis of distribution for sleeping bags, issuing them to all except troops in the front lines, who slept with their boots on.

By the end of November 1944, the problem of the oversized shoepac was partially solved by redistribution so as to provide each man with shoepacs of the same size as his combat boots, and by increasing the allowance of ski socks and felt inner soles, which provided much better insulation and absorbed perspiration. Still it was found that the lack of arch support in the shoepac produced sore feet among infantrymen who trudged along in springy rubber soles on lengthy marches. Mud also stuck to the rubber cleats on the soles, adding excessive weight. In contrast, the shoepac was praised by artillerymen and others

---

[68] (1) Journals cited n. 67 (3). (2) Msg, CG Fifth Army to CG PBS, 29 Oct 44; Requisition 5A QM–199–44–X–1, Sullivan to Bare, 29 Oct 44; Inds, Bare to Ramsey, 29 Oct 44; Ltr, McNarney to Truscott, 24 Dec 44, sub: Issue of Jackets, Field, Pile. All in Sullivan Papers.

[69] Memo, Capt E. C. Beyer for Surgeon Fifth Army, 11 Oct 44. Sullivan Papers.

in rear areas, where less walking was required.[70]

Near the end of the war, one new QM item—a Doron type, lightweight steel vest—captured the soldier's imagination. It was not available for army-wide issue, but the word spread from the few who chanced to test it that they would never be without their bulletproof vest, if only for its psychological effect, in time of action.[71]

Closely related to the supply of adequate wet-cold weather clothing was the need for portable shelters and heating stoves. When the first wintry blasts were felt in November 1943 the Fifth Army made repeated calls for storage tents to replace the inadequate covering over field kitchens, for tents where men coming off extra duty could warm and dry themselves and change clothes, and for extra shelter halves to be used as ground sheets. As the weather worsened and shelter halves became scarce, the Fifth Army asked SOS NATOUSA for the recently standardized mountain tent, a two-man unit with a cloth floor and a white reversible lining for snow camouflage.[72]

During the second winter the supply of tentage in Fifth Army threatened to be inadequate because part of SOS NATOUSA's stocks had been contributed to DRAGOON troops and because the Fifth Army was obliged to compete with ETOUSA demands at NYPE. Furthermore, the Fifth Army seemingly was unable to convince support commands that its consumption of tentage exceeded War Department maintenance factors owing to adverse tactical and climatic conditions. In mountain operations the constant relocation of troops was particularly hard on tentage. In heavy winds and damp air frequent pitching and striking of canvas, even when handled by a veteran, weakened the tent's fabric. Depletion from this cause was aggravated by the heavy losses at Anzio where hundreds of tents were steadily subjected to shellfire and bomb fragments for almost four months.

By issuing a single tent to a larger group of men—in the case of pyramidal tents the basis of issue was changed from 1 for 6 men to 1 for 8 men—and by a notable improvement in SOS NATOUSA and Fifth Army salvage procedures, enough additional tents were made available to avoid an acute shortage. Another help was the stabilized tactical situation in the northern Apennines that permitted a large-scale winterization of living quarters. Buildings were used wherever possible; combat troops trans-

---

[70] (1) Memo, IG Fifth Army for CofS Fifth Army, 7 Nov 44; Memo, IG Fifth Army for IG 1st Armd Div, 11 Nov 44; Ltr, IG 34th Inf Div to IG Fifth Army, 18 Nov 44, sub: Shoepacs and Combat Jackets; Ltr, IG IV Army Corps to IG Fifth Army, 22 Nov 44, sub: Complaints Relative to the New Shoepac and Field Jacket; Ltr, IG 88th Inf Div to IG Fifth Army, 26 Nov 44, sub: Special Winter Clothing and Equip; Memo, IG for CofS Fifth Army, 28 Nov 44; Ltr, Asst IG MTOUSA to IG MTOUSA, 1 Dec 44, sub: Check Made on New Type Field Clothing; Msg 72493, CG Fifth Army to CG PBS, 22 Dec 44; Msg 9287, CG Fifth Army to CG MTOUSA, 25 Jan 45. All in AG 420, Misc MTOUSA. (2) Ltr, CG II Corps to CG Fifth Army, 24 Nov 44, sub: Additional Blankets for Pers. Fifth Army, AG 427.

[71] Ltrs, Bates to Doriot, 1 Apr, 15 Apr, 3 May 45; Ltrs, Doriot to Bates, 21 Apr, 7 May 45. Both in OQMG MTO 319.25.

[72] Ltr and Inds, Clark to Larkin, 15 Oct 43, sub: Storage Tents for Kitchens During Winter Opns; Ltr, CG VI Corps to CG Fifth Army, 18 Oct 43, sub: Tentage; Msg [no number], CG Fifth Army to CG NATOUSA, 26 Nov 43; Msg 8607, Clark to Larkin, 8 Jan 44. All in Fifth Army, AG 420.

formed foxholes into reasonably comfortable accommodations; reserves lived in pyramidal tents; and hospital corpsmen provided their field evacuation tents with floors and sidewalls. In some places the engineers were able to replace tents with Nissen huts or prefabricated structures.[73]

Neither tentage nor improvised billets could alone provide protection from the elements in the northern Apennines, where, from December to March, temperatures dropped below freezing ten to fifteen days each month. Many stoves were needed. The Quartermaster responsibility for space heating was restricted to tents.[74] To install stoves in field hospitals, which always had first priority on space heaters, in command posts, in shelters where troops dried themselves and changed clothes, in administrative offices or workshops of maintenance units, and in the quarters of nurses and Wacs, the Fifth Army calculated in the early fall of 1944 that more than 14,000 tent-type heating stoves would be required. To this estimate SOS NATOUSA offered no encouragement. Middleswart wrote to Sullivan that "Additional troops . . . being dumped in our laps total considerably more than the total number in Fifth Army, so if you do not get all of the things to which you feel you are entitled, you can readily understand." [75]

On 18 October 1944 Sullivan adjusted his basis of issue, reducing it to 12,500 stoves. Notwithstanding this concession and having received less than 8,000 stoves by then, the Fifth Army on 19 October sent a blunt note to Headquarters, NATOUSA:

This headquarters cannot relax its efforts to obtain the stoves . . . as it is our firm conviction that the efforts of all the supply echelons to provide our men with warm winter clothing will go for naught unless facilities are provided to dry this clothing and give combat troops the opportunity to warm themselves. . . .[76]

Over the next few weeks the Fifth Army received almost 3,000 more stoves from its Neapolitan and Leghorn bases, and Sullivan made arrangements to secure an additional 4,000 from Italian factories around Florence and Pistoia. By 20 November 1944 local stoves were being delivered, and Fifth Army, now more confident that its requirements would be met, indulged in the rare practice of voluntarily canceling about two-thirds of its stove requisitions at SOS NATOUSA.[77]

While the new clothing and equipment of the December 1943 and June 1944 T/E 21 were imperfect in some respects, and standard items could not always be delivered when and where they were needed, troops in the northern Apennines were undoubtedly better clothed and equipped than those who had fought in the valleys and mountains beside the Volturno and Garigliano Rivers in the winter of 1943–44. With

---

[73] (1) Rads L–46098, L–50002, CG COMZ NATOUSA to CG Fifth Army, 8 Oct, 30 Oct 44. Sullivan Papers. (2) Memo, CofS Fifth Army for CG COMZ NATOUSA, 1 Nov 44. Fifth Army, AG 424. (3) *Fifth Army History*, VIII, 24–25. (4) Sullivan MS, p. 141.
[74] Cir 49, Hq SOS NATOUSA, 9 Oct 43.
[75] Msg, Clark to Pence, 17 Sep 44; quoted from Ltr, QM COMZ NATOUSA to QM Fifth Army, 3 Oct 44. Both in Sullivan Papers.

[76] Msg 6369, Clark to Devers, 19 Oct 44. Sullivan Papers.
[77] Msgs 1701 and 3526, G–4 Fifth Army to CG MTOUSA, 7 Nov, 20 Nov 44. Sullivan Papers.

staged supply working to perfection out of Naples and Leghorn, the Fifth Army's complaints subsided, replacement rates dropped, quality improved, and trench foot casualties dropped 70 percent. Such statistics were all the more impressive in view of the fact that the weather was severer during the winter of 1944–45 than in the previous one and that the number of combat troops in the Fifth Army in 1944–45 was greater by more than one division than in 1943-44.

The effect on Mediterranean Quartermaster supply of the loss of three veteran U.S. divisions to Seventh Army in France and the gain of three uninitiated divisions, arriving with new equipment, is not known. But certainly tactical factors—in contrast to those in northwestern Europe at the time—were influential in Sullivan's improved supply situation. The M1943 items had just been issued when the Fifth Army pulled most of its strength from the line. The stabilized front from 2 November 1944 to 1 April 1945 permitted troops to dig in and construct crude but comfortable quarters from empty shell cases, food containers, and scrap materials. Rest hotels opened in Florence and Montecatini. With regrouping going on after 2 November 1944, troops rotated in and out of static front lines to reserve areas where they could obtain better food, baths, and clean clothes.[78]

Outfitting the DRAGOON Forces

As already noted, the three U.S. divisions that landed in southern France were all carefully re-equipped at Naples

before embarking, and the Seventh Army quartermaster had provided a clothing reserve for each unit. As the divisions advanced inland, they continued to send their own organic trucks back to the beaches for rations, POL, and ammunition, but clothing and equipment were not needed in significant quantities, and are not even mentioned in unit reports. Class II and IV supplies therefore piled up at the beaches and in Marseille. By 18 September 3,198 tons had been received, and only 387 tons issued, including 121 tons to base troops. But by this time the rapid advance had carried the combat units into an entirely different climatic zone, nearly 400 miles from the coast. During the next week, 1,065 tons of Class II and IV supplies were issued from continental base section dumps. The most critical items, blankets and overcoats, were shipped by air, and by 26 September Seventh Army's initial requirements had been filled.[79]

French units in southern France did not fare so well. Since some embarked from North Africa and others from British-administered ports in southern Italy, there were difficulties in inspecting the units before embarkation, and some sailed with incomplete equipment. Difficulties in co-ordination between U.S. agencies and French Base 901, which was theoretically responsible for supply of French units, have already been mentioned. The system whereby Seventh Army supplied 1st French Army was not very efficient, and became even less so after CONAD, an additional link in

[78] (1) QM Fifth Army, pp. 82-83. (2) Fifth Army History, VIII, 23–25, 42–45, 48.

[79] (1) See p. 120, above. (2) CONAD History, I, 60; II, 520. (3) Unit histories, 3d, 36th QM Companies. Hist Br OQMG.

the chain of supply, was established on 1 October. The deteriorating situation was given dramatic emphasis when, at about the same time, General de Lattre de Tassigny announced that unless wool clothing could be provided immediately for his troops he would be forced to withdraw them from combat.[80] Investigation revealed that at least part of the trouble could be traced to the inexperience and dilatory operating methods of French Base 901. Although seriously understrength, that organization had been forced to split its staff between Marseille and Dijon. On 12 September Brig. Gen. Georges Granier became its new commander, and he arrived at Dijon four days later. During the following week Granier, General Wilson of CONAD, and General de Lattre de Tassigny reached an agreement. Granier would become Wilson's deputy, and the two supply organizations would be completely integrated, except for Base 901's special responsibilities to the French Forces of the Interior and its local procurement functions. The new combined headquarters, still known as CONAD, would support Seventh Army and 1st French Army directly, on an equal basis. Actual issues of clothing and equipment by CONAD during the period 2 October–31 December 1944 demonstrate that the Americans more than lived up to their agreement. A total of 6,144.3 long tons of QM Class II and IV supplies were issued to a force which

grew quickly from 350,000 men in October to 618,775 men at the end of the year. The breakdown of issues was as follows: to Seventh Army, 1,263.3; to base troops, 1,775.8; to 1st French Army, 2,900.4; to air forces (U.S. and French), 205.8.[81] Thus it can be seen that 1st French Army received more than twice as much clothing and equipment as Seventh Army. Moreover, about 11 percent of base troops were French, and an undetermined proportion of German prisoners and Italian service personnel, also included among base troops, were supporting the French military effort. In addition to making good the shortages in initial equipment of their units, these heavy requirements undoubtedly reflect the unofficial support the French were providing to volunteer units with their army.[82]

Local Procurement

Along the shores of the Mediterranean, support and combat quartermasters alike had to dismiss thoughts of setting up an elaborate and centralized purchasing system for Class II and IV items. Many complications were involved in this method of supply. Since industrial facilities, skilled technicians, and basic raw materials were scarce, if available at all, quartermasters made no concerted effort to procure locally such end items as trousers, shoes, towels, and jerricans. When facilities were intact, labor was often lacking; when labor was available, raw materials might be unob-

---

[80] (1) Littlejohn, ed., Passing in Review, ch. 43, "Quartermaster Operations in CONAD." (2) Dr. Marcel Vigneras, an authority on supply to the French, has never heard of this episode. He suggests that de Lattre was referring to his French Forces of the Interior units, which were not officially entitled to U.S. support. Interv, Ross with Vigneras, 20 Aug 58.

[81] (1) CONAD History, I, 82–83; II, 534–631. (2) Vigneras, *Rearming the French*, pp. 187–88. (3) Official Diary for CG Seventh Army, vol. II, 15 Aug 44 to 31 Jan 45, entry for 1 Oct 44. OCMH.

[82] See above, ch. IV.

tainable. Thus, soapmakers in Casablanca had peanut oil and wood ash, but caustic soda had to be imported before quartermasters could obtain a suitable cleansing agent. Seamstresses in Bizerte made nurses' undergarments from linen fabric, but nurses preferred silk underwear.

A factory in Tunis was capable of manufacturing bungs for 55-gallon drums, but the company needed scrap aluminum that lay miles away in a salvage yard.[83] The local purchase of office furniture for Headquarters, AFHQ, was a constant source of worry to its quartermaster purchasing and contracting officer. In Algiers, special missions, planning groups, and staff sections were constantly being organized and reorganized, and the prompt delivery of furniture and office equipment was ordered rather than requested. The purchasing officer described his difficulties this way: [84]

Supply of many raw materials has been extremely limited and it has usually been necessary to obtain these . . . with necessary releases from agencies of the French Civil Government for the manufacturers. For instance, before letting a contract for manufacture of a few items of furniture it has been found necessary to locate a manufacturer to fabricate required articles, determine kind and amount of material necessary, locate the supply of lumber, glue, nails, finishing materials, arrange release of each of these materials from individual Control Boards, provide transportation for these materials, and provide transportation for the finished products.

Suggesting that this was more typical than exceptional, the officer estimated that each of the 1,334 vouchers he had handled to date, covering the purchase of 2,000 different items and services, required an average of at least ten personal contacts.

After the invasion of Sicily, quartermasters had an added incentive to live off the shores and islands of the western Mediterranean. Strategically, their war no longer enjoyed a favorable supply priority. Quartermasters assembling at Naples in late 1943 understood this situation and more and more officers became conversant with local procurement matters. Quartermasters found that Italy was a better source for Class II and IV items than North Africa and Sicily. Naples ultimately restored fifty factories as a basis of local procurement, but only after early difficulties were resolved.

Early contact with manufacturers was essential to ameliorate such conditions. But this was difficult for purchasing agents who did not speak the language or understand Italian business methods. Interpreters with an appreciation of the urgency and size of a military purchase were hard to find. Asked to assist in locating someone to make 50,000 Fifth Army insignia, one interpreter escorted a purchasing agent into the back alleys of Naples in his search for the homes of seamstresses and the shops of tailors. Such shops, the contractor found, could each produce only ten to thirty shoulder patches in a day. At this rate delivery would be completed in three months. Fortunately, the quartermaster with this mission found a Caserta manufacturer who could make 50,000 insignia in a week. By July 1945 this company had turned out five million shoulder patches.[85]

[83] (1) Hist QM ABS, p. 20. (2) Hist Rpts, OQM EBS, Mar–May 44. AG 314.7, Mil Hist EBS–MTO.

[84] Memo, P&C Off Hq Comd AFHQ for Maj Murdock, 1st Gen Depot, 21 May 43. AG 400.12 NASC, 1943–45.

[85] Hist QM PBS, p. 219.

A war of attrition produces a change in the attitude of a spigot quartermaster, who much prefers the routine of staged supply. While at Caserta—twenty-five miles away from Naples by the daily train—Sullivan encouraged his staff and divisional quartermasters to turn the modest resources of the countryside to their use. Graves registration officers especially, Sullivan believed, would benefit thereby, chiefly on the grounds that the added task of purchasing goods locally would prove a welcome diversion from the duties normally performed by these officers. The plan took root and more and more divisional rosters listed "purchasing and contracting officer" beside the name of the graves registration officer. As they moved around the countryside, these men under two hats cheerfully reported what items could be locally procured.

When Fifth Army was deadlocked south of Cassino and the mountains resisted even the versatile jeep, Sullivan sought packboards which would enable the soldier to carry ammunition, water, rations, and medical supplies on his back. Although the army quartermaster's office recruited local manufacturers who during the campaign produced 45,000 packboards, the Italians first had to be supplied with canvas and wood and taught assembly line production methods. Just as caustic soda had to be imported for Casablanca soapmakers, a large Florentine cleansing agent manufacturer could not resume soap production until Sullivan supplied fats and greases from the Fifth Army's company kitchens. Similarily, Sullivan needed 100,000 pieces of tableware for rest camps, but the contract went unfilled until he sent several hundred tons of

coal to the Sesto kilns to fire the porcelain.

By Salerno's first anniversary, factories in Naples and Rome had been turned to full account in providing quartermaster goods and services. Each week a foundry in Naples produced 14,000 bungs for 55-gallon drums, a hosiery mill manufactured 150,000 shoulder patches and overseas stripes, and a glass works turned out 75,000 drinking tumblers. In Rome, where there were no major depots, quartermasters emphasized services to the troops, operating laundries, dry cleaning plants, and shoe, typewriter, clothing, and tentage repair shops.[86]

Around Leghorn and Florence various manufacturing facilities were converted to military uses and procurement opportunities were fully exploited. A few of the items obtained were hospital bed trays, mattresses, cotton thread, inner soles for shoepacs, coat hangers, military decorations, sleds, skis, and snowshoes. One stove factory turned out heating units for pyramidal tents and mess gear refinished in nickel plate. A woodworking shop replaced broken shovel handles; a steam pressing plant in Florence, supervised by an American corporal, employed more than forty women to press and patch 4,000 shirts and trousers daily. A Florentine industrialist developed a reputation for versatility and adaptability to mass production techniques by making 10,000 ice creepers for a mountain division, 45,000 cigarette lighters out of empty shell cases, 8,000 stoves, and 50,000 stovepipes. When this same manufacturer could not produce convoy flags or boxing togs, his

---

[86] Memo, QM for G-4 PBS, 11 Sep 44, sub: Compilation of Data for G-4 Rpt to War Dept. G-4 MTOUSA, 319.1.

sister, who was better known in the community as a corsetière, filled the order in record time.[87]

For a variety of reasons, local procurement of clothing and equipment for U.S. units in southern France was very nearly nil. First of all, the area had been thoroughly exploited by the Germans and was so short of clothing that AFHQ planning for the ANVIL operation had included 300,000 blankets and 350,000 sets of Red Cross relief clothing for civilian use. Clearly, any far-reaching local procurement program would have to await the arrival of imported raw materials and the rehabilitation of mines and factories. Steps were taken as quickly as possible, but before concrete results were achieved the area had come under the jurisdiction of ETOUSA, whose local procurement activities are described below. A second major consideration was the priority claimed by the French armed forces within their own territory. Supplies actually on hand were requisitioned by the volunteers who joined First French Army immediately after the landing, and proved to be quite inadequate even for these units. Moreover, such productive capacity as existed was earmarked to support the activation of additional French units, an overly ambitious program undertaken for reasons of prestige despite the opposition of SHAEF. In any event, French production never reached expectations, and while a considerable number of replace-

ments for French units and a few new units were recruited in metropolitan France, virtually all their clothing and equipment had to be provided from other Allied sources.[88]

Clothing and Equipment for Allies and POW's

The same groups drawing rations from the Americans looked to them for a certain amount of clothing and equipment. Plans to rearm and supply Allied forces were on the agenda of the Casablanca Conference in January 1943, when the decision was made to equip eleven French divisions. Subsequent conferences throughout the year confirmed the general agreement. It was understood that initial supplies for all such forces would be shipped from the United States and specifically earmarked for delivery to Allied groups. Since the French forces, to be followed by the Brazilian and Italian, were organized in conformity with American T/O&E's, it would be feasible to provide various items of supply on the same basis and from the same supply points as those for American forces. As much as possible, AFHQ hoped that the duplication of supply channels would be obviated.[89]

Theoretically, this system left Ramsey and Middleswart responsible only for providing American clothing and equipment on a replacement basis, but when the special stocks from the United States were delayed these forces had to be

---

[87] (1) "Italian Factories Serve Fifth Army," *QMTSJ* (30 March 1945), p. 8; "Fifth Army QM's Reopen Italian Soap Plant," *QMTSJ* (4 May 1945), p. 28. (2) Hist QM ABS, p. 20. (3) Memo, Depot QM for G–4 Fifth Army, 14 Mar 45, sub: Rpt on Ginori Situation. Sullivan Papers. (4) Sullivan MS, pp. 157–58.

[88] (1) See below, ch. XVII. (2) Vigneras, *Rearming the French*, pp. 335–38, 347–50. (3) Komer, Civil Affairs, ch. XXI.

[89] (1) Vigneras, *Rearming the French*, ch. II. (2) Hist of Plng Div ASF, vol. II, pt. IV, pp. 227ff. OCMH. (3) *Logistical History of NATOUSA–MTOUSA*, pp. 366–67, 374–75.

equipped with supplies from available reserves. In the summer of 1944 the Brazilians, for example, had to be provided with field ranges, spare parts, one-burner stoves, service caps, helmets and leggings, ammunition bags, and mattress covers.[90] Because of too little demonstration in the use of quartermaster items some misuse and mishandling resulted. Instruction sheets, printed in English, meant nothing to Brazilian supply personnel. The Brazilian uniform had not been designed for the cold weather frequently encountered in northern Italy and did not include items comparable to the American wool knit caps, gloves, and sweaters. The soldier's needs increased still more when woolen underwear and socks proved inferior and had to be replaced by American garments. Later, combat suits and kersey-lined trousers were supplied as organizational equipment, making it possible for the Brazilian commander to transfer these items as needed. By mid-February 1945 there was no longer any doubt that the Brazilians could scarcely meet their minimum needs. American quartermasters in consequence undertook to supply them with almost everything a soldier wore beneath and outside of his shirt and trousers.[91]

Soon after Italy's surrender in September 1943, SOS NATOUSA prepared elaborate tables authorizing the complete supply of Italian service units with all their personal and organizational equipment, and an attempt was made to use whatever distinctive clothing was found in Italian depots. So long as the latter was available, American quartermasters provided only the items needed for specific work.[92] Shortages included pyramidal and individual tents, woolen gloves, wool knit caps, raincoats, and overshoes. Since Italian hobnailed footwear was a fire hazard around POL dumps, the Quartermaster Corps furnished smooth-soled American shoes to men working at such installations. Unfortunately for the Italian soldiers, the clothing which was inadequate for the wet weather was too warm in summer. Relief was nowhere in sight, for the Italians were unable to provide a lighter substitute and the American supply of cotton khaki did not permit the diversion of any part of it to cobelligerent forces.[93]

Determined that assistance to the Italians should not add to the burden of imports into the theater, American quartermasters gave them mostly second-

[90] (1) Supply Memo 54, Hq PBS, 26 Jul 44, sub: Supply of Brazilian Units; Ltr, Lt Col John R. Currey to G–3 Sec Fifth Army, 21 Aug 44, sub: Inspection—Combat Team BEF. Sullivan Papers. (2) Logistical History of NATOUSA–MTOUSA, p. 374. (3) Rpt, 1st Inf Div BEF, 16 Jul 44–May 45. OCMH.

[91] (1) Msg 4319, MTOUSA to CG Fifth Army, 3 Dec 44; Ltr, CG Fifth Army to CG 1st BID, 11 Jan 45. Both in Fifth Army, AG 420. (2) Memo, CG 1st BID for CG Fifth Army, 24 Dec 44. IV Corps, AG 400. (3) Ltr, Maj G. H. Munn to CG USAFSA, 27 Feb 45, no sub. Fifth Army, AG 319.1. (4) Ltr, CQM MTOUSA to QM PBS, 18 Feb 45, sub: U.S. Individual C&E for Brazilian Repls. Sullivan Papers.

[92] (1) T/E, Italian Units, Hq SOS NATOUSA, 19 Oct 43. OQMG MED 319.25. (2) Ltr, Deputy CofS NATOUSA to CG Fifth Army, 31 Jul 44, sub: Supply of Italian Armed Forces; Admin Instr 9, Army Sub-Comm (MMIA), 12 Aug 44, sub: Supply of Italian Army. Sullivan Papers.

[93] (1) Ltr, CO 337th Engr GS Rgt to Clark, 17 Mar 44, sub: Request for Tentage for Italian Troops. Fifth Army, AG 424. (2) Ltr, ExO 204th QM Bn (M) to Sullivan, 6 Aug 44, sub: Issue of Shoes for Italian Soldiers; Ltr, CO 1108th Engr Combat Group to CG Fifth Army, 10 Jan 45, sub: Clothing for Italian Unit; Ltr, CO 6th Mil Guards Regt to Hq 210th Inf [Italian] Div, 16 Jan 45, sub: Status of 512th Guards Bn. All in Sullivan Papers.

hand items unsuitable for further use by U.S. troops or beyond the facilities of the salvage repair program. Dyed spruce green and stripped of distinctive buttons and rank and organizational insignia, such clothing was delivered to the repair installations of the Italian Army and put into the flow of Italian supply.

To a lesser extent quartermasters furnished clothing to Italian civilians who worked for the Americans.[94] Just as noon meals or extra ration allowances served as incentives for recruiting native civilians in North Africa and Italy, so did blue denim suits, black wool shirts and trousers, and Class C shoes add to the attractiveness of the jobs offered. Early in TORCH planning, the Americans had foreseen the need for local labor. Thus quartermasters brought with them cotton goods to be used in partial payment for such services. As stocks of used clothing accumulated, their judicious distribution in areas where consumer goods were at a premium was actually an act of economy and enlightened self-interest.

In southern France, as already noted, some 225,000 troops of First French Army were included in the approved troop basis, and were clothed and equipped by American quartermasters. Members of the French Forces of the Interior in the DRAGOON area and young volunteers who joined the French units numbered over 100,000 more, but without proper authority it was impossible to provide them with supplies of any kind. Generals Devers and de Lattre urged that

60,000 be added to the troop basis, but SHAEF demurred. The Frenchmen all wanted to fight, but the current need was for service troops. At the end of September, the Americans provided combat equipment for 12,000 recruits, but there was no corresponding concession from the French. The distaste of their men for duty with service units was genuine, and was reinforced by the conviction that only a large French fighting force, engaged in actual combat against the Germans, could restore the damaged prestige of France. Since these troops were not being used in accordance with the wishes of SHAEF headquarters, any support they received had to come from the meager resources of liberated France. Their status was rather similar to that of the "ITI-ITI's" already described.

Because of the shortage of French labor, the Americans enlarged their original plans to use Italian units in southern France, ultimately bringing in about 28,000 who were also employed in the north. The ISU personnel required additional clothing in the severe winters of central and eastern France. Another source of labor was German prisoners, most of whom needed to be completely re-equipped before they could be put to work. The CONAD labor force at the end of 1944 was composed of the following: [95]

U.S. service units	32,194
French service units	7,003
Italian service units	10,350
POW's	8,350
Civilian employees	3,162

Securing clothing and equipment for

---

[94] Ltr, Actg AG AFHQ to All Concerned, 22 Sep 44, sub: Supply of Italian Armed Forces. QM 400.3295, NASC.

[95] CONAD History II, 623.

non-American personnel was an extremely difficult problem, and no completely satisfactory solution was ever found. The little that actually became available for this purpose was principally captured enemy material, and is discussed in Chapter XX, below.

Combat experience with clothing and equipment in the Mediterranean theater antedated similar experience in western Europe by nearly two years, and undoubtedly influenced plans and procedures in the latter area. But the lessons of Mediterranean experience were complicated and unclear, and were subject to differing interpretations, as exemplified by the Sullivan-Middleswart controversy and by later differences of opinion between the OQMG and the Office of the Chief Quartermaster, ETO. These disagreements involved replacement rates as well as basic clothing design, but the latter subject of debate always tended to be the major area of conflict. Probably the explanation is that a uniform is an extremely personal category of equipment. Under conditions of tension, an individual tends to become convinced that a particular uniform either reduces or aggravates the inevitable bodily discomforts of combat, and he often favors what he knows best.

Conversely, he may have preconceived prejudices against familiar items, and accept makeshift substitutes too readily. Time and experience are the only reliable antidotes for such errors, and unfortunately there was never enough time for deliberate, thorough testing in the Mediterranean theater. In this connection, it should be noted that the M1943 uniform was *not* based on Mediterranean experience, but upon an appraisal of Mediterranean requirements formulated in the zone of interior. This was normal and even desirable. Most combat zone innovations are stopgaps and minor modifications. Really new ideas usually originate at research centers, and not in the heat of battle. But once conceived, a promising new concept deserves development, and especially combat-testing, as speedily as possible. To miss the opportunity for such a test through procrastination, excessively elaborate staff co-ordination, or niggling perfectionism is an irretrievable blunder. For Class II and IV specialists, the main lesson to be derived from Mediterranean warfare is that an overseas theater of modest size represents an invaluable testing laboratory, to be exploited quickly before the opportunity disappears.

CHAPTER VIII

Essential Services to the Line

In addition to provisioning and equipping the American Army, the Quartermaster Corps had the collateral mission of furnishing services which contributed to the welfare and morale of the troops, promoted the economy of supply, and augmented the labor force. In a protracted campaign, seriously handicapped by shipping shortages and by a relatively low supply priority, a systematic program of recovery, repair, and reissue of all repairable equipment was an absolute necessity. Other QM services, while provided on a scale that appeared luxurious to the less fortunate soldiers of other nations, more than paid for themselves in terms of health, morale, and increased combat efficiency. American civilian standards and concepts of human dignity, sanitation, and material comfort were retained in the U.S. Army; indeed one could argue that they had been reinforced during military training. Under the circumstances, the Army would have been shortsighted and wasteful had it ignored such essential services as graves registration, salvage, baths, and laundries. The highest tribute to their worth was indicated by postwar plans to integrate these services more effectively and permanently into the Quartermaster Corps.

Traditions in Caring for the Dead [1]

In honoring men who give their lives on the battlefield, the American Graves Registration Service can look back upon the ancient Mediterranean world for the origin of many of the traditions which pervade present burial customs. Accounts of funerary rites and of rudimentary systems of recovery and identification occupy an honored place in the literary works of the Egyptians, Hebrews, Greeks, and Romans. Yet, from ancient to modern times, homage was usually reserved for a famed commander or for a group of anonymous dead who had saved the day for their people. As recently as Napoleon's day most of the rank and file had been either cremated or buried in unmarked graves, interred en masse under mounds of limed earth, or dumped unceremoniously into abandoned wells.

The American soldier was subject to the same fate until about a century ago. In 1850 Congress created a precedent for the establishment of permanent cemeteries abroad when it appropriated

[1] Except where otherwise noted, this section is based on a monograph written by Edward Steere, *Graves Registration Service in World War II* QMC Historical Studies, 21 (Washington, 1951).

funds for the erection of a Mexican War shrine. It stood at the head of a common grave wherein 750 American dead were interred after they had been exhumed from their battlefield graves along the road to Mexico City. Today this monument stands as a reminder that American burial procedures of that day were hopelessly inadequate. In 1862, for the first time, the United States took steps to provide each of its soldier dead with what might be regarded as an individual shrine in the midst of a larger, if less personal, national cemetery.

In 1876 another step was taken. The Secretary of War formally charged the Quartermaster General with the responsibility of supervising the national cemetery system, and centralized all mortuary records in the Quartermaster's Department. Unquestionably, the records themselves began to acquire a more profound meaning to those who analyzed them than was attached to a mere file of the names and ranks of deceased soldiers. The burial lists not only fulfilled their role of building morale among the relatives and friends of the dead, but as time passed these records also came to have considerable value as operational statistics. Gradually, all echelons of command built up figures on their loss experiences, and this information entered more and more into plans for providing replacements. Commanders began to realize that it was to their advantage to perfect procedures for the recovery and identification of the dead. Metal identification tags had been sold to individual soldiers during the Civil War, and were officially sponsored at the regimental level within many units during the Spanish-Ameri-

can War. That conflict demonstrated the need for a uniform, Army-wide procedure, and a general order of 1906 directed the Quartermaster's Department to issue an aluminum identification tag to each officer and enlisted man.[2] The end of the war with Spain marked another precedent in that pains were taken to return as many of the dead as possible from an overseas theater, a program that was greatly expanded after World Wars I and II.

World War I brought a theater graves registration service into being. For the first time such a service provided units to act in direct support of combat troops and a headquarters staff section at the chief quartermaster's level to keep systematic mortuary records and to supervise the maintenance of temporary cemeteries. In 1924, a series of regulations appeared in the Army Regulation series 30, representing a serious effort to evaluate the lessons of World War I. The authors attempted to anticipate future demands for such a wartime service and to define the mission that a chief quartermaster would have under a theater commander. These regulations further called for the development of a specialized service unit suited to carry out the necessary work in the field. Nevertheless, American graves registration service on the eve of Pearl Harbor had made only a few paper improvements over the system of 1917 and 1918.[3]

When the United States became in-

---

[2] GO 204, 20 December 1906.

[3] By early 1945 the following regulations governed burials and graves registration in the Seventh Army area: TM 10–630, AR 600–50, AR 30–1805, AR 30–1810, AR 30–1815, AR 30–1820, AR 30–1825, AR 30–1840; WD Cirs 79, 195, 206, 235 (1943); COM-ZONE ETOUSA SOP 26.

volved in World War II an overseas quartermaster had two primary tools to carry out his graves registration mission. The first was a regularly constituted service unit. Based on T/O 10–297, dated 1 November 1940, a QM graves registration company, consisting of a headquarters section and four platoons, was theoretically to support a corps of three divisions. It had an aggregate strength of 130, of whom five were officers. They were not responsible for the collection of battlefield dead. This mission remained with tactical units. The other tool, Technical Manual 10–630, appeared on 23 September 1941, at a time when neither a G–1 nor a G–4 officer at any staff level clearly understood which officer would have the overall supervision of the burial function within a command. Unfortunately, the 1941 manual failed to reflect German field experience after the speedy victories over Poland, France, and Norway. By the time of Pearl Harbor, German doctrine had developed to the point where graves registration service, in both its command and staff arrangement, was placed at the highest field level.[4] The German system had the dual advantage of building morale at home and of providing operational data. German manuals repeatedly warned every commander of the danger of allowing graves registration service troops to become calloused or emotionally disturbed because of their tasks. Staffs of supervisory personnel were to be changed frequently, rested, and returned to the field, but never to their old duties. In contrast, American graves registration service re-

mained a staff function and the major advantage it enjoyed over other field work was that of having little, if anything, to unlearn.

Development of Graves Registration Service

The fighting forces of 1942 and early 1943 in Bataan, the Solomons, and North Africa were obliged to improvise their graves registration service at every step. TORCH field orders specified that tactical units would collect and bury their own dead, that graves were to be carefully marked and reported to unit commanders, that unit commanders would provide the blanks for reporting burials, and that unit commanders were to make frequent checks to see that the troops had identification tags, properly marked and worn. Plans for the Western Task Force included the assignment of the recently activated 46th and 47th Graves Registration Companies, but because of shipping restrictions these units remained behind in the United States. Consequently, graves registration became an added responsibility of combat commanders whose primary concern was with their living men. Before sailing, most commanders had no time to familiarize themselves with TM 10–630 or the AR 30 series of 1924. In fact, most of this literature was not in unit files at sailing time. Even with it, commanders would have been handicapped because there was no over-all staff agency to interpret the procedures or supervise a graves registration service.[5]

On 8 November 1942, French resist-

[4] Service Regulations for the Armed Forces Graves Registration Officer, 25 January 1942. OKW–1642–GRS.

[5] Ltr, Pounder to Cowles, 4 Apr 43. OQMG MED 319.25.

ance demanded the undivided attention of TORCH commanders. Unit chaplains handled graves registration with the assistance of noncommissioned officers and enlisted men from either the combat elements or medical detachments. After action reports revealed that commanders objected to the employment of combat soldiers for the recovery and burial of their own dead, and desired the assignment of specialized graves registration units. At Oran, McNamara, after his G–3 had disapproved a graves registration platoon on his original troop list, was immediately confronted with the task of reburying 400 dead who had been slaughtered in Oran Harbor. On the outskirts of Oran he selected a site near a civilian cemetery, obtained the services of engineers, and turned the detailed work over to an assistant, who laid out the military cemetery at Sidi Chami and supervised and reported the burials. The assistant had one complaint against TM 10–630. It was ideal for the superintendent of Arlington National Cemetery, but worthless for telling how a temporary burial ground should be laid out.[6]

In the hasty planning for SATIN Task Force, the II Corps did not entirely overlook the lessons of the TORCH landings. On 20 December 1942 it distributed a three-page pamphlet which outlined procedures to be followed in Tunisia. This document stressed stricter compliance with the requirement for reporting burials and assigned this responsibility to a graves registration officer who was to be appointed in each regiment, separate battalion, or com-

pany. But this vaguely worded pamphlet made no provisions for the assignment of burial details, for transportation in evacuating the dead, or for methods of identifying remains. As in TORCH, the authors assumed that all graves registration officers were familiar with the basic manuals. In December 1942, few, if any, such publications had reached the theater.

Once again, during the Tunisian fighting, assignments as graves registration officers fell largely to chaplains. Only in the Eastern Base Section were quartermasters available for this duty and even they always performed it in addition to other work. Both chaplains and base section quartermasters continued to lack technically trained personnel needed to assist them. In Tunisia, Lt. Col. Edward R. Martin, Chaplain Corps, became the 1st Infantry Division's graves registration officer and excerpts from his after action reports indicate that his subordinates hired native laborers to dig and fill the graves and to evacuate the dead by pack train to collecting points. Martin reported that his chaplains often personally supervised the details of evacuation and burial, not infrequently ending their work late at night.

Under this system the II Corps improvised graves registration until early 1943, when two events alleviated the situation. First, the 46th Quartermaster Graves Registration Company, which had originally been earmarked to make the TORCH landing in November 1942, arrived at Constantine on 2 March 1943. Working under the supervision of the II Corps G–1, one platoon of the 46th, perhaps the first to be committed in the war with Germany, supported the 1st

---

[6] (1) McNamara *Memoir,* pp. 27–28. (2) Pounder Rpt, p. 68.

Division in the Gafsa-El Guettar sector from 16 March to 6 April 1943. Secondly, coincident with the 46th's appearance, NATOUSA announced a theater graves registration service on 1 April 1943. To head it, Middleswart later named Col. Thomas R. Howard, QMC, as theater graves registration service officer, and subordinates soon were designated in each base section. Colonel Howard's duty was to co-ordinate field activities and maintain control of the theater's burial files. Howard did not assign units to combat organizations because this was a G–1, NATOUSA, function. Graves registration officers within divisions and higher units and graves registration companies were responsible to unit quartermasters who, in turn, co-ordinated with a base section quartermaster.

Benefits from the new organization were not felt until the II Corps moved into northern Tunisia. In the meantime, the graves registration service in base sections settled down into operating on standard procedures for securing mortuary supplies, temporary sites, and a mortician's services. But within the II Corps there still were not enough regularly constituted units, with adequate transportation, to relieve the combat troops of their role in graves registration. The most advanced positions reached by specialists were collecting points. While this situation did not satisfy those who wanted to spare the combat troops the demoralizing experience of handling their own dead, the establishment of collecting points was a giant stride in improving the evacuation of remains. The system set a precedent to be adopted in subsequent campaigns and made for speedier and more

efficient identification, which in turn reduced the number of unknown dead.

Graves registration planning for Sicily began early in 1943, before all the lessons of the Tunisian campaign had come to hand. The Seventh Army therefore studied the shortcomings of TORCH and hoped that trained Quartermaster graves registration platoons would be on hand for the invasion of Sicily. Planners also had reason to expect that the infantry and armored divisions to be redeployed from Tunisia would by trial and error obtain experience that could be properly applied to an amphibious operation. Dated 20 June 1943, plans for HUSKY's task force assigned responsibility to each company, battalion, regiment, and division, as well as to hospitals, depots, and other separate establishments for the appointment of a graves registration officer, who, in turn, was to be responsible to the unit quartermaster. In addition to these staff officers, each subtask force was to create a provisional graves registration platoon if regularly constituted platoons were not available from the United States. A provisional platoon was to consist of a headquarters and three seven-man sections.

By D-day, six platoons were available, providing at least one in support of each of the assault divisions. Between D-day and D plus four, each subtask force, with the exception of one infantry division, fielded a platoon from the 48th Graves Registration Company. This time the continuous evacuation of the dead was facilitated by more vehicles. The relatively prompt establishment of collecting points demonstrated that the divisions which came out of Tunisia had learned their lessons well.

In sharp contrast, the uninitiated 45th

Infantry Division, which had staged for HUSKY in the United States and only briefly touched North Africa, reflected its lack of experience. Not until it arrived at Oran did this unit give serious thought to the problem. When the division commander finally appointed a graves registration officer, the man had neither the requisite training nor experience for his assignment. When he distributed mortuary supplies such as temporary markers, bed sacks, and personal effects bags among the units, they failed to understand their use. Furthermore, the 45th repeated the errors of TORCH by assigning a special service officer and two chaplains as regimental graves registration officers—men who by profession, temperament, and supply experience were the least fitted for the task. The 45th also failed to provide vehicles or fatigue details at the assault beaches. The results were unsatisfactory in the extreme and, reviewing his experience, the division graves registration officer recommended that for an amphibious operation trained platoons together with their vehicles should arrive on D-day, that graves registration functions should be assigned to the division quartermaster, and that a special Quartermaster service unit should be on hand to dig graves. With the exception of the 45th Division's graves registration experience, the Sicilian campaign marked the end of improvisation.

The Italian campaign taken as a whole represents a special case in the development of graves registration service. From Salerno to Leghorn the Fifth Army used the divisional system of evacuating and burying the dead in army cemeteries. Combat units evacuated their dead to divisional collecting points located very close to Quartermaster supply points where attached graves registration platoons assumed responsibility for further identification of the remains, prepared mortuary records, and attended to burials in army cemeteries. In part the relatively low number of isolated burials and a corresponding high percentage of positive identification in Italy may be attributed to Fifth Army's superior planning for the use of combat personnel in the recovery of 22,953 American dead and to the efficient evacuation work of the veteran 46th, 47th, and 48th Graves Registration Companies. This system prevailed until August 1944 when the companies reverted to army control. In Italy the tactical situation also assisted the recovery and evacuation system. Most of the battles were positional. Despite transport difficulties over mountainous terrain, stationary warfare favored Quartermaster efforts to restrict isolated burials—twelve by V–E Day—and afforded opportunities for identification of unknown dead that seldom obtained in a war of movement.

Reconstitution of the Seventh Army in June 1944 took VI Corps headquarters with three veteran infantry divisions, the 3d, 36th, and 45th, for the southern France operation. Three platoons of the 46th Graves Registration Company, each attached to a division, were expected to evacuate the dead through independent collecting points to a division cemetery. In the first week ashore, each division established a cemetery. Within a week of laying out its cemetery, each division was sixty miles beyond its collecting point. Evacuation of the dead lagged. On 27 September 1944 the VI Corps took action, establishing a cen-

TEMPORARY AMERICAN CEMETERY *near Cassino.   Flag is at half-mast for the late*
President Franklin Delano Roosevelt. 16 April 1945.

trally located corps collecting point, and thus for a time ended the classic Mediterranean concept of divisional unity. After the war of movement was over, the corps system was dropped.

On 5 October, the Seventh Army established a cemetery at Épinal. But the location was only accessible to the VI Corps, not to the XV Corps, which with the attached 3041st Graves Registration Company recently had been shifted from the Third to the Seventh Army. Organizationally, the XV Corps used an evacuation system different from that of the VI Corps. The 3041st established a corps collecting point at Charmes, and after detailing 43 men to handle burial operations at Épinal divided its remaining strength among detachments of 5 to 11 men for operating several collecting points, but they were identified more with corps sectors than with specific divisional areas. Meantime

the VI Corps retained its organization of platoon attachments to divisions. As more and more divisions joined these two corps, the development of the 3041st's method of operations was arrested. The system of an attached graves registration platoon behind each division became a uniform one. In effect, the Seventh Army adopted the battle-tested procedures of the Mediterranean war.

*Identification Procedures
and Cemeteries*

While conforming to the humanitarian premises of the Geneva Convention, the American Graves Registration Service had to provide an evacuation system swift enough to prevent demoralization of troops but slow enough to assure the most accurate identification possible. Success depended largely on technical competence. Notwithstanding the zeal of chaplains who were assigned graves registration responsibilities in North Africa, untrained combat personnel were not qualified and in subsequent campaigns the task of identification was relegated to specialists in the rear.

Experience in the Tunisian campaign demonstrated the need to revise current identification procedures. Regulations dating back to prewar days provided that reports of interment would bear the fingerprints of only one hand of the deceased, while the fingerprint files of The Adjutant General's Office and the Federal Bureau of Investigation were based on mathematical formulae which required the prints of both hands. If ten prints were available, a positive identification could be made by a final search of less than 200 separate files, but the fingerprints from one hand alone required a search through many thousands of files and presented an unsurmountable task in time of war. By mid-March 1943 the War Department had sent revised instructions to all theaters.[7] Normally, the existence of two dog tags was sufficient to establish a positive identification. But men were known to exchange tags and it became customary to check a man's tags against his personal letters, driver's license, and membership cards. If no discrepancies were revealed, the body was wrapped in a mattress cover and evacuated. The absence of dog tags meant the beginning of a wider search. After all papers on the body were carefully studied, the time and place of death were checked against operational records to determine which unit had been in the area. The likeliest parent organization was asked to report the names of all missing persons on the specified day and to send someone to the collecting point to examine the unidentified body.[8]

In addition to the study of tooth charts, fingerprints, and other physical characteristics, Capt. Steven F. Capasso of the 47th Graves Registration Company developed new techniques for obtaining legible fingerprints from bodies long interred. Another technique made it possible to cleanse the clothing of those interred as unknowns. Previously such garments were disposed of after a cursory examination. Upon being cleaned, clothes often revealed hidden laundry marks. Because the likelihood of duplicating a laundry mark was less than one in a quarter of a million, this was a useful clue to the identity of a body. Recognizing the importance of such clues, before the Salerno landing Truscott ordered his 3d Division infantrymen to place their serial number inside both leggings.

Reviewing the success of identification procedures, Sullivan and his graves registration officer noted that the problem of identifying remains taken from badly damaged tanks was another that had been largely solved. Useful data included the tank's serial number, the position of the remains within the wreckage, and the status of other crew members. As always, familiarity with the units and troops within the area was another aid in successful identification which, by the end of hostilities, had

---

[7] (1) Ltr, Brig Gen F. N. Pope, Asst QMG, to CG ASF, 6 Mar 43, sub: Identification and Burial of Deceased. AG 293, WW II, FRC. (2) WD Cir 79, 1943, sec. 4.

[8] Ltr, Ramsey to Littlejohn, 4 Feb 44. OQMG MED 319.25.

brought the Fifth Army's factor of "un-identified remains" to an all-time low of 1.1 percent.

The final phase in wartime graves registration activities involved the burial of the dead in accessible and attractive temporary cemeteries. Every measure was taken to reduce the number of isolated burials, both by rapid evacuation of remains and by constant search for and disinterment of those decedents who had been individually buried either by civilians or the enemy. A limited number of isolated burials was inevitable, particularly in beachhead operations. Center Task Force, for example, buried its dead in eight different places during the first few days ashore, but McNamara concentrated all bodies in military cemeteries at Arzew and Oran before the end of the first week. At Gafsa in Tunisia, for five dollars in cash and ten pounds of tea, a regimental chaplain of the 1st Infantry Division "bought" a tract of land which later became the Gafsa cemetery. The effort to minimize isolated burials was demonstrated again in Sicily by the 3d Infantry Division, which opened a burial ground at Licata on D plus 1, and continued to evacuate remains to this cemetery until it was a hundred miles behind the front. Not until the 3d Division reached Palermo was another cemetery established. Meanwhile the 1st Division opened a burial site at Gela on D plus 1, and buried, in the following three weeks, fifteen hundred American, Allied, and enemy dead. During the eastward thrust of Seventh Army, when the enemy retired across the Strait of Messina, the attacking divisions opened at least five temporary burial grounds, one of which, Caronia, later became the concentrated burial plot.

To students of military history, a map of U.S. military cemeteries in Italy reveals a great deal about the nature of the Fifth Army's campaigns. Noting that seven of the thirteen cemeteries were clustered in the 150 miles between Paestum and Anzio, one might correctly conclude that actions over this western watershed of the Apennines were prolonged and costly. Since the 150–200-mile stretch north of Rome included only two cemeteries—at Tarquina and Follonica—and these largely held the remains of airmen, it was apparent that the Fifth Army had swept to the Arno quickly. The Gothic Line battles forced the opening of large cemeteries again, at Castelfiorentino, Mount Beni, and Mirandola. That there were only half as many burial sites along the Gothic Line as along the Winter Line may be attributed to the stabilization of the front as well as to the fact that in August 1944 the Fifth Army had assumed control over burial sites as part of a personnel economy drive.[9] Similarly, a map of France will reveal that, after the initial landings east of Marseille, Seventh Army encountered little resistance in the Rhône valley except at Montélimar. Cemeteries at Épinal, at Saint Juan near Besançon, and at Hochfelden near Saverne commemorate the Seventh Army's winter battles in the Vosges.[10]

In the base sections, a graves registration company rarely, if ever, worked as a unit in one cemetery. Three of the companies which saw the longest service in the theater were broken down into detachments and platoons and scattered

---

[9] (1) See Map 1 in Steere, *Graves Registration Service*, p. 91. (2) Hist QM PBS, pp. 260–67. Middleswart Papers.

[10] Steere, *Graves Registration Service*, Map 2.

over widely dispersed locations. The 47th, which arrived in North Africa in the spring of 1943, was subdivided into twenty groups, several of which consisted of only two enlisted men who were assigned to inactive cemeteries. The 602d Graves Registration Company detailed its members late in the summer of 1943 to sites throughout eastern Algeria and Tunisia. One detachment took over the II Corps cemetery on the Mateur-Bédja highway, another went to the cemetery at Tunis, the third to Constantine, while the fourth remained in Mateur with the company headquarters to search the countryside for isolated graves and to evacuate the dead from the many hospitals nearby. On occasion cemeterial work was of an emergency nature. Such was the case when elements of the 602d raced to Bougie, Algeria, in anticipation of establishing a cemetery for dead expected to be washed ashore from a sunken transport. When the unit left North Africa, its various detachments deployed over a large area, including Corsica, the islands of Ischia, Ponza, and Ventotene off Naples, and along the eastern watershed of Italy. In November 1944 the 602d airlifted several teams to Greece, Bulgaria, and Rumania to investigate the fate of American pilots who failed to return from sorties over Balkan oil fields. In Italy, the work was shared with the 3044th, the 2611th, the 2612th, and 2613th Graves Registration Companies. Behind Seventh Army, the 48th, 605th and 610th Graves Registration Companies searched the countryside and maintained cemeteries in southern France.

Detachments assigned to temporary cemeteries conducted all activities except the performance of religious rites.

In normal cases, they identified the deceased before the body was evacuated to the cemetery. If both dog tags were still available, one was left on the body, the other nailed to the grave marker. If not, embossed metal plates were secured to each marker, while copies of the interment report were placed in sealed waterproof containers and deposited in each grave. This report contained a complete history of the decedent, including all details relative to the manner of death, objects found on the body, tooth charts, fingerprints, and other pertinent information.

In addition to preparing the bodies for and fulfilling the task of burial, and mailing personal items to the Quartermaster Personal Effects Depot in Kansas City, Missouri, cemeterial units beautified the grounds as quickly as possible. Landscaping, installation of lawn sprinkler and drainage systems, planting of shrubbery and trees, erecting of flagpoles, and constructing of ways, walls, and walks were all part of standard engineering procedure. Progress was frequently delayed by adverse weather, inadequate facilities for grading roads, lack of trucks for hauling rocks, and the limited number of grave markers.

Although handicapped by scant information on men who were missing and perhaps buried in isolated graves, if indeed the lone casualty was buried at all, base section cemeterial units pursued all clues as to the whereabouts of such soldiers. Sometimes graves were found in the fields where wild growth obscured them from view; others, particularly those of air force casualties, were occasionally found in small-town cemeteries where bodies of a single crew rested in a common grave. Seeking the victims of airplane accidents, graves registration troops climbed the rocks and peaks of mountains. The successful removal of bodies from such inaccessible places frequently required pack mules as well as the strong backs of human beings. Often searching parties learned that battlefield dangers persisted long after the combat forces had left. Where the fighting was bitter and the snows were deep—as in the precipitous peaks around Mignano—teams postponed recovery work until spring, when mechanical detectors would work more effectively against mines and precautionary measures could be taken before booby-trapped bodies were removed. While crossing part of the Anzio beachhead which was known to be mined, for example, one such party lost three of its members as the result of an accidental detonation. As late as January 1945 the 3044th Graves Registration Company at the Nettuno cemetery reported that "the search of battlefields for and the conducting of investigations into the isolated burials . . . constitute the intensified operational program with which this organization was and is still occupied." The monthly rate of recoveries and interments at this one cemetery, by that time some 200 miles behind the front, amounted to approximately 100 American, Allied, and enemy dead.

Salvage, Recovery, and Repair Programs

If supply inventories were to be maintained, financial and shipping economies effected, and training and intelligence advantages gained from captured enemy matériel, a systematic procedure for recovery, segregation, and classification of repairable equipment was indispen- sable. In addition to its value for supplying the combat zone, prisoners of war, and direct civilian relief, an active salvage program served as a source of scrap lead, brass, copper, and rubber, vital to production in the United States. Scrap metals, paper, and lumber that were not needed by American producers or by the Army could be sold locally, thereby providing a monetary return. Such sales were also a small stimulant to industrial recovery and personal comfort in North Africa and Italy. Because the enemy had swept these areas of raw materials, irrepairable salvage usually brought high prices. Torn flour sacks and worn-out barracks bags sold for one dollar each, waste cardboard and paper brought five cents per pound, and natives frequently offered to buy worn shoes and clothing at triple the price of new articles in the United States.

The supervision exercised by Ramsey at the AFHQ and NATOUSA levels and by Middleswart at SOS NATOUSA became an integral part of a continuous and concerted program calling for the prompt recovery, repair, and re-use of unserviceable property, whether Allied or enemy, and for the utilization of battlefield scrap. Throughout the theater their supervision in no way relieved the commanders of salvage discipline. Organizationally, Ramsey was exclusively concerned with captured enemy matériel and Middleswart with United States property. On 1 March 1943 Middleswart assumed responsibility for the salvage and disposal of all waste materials except lumber, ammunition, and ammunition components. The latter two materials moved through ammunition supply channels, and scrap lumber was an Engineer responsibility. Middleswart set forth the objectives of War Department policy, laid down the conditions to be satisfied, and decentralized operations to each base section.[11]

A system of categories was set up to accelerate the evacuation of salvaged properties. New supplies were designated as Class A, used but still serviceable supplies as Class B, and unserviceable but repairable property as Class C. Supplies that were neither serviceable nor fit for reclamation were put in Class D. The first three classes were ultimately returned to the parent supply service for processing and reissue, while the quartermaster salvage officer in each base section retained Class D. To refine salvage procedures still further, priorities were set up to govern the recovery of Allied and enemy supplies alike. Generally, AFHQ assigned jerricans and optical, signal, and electrical equipment the highest value, and the theater commander was permitted to retain any captured materials or equipment he desired for training purposes.

Before anything could be done with salvage it had to be cleared from the battlefield. Like all other aspects of logistical support, recovery work varied with terrain and tactical conditions. In a war of rapid movement or in mountain warfare problems were magnified, and when combat troops were too busy to clear their own sector this responsibility was given over to semimobile Quartermaster salvage collection companies. To effect a smoother transfer, a steady effort was made to move Quar-

termaster salvage collectors closer to the front and also to lighten their work by sending into the advance areas mobile salvage repair companies capable of making repairs on the spot. Two other types of Quartermaster units—laundry companies and sterilization and bath companies—became partners in the salvage program.[12]

Salvage recovery lagged behind all other Quartermaster services in North Africa. A year after TORCH the War Department was alarmed at the mounting piles of unprocessed scrap metal in Oran, Bizerte, and Palermo. The scrap was not flowing to the United States. An Army Service Forces officer arrived in Oran to survey the situation and found that recovery techniques had long been the heart of the problem. He challenged NATOUSA's policy of continuing to make the Quartermaster organization completely responsible for the recovery program. Specialists at Eastern Base Section had for a considerable period been aware that salvage in Tunisia consisted largely of ordnance matériel, most of which proved too large, too heavy, and too specialized to be handled by the two collecting companies as they were then staffed, equipped, and trained. Company four-ton salvage wreckers could not move tanks, airplanes, and bridging equipment from the countryside to major roads and from the roads to salvage yards. To help them, the collectors had

---

[11] (1) QM FM 10–10, QM Service in Theater of Operations (Washington, 1942), p. 44. (2) *Logistical History of NATOUSA–MTOUSA*, pp. 414–15. (3) Pounder Rpt, p. 63. (4) Ltr, Ramsey to Littlejohn, 4 Feb 44. OQMG MED 319.25.

[12] (1) Cir 22, Hq NATOUSA, 1 Mar 43, Collection and Evacuation of Salvage. (2) CCS Dir, Disposal of Material Captured in North Africa, 23 Apr 43. AG 400.93, EBS. (3) The first opportunity to return enemy QM items for technical intelligence purposes came in April 1943. Pounder himself initiated this program. (4) Cir 100, Hq MBS, 27 Jul 43. (5) Ltr, Middleswart to Col Joseph C. Odell, 16 Jun 44. Littlejohn Collection.

borrowed ordnance wreckers and recovery vehicles as well as signal and engineering equipment. Without cutting
torches, bolt clippers, and heavy jacks,
as well as technicians capable of cutting
heavy metals or deactivating the ingenious mines and booby traps frequently
attached to abandoned equipment, the
work was slow.

For a long time NATOUSA resisted
suggestions that heavy salvage work be
transferred to the Ordnance Department. It proposed instead to create a
Quartermaster salvage recovery company
(special) which would have the personnel and tools to move tank hulks,
disassemble them, cut armor plate, bolts,
and rivets, and strip, recover, and prepare scrap for shipment. NATOUSA
planned to use the special unit for completing the job in Tunisia, then in
Sicily, and finally in Italy. But on 8
September 1943 NATOUSA itself restricted the activation of provisional
units, and the special recovery company
stayed on paper. A fortnight later, the
War Department revised the Table of
Organization of the regular collecting
company. While a step in the right
direction, this change still left the company woefully inadequate to handle
heavy salvage jobs such as had been
encountered in Tunisia.[13]

It was mid-February 1943 before the
226th Salvage Collection Company arrived in Tunisia. Since the II Corps

was withdrawing behind Kasserine Pass
and an effective recovery program was
impossible, the 226th had little to do at
first. McNamara clung to his original
salvage plan. Once fighting had dwindled, this called for the divisions to recover and evacuate their own salvage.
Then rear-bound trucks would reduce
the divisional piles by hauling scrap to
Tébessa, where the 226th would classify
and repair it. But if the plan was
simple, its execution was not. By mid-
April the II Corps had left behind an
area in central Tunisia covering more
than 3,000 square miles, twice fought
over and littered with damaged and
abandoned equipment. Shuttling combat troops to the Bizerte front had left
little time for salvage recovery.

Salvage discipline within the 1st
Armored Division, to cite only one example, was poor. Units failed either to
deposit their waste materials along the
main supply routes or evacuate them to
corps dumps. A month after Bizerte's
fall the El Guettar–Gafsa battlefield was
still strewn with hundreds of tons of
valuable property. One officer wrote:
"We are wasting millions of dollars in
failing to pick up material from the
battlefield . . . our trucks carry ammunition and supplies to the front and then
return unloaded." Another quipped
that the evacuation program would have
been considerably improved if soldiers
had hunted for salvage as they did for
souvenirs. Hungry for battlefield me-
mentos, American soldiers stripped prisoners, dead or alive. One soldier was
seen removing the Nazi swastika from
a Messerschmitt's tail with the aid of a
kitchen type of can opener. In their
search for altimeters, clocks, speedom-
eters, and name plates on newly cap-

[13] (1) Tab G, Memo, Salvage Off EBS for QM
EBS, 23 May 43, sub: Salvage Activities in EBS;
Memo, Chief Redistribution and Salvage Br ASF
for Dir Prod Div ASF, 1 Oct 43, sub: Status of
Salvage in NATOUSA. Both in Littlejohn Collection. (2) Frink Rpt. (3) Ltr, AGWAR to CG
NATOUSA et al., 22 Nov 43, sub: Recovery, Reclamation, and Salvage in Theater of Opns; 3d Ind
to Ltr, CG ASF to CG NATOUSA, 11 Jan 44. Both
in AG 400.93, NATOUSA.

tured airplanes, looters often left behind a mass of unidentifiable junk for intelligence teams to survey.[14]

After Bizerte fell, SOS NATOUSA instituted an elaborate battlefield clearance program. At first the mission was assigned to the few remaining combat troops. But without making much progress the infantry left for Sicily. The job then fell to Eastern Base Section's General Depot 4. Under a single command, teams of ordnance, engineer, transportation, signal, and medical troops worked side by side with the 226th and 227th QM Salvage Collection Companies. The battlefield was marked off into sectors following the grid system found on military maps. Eastern Base Section assigned each surveying team a sector to reconnoiter. Teams were instructed to provide overlays indicating the location and nature of salvage. By making a map mosaic, recovery points were determined. When the 226th and 227th completed their task, 20,000 long tons had been evacuated, the bulk of it spent ammunition. Of the remaining tonnage, 10 percent included motor parts, 10 percent gasoline containers, 2 percent clothing, and 15 percent miscellaneous scrap. From metals unwanted in the United States, NATOUSA realized a sum of almost two million dollars by sales to French authorities.[15]

Salvage collection in Sicily during the course of the campaign improved slightly. The first collecting company, the 232d, landed in Palermo on 6 August 1943. A backlog of accumulated clothing, shoes, and typewriters for repair—not collecting—faced the 232d. To the combat units "QM's were QM's" and it made no difference that the 232d was a collecting unit if there was a big repair job to be done. So without any trained repairmen, without equipment, and without directions, the 232d began collecting spare parts, secondhand machines, and tools to repair clothing, shoes, and typewriters. Late in August, the men of the 232d became collectors once again. Even then the unexpected dogged their steps. The 232d was a light salvage company, but heavy work faced it beyond Palermo. As in Tunisia, quartermasters found that more trucks and larger wreckers were needed to handle battered tanks, field guns, and self-propelled artillery. Cutting through this heavy material with torches was barely possible, but took too long and was too expensive; demolition was faster and easier. Two experts from a nearby Ordnance bomb disposal company therefore were attached to the 232d. Teamwork had the happy effect of helping both services. In blowing heavy scrap into pieces, the concussions in the junk piles set off a few hidden booby traps and land mines.

Searching teams, augmented by Italians, hunted for scrap steel and aluminum on the basis of sections marked off on a map of Sicily by the base section salvage officer. The 232d searched the Italian quartermaster depot at San Cataldo, the ration dumps at Prizzi, the rail yards at Napola, and the airfield

---

[14] (1) Pounder Rpt, p. 63. (2) McNamara *Memoir*, pp. 58–59. (3) Quoted from OQMG Intel Bull 13, 5 May 43. Hist Br OQMG. (4) Frink Rpt. (5) Ltr, Sullivan to Ramsey, 4 May 43. Sullivan Papers. (6) Rpt, CG 1st Armd Div to CG NATOUSA, 26 Jun 43, sub: Adequacy of Pers and Transport for Supply of a Div in Combat. Hist Br OQMG. (7) Ltr cited n. 11 (4).

[15] (1) Ltr, Ramsey to Gregory, 2 Jun 43. Hist Br OQMG. (2) *Logistical History of NATOUSA–MTOUSA*, pp. 412–15.

complex around Trapani. All salvage collected was hauled daily to the nearest railroad siding and loaded on flatcars. At Palermo, the 232d cut the metal scrap to size and prepared it for shipment to other ports for final disposition.[16]

The Italian campaign provided a better example of battlefield clearance and, even more, of salvage repair in combat than had that in North Africa. Commanded by Capt. Harris J. North, the 230th Salvage Collecting Company was the key organization of its type under Sullivan's command. The 230th came to be known respectfully as "Fifth Army's junkmen." Arriving in Naples on 10 October 1943, it sent one platoon to Avellino and left another in Naples. The remainder of the company moved to Caserta where it operated the Fifth Army base salvage depot until April 1944. North subdivided his base depot into three operational sections. A receiving section segregated such items as headgear, webbing, and herringbone twill clothing; the classification section determined the serviceability and repairability of individual pieces; and the shipping section moved the materials to the next destination. Two new classifications were added by Fifth Army to the four used in North Africa: enemy salvage, now obtained in ever-increasing quantities, was designated Class I; Class X was a further refinement of Class C, and included those items which were to be repaired but distributed only to noncombat groups such as Italian service troops and working civilians.

The evacuation of salvage utilized the return trip of the ration transport system. At ration railheads troops of the 230th maintained well-guarded and sheltered salvage dumps, where they could sack or bundle unpackaged materials. From these recovery points they delivered clothing which could be readily used to the nearby mobile laundries for cleaning. These in turn transferred laundered articles to the clothing exchanges. Salvage requiring additional processing moved from the ration railheads to the army base dump aboard homebound trucks or freight cars. Teams from the 230th often received special assignments. As in Tunisia, they plotted the fields over which the Fifth Army had passed. Section by section, village by village, house by house, they carried out their assignments. The teams promptly transmitted to ordnance experts information as to the location of ammunition dumps, unexploded bombs, projectiles, booby traps, and wrecked vehicles.

South of Cassino combat salvage operations assumed proportions which Sullivan described as "tremendous, apparently far beyond our capacity to handle. The stuff is coming down off the mountains at the rate of about twelve to fourteen truckloads a day." During two weeks in January 1944 his teams recovered and repaired more than a million dollars worth of quartermaster supplies. Because divisions encountered difficulties in clearing their sectors, corps troops helped them. From December 1943 to March 1944, the II Corps dispatched special trucks to divisions possessing salvage in quantities beyond the transport means of the quartermaster company and sent out another fleet of vehicles to

---

[16] (1) Ltr, CO 232d QM Salvage Collecting Co to CO IBS, 24 Jun 44, sub: Orgn Hist. Hist Br OQMG. (2) Rpt of Opns SUSA in Sicilian Campaign, p. 3. (3) "Supply in Sicily—II," QMTSJ, III, No. 21 (3 December 1943), 16.

police roadsides. For almost a month in the spring of 1944 the II Corps detailed 150 Italian service troops to battlefield clearance while another group of Italians using pack trains evacuated salvage from advance positions. Salvage teams reconnoitered mountain trails as well as roads for supplies which had been abandoned or scattered when vehicles overturned or mules bolted. In these relatively remote regions salvage parties arranged for speedy evacuation of property lest it be lost to the vagaries of the weather or to battlefield scavengers.[17]

At Anzio, where the full complement of services could not be maintained, the recovery program was necessarily less thorough. Here collectors were so few that they could not be used to locate or evacuate discarded supplies. Fatigue details could only separate the salvage brought in by the combat units and ship by LST's bound for Naples that which required repair.[18]

Throughout all these recovery operations one work steadily progressed: salvage repair. The Fifth Army advanced what the 232d had begun in Palermo. Although Sullivan received no repair companies during the first nine months in Italy, he knew that sufficient quantities of quartermaster equipment would

be available to him only if he conducted processing and renovation work. Secondhand items rather than new supplies could be used while older equipment was being repaired. To this end, the 230th initiated a program far beyond its original mission. By exploitation of local resources, by improvisation of sundry types of equipment, and by using space wherever it could be found, this versatile unit began the repair of clothing, tools, office machines, helmets, mess kits and canteens, stoves, saddles and harnesses, gasoline and water cans, webbing, cots, and tents. Indeed the Fifth Army to a considerable extent liberated itself from Peninsular Base Section's reclamation program.[19]

Sullivan's first salvage repair depot opened at Caserta in October 1943. From the receipt and classification of the various items to their ultimate disposition, it operated on an assembly line plan. For the renovation of clothing, by far the most extensive of repair activities, space was utilized wherever it was found. A spaghetti factory provided shop space for drying thousands of pieces of clothing under heating pipes. In terms of volume, starting with field jackets and continuing in successive order, wool trousers, fatigue trousers, fatigue suits, fatigue jackets, wool shirts, wool underwear, overcoats, and combat jackets were the major clothing items repaired. Many obstacles had to be overcome before the clothing repair depot worked smoothly. Caserta lacked electricity. Flatirons had to be heated

---

[17] (1) Opn Memo 38, OQM Fifth Army, 11 Feb 44, sub: SOP Fifth Army Salvage Procedures; Opn Memo 46, 19 Mar 44, sub: Class B Clothing Issue Policy. Both in Sullivan Papers. (2) Quoted from Sullivan Diary, 5 Jan 44. (3) Ltr, CG II Corps to CG Fifth Army, 4 Apr 44, sub: Status of Salvage Collection in Corps Sector, Cassino Area. II Corps, AG 400. (4) "Mountain Operations Are a War of Supply," QMTSJ, IV, No. 25 (23 June 1944), 4.

[18] (1) "Anzio Quartermasters Battle Proved," QMTSJ, IV, No. 19 (12 May 1944), 7. (2) Hist 36th QM Co, May 44. Hist Br OQMG. (3) Sullivan MS, pp. 88–89.

[19] (1) Sullivan MS, p. 26. (2) Memo, Sullivan for QM Staff, 12 Dec 43, no sub; Ltr, Sullivan to Clark, 4 Nov 44, sub: Bronze Star Medal Recommendation. Both in Sullivan Papers. (3) Hist QM PBS, p. 170.

over crude charcoal stoves which required constant fanning. Mending of clothing depended on the employment of Italian women who either brought their own sewing machines to the factory or took work home. In either place the seamstresses worked in unheated rooms. At the factory the stone floors and glassless windows added to the workers' chill and discomfort. Quartermasters provided partial relief by covering the factory's open windows with cellophane from salvaged protective gas capes and by permitting the seamstresses to wear some of the mended clothing.

All branches of the salvage depot demonstrated their ingenuity in the recovery of serviceable parts from irrepairable equipment and their placement in usable equipment—a process which was known as "cannibalization"—and in the improvisation of new items and tools. By using wool from a badly worn blanket and the zipper from an old field jacket, seamstresses tailored vests for combat infantrymen. The workers exploited the smallest of scrap goods. To cushion the telltale jingle of two clanging aluminum dog tags swinging freely around the neck chain of men on night patrols, needleworkers fashioned tiny cloth pouches. Every week, on the average, artisans thumped out dents in 1,500 aluminum mess kits and reclaimed 800 canteen cups. Corroded kits were dipped in a lye solution, then rinsed, redipped in a weak nitric acid solution, rinsed again, and hung up to dry. Soldiers who passed the shop were unaware that the shiny, new-looking kits had been a heap of blackened scrap metal a few hours before. Eighty-five percent of all aluminum kits could be repaired and returned to stock. By dint of 145 pounds

of compressed air per inch, workers restored depressed aluminum canteens. In a separate yard, tents—critical items throughout the war—were dried, classified, patched, strengthened in the seams, provided with new rope, and waterproofed, sometimes within a matter of hours. A single typewriter shop, employing skilled Italian repairmen, boasted that it drew no new spare parts. All were cannibalized from Class D machines.[20]

Repair projects eventually exceeded the 230th's capacity. The strain was even greater during the sweep to the Arno. To lend assistance, Peninsular Base Section released the 299th Salvage Repair Company from the depot at Secondigliano in July 1944. Sullivan pressed the company into work at his army depot and restored the 230th to its collecting chores. Accompanying Fifth Army up the peninsula, stopping temporarily at Civitavecchia and Piombino, the 299th finally settled in Florence where it passed the second winter, training and supervising fifteen hundred employees and amassing approximately 400,000 square feet of working space.

Late in 1944 MTOUSA believed that the Fifth Army should be relieved of all those facilities which Peninsular Base Section could staff and operate. Sullivan fought the proposal; insisting that he was unprepared to relinquish his repair train until the army advanced, he argued:

---

[20] (1) QMTSJ, IV, No. 17 (28 April 1944), 10; QMTSJ, IV, No. 19 (12 May 1944), 14–15. (2) Rpt, Repair Activities of the 230th QM Salvage Collecting Co, n.d.; Memo, Sullivan for Tate, 2 Mar 45, sub: QM Equip. Both in Sullivan Papers. (3) Fifth Army History, III, 71. (4) "QM Salvage Company Renews Damaged Equipment in Italy," QMR, XXIII, No. 5 (March–April 1944), 103–04.

. . . If I can repair every last item of Fifth Army Salvage within the Army area and still keep my installations mobile, I intend to do so. If PBS would follow us closely with closely supporting installations where evacuation would be simplified, I would have no objection to reducing my activity to the minimum. My salvage has immediate value to the Army. If long lines of communication with no intermediate base establishments are in the picture, I think a plan to ship everything to the rear is ridiculous. Also if salvage were shipped to the rear and I could get resupply without voluminous requisition, verification, reverification and long waiting I would not object. I haven't been convinced to date that such will ever be the case while PBS operates as it does.[21]

The 900,000 articles of Class C equipment repaired within the army's boundaries, Sullivan held, represented stores which were either in constant demand or essential because of seasonal or sudden weather changes. Local repair meant a speedier turnover of used equipment and a reduction in calls for new supplies. Furthermore, Sullivan issued Class C clothing in response to urgent unfilled requisitions. The Fifth Army, for example, issued field jackets, underwear, shoes, and leggings to French, Brazilian, and Italian troops within hours after NATOUSA had approved the delivery of equipment originally intended for American troops alone. Similarly, Sullivan replenished without delay all the 88th Division's stocks which had been burned by an incendiary bomb. Finally, the savings in transportation provided him with another justification. In little more than a year

2,200 truckloads of Class C clothing had been renovated within Sullivan's salvage works. Considerable quantities now lay in the Class II and IV depot awaiting issue. To the Fifth Army, this represented a saving of 341,000 truck-miles.[22]

Improvements in combat zone salvage repair did not end with the establishment of repair works inside the army area. Experience in North Africa, where the field range became clogged because of prolonged use of leaded gasoline, taught that substantial savings of time and supplies could be achieved if mobile repair sections roved among the commands. Shortly after arriving in Naples, Sullivan formed a mobile four-man team equipped with adequate tools and parts to visit units on a prearranged schedule and help them inspect and maintain field ranges. A 2½-ton truck bed was rebuilt as a workshop fitted out with a bench, a parts cabinet, and a rack for welding and cutting tools. Enlisted men who had been given specialized training at one of the depots took their journeymen's training with a regiment in the 34th Infantry Division. Sullivan put them to work on the field range project, and between December 1943 and April 1944 they restored almost fifteen hundred ranges to service. In May and June the team reconditioned every field range belonging to the 88th Infantry Division.

Sullivan inaugurated two other programs in 1944. Both were rewarding. A typewriter and office machine repair team, carrying tools, an air compressor, and a trailer-mounted work bench, traveled among the units of the II and IV

---

[21] (1) Quoted from Ltr, Sullivan to Ramsey, 6 Dec 44; 2d Ind, QM Fifth Army for QM 92d Inf Div, 22 Jan 45. Both in Sullivan Papers. (2) Sullivan Diary, 20 Dec 44.

[22] (1) Sullivan Diary, 14 Dec 44. (2) Rpt, Army Salvage System with QM Base Salvage Depot Eliminated [ca. 1 Jan 45]. Sullivan Papers.

Corps. The mechanics repaired ten machines a day. In northern Italy Sullivan organized two mobile shoe repair teams, one of which was assigned to each of the corps. During a thirty-four day period in October and November 1944, the unit working for the II Corps in the vicinity of the ration dump received 4,000 pairs of shoes, of which 2,700 were repaired and 1,300 classed as salvage. Its accomplishments received well-deserved publicity through the armed forces' radio network.[23]

Although the Fifth Army's programs were the more praised because they reflected what could be achieved along a static, mountainous front, salvage and repair activities in the base sections yielded greater returns in volume. While fighting raged in Tunisia, Mediterranean Base Section operated nine salvage dumps, one in each of the major supply centers at Oujda, Arzew, Mostaganem, Perrégaux, Relizane, Orleansville, and Algiers, and two in Oran. One of the Oran depots specialized in cloth and leather items, the other in scrap metals of all shapes and sizes, including even toothpaste tubes.

Lacking organic repairmen for the renovation and repair of clothing and equipment during the first few months in North Africa, the Mediterranean

Base salvage officer negotiated with contractors for laundry and dry cleaning at Oujda, for shoe repairing at Sidi Bel Abbès and Oran, and for both services at Algiers. Later, when space and equipment from several semimobile trailers became available, he terminated the contracts and combined a variety of services in a single plant. This effort was short-lived. The quantity of salvage increased the longer Tunisian operations continued, and soon the job exceeded the capabilities of military manpower. Again, the salvage officer resorted to civilian contracts. Algerian and Moroccan natives, French and Spanish refugees, and Italian prisoners of war comprised the labor forces. Their work was satisfactory only when supervision was strict and sustained. Because of language barriers, American methods and work standards were difficult to communicate. Since there was no alternative to using whatever labor was available, the salvage program was often inefficiently carried out. Workers in the coastal cities were unable to cope with the muddy and torn tents retrieved from southern Tunisia, which accumulated in mounting piles. Finally, during several trips into the desert the salvage officer recruited nomadic Arab tentmakers whose methods were primitive but fairly effective. Adding their handiwork to that of day laborers who either brightened the tents with brushes and on scrubbing boards or folded and packed them for reissue, quartermasters soon restored what had once been a deteriorating heap of canvas and cord.

Salvage developed into a big business at Naples. Lt. Col. William E. Ela, having arrived on 3 October 1943 from Casablanca, was named Chief, Salvage

---

[23] (1) Opn Memo 57, OQM Fifth Army, 18 Apr 44, sub: SOP Field Range Inspection Group. Sullivan Papers. (2) Hist 88th QM Co. Hist Br OQMG. (3) "Troubleshooters Service Fifth Army Field Ranges," QMTSJ, V, No. 7 (18 August 1944), 3. (4) Sullivan MS, pp. 30–33, 64. (5) Hist 34th QM Co, Apr 44. Hist Br OQMG. (6) Ltr, Sullivan to Middleswart, 21 Sep 44; Memo, Salvage Off OQM to Sullivan, 14 Nov 44, sub: Résumé of Activities of Mobile Shoe and Typewriter Units in II Corps; Memos, CO 230th QM Salvage Collecting Co for Sullivan, 17 Nov 44; 17, 31 Jan 45, sub: Contact of II Corps QM. All in Sullivan Papers.

and Reclamation Branch, Quartermaster Section, Peninsular Base Section. Subsequently Ela supervised 8 laundry companies, 5 salvage repair companies, 4 salvage collecting companies, 1 sterilization company, and 2 fumigation and bath companies. Later 6 Italian POW companies, 7 Italian service units, 23 German POW companies, and 4,000 civilians joined in Ela's program. At Bagnoli, west of Naples, the 819th Sterilization and Bath Company became the first to engage in salvage work by receiving and classifying clothing and equipment ten days after the fall of Naples. Because Ela's spreading works attracted enemy aircraft and jeopardized the safety of the nearby medical center, he moved his depot ten miles inland to a former Italian barracks in Secondigliano, on the highway leading out of Naples to Aversa. Here the depot lay close to Sullivan's salvage dump. On 16 November 1943 the 299th Salvage Repair Company arrived at Secondigliano, and within ten days it was repairing 500 pairs of shoes daily, processing 600 garments, servicing 220 office machines, and renovating 90 tents. By the first week in December more than 2,000 tons of clothing in need of mending had accumulated at the depot. Meantime Ela rented 30 sewing machines from an Italian merchant, canvassed Naples for typewriter repairmen, advertised for baling machines, and imported a surplus shoe repair trailer and crew from Atlantic Base Section in Morocco.

With each passing month the 299th encountered extraordinary problems and additional tasks. Within minutes enemy bombers in December converted 500 tons of quartermaster equipment into 250 tons of salvage. Of this re-

mainder the 299th reclaimed 80 percent. The incident gave birth to Ela's first Neapolitan labor force, which mushroomed from 200 employees in 1943 to a maximum of 2,200 in 1945. In January 1944 whipping winds weakened and wrenched more than 4,000 wall tents. These were promptly patched by the 220th Salvage Repair Company, which had recently arrived from Tunisia. From Anzio the 299th and 220th received daily as many as 100 trucks, loaded indiscriminately with battlefield litter which had to be sorted and classified before moving along the repair cycle. In April salvage tonnage rose. Relief was provided by the addition of the 219th Repair Company. May brought a tidal wave of winter woolens as the troops donned summer-weight uniforms. On the eve of the taking of Rome, Ela reported to Bare that well over 80 percent of all salvage at Secondigliano had gone back into stock. Although the results of his first six months in Naples were impressive, Colonel Ela concluded that "the salvage program is still in its infancy. As the campaign is well in its second year, the quantity of clothing and equipage that require salvage is constantly increasing."[24]

There was a lull in the fighting in July 1944, following the capture of Leghorn. As already noted, the opportunity was taken to shift the 299th forward to the Fifth Army. Meanwhile the 219th and 220th Salvage Repair Companies, the 819th Sterilization and Bath Company, and the 2d Italian Salvage Repair Company carried the heavy load at Naples, where most of Seventh Army

---

[24] Ltr, Ela to CO 6698th QMBD, 27 Mar 44, sub: Sketch of Salvage Activities to Date. Sullivan Papers.

Table 5—Salvage Repair by Peninsular Base Section: Selected Items
1 December 1943–30 June 1945

Item	Number	Estimated Savings[a]	Unit Cost
Total......................	5,830,488	$15,134,506	.....
Shirts, cotton khaki..............	1,193,412	1,766,433	$1.89
Trousers.......................	1,034,175	2,044,276	2.40
Shirts, wool....................	866,702	2,093,511	4.35
Trousers, wool..................	1,064,052	2,777,770	4.85
Boots, combat..................	1,318,267	2,260,535	6.74
Raincoats......................	280,720	291,589	4.51
Tents, pyramid.................	73,160	3,900,392	80.00

[a] Estimated savings were based upon difference between cost of making repairs and the value of new items in the zone of interior. Thus even the cost of transatlantic shipping was excluded, and the *value* of supplies at the far end of a long and hazardous logistical pipeline was completely ignored. Possibly the prices paid by Italians at U.S. Army auctions of "unrepairable" salvage reflected true values more accurately. At Naples late in 1943, shoes, service, Class D, were sold for $15.00 a pair. The unit cost (new) for this item was $3.95.

Source: (1) Hist QM PBS, p. 165. (2) Price List, AR 30–3000, 16 Oct 44.

embarked for the DRAGOON operation. During this same period the capacity of the 220th was multiplied many times by converting it from a mobile to a fixed unit. This step elevated most of its men to foremen over Italian workers, but the 220th retained its mobile trailers, sending them forward to Leghorn with a skilled cadre in September.[25] During the next month the major portion of the unit was reunited in that city and two Italian repair companies also arrived, taking over the operation of the tent, shoe, and webbing shops. At Leghorn, Ela's repairmen and supervisors had an excellent location with covered shop space exceeding 70,000 square feet. It was laid out to permit production line operations. Gradually more equipment was obtained including cranes and con-

veyors to handle the mounting stacks of jerricans and oil drums. Within a few months the workload at Leghorn justified the construction of two large temporary buildings, expanding the indoor working space to more than 100,000 square feet. Repair of jerricans passed the 800-cans-a-day mark in February 1945, and by April the Leghorn depot was returning 1,000 bales of salvage clothing a day to stock.[26]

Peninsular Base Section conservatively estimated that during the period from 1 December 1943 to 30 June 1945 a representative portion of its salvage operations, involving only seven major items, had saved the U.S. Army over $15,000,000. (*Table 5*) While Ela's program had stressed reclamation and return of articles to stock, the disposal of goods that had either outlived their usefulness or were

---

[25] The mobile element of the fixed salvage repair company was a useful innovation, later imitated by other converted repair companies in the Mediterranean theater. It made possible a flexible forward movement by echelons to give closer support to the combat troops. Col. Hugh S. Harpole, "Salvage in the Mediterranean Area," *QMR*, XXIV. No. 3 (November–December 1944), 20.

[26] (1) MBS Cir 49, sub: Salvage and Reclamation, 1 Apr 43. (2) *QMTSJ*, IV, No. 9 (3 March 1944), 4. (3) Lt. Col. Karl Detzer, "The Mop-up Crews Take Over," *QMR*, XXIII, No. 1 (July–August 1943), 18–19. (4) Article cited n. 25, above. (5) Hist QM PBS, pp. 165–70.

unwanted in the United States was an activity not to be ignored. From an initial sale of $50.00 worth of fats and greases to a Neapolitan soapmaker in December 1943, Ela's sales activities expanded to an enterprise that had grossed two million dollars by May 1945. At public auctions quartermasters gave Italians the opportunity to obtain bottles, rags, tin cans, scrap rubber, and even heavy metal plates. Aircraft provided Italian industry with a sizable amount of scrap aluminum. Garbage and spoiled foods were sold for feed to animals and for the manufacture of soap. In February 1944, the Remount Service rejected 110 horses and mules. The animals were herded into a rural district. Handbills were circulated. The first auction proved as popular with the Italians as it was profitable ($50,000.00) to the Americans. So Ela repeated the auctions at six-week intervals.

In November 1944 Allied commissioners replaced the auctions with a different system. In order to obtain a wider and more equitable distribution than had proved possible by public sales, which unavoidably favored a comparatively few high bidders, Italian authorities designated the industries which could buy Class D salvage. Although the larger part of the scrap metals went into Italian industrial rehabilitation, much was returned to the U.S. Army in the form of aluminum pistons, butcher knives, chisels, space heaters, grates, drawbars and spare parts.[27]

Salvage units had low priorities for the DRAGOON operation, and arrived rather late in southern France. When separate troop lists were set up for CONAD and Delta Base on 25 September

ber 1944, only three salvage repair companies and no collecting companies were available to the two headquarters. By late October, typewriter, clothing, and shoe repair installations were operating in the Dijon area, but the major salvage center of CONAD was established at Vesoul during the following month. Here the 223d Salvage Repair Company supervised the activities of two service companies, and ultimately of five Italian salvage companies, received the valuable assistance of several laundry units, and co-ordinated activities with a French salvage installation. It repaired tents, mess kits, field ranges, and jerricans and received an average of forty carloads of salvage each week from Seventh Army and three carloads from 1st French Army. Meanwhile the 227th Salvage Collecting Company and the 232d and 592d Salvage Repair Companies operated still farther forward, at Sarrebourg, Nancy, and Lunéville. Because of transportation shortages, salvage repair operations were concentrated in the forward area to a maximum extent. In October and November, when the new M-1943 clothing was being issued and vast amounts of older garments were turned in, Delta Base loaned the 3068th Salvage Repair Company to CONAD. By early December this unit had returned from Vesoul to Marseille, where its main duties were repairs for service troops within the base section.[28]

Spare Parts

Of the many logistical lessons, one of the most difficult to communicate was

[27] Hist QM PBS, pp. 182, 184–88.

[28] (1) CONAD History, II, 563–681, 835–873. (2) Littlejohn, ed., Passing in Review, ch. 43. (3) Unit History Files, Hist Br OQMG.

that a highly mechanized army depended almost as much on an uninterrupted flow of spare and interchangeable parts as it did on rations, fuels, and ammunition. For quartermasters, the lesson came early in North Africa when mechanical difficulties of the field range and bakery oven were compounded by the absence of replacement parts. After Tunisia the first replacement factor study which Middleswart presented to the War Department embraced parts for the field range. He listed ninety-five separate items that were in short supply, presumably because War Department allowances as of June 1943 did not reflect Tunisian experience. Shortages reappeared in Sicily. Even when the theater was eighteen months old and machinery was that much more worn, little improvement could be claimed.[29] In a tone of desperation Sullivan wrote to Middleswart on the eve of the breakthrough toward Rome:

The question of repair parts for our laundry, bakeries, S&B units, etc., has been brought to my attention. I have written you regarding the problem and discussed it with you on your visits here. . . . Why can't you get repair parts? We have requisitions still outstanding from as far back as October of last year, with requisitions for each month thereafter submitted and no parts received. . . . We have been able to keep our units going by improvisation and sheer luck. . . . However this cannot go on indefinitely.[30]

Unpleasant as this situation was, Sullivan made no attempt to keep it a secret; only the day before he had dispatched a stern note to OQMG:

. . . the flow of spare parts for the present laundries, British bakeries, sterilization and bath units, and for other mechanical units put out by the Quartermaster is terrible beyond words. . . . Now please, find out who is responsible for the supply of spare parts to the mechanical units . . . go around to this gentleman and tell him that we don't need any more production until they get caught up on spare parts.[31]

The Quartermaster General sought to determine whether the spare parts had been shipped to NATOUSA or sidetracked at New York. From the available records, General Gregory claimed that enough parts had been shipped to provide for one year's maintenance. He concluded that the shortage was attributable to a faulty distribution system within the theater, to a high mortality rate resulting from continuous operation of equipment, and to a lack of efficient maintenance and operating personnel. NATOUSA did not deny that logistical hazards contributed to the lag between the submission of requisitions and the delivery of parts. Time was lost Sullivan pointed out, when vessels were diverted from their original destinations. The relatively few boxes of spare parts were difficult to spot amidst the thousands of commodity containers. Quartermaster operations were often seriously handicapped and at times suspended because spare parts failed to arrive. For example, in January 1944 Sullivan submitted requisitions to ETOUSA for a stock of spare parts for

[29] (1) Pounder Rpt, pp. 20–22. (2) Memo, Sullivan for Tate, 19 Dec 43, no sub; Memo, 2d Lt Ernest E. Ballard, Class II and IV Off, for Col. Victor J. MacLaughlin, OQM Fifth Army, 24 Dec 43, sub: Field Range Parts. Both in Sullivan Papers.

[30] Ltr, Sullivan to Middleswart, 14 May 44. Sullivan Papers.

[31] Ltr, Sullivan to Doriot, 13 May 44. OQMG MED 400.4.

British-made bakery equipment. After waiting for the parts for almost six months he was ready to replace the trailer-mounted British equipment with the far less mobile M1942 model. To Littlejohn, Sullivan wrote: "I do not intend to continue to be responsible for the maintenance of equipment for which I am unable to obtain spare parts." [32] Although Sullivan had repeated his order with regularity, the shipment was not made until June 1944, and then the containers were lost in transit. Not until November—ten months after the original request—were the parts successfully shipped by air. Difficulties originated in another quarter. In August 1944, a 66,000-pound shipment of spare parts for laundry equipment, presumably unloaded at Civitavecchia, was misplaced, and an extensive search of Fifth Army's dumps failed to locate these urgently needed supplies. Middleswart's remedy, in part at least, lay in the recommendation that his 75-day level of spare parts be raised to a 6-month level. This had the support of the OQMG but it was denied by Army Service Forces. [33]

Two spare parts depots, one in Oran and the other at Naples, were opened by NATOUSA in the spring of 1944. The former, Middleswart designated as his central depot, much to the chagrin of those who thought this vital stock should be situated "where the fighting is going on" and close enough to eliminate the two-month period in which spare parts were ferried from North Africa to Italy. The Neapolitan depot opened on 1 April 1944 and remained there until 1 January 1945, when it moved to Leghorn. Designed to issue salvaged supplies and spare parts for fixed laundries, typewriters, and office machines, as well as equipment for mobile laundries, sterilization and bath trailers, and refrigeration, bakery, and salvage repair vans, the depot ultimately carried twelve thousand different spare parts for almost sixty major items of Quartermaster equipment. [34]

Indicating how new problems grew out of solutions to old ones, the purchase of Italian machinery also led to the search for appropriate spare parts. A chore from the outset, this search became even more difficult as the demand rose. Not only were stocks more precious but parts dealers were also known to charge from five to ten times the original price; indeed, in some instances, the Quartermaster Section suspected that many errant parts appearing on the market had recently rested in their own depot racks. An attempt to fashion spare parts locally, on a contractual basis, was an imperfect solution since the prices were again high notwithstanding

[32] Ltr, Sullivan to Littlejohn, 22 May 44. Littlejohn Collection.

[33] (1) Ltrs, Sullivan to Middleswart, 8, 27 Jul 44; Msgs, Clark to Larkin, 22 Feb 44, 10 Sep 44; Rad L–38824, Larkin to Clark, 25 Aug 44; Memo, Middleswart for Sullivan, 28 Aug 44; Msg L–48049, Larkin to Lee, 1 Oct 44. All in Sullivan Papers. (2) Memo, Actg Chief Maint Br ASF for Dir Sv Instl Div ASF, 20 May 44, no sub; Memo, TQMG for Dir Sv Instl Div ASF, 23 May 44, no sub; Memo, Dir Sv Instl Div ASF for TQMG, 6 Jun 44, sub: Spare Parts for Mechanical Equip; Ltr, Gregory to Sullivan, 9 Jun 44. All in OQMG MED 400.4. (3) Rad F–65896, CG NATOUSA to WD, 29 Jun 44; Rad WAR 61901, Somervell to Larkin, 7 Jul 44. Both in OQMG NATOUSA 451.31.

[34] (1) Ltr, Sullivan to Middleswart, 22 May 44; 1st Ind, AG SOS NATOUSA for CG NATOUSA, 6 May 44. Both in Sullivan Papers. (2) Hist QM PBS, p. 156.

the fact that the Americans furnished raw materials. Furthermore, the finished product was rarely engineered with sufficient precision to function properly when assembled in the larger piece of machinery.[35]

If the situation had improved by the end of 1944 or early 1945, it cannot be demonstrated by the evidence. Spare parts teams sent to the theater noted that the Fifth Army was not permitted to maintain stocks of replacement parts and that deliveries to Sullivan were still delayed by inadequate inventories at Peninsular Base Section. This was especially true of spare parts for mobile laundries, bakeries, clothing and textile repair units, and sterilization, bath, and shoe repair trailers. All too often, another observer noted, machinery worked only through the mending of tinkers or the improvising of technicians. Concluding that the spare parts problem was not generally understood, he thought it small consolation that "this feeling of frustration was not evident . . . in any of the other Quartermaster activities." [36]

Spare parts organization in the south of France followed the Mediterranean pattern. A single warehouse at Marseille contained all spare parts received from the United States. They were controlled items, sent forward only after requisitions were approved by the SOLOC quartermaster. After inspecting the installation in February 1945, General Littlejohn noted that it was "well or-

ganized, but has insufficient stocks. Specifically, has no bakery parts." Meanwhile the CONAD quartermaster had arranged for the Ordnance Section to provide parts and to perform repairs on field ranges, stoves, and similar equipment. Beginning in mid-December 1944, both salvaged and captured matériel in these categories were turned over to that organization, which had requisitioned several French arsenals and automotive factories and had ample workshop facilities. The amounts involved, never more than thirty tons in a two week's reporting period, were too small to appear in Ordnance activity reports, but represented a major service to the Quartermaster Section.[37]

Four-Legged Soldiers

In an Army moving toward complete mechanization, the reversion to pack trains and the use of war dogs appeared rather anomalous. The War Department had long debated the utility of horses and mules and procured fewer and fewer of them, but beginning early in 1942, it procured dogs in mounting numbers. In North Africa the Quartermaster Corps introduced the first of its four-legged soldiers—trained sentry dogs —to the battlefield on 8 November 1942. The 3d Battalion, 30th Infantry, 3d Division, had obtained four dogs from the Canine Section, Quartermaster Remount Depot, Front Royal, Virginia, before sailing. On board ship, handlers saw

[35] Hist QM PBS, p. 178.
[36] (1) Memo, QM Spare Parts Team for TQMG, 24 Dec 44, sub: Fifth Army QM Opns. Sullivan Papers. (2) Quoted in Memo, Asst ExO G–4 for QM AFHQ, 9 Jan 45, sub: Rpt of QM Spare Parts and Maint Activities. AG 319.1 NATOUSA.

[37] (1) Memo, CQM ETO for Brig Gen John B. Franks, 23 Feb 45, sub: Inspection of SOLOC Area and Action Required. Littlejohn Reading File, vol. XXXIII, item 124. (2) CONAD History, II. 617, 631, 646.

their dogs for the first time, fed them C rations, and engaged in last-minute training. On D-day the dogs proved gun-shy and flinched with fear when the convoy was subjected to aerial bombardment and naval gunfire. Once ashore, each canine sentry clawed out his own foxhole immediately. Behind the lines in the stillness of the next two nights, the dogs walked post. Handlers now praised their sentry work, feeling that the war dogs had remained alert for a greater period of time than the men had. The 3d Battalion's commander, Maj. Charles E. Johnson, recommended that in the future dogs should have an opportunity to become accustomed to battle noises, training which he believed had been overlooked at Front Royal. Later, in Italy, a mine dog platoon failed at mine detection work, and commanders reported that they much preferred engineer experts with technical devices for the job. At the war's end, five war dog platoons, the 33d, 34th, 35th, 37th, and 38th had served with the Fifth Army, mostly in the Gothic Line. Judging from reports and statements by handlers, messenger and scout dogs were only desirable in static warfare.[38]

Interest in pack animals as carriers first became pressing when the II Corps deployed on the approaches to Bizerte. With the main roads of the Sedjenane valley interdicted by mines, the 6oth Combat Team, 9th Division, ascended narrow trails so overgrown with scrub brush as to be impenetrable to vehicles. If the Bizerte offensive was to continue on terrain that was more suited to defensive operations, a less conventional method of supply had to be improvised.[39] Describing the same problem after similar experience in Sicily, Maj. Gen. Clarence R. Huebner, commander of the 1st Infantry Division, wrote:

It is impossible for infantry to operate exclusively in tank country when there is danger of an enemy tank attack; therefore, infantry must seek out tank-proof localities. The tank-proof localities normally include commanding terrain. To enable the 81mm. mortar and its ammunition to follow the infantry into rough country, mules, equipped with . . . pack saddles must be available.

Engineers normally follow closely behind the advancing infantry preparing trails which will permit supplies to be carried by $\frac{1}{4}$-ton C&R trucks. Until these trails are built, the only means of providing ammunition and rations is by mule or light animal transportation. Once these trails have been completed, the only use for the mule is to supply isolated patrols or detachments and to further the advance of the infantry elements.[40]

In Tunisia commanders and Quartermaster planners had not fully anticipated the use of pack animals. The beasts could not come from the United States. Shipping was already scarce and if vessels were altered to transport livestock and their forage, the problem of shipping would become even more involved. For

---

[38] (1) Ltr, CO 3d Bn 30th Inf to CG 3d Div, 25 Nov 42. Seventh Army, AG 454. (2) Rpt 419, AGF Bd Hq MTOUSA, 9 May 45. OQMG MED 319.25. (3) Erna Risch and Chester L. Kieffer, *The Quartermaster Corps: Organization, Supply, and Services,* Volume II, UNITED STATES ARMY IN WORLD WAR II (Washington, 1955), p. 336.

[39] (1) Ltr, CG 3d Inf Div to CG Seventh Army, 21 Sep 43, sub: Authority for Proc of Mules. Seventh Army, AG 454. (2) *To Bizerte With the II Corps, 23 April–13 May 1943,* AMERICAN FORCES IN ACTION SERIES (Washington, 1943), pp. 31–33.

[40] Ltr, Huebner to Patton, 19 Sep 43, sub: Rpt on Pack Equip and Animals. Seventh Army, AG 454.

that reason animals, forage, and equipment had to come from the countryside. Finding offspring of the male donkey and mare was just the beginning of the problem. Few quartermasters reared in a machine age knew how to organize a pack train. Nor could they find many experienced muleteers among the combat troops. For the Sedjenane valley advance, the G–4 of II Corps provided a remount fund of $150,000. McNamara's agents successfully negotiated in the towns of Le Kef, Souk el Arba, Aïn Draham, Bédja, Tabarka, Souk Ahras, and Bône for 218 mules, 95 donkeys, 28 horses, 285 packsaddle sets, and 24 tons of forage. The prices paid for animals and remount supplies mainly reflected their local value and the willingness of Arab owners to sell or rent them. Mules and horses rented for 50 francs ($1.00) per day, donkeys were purchased at prices ranging from $295 to $385, packsaddles were borrowed, and forage was furnished by the British as reciprocal aid.[41]

In Sicily, west of Mount Etna where the terrain was mountainous, the Seventh Army used mule trains even more extensively than the II Corps had done in Tunisia. A small number of animals came from Bizerte, but most of Patton's 4,000 beasts of burden bore the brand of Mussolini's army. Others were commandeered along the route of advance or were bought or rented from liberated Sicilians. The latter transaction marked an improvement over the II Corps' methods. In company with an American veterinarian, procurement officers of the divisions traveled from town to town—Alimena, St. Caterina, Sierra di Falco, and San Catelda, to cite the itinerary of the 3d Infantry Division's procurement section—directing the native police to corral pack animals. In the presence of an official, an Italian veterinarian, and the animal's owner, arrangements were made for the animals' sale or rental. The customary fee was 50 lire per day, but each animal was appraised and an agreement reached that the owner would be paid a specified amount if the animal was lost or killed. The average prices were $150 per mule, $120 per horse, and $40 per donkey. The 3d Division also rented carts and wagons at $60 and saddles at $40. With the understanding that their property would be returned, most owners painted or branded their animals. In Sicily, more than a third were killed by enemy action and many other animals were rendered unserviceable because of bad feet, saddlesores, or general debility.[42]

Animal transport also proved to be necessary in Italy. With years of experience behind them, the Germans were demonstrating the advantage that 4,000 animals per infantry division could give in terrain unfavorable to mechanized trains. General Clark saw the lesson. Having been in Italy less than a week, he told his chief of staff: "I am impressed with the pack train which the 3d Division has. We are going to need more of this type of transportation."

[41] Ltr, G–1 II Corps to CofS II Corps, 27 Apr 43, sub: Rpt of Animal and Equip Proc Activities; Memo, G–4 II Corps for Finance Off, 19 Apr 43. G–4 Jnl II Corps, 16 Apr–14 May 43.

[42] (1) Rpt of Opns SUSA in Sicilian Campaign, p. E–37. (2) Ltrs, 2d Lt Chester to CG 3d Inf Div, 2, 5, 7 Aug 43, sub: Convoy; Ltr, 2d Lt Clyde F. Howe to CG 3d Div, 17 Aug 43, sub: Mule Trip. Both in Hist Br OQMG. (3) 1st Lt Richard L. Walk, "Purchasing and Contracting Overseas," QMTSJ, VII, No. 2 (12 January 1945), 20–21.

From Caserta, initially, Tate set the Fifth Army's estimate at 1,300 mules. Filling the G–4 request was another matter. Sullivan's first call on Painter asked for 900 pack animals. For these the Quartermaster Section, Peninsular Base Section, wholly unfamiliar with animal matters, scoured the Neapolitan area for three weeks, sent agents to Sicily, and called upon the inexperienced Civil Affairs commissioners of AFHQ to set up an allocation policy on animals, forage, and equipment. Because of these hampering factors only 316 mules reached the Fifth Army during November 1943. Concurrently, the French Expeditionary Corps arrived, ascended into the Apennines, and, being more familiar with animal trains, insisted on receiving good remounts. In Naples, Painter immediately raised his estimates to 20,000 animals, searched for excavalrymen to tend his animal lines, sought veterinarians, and called on Middleswart to obtain a remount squadron from the United States.[43]

Painter was attempting to establish a remount service when most minds were on jeeps, trucks, and petroleum. The War Department, Middleswart reported, carried no remount squadrons on its active rolls. Painter immediately sought relief from Italy's manpower and U.S. replacement depots. Shoes, nails, halters, and saddles were just as scarce as men and mules, and at first a weird assortment of tack and gear was assembled. Initially, such good grain stocks as had not been carried off by the Germans

were claimed by Allied commissioners. Fields of local forage yielded roughage of poor quality. Having consumed poor Italian feed, the 3d Division's ill-shod mules lost some fifty pounds each during their first November fortnight of work. Two months later the situation was no better, and Clark wanted action. Each ascending ridge of the Apennines had cost many lives, and the squads holding the gains had to be supplied by pack animals or the outposts sacrificed.

Such persuasive appeals prodded the Fifth Army and Peninsular Base Section to accelerate the delivery of sound pack trains. Sullivan exhausted all local resources. Allied commissioners, who necessarily had to screen and control all animal bidders, hurried plans to obtain mules outside Italy. Two Sardinian trains, each containing 600 animals, arrived on the mainland. Yet Italy itself remained the prime source of supply. Early in December 1943 Painter finally found an American officer to head the Quartermaster Remount Service, Peninsular Base Section. This man was Lt. Col. Sebe J. Houghton, an excavalryman, who had served five years on the Cavalry Board in Washington.

Painter had created the Remount Service without the guidance of a War Department Table of Organization and Equipment or the established experiences of predecessors. Houghton quickly expanded the service. The 2610th and 6742d Remount Depots, both overhead units, operated stations at Persano, Bagnoli, and Santa Maria. At the end of January Houghton's agents were purchasing an average of 200 animals each week. On 27 February 1944 the 6742d established the policy of keeping in its yard 10 percent of the total animal

[43] (1) Quoted in *Fifth Army History*, II, 67. (2) Poore Journal, Nov–Dec 43. (3) *QM Supply in Fifth Army*, pp. 18–19.

strength of Fifth Army animals as replacements. Chutes, racks, fences, troughs, and cutting pens were built, and slowly from a small picket line the Remount Service began to grow until eventually it accumulated 15,000 pack animals, of which 11,000 were issued to combat troops. Thousands of animals also went through remount depots for reconditioning or disposal. Less than 2,900 animals arrived from the United States, and these did not work in the field until the last weeks of the war. The 10th Mountain Division had a strength of 200 French and Sardinian horses, 560 American horses, and 500 American mules. The 6742d and the 2610th also struggled to fill their personnel rosters. Initially, Painter found all replacement depots closed to him. Gradually he received the men, but they were inexperienced and had to be trained on the job. Veterinarians were lacking until May 1944, when the first of them, Maj. Herbert F. Sibert, reported to Houghton. At the same time the first equipment arrived from the United States, consisting of medicines, nails, shoes, and clipping machines. Then the push for Rome began, trucks were used, and the Remount Service momentarily breathed more easily.[44]

In Italy, the requisitioning and pricing policy was similar to that in Sicily, but initially the scarcity of animals forced Houghton to modify the Army's traditionally high physical standards. His agents paid as much as $250 for a horse or $300 for a mule that might carry one load of ammunition and then be suited only for the auction block.

It might then be sold at a 300 percent profit, its carcass later to appear in the black market. In the interests of expediency, too, Houghton had sacrificed his regard for camouflage. In Italy, black and brown mules were rarer than white and grey ones. Initially, pack trains of light-colored animals presented conspicuous targets on ground once held by the enemy and now carefully pinpointed by German artillery. Until an ingenious quartermaster conceived the idea of spraying the animals with a 5 percent solution of potassium permanganate, which effectively darkened and perfumed hair and hide for a month or more, white mules suffered high casualties.

Like good mules, good hay was also at a premium. Toward the end of April 1944 rather daring plans were worked out to get forage from the other side of the Volturno River. Special permission had to be obtained from the Fifth Army for a thousand "hay raiders"—Italian volunteers—to cross the river and enter the combat zone. The operation involved many carts, trucks, baling machines, and other equipment, but the harvest was worth the effort as some 3,500 tons of very scarce hay were gathered. It was placed in a new depot at Falcione Monragoni very close behind the lines.[45]

For the remainder of the war in Italy, Remount Service was essentially an American co-ordinating agency to insure that Italian mules and equipment were provided in sufficient quantities for Italian pack units. By the end of 1944, the muleteers of the Fifth Army's fifteen pack companies, organized according to

[44] (1) Hist QM PBS, pp. 232–33, 237–38, 245, 248–49. (2) QM Supply in Fifth Army, p. 41.

[45] (1) Hist QM PBS, p. 237. (2) Hist PENBASE, III, 81.

AMERICAN PACK UNIT *waiting for Italian muleteers to clear the trail. February 1944.*

Italian T/O's and administered by the 210th Italian Infantry Division, were almost entirely Italian. The fifteen companies were organized into five battalions which in turn were under the 20th Pack Group. In addition to muleteers, these units provided porters for the final stage of delivery to combat units. Each company contained an average of 11 officers and 380 enlisted men, and 260 mules and 12 riding horses. It normally supported a U.S. infantry battalion. There was little that was not of Italian origin. Peninsular Base Section's stables at Persano, Santa Maria near

Capua, Bagnoli, Grosseto, and Pisa were former Italian breeding agencies or race tracks. Most animal equipment was locally made. Feed bags, breast straps, bridles, canvas buckets, halters, and harness buckles originated in the small saddleries of Naples. Even the small and lightweight Italian pack carrier was preferred over the American cargo saddle that was too large for Italian breeds. As was the case in procuring other Class II and IV supplies, Painter, and later Bare, assisted Italian contractors by furnishing them raw materials. Canvas for feed bags was supplied. Coal and iron were furnished those who forged snaps, rings, rivets, and mule and horse shoes, although the contractor sent his own labor to salvage yards for scrap metal. Similarly, the contractor who agreed to supply oats hired his own help for sacking feed, but the quartermaster provided the bags as well as the transportation to deliver the laborers to and from the job.

At the close of the Po valley campaign, there was an excess of animals. Having retreated hastily, the enemy abandoned thousands of fine draft and riding horses. Many had been brought from Germany and Austria early in the war. Others were of finest Italian breeds. When hostilities ended the Remount Service corralled all animals at San Martino De Spino, formerly an Italian cavalry school. Ultimately Allied commissioners distributed the captured animals among those farmers who had assisted in the liberation of Italy.[46] The fact that the last stable closed without one epidemic ever having scourged Remount Service's herds is evidence enough that quartermasters and veterinarians had accomplished their remount mission in Italy, especially when the multitude of stock sources is considered.

Remount service in southern France dated from 20 October 1944, when Col. Louis G. Gibney landed at Marseille with half of the 6742d QM Remount Depot. Movement orders from Persano, Italy, had been issued at the beginning of the month, but covered only the ten

officers and fifty enlisted men of the detachment. There was a two weeks' delay until shipping space could be found for 700 mules, an integral and invaluable part of the unit. At the Delta Base staging area, the depot assumed command over an Italian service unit, and was shortly redesignated the 6835th QM Remount Depot. After a month of comparative inactivity in the coastal area, the 6835th moved to Is-sur-Tille, a rail center near Dijon, where it came under CONAD command and was attached to the 71st QM Base Depot. On 25 November it received the designation Remount Depot Q–581, which had previously identified a similar installation at Pisa, Italy. At Is-sur-Tille, and later at Chaumont and Rambervillers, the 6835th kept a reserve of 600 mules and 50 horses at all times, and maintained a large veterinary hospital and rehabilitation farm. Horses were obtained by local procurement through French agencies and many more were captured and turned in by the combat units. There was an actual surplus of horses and a considerable number were shipped to Italy, but mules were scarce, most of them coming from the United States. Hay and forage were at first procured through French channels, but the quality was unsatisfactory, and beginning in December the depot obtained such supplies through the CONAD purchasing officer.[47]

Beginning in October 1944, Seventh Army troops in the Vosges encountered conditions similar to those in the moun-

---

[46] (1) *Fifth Army History*, III, 68. (2) *QM Supply in Fifth Army*, pp. 75–76. (3) Msg L–16628, Larkin to WD, 22 Apr 44. OQMG MED 311.2. (4) Ltr, Maj H. M. Rhett to Remount Br OQMG, 3 Jan 45, sub: Pack Mules MTO. OQMG MED 319.1. (5) Memo, Asst Remount Off PBS for Houghton, 1 Apr 44, sub: Harness Gear. Sullivan Papers. (6) Hist QM PBS, pp. 245, 248–49.

[47] (1) Hist QM PBS, pp. 232, 237. (2) Unit History, 6835th QM Remount Depot. Hist Br OQMG. (2) Littlejohn, ed., Passing in Review, ch. 43.

tains of Italy, and requested pack units for forward support. The 513th QM Pack Company, a Negro unit, was transferred from Italy to the DRAGOON area, arriving in late November. It provided support for the infantry of the 45th and 103d Divisions, and was the only unit of its type in the European theater.[48] Organized under T/O 10–118, this unit had two officers and seventy-five enlisted men, or about one quarter of the strength of the Italian-type units. Since the U.S. unit did not perform porter service, its manpower was ample to handle its T/O allowance of 298 animals. The 513th proved able to handle its rated cargo capacity of twenty tons (five tons per platoon) with excellent efficiency as long as the round trip for the pack animals did not exceed one day.[49]

Clean Linens and Showers

Among the varied housekeeping duties performed by the Quartermaster Corps, helping the soldier to keep his body and his clothes clean was one of the most basic. But if this service was an obvious one, it was also relatively new. Before the turn of the twentieth century, a detachment at a post, camp, or station hired its own laundresses or made contracts with commercial laundries. In 1909 the Quartermaster Corps established post laundries with funds appropriated for general supplies. During World War I the overseas program expanded to provide delousing and bathing facilities as well. The American Expeditionary Forces realized considerable success with fixed laundries in the communications zone where they were established at the dozen largest salvage depots between Marseille and Brest, but in the use of mobile field units and mechanical devices the Americans lagged far behind the British and French. The best that could be done for the front-line soldier was to replace his soiled outer garments. Washing undergarments and socks remained an individual responsibility. Nothing illustrated the poverty of the bath and laundry program in the combat zone as dramatically as the results of inspections that followed the 1918 armistice. Reports showed that 90 percent of the fighting force had body lice, and a typhus epidemic was feared imminent.

Mobile and Static Laundries

In spite of this ominous development, the War Department gave only desultory consideration after the war to mobile laundries. Everyone knew that immaculate linen had never won battles. When the Medical Department sought assistance in planning for hospital laundry service, the Quartermaster Corps referred The Surgeon General to a laundry machinery manufacturer. This firm indicated that no mobile laundry blueprints were available. Not until after the fall of France in June 1940 did the War Department allocate funds for the purchase of experimental laundries. Shortly afterward new designs assembled a 6-unit laundry on a single vehicle, easily concealed and less vulnerable to air attack. In subsequent months, Quartermaster designers standardized a 10-unit semitrailer, capable of washing 125 pounds of clothing per hour. The War Department then activated laundry com-

---

[48] (1) *Fifth Army History*, II, 249–50. (2) *QM Supply in ETO*, VIII, 88–89.
[49] *QM Supply in ETO*, VIII, 222–23.

panies, each with 16 semitrailer units, in increasing numbers.[50]

Throughout the TORCH operation, laundry and dry cleaning services were sadly inadequate. The earliest service units were few in number and NATO-USA necessarily assigned them to the large base section hospitals. Not until the restoration of facilities at major ports were the mobile laundries taken forward, and even then they moved with field hospitals as attachments. Only after cleaning hospital linens could laundry units serve the field forces, and the laundry's sporadic assistance proved more a hindrance than a help when haste forced the return of loose and scrambled wash. For the most part, the field soldier scrubbed his own things or hired natives, who insisted that soap be provided and charged high prices.

By mid-April 1943 Middleswart had a total of 17 vans at his disposal, but these were too few to provide adequate service within three base sections. Most of the vans remained in Morocco where they had been combined with commercial laundries. With only 11 of its authorized

16 vans, Company D, 61st Laundry Battalion, was the first of its type to operate in Atlantic Base Section. At Casablanca this unit operated a large fixed laundry to which four semitrailers were attached. In January 1943 Company D deployed its other vans to Rabat, Fedala, Safi, and Casablanca when it appeared that the I Armored Corps would play a major security role in that part of Africa.

Initially, D Company refused to accept individual laundry bundles. On a scheduled day of each week, each unit of the I Armored Corps assembled its fatigues, white cottons, and woolens in separate mattress covers and hauled them to the laundry. Thirty-six hours later the roughdry wash was ready. Then the unit separated each individual's bundle according to the standard Army laundry mark of the soldier's surname initial and the last four digits of his serial number. By this process once a week each soldier received a laundered shirt, a pair of trousers or a complete fatigue suit, a pair of socks, a towel, an undershirt, and a pair of underdrawers. Daily linen service was given only to dispensaries and hospitals. To handle one large hospital's laundry, French authorities scheduled an evening shift of workers at one of their military laundries. In the summer of 1943, Atlantic Base Section received equipment for several large laundries, each capable of serving 10,000 men, and a 2,500-man dry cleaning plant. Using packing and crating materials, engineers erected a fixed plant to house the new equipment.

In areas as comparatively undeveloped as North Africa and Sicily, laundry officers encountered countless difficulties in using commercial facilities. Soap powders, bleaches, and soda ash had to be

---

[50] (1) Technical improvements in equipment continued throughout World War II, but the organization based on a company of 4 platoons, each of 2 sections, each with 2 trailers, was retained. T/O 10–167 of 21 April 1944 authorized a semimobile laundry company of 5 officers and 262 enlisted men. Operating 2 shifts a day, it could serve 48,000 men per week, providing each man with a clean shirt, a pair of socks, a towel, trousers, undershirt, and underdrawers, or roughly 200,000 pounds of wash. Normal assignment of these units was 1 per corps or 2 per army. QM Supply in ETO, VIII, 227–28. (2) For the best general history of laundry activities, see Louis Filler, Laundry and Related Activities of the Quartermaster General, QMC Historical Studies, 13 (Washington, 1946). (3) Operations of the Quartermaster Corps, U.S. Army, During the World War, Monograph 4, Notes on Salvage Activities, AEF., France (Schuylkill Arsenal, Philadelphia, Pa., 1929), p. 25.

imported as well as steamfitters to repair antiquated boilers and plumbing. So inadequate were the local plants that even the smallest were commandeered. In Casablanca, a shop operated by one laundress was taken over, notwithstanding the need to assign two soldiers who saw that her operations were not interrupted, correct amounts of soap were measured, only soldiers were served, and just prices were charged. Local conditions were not always at fault. In TORCH planning quartermasters had completely overlooked one aspect of the dry cleaning trade. Civilian shops refused to accept orders unless first issued cleaning fluid. Quartermaster sought such solvents in Ordnance shops. Politely, the issue was refused because solvents were needed for cleaning weapons and engines. When the first two convoys failed to bring Quartermaster cleaning fluids, laundry officers lost their contracts. In Sicily the unsanitary condition of village laundries made it impossible to use them even temporarily. Military laundries assigned to repair and salvage work had to ask that their full load of equipment be forwarded from North Africa.[51]

In Italy the laundry and dry cleaning service developed tremendously under Colonel Ela's guiding hand. His laundries had a dual purpose within the salvage program, that of providing clean linen for hospitals, troops, and organizations, and that of washing clothing and equipment turned in for renovation or rags. On 6 October 1943 the first unit in Naples, the 496th Laundry Company, arrived at the site of Mussolini's fairgrounds near Bagnoli. Bags of soiled hospital bedclothes greeted them. For a time a lily pad pool was the only source of water, and sixteen trailers dropped their hoses into this single reservoir. Three weeks later, the 497th debarked at the Bagnoli pier, and in the absence of its own vans it commandeered two civilian laundries in order to help the 496th.

Because of the widespread destruction in Naples—where boiler rooms had been blasted by bombs, buildings gutted by fire, and equipment rusted from exposure —engineers completely reconstructed several laundries. In others, they replaced roofs, floors, and windows. Extractors and steamers were rebuilt from salvaged sheet metal and plate. Gears were redesigned and cut in local machine shops. Searching for sources of electricity, Ela learned that weeks would pass before high-tension lines could be restrung to his main plant. Further investigation revealed that an underground conduit had once been laid in the vicinity. Engineers located the line, found it usable, and averted considerable delay.

The 497th opened the first fixed military laundry in Naples on 29 November 1943. Two days later the first ironed sheets and pillowcases brightened beds of base section hospitals. Working around the clock, seven days per week, the 497th eventually freshened linens for thirty-two hospitals, all of which received twenty-four-hour service. Notwithstanding the relief afforded by the renovated plants, construction began in June 1944 to house a 10,000-man laundry. It eventually became one of the largest works of its kind in the theater. Elements of the 424th operated it.

[51] (1) Pounder Rpt, p. 87. (2) Frink Rpt. (3) Cir 49, Hq MBS, 1 Apr 43. (4) Ltr, Larkin to Eisenhower, sub: Quarterly Rpt on Laundry and Dry Cleaning Opns. Hist Br OQMG. (5) Hist IBS QM Sec, p. 4. Hist Br OQMG.

Until the Anzio front became static, casualties there were high and hospitals busy. Enemy shellbursts seriously damaged both the hospital and its attached laundry thereby adding to the workload of Neapolitan laundries. Nevertheless, it was decided not to replace the expensive and scarce washing machinery on the beachhead. Thereafter Ela took advantage of the LST shuttle service. When working at maximum efficiency, fifteen 2½-ton trucks relayed the complete linen supply of one Anzio hospital to Naples and returned a fresh stock to the beachhead twenty-four hours later.[52]

Ela's laundrymen, collecting the woolens of winter, followed the Fifth Army to the Arno. In July and August base section laundries handled twelve million pounds, the highest figure of the campaign. The 496th was one of the few Quartermaster units to halt in Rome, where it served a large base hospital and one of Italy's favorite rest camps. When the enemy retired from Leghorn and Pisa, Ela's search for commercial laundries was complicated by the widespread devastation. In all of Leghorn, a city of 125,000, he found one small laundry and dry cleaning plant intact. In historic Pisa, on the other hand, a former clothing factory was undamaged and fourteen woolpresses remained in the building. Operations were temporarily thwarted when the Arno inundated Pisa with four feet of water. Installation of new equipment for a 10,000-man plant was shortly undertaken thereafter. By mid-December, the 631st Laundry Company had tested the machinery, hired Italian operators, and trained them as sorters, markers, and ironers. Business

opened on 1 January 1945. Using a floor plan which permitted a circular flow of work, the 631st supervised production with a minimum of interference, reaching an output of 8,000 pieces daily, plus 2,000 to 3,000 salvaged garments returned to stock. For a while the Pisa plant was close enough to the front to handle dry cleaning for the combat soldier. Over the plant's counters, combat air crews and base section troops enjoyed a considerable amount of personalized service. In Florence, which, like Pisa, had suffered comparatively little damage, another civilian plant was utilized. By the end of the Italian campaign nine companies, plus a separate platoon, were operating laundries which stretched from Naples to Pistoia. Supplementing the many fixed laundries were mobile units supervised by several American enlisted men and one officer and employing Italian Army service units and later German prisoners of war. In Italy the monthly wash of Peninsular Base Section's laundries rose from a half-million pounds in January 1944 to more than ten million pounds in May 1945.[53]

Although the bulk of laundry work was performed in the base section, and troops there were the beneficiaries of a laundry and dry cleaning service which closely resembled that in the United States, the combat soldiers were not altogether neglected. Mobile laundries went into the combat zone, but primarily to supplement a shower program. The roughdry wash and issue of used items were necessary features of a large-scale field operation. Nevertheless it was possible to provide a degree

---

[52] Hist QM PBS, p. 174.

[53] *Ibid.,* pp. 174–75.

of cleanliness under field conditions that virtually eliminated louse-borne diseases from the Italian front.

Since the first laundrymen ashore in southern France were veterans of North Africa, Sicily, and Italy, they brought typical Mediterranean procedures to the DRAGOON area. The 549th QM Laundry Company, a VI Corps unit, landed on D-day and kept close behind the combat troops during their swift northward advance. The headquarters and two platoons of the 498th QM Laundry Company, also Mediterranean veterans, had two civilian laundries in operation in Marseille by mid-September. By the end of that month the 3d Platoon had been assigned to CONAD and departed for Dijon. There it operated a civilian laundry and assumed control over two Italian laundry companies, the 7159th and 7169th, during October. For closer co-ordination with the salvage repair program, which involved a large-scale renovation of clothing, most of these laundry units moved to Vesoul in late October. The 898th Semimobile Laundry Company from northern France and the 7172d Italian Laundry Company had also assembled there by the time that southern France became part of the European theater.[54]

Bath and Clothing Exchange Program

In the combat zone—where soldiers were constantly exposed to dirt and sand, water and oil, sweat and blood—the bath program was as difficult to implement as was the laundry program. Few of the

100,000 men in the II Corps could bathe in Tunisia, and fewer still in Sicily, where no shower equipment was available. This lesson was not lost to Sullivan and, while still in French Morocco, he sought ways of providing a 300,000-man force with a bath and clean clothing program. As each soldier was necessarily burdened with a resupply of barracks bag clothing, most of which would be better used if part of a steadily rotating inventory, Sullivan proposed to combine the features of a clothing exchange and a bathing system.[55]

This concept became even more compelling after the Fifth Army landed at Salerno. The first sterilization and bath company did not arrive for two months, few divisions were in rest areas, and the bath unit could be exploited only by service and rear echelon troops. To compound the frustrations, when the 3d Infantry Division retired from the line after the hard-fought Volturno battle, the heavy rains made it impossible to use the existing equipment and the men bathed only under a shower improvised by engineers.[56]

By this time, Colonel Tate, the G–4 of Fifth Army, was echoing Sullivan's sentiments for a bath-clothing exchange program. Presenting the idea to the G–4's of the II and VI Corps, Tate wrote:

I am confident that under the present system, there is a great waste of clothing due to: (1) The individual soldier discarding all but his most immediate needs when under pressure of combat; (2) throwing away soiled clothing when changes are made due to inability to have such clothing laundered in forward areas. . . . I am convinced that all clothing, except that worn

[54] (1) Unit Histories, 498th, 549th QM Laundry Cos. Hist Br OQMG. (2) CONAD History, II, 835–60.

[55] Sullivan Diary, 30 Jun 43.
[56] Ltr, Dill to OQMG, Nov 43. OQMG MED 457.

by the soldier, plus one change of underwear and socks, should be withdrawn . . . and carried in bulk, split between Regimental and Divisional trains, as a reserve to replace soiled and worn clothing as needed.[57]

Sullivan promptly instituted this system in the Naples rest area. He directed Colonel Currey of the 94th Quartermaster Battalion to carry out the program "in spirit as well as in word." In the interests of speed Sullivan set aside a basic supply of clothing for 5,000 men. Eager that every man derive the benefits of the new program, he encouraged Currey to station guards at all tent exits and prevent any soldier from departing with his dirty clothing. Exchanges opened in the Fifth Army's rest centers on 20 November 1943 and, after the second week, Colonel Currey reported to Sullivan that more than 4,000 men had used the facilities. To these men, the 94th had issued fifteen different types of clothing, from shoelaces to overcoats, in quantities varying from two bath towels to 3,243 pairs of wool socks. Noting the contribution of this innovation to the health, welfare, and morale of this command, Clark acknowledged its immediate success in a letter to The Quartermaster General.[58] Reflecting his own pleasure, General Ryder, commander of the 34th Infantry Division, spelled out the earliest details of the program. He wrote to Clark:

The soldier walked into the undressing tent, where he disrobed, placing the cloth-

ing for which he required no replacement, together with his valuables or personal property, in a bag which he would redeem by means of a tag prior to leaving the unit. He was then given a cake of soap, took his shower, came out, was given a towel, and then was given clean clothes from the skin out, consisting of underwear, sox, shirt, and trousers, and, if required, field jacket, leggings and shoes. The entire operation took place under canvas and the tents were well heated, including the dressing tent. The unit, operating in this manner, serviced two thousand individuals per day.

Hoping that the tents could be brought closer to the front, Ryder recommended that a similar unit with a capacity of 900 to 1,000 individuals per day be attached to each infantry division. Given such facilities and a favorable tactical situation, every soldier could be processed through the exchange once every two weeks. Other division commanders were interviewed. They concurred with Ryder on the project's desirability, but most did not want the responsibility of having such a unit added to their train. In January 1944 the exchange unit was made available to British and French troops serving under General Clark's command, and they similarly applauded it.[59]

While the exchanges became a fixture at rest areas, a miniature program was started in the army area on 14 December by the 62d Quartermaster Battalion, Lt. Col. Lawrence C. Page, Jr., commanding. Eventually composed of two laundry companies and four sterilization and bath companies, the 62d served more than 900,000 men in its first six months

---

[57] Memo, Tate for G–4 II Corps and G–4 VI Corps, 13 Nov 43. Sullivan Papers.

[58] Quotation from Ltr, Sullivan to Currey, 18 Nov 43, sub: Clothing Exchange for Troops in Rest Areas; Ltr, Currey to Sullivan, 11 Dec 43, sub: Rpt, Clothing Exchange Opns in Fifth Army Rest Centers; Ltr, Clark to Gregory, 18 Dec 53. All in Sullivan Papers.

[59] Quotation from Ltr, Ryder to Clark, 30 Dec 43, sub: Recommendation for Continued Use of Bath-Laundry-Clothing Exchange Unit; Memo, Sullivan for Tate, 29 Dec 43; Ltr, Sullivan to Tate, 9 Feb 44, sub: QM Hist Data. All in Sullivan Papers.

of operation, from December 1943 to June 1944. Because field hospitals had the highest priority, Colonel Page deployed his laundry platoons so that they could simultaneously handle hospital linens and the clothes turned in to his eight bath and clothing exchanges. In the army area this required constant and careful reconnaissance—not without its difficulties. Page did not control selection of hospital sites, yet each of his bathing or laundry points required a water supply capable of serving 3,000 men per day.[60]

Pleased as he was that the fighting man welcomed these services and wanted them at hand, Sullivan preferred that exchanges should be located in rest areas where a water supply was accessible and to which men could repair. Not a minor consideration was the fact that the semi-mobile units, weighing ten tons or more, were restricted to surfaced roads and reasonably level terrain. The satisfactory shower and clothing exchange required a clear water supply of 20,000 gallons for every sixteen hours of operations, heavy tentage, additional space to store several thousand clothing sets, and portable lighting facilities. Sullivan contended, too, that each operating unit was noisy, had a telltale silhouette, and would be far removed from any replacement parts if machinery was damaged by enemy artillery.[61]

These unwieldy features led Colonel Page to recommend in November 1944

that a new and more compact company be organized, capable of rendering closer combat support. Although the fumigation and bath company—a small unit and one which broke down into self-contained platoons—had been recently introduced into Fifth Army, it still depended on an attached laundry platoon. By combining them Page felt that each bath platoon would be self-sufficient. It was to serve 225 men an hour. Because it would not be pulling heavy trailers and vans, the proposed bath and clothing exchange company could move more rapidly, and excessive travel by all parties would be eliminated. For his proposal, Colonel Page earned a medal. But the War Department rejected the suggestion on the ground that its applicability was limited. Meanwhile, General Sullivan felt that he could not advance the shower facilities to railheads, but he brought the clothing exchange system there. Truck drivers reaped the first benefits in February 1944. "A wet cold truck driver," he maintained, "who can be given a hot bowl of soup and fresh clothing has less chance of a wreck and thereby contributes to the war effort." [62]

Meanwhile the divisions improvised their own relief. In February 1944 the 34th Division established its own shower program in its rest area, with quartermasters operating the clothing exchange and engineers operating a 24-head shower. Within the next six months the 3d and 88th Infantry Divisions started similar programs. On the day following its first combat mission in February 1945,

[60] Ltr, Sullivan to Clark, 12 Dec 44, sub: Recommendation for Award of Bronze Star Medal. Sullivan Papers.

[61] Sullivan Diary, 11 Jan 44; 3d Ind, Sullivan to Tate, 30 Jun 44, sub: Laundry and Bath Units. Both in Sullivan Papers.

[62] (1) Ltr and Inds, Page to Sullivan, 10 Nov 44, sub: Recommended Bath and Clothing Exchange Co. Sullivan Papers. (2) Quoted in Sullivan Diary, 3 Feb 44.

the 10th Mountain Division began a comparable service. The improvised divisional shower equipment was compact and easily moved. Unlike the semimobile sterilization and bath unit, which provided less shower space, this equipment could be brought to the troops and put into operation in twenty minutes. For one division's experiment Sullivan sent 500 units of clothing. Another division was unable to institute a shower program immediately, but it experimented with the issue, two to three times weekly, of clean, dry socks, making deliveries through the ration railheads.

By the fall of 1944, the army quartermaster standardized his clothing exchange program for the forward units. Each exchange was equipped to maintain a daily turnover of 1,000 shirts, trousers, drawers, and undershirts, and 5,000 pairs of socks. Each corps was directed to regulate the use of these exchanges by the separate units. The organizations so designated brought their soiled garments to a laundry where they were provided with a receipt authorizing the exchange or initial issue of a like quantity of clean clothes.

One of the obvious results of the clothing exchange was to eliminate the "bundle" system of laundry and to reduce the difficulties of personalized service under combat conditions. Equally significant—as an economy measure—was that troops accepted stocks of used clothing they normally were reluctant to wear. In the interests of speedier handling the Fifth Army established a new sizing policy for items which had passed through the clothing-exchange, laundry, and salvage systems. Instead of issuing by the conventional tariff—which con-

sisted of about thirty sizes for shirts and forty for trousers—clothing was assembled into three broad categories: small, medium, and large. Traditionally, this practice was repulsive to troops, but a survey of divisions elicited approval of three sizes. The soldier who had not bathed for several weeks, and whose clothing was offensive, was not likely to complain about the minor inconvenience of wearing garments not his own or loose fitting as long as they were well sterilized and freshly laundered.[63]

By contrast with Italian conditions, warfare in the south of France was extremely mobile, at least in the early stages, and it was impossible to provide comparable comforts for the combat troops. Seventh Army's veteran divisions had outrun their service units as well as their supplies, and could not expect the services they had enjoyed in Italy the previous winter. Having left the mild Riviera zone for forested subalpine terrain, they needed extra clothing rather than an exchange, and such fuel as they could obtain was used for heating tents and billets rather than for baths. The 36th QM Company reported in early November that it was organizing a sock exchange for the 36th Division. Public baths were a feature of most French cities, and were used by the troops whenever possible, especially when they were rotated out of the line for a brief rest. CONAD provided as much assistance as possible. The 814th Sterilization Company, at Vesoul and later at Strasbourg, speeded up the clothing salvage operations already described, and the 865th and 7164th Fumigation

---

[63] Ltr, Sullivan to Ramsey, 8 Apr 44; Ltr, Bates to Doriot, 1 Aug 44. Both in Sullivan Papers.

and Bath Companies, the latter an Italian service unit, were sent to Vaivre near Vesoul in November, and on to Lunéville in January.[64]

The contrasts between climate, terrain, and tactics in the successive combat areas of North Africa, Sicily, Italy, and southern France emphasize the variable conditions and flexible procedures characteristic of the Mediterranean theater. This flexibility was also a favorable result of comparatively small-scale operations, in which one base section supported one army and was able to adjust rapidly to the special needs of that army. The succeeding chapters describe large-scale operations in which those elements of flexibility and rapid adjustment were notably lacking.

[64] (1) Unit History, 36th QM Co. Hist Br OQMG. (2) *CONAD History,* II, 835–60.

CHAPTER IX

The Quartermaster Establishment in the United Kingdom

During 1943 the Americans in the British Isles followed the shifting fortunes of war in the Mediterranean with intense interest. Successes or disappointments there had a very direct effect on ultimate plans for their own theater. ROUNDUP had been scheduled for April, but all concerned were agreed that the TORCH operation would delay a cross-Channel attack by at least a year. Secretary of War Henry L. Stimson, one of the strongest advocates of ROUNDUP, had seen this clearly as early as July 1942, and had vainly used that argument in urging cancellation of the TORCH operation.[1] Even when enthusiasm over Mediterranean successes was at its height, there were no serious proposals to cancel the BOLERO build-up permanently. Yet Americans on the spot found the vacillating troop basis, unfirm shipping schedules, and low priority of their theater almost worse than an outright repudiation. They gloomily referred to BOLERO as "in limbo." The various British headquarters in the United Kingdom were considerably more optimistic about BOLERO, although opinion on ROUNDUP was sharply divided. Englishmen who disapproved of ROUNDUP as a suicidal venture nevertheless welcomed the American build-up in the United Kingdom. It helped secure their home territory against the possibility of a German invasion, and even permitted British troops to be sent to other theaters. All were in agreement on the need for an American bomber offensive, which could not be launched from any other base. Finally, the continuance of BOLERO guaranteed the presence of a combat reserve in a location where it could quickly exploit any sudden strategic or political crisis that might occur within Axis territory. Further than that, the more conservative British strategists would not go.[2] They had seen British armies driven off the Continent four times since 1939. These were sobering facts that many Americans had not completely grasped before they arrived in the British Isles. Therefore the newcomers were all the readier to admire the courage of those Englishmen, fortunately a majority, who were willing

[1] Henry L. Stimson and McGeorge Bundy, *On Active Service in Peace and War* (New York: Harper and Brothers, 1947), p. 426.

[2] Gordon A. Harrison, *Cross-Channel Attack*, UNITED STATES ARMY IN WORLD WAR II (Washington, 1951), pp. 95–96. The possibility that German troops might be withdrawn from all occupied areas in the west was taken very seriously in ETOUSA headquarters, and even the possibility of a wholesale German surrender was provided for. The plans to take care of these eventualities were given the code names RANKIN B and RANKIN C, respectively.

to ignore past defeats and try again.

Until the end of January 1943, ETO-USA was essentially a subtheater commanded for Eisenhower by his deputy, Maj. Gen. Russell P. Hartle, whose major duty was to forward promptly from Great Britain to North Africa whatever personnel and supplies were required. Early in February ETOUSA became a separate theater and Lt. Gen. Frank M. Andrews, an Air Corps officer, assumed command. During that month the U.S. forces in the theater dwindled to a low of 104,510, including about 35,000 service troops, but thereafter came a very slow increase in strength.[3]

Revived Plans for Combat

General Lee returned from the Casablanca Conference in January 1943 full of optimism for a renewed BOLERO build-up, but his hopes were dashed when, at the end of February, Eisenhower announced that he would need 160,000 additional troops for HUSKY (the coming campaign in Sicily.) Clearly, this meant another postponement. In April and May there was a series of dramatic successes in antisubmarine operations in the Atlantic, arousing the hope that shipping could be found to support simultaneous campaigns in the Mediterranean and in northern Europe. Also in April one of the few firm decisions of the Casablanca Conference favorable to BOLERO was implemented: a planning staff called COSSAC (Chief of Staff to the Supreme Allied Commander (Designate)) was set up under British Lt. Gen. Sir Frederick Morgan, and began an intensive study of cross-Channel operations. Morgan and his American

deputy, Brig. Gen. Ray W. Barker, were comparatively junior officers and, as assistants to a nonexistent Supreme Commander, wielded little authority. But they had a talent for conceiving aggressive combat plans and working them out to the point where co-ordination with other headquarters became necessary, thereby arousing the interest of other commanders. Morgan, especially, was a strong personality, and firmly opposed to the conservative school of British strategy. Above all, if these men felt that the forces or supplies allotted for any aspect of the contemplated cross-Channel operation were too small, they were quick to demand reinforcements or higher priorities. Their anomalous position as aides to an undesignated Supreme Commander made it possible to forward such recommendations direct to the very highest echelons. Thus the activities of COSSAC had a vitalizing effect upon BOLERO planning everywhere, but especially within ETOUSA headquarters.[4]

In May 1943 General Andrews was killed in an aircraft accident, and was succeeded by General Devers, former commander of the Armored Force at Fort Knox, Kentucky. The choice was significant. Before his death, General Andrews had virtually completed preparation of a detailed troop basis to replenish the weakened Eighth Air Force, and of plans to resume the air offensive against the Continent. Now an expert on armored forces would perform the same services for ground combat troops. In accordance with the figures developed during the TRIDENT Conference at Washington in late May, Devers called on his staff for a detailed troop basis to support

---

[3] Ruppenthal, *Logistical Support,* I, 129.

[4] Harrison, *Cross-Channel Attack,* pp. 47–54.

a force of twenty-one divisions. Early in July, SOS ETOUSA submitted a troop basis calling for 490,000 men in service units, including Littlejohn's requirement for 56,000 Quartermaster troops. This estimate, based more on BOLERO requirements than on a forecast for continental operations, involved several considerations. The time for mounting a cross-Channel attack in 1944 was getting very short, and all available British port capacity (150 ships a month) would have to be utilized fully. But this was possible only if the U.S. Army could provide half of the necessary dock labor. British construction programs, especially for troop accommodations and hospitals, had been curtailed during the lean months, and timely completion of these necessary buildings would now require large numbers of U.S. construction troops. Under an accelerated program, depots and sorting sheds would require more operating personnel than was used at the height of the 1942 build-up. The British would require much labor for their own OVERLORD effort. Finally, there had been a noticeable attrition of the British civilian labor force during the past year; at Liverpool, the average age of stevedores was fifty-two.[5]

Devers directed that temporary and local needs for labor, before the combat phase of OVERLORD began, were to be met by drawing on the service elements of combat units. He warned against planning to maintain a large supply organization in England after a French base had been secured. The maximum strength of service troops, he decreed,

would be 375,000 men, and the various technical services must trim their estimates to meet this figure. On 18 July he presented a troop basis of 375,000 service troops and 635,000 ground combat troops to the War Department for approval. Of this number, 49,950 would be QMC personnel.[6] The service troop portion of this estimate, as approved by both Army Ground Forces (AGF) and ASF, was a figure that remained fairly firm until COSSAC forced a general reconsideration of all troop strengths late in 1943. In the kaleidoscopic story of the troop basis, this is just a fleeting episode, but it reveals the SOS estimate of the dimensions of the OVERLORD logistical mission and the combat commander's view that the proportionate strength of service troops could and should be regulated by fiat.

Organizational Changes in SOS ETOUSA and the OCQM

In the meantime certain changes had taken place in organization within Headquarters, ETOUSA. General Order 16 of 26 March 1943 represents General Andrews' effort to redefine ETOUSA-SOS relationships. Lee had made a determined but unsuccessful effort to eliminate the G–4 position from the ETOUSA staff. G–4 remained as the agency to "guide SOS according to broad phases of plans by theater and higher headquarters," but all of the technical services were unequivocally assigned to SOS. The Inspector General, Adjutant General, Judge Advocate, and Provost Marshal remained under ETOUSA. Lee and his service chiefs were moved to

---

[5] W. K. Hancock and M. M. Gowing, *British War Economy*, "History of the Second World War" (London: His Majesty's Stationery Office, 1949), p. 449. The annual wartime attrition of the British civilian labor force was about 150,000.

[6] (1) Ruppenthal, *Logistical Support*, I, 125–28. (2) *QM Supply in ETO*, VIII, 8.

London to assist ETOUSA headquarters in its planning functions. Operations would continue at Cheltenham under deputy service chiefs, thus reversing the previous arrangement. In April this concept was carried still further: the Cheltenham organization was placed under Brig. Gen. William G. Weaver as Field Deputy Commander, SOS, and became almost a separate headquarters. It assumed direct control over the base sections and was responsible for the training and combat readiness of SOS troop units. London Base Command of ETOUSA became Central Base Section, SOS. Thus there were again four base sections (Northern Ireland Base Section had been downgraded to a district of Western Base Section in December 1942).

Late in May General Devers, the new theater commander, made still more changes. To Lee's satisfaction the position of G–4 was consolidated with his own office. SOS also assumed control of the Judge Advocate and Provost Marshal Divisions, the Claims Commission, and the new Area Petroleum Service. SOS now proceeded to modify its own structure, first eliminating the G sections.

In the organization that was in force by the end of August 1943, the four former G sections of the staff had been upgraded to "chiefs" (not to be confused with the chiefs of technical services), and all activities of SOS headquarters were now channeled through them. Under this system, in theory, Littlejohn had access to General Lee only through Col. Royal B. Lord, Chief of Operations. Although the Chief Quartermaster continued to be in charge of general depots, theoretically he could only contact them through General Weaver, Field Deputy

Commander at Cheltenham, and then through the base section commanders. Similarly, his access to Quartermaster units was through the Chief of Training and Security, and to the Army Exchange Service through the Chief of Administration. In practice, only junior officers and official correspondence followed these rigid channels. Littlejohn continued to fulfill his responsibilities by simple, direct action as the situation required. His staff saw to it that the proper agencies were informed of all action taken.[7] The arrangement was eminently satisfactory to Lee, who was able to reduce the amount of paper work and routine policy making requiring his personal attention and yet retain control over the whole SOS organization through four deputies who knew in detail all that was happening.

Initially the reorganization was less pleasing to the technical services, which lost a good deal of authority to the "chiefs" and to the base section commanders. For example, the Transportation Service lost direct control of ports and sorting sheds, and base section commanders assumed almost complete control over personnel assignments within their areas. At the same time the OCQM lost control of motor transport units to the ETO Transportation Service, headed by Brig. Gen. Frank S. Ross. This was largely a matter of technical training and inspections, since the base section commanders had also assumed a large measure of operational control over these units.[8]

These developments did not arouse

---

[7] Littlejohn became a major general on 3 November 1943.

[8] Bykofsky and Larson, *The Transportation Corps: Operations Overseas*, p. 128.

the opposition they might have engendered earlier, for by the fall of 1943 the technical service staffs were furiously busy with more important matters. The BOLERO build-up had recommended and OVERLORD logistical planning—no ivory tower staff problem, but a real plan for combat—was in full swing. On 18 October Lt. Gen. Omar N. Bradley formally activated Headquarters, First U.S. Army, at Bristol. Most of the staff were drawn from his old II Corps headquarters. Several of them, including his quartermaster, Colonel McNamara, had already been in Great Britain more than a month studying the OVERLORD plans prepared by COSSAC.[9]

The renewed emphasis on planning was also reflected in changes in the organization of the OCQM. The biggest change came in August 1943 when all elements of the OCQM in any way concerned with planning were moved to London. This move encouraged closer co-ordination between BOLERO and COSSAC planners. An enlarged Plans and Training Division, headed by Col. Albert G. Duncan, became the most important element in the London office. Its training responsibilities had at first been confined to training literature, but were later extended to actual training and inspection of Quartermaster units that would participate in combat operations. Meantime the inspection functions of the Field Service Division in Cheltenham were reduced to overseeing depots, installations, and units to remain behind in the United Kingdom. A corresponding shift in emphasis between London and Cheltenham also changed the functions of other staff divisions. But despite its greater impor-

tance, London remained numerically the smaller of the two offices. In November 1943 there were 72 QM officers and 86 enlisted men in the London headquarters, and 84 officers and 320 enlisted men at Cheltenham. At that time 124 British civilians were employed in London and 69 in Cheltenham.[10] Coordination between the two offices, situated about ninety miles apart, was achieved by rapid courier service, frequent exchanges of staff personnel, and careful planning. In some respects the separation was actually beneficial, constituting a rehearsal for a combat situation where two echelons of the OCQM would inevitably be separated by the English Channel. The organization of the OCQM on D minus 3 is shown in Chart 1.

The Depot System

Largely a Quartermaster responsibility, U.S. depot operations in the United Kingdom began very modestly in rented warehouses. The War Department's oft-repeated directives to conserve shipping and strategic materials, make maximum use of local resources, and respect British wartime rationing regulations applied with particular stringency to authorizations for new construction in the British Isles in 1942. Besides the hundred thousand homes and other buildings totally destroyed in the blitz, over a million more had been damaged. In Britain's moist climate, prompt repairs were necessary to save the contents of damaged buildings and even to preserve the structures themselves. Except for essential war industry, no new building whatever was allowed. Authorities pro-

---

[9] McNamara *Memoir*, ch. VII.

[10] *QM Supply in ETO*, VIII, ch. 4.

CHART 1—OCQM ORGANIZATION: 3 JUNE 1944

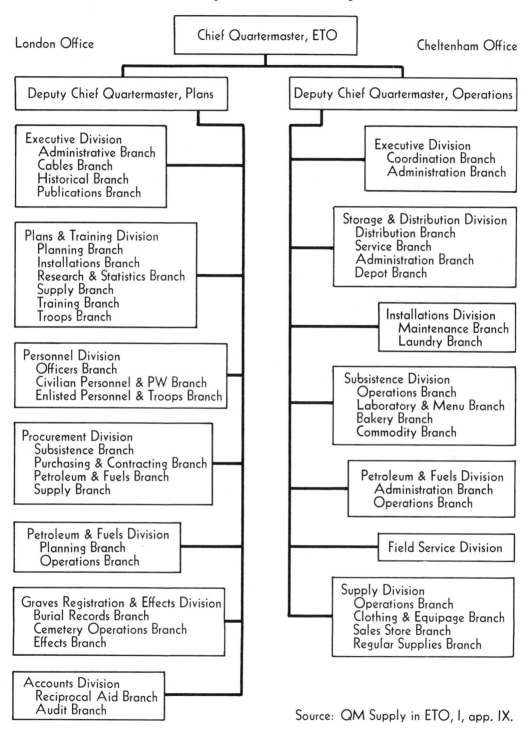

London Office

Chief Quartermaster, ETO

Cheltenham Office

Deputy Chief Quartermaster, Plans

Executive Division
   Administrative Branch
   Cables Branch
   Historical Branch
   Publications Branch

Plans & Training Division
   Planning Branch
   Installations Branch
   Research & Statistics Branch
   Supply Branch
   Training Branch
   Troops Branch

Personnel Division
   Officers Branch
   Civilian Personnel & PW Branch
   Enlisted Personnel & Troops Branch

Procurement Division
   Subsistence Branch
   Purchasing & Contracting Branch
   Petroleum & Fuels Branch
   Supply Branch

Petroleum & Fuels Division
   Planning Branch
   Operations Branch

Graves Registration & Effects Division
   Burial Records Branch
   Cemetery Operations Branch
   Effects Branch

Accounts Division
   Reciprocal Aid Branch
   Audit Branch

Deputy Chief Quartermaster, Operations

Executive Division
   Coordination Branch
   Administration Branch

Storage & Distribution Division
   Distribution Branch
   Service Branch
   Administration Branch
   Depot Branch

Installations Division
   Maintenance Branch
   Laundry Branch

Subsistence Division
   Operations Branch
   Laboratory & Menu Branch
   Bakery Branch
   Commodity Branch

Petroleum & Fuels Division
   Administration Branch
   Operations Branch

Field Service Division

Supply Division
   Operations Branch
   Clothing & Equipage Branch
   Sales Store Branch
   Regular Supplies Branch

Source: QM Supply in ETO, I, app. IX.

vided shelter for the thousands made homeless by repairing, renovating, and adapting existing structures. The necessary construction materials were doled out under the strict supervision of the Ministry of Works.[11]

These had been the local conditions when in May 1942 British General Wooten was directed to provide accommodations, including storage space, for 1,000,000 Americans before 1 April 1943. Wooten was Deputy Quartermaster General (Liaison), commonly referred to as Q (Liaison), a post specially created to coordinate logistical matters with the U.S. Army. Since the British system gives its quartermasters broad responsibilities for logistics, Wooten was generally regarded as Lee's opposite number. He was also the British Army member of the BOLERO Combined Committee (London), and the BOLERO Key Plans were issued by his office.[12]

In the First BOLERO Key Plan, Wooten estimated the American storage requirement at 14,000,000 square feet of covered space and 26,000,000 square feet of hardstand—paved, drained, open storage. The rate at which this space would actually be used was uncertain, depending entirely upon available shipping. On 24 June, SOS ETOUSA estimated that 300,000 to 560,000 tons of cargo would reach the United Kingdom by 1 September. These uncertain figures were largely based on an equally tentative estimate by the Washington BOLERO Committee that 105,000 to 150,000 troops would arrive by the same date. Allowing 30 percent as a probable Quarter-

master share of this tonnage, and 12 square feet per ton of cargo, ETO Quartermaster Service would have to occupy and organize between one and two million square feet of depot space in the next two months.[13] Construction at such short notice would be impossible, even if materials were available. Since the brewing and tobacco-processing industries were hard hit by rationing and labor shortages, a considerable number of breweries and warehouses were not in use. Wooten arranged to requisition several of these, and also evacuated four British Army depots and turned them over to the Americans. The deadline was easily met, and because of the sudden shift in supply operations to support TORCH not all of the space was needed. In December 1942 the U.S. forces began to transfer small amounts of storage space back to the British.[14]

Pressed by time, the U.S. Chief Quartermaster and the other technical service chiefs had meanwhile accepted and occupied the only space available, irrespective of its suitability, convenience, or even compliance with U.S. minimum standards for safety. Many sites were poorly located with reference to planned

[11] (1) Ruppenthal, *Logistical Support*, I, 61. (2) Hancock and Gowing, *British War Economy*, pp. 496–97.

[12] Ruppenthal, *Logistical Support*, I, 62–64.

[13] DQMG (L), Notes of a Meeting Held . . . on 24 Jun 42. USFET AG 633.

[14] By informal agreement between Generals Wooten and Lee, command of a military depot was transferred from the senior British to the senior U.S. officer present when more than half the available storage space had been occupied by the Americans. Even this apparently simple arrangement caused difficulties because of differences in British and American methods of computing storage space. (1) Memo, CO SBS to CG SOS ETO, 22 Sep 42, sub: Command at Gen Depot G–45. USFET AG 323.7. (2) Ltr, Lee to Wooten, 1 Aug 42; Memo, SOS ETO for Wooten, 25 Dec 42, sub: Glasgow QM Depot; Memo, CQM for G–4 ETO, 21 Jan 44, sub: Asgmt of Storage Space; Memo, SOS ETO for CO WBS, 27 Dec 43, sub: Release of Covered and Open Storage Space. All in USFET AG 400.242.

TYPICAL WAREHOUSE. *Depot G–20 at Burton-on-Trent, Staffordshire, England. January 1944.*

U.S. troop locations. Some of the facilities taken over, particularly the civilian establishments, were badly constructed and insufficiently equipped for heavy military use. Many were old multistoried buildings with inadequate elevators and poor accessibility by road and rail. Often they were situated in areas of dense traffic. Even new construction was not always in the best locations to serve American needs because the British encouraged development of facilities in line with their own future requirements.[15]

To reduce the heavy demand from all services for closed space, Lee agreed to use open storage whenever the nature of the supplies would permit. About a third of QMC supplies could be placed outdoors. Pending the arrival of storage tents from the United States, Littlejohn borrowed 27,000 from the British.[16] Even this expedient presented new difficulties.

---

[15] 1st Ind, OCQM, 12 Oct 43, on Memo, Hq WBS for CQM, 20 Sep 42, sub: QM Missions of Depots in WBS. USFET QM 400.24, Storage.

[16] SOS ETOUSA, Staff Mtg, 4 Jul 42. USFET AG 337.

Not every open field could be used. In most cases roads had to be built, rail lines brought to the site, and the ground surface conditioned to support heavy loads and provide rapid drainage. Utilization of open storage was also limited because it was harmful for many kinds of Quartermaster supplies, especially in the period before special overseas packing became customary. By mid-1943 improvements in overseas packaging and new techniques of outdoor storage under canvas made it possible to store even sugar and flour in the open for extended periods.[17]

Once it was clear that the original BOLERO program was being postponed and that a local emergency no longer existed, the Americans began to demand better storage facilities, but this was still impossible. The British had begun an extensive building program, but none of the new depots would be ready until the summer of 1943. Moreover, their policy was to use all available space. The new construction was designed to supplement and not to replace the older buildings. The Americans therefore began an intensive program of renovation and enlargement. Engineer troops provided most of the labor, and the Chief Engineer co-ordinated all requisitions for locally procured building materials with Quartermaster (Liaison) and the Ministry of Works.

Engineer personnel also contributed materially to the program of new construction, especially of paved concrete hardstands. Their training and equipment made them particularly suited to this task. But several large and completely new depots were also needed. The British provided corrugated sheet steel for Nissen huts but the Americans had to ship ingots from the United States to replace the steel reserves.[18] Construction began late in 1942, and during the following year seven general and six Quartermaster depots were completed. Several sites were occupied and used for open storage before construction work began. The location of general and Quartermaster depots and the amount of space in them assigned to OCQM in November 1943 and May 1944 are shown in Table 6. It should be noted that by the latter date initial issue to troops had materially reduced QM space requirements.

The first of six new depots, all constructed on one standard design, was built at Wem, near Shrewsbury in western England, by British contractors. Begun in December 1942, construction at Wem (G–16) was completed in the following June at a cost of $2,360,000. It contained 450,000 square feet of covered storage, mostly in steel huts, 1,375,-000 square feet of hardstand, and barracks for 1,250 men.[19] Histon (G–23) and Lockerly Hall (G–55) were built on the Wem design entirely by Americans. U.S. troops also assisted in the construc-

---

[17] (1) Personal Memo, Littlejohn for Cound, 10 Sep 43. Littlejohn Reading File, vol. XVI, item 27. (2) At Hilsea Depot (G–65) Lt. Col. Harold Florsheim developed a modified outdoor storage method which economized on canvas—a commodity in critically short supply. Because of his lively interest in depot management and his excellent administration of Hilsea, Florsheim in September 1943 was placed in charge of the OCQM Storage and Distribution Division.

[18] Cable 165, AGWAR to USAFBI, 31 Mar 42, sub: Engr Constr. USFET AG 400.242.

[19] During early 1942 SOS devised a block system for numbering QM depots (Q–100 to Q–199 for Classes I, II, and IV, and Q–300 to Q–399 for POL) and later general depots (G–1 to G–99) in the United Kingdom.

TABLE 6—QM STORAGE SPACE IN THE UNITED KINGDOM: GENERAL DEPOTS AND QM DEPOTS

(Thousands of square feet)

Depot	Activated	November 1943				May 1944			
		Space Assigned		Space in Use		Space Assigned		Space in Use	
		Covered	Open	Covered	Open	Covered	Open	Covered	Open
Grand Total: Quartermaster Storage Space		7,967	6,303	5,420	1,816	4,159	3,195	3,242	2,005
Total QM Space in General Depots		6,363	5,210	3,620	1,424	3,262	2,482	2,598	1,584
G-10 Belfast[a]	15 Dec 42	744	518	207	23	—	—	—	—
G-10 Wilmont[a]	16 Dec 42	999	220	614	205	—	—	—	—
G-14 Liverpool[a]	23 Aug 42	135	299	—	—	478	177	379	91
G-15 Boughton[b]	5 Nov 43	95	100	97	81	71	77	45	19
G-16 Wem[b]	1 Jun 43	242	268	204	177	65	72	54	57
G-18 Sudbury[b]	25 Sep 42	468	397	334	183	178	181	96	130
G-20 Burton-on-Trent	11 Jul 42	134	184	21	—	266	115	198	77
G-22 Moreton-on-Lugg[b]	11 Jul 43	125	200	—	—	98	82	88	69
G-23 Histon[b]	15 Nov 43	140	200	—	64	80	133	68	19
G-24 Honeybourne[b]	29 Oct 43	77	80	66	147	95	119	68	34
G-25 Ashchurch[c]	11 Jul 42	630	340	461	7	51	40	46	15
G-30 London	17 May 43	489	186	204	71	272	128	244	108
G-35 Bristol	11 Jul 42	372	320	249	192	339	137	279	55
G-40 Barry[c]	14 Aug 42	509	647	440	—	201	272	179	234
G-45 Thatcham-Newbury[c]	11 Jul 42	228	200	—	58	353	200	338	147
G-47 Westbury	15 Oct 42	522	451	450	—	148	116	68	54
G-50 Taunton	11 Jul 42	100	200	—	—	284	195	233	192
G-55 Lockerly Hall[b]	22 Nov 43	—	—	—	—	66	95	36	34
G-65 Hilsea[c]	7 Oct 42	244	300	181	186	156	225	123	138
G-75 Coypool	12 May 43	110	100	92	30	61	118	56	111

Total Space in Quartermaster

Depots									
		1,604	1,093	1,800	392	897	713	645	421
Q-101 Kettering-Wellingborough	15 Jul 42	132	106	113	44	93	61	48	24
Q-103 Glasgow	27 Oct 42	100	78	21	12	63	24	31	5
Q-104 Bungay-Ditchingham	16 Apr 43	94	56	120	26	63	60	45	10
Q-105 East Harling	16 Aug 43	81	81	—	—	34	5	24	5
Q-107 Stowmarket	13 Sep 42	145	131	—	—	82	112	53	14
Q-108 Great Dunmow	27 May 43	84	60	74	21	57	47	34	18
Q-111 Belfast[a]	23 Nov 43	466	207	778	28	295	132	224	94
Q-125 Weyhill	1 Aug 43	107	86	105	51	52	24	39	23
Q-134 Exeter	25 Sep 42	55	54	67	19	35	27	33	23
Q-140 Lydney	27 Oct 42	249	187	400	159	58	156	55	155
Q-150 Shepton Mallet	14 Jul 43	57	47	88	32	31	65	25	50
Q-152 Gloucester[d]	23 Sep 43	20	—	20	—	20	—	20	—
Q-160 Street[d]	12 Jan 43	14	—	14	—	14	—	14	—

[a] General Depots G-10 Belfast and G-10 Wilmont were combined and designated Quartermaster Depot Q-111 Belfast on 23 November 1943.
[b] New depots—specially built for the U.S. forces.
[c] Depots transferred by the British Army.
[d] Salvage depots.

Source: For November 1943: Plans and Training Division, OCQM ETO, Work Sheet, 10 November 1943. For May 1944: Plans and Training Division, OCQM ETO, Current Operating Data Book, 8 May 1944.

tion of three more such depots. The building program was pushed through despite serious doubts about the future of BOLERO and ROUNDUP. The total cost was about fifty million dollars.[20]

By mid-1943, the U.S. depot system covered most of the United Kingdom, with Quartermaster branch depots, functioning mainly for direct support of combat units, concentrated largely in areas where most U.S. troops were stationed. Geography itself imposed conditions on each base section which forced quartermasters to develop certain specialties. In Northern Ireland they gained experience in staging troops for shipment to other parts of the British Isles. At Western Base Section, which contained some of the finest ports on the Irish Sea and Bristol Channel, quartermasters developed depot management as a specialty.[21] Eastern Base Section, embracing relatively flat terrain adjacent to the continent of Europe, contained most of the U.S. air bases. Quartermasters there worked very closely with the Quartermaster, Eighth Air Force, and specialized in techniques peculiar to the job of supporting the air arm.[22] Knowledge and skill in assisting corps commands developed among quartermasters in Southern Base Section, which accommodated large bodies of troops in training or in concentration areas adjacent to English Channel ports. In all the coastal areas there were Navy personnel who drew common items directly from U.S. Army depots. In all base sections, including the small one later established for greater London, quartermaster activities became more and more decentralized, with operations patterned on OCQM procedures.[23]

Reserves of Quartermaster supplies were maintained in the Quartermaster sections of general depots. It was not necessary to activate as many QM branch depots as originally planned, since as a result of the energetic British building program of 1943 general depots were scattered almost as widely as the branch depots. During 1943–44 the branch depots declined in size. Although some effort was made to avoid the dangerous areas on the south and east coasts, important general depots were set up near Southampton and Plymouth in addition to those at Liverpool, on the Bristol Channel, in London, and at inland points.

A major consideration in locating depots, especially in the early days, was accessibility of civilian manpower. The four military depots surrendered by the British Army each had a standard complement of 690 civilians. Depots in port cities were soon employing twice that number, but the newly constructed installations in rural areas had to rely on military personnel, plus a small number of laborers and clerks hired in the neighborhood. Because of transportation

---

[20] (1) Ruppenthal, *Logistical Support*, I, 247–48. (2) *Final Report of the Chief Engineer, ETO, 1942–45* (Paris: Hervé et Fils, n.d.), vol I, pp. 244ff and app. 26.

[21] Cols. Bernard E. McKeever (Bristol General Depot) and James E. Byrom (Burton-on-Trent General Depot) pioneered in this field and their standards were adopted widely. Ltr, Littlejohn to CofS SOS, 30 Jul 42. Littlejohn Reading File, vol. II, item 69.

[22] AAF combat units drew common-use items, notably food and clothing, direct from SOS depots, but VIII Air Force Service Command consolidated requisitions and prepared estimates of future requirements, and assisted the base commands by loans of work details and truck transportation. See Craven and Cate, eds., *Europe TORCH to POINTBLANK*, ch. 18.

[23] Min, OCQM Mtg of All Div Chiefs OCQM and Depot Comdrs and All QMSO's, 31 Jul 42. Littlejohn Reading File, vol. II, item 72.

THE "WEM WRAP" *developed to protect supplies stored out of doors.   Wem Depot, July 1943.*

shortages, it was never possible to arrange for large numbers of civilians to commute to these depots. By early 1944 there was a labor shortage at all depots. About 2,000 Irish laborers were hired on 90-day contracts, but housing them was a problem never satisfactorily solved, and plans to hire 3,000 more were stopped. Housing was available only in urban areas, where the need was least pressing. Because temporary housing was expensive, the Irish were paid more than prevailing British wages, which inevitably led to friction. At the insistence of the British authorities, English and Irish laborers were not employed at the same depots. By May 1944 OCQM had some 8,000 British and 2,000 Irish employees, with no immediate prospect of obtaining more. Arrangements had been made with NATOUSA for 7,000 Italian ex-prisoners, organized into Italian service units, to be sent to the United Kingdom, but they would not arrive until after D-day. Meanwhile, the entire 5th Armored Division and several smaller combat units were used temporarily as laborers. By September 1944, over 5,000 Italians had arrived, and local civilians were again available in large numbers. On 11 September some 11,000 British civilians—laborers and clerks—were employed, mostly in urban areas.[24]

Quartermaster storage functions were carried on in much the same way throughout the United Kingdom in both Quartermaster and general depots. Stocks of a single item were often spread through many depots rather than concentrated at a minimum number of locations, as efficiency and Quartermaster Corps doctrine directed. Each depot was assigned a retail "mission" of providing for supply of troops stationed in its vicinity and for storage of calculated amounts of bulk stocks forming part of the theater reserve. The close supervision required to keep the system in balance was provided by the Office of the Chief Quartermaster. In the first rush to get stocks into storage, General Littlejohn had personally taken care of many details that later became responsibilities of the base section. The OCQM, although itself still in process of formation, took the initiative among the technical services in regard to storage of supplies, settled details of depot locations with the British, moved officers and men to staff depots, and directed shipments from the ports. By early 1943 responsibility for these functions had been definitely assigned. The Engineers coordinated acquisition of storage space, the base section commanders provided personnel and services, and the Transportation Service controlled all shipments.

In the original SOS ETO organization, depot administration had been assigned to a General Depot Service under SOS G–4. This arrangement paralleled the organization at SOS headquarters in Washington. The General Depot Service was abolished in the zone of interior in July 1942 and SOS ETO followed suit, leaving the function directly under G–4.[25] It soon developed that G–4 was not equipped to deal with the details of depot operations. Accordingly, again paralleling the zone of interior, the functions of the General Depot Service in the ETO were transferred to the Chief Quartermaster.[26] This gave the OCQM supervision of all general depots as well as Quartermaster branch depots.

OCQM eventually assumed responsibility for supervising and staffing four types of depots: general depots with stores and provisions for two or more of the technical services, Quartermaster branch depots, salvage depots, and POL depots. The British controlled all depots and commercial establishments which contained cold storage space for perishable subsistence items. Because cold stores were largely located in port cities, such items as beef and butter were separated from nonperishable foods, which caused some difficulty in assembling a balanced menu.[27]

The U.S. forces in the United Kingdom drew their liquid fuels and lubricants direct from the British through a

---

[24] (1) *QM Supply in ETO*, VIII, 55–58, and app. XXXVI. (2) DA Pamphlet No. 20-213, *History of Prisoner of War Utilization by the U.S. Army, 1776-1945* (June 1955), pp. 211–12.

[25] SOS ETOUSA Cir 13, 19 Aug 42.
[26] (1) Memo, Asst CofS G–4 for CG SOS, 24 Sep 42, no sub; Memo, DCQM for CG SOS through G–4, 30 Sep 42, no sub. Both in USFET AG 400.21. (2) SOS ETOUSA Cir 38, 27 Oct 42. (3) See ch. I, above.
[27] *QM Supply in ETO*, I 168–70.

OPEN STORAGE OF PACKAGED GASOLINE *at Highbridge, England.   March 1943.*

common pool arrangement. Consequently, the main purpose of Quartermaster POL depots was supply for cross-Channel operations, and many of them were activated late in 1943. Because of the fire hazard, POL depots were normally kept separate from other depots and were dispersed over large areas— sometimes more than fifty acres. Only packaged POL was a QMC item; bulk POL was handled by the Transportation Corps or the Corps of Engineers. Thus a POL depot was primarily a place where filled 5-gallon cans were stacked in the open, usually camouflaged under trees. Each stack was normally on a "base," a hardstand of 56x56-foot dimensions. Each base held 340 long tons of gasoline, or about 19,000 cans. Bases were never less than 100 feet apart.

Kerosene and diesel oil were also stored in such stacks. Greases and lubricants were packed in tin cans and were stored in corrugated steel huts, but the number of huts at a POL depot was always very small compared to the number of huts at other depots. Tentative sites for twenty-two POL depots were part of the first BOLERO Key Plan, but only fourteen of these depots were activated. (*Table 7*) Most of them were located near the south coast of Britain, ten or fifteen miles inland from the embarkation ports assigned to the American troops. By 1 October 1943 eight depots had been activated, but since there were only three gasoline supply companies in the British Isles to man them, civilian labor was used as at other depots. Although the Engineers were confident that bulk gas-

TABLE 7—QUARTERMASTER POL DEPOTS: 31 DECEMBER 1943

Number	Location	Open Space		Closed Space		Activated
		Long Tons	Bases^a	Square Feet	Huts	
Q–305	Altcar	7,140	21	3,360	1	8 Apr 43
Q–304	Trefnant	7,140	21	2,240	1	26 Dec 43
Q–303	Eardisley	21,420	63	10,000	3	17 Oct 43
Q–331	Highbridge	18,700	55	51,007	(b)	26 Oct 42
Q–316	Masbury	15,640	46	2,100	1	23 Sep 42
Q–328	West Moors	47,260	139	33,450	(b)	27 Jul 43
Q–329	Wimborne	25,280	74	10,080	3	6 May 43
Q–324	Dorchester	14,280	42	10,080	3	15 Apr 43
Q–321	Wrangaton	14,280	42	8,400	3	1 Nov 43
Q–323	Bovey-Tracey	18,020	53	8,400	3	1 Jun 43
Q–317	Newbury	11,900	35	2,240	1	15 Oct 43
Q–318	Everleigh	7,140	21	2,240	1	15 Aug 43
Q–320	Porton	7,140	21	2,240	1	16 Aug 43
Q–326	Droxford	16,660	49	2,240	1	1 Nov 43
	Total	231,880	682	148,077	22^c	

a Base = 3,136 sq. ft. (56' × 56') hardstand, capable of storing 340 long tons of gasoline in 5-gallon cans.
b Existing buildings.
c Plus existing buildings.
Source: POL Plan, Petroleum and Fuel Division, 1 August 1943, and Current Operating Data Book, OCQM, June 1944, p. 48.

oline would be available on the Continent by D plus 30, the OCQM decided to accumulate a packaged reserve to support the invasion through D plus 90, and the POL depot system was organized on that basis. The depots were filled to capacity by 30 April 1944, and enough gasoline supply companies had arrived by then so that one company could be assigned to each POL depot, in addition to those earmarked for First Army.[28]

The Chief Quartermaster's technical supervision involved frequent inspections of the general and Quartermaster branch depots to insure maximum efficiency through compliance with authorized procedures. Methods of storage and stock control were under continuous scrutiny, and results of depot operations in terms of tons moved per man per month were carefully checked and compared.[29] Full instructions from OCQM appeared in a depot operations manual that covered in detail warehousing operations, stock control procedures, and reports. The OCQM computed model stocks and storage space requirements on the basis of the depot mission and sent this data to the Quartermaster supply officer at each general and branch installation.[30] But frequent changes in depot missions, and local conditions over which depot quartermasters had no control,

often made compliance with these instructions impossible.[31]

U.S. Quartermaster storage doctrine was based on larger, more concentrated facilities than were generally available in the United Kingdom. Efforts to increase efficiency by making the depots' arrangement conform more closely to U.S. standards led to almost constant rebuilding and expansion. The resultant shifting and rewarehousing of supplies made for even more intradepot movement than arose from actual receipt and issue of supplies. Since labor was scarce and, in most cases, extensive use of mechanical equipment was not feasible due to the layout and condition of floors, the normal difficulties of achieving neat and accurate storage were multiplied. Despite continuous effort to make activities conform to storage manual principles, operations were often not completely satisfactory when measured by United States standards.[32]

Many early difficulties of depot location and operation are illustrated in the experience of the depot at Liverpool, G–14. Planners had seen from the beginning that the Mersey River area, with Liverpool as its chief port, would be an important point of entry for U.S. supplies. Accordingly, in late July 1942 American and British officers were sent there to establish a Quartermaster depot. Within a few days they had acquired their main facility, the Stanley Tobacco Warehouse, a large fourteen-story building, with access by road, rail, and canal.

---

[28] (1) Littlejohn, ed., Passing in Review, ch. 18. (2) QM Supply in ETO, IV, 13–15.

[29] IRS, Depot Comdrs [SOS] to IG [SOS], 27 Apr 43, with additional comments by IG and OCQM; Memo, CG G–25 for IG [SOS], 4 May 43. Both in USFET AG 333.

[30] (1) Memo, OCQM for QMSO Depot G–25, 12 Feb 43, sub: Model Stock. USFET QM 400.164. (2) The depot operations manual was revised and published in several mimeographed and printed versions. Copies are in the Littlejohn Collection and in the Historical Branch, OQMG.

---

[31] Memo, Subs Off for CG QM Depot Q–101, 18 Feb 43, sub: Model Stock. USFET QM 400.164.

[32] Memo, OCQM for Hq SOS, 3 Jun 43, sub: Answers to Questions (From WD to CG SOS), sub: Opns in U.K. USFET AG 310.1.

Aside from the fact that the Mersey Docks and Harbour Board retained part of the warehouse for its own use, there were other drawbacks. The building was situated in an area of heavy traffic; the fourteen stories and the basement were served by only four slow elevators; and windows were broken, lights were few, and there was no blackout equipment to permit night work. Despite these handicaps the depot started to function, using local civilian labor exclusively, when the first supplies arrived on 17 August.[33] When formally established a few days later, it was set up as a general rather than a Quartermaster depot as had been originally planned. Eventually it contained medical, chemical, engineer, post exchange, and adjutant general supply sections, but QMC supplies were always the depot's main concern.

Supplies immediately began to pour in. Within a few weeks the 900,000 square feet of Stanley Warehouse were used up and expansion had begun. By the end of September the depot had acquired additional space in a railway warehouse, in railway sorting sheds, and in two private warehouses. In addition to this closed space the depot had an open storage area of approximately one million square feet. With the exception of Stanley Warehouse and the open area, operated by a combination of American military and local civilian personnel, these facilities were managed by British public or private organizations on a fee basis for freight handling and space rental.[34]

In the next year and a half, in the midst of constantly expanding operations, the efficiency of the depot was gradually built up. British civilian labor and U.S. troops, working together, repaired Stanley Warehouse and installed blackout fixtures. Offices and accommodations for troops were provided by Quartermaster (Liaison). Methods of operation were standardized and perfected by close supervision of the Commander, Western Base Section, and inspections by OCQM. Even the handicap of multistoried buildings was partly overcome by the installation of chutes, hoists, and conveyors. By April 1944, just before the climactic preparations for the cross-Channel attack, the Liverpool depot had progressed to the point where 1,500 military and civilian workers were handling every day 2,000 tons which arrived and left by rail, barge, and truck.

In contrast, the development of General Depot G–45 at Thatcham near London was typical for military depots transferred to the United States Army by the British Army. It was a modern manufacturing plant which had been requisitioned soon after completion in July 1940. It contained 600,000 square feet of covered storage and was operated by 600 civilians. In keeping with British dispersal practice, the storage areas were scattered over 152 acres.[35] An American depot was officially activated there on 11 July 1942. The transfer was gradual,

---

[33] This account of the origins of G–14 is drawn, except as indicated, from General Depot G–14, APO 507, A Short History From Activation to 1 April 1944, 14 Apr 44. Hist Br OQMG.

[34] Memo, CO Gen Depot G–14 for CG SOS ETO-USA, 29 Sep 42, sub: Storage Facilities and Change in Address "Stanley Warehouse" to "General Depot G–14." USFET AG 400.242.

[35] This account is drawn from General History, G–45 [ca. February 1944]. Hist Br OQMG.

proceeding by weekly increments until the U.S. Army took over the entire installation and the military command in November.

The transfer went off smoothly as far as Anglo-American relations were concerned, but not without some physical problems. The dispatch of British supplies and the influx of U.S. supplies taxed the transportation and handling capacity of the depot. At the same time a number of important changes were made in the plant: new open storage areas were prepared to receive supplies, new roads built, new railroad tracks installed, and some of the warehouses reconstructed along lines more suitable to U.S. storage operations. U.S. Engineer troops constructed most of the hardstands with mechanized equipment. British civilian workers renovated the buildings. In January 1943 the Newbury Race Course, a tract of 220 acres, six miles from the establishment, was added to the G–45 open storage area. The depot began to operate almost immediately. In September 1942 it supplied an average of 5,000 troops; the next month it supplied 23,000. Supply of North Africa, in which the depot was heavily engaged, caused considerable fluctuation in its activities. By the beginning of 1944, it was serving over 70,-000 troops and plans were under way to increase its mission to 100,000 troops.

The Base Sections

The base sections, territorial subdivisions of SOS, came into existence later than the depots. Their structure developed more slowly, reflecting the evolution of service commands in the United States. Northern Ireland Base Command, a provisional headquarters organized in February 1942, was not a territorial organization, despite its name, but a support echelon of V Corps. Lee formally activated four base sections on 20 July 1942 but Northern Ireland Base Section retained its subordinate role with respect to V Corps, and was inactivated when that headquarters moved to England in December. *(See Map 1.)* The other three base sections, beginning with considerable autonomy, developed the concept of "host" organizations to whom combat units were "guests." [36] By July 1943 an informal booklet published by OCQM for supply officers of newly arrived units declared that: "A base section corresponds basically to a service command in the United States." [37]

Since the technical services had created and staffed the depots and had dictated their methods and standards of operation for several months, they put up considerable resistance to the establishment of a new chain of command. The technical services tended to retain control over not only purely technical matters, but everything pertaining to more than one base section, especially operational control of transportation units. Technical service representatives on each base section headquarters staff were capable of performing many of these

---

[36] Eastern, Western, and Southern Base Sections remained in continuous existence until after D-day. London Base Command became Central Base Section in April 1943. Northern Ireland Base Section was reactivated in October 1943. Thus at various times there were three, four, or five base sections.

[37] Headquarters, SOS ETOUSA, OCQM, A Guide to Functions Performed by the Quartermaster Service in the European Theater of Operations (1 July 1943). Hist Br OQMG.

functions, and in some cases did so, but under technical service direction. As the base section organization was built up in the fall of 1942, the base section commanders tended to expand their jurisdiction to all SOS installations in their territories. Lee gave them considerable support, and gradually reduced the number of "exempt" installations and activities.[38] Their staffs matured and assumed increasing responsibilities. For example, once the location and size of new depots had been agreed upon, the Engineer Sections of the base section staffs took over direction of American construction activity, co-ordinating details of the work with local representatives of British agencies and initiating requisitions for building materials from the United States if necessary, or from such local military agencies as the Directorate of Fortifications and Works. Instructions to unit supply officers in July 1943 stated that "Each base section has a suitable quartermaster staff located at the base section headquarters. The base section quartermaster and his staff are equipped to provide a solution to most of the local quartermaster supply problems." [39]

Littlejohn's dual position as Chief, Quartermaster Service, and Chief, General Depot Service, gave him great influence with the base section commanders. This was reinforced by his temporary position as Deputy Commander, SOS, in November and December 1942, and by his seniority and informal position of leadership among the technical service chiefs. But his personal position confused rather than clarified the demarcation of authority between base section commanders and chiefs of technical services in their relations with depot commanders and supply units. In all disciplinary and administrative matters, including personnel assignments, SOS headquarters assigned increasing authority to the base section commanders, finally abolishing all "exempt" activities in August 1943.[40] Base Section commanders thus won jurisdiction in August 1943 over all general depots, except for certain matters involving internal management and technical operations. Such matters could be handled best by direct communication between depots and the technical service staffs at SOS headquarters.[41]

The increasing responsibility for housekeeping and general administration which the base sections took over from the depots was delegated to districts. Southern, Western, and Northern Ireland Base Sections were each subdivided into four districts. But Eastern Base Section, which delegated many functions to VIII Air Force Service Command, and Central Base Section, a small unit which supervised supply administration in greater London, were not so subdivided. The districts became of major importance just before D-day, when they assumed command of service units at the embarkation points to pro-

[38] Ruppenthal, *Logistical Support*, I, 168–70.
[39] Booklet cited n. 37.

[40] SOS ETOUSA Cir 49, 24 Aug 43. This circular charged base section commanders with "all SOS operations."
[41] (1) Memo, OCQM for G–4 [SOS ETO], 14 Oct 42, sub: Asgmt and Reasgmt of Labor Pers for Depots. USFET QM 370.5. (2) QM History of ETO, May 1941–June 1944. USFET AG 568A. (3) Memo, SOS ETO for CG WBS, 29 Sep 43, sub: Admin of Depots. USFET AG 400.21.

vide last-minute support and services to the departing combat troops.[42]

Automatic Supply and Requisitions

The aim of supply planning in an overseas headquarters is to maintain all stocks within the minimum and maximum supply levels prescribed by higher authority. During World War II this objective, so easily defined, was surrounded by pitfalls and proved very difficult to attain. A major element in the problem was the "lead time" of 90 to 120 days between preparation of a requisition and arrival of the requested items. After some experiment it became normal procedure in the ETO to submit requisitions to cover requirements for a 30-day period, but that period would begin 90 days or more in the future. Requisitions therefore had to take into account anticipated consumption and anticipated arrivals of supplies in the interim period. An even more uncertain element was the anticipated troop strength of the theater at the time the supplies were to arrive. Enemy action, especially submarine and air attacks against shipping, provided another factor of uncertainty. This is by no means a complete catalogue of all the variables involved and the inevitable result was that ETO supplies were always somewhat out of balance. Stocks of some items were too large, and of others too small, and slow corrective action could not overtake the new complications that constantly emerged.

The source of supplies for the ETO, as well as for predecessor commands during World War II, was the New York Port of Embarkation.[43] After 6 June 1942, NYPE was also the agency controlling priorities, size of shipments, and theater levels of supply. The necessary authority, previously exercised by the War Department, had been delegated to NYPE as part of a general process of decentralization. Control was exercised by "editing" theater requisitions—that is, by careful checking to ensure that they contained no technical errors, were in accord with War Department policy directives, and took into account the most recent revisions of strategic plans and the troop basis. NYPE exercised considerable autonomy in modifying regulations to meet current problems. For example, minimum theater supply levels were the basis of strategic planning, and were only changed with the approval of the War Department, but maximum levels were modified to conform to the current shipping situation, or to meet special theater needs.

During the gradual preparation of a forward base for a continental operation, economy of supply and shipping indicated a low supply level as desirable, while to make possible efficient service to the troops, orderly procedure, and American self-sufficiency in a British theater, a high level was called for. General Littlejohn, as the man who would have to cope with local problems and keep the troops supplied, favored the higher levels. This meant that each of his many small depots would have an ample reserve, even if his inexperienced and overworked depot personnel made

---

[42] Ruppenthal, *Logistical Support*, I, ch. IX.

[43] Functions and organization of ports of embarkation are discussed in detail in Chester Wardlow, *The Transportation Corps: Movements, Training, and Supply*, UNITED STATES ARMY IN WORLD WAR II (Washington, 1956), pp. 99–105 and 341–57.

occasional mistakes in inventory accounting. Crosshauls between depots to correct local shortages would be minimized, and the theater itself would have a reserve to offset losses in transit or to meet unexpected demands. To him, these advantages outweighed the fact that ultimately all supplies not locally consumed would have to be hauled to ports and transshipped to a combat zone across the Channel.[44]

The War Department had established a 60-day level for all supplies in the United Kingdom in January 1942, as already described. This was a minimum level and no maximum was set at that time. In July the minimum was increased to 75 days, and in August a maximum level of 180 days was authorized. TORCH requirements were given priority over BOLERO during the following month, and in November the War Department reduced the ETO maximum supply level to 75 days for subsistence, 90 days for clothing, and 60 days for other supplies. It should be borne in mind that the only place where such a directive had an immediate effect was in the Overseas Supply Division of NYPE, where it was used in editing requisitions. It did not affect supplies already in the pipeline. In the ETO, General Lee reacted to the November directive by announcing that an additional 45-day combat maintenance factor would be added. This, he felt, was needed to maintain the established levels in the United Kingdom and at the same time support the North African operation.[45]

During the next three months troop departures more than offset the decrease in cargo arrivals so that the theater supply levels rose sharply. At the end of February, the month in which ETO-USA and NATOUSA became separate theaters, Quartermaster supply levels in the United Kingdom were as follows:

DAYS OF SUPPLY FOR 125,000 MEN

Class I

A Ration	75	*Remarks*
B Ration (balanced)	34	Surplus of perishable components of the A ration:
B Ration (unbalanced)	132	Beef .... 7,838,075 pounds
C Ration	7.7	Pork .... 1,003,775 pounds
D Ration	4.6	Butter .... 628,750 pounds
K Ration	9.4	
5-in-1 Ration	0	

Class II

Clothing	249	Clothing tariffs are somewhat unbalanced.
Equipage	206	Certain deficiencies as well as excesses in equipage.
Regular Supplies	188	

Class III

POL	60	POL assured from British sources; also 22 days
Coal	105	packaged oils and greases in U.K. depots for
Coke	77	TORCH.
Army Sales Store Supplies	90	

Source: Hq, SOS ETOUSA, G–4 Special Monthly Rpt, QM Sv as of 28 Feb 43. USFET AG 319.1.

---

[44] Littlejohn, ed., Passing in Review, Operational Study 3.

[45] (1) See above, ch. II. (2) Cable SPAOG–600, AGWAR to USFOR, 22 Aug 42; Ltr, CG ETOUSA to Chiefs Tech Svs . . ., 8 Nov 42, sub: Levels of Supply; Cable R–3404, AGWAR to ETOUSA, 22 Nov 42. All in USFET AG 400.32.

But these high levels could be regarded as transitory, arising from a temporary manpower shortage, or even as illusory, since the supplies included items unwanted or actually discarded by the troops who had departed for North Africa. Both the War Department and SOS ETOUSA headquarters were preoccupied with long-range plans, and especially with projected minimum levels. In April 1943 General Marshall suggested a 45-day minimum level for all classes of supply, pointing out that shipping was critically short and other theaters were also reducing their levels. Littlejohn declared that a 45-day level was entirely inadequate, and recommended that the current levels be maintained. Nevertheless, in June the War Department reduced the levels for food and clothing to 60 days, and for all other classes to 45 days. In November 1943 the War Department again suggested reducing all minimum levels to 45 days. Littlejohn agreed to accept that figure for rations but insisted that the level for clothing remain unchanged.[46]

Throughout 1943 the operating level for all classes of supply remained fixed at 30 days, reflecting the standard procedure of requisitioning once a month to replace 30 days of consumption. Thus the maximum level was 30 days more than the minimum level. In the theater, the War Department's concept of minimum, operating, and maximum levels was largely ignored. Stocks were not segregated on that basis and requisitions were computed to bring stocks up to the maximum level on the estimated date of arrival. Early in 1944 the War

Department adopted the theater's method of computation, agreeing that thereafter authorizations would refer only to maximum levels. On 20 January maximum levels for the ETO were reduced to 60 days for Class I and Class III, and 75 days for Class II and Class IV.[47]

As troops began to arrive in the United Kingdom in the early spring of 1942, automatic issue of Class I and III supplies from NYPE went into effect, as provided by Quartermaster doctrine and current regulations.[48] Quantities of food and fuel to be shipped were calculated by multiplying the troop strength, a figure obtained from sources in Washington, by the authorized days of supply. Automatic supply was thus based on the belief that consumption of Class I and III supplies was not significantly affected by local or temporary conditions, and could be accurately predicted by the shipper.

As early as mid-1941 the SPOBS quartermaster had made arrangements for local procurement of fuels and lubricants, but NYPE, a new organization groping its way toward efficient procedures, was apparently unaware of this. The port authorities shipped considerable quantities of Class III items in the first half of 1942 before they were informed that such supplies were not required.[49]

In the case of food (Class I), automatic supplies became unbalanced at the very beginning. The 90-day reserve of subsistence which was to accompany or closely follow the first U.S. troops to the

[46] Cable R–7894, AGWAR to ETOUSA, 28 Apr 43; Cable R–9743, AGWAR to ETOUSA, 20 Jun 43; Cable W–7545, ETOUSA to AGWAR, 22 Nov 43. All in USFET AG 400.32.

[47] (1) *History of Planning Division, ASF,* II, 203. (2) *QM Supply in ETO,* I, 44.
[48] Ltr, TAG to CG's . . . Base Comds, 28 Apr 42, sub: Supply of Overseas Depots, Theaters. USFET AG 400.
[49] Memo, Middleswart for G–4, 29 Jun 42, no sub. USFET AG 400.

United Kingdom did not arrive on schedule and the troops had to be fed by the British Army. By the time American rations had begun to arrive in quantity, arrangements with the British Ministry of Food were in effect whereby the U.S. forces would receive many food items over an extended period. Since NYPE shipped Class I supplies on the basis of a ration established by the Office of The Quartermaster General, local ETO food procurement obliged NYPE to adjust shipments to avoid duplication. Such adjustments could only be made on the basis of ETO local procurement reports, which came to be almost equivalent to "stop orders" canceling shipments of various items.

Preparations for the North African invasion further disrupted the automatic system. Food supplies for troops sailing from the United Kingdom were withdrawn from local stocks in accordance with combat requirements rather than in the same proportions called for by the menu used in assembling shipments from the United States. Some stocks, especially of operational rations, were reduced to very low levels, while others mounted rapidly because of underconsumption. Stocks were further unbalanced by nondelivery of requested quantities, by sinkings and damage en route, by local distribution difficulties within the theater, and by substitutions at the port for items unobtainable at the time of shipment. The cumulative effect of all these various factors upon what was supposed to be a simple system led to a suspension of the automatic supply of rations in October 1942.[50] Extensive

requisitions then had to be submitted to bring food stocks into the balance called for by the planning menu.[51]

Discontinuance of automatic shipments put all ETO quartermaster supplies on a requisition basis. Supply by requisition was in theory a simple procedure. Using authorized theater levels as the limit of what might be requisitioned and subtracting stocks that were on hand and on the way, each technical service submitted requisitions at regular intervals—usually one month—through G–4, SOS, to NYPE for the specific items and quantities needed to replace current consumption and maintain the authorized reserves. The port received the requisitions, edited them for possible mistakes in computation, called forward the supplies from designated depots, and shipped them in time to meet current requirements. When the theater requisitioned items that were not available to the port from its own supporting depots, the port called on the appropriate technical service to arrange for supply from another depot, or by special procurement if necessary. If there was a prospect of delay and a substitute item was available, the port made a substitution on its own authority. When requisitioned items were unauthorized for the theater or exceeded the authorized allowance, the port referred the matter to the War Department for decision. Certain critical items were controlled by the War Department and released for shipment only on specific authorization.

---

[50] Cable SA–1531, Lee to PEMBARK, 13 Oct 42. USFET AG 319.1.

[51] (1) Memo, OCQM for Actg CofS SOS, 5 Nov 42, sub: Levels of Class I Supplies by Groups. USFET QM 430. (2) See OTCQM TSFET Operational Study 9, page 2, for a postwar reaffirmation of the disadvantages of automatic supply.

In practice this procedure proved to be full of complexities, which the OCQM had anticipated and attempted to overcome. Briefly stated, the simple mathematical computations of the requisition were based on statistics, which in turn were derived from a wide variety of sources of varying reliability, and were subject to varying interpretations. Troop strength, for example, a basic figure for translating levels of supply into specific quantities, was interpreted in the theater to mean the troop strength expected to be present during the period covered by the requisition, which was usually several months in the future. The War Department objected that this interpretation led to duplication of supply, since supplies for 90 days' maintenance were supposedly shipped with or immediately following each troop unit sent overseas.[52]

Many conditions contributed to mutual lack of understanding in this early period. Cables were overloaded and airmail was slow and uncertain. Cargoes were delayed or lost at sea, and when they did arrive there was nothing to indicate whether they were in response to requisitions, automatic supply, specific maintenance for new units, or preshipments. But uncertainty was not confined to the theater. NYPE sometimes found ETO reports of local procurement possibilities overoptimistic. Even formal contracts were not always fulfilled, and there was the constant possibility that agreements with the various British supply ministries might be repudiated by either government.

When a major change in plans occurred, the forecast of troop strength temporarily became very uncertain. During the shift to the TORCH operation, for example, the future of the forces in the United Kingdom was so uncertain as to cause a cancellation of all outstanding requisitions.[53] When the theater was using a troop strength figure, either current or projected, which differed significantly from that used by NYPE or by other zone of interior agencies, the editing of requisitions was fraught with numerous delays. This problem was not resolved until July 1944, when the War Department began to issue a Troop List for Operations and Supply (TLOS).[54]

The rate at which Class II and IV supplies had to be replaced—the "replacement factor"—was another troublesome matter. Some of the confusion in the early days of the build-up was caused by the incomplete equipment of incoming troops.[55] In theory all soldiers were to arrive fully equipped according to the appropriate Tables of Basic Allowances, with the theater replacing articles only as they were worn out, used up, or destroyed. In reality the theater frequently had to make initial issues of items that incoming troops were short of. If these initial issues were simply counted with other supplies turned over to

---

[52] Memo [W35–1–42], TAG for CG's . . . Overseas Bases . . . , 21 Aug 43, sub: Elimination of Requisitions for Excessive Supplies. USFET AG 319.1.

[53] Memo, Asst CofS G–4 for CG SOS ETO, 17 Sep 42, sub: Status of Supply Technique and Its Effect on This Theater. USFET AG 400, vol. I.

[54] The TLOS is discussed in detail in Chapter XII, below.

[55] (1) Memo, CQM to ACofS G-4 SOS ETO, 14 Jun 42, sub: Clothing Enlisted Men. USFET QM 421. (2) War Department Circular 297, 13 November 1943, directed that the term "replacement factor" be used to describe replacement of matériel; thereafter "maintenance" would refer to upkeep.

troops, the figures for replacements would be inflated to that extent. For planning purposes at the War Department level it was therefore most essential to distinguish between initial issue, which would not recur, and replacement, which would be repeated at foreseeable intervals. The overseas depots found it extremely hard to make this distinction.

Regular requisitions were supposed to cover replacement issues only, with special requisitions to cover initial issue. Since the latter issues nearly always consisted of unforeseen expenditures, they had to be drawn from theater stocks and replaced later. But enough experienced personnel, trained to interpret Tables of Basic Allowances, were not available in the theater at that time. Depots thus could not cope adequately with the complex problem of distinguishing between initial and replacement issues. Moreover, tables showing authorized equipment of units were not always on hand, and up-to-date changes in such tables were almost invariably lacking. Under such conditions, far beyond staff control, the accuracy of replacement statistics was highly questionable. To the theater, interested chiefly in having supplies on hand when needed, the difference between the two types of issues was in any event secondary. To zone of interior agencies, concerned with long-range forecasting of requirements, the distinction was of primary importance.

The question was further complicated by misunderstandings with respect to details of allowances. The OCQM, SOS ETOUSA, NYPE, The Quartermaster General, and the Commanding General, ASF, were all involved in determining allowances of clothing and equipment. At times tactical commanders, AGF

boards, and other technical services were also involved. Agreements affecting these allowances were sometimes reached between certain agencies without proper notification to the others. Resolution of the ensuing confusion occasionally demanded weeks of correspondence and consultation. Efforts were made to fix allowances on a firm basis and to maintain the required distinctions in statistical reports, but the problem was never entirely solved.[56]

Another basic factor in calculating quantities needed to maintain stocks for reserve and current use was the inventory on hand and expected. This had to be noted on the requisition itself. For stocks on hand, the theater was the source of information, but NYPE also calculated overseas stocks on the basis of the shipments it had made, less presumed consumption. When there was a wide discrepancy, an adjustment had to be made before the port would honor the requisition.[57] For the calculation of stocks expected in the theater, the theater was ultimately dependent on the port. In the early days of the ETO, information on supplies in transit was late and fragmentary. The outstanding requisitions canceled in August 1942 during the build-up for TORCH could not be immediately reinstated when the interim troop basis for BOLERO was clarified because three weeks after the cancellation order the ETO still did not know what

---

[56] (1) Ltr, NYPE Overseas Supply Div to CG SOS ETO, 19 Dec 42, sub: Editing Procedure for Requisitions From U.K. 430.2 ETO. (2) SOS ETO-USA, Notes on Staff Conf, 8 Mar 43, 14 Jun 43, remarks by Gen Littlejohn. USFET AG 337. (3) Memo, OQMG for CQM ETO, 26 Jul 43, sub: Maint Factors and Supply Levels. 400 ETO.

[57] Ltr cited n. 56 (1).

supplies had been shipped before the cut-off date.[58]

Even minor technical details caused difficulties in processing requisitions. Apparently erroneous theater calculations could not always be easily rectified, for the receiving office in the zone of interior did not know enough about theater conditions to risk a correction without time-consuming correspondence.[59] Attempting to avoid the delays involved in dealing with the New York Port of Embarkation, the OCQM sometimes dealt directly with the Office of The Quartermaster General and the Army Service Forces. But direct negotiation with agencies to the rear of the port often caused more rather than less delay. NYPE was not hostile to OCQM, though at a distance of more than 3,000 miles this sometimes seemed the case, and the port's intimate knowledge of theater requirements usually led to speedier action than the special pleading of Quartermaster officers in Washington.[60]

How to deal with the flow of initial equipment for units arriving in the theater was another perplexing matter. At first, units and groups of units, temporarily designated task forces, arrived with cargo specifically marked for each of them. This cargo consisted of their organizational equipment and a 90-day allowance of maintenance supplies. As

early as June 1942 the OCQM requested that the maintenance supplies not be "force marked," that is, assigned to a specific unit, but instead be included in ordinary depot stocks for maintenance issue. This procedure made sorting and control of supplies so much easier that it was applied by most supply services in the ETO even before the War Department approved it.[61]

But when the War Department suggested applying the bulk system to organizational equipment as well as to maintenance supplies, Littlejohn strenuously objected.[62] Such equipment could be shipped in sets for type units or in bulk. The chief argument advanced against the first alternative was that units arriving without equipment would be unable to carry out operations pending their "marrying up" with their equipment. A similar argument applied to the bulk system, with the additional objection that the ETO depot system did not have enough qualified people to deal properly with the enormous quantities and manifold problems involved. In December OCQM was still opposed to bulk shipments. As an alternative to force marking of organizational equipment, Colonel Sharp of the Depot Branch proposed combat loading of units, that is, putting the unit and all its equipment on the same ship, so stowed that both troops and equipment could be simultaneously unloaded ready for immediate operations. This method, used by Patton's Western Task Force in

---

[58] Memo, ACofS G–4 for CG SOS ETO, 17 Sep 42, sub: Status of Supply Technique and Its Effect on This Theater. USFET AG 400, vol. I.

[59] (1) Memo, DCQM for Chief P&T Div, 24 Jan 44, sub: Requisitioning Procedure. USFET QM 400.311. (2) SOS ETOUSA Notes on Staff Conf, 7 Jun 43, remarks by Gen Styer. USFET AG 337.

[60] SOS ETOUSA, Notes on Staff Conf, 14 Jun 43, remarks by Brig. Gen. Calvin DeWitt. USFET AG 337. For later developments in OCQM-NYPE relationships, see below, Chapter XII.

[61] Memo, OCQM for CG SOS ETO, 16 Jun 42, sub: Disposition of QM Supplies Allocated to Task Forces. USFET QM 475.

[62] Memo, CQM for ACofS G–4 SOS, 12 Jun 42, no sub; Memo, DCQM for CQM, 5 Jul 42, no sub. Both in USFET QM 475.

Morocco, was considered too wasteful of space to be justified in a theater where there were no combat operations.[63]

Force marking of organizational equipment was meanwhile continued, but within a month the theater reversed its earlier opposition.[64] In January 1943 it formally recommended a change to bulk shipment. The reason was that 80 to 120 days and sometimes more elapsed between the arrival of troops and that of their force-marked equipment. Force marking of equipment had proved a hindrance rather than a help. A lag in shipments from the zone of interior could be overcome by maintaining an emergency reserve of complete sets of equipment for type combat units. It should be remembered that the ETO was now a quiet theater, with a surplus of service troops. SOS felt that these troops had received the training to effect initial issues to troop units, although OCQM was dubious.

In early 1943 the War Department hesitated to approve the bulk system it had advocated in 1942. Organizational equipment was no longer available in zone of interior stocks or from current production in sufficient quantities to allow for both the equipment of units training in the United States and the movement of large stocks to the theater much in advance of the troops. In addition, bulk shipments would have to be made on uncertain long-range forecasts of troop movements. If the plans changed significantly after equipment had been shipped, equipment already on its way to or in the ETO might have to be duplicated in other theaters. The adjustments required to implement TORCH served as an object lesson. The War Department therefore continued to force mark shipments.

Its position was modified by an important change in the shipping situation in the late spring of 1943. The successful conclusion of the North African campaign and naval successes against U-boats in the Atlantic permitted renewal of the build-up in the United Kingdom for cross-Channel operations. However, the schedule of troop availability was such that troop movements would be light until the last quarter of the year. This created an "excess" of cargo capacity during the summer and afforded an opportunity to ship in advance of need both maintenance supplies and organizational equipment for troops who would be arriving later.[65] On 19 May, therefore, the theater was notified that bulk shipment of organizational equipment would be instituted for units sailing after 1 July 1943.[66]

As the OCQM had foreseen in the preceding year, the handling of bulk shipments presented some troublesome problems. Issue of organizational equipment to units was handicapped by

[63] Memo, SOS ETO for Chief Supply Svs, 1 Dec 42, sub: Issue of Organizational Equip in This Theater; Memo, OCQM for Supply Div Stock Control, 4 Dec 42, same sub; Memo, DQM for G–4, 8 Dec 42, same sub. All in USFET QM 400.34.
[64] This and the following paragraphs pertaining to T/BA equipment for units debarking in the United Kingdom are based largely on a résumé of cables quoted in SOS ETO Tentative Over-all Plan for Supply and Administration, 20 June 1943 (hereafter cited as SOS ETO Plan), Section 7C. USFET AG 381.

[65] Cable R–7742, WAR to USSOS [Andrews for Lee from Somervell], 21 Apr 43, SOS ETO Plan, bk. I, sec. 1A. USFET AG 381.
[66] Cable R–8592, WAR to USSOS [Devers for Lee from Somervell], 21 Apr 43, SOS ETO Plan, bk. I, sec. 1D. USFET AG 381.

lack of proper information on Tables of Equipment.[67] There were only vague distinctions between initial issue and replacement supplies, with resulting uncertainty as to the actual quantities of bulk-shipped organizational equipment that had been received and issued. This in turn made for uncertainty in calculating replacement items on hand.[68] Supplies, moreover, did not arrive in accordance with requirements. U.S. industry, already working at full capacity, could not produce the necessary quantities of additional matériel on such short notice. These delays were particularly critical for units activated in the theater, which were sometimes overlooked in the preparation of planning lists by the War Department. The result was a severe drain on theater stocks.[69] But despite the handicaps, the bulk shipment system did work; tonnages discharged rose from 348,900 in June 1943 to 1,008,150 in December. The troop build-up passed the 1,000,000-mark in January 1944, and by May, as noted earlier, initial issues to troops had reduced QM stocks in the depots very noticeably. *(See Table 6.)* When the war was over, the ASF Planning Division considered that this procedure had been an important factor in making possible the timely equipment of the ETO fighting forces.[70] The Transportation Corps agreed that bulk shipments were desirable, but criticized inadequate coordination of arms production, troop training, and transportation programs. Because of various shortages and delays less than 50 percent of the 1943 shipping space earmarked for preshipments was actually utilized, and the inevitable result was a severe congestion of U.K. ports in the spring of 1944. Outloading for OVERLORD therefore proceeded under serious handicaps, and, of necessity, the OVERLORD supply arrangements included a wasteful use of shipping as floating warehouses.[71]

Transportation and Storage

Difficulties involved in moving supplies into United Kingdom ports, whether by automatic shipment or on requisition, were aggravated by wartime congestion of transportation facilities in the United Kingdom which put a high premium on maximum efficiency in handling stocks. The greatest care had to be exercised to avoid unessential transportation of goods by rail, road, or canal.[72] Ideally, all movements of supplies would have begun with the arrival of cargo on ships directed to the most logical port for the discharge of the particular supplies they carried. Cargo so landed could have been loaded directly into freight cars, trucks, or barges and sent immediately to the depot of ultimate destination. Unfortunately, lack of ad-

[67] Memo, OCQM for QM SBS, 10 Aug 43, sub: Initial Issue of T/BA Equip. USFET QM 400.34.

[68] Memo, Chief Supply Div OCQM for Chief P&T Div, 29 Dec 43, sub: Calculation of Status of Initial T/E Equip, and reply, 10 Jan 44. USFET QM 400.34.

[69] ETO G-4 Periodic Rpt, quarter ending 31 Mar 44. EUCOM 319.1.

[70] (1) *History of Planning Division, ASF,* I, 98; (2) Logistical Build-up in the British Isles, USFET Gen Bd Rpt 128, p. 22.

[71] Bykofsky and Larson, *The Transportation Corps: Operations Overseas,* pp. 106–08.

[72] (1) Memo, USAFBI for CG USANIF, 13 Mar 42, sub: Conservation of Shipping. USFET AG 430. (2) Memo, CQM ETO for CofT ETO, 26 Jul 42, no sub. USFET QM 400.2. (3) 1st Ind, QMSO G-40 to CQM ETO, 16 Feb 43. USFET QM 400.21, G-40.

vance information and improper marking and packing of goods often precluded this ideal procedure.

In order to give the Transportation Service timely advice on where to send its cargo, OCQM needed detailed advance information on the arrival date and the cargo of each ship carrying Quartermaster supplies. This information was supplied by NYPE, and supposedly reached OCQM by air courier some five days before the ship was to dock, in the form of the ship's manifest. But manifests often arrived too late to be of any value in planning and sometimes were not received at all.[73] When they did arrive, all too often the manifests were useless because they lumped many supply items together under one heading for the sake of brevity. One manifest, quoted by the OCQM, simply listed "1,298 cases Clothing, Meat, Vegetables 102,540 lbs." [74] More common listings were "2,000 pieces Subsistence" and "3,000 pieces Tomatoes, Peas, Corn, etc." [75]

When the information supplied by the manifests was too late or too vague, the cargo on the ship or on the dock had to be inspected by port authorities. This procedure was hampered by inadequate marking and packing. Littlejohn sent personal representatives to meet undocumented shipments whenever possible, but even they had difficulty in identifying supplies. It was sometimes necessary to open cases and bundles to determine their contents; then the inspecting officer notified OCQM and received instructions regarding shipment from the port. This time-consuming process was frowned upon by port authorities since Irish Sea ports suffered occasional German air raids and were under constant pressure to speed the turnaround of ships and clear discharged cargo out of the ports. They resisted cargo sorting by the quartermaster if any delay in unloading or port clearance was involved, as it almost always was. In the absence of instructions, the Transportation Service tended to ship quartermaster items as quickly as possible to what was considered the most logical Quartermaster installation, regardless of the possible necessity for rehandling and reshipping.[76] Packing and marking, as well as manifest listings, improved gradually, but the need for maximum haste in clearing the ports remained a major impediment to the efficient handling of quartermaster materials.[77]

Early shortcomings in the movement of supplies through the ports into the depots were gradually corrected. In the zone of interior efforts of NYPE and of the technical services to improve the preparation of ships' manifests and of the Air Transport Command to hasten their delivery attained notable success. In January 1943 only 40 percent were received on time, but by May 1943 this figure had risen to 91 percent.[78] Cable-

---

[73] Chart, Time of Receipt of Manifests . . . , data covering 1–31 Jan 43, from SOS ETO Plan, bk. II, sec. 5F. USFET AG 381.

[74] Memo, CQM for Chief Transportation Svs SOS, 5 Aug 42, sub: Info Pertaining to Supplies Arriving in Ports of Debarkation. USFET QM 560.

[75] Memo, OCQM for Goodman [Overseas Supply Div NYPE], 12 Sep 43, sub: Problems Concerning the QMC Sv. ETO 319.25.

[76] Memo, Chief Subs Div [OCQM] for DCQM, 3 Dec 42, sub: Distr of Subs From Shipside. USFET QM 430.

[77] Memo, DCQM for OCT, 1 Mar 44, sub: Misdirected Shipment of QM Supplies ex Ship. USFET QM 400.22.

[78] Charts, Time of Receipt of Manifests, 6 Apr, 7 May, and 7 Jun 43, from SOS ETO Plan, bk. II, sec. 5. USFET AG 381.

grams and other speedy means of communication were used to convey the essential information to the theater if manifests did not arrive on time.[79]

To improve the handling of cargo from ports to depots in the United Kingdom, SOS ETO asked the zone of interior agencies concerned to set up a new system of marking cargo specifically tailored to ETO needs. The "UGLY" system—named after its code word for United Kingdom—also provided a rudimentary division of shipments according to destination. The United Kingdom was to be divided into two zones. Requisitions would direct movement to the zone in which the depot of destination was located and thus reduce crosshauls between ports and depots. In addition, each package or shipment would be marked with a combination code tying it directly to a specific requisition, speeding identification in the port, and simplifying decisions on depot destination.[80]

The cargo marking part of this proposal was adopted by NYPE and the technical services in the zone of interior on 23 March 1943. But ASF viewed the zoning of the United Kingdom as unjustified. Maj. Gen. LeRoy Lutes, Chief of Staff for Operations, objected to thus assuming partial responsibility for supply distribution in the United Kingdom

and felt that it would lead to worse confusion than ever. He believed that the solution lay along the lines of improved manifests and the use of branch depots close to the United Kingdom ports to act as wholesale supply points for each technical service.[81] General Lee countered that storage space for such "wholesale" depots at portside was simply not available, and that British railways would be unable to handle cargo from 150 ships per month, as was planned for the full BOLERO build-up, unless the zoning system or its equivalent was adopted.[82] But meanwhile the British War Office and the Chief of Transportation, United States War Department, had concluded an agreement on zoning early in March, which was put into effect three months later. This was based on a series of conferences between representatives of the British Ministry of War Transport, the British Railways, the U.S. War Shipping Administration, and SOS ETOUSA. All these agencies had become convinced that such a plan was essential. The plan provided for three zones, and their code names, SOXO (Zone I, North Britain), GLUE (Zone II, South Britain), and BANG (Zone III, Northern Ireland), were substituted for UGLY, except for cargo directed to any British port.[83] Service chiefs in the United Kingdom were to requisition for

[79] SOS ETO Notes on Staff Conf, 13 Sep 43, remarks by Gen Goodman. USFET AG 337.

[80] (1) Memo, CG SOS ETO for CG ASF, 5 Apr 43, sub: Zoning of U.K. for Receipt of U.S. Army Cargo, quoted in SOS ETO Plan, bk. II, sec. 4C. USFET AG 381. The CQM advocated directing shipments to a specific port when a single depot was to receive the entire ship's cargo but this refinement was not seriously considered. (2) Memo, OCQM for G–4, 29 Mar 43, sub: Proposed Area Loading. Littlejohn Collection, sec. II. (3) Ltr, Littlejohn to G–4 SOS, 16 Jul 42, no sub. Littlejohn Reading File, vol. II, item 59.

[81] Ltr, Lutes to Lee, 6 Mar 43, in SOS ETO Plan, bk. II, sec. 5C. USFET AG 381.

[82] Ltr, Lee to Lutes, 1 Apr 43; Memo, Lee for CG ASF, 5 Apr 43. Both in USFET AG 381.

[83] The two zones in Great Britain were of approximately equal port capacity. Barry, Bristol, and London, each capable of unloading twenty ships for the U.S. forces each month, were the important ports of Zone II. Liverpool, with thirty-five ships per month, was by far the most important port in Zone I.

a particular zone, and ships were to be loaded in the United States so far as possible with cargo for that zone.[84]

Personal inspection of the traffic situation in the United Kingdom convinced doubtful ASF officers that this system was essential despite its added burdens on zone of interior agencies.[85] During the summer of 1943 details were ironed out by conferences and correspondence between representatives of New York Port of Embarkation and the ETO supply services.[86] By the time cargo movement for OVERLORD reached its peak, the system was working smoothly.

Efforts were also made to improve the handling of supplies at ports in the United Kingdom. As early as August 1942 the OCQM had proposed that facilities for sorting and reclassification of cargoes be installed near the most important ports.[87] Such facilities were essential if the Transportation Service was to distribute balanced quantities of various components of the ration and sized items of clothing directly to their final destination without wasteful rehandling and crosshauling. Facilities of the type needed existed in the form of emergency storage sheds behind the large ports. These sheds had been set up by the British primarily for rapid clearance of ports in the event of air attack, but also to serve as equipping points for embarking task forces. With both functions in mind, the Ministry of War Transport categorically refused to risk congesting these emergency facilities by allowing them to be used for permanent storage.[88]

But ever since the fall of 1942 a few of these sheds had been employed for sorting by individual American units, notably of the Air Forces, on the basis of specific and temporary agreements.[89] A series of conferences between the interested U.S. and British agencies held in May 1943 produced an understanding whereby the American technical services were granted conditional use of shed space behind major port areas at Liverpool, Bristol, Cardiff, and Glasgow. Supplies were not to be permanently stored there, and assigned space was subject to withdrawal on seventy-two hours' notice. If the sheds had to be cleared, the labor force, civilian and military, ordinarily employed by each service would assist in the emergency clearance and remain to help the British.[90] In the sorting sheds, the Quartermaster Corps received the largest share assigned to any single service, since one of their chief uses would be the sorting and reconsignment of sized clothing in balanced lots direct to depots issuing to

[84] (1) Memo, Actg CofT for G–4 SOS ETOUSA, 13 Mar 43. USFET G–4. (2) Ruppenthal, *Logistical Support*, I, 144. (3) Notes on Conf Between Devers, ASF, and Chiefs of Svs, 7 May 43, remarks by Gen Lutes. USFET AG 337. (4) Memo, Chiefs of Svs SOS ETO for Gen Collins, 14 Jun 43, sub: UGLY System of Marking and Forwarding Supplies, SOS ETO Plan, bk. II, sec. 52. USFET AG 381.

[85] SOS ETO Notes on Staff Conf, 19 Jul 43, remarks by Col Ottzenn, Superintendent Army Transport Sv, NYPE. USFET AG 337.

[86] Memo, Chief of Opns 871 for QM Sv, 22 Oct 43, sub: Gen Info From NYPE. USFET QM 319.1.

[87] Memo, Stock Control Div for CQM, 5 Aug 42, sub: Distr USFET QM 475.

[88] (1) Memo, CofT for CQM, 2 Mar 43, sub: Use of Sorting Sheds by QM. USFET QM (600. (2) Interv with Littlejohn, 3 May 60.

[89] Memo, Deputy Comdr SOS for CG Eighth Air Force, 21 Apr 43, and Inds, sub: Sorting Sheds. USFET AG 633.

[90] (1) Inland Sorting Sheds, Notes on a Mtg . . ., 12 May 43. USFET AG 337. (2) Memo, CG SOS ETO for Chiefs of Supply Svs, 15 Aug 43, sub: Inland Sorting Sheds. USFET QM 567.

troops.[91] It was estimated that reshipment of about 90 percent of sized clothing would have been necessary if the clothing had been sent directly from shipside to the nearest depot.[92]

As already described, the almost disastrous confusion that accompanied outloading for the TORCH expedition had taught Littlejohn a bitter lesson. Consequently, as the Transportation Corps' port units came into the United Kingdom, the OCQM attempted with indifferent success to instruct them in specialized QMC cargo sorting and inventory techniques. Although each port organization included QMC personnel who should have been used for this purpose, most port commanders insisted on using them as housekeeping or station complement troops. Moreover, few of these port quartermasters were trained for their real duties. Littlejohn was therefore obliged to provide extra personnel to perform these specialized functions, and even then had to overcome considerable resistance from port commanders who believed that cargo sorting was unnecessary. It should be noted that General Ross found many of his original port commanders lacking in the required flexibility for duty under foreign conditions and had to relieve more than half of them before D-day. Littlejohn found General Ross himself somewhat unsympathetic to the Quartermaster point of view, and had to appeal to the SOS commander to lay down rules for effective co-operation.[93]

On 15 August 1943 General Lee directed each service to furnish a liaison officer and enlisted assistants to the staff of each port commander. This directive regularized arrangements to control movement of supplies from the ports via sorting sheds to depots. Thereafter, the Quartermaster port representative and his assistants served as a direct personal liaison between the OCQM and each port commander to speed the movement of supplies by action on the spot. Before the arrival of a ship, the Quartermaster representative or his men examined the manifest or loading cable sent him by OCQM that indicated the destination of supplies. He planned with Transportation Service the methods of handling these supplies. When the ship arrived, he checked the actual cargo, taking particular note of items not listed on the manifest or not properly marked, phoned information on such undocumented cargo to OCQM, and requested appropriate disposition instructions. These teams also inspected rail cars as they were loaded and dispatched in order to eliminate as far as possible mixed loads and improper waybills, and checked notices of shipments to the depots to make sure that all useful information was transmitted correctly and on time. They advised the port commander on items requiring sorting, supervised all shipside documentation of supplies, and notified the sorting sheds of goods on the way to them. Finally,

---

[91] On 22 March 1943 OCQM requested 150,000 square feet of shed space at Liverpool, 100,000 square feet at Bristol, and 50,000 square feet each at Newport and Glasgow. *QM Supply in ETO*, I, 60.

[92] Memo, CO G–35 for CQM, 2 Nov 43, sub: Sorting Sheds. USFET QM 000.4.

[93] (1) Bykofsky and Larson, *The Transportation Corps: Operations Overseas*, p. 110. (2) Littlejohn's Memo 4 for Dr. Stetson Conn, OCMH, 27 Sep 59. Hist Br OQMG.

the teams made detailed reports on each day's activities to OCQM and summarized them weekly.[94]

Even after General Lee's directive had clarified the status of port liaison personnel, Littlejohn continued to encounter some opposition. But these representatives, in close touch with both the OCQM and the Transportation Service, proved their worth and filled a major gap in the supply chain. As the flow of supplies accelerated late in 1943, their assistance was most important, especially in connection with items requiring sorting before shipment. Despite the improvements effected by the UGLY system, there remained an apparently irreducible minimum of Quartermaster supplies, in the neighborhood of 25 percent, for which the destination could not be determined on the basis of documents in advance of arrival. These supplies the port representatives identified and speeded on their way. In addition, they provided information valuable to the receiving depots in their day-to-day operations.[95]

Pilferage in transit and in storage was another problem of overseas supply. Wartime shortages made quartermaster items very tempting to those in touch with black market dealers, both British civilians and U.S. soldiers. This situation, combined with relatively poor

guarding of supplies both in transit and in storage, made losses inevitable. As early as September 1942 reports reached General Lee indicating that pilferage had mounted to serious proportions.[96] Investigation indicated that poor packing and rough handling, which exposed the contents of cases, and storage in remote locations where they were hard to protect, plus the indifferent attitude of U.S. troops, made pilfering of goods in transit temptingly easy. Obvious remedies were increasing the number of guards at docks and other exposed places, more careful handling and checking of goods in transit, and closer co-operation with the British civilian and military police.[97] Such measures were in effect by the end of 1942 and by the following April Lee was able to assure Somervell that the pilferage problem was well under control.[98]

Despite these assurances the ETO Provost Marshal reported in May 1943 that "the amount of goods stolen is tremendous and that the fault is due largely to the failure of our own people to take reasonable adequate measures to safeguard the property."[99] But it appeared that those most worried about pilferage might be exaggerating the

---

[94] (1) Memo, S&D Div OCQM for Littlejohn, 7 May 43, sub: Distr Control Plan. Littlejohn Collection, sec. II. (2) Memo, CG SOS ETOUSA for Chief of Svs, 15 Aug 43, sub: Port Representatives. USFET AG 381. (3) Memo, S&D Div OCQM for Littlejohn, 27 Oct 43, sub: Port Representatives and Sorting Sheds. USFET QM 600.

[95] (1) Memo, CO G–35 for CQM, 2 Nov 43, sub: Port Liaison Representative. USFET QM 000.4. (2) Memo, CQM for CO WBS, 5 Nov 43, and Inds, sub: Opn of Sorting Sheds and Utilization of Port Liaison Offs. Hist Br OQMG.

[96] Memo, ACofS G–1 for Lee, 3 Sep 42, sub: Pilfering. USFET AG 400.73.

[97] (1) Memo, PMG ETO for CofS SOS ETO, 16 Sep 42, sub: Prevention of Pilfering and Police of Docks; Memo, SOS ETO for CO's of Ports, 27 Sep 42, sub: Prevention of Pilfering of U.S. Stores at Ports. Both in USFET AG 400.73. (2) Memo, ACofS G–4 for CG SOS, 29 Oct 42, sub: Losses and Pilferage at Docks, Depots, and in Transit. USFET QM 400.73.

[98] Cir 58, Hq SOS ETO, 1 Dec 42, Prevention of Pilferage; Ltr, CG ETO to Somervell, 5 Apr 43, no sub. Both in USFET AG 400.73.

[99] Memo, PMG ETO for AG ETO, 28 May 43, sub: Theft of Stores From Warehouses. USFET QM 400.73.

losses. Reports of goods missing were often based on discrepancies in the records rather than on physical evidence of loss. Investigation revealed that many supposed losses were paper shortages rather than actual thefts. Blankets, for instance, were usually tallied into warehouses in bundles that were not broken down and counted until later. Inaccurate record keeping, rather than theft, was clearly the cause of some of these shortages.[100]

One measure against pilfering that might possibly have been exploited to a greater degree was the use of guard dogs. They were especially effective for patrolling outdoor storage areas at night. One man and one dog were considered to be as effective as six or eight ordinary guards. Teams of eight men and eight dogs were trained by the Ministry of Aircraft Production in a five-week course in a school at Cheltenham. The dogs were loaned to the Americans for the duration by British civilians; no American dogs arrived in the British Isles, although some were used on the Continent later. The men were all American volunteers. By the end of 1943 there were twenty-two such teams. An American guard dog school, also at Cheltenham, was organized late in 1943 under the Depot Branch of OCQM. The maximum number of teams, fifty-six, was reached shortly before D-day. They were considered Quartermaster units, but were used by all of the technical services and many combat units.[101]

Actually, combined efforts along all lines proved reasonably successful in checking losses. A number of civilians and U.S. soldiers were arrested at Liverpool in January 1943 and at Glasgow in May. Organized black market rings were broken up by co-operative action of the ETO Provost Marshal and the British Special Investigations Branch (Ports). Security in transit and in the depots was tightened and recording of supply movements improved to a point where losses were detected early enough for effective follow-up.[102] These measures could not eliminate pilferage entirely, but they did prevent the large-scale losses that the U.S. Army suffered in other theaters.

During the thirty months of logistical preparations that culminated on D-day, the United Kingdom was at once a sovereign Allied power, largely preoccupied with its own contribution to OVERLORD, a densely populated country with a highly complex civilian economy, and an American forward base area reasonably secure against enemy interference. From the narrow viewpoint of American Quartermaster operations, only freedom from enemy interference was a clear and unmistakable asset; the other conditions engendered irritating complications. There were compensating advantages, of course, but they could only be exploited by an elaborate process of inter-Allied co-ordination and

---

[100] Memo, CO Depot G–30 for McKeever, OCQM, 5 Jun 43, sub: Pilferage. USFET QM 400.73.

[101] (1) Ltr, Hq SOS ETOUSA to CG ETOUSA, sub: Guard Dogs, 10 Jul 43. AG 454.3 MT&SD. (2) IRS, Depot Br S&D Div to Hist Records OCQM, sub: Guard Dog School, 3 Jan 44. USFET QM 353.5. (3) QM Supply in ETO, VIII, 96–97.

[102] (1) Memo, PMG for AG ETO, 28 May 43, sub: Theft of Stores From Warehouses; Memo, Hq SOS ETO for CG WBS, 10 Jul 43, sub: Theft and Sale of Government Supplies. Both in USFET QM 400.73. (2) Memo, Chief S&D Div for CQM, 14 Feb 44, sub: Investigation of Discrepancies in Incoming Shipments, Depot G–25. USFET QM 400.61.

liaison, requiring many competent and experienced staff officers.

In retrospect, it appears likely that the difficult problems inherent in BOLERO were precisely the ones that contributed valuable lessons and useful precedents for the future. Members of the American technical services had never previously encountered real problems in the matter of working space. Even in such small and heavily industrialized states as Maryland and Delaware, military installations were usually of ample size and equipped with every facility. In the United Kingdom quartermasters learned how to operate small depots, dispersed during the period of German air superiority, and located in densely populated areas. For them BOLERO was an intensive course in how to "do without." They learned how to use open storage instead of covered warehouses, and how to get along with a minimum of materials-handling equipment, with limited civilian labor, with a meager ration of gasoline, and with severely curtailed rail services. They demonstrated that the problem of sharing docks, railways, highways, and manpower pools with civilians, while simultaneously supporting large combat forces, can be solved, although not easily. In a nation which had converted almost its entire industry to essential military purposes, it was often difficult to establish priorities between purely military activities and industrial programs of equal importance. Americans had to learn that the regimentation of British industry, which made it completely subservient to the national war effort, by no means implied that individual industrial operations would be modified to suit the local convenience of American

military installations. Such matters were decided by representatives of the various supply ministries of the British Government, which maintained a very considerable degree of ascendancy over both the British and U.S. military forces as long as those forces remained in the United Kingdom. Despite initial misgivings and occasional inconveniences, quartermasters found this arrangement to be a practical one. Indeed, the necessary co-ordination between American soldiers and British civilians could hardly have been achieved in any other way.

Direct liaison between British and American technical services during the BOLERO period did not present any new or unfamiliar problems, but during a logistical build-up of unprecedented size lasting more than two years, old problems inevitably took on new dimensions. The intimacy of co-ordination that proved to be necessary and the sheer volume of international dealings which had to be transacted exceeded all previous experience. The various British logistical headquarters had to set up separate staff sections solely to deal with the Americans, and the U.S. services found that their requirements for competent staff personnel far surpassed expectations. In this relationship British responsibilities were more exacting than the corresponding American ones, but the situation demanded revised standards of competence for liaison personnel of both nations. Staff officers had to be trained not only in their own specialties, but also in the completely different staff and supply procedures of a foreign army. One other essential qualification of such officers should also be noted. At AFHQ and later at SHAEF General

Eisenhower maintained the principle that only officers who were able and willing to co-operate with Allies were suitable for positions on his staff. Although at lower levels and among the technical services there was no official enforcement of this principle, a co-operative spirit was in fact an essential qualification for all liaison and made the solution of technical problems comparatively easy. Unofficial, personal contacts involved problems of a different kind, which are discussed in the following chapter.

CHAPTER X

Living in Britain

The first sizable contingent of U.S. troops (4,058 men of the 34th Division) reached Northern Ireland on 26 January 1942, and by D-day there were more than one and one-half million Americans in the United Kingdom. The earliest units arrived ready for combat in a theater where a German invasion was still a lively possibility, but their own mounting numbers and favorable events in other theaters during 1942 made such an event less and less likely. The realization that major combat in the theater would come only on Allied initiative brought some slackening of tension, and after the TORCH operation —one of the best-kept secrets of the war —had been unveiled, even amateur strategists could foresee that an assault on the Continent would have to be postponed. Thus during 1942–43 ground and service troops in the British Isles found themselves in a very quiet theater, almost like an extension of the zone of interior. But the blackout, occasional enemy air raids, and the operations and combat losses of the Army Air Forces were reminders that the enemy was within striking distance.

Training—much of it basic training for incompletely trained troops—was a major activity in the United Kingdom, especially among service units. As early as May 1942 General Lee had reluctantly accepted partially trained units because of the world-wide shortage of service troops. The shortage continued through 1943, and very few of the service units arriving in the ETO were adequately trained. Time had to be found for close-order drill and weapons familiarization, although the men were working long hours on the docks or in the depots. Ground combat troops likewise came into the theater incompletely trained and went through field training exercises of mounting complexity. Life in Britain was neither soft nor idle, but activities were considerably different from those in the rear areas of an active theater of war.[1]

Foreign uniforms and accents were no novelties in the United Kingdom. Troops from most of the dominions and colonies of the Empire had been present almost since the war began. Each successive disaster on the Continent had brought in a wave of what were, in reality, refugees in uniform, so that Poles, Free French, Norwegians, and Netherlanders were seen everywhere. Americans were something else again, emphatically not refugees or colonials, but guests who felt very much at home, persistent in the delusion that they spoke the language of the country, and with money in their pockets. The high

---

[1] (1) See above, p. 28. (2) Ruppenthal, *Logistical Support*, I, 57. (3) *QM Supply in ETO*, VIII, 6.

pay scale and spendthrift habits of U.S. personnel were sources of irritation to their British hosts. By giving large tips and paying exorbitant prices, U.S. servicemen received considerably more than their share of personal services and of the few articles that were not rationed. On the other hand, their spending was a valuable source of dollars to the hard-pressed British Treasury. Troubled by the very clear relationship between reckless spending and troop disciplinary problems, SOS headquarters launched an intensive campaign to encourage increased family and other allotments and purchases of war bonds. By September 1943 SOS troops had been persuaded to save more than half their pay, and during the following spring a similar campaign among First Army troops was even more successful. By May 1944 American troops were sending home 73 percent of their pay, and spending much of the balance in U.S. post exchanges, so that the inflationary impact upon the British economy was reduced.[2]

Inevitably several hundred thousand American troops fresh from training camps in the zone of interior, where they had been sheltered from the modest beginnings of U.S. civilian rationing, made a severe impact on the war economy of Great Britain in its fourth year of conflict. The "Yanks"—including many southerners who never became reconciled to that nickname—were coming into an English-speaking area where they expected to find many of the comforts and conveniences of their accustomed civilian environment. Instead they found no ice cream, no Coca Cola, and very little beer; candy, razor blades, soap, writing paper, and even toilet paper were rationed. The widespread drafting of women was both a shocking fact and an inconvenience—in many towns it was hard to find anyone to press trousers, iron shirts, tend a bar, or even sell postcards. Trains were unheated and taxis almost nonexistent. The newcomers were admitted to the NAAFI store, the British soldier's PX, but found its contents unfamiliar, meager, and unsatisfying. Naturally, the troops and their commanders demanded that the Quartermaster Service supply all their wants. Some of these demands could be met by imports from the United States, but others could not be met at all in wartime. Ultimately, rationed local resources produced far more than the OCQM had originally expected, partly because U.S. requirements were different and not entirely in competition with the demands of British troops.

Subsistence

The first American troops to land in Northern Ireland found that the ninety-day supply of rations which should have accompanied them had not arrived. No American rations were available in the theater, and it took several months to build up a depot system to the point where reliable distribution of rations was possible. Meanwhile the Royal Army Service Corps (RASC) supplied American troops with the regular British Army ration, which quickly became unpopular. Reflecting British tastes and the available resources of the United Kingdom, its basic ingredients were dark

---

[2] (1) See above, ch. II. (2) Notes on Comd and Staff Conf, Hq SBS, 2 Nov 43. USFET AG 337. (3) *FUSA Rpt of Opns*, 20 Oct 43–1 Aug 44, VII, 216. (4) Hancock and Gowing, *British War Economy*, p. 353.

whole-wheat bread, potatoes, tea, mutton, and smoked fish. Moreover it was skimpy, weighing three and one-fourth pounds in contrast to the five and one-half pounds of the standard American ration. Actually, the British "regular" (Home Forces) ration was similar in concept and purpose to the prewar garrison ration of the U.S. Army, which had also been augmented by a monetary allowance. A British unit received two and a half pence (four cents) per man per day while in garrison, and its unit mess funds also benefited by receipts from unit gardens, and from money-making schemes such as sale of surplus fats and garbage. Most of these benefits were contrary to current U.S. Army regulations, and initially none of them were available to U.S. units in Great Britain.[3]

Reverse lend-lease enabled American units to become customers of the Navy Army Air Force Institute where British units spent a good deal of their available cash in purchases of fruits, vegetables, and other foods, supplied practically at cost. NAAFI has been compared to the U.S. Army Exchange Service (AES), but was actually a larger, more versatile, and more autonomous organization—a military version of the powerful co-operative chains familiar in British civilian life. NAAFI was equipped to supply many foods preferred by Americans; in co-operation with the RASC and the OCQM, the British modified their basic ration, reducing the quantities of bread, potatoes, mutton, and tea, and increasing the

amount of beef, vegetables, fruit, and coffee.[4] With these changes, the so-called British-American ration was evolved, weighing four and a half pounds and containing 4,100 calories. Even this augmentation did not provide a fully adequate diet for all troops, and the Chief Quartermaster persuaded the British to increase the allowance another 15 percent for men engaged in hard labor.[5]

As the inventories mounted American troops gradually changed over from the British-American to a straight American ration. This switch occurred in Northern Ireland as early as March 1942, only about two months after the first U.S. troops arrived there. In England the transition took place as the subsistence depots began to function in the late autumn of 1942.[6] An important part of the change involved replacing British mess and subsistence depot personnel. The process was hastened by criticism from the War Department, which was dissatisfied with a policy of calling on the British without employing U.S. serv-

[3] (1) Ltr, CO Hq Comd ETOUSA to CG ETOUSA, 21 Aug 42, sub: Rations. USFET AG 430.2. (2) *QM Supply in ETO*, II, 88–89.

[4] Memo, Maj Herman for Col Carter, Subs Div OCQM, 28 Aug 42, sub: Facts Concerning British-American Ration. Hist Br OQMG.
[5] (1) Memo, CQM to G-4 SOS (Opns), 29 Jul 42, sub: Additional Allowance of Rations; Memo, Chief Subs Div to CQM, 11 Aug 42, sub: Basis for 15 percent Increase in Rations; Ltr, CQM to Deputy Dir Supplies and Transport, War Office, 9 Aug 42, no sub. All in USFET QM 430.2. (2) Maj. Gen. Thomas W. Richardson, RASC, the Deputy Director of Supplies and Transport, War Office, provided invaluable assistance, both administrative and technical, in the development of a British-American ration. Cf. Ltr, CQM ETO to CG ETO, 16 Jun 45, sub: Recommendation for Award of Legion of Merit. Littlejohn Reading File, vol. XXXVII, item 50.
[6] Memo, CO Depot G-14 for CG WBS, 5 Oct 42, sub: American Rations, Liverpool Area. USFET QM 430.2.

ice troops to full advantage. Lee had reported on 6 October that, because of the continued shortage of suitably trained U.S. personnel, the British Army was still feeding about 50,000 American troops. The base sections were directed to correct this situation with all possible speed and report progress monthly. By the end of the year the number of U.S. troops still subsisting permanently on the British-American ration was less than 1,000, and consisted mainly of very small technical detachments working in British installations and too isolated to draw on American depots. But this ration continued to be supplied to U.S. units and individuals temporarily located in predominantly British areas, and in many cases to newly arrived units.[7]

With the aim of combining subsistence imported from the United States and items procured locally into a series of menus that would offer the American soldier the most suitable diet, the OCQM undertook the revision of the current American Type A ration in co-operation with the theater Chief Surgeon. The initial flow of subsistence from the zone of interior was based on OQMG Expeditionary Force Menu 1, a Type B field ration that used only canned, dehydrated, and other nonperishable items.[8] Even the British-American ration was superior to the Type B, but

Littlejohn was convinced that for reasons of morale as well as nutrition, American troops should receive a diet as similar as possible to the Type A ration served in the United States, despite the added difficulties in storage and distribution. The OCQM studied the problem carefully and found that the required items fell into two main categories: fresh meats and fats, which were in short supply in the British Isles, and fruits and vegetables, which might be procured locally.

Since a large proportion of Britain's meats and fats were imported, additional imports would be needed to provide for the American troops. The British suggested that a common store be set up, pointing out that this would economize on transportation, labor, and storage space. The OCQM rejected this solution for several reasons. First, it would deplete British reserves and temporarily reduce the meager meat ration of British civilians. In the current situation, even a temporary decrease in civilian rations was undesirable. Second, the staple British meat was mutton; Americans preferred beef. And finally the ETO quartermasters were eager to set up an independent supply line and practice the procedures that would become necessary if an American force ever secured a lodgment on the Continent. But the two supply systems could not be completely independent; construction of separate refrigerated storage to be used for only a few months was clearly unjustified, and the QMC agreed to share British cold storage facilities. Frozen meats, fats, and cheeses moved in British freight cars from the ports to British refrigerated warehouses near the principal U.S. troop centers, where they were

[7] (1) Ltr, Lee to CG ETOUSA, 6 Oct 42, sub: SOS Troops and Labor Situation. USFET AG 320.2. (2) Memo, OCQM for QM SBS, 16 Dec 42, and 1st Ind, sub: British-American Ration. Littlejohn Collection, sec. II. (3) Ltr, CG SBS to CG SOS ETO, 4 Jan 43, sub: British-American Ration. USFET AG 430. (4) Ruppenthal, *Logistical Support*, I, 111. (5) Memo, CQM for CG SOS, 3 Jun 43, sub: Answers to Questions. USFET AG 310.1.

[8] Risch, *The Quartermaster Corps: Organization, Supply, and Services*, I, ch. V, *passim*.

BRITISH WOMEN WAR WORKERS *unloading American supplies at Thatcham Depot, October 1942.*

held until distributed to the consuming units.[9]

Inevitably, shortages of refrigerated transportation caused some difficulties. During 1942 and 1943, for lack of such equipment, perishables were often shipped in freight cars and trucks which were insulated but not refrigerated. If these trips were short, taking no more than two to three days, such transportation was generally satisfactory. Even-

tually, improved handling procedures and the importation of refrigerated rail cars made for a better system of moving perishables. A by-product of this shortage was the British ban on all production of ice cream. A ready ice cream mix, requiring only water, was available in the zone of interior, and considerable quantities were actually shipped to the United Kingdom. This could have been manufactured locally without adding to the transport burden. Nevertheless, out of deference for British feelings, General Lee personally forbade the making and serving of ice cream in Great Britain.

[9] Ltr, OCQM to CO Depot G–25, 7 Sep 42, sub: Proc Storage and Withdrawal of Perishable Subs Items. USFET QM 430.

The ban was lifted shortly after Lee departed for Normandy in August 1944.[10]

Since fresh produce was available locally, arrangements were made for U.S. troops to get a proportionate share of the fruits and vegetables commonly grown in the United Kingdom. Thus cabbage, brussels sprouts, potatoes, lettuce, beans, root vegetables, and small quantities of apples and pears were obtained on reverse lend-lease from local commercial sources and from NAAFI. Beginning in the summer of 1942, U.S. troops also participated actively in British gardening activities. On 11 August 1942, Littlejohn became ETOUSA agricultural officer, and shortly thereafter established an Agricultural Branch in the Service Installations Division of OCQM. The branch maintained liaison with a corresponding agency in the British Army and with the Ministry of Agriculture to obtain seeds, tools, and expert advice for the agricultural officers of American units, maintained statistical records, and prepared informational literature for the troops. Produce might be used locally or sold to NAAFI. In either case a profit was credited to the post, camp, and station fund for the benefit of the troops. Exact accounting was very difficult because of frequent shifts of troop units, so that U.S. troops harvested crops planted by British soldiers, and vice versa. Americans cultivated nearly 8,000 acres in 1942 and over

15,000 in 1943. The Eighth Air Force was particularly active in this work and continued it during 1944, after the bulk of the ground forces had departed for the Continent. In that year the product of combined British and American military agriculture was estimated at 50,000 ship tons.[11]

The main problem in handling fresh fruits and vegetables stemmed from the irregularity of supply and variations in quality. Kinds and quantities varied with the season, weather, and crop conditions. Complaints were frequent that the lettuce was tough, the apples and pears woody, and the cabbage rank and stringy. Irrespective of quality, Americans disliked parsnips and brussels sprouts. Depot subsistence officers did not always know the amounts forthcoming, and since their stocks often had to be issued quickly to avoid spoilage, receiving units frequently refused the vegetables rather than go to the trouble of revising the menu to include them.[12]

A relatively small but occasionally troublesome problem was the controlled distribution of shell eggs, oranges, and milk. These highly nourishing foods were required for treating hospital patients and were supplied, for reasons of health as well as morale, to U.S. Navy submarine crews and to air crews on combat duty or in training. Surplus

---

[10] (1) Memo, OCQM for Chief Transportation Div, 4 Aug 42, sub: Transportation of Perishables; Ltr, OCQM to Ministry of Food, 7 Jan 44, no sub. Both in USFET QM 430. (2) Memo, DCQM for CQM [ca. Jan 44], sub: Reefer Rail Cars. USFET 004. (3) Hancock and Gowing, *British War Economy*, p. 485. (4) Littlejohn, ed., Passing in Review, ch. 33, p. 25. (5) Interv with Col Leo J. Meyer, TC, 25 Oct 57.

[11] (1) *QM Supply in ETO*, VI, 97–99. (2) ETOUSA Cirs 81 (6 Dec 42) and 31 (23 Mar 43). (3) ETOUSA Agricultural Bulls, 1942–43. USFET AG 331.6.
[12] (1) Memo, Actg CQM for QM WBS, 3 Apr 44, sub: Use of Fresh Vegetables. Littlejohn Collection, sec. II. (2) Ltr, OCQM Subs Div to NAAFI, 23 Jun 43, no sub; Memo, CQM for DCQM, 19 Nov 43, sub: Review of Subs; Memo, Chief Subs Div for DCQM, 5 Feb 44, sub: Complete Survey of Subs Situation in U.K. All in USFET AG 430.

ships' stores were occasional but irregular and unreliable sources of these items. NAAFI provided 1 egg per day for hospitalized stomach cases, 2 eggs per week for other hospital patients, and 3 eggs and 3 pieces of fruit per week for all submarine, air force combat, and flight training crews.[13] A special in-flight ration for aircraft crews, in large part locally procured hard candies, was supplied by the OCQM until mid-1943, when it became a standard Air Forces item, supplied by AAF technical depots.[14] The use of fresh milk, although it was available in small quantities from British production, was prohibited by the ETO Chief Surgeon because the British did not test their cattle for tuberculosis in accordance with U.S. standards. Milk requirements therefore had to be met by importing canned, evaporated, and dried milk.[15]

The ETO A ration, which became effective in March 1943, established a pattern that remained constant until V–E Day despite minor changes in detail.[16] Quantitatively, it was devised to be adequate but not excessive and totaled 4,050 calories per man per day as against the earlier ration's 4,500 calories, which in practice had proved wasteful. The inevitability of substitutions at various points in the supply chain was recognized, and foods were listed in nutritional groups within which one item could be substituted for another with the least damage to nutritional balance. A special ration scale was set up for hospital patients, which provided a lower caloric intake by reducing starches and fats but which increased those items useful in special diets, such as boned chicken, strained fruits and vegetables, fruit juices, and milk.[17]

U.S. Navy personnel in the British Isles had evolved their own British-American ration, using components supplied by the British Admiralty in a manner closely parallel to Army experience. As soon as a purely American ration became available, it was supplied to naval shore installations from the nearest QM Class I depot exactly as it was to Army units. Ships, especially those operating at sea for extended periods, demanded a slightly different menu, but the OCQM was able to meet their requirements too. Experience showed that smaller ships, like small Army messes, inevitably utilized food less efficiently than larger units, and a 10 percent allowance was made for this. But the OCQM had not foreseen that tactical movements of naval combat units might result in sudden and very heavy demands for rations at a single depot. On one occasion in the spring of 1943 a large part of the fleet pulled into southern England and asked to be provisioned immediately for a cruise of several weeks. The OCQM had received no advance information, and the local depot was stocked to supply only a

[13] (1) Memo, OCQM for QM NIBS, 8 Nov 43, sub: Distr of Surplus Ships' Stores. USFET AG 430. (2) Memo, Chief Subs Div for CQM, 17 May 43, sub: Fresh Eggs for Hospital Patients and AF Combat Crews. USFET QM 434.

[14] Interv with Littlejohn, 29 Oct 57.

[15] Memo, Chief Surgeon for AG ETO, 29 Jul 42, sub: Instrs Governing the Use of Cow's Milk in ETOUSA. USFET QM 434.

[16] (1) Cir 13, Hq ETOUSA, 11 Feb 43. Reproduced in full in Littlejohn, ed., Passing in Review, ch. 33, vol. II, app. 3A. (2) See Table 17.

[17] (1) Memo, CQM and Chief Surgeon for CG ETO, 14 Jan 43, sub: Proposed Revised Ration Allowances. USFET AG 430.2. (2) Memo, CQM for QM's of Base Secs, 21 May 43, sub: Conservation of Food; Memo, CQM for DTQMG, 22 Jun 43, sub: Situation Rpt Subs. ETO 430.

limited number of troops. Littlejohn recalled later that:

A squawk went to the "top salt" and I got sent for. The "top salt's" Chief of Staff and I had a very firm but pleasant conversation. Out of it came the appointment of Captain Polatti, USN, as aide to the Chief Quartermaster. His job was to advise the Quartermaster Service what the Navy wanted, when they wanted it, and where they wanted it. From then on the Navy got what they wanted.

The original difficulty, of course, stemmed from the fact that the Navy could not conceive of a major port which was not the site of a major depot. Littlejohn, also, would have liked to locate depots at major ports, but this had been impossible for reasons already described.[18]

During the build-up period, a number of minor problems interfered with the most efficient operation of the subsistence program. In the summer and fall of 1942, large stocks of subsistence had been accumulated in the United Kingdom to provide for the troops later sent to North Africa. The most perishable and most desirable items were issued first, while very large stocks of other items accumulated. Some of these overstockages, such as canned hash, stew, Spam, and chili con carne, were offered to the forces in North Africa in May 1943, but these were B ration items practically identical with the current C ration.[19] No one was surprised when they were not accepted. Overstocks of flour, dry skimmed milk, and pork luncheon meat in danger of spoilage were transferred to the Ministry of Food for rapid

disposal to civilians. Eventually these excesses were used up.

In the fall of 1943 SOS ETOUSA hoped to return to a single menu as the basis for both requisition and distribution. A new ration, reflecting minor changes in availability of various foods and increased knowledge of troop preferences, went into effect in November.[20] Like the previous A ration, this one contained a large proportion of locally procured items. The amount of pork and prepared pork products was increased, with a corresponding decrease in consumption of beef. The caloric value of the ration was not changed. But certain shortages (notably tin for cans) were now developing in the United States, and NYPE was forced to make frequent and large-scale substitutions of ration items, with the result that depots could not follow the menu in making issues. Substitutions were passed down the supply chain until meals bore little resemblance to the prescribed menu. The theater was forced to recognize that the difference between a basic requisitioning menu and a short-term distributing menu is a permanent one, not to be eliminated by closer liaison with the zone of interior or by improved staff methods. The requisitioning menu represents what is desired, while the distribution menu must reflect what is available. Requisitions are superior to automatic supply, but neither can be completely satisfactory, especially in an overseas theater partially dependent upon local procurement. The November 1943 ration represented a permanent long-range A ration for theater planning purposes and for requisitions on the zone of interior, varied enough to enable

---

[18] (1) Interv with Littlejohn, 29 Oct 57. (2) Quotation from Littlejohn, ed., Passing in Review, ch. 5, p. 7.

[19] The problem of monotony in operational rations is discussed in Chapter XV, below.

[20] Admin Cir 85, SOS ETOUSA, 21 Nov 43.

quartermasters to take into account, on a monthly basis, actual stocks on hand.[21]

Distribution and food-processing menus required constant revision, but this was only a small part of OCQM's supervisory responsibility at the unit mess level. Cooks and bakers, like other service troops, came to the ETO only partially trained. Basic training courses for mess personnel were started at Shrivenham and Tidworth in September 1942. An advanced mess management course, stressing the use of British food and equipment, and a subsistence laboratory, which was instrumental in developing the successive ETO rations, were both established in the American School Center at Shrivenham in December. The OCQM also initiated a Mess Advisory Service to aid unit mess officers and mess sergeants in solving their problems on the spot. The mess advisers combined demonstration with informal instruction, and their visits were followed up by instructional literature, much of it prepared by the subsistence laboratory, and by regional conferences of mess officers. Contests were carried on in each base section, and model messes were selected to illustrate what could be accomplished with the standard facilities and food ingredients available in the theater. All these activities resulted in improvements in nutrition and palatability of the ration, reduction of waste, and a perceptible improvement in troop morale.[22]

One famous landmark of American life in Great Britain was the consolidated officers' mess at Grosvenor House in London. Operated as a cafeteria beginning in December 1943, it could seat nearly 1,000 officers at a time, and during most of 1944 it served over 6,000 meals a day. Capt. Walter A. Stansbury ran the restaurant, which was given the nickname of "Willow Run," with a staff of more than 400 British civilians. He was so successful in overcoming the technical and personnel problems involved that Littlejohn recommended him for the Legion of Merit. "Willow Run" contributed greatly to the prestige of the Central Base Section, and when General Rogers was appointed to the new headquarters command in Paris, one of his earliest requests was that Stansbury, by this time a major, be assigned to his command.[23]

Clothing

By War Department directive, troops arriving in the ETO brought with them the full set of clothing provided by the current Table of Basic Allowances. This included all elements of the normal uniform issued in the zone of interior except the cotton outer uniform, which even in summer was not worn in the United Kingdom. The quartermaster was therefore charged primarily with the replacement of lost or worn clothing and with repairing clothing turned in for salvage.

Prior to D-day, the clothing maintenance problem centered on the source of clothing stocks. At the outset the zone of interior was prepared to supply the

[21] Littlejohn, ed., *Passing in Review*, ch. 33, vol. I, p. 54.

[22] (1) *Ibid.*, ch. 33, pp. 146–56. (2) *QM Supply in ETO*, II, 70–72.

[23] (1) History of QM Section, Central Base Section. Hist Br OQMG. (2) Personal Ltr, Littlejohn to Rogers, 22 Aug 44; Ltr, CQM to Gen Vaughan, 4 Sep 44, sub: Release of Mess Officers From U.K. for Continent. Littlejohn Reading File, vol. XXVII, item 101; vol. XXVIII, item 33.

theater with all its requirements, but transatlantic shipping was desperately short and deliveries were uncertain. The quartermaster of SPOBS opened negotiations with the British for the local production of needed clothing. Since facilities and cloth were available, the OCQM placed trial orders as early as July 1942, but fundamental differences of opinion quickly developed. Unless American orders were sufficiently large and definite to justify changes in their manufacturing processes, the British preferred to maintain their existing production facilities. This meant that American clothing would be produced according to British specifications as to color, cloth, and design. On the other hand, American officials were not prepared to commit themselves to sizable orders (involving tens of thousands of items) until they were satisfied that British samples conformed to their needs. Moreover, improvements in the shipping situation and in U.S. production might lead to cancellation of many orders. As a result the only clothing produced locally in significant quantities consisted of such items as underwear, socks, mufflers, mackinaws, and officers' battle-dress jackets and trousers, which did not require rigid conformity to War Department specifications.[24]

Although large amounts of special clothing were procured from the British, the bulk of regular clothing for U.S. enlisted personnel in the United King-

dom came from the United States. The quantities shipped were based on two factors: the Tables of Equipment issued by the War Department, specifying the items and quantities to be issued to each soldier, and the replacement factor based on the calculated rate of replacement for items worn out, lost, or destroyed. Before D-day, theater replacement factors were based on a modified combat scale, and thus were ample to maintain authorized allowances of clothing. But although conditions in the United Kingdom were more like those in the zone of interior than in an active theater of operations, they were still different enough to require a more generous initial issue than was authorized. An allowance of a single overcoat, one service coat, two shirts, two pairs of trousers, and two sets of underwear presupposed a speedy and efficient laundry and dry cleaning service not available in Great Britain in time of war. Soldiers working outdoors, particularly in the winter, at the end of the day found their clothing soaked through to such an extent that it would not dry overnight without artificial drying facilities, which ordinarily were not available. With laundry slow and dry cleaning slower, even the soldier who worked indoors had only one set available at any given time. Unable to buy clothing in a country where such items were strictly rationed, troops were entirely dependent on issued allowances. As a result the Quartermaster Service received a never-ending stream of requests from commanders to increase the soldier's clothing allowances. Units working outside asked for three pairs each of herringbone twill fatigues, woolen underwear, and shoes, for wool socks instead of cotton socks, for eight

[24] (1) Memo, Chief Proc Div OCQM for GPA, 13 Sep 42, sub: Rpt on Proc of Clothing; Ltr, OCQM to War Office, 26 Nov 42, sub: Clothing for Enlisted Men; Ltr, GPA to Ministry of Supply, 2 Apr 43, no sub. All in USFET GPA 420. (2) Memo, CQM to Under Secy of State for War, 22 Jul 42, sub: Proc of Items of Clothing. USFET QM 421. (3) QM Supply in ETO, III, 27.

handkerchiefs instead of four, and similar increases.[25] Units assigned to higher headquarters, where they wore class A uniforms at all times, were particularly hard pressed by the inadequacy of laundry and dry cleaning services. They asked for higher allowances of coats, shirts, and trousers.

The Office of the Chief Quartermaster was well aware of the conditions which led to such requests, but was unable to remedy the situation on its own. It had to work within allowances set by the War Department, and only the theater commander could authorize variations or recommend changes to Washington. The problem was further complicated by theater policy, which authorized only such increases as would benefit all troops equally. While stocks of a particular item might suffice for extra issues to a small group, they were usually not large enough to permit additional issues to all troops. Even when the theater commander authorized such increases and the OCQM submitted requisitions based on them, NYPE could not make shipments without War Department approval. Some relief from this dilemma came by local procurement, but not enough to make a significant difference.[26]

Continued pressure from the troops and their commanders gradually brought about the practice, if not the policy, of permitting excess clothing issues whenever an available margin of stocks existed. Thus the allowance of herringbone twill coveralls was raised slowly until almost all troops were benefited. British production made it possible to provide each man with a third set of wool underwear. In the course of 1943, most men working under exposed conditions acquired both an overcoat and a mackinaw, and troops at higher headquarters received extra coats, shirts, and trousers.[27] This practice was continued until the first months of 1944, when the number of troops in the United Kingdom passed the million mark. At this point, authorization for excess issues would have involved such major quantities of each item as to threaten the theater's ability to make ordinary issues. Accordingly the OCQM returned to a rigid interpretation of those allowances recognized by NYPE as the basis for requisition.[28]

The War Department policy of supplying overseas troops with antigas protective clothing by chemically impregnating their flannel shirts and wool trousers proved irksome and futile. Impregnated clothing was clammy and malodorous and soiled rapidly because it was sticky. Moreover, there were not enough facilities for rapid cleaning and reimpregnation in the theater. It is an understatement to say that these items were universally detested by the troops,

---

[25] (1) Memo, CG Eighth AF for CG ETOUSA, 12 Nov 42, sub: Revision of Allowances of Clothing; Memo, Engr EBS for CG SOS, 16 Nov 42, sub: Individual Clothing Allowances. Both in USFET QM 420. (2) Memo, QM WBS for CQM, 14 Nov 42, sub: Handkerchiefs to Enlisted Men. USFET QM 425.

[26] Memo, SOS ETO for CG ETO, 18 Feb 43, sub: Clothing Allowances. USFET AG (C&E) 400.34.

[27] (1) IRS, DCQM to Supply Div, 11 Sep 43, sub: Leggings; Memo, CO AAF Station 586 for QM USSAFE, 27 Jan 44, sub: Additional Clothing for Enlisted Pers. Both in USFET QM 421. (2) Memo, OCSigO for CG SOS ETO, 30 Nov 43, sub: Overcoats. USFET QM 000.4.

[28] (1) Memo, DCQM to CQM, 4 Feb 44, sub: Initial Issue of Overcoats. USFET QM 422. (2) IRS and Inds, DCQM London to DCQM Cheltenham, 2 Mar 44, sub: Additional Coats, Wool Olive Drab for Enlisted Men. USFET QM 420.

who had no other such clothing. They either had to wear one set for overly long periods of time or switch to non-impregnated items drawn from theater stocks. The latter alternative was by far more popular and was adopted with the consent of the OCQM and the theater chemical officer. On 5 May 1943 ETOUSA directed that fatigue clothing, rather than wool clothing, was to be impregnated. At first glance this directive did not seem to improve matters, since herringbone twills were in as short supply as woolens. But the factor of appearance was of minor importance in work clothing, and in Britain's raw climate fatigues were worn over woolens, so that there was no direct contact with the skin. In actual practice, this clothing combination was very satisfactory. The impregnating chemical made the twill windproof and fairly water-repellent, and increased its resistance to abrasion and tearing. By the spring of 1944 the Chemical Warfare Service had facilities capable of impregnating 20,000 uniforms a day, and before D-day more than 75 percent of the troops were thus equipped. But troops continued to arrive overseas in impregnated woolens until May, when the Supreme Commander requested that this policy be changed.[29]

Supply of officers' clothing also gave

rise to major problems. In theory, all officers arrived in the ETO completely outfitted and required only replacements for those items which wore out or were lost. But the ETO quartermaster was required to furnish initial as well as replacement items to several categories of personnel. Officers commissioned in the theater had to outfit themselves there, as did the many civilians serving the U.S. forces who often needed all or part of an officer's wardrobe. Moreover, the many officers who traveled to the ETO by air, especially Air Forces personnel and casuals, were permitted to carry only limited amounts of baggage. Many officers therefore had to obtain additional clothing as soon as they arrived. In addition, the official replacement factor for officers' Class A uniforms in the United Kingdom was identical with the zone of interior rate —one-half uniform per year. Littlejohn found this quite unrealistic, but could never get it changed. He later wrote: "It seemed to me during the two years in Britain that every officer, nurse, and Wac came over completely naked. They all came to London and lined up for blocks at the Quartermaster sales store. It was impossible to keep any stock on hand." [30]

Since the British rationing system severely limited commercial purchases it was up to the OCQM to see that, somehow or other, these officers and civilians were supplied well enough to make a favorable appearance. The normal source was the United States, but officers' clothing was available there

[29] (1) Memo, CG SOS for CG ETO, 26 Oct 42, sub: Protective Clothing; Memo, 505th CA (AA) for CG ETO, 12 Jan 43, sub: Gas Protective Impregnated Clothing. Both in USFET AG 420. (2) Memo, SOS G–4 for OCQM, 24 Jan 43, sub: Status of Protective Clothing. USFET QM 422. (3) ETOUSA Admin Cir 17, 5 May 43. (4) IRS, P&T Div to DCQM, 9 Feb 44, sub: Impregnated Clothing and Impregnation Facilities. USFET QM 422.3. (5) *QM Supply in ETO*, III, 70–71. (6) 12th Army Group Rpt of Opns, XII, 185. (7) Cable E–29064, ETOUSA to AGWAR, 22 May 44.

[30] (1) Quotation from Littlejohn, ed., Passing in Review, ch. 4, p. 5. (2) Ltr, CQM to Evans, 4 Jan 44, sub: Maint Factor for Offs' Clothing. Littlejohn Reading File, vol. XX, item 10.

only in small quantities until after the middle of 1943. When the OCQM turned to the British as an alternate supply source, it ran up against the same difficulties encountered with enlisted men's clothing. But even though British design and materials differed from U.S. Army standards, British output had to be used. During the first two years of the ETO, therefore, officers' uniforms showed notable variations in cut and color.

An officer could obtain coupons to buy from British stores if he certified that his purchase did not provide him with more clothing than permissible under published allowances. But experience proved that the honor system would not work here. While on garrison-type duty in a friendly foreign country, all U.S. troops were ordered to look their best, and naturally found it easier to do so in new clothing. Within SOS headquarters, a smartly-tailored appearance was regarded as a prerequisite for promotion. One visitor from the OQMG observed "Without doubt, this is a Beau Brummel theater. An officer must be dressed up." [31]

By the end of 1943 stocks of regulation items in Quartermaster sales stores had been built up to the point where most officers could be fitted, and reliance on rationed British clothing was no longer essential. Thereafter, British clothing coupons were issued only when sales stores experienced temporary shortages of certain items, and to officers who

could not be fitted from the normal tariff of sizes. Ultimately, the mounting number of American officers in the ETO led to rigid rationing in the sales stores.[32]

Clothing the women in the United States forces was seemingly a simple matter because of the small numbers involved. Actually, a small group was harder to clothe than a large one, and the problem was also complicated by the adoption of new uniforms. This difficulty is illustrated by the nurses' uniform introduced in mid-1943. The blue outfit worn earlier had been criticized as inadequate for field use. While making alterations to overcome these drawbacks, the OQMG also changed the color to olive drab. Except for buttons and insignia, most items were made identical with the WAAC officers' uniform, thereby simplifying manufacture and distribution. Since this was a completely new uniform, nurses were to receive a free initial issue, and the first distribution was to be made about 1 July 1943.

There were two obstacles to an easy change-over. Though new uniforms for the 1,500 ETO nurses were requisitioned in March, they did not begin to arrive until September, and then only piecemeal in small mixed lots, poorly marked, and often in broken containers. In addition, the OQMG size tariff did not fit the ETO nurses, providing too many large garments and too few in small sizes. The difficulty was not with the tariff itself, but the small number of

---

[31] (1) Ruppenthal, *Logistical Support*, I, 267. (2) Interv with Col Meyer, TC, 25 Oct 57. (3) IRS, CQM to Brumbaugh, 30 Oct 43, sub: Promotion of Maj Keener. Littlejohn Reading File, vol. XVII, item 105. (4) Quotation from Ltr, Pounder to Doriot, 13 Mar 44. Hist Br OQMG.

[32] (1) Memo, CQM for DTQMG, 27 Jun 43, sub: Uniforms for Offs. ETO 421. (2) ETOUSA Cir 10, 1 Feb 43; Memo, CO LBS for CG ETOUSA, 12 Mar 43, sub: Clarification of Issue of Clothing Coupons and Instrs Pertaining to Issue. Both in USFET AG 420.

persons to whom it was applied. Like most statistical concepts, a tariff is only valid when applied to large quantities. Recognizing this, Littlejohn had requested a 100 percent distribution factor, but because of shortages the OQMG was able to allow only 25 percent. To speed the distribution of the new uniforms, an emergency mobile sales unit carried them to each medical installation and attempted to fit the nurses on the spot. Despite this unusual effort, many nurses were still not adequately outfitted at the end of the year. Consequently it was necessary to concentrate all stocks in London, bring the nurses there for fitting, and manufacture special sizes. By the end of March 1944 the problem had been solved, at least for the moment.[33]

WAAC officers had problems somewhat similar to those of nurses, although less serious and on a smaller scale. WAAC officer casuals began to appear in the ETO in April 1943, and the first WAAC unit arrived in July. Since enlisted Waacs brought their T/BA clothing allowance with them, the problem of initial issues did not arise for them. But the slowness of British laundry and dry cleaning service made extra clothing extremely desirable, especially since Wacs were expected to present a smart military appearance. During the winter, Wacs working in unheated offices suffered almost as much as those whose duties kept them in the open. The

WAC winter uniform was inadequate in both cases.[34]

British Laundry and Salvage Services

Except in combat, the individual U.S. soldier has always been responsible for cleaning and minor repair of his clothing. Since before World War I, the QMC has aided the soldier by providing laundry and dry cleaning service approximately at cost.[35] In the United Kingdom such assistance was a necessity. Quartermaster laundry units had a very low priority; those in the theater were not even able to supply all the needs of Army hospitals, so that no help was available from that source. Soldiers tried, with limited success, to solve their problems on an individual local basis, but British wartime conscription of both men and women, and rationing of necessary supplies, brought about so drastic a decrease in ordinary commercial facilities that satisfactory service could be arranged only on official levels. That the QMC, which had experience in negotiating laundry contracts as well as in operating laundries in the United States, should undertake the arrangements, was but natural. In this field the British co-operated to the limit of their ability in an effort to supply regular laundry service to as many as 600,000 troops on the same scale of nine pieces per man per week authorized to the British

[33] (1) Ltr, OCQM to NYPE, 16 Nov 43, no sub. ETO 420. (2) Memo, OCQM for QMSO Depot G-30, 8 Sep 43, sub: Distr of Initial Issue of Nurses' OD Uniforms. USFET QM 421. (3) Memo, DCQM for CQM, 5 Feb 44, sub: Status of Initial Issue of Nurses' OD Clothing. ETO 421.

[34] (1) Mattie E. Treadwell, The Women's Army Corps, UNITED STATES ARMY IN WORLD WAR II (Washington, 1954), pp. 381, 396–97. (2) The WAAC was officially redesignated the WAC on 1 September 1943.

[35] (1) Filler, Laundry and Related Activities of The Quartermaster General QMC Historical Studies, 13, pp. 1–2. (2) U.S. laundry operations in the ETO are described in Chapter XX, below.

Army. Use of British laundries raised a thorny issue regarding payment. Since arrangements were made for the provision of this service under reverse lend-lease—ostensibly without cost to the United States—the Chief Quartermaster and troop commanders felt that no charge should be made against the troops. On this premise soldiers received free laundry service until War Department directives required payment. Accordingly, after mid-1943 a small flat fee was charged for the weekly nine-piece bundle.[36]

Free or paid for, laundry service in the United Kingdom was poor and dry cleaning poorer. The troops were located mainly in rural areas and transportation problems hampered access to the superior laundry facilities in the large cities. Commercial facilities suffered continuing labor shortages and the British were therefore unable to meet all of their original commitments. To aid soldiers in maintaining a presentable appearance notwithstanding these obstacles, the OCQM offered several self-help expedients. The QM depots issued carbon tetrachloride and brushes for cleaning, several thousand electric hand irons for pressing uniforms were requisitioned from the United States and distributed, and locally procured sewing kits were issued for minor repairs. But these improvisations did not solve the problem. If the laundry situation did not become truly critical, it was because anticipated demands for laundry service did not materialize in the spring of 1944. Expectations had been that between January and May, requirements would

rise rapidly from seven and a half million pounds weekly to eleven million pounds. For a variety of reasons, requirements fell below 50 percent of these estimates. A substantial proportion of American troops were often on training exercises in remote areas, and could not make use of official services. Many did their own laundry. Fortunately, by one expedient or another, the troops in Britain managed to stay clean enough to preserve their health, although in some instances their soldierly appearance suffered.[37]

Most of the necessary cleaning, repair, and redistribution was handled on a unit basis with no attempt to return items to their original owners. Clothing and equipment not in condition for immediate use flowed into a theater-wide salvage organization. In contrast to World War I, when the salvage organization developed late, the ETO Quartermaster Service from the outset promoted conservation of materials. Owing partly to the concentration on building up combat strength and partly to the shortage of trained U.S. salvage units, early salvage operations used British military and civilian facilities almost exclusively. The British cooperated fully, making all arrangements with civilian firms and meeting all payments to these firms.[38]

---

[37] (1) Memo, OCQM for TQMG, 1 Sep 43, sub: Dry Cleaning and Laundry Facilities; Memo. Laundry Br Sv Instls Div for Opns Br Mil Plng Div, 8 Sep 43, same sub. Both in ETO 486.3. (2) Memo, Actg Deputy for Opns for P&T Div OCQM, 22 Oct 43, sub: Situation Rpt Dry Cleaning in U.K. USFET QM 319.1. (3) Instls Br P&T Div, 22 Jan 44, Analysis of Laundry Situation in U.K. USFET QM 331.51.
[38] (1) Memo for Record Only [ca. July 1942]. USFET AG 486.3. (2) U.S. Salvage operations in the ETO are described in Chapter XX, below.

---

[36] Memo, Dir Opns ASF for TAG, 23 Jul 43, sub: Laundry Sv. ETO 331.5.

Experience in the British Isles during the two years before D-day illustrated the tremendous possibilities of a salvage program. Here some 60,000,000 pieces of American salvage had been processed, largely by British commercial firms under contract to the Ministry of Supply. Wages were high in the United Kingdom, and the "profits" of this undertaking had been only $45,000,000, or 75 cents per item, compared to about $2.60 per item realized in similar Italian operations.[39] (See Table 5.) But in both cases ability to make available scarce clothing and equipment, much of it made from rationed raw materials, outweighed financial considerations. An additional benefit from salvage operations in Britain was a saving of 2,000,000 ship tons of precious transatlantic cargo space.[40]

A prime example of successful Anglo-American co-operation in the salvage field was the shoe repair program. On coming to the United Kingdom the OCQM found that availability of shoe repair facilities made possible the immediate, though temporary, reduction of shoe repair companies scheduled for arrival and the cancellation of shoe machinery on requisition.[41] For bulk repair and rebuilding of shoes the British provided a factory near Bristol and the

necessary labor to turn out 5,000 pairs of shoes a week. This plant, it was estimated, could handle shoe rebuilding for a force of one million men.[42] Minor repair of shoes for return to the individual wearer was handled through local contracts arranged by the British with civilian shoemakers. But sole leather and rubber heels had to be imported from the United States for all repairs. As the U.S. forces rapidly increased during the second half of 1943, British facilities could no longer handle the workload, but by that time American units were available.[43]

Post Exchange Supplies

The post exchange, or PX, which sold luxury and comfort articles to the troops, usually at less than current retail prices, was an old Army institution operated by the Army Exchange Service. As in all overseas theaters, the PX took on an importance which it did not enjoy in the zone of interior because many items were either strictly rationed or unavailable from ordinary commercial sources. Realizing the value of well-run PX's in maintaining troop morale, the OCQM from the outset gave close attention to this problem, helping the AES with its distribution functions and in its dealings with the general purchasing agent.

The initial unit PX's were established soon after the first American troops ar-

---

[39] Estimates of savings from salvage operations reflected peacetime bookkeeping procedures in the zone of interior.

[40] QM Salvage Operations, article by Col. R. T. Bennison, Chief Instl Div OCQM, and Richard S. Hore, civilian technician, 14 Sep 44. Littlejohn Reading File, vol. XXVIII, item 111.

[41] (1) Ltr, CQM to CG NYPE, 19 Aug 42, sub: Shoe Repair Supplies. ETO 413.193. (2) Sir Cecil M. Weir, Director General of Equipment and Stores in the Ministry of Supply, was especially helpful in providing this service. Interv with Littlejohn, 1 Dec 59.

[42] 2d Ind, SOS ETO to CG ETO, 11 Nov 42, on Ltr, TAG to CG's All Theaters, etc., 10 Aug 42, sub: Disposition of Worn Shoes. USFET AG 421.

[43] (1) Memo, CQM for DTQMG, 23 Jun 43, sub: Repair of Shoes in U.K. USFET GPA 321 (QMC). (2) Memo for Record Only [ca. July 1942]. USFET AG 486.3.

rived in Northern Ireland. At that time, they drew their supplies from and functioned under the general supervision of the AES, which operated as an independent supply service, procuring comfort items in the United States or locally and shipping and distributing them through the general depots and distribution points. With insurance costs of 15 percent and other AES overhead expenses added in, PX retail prices were high. Moreover, since the PX's were unit activities, there were wide variations in procedure and efficiency of management. AES, a tiny organization without the prestige or authority of a technical service, was hampered in exercising supervision over unit exchanges. It could not enforce uniform procedures or even supervise the warehousing of its own supplies. General Chaney, the SPOBS commander, had noted the scarcity of items desired by U.S. troops (especially soft drinks, razor blades, and chewing gum), and had requisitioned a large allowance of PX supplies. Authorities in the United States had minimized the importance of such items, and given them a very low shipping priority.

During the summer of 1942 all these factors led to widespread dissatisfaction with PX service. At the same time, the world-wide shortage of service troops had become evident. Clearly, it was impossible for AES to obtain a large personnel allotment to run PX's throughout the United Kingdom. For these reasons AES functions were transferred in October 1942 to the Quartermaster Corps. Colonel Barnum, former theater AES officer, became head of the Exchange Service Division, OCQM. Thereafter PX supplies were handled by the regular Quartermaster storage and dis-

tribution system and turned over to unit exchanges and sales stores at cost plus a small mark-up, without any addition to cover the heavy insurance and overhead charges. Low as the prices were, enough revenue came in within five months to liquidate the $5,000,000 debt to the AES for merchandise and premiums and still show a profit of more than $1,000,000.[44]

Since under OCQM management all profits accrued to the U.S. Government and could not be used, as when under AES, to pay for help and overhead in individual exchanges, the unit stores were often shorthanded and housed in unsuitable quarters. Because Quartermaster personnel could not be spared for this activity and because The Quartermaster General was anxious to avoid becoming involved in overseas retailing operations, a new world-wide policy was established in the spring of 1943, under which the Quartermaster Corps retained the role of wholesaler but restored to the AES some of its former retailing functions. In the ETO, the QMC procured, shipped, and distributed PX supplies, issuing them to units but charging the AES. That agency collected from the units which sold PX supplies in the stores that they themselves maintained. At the end of March 1943, U.S. Navy exchanges became part of this system, and agreed to abide by the U.S. Army rationing regulations.[45]

---

[44] (1) Orgn, Opn, and Supply of the AES, USFET Gen Bd Study 57, *passim*. (2) Memo, CQM for CofS, SOS, 21 Sep 42, sub: Transfer of AES to QM. Littlejohn Reading File, vol. IVA, item 19. (3) AES Rpt, 31 Aug 43, sub: AES Activities; Memo, Supply Div for CQM, 17 Feb 43, sub: Revision of Selling Prices on Sales Store Items. Both in USFET QM 331.3. (4) *QM Supply in ETO*, V, 29–33.
[45] Ltr, GPA to CQM, sub: PX Items for the Navy, 30 Mar 43. USFET QM 331.3.

Ordinary PX supplies—candy, soft drinks, cigarettes, toilet articles, and gifts—were drawn from depots and distribution points by units using their own transportation. Financial details, prices, and transfers of cash and credit were calculated by a central office. The AES acted as co-ordinator, providing a revolving fund, supervising the unit exchanges, and advising the Chief Quartermaster on types and quantities of items to keep in stock. Only the large central PX's at major headquarters such as Cheltenham and London were operated directly by the AES.

PX supplies, like most other Quartermaster supplies in the United Kingdom, came from both U.S. and British sources. For items derived from local sources, the OCQM dealt directly with the British. Most of these articles were covered by a general agreement with NAAFI providing that PX's must sell British items at the same price as NAAFI canteens and that the British manufacturer could deviate from the specifications when war conditions made this necessary. The latter provision meant that many PX supplies did not meet the standards of quality and packaging that Americans were accustomed to. British items became increasingly unpopular and the troops exerted constant pressure for increased importation from the United States.[46]

Nevertheless, the United Kingdom was a source of post exchange supplies on a scale that certainly could not have been duplicated through imports, espe-

cially during the period of shipping shortages. From September 1942, when the OCQM took over the function of procuring PX supplies from the Army Exchange Service, to the end of December 1944, the major procurements from the British in this field were:[47]

Beer, gallons	a 54,000,000
Brushes, tooth	2,258,310
Candy, chocolate bars	94,945,728
Cookies, 4-oz. packets	79,828,400
Handkerchiefs	2,350,836
Kits, sewing	393,175
Matches, box	55,322,488
Prophylactics	15,112,400
Soap, toilet	57,752,014
Soft drinks	35,819,875

a Estimated figure for entire period of hostilities.

American magazines were among the articles most frequently demanded by the troops. A plan to print various magazines overseas from plates flown over from the United States was opposed by the Ministry of Supply, which controlled Britain's meager wartime imports of wood pulp. Littlejohn proposed the use of a low-grade paper made of wheat straw, but the British paper industry had lost most of its labor force to more essential activities, and nothing came of this suggestion. The program finally succeeded through the personal intercession of Ambassador Averell W. Harriman, who undertook to provide pulp or finished paper as required. Thereafter, His Majesty's Stationery Office, the agency in charge of paper rationing, provided paper for printing *Stars and Stripes* and allowed *The Reader's Digest* to print 5,000 extra copies of its British edi-

---

46 (1) Ltr, OCQM to NAAFI, 31 Mar 43, sub: Gen Conditions. USFET QM 400.314. (2) Memo, PX Bulk Distr G–45 for OCQM, 27 Oct 43, sub: Faulty Packing. USFET QM 681.

47 Littlejohn, ed., *Passing in Review*, ch. 41, pt. I, p. 49.

tion for sale to U.S. troops. *Yank* was printed on paper especially imported from the United States. *Time* and *Newsweek* printed special lightweight editions and sent them to the ETO by fast ships. American soldiers overseas seemed to have an avidity for writing letters, and demanded enormous quantities of writing paper. By special agreement, the Stationery Office allowed them to have slightly more than the British allowance of this rationed item.[48]

Inevitably, some PX supplies found their way into the British black market. The British Government was determined to prevent this illegal activity and insisted, for example, that all soap made in Britain for Americans bear a special United States marking and that every package of cigarettes sold in a PX be marked to indicate that it had entered the country duty-free. In an effort to co-operate with the British, American exchanges set up a strict rationing system intended to give the U.S. soldier enough supplies for his weekly needs but little if any surplus that might find its way into civilian hands.[49]

The cigarette supply provided a noteworthy example of the trouble experienced in disposing of unpopular brands. Early in 1943, ETO had on hand a very large accumulation of cigarettes which NYPE had shipped to the theater despite protests of General Littlejohn, and which American troops would not consume. Fortunately, the Canadians and Australians, for whom only a limited supply of cigarettes had been provided, agreed to take 10,000,000 packages of the unpopular brands.[50]

Just before D-day, in an unusual development in marshaling areas of Southern Base Section, the section through which the bulk of United States ground troops were staged, mobile canteens began to sell PX supplies to the departing troops. This activity was similar to that of the mobile sales stores, but was under AES rather than Quartermaster control. At the retail end of the supply system, the Quartermaster Corps retained direct control of the sales stores which sold clothing, and occasionally incidental items like luggage, to officers and other authorized purchasers. These stores, located at three or four troop centers in each base section, were supplemented by mobile sales units that circulated among the troops who did not have ready access to static stores. At the peak of activity in the United Kingdom just before D-day there were sixteen static and eight mobile sales units. Both types were gradually reduced in number after D-day as American troops left for the Continent and sales activities came to center more and more in London.[51] Though American troops were not com-

[48] (1) *QM Supply in ETO*, I, 156; V, 47–49. (2) Ltr, CQM to G–4, 1 Apr 43, sub: Local Proc of Newsprint for Reprinting American Magazines in U.K. Littlejohn Reading File, vol. XI, item 6. (3) Interv with Littlejohn, 1 Dec 59.

[49] (1) Memo, Proc Div for Supply Div OCQM, 27 Oct 42, sub: Marking of 12,000,000 Bars of Toilet Soap. USFET QM 438. (2) Memo, DCQM for AES, 30 Dec 43, sub: Drawing of Rations. USFET QM 430.2. (3) Memo, British Ln Off SOS for Chief of Admin SOS, 17 Aug 43, sub: Sale of U.S. Army Cigarettes to British Subjects. USFET AG 439.

[50] (1) 1st Ind, Memo, DCQM for CQM, 15 Jan 43, sub: Receipt of Requisitioned Cigarettes; Ltr, Maj Gen P. J. Montague, Senior Off Canadian Mil Hq to CG SOS, 31 May 43, sub: Purchase of U.S. Cigarettes by Canadian Army. Both in USFET AG 439. (2) Marginal note by Colonel Florsheim on a draft version of this MS.

[51] Memo, CQM for G–4, 3 Mar 44, sub: Sales Stores and Mobile Sales Units. USFET QM 331.3.

pletely satisfied with PX services, theirs were typical soldiers' "gripes" rather than serious expressions of discontent. Considering all the circumstances the Americans were reasonably well provided with both comforts and luxuries.

Liquor

Unlike beer, liquor was sold only to officers in the ETO. Shortly after SOS was organized, General Lee directed Littlejohn not to bring any liquor into the United Kingdom from the United States or Canada. Accordingly the Chief Quartermaster appointed Mr. Charles J. Lytle, an American residing in London, as his representative to deal with the British liquor industry. By early August 1942, an arrangement had been made with the Scotch Whiskey Association whereby the liquor requirements of U.S. officers' messes in the theater were to be reported monthly to SOS headquarters in London. After mess officers had deposited the correct amount in Lloyd's Bank, Mr. Lytle would inform the association of the total amount required and the distilling firms would make bulk deliveries to QM depots. A condition of this arrangement was that sales were to be made to messes for consumption within the mess; no bottles were to be sold to individuals, and the ration basis was the same as in British messes—one-half bottle per officer per month.[52]

Some messes found this allowance inadequate, and proceeded to import American liquor on their own initiative. Since General Lee's policy directive to Littlejohn had never been formally published, this procedure was not actually illegal. On visiting the zone of interior in November 1942, Littlejohn discovered that 500 cases of tax-free liquor were in storage at NYPE, awaiting transportation to the United Kingdom as filler cargo. But General Goodman, commander of the New York port, did not wish to forward this liquor, and its presence in New York had received critical notice in the press. On being informed of the situation, General Hartle, Eisenhower's deputy in the United Kingdom, ruled that any liquor actually en route might be delivered to the messes which had ordered it, but all future shipments would be confiscated and sold, the proceeds going to the U.S. Treasury.[53]

While the publicity aspects of this incident vindicated General Lee's stand on bringing U.S. liquor into the theater, it was also clear that American officers wanted a larger liquor ration and had the money to get it by one means or another. In August 1943, after repeated conferences with higher authorities both American and British, Littlejohn was finally able to arrange for a direct ration of liquor to American officers from the Ministry of Food. Distribution was handled on an equitable basis by NAAFI, the same organization which issued liquor to British officers. This arrangement had at least two major advantages. It provided officers, as individuals, with an increased liquor ra-

[52] (1) Littlejohn Reading File, Special Personal Cases File, vol. VII, items 1, 2. (2) IRS, CQM to CG SOS ETO, 4 Dec 42, sub: Shipment of Liquor into U.K. Littlejohn Reading File, vol. VII, item 1.

[53] Ltrs, CQM to Gen Collins and Col Woellner, 5 Oct 42, sub: Liquor. Littlejohn Reading File, vol. VI, items 22, 23.

tion, and it removed the U.S. Army from the liquor business.[54]

Practical experience made Littlejohn a convinced partisan of NAAFI. This co-operative interservice organization performed roughly the same functions as the AES but had an entirely different organization and far greater autonomy and influence. NAAFI's foremost merit was an established and efficient distributing system which made no demands on the Quartermaster's meager pool of manpower. Also, in transactions regarding liquor there were obvious advantages in dealing with an organization dedicated to service rather than profits, and directed by eminent retired officers of unassailable reputation. The agreement between the OCQM and NAAFI was extended to the Continent with very satisfactory results. In October 1944 Littlejohn directed that captured German wines and spirits, turned over to COMZ by the armies, be sold to senior officers for official entertainment, and to officers' messes in accordance with established allowances. Whatever was left after twenty days was to be sold to NAAFI, at prices established by the French Government, for subsequent resale to U.S., British, and French messes. By January 1945 Littlejohn had entered an agreement with the French Government to buy 500,000 bottles of brandy per month, plus unspecified amounts of wines and liqueurs. This was for the entire Allied force on the Continent,

and again the distributing agent was NAAFI. In the meantime, SOLOC messes had been supplied with one bottle of American whiskey per officer each month through Mediterranean theater channels, an arrangement which was continued after the two lines of communication were consolidated. At first NAAFI objected to this additional source of supply. Liquor was scarce in Europe, and it seemed probable that under this arrangement many American officers would enjoy two rations, a form of discrimination which a British organization could not be expected to condone. Since the alternative was for the Chief Quartermaster to organize an extensive system of guarded warehouses and elaborate distribution facilities, Littlejohn managed to placate NAAFI by maintaining a strict territorial separation between the two distribution systems. On 11 May, three days after the German surrender, he declined to help General Rogers, the commander of the Seine Base Section, to obtain cognac and champagne for Army-sponsored night clubs in Paris. Neither the OCQM nor NAAFI was equipped to undertake an operation of the size proposed by Rogers. Three days later Littlejohn wrote to General Lee that "The two systems must eventually be combined," but apparently this very desirable development never materialized.[55]

---

[54] (1) Personal Ltrs, Littlejohn to Gen Pulsifer and Gen Hawley, no sub, 17 Nov 43. Littlejohn Reading File, vol. XVIII, items 48, 52. (2) IRS, CQM to G–1, 14 Feb 44, sub: Final Result of Negotiations With Ministry of Food. . . . Littlejohn Reading File, Special Personal Cases File, vol. VII, item 12.

[55] (1) Quotation from Personal Ltr, CQM to CG SOS, 14 May 45. Littlejohn Reading File, vol. XXXVI, item 35. (2) IRS, CQM to Actg DCQM (Duncan), 14 Aug 44, sub: Liquor From Spain; IRS, CQM to Chief Proc Div OCQM, 2 Oct 44, sub: Disposition of Captured German Stocks of Wines and Spirits; Personal Ltr, Littlejohn to Hardigg, 13 Oct 44; Ltr, CQM to CG Seine Sec (Rogers), 11 May 45, sub: Liquor. Littlejohn Reading File, vol. XXVII, item 60; vol. XXIX, items 3, 64; vol. XXXIV, item 30.

After the end of hostilities every transaction and policy decision regarding liquor was subjected to criticism. Officers in SOLOC were convinced that their ration was too small, while officers in northern France were equally convinced that Littlejohn's decision to utilize NAAFI was base subservience to British economic imperialism. Few enlisted men agreed that Eisenhower's directive of 1 July 1945, authorizing a liquor ration for NCO messes, was equitable. It meant that only noncommissioned officers of the first three grades would receive a liquor allowance. Lt. Col. Floyd W. Oliphant, who was in charge of procuring liquor for the troops in southern France, wrote in May 1945: "I would prefer to go to the Pacific rather than handle this 'red hot' theater program which requires such exactitude, and is subject to condemnation by all ranks with the minimum amount of credit for efforts expended." To Littlejohn the real crux of the liquor problem, as of so many other problems, was competent and reliable personnel to supervise distribution. Liquor was undoubtedly one of many considerations he had in mind in August when he wrote: "What troops have we loaned to the Post Exchange or what troops have been transferred to the Post Exchange without my authority? The day of reckoning is here in this case . . . . Colonel Marshburn [Chief, AES] . . . . must immediately ask for the creation and assignment to him of proper T/O units . . . ." [56]

But the plan to transfer responsibility for liquor to the AES was never consummated. Procurement of Class VI supplies, a designation which apparently originated in the OCQM in April 1945, remained a Quartermaster function, and distribution was still being performed by NAAFI at the end of the year.

Arrangements for Local Procurement

The beginnings of U.S. local procurement in the United Kingdom have already been noted. At the end of August 1942 Colonel Allen, formerly Chief of the Procurement Division, OCQM, and Quartermaster representative on the SOS General Purchasing Board became general purchasing agent.[57] The OCQM now had an influential friend at the head of this important agency, and found that its purchasing operations proceeded more smoothly. It should be noted that Colonel Allen himself had made the initial investigation into the possibilities of local QMC procurement in the ETO, so that he was well acquainted with the OCQM's requirements. The general purchasing agent co-ordinated local procurement by U.S. supply services, made over-all arrangements with the British, recorded agreements, and passed to the appropriate agency on either side complaints regarding the execution of agreements. Operating under the general policies worked out by the agent, the individual supply service dealt with the details of actual procurement. The British ar-

---

[56] (1) QM Supply in ETO, V. 54. (2) Quotation from Memo, CQM for Middleswart, Franks, and Odell, 3 Aug 45, sub: Sales Store Program. Littlejohn Reading File, vol. XXXIX, item 2.

[57] (1) See above, ch. II. (2) He was succeeded as Chief, Procurement Division, OCQM by Lt. Col. Michael H. Zwicker (August 1942–October 1943) and Col. Thomas V. Barber (November 1943–August 1945).

ranged with the agent for each service to procure its special supplies but items common to two or more services would be assigned to one service acting for all.

Despite the difficulties of initial organization, by the end of 1942 the ETO supply services had confidence in the dependability of local procurement. Lists of items available in the United Kingdom were drawn up and used as the basis for canceling items requisitioned from the United States. While at first such cancellations were effected only after the approved supply level was actually on hand, by mid-December it was decided that items on requisition could be canceled if the British had made a commitment to supply on demand.[58] By mid-1943, confidence in British commitments reached such a point that special justification had to be made before an item listed as available in the United Kingdom could be requisitioned from the United States.[59]

The basic arrangement for American procurement of goods in Britain was that all purchasing would be done through central agencies of the British Government. The U.S. Army, Air Forces, and Navy would deal with the British War Office, Air Ministry, and Admiralty, respectively, and would call in representatives of other agencies, British and American, only when the procurement under discussion involved such matters as raw materials or labor which were be-

yond the control of the military agencies.[60]

Planners agreed that U.S. requirements for British goods would be consolidated and presented to the British in large enough quantities to cover needs for six months at least in order to help production agencies fit U.S. needs into their long-range plans. If accepted by the British, these became "programed requirements" against which the U.S. supply services could draw.[61] Until the routine was well established, requirements were sometimes presented at irregular intervals and for small quantities covering shorter periods. Such irregular requests drew protests from the British, who urged more careful planning.[62] With increased experience on both sides, programing for local procurement improved so much that after mid-1943 few complaints were made on that score.

Occasionally the British were also provoked by a tendency of American procurement officers, particularly those in the field, to bypass official channels and deal directly with the private manufacturer or supplier.[63] The manufacturer almost always needed raw materials to fill the order, and such officers sometimes gave unauthorized assurances that raw materials imported from the United States would be furnished outside the British rationing system. A long ex-

---

[58] Memo, CG SOS ETO to Chiefs of Supply Svs, SOS ETO, 14 Dec 42, sub: Cancellation of Items Appearing on Revised List of Items Available in U.K. USFET AG 400.

[59] Memo, GPA ETO to CG NYPE, 22 Jul 43, sub: Equip and Supply Available for Local Proc in the U.K. USFET AG 400.12.

[60] Memo of Conf, 15 Jun 42, sub: Procedure in Proc of Supplies for American Forces in the U.K. USFET GPA 091.

[61] SOS ETOUSA Proc Dir 1, 15 Feb 53. USFET AG 310.

[62] Ltr, Dir Ord Svs [Brit] to Deputy Chief QM ETOUSA, 11 Sep 42, no sub. USFET QM 421.

[63] Memo, Chief Proc Div OCQM for Office Ord Svs, 18 Aug 42, sub: Field Desks. USFET QM 414.1.

change of correspondence on the subject and gradual realization of the effectiveness of official British co-operation brought the Americans closer to the British position. By February 1943 agreement was reached whereby American agents could contact British concerns for information only, with the knowledge and consent of the War Office. Thereafter both sides co-operated to force U.S. procurement into the prescribed channels, while the British were always willing to make exceptions for occasional small emergency purchases.[64]

In a number of cases the British persuaded the Americans to accept as a guide the ration allowances of the wartime British Army. Usually the items involved were minor issues, like matches and toilet paper, and compromises were easily reached. Food presented more difficulties, bread being one of the troublesome items.

In the absence of American baking facilities, the British had agreed to supply the U.S. troops with bread. For their own use, both civil and military, they produced one type of bread only: the national wheatmeal loaf. This was a graham type of bread of very high nutritional value. It was made from flour that utilized about 85 percent of the whole-wheat kernel, plus small amounts of barley and oats. It had been developed to permit the fullest use of local grains and thus to decrease grain

imports.[65] To avoid local discontent and save additional shipping space, the British proposed that the United States Army give up white bread and accept the national wheatmeal loaf.[66]

Because it prevented an unnecessary duplication of storage space and avoided the problem of controlling the use of white flour by civilian bakeries, the Chief Quartermaster favored the British proposal. Accordingly, orders were issued for the use of national wheatmeal in all bread baked for U.S. personnel, and all white flour was turned over, on an exchange basis, to the British, who mixed it with the common stock.[67] The only reservation was that the Ministry of Food should agree to supply on demand any white flour the ETO might require for forces outside the United Kingdom.[68]

For all of its apparent advantages, this arrangement did not work well. American troops disliked the British bread and ate so little of it that the nutritional balance of their diet was upset, and supplies mounted. To overcome this, the

---

[64] (1) Ltr, Actg GPA to War Office, 27 Jan 43, no sub. (2) Extract Min of U.S. Reqmts and Supply Com Mtg, 19 Feb 43, sub: Relations of SOS with Civilian Firms. (3) Corresp Between GPA and War Office, 3 Apr, 8 Apr, 5 Jun, 16 Jun, and 19 Jul 43, sub: Direct Contact with Civilian Firms. All in USFET GPA 091.

[65] Hancock and Gowing (British War Economy, page 423) estimate the annual saving in shipping at 400,000 tons, beginning in March 1942 when the plan went into effect.

[66] Ltr, Lord Woolton, Minister of Food, to Lee, 5 Sep 42, no sub. USFET AG 312.1.

[67] (1) Memo, CQM for CG SOS ETO, 14 Sep 42, sub: National Flour. USFET QM 430. (2) Ltr, Lee to Woolton, 8 Sep 42, no sub. USFET AG 312.1. (3) Memo, DCQM for Chief Subs Div 7, Sep 42, no sub; Cir 18, OCQM, 9 Sep 42, Required Use of National Wheatmeal Flour; Ltr, CG SOS ETO to Ministry of Food, 13 Oct 42, no sub. All in USFET QM 433.

[68] Ltr, Ministry of Food to Proc Div OCQM, 5 Nov 42, no sub; Memo, Proc Div OCQM for Subs Div OCQM, 6 Nov 42, sub: White Flour; Memo, Subs Div for Proc Div, 2 Feb 43, sub: Proc of White Flour in U.K. for NATOUSA. All in USFET QM 433.

OCQM tried numerous ways of improving the texture and flavor of the bread. The Ministry of Food agreed to eliminate oats from flour supplied to the U.S. Army and also considered the elimination of barley. At the same time the ETO Quartermaster subsistence laboratory developed a formula which, by adding shortening and sugar to the dough, produced a loaf more acceptable to American tastes. Meanwhile the number of American bakery companies in the United Kingdom increased rapidly during the late fall of 1943. Only the personnel were brought across the Atlantic, and the units were provided with locally procured baking equipment. The new bakeries provided both on-the-job training for their own men and bakery support in many troop areas, so that the proportion of U.S. troops receiving the improved bread rose until by the end of the year it included a majority of those in the United Kingdom.[69]

Candy sold by post exchanges brought other problems. "Sweets" were severely rationed in the United Kingdom but to save the shipping space taken up by manufactured articles and to avoid transshipment of raw materials through the United States, the British offered to supply candy if the American allowance did not significantly exceed the British. This agreement provided the Americans with two bars of chocolate and one package of chewing gum or roll candy per week. Special arrangements for temporary increases in this ration were occasionally made, but if a PX made unauthorized sales, as sometimes happened,

official British protests soon reached the Chief Quartermaster.[70]

American soldiers found this candy allowance very skimpy, and their commanders pressed for an increase to seven bars a week, or three more than authorized even by the War Department. The OCQM therefore entered into negotiations with both the British and the zone of interior aimed at maintaining the supply from the British and importing the difference. But the matter was still unresolved when the bulk of U.S. troops moved to the Continent and the agreement with the British ceased to operate.[71]

Another type of local procurement problem stemmed from the range of sizes provided for the various parts of the American uniform. The British used suspenders with loose-fitting trousers and thus reduced the tariff of sizes. In shirts, the British provided two sleeve lengths for each collar size and did not wish to use scarce manpower to give the Americans their accustomed four sleeve lengths. The Chief Quartermaster agreed to this limitation, but in the case of shoes no agreement could be reached. The British equipped their troops with 18 sizes, the Americans required 105 sizes.[72] The U.S. require-

---

[69] (1) Memo, CQM for CG SOS ETO, 15 Oct 43, sub: Situation Rpt—Bread Supply in ETO. Littlejohn Collection. (2) Littlejohn, ed., Passing in Review, ch. 36, pp. 41—47.

[70] Memo, Proc Div OCQM for Sales Store Div, 24 Nov 42, sub: Sale of Distressed Stocks of Sugar Confectionery During Month of December; Memo, GPA for CQM, 16 Jan 43, sub: Sale of Candy in U.K. Both in USFET QM 436.
[71] Memo, CQM for GPA, 10 Jan 44, sub: Increase in Allowance of Candy Bars; Memo, CQM for CG SOS ETO, 13 Jan 44, sub: Increase of Candy Ration. Both in USFET QM 000.4.
[72] (1) GPA Rpt on Mtg With . . . War Office and Ministry of Prod Concerning U.S. Reqmts of Clothing, 4 Nov 42. USFET GPA 420. (2) IRS, IG SOS to CQM, 24 Mar 43, and Ind by CQM, 29 Mar 43. USFET QM 421.

ment, based on civilian procedures in the zone of interior, was reinforced by Army regulations on the correct fitting of service shoes, and could not be readily modified. Therefore large-scale manufacture of shoes for enlisted men could never be satisfactorily arranged in the United Kingdom. But the British supplied over 152,000 pairs of officers' shoes in 1942–43, and about 75 percent of all shoes for officers, nurses, and Wacs in the ETO during hostilities.[73]

With respect to the magnitude of American requirements for items of clothing and individual equipment, the British also raised the question of "scale." They did not favor the diversion of their facilities to production for the Americans unless requirements approximated British rates of issue, which were generally lower for corresponding items. Replacement factors posed another problem. The British applied to their home forces garrison allowances for wear similar to those used in the United States, while the ETO Quartermaster used overseas combat replacement factors. The Chief Quartermaster refused to cut maintenance requirements to the British scale and, in general, the British yielded on specific requirements, but the question was a persistent one.[74]

Most of these difficulties were resolved during the spring of 1943, and May to November of that year was the most fruitful period for local procurement of clothing and individual equipment, especially of wool knit goods. The fact that the International Division, ASF, had decided to adopt the exchange basis rejected a year before, and to ship woolen goods to British troops in the Pacific, greatly eased these arrangements. Although the British at first believed that their own military contribution to OVERLORD would curtail their industrial capacity severely in 1944, they were prevailed upon to continue large deliveries to the U.S. forces during that year. The following items are representative of deliveries from reverse lend-lease by the middle of 1944:[75]

Clothing

Coats, mackinaw	328,802
Drawers, wool	2,286,190
Gloves, wool	871,690
Mufflers, wool	1,200,000
Socks, wool, light and heavy	8,604,180
Trousers, battle-dress	417,785
Undershirts, winter	2,242,151

Equipment

Bag, canvas, field	378,204
Belt, cartridge, cal. 30	186,294
Belt, pistol	381,646
Blanket, wool, OD	640,000
Carrier, pack	369,024
Cover, canteen	823,209
Pouch, first-aid	1,554,875

The British supplied a considerable amount of heavy mobile and semimobile equipment used in the field by U.S. Quartermaster units. This is described in connection with the continental

---

[73] (1) Littlejohn, ed., Passing in Review, ch. 41, pt. I, pp. 32, 119. (2) Interv with Littlejohn, 1 Dec 59.

[74] Memo, War Office for GPA, 2 Apr 43, no sub; 1st Ind, DCQM to Chief Proc Div, 13 Apr 43; Ltr, GPA to War Office, 16 Apr 43, no sub; Ltr, GPA to Anglo-American Co-ordinating Committee (Supply), 27 Apr 43, no sub; Ltr, GPA to Mr. Averell Harriman, 27 Apr 43, no sub. All in USFET GPA 420.

[75] (1) See above, p. 37. (2) *QM Supply in ETO,* III, 24–27, 125. (3) Clothing figures are cumulative, 1942–31 June 1944; equipment figures are for 1943 and 1 January–31 August 1944.

operations in which these items were used but also deserves mention here.[76] Equipment for a total of 69 mobile bakery companies was procured locally. Similar items procured were laundries (3 fixed, 21 mobile), shoe repair (3 semi-mobile, 19 mobile), and dry cleaning units (3 fixed). A much larger mobile laundry program (100 units) finally had to be canceled because of increased requirements for British troops in North Africa and the Middle East. Jerricans were another very large item: the British supplied 10,500,000 by D-day, and over 18,000,000 by May 1945.[77]

Liquid fuels presented an unusual procurement problem, since in many cases the original source was the United States. Within the United Kingdom, POL was provided directly to the U.S. forces by the British Army. Bulk POL reaching the United Kingdom from whatever source went into a common Anglo-American pool, which served civilians as well as the armed forces, and was in fact controlled by the British Petroleum Board in close liaison with the U.S. Area Petroleum Board. The Quartermaster Corps was theoretically entitled to draw up to half of this common pool, but during 1942–43 did not actually maintain an independent reserve except for a relatively small quantity held in Quartermaster POL depots for emergency shipment to North Africa, for troop training, and for training its own units in Class III supply proced-

ures. American units requiring POL drew it from British military sources on a simple requisition form—either in containers or in bulk from roadside pumps.[78]

Such a smooth relationship between two military systems was not achieved without mutual concession and careful co-ordination. Because of the heavy consumption by the Americans, both countries followed United States Army and Navy specifications with few exceptions. POL storage and distribution problems were further simplified by agreement to use MT80 gasoline (80-octane motor vehicle type) for all military and civilian engines in the United Kingdom except those of aircraft. Use of MT80 with its relatively high lead content created a serious maintenance problem for the British, most of whose motors were not designed to use highly leaded gasoline. The British accepted this burden to avoid the reduction in military reserves that would have resulted from a division of storage and distribution facilities between two varieties of gasoline. When, in 1944, a temporary shortage of tetraethyl lead forced consideration of a return to 72-octane gasoline for civilian users in the United Kingdom, the single-variety system was so well established that it was found uneconomical to attempt to differentiate between civilian and military users.[79]

---

[76] See below, chs. XV, XVIII, and XX.

[77] (1) Littlejohn, ed., Passing in Review, ch. 41, *passim*. (2) Ltr, Chief Proc Div to CQM, sub: Some Facts on Local Proc, 21 Jan 43 (reprinted in full in *QM Supply in ETO*, vol. I, app. XXIV). (3) Ltr, CQM to Somervell, 15 Apr 45. Littlejohn Collection. Bakery Study, app. A, item 6.

[78] (1) SOS ETO, Cir 4, 22 Jul 42, sub: Storage and Issue of Fuels, Oils, and Lubricants. USFET GPA 334. (2) Comment 2, CQM to Chief of Opns SOS, 18 Sep 43, on IRS, Chief of Opns to CQM, 16 Sep 43, sub: Definition and Understanding of "Joint Stockpile." USFET QM 400.23.

[79] (1) Memo, Area Petroleum Off for CG SOS WD, 4 Nov 42, sub: Motor Fuel All Purpose. USFET AG 463.7. (2) Ltr, Deputy Chief Petroleum Off to Ministry of Fuel and Power, 10 Aug 44, sub: Lead Content of Gasoline; Cable E–43353, Lee to ANPB, 15 Aug 44. USFET Petroleum Off 463.72.

The U.S. Army, too, was confronted by maintenance problems arising from the universal use of highly leaded gasoline. Field ranges and gasoline lanterns operated very poorly on leaded gasoline and caused serious maintenance and repair problems. The Quartermaster Corps nevertheless insisted on the advantages of simplified supply and refused to provide any other fuel. But unleaded gasoline always remained superior to MT80 for certain types of specialized engines, notably those of liaison aircraft and the small gasoline-powered electric generators used by signal and medical units. The pressure on the Chief Quartermaster to provide such gasoline was so persistent that when small quantities occasionally became available their issue was carefully controlled.[80]

The OCQM looked to Eire, Spain, and Portugal as possible sources of such supplies as vegetables, towels, blankets, gloves, and sweaters, but none of these countries ever provided more than an insignificant fraction of what was needed. The British, with their tightly knit economic relations with the Irish, were cool to the suggestion that Americans enter the Irish market for this move would cause prices to rise. At first the Irish were equally cool to a proposal that might compromise their position as neutrals. But Littlejohn visited President Eamon de Valera and obtained a personal commitment that the U.S. orders could and would be filled. Only by the persistence of the Chief Quartermaster, after the OQMG was unable to provide sufficient cotton yarn for towels and handkerchiefs, were the British persuaded to supply 125 tons of surplus long-staple cotton for such production in Ireland. This figure barely amounted to 25 percent of U.S. Army requirements. In this transaction, as in many others, Sir Cecil Weir, the British Minister of Supply, was very sympathetic and helpful.[81]

Meanwhile a survey of Spanish production facilities by the U.S. military attaché disclosed that clothing prices were high and quality low. This discouraging report caused the ETO Quartermaster to lose interest in Spanish goods except for oranges, winter vegetables, and miscellaneous emergency purchases. At the same time purchases of wool and leather items suitable for military use were made in Spain and Portugal by the United States Commercial Corporation (USCC), a federally owned U.S. agency engaged in preclusive buying—that is, in purchasing supplies to prevent the Axis Powers from acquiring them. Naturally, such activities involved competitive bidding, and prices were high. At first, most of these supplies were stored in the country of origin, but in the latter half of 1944 it

---

[80] (1) Memo, P&T Div for DCQM, 25 Jun 43, sub: Rpt on Opn of Coleman Lamps on Leaded and Unleaded Fuel. USFET QM 319.1. (2) IRS, DCQM to Chief of Svs SOS, 24 Aug 43, sub: Lanterns. USFET QM 000.4. (3) Memo, ACSigO ETO for Area Petroleum Sv, 18 Jan 44, sub: White Gas; Memo, Area Petroleum Off for Lt Comdr Lamont, USN, 18 Jan 44, sub: Unleaded Petroleum for U.S. Army Field Ranges. Both in USFET Petroleum Off 463.72.

[81] (1) File on Irish Free State, *passim*, especially 17 Jun, 9 Jul, 17 Aug, 29 Sep 42. USFET GPA 091. (2) Memo, Chief Subs Br for CQM, 7 Jan 43, sub: Prod of Fresh Vegetables in Eire. Littlejohn Collection. (3) Cable LN–2565, CQM to TQMG, 3 Jul 43; Cable R–392, TQMG to CQM, 7 Jul 43. Both in USFET AG 426. (4) Interv with Littlejohn, 1 Dec 59.

became evident that there would be serious shortages, particularly of blankets, in the ETO during the approaching winter. The OCQM arranged to acquire these supplies, many of which were used in rest camps and leave centers where first-class equipment was not vitally necessary. In November 1944, Colonel Brumbaugh visited Spain and Portugal to negotiate for additional supplies through military attaché and USCC channels. In Spain he acquired 300,000 blankets that had been manufactured specifically for the German Army, and in Portugal the USCC obtained for him 500,000 blankets, 3,000,000 unbleached cotton towels, 1,500,000 terry towels, 300,000,000 handkerchiefs, and 3,000,000 meters of sheeting. Delivery was to be completed by May 1945.[82]

Local procurement was a complicated process, involving an exasperating amount of attention to minor detail and requiring a large and highly qualified staff. But arrangements finally perfected after a period of adjustment resulted in significant savings in transatlantic shipping. During 1942 the Quartermaster Service procured in the United Kingdom supplies of all types amounting to 259,000 ship tons. These figures increased in 1943 to a total of 1,389,000 ship tons. During the first eleven months of 1944, total deliveries amounted to 2,319,-

000 ship tons. This total, broken down by category, included: Class I, 307,000 ship tons; Class II, 32,000 ship tons; Class III, 146,000 tons of POL plus 1,309,000 tons of solid fuels; and Class IV, 525,000 ship tons.[83]

In assessing the importance of the local procurement program, the limited port capacity of the British Isles should be considered as well as the direct saving in shipping. The average capacity of an Atlantic Ocean freighter was roughly 10,000 ship tons. By mid-1943 the crisis in shipping was largely overcome, but the unloading rate at British docks remained a limiting factor. The absolute maximum available to all U.S. forces in the United Kingdom was 150 ships, or 1,500,000 ship tons of imports per month, of which the Quartermaster Service received about one-third. Littlejohn's estimate of July 1943 that he could procure 40 percent of his vital needs in the United Kingdom was actually far short of reality. It was estimated that for the period June 1942–June 1944, 63 percent of QMC requirements were locally procured.[84] Such procurement provided welcome relief to the OCQM in the last hectic months before D-day, when the other technical services were badly hampered in their operations, and ships waiting to be unloaded threatened to clog every British port. Thus local procurement alleviated the ill effects of an almost disastrous bottleneck.[85]

---

[82] (1) Memo, GPA for CQM, 7 Sep 42, sub: Purchases and Proposed Purchases in Spain and Portugal; Memo, Maj Giblin OGPA for GPA, 11 Sep 42, sub: Mtg Held With Economic Warfare Sec in American Embassy. Both in USFET GPA 334. (2) Memo, CQM ETO for CG SOS WD, 9 Oct 42, sub: Investigation of Availability of Woolen Cloth in Spain. USFET AG 423. (3) Memo, Proc Div OCQM for USCC, 25 Jan 44, sub: Gloves, Spanish; Memo Supply Div OCQM for DCQM, 31 Jan 44, no sub. Both in USFET QM 422. (4) QM Supply in ETO, I, 37–38.

[83] (1) Proc in U.K., 1942. QM ETO, Lend-Lease File. (2) QM Supply in ETO, I, 29–34.
[84] Memo, CQM for CG SOS, 8 Jul 43, sub: Local Proc by QM Sv in U.K. USFET GPA 400.1911. (2) Ruppenthal, Logistical Support, I, 257.
[85] Ruppenthal, Logistical Support, I, 234, refers to this problem as "an aggravating stricture which dominated the course of the supply build-up in the final months before D-day."

Maintaining a military base within a sovereign foreign nation involved certain unavoidable complications and inconveniences, but the British Government and people made unprecedented efforts and concessions to reduce these disadvantages to a minimum. Such official actions as Parliament's granting extraterritorial privileges to the U.S. forces in the British Isles, and relaxation of wartime rationing restrictions by the various Ministries, became significant through general public acceptance of these measures. It might be said that the Americans came to appreciate Great Britain fully only after they had left it. Minor problems caused by differences in speech and by the unfamiliar technical vocabulary of the British Army assumed their true proportions once the Americans had experienced real language difficulties on the Continent. After making laborious efforts to achieve satisfactory contacts with people whose basic attitudes and fundamental institutions were widely different, they reached a better understanding of the value of a common English heritage, of which language was only one aspect. That heritage made possible a degree of mutual understanding which could never be duplicated in any of the continental countries, despite unlimited good will on both sides. For that reason, both official and personal relationships between the British people and the U.S. Army remained close, even after most U.S. troops had crossed the Channel. Great Britain remained the chief source of local procurement for the European theater until V-E day, not only in textiles and hardware, but even in many foodstuffs. This fact is only partially explained by economic chaos and devastation on the Continent; the ease of doing business in English with men whose methods and working habits were familiar was a powerful incentive. Individual Americans were apparently swayed by similar considerations. Despite the rival attractions of Paris and the Riviera, London remained the favorite leave center for U.S. troops in the ETO.[86]

---

[86] (1) *A Short Guide to Great Britain*, prepared by Special Services Division, SOS, U.S. Army (Washington, 1942). (2) Mary Welsh, "U.S. Troops Set Up Housekeeping," *Life*, (February 23, 1942), p. 39. (3) "Parliament Grants U.S. Forces Courtmartial Jurisdiction," *Newsweek* (August 17, 1942), p. 20.

CHAPTER XI

The Build-Up for Overlord

By the end of 1943 it seemed reasonably certain that BOLERO would be completed on schedule and that the reserves of manpower, matériel, and supplies for ground combat would be more than enough for the OVERLORD operation. But suitable shipping, especially landing craft and crews trained in landing operations, were in critically short supply. Ultimately plans for amphibious operations both in the Pacific and in the Mediterranean had to be curtailed to provide more landing craft and to help ensure the success of OVERLORD. Moreover, British ports facing the Continent were of limited capacity, with their use further restricted by the heavy tides of the area. Lack of warehouse space and open storage areas immediately adjacent to these ports were also limiting factors, since speedy loading and turnaround of ships were essential. All major French ports had been turned into fortresses and their German garrisons had been ordered to defend them to the last man.

Thus the initial assault would have to be made from landing craft over open beaches, and only a fraction of the potential Allied power could be brought to bear at the landing points. Since preparations for an operation of this magnitude were too massive to conceal, only the exact time and the actual landing places would be a surprise. A great logistical race would begin at the instant the first troops went ashore, and would continue until it became clear that the immediate tactical operation was either a success or a failure. In this race the Germans would match land transportation against Allied water and air transportation, and would attempt to keep the railroads in operation and the highways open despite Allied air interdiction. Since the enemy could also bring combat units into the area by cross-country foot marches at night, Allied air superiority would not guarantee a complete isolation of the invasion sector, although strategic as well as tactical aircraft had this main mission in the last weeks before D-day. At first all means of transport would be used by both contenders primarily for combat troops and their fighting equipment, but the need for supplies would mount rapidly as the concentration of troops in the area increased. The first days of the assault would undoubtedly involve very heavy combat, with rapid rates of consumption for all supplies.[1]

The British had constructed MULBERRIES—movable artificial ports of revolutionary design—so that even in the initial phase the Allies would be able to utilize a certain number of conventional

---

[1] Forrest C. Pogue, *The Supreme Command*, UNITED STATES ARMY IN WORLD WAR II (Washington, 1954) ch. VI.

freighters, but landing craft would have to bear the brunt of the transport mission until French ports could be captured and put into operation. However large the reserves on hand in the United Kingdom, only men and matériel actually on the beachhead when the enemy counterattacked could influence the tactical situation. Before the enemy became strong enough to mount a major counteroffensive, the lodgment area had to become deep enough to place the beaches out of artillery range, and strong enough to prevent enemy reinforcements from piercing its defensive lines. This requirement implied a heavy emphasis on combat troops in the initial phase, and a continuous shuttle service by all available shipping over a period of several weeks. From staff planners it called for a careful distinction between the essential and the nonessential, with regard to both units and supplies, and a meticulous system of priorities for every item and every individual found to be essential for both the initial assault and the early build-up. If ordinary military standards for minimum supply were used, the operation would be impossible because of sheer inability to lift all the necessary combat units with their normal complements of vehicles, supplies, and support units.[2]

For guidance in their crucial selection of supplies and manpower, staff officers turned to lessons of recent comparable support operations. Quartermasters were sent to study the problems of amphibious, fast-moving, and attritional

warfare, all three types of which had developed in the western Mediterranean, and to learn which solutions had been most successful. But of greater importance were the lessons carried back by quartermasters who had actually fought in North Africa, Tunisia, Sicily, and Italy and who had been part of a team which had grown in a single year from a small task force to a field army. Through these sources, the Quartermaster Service in the ETO was able to confirm much of its evolving field doctrine and to develop new points of emphasis.[3]

A knotty and unsolved problem was involved in logistical support for rapidly moving forces. Previous experience was mainly useful only in pointing out mistakes that should not be repeated. When the TORCH landings developed into a race for Tunis, the base sections echeloned along the North African coast were slow in recognizing the implications of the changed situation and the changed axis of advance. Deficiencies in co-ordination with one another, and with the combat units, were very conspicuous. Apparently army-level planners drew the moral that logistical headquarters were by nature cumbersome

---

[2] (1) Ruppenthal, *Logistical Support*, I, 178–89, 270–71. (2) *QM Supply in ETO*, I, 6–9. (3) Harrison, *Cross-Channel Attack*, pp. 62–68. (4) IRS, G–4 to CQM, 4 Feb 44, sub: Storage Reqmts OVERLORD. USFET AG 400.242 (QM).

[3] Colonel Sharp, former Deputy Chief Quartermaster, went to North Africa with the TORCH forces and returned to the ETO during the summer of 1943. Colonel Zwicker, former executive officer of OCQM and QM-designate of ADSEC, toured the Mediterranean theater with several other ADSEC staff officers in the spring of 1944. Colonel McNamara, former QM, II Corps, and QM-designate, First Army, brought 2 officers, 1 warrant officer, and 3 enlisted men with him to England in September 1943. Colonel Eymer, G–4 1st Division, had extensive combat experience in the Mediterranean; he lectured at several SOS staff conferences. Colonel Beny Rosaler, for a time QM, Twelfth AF Service Command in the MTO, returned to the OCQM in early 1944 and became Chief, Field Service Division.

and slow to respond, and that under certain circumstances the combat forces could get along without them. Based on this premise, HUSKY, the next Mediterranean operation, may be called an experiment in simplicity. The logistical organization was placed directly under the tactical commanders. The G–4 sections of Seventh U.S. Army and the subordinate Corps headquarters were given very limited missions. Their principal functions were to initiate and publish administrative paragraphs for the field orders, and then to act as liaison officers during the operation. Implementation of the entire logistical plan for the operation was entrusted to the 1st Engineer Special Brigade. This headquarters, with its organic amphibious transport units, was admirably equipped and trained to support the initial assault, but lacked the administrative machinery to supervise all the service units temporarily attached to it. With all attachments, the brigade numbered about 20,000 men for the Sicilian campaign, and although this number was rather scanty for support of a field army, the more serious deficiencies that emerged were not in actual numbers of service troops. A larger administrative staff was plainly needed. As the supply lines lengthened, the furious activity and final exhaustion of the brigade staff, and the comparative idleness of G–4's and technical service officers on army and corps staffs, became clearly evident. Apparently this organization was an attempt to achieve flexibility by reducing the size of the command structure, but Sicily was a large island, unlike the Pacific atolls where similar concepts had been successful. What was needed was a chain of subordinate logistical headquarters to ad-

minister intermediate depots along the supply pipeline, but regularly constituted units for this purpose were not yet available.[4]

Colonel McNamara, the II Corps quartermaster, was an interested and critical observer of the Sicilian operation. He was particularly irked by the role of passive onlooker forced on him by the HUSKY plan. Later, when he was appointed First Army quartermaster and participated in OVERLORD planning, he insisted upon both an adequate number of QM troops and upon an adequate organization to control them. Quartermaster troops for First Army, including assigned motor transport, numbered more than 22,000 men and were administered by three QM group headquarters (a new type of organization) and fourteen battalion headquarters. The army quartermaster could locate subheadquarters where they were needed and still maintain an intact organization close behind the combat troops.[5]

McNamara's solution applied only to the field-army-level organization: COMZ ETOUSA would have to build an organization to support several armies. In considering this aspect of the problem, the familiar QMC metaphor of spigot and pipeline quartermasters may be helpful. The COMZ ETOUSA plan provided that when the combat troops moved forward, ADSEC, the spigot organization, followed to serve them, but the pipeline already in place did not move; additional lengths of pipe were added to span the increased depth of the communications zone. Each length of

---

[4] (1) See ch. III, above. (2) McNamara *Memoir*, pp. 39–40, 84–86.
[5] McNamara *Memoir*, pp. 93–95.

pipe represented an additional increment of service units, and each joint an additional SOS subheadquarters. But the intention was not for these units to settle down to improve their installations and organize the countryside like Pershing's superficially similar organization of 1917–18. As the armies advanced toward the northeast, newly acquired coastal bases on the left flank would pour in additional streams of supplies, so that constant readjustment and reorganization of the whole territorial supply organization would be necessary. Certainly this concept predicated a massive organization, but one that was flexible and not out of proportion to its mission. To operate efficiently, such an organization needed sound doctrine and thorough training; its size was an inevitable corollary of the amount of support it had to provide.[6]

The Command and Logistical Organization

Normal staff procedure in World War II required that insofar as possible an operation should be carried out by the same staff that had planned it. A major aspect of planning at the highest levels involved the activation of subordinate headquarters and the allocation of subsidiary planning responsibilities to them. The best proof of the essentially tentative and theoretical nature of ROUNDUP was the absence of a subordinate structure to implement it. OVERLORD, by contrast, speedily called into being an elaborate command and logistical network, and even the plan itself was subdivided as an aid to clarity in the necessary detailed planning. NEPTUNE was originally a security designation for papers which named the specific assault areas and the target date. By a natural extension, it came to be the code name for the assault phase of the operation.[7]

The operation would be conducted in three phases: in Phase I (D-day to D plus 14) one U.S. corps and a British Army of two corps would hold off German attacks from the east while two other American corps captured Cherbourg; in Phase II (D plus 15 to D plus 40) one British and one Canadian army would defend to the east, one U.S. army would face south, and another U.S. army would capture the seaports of Brittany; in Phase III (D plus 41 to D plus 90), two Allied army groups controlling four armies would push eastward to the Seine, and southward to the Loire. Post-OVERLORD plans were revised so often, both before and after the landings, that no detailed description will be attempted. But one basic assumption was common to them all: the Germans would contest all major river crossings and attempt to hold every favorable terrain feature. The Allies would probably have to make a thirty-day pause at the Seine while supplies were built up for a further advance; possibly another pause at the Somme-Aisne line would be necessary. The advance to the Rhine would require a full year, at an average rate of less than two miles per day. This forecast was not an inflexible plan, but primarily a yardstick for computing requirements. It was conservative, even pessimistic, and the derived require-

_____

[6] Ruppenthal, *Logistical Support*, I, 452.

[7] Unless otherwise noted, this outline of the organization and planning for OVERLORD is summarized from Ruppenthal, *Logistical Support*, I, 190–230.

ments for combat units, replacements, and supplies were very high. This was, on the whole, an advantage; but all the forecasts contained one serious error. The expected slow rate of advance implied that there would be ample time to repair railroads and bridges and that there would be no unusual requirements for motor vehicles.[8] An example of the influence of these studies upon specific plans was the COMZ action on a recommendation by the Transportation Corps during the BOLERO period. General Ross had estimated that 240 truck companies would be required, but the G–4 Section decided that 160 would be sufficient.[9]

General Eisenhower was appointed Supreme Allied Commander in December 1943, and COSSAC was renamed Supreme Headquarters, Allied Expeditionary Force, on 15 January 1944. Two days later ETOUSA and SOS ETOUSA were combined into one headquarters, now officially designated ETOUSA–SOS. Eisenhower retained the title of theater commander, but Lee as his deputy gradually assumed most of the administrative duties of a theater commander. Almost from the beginning, this headquarters was unofficially referred to as the Communications Zone, which became its official title on D–day. Since Eisenhower moved many of the senior ETOUSA officers to his new SHAEF headquarters, Lee as deputy theater commander continued to operate with largely the same staff as before. One notable exception was Maj. Gen. Walter Bedell Smith, chief of staff of both SHAEF and ETOUSA-SOS. But both Eisenhower and Smith as SHAEF officers would be physically absent from theater headquarters, an arrangement strongly reminiscent of the separation of BOLERO and ROUNDUP planning staffs in 1942.[10]

For ground combat troops, the next lower echelon was provided by an army group headquarters. Initially, British 21 Army Group commanded by General Sir Bernard L. Montgomery would direct all ground force operations in the beachhead. The 1st U.S. Army Group (FUSAG) would become operational at a later stage. The senior U.S. headquarters in the assault was First U.S. Army (FUSA), commanded by Lt. Gen. Omar N. Bradley. Under the principle of separate national logistical systems, supply and administrative support would flow directly from COMZ to FUSA. In terms of geography, American bases in southwestern England would support U.S. troops in the western part of the beachhead. This relationship would be largely retained even after an American army group headquarters was inserted into the command chain, since at army group level the G–4 and technical services staff had co-ordinating and supervising, rather than operating, functions. Subordinate to First Army were two corps headquarters, V and VII Corps; a third (XIX Corps) was to be added later. The eastern U.S. objective was OMAHA Beach, directly adjacent to the lodgment of Second British Army, still farther to the east. Here V Corps would direct a landing by two divisions, supported by two

---

[8] (1) Ruppenthal, *Logistical Support*, I, 189, 553–54. (2) A composite map of the various forecasts is given in Eisenhower, *Crusade in Europe*, pages 224–25.
[9] Bykofsky and Larson, *The Transportation Corps: Operations Overseas*, pp. 239–40. (2) Ruppenthal, *Logistical Support*, I, 315.

[10] See ch. II, above.

Engineer special brigades. In the west, slightly separated from the V Corps zone, VII Corps would direct the initial assault by one infantry division supported by one Engineer special brigade on UTAH Beach. The 82d and 101st Airborne Divisions, directly subordinate to First Army, were to land on drop zones inland from UTAH Beach before dawn of D–day, and were then to come under the command of VII Corps. As the initial lodgment area was enlarged, more units and headquarters would be brought ashore until a conventional balanced force of combat and service troops was established. The airborne troops would be withdrawn during Phase II.

Plans for logistical support of the operation were worked out in even greater detail. During Phase I, COMZ would be represented on the Continent by an Advance Section (ADSEC). To ensure co-ordination of supply in the initial assault, ADSEC was to be directly subordinate to First Army during Phase I. In Phase II, First Army was to establish a rear boundary, separating itself from ADSEC both organizationally and geographically. At this time ADSEC would become a normal area headquarters of service troops, differing from a base section only in that it was mobile, and thus able to maintain immediate contact and provide direct support for an advancing army. At the same time all service troops on the Continent not organic or permanently assigned to combat units would revert to ADSEC control, and ADSEC itself would come under the control of COMZ, exercised on the Continent by personnel of its Forward Echelon (FECZ). During Phase III (about D plus 90), SHAEF and COMZ would become operational on the Continent;

FECZ would be absorbed by COMZ, and COMZ as an independent headquarters of equal rank would assume responsibility for logistical support of 1st Army Group.

Specific and detailed planning by these new headquarters had to proceed by echelons—decisions at the higher levels were a necessary preliminary to the formulation of plans at lower levels. A very stringent security system known as BIGOT made informal liaison and exchange of ideas almost impossible. To save time, so that lower levels could go to work before higher level plans were completed and formally published, a system of formal liaison and interheadquarters briefings was instituted. Thus NEPTUNE, the initial plan for a combined assault by British and American armies, navies, and air forces, was published on 1 February 1944 by SHAEF. Members of the First Army Planning Group from Bristol had been in London since 19 December, and had assisted in preparing certain portions of this plan.[11]

ADSEC also prepared a separate plan for the period when it would be independent of First Army, especially for Phase II when it would be the senior logistical headquarters on the Continent. The main problems to be solved in this plan were how to accomplish an orderly transfer of service troops temporarily attached to First Army, and how to select depot sites with an eye to their use in

---

[11] The First Army NEPTUNE plan was published on 25 February, and included as annexes a Quartermaster Plan (Annex 7) and an ADSEC Plan (Annex 17), both printed in full in *First United States Army Report of Operations*, 20 October 1943–1 August 1944, 7 vols. (Europe, 1946). (Hereafter cited as *FUSA Rpt of Opns*, 20 Oct 43–1 Aug 44.) (See Bibliographical Note.)

later operations. During Phase II the axis of advance would be southwestward to enlarge the lodgment area, capture additional ports, and establish a major complex of U.S. depots in the Rennes-Laval area. But the main thrust would eventually be toward the east and ADSEC would soon follow the armies in that direction, leaving the rear support areas to be administered by other logistical headquarters. ADSEC would receive support out of the administrative network it left behind but could not count on others to correct its mistakes and therefore planned this phase carefully and in detail. Because Allied bombing had destroyed most large warehouses, there would be no general depots. Thus the selection of depot sites was the separate responsibility of each ADSEC technical service section.

SOS also had a very active part in operational planning. SOS troops had to be trained and prepared; detailed plans had to be made to pack and crate all supplies for a sea voyage; all supplies and all troops had to be moved forward to marshaling areas, then to embarkation areas, and finally loaded on ships. Meanwhile, although stripped of troops and forced to activate additional base sections for service on the Continent, SOS had to keep the original base sections operating in the United Kingdom to fill the requisitions from units on the far shore, and to receive the torrent of supplies still arriving from the United States. SOS was a "going concern," whereas the other headquarters were waiting to become operational, and this meant that the main burden of actually implementing interstaff agreements fell on SOS. Naturally, this SOS responsibility was parceled out to a maximum

extent among the technical services. The OCQM, the base section quartermasters, and the Quartermaster depot organizations were all vitally concerned. One particular difficulty was the extreme scarcity of Quartermaster units. Many would have to work in the depots until the last minute and then proceed directly to the marshaling areas for movement to the Continent. The marshaling areas themselves required large quartermaster staffs to provide a variety of services to the troops passing through.[12]

As might have been expected, the first requirement of the various new headquarters was personnel—initially staff personnel for planning, and later units, especially logistical units, to implement the plans. Littlejohn was called on for a large number of experienced, competent, senior officers to fill key posts. Colonel Zwicker became Quartermaster, ADSEC, in January 1944, and Col. John B. Franks, former DCQM, became Quartermaster, FECZ, during the next month. Many of the first units called for in connection with NEPTUNE were QM group or battalion headquarters, used initially as staff augmentations to help in the planning phase at army and corps levels. Here again the unit commanders had to be hand-picked to suit the tactical commanders, since they would also serve as special staff officers all through the operation. Littlejohn found that even superior officers of wide experience needed prolonged orientation in the peculiarities of the European theater before they could be used in key positions. Most of

---

[12] The SOS Plan for Mounting OVERLORD was published on 20 March 1944, and Annex 10 (Quartermaster) on 30 March 1944. See *QM Supply in ETO*, I, 8.

these posts were filled by promoting junior officers who had demonstrated their capacity in the ETO. The vacancies thus created were easily filled. Littlejohn had obtained a special allocation of more than 300 second lieutenants from the Office of The Quartermaster General.[13]

Detailed Quartermaster Planning

Whatever the merits of the operational plans, they were completed late—even dangerously late—from the logistical point of view.[14] In a more conventional and more favorable situation, the SOS technical services would first have helped the supply officers of the army group, armies, and air forces compute their requirements, based on operational plans; then, adding a reasonable amount for the needs of the SOS itself, planners could forward the total figures to the zone of interior as the estimated theater supply requirements for a future campaign. But since the necessary lead time for routine requisitions was three to four months, clearly a requirement of this magnitude could only be filled over a period of many months, or even years. BOLERO had filled this need for advance notice, but only in a very rough and general way. From a planner's point of view, BOLERO comprised a tentative and fluctuating troop basis, supported by a fluctuating and tentative level of author

ized supply. Moreover, the trend of revisions in the troop basis was upward, and in the supply levels, downward.

With the inexorable time limitations in mind, the technical services could not wait for the completion of operational plans by newly activated headquarters. However meager the knowledge on which they acted, they still had to come to grips with the problem of detailed supply requirements, revise the crude BOLERO forecasts item by item, and make decisions that would probably be final.[15] Three elements entered into every equation: the troop basis, the authorized days of supply, and the replacement factor for a specific item. The troop basis was not in the province of Quartermaster planners—they considered themselves fortunate if their information on the subject was fairly complete and up-to-date. Authorized days of supply were policy matters, decided at the highest War Department levels. Changes in this element of the supply equation were nonselective: they affected all items of a given class. Still, Littlejohn believed that recent reductions in the level of QM supply—particularly the drastic one of 20 January 1944—had been excessive. He drafted a letter to the War Department, which went out practically unaltered over the signature of

---

[13] Personal Ltr, CQM to Col O. E. Cound, 15 Oct 43; Ltr, CQM to CG SOS, 23 Nov 43, sub: Casual Comments Pers of QM Sv ETO. Littlejohn Reading File, vol. XVII, item 52; vol. XVIII, item 63.

[14] Ruppenthal, *Logistical Support*, I, 262. General Lutes, Chief of Operations, ASF, who inspected the theater in April–May 1944, was very critical of SHAEF in this respect.

[15] The OCQM developed three basic supply plans: one for Class I, one for Class II, IV and PX, and one for Class III. These were generalized plans, not intended to support any specific continental operation, but formulated to enumerate and locate the QM resources that were available, and to provide concrete suggestions as to how they might be utilized by a tactical headquarters. First Army found these suggestions extremely helpful, and adopted most of them. The three plans are reprinted in full in OTCQM TSFET Operational Study 14, Appendixes A, B, and C.

General Lee, recommending that this latest change be rescinded.[16] There was no immediate reply, and Col. Ira K. Evans, the control officer in Overseas Supply Division, NYPE, writing on 11 March, warned Littlejohn that the response would probably be unfavorable: "It seems that they intend to be quite hard-boiled on this levels business. If the levels stick, then it seems to me that the only way in which you are going to get needed supplies is by complete revision of replacement factors. . . ."[17] The same idea had already occurred to Littlejohn, as it probably would to any experienced supply officer, for the replacement factor is the third element of the supply equation, the one easiest to modify in the light of professional knowledge and experience. In fact, since the troop basis was still fluctuating and detailed operations plans were not available, detailed supply planning was largely concerned with correcting, refining, and applying replacement factors.

All the replacement data collected on previous American operations in World War II were available to the NEPTUNE planners, but Mediterranean experience was considered most nearly applicable, and was also most readily accessible. Littlejohn had maintained a regular correspondence with Middleswart at SOS NATOUSA and Sullivan at Fifth Army, and both these men had sent him copies of their more important reports to Washington. In the more leisurely atmosphere of the ETO in early 1943, staff members were able to collate and systematize this information, which was then returned to the Mediterranean theater in the form of the 100,000-man plan and related QM reference data.[18] These were enthusiastically received in NATOUSA and prompted further correspondence with all the senior Mediterranean quartermasters. In the period November 1943–January 1944, revised printed editions of these studies were published in London.[19] Littlejohn sent copies to all his contacts in active theaters, requesting comment, and received prompt replies, principally in tabular form, which were reproduced and distributed to the QM sections of all the headquarters engaged in NEPTUNE planning. Sullivan (the Fifth Army quartermaster) also made some general observations:

. . . We wish to reciprocate for the wonderful aid that your Basic Manual has been in the planning stages; without it we would have been sunk. . . . I am sending you our maintenance studies for October 1943 through February 1944. Also we found that maintenance requirements on items such as shoe strings, BAR belts, socks wool light, command post tents, hospital tents, and meat cans should be revised upward; intrenching tools should be revised upwards to a very substantial degree. . . . We have had rather a rich field experience in this operation and have compiled some data which may be valuable to others. . . .[20]

Littlejohn sent this letter to Col. Max Brumbaugh, currently DCQM (Lon-

---

[16] (1) See ch. IX, above. (2) Ltr, Deputy Comdr ETOUSA to AG WD, 29 Feb 44, sub: Levels of Supply. ETO 400.

[17] Personal Ltr, Evans to Littlejohn, 11 Mar 44, no sub. Evans' Staybacks, 291.

[18] See ch. III, above.

[19] The most important of these publications was *Quartermaster Service Reference Data, vol. II (rev.): Operations—Planning, 1 January 1944* (Hq SOS ETOUSA, OCQM). (Hereafter cited as *QM Sv Reference Data,* vol. II.) Copies on file at Hist Br OQMG and at Ft. Lee, Va.

[20] Ltr, Sullivan to Littlejohn, 9 Mar 44, no sub. Littlejohn Reading File, vol. XXII, item 53.

don), with the notation: "Please note the attached correspondence. . . . I want the maintenance factor problem brought [from Cheltenham] to London immediately and put into the Plans & Training Division, and some action obtained, so that we will at least be ahead of that gang of professors in the Quartermaster General's Office, instead of behind as at present."[21] These papers illustrate a typical controversy between an overseas technical service and the zone of interior. Replacement factors were not merely statistical data based on observation; they were also policy matters. For example, approved theater replacement factors were used by NYPE in editing theater requisitions. The factors currently authorized for the ETO in 1943 were ample, and even excessive, for forces while they remained in the United Kingdom.[22] They were based on experience of maneuvers and training, only slightly modified by the meager information on actual combat experience available when they were compiled. If combat operations experience in North Africa and Italy was pertinent, and Littlejohn emphatically believed that it was, the authorized factors were not combat factors at all, and were entirely inadequate for a cross-Channel attack and continental operations. He therefore forwarded his *QM Service Reference Data* to The Quartermaster General, and proposed to use them in computing and assembling stocks to support the assault forces.[23] This proposal was received rather coolly in Washington. The statisticians Littlejohn referred to as "that gang of professors" had a viewpoint fundamentally different from that of a theater quartermaster. Analyzing the expenditures upon which the proposed new rates were based, they found special and nonrecurring issues lumped in with true replacement figures—the same practice they had objected to in connection with initial issues to Bolero units a year before. They recommended that no changes be made in replacement and maintenance factors until actual combat of sufficient duration had demonstrated a permanent trend.[24] This emphasis on long-range trends was natural, since the OQMG used replacement and maintenance factors primarily for long-range forecasting of procurement requirements for a global war effort.[25] The OCQM, on the other hand, was primarily interested in meeting the specific demands of theater forces during combat. The thought will instantly occur that here were two staff agencies, compiling statistics for different purposes from different data, and yet trying to reconcile the results. Evans wrote that the War Department was "playing around with" the idea of allowing each theater to decide its own maintenance factors.[26] It seems highly probable that

[21] Ltr cited n. 20, with IRS, Littlejohn to Brumbaugh, attached.

[22] Memo, OCQM for CG SOS ETO, 4 Jun 43, sub: Answers to Questions to CG SOS from WD. USFET AG 310.1.

[23] Memo, CQM for TQMG, 13 Jan 44, sub: Combat Consumption Factors. ETO 400.6.

[24] OQMG Rpt, 15 Apr 45, sub: Supply of C&E to ETO 1944, pt. 2, sec. III, Replacement Factors. ETO 420.

[25] The methods and objectives of OQMG statisticians and the use they made of data from overseas theaters are discussed in Donald F. Bradford, *Methods of Forecasting War Requirements for QM Supplies*, QMC Historical Studies, 14 (Washington, 1946). See especially pp. 85–88.

[26] Personal Ltr, Evans to Littlejohn, 11 Mar 44, no sub. Evans' Staybacks, 291.

the idea had originated in his own office, where the troublesome factors had to be used daily in editing requisitions from overseas. But the proposal was not adopted at the time. Littlejohn's estimates later proved to be considerably more accurate than those of the OQMG, but they were still only estimates, and the OQMG had revised its factors as recently as 15 December.[27] If a change were made at this point, actual continental campaign experience would require still more changes at a later date in the complicated and cumbersome U.S. procurement program. There was much to be said for ASF's wait-and-see attitude, particularly since steps were being taken to increase the margin of safety for all supplies. On 26 April the War Department approved Lee's recommendation (actually initiated by Littlejohn) for an increase in the ETO level of supply, but for the preinvasion and NEPTUNE periods only—that is, through D plus 90.[28]

Another means of obtaining sufficient supplies for combat purposes was provided by PROCO (Projects for a Continental Operation), a procedure instituted by ASF in June 1943. As originally conceived, this was a long-range production program to cover procurement of special items of major equipment required for OVERLORD but not provided for under current allowances or Tables of Equipment. Most of the items were Engineer or Transportation Corps responsibilities; the only applicable QMC items under this definition were materials-handling machinery. But the original PROCO projects ran into serious difficulties, largely because of the lateness of operational planning already mentioned. Meanwhile all the technical services had noted that PROCO provided a method of securing supplies for OVERLORD in excess of ordinary allowances and, since the requirements were nonrecurring, without disturbing the calculation of normal replacement factors. Moreover, PROCO supplies were not counted as part of the authorized theater level.[29]

The Quartermaster Corps, like other technical services in the ETO, adopted an interpretation of PROCO to cover all OVERLORD requirements in excess of ordinary allowances, and submitted projects accordingly. ASF immediately objected that this procedure made PROCO useless. On 19 September 1943 it advised the theater that most of the projects submitted were being reduced to ordinary requisitions.[30] The theater replied that common items of supply had been included because the planned operation would require exceptional issues in excess of ordinary allowances. The War Department withdrew its objections and on 10 October announced that the ETO interpretation would be followed. Presumably ASF had viewed the original PROCO concept as a failure, and had decided to use the available administrative machinery for other purposes. PROCO thus became the vehicle for the acquisition of all supplies needed for Operation OVERLORD in excess of normal

---

[27] Ibid.

[28] QM Supply in ETO, I, 44.

[29] QM Supply in ETO, I, 47–48.

[30] (1) Summary, Development of Procedure in Submitting Projects for a Continental Operation, in Plan for SOS ETO, vol. II, 1 November 1943, sec. 1D. USFET AG 381. (2) OTCQM TSFET Operational Study 14, 1 November 1945, pp. 1–2.

allowances and outside authorized theater levels.[31]

Use of the PROCO procedure by the Quartermaster Corps is illustrated by the example of operational rations. The authorized theater level for C, K, and 10-in-1 rations combined was only eight days in the spring of 1944. This was hardly enough to supply the amphibious exercises before D–day. Elaborate special preparations had to be made to support the assault forces. Quantities of B and operational rations had to be set aside months in advance so as to have them specially packed and ready for loading at the proper time. Another drain on reserves was caused by the rapid shifting of large bodies of troops across the United Kingdom just before D–day. These movements involved last-minute exercises and rehearsals as well as the final staging for the assault. Transient troops consumed an unusually high proportion of operational rations. The fact that some other depot would be supplying fewer troops at the same time did not balance the situation because troops moved more rapidly from one depot area to another than did supplies. This meant that an unusually large proportion of stocks had to be held in depot reserves and could not be considered fully available to the whole theater. The temporary increase in theater ration levels from 45 to 60 days authorized for the mounting of Operation OVERLORD was not enough to meet these additional demands, especially as the 15-day increase was all in A rations. The Chief Quartermaster therefore requisitioned a special 15-day supply of combat rations, which was considered a PROCO project not charged against the theater ration level. The War Department agreed on condition that the additional rations would not permanently increase the theater level and that they would be absorbed within the first six months of the operation.[32]

Similar problems arose because of the special demands for tentage, field ranges, and other housekeeping equipment at the concentration, marshaling, and embarkation areas used in training for and mounting the operation. These supplies were also furnished under the PROCO procedure. Still a third category supplied through this procedure consisted of items of ordinary equipment needed during combat in quantities greatly exceeding regular allowances. A notable example was the intrenching tool, which, as experience in North Africa, Sicily, and Italy amply demonstrated, was required by each individual soldier as a means of digging his own shelter.[33]

Information received from General Sullivan, the Fifth Army quartermaster, convinced Littlejohn that War Department replacement factors for clothing were inadequate for combat. Since his own reference data had been rejected,

[31] (1) Summary cited n. 30(1). (2) ASF, *History of Planning Division, ASF,* II, 213ff. (3) Ruppenthal, *Logistical Support,* I, 260–61.

[32] (1) Memo, WD for CG ETO, 8 Mar 44, sub: QM Project A–59 for the ETO. EUCOM 400.312/4, vol. II. (2) *QM Supply in ETO,* II, 4. (3) Evans Ltr cited n. 26, above. Colonel Evans' comment was, "It was quite a battle to get A–59 through."
[33] (1) Memo, CG FUSA for CG SOS ETO, and Inds, 26 Feb 44, sub: Projects for a Continental Opn; Carrier Sheet, AG Opns ETO to G–3 and G–4, 2 Jun 44, same sub, and additional notes. Both in EUCOM 400.312/4, vol. II. (2) A complete list of PROCO projects for QM Class II and IV supplies is given in OCTQM TSFET Operational Study 14, exhibit B.

he submitted a rather large PROCO requisition (3,669 long tons) for extra quantities of regular clothing, basing his request largely upon NATOUSA factors. The War Department approved this project only to the extent of 33 percent, withholding approval of the balance until further study could be made. Ultimately, the remaining two-thirds was canceled by ASF because of production considerations. Meanwhile the need for this clothing had been partially met by increasing the over-all supply level. This experience developed in Littlejohn a distaste for special requisitions based upon the exigencies of combat. Henceforth, he was determined to procure his combat requirements by requesting a modification of regular replacement factors.[34]

The objectives of Quartermaster planning for OVERLORD were a 4-day reserve of all classes of supply by D plus 14, and a 14-day reserve by D plus 41 for all troops in the beachhead. Only the first (Phase I) objective was a First Army responsibility, since after D plus 14 (Phase II) ADSEC would relieve First Army of support for nonorganic units.[35] These modest-sounding goals actually involved tremendous quantities of supplies because of the rapid troop build-up. The SHAEF G-4 Division esti-

mated that to achieve them resupply would have to be maintained at 150 percent of daily consumption, and questioned whether this was possible.[36]

Special Supplies for the Assault

Combat Rations

Mediterranean experience had demonstrated both the advantages and the limitations of the various operational rations.[37] Briefly stated, all of them were compact, fairly nutritious, waterproof, and resistant to rough handling. These features made them very convenient to transport and issue, and well-nigh indispensable for amphibious assaults and other periods of rapid movement or intense combat. On the other hand, they were not very palatable, and after a very few days became monotonous. Thereafter, loss of appetite rapidly led to malnutrition, loss of combat efficiency, and lowered morale. Technically qualified QMC officers were well aware of these disadvantages, and made plans to shift over to A or B rations at the earliest possible stage of each operation. But the major ETO problem in this field stemmed from the gigantic scale of the OVERLORD operation. MTOUSA had experienced repeated amphibious assaults and brief campaigns, with pauses in between. There was small prospect of such pauses on the Continent; it appeared likely that many of the combat troops and some of the close-support units would be continuously on the

[34] (1) General Sullivan's disagreement with higher QM echelons within his theater regarding replacement factors are described in Chapter VII, above. (2) Ltr, OCQM to AG WD, 21 Jan 44, sub: QM Project 242-A (Projects for a Continental Operation). EUCOM 400.312/4, vol. II. (3) Cable SPTAA-17080, PEMBARK to ETOUSA, 10 Mar 44.
[35] The detailed planning required at tactical levels to implement such logistical objectives is described in detail in McNamara *Memoir*, pp. 106-10.

[36] (1) McNamara *Memoir*, p. 111. (2) Ruppenthal, *Logistical Support*, I, 306-12.
[37] See ch. V, above.

move for months at a time. Such troops would receive the 10-in-1 ration, nutritionally the most satisfactory of the operational rations, plus whatever supplements of fresh foods could be sent forward to them under combat conditions.

The 10-in-1 ration was developed in the late summer of 1943, and when OVERLORD plans were being formulated it was still not completely tested in combat. It was essentially a simplified B ration for use in areas where the bulk-packed ordinary B ration could not be issued.[38] Two major points of criticism were directed against the 10-in-1 ration. Based on information furnished by OQMG, the new ration provided an average of 3,377 calories per man per day while the OCQM estimated that a combat soldier would require about 4,000 calories.[39] Accordingly, the ETO proposed to issue one case of 10-in-1 to eight soldiers engaged in strenuous activity, or 1.25 rations per man per day. Littlejohn also felt that field conditions on the Continent made it mandatory to provide some means of heating the ration.[40]

During October 1943 a field test was held in the ETO in which the 10-in-1 ration was used both alone and with various combinations of supplements. A ration board, made up of Quartermaster and Medical officers, conducted this test and concluded that 500 calories per man per day should be added to the ration, that additional hot beverages should be provided, and that the ration pack should include heating facilities.[41] The ETO proposal to requisition 10-in-1 rations on a basis of ten for eight men had been turned down by NYPE. The OCQM now proposed to achieve the increase in calories through a supplemental issue of the D ration chocolate bar.[42]

Though questioning whether the average soldier required as much as 4,000 calories, the OQMG had, in the interval between the original development of the ration and the end of 1943, raised the average content of the ration to 3,850 calories. It recognized the extra value of the heated ration but argued that the inclusion in each 10-in-1 pack of heat tablets or small stoves would be extremely wasteful. The ration would often be employed in situations where other sources of heat were available. The OQMG therefore planned to provide means of heating by making sep-

[38] Thatcher, *Development of Special Rations,* ch. VI.

[39] Early in 1943, the OCQM experimented with a 12-in-1 ration, locally assembled from B ration components and locally procured items. The project was handicapped by the unsuitable size of available components, and was abandoned when the OQMG's new 10-in-1 ration was announced. But while assembling and testing the 12-in-1, the OCQM had developed some ideas on nutrition, and as usual those ideas were at variance with the concepts of research and development personnel in the OQMG. Ltr, CQM to TQMG, 27 Apr 43, sub: Composite Ration for ETOUSA. ETO QM 430. Reprinted in full in USFET Gen Bd Study 109, app. 9.

[40] Ltr, Littlejohn to Frink, 23 Jul 43, no sub. MED 430.

[41] (1) Memo, CQM ETO for TQMG, 19 Nov 43, sub: Type 10-in-1 Rations. Littlejohn Collection, box 2, item 29. (2) Memo, Col. R. A. Isker, Dir QMC Subs Research Lab, for TQMG, 30 Nov 43, sub: Rpt on Tests of 10-in-1 Ration in the U.K. ETO 430.2.

[42] Memo, DCQM for President Ration Bd, 14 Nov 43, sub: Proposed Augmentation of Types 10-in-1, C, and K Rations; Memo, CQM for CG SOS ETO, 20 Nov 43, same sub. Both in USFET QM 400.3121.

arate issues of expendable supplies.[43] By the end of 1943 the form and size of the various operational rations used in the ETO were well stabilized. When the tactical plans became firm enough to permit detailed supply planning, the OCQM and lower quartermaster echelons knew what rations they had to work with.

A major problem remaining with respect to all nonperishable rations was to make them palatable. As already noted, First U.S. Army was the senior American headquarters in the assault, and Colonel McNamara was thus responsible for ration planning in the initial phase of operations. He regarded the 10-in-1 as superior to C and K rations in respect to both palatability and nutrition, but inferior to the B ration. He therefore planned to furnish the full B ration as early as possible and to as many troops as possible, using the combat rations only as long as transportation shortages and lack of handling facilities made this absolutely necessary. He also made plans for early supply of bread and perishables to augment the combat rations. This plan made it possible to issue whatever refrigerated food actually arrived in the forward areas, without waiting for the accumulation of balanced stocks necessary to issue an A ration.

Each individual was to carry one D and one K ration and four candle-type heat units on his person when disembarking, and each organization carried three C or K rations for its members. No unit was to draw rations until its third day ashore. During the first three days, maintenance and build-up rations would be shipped in the proportion of 60 percent C rations and 40 percent K rations. On D plus 4, 10-in-1 rations would begin to arrive, and on D plus 15, the first B rations, bread ingredients, and fresh coffee were scheduled. By the end of the first month, it was estimated, 50 percent of consumption would be B rations, 25 percent 10-in-1, and 25 percent C, D, and K rations.[44] After D plus 15 fresh bread at the rate of eight ounces per ration would be available for 40 percent of the troops, and by D plus 30, enough perishable foods to provide a rough equivalent of the A ration for 40 percent of all personnel on the far shore.[45]

Hospitals were to be provided with the 5-in-1 until the B ration became available. This was augmented by a 25-in-1 hospital supplement pack containing sugar, cocoa, and coffee, and canned milk, soup, and fruit juices. Requisitions of the hospital supplement were to build up during the first eleven days to 25,000 rations per day, and of the 5-in-1

---

[43] (1) Ltr, CQM to TQMG, 19 Nov 43, sub: Type 10-in-1 Rations, with 1st Ind, Doriot to CG ETO, Attention CQM, 9 Dec 43. Hist Br OQMG. (2) For operational rations, the final solution was to requisition one 1½-ounce heating candle with each C ration, and four 3-ounce candles with each 10-in-1 ration. A 4-ounce can of solidified alcohol was also available in limited quantities, and was to be issued as a substitute for the 3-ounce candle. No heat units were requisitioned with K rations because it was anticipated that a surplus from the C rations would be available at supply points if the troops desired them. Experience vindicated this ratio of heat units to operational rations. Cf. OTCQM TSFET Operational Study 14, exhibit A, p. 11, and ADSEC QM Estimates of Situation (10-day intervals), Oct 44–May 45.

[44] (1) Memo, QM FUSA for CQM, 2 Mar 44, sub: Class I Plan for an Opn on the Continent. Littlejohn Collection, sec. I. (2) FUSA Rpt of Opns, 20 Oct 43–1 Aug 44, III, 85.

[45] OTCQM TSFET Operational Study 14, exhibit A, sec. 3.

to 27,500 per day. These figures represent about 1.2 and 1.4 percent of anticipated troop strength respectively.[46]

Clothing and Equipment

The original date for D-day was 1 May 1944, so that plans provided for troops to take the field in clothing suited to late spring in a temperate zone climate. The First Army QM plan directed that all personnel go ashore in antigas protective clothing. The typical assault uniform was treated herringbone twill, either jacket and trousers or coverall, worn over untreated flannel olive drab shirt and woolen trousers. Less popular, but also worn by many of the men were impregnated woolen shirts and trousers. Since the weather would still be cool, the wool shirt and trousers would usually be worn with a jacket, either the 1941 Parsons type or the winter combat jacket. The Type III combat shoe was to be worn with protective socks and impregnated canvas leggings. Everyone wore untreated wool undershirts and drawers. The troops would carry, but not wear, protective hoods and gloves.[47]

An unmistakable lesson of Mediterranean combat was that too much clothing and equipment had been issued. The authorized allowance filled two barracks bags and weighed down the disembarking troops, who promptly abandoned most of it. All ETO headquarters were agreed that something should be done, but the final decision on specific items of equipment to be carried

ashore by the assault troops was made by General Bradley, on the advice of his army quartermaster, Colonel McNamara.[48] McNamara's concept centered on two main ideas: first, all troops should turn in their winter clothing to QM depots of SOS, which would reissue it on the Continent when needed; second, the combat troops in the assault should cut down their equipment to an absolute minimum. Troops of divisions, tank destroyer, field artillery, reconnaissance, and tank units fell into this category. The list of what they would wear and carry is very brief. (*Table 8*) They were directed to turn in all additional clothing and equipment at the nearest SOS Quartermaster installation on being alerted. Although the newly issued duffle bag was an improvement over the two barracks bags carried in North African operations, even this was judged too bulky for combat troops. Apart from items on their belts or in haversacks, they were to carry their equipment in a blanket roll on their organizational vehicles. Some troops in the first wave wore an assault jacket with six pockets to carry extra articles. Personal belongings, except items that could be carried in the pockets, were to be sent home or

---

[46] *FUSA Rpt of Opns*, 23 Oct 43–1 Aug 44, III, 86; VI, 199–201.

[47] *Ibid.*, III, 86.

[48] (1) See ch. VII, above. (2) According to T/E 21, 1 June 1944, the combined summer and winter allowances weighed 131 lbs. (3) Littlejohn had prepared a plan very similar to McNamara's. (See OTCQM TSFET Operational Study 14, app. B.) The best proof for the statement that the decision was made at army level is the fact that for Third Army, Patton and his quartermaster, Col. Everett Busch, permitted several units to bring along a complete outfit in a duffle bag for each soldier, on the insistence of their division commanders. But Busch later regretted this, for just as in North Africa, these bags had to be left behind, and not all of them could be found when they were needed.

PREINVASION TRAINING.   *Combat engineers aboard an LCI show the minimal clothing and equipment to be used for assault operations.   Slapton Sands, Devon, England, May 1944.*

to the QM Personal Effects Depot in Kansas City.   In his account of the episode, McNamara notes that these instructions evoked considerable surprise.   Some units ignored them entirely, and had to be relieved of their excess equipment in the staging areas.[49]

An analysis of Table 8 reveals that this was a very frugal allowance.   In addition to such parade ground items as neckties, garrison caps, and serge coats,

each man was to turn in two blankets, one wool undershirt, one pair of wool drawers, and a barracks bag.   The men in the combat units category would also give up two cotton drawers and two cotton undershirts, one herringbone twill jacket and trousers, one wool olive drab shirt and trousers, a duffle bag, and a pair of leggings.   Certain articles retained or added are also of interest.   Every man would have a raincoat—a necessity in the wet climate of northern France.   The direct issue of four heat tablets to each man indicated that the OQMG had turned down Littlejohn's urgent request that this item be included in the opera-

[49] (1) McNamara *Memoir*, pp. 40, 120. (2) Joseph H. Ewing, *29 Let's Go! A History of the 29th Infantry Division in World War II* (Washington: Infantry Journal Press, 1948), p. 36.

TABLE 8—EQUIPMENT OF ASSAULT TROOPS FOR NEPTUNE
(D-day to D-plus-44)

Items Worn by Individual

Number and Item
1 Belt, web, waist
1 Drawers, wool
1 Gloves, cotton, protective[a]
2 Handkerchiefs
1 Helmet, steel with liner
1 Hood, wool, protective[a]
1 Jacket, field, or jacket, combat, winter (when authorized)
1 Leggings, canvas, protective
1 Shirt, flannel, protective
1 Shoes, service, pair
1 Socks, wool, protective
1 Trousers, wool, protective
1 Undershirt, wool

Items Carried by Individual

Number and Item
1 Bag, canvas, field, with strap and suspenders when authorized
1 Belt, cartridge, pistol or BAR
1 Canteen
1 Cover, canteen
1 Cup, canteen
1 Haversack
1 Pack carrier
1 Pocket, magazine, double web or pocket, carbine
1 Pouch, first aid
2 Tags, identification, with necklace

Items in Haversack or Field Pack

Number and Item
1 Can, meat
1 Bottle halazone tablets
2 Handkerchiefs
4 Heat units—1½-oz.
1 Insecticide, 2-oz. can
1 Knife
1 Raincoat
3 Socks, wool, light, pairs
1 Socks, wool, protective
1 Spoon
  Toilet articles
1 Towel, huck

Items Carried in Blanket Rolls on Vehicles of Assault Units[b]

Number and Item
2 Blanket
1 Can, meat[d]
1 Drawers, cotton, short
1 Fork[d]
2 Handkerchiefs
1 Jacket, herringbone twill[c]
1 Knife[d]
5 Pins, tent, shelter half
1 Shoes, service
2 Socks, wool
1 Suit, herringbone twill[c]
1 Tent, shelter half and pole
1 Towel, bath
1 Trousers, herringbone twill[c]
1 Undershirt, cotton

[a] Items to be worn when and if ordered.

[b] Defined as divisions and tank destroyer, field artillery, reconnaisance, and tank units.

[c] If herringbone twill protective clothing was worn, it would be worn over regular OD flannel shirts and OD woolen trousers. Each unit would be initially clothed in either OD protective or herringbone twill protective clothing.

[d] Not carried by assault troops.

Source: Operation OVERLORD, First United States Army Plan, NEPTUNE, Annex 7, 25 February 1944.

tional ration. The insecticide and the halazone tablets used to purify drinking water were normal issues to men going into combat.

Men as lightly equipped as the assault troops would need prompt and adequate maintenance, and this was provided by beach maintenance sets. (*Appendix A*)

Starting on D plus 4 and continuing for 10 days, these sets were very successful in replacing lost, worn-out, or expended items of clothing, equipage, and general supplies. Each set contained 75,000 mandays of Class II and IV supply, but only on a scale to re-equip the troops with the items they had carried ashore. To quote the First Army after action report: "The articles were essential rather than ornamental, and the factors were accurate."[50] Here, then, was a combat-tested list of minimum requirements for an amphibious assault followed by two weeks of hard combat. While it is true that this scale of maintenance was adequate for a short time only, it represented a tremendous saving in supply and shipping space. As a specific instance, the per-man-per-day factor for this set was .3859 pounds, whereas the corresponding figure from earlier ETO planning tables was .8503 pounds.[51] Each set, consisting of 422 waterproofed packages weighing an average of about 68 pounds, totaled almost 13 long tons and was loaded on 18 skids for faster handling during the initial phase. By D plus 14, a total of 61 sets was scheduled to arrive, and on that day this system of supply would be discontinued.[52]

From D plus 14 through D plus 41, a considerably larger variety of Class II and IV supplies would be furnished through follow-up maintenance sets.[53]

(See Appendix A.) These sets, weighing 100 tons each, furnished replacement supplies for 450,000 man days. These packages were not assembled on skids. The additional articles were principally major nonexpendable items of equipment. The allowances of expendable supplies were considerably more generous, but the per-man-per-day factor was still only .485 pounds. By D plus 41 a total of 32 follow-up sets would be received in the beachhead. In general, the belief was that they were nearly as accurate as the factors for beach maintenance sets.[54] Beginning on D plus 43, full-scale maintenance requirements would be met by conventional supply methods.[55]

Liquid Fuels

Planning for motor fuels and lubricants for vehicles of the assault force did not begin as promptly as planning for food and clothing. The division of responsibilities for POL was not determined until mid-1943, and definitive directives were not issued until December 1943. This unstable situation paralleled that in the United States, where the exact function of the SOS, the Army-Navy Petroleum Board, the Quartermaster Corps, the Transportation Corps, and the Corps of Engineers with respect to

---

[50] FUSA Rpt of Opns, 20 Oct 43–1 Aug 44, an. 14, p. 134.

[51] QM Sv Reference Data, vol. II, 1 Jan 44, p. 83. The total was arrived at by combining Class II and IV factors.

[52] FUSA Rpt of Opns, 20 Oct 43–1 Aug 44, an. 14, p. 247.

[53] FUSA Rpt of Opns, 20 Oct 43–1 Aug 44, an. 14, pp. 242–46. In contrast to the 58 articles of the

beach maintenance set, the follow-up list comprised 128 items, plus special articles for tank crews, parachutists, and nurses.

[54] (1) FUSA Rpt of Opns, 20 Oct 43–1 Aug 44, an. 14, pp. 135, 247. (2) Before the last set was delivered, similar supplies began to arrive direct from the United States, making it impossible to evaluate accurately the effectiveness of the estimates.

[55] (1) OTCQM TSFET, Operational Study 14, an. B. (2) Littlejohn, ed., Passing in Review, ch. 14.

liquid fuels for a time remained uncertain. When the situation clarified in the zone of interior, POL at the army level became a Quartermaster Corps responsibility.[56] Parallel to developments in the Mediterranean theater, an Area Petroleum Board under General Lee came into being to represent all U.S. military agencies in dealing with the British and the Washington Army-Navy Petroleum Board and to decide questions about importation, storage, and use of POL. On 26 July 1943 the Chief Quartermaster, ETO, was charged with establishing combat requirements and making plans for control, storage, and distribution of all POL for U.S. forces on the Continent, except for items peculiar to the Army Air Forces.[57]

The chief problem facing Quartermaster Corps planners was determination of POL requirements for the assault and later operations on the Continent. Here the main obstacle was the absence of applicable data on which to base predictions of expenditures. Although planners could draw on British consumption figures for various campaigns since 1939 as well as on American experience in North Africa, Sicily, and the current campaign in southern Italy, they found that expenditure figures were not broken down in sufficient detail to be very useful. Moreover, such statistics could serve only as general rather than as specific guides. Basic factors in calculating requirements were the rate of consumption of each type of vehicle, the number of vehicles, and the so-called duration factor, which might more accurately have been called a mileage or distance factor. Vehicular consumption was the only factor in the equation that could be figured out with fair accuracy. The number-of-vehicles factor remained uncertain because the size and composition of the forces were subject to endless changes down to the last week before D-day. Moreover, tactical commanders had discretion to modify the organization of their units for the assault and to decide how many organic vehicles would accompany the initial waves of the landing. Motor vehicles would be among the largest and most vulnerable items of equipment in the assault. No estimate of vehicle losses during the first days could be more than a guess. Given all these variables, the conventional procedure of adding together vehicle totals derived from T/O&E's was virtually useless. Consequently, in the *QM Service Reference Data* which Littlejohn sent to the OQMG in January 1944, POL requirements were computed on a pounds-per-man-per-day basis.[58] This concept was predicated on the assumption that, in very large forces, the ratio of men to various types of vehicles would be fairly constant. It had already been adopted by Fifth Army in Italy.

The duration-of-operations factor was at once the most important and the most difficult to determine. It depended on the character and outcome of future

[56] (1) Memo for Record, CofS SOS ETO, 11 Jun 43, sub: ETO Staff Conf, 8 Jun 43, remarks of Gen Styer. USFET AG 337. (2) Risch, *Fuels for Global Conflict* (rev. ed.), pp. 8–10.

[57] (1) Memo, CQM for DTQMG, 30 Jun 43, sub: Pers for . . . the Supply of Petroleum Products. ETO 210.321. (2) Hist of POL in the ETO. ETO Admin 568. (3) Cir 46, SOS ETO USA, 26 Jul 43. (4) See ch. VI, above.

[58] (1) Ltr cited n. 21, with IRS, Littlejohn to Brumbaugh, attached. (2) *QM Sv Reference Data*, II, 51. (3) McNamara *Memoir*, p. 109.

TABLE 9—FORECAST OF POL CONSUMPTION PER MAN PER DAY

Typical Force[a]—Combat Conditions

	Percent	U.S. Gallons	Lbs. (Gross)	Net Weight (Lbs. Per Gallon)	Gallons (Per Net Long Ton)	Gallons (Per Gross Long Ton)
Gasoline (MT80)..........	81.75	[b]1.56	[b]12.68	6.1	368	276.57
Diesel fuel...............	14.15	[b].27	[b]2.12	7.115	315	267.82
Engine oils..............	3.67	.07	.605	7.466	300	259.58
Kerosene................	.26	.0049	.042	6.686	335	270.18
Greases.................	.17	.0032	.0318	7.5	298	231.02
Total POL...........	.....	1.9081	15.4788	.....	...	......

[a] Composition: 71 percent field forces, 8.7 percent Army Air Forces, 20.3 percent Services of Supply.

[b] Including fuel for powered equipment, cooking, and heating.

Sources: QM Service Reference Data, 1 Jan 44, II, 86; Littlejohn, ed., Passing in Review, ch. 18, an. B, Activities of the P&F Div, OCQM, by Col. Lyman R. Talbot and Lt. Col. Claud Ettele.

operations, with all the attendant variables and uncertainties. Important unknown elements in the equation were weather, length and development of lines of communication, and duration and effectiveness of enemy resistance. In an operation as big as OVERLORD, these elements would probably vary from place to place within the combat area. They were imponderables which could be estimated only roughly.

In July 1942 the ETO Chief of Transportation, at that time charged with POL supply, estimated the duration factor at 150 miles per day.[59] A year later—largely on the basis of experience in Tunisia— this figure had been much reduced. The British calculated an average vehicle range of fifty miles per day in combat and the OCQM substantially agreed.[60] By the end of 1943 more information was available on the numbers and types of vehicles that were to be employed on the Continent, and Lt. Col. Claud Ettele, the OCQM POL statistician, was able to submit some preliminary figures. Official consumption rates were available for each type of vehicle, but he decided that 20 percent should be added to allow for partially worn-out motors and other unfavorable conditions. On that basis he arrived at an average daily consumption of 8 U.S. gallons per wheeled vehicle, 24 per half-tracked vehicle, and 52 per full-tracked vehicle.[61] Estimates of the composition of the force and its fuel-consuming equipment suggested an average consumption of 1.9081 gallons per man per day. (*Table 9*)

Although these figures were still only approximations they were accepted by the Engineers, the Transportation Corps, and the COMZ G-4 for planning purposes. They were based on a heterogeneous force, composed of 71 percent

[59] Memo, OCOT ETO for G-4, 8 Jul 42, sub: Proposed System of Gasoline Supply. USFET AG 463.7, vol. I.

[60] (1) Memo, OCQM for CG SOS, 4 Jun 43, sub: Answers to Questions From War Dept. USFET AG 310.1. (2) See ch. VI, above.

[61] Ruppenthal, *Logistical Support*, I, 322.

field forces, 8.7 percent air force, and 20.3 percent SOS troops. If such a distribution did not materialize, consumption might be quite different, the estimates ranging from 2.10 gallons per man per day for field forces personnel alone to 1.14 gallons for SOS units. This meant that a variation in the composition of the force, all other factors remaining constant, could result in a difference of as much as 50 percent or more in POL consumption. Under the circumstances, refinements in estimating techniques meant relatively little. The OQMG questioned the validity of a 50-mile per day operational estimate, but approved a 20 percent allowance for age of vehicles and adverse conditions. Littlejohn pointed out that he had made no other allowance for loss from various causes, such as fire, leakage, pilfering, or enemy action. He contended that a rough rule-of-thumb estimate was likely to prove as accurate as a most carefully elaborated one.[62]

Even when tactical plans had matured to the point where the number and types of vehicles could be counted day by day, accuracy of consumption estimates could never be precise. Only as operations proceeded could estimates be brought into line with actual expenditures. In the end, planning was based on what appeared to be the best guess as to operational needs: 25 miles per day up to D plus 15, 50 miles per day thereafter.[63]

Roughly estimated in terms of gallons per man per day, this amounted to an expenditure rising from about 100,000 gallons (360 long tons) on D plus 1 to 450,000 gallons (1,600 long tons) on D plus 14. Moreover, these figures applied only to current requirements for ground operations. Total daily requirements including reserves would exceed 5,000 long tons by the latter date, and reach 7,350 tons by D plus 41.[64]

With such large quantities under consideration, the question of transportation was paramount. Experience in other theaters indicated that the ultimate solution lay in the movement of bulk gasoline by tanker ships, pipelines, tank cars, and tank trucks as far forward as the tactical situation would permit. Once a lodgment area had been secured and organized, responsibility for this rearward phase of the problem would be shared by the Engineers and the Transportation Corps.[65] The Quartermaster Corps was entirely in accord with this arrangement. Its own POL units were trained and equipped to decant gasoline into five-gallon jerricans, and to move it forward as dry cargo to the combat units.[66] But one major question remained unanswered. How soon could a

---

[62] (1) Littlejohn, ed., Passing in Review, ch. 18, Activities of the P&F Div, OCQM, p. 6. (2) Memo, OQMG to OCQM, 1 May 44, sub: Comments on QM Sv Reference Data, and 1st Ind. ETO 463. (This was in answer to Littlejohn's Memo of 13 January, cited in n. 23, above.)

[63] Opns Plan NEPTUNE, an. 7, QM Plan (printed in FUSA Rpt of Opns, 23 Oct 43–1 Aug 44).

[64] (1) Computed by the author from personnel build-up figures as given in Ruppenthal, Logistical Support, I, 298. (2) Hq FECOMZ, Communications Zone Plan, 14 May 44, app. P (POL). ETO Admin 376.

[65] Engineer and Transportation responsibilities, plans, and operations with regard to POL for NEPTUNE are discussed at length in Ruppenthal, Logistical Support, I, especially pages 319–26, and in Bykofsky and Larson, The Transportation Corps: Operations Overseas, Chapter VI.

[66] The jerrican and Mediterranean decanting operations are described in Chapter VI, above. See also Chapter XVIII, below.

bulk system be placed in operation? For quartermasters this really meant: how long will jerricans, brought in over the beaches, remain the source of POL supply on the Continent?

The Engineers and the POL Section, G–4, were confident that bulk POL would be available on the Continent in sufficient quantities for all purposes by D plus 30, but the various Quartermaster organizations concerned decided to provide packaged supplies for current consumption and reserves through D plus 90 if possible. The required quantities were computed at approximately 275,000 long tons, and the limiting factor was the supply of jerricans. The decision finally reached was that packaged POL would be supplied in sufficient quantities to carry the entire force through D plus 41, in case the Engineer plan could not be carried out on schedule. Moreover, all available jerricans were to be filled before being transported across the Channel, and were to arrive during the first 90 days. Subdividing their responsibilities by phases, the various Quartermaster agencies requisitioned the following quantities of POL for delivery to QM depots in the United Kingdom: [67]

Period	Agency	Long Tons (All Products)
D to D plus 14	QM First Army	48,576
D plus 15 to D plus 41	QM ADSEC	85,998
D plus 42 to D plus 90	QM FECOMZ	60,403
Total		194,977

Fifth Army experience in Italy indicated that combat units in action received 88 percent of their gasoline in five-gallon cans.[68] This confirmed earlier British experience, demonstrating that the jerrican was a combat item of major importance and would have to be provided in adequate quantities. The determination of can requirements involved the consideration of two factors: the number of cans needed for initial equipment of vehicles and the number required to maintain forward distribution of gasoline. The first factor was relatively simple; it could be calculated from unit T/O&E's once the composition of the force was settled. The second factor depended on the time that would elapse between the issue of a full can and its return empty to the refilling point. This would determine the number of cans in circulation at any given time and the rate of loss through various causes. The loss factor could be calculated, though only roughly, on the basis of past experience. But the circulation factor, depending as it did on the character of the fighting, was subject to such wide variations as to defy advance calculations. Predictions of can requirements were as uncertain as estimates of gasoline requirements, and in defiance of logic came to be influenced by can production capacity as well.[69]

---

[67] (1) Littlejohn, ed., Passing in Review, ch. 18, pp. 8–12. (2) These requisitions amounted to about 52,000,000 gallons, or enough to fill 10,400,000 jerricans. (3) See Table 7.

[68] The balance was provided: 3.5 percent in 55-gallon drums; 3.2 percent in tank trucks or trailers; 5.1 percent directly from bulk containers at roadside. See ch. VI, above.

[69] (1) Colonel Evans commented bitterly on this irrational tendency in high-level logistical planning. Ltr cited n. 17, above. (2) Leighton and Coakley (Global Logistics, 1940–1943, page 435) referred to a similar situation involving shipping as "cutting the foot to fit the shoe," and noted that in modern warfare it is hardly ever possible to make good such deficits at a later date.

Estimates in August 1942, based on a cross-Channel operation around 1 April 1943, arrived at a can requirement of 6,000,000, including 400,000 to be used for water. The OCQM was still using this figure in November 1942, although there was a growing recognition that the five-gallon can would probably be used more extensively than had first been thought.[70] By June 1943 strategic plans had greatly changed and can requirements had been completely revised. These were now calculated at 11,500,-000 through the first quarter of 1944, the total quantity expected from British and United States sources. All but 1,000,000 cans were being manufactured in the United Kingdom.[71]

This total appeared so high to the OQMG that it suspected the ETO of preparing to use its resources for the direct supply of other theaters, notably North Africa. But all 11,500,000 were intended for the ETO alone.[72] This figure, which represented the maximum available supply for D-day, was justified by estimates based on a 10 percent loss factor and a 7-day turnaround. British staff planners, meanwhile, using 15 percent for loss and 13-day turnaround, calculated that American requirements through 1944 would amount to nearer

20,000,000 cans. This estimate was rejected by the OCQM, partly because no such quantity could be procured within the time limits, but both calculations, while they could be refined ad infinitum, were admittedly uncertain.[73] The final decision had to be made on the basis of the best judgment of those responsible. This is what Littlejohn meant when he wrote later to Brig. Gen. Wayne R. Allen, who, as general purchasing agent, had made all production arrangements with the British, "I wish to recall the day that you and I stood in London, threw our slide rules and computors out of the window, got down to facts, and estimated 15½ million jerricans as required to mount an operation on the Continent. This figure has been so accurate that it has been astounding."[74]

Special Arrangements for Support of the Beachhead

The authorized stock levels, supplemented by PROCO projects, furnished the Quartermaster Corps with necessary supplies, but the responsibility for moving these supplies to the Continent lay with the Transportation Corps. Since the availability of required items on the far shore would determine the success or failure of its mission, the ETO Quartermaster Service co-operated closely with the Transportation Corps in trying to make shipment plans successful. To facilitate the movement of supplies over open beaches and to protect supplies stored in the open, the decision was made early that all items for the assault

---

[70] Memo, G–4 ETO for Reqmts Div SOS WD, 22 Aug 42, sub: Gasoline Distr Equip; Comment 3, OCQM to G–4, 7 Nov 42, on IRS, Supply Br G–4 ETO to QM Sec, 4 Nov 42, sub: Revised Status of 5-Gallon Returnable Petrol Containers. Both in USFET AG 463.7.

[71] Memo, OCQM for TQMG, 11 Jun 43, sub: Petrol Containers. ETO 457.

[72] (1) Memo, Col. H. E. Rounds, OQMG, for Col. W. E. R. Covell, 16 Jun 43, sub: Gasoline Containers Manufactured in U.K. ETO 457. (2) Memo, Area Petroleum Off for GPA ETO, 28 Jun 43, sub: Containers, and 3d Ind, OCQM to Area Petroleum Sv, 8 Jul 43. USFET Petroleum Off 458.1.

[73] QM Supply in ETO, IV, 32.

[74] Memo, CQM for GPA, 27 Mar 45, no sub. USFET GPA 457.

phase must be packed in containers which, if not completely waterproof, were at least reasonably impervious to water; also, as far as the divisibility of supplies permitted, all packages must be small and light enough to be moved without mechanical aids, 100 pounds gross per package being considered the maximum.[75] The OCQM lacked labor, materials, and depot space for repacking in the United Kingdom and therefore requested that the OQMG give most careful attention to the requirement for waterproof packing.[76] The OQMG eased this problem somewhat by developing waterproof laminated burlap tubing for use in repacking supplies that were not in acceptable containers.[77] On hearing about this development the ETO Quartermaster Service immediately requested shipment of 15,000 yards of the tubing but reiterated its general requirements for amphibious packing.[78]

The flow of amphibiously packed supplies into the theater in itself created new problems. To have these supplies readily available when needed and to prevent their dissipation by issue for current consumption, depots in the United Kingdom were instructed to inventory amphibiously packed supplies separately from ordinary stocks and to keep them physically apart. This stipulation added substantially to the physical and bookkeeping burdens of the depots. Depot commanders and base section quartermasters complained that such special stock control was almost impossible because of constant addition of new items and also because of labor and space shortages. Furthermore, they alleged that the program was hindered by the difficulty of distinguishing between amphibious and ordinary varieties of packages and also by the poor quality of much of the special packing. Admitting the validity of such complaints, the OCQM maintained that the quality of amphibious packing would shortly improve and insisted that, despite the added effort, the segregation of amphibious stocks was indispensable to the rapid movement of these supplies once the details of the offensive operation were settled.[79]

To improve control of amphibious stocks and reduce demands on transportation, supply planners decided in January 1944 to concentrate them in depots G–35 at Bristol and G–40 at Barry, on either side of the Bristol Channel. This area was to be the center for U.S. supply to the Continent in the early phases of OVERLORD, and these depots were selected as the major Quartermaster reserve installations for the first thirty days of the operation. To enable the two depots to perform this special mission, involving the storage and rapid dispatch

---

[75] Memo, OCQM for CG SOS ETO, 4 Jun 43, sub: Answers to Questions From WD to CG SOS. USFET AG 310.1.

[76] Memo, DCQM for TQMG, 15 Jun 43, sub: Packing of Supply . . . From the U.K. USFET QM 400.162.

[77] Ltr, OQMG to CQM, 17 Jun 43, no sub. USFET QM 457.

[78] Ltr, OQMG to CQM, 9 Jul 43, no sub. ETO 420.

[79] (1) Memo, QM SBS for OQMG, 23 Sep 43, sub: Warehousing Amph-Packed Rations, and 1st Ind. USFET QM 400.2. (2) Memo, OCQM for Chief of Opns SOS, 1 Dec 43, sub: Situation Rpt—Specifications for Amph-Packed Supplies. USFET QM 000.4. (3) Memo, OQMG for CQM, 23 Dec 43, sub: Amph-Packed QM Supplies. ETO 400.162.

of over 28,000 tons of operational supplies, part of their responsibility for current supply had to be shifted to other depots.[80]

"Type loading" was another improved transportation technique. The Quartermaster Corps and other technical services co-operated with the Transportation Corps in developing this plan for loading supplies for direct shipment from the United States to the Continent without intermediate storage in the United Kingdom. The procedure involved loading the holds of ships with balanced lots of each supply category needed to support the assault forces at different operational stages. Items destined for the United Kingdom could be loaded on the decks of the transatlantic vessels, while special "bricks" of balanced supplies were stored in the holds. These were not unloaded in England but taken directly to the Continent as soon as the beachhead could receive them. The ETO technical services estimated that about 150,000 tons could be handled in this way and that the QMC share would be 40,000 to 50,000 dead-weight tons.[81]

The ultimate value of the type loading procedure depended on skillful selection of the supplies making up the bricks. The OCQM therefore calculated very carefully the needs of the assault force in the period between D plus 31 and D plus 90 when the type

loaded cargoes would be available on the Continent. Two types of ration bricks were decided on, one for delivery from D plus 31 through D plus 60, containing 57 percent balanced B ration components, 23 percent 10-in-1, 10 percent C, and 10 percent K rations, plus supplementary D rations and heat units. The second type, for the period D plus 61 through D plus 90, contained 68 percent B rations, 14 percent 10-in-1, 9 percent C, and 9 percent K, plus D rations and heat units. Each brick weighed 500 tons; the first type contained 210,000 rations, the second 220,000. For clothing and equipage only one type of brick was provided. It contained a slightly more varied list of items than the follow-up maintenance sets, weighed 626 tons, and provided maintenance for 50,000 men for 30 days.[82]

To speed handling of supplies in the assault, the Transportation Corps proposed that they be loaded on skids for use in the phase immediately following the landing of the assault waves. This technique provided that a quantity of supplies—not more than 3,000 pounds because of the limited carrying and handling facilities of the vessels and vehicles involved—should be attached with metal straps to a wooden platform mounted on wooden runners, making it possible to treat the supplies as a unit rather than as individual packages. It will be recalled that skids had been used successfully in the invasion of Sicily. In October 1943 the OCQM agreed to co-operate in experiments to determine the usefulness of skidloads for

---

[80] IRS, DCQM London to DCQM Cheltenham, 27 Jan 44, sub: Distribution of Amph-Packed Supplies, and Comment 2, 10 Feb 44. Littlejohn Collection, sec. II.

[81] (1) Memo, Chief P&T Div for DCQM, 21 Dec 43, sub: Type Loading of Cargo Ships for Shipment to Continent. USFET QM 000.4. (2) Memo, CG SOS ETO for CG NYPE, 21 Jan 44, sub: Type Loading. USFET QM 400.3.

[82] OTCQM TSFET, Operational Study 14, exhibit A, app. E.

cross-Channel operations.[83] Tests in the United Kingdom led the Transportation Corps to conclude that skidloads would make for more rapid handling, simplified control procedures, and better protection of supplies than was possible in moving separate packages. That service believed that the additional labor required to assemble the skidloads in the United Kingdom would be more than offset by the greater ease of handling on the beachhead.[84] Quartermaster personnel, on the other hand, were less enthusiastic about skids.[85] The OCQM, better acquainted than the Transportation Corps with depot labor and space problems, was particularly concerned about the unavoidable loss of cargo space —estimated at 25 percent—caused by the fact that large units could not be stowed aboard ship as advantageously as smaller separate packages. But recognizing that skidloads permitted faster handling (provided the essential fork-lift trucks, cranes, and winches were available as planned), it agreed to adopt the procedure.[86]

A conference in January 1944 between OCQM officers and Colonel McNamara resulted in the decision to use skidloads for packaged combat rations up to D plus 10. Clothing and equipage, in the form of beach maintenance sets, which were made up of tight bales and shoe boxes and therefore better adapted to strapping than ordinary packages, would also be loaded on skids until D plus 14. POL in cans and drums would be transported in skidloads after D plus 3. In all, 4,448 tons of rations, 386 tons of clothing and equipage, and over 16,000 tons of POL were involved.[87]

Experiments with various sizes and types of skidloads continued through the spring of 1944, but no change was made in the original decision to limit their weight to about 3,000 pounds so that the skids could be handled by cargo gear on small ships, and so that two skids would make a load for a Dukw or a 2½-ton truck.[88] But when the proposal was made to extend the use of skidloads to D plus 120, the OCQM objected. It felt that the additional drain on depot labor, facilities, and materials would not be justified once the special unloading problems of the initial assault phase had been overcome.[89]

Special arrangements for support of the airborne troops were limited in scope, since these troops were expected to link up with the seaborne forces very early. Like other assault troops, the parachutists packed blanket rolls to be

[83] (1) See ch. III, above. (2) Memo, S&D Div OCQM for DCQM, 16 Oct 43, no sub. USFET QM 427. (3) The Seventh Army did not, however, consider palletizing loads an unqualified success, at least for combat-loaded vessels. See Memo, CG Seventh Army for CofT AFHQ, 7 Sep 43, sub: Palletizing Supplies. Seventh Army AG 400.16.

[84] Memo, OCT for CofT ETO, 25 Nov 43, sub: Proposal to Skidload Supplies Moving in the Initial Stages of Continental Opns. SOS TC 400.2.

[85] Memo, S&D Div OCQM for DCQM, 10 Mar 44, sub: Skidloads Class II and IV Supplies. USFET QM 400.2.

[86] Memo, Capt R. M. Walrath for Col Stevens, Chief S&D Div [ca. Nov 43], sub: Rpt on Amph Unloading Skidloads. USFET QM 400.112.

[87] Memo, P&T Div OCQM for Supply Div et al., 29 Jan 44, sub: Skidloading Supplies; Memo, same to same, 12 Feb 44, sub: Skidloading; Table Plan for Skidloading of OVERLORD. All in Hist Br OQMG.

[88] Memo, QM WBS for OCQM, 13 Mar 44, sub: Skidloading of Class I Supplies; Memo, S&D Div OCQM for DCQM, 26 Mar 44, same sub. Both in USFET QM 400.2.

[89] IRS, G–4 SOS to OCQM, 19 Apr 44, sub: Proposed Extension of Skidloading Program, and reply, 22 Apr 44. Littlejohn Collection, box 13.

brought to them later on unit vehicles. As already noted, First Army's follow-up maintenance sets included special airborne Class II items. Since the organic airborne Quartermaster companies of the divisions were included in their seaborne echelons, supply support at the take-off airfields was provided by units of IX Air Force Service Command. The 2d QM Depot Supply Company had been earmarked for aerial resupply support, and its men packed supplies in canvas containers for parachute dropping. The XVIII Corps (Airborne) had arranged for five days of supply (packed) and three days (unpacked) for each division to be held at the take-off airfields to cover any emergency. At dusk on D-day gliders were to land reinforcements and supplies for the two divisions. Only one parachute resupply was planned—a daylight drop on D plus 1. This was automatic supply, to be landed on prearranged drop zones. Each division was to receive about 240 tons, to be dropped by the 50th and 52d Troop Carrier Wings.[90]

As the date for launching the cross-Channel assault approached, storage and distribution problems, already intensified by the accumulation of huge quantities of supplies, were further complicated by special preparations for supporting the forces on the far shore. Quartermaster tonnage arriving in the United Kingdom increased from 69,000 in January 1944 to 139,000 in May.[91]

Transportation Corps attempts to deal promptly with vastly increased imports led, unavoidably, to a partial breakdown of the expert handling procedures ETO had been accustomed to. There were complaints, reminiscent of early 1943, about the strain on depot operations as well as the need to re-sort and reshuffle misdirected supplies, but the improved efficiency of the Transportation Corps and the validity of the system of using sorting sheds were demonstrated by the steady decline in the proportion of inter-depot shipments to total tonnage received.[92] To achieve this improvement despite rapid unloading in ports and depots, road and rail congestion, and special embargoes on movement into southern England, required careful cooperation between British and American agencies.[93]

OCQM Plans for Use of Quartermaster Troops

Just as supply planning was carried on even before the detailed tactical plan for OVERLORD was worked out, so was planning for the use of Quartermaster troops. Organization and training of troop units took so long that they could not have been achieved in time had they not started long before final decisions were made on the cross-Channel assault. Personnel for Table of Organization units, the regular organizations which made up the great mass of the Quartermaster Service, involved the question of

---

[90] (1) John C. Warren, Airborne Operations in World War II, European Theater, USAF Historical Study 97, (The Air University, 1956), pp. 75–76. (2) Maj. James A. Huston, Airborne Operations, ch. VII, p. 96. Draft MS, n.d., OCMH.

[91] IRS, Exec Div OCQM to CQM, 17 Jun 44, sub: Better Utilization of Sorting Sheds. Littlejohn Collection, sec. II.

[92] IRS, Chief S&D Div to CQM, 7 Jul 44, sub: Proposed IRS to CofT. Littlejohn Collection, sec. II.

[93] Special Monthly Report, CofT to G-4 SOS, 2 May 44, sub: Congestion of Ports and Depots and Unusual Long or Cross Hauls. EUCOM 319.1.

the whole theater troop basis and the fluctuating QMC portion thereof. The total number of American troops coming to the United Kingdom at any given time was determined by the transportation available and by current commitments in other parts of the world. This figure was calculated at the highest levels of strategic planning and announced to the theater on appropriate occasions. The theater staff could do little to influence its size, but it could, in agreement with the War Department, establish priorities for the movement of units of different types within the planned totals.

The proportion of service troops in the whole force was subject to pressure arising from the high command's desire to build an effective fighting force as rapidly as possible and from the prevailing attitude of judging effectiveness largely by the number of troops available for direct combat with the enemy. That the full impact of a fighting force depended heavily upon the efficiency of its supply system was a fact which received inadequate recognition outside SOS ranks.[94]

When plans were being made for the build-up in the United Kingdom, the technical services had little to support their arguments for a given proportion of the troop basis. Such information on the support capability of specific Quartermaster units as existed in 1942 and

1943 was not derived from extensive combat experience in World War II and the OCQM often fell back on World War I observations which were not available in detail and were not strictly comparable. Even within SOS some of the other technical services could point out the greater technical proficiency required of their personnel, and make a stronger case for their units as essential in combat. Consequently, whenever pressure was exerted to reduce the SOS proportion of the troop list, the less skilled troops of Quartermaster Service suffered, and the miscellaneous personnel who were assigned to quartermaster duties in emergencies were rarely satisfactory.[95]

The first BOLERO plan of May 1942 provided that 53,000, or slightly more than 5 percent of the total force and 19 percent of the SOS, were to be Quartermaster troops. The second BOLERO plan of July 1942 increased the total United States forces expected in the United Kingdom by April 1943 to 1,147,000 but reduced the Quartermaster component to 39,000, or 15 percent of SOS and 3.5 percent of the whole force. This figure, the all-time low for the ETO Quartermaster Service, was far short of the 51,-324 Quartermaster troops that the Chief Quartermaster considered essential for a force of this size.[96] From the spring of 1943, when plans were drafted anew for the creation of a large striking force in Britain, the Quartermaster proportion

---

[94] (1) General Middleswart, QM NATOUSA, agrees emphatically with this statement. (2) Brig. Gen. Everett Busch, QM Third Army, remarks in this connection: "Too many in responsible command assignments took supply—even over-supply—for granted." Critical comments on preliminary MS version of this history, 10 Oct–15 Nov 54. Hist Br OQMG.

[95] USFET Gen Bd Study 128, pp. 29–30.

[96] (1) Memo, CQM for TQMG, 8 Aug 42, sub: Troop Reqmts, QM Sv SOS ETO. ETO 320.2. (2) See Ruppenthal, *Logistical Support*, Volume I, Chapter III, for an analysis of early difficulties in computing a satisfactory troop basis for the SOS.

of American troops was alternately raised and lowered in successive revisions.[97]

In calculating the Quartermaster troop list the Chief Quartermaster was confronted with a twofold problem: he had to provide quartermaster services for the troops involved in the prelanding build-up and also for the force ultimately to be engaged in the liberation of Europe. The War Department placed major emphasis on preparations for the assault, and directed the Chief Quartermaster to pattern his build-up force closely on the needs of the assault force. This task was made difficult both by the vagueness of the assault plans, which did not really begin to crystallize until six months before D-day, and by the drawn-out period of the build-up, which put substantial numbers of troops and immense quantities of supplies in the United Kingdom long before the assault.

The interval between the arrival of Quartermaster units and the troops they were to support was always too short, and sometimes all troops arrived simultaneously.[98] While ASF appreciated the importance of getting service troops to the theater ahead of the combat troops, the heavy demands from other theaters and the shortage of selectees made it impossible to carry out this policy.[99] Since the OCQM had intended to use the same service units scheduled for OVERLORD to assist also in the final preparations for the assault, their delayed arrival threatened to disrupt the schedule of the mounting operation.[100]

The technical services tried to distribute their limited numbers so as to give the highest priority to support of the assault, but they were handicapped by the tardy development of definitive operational plans. Although service programs were based on the best available estimate of tactical plans, as late as April 1944 new tactical plans were being developed which called for a 50 percent rise in the rate of build-up and double the rate of advance scheduled by the technical services. These new plans necessarily caused a severe strain on scarce service personnel.[101]

A partial solution to the shortage of Quartermaster units was found in the employment of British and North Irish civilian labor, as already described, but most SOS demands had to be met by U.S. troops. Quartermaster strength rose from just over 30,000 at the end of 1943 to more than 72,000 by the end of June 1944, but because of the rapid influx of other troops during the same period the Quartermaster proportion of military personnel rose only from about 4 percent to something less than 4.5 percent.[102]

---

[97] (1) Memo, CQM for CG SOS ETO, 18 Mar 43, sub: Flow Chart for QMC Troops. Littlejohn Collection, sec. II. (2) See also p. 254, above.

[98] (1) Memo, CQM for CG SOS ETO, 18 Mar 43, sub: Flow Chart for QMS troops. Littlejohn Collection, sec. II. (2) Memo, Sv Troop Br for ExO G–4, 3 Jul 44, sub: ETO Sv Troop Build-up for Operation OVERLORD. ETO 370.092, Admin 145A.

[99] Notes, Conf Between Devers and Chiefs of Svs, 7 May 43. USFET AG 337.

[100] (1) IRS, G–3 to CG SOS, 14 Dec 43, no sub. USFET QM 000.4. (2) Memo, Sv Troop Br for ExO G–4, 3 Jul 44, sub: ETO Sv Troop Build-up for Opn OVERLORD. ETO 370.092, Admin 145A. (3) Comment 3, CQM to Chief Opns SOS, 16 Dec 43, on IRS, G–3 to CG SOS, 14 Dec 43, no sub. USFET QM 000.4. (4) Comment FECZ, n.d., on Ltr, FUSAG, 28 Feb 44, sub: U.S. Cargo Shipping Reqmts Opn OVERLORD. ADSEC COMZ 384.

[101] Cable E–24140, Lee to AGWAR, 20 Apr 44, no sub; Cable E–25349, Eisenhower to AGWAR, 28 Apr 44, no sub.

[102] Memo, CQM for Chief Pers Div, 7 Oct 44, no sub. Littlejohn Reading File, vol. XXIX, item 42.

These figures embraced all Quartermaster troops in the theater, those earmarked for tactical units as well as those permanently assigned to SOS. Eventually about 70 percent of these troops would be in the SOS and 30 percent in the field forces, but the situation in the United Kingdom prior to D-day compelled the OCQM to delay assignments of Quartermaster troops to field forces and retain a high percentage for SOS functions. This was possible because the geographical intermingling of SOS and field force units, otherwise often disadvantageous, enabled most of the field troops to draw their support direct from SOS installations, without the use of their organic Quartermaster units. While the practice had some harmful effects on the co-ordination of training between the combat elements of the field forces and their organic Quartermaster units, it was often possible to postpone the actual assignment of the service units until the combat forces completed their training and braced themselves for the cross-Channel attack.

Quartermaster units were also shifted among organizations scheduled to reach the Continent at different times. Units destined, for example, for eventual assignment to Third Army, scheduled not to go into action until the end of July, were used by the Engineer special brigades or First Army units which participated in the first phase of the assault. In the same way service units earmarked for the Ninth Army were used temporarily by the Third Army pending activation of the former organization.[103]

The reassignment procedure did not always proceed smoothly. Planners agreed that the best trained and most experienced QM units would be turned over to organizations going into combat —the armies, corps, and divisions, the Engineer special brigades, and ADSEC. But it was precisely these units which the hard-pressed rear installations wanted most to keep. The OCQM tried to arrange transfers so as to do the least possible damage to the losing organizations, taking into account current and future operations and going so far as to suggest, as late as 15 April 1944, that valuable units assigned to First Army be permitted to remain at work in SOS installations and there be given whatever additional tactical training the army thought necessary. This careful juggling of unit assignments and reassignments complicated administration, but it allowed the OCQM some leeway in performing essential functions.[104]

Meanwhile, in an attempt to reduce the size and increase the flexibility of all service organizations, the Quartermaster Corps in the summer of 1943 had acquired several new types of administrative units.[105] The need for such units to provide a system of subordinate logistical headquarters has already been noted. The newly authorized organizations were a revised headquarters and headquarters detachment, QM battalion, a similar mobile QM battalion headquarters, a QM group headquarters, and a headquarters and headquarters com-

---

[103] Memo, CG TUSA through CG FUSAG for CG ETO, 27 Jun 44, sub: QM Units for Third Army, plus Inds. USFET AG 322 (QM).

[104] (1) Memo, QM WBS for CQM, 29 Nov 43, sub: Priority of Alert for Depot Supply Cos. USFET QM 000.4. (2) Memo, QM WBS for CQM, 1 Apr 44, sub: Reassignment of QM Troops From SOS to Field Forces, and 1st Ind. EUCOM 322.

[105] WD Cir 256, 16 Oct 43.

pany, QM base depot. The new battalion headquarters could each supervise and administer as many as ten Quartermaster companies. In theory, the battalion headquarters detachment (mobile) would administer mobile-type Quartermaster units, especially truck companies, but in many cases the two types of battalions were used interchangeably. They replaced headquarters of salvage, service, bakery, truck, and gasoline supply battalions, so that henceforth any QM battalion could be homogeneous or mixed. The strength of the two units was nearly the same: the battalion headquarters detachment contained 5 officers and 12 enlisted men; the mobile type had 2 more enlisted men. The group headquarters replaced various types of regiments; with 10 officers and 25 enlisted men, it could supervise and administer three or more QM battalions, irrespective of their type or functions. These battalions and groups were assigned to armies as well as to COMZ and the base sections.[106]

The headquarters and headquarters company, Quartermaster base depot, was also a new organization, authorized only since July 1943. These units were to be assigned within COMZ only; they were designed to provide administrative personnel for the Quartermaster section of a general depot or a major Quartermaster depot. Mediterranean experience indicated that such an organization was able to provide most of the Quartermaster staff of a base section headquarters, handling all inspections, training, local procurement, and supply control, as well as ad-

ministering subordinate QMC units. These new organizations were capable of assuming responsibility for routine administrative detail, promoting a desirable degree of decentralization and reducing the burden of the OCQM and the base sections.[107]

The advantages of all these innovations in active operations were immediately evident to the OCQM, which had already proposed an organization along similar lines.[108] That office asked permission to activate two headquarters and headquarters companies, QM base depot, without waiting for such units to be trained in the zone of interior. The stated purpose was to provide a suitable QM organization for Eastern and Western Base Sections when they followed combat troops across the Channel, and incidentally to convert casual personnel to T/O status.[109]

Attempts to secure the men to make up units of the new types by drawing on the SOS in the theater or direct from the zone of interior were only partly successful because of the theater personnel ceiling. The OCQM therefore resorted to breaking up or reducing one type of unit to get the "bodies" needed to activate or increase units of another type. For this purpose the large field bakery units

---

[106] Detailed descriptions, T/O&E's, and evaluations of these units are given in OTCQM TSFET Operational Study 10.

[107] (1) Memo, CQM for QM FECZ, 19 May 44, sub: Orgn and Functioning of the QM Sv in the Theater of Opns. Littlejohn Reading File, vol. XXIV, item 63. (2) Ltr, CQM to TQMG, 2 Jan 45, sub: Transmission of Hist Data Concerning QM Opns in the ETO. ETO 321. (3) See ch. IV, above.

[108] Ltrs, CQM to CO's WBS, SBS, EBS, 3–4 May 43, no sub. Littlejohn Reading File, vol. XII, items 9, 15, 16.

[109] Memo, CQM for Chief of Admin SOS, 30 Oct 43, sub: Activation of Hq and Hq Co, QM Base Depot. Littlejohn Reading File, vol. XVII, item 104.

furnished a timely reservoir of man-power, thanks to the ability of the British to supply the Americans with some of their excellent labor-saving equipment. By disbanding 14 American bakery companies of 168 men each and activating 19 British-equipped bakery companies (mobile), the OCQM simultaneously raised the bread-baking capacity and obtained 756 men for use elsewhere.[110] This procedure also accelerated the building up of the Quartermaster Service in the ETO, since the personnel credit came from companies due to arrive in October and November 1944, and the base depot headquarters units, using available non-T/O personnel, were to be activated immediately.[111]

To form new units and overcome the lag in shipment of QM troops from the zone of interior, Littlejohn arranged for the transfer to the Quartermaster Corps of 2,300 surplus replacements who had accumulated in the theater ground force replacement system by June 1944, and to these were added approximately 3,200 men obtained through a 10 percent reduction in basics in all types of Quartermaster units. The reduction made soldiers, even though relatively untrained available without depriving the

losing units of their specialists. During the summer of 1944 a training program was inaugurated in the United Kingdom which processed these men into eighty-eight units, including group headquarters, fixed and mobile battalion headquarters, railhead companies, service companies, and a variety of composite units.[112]

Local activations, while helpful, were only a minor factor in the build-up of Quartermaster units. All planning for the use of Quartermaster troops had to be based on lists of units actually present, or definitely scheduled to arrive in the theater. (Table 10) Naturally, First Army, about to be committed in combat, had received a generous allocation, including troops to be transferred later to ADSEC and others on loan from SOS to be attached to the Engineer special brigades. In comparison, the meager allocation to Third Army is clearly evident. By the time Third Army was scheduled to become operational (about D plus 60), the hope was that troop arrivals from the United States would make up this deficit.

The Third Army requirements for QM units as shown in Table 10 present a typical Army-level QM organization in the European theater at the time. Such allocations varied slightly from army to army, in accordance with the desires of the individual army quartermaster and the current availability of units.[113] The

[110] This was merely a first installment of manpower dividends from this procedure. Ultimately, the OCQM organized a total of 55 mobile-type bakery companies, representing a personnel saving of 4,620 men, with additional advantages of efficiency and mobility. See ch. XV, below.

[111] (1) Memo, CQM for CG SOS, 10 Mar 44, sub: Modification of Troop Basis. Littlejohn Reading File, vol. XXII, item 24. (2) Ltr, Col A. Bliss, OCQM, to Col K. L. Hastings, OQMG, 10 Mar 44, no sub; Memo, OCQM for G–4 and G–3, 17 Mar 44, sub: Reorgn of QM Bakery Co. Both in Littlejohn Collection, sec. II.

[112] (1) AGF Rpt 974, 22 May 45, sub: Activation and Training of QM Units in the U.K. ASF 319.1 EUCOM. (2) Memo, CQM for G–1 and G–4, 20 Jun 44, sub: Conversion of QM Sv non-T/O Allotments Into T/O units. Littlejohn Reading File, vol. XXV, item 52.

[113] IRS, CQM to G–4, COMZ, 25 Jun 44, sub: QM Troop Basis for Third Army. Littlejohn Reading File, vol. XXV, item 60.

Table 10—QM Units Assigned to First and Third Armies and SOS ETOUSA
2 June 1944

	Total in U.K.	First Army Required	First Army Assigned	Third Army Required[c]	Third Army Assigned	SOS Assigned	SOS Unassigned	WD Authorized Allocation Per Army
QM Group Hq/Hq Det.........	15	3	3	3	1	11	0	0
QM Bn Hq/Hq Det............	66	10	4+(8)[b]	4	4	56	2	4
QM Bn(M) Hq/Hq Det........	14	[a]15	[a]3+(8)	2	1	10	0	1
QM Gas Sup Co..............	39	13	11+(2)	9	7	20	1	8
QM Dep Sup Co..............	27	2	1+(1)	2	(1)	23	3	1
QM Rhd Co..................	25	15	13+(2)	6	4	8	0	0
QM GR Co...................	12	5	3+(2)	3	2	5	2	0
QM Serv Co.................	137	43	28+(15)	19	10	85	14	19
QM Salv Coll Co.............	6	3	1+(2)	3	(1)	3	2	0
QM Salv Rep Co (SM)........	10	(3)	(3)	(3)	(1)	7	3	0
QM Bkry Co (Spec)..........	42	(5)	(5)	(6)	(2)	37	5	0
QM Ldry Co (SM)............	16	(5)	(5)	(5)	(1)	10	6	0
QM Sales Co.................	3	(1)	(1)	(1)	0	2	1	0
QM Refrig Co (M)............	5	(1)	(1)	(1)	0	4	1	0
QM Fumig & Bath Co.........	6	(2)	(2)	(3)	0	4	2	0
QM Pet Prods Lab...........	3	(1)	(1)	(1)	0	2	1	0

[a] Includes Transportation Corps units (organization identical with that of QM Bn(M) Hq/Hq Det).

[b] ( ) represent SOS units attached to Field Forces.

[c] This was the OCQM estimate of requirements; Third Army's estimate was higher, especially for administrative units.

Sources: Chart, Personnel Div, OCQM SOS ETOUSA, 2 Jun 44. USFET QM 322. IRS, CQM to G–4 COMZ, 25 Jun 44, sub: QM Troop Basis for Third Army. Littlejohn Reading File, vol. XXV, item 60.

War Department was not directly consulted, and exercised only indirect control by imposing a numerical ceiling for all QMC personnel in the theater, irrespective of units. Littlejohn felt that the War Department scale of authorized unit allocations, unchanged since 1942, should be revised upward. First Army requirements were extraordinary, but even if the ETO scale as applied to Third Army was maintained, and several more armies were activated, the theater ceiling would have to be raised.[114] This ETO scale was a direct result of Mediterranean experience, which had demon-strated that field armies needed a wide variety of Quartermaster units to provide direct support in the combat zone. McNamara later stated that the QM troop requirements for First Army which he had presented to Littlejohn in the fall of 1943 were equal to the number OCQM was then planning for the entire theater.[115]

Unlike Third Army, First Army had no transportation officer; motor transport units were directly under the army quartermaster. That was the way Bradley and McNamara had operated in the Mediterranean, and neither of them had any desire to entrust this important

[114] For later experience on the Continent and Littlejohn's recommendations at the end of World War II, see chapter XIV, below.

[115] McNamara *Memoir*, p. 169.

function to what was, in late 1943, a new and inexperienced organization. Accordingly, 8 QM battalion headquarters (mobile), 34 QM truck companies, and 9 QM troop transport companies, all of which were actually Transportation Corps units, were assigned to the First Army quartermaster, and 7 more truck companies were attached to his command through D plus 14.[116]

Troop Training

While the build-up of Quartermaster forces in the United Kingdom was under way, the OCQM, in co-operation with SOS, the base sections, and the tactical commands, attempted to assure the readiness of Quartermaster units for OVERLORD. Two principal activities were involved: quartermaster operations with the tactical forces on the Continent, and quartermaster participation in mounting the assault.

Co-operation with the field forces in training for active operations was a fundamental part of Quartermaster doctrine, although somewhat neglected in the ETO, where there was time for very little besides on-the-job training. Training with particular regard for anticipated tactical conditions and actual experience in working with specific field units were essentials that could not be omitted. Recognizing the importance of further field training, all echelons of command co-operated to create realistic operational situations. Thus as early as April 1943 supply of the 29th Division, stationed in southwestern England, was organized on a field basis, with distribu-

tion by daily train through railheads.[117] Similarly, Quartermaster organizations assigned to First Army and ADSEC were attached to SOS installations where they engaged in activities closely resembling their assignments in the forthcoming operation and worked as much as possible with the units they would later serve. In the early spring of 1944, the First Army quartermaster assumed direct responsibility for training these units.[118]

To speed up the integration of new Quartermaster units into the theater organization, OCQM took the lead in working out systematic co-operation with SOS and the base sections for the reception and inspection of newly arrived units. Within ten days of a unit's arrival it was visited by a combined OCQM base section team which helped the commander orient himself and at the same time determined the status of his troops with respect to equipment and technical and basic training. Information thus collected enabled the OCQM and the base section to correct deficiencies much more rapidly. Early in 1944 Littlejohn decided that QM units needed active assistance in their training programs. He therefore arranged to lend one QM battalion headquarters to each base section for that purpose.[119]

Follow-through on the status of Quartermaster units was systematized in the Training Branch, OCQM London Office, in much the same way as central

---

[116] (1) *QM Supply in ETO*, VIII, 136–42. (2) Interv with Littlejohn, 29 Oct 57.

[117] SOS ETOUSA, Notes on Staff and Comd Conf, 26 Apr 43, remarks of Littlejohn. USFET AG 337.
[118] (1) *FUSA Rpt of Opns*, 20 Oct 43–1 Aug 44, I, 21. (2) McNamara *Memoir*, pp. 100–101.
[119] (1) Memo, OCQM for QM SBS, 9 Nov 43, sub: Plan for Mtg Newly Arrived Units. USFET QM 000.4. (2) Ltr, CQM to Lt Col Chapin Weed (QM SBS), no sub, 11 Feb 44. Littlejohn Reading File, vol. XXI, item 16.

control of the supply situation. A current report book was set up indicating for each unit the date of its arrival and its location, strength, training, and utilization. Changes in the book were made weekly on the basis of reports from base section quartermasters and OCQM observers. This information was summarized by a monthly analysis of the state of readiness of all Quartermaster units in the theater.[120]

Plans for the movement of supplies in OVERLORD were rehearsed in a series of field and amphibious exercises. These began with experiments and small-unit maneuvers in January 1944 and culminated in corps level dress rehearsals, including practically all units and equipment, in early May. The OCQM suggested a number of special tests, such as loading of clothing and equipage on skids, use of field ranges on landing craft, adequacy of the reserve stocks planned for transit areas, and the efficiency of the Type III shoe in an assault landing.[121] Quartermaster observers at the exercises noted especially the handling of skidloads of Class II supplies, carrying their investigations as far back as the preparation of the special waterproof packages in the depots. Final procedures for packing and handling skidloads of the various types of supplies were arrived at only after much experimentation.[122]

The exercises, particularly the final ones preceding the assault, also tested the plans for the movement of troops. Quartermaster observers were particularly interested in the arrangements for supplying rations, clothing, equipage, and POL to units in transit. Unless the troops were already stationed near the south coast of England, they were first moved to concentration areas, where they received special equipment and lost certain administrative overhead not considered essential for the assault. A second move brought them to marshaling areas close to the embarkation points. There, final supplies were issued for the voyage, and the units were broken down into boatloads. Maintenance stocks were provided and ordinary housekeeping functions performed for troops in transit by the personnel attached to the camps. The mounting-out operation called into being a temporary but huge organization, largely for housekeeping purposes. The various districts of Southern Base Section bore the brunt of this responsibility, and since the functions were largely those of the Quartermaster Service, the Southern Base Section Quartermaster staff, headed by Col. Carroll R. Hutchins, was very actively engaged in supervision. But because of the shortage of QM units, personnel of every type were used, including, for example, the entire 5th Armored Division. The magnitude of the problem can be illustrated by a few statistics. About 60,000 men were required to establish and maintain in-

---

[120] Memo, Training Br for CQM, 14 Dec 43, sub: Summary of Major Projects of Training Br; Memo, Training Br for DCQM, 15 Jan 44, sub: Analysis of Monthly Rpts on Status of QM Units. USFET QM 319.1.

[121] Memo, OQM for Chief of Opns, 1 Dec 43, sub: QM Items To Be Tested in DUCK Exercise. USFET QM 000.4.

[122] (1) Memo, S&D Div for Brumbaugh, OCQM, 6 Nov 43, sub: Rpt of Detached Sv; Memo, Walrath for Florsheim, OCQM, 12 Dec 43, sub: Rpt on Observations of Beaching Skidloads. Both in USFET QM 319.1. (2) Memo, Brumbaugh for Franks, OCQM, 26 Mar 44, sub: Skidloading of Class I Supplies. USFET QM 400.2.

stallations for the seaborne assault forces and perform services necessary to make them ready for sailing. To cook their meals, more than 4,500 new cooks were trained during the spring of 1944. Southern Base Section operated over 3,800 trucks to transport them and haul their supplies.[123]

With inexperienced personnel, repeated rehearsals were a necessity. The chief weaknesses of QM units were lack of detailed instructions and failure of subordinate commanders to understand their instructions. These shortcomings caused irregular supply procedures, ineffective use of field ranges, relatively poor ration preparation, and failure to provide a fully operative salvage organization, a defect which threatened to raise consumption of available equipment to alarming figures. As a result of these exercises, changes were initiated at all quartermaster levels to improve performance.[124] Participation in the numerous exercises, especially the final ones which were on a very large scale, gave the Quartermaster units and their amateur assistants so many dry runs of their duties that the actual mounting of OVERLORD was in many respects little different from just another rehearsal.[125]

The tactical Quartermaster units participated actively in the amphibious training exercises. For example, units assigned or attached to the Engineer special brigades went to sea repeatedly in LST's, transferred to landing craft, received cargo brought ashore in Dukws, transferred skidloads from Dukws to trucks, and actually established Class I and III dumps near the beach. During Exercise TIGER, the last VII Corps rehearsal before D-day, German E-boats intercepted a convoy off Portland in the early hours of 28 April. Two LST's containing troops of the 1st Engineer Special Brigade, with the 3206th QM Service Company and the 557th QM Railhead Company attached, were sunk with great loss of life. The two QM units had over 300 casualties and had to be withdrawn from the NEPTUNE assault force. The disaster revealed serious deficiencies in command arrangements and emergency procedures.[126]

Although the QM units assigned or attached to the divisions, corps, and Engineer special brigades went through the great maneuvers with their respective tactical commands, the bulk of logistical support units for OVERLORD were concentrated directly under First Army and ADSEC. These were precisely the skilled cargo-handling units that were desperately needed in the U.K. depots and ports until the last minute, and only a few of them could be spared to participate in the exercises. Since these troops were not scheduled to land during the assault phase, their on-the-job training was appropriate to their future mission on the far shore.

---

[123] (1) Southern Base Section History, pp. 17–18. ETO Admin 601. (2) McNamara *Memoir*, p. 117.

[124] (1) Ltr, Thrasher, CO SBS, to Littlejohn, 7 Jan 44, no sub. USFET QM 331.4. (2) Memo, QM to CO XIX District SBS, 7 Jan 44, sub: Rpt of QM Sv on Exercise Duck; IRS, Lt Col Hower to Franks, OCQM, 27 Dec 43, sub: Brief on Exercise Duck; Memo, G–4 ETO for OCQM, 1 Feb 44, sub: SOS Participation in Exercise Duck. All in USFET QM 353. (3) IRS, Maj Scott to Zwicker, QM ADSEC, 6 May 44, sub: Exercise Fabius I. ADSEC COMZ 384.

[125] (1) Ruppenthal, *Logistical Support*, I, 345–54. (2) Hist of 3627th QM Truck Co. Hist Br OQMG.

[126] (1) Clifford Jones, NEPTUNE, vol. I, ch. VII. OCMH. (2) McNamara *Memoir*, p. 115.

Final Preparations for the Assault

As tactical troops assembled, preparatory to landing in Normandy, representatives of the OCQM and the First Army quartermaster took final steps to insure that all required quartermaster equipment would be on hand. Inspectors visited field force units to check the adequacy of their stocks. These visits showed that the tactical commanders had few if any criticisms of Quartermaster Service and in general had secured their full requirements. The few supply weaknesses were of minor significance and involved mainly items authorized after the initial organization of the units. Shortages of personal equipment were corrected by an elaborate system of showdown inspections and shortage reports, prescribed by the First Army quartermaster and issued to the troops as part of the Administrative Instructions Preliminary to Mounting.[127]

During the spring of 1944 Littlejohn demanded repeated surveys of the overall theater supply position of quartermaster items, and sent frequent reminders of the need for constant review of requirements to the various divisions of his office. Some shortages were found, but they involved primarily the possible reduction of theater stocks below safe maintenance levels rather than the absence of supplies for immediate issue. As the build-up approached its climax, contact between OCQM and the New York Port of Embarkation became practically continuous, both by message and by reciprocal visits of key officers. These efforts on both sides of the Atlantic enabled NYPE to ship all items requisitioned or furnish suitable substitutes.[128]

All services concerned in the staging of OVERLORD through southwestern Britain realized the pressing need for flexibility and speed. To achieve these objectives, authorities decentralized responsibility among the districts of the Southern and Western Base Sections. Each district was provided with a technical staff capable of carrying out the staging activities assigned to it. Outloading of cargo, concentrated in the Bristol Channel ports, was handled largely by the XXIX District of Western Base Section. POL presented an especially difficult problem. The original BOLERO Plan had provided that POL would be shipped out from the same ports used by the combat troops. Repeated increases in the scale of OVERLORD soon made this arrangement impossible —the south coast ports had barely enough capacity for the troops and their vehicles. The POL depots were conveniently located to supply the basic loads of the departing vehicles, but this service was only a small portion of their responsibility. Most of the POL reserves would have to go by rail from the areas behind Southampton and Plymouth to ports in south Wales, moving diagonally across the main southward flow of outgoing traffic. The desired schedule amounted to about 4,000 tons

---

[127] (1) Memo, Stevens for Brumbaugh, OCQM, 9 Dec 43, sub: Visits to Units; Memo, OCQM for G–4, 4 Mar 44, sub: QM Representative's Inspection Trip. USFET QM 333.3. (2) *FUSA Rpt of Opns*, 20 Oct 43–1 Aug 44, an. 14, p. 207.

[128] (1) IRS, ExO OCQM to Chief S&D Div, 23 Feb 44, sub: Rpt to CQM on Completeness of Requisitioning for Opns. USFET QM 319. (2) Ltr, Evans, NYPE, to Littlejohn, 31 May 44, no sub; IRS, DCQM to CQM, 9 Jul 44, sub: Supply Action Taken on Items Reported to Evans. Both in Littlejohn Collection, box 17.

per day between D minus 30 and D plus 30, and bearing in mind the other tonnage requirements during the same period, the Petroleum and Fuel Division, OCQM, judged this to be impossible. Despite the fire hazards involved, the only solution was to move a portion of the POL to dumps near Llanelly, Port Talbot, and Sharpness before the rush of pre-D-day traffic began. As much gasoline as possible was loaded on small coaster vessels, which then anchored in the outer harbors. Fortunately there were no accidents.[129]

Virtually all seaborne personnel were staged through XVIII and XIX Districts of Southern Base Section. During the staging, the districts could call on the base section and even on SOS headquarters for assistance, but while the troops were moving to the Channel the district was the hub of activity. The XIX District, covering Devonshire and Cornwall, the southwest corner of England, and staging a considerable part of the UTAH Beach invasion force, was fairly representative.[130] In January 1944 it set up a planning and operations group of five officers to co-ordinate quartermaster district activities with respect to tests and operations. This group participated in the preinvasion exercises (the main training beach at Slapton Sands and the chief embarkation points for training were in its area) and moved smoothly into the mounting of OVERLORD. As the transit camps in XIX District filled up,

the group acquired a field staff which expanded to a peak of 111 officers, 7 warrant officers, and 2,250 enlisted men. Organizationally, it consisted of all or parts of 3 QM battalion headquarters, 2 railhead companies, 2 refrigeration companies, 7 service companies, 3 bakery companies, 2 fumigation and bath companies, 3 laundry companies, and 2 graves registration companies. These organizations drew on the general depots in the district and supported the troops in the camps chiefly through three combination railheads and distribution points, each of which handled all classes of supply. Certain very special items were issued here, notably antiseasickness pills, insecticide powder, vomit bags, heating tablets, life belts, and antigas impregnite paste for shoes. The troops also drew a 7-day free issue of PX items —principally tobacco, candy, and razor blades.

Ration distribution was one of the most important QM functions of the districts. The inevitable difficulties of supplying large and constantly fluctuating numbers of men in scattered camps without extensive storage facilities were aggravated by General Bradley's determination to feed the transient troops a ration of the highest quality. When movement into the camps began, the troops were served the full ETO ration, including perishable meats and vegetables, fresh bread, and freshly roasted and ground coffee. Once the troops reached the marshaling areas and were briefed, maximum security measures were imposed. Since the men were now cut off from contact with British troops and civilians, the menu that had been somewhat modified out of respect for

---

[129] (1) See Table 7. (2) Littlejohn, ed., Passing in Review, ch. 18.

[130] (1) XIX District Hist of QM Activities in Opn OVERLOAD. USFET Hist Sec 314.7. (2) Ruppenthal, Logistical Support, I, 257–63.

SETTING UP A POL DUMP *on the beach during training exercises at Slapton Sands, April 1944.*

British sensibilities no longer had any point. Thereafter, both in the cross-Channel assault and on the Continent, only American resources and American preferences affected the variety and quantity of food served. During the last phase of staging in XIX District, beginning on 24 May, a special menu was provided, containing such traditional. American favorites as steak, chicken, roast beef, and, for the first time since the early days of the ETO, white bread.[131]

[131] Littlejohn, ed., Passing in Review, ch. 33, (vol. II) app. 2A, p. 10.

Ironically, owing to inadequate sanitary facilities in overcrowded mess halls and the unaccustomed richness of the fare, limited outbreaks of digestive disturbances occurred, and because of unexpected arrivals and departures of troops, distribution points could not always furnish the special menu. Occasionally they were forced to issue 10-in-1 rations instead. Also, in the first phase of the embarkation, when the hour was of no consequence and full meals were served regardless of the time of day, there was a high wastage rate. But all obstacles considered, the feeding of troops in transit was a superior accomplishment.[132]

The supply of Class II and IV items presented several problems. While the camps were being built, there were heavy demands both for maintenance of the construction troops and for supply of the camps. Requirements estimates generally exceeded actual needs and districts were thus easily able to meet most demands as they arose. But at times there were special requirements difficult of fulfillment, as when XIX District was notified on a Sunday afternoon that twenty-five 230-man camps would have to be erected and be ready to serve a meal by Tuesday at noon.

When the troops in transit began to go through the camps, other unforeseen demands arose. The mounting plan provided that the assault troops should be completely equipped before they left their home stations. For that reason clothing and equipment stocked for transient troops provided only minimum maintenance requirements for the short time the troops were expected to be in transit. But troops were often kept in marshaling areas longer than was anticipated and made unexpected demands. In addition, despite instructions, units sometimes arrived in the marshaling areas without their full equipment, expecting to fill out their allowances while in transit. Antigas impregnated cloth-

ing suddenly became very popular, reversing a two-year trend.

These demands were usually filled since there was no intention of penalizing errors by allowing the troops to proceed to the assault without necessary equipment. To meet this situation, ordinary supply routine was modified in XIX District, permitting the distribution points to deal directly with all accessible depots. In the Eastern and Western Base Sections, where airborne troops bound for the Cotentin Peninsula were being mounted, QM units supporting them were allowed to deal directly with any depot in the British Isles. Though these procedures caused inefficient use of transportation, they enabled all essential requirements to be filled.[133]

The most common criticism of the mounting operation concerned waste—of food as well as clothing and equipment. Although some waste was unavoidable because of last-minute changes in plans, the chief cause was inability of QM officers to enforce supply discipline.[134] Troops were inclined to use supplies freely, discard what they did not want wherever they might be, and leave policing of the staging area and the immense salvage problem to the stationary service troops. The high wastage rate was an important factor in the unexpectedly heavy demands for clothing and equipment. The local quartermasters, base section commanders, and

[132] (1) Memo, Chief Subs Div for CQM, 20 May 44, sub: Menu in the Marshaling Areas; Memo, IG for CG ETO, 12 Jul 44, sub: Inspection of Conditions in Marshaling and Embarkation Areas. Both in Littlejohn Collection sec. II. (2) QM Sv, Opn OVERLORD, in History of the Western Base Section, vol. II. USFET 314.7. (3) Ltr, CQM to TQMG, 3 Jul 44, sub: Poultry for ETO. Littlejohn Reading File, vol. XXVI, item 17.

[133] MS history cited n. 130 (1).
[134] Critical comment by Gen. Busch, QM Third Army, dated 15 Nov 54: "Supply discipline should not be regarded as something apart from ordinary discipline. . . . Supply training and standards of discipline in all echelons, starting with the highest level, will go far toward improving this dangerous American habit." Hist Br OQMG.

other high-ranking officers, repeatedly called attention to this fact. But with camp commanders generally lower in rank than commanders of units in transit, and with assault troops for NEPTUNE taking precedence over all others, little could be done to improve supply discipline. Even after D-day, when troops passing through the camps were no longer under the same strain as the initial assault force, only slight improvement could be effected. Units left behind a mass of salvage that taxed U.K. facilities for months. To this mass was soon added the camp equipment that was no longer needed after mounting operations had been completed. As Littlejohn put it a week after D-day, "we are confronted with the largest salvage problem in history." [135]

After the assault units left the docks and hards of southern England,[136] they put themselves in the hands of the Navy. But, although the Navy fed the troops during the crossing and delivered them to the Normandy beaches, the Quartermaster Corps selected and provided food suitable for feeding troops at sea. The "sea passage menu" varied according to the facilities available on each type of vessel, but a special effort, in response to General Bradley's personal request, was made to provide bland and easily digestible foods to counteract seasickness and the emotional tension of preparing for combat. Before the crossing the Quartermaster Corps and the Navy had made detailed plans for special cooking facilities to avoid as far as possible feeding cold processed rations to the troops. But as it finally worked out, only the larger naval cargo and personnel vessels were able to serve the A ration; LST's used a modified B ration. These three types of ships carried most of the troops. The smaller landing craft, transporting 200 men or less, were furnished a 10-in-1 ration. All vessels carried a reserve of C and K rations lest cooking facilities be damaged in action. This precaution was fortunate since D-day was postponed, and many ships were at sea more than a week.[137]

As the convoys moved toward the coast of Normandy on the night of 5–6 June, the Channel was smooth for the first time in several days, and many of the men were asleep. Even among their officers, few shared the forebodings of the senior logistical staff officers. Calculated wartime propaganda reminded them that they were backed by the most productive industrial system ever developed. They themselves had seen the loaded trucks and stacks of supplies along every road leading down to the embarkation points, and the huge fleet of vessels loaded down with supplies, top-heavy with their deckloads of vehicles. Logistical experts may have noted the relative scarcity of small landing craft, but only a few staff officers with extremely high security clearances

[135] IRS, CQM to DCQM, 14 Jun 44, sub: Salvage. Littlejohn Reading File, vol. XXV, item 28.

[136] Originally, hards were simply stretches of hard, gravelly beach where a wagon could come alongside a beached small craft at low tide. For NEPTUNE, engineers laid concrete aprons on designated beaches so that landing craft could take motor vehicles aboard more easily, and these were also called hards.

[137] (1) Memo, CG FUSAG for CG SOS, 27 Nov 43, sub: Feeding During a Cross-Channel Voyage. USFET AG 430.2. (2) Memo, DCQM for CG, 22 Feb 44, sub: Modified B Ration Menus for Use on LST. USFET QM 430.1. (3) Memo, P&T Div for Subs Div OCQM, 12 Apr 44, sub: Issue of Opnl Rations to U.S. Navy. Littlejohn Collection, sec. II.

wondered about the effectiveness of the untried MULBERRIES. And yet the whole operation hinged on three things: the MULBERRIES, the landing craft, and the weather.

Security hid these doubts from the assault quartermasters, who checked over their reams of mimeographed instructions and pondered their personal responsibilities in the coming operation. The logistical skill of General Littlejohn and the tactical experience of Colonel McNamara did much to assure that Quartermaster plans covered every fore-seeable contingency. Requisitions had been prepared in England to provide for each of the first ninety days on the Continent, and Standing Operating Procedures governing every quartermaster activity had been issued both to the participating Quartermaster units and to the combat units they were to support.[138] Few service troops went ashore the first day; for most of them, there was nothing to do but wait.

---

[138] These SOP's are printed in full in *FUSA Rpt of Opns,* 20 Oct 43–1 Aug 44, an. 14, pp. 156–92.

CHAPTER XII

Rear Area Support on the Continent: Administration

Logistical Implications of the Allied Invasion

Allied plans for logistical support on the Continent were strongly influenced by World War I experience, and the first objective of Operation OVERLORD —securing Cherbourg and the Britanny ports—might be defined as restoring part of the familiar transportation network of the AEF. The Germans were very conscious of this objective, and set themselves resolutely to oppose it. Moreover, they attained a large measure of success; none of the major ports were captured on schedule. That the Allies were nevertheless able to bring large forces to the Continent across open beaches and support them from those beaches as far as the German frontier was a surprising technological development that upset the calculations of Germans and Allies alike. Of nearly equal import was the technique developed by the Germans for demolishing and mining major ports so that they could not be used at maximum capacity for months even after being captured. Another thing that upset calculations was the effect of Allied bombing on railroads and bridges before D-day in the effort to isolate the battlefield. While this attempt was essential for tactical reasons it was almost too successful, and Engineer requirements for supplies to repair the damage distorted transportation priorities for months thereafter.

Despite all these difficulties, the Allies were able to reach the German frontier in three months, instead of a year as originally estimated. Tactically, this was a resounding victory. Logistically, it was something of a mixed blessing. It meant that future battles would have to be fought at the end of a long and warscarred line of communications, on terrain of the enemy's choosing. These unexpected developments had both direct and indirect bearing on quartermaster operations. They deeply influenced the nature of the warfare, thus modifying requirements for quartermaster support, and sharply restricted the types of land and water transportation that might be used to move supplies. Above all, for six months they imposed severe limitations upon transportation capacity, and thus transformed an important part of the OVERLORD logistical plan into a disorderly contest for tonnage allocations. Ships, trains, trucks, and aircraft all came to be rigidly controlled, with G–4,

COMZ, acting as arbiter for the U.S. forces. Each army and each technical service, the Air Forces, the Navy, base sections, the civil affairs organization, AES, and even the Red Cross, had to bid for its share of the available tonnage and be ready to justify its bids in detail.[1]

The original OVERLORD plan had provided that Headquarters, COMZ, move to the Continent early in September 1944 (about D plus 90). Military leaders assumed that by then the lodgment area would extend from the Seine to the Loire and that three base sections—Normandy, Britanny, and Loire—would be operative. They expected that Brest and Quiberon Bay, and possibly other Brittany ports, would be in full operation and that a depot complex in the Rennes-Laval area, designed to give all necessary support to U.S. combat forces on the Continent, would be nearly completed. Meanwhile ADSEC, about a hundred miles farther east, was to support the combat organizations as they crossed the Seine.

By mid-July it was painfully clear that this plan would not be realized. U.S. troops, barely twenty miles inland from the beaches, were receiving a costly lesson in the tactical importance of hedgerows, and measuring their daily gains in yards. Cherbourg harbor, in American hands since 26 June, was still blocked by mines and sunken ships, and all supplies were still coming ashore over the beaches.[2]

Paradoxically, lack of tactical success had helped the supply situation. Despite delays caused by the great storm of 19–22 June, the 14-day reserve of Class I and III supplies scheduled for D plus 41 (17 July) was actually on hand. But room had to be found for these supplies in a lodgment area only one-tenth the planned size. Local soil conditions were such that secondary and improvised roads were quickly worn out by heavy military traffic. Consequently, vehicles moved almost exclusively on the main Valognes-Bayeux highway, which was the only good paved road on the beachhead until mid-July. Traffic became seriously congested, the more so since the main depots were also strung along this highway, in the same locations where the assault troops had established their first inland dumps. All these depots were twenty miles or less from the front lines, and supplies controlled by ADSEC, by First Army, and by the combat divisions were crowded into the same small area. Sorting and inventory of supplies in these depots was far from satisfactory, a fact which COMZ attributed to uncontrolled and undocumented withdrawals by First Army units. First Army rejected this explanation and was very reluctant to implement the plan for drawing a rear boundary and releasing these depots to COMZ control. That plan had anticipated a geographical expansion which had not yet taken place, and the organization of new army depots on territory which was still in enemy hands. Since the depots administered by ADSEC were the only ones in existence on the Continent, First Army contended that it should continue to control them. Moreover, ADSEC had not yet demonstrated that it could ad-

---

[1] The influence of tactics upon logistics, and vice versa, are discussed in some detail in Roland G. Ruppenthal, *Logistical Support of the Armies,* Volume II, UNITED STATES ARMY IN WORLD WAR II (Washington, 1959), Chapter I, and in Eisenhower, *Crusade in Europe,* Chapter 16.

[2] Ruppenthal, *Logistical Support,* I, 430–48.

minister depots efficiently, and provide reliable support for combat units.[3]

Since First Army refused to surrender control of ADSEC and the tactical situation indicated that plans to organize a base section in Brittany would have to be postponed, the Forward Echelon, Communications Zone, was left without a function. Personnel of that headquarters began to reach Valognes, south of Cherbourg, as early as 18 June, and Brig. Gen. Harry B. Vaughan, Jr., the FECZ commander, was a somewhat tactless participant in the debate over First Army's rear boundary. Apparently COMZ decided that it had been a mistake to allow a forward echelon to develop into an independent headquarters, for by 12 July General Vaughan had departed for a new assignment.[4] Two days later, SHAEF rendered a somewhat complicated compromise decision on the role of ADSEC—it was to be administratively under COMZ, but General Bradley personally was to pass on all its major policy decisions. This arrangement reflected plans to activate the 12th Army Group and appoint Bradley to this command with control over First Army (Lt. Gen. Courtney H. Hodges) and Third Army (General Patton); 12th Army Group and Third Army became operational on 1 August 1944. All these headquarters had been displeased when FECZ attempted to insert itself into the chain of command. The solution adopted was for COMZ to move to the Continent immediately and absorb FECZ; this was done during the first week in August 1944.[5]

Lee's decision to move COMZ to the Continent ahead of schedule was also influenced by Bradley's tactical plans. Hopes were that Operation COBRA, launched on 25 July, would provide room for tactical maneuver as well as for a base section organization similar to the one originally planned. But plans made for an orderly expansion would undoubtedly need modifying to fit a sudden breakout, and COMZ naturally wanted to be closer to the scene of action and thus better qualified to prepare new plans. Tents and huts were quickly erected to supplement several chateaux taken over by FECZ in the Valognes area, and signal communications, including direct teletype with the United States, were hastily installed.

Office of the Chief Quartermaster

The FECZ Quartermaster Section had operated as an advance party of OCQM rather than as part of a separate headquarters, so that the move to the Continent was an orderly transition for the Quartermaster Service. Littlejohn had paid repeated short visits to France in June and July, and considered Valognes to be his forward command post.[6] Since the OCQM did not recognize its for-

---

[3] (1) *Ibid.* (2) IRS, Willkie to Littlejohn, 5 Jul 44, sub: Trip to Far Shore. Littlejohn Reading File, vol. XXVI, item 23.

[4] Shortly before D-day Vaughan asked Littlejohn to design a distinctive shoulder patch for FECZ. The Chief Quartermaster found this request highly symbolic of FECZ thinking. His view of FECZ plans was that they were certainly broad, and cut across everything; but Littlejohn, intended to resume control of QM units and QM operations upon arriving on the Continent. *Cf.* Littlejohn, ed., Passing in Review, ch. 19, p. 10.

[5] (1) Ruppenthal, *Logistical Support*, I, 436–37. (2) Littlejohn, ed., Passing in Review, ch. 19, p. 12.

[6] Memo, CQM for Franks, no sub, 27 Jul 44. Littlejohn Reading File, vol. XXVIA, item 110.

ward echelon as a separate entity it is difficult to assign an exact date for its arrival on the Continent, but the bulk of its military personnel, about 425 officers and men, had reached Valognes by 15 August. By that time all Brittany except the coastal ports and most of Normandy had been cleared of the enemy. The First Army and the British were converging on German forces at Argentan, and the Third Army was approaching the Seine both north and south of Paris. Supply to the armies was still barely adequate, and growing more difficult each day. Normandy and Brittany Base Sections were formally activated on 16 August, but except for Cherbourg their depots did not contain enough supplies for even their own service troops. ADSEC also lacked reserves, and moreover its depots were so far behind the front that they served only air forces and service units. Supply of the combat troops was still a hand-to-mouth affair based directly on OMAHA and UTAH Beaches, and on Cherbourg which had begun very limited operations on 16 July.[7]

Headquarters Staff

On 19 September, three weeks after the liberation of Paris, the OCQM moved from the tent city at Valognes to more commodious quarters in the Hotel Astoria on the Champs Elysées. With a staff of 209 officers, 553 enlisted personnel, men and women, and 82 British civilians, it was nearly up to authorized strength. In addition to professional officers with lengthy military service, Littlejohn's key assistants included a large percentage of able young business executives, most of them with mercantile or manufacturing experience. This background had enabled them to absorb the intensive specialized training courses given to a maximum number of QMC officers in the United Kingdom. The purpose of these courses was selection as well as training; those who passed formed a competent group of subordinates, but events during the next three months demonstrated that there were not enough of them.[8]

To cope with the perennial personnel shortages within the OCQM, as a non-T/O organization and to provide overhead to administer its enlisted personnel, several T/O units were attached to the office. The Headquarters and Headquarters Company, 67th Quartermaster Base Depot, activated in the ETO early in 1944 to serve as the Quartermaster component of FECZ during the early days on the Continent, remained with the OCQM throughout the continental campaign. The 537th, 549th, and 551st Quartermaster Groups were also valuable reinforcements of the OCQM with such specific assignments as the operation of a Quartermaster Subsistence Laboratory, schools for Quartermaster officers, and the formation of technical intelligence teams which traveled with combat units, observing and reporting on the serviceability of captured and U.S. quartermaster items. These units were quartered outside Paris at the Isle St. Germain, which came to be an important center of QMC activities.[9]

---

[7] Ruppenthal, *Logistical Support,* I, 493–97.

[8] *QM Supply in ETO,* VIII, 48.
[9] OTCQM TSFET Operational Study 16, Planning for Non-T/O Quartermaster Units, 1 Nov 45, p. 7.

The ever-lengthening lines of communications demanded a continuous program of setting up new QM installations. Fortunately, the units to man them were available, but the training and experience of these units did not equal the demands of the situation, which required that each new installation immediately begin to operate at full capacity. As already noted, SOS ETO-USA had been forced to accept untrained service units for duty in Great Britain.[10] Some of these units had received limited on-the-job training in the United Kingdom, but the majority were activated so late that on arrival in the ETO they were immediately phased through the marshaling areas and sent to the Continent. This undoubtedly contributed to the difficulties of the new installations, most of which were in trouble shortly after they were activated. Littlejohn's policy of rotating personnel so that experienced officers went to the field to command these units and others newly arrived from the United States received intensive training in the OCQM alleviated these problems without really solving them.[11]

In retrospect, Great Britain did not turn out to be a completely satisfactory training ground for continental logistical operations. The willing co-operation of the British was, in this particular respect, a disadvantage. Whatever their deficiencies, the roads, railroads, docks, and warehouses placed at the disposal of the Americans were in usable condition, and located in a well-organized country where raw materials, services, and labor were made available through official channels. This was poor preparation for operating in newly liberated territory where a foreign language was spoken, civil authority was in process of reorganization, and all economic initiative and most raw materials had to be supplied by the occupying troops.

In the United Kingdom the OCQM had evolved an orderly supply routine, based on co-operation with British civil authorities and consistent with a static situation. On the Continent, its initial mission was support for a headlong tactical advance by whatever means could be improvised. But simultaneously it had to create a new field organization against the day when a more conventional type of logistical support would be possible. Thus the OCQM continued to be both a planning and an operating agency, but naturally emphasis had shifted very strongly toward the latter function. Although organization had been simplified only slightly when the entire office was assembled under one roof in Paris, Littlejohn felt that practical working efficiency had been greatly improved. *(Chart 2)*[12] This was fortunate, for while the enumerated responsibilities of the OCQM had changed only slightly since the BOLERO period, their scope and complexity had increased enormously. Active combat operations demanded different working methods and a changed subdivision of functions. The following review of these functions and of the handicaps under which they were performed affords an insight into OCQM operating methods on the Continent.

---

[10] See ch. X, above.

[11] (1) Personal Ltr, Evans to CQM, 24 Nov 44. Littlejohn Collection. (2) *QM Supply in ETO*, VIII, 42–51.

[12] Compare this organizational chart with Chart 1.

CHART 2—OFFICE OF CHIEF QUARTERMASTER: 1 SEPTEMBER 1944

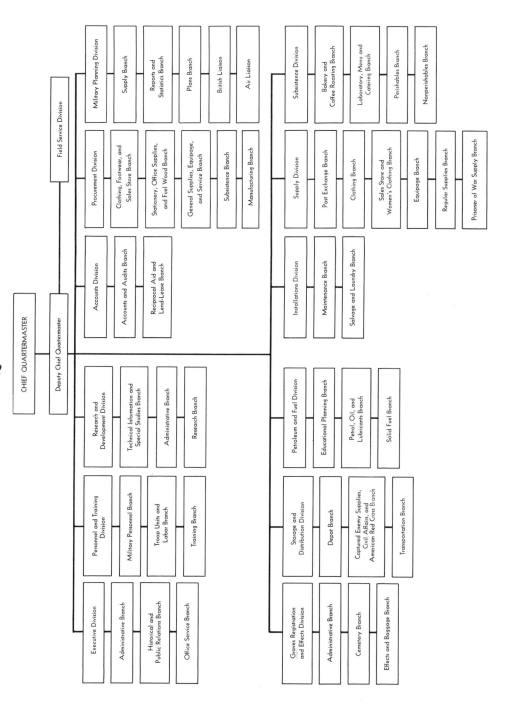

*Changes in the Organization
of the OCQM*

As in Great Britain, the Military Planning Division was the key unit of the OCQM organization. Littlejohn considered it his "general staff" and assigned it his most pressing problems.[13] On the far shore, the first of these was keeping track of maritime tonnage, since QMC supplies began to arrive off the coast much faster than they could be unloaded. G–4, COMZ, allocated berthing and unloading priorities at major ports among the technical services, but each service had to solve its own internal priority problems and arrange for ships carrying low-priority cargo to proceed to minor continental ports or to Marseille, to unload in the United Kingdom, or simply to wait. There was almost unlimited discharge capacity at small, shallow-water ports all along the French coast, but the landing craft and coasters from England that could ply such ports were scarce and strictly controlled. The Military Planning Division kept track of inventories in the United Kingdom, procured cross-Channel tonnage allocations for needed items, and saw to it that they were not duplicated in requisitions on the zone of interior.

QMC personnel, units, installations, and responsibilities had all expanded enormously on the Continent, but because the nucleus of able QMC officers was very small, Littlejohn concentrated them in the Military Planning and Field

Service Divisions of his office and gave them trouble shooting assignments. Once a crisis was passed, routine functions were consolidated and assigned to other divisions. For example, the acute shortage in port facilities was not overcome until December 1944, when Antwerp became fully operational. In the same month responsibility for marine tonnage was consolidated in the Storage and Distribution Division, which already handled all other transportation matters. Such an abrupt shifting of functions among subordinate offices was typical of OCQM during the continental period. Littlejohn himself considered this an efficient and economical use of personnel, but other staff agencies were inclined to regard OCQM as an unstable organization, with which it was difficult to establish time-saving routines based upon personal contacts.[14]

A typical case, about which Littlejohn apologized to Colonel Evans in a personal letter, concerned a requisition for blankets. After sending three increasingly urgent cables to NYPE, the Supply Division of OCQM discovered that a shipload of blankets had been awaiting discharge in European waters for thirty-eight days. Military Planning Division had made unceasing efforts to get the ship unloaded but had neglected to inform the Supply Division that it had arrived.[15]

[13] IRS, CQM to P&F Div, 10 Jul 44, sub: Coordination of P&F Div Activities with Plans and Training Div; IRS, CQM to DCQM, 28 Dec 44, sub: Matters Pertaining to Transportation. Littlejohn Reading File, vol. XXVI, item 42; vol. XXXI, item 100.

[14] (1) Personal Ltr, Evans to Littlejohn, 24 Nov 44. Littlejohn Collection. (2) *QM Supply in ETO*, VIII, 48–51. (3) Critical comments by Col T. R. J. Hickey on draft version of this MS, 14 Jan 54. Hist Br OQMG.
[15] Ltrs, Littlejohn to Evans, 14, 15, 17 Sep 44; Memo, CQM for Col Odell, 29 Nov 44, sub: Committee for Evaluation of Tonnage Allocations. Littlejohn Reading File, vol. XXVIII, items 91, 103, 126; vol. XXX, item 106.

However much the frequent shifts in personnel sacrificed continuity and even efficiency in relations with others, they strengthened OCQM internally. At staff conferences Littlejohn repeatedly spoke of "getting on the team" and "moving around to exchange ideas, and insure that we all speak the same language." The informal phrases should not obscure the important fact that these objectives were achieved. One of the OCQM's ablest officers, Col. Albert G. Duncan of Military Planning Division, later recorded his regret that, because of his excessively specialized assignment, he had been unable to participate in this very educational interchange.[16]

Research and Development—a new division organized on the Continent—was headed by Col. Michael H. Zwicker. It evaluated U.S., Allied, and enemy quartermaster equipment under combat conditions. It also reported quantities and locations of captured enemy equipment and supplies to the OCQM, which urgently needed such items for the support of POW labor units, used by all the technical services to conserve military manpower. The Storage and Distribution Division and the Supply Division organized branches to deal with captured items. The Subsistence Division developed a special POW menu, falling back on captured stocks and a few surplus U.S. items to provide the prisoners with an adequate diet. Ultimately, all these POW activities were centralized under Col. Beny Rosaler in the Installations Division. Col. Thomas V. Barber headed the Procurement Division. Since its activities affected the civilian economies of the liberated countries, they were closely controlled by a theater-level procurement organization which is described separately below.

Shortages in land transportation had developed almost immediately after the breakout from Normandy, and early in August the Transportation Branch of the Storage and Distribution Division developed into an information center on such matters as progress in railroad repair, location of tank and reefer cars, and the number of trucks available in COMZ. Such information was essential since G–4, which controlled all transportation, merely allocated gross daily tonnage to each army and major installation, subdivided by technical service and class of supply, without specifying what types of cars or trucks were available, or how far forward rail service had been established. In the confused period of the pursuit, Transportation Branch frequently had the latest and best information available. G–4 and the other technical services often relied upon it, and the OCQM found it especially helpful in preparing the daily bids for tonnage. The many-sided job of getting supplies forward from the docks and beaches to the combat units and intermediate depots demanded that no assets be overlooked. The Transportation Branch occasionally brought to light tonnage capacity unknown to G–4, and therefore not allocated. The OCQM arranged to share this tonnage equitably between the First and Third Armies and to include all classes of QM supplies in the shipments.[17] In January

---

[16] Littlejohn, ed., Passing in Review, ch. 19.

[17] OTCQM TSFET Operational Study 5, p. 14, and exhibit D, Ltr, CQM to QM Normandy BS, 25 Sep 44, sub: Additional Rail and Truck Transportation.

1945 G–4 began to allocate overland tonnage on a monthly rather than a daily basis and turned over detailed operations to the Transportation Corps. The OCQM found this a much more efficient method of operating and dissolved its Transportation Branch shortly thereafter.

A major function of the Field Service Division was to compensate for poor communications. Signal communications rearward, to the United Kingdom and the zone of interior, were fairly satisfactory, but signal service forward was a constant problem as long as the pursuit lasted. Use of the overloaded lines was severely limited, and the brief daily telegram from the armies was often the only official contact with the combat zone. Littlejohn set up an elaborate courier service by jeep and liaison aircraft to expedite reports from the combat units and from his liaison teams, but the supply situation was confused and the reports themselves were sketchy. For example, during the last fortnight in August, the Third Army quartermaster knew neither his daily requirements nor what he was actually receiving each day.[18]

Clearly, this was a situation requiring vigorous action by a central authority. At Littlejohn's insistence a single theater-wide stock record file of quartermaster supplies was set up in the Military Planning Division, and provision was made to maintain it accurately thereafter through a standardized system of documentation for each shipment, periodic reports from all concerned, and

continuous supervision by Field Service Division. Littlejohn considered this central stock record his main instrument for staff control of operations on the Continent, and never allowed it to be decentralized even after the logistical situation had become stabilized.[19] ADSEC was part of this inventory system, but the armies were not. Consequently, when the armies moved forward and transferred depots to ADSEC, their contents again became theater "assets." Counting and sorting the vast accumulation of supplies left behind in Normandy by the First Army was a major task.

The Field Service Division acquired other new functions on the Continent. A basic consideration was that all field installations were newly organized and just beginning to operate. They needed active assistance and expert advice rather than inspections and criticism, and at first these aids were provided by all the divisions of OCQM as required. The result was confusion, lack of co-ordination, and an excessive number of liaison officers absent from OCQM, so that in September 1944 all such activity was centralized under Colonel Rosaler of Field Service. The number of liaison officers was drastically reduced. To correct the weaknesses that had been reported, as many as possible of the less experienced QMC officers were sent in rotation to attend short supply courses, first at UTAH Beach and later at the QM school already mentioned. Inspection reports and Littlejohn's correspondence with base section and depot quarter-

---

[18] (1) Ltr, CQM to QM Normandy BS, 24 Sep 44, sub: Orgn and Methods of Functioning. Littlejohn Reading File, vol. XXVIII, item 183. (2) Ruppenthal, *Logistical Support*, I, 507.

[19] OTCQM TSFET Operational Study 9, p. 2. (2) Ltr, CQM to DCQM Forward (Col Franks), 2 Sep 44, sub: Rpts on Stock Status of Supplies. Littlejohn Reading File, vol. XXVIII, item 3.

masters during the fall of 1944 indicate that all the mistakes made previously in England were being repeated by the new units fresh from the zone of interior. Perishable supplies were left exposed, and shiploads of balanced rations and sized clothing were scattered and had to be laboriously rebalanced. Inventory and proper documentation of supply actions were neglected. Many units had lost or abandoned the libraries of basic Quartermaster reference data issued to them before D-day and were unable to perform their technical staff functions. Most serious of all, none of the base section commanders, despite their seniority and professional experience, were willing to assert their authority over the port headquarters and insist upon applying the lessons learned at the sorting sheds adjacent to British ports. On the beaches, at first operated by tactical personnel, this reluctance was understandable, but Cherbourg began to operate in July, Dieppe in September, Le Havre and Rouen in October, and Antwerp in November. In no case were effective sorting procedures set up until after the port had become seriously clogged.[20]

Unfortunately, the cure for some of these ills involved indoctrinating persons and agencies outside the Quartermaster Corps. Littlejohn's letters to base section commanders and COMZ staff officers frequently presented the whole ETO supply situation from the Quartermaster point of view, as a pre-liminary to requesting co-operation or concurrence on some specific point. Within the OCQM, indoctrination was a very direct and accelerated process, centering in the QM school on the Isle St. Germain. Supervision of this school and of training courses offered in various base sections at different times was a major responsibility of the Personnel and Training Division, headed by Col. Joseph C. Odell. The transfer of the training function, formerly supervised by the Plans and Training Division, was a significant development. Senior officers of newly arrived QM units, it often turned out, were recently transferred from the combat arms and had to be replaced, at least temporarily, for the units were urgently needed for immediate operations. Many of these officers could be utilized to advantage after brief courses of orientation in ETO practices, but others, less adaptable or of inferior physical stamina, had to be reclassified, used in posts of minor responsibility, or assigned in the United Kingdom, where conditions were less strenuous. Under ETO conditions, training and personnel assignments were closely connected functions.[21]

The Personnel and Training Division was responsible for assignment of QM units as well as individuals. Littlejohn insisted that the Field Service Division maintain continuous surveillance to insure that QM units were being used efficiently, and he ordered prompt transfers whenever the tempo of activity slackened in any portion of the COMZ.

---

[20] (1) Memo, CQM for Franks, 28 Aug 44, sub: Comments on Conf of OCQM Div Chiefs. Littlejohn Reading File, vol. XXVII, item 137. (2) Littlejohn, ed., Passing in Review, ch. 27, pp. 5–6. (3) Personal Ltr, CQM to CG Channel BS, 11 Dec. 44. Littlejohn Reading File, vol. XXXI, item 24.

[21] Personal Ltr, Littlejohn to Gregory, 4 Sep 44; Ltr, CQM to Col Weed (CO 56th QMBD), 15 Oct 44, sub: School at Cherbourg. Littlejohn Reading File, vol. XXVIII, item 29; vol. XXIX, item 77.

Moreover, units as well as individuals were given periods of orientation and training in quiet rear areas, and then sent forward nearer to the front. But there were repeated crises and unexpected demands for U.S. units which could be met only partially by surveying the whole theater basis of QM troops and dividing them up as equitably as possible. Every change in tactical plans increased the demand, especially for service companies. Delay in phasing out U.K. supply operations, activation of two extra base sections, and the additional support required for an expanded 6th Army Group were only the most conspicuous of these problems.[22] The steady increase in the ETO troop basis and the considerably slower increase in the number of Quartermaster units in the theater are illustrated in Appendix B.

An obvious and yet persistently unpopular solution of this difficulty was the use of foreign personnel. Taking a realistic tack Littlejohn set up a Troop Units and Labor Branch within the Personnel and Training Division shortly after D–day. The OCQM found that the French Government's regulations on such matters as regional wage differentials and the payment of special family allowances to married employees were extremely complicated and cumbersome. It recommended that prisoners of war be used instead, since they were good workers, easily administered, and could be moved about at will within the communications zone. But installation commanders were extremely reluctant to use any type of nonmilitary labor, and especially POW's. They exaggerated the se-

curity problems involved. This attitude probably originated in June and July, when ADSEC units were subordinate to First Army and the entire beachhead was, technically, a part of the combat zone. Moreover, during the OVERLORD planning period the ETO Judge Advocate (JAG) had favored a very narrow interpretation of the Geneva Convention, which severely limited the use of prisoners. By August 1944 the Judge Advocate had modified his ruling, and COMZ was urging a wider use of prisoners. The OCQM was particularly anxious to substitute prisoners for service units in the rear areas, since military labor was more suitable for use in newly established installations farther forward, and could be used in the combat zone where prisoners were not permitted. The OCQM pursued this program so persistently that at the end of hostilities prisoners comprised 46 percent of Quartermaster personnel in COMZ, or about some 115,000 men. The majority of Quartermaster troops had been transferred to the armies, and Littlejohn only controlled 57,800 men in regular QM units—some 21 percent of his available labor force.[23]

An even more perplexing problem was the theater troop basis to be used in computing requisitions. Uncertainty and lack of co-ordination in this field had caused endless difficulties during BOLERO. Beginning in July 1944 a Troop List for Operations and Supply was published by the War Department. This provided invaluable guidance as

---

[22] QM Supply in ETO, VIII, pp. 21–26.

[23] (1) DA Pamphlet 20–213, *History of Prisoner of War Utilization by the U.S. Army, 1776–1945*, pp. 77–89, 208–223. (2) OTCQM TSFET Operational Study 11, p. 1; Study 15, pp. 9–10.

TABLE 11—ETOUSA STRENGTH FORECAST FOR QM REQUISITIONING
28 FEBRUARY 1945 AND 31 JULY 1945[a]

(In Thousands)

Category	Continent (Less SOLOC)		SOLOC		United Kingdom		Totals	
	28 Feb	31 Jul	28 Feb	31 Jul	28 Feb	31 Jul	28 Feb	31 Jul
U.S. Military:								
Ground Forces.............	1161	1207	369	370	40	—	1507	1577
Service Forces.............	359	378	93	124	101	58	553	560
Air Forces.............	175	190	28	32	230	215	433	437
Reinforcements.............	85	90	18	18	20	10	123	118
Others[b].............	113	121	30	56	119	117	262	294
Total	1893	1986	538	600	510	400	2878	2986
Total includes:								
Officers.............	140	145	45	50	52	46	237	241
Nurses.............	9.68	11.65	2.29	2.34	7.7	6.7	19.67	20.69
WAC Officers.............	.27	.27	.002	.002	.135	.135	.406	.41
Other U.S. and British Personnel:								
U. S. Navy.............	9	9	4	4	58	38	71	51
Merchant Marine.............	—	—	—	—	2	2	2	2
UNRRA.............	1	10	—	—	—	—	1	10
British & Allied Military.............	17	17	—	—	3	3	20	20
British & Allied Civilian.............	11	11	—	—	4	4	15	15
Others[c].............	6	7	—	—	6	6	12	13
	44	54	4	4	73	53	121	111
Liberated Manpower:								
Type A—French Combat Forces[d].....	—	—	273	557	—	—	273	557
Italian Service Units........	3	7	30	31	4	—	37	38
Slav Service Units.........	—	—	2	5	—	—	2	5
Type B—Security & Service Units[e]....	70	156	105	148	—	—	175	304
Type C—Misc. Security Units[f]	51	106	—	—	—	—	51	106
	124	269	410	741	4	0	538	1010
Civilian Labor, Mobile[g].............	29	95	—	—	—	—	29	95
Civilian Labor, Static[g].............	75	79	30	32	22	22	127	133
POW, Labor	155	160	115	264	18	18	288	442
POW, Others	170	850	—	—	6	8	176	858
Allied POW.............	—	570	1	162	—	—	1	732
Displaced Persons.............	—	3000	—	—	—	—	—	3000
Total.............	2490	7063	1098	1803	633	501	4158	9367

[a] This table is a summary only. The original included monthly estimates.
[b] Principally hospital patients and theater overhead.
[c] Includes Red Cross, USO, Technicians, Special Service, Press, guests.
[d] Includes direct support troops.
[e] French, Belgian, and Dutch personnel.
[f] French only—Gendarmerie, FFI, Miscellaneous.
[g] Mobile civilian labor received clothing and all meals; static civilian labor received a mid-day meal only.
Source: Ltr, CQM to CG ComZ, 16 Feb 45, sub: QM Supply Responsibilities to Agencies other than U.S. Army. LRF XXXIIIA, 123.

far as U.S. troops were concerned, and seemed to solve the problem. But ultimately support of non-U.S. personnel became the larger portion of the QMC mission, and estimates regarding such personnel remained highly uncertain until after V–E Day. Littlejohn believed that such forecasts should be made by the G–4 or G–1 Section of COMZ, but the responsibility was given to G–3, which apparently failed to recognize its importance. Within his own organization, the Personnel and the Military Planning Divisions were made jointly responsible for forecasts to be used in all computations prepared by the OCQM.[24] The complexity of the problem was dramatically displayed in February 1945, when the OCQM submitted its own six-month forecast to General Lee, with a request that the estimate be approved or alternate figures provided by his headquarters. Except for the TLOS, all figures had "been obtained through unofficial channels, informally from various agencies." The estimate was broken down into fifty-five categories of personnel, each to receive different treatment with regard to rations, clothing, or PX privileges, and separate figures were provided for the end of each month, from February through July. The accompanying summary gives only major subtotals for the first and last month-end of the forecast. (Table 11) In February the OCQM was supporting 4,220,000 persons. At the end of July 1945 it expected to be giving direct support to 6,367,000 plus an undetermined amount of indirect support to 3,000,000 displaced persons, who were

a responsibility of Civil Affairs. On 5 March, COMZ concurred in the manpower estimate with minor exceptions. It should be noted that this forecast was actually overconservative in several respects. Peak requirements came in May instead of July, and Littlejohn's actual direct-support responsibility then totaled a staggering 7,629,000 persons, including 2,835,000 prisoners of war. At the same time some 340,000 long tons of supplies in Quartermaster depots were earmarked for Civil Affairs.[25]

Relations with NYPE

During the early part of the OVERLORD operation, the War Department shaped all supply policy and controlled certain critical items, releasing them for shipment by specific authorization. But by the end of 1944 recommendations from the Overseas Supply Division of NYPE were the controlling factors in such authorizations.[26] By that time OSD had become a clearing house for information on the progress of the procurement program, the stock levels of all the services in the zone of interior depots, and rail traffic and maritime tonnage availabilities, as well as the requirements of the European and Mediterranean theaters. Apart from high-level policy decisions on such matters as levels of supply, OSD decided what would

---

[24] OCQM Office Memo 44, 6 Dec 44, sub: Pers Forecasts. Littlejohn Collection, sec. II.

[25] (1) Quotation from Ltr, CQM to CG COMZ, 16 Feb 45, sub: QM Supply Responsibilities to Agencies other than U.S. Army; Memo, CQM to G–4 COMZ, 25 Mar 45, same sub. Littlejohn Reading File, vol. XXXIII, item 123; vol. XXXIV, item 86. (2) OTCQM TSFET Operational Study 8, exhibit A. (3) QM Supply in ETO, I, app. XLV–B.
[26] See discussion of the origins of NYPE and its growing authority within the zone of interior logistical organization in Chapter IX, above.

actually be shipped to those theaters, and in what priority.[27]

It will be recalled that shortly before D-day OCQM submitted detailed requisitions covering the first ninety days of OVERLORD.[28] Support for the invasion was not, therefore, strictly speaking, by automatic supply, but the distinction was largely academic. A headquarters directing an assault had no time to recompute its requirements from day to day; whether the staff computed its own requirements in advance (preplanned supply) or delegated that function to another headquarters nearer the source of support (automatic supply), the initial flow of supplies had to follow a prescribed plan until combat experience indicated what adjustments should be made. Supply to the individual combat units was, or course, completely automatic, apart from emergency requirements. The OVERLORD plan had provided a reserve in Great Britain to cover such requirements, and airlift to deliver them to the requesting units.

During the first weeks after D-day, the Military Planning Division of OCQM kept its eyes on the reserve levels and attempted to translate day-to-day fluctuations into intelligent trends. Inevitably, combat brings logistical as well as tactical surprises, and some of them are so far-reaching that they cannot be compensated for by the over-all margin of safety provided in the supply level. The first readjustment requiring action by NYPE was a direct result of the hedgerow fighting in Normandy. In the heavily compartmented terrain, each enclosed field was a separate strongpoint to be attacked, captured, and abandoned in rapid succession. During the first six weeks, requirements for clothing and such Class II items as blankets, mess gear, and shelter halves were at about two and a half times the expected rate.[29]

Then, during the pursuit in August and September 1944, there was little time to cook field rations, and operational rations, especially the 10-in-1, were consumed at about twice the projected rate.[30] As further by-products of the pursuit and the early liberation of Paris, French civilians became dependent upon Civil Affairs supplies in unexpected numbers, and German prisoners of war, including deserters and whole units surrendered by their commanders, totaled 400,000 by late September, exceeding estimates by about 100 percent. These huge requirements produced a real emergency, necessitating not merely a drastic upward revision of procurement programs but also a change in priorities and expedited shipments from the zone of interior.

When Quartermaster requisitions reached the OSD, they were sent to the Quartermaster Section of the Operations Branch. Here, a staff of more than 300, working under Lt. Col. Terrence R. J. Hickey, edited these requests on the basis of authorized levels, theater strength figures, maintenance factors, and current and projected availability

---

[27] Critical comments by Col Hickey, 19 October 1954, on a preliminary draft version of this volume. Hist Br OQMG.

[28] See ch. XI, above.

[29] Personal Ltr, Littlejohn to Feldman, 4 Sep 44; Ltr, CQM to OQMG, 6 Oct 44, sub: Continental Replacement Factors. Littlejohn Reading File, vol. XXVIII, item 29; vol. XXIX, item 41.

[30] Personal Ltrs, CQM to QM's Brittany, Loire, and Oise Secs, 7 Sep 44. Littlejohn Reading File, vol. XXVIII, items 50, 51, 52.

of materials. This review was by no means routine, since OSD was in reality the executive agency implementing ASF supply policy. It had the authority to make substitutions when necessary as well as on-the-spot changes in authorization. Particularly knotty problems could be resolved by direct teletype conference between the theater and the port.[31]

Aside from these formal means of communication, the Chief Quartermaster profited from his friendly personal relationship with Colonel Evans, Chief of the Planning and Control Branch in OSD. Evans, himself a regular Quartermaster officer of wide experience, who had won high respect on both sides of the Atlantic, was in an excellent position to keep Littlejohn up to date on shifts in logistical policy in the zone of interior and, in turn, to transmit the Chief Quartermaster's viewpoint to the ASF and The Quartermaster General. Littlejohn discovered that Evans could predict fairly accurately how Gregory's and Somervell's staffs would react to any proposals from overseas, and moreover was willing to give prompt answers to informal inquiries about the probable fate of official requests. Littlejohn found Evans' letters so useful that by early September 1944 he requested that they be sent regularly each week. Obliging the Chief Quartermaster as best he could, particularly during the period when the logistical pipeline was under unprecedented strain, Evans communicated with Littlejohn on such subjects as maintenance factors, winter clothing, tentage, clothing for prisoners of war, and reefer

tonnages. Each of these was a pressing ETO problem awaiting official action in the zone of interior.[32]

At the end of September 1944, Littlejohn called upon Evans to perform a task that bordered upon the impossible. During the preceding two weeks, as the pursuit across France came to a halt and the quartermasters of combat units surveyed their clothing shortages, unseasonably cold weather set in. Thus unexpectedly early demands for initial issue of winter clothing were piled upon the accumulated demands for replacement of regular clothing, and the theater's official forecast of Class II and IV requirements abruptly increased by nearly 250 percent. Simultaneously, the congestion of shipping in European waters made it necessary to cut ten ships from each transatlantic convoy. Littlejohn's share of this cut in September was 77,000 measurement tons, or about 13 percent, and the prospect was that this deficit would be doubled in October. Having reviewed every outstanding requisition and weighed its relative importance, on 26 September Littlejohn asked Evans' advice and assistance in completely rescheduling his October shipments from NYPE. The changes necessary were so drastic that Littlejohn suggested canceling all outstanding requisitions and starting afresh. Evans advised against such a procedure, since "it would take thirty to sixty days to get you back on a sound supply basis. There are unquestionably items which, regardless of tonnage allocations or shipping situation, are

---

[31] Interv, Irving G. Cheslaw, OQMG, with Col Hickey, 6 May 52.

[32] (1) Personal Ltrs, Evans to Littlejohn. 4 Oct; 8, 27 Nov 44; 3 Feb 45. Littlejohn Collection. (2) Extracts of Personal Ltrs, Littlejohn to Evans, 8, 14, 18, 26 Sep; 3 Oct; 5 Dec 44. Evans' Staybacks, Hist Br OQMG.

absolutely essential for you to have in order for you to support the minimum of operational requirements." [33] Instead, he proposed that Littlejohn cable immediately a list of specific requisitions to be canceled, and later the new priorities for those to be retained. He personally undertook to cancel shipments at the depots, en route to the port and in the port itself, although he explained apologetically that ships more than 50 percent loaded when the cancellation order arrived could not be unloaded. Even beyond this far-reaching compliance with Littlejohn's wishes, Evans successfully presented the ETO point of view while awaiting specific cabled instructions. He managed to resist pressure from ASF to cancel whole categories of QM requisitions, offering instead to delete specific items that he believed the ETO could readily get along without. Littlejohn found these decisions to be entirely sound, and on 9 October wrote: "As usual, you have been very helpful in assisting me to solve my problems. Many Thanks." [34]

Despite this cordial and efficient personal relationship with Evans, Littlejohn was convinced that in certain respects NYPE had been accorded too much authority, with unfortunate results. This applied particularly to long-term requirements, which after editing were forwarded direct from NYPE to

ASF and incorporated into the Army Supply Program. Only then was the OQMG informed and directed to deliver the supplies. Littlejohn contended that the OQMG, which had to arrange procurement, needed information on such requirements earlier than NYPE, which merely called the supplies forward from the depots for loading. When ASF called all the ETO service chiefs home to Washington in March 1944 for a last preinvasion review of the supply situation, Littlejohn went straight to Somervell about the matter. The result was an informal agreement that Littlejohn would state his long-term requirements in personal letters to The Quartermaster General, with information copies to the appropriate division of ASF and to NYPE. Short-term and immediate requirements were to be transmitted as formal requisitions to NYPE. The Overseas Supply Division of NYPE was formally directed to forward an edited copy of each QM requisition from the ETO to The Quartermaster General, in order to expedite action on critical items and new items requisitioned. It was unfortunate that the procedure for estimating long-term requirements was not similarly formalized. Most officials in ASF, at NYPE, and even in the OQMG appeared to regard Littlejohn's letters on the ETO supply situation as informal expressions of opinion, rather than as providing authority to initiate procurement. Moreover, these officials regarded their own estimates of what could be sent as statements of industrial practicability, and not as hard-and-fast commitments to deliver. Conversely, Littlejohn felt that since he had provided ample time for procurement, the "lead time" on formal requisitions to NYPE might

---

[33] (1) Quotation from Ltr, Evans to Littlejohn, 4 Oct 44; OCQM Directive 1, Review of Requisitions, 25 Sep 44; Ltr, Littlejohn to Evans, 26 Sep 44, sub: Request for Advice re . . . Essential Changes in Requisitions. . . . Littlejohn Reading File, vol. XXIX, item 16; vol. XXVIIIA, item 192; vol. XXVIII, item 197. (2) Ruppenthal *Logistical Support,* II, 128.

[34] Personal Ltr, Littlejohn to Evans, 9 Oct 44. Littlejohn Reading File, vol. XXIX, item 50.

be materially reduced—a view emphatically not concurred in by the New York
Port.[35]

Apparently even Evans failed to understand the full scope of the franchise
that Littlejohn conceived himself to have
received from General Somervell. Certainly Evans felt that whatever authority
Littlejohn might have been given to bypass NYPE it was unwise to do so as a
matter of routine, and moreover that the
tone adopted in some of these direct-
action letters was unfortunate. On 24
November he wrote:

I am certain that you will allow me the
liberty of making a couple of observations
which I can assure you are made with your
best interests in mind. . . .

Your technique of bombarding The
Quartermaster General, individuals in the
OQMG, Headquarters, ASF, and the port
with emphatic demands for action in connection with those matters of Quartermaster
supply which are not satisfactory to you to
date, I believe, has had excellent results.
However, there have been informal rever-
berations from Washington to the effect
that a continuation of this technique will
probably result in the development of dis-
inclination to be sympathetic with some of
your future demands. I have talked this
over with General Goodman and we agree
that in order to prevent such a procedure
from operating to your disadvantage, it
would be advisable to, at least temporarily,
channel your complaints and special requirements through the port, except for
those items of a purely technical nature and
perhaps occasionally a vital problem. I am
sure you will say that you don't give a
damn what they think or what they say as

long as you get what you want. On the
other hand a gauge of their tempers indicates that in the final analysis you may not
get what you want.[36]

Littlejohn's reply, expressing be-
wilderment at Evans' admonition, reveals the extent to which he was engrossed in his mission and indifferent
to considerations involving personalities. Moreover it reiterates his conviction that, while formal requisitions
could best be handled through the port,
satisfactory action on broad policy matters—notably maintenance factors—demanded precisely those vigorous methods which Evans decried:

I have gone very carefully over your letter of 24 November. As a matter of fact, I
have read it three times as you have sort of
caught me off base.

Cotulla raised the question of staying in
the groove on requisitions the other day. I
do not recall any specific instance except.
. . . my 5,000,000 yards of cloth and the
manufacture of the ETO field uniforms.
Frankly, I am not proud of the action
which I have obtained on either of these
. . .

I have been very much embarrassed over
our inability to secure the ETO uniform.
Goodman suggested that I write on this
matter to Lutes, which I did . . . Some weeks
ago it became apparent to me that on
clothing and equipage . . . I was headed
for disaster.[37]

Clearly, Littlejohn considered his supply position to be precarious, and was
ready to ride roughshod over all opposi-

---

[35] Memo 2, Littlejohn for Stetson Conn, OCMH,
29 July 59, p. 6. Hist Br OQMG. (2) Memo,
Styer for CofT, ASF, 14 April 44, sub: QM Overseas
Requisitions. Reprinted as exhibit E, OTCQM
TSFET Operational Study 9, 1 Nov 43. (3) Interv,
W. F. Ross with Littlejohn, 24 Jun 59. (4) Hickey
comments on draft MS.

[36] Personal Ltr, Evans to Littlejohn, 24 Nov 44.
Hist Br OQMG.

[37] (1) Personal Ltr, Littlejohn to Evans, 5 Dec 44.
Hist Br OQMG. (2) Cotulla and Goodman were,
respectively Commanding General and Deputy Commanding General, PEMBARK. Lutes was Chief of
Operations, ASF.

tion to improve it. Evans hastened to agree and gave assurance of his personal support, but again warned that such a policy would probably arouse some hostility:

. . . Goodman and myself are entirely in sympathy with your outlined position and your stated objectives with respect to your unparalleled mission and that you are assured of our best efforts in your behalf . . . we feel that in many cases because of our specific responsibility to your theater we have a more sympathetic understanding and attitude toward your problems than that . . . of those in the OQMG. In our dealings with them rightly or wrongly, we . . . attempt to secure action for you regardless of other theaters. . . . We fully realize that . . . our capabilities are limited and that in the final analysis the channels of communication utilized by you are a matter for your decision. Perhaps you will remember that . . . I indicated to you that in some instances it might be necessary to effect a cable direct from Eisenhower to Marshall. Normally the boys in the lower echelons do not like to see this type of cable. . . . However, to date I know of very few instances when cables like that have come through that the request was not complied with.[38]

The mechanics of co-operation between NYPE and the ETO improved considerably in the course of time. An agency preoccupied with maritime aspects of supply, NYPE favored decentralization of requisitions among overseas areas served by different ports. COMZ generally agreed with this view, and supplies destined for delivery to Marseille were requisitioned by SOLOC although the requisitions were reviewed by the appropriate technical service within COMZ. In November 1944, reflecting the increasing autonomy of the United Kingdom Base, a similar arrangement was set up for supplies destined for Great Britain. Littlejohn laid down stringent rules governing the Quartermaster aspects of these decentralized procedures. He demanded that requisitions show stocks on hand for each requisitioned item, amounts due in, and projected future requirements over a considerable period. This procedure was not merely a matter of supply discipline but also provided invaluable information to NYPE. After inspecting the ETO in January 1945 General Somervell directed that all the technical services adopt and standardize such procedures. Another result of Somervell's January tour was of considerable interest to the OCQM; early in April, Evans came to COMZ as Deputy Chief of Staff for Planning and shortly thereafter was promoted to brigadier general.[39]

The Organization for Procurement on the Continent

To supplement their requisitions on the zone of interior, the U.S. forces made elaborate plans for procurement of continental labor, supplies, and services. During the spring of 1944 SHAEF concluded agreements on reciprocal aid, or reverse lend-lease, with the governments-in-exile of most of the continental nations. An agreement with the French broke down on the thorny issue of recognition for Gen. Charles de Gaulle's provisional government, but most of the technical details had already been worked out and the Supreme Com-

---

[38] Personal Ltr, Evans to Littlejohn, 20 Dec 44. Hist Br OQMG.

[39] (1) Ltr, CQM to QM UKB, no sub, 29 Nov 44. Littlejohn Reading File, vol. XXX, item 108. (2) Ruppenthal, *Logistical Support*, II, 353, 383.

mander decided to ignore the diplomatic aspects of the situation for the time being. For Eisenhower's own troops this made no difference; their orders had already been written and would be obeyed. Initially, there were some fears about the attitude of civilian officials in newly liberated areas. These proved groundless, but an accord with the French Committee of National Liberation before the landing would doubtless have speeded up co-ordination of effort at the tactical level. Lack of an accord caused various minor complications. For example, it was something of a paradox that each U.S. soldier landing in France, a supposedly friendly country, carried 400 francs ($4.03) in invasion currency secured only by military fiat and angrily repudiated by de Gaulle. Norman farmers and French bankers alike accepted the paper money without protest, but for several weeks the finances of the liberated areas were in a state of confusion that could have been prevented. Littlejohn, visiting the Continent on 22 June, found that his purchasing and contracting officers were buying produce at prices fixed months earlier by the Germans. While the prices seemed slightly high, the lack of an ETO policy on prices was far more serious and Littlejohn asked the general purchasing agent to establish one immediately. The general purchasing agent was well aware of the need for fixed prices to prevent competitive bidding and inflation, but for lack of an over-all agreement his agents had made slow progress in concluding separate and temporary agreements with individual regional officials. On 25 August 1944, when all the military orders to Allied troops regarding civil affairs, local pro-

curement, and similar matters received the sanction of international agreement, the invasion currency was retroactively validated.[40]

The organization for local procurement employed in the United Kingdom was brought to the Continent intact. General Allen, the general purchasing agent, had become subordinate to the G–4 Section of COMZ in January 1944, but without change in duties. Colonel Barber continued as chief of the OCQM Procurement Division after it moved to France, but it should be noted that many important functions of his office remained behind in London. The program of purchasing British products, especially wool clothing and vegetables, was expanded to include exports to U.S. troops on the Continent.

Reflecting earlier experiences in the Mediterranean theater and the wishes of the governments-in-exile, an ETO directive of April 1944 provided guidance on policy and operating procedures for the procurement of supplies and services. Aware that four years of German occupation had stripped the economies of the liberated countries, the general purchasing agent sought to prevent any local procurement that would result in compensating imports to support the civilian population. He specifically prohibited local requisition of medical supplies and soap, POL, and all foods except fresh fruits and vegetables. Allied

---

[40] (1) Pogue, The Supreme Command, p. 233. (2) Komer, Civil Affairs, ch. XXI, p. 14. (3) FUSA Rpt of Opns, 20 Oct 43–1 Aug 44, VI, 218–20. (4) IRS, CQM to GPA, 23 Jun 44, sub: Price Policies in France. Littlejohn Reading File, vol. XXV, item 55. (5) Accords relatifs aux questions . . . financières, entre le Gouvernement Provisoire de la République et les États-Unis . . . signés le 25 Aout 1944 (Paris: Imprimerie Nationale, 1944).

personnel were expressly forbidden to buy food in restaurants, though night clubs were excepted. No fuel could be purchased except firewood released by local forestry officials. This provision, included at the insistence of the French, later had to be modified. Although coal was in short supply, it was required by the combat forces and requisitioned as a matter of military necessity. The directive further provided that, before the re-establishment of recognized central governments in the liberated countries, U.S. forces could either requisition through the local regional officials, with ultimate settlement to be left to the national authorities, or make direct cash purchases. Once the central governments became operative, procedures were to be revised, and the bulk of procurement was to be handled through a central agency—in France, the *Service D'Aide Aux Forces Alliées (SAFA)*. For practical purposes, a distinction was also made between day-to-day operational needs, which could be met by "field procurement" of surplus civilian supplies and "headquarters procurement" covering long-term or recurrent requirements for supplies not immediately accessible and involving the initiation of manufacturing or other productive processes.[41]

Notwithstanding that the area to be liberated was one of the highly industrialized regions of the world, it was doubtful from the start how much local support the Allies might draw from it. Industry and transport had been exploited by the Germans and bombed by the Allies. Inadequate transportation aggravated a severe food shortage in the whole area. Labor was plentiful, although rendered inefficient by malnutrition. Any major continental procurement program would need food for the workers, parts or materials to renovate transportation and industrial plants, and raw materials to be manufactured for delivery to the Allies. This implied a complicated long-term program requiring multilateral agreements. Thus in headquarters procurement the OCQM Procurement Division had little freedom of individual action. Littlejohn was an enthusiastic proponent of the continental program, but he wisely refused to cancel any requisition on NYPE until deliveries from continental sources had actually begun.[42]

Within a month after the liberation of Paris, representatives of *SAFA*, the French Ministries of Finance and Labor, SHAEF, and the general purchasing agent agreed upon the procedures for American procurement of supplies and civilian labor. Henceforth American procurement officials were in daily contact with *SAFA*, and whenever a sizable order was placed—for jerricans, cotton duck, or fuel wood, to mention several typical Quartermaster projects—representatives of the interested technical service and of the general purchasing agent conferred with both *SAFA*

---

[41] (1) ETO SOP 10, Proc Regulations in Occupied and Liberated Territory, 1 Apr 44; Change 1, 1 Jul 44, Incl, SHAEF Admin Memo 60; Amendments 10F, 23 Sep 44 (France), 10B, 5 Oct 44 (Belgium), and 10G, 15 Dec 44 (Germany). All in AG 400.12. (2) International Div ASF, History of Reciprocal Aid, 9 May 41–31 Dec 45, pp. 45–46. MS OCMH. (3) Continental Operating Instructions, OCQM, 19 Feb 45, p. 21. Hist Br OQMG. (4) Ltr, Deputy GPA ETOUSA to Dir Prod Div ASF, n.d., sub: Prod in France. GPA 004.03.

[42] (1) Ruppenthal, *Logistical Support* II, 474–75. (2) Pentagon Conf on ETOUSA Proc, 3 Jan 45. GPA 004.03.

and the French ministry having jurisdiction over the particular supplies under consideration.[43] Similarly, as soon as the enemy was cleared from Belgium and Luxembourg, the governments of these countries established offices comparable to *SAFA,* and the general purchasing agent sent deputies to the various capital cities, to determine what facilities could be readily put into operation that would be of either direct or indirect benefit to the military forces. Rivalry with the British for the use of continental facilities added to the complications of procurement. After creation of the British-American Mission for Procurement on the Continent in September 1944, General Allen and Sir Cecil Weir, the senior British member, easily reached an amicable settlement of most problems of that nature.[44]

Except for temporary and emergency requirements, services and supplies received by the American forces were paid for by the individual European governments in accordance with lend-lease and reciprocal aid agreements concluded at the diplomatic levels. While superficially this arrangement seemed simple, procurement activities were barely beyond the blueprint stage before delays were caused by conflicting interpretations of reciprocal aid agreements, by the refusal of suppliers to participate in

the program until they were sure payment would be promptly forthcoming from the French authorities, and by the inability of French manufacturers to obtain needed raw materials through their accustomed channels.[45]

Among Quartermaster field installations, the responsibility for short-term procurement was separated from the various supply sections and given to a purchasing and contracting officer in the administrative or executive division. To assure a reasonable orderliness in procurement procedures, the OCQM issued explicit instructions that only duly designated purchasing and contracting officers would engage in such activities. But field procurement was not exclusively concerned with supplies which were unavailable from military sources; regulations provided that local procurement could be employed "when the time element and exigencies of the service did not permit acquisition through regular channels." [46] Monetary limitations, originally $1,000 and later $2,000, were put on the amounts that base section purchasing and contracting officers could spend without going through the OCQM, while in the combat zone officers were obliged to obtain army-level approval for all purchases above $100. The First Army controlled pro-

[43] Ltr, GPA to Chief Ln Sec Hq ComZ, 22 Sep 44, sub: Relations With French Authorities. GPA 091.1 France.

[44] (1) Ltr, Deputy GPA to GPA, 21 Oct 44, sub: Belgium—Proc and Labor; Memo, GPA in Belgium for Purchasing Agent CBS, 22 Oct 44, sub: Hq Proc Program in Belgium; Daily Rpts, OGPA USA 21 Army Group (Rear), 19, 30 Oct, 2 Nov 44. All in USFET GPA 319.1. (2) IRS, GPA to CQM, 24 Sep 44, sub: Prod of Garments in France. USFET GPA 432.

[45] (1) Ltr, Deputy GPA to Dir Prod Div ASF, n.d., sub: Prod in France. 004.03 GPA. (2) Personal Ltr, Deputy GPA to Chief *SAFA,* 3 Oct 44; Ltr, OGPA Oise Sec to GPA COMZ, 11 Dec 44, sub: Payment to French Civilian Vendors by French Authorities. Both in GPA 091.1 France. (3) *CONAD History,* I, 146. (4) Hist of 63d QMBD, p. 8. Hist Br OQMG. (5) Littlejohn, ed., Passing in Review, ch. 41, "QM Procurement in the ETO," by Col. T. V. Barber, pt. 2, p. 9.

[46] Continental Operating Instructions, OCQM, 19 Feb 45, p. 21.

curement through its G–5 Section, while Third Army used the Fiscal Branch of its G–4 Section for this purpose. Once the reciprocal aid procedures were improved by experience, direct expenditures of cash dropped perceptibly. At the 62d Quartermaster Base Depot in Verdun, for example, less than one-fourth of one percent of total procurements before V–E Day were cash transactions.[47]

As the forward liaison office of the OCQM Procurement Division, the ADSEC quartermaster was the most active field procurement agency. The Procurement Branch at this echelon supervised and co-ordinated purchasing and contracting activities of all ADSEC Quartermaster depots, and participated with regional deputies of *SAFA* and liaison officers from the Low Countries in surveys and contract negotiations of procurable facilities. No less than in the areas farther to the rear, these tasks had their trying moments. It was necessary to arbitrate conflicts between military and civilian priorities, educate Europeans in American business methods, outline efficient work plans for the suppliers, and settle the claims of civilians and members of former resistance movements against needed stocks. So that future procurement would not suffer, such friction as occurred between the American military and Allied nationals in the course of these negotiations had to be eliminated by tact and diplomacy. Even when relations were at their best, local procurement was complicated by inadequate transportation, inexperienced civilian labor, and an absence of weighing and packaging equipment. If the Americans had not been able to provide Army transport to the suppliers, or at least gasoline, tires, and oil for their vehicles, as well as sacks, cartons, and crates, the procurement program would have been even further handicapped.[48]

The Ordnance Service arranged the first large importation of U.S. raw materials on the Continent for military purposes—rubber required for retreading tires after the pursuit across France. Brig. Gen. Hugh O. Minton, chief of the Production Division, ASF, came to Europe in October 1944 to get the program under way. With this exception, Ordnance procurement activities, mainly repair of vehicles and modification of equipment, required skilled labor rather than raw materials. Engineer procurement, largely concerned with construction, used locally available materials. The OCQM initiated most of the procurement that required importation of raw materials from the United States. Late in December 1944 Colonel Barber and General Allen went to Washington to arrange for an allocation of about 100,000 tons of materials, largely sheet steel, cotton, wood pulp, and wool. They traveled on the same aircraft with General Minton, who gave them considerable support during a conference with General Somervell on 3 January 1945.[49]

---

[47] (1) *Ibid.* (2) Hist of 62d QMBD, p. 40. (3) TUSA AAR, II, G–4 40.

[48] (1) Hist of QM Sec ADSEC, p. 33. (2) Hist of 63d QMBD, pp. 6–7. (3) QM Procurement on the Continent, January–June 1945, pp. 1, 13–14. MS, Hist Br OQMG. (4) The detailed results from continental procurement are reported separately for each category of QM supply in succeeding chapters.

[49] (1) Pentagon Conf on ETOUSA Proc, 3 Jan 45, GPA 004.03. (2) Ruppenthal, *Logistical Support*, II, 489.

On 28 February a Production Branch was set up within the OCQM Procurement Division to assist the general purchasing agent in the many-sided production program. This branch expedited raw materials from the ports to its own warehouse within Depot Q-177 at Paris, allocated them to manufacturers, checked on the manufacturing process, and inspected items before acceptance. It maintained careful stock control and consumption records which contributed to improved accuracy in computing raw materials requirements. The branch also controlled captured German raw materials and raw materials requisitioned from private German sources, insofar as these were in Quartermaster categories. On 29 April 1945 the Production Control Agency, ETOUSA, was established, and thereafter the activity of this branch within Germany was controlled by that agency. Since the U.S. zone of Germany was to be administered by military districts under the armies, and no base sections were to be organized, this implied a new channel of command, but the channel of technical supervision was not materially modified. Subject to co-ordination by G–4 and G–5, the Quartermaster Service was assigned responsibility for the German industries producing most of those items procured by the QMC in the zone of interior. POL was not included, but the OCQM found itself concerned with both basic and final processing in textiles, food, leather, office equipment and supplies, containers and household goods, and ceramics. To handle these tremendous responsibilities the Quartermaster Production Control Division, staffed by 762 officers and enlisted men and headed by Brig. Gen. John B.

Franks, was set up at Frankfurt. This unit provided most of the personnel for the Office of the Quartermaster, Occupation Forces, Germany, which was established at the same site and under the same commander on 20 June 1945.[50]

In terms of actual deliveries to the U.S. forces before V–E Day, the production program on the Continent was disappointing. Scheduled deliveries of QM supplies for the entire year 1945 from Allied countries on the Continent and neutrals had a total value of $210,000,000. Supplies actually received through 30 June were worth only $14,510,377. None of the major programs based on processing of imported raw materials had produced any large volume of deliveries before V–E Day. Littlejohn and Somervell were aware that delays were inevitable, and that these projects had more humanitarian significance for the rehabilitation of the continental economy than strictly military importance. Some of them were undertaken at the specific insistence of War Production Board representatives.[51]

Shipping shortages and congestion in continental ports delayed the arrival of raw materials, but the major difficulties stemmed from the disorganized economies of the Allied countries. Government administration, production, distribution, and currencies were all re-

[50] (1) Ltr, CQM to QM ADSEC, 19 Dec 44, sub: Proc in ADSEC; Personal Ltr, Middleswart to Littlejohn 5 Dec 44, and Ltr, CQM to SOLOC QM, 19 Dec 44, sub: Proc on Continent. Littlejohn Reading File, vol. XXXI, items 64, 66. (2) QM Supply in ETO, I, 24, 37–38.

[51] (1) MS cited n. 48 (3), above. (2) Ltr, CQM to Dr. W. Y. Elliott, 14 Jan 45, sub: Prod Program for Europe; Memo, CQM for Somervell, 15 Jan 45, same sub. Littlejohn Reading File, vol. XXXII, items 65, 66.

covering slowly from a complete collapse. Under strict military controls such as were imposed initially in Italy, it might have been possible to shore up specific enterprises by stopgap measures and compel them to produce. In free countries where the needs of the civilian population came first, the U.S. technical services had to be content with their allocated share of the slowly reviving industrial potential. To an American procurement officer, the machinery of reciprocal aid appeared to be primarily a means of curbing U.S. procurement activity, and only secondarily a method of recompense for lend-lease supplies. Moreover, he often found himself in competition with the French national rearmament program, which received favorable priorities from local officials because it enhanced the military prestige of France. But probably the most important cause of failure to complete the large industrial procurement projects was lack of coal. It had been estimated that the 100,000 tons of American raw materials already mentioned would require a direct supplement of 180,000 tons of European coal to complete the QM procurement program. That estimate had ignored the needs of an urban population for light, heat, and transportation, which were also dependent upon coal.[52]

The end of hostilities on 8 May came just as seasonal requirements of coal for civilian uses were declining. During late May and early June most of the large industrial projects were canceled, and the rest were materially reduced in size. Large shipments of U.S. raw ma-

terials had arrived and were reported as surplus at the end of June. General indications are that the industrial procurement program was just beginning to show results when it was cut off.[53]

The Supply and Relief Operations of G–5

Some mention has already been made of the ETO Civil Affairs organization in connection with local procurement. Very briefly stated, Civil Affairs was the established channel for all communication between military commanders in liberated territory and the civilian population. In conquered enemy territory, a very similar function called Military Government was performed by the same organization. A special staff section, commonly called Civil Affairs–Military Government was attached to every major tactical and logistical headquarters in the theater. Its aims were to prevent disease and unrest among the civilian population that might impede military operations and also to make available manpower and resources for military objectives. In the Mediterranean theater these functions had been rather narrowly interpreted, and a separate Civil Affairs–Military Government chain of command had been set up to implement them. Moreover, requisitioning, storage, and distribution of relief supplies were a separate Civil Affairs responsibility in which the technical services did not participate. In the European thea-

---

[52] QM Procurement on the Continent, Jan–Jun 45.

[53] For example, production of jerricans is often cited as one of the less successful projects, but output for May 1945 was estimated at 150,000 cans, and a 300 percent increase was forecast for June. IRS, GPA for CQM, 7 May 45, no sub. USFET GPA 457.

ter, COSSAC planners had envisioned a Civil Affairs–Military Government organization more closely tied to the tactical chain of command at each level, culminating in a close control over liberated and occupied areas alike by SHAEF. These views, codified as a proposed Civil Affairs–Military Government handbook for civil affairs units in the field, provoked an acrimonious debate between Mediterranean and north European theorists which transcended nationality. General Morgan later admitted that COSSAC set off entirely on the wrong foot in regard to its civil affairs planning, and one of his harassed subordinates observed that "there were plenty of affairs, but the difficulty was to keep them civil." [54]

President Roosevelt widened the area of debate when he directed Secretary Stimson to plan for initial relief and rehabilitation operations by the Army in all areas evacuated by the Germans, whether those areas were of military importance or not. That directive insured that the Civil Affairs–Military Government function would be very broadly interpreted in the ETO, and involved the new organization in a wide range of logistical, economic, fiscal, and diplomatic activities. The plan finally settled upon was a compromise. Military Government (in Germany) would conform to the original close control concept; in the combat zone within liberated areas, close control would also be exercised by tactical commanders, but in close co-ordination with liaison officers of the Allied nation concerned. In the

communications zone and in other rear areas control would be turned over to restored Allied governments as rapidly as possible, and such relief activities as were still necessary would be assumed by the United Nations Relief and Rehabilitation Administration (UNRRA). As long as any Civil Affairs functions in rear areas remained in military hands, they would be administered through command channels—primarily by Civil Affairs–Military Government officers in each base section.

Any possibility of a separate Civil Affairs–Military Government chain of command in the ETO was definitely eliminated in February 1944, when the Civil Affairs Division of SHAEF was upgraded to a general staff division, and redesignated G–5. Lt. Gen. Arthur E. Grassett, a Canadian, was appointed Assistant Chief of Staff, G–5, with Brig. Gen. Julius C. Holmes as his American deputy. These officers brought about a basic revision of the controversial handbook, and later exercised technical supervision over the Civil Affairs—Military Government units deployed in the field. By virtue of their position in the command structure, the two officers could call on the COMZ technical services for support in fulfilling their mission. [55]

Quartermaster Support for G–5

The procedure followed in obtaining and delivering relief supplies involved close co-operation. Requirements were

---

[54] Lieutenant-General Sir Fredrick E. Morgan, *Overture to OVERLORD* (New York: Doubleday & Company, Inc., 1950), p. 227.

[55] (1) USFET Gen Bd Study 32, pp. 46–51. (2) OTCQM TSFET Operational Study 12, pp. 1–4. (3) Ltr, Roosevelt to SW, 10 Nov 43. (4) Pogue, *The Supreme Command*, pp. 79–83. (5) *QM Supply in ETO*, IX, 2–11.

computed by G–5, and SHAEF divided procurement responsibility for specific items between Great Britain and the United States. The OCQM forwarded to NYPE such requisitions as were referred to it for that purpose. Editing requisitions and designating shipping priorities were G–5 responsibilities. Once they arrived in the theater, all supplies of a quartermaster nature were stored in Quartermaster depots. Furthermore, the OCQM assumed full responsibility for distribution from ports to depots, and between depots, but G–5 designated the locations of supplies and arranged intratheater shipping priorities. Issue was made in bulk to Civil Affairs units or officers at depots or truckheads. G–5 edited the requisitions of its own subordinate units. Civil Affairs supplies were segregated from other supplies, but were stored at the same depots that handled Quartermaster supplies of the same category. By military standards, the packing of Civil Affairs supplies was inferior, so that they deteriorated rapidly when stored in the open. This applied especially to food and clothing, which were by far the largest categories of relief supplies. From modest beginnings, Civil Affairs tonnages in Quartermaster Class I, II, and IV depots rose to nearly 350,000 tons—some 15 percent of all such supplies—in April 1945.[56]

At first glance, computing relief requirements may seem a technical matter suitable for transfer to the various technical services, but Civil Affairs–Military Government requirements differed from all others in one important respect: relief issues were supplementary and not intended to supply all the needs of a nation, or even of an individual except on a temporary basis. Requirements were therefore based on anticipated deficits in local sources of supply. Such computations were made from specialized economic intelligence data and included such imponderables as the amount of "scorching" the Germans might perform before they evacuated various areas. Civil Affairs supplies fell into four general categories:[57]

Items necessary for immediate relief, consisting of food, clothing, medical, and sanitary supplies.

Items necessary for distribution of relief, consisting of emergency feeding equipment, fuel, and initial repairs to public utility, communication, and transport systems.

Items required to re-establish production of natural resources, such as coal, oil, etc., for military purposes.

Items which will have the effect of reducing the relief burden at the earliest possible date, consisting of agricultural implements and seeds and raw materials for rehabilitation of the textile industry.

The President's decision to provide this type of support through military channels involved the Quartermaster Corps in many new and unfamiliar responsibilities. For example, before D-day the OCQM requisitioned some 73,000 items of agricultural equipment and over five million pounds of seeds for delivery by D plus 180. Beginning

---

[56] (1) Each category of Civil Affairs supplies is discussed separately in connection with similar Quartermaster supplies. (2) The OCQM reported that at the end of hostilities roughly one-third of all QM supplies in the theater were earmarked for Civil Affairs. See OTCQM TSFET Operational Study 8, p. 2. (3) OTCQM TSFET Operational Study 12, p. 3. (4) QM Supply in ETO, I, 193–96; IX, 27.

[57] ETO SOP 28, Civil Affairs Supply Procedures, 2 Jun 44. AG 400.

in November 1944 a French Civil Import Program, presented to ASF by Jean Monnet and co-ordinated by the general purchasing agent, gradually relieved the OCQM of its responsibility for long-term rehabilitation in France.[58]

The OCQM was engaged in providing identical items of food, clothing, and sanitary supplies to two general categories of personnel through two different supply channels. Needy local civilians and refugees received Quartermaster supplies from the Civil Affairs organization, either from CA field units or through local governmental agencies. The OCQM supplied the same articles directly to people for whom the U.S. Army was exclusively responsible—prisoners of war, recovered Allied prisoners (including Russians), Italians and Slavs in service units, and civilian laborers. The Civil Affairs ration, since it was supplementary, was rather meager. The OCQM ration for prisoners of war was considerably larger, and that for recovered Allied prisoners was still more generous. Displaced persons were a particular source of confusion. Many had fought on both sides in the war, and could describe themselves as POW's, Allies, or civilian refugees, according to the exigencies of the moment. Three months after the end of hostilities Littlejohn estimated that the Army was still feeding some 1,500,000 displaced persons from military stocks, partly because of confusion regarding their status, and partly because G–5 stocks had been exhausted. The Chief Quartermaster recommended that, in any future conflict, policy on support for all non-U.S. personnel, including careful statistical con-

trols, be the subject of earlier and more centralized planning, and that the actual computation of requirements should be an exclusive QMC function.[59] (See Table 17.)

The OCQM normally computed requirements for storage of Civil Affairs supplies as part of its successive over-all storage plans. In December 1944, space was allocated for 20,000 long tons each at Liège, Charleroi, and Verdun, 17,000 tons at Paris, and 10,000 tons at Cherbourg. By February 1945 these allocations had been materially exceeded, but no new locations had been designated. On 13 March, G–4 requested Civil Affairs storage space for 260,000 long tons at new sites nearer to the Rhine, capable of issuing more than 9,000 tons daily. Four days later the OCQM submitted the following plan:

Depot	Storage capacity	Daily issues
Verdun-Esch subdepot	90,000	3,400
Liège-Lutterade subdepot	75,000	2,800
Charleroi depot	45,000	1,400
CONAD depots	35,000	1,350
Total	245,000	8,950

At the end of April all these allocations except CONAD's had been exceeded, and over 300,000 long tons were on hand east of Paris. By June 1945 Quartermaster responsibility for Civil Affairs storage was restricted to Germany, where space for 100,000 tons each was required in the Eastern and Western Military Districts, 5,000 tons in Berlin, and 35,000 tons in Bremen.[60]

---

[58] QM Supply in ETO, IX, 29–32.

[59] (1) OTCQM TSFET Operational Study 8, exhibit C–9. (2) OTCQM TSFET Operational Study 12, p. 5.

[60] QM Supply in ETO, I, 187, 193, 196; IX, 20.

ETO Requisitioning Procedures

As long as the supply situation remained critical, the OCQM was forced to maintain careful supervision over base sections, depots, and other field installations. Littlejohn and his staff realized that centralized control of supply in the OCQM was a cumbersome, slow, and unwieldy method of meeting demands from the combat troops. Gradually, the depots were given greater autonomy in editing and filling requisitions, and part of the task of monitoring these activities was delegated to base section quartermasters. But progress along these lines had to go hand in hand with improvement in the training of Quartermaster troops, which was a responsibility of the Field Service Division. Irregular and unreliable transportation presented another obstacle to the OCQM objective of delegating authority over supply, since the Storage and Distribution Division had to intervene frequently. Moreover, as long as port discharge was confined to Cherbourg and the beaches, there was a natural tendency to maintain centralized control over centralized operations.[61]

The daily allocation of transportation tonnage by G–4, COMZ, to the armies remained the controlling factor in all supply operations until early January 1945. Requisitions flowed from the armies through the regulating stations to the G–4 Section, COMZ, which was interested only in tonnage and directed that only unitemized gross tonnages of each class of supply should be requested. As long as the armies were in motion they were able to justify demands for most of the available tonnage, and received it in the form of a specific number of railroad trains for each class of supply. The base sections received barely enough to supply the air forces and their own personnel, and nothing at all to build up stocks in the depots.

A characteristic episode of this period concerned winter clothing. Littlejohn warned the army quartermasters that such clothing was available at the ports, but if they wanted it they would have to make their desires known by way of the army G–4's to 12th Army Group and G–4, COMZ, for the OCQM had no control over transportation. Moreover, in view of slow and uncertain deliveries he recommended that they request air transportation.[62] Under prevailing conditions, such action meant that clothing went straight from the beaches to the armies, but none was added to the meager stocks in the depots.

Since specific items, not tonnages, were needed to supply the troops, OCQM maintained close contact with the army quartermasters to learn their actual needs. On 16 September 1944, an OCQM circular letter directed that army and base section quartermasters submit periodic estimates of their future needs—for rations every ten days, and for clothing every fifteen days.[63] These estimates were in detail, with separate tonnage listed for each item, and indicated the desired priority. They were used in making up loads for the daily trains allocated by G–4. As an aid to

---

[61] OTCQM TSFET Operational Study 5, p. 12.

[62] Personal Ltrs, CQM to QM's First and Third Armies, 7 Sep 44. Littlejohn Reading File, vol. XXVIII, item 48.

[63] OCQM Cir Ltr 52, 16 Sep 44, sub: Procedure for Supply of QM Items on the Continent. Hist Br OQMG.

estimating Class II requirements, OCQM prepared and circulated a basic maintenance set, listing probable requirements of various items and sizes of clothing. (*See Appendix A.*) But the estimates and the more detailed telegram were merely for the convenience of the OCQM. Despite Littlejohn's objections, G–4, COMZ, continued to receive the official daily telegram and to make rigid allocations of tonnage to each army for each class of supply. Significantly, the OCQM's circular letter prescribed an elaborate courier system to insure prompt delivery of the estimates.[64]

Although rapid pursuit came to an end during September 1944, the armies held obstinately to their optimistic estimate of the situation. With the same obstinacy, G–4 as their agent retained exclusive control over tonnage allocations. Each day it seemed that one more division committed to combat or one more day of hard driving would crack the stubborn German resistance and end the war. Littlejohn believed that the time had come to establish intermediate depots nearer the combat zone. Even in victory the troops would have to be fed and clothed; Quartermaster responsibilities might even be increased. A resupply of the armies had just been completed, but this merely replaced clothing and equipment lost or worn out during the pursuit. It provided few heavy winter items and no reserve at all for cold weather. On 7 October Littlejohn urged the G–4, COMZ, to establish a Class II and IV depot at Reims, perishable Class I and PX supplies at Paris, and all classes of supply at Nancy and

Liège-Namur. He pointed out that the line of communications was now over 400 miles long. UTAH and OMAHA beaches would soon have to shut down because of winter storms, and Cherbourg could hardly be expanded to make good the deficit. The system of hand-to-mouth supply over long distances was completely unsuited to proper distribution of sized items of clothing—an absolute necessity as winter set in. Pilferage was growing, encouraged by the disorderly current procedures. Littlejohn understood that Oise Intermediate Section would be activated in the very near future and recommended that ADSEC's two base depot companies be sent forward immediately to establish depots at Liège and Nancy. His recommendation was ignored. During the next few days the G–4's of the armies and Brig. Gen. Raymond P. Moses, G–4 of the 12th Army Group, all refused to allocate Class II tonnage to the Chief Quartermaster. A personal appeal to General Bradley brought a similar refusal. The 12th Army Group commander felt that other supplies were more urgently needed. Possibly he misunderstood the inadequacy of the recent clothing issue. He said that "The men are tough and can take it." [65]

In late October a shortage developed of the ration accessory convenience kits distributed to combat troops with operational rations. These kits were considered an integral part of the operational

---

[64] OTCQM TSFET Operational Study 5, p. 12, and exhibit C–3.

[65] (1) Ltr, CQM to G–4 COMZ, 6 Oct 44, sub: Establishment of Intermediate QM Depots; Ltr, CQM to CG ADSEC, 7 Oct 44, same sub. Littlejohn Reading File, vol. XXIX, items 43 and 43a. (2) Littlejohn, ed., Passing in Review, ch. 21, p. 9. (3) Quotation from Ltr, CQM to Busch, 18 Jan 45. Littlejohn Reading File, vol. XXXII, item 94.

ration and enjoyed the latter's high priority for transportation. The most important item in the kit, from the viewpoint of the combat soldier, was a package of cigarettes. It would have been simple to requisition bulk citgarettes from PX stocks in Great Britain, reclassify them as emergency Class I supplements to operational rations, and bring them to the Continent under high transportation priorities. Littlejohn refused to do this; he directed that the few cigarettes remaining on the Continent be reserved for combat troops, but otherwise he took no action whatever for nearly a month. On 27 November there were no cigarettes in the rear areas, and only a three-day reserve with the armies. The shortage received considerable publicity in the press, both at home and in the ETO, and a Congressional delegation when in Europe demanded an explanation. Now assured of a wide audience, the Chief Quartermaster submitted a report showing that there were nearly 150 million packages of cigarettes en route, in the United Kingdom, or awaiting discharge off continental ports. He stated that he did not feel justified in requesting special priorities for cigarettes as long as there were shortages in operational rations and winter clothing. As a specific example, he called attention to a ship loaded with 1,200,000 blankets. This ship had been berthed at Le Havre seven times, but each time had been removed without unloading to make way for other cargo with higher priorities. General Lee conceded the validity of the argument, and personally guaranteed the QMC a special allocation of tonnage to move Class II supplies. But Littlejohn failed to achieve his real objective—a permanent allocation of five extra un-

loading berths for the Quartermaster service at Rouen.[66] (See Table 19.)

This episode presents only one facet of a many-sided struggle over tonnage allocations. Inevitably, the SHAEF G–4 Section became involved and began assigning allocations to all subordinate headquarters on 5 November. Meanwhile the supply situation had eased considerably and a build-up of reserves had become possible. But the armies, blaming COMZ for the recent shortages, were determined to have the reserves built up in their own dumps rather than in COMZ depots. Therefore they favored continuing the allocation system as long as SHAEF administered it to their advantage. They were only partly aware of the inherent clumsiness and inflexibility of the daily allocations that often provided them with supplies they had not requisitioned and could not use, and were inclined to blame COMZ for these misdirected supplies. COMZ contended that it should receive a much higher proportion of the tonnage to build up reserves in its own intermediate and advanced depots, which could then provide better supply service to the armies. But COMZ was consistently overoptimistic over its own movement capabilities, and the resulting deficits in deliveries weakened its arguments in opposition to SHAEF and the armies. To a large extent, those deficits cut into the overinflated requisitions of the

---

[66] (1) Littlejohn, ed., Passing in Review, ch. 21, pp. 10–11. (2) Memo, Chief of Supply Div for CQM, 27 Nov 44, sub: Supply Status of Cigarettes in France; IRS, CQM to G–4 COMZ, 30 Nov 44, sub: QM Items Currently in Short Supply. Littlejohn Reading File, vol. XXX, items 104, 111. (3) Transcript of Daily [COMZ] Conference, 29 Nov 44.

armies rather than their actual needs. The build-up of supplies in the army areas continued despite paper "deficits." [67]   SHAEF discontinued allocations in December, but COMZ retained this practice until January 1945.[68]

By December the tactical situation was less critical, the OCQM had assembled considerable information on the size and location of its supply assets, and current requirements were fairly steady and predictable. Moreover, the armies and base sections were becoming increasingly dissatisfied with the whole concept of daily telegrams and daily allocations. The main reason for this, was the delay in filling requisitions. Unfilled requisitions were placed in a "back-order" file in the port depots, but frequently the armies were not informed. The armies then assumed that the original requisition had not arrived and placed another one. This made for overlapping of requisitions—multiple back orders for the same items—and much confusion. With the consent of G–4, COMZ, the OCQM published a new procedure on 5 December 1944, whereby Class II, sales store, PX supplies, and solid fuel were to be omitted from the daily telegram. Using these estimates, the OCQM established credits for the various major commands at intermediate depots, and the depots could honor all requisitions without reference to OCQM as long as the credits were not exceeded. The only exceptions were solid fuels, spare parts, and certain scarce items of clothing officially designated "controlled items."

The OCQM controlled the whole process through distribution directives issued to base and intermediate depots, and designed to maintain the levels needed in the advance depots to meet established credits.

In January 1945 COMZ finally abandoned the daily allocation of trains, and the whole transportation procedure was put on what Littlejohn regarded as a "concrete, business-like basis." [69]   Thereafter, G–4 allocated available transportation to the technical services on a monthly basis, and left all operating details to the theater chief of transportation.[70] Under Transportation Corps control, supply movements were coordinated all the way from shipside to the army dumps. Volume of freight was regulated to fit the unloading capacities of the depots, and the urgent daily needs of the combat forces could be met by rail, truck, or air transport, whatever means were most convenient. The OCQM likewise relaxed its control— ADSEC now designated the advance depots to supply the individual armies.

On 9 February, the OCQM issued Circular Letter 14, which prescribed new procedures for operating base, intermediate, and advanced depots. Decentralization of supply was developed to the maximum by putting the burden of editing requisitions on the depots desig-

---

[67] Ruppenthal, *Logistical Support*, II, 172–180.

[68] (1) Cir Ltr 97, OCQM, 5 Dec 44, sub: Procedure for Distr of QM Supplies to Armies, ADSEC, and Secs. (2) USFET Gen Bd Study 109, QM Supply Opns in an Overseas Theater. OCMH.

[69] Ltr, Maj Gen Royal B. Lord to G–4 and Chiefs of Tech Svs, 10 Jan 45, sub: Procedure for Planning Reception and Movement of Supplies, Equip, and Pers. Quoted in OTCQM TSFET Operational Study 5.

[70] It appears likely that this change was made at the urging of Generals Somervell and Lutes of ASF, who inspected the COMZ organization in December 1944. At their insistence, the influence and authority of Transportation was enhanced. Ruppenthal, *Logistical Support*, II, p. 391.

nated to receive the requisitions. Review of requisitions for controlled items was delegated to base section quartermasters. Intermediate depots were to carry the bulk of balanced stocks of all Quartermaster items for the entire theater; limited model stocks for local issue and the unbalanced reserve of all classes of supply would be held in the base depots. Advance depots would carry only limited quantities of carefully selected fast-moving items. Their stocks were also to be exactly balanced so that the supply units could close out depots rapidly and move forward. The requisition period for Class II, IV, and PX supplies was lengthened to twenty days to decrease still further the probability of overlapping requisitions. The regulating stations that received the requisitions from the armies and the depots that filled them were made jointly responsible for informing the armies promptly of action taken on requisitions and when the supplies would arrive.[71]

This plan was received by combat zone quartermasters with a certain amount of trepidation. Col. James W. Younger, the 12th Army Group quartermaster, feared that editing of requisitions at the level of the intermediate depot would be interpreted too literally and would jeopardize the liberal screening policy practiced by the OCQM. "There must be no headquarters or agencies interposed between the echelon needing the supplies and the echelons furnishing the supplies," wrote Younger. Direct contact had to be maintained between the army quartermaster and the supplying depots. He wanted to be reasonably sure that the new procedure would not delay the front-line receipt of supplies and reiterated the obvious advantages of being over rather than under supplied. Littlejohn answered that the new procedure was designed to speed up the receipt of supplies by reducing the number of agencies that reviewed requisitions. He suggested that until all concerned were familiar with the new procedures an officer hand-carry each major requisition to the depot and remain until it had been approved.[72]

Regulating Stations

Regulating stations were vital links in the supply chain since they both forwarded requisitions and monitored the delivery of supplies.[73] A heritage of World War I, regulating stations were described in the 1943 edition of Field Service Regulations as traffic control agencies of the theater commander on the line of communications, through which supply and personnel movements were directed. Situated near the boundary between the communications zone and the combat zone, preferably at the junction of several rail lines, the regulating stations were expected to determine priorities of traffic moving into army areas. It was assumed that one regulating station would be assigned to

[71] Cir Ltr 14, OCQM, 9 Feb 45, sub: Procedure for Distr of QM Supplies on Continent. Quoted in full in OTCQM TSFET Operational Study 5.

[72] (1) Memo, QM 12th Army Group for G–4 12th Army Group, 8 Feb 45, sub: Levels of Supply; OCQM Cir Ltr 14, OCQM, 9 Feb 45, sub: Procedure for Distr of QM Supplies on Continent; Memo, QM 12th Army Group for CQM, 12 Feb 45, sub: Comments on Cir Ltr 14. All in Littlejohn Collection. (2) Ltrs, CQM to QM 12th Army Group, no sub, 16 and 18 Feb 45. Littlejohn Reading File, vol. XXXIII, items 80, 100.

[73] USFET Gen Bd Study 27, pt. III.

each army and that the principal means of transportation would be rail.[74]

Whether there was actually a need for regulating stations under World War II conditions, and if so what ought to be their areas of jurisdiction, were subjects of considerable debate. In the ETO, G–4, COMZ, as already noted, had assumed the responsibility of determining priorities and allocating transportation, depriving the regulating stations of their most important function. Under that procedure there was little reason for the regulating officer to be a personal representative of the theater commander, as prescribed in Field Service Regulations. Responsibility for establishment and management of regulating stations was delegated successively from SHAEF to COMZ, to ADSEC, and finally to the Transportation Section, ADSEC. Regulating stations—one for First Army and another for Third Army—became operational in August, after the drawing of an army rear boundary. ADSEC immediately appointed a representative to each army headquarters to act as regulating officer, advise the army on general supply policies, and suggest the location of service areas.[75] From the viewpoint of army commanders and their staffs, the chief function of the regulating station was to provide information on how soon requisitioned supplies would arrive.

In September, all ADSEC railheads and truckheads serving the armies were put under the control of these regulating stations. To each was attached a railhead team of Quartermaster service companies, a depot supply platoon, railhead platoon, and a complement of approximately five hundred POW's. The job of this team was to operate the transfer point and to move supplies from train to truck or from COMZ truck to army truck. It should be noted that this was an operating function and according to current doctrine should not have been performed by a staff section. Col. Samuel W. Smithers, the ADSEC quartermaster, was dissatisfied with the initial operations of the regulating stations, claiming that they did not make available to the armies enough information about shipments en route. This sentiment was echoed by both Colonel McNamara of the First Army and Colonel Busch of the Third Army. These army level quartermasters had very satisfactory relationships with G–4, COMZ, and felt that the regulating stations should be primarily information centers and documentation offices. They held that routing requisitions through the regulating station was time-consuming and unnecessary. They also noted and strongly disapproved a tendency of the regulating stations, as agencies of ADSEC, to take over railheads and transfer points in the army service areas.[76]

Littlejohn also, for different reasons, considered the early performance of the regulating stations so unsatisfactory that he was willing to see them dissolved. He felt that the Quartermaster representa-

---

[74] FM 100–10, Field Service Regulations, Administration, 15 November 1943, pp. 39–44.

[75] (1) USFET Gen Bd Study 27, pp. 48–49. (2) Ruppenthal, *Logistical Support*, I, 497–99.

[76] (1) Personal Ltrs, Littlejohn to Smithers, 3, 9 Sep 44; Personal Ltr, Smithers to Littlejohn, 12 Sep 44; Memo, CQM for Chief Field Sv, 16 Sep 44, no sub. All in Littlejohn Collection. (2) Critical comments on preliminary MS version of this history by General McNamara and Colonel Busch. Hist Br OQMG files.

tive in the regulating station should edit army requisitions critically, rather than merely give a "rubber-stamp approval" and forward them. Specifically, he felt that in a stringent supply situation combat units should receive only what they actually needed to fight with, rather than everything they were entitled to according to Tables of Equipment. Moreover, regulating stations were in an ideal position to know the actual strength of the units they served. They should never tolerate the common practice of submitting inflated strength reports for rations. To underline his conviction that regulating officers should have an intimate knowledge of the units they regulated, Littlejohn requested that ten jeeps be assigned to each regulating station, to be used for regular inspections and courier service to the rear.[77]

With the improvement in transportation and the development of a reliable communications system, regulating sta-

tions also began to operate more effectively. Late in November, daily ration and POL telegrams went to the appropriate station, which, in turn, sent them to the supplying base depot. The shipments forward were made by ADSEC. In February, this system was broadened to include the twenty-day requisition for clothing and equipage, which previously had been sent through ADSEC to the Class II and IV depot at Reims. The regulating officers and the quartermasters of the armies and of ADSEC met periodically to exchange information on their supply problems and to work out supply procedures. By the end of the year Colonel Smithers reported that the requisitioning procedures were working smoothly. The combat elements, confident that the supply organization behind them was operating efficiently, were preparing to renew the offensive against Germany.[78]

---

[77] Memos, CQM for Franks, 2 Sep 44, sub: Regulating Stations. Littlejohn Reading File, vol. XXVIII, items 13, 14.

[78] (1) Rpt, 24th Regulating Station, 10 Dec 44, sub: Processing of QM Class I Telegram. ADSEC 430. (2) TUSA AAR, II, QM 10, 13, 19.

CHAPTER XIII

Rear Area Support on the Continent: Operations

The operating agencies of the Communications Zone, responsible for moving supplies forward and delivering them to the combat units, were territorial subdivisions known as base sections, intermediate sections, and advance sections. Base sections on the Continent had almost exactly the same function as those in the United Kingdom. Intermediate sections also remained very much the same, except that they received supplies from a base section instead of from a port, and sometimes provided direct support to combat troops. Advance sections were direct-support agencies which concentrated their operations at the boundary between the communications zone and the combat zone. During an advance they were in constant motion, taking over and expanding the supply installations abandoned by the armies. Under such circumstances an advance section was primarily a traffic expediting and reconsignment agency, which only engaged in storage and distribution activities to a very limited extent. In a static situation, an advance section operated very much like an intermediate section. The European theater ultimately included two advance sections: the Advance Section, Communications Zone (ADSEC) which landed in Normandy in June 1944 and supported the 12th Army Group; and the Continental Advance Section, Southern Line of Communications (CONAD), which landed in southern France two months later and supported the 6th Army Group.[1]

Advance Section

According to plan, personnel of ADSEC were attached to the supply echelons of First Army, and began to arrive in Normandy about D plus 10. First Army retained control over its own logistical support as long as geographically feasible, and the ADSEC Quartermaster staff under Colonel Zwicker spent the first month on the continent largely observing supply operations under combat conditions. Gradually, ADSEC began to take over installations, first at Cherbourg and later on the beaches, while the armies readied themselves to break out of Normandy.[2]

Inextricably concerned with ADSEC's mission, Littlejohn visited the beach-

---

[1] Early activities of CONAD are described in Chapter IV; the role of Headquarters, ADSEC, in preinvasion planning is discussed in Chapter XI.

[2] Hist of QM Sec ADSEC, pp. 6, 8, 14. Hist Br OQMG.

head repeatedly in June and July. The First Army, with its front lines still almost in sight of the beach, relinquished its supply responsibilities grudgingly, one at a time. The commander of the Provisional Engineer Special Brigade Group, a brigadier general, retained many Quartermaster functions that should properly have been assumed by Colonel Zwicker. The result was that depots were located at the sites of the original dumps and that they were arranged primarily to speed the turnaround of amphibious trucks (Dukws), but without regard for segregation and inventory of quartermaster supplies. Statistical control over supply had disappeared. Littlejohn temporarily appointed himself quartermaster of ADSEC to solve the command problem, but the damage had already been done. Certain categories of scarce but important quartermaster items became lost and were not found for eight months.[3] After his third trip to the Continent, on 16 July, Littlejohn got Col. John B. Franks, the FECZ quartermaster, also to serve as acting quartermaster of ADSEC. He felt that on the eve of the crucial COBRA operation to break out from the constricted beachhead the ADSEC Quartermaster Section required aggressive leadership. Colonel Zwicker's extensive Quartermaster experience could be better utilized as a combat observer and as a judge of Quartermaster equipment under combat conditions. He was therefore made chief of the Research and Development Division of OCQM.[4]

Littlejohn found faults in his own staff as well as in ADSEC. One of the first QM base depot companies to reach the far shore reported the arrival of 11,073 corn brooms and 12,789 cotton mops, enough to sweep the battlefield. It questioned the immediate usefulness of 5,269 large garbage cans and 32,616 reams of mimeograph paper at a time when the main need was for rations, POL, and combat clothing. The Chief Quartermaster demanded more care and better judgment in the mechanics of quartermaster supply.[5]

Support of the Armies in the Pursuit

On 1 August, when the 12th Army Group and the Third Army became operational, ADSEC was detached from the First Army and assumed responsibility for support of both First and Third Armies through the 12th Army Group. By this time the breakout from the beachhead had succeeded, the armies were picking up speed, and ADSEC was soon hard pressed to follow them. It moved forward three times in as many weeks, establishing successive headquarters and supply installations at Le Mans on 20 August, Étampes on 31 August, and Reims on 8 September. What this pace meant to the Quartermaster Section can be more fully appreciated by realizing that the life of the average Class I and Class III supply point during this turbulent period was sixteen and ten

[3] (1) Interv with Littlejohn, 29 Oct 57. (2) Memo, CQM for Actg QM ADSEC, 17 Jul 44, no sub. Littlejohn Reading File, vol. XXVI, item 76.
[4] (1) *QM Supply in ETO*, VIII, 48. (2) Personal

Ltr, CQM to Col Zwicker, no sub, 8 Aug 44. Littlejohn Reading File, vol. XXVII, item 25. (3) OCQM Office Order 23, 2 Aug 44.
[5] Memo, CQM for DCQM, 20 Jul 44, no sub. Littlejohn Reading File, vol. XXVI, item 85.

days, respectively.[6] These sites were in fact little more than transfer points where supplies, largely operational rations and POL, were quickly relayed to eager and poised combat units. Two QM base depots, the 55th and 58th, worked feverishly to support ADSEC. At the end of August, when according to plans supplies should have been building up in the advance depots, 90 to 95 percent of continental supplies still lay on the beaches, 300 miles behind the army dumps. To complicate the situation further, ADSEC's transportation facilities were inadequate to meet the full needs of the combat units and the armies had to send some of their own vehicles back to the beaches as well as to the ADSEC transfer points.[7]

Colonel Smithers, the new ADSEC quartermaster, called for able and aggressive POL experts to aid him in this, the most important aspect of his mission. As usual at this level, information on what supplies would arrive, when, and where was even more important than the mechanics of unloading and forwarding. Smithers found that for lack of a liaison officer with the Transportation Corps to provide such information, the ADSEC G–4, a staff officer who should not have engaged in operations, was invading his domain and creating considerable confusion. The ADSEC quartermaster also wanted about 2,000 POW's to expedite unloading of trains and trucks. The OCQM was able to meet his requests.[8]

As evident in retrospect, there was not only feverish activity at ADSEC headquarters, but also a strong feeling of frustration and exasperation with COMZ headquarters because of its consistent overoptimism and failure to deliver. It was quite true that combat needs were not being filled and that ADSEC's efforts met with angry recriminations from various tactical headquarters. This state of affairs was inevitable, since German resistance was slight and the senior Allied commanders had placed no limitation whatever upon the advance of the combat forces. On 27 August, Bradley's official instructions read in part: "It is contemplated that the armies will go as far as practicable and then wait until the supply system in rear will permit further advance."

In other words, a breakdown of the supply system had been anticipated and even courted. Littlejohn was not a party to this controversy but found deficiencies in both headquarters. Certainly he held no brief for the G–4, COMZ, whose rigid system of controls and slow response to changing conditions had put a straitjacket on Quartermaster operations. But he held that ADSEC was not content merely to advocate the point of view of the combat units: it actually tried to act like a combat zone organization and carried the principles of close support and extreme mobility much too far. In particular, he criticized its efforts to operate exclusively as a reconsignment agency and its patent lack of interest in establishing large or efficient dumps. This weakness was particularly evident during the period of static warfare in September–November 1944, when the OCQM had to step in and assume direct command over the two QM base depots

[6] Computed from data in Hist of QM Sec ADSEC, an. F, pp. 1–2.

[7] Ruppenthal, *Logistical Support*, I, 491.

[8] Personal Ltr, QM ADSEC (Smithers) to CQM, 20 Aug 44, no sub; Ltr, CQM to QM ADSEC, 29 Aug 44, no sub. Littlejohn Reading File, vol. XXVII, item 158.

newly located in ADSEC territory at Liège and Verdun.[9]

The Red Ball Express

In a desperate effort to bridge the widening gap between the armies and the stocks in Normandy, the ADSEC Motor Transport Brigade and the Transportation Section, COMZ, jointly inaugurated the widely publicized Red Ball express on 25 August 1944. The decision to pursue the enemy beyond the Seine had still further inflated combat requirements; the immediate need was now estimated at 100,000 tons (exclusive of bulk POL) to be delivered to the Chartres-Dreux area by 1 September. The railways could haul less than one-fifth of these supplies and planes only about 1,000 tons per day. Trucks would thus have to move more than 75,000 tons, mostly from St. Lô to Chartres, in seven days. This objective was not quite achieved, but the Red Ball express did demonstrate that it was an effective instrument at a time of extreme stringency in transport. Starting with 67 "Quartermaster" (actually Transportation Corps) truck companies of ADSEC, it reached a peak on the fifth day of 132 companies with nearly 6,000 vehicles, which moved 12,000 tons. These included provisional truck companies formed from engineer, heavy artillery, chemical, and antiaircraft artillery troops. Three infantry divisions were immobilized, all their vehicles going to Red Ball. These units provided a steady stream of fast freight vehicles which rumbled over reserved one-way highways twenty-four hours a day, averaging twenty-five miles an hour. On 10 September the route was extended, forking at Paris to serve the Third Army at Sommesous and the First Army at Soissons (later extended again to Hirson).[10]

The scale of these motorized operations was a complete surprise to the enemy and upset his calculations, but there were also disadvantages. The operation required a very heavy overhead of military police, engineer road maintenance crews, ordnance automotive repair units, signal troops and equipment, and specialized supervisory personnel. Attrition of equipment was very great, especially among the untrained provisional units. Some of them neglected preventive maintenance to the point where they were derisively called "truck destroyer battalions." Moreover, on the extended routes Red Ball vehicles daily consumed about 300,000 gallons of gasoline and wore out more than 800 tires. As the commander of the COMZ Motor Transport Service observed, trucks can haul whatever the railroads do, but at a much greater cost in manpower and equipment. Red Ball, begun as a desperate gamble to hasten victory, had to be continued until other transport means could support the combat units in their extended positions on the German frontier. It was terminated in mid-November as soon as large-scale rail and barge facilities became available.

Littlejohn's objections to excessively rigid control of all transportation by the

[9] (1) Ruppenthal, *Logistical Support,* I, 489–99. (2) Quotation from 12th Army Group Admin Instr 13, 27 Aug 44. 12th Army Group Mil Objectives, 271.3, I. (3) Interv with Littlejohn, 1 Dec 59.

[10] (1) Ruppenthal, *Logistical Support,* I, 553–73. (2) Bykofsky and Larson, *The Transportation Corps: Operations Overseas,* pp. 330–35.

G–4, COMZ, applied with particular force to the Red Ball operation. At the time, this was the only effective means of getting supplies forward, and the Chief Quartermaster contended that all the technical services should have had a voice in deciding how Red Ball tonnage was to be utilized. The Motor Transport Brigade should have been concerned exclusively with such matters as traffic control, highway discipline, and motor maintenance. Actually, as the chosen instrument of the G–4 at COMZ and in the headquarters of the armies, the brigade also exercised authority over supply at the initial and final Red Ball traffic control points. Attempting to interpret broad policy as best they could, officers of the brigade were making decisions on supply priorities and final destinations. The results were impressive tonnage statistics, accompanied by a regrettable lack of selectiveness in the supplies moved forward. Some of the Red Ball trucks could more profitably have been allocated for use within the coastal dumps and depots to rearrange their disorderly heaps of unsorted supplies. Such action would have gone far to insure that the supplies received by the armies were those that had been requisitioned.[11]

Progress of the Build-up

Vitally interested in ADSEC's forward movement, the OCQM maintained a careful surveillance of the rapidly shifting supply situation through its system of liaison visits and reports. The activation of new base sections kept pace with the pursuit even though supplies did not.

---

[11] Interv with Littlejohn, 1 Dec 59.

For example, the original Red Ball route was entirely within ADSEC territory, since Normandy Base Section had not yet taken over the St. Lô area, but by 1 October the route passed through five different sections. (*See Table 12.*)

To implement its own forwarding program, less spectacular than Red Ball but possibly of equal importance, the OCQM transferred to ADSEC and to the new base sections experienced QM base depot headquarters, railhead, service, and depot supply companies over the protests of commanders in Normandy, Loire, and Brittany Base Sections. They were replaced by green units from the United Kingdom and by many prisoners of war. Littlejohn asked the Provost Marshal to delay shipping POW's to Great Britain until the needs of the technical services on the Continent had been met, and he then insisted that each base section quartermaster put in a request for several hundred, warning them they would soon lose most of their service companies.[12]

Unfortunately, the critical situation in regard to land transportation was accompanied by a simultaneous crisis in port capacity, which was also largely ignored by the tactical commanders. Although not explicitly stated, Bradley's objective in late August 1944 was undoubtedly the Rhine, as already noted, which the 12th Army Group actually reached in Febru-

---

[12] (1) Ltr, CQM to Franks, 20 Jul 44, sub: Utilization of POW's. Littlejohn Reading File, vol. XXVIA, item 86. (2) Ltr, QM ADSEC to CQM, 20 Aug 44, and Ltr, CQM to QM ADSEC, 29 Aug 44, no sub. Littlejohn Reading File, vol. XXVIIA, item 158. (3) Ltr, CQM to G–4 COMZ, 29 Oct 44, sub: Additional Sv Cos for 12th Army Group; Ltr, CQM to QM Normandy BS, 17 Nov 44, sub: Release of QM Units for Duty at the Front. Littlejohn Reading File, vol. XXIXA, item 134; vol. XXX, item 58.

ary 1945. How overoptimistic this objective was can be illustrated by comparing the 12th Army Group's estimated requirements and COMZ capabilities at the end of September. On the 25th, the army group G–4 estimated that the field forces would require 650 tons per division slice per day. Currently, there were 10 divisions in the First Army, 8 in the Third, and 2 in the Ninth—a total of 20. Adding the requirements of ADSEC and Ninth Air Force, and including the contemplated build-up, brought the total to 18,800 tons a day in early October (22 divisions); 20,750 tons in late October (25 divisions); and 22,700 tons by 1 November (28 divisions). Other ETO requirements were not included. The G–4 estimated that an additional 100,000 tons would be required by 1 November to meet deficiencies in equipment and build up a reserve of three days of all classes of supply. He inquired how soon COMZ could deliver the additional 100,000 tons and also establish depots in ADSEC that could maintain the armies.[13]

The COMZ reply was most discouraging; even using the more frugal SHAEF figure of 560 tons per division slice would mean a deficit below daily maintenance for the proposed forces all through October. COMZ planned to build up 10,000 tons of reserves for the First Army in October and 20,000 more in early November, but only at the expense of daily maintenance for the other armies. The required 100,000 tons might be available at the end of November. Even this estimate proved overly optimistic, based as it was largely on an impossible 20,000 tons per day from Cherbourg and the

beaches. Actual discharge there was about 12,000 tons per day in October and 14,300 in November. A surprising 6,000 tons a day from Le Havre and 2,000 tons from Rouen, achieved by the end of October, allowed Bradley to maintain 23 divisions after a fashion, although fortunately only 13 were actively engaged in combat.[14] The troop build-up had outstripped port capacity as well as overland forwarding capacity. Clearly, everything now depended on the opening of Antwerp, a tremendous port capable of maintaining all Bradley's divisions, and Montgomery's as well. Moreover, it was a port in an advanced location, practically on the edge of the combat zone. The following comparative mileages emphasize dramatically the advantages of Antwerp: Cherbourg to Liège, 410 miles; Antwerp to Liège, 65 miles; Cherbourg to Nancy, 400 miles; Antwerp to Nancy, 250 miles.

Advance Depots

In the course of its advance across Europe, the Quartermaster Section of ADSEC operated about 175 storage and service installations of all types in five countries, most of them for periods of less than 60 days. Nearly half of these were POL sites, and approximately a quarter were Class I sites. Salvage, laundry, and baths were also important activities of ADSEC, but for several reasons it handled only small quantities of Class II and IV supplies. During the early stages of continental operations these items had low priorities and few arrived. Later, the specific needs of the combat troops in clothing and equip-

---

[13] Ruppenthal, *Logistical Support*, II, 18.

[14] *Ibid.*, II, 100.

ment were shipped to them direct without being stored in advance depots.

After the impetus of the pursuit was checked in mid-September 1944, ADSEC settled down for nearly six months to a more static type of operations. On 1 October, Class I and III depots were opened at Liège (Q–179) and Verdun (Q–178). On paper, their initial Class I missions were eight million A rations each, but supplies arrived slowly, and ADSEC was not experienced in the operation of large fixed depots. An improvement in transportation and the loan of supply specialists from the OCQM made it possible for these depots to begin supplying the field armies late in November. During the next five months each depot handled daily averages of Class I and III supplies approaching seven thousand tons.[15]

Since size tariffs made distribution of clothing complicated and multiple depots were wasteful, Littlejohn believed that Class II should be handled for all the armies at a single large depot under close supervision. At his direction Q–180, the first large inland Class II and IV depot, was established at Reims on 1 October. Reims was in ADSEC territory at the time, but it was transferred to the jurisdiction of Oise Intermediate Section before the end of the month. Although later surpassed in storage capacity by Charleroi-Mons, Q–180 at Reims, commanded by Col. Carroll R. Hutchins, remained the major active distribution depot for clothing in the ETO until after the end of hostilities. Situated at a rail junction, it could support the First and Ninth Armies advancing

through Liège to the lower Rhine and the Third Army moving through Verdun to the Saar. To increase its potential, Littlejohn set up Q–256, a separate salvage and clothing repair depot, also at Reims. Both these installations employed very large numbers of POW's; in fact Q–180 was operated largely by some 10,000 Germans, headed by a captured colonel. The American supervisory and security staff at Q–180 was limited to the 55th QM Base Depot and attached personnel—a total of less than 300—commanded by Colonel Hutchins.[16]

Liège and Verdun, handling Class I and III supplies, and Reims, responsible for Classes II and IV, formed a strategic triangle to provide advance support for the 12th Army Group. This was the heart of Littlejohn's organization to back up the main combat effort in the ETO. He had proposed this plan to the COMZ G–4 as early as mid-September, but at that time neither supplies nor Quartermaster operating units were available. Liège Depot was commanded by Col. Mortlock Petit. In December, its mission was expanded and redefined as 40 days' rations and 13 days' POL for 925,-000 men of First and Ninth Armies. Verdun was commanded by Col. Roland T. Fenton; it was to support 450,000 men of Third Army with 40 days' nonperishable rations, 22 days' cold stores, and 16 days' POL. Reims was to provide 40 days Class II for 2,225,000 men. These included the three armies, Ninth Air Force, ADSEC, and some 300,000 non-U.S. troops.[17]

Until the end of 1944 this triangle was

[15] (1) Hist of QM Sec ADSEC, an. G. (2) 12th Army Group Rpt of Opns, VI (G–4), p. 48.

[16] (1) Littlejohn, ed., Passing in Review, ch. 5, p. 10. (2) QM Supply in ETO, VIII, 108.
[17] QM Supply in ETO, I, 82.

supplied mainly through Cherbourg and Le Havre. The German Ardennes offensive, directed largely against Liège, succeeded neither in capturing that city nor in cutting the supply lines to these depots. After Antwerp began large-scale operations in late December, it supplied much of Liège's needs, but Verdun and Reims were still partly dependent on Cherbourg, Rouen, and Le Havre. Early in April ADSEC moved forward into Germany and the Liège and Verdun depots were turned over, respectively, to Channel Base Section and Oise Intermediate Section. Thus in theory the triangle had become an intermediate depot system, but ADSEC was racing across Germany after the victorious armies and never had time to set up more than temporary distributing points. Reims, Verdun, and Liège (along with Q–186 at Nancy, supporting CONAD) therefore actually continued to be the forward depots of the ETO until after the German surrender.[18]

The final campaign in Germany confirmed the experience gained in the pursuit across France: advance depots provided necessary reserves and take-off bases for a pursuit, but the depots themselves could not be moved forward until after the pursuit had ended. The sixty-day interval between the date of formal activation of depots at Verdun and Liège and the time when they actually began to support the armies represents the crux of the problem. Since the Communications Zone could not operate at full capacity and extend itself at the same time, the expansion had to take place in the combat zone. Air transport could and did provide considerable relief, but did not solve this problem.[19] By the end of World War II the Allied armies had greatly improved their mobility, even surpassing their German models in this respect, but geography still imposed a definite limit upon the duration of an uninterrupted pursuit.[20]

Base Sections and Base Depots

Located behind ADSEC were the base sections and their depots, the major installations engaged in large-scale storage and wholesale distribution operations. A base section was a comparatively static organization which, unlike ADSEC, did not continually move forward as the troops advanced. Rather, separate base sections were designated for the various areas to be liberated, and each was brought in to take over installations left behind by ADSEC. The RHUMBA plan, originally called Reverse BOLERO, provided that the continental base section system would be organized by progressive transfer of the United Kingdom base

---

[18] (1) Littlejohn, ed., Passing in Review, ch. 5, pp. 9–10. (2) Interv with Littlejohn, 29 Oct 57. (3) Personal Ltr, CQM to QM ADSEC, 17 Oct 44. Littlejohn Reading File, vol. XXIXA, item 90.

[19] By definitely canceling all plans for airborne operations, an airlift of 1,600 tons per day, about 30 percent of the requirements of a field army at current rates of expenditure, was made available. Third Army received most of this. Ruppenthal, *Logistical Support*, II, 427.

[20] (1) The maximum practicable depth of the combat zone is discussed in detail in Chapter XIV, below. (2) German views on the limitations of blitzkrieg are very well summarized in Department of the Army Pamphlet 20–290, *Terrain Factors in the Russian Campaign*, by General der Infanterie Karl Allmendinger (Washington, 1951). Allmendinger points out that during the 1940 campaign purely logistical considerations compelled the German forces to halt for ten days at the Somme, although French resistance was virtually broken.

sections to the far shore.[21] Personnel in the Eastern Base Section in Great Britain were earmarked for Base Section 1 on the Brittany Peninsula, which was expected to bear the main burden of logistical support for the American forces. Another headquarters was formed in North Ireland, activated as Base Section 2, and designated to assume control of supply in the Cherbourg area.

In the first six months on the Continent, six base sections—one more than originally planned—were established along the northern line of communications. The main axis of supply developed from Cherbourg and the beaches instead of from Brittany as anticipated. Until Antwerp could be opened, the British made Le Havre and Rouen available to the U.S. forces—an arrangement that actually lasted until after V–E Day. Use of these ports involved setting up Channel Base Section, an organization within the British administrative zone, and therefore with very limited territorial functions. An extra headquarters was available for this purpose because Cherbourg Area Command, which had demonstrated its abilities under difficult conditions in the original lodgment area, was reinforced and designated Cherbourg Base Section. (*Table 12*)

The organization of the Quartermaster staff in a base section was much simpler than that of the OCQM, though all of the essential services were provided for. All the commodity responsibilities came under a consolidated Supply Division, with subordinate branches handling storage and distribution and the various classes of supply. Services were handled by an Installations Division.

Since the base section quartermaster's problems involved co-ordination of activities in the scattered depots, dumps, distributing points, and other field installations, the Field Service Branch, acting as liaison and trouble shooting agency, was extremely important.

Like all senior Quartermaster organizations, the base section QM staffs were plagued by shortages of trained manpower. Before D-day, a T/O of 33 officers and 88 enlisted men had been authorized, and ADSEC actually attained this strength for a brief period. But continental base sections were organized considerably faster than U.K. bases were inactivated, and the available personnel had to be shared. Late in August Littlejohn proposed to break up Base Section 3 and form three "Class I QM Base Section Staffs." [22] With 11 officers and 25 enlisted men each, he considered them adequate for initial operations of Normandy, Brittany, and Paris (Seine) Base Sections. He felt that ADSEC could operate as a Class II staff with 23 officers and 60 men.[23] By V–E Day, the average official strength of a base section was about 75 persons. There were usually a good many more actually present, for from the first it was planned to attach a QM group to each staff, and as they became available one or more base depot headquarters companies were assigned within each base section.[24] (*Appendix B*)

---

[21] Ruppenthal, *Logistical Support*, I, 216–17.

[22] Ltr, CQM to OQMG, 16 Jun 44, sub: Orgn of QM Base Sec Group; Ltr, CQM to CG COMZ, 28 Aug 44, sub: QM Staff for Base Sec Hq. Littlejohn Reading File, vol. XXV, item 24; vol. XXVIIA, item 127.

[23] Personal Ltr, CQM to Smithers (QM ADSEC), no sub, 24 Aug 44. Littlejohn Reading File, vol. XXVIIA, item 121.

[24] *QM Supply in ETO*, VIII, 39.

TABLE 12—BASE, INTERMEDIATE, AND ADVANCE SECTIONS

Section	General Area of Responsibility	Headquarters	Date Activated	Inactivated or Absorbed
Advance Sec (ADSEC)	Area immediately behind 12th Army Group[a]	Catz (France) Le Mans Étampes Reims Namur (Belgium) Bonn (Germany) Fulda	18 Jun 44 (operational) 1 Aug 44 (released by First Army)	Inactivated 15 Jul 45
Normandy Base Sec (NBS)	Normandy; absorbed BBS and LBS and acquired Rouen–Le Havre area from CBS 1 Feb 45	Cherbourg Deauville	21 Jul 44 (as Cherbourg Command; redesignated NBS 16 Aug 44)	Absorbed by CHANOR 1 Jul 45
Brittany Base Sec (BBS)	Brittany (later absorbed LBS)	Rennes	16 Aug 44	Absorbed by NBS 1 Feb 45
Seine Sec	Paris and environs	Paris	24 Aug 44	Became subsection of OIS 2 Jul 45
Loire Base Sec (LBS)	Between BBS and left bank of Seine	Le Mans	5 Sep 44	Absorbed by BBS 1 Nov 44
Channel Base Sec (CBS)	Rouen–Le Havre; later shifted to Belgium	Le Havre Lille Brussels	10 Sep 44 1 Feb 45 (lost Le Havre to NBS)	Absorbed by CHANOR 1 Jul 45
Oise Intermediate Sec (OIS)	Area between Seine Sec and ADSEC; later absorbed all ADSEC and CONAD territory	Reims	15 Sep 44	(b)
CHANOR Base Sec	Former CBS and NBS territory	Brussels	1 Jul 45	(b)
Continental Advance Sec (CONAD)	Area immediately behind 6th Army Group[a]	Dijon Nancy Kaiserslautern	1 Oct 44	Inactivated 15 Jul 45
DELTA Base Sec	Rhône Valley and all SW France	Marseille	1 Oct 44	(b)
Burgundy District (of CONAD)	Burgundy, Lorraine	Dijon	9 Feb 45	Absorbed by OIS 21 Mar 45

a ADSEC and CONAD began to operate exclusively in Germany on 1 and 7 April 1945, respectively. On those dates they transferred territory in Allied countries to Channel or Oise Sections. Territorial functions within Germany were performed by armies, not by advance sections.

b Continued to operate during 1945–46 for redeployment and support of U.S. forces in Germany.

Source: Administrative and Logistical History of the ETO, pt. II, vol. II, pp. 187–202. OCMH.

When a new base section became operational and prepared to assume control of branch installations released by ADSEC, the various technical services hastened to make contact with their opposite numbers in ADSEC for orientation on the logistical and tactical situation. They would normally confer with the G–5 (civil affairs) officers and town mayors regarding additional storage and depot sites, salvage and cold-storage facilities, marshaling yards, and the exact location of abandoned or captured enemy material. It could usually be assumed that ADSEC had made a hurried beginning of such activities, which would now be carried out more thoroughly. The degree of co-operation between quartermasters of a base section and ADSEC was variable. During the pursuit, ADSEC gave incoming base section personnel no more than a very hasty briefing. But when Oise Intermediate Section "understudied" ADSEC at Reims during most of October, several of the incoming base section officers and noncommissioned officers were taken on temporary duty for informal training with ADSEC, and for a time each section supplied the other's troops when storage sites or stock levels made such an arrangement advantageous.[25]

Such a smooth and orderly transition was exceptional. Indeed Littlejohn questioned the validity of the whole ADSEC concept. He doubted that a headquarters that was "always rushing off somewhere" could give efficient direction to a territorial type of organization. The "understudy" concept was useful, but when an additional base section was needed, the understudy, rather than the original base section, should move forward to administer it. A permanent base section immediately behind the combat zone, which was not preoccupied with trying to retain its mobility, could establish really large dumps at the outset and give efficient support from them. Thus the armies would not be tempted to establish large dumps of their own— as actually occurred in the ETO, seriously disrupting supply operations.[26]

Brittany Base Section

In Brittany, where ADSEC had not followed the tactical units, the Quartermaster Section, Brittany Base Section, had to search out its own depot locations. Here, also, the base section staff selected minor ports for temporary use, and arranged for the development of port storage and transshipment facilities. For example, even before the reduction of Brest, the base section quartermaster took the initiative in developing north shore offloading potentialities at Morlaix, St. Michel en Grève, St. Brieuc, and St. Malo. The capacities here were small; Morlaix, the largest of the four ports, could anchor only seven Liberty ships and handle but three thousand tons per day, and St. Brieuc was limited to coasters with no more than a ten-foot draft. By 23 September Brittany Base was getting its Class I supplies from Morlaix and was preparing to relieve the

[25] (1) Ltr, Maj Charles E. Johnson to ACofS G–4, Hq BBS, 10–11 Aug 44, sub: Rpt of Reconnaissance; Memo, Chief Field Installations for Chief P&T Div, Hq Base Sec 1, 15 Aug 44. Both in Lorraine District 314.7. (2) Admin and Log Hist of ETO, pt. II, vol. II, pp. 202–06.

[26] OTCQM TSFET Operational Study 13, p. 4.

congestion on the Normandy beaches and at Cherbourg.[27] But if Morlaix sought to take pressure off Cherbourg, it soon encountered its own difficulties. In the absence of equipment for the steady unloading of vessels, railroad cars had piled up. Littlejohn found the plan whereby Morlaix was to feed six daily trains into the Red Ball program for the support of forward areas wholly unrealistic and directed that his Storage and Distribution Division consult him before issuing such orders to base sections. This was but one example of inflexible thinking and stubborn adherence to plans made before D-day. Clearly, Brest was not available as a port and Morlaix would barely be able to make Brittany self-sufficient in Class I supplies.[28] Developments in Brittany Base Section, commanded by Brig. Gen. Roy W. Grower, illustrate admirably Littlejohn's thesis that even territorial organizations had to maintain a certain mobility and flexibility under modern conditions and be prepared to break the precedents of World War I. Patton's Third Army had swept through Brittany in August and left VIII Corps behind to reduce the coastal fortresses Brest was finally captured on 19 September, after four weeks of intensive siege but the port was virtually useless. Combat operations in Brittany had been supported largely from the Cotentin, involving a westward movement of supplies, instead of the eastward movement planned before

D-day. Meanwhile Ninth Army had been activated and had assumed control of VIII Corps on 5 September, remaining in the area until it was transferred to Belgium early in the following month. Brittany absorbed Loire Base Section on 11 November, but even the enlarged unit was an inactive backwater; while the main current flowed from Cherbourg northeastward, the depots at Rennes and Le Mans remained nearly empty. The Brittany Base Section staff turned over its territory to Normandy Base Section on 1 February 1945 and eight days later assumed command of the Burgundy District, with headquarters at Dijon, thus permitting CONAD to move forward to Nancy. Burgundy District was transferred to Oise Intermediate Section on 2 April, and on 7 April it assumed control over all territory formerly administered by CONAD. A bit later it was renamed Lorraine District after the newly acquired territory.[29]

Miscellaneous Base Section Responsibilities

In addition to supporting the COMZ and Air Forces personnel stationed in rear areas, the base sections also had certain direct responsibilities for Ground Forces personnel, both units and casuals. The temporary location of Ninth Army in Brittany Base Section has already been mentioned. Late in December the Fifteenth Army was activated and assumed

[27] Ltr, Ln Off to Storage and Distr Div OCQM, 23 Sep 44, sub: Ln Rpt, BBS. Hist Br OQMG.

[28] (1) Memo, CQM for DCQM, 13 Sep 44, sub: QM Supply Situation on Brittany Peninsula. Littlejohn Reading File, vol. XXVIII, item 80. (2) Ltr, ACofS G–4 to CO BBS, 25 Sep 44, sub: Red Ball

Supply Movement—Function of BBS. Lorraine District 400. (3) Daily Jnl QM Sec Hq BBS, 3 Oct 44. Lorraine District 314.17.

[29] (1) Admin and Log Hist of the ETO, pt. II, vol. II, pp. 180, 238–43, 277–79. (2) CONAD History, vol. I, pp. viii–ix (Chronology).

a similar role over the forces hemming in the German garrisons on the lower Loire. But this was incidental; the army's main duty was to serve as a headquarters for U.S. units in the SHAEF reserve, and to stage, equip, and train new units entering the Continent. Each of these responsibilities required considerable assistance from the base sections and their Quartermaster elements.

The Red Horse staging area, with a capacity of 70,000 men, was formally designated as the main installation of this type on 26 October 1944. During succeeding months various camps, all in the Rouen–Le Havre area, were built up to a total capacity of 138,000 men. Camp Lucky Strike near Dieppe, used principally for staging units from the United States, was the largest. Camp Twenty Grand near Rouen was both a staging area and a replacement depot, and other installations in the area specialized in processing personnel going to the United Kingdom on leave and to the zone of interior on rotation. These were large and unexpected commitments and the OCQM was hard pressed to provide camp equipment. British cots and other accommodation stores were forwarded in large quantities, and also British and Spanish blankets, which had not been considered suitable for combat. Littlejohn felt that a requisition from the Quartermaster, Channel Base Section, for 2,500 field ranges, submitted quite without warning at a time when maintenance parts for this item were a major problem, betrayed a lack of contact with reality. He promised to obtain whatever substitutes were available, and authorized the Channel Base Section quartermaster to make local purchases. Moreover, he pointed out that men passing

through the areas were field soldiers and presumably able to improvise.[30]

With its headquarters at Reims, the Fifteenth Army, commanded by Maj. Gen. Leonard T. Gerow was admirably situated to insure that Depot Q–180 at the same location provided the necessary Class II and IV equipment for newly arrived units. Its training installations were scattered all through the rear areas. Beginning late in January 1945, many of these functions came under Lt. Gen. Ben Lear's Ground Forces Reinforcement Command. This high level theater-wide organization was largely concerned with reassignment and retraining of ETO personnel to provide an adequate number of infantry riflemen. Casualties in this category had been far higher than anticipated, and all ETO organizations —including the QMC—had to provide their share of able-bodied troops. The COMZ quota was increased from 5,750 men in December to 17,700 in March. Theoretically, limited-service personnel were to replace the men "combed out" for infantry service, but these replacements were always slow to arrive, which made the manpower losses even more serious for the technical services. On 31 March, the commanding general of ADSEC reported that losses from this cause had reduced the efficiency of his supply units by 18.8 percent. During March and April the QMC lost all able-bodied replacements except a few highly qualified specialists, but otherwise the losses were disruptive rather than nu-

---

[30] (1) *QM Supply in ETO*, I, 72. (2) Ltr, CQM to QM's Base Secs, 8 Aug 44, sub: Accommodation Stores; Ltr, CQM to Col Hoss, QM CBS, no sub, 27 Dec 44. Littlejohn Reading File, vol. XXVII, item 23; vol. XXXI, item 95.

merically serious. For example, all members of salvage units were considered exempt specialists, but several service units suffered such heavy drafts that they could not operate at all. The Oise Section quartermaster reported at the end of March that he had lost 469 general assignment men and had received 245 limited assignment replacements. But personnel were called out at the beginning of the month and replaced toward the end of the month, so the actual loss of effective manpower was considerable. However, the end of hostilities curtailed the reconversion program. The OCQM had estimated that by June it would impair the efficiency of ETO Quartermaster operations by as much as 40 percent.[31]

In April the Fifteenth Army moved into Germany, where it assumed occupation duties west of the Rhine to decrease the 12th Army Group's security responsibilities. In the same month the Assembly Area Command (AAC) was activated at Reims under Maj. Gen. Royal B. Lord to assume control over redeployment after the fighting was over. Thus its duties were strikingly similar to those relinquished by the Fifteenth Army and it controlled much the same complex of camps and staging areas as well as several large transient camps built near Reims. To support these installations, Q–180 and Q–256 had to expand their activities despite the fact that many of their own subordinate units were also being redeployed. By July 1945, these two depots had a strength of

57,000 men, of whom only 6,700 were Americans.[32]

Main Depots

The story of base section operations cannot be separated from that of the main depots, for such depots carried out the actual task of wholesale and retail distribution of quartermaster supplies. Plans for the move to the Continent had involved abandoning the general depot in favor of branch depots as already described. According to contemporary official doctrine, a general depot had to be concentrated in a small area to operate efficiently. Even in the United Kingdom, where conditions were far from ideal, the installations of a general depot were usually all within a ten-mile radius. But Littlejohn argued that a system of branch depots permitted greater dispersion and decreased vulnerability to air attack. Moreover, intelligence sources reported that limited storage facilities on the Continent would seldom permit the establishment of large concentrated installations. Branch depots evolved into elaborate administrative organizations on the Continent, each one controlling many subinstallations scattered over a wide area. Also, the shortage of administrative personnel was a major consideration. In a branch depot, technicians could handle command functions also, an important saving in trained QMC officers, whereas in a general depot a separate depot commander was needed.

As a contribution toward BOLERO in 1942, the OCQM had provided most of

[31] (1) Ruppenthal, *Logistical Support*, II, 329–34, 461–65. (2) Hist of Activities QM Sec Oise Intermediate Sec, ch. V, 1–31 Mar 45. Hist Br OQMG.

[32] (1) *QM Supply in ETO*, X, 33. (2) R. M. Littlejohn, "QM Service in the Assembly Area," *QMR*, XXV (November–December 1945), 18–20.

the overhead for a General Depot Service,[33] only to lose these well-trained men permanently to the evolving U.K. base sections. In the spring of 1944 the designated commanders of future continental base sections cast covetous eyes on the newly authorized Headquarters and Headquarters Company, QM Base Depot. On 19 May, Littlejohn wrote these commanders that the new units would not be available as overhead for general depots on the Continent. He declared that "Branch depots, distributed over wide areas and receiving direct orders from . . . the Chief of Service, have been determined to be the most efficient type of organization." [34] Naturally, the base sections were opposed to this idea. They repeatedly proposed a return to general depots as an alleged cure for the never-ending distribution difficulties of an active campaign, and usually received some support from the G–4 Division of COMZ. Probably the most plausible case was advanced by Brig. Gen. Charles O. Thrasher, the commander of Oise Intermediate Section, who proposed the establishment of a general depot at Reims in November 1944. Every technical service had installations in the area at that time, and thus the change would have been largely administrative. Littlejohn retorted that his plans called for only a Class II depot at Reims. He pointed out that the situation at Reims was fluid and should be allowed to remain so to meet the future demands of the tactical situation. A general depot, he maintained, lacked mobility. Though Thrasher's proposal was shelved, it was never completely abandoned.[35]

How the establishment of main Quartermaster depots followed the axis of advance is most clearly apparent from the trail of the American armies as they moved south and east in the summer and fall of 1944. The line, Cherbourg, Rennes, Le Mans, Paris, Reims, Liège— with a major subsidiary, Reims, Verdun —generally described the inland axis of communications. As this line lengthened, measures were also taken to develop the Channel ports and those parallel depots at Le Havre, Charleroi, and Lille, from which supplies could be brought in along the left flank.[36]

Of necessity, OCQM revised the depot plan repeatedly in order to fit the unfolding tactical situation. Operation OVERLORD may be regarded as having terminated on 24 August, when the armies closed up to the Seine eleven days ahead of schedule. But that landmark went unnoticed in the forward rush that carried troops eastward across 260 phase-line days in 19 actual days.[37] Understandably, the over-all plan that Littlejohn requested from his staff on 31 August reflected some of the heady optimism of the SHAEF G–2, who considered "the end of the war in Europe within sight, almost within reach." That

---

[33] See ch. IX, above.

[34] (1) USFET Gen Bd Study 27, p. 32. (2) Ltr, CQM to CG's FECZ, ADSEC, and Base Secs, 19 May 44, sub: Orgn and Functioning of QM Sv in Theater of Opns. Littlejohn Reading File, vol. XXIV, item 63.

[35] Ltr, CG Oise Sec to CG COMZ, 21 Nov 44, sub: Formation of a Gen Depot; 1st Ind, Memo, Chief Storage Br G–4 COMZ for Chiefs All Tech Svs, 29 Nov 44, same sub; 3d Ind, Memo, CQM for G–4, 2 Dec 44, sub: Nonconcurrence. Littlejohn Reading File, vol. XXXI, item 2.

[36] Rpt, QM Depots on Continent, n.d. Littlejohn Collection.

[37] Ruppenthal, *Logistical Support*, I, 488.

11TH PORT, ROUEN, *showing a variety of supplies stored in the open.   December 1944.*

opinion goes far to explain a proposal by Littlejohn to locate main depots at Paris, Metz, and Koblenz, despite the fact that only the first of those three cities was in Allied hands.[38]

Although the details of the new plan were overoptimistic, it was clear that current plans were nonetheless badly outdated. When the front lines were 150 miles east of the Seine, a principal storage area in Brittany was useless. The demand for revision was all the more urgent because, amazingly, Brest was still in German hands. By the time the stubborn defenders had demolished the port and finally surrendered on 19 September, Antwerp had been occupied by

the British for two weeks. Moreover, there had been no fighting in the area so that Antwerp, one of the great ports of the world, was intact except for the continuous but haphazard damage of flying bombs. But here was another disappointment; access to the sea, fifty miles in a straight line and twice as far down the winding Schelde estuary, was blocked by fortified German positions. Meanwhile Antwerp's civil population, even its 20,000 skilled dock workers, were merely a liability and a problem for G–5. Both SHAEF headquarters and the logistical planners required time to comprehend all the implications of this situation. During October Eisenhower became both impatient and alarmed by Montgomery's preoccupation with the unsuccessful MARKET operation at Nij-

---

[38] (1) SHAEF Weekly Intel Summary 23, 26 Aug 44. (2) *QM Supply in ETO,* II, 68.

megen, and his neglect of the Schelde estuary. To a logistician, the eighty-five-day interval between the capture of Antwerp and its opening to Allied shipping was the most unfortunate development of the European campaign—the bitter fruit of a decision hard to understand in retrospect. There is some evidence that the enemy understood the importance of major ports better than the Allied command.[39]

Rouen had been captured on 30 August, but here too the Germans held the Seine estuary and the port of Le Havre. After a stubborn defense involving much damage, Le Havre fell to the British on 12 September. Despite the damage, this port was a valuable prize for reasons of geography. The plans officer of G–4, SHAEF, noted that every 5,000 tons discharged there instead of at south Brittany ports would save the equivalent of seventy truck companies in vehicle turnaround time.[40] Although Le Havre and Rouen were in the British zone, Maj. Gen. Charles S. Napier, the British officer in charge of movements and transportation at SHAEF, recommended on 11 September that they be turned over to the U.S. forces, since Dieppe and Calais had also fallen into British hands. But conflicting recommendations from various headquarters as to whether to develop Brest or Quiberon Bay or wait for the opening of Antwerp delayed a clear-cut decision on use of Engineer and

Transportation Corps units for rehabilitating the Seine ports.

Meanwhile temporary dumps were located where the need was greatest and tentative depot plans, reflecting current optimism or pessimism and the latest tactical gains or losses, followed one another without time to implement any of them. In retrospect it appears that most of these depot plans suffered from over-optimism. Although true intermediate depots such as Rennes, Le Mans, and Paris had been established, they remained of minor importance. As much transportation as became available was used to concentrate stocks in such forward depots as Nancy, Verdun, and Liège, with the expectation that with continued tactical successes, they would soon become intermediate depots. This is the essential element of the OCQM supply plan published on 1 December 1944.[41] (Table 13)

Actually, despite optimism all through the autumn, there were no outstanding Allied successes until March 1945, and meanwhile the lack of a supply system echeloned in depth hampered support for the combat forces. The most serious deficiency was at Liège. For lack of a base installation at Antwerp, this site had to function simultaneously as base, intermediate, and advance depot all winter. General Somervell, who visited the ETO in January 1945, pointed out these defects, and laid most of the blame on the system that gave the armies control of transportation.[42] Transportation Corps historians are inclined to agree. But they contend that an absolute short-

[39] (1) R. W. Thompson, *The Eighty-Five Days* (London: Hutchinson & Co., Ltd., 1957), pp. 19–21, contains a blistering indictment of Montgomery's decision regarding Antwerp. (2) Pogue, *The Supreme Command*, pp. 294–98. (3) Ruppenthal, *Logistical Support*, II, 104–10.

[40] Ruppenthal, *Logistical Support*, II, 49.

[41] Ltr, OCQM to Base Sec Comdrs, 1 Dec 44, sub: QM Supply and Storage Plan. ADSEC 400.

[42] Ruppenthal, *Logistical Support*, II, 355–56.

TABLE 13—DEVELOPMENT OF THE QM DEPOT SYSTEM ON THE CONTINENT

(Thousands of Long Tons)

Depot and Location	Required 1 Dec 44	On Hand 13 Jan 45	Capacity* 20 Jan 45	Capacity* 30 Apr 45	Required Jun–Jul 45	Opening Dates	Mission[a] and Classes of Supply Handled
Q–171 Cherbourg	(b)	c40	(191)	(89)	d0	e16 Jul 44	Port depot; all classes until Q–181 took over Class II and IV
Q–172 UTAH Beach	(b)	c10	d(166)	—	—	f8 Jun 44	Base dump, all classes; reserve after Nov 44
Q–173 OMAHA Beach	(b)	c22	d(22)	—	—	f8 Jun 44	Base dump, all classes; reserve after Nov 44
Q–174 Rennes	(b)	c15	(79)	d(79)	—	f6 Aug 44	Staging area; Class I and coal
Q–175 Le Mans	(b)	(b)	(13)	d(13)	—	f17 Aug 44	Captured enemy matériel; CWS clothing
Q–177 Paris	(b)	c41	(47)	(91)	d36	fOct 44	Leave center; cold stores; PX and CA supplies
Q–178 Verdun	99	c61	(63)	(207)	121	e1 Oct 44 / f27 Nov 44	Class I and III for TUSA
Q–179 Liège	192	c27	(102)	(235)	d0	e1 Oct 44 / f25 Nov 44	Class I and III for FUSA and NUSA
Q–180 Reims	123	c34	(65)	(169)	d0	f23 Sep 44 / eOct 44	Class II and IV, northern armies
Q–181 Le Havre	(b)	c12	(15)	(116)	100	e2 Oct 44 / f16 Oct 44	Port depot; class II and IV
Q–183 Charleroi	80	c39	(216)	(322)	225	f15 Dec 44	Overflow depot, class I, III, PX
Q–184 Luxembourg	106	—	(91)	—	—	e10 Dec 44	Never active (TUSA dump)
Q–185 Lille	—	—	(57)	(185)	d0	e30 Dec 44 / f16 Jan 45	Overflow depot, class II and IV
Q–189 Antwerp	—	(b)	c32	(64)	200	f2 Dec 44 / e25 Apr 45	Port depot, all classes
Q–191 Rouen	—	(b)	(b)	(6)	d0	f15 Oct 44 / e30 Apr 45	Port depot, all classes
Q–186 Nancy	—	—	—	(85)	d0	e9 Feb 45	All classes for SUSA
Q–187 Dijon	(b)	c18	c32	d(146)	—	e20 Nov 44	Intermediate depot for SOLOC, all classes
Q–188 Marseille	180	—	c120	(388)	112	f1 Sep 44 / e1 Oct 44	Port depot, all classes
Western Mil Dist	—	—	—	(26)	171	e22 Jun 45	Occupation forces main depot, all classes
Eastern Mil Dist	—	—	—	—	203	e22 Jun 45	Occupation forces main depot, all classes
Berlin	—	—	—	—	34	e22 Jun 45	Occupation forces retail depot, all classes
Bremen	—	—	—	—	770	e22 Jun 45	Port depot, all classes
TOTALS	—	—	—	(2221)	1973		

* Figures in parentheses represent total capacity.

a In each case includes retail support for local units.

b Data lacking, but depot known to be operating.

c Tonnage currently on hand, excluding Class III.

d Depots to be inactivated.

e Date of formal activation.

f Approximate date operational.

Source: QM Supply in ETO, I; CONAD History; Hist of QM Sec ADSEC.

693–028 O—65——28

age of transportation facilities, irrespective of how they were administered, contributed materially to this situation.[43] Geography constituted an additional source of difficulty. Antwerp was in the extreme northeast corner of Allied territory in Europe, conveniently close to enemy-occupied territory. With land transportation facilities so scanty, it went against the grain to move supplies away from the front; yet the area between Antwerp and the combat zone was so constricted that such action was occasionally necessary. The major example was Lille (Q–185), an overflow depot located some fifty miles southwest of Antwerp. This Class II and IV depot was established in January 1945 to complement Q–183, the Class I and III depot which had begun to operate at Charleroi a month earlier. Dijon (Q–187) became an intermediate depot in February, when CONAD moved forward to Nancy.

But a major feature of the December plan was retained in planning the spring offensive—the current advance depots were to become the main intermediate depots as soon as the armies had moved forward. This aspect of the depot plan was sound and operated smoothly. Even in December it had been a good plan, and in retrospect General Somervell's criticism of it does not seem completely justified. It is true that excessive stocks of Class I supplies had been concentrated in the forward areas, but these were unbalanced stocks that had accumulated because of poor transportation practices as the advance depots tried to achieve their assigned levels of balanced rations. Those levels were part of an Allied plan

for offensive action, and in that context the excesses in the forward area were an asset rather than a liability. That they were also a tempting target was a minor consideration. In all military operations, an enemy "spoiling attack" against one's own offensive preparations is a constant possibility, but the threat is a responsibility of tactical rather than logistical headquarters. It was not reasonable to demand that COMZ be more cautious than SHAEF in estimating enemy capabilities.

Base Depots

General Somervell's criticism of port and base depot operations was entirely justified, although here, too, SHAEF must bear part of the blame. Two major ports, Le Havre and Antwerp, were in the British zone, and the British permitted use of them only under arrangements which COMZ considered ill-advised and hampering to its operations. The heart of the problem was the absolute necessity for a transit depot immediately adjacent to each major port, where supplies could be inventoried and stored at least temporarily. In the United Kingdom, this need had been met by sorting sheds, as already described. At Cherbourg, the advice of the ADSEC quartermaster was ignored since initially this was the only large port available. Under combat conditions Transportation Corps officers regarded segregation and inventory as unnecessary and time-consuming. Cargoes were dumped on the docks and segregated by technical service and class of supply only. Shipments inland were measured in tons rather than items. Selective loading was the exception

---

[43] Bykofsky and Larson, *The Transportation Corps: Operations Overseas*, pp. 239, 242, 302.

rather than the rule, and brooms, soft drinks, and fly swatters were sometimes shipped at a time when there was a crying need for winter clothing. Furthermore, supplies were unloaded from ships' hatches directly into railroad cars and dispatched to interior depots without shipping documents. When the forward depots received equipment for which there was no immediate need at the same time that shortage of transportation prevented interdepot exchanges, it meant that valuable space was burdened with slow-moving stocks.[44]

In November, operations at Cherbourg were reorganized under the direction of Maj. Gen. Lucius B. Clay, but similar practices persisted at other ports into 1945. The beach depots at OMAHA and UTAH would shortly be closed by winter weather, and interior depots were needed to drain off the rapidly accumulating surpluses at Cherbourg. Despite the disadvantages involved, inland installations would have to serve as sorting points where, for example, forty million pounds of unbalanced B rations, many of them left behind by the First Army, could be converted into five million balanced rations and where items unnecessary for active combat could be segregated.[45] For sized items of clothing, the solution was to concentrate all Class II operations at Reims. Other supplies could not be handled at any single depot, and the problem of efficient sorting and inventory remained unsolved until after V–E Day. (Chart 3)

In an effort to reduce the necessity for inventory, NYPE initiated commodity loading of ships. For example, all the ingredients for two million B rations, loaded on a single ship in New York in the correct proportions, could be shipped to a single port with a minimum of paper work. But a shipload made about sixteen trains, and if all these trains were not dispatched to the same destination the balance was destroyed, and the inland depot received food, but no balanced rations. Sized items of clothing presented the same problem. G–4's tight control over trains frustrated the efforts of technical services to control items. When Littlejohn obtained small consignments of specific items from the United Kingdom to balance rations or clothing tariffs, he always asked for direct delivery by air. If this was impossible, such shipments were sent by small coaster to a specific port with an officer escort to insure that the supplies were not lost or diverted.[46]

Antwerp

As already noted, Antwerp was the great port on which all plans had hinged even before its capture in September. Since Antwerp was west of the inter-Allied administrative boundary, the Supreme Commander decided that it would be opened under British control, although slightly more than half the facilities were assigned to the Americans. The detailed technical agreement regarding operations was worked out by Maj. Gen. Miles H. Graham, Chief Ad-

[44] (1) QM Supply Opns in COMZ During Combat. OTCQM TSFET Operational Study 5, 1 Nov 45, pp. 7–10, 17. (2) USFET Gen Bd Study 27, ch. 2.

[45] IRS, CQM to G–4, 6 Oct 44, sub: Intermediate Depots. Littlejohn Collection, box 13, Depot Pers Data.

[46] (1) See n. 44 (1), above. (2) Memo, Lt Col Snow for Gen Ross, 30 Oct 44, sub: Mtg, Held at OCQM This Date. Hist Br OQMG.

CHART 3.—*Progress in Inventory of QM Supplies*

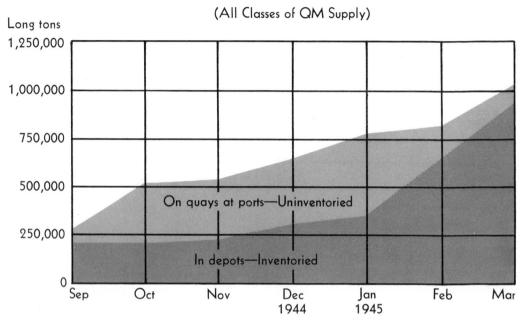

(All Classes of QM Supply)

Source: OTCQM TSFET Operational Study 5, p. 7.

ministrative Officer, 21st Army Group, and Col. Fenton S. Jacobs, Commanding Officer, Channel Base Section. It was obvious from the start that port clearance would be a major problem, and plans were made to use less than half of the tremendous port capacity (242 berths). In peacetime, the Belgians had operated the port on a tight schedule with a minimum of delay and had provided only very limited local storage space. Military operations demanded far more flexibility, and by mid-December, when the 13th Major Port was unloading 19,000 tons per day of American cargo, the backlog was already troublesome. The G–4 plans officer had estimated that any accumulation of more than 15,000 tons would hamper operations, but 85,000 tons were already stacked under tarpaulins back of the quays and no relief was in sight. At the end of the month the British granted space for another 50,000 tons, but estimates were that this would be filled up by 19 January. The Battle of the Bulge was then at its height. COMZ had ordered an embargo on freight to Liège and Namur, which Littlejohn considered overtimid and ill-advised. Ultimately, alternate overflow depots were selected and organized at Charleroi (Q–183) and Lille (Q–185). But meanwhile the performance of this great port had been most disappointing. During January the tonnage actually cleared in the American side of the port averaged less than 11,000 tons per day.[47]

_____

[47] Ruppenthal, *Logistical Support*, II, 111–13.

LOW-PRIORITY SUPPLIES *at Antwerp awaiting rail transportation, January 1945.*

Littlejohn was extremely critical of the "Treaty of Antwerp," whereby the U.S. forces agreed not to establish a depot in that city, and contended that the congestion could not be corrected in any other way. The necessary space was already occupied by American supplies, which a depot organization could inventory and dispatch inland. But the British feared that this process would slow down the clearance of the port and constitute a precedent for formal and permanent admission of U.S. supply services into port areas. They refused for several months to permit establishment of a depot, but meanwhile General Somervell, during his visit to the theater in mid-January 1945, asked General Littlejohn to remedy the situation if possible. Thus assured of at least tacit approval, Littlejohn set up a completely unofficial branch of the Le Havre depot at Antwerp under Col. George L. Olander. On 2 March this branch was formally activated as Depot Q–189. On investigation, a major depot site within the city proved to be neither possible nor desirable. Depot Q–189 acquired 2,750,-000 square feet of open storage along the Albert Canal outside Antwerp, which was used principally to store heavy tentage and similar low priority articles which had clogged the port. Thereafter, Q–189 operated primarily as a sorting and inventory center, advising the port quartermaster on the desired disposition of QMC supplies, segregating low priority articles, and expediting critical items direct to the armies.[48]

While a transit depot at each major port was essential for orderly QM operations, proper co-ordination with the Quartermaster Section of the Port Headquarters was equally important. In a major port, this was a unit of seven officers and twenty-nine enlisted men. Littlejohn considered the port quartermasters the least satisfactory of the QM personnel in the ETO. They had been placed on detached service with the Transportation Corps before leaving the United States, and neither service had taken much pains with their selection or their training for these key assignments. The Transportation Corps manuals defined their duties quite correctly, but both port quartermasters and port commanders either ignored these instructions or failed to understand them. Most port quartermaster sections functioned merely as station supply or mess personnel, and did not participate in the port operation of accounting for and forwarding quartermaster supplies.

Despite the shortage of experienced officers in the OCQM, Littlejohn found it necessary to replace the senior port Quartermaster officers at Cherbourg, Rouen, and Antwerp. In the case of Antwerp, this action encountered active resistance from Col. Doswell Gullatt,

Commanding Officer, 13th Major Port. Early in December Littlejohn had arranged informally with the chief of the ETO Transportation Service, General Ross, to replace the current Antwerp port quartermaster with Col. Edwin T. Bowden, an extremely well-qualified storage and distribution expert. Colonel Gullatt maintained that the transfer had not been processed through proper channels, and, moreover, that he was satisfied with his port quartermaster. He appealed to General Lee, who found that Generals Littlejohn and Ross were in agreement and decided in their favor.

The incident illustrates the significant fact that ports were units almost equal to base sections in importance, and equally inclined to resist personnel actions taken through technical service channels. Nevertheless, Littlejohn was able to establish that port quartermasters were "part of the QM team," and thereafter included them on his distribution lists and in QMC conferences and inspections.[49]

Headquarters and Headquarters Company, QM Base Depot

The major role assigned to the Headquarters and Headquarters Company, QM Base Depot, in the Italian campaign has already been described.[50] These were senior command organiza-

---

[48] (1) Littlejohn, ed., Passing in Review, ch. 5, p. 13. (2) Memo, DCQM for ACofS G–4 COMZ, 11 Dec 44, sub: Clearance of the Port of Antwerp. Hist Br OQMG. (3) IRS, Potter to CQM, 8 Mar 45, sub: Assignment of Space to QMS, with reply, CQM to G–4, 14 Mar 45. Littlejohn Reading File, vol. XXXIV, item 37.

[49] (1) Personal Ltr, CQM to Jacobs (CG CBS), 11 Dec 44; Personal Ltr, CQM to Hoss (QM CBS), 13 Dec 44; Personal Ltr, Jacobs to Littlejohn, 17 Dec 44; Personal Ltr, Hoss to CQM, 18 Dec 44; Memo, CQM for Ross, 21 Dec 44, sub: Port QM Antwerp; Memo, Ross for CQM, 22 Dec 44, same sub. Littlejohn Reading File, vol. XXXI, items 24, 35, 55, 60, 67, 72. (2) Littlejohn, ed., Passing in Review, ch. 27, pp. 5–6.
[50] See ch. IV, above.

tions, designed for the administration of widely dispersed activities. The official organization as originally authorized by the War Department was somewhat inflexible and not altogether in harmony with the ideas of ETO quartermasters, who had been experimenting along similar lines since 1943.[51] Colonel Sharp, former Deputy CQM, ETO, drafted the first experimental T/O while serving in North Africa in August of that year. Unlike the official table, his proposed organization had provided for the elaborate storage and distribution functions necessary under overseas conditions of wide dispersion. Moreover, dispersion implies presence of a large local military population, requiring retail support and local services, which must also be provided by the base depot. In the ETO this military force included AAF as well as COMZ personnel, and sometimes such local responsibilities were one quarter or more of the total mission. The OCQM also found the official War Department table, with its 4 colonels and 8 lieutenant colonels out of a total of 36 officers, somewhat top-heavy from the standpoint of rank. This was extremely inconvenient if the senior officers assigned to the unit in the United States were lacking in field experience and had to be transferred. But despite these minor faults the organization filled an urgent need. It provided official recognition that a Quartermaster depot was a major activity requiring a large amount of specialized senior personnel, and Littlejohn wrote to The

Quartermaster General early in 1945 that "this depot organization has undoubtedly proven one of the greatest assets developed for the Quartermaster Service."[52]

With the tacit consent of the G–1 Section, the OCQM modified the organization and grade structure of each of these units to fit the particular mission of the installation to which it was attached. Thus, at Verdun, essentially a rations and POL depot, the Headquarters Company, 62d Quartermaster Base Depot, elevated subsistence matters from a branch of the Supply Division to an independent Subsistence Division, and assigned more than a quarter of its officers to this operation. At Reims, on the other hand, the 55th Quartermaster Base Depot assigned less than one-seventh of its officers to subsistence activities while 21 officers concerned themselves with all phases of the Class II and IV mission. Had it not been for such flexibility, which Littlejohn felt had been too long absent from the QMC, it would have been impossible for a single unit such as the 62d Headquarters and Headquarters Company to administer a "depot" like Verdun, which actually consisted of 41 subinstallations spread over a territory of 6,400 square miles. This depot complex contained nearly fourteen million square feet of storage space, and in addition to POL handled up to 450,000 long tons of freight in a single month. It controlled 39 Quartermaster companies of various sorts, and had a strength of 13,000, of whom less than half were U.S. personnel. Yet the 62d QM Base Depot

[51] T/O 10–520–1, 11 August 1943, is printed in full in OTCQM TSFET Operational Study 10, 1 November 1945, QM Units, Organizations and Personnel, pp. 92–95.

[52] Ltr, CQM to TQMG, 2 Jan 45, sub: Transmission of Hist Data Concerning QM Opns in the ETO. OQMG ETO 321.

itself numbered only 36 officers and 118 enlisted men.[53]

These units were used in the communications zone only. At advanced depots, one QM base depot plus one QM group was able to administer supply operations for a field army. In intermediate and base sections, their responsibilities were sometimes considerably greater, but more subunits were attached. Seventeen QM base depots served in the ETO, including one permanently attached to OCQM headquarters.[54] (See Appendix B.)

Depot Facilities

The performance of base depots in the ETO was affected by conditions which apparently were not anticipated in the zone of interior training of Quartermaster troops and only partly foreseen in OVERLORD planning. The reports of base depots, from Cherbourg to Liège, refer again and again to shortages of closed and weatherproof storage space, weak or uneven floors that made it impossible to use fork-lift trucks, lack of other materials-handling equipment, poor lighting facilities, rutted roads, muddy or flooded fields, insufficient dunnage, bombed out rail trackage, and scarcity of rail equipment and of responsible civilian labor. Though their facilities were conspicuously inferior to those of the zone of interior, the inland installations were better than those at the original beachhead depots at Bouteville

(Q–172) near UTAH and Le Molay (Q–173) near OMAHA, with their stocks piled in open fields, where hot weather melted lard and chocolate, and rain spoiled other stores. Here the shortage of truck transportation to railheads had been chronic, and occasionally horse and donkey carts carried stocks to rail sidings. Topography prevented real improvements at these sites, but for lack of better facilities the beaches continued to operate until mid-November. The storage areas were then turned over to Cherbourg (Q–171), which did not completely clear them until late March 1945.[55]

As the troops moved inland depots were located at leading rail centers. Wherever possible, warehouses and sheds in proximity to rail yards were converted to quartermaster uses, but too often such facilities had been Allied bombing targets. Now they suffered from leaking roofs, weak flooring, and exposure to pilferage, and usually had to be cleared of much debris. For these reasons the bulk of supplies at all depots in France were stored in the open in accordance with techniques developed in Great Britain. At Paris, Charleroi-Mons, Liège, and Verdun, tremendous quantities of quartermaster supplies were stacked in the freight yards. At Liège, eight million gallons of gasoline were lined along the Meuse River for two miles.

In the absence of concentrated facilities, every depot became a cluster of subdepots distributed around the various centers. The installations of the Charleroi-Mons Depot were dispersed

---

[53] (1) *Ibid.* (2) OTCQM TSFET Operational Study 10, pp. 93–98. (3) Hist of 62d QMBD. Hist Br OQMG. (4) "QM Functions in the Theaters of Operations," *QMR*, XXIII, No. 5 (March–April, 1944), 41.

[54] *QM Supply in ETO*, VIII, 105–08.

[55] (1) Hist of 54th QMBD. Hist Br OQMG. (2) Ruppenthal, *Logistical Support*, II, 86-88.

OPEN STORAGE OF FLOUR *at Verdun, December 1944.*

over an area of 4,700 square miles, while Liège Depot controlled warehouses and open storage scattered across the entire width of Belgium from Herbesthal westward to Givet, France. Similarly, the 62d Quartermaster Base Depot, sent into Verdun before the Third Army had evacuated that city, found that the most desirable storage sites had not been released by army units. It established eight Class I and eight Class III subdepots using all rail sidings within a thirty-mile radius of Verdun. Usually, the exploitation of open space required the assistance of the Corps of Engineers. Areas had to be graded, rubble cleared, and road networks laid out. In addition, fences had to be constructed for security, lights for night work installed, and cranes set on concrete bases.[56]

Not all of a depot's difficulties resulted from such physical handicaps.

Allowance had to be made for the difficulties of adjusting to economic and topographical conditions on the Continent, all of which were aggravated by the pressure of combat. After several inspection tours through the depot system, the CQM set up short courses of instruction, notably at Reims, to give key personnel additional training in better supply and storage procedures. At UTAH Beach, a Quartermaster Orientation School conducted evening classes for transient Quartermaster officers, emphasizing the operation of continental depots and depot headquarters.[57]

Experience had convinced Littlejohn that technical training in an overseas theater had to be directly under the

---

[56] Histories of 52d, 54th, 56th, 58th, 63d, and 68th QMBD's. Hist Br OQMG.

[57] Ltr, CO 56th Hq Base Depot to QM NBS, 8 Oct 44, sub: Conditions Preventing Efficient Opn of Depot; Memo, CQM for QM Oise Section, 29 Dec 44, sub: 55th QM Base Depot Co; Ltr, CQM to QM ADSEC, 9 Nov 44, sub: Observations Concerning Visit to QM Instl at Vendun; Memo, CQM for CG Oise Base Sec, 20 Feb 45, sub: Survey of Depot Q–180. All in Littlejohn Collection.

supervision of each chief of service. The Quartermaster Section of the American School Center at Shrivenham had proved to be completely ineffective in solving the current problem—providing a large number of competent Quartermaster officers trained to perform specific tasks. When the QM School was transferred to the Continent late in 1944, he insisted that it be placed under his immediate control. Col. Henry A. Wingate commanded the school, first at the Isle St. Germain and later at Darmstadt, Germany. He was an experienced QM officer who had previously commanded various general depots in Great Britain and had been quartermaster of Northern Ireland Base Section and Loire Base Section. Wingate kept the curriculum of the school flexible to meet the changing needs for various types of QM specialists. He insisted upon a practical approach to current problems, and endeavored to provide instruction in up-to-date solutions and techniques. Lectures by outstanding experts in various QM specialties were a notable contribution to that end. Such men invariably held key positions from which they could be spared but very briefly. They were made available primarily because the school, like the installations to which they were assigned, was a part of the Quartermaster Service, so that cumbersome staff liaison was not needed to secure their services.[58]

The United Kingdom Base

With the development of the COMZ on the Continent and the influx of men

and matériel into France directly from the zone of interior, the United Kingdom, once the center of activities in the European theater, was relegated to the role of a base section somewhat isolated from the main axis of supply. The eleven months of the major campaign against Germany saw Britain, which, according to the contemporary jest, had been sinking under the load of Yankee supplies, start on its way back to normal conditions. But manifold problems still confronted Quartermaster personnel remaining in the United Kingdom.

The RHUMBA plan provided not only for the transfer of base sections to the Continent but also for progressive inactivation of supply depots and reduction of stocks in the United Kingdom. Installations were to be either closed down completely or returned to the British. Depots and maintenance, reclamation, and salvage facilities were to be consolidated in order to conserve military manpower.

During 1944 the Eastern, Western, and Southern Base Sections became districts under the single United Kingdom Base, and Northern Ireland Base Section was inactivated and absorbed by Western Base Section, later Western District. In April 1945 all the districts were disbanded and their responsibilities transferred to the various depots. In the "Little America" (Grosvenor Square) section of London, Central District served both the U.K. Base headquarters and COMZ Rear. The Quartermaster officer here represented the Chief Quartermaster in miscellaneous functions, which included operation of the London Sales Store, the London Baggage Bureau, and the outlying Brookwood Cemetery. The U.K. Base quartermaster also co-operated with Special Services and the Red Cross to provide services for combat troops on leave from the Continent.[59]

Depot Closing Program

RHUMBA was barely two months old when Col. Aloysius M. Brumbaugh, the quartermaster of U.K. Base, informed General Littlejohn that the scheduled closing dates for the depots could not possibly be met and that perhaps as much as a ninety-day delay was unavoidable.[60] The most serious problem was Transportation Corps' inability to furnish shipping for the movement of stocks to the Continent. Backlogs at closed installations and in open depots, including civil affairs supplies, totaled 131,000 long tons. These had to be moved before the closing program could be carried out. Meanwhile the inactivation of depots was delayed by an order from U.K. Base headquarters prohibiting interdepot shipments except to balance inventories. Under these circumstances, the close-out of Quartermaster Sections at general depots was postponed thirty days, but any prospective relief was almost immediately offset by the sudden and unanticipated diversion of four divisions and 17,000 nondivisional troops to the United Kingdom.[61]

By the end of November, 9 of the original 18 general depots had suspended operations and a month later only 4 of the 11 original QM branch depots were still open.[62] But the general depots were not closing fast enough to suit the OCQM. Pointing to the lengthening lines of communication and the imminent entry of American forces into enemy territory, Littlejohn reiterated the urgent need for Quartermaster personnel on the Continent. To hasten the close-out program, he urged that the directives against interdepot shipments be modified and that surveys be inaugurated to determine what stocks could be transported to the Continent, what ought to be shipped back to the United States or to other theaters, and what could be disposed of locally in Britain.[63]

Base of Supply

Meanwhile U.K. Base served as a supply base for the forces on the Continent, particularly for fresh fruits and vegetables and for Class II items. But in the realization of this mission the theater-wide shortage of transportation was a severe handicap. The crux of the problem was securing an adequate allocation of cross-Channel shipping for quartermaster items. When the U.K. Base quartermaster's tonnage allocation for September 1944 was set at 62,000 long tons, the OCQM pointed out that it

[59] Hist of Central District UKB [ca. 31 Dec 44]. Hist Br OQMG.

[60] Ltr, QM UKB to CQM Hq COMZ (Forward), 9 Sep 44, sub: Current Situation on Depot Closing Program. Littlejohn Collection.

[61] (1) 1st Ind, Chief Storage and Distr Div OCQM for Chief Subs Div, 18 Sep 44, sub: Closing of Depots in U.K. Littlejohn Collection. (2) Notes on U.K. Base Conf, 15 Oct 44; Hist Rpt OQM UKB, 1 Sep 44–30 Sep 44. Both in USFET 314.7.

[62] Hist Rpts OQM UKB, 1–20 Nov 44, 1–31 Dec 44. USFET 314.7.

[63] Personal Ltr, CQM to Chief Ord Off, 7 Sep 44, no sub; Memo, Chief Storage and Distr Div OQMG for QM UKB, 14 Nov 44, sub: Current Status of U.K. Depots; Ltrs, CQM to CG COMZ, 20–23 Nov 44, sub: UKB Depot Closing Program; Personal Ltr, CQM to QM UKB, 25 Nov 44. All in Littlejohn Collection.

needed 88,000 long tons. It predicted that this shortage would hurt the winter clothing program. Moreover, it complained of delays and pilferage of critical supplies, and requested permission to overcome this handicap by the use of airlift. This request was denied, for at the moment POL was the most critical item on the Continent. The Red Ball express was operating at full capacity and all available airlift was being used to move the fuels continually demanded by the armies.[64]

In October the Quartermaster tonnage allocation for shipments out of the United Kingdom was increased 50 percent, to 92,000 long tons, but even this figure was only half what had been promised. Fortunately, the stabilized tactical situation had reduced POL requirements, and winter clothing and equipment began to enjoy higher transportation priorities.[65] By this time, the need for winter clothing and equipage had become so critical that the OCQM authorized U.K. stocks of such items to be reduced to zero, and it even directed that service and AAF units in Great Britain turn in overcoats and arctics for the use of front-line troops. By November, U.K. Quartermaster depots were actually having trouble finding the supplies to fill allocated tonnages.[66]

During the last six months of 1944, Colonel Brumbaugh ran into personnel and labor problems similar to those of his colleagues on the Continent. Shortages of military and civilian workers resulted in poor warehousing, inaccurate inventory records, and a laxity growing out of the realization that the job could not be properly accomplished. His own office was subjected to repeated drafts by OCQM, beginning with instructions on 19 August to reduce his overhead to 68 officers and 225 enlisted men by September.[67]

But these personnel problems were not merely quantitative. Having added German POW's and Italian service units to the British civilians and Irish "industrials" hired before D-day, the Quartermaster Corps found itself with a labor force of mixed and conflicting national loyalties. Moreover, the Continent was calling for the transfer of all Italian service unit troops, numbering nearly seven thousand, and offering only three thousand German prisoners as replacements.[68] Luckily, these multiple pressures on the U.K. Base quartermaster were alleviated by measures to get more British workers, by delaying the departure of the Italian service units, and by the action of the Commanding General, U.K. Base, in prohibiting the transfer of personnel to the Continent if such a shift endangered the local mission. The in-

[64] Ltr, CQM to CG COMZ, 7 Sep 44, sub: Sep Lift from U.K.; Ltr, Actg CofS G–4 COMZ to CQM COMZ, 8 Sep 44, sub: Tonnage Lift ex U.K. Both in Littlejohn Collection.

[65] Notes on UKB Confs, 1 Oct, 8 Oct, 15 Oct 44. London Area Office 337.

[66] (1) Hist Rpt OQM UKB, 1–30 Sep 44; 1–30 Nov 44. USFET 314.7. (2) McNamara Memoir, p. 149.

[67] (1) Personal Ltr, QM WBS to CQM COMZ, 4 Jul 44; Ltr, Chief Field Sv Div OQM UKB to QM UKB, 7 Sep 44, sub: Inspection of Depot 107. Both in Littlejohn Collection. (2) Memo, CQM for Deputy, Forward, 19 Aug 44, sub: High Points of Conf. Littlejohn Reading File, vol. XXVIIA, item 85.

[68] Personal Ltr, QM UKB to CQM, 11 Oct 44; Memo, QM UKB for G–1 Civilian Pers UKB, 31 Oct 44, sub: Release of British Civilians at U.S. Instls; Memo, Chief Pers Div OQM UKB for QM UKB, 3 Nov 44, sub: Reduction in Pers in U.K.; Memo, Asst QM UKB for Troops Br OCQM, 18 Nov 44, sub: Advance Phasing of QM T/O Units. All in Littlejohn Collection.

creasing autonomy of the U.K. Base was demonstrated in December, when Colonel Brumbaugh began to prepare independent requisitions on PEMBARK.[69]

By the first anniversary of U.K. Base, Quartermaster activities had decelerated, keeping pace with the base as a whole. Incoming QM supplies from the United States during August 1945 dropped to a mere forty-five tons, the lowest in the three years of American military activity in the United Kingdom. This virtual termination of receipts led to notable decreases in interdepot shipments; the outloading of quartermaster supplies continued, but on a very modest scale. Local procurement was drastically cut, and salvage installations either closed down or were turned over to organizations scheduled to retain a permanent location in Great Britain.

On 30 April 1945 (the nearest month-end to V–E Day), there were 431,860 American troops in the U.K. Base, and U.S. supplies still exceeded 1,000,000 tons, including many items no longer needed on the Continent. Cross-Channel shipments had reached 392,000 tons in April, but dropped to 150,000 tons in June. Shortly after V–E Day, embargoes on shipping both into and out of Great Britain were applied to all supplies not needed for redeployment or for civil affairs purposes.[70]

Quartermaster Support During the Battle of the Bulge

On 16 December, the combined British, Canadian, American, and French forces stood generally along the German border, although the First Army had captured Aachen and the Germans held out in Colmar. Military leaders had decided to resume the offensive toward the Rhine by attacking in the direction of the Roer dams on the north and the Saar on the south. In deploying his forces to bolster this double threat, Bradley directed Hodges to reduce his strength along the eighty-mile Ardennes front to four divisions. Rather than assume a defensive winter position, the high command took a calculated risk and determined to renew the offensive toward the enemy's homeland.[71] The organization of the supply system for close support of this advance had been completed during November. COMZ had built up stocks in Liège (Q–179) for the First and Ninth Armies and in Verdun (Q–178) for the Third Army. Army depots were equally well prepared. But when the enemy's panzer divisions struck in force through the Ardennes, hoping to capture or destroy the large stocks which the Americans had concentrated in the forward areas for their own projected offensive, these supplies had to be rapidly evacuated.

On 20 December SHAEF, having noted how the German thrust disrupted lateral communications, extended Third Army's left boundary northward to the line Givet–St. Vith and transferred the battered remnants of VIII Corps from

---

[69] (1) 1st Ind, QM UKB to CQM COMZ, 24 Nov 44, sub: Present and Future Utilization of Troop Units and Other Types of Labor in ETO. Littlejohn Collection. (2) Memo, Pers Div QM UKB for G–1 UKB, 29 Nov 44, sub: 1945 Civilian Allocation; Notes of Mtg, G–1 and GPA, 9 Dec 44. Both in USFET GPA 230. (3) Memo, CQM for QM UKB, 14 Dec 44, sub: Preparation of Requisitions in U.K. Littlejohn Reading File, vol. XXXI, item 51.

[70] Ruppenthal, *Logistical Support*, II, 402–04.

[71] (1) Eisenhower, *Crusade in Europe*, pp. 337–41. (2) Bradley, *A Soldier's Story*, pp. 451–55.

Hodges to Patton. Third Army performed a remarkable feat in disengaging from combat in the Saar and shifting northwestward to relieve Bastogne. Colonel Busch, the Third Army quartermaster, reported that although his new QM dump and truckhead sites were selected solely by map reconnaissance, all of them proved to be satisfactory.[72]

On 21 December, General Lee's service troops began fortifying a Meuse River line as a reserve position.[73] Though the First and Ninth Armies were temporarily transferred to the tactical command of Montgomery's 21 Army Group, they remained under Bradley for administrative support and drew their supplies from American sources. In the First Army area, largely in Belgium, POL stocks were evacuated from the main reserve dumps between Spa and Stavelot, the Welkenraedt Class I dump was completely evacuated, and four thousand tons of Class II and IV items were removed from Eupen. Meanwhile First Army was supplied directly from Liège, which was closer to many army truckheads and railheads than the relocated army depot near Gembloux.[74]

The combat zone evacuation process was executed with remarkable speed, priority being given to the clearance of fuels and lubricants. Third Army lost 100,000 gallons of gasoline by hostile bombing, First Army ignited 134,000 gallons at Stavelot to serve as a roadblock against enemy tanks, and flying bombs and enemy aircraft hit 650,000 gallons of ADSEC gasoline near Liège.

Actually, only a negligible quantity of gasoline fell into enemy hands as a result of the Germans overrunning American dumps.[75] Meanwhile ADSEC headquarters, confronted with 3,700 tons of balanced B rations, 16,000 tons of operational rations, 31,000 tons of unbalanced B's, 10 million packages of cigarettes, and 5 million gallons of packaged MT80 gasoline, all located in the Liège area, made hasty plans for removal or destruction of this property. All operational rations and such special items as cigarettes, coffee, yeast, fats, and flour were to be evacuated to a secure storage point. Fresh meats, lard, certain canned foods —butter, cheese, sausage, meats—and dehydrated eggs were to be distributed to the civilian population. Perishables were to be spoiled by shutting off the power on the refrigeration equipment and other foodstuffs were to be soaked in gasoline and ignited.[76] Plans were made to contaminate 1,500,000 gallons of bulk aviation gasoline, since the surrounding area was inhabited and burning was impossible.[77]

As it happened, the enemy never came within thirty miles of Liège, and although a few supplies were evacuated, Maj. Gen. Ewart C. Plank, the ADSEC commander, never ordered any part of the destruction plan to be put into effect. Littlejohn considered the evacuation plan completely unrealistic, and the fact that after a maximum effort

---

[72] Critical comment upon a preliminary MS version of this narrative by Brig Gen Everett E. Busch, 1 Dec 54. Hist Br OQMG.

[73] Pogue, *The Supreme Command*, pp. 376, 382.

[74] *FUSA Rpt of Opns*, 1 Aug 44–22 Feb 45, II, 119–29; IV, 66.

[75] (1) *Ibid.*, IV, 72. (2) 12th Army Group Rpt of Opns, XII, 203–04; VI, 52–53. (3) OCQM Field Obsvn Rpt 16, app. A [ca. 25 Jan 45], sub: QM in FUSA During German Counteroffensive. (4) Hist of QM Sec ADSEC, p. 19.

[76] Memo, Chief Subs Div for CQM, 22 Dec 44, sub: Destruction of Subs. Littlejohn Collection.

[77] Personal Ltr, QM ADSEC to CQM, 23 Dec 44, no sub. Littlejohn Reading File, vol. XXXI, item 77.

only nine trainloads of rations were moved out of Liège bears out his contention. As usual in the ETO, transportation was the decisive factor, and most of the available trucks and trains had been allotted to the armies to evacuate their own reserves. In the uncertain tactical situation, the army quartermasters preferred to keep these reserves loaded on cars or vehicles, so that very few trains were emptied and released to ADSEC. Littlejohn could have secured a prior allotment of transportation if he had desired it, but under the circumstances he felt that the armies should have first priority, since their success in evacuating their own dumps was a vital factor in slowing down the enemy attack. He refused to take action despite repeated urging by General Plank, by his own staff, and even by the G–4 of the 12th Army Group, General Moses. Littlejohn contended that the supplies at Liège (mostly Class I and III) could be destroyed in time to prevent capture, and that if necessary the theater could operate without them for thirty days. In that length of time more supplies could be discharged from ships offshore. (This evaluation was based on exact knowledge; it demonstrates the value of an up-to-date theater-wide inventory.) But his major consideration was that evacuation was an admission of defeat. If the Allied armies intended to counterattack, they would require large reserves of supplies in the forward portion of the communications zone. Events vindicated this view. Entrusted to civilian railroad crews the "rolling reserve" of the First Army was carried too far to the rear and caught in the inevitable congestion that plagues rear areas after a surprise attack by the enemy. For

several weeks Liège depot had to expand its retail distribution activities greatly and issue supplies direct to combat units.[78]

To adapt it to the radically altered tactical situation, many changes were made in the COMZ supply plan. A first step was the suspension of shipments to Liège. Rations and gasoline were diverted to Charleroi, about fifty miles to the west, while rations for Luxembourg were sent instead to Verdun. The space saved was used for ammunition. Meanwhile the offloading of supplies was continued at the Channel ports to prevent a jam of unloaded vessels in the ports. But the embargo on forwarding supplies, especially from Antwerp, created a backlog which forced a search for storage space east of Antwerp. Charleroi-Mons (Q–183) and Lille (Q–185) accepted most of this overflow, and became very large depots at this time.[79]

The OCQM also faced the possibility that Liège might be overrun and that Charleroi, Antwerp, and even Reims might have to perform retail distributing functions for the combat troops. Colonel Rosaler of Field Service and ten officers and fifty enlisted men from the 72d QM Base Depot were temporarily detailed to Channel Base Section for that purpose.[80]

[78] (1) Ibid. (2) Hist of QM Sec ADSEC, pp. 11, 19, 20, 30. (3) Littlejohn, ed., Passing in Review, ch. 21, p. 3. (4) Interv with Littlejohn, 29 Oct 57.
[79] (1) Cable EX 77256, Lee to 4th Port et al., 21 Dec 44. TSFET G–4 Mtgs, Nov 44–25 Jul 45. ETO 337. (2) Ltr, CQM to ADSEC et al., 23 Dec 44, sub: Immediate QM Plan for Supply of Armies. Littlejohn Reading File, vol. XXXI, item 75.
[80] (1) Ltr cited n. 79 (2). (2) Ltr, CQM to Brig Gen Fenton S. Jacobs, CG CBS, 23 Dec 44, sub: Establishment of Distr Points for QM Supply. Littlejohn Reading File, vol. XXXI, item 76.

By 1 January the enemy's counter-offensive had been checked, and the salient began to shrink. Rations, clothing, and equipment were particularly scarce and the depleted reserves had to be restored before the offensive into Germany could be renewed. Because Liège had received none after 18 December, it was particularly low on rations. If that depot was to reach its prescribed 15-day supply level, while also maintaining the troops in its area, it would require 2,150 tons per day throughout January. While the levels of gasoline were low in the forward areas, the situation was not considered alarming because one thousand rail cars loaded with gasoline were available on short notice to either Liège or First Army.[81]

Reorganization for Offensive Action

With the reduction of the Bulge in the north and the Colmar Pocket in the south by 15 February, the entire Allied front again ran along the western boundary of Germany. Since orders were that only ADSEC behind 12th Army Group and CONAD behind 6th Army Group would follow the armies into the enemy's homeland, and that the armies would retain all territorial control in Germany, the Communications Zone organization had to be developed to provide maximum support for what was to be the decisive tactical effort.[82]

As a transitional headquarters to facilitate the transfer of supplies to exclusive COMZ control, SOLOC had assumed responsibility for supply regulation from Advance Echelon, MTOUSA, on 20 November 1944. Its mission was the administrative support of 6th Army Group and attached air forces, and as such it had control over CONAD at Dijon and Delta Base Section, which reached northward from Marseille. Rear support was provided by depot Q-187 at Dijon and depot Q-188 at Marseille.[83] As CONAD readied itself to follow the combat elements into Germany, SOLOC prepared to establish an Intermediate Section in its former location, though initially, and for the purpose of expediting the build-up, this section would be an administrative district of CONAD. A new depot (Q-186) was officially opened in the Toul-Nancy-Lunéville-Metz area on 5 February. By 1 April it would be capable of supporting forty divisions and handling 300,000 tons of supplies, of which 140,000 tons of storage space were to hold quartermaster matériel. CONAD moved its headquarters from Dijon to Nancy on 17 February, but Nancy was only a way station on the road to Germany. As already noted, Dijon had become headquarters for the new Burgundy District, formerly the Loire Base Section, on 9 February. In March the month-old Headquarters, Burgundy District, was transferred from CONAD to Oise Section. Oise Intermediate Section now stretched from the Belgian to the Swiss border and was responsible for the storage of more than half the theater stocks. Before the cessation of hostilities, the Quartermaster Section of Oise Section

---

[81] (1) Memo, QM ADSEC for CG ADSEC, 3 Jan 45, sub: QM Supply Situation ADSEC. Hist Br OQMG. (2) Memo, CQM for G-4 COMZ, 6 Jan 45, sub: Port Offloading and Inland Movement of Class I Supplies. Littlejohn Collection.

[82] Admin and Log Hist of ETO, pt. II, vol. II, p. 274.

[83] SOLOC is discussed in detail in Chapter IV, above.

comprised 17,000 military and 58,000 nonmilitary personnel, 7 major depots, and more than 100 specialized Quartermaster units. On 12 February, SOLOC was dissolved, and thereafter five base sections and two advance sections were directly under Headquarters, COMZ.[84] (*See Table 12.*)

The unification of supply control facilitated the exchange of supplies and service troops between north and south. Exchange of quartermaster goods had begun on a small scale in the fall of 1944, but it was soon evident that shortages in both areas were too similar for substantial exchanges.[85] Between 15 December and 25 January 1945, ETO depots sent 4,300 long tons of Class I and 75 long tons of QM Class II, IV, and PX supplies to SOLOC intermediate depots and received 600 tons in return.

The situation with respect to service troops was somewhat different. In February, SHAEF sent 12,000 such troops to the south in support of the four combat divisions temporarily diverted to the 6th Army Group for the Colmar offensive, and COMZ agreed furthermore to release 7,500 of its own service personnel to SOLOC to help back up this effort.[86]

In addition, SHAEF directed the 12th Army Group to transfer certain service troops, including the following QM units, direct to 6th Army Group by 1 March:[87]

- 1 Gasoline Supply Company
- 1 Salvage Collecting Company
- 2 Service Companies
- 1 Salvage Repair Company
- 1 Platoon, Sales Company (M)

The adjustment of troop allocations between the two army groups was merely one aspect of the differences between them that made co-ordination difficult. The 6th Army Group included 8 French as well as 12 U.S. divisions, but the French contributed considerably less than their proportion of service troops. This was partly compensated for by the assignment of Italian service units, but the Italian units were not completely satisfactory substitutes for corresponding U.S. units. Base 901, the French logistical organization subordinate to SOLOC, became an independent subcommand of COMZ on 19 February 1945. Although by U.S. standards it should have numbered 112,000 men to support an 8-division army, its strength never exceeded 29,000.[88]

Smoother liaison between COMZ and the former SOLOC area was accomplished in several ways. CONAD and Delta Base were furnished complete files of ETOUSA Standard Operating Procedures and directives and were expected to adapt their procedures accordingly. For example, CONAD adopted the ETOUSA depot numbering system at this time. COMZ also absorbed much of the SOLOC staff. Thus General Lar-

[84] (1) Admin and Log Hist of ETO, pt. II, vol. II, pp. 238–43, 271, 277–79. (2) Ltr, Chief Plans Br SOLOC to CG SOLOC, 1 Feb 45, sub: Estimate of Supply Situation. Littlejohn Collection. (3) *CONAD History*, I, 111–12, 166, 169, 198–200. (4) Hist of QM Sec Oise Intermediate Sec. 1–30 Apr 45. WBS 314.7.

[85] Memo, G–4 for CQM, 21 Jan 45, sub: Shipments to SOLOC; Memo, DCQM for G–4, 25 Jan 45, sub: Movement of Supplies Between Northern Line of Communications and SOLOC. Littlejohn Collection.

[86] Memo, DCQM for G–4, 25 Jan 45, sub: Movement of Supplies Between Northern Line of Communications and SOLOC; Ltr, Chief Plans Br SOLOC to CG SOLOC, 1 Feb 45, sub: Estimate of Supply Situation. Littlejohn Collection.

[87] (1) *QM Supply in ETO*, VIII, 25.

[88] (1) Ruppenthal, *Logistical Support*, II, 297–302. (2) Vigneras, *Rearming the French*, p. 188.

kin, commanding general of SOLOC, became deputy commander of COMZ, and Brig. Gen. William H. Middleswart, the SOLOC quartermaster, moved to Paris as Deputy Chief Quartermaster. These changes brought COMZ into closer contact with units, personnel, and procedures on the southern flank.[89]

Immediately after the dissolution of SOLOC, and as part of his plan to standardize and decentralize supply procedures, Littlejohn sent Colonel Rosaler, his chief of Field Services, to CONAD and Delta Base Section to acquaint those staffs with OCQM policies and practices. In conformity with the directive issued to ADSEC on 9 February, CONAD also got authority to designate the depots to receive requisitions from the 6th Army Group, and those depots made deliveries against credits without prior approval from higher headquarters. OCQM would only review requisitions calling for items in critical supply. The last and most conspicuous change shifted the bulk of stocks for the southern area from Marseille and Dijon to the Metz-Nancy area, with Marseille holding only supplies for troops in Delta Base.[90]

[89] This transfer marks the final change in the internal organization of the OCQM before V–E Day. On 17 March General Middleswart was formally designated Deputy for Administration, supervising the activities of the Executive, Accounts, Graves Registration and Effects, Personnel and Training, and Research and Development Divisions. Simultaneously, Brig. Gen. John B. Franks became Deputy for Operations, supervising the Installations, Petroleum and Fuel, Procurement, Storage and Distribution, Subsistence, and Supply Divisions. Littlejohn retained personal direction of the Control and Military Planning Divisions. QM Supply in ETO, I, 23; VIII, 51.

[90] Memo, DCQM for Chief Supply Div [ca. 30 Jan 45], sub: Controlled Items; Memo, CQM for Chief Field Sv Div, 22 Feb 45, sub: Integration of Hq; Memo, CQM for DCQM, 23 Feb, no sub. All in Littlejohn Collection.

By the end of January, when the front was deployed to its full width, plans envisioned the eventual support of three million persons, American, Allied, and prisoners of war, in the forward areas —that is, in the combat zone plus the ADSEC and CONAD areas. To facilitate the execution of the Quartermaster role in this vast supply program, General Littlejohn drew on the experience of the recent Ardennes campaign and concluded that the front had to be divided into several sectors, each having a vertical depot system in depth that would be capable of furnishing all classes of supplies. At this time improvements in transportation facilities and the unloading capacities of the Channel ports, and COMZ development generally, had reached the point where conventional and orderly Quartermaster procedures, calling for staged supply through base, intermediate, and advanced depots, could be applied. From the Quartermaster point of view, reduction of the levels of supply held within the armies was now desirable. The OCQM had found that the armies seldom reported their reserves accurately and tended to leave supplies behind when they moved forward. Late in January it recommended that army supply levels be reduced to three days of supply for gasoline, and five days for all other classes, contending that the build-up in the depots, especially intermediate depots, justified these reductions. (Chart 4)

But the armies objected to this proposal, pointing out that serious shortages had been overcome only in the last few weeks. COMZ and 12th Army Group agreed that the level in the armies should be seven days for Classes I and III and fifteen days for Classes II and

CHART 4—DISTRIBUTION OF QM STOCKS IN BASE, INTERMEDIATE, AND ADVANCE SECTIONS: AUGUST 1944–MAY 1945

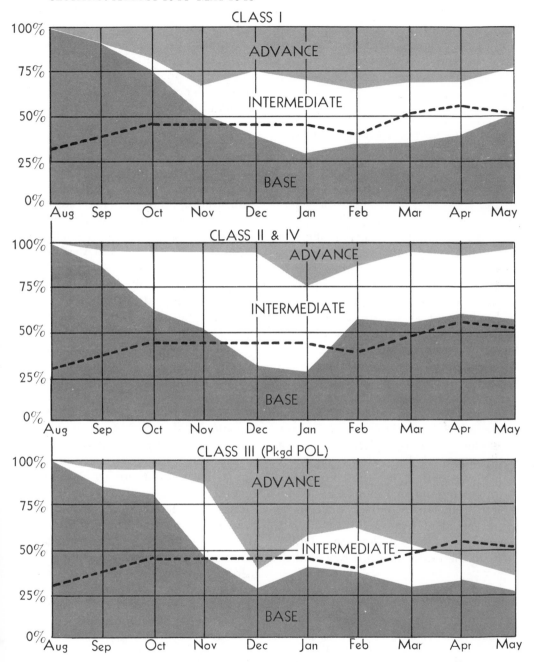

- - - Represents the division of ETO troops along a line drawn at the rear of advance sections.
Percent above—those in and forward of advance sections.
Percent below—those in rear.

Source: OTCQM TSFET Operational Study 5, 1 Nov 45.

IV. Shortly after SOLOC was dissolved, the same levels were extended to 6th Army Group, and were continued until after the end of hostilities. Thus on V–E Day the theater levels were as follows:[91]

Class of Supply	Total Theater	Army Depots	Advance Depots	Inter-mediate Depots	Base Depots
I	50	7	10	18	15
II	60	15	15	20	10
III*	45	7	10	18	10
Gasoline ...	30	7	10	10	3
IV	60	15	15	20	10

* Less gasoline.

In planning for the spring offensive Liège and Verdun, currently advance depots, were to become intermediate depots for rations and petroleum supplies. Stocks of clothing and equipment were to be brought closer to the front by establishing a Class II and IV depot at Mons for the north side of the 12th Army Group line and possibly another on the south side more accessible to the Third Army than the depot at Reims. As already indicated, the intermediate depot on the south flank of the Allied line was to be located in the Metz-Nancy area. Smaller than the Liège depot, the Metz-Nancy site alone would not be capable of supporting the operations planned for the 6th Army Group, but any deficiencies would be filled from Verdun.[92] Plans were also made to follow any deployment to the north or south by establishing additional depots in the Maastricht or Luxembourg areas.

General Littlejohn's original plan for supply in depth called for a separate advance depot for each army. But these advance depots were never intended to be main installations in the forward flow of supply. The normal flow would be directly from the intermediate depots to the armies, with the advance depot serving essentially as an auxiliary agency to meet emergency requisitions and ensure a continuing flow of essential supplies.[93] Generally, this had been the practice with Class I and III supplies since the establishment of Liège and Verdun, but Class II and IV items, many of which were in scarce supply, had been centralized in the single depot at Reims to conserve clothing and equipage and reduce the distribution factor. Now that Class II and IV levels were rising, thanks largely to the improved transportation system, it was possible to consider the decentralization of clothing and equipage, particularly those items in steady demand by the combat elements. Advance depots were to stock not only a 10 to 15 days' level of rations but also a similar level of fast-moving clothing and general supplies and a 5-day level of fuels. The latter stocks would come from Reims or from the new intermediate clothing depot at Lille in balanced shipments, some of which could be immediately reconsigned to the armies without unloading and rehandling. The first advance depots were to be located at Aachen and Luxembourg as soon as the

[91] QM Supply in ETO, I, 83.

[92] Personal Ltr, CQM to QM ADSEC, 5 Jan 45, no sub; Memo, CQM for G-4 COMZ, 5 Jan 45, sub: Current and Future Supply and Storage Plan, QM Sv, and Inds; Memo, QM ADSEC for G-4 ADSEC, 7 Feb 45, sub: Plan for Selection and Activation of ADSEC QM Depots; Memo, G-4 COMZ for CQM, 13 Feb 45, sub: Current and Future Supply and Storage Plan. All in Littlejohn Collection, sec. I.

[93] Ltr, DCQM to G-4 COMZ, 27 Feb 45, sub: Emergency Plan for Support of Rapid Advances; Memo, CQM for QM's ADSEC and CONAD, 4 Mar 45, sub: Establishment of Advanced Depots. Both in Littlejohn Collection.

tactical situation permitted. It was anticipated that they would be semimobile and would move forward immediately behind, or even in, the army areas to take over and expand existing Quartermaster dumps and railheads.[94]

The plan for an advance depot behind each army was modified in February and March while COMZ waited for the combat forces to cross the Rhine so that the first of these depots could be brought as close as possible to that river. Instead of one advance depot for each army, the plan now provided one for every two armies: the ADSEC–12th Army Group area (with four armies in Germany) would contain two advance depots and the CONAD–6th Army Group area would have one. Their specific locations would be recommended by the advance sections after consultation with quartermasters at all echelons between army and OCQM. Anticipating the assumption of technical control of perhaps a hundred German manufacturing plants having useful storage facilities, the Quartermaster Corps was to reinforce advance depots with specialized personnel who would inventory and control captured stocks and space.[95]

The Advance into Germany and Redeployment

The March offensive speedily gained full impetus after the Rhine, the final geographical obstacle to the complete conquest of Germany, was crossed with relatively little difficulty. The forward thrust now turned out to be too rapid to permit the establishment of advance depots, and all the elaborate planning proved academic. In this setting the deteriorating transportation system would have been worsened by a depot system that called for the successive shuttling of supplies from rear base to intermediate section and from intermediate to advance section. By 12 April no advance depots had been established.[96] ADSEC had moved its headquarters forward to Bonn on the Rhine on 7 April, but had no time to establish depots of any sort; its new supply sites were little more than transfer points between intermediate depots and the armies. In a tactical situation of rapid pursuit resembling that of the summer before, ADSEC's control of Class I and III installations in March and early April seldom lasted longer than two weeks. The major difference was that instead of being turned over to another COMZ echelon the installations were now closed out.[97]

As usual in rapid forward movements, the primary requirements in the spring offensive were gasoline and rations. Motor fuel had been the most critical item during the previous summer. Now,

[94] (1) Memo, CQM for CofS COMZ, 25 Jan 45, no sub; Memo, CQM for G–4 COMZ, 1 Feb 45, sub: Current and Future Supply and Storage Plan, QM Sv, and Ind; Memo, Chief Mil Plan Div for Chief Pers Div, n.d., sub: Establishment of Advance Depots. All in Littlejohn Collection, sec. I. (2) OCQM Cir Ltr 14, 9 Feb 45, sub: Procedure for Distr of QM Supplies on the Continent (reproduced in OTCQM TSFET Operational Study 5, exhibit C–5).
[95] Memo, DCQM for QM FUSA, 20 Feb 45, sub: QM Opns Under ECLIPSE Conditions; Memo, CQM for QM's ADSEC and CONAD, 4 Mar 45, sub: Establishment of Advance Depots. Both in Littlejohn Collection, sec. I.

[96] (1) Memo, Chief Control Div for Deputy for Opns, 12 Apr 45, sub: Rpt of Trip Forward by Col Phillips; Monthly Narrative Hist, CONAD, 30 Apr 45. Both in Littlejohn Collection. (2) USFET Gen Bd Study 27, p. 40.
[97] Hist of QM ADSEC, an. F, pp. 1, 3.

with their increasing responsibility of feeding thousands upon thousands of prisoners of war, displaced persons, and liberated Allied prisoners of war, quartermasters found that rations, too, had become scarce items.[98] Fortunately, the arrival of warm weather early in March not only cleared the snowbound road and rail networks but also reduced the demand for coal and winter clothing.

The last seven weeks were a hectic period logistically. As in the previous August, the 12th Army Group's situation maps again revealed the yawning gap between the army service areas and the front lines. Late in February, the depth of the army areas rarely exceeded 50 miles; toward the termination of hostilities it was closer to 250 miles. By 4 April, two weeks after the first Rhine crossing, the First, Third, and Ninth Armies were more than a 100 airline miles east of that historic river. While the COMZ transfer points struggled to keep up, some 25 emergency airstrips were opened for the delivery of unprecedented amounts of rations and gasoline to the forward areas of 12th Army Group.[99]

Around 1 April, increasing distances and congestion on the floating bridges across the Rhine caused the turnaround time of trucks moving between Trier and the advanced areas of the Third Army to reach thirty-six hours. Colonel Busch of Third Army was hesitant about setting up a Class II and IV depot at Frankfurt. It would probably be too

far to the rear before it began to operate. He summarized his view in a letter to General Littlejohn: "Only God and General Patton know where the Army is and whither bound." [100] Meanwhile the First and Ninth Armies were no better off; trucks were traveling 400 miles to pick up and deliver gasoline, and the monthly mileages reported were the highest in the history of continental operations. Divisions were calling for gasoline deliveries to the forward truck-heads, and to help make this possible a pipeline was laid under the Rhine behind each army and ADSEC decanting farms were opened east of the Rhine. But these expedients quickly proved inadequate as the supply lines lengthened. The armies having run far beyond the limits of the pipelines, their receipts of gasoline were threatened by a shortage of jerricans, an almost inevitable byproduct of rapid pursuit.[101] Jerricans were not only dispersed; they were wearing out from hard usage. In March, Littlejohn estimated that 50 percent of all jerricans would have to be replaced by June.[102]

Meanwhile 6th Army Group made somewhat less rapid progress, but it crossed the Rhine late in March, and the Danube by mid-April. CONAD's supply points were not closed out as rapidly as ADSEC's, and one of them, Q–190 at Mannheim, was formally organized on 16 April as an advance depot.[103]

---

[98] (1) 12th Army Group Rpt of Opns, VI, 66, 72–73; XII, 208–09. (2) CONAD History, I, 257–70.
[99] (1) 12th Army Group, Rpt of Opns VI, 72–73, an. F, G, J, K. (2) Hist Rpt G–4 Sec SUSA 1–30 Apr 45. Hist Br OQMG.

[100] Personal Ltr, QM TUSA to CQM, 1 Apr 45. Hist Br OQMG.
[101] OQM NUSA AAR, 16–30 Apr 45; Ltr, G–4 to AG XX Corps, 7 May 45, sub: G–4 AAR 1–30 Apr 45. Both in Hist Br OQMG.
[102] Memo for Record, CQM for DCQM, 13 Mar 45. Littlejohn Reading File, vol. XXXIV, item 32.
[103] CONAD History, I, 203–05.

Meanwhile transportation difficulties had been considerably eased by the XYZ express, the last and greatest of the long hauls by motor truck in the ETO. It began operations on 25 March 1945, exactly seven months after Red Ball. The four XYZ routes extended eastward from Liège, Dueren, Luxembourg, and Nancy to support respectively the Ninth, First, Third, and Seventh Armies. The truck operations were from railheads forward to army service areas, and rail repairs were completed behind each army so that the truck routes seldom extended more than 175 miles, which proved to be the maximum efficient operating range. A force of 128 truck companies, equipped principally with 10-ton trailers and 2,000-gallon bulk tankers, averaged a daily lift of 12,859 tons during April and May 1945. Each army was supported by a provisional highway transport division, a Transportation Corps headquarters which provided supervision and maintenance, traffic control, and co-ordination with rail service to the rear and combat units to the front. Since ADSEC and CONAD did not assume territorial responsibilities within Germany, each operation was entirely within a single army area, greatly simplifying administration. The XYZ express was the most orderly and efficient, as well as the largest, of the motor express operations. Notable improvements over Red Ball were in administration, traffic control, equipment, and co-ordination with other means of transportation, especially rail.[104]

One of the problems immediately confronting quartermasters everywhere as the armies swarmed over Germany was the manning of the dispersed dumps and transfer points. Heavy demands were made on base sections for service troops and transportation facilities. Normandy Base Section, the rearmost installation of its kind, closed all Quartermaster installations except those at Cherbourg and Rouen and thereby released 20 units, including service and supply companies, and 2 base depot headquarters. Littlejohn was able to supply a small number of Wacs to replace administrative personnel, and the base section substituted prisoners for the service troops sent forward.[105] By mid-March, the Seventh Army had received 10 additional truck companies and an administrative Quartermaster group improvised from a former headquarters of an antiaircraft artillery battalion. Third Army obtained additional truck companies in March, and in the same period First Army was given another Quartermaster battalion of gasoline supply and service companies. Once the Rhine was crossed, 10 more service companies were added to General Hodges' forces to help bridge the gap between dumps and distributing points. Similarly, the Ninth Army's quartermaster strength was steadily augmented by the addition of railhead, service, gasoline supply, and truck companies, as well as by several Quartermaster battalion headquarters detachments.[106]

---

[104] Bykofsky and Larson, *The Transportation Corps: Operations Overseas*, pp. 337–39.

[105] (1) Memo, CQM for Middleswart, 13 Feb 45, sub: Current Pers Problems; Personal Ltr, CQM to CG NBS, 4 Mar 45, no sub; Memo, G–3 for CQM et al., 4 Mar 45, sub: ADSEC Troop Reqmts, and 1st Ind. All in Hist Br OQMG. (2) Memo, G–3 COMZ for CofS COMZ, 13 Mar 45, sub: Withdrawal of QM Units From NBS to Meet Reqmts in Forward Areas. EUCOM 322.

[106] (1) *SUSA Rpt of Opns*, III, 884–85. (2) *FUSA Rpts of Opns*, 23 Feb 45 to 8 May 45, an. 10, 56–58, 64–65, 75–77. (3) OQM NUSA AAR's, for periods 1–15 Mar 45, 1–15 Apr 45, 16–30 Apr 45.

The effect of the quartermaster manpower shortage in this period of rapid advance was felt along the whole axis of supply. A survey of eighteen ADSEC and Channel Base Section installations by the G–4 Section revealed that the depots were "getting the supplies out, but many of them are doing it the hard way."[107] Prisoners of war were being used inefficiently, and military personnel were wasting time dressing up installations that were too frequently inspected. Continuity of operations broke down because of the rapid turnover of units, so that the depots were not able to maintain uniform organizations or procedures. At all the installations visited, stocks of clothing and equipment were found in the poorest state of care, and it was predicted that further depletion of manpower would aggravate conditions.[108]

In the combat zone, meanwhile, the frequency of forward displacement demanded rapid opening and closing of railheads and truckheads which, in turn, resulted in the loss of considerable working time and compounded the difficulties arising from the shortage of personnel.[109] In Littlejohn's view, the only discernible relief was either to convert combat divisions to security activities or to employ French, Belgian, and Dutch light infantry battalions as guards for depots and POW laborers. While the First Army temporarily utilized three companies of Belgian fusiliers, such Allied military units never became a significant factor in Quartermaster activ-

ities in the ETO.[110] Littlejohn's suggestion on the use of U.S. combat divisions for security was followed almost immediately when the Fifteenth Army took over occupation duties for Germany west of the Rhine from the 12th Army Group.[111]

The shortage of manpower for quartermaster operations was not only related to the difficulties of supply in a period of rapid movements but was also an outgrowth of the theater prohibition against bringing Italian nationals, French civilians, or German prisoners into the enemy's homeland. This policy decision was finally reversed in April, but meanwhile curtailing the forward displacement of those sources of depot labor made necessary the use of increasingly scarce Quartermaster service troops as guards for the tremendous quantities of captured German equipment, ADSEC supplies, and prisoners of war. In addition to the scarcity of laborers, a shortage of supervisors was threatened by the prospect that the QMC would have to contribute its share of general assignment personnel for infantry retraining.

The formal program of organizing nonmilitary labor companies—Italian service units and German prisoner of war work units—into organizations closely resembling U.S. Army units, but under the training and supervision of American cadres, was initiated by the ETO Military Labor Service (MLS) late in December 1944. The OCQM had been using Italian units in Great Britain since before D-day and began to

---

[107] Summary of Br Chiefs' Mtg, G–4 COMZ, 15 Mar 45. USFET G–4, 337.

[108] Ibid.

[109] SUSA Rpt of Opns, III, 895.

[110] (1) Memo, CQM for G–3, 1 Apr 45, sub: ADSEC Request for Troops for Handling of Captured Enemy Material; Hist of 471st QM Group, 1 Jan–8 May 45, p. 9. Both in Hist Br OQMG. OTCQM TSFET Operational Study 11, p. 5.

[111] Ruppenthal, Logistical Support, II, 378.

make use of German POW labor in August after overcoming the objections of the Provost Marshal and the army commanders. The Quartermaster Service pioneered in the use of POW labor because of the extreme shortage of other sources of labor, and for the same reason attached the POW's to its own regular units, rather than form regular prisoner units with their own cadres. By the end of 1944, informally organized prisoner of war units were cutting wood, handling freight, and working in cemeteries, bakeries, laundries, and salvage depots. On 19 February 1945 COMZ directed that all prisoners be organized into POW labor companies under T/O&E 20–20T, which required a cadre of two officers and seven U.S. enlisted men for each company. Since the Quartermaster requirement was at least 250 companies, this was a severe drain on supervisory personnel, especially in view of the shortages already mentioned. But the purpose of this program was to organize technically proficient units capable of independent operations, a step which would release gasoline supply, depot supply, salvage repair, and other regular Quartermaster units for duty elsewhere. These technical units were highly satisfactory, and by a fortunate coincidence they became available just before V–E Day, so that Quartermaster units could be redeployed to the Pacific. On that day 92,279 POW's, 46 percent of all Quartermaster strength in COMZ, were being employed by the Quartermaster Service, principally in the Normandy and Oise Sections.[112]

Toward the end of April, it became clear that the termination of hostilities was near at hand. For combat troops this promised a respite from the anxieties and dangers of active operations but for Quartermaster troops it offered only a continuation of their strenuous routine. Months before V–E Day, the OCQM had started to plan the posthostilities organization of Quartermaster activities. The future role of the Corps would be twofold: the equipment of ETO personnel and units earmarked for direct or indirect redeployment to the Pacific theater and the support of the armies occupying the U.S. zone in Germany. Some consideration was given to redeployment as early as 15 September 1944, but the final program was outlined in December, and the details of support were worked out in March. They provided that at any given time 250,000 transient troops would be in the camps of the Assembly Area Command around Reims for processing before going on to the staging areas at Marseille or Le Havre, and that the QMC would be responsible for equipping these troops for duty at their next station as well as for rendering the full complement of other quartermaster services.

Besides planning the support of the AAC, the OCQM drafted a tentative program for the interim support of the U.S. forces temporarily deployed over much of central and northwest Germany as well as in the designated American zone of occupation in the south. The forces involved were estimated at 1,000,000 Americans and 500,000 other military personnel. Tentative plans called for forty-five days of supply within Germany, to be located in temporary dumps in the north and perma-

---

[112] (1) *QM Supply in ETO*, VIII, 67–72. (2) Personal Ltr, QM ADSEC to DQM, 9 Mar 45. Littlejohn Collection. (3) Hist of QM Sec Oise Intermediate Sec, 1–28 Feb 45, 1–31 Mar 45. WBS 314.1.

nent depots in the U.S. zone. In addition to retaining the depots at Le Havre and Marseille, largely preoccupied with problems of redeployment, military authorities planned to keep Antwerp and Charleroi as base depots and Verdun as a convenient intermediate location on the main rail line into the U.S. zone. Cherbourg, Liège, Reims, and Nancy-Metz were to be closed down as soon as their stocks were exhausted and Paris was to be reduced to a minor issue depot for the rear headquarters. As soon as possible Bremen, a U.S. enclave in the British zone, was to be developed to the point where it could serve as a base for all American occupation forces. The U.S. zone would be divided into two districts. The Eastern Military District, occupied by Third Army, would include the U.S. zone of Austria for logistical purposes. It was to be supported from depots at Munich, Nuremberg, and Salzburg. The depots initially selected for the Western Military District, supporting troops of Seventh Army, were at Kassel, Stuttgart and Ulm. These locations, at the northern and southern extremes of the area, proved inconvenient even before the final surrender, and were replaced by Giessen and Hanau, north and east of Frankfurt respectively, and by Mannheim, an important barge terminal and site of a major railroad bridge over the Rhine. It was here that CONAD had established its last numbered QM depot, Q–190, in April 1945. Bremen and Berlin, the latter primarily a headquarters location, also officially bore the designation of districts.[113] Unlike Burgundy Dis-

trict and similar COMZ units, these districts were administered by the tactical troops in the area. This arrangement left ADSEC and CONAD without a function, and they were inactivated on 15 July.

During the six months after V–E Day Quartermaster responsibilities were almost as pressing as during the mighty sweep across Europe. Requirements for support of non-U.S. personnel were very great, actually exceeding the enormous estimates which the OCQM had presented in February. (See Table 11.) Redeployment was not only a problem of feeding, housing, and clothing transient troops; Quartermaster units, to a total of more than 46,000 men, were also redeployed, so that the Personnel Division continued its old wartime practices of adjustment and substitution of prisoners and civilians to overcome the labor shortages. Redeployment involved equipment and supplies as well as men, and quartermasters again found themselves engaged in packing and crating, as in Great Britain before D–day, and loading supplies instead of unloading them. Moreover, the staging areas that embarked U.S. troops for the Far East or the zone of interior also had to make preparations to receive 371,000 German prisoners of war traveling in the opposite direction.

But the greatest need for quartermaster services simply arose from the fact that soldiers have to be fed, clothed, and housed whether they are fighting or not. Indeed their scale of demands, if not of actual requirements, increases manyfold after the end of hostilities. The commanders of units engaged in occupation duties rightly insisted that their men look neat and soldierly, and

---

[113] (1) *QM Supply in ETO,* I, 75–79. (2) The final depot plan is summarized in the last column of Table 13.

REDEPLOYMENT STAGING AREA *near Marseille, June 1945. Note extensive use of tents.*

above all avoid a motley appearance. In practice, this meant providing several of the new ETO-type field uniforms for each of 400,000 soldiers in the occupation forces, plus laundry and dry cleaning service on a scale never attempted during combat. Meanwhile directives from the zone of interior emphasized the importance of complete and correct documentation for each man returning home; if his service record was in order, zone of interior depots could and would provide him with a clean new uniform to wear until he was discharged. But shipping was again a problem, and at an average rate of 300,000 men per month the redeployment program took nearly a year to complete. Thus ordinary maintenance requirements continued for a very large force, and in a period of comparative idleness demands for sales store and PX supplies and items to be used at recreation centers reached astronomical proportions.[114]

After V–E Day, organizational changes modifying the command structure and Quartermaster supply responsibilities came thick and fast. The First Army

[114] (1) Bykofsky and Larson, *The Transportation Corps: Operations Overseas*, pp. 352–74. (2) *QM Supply in ETO*, I, 72–83. (3) Robert E. Molyneux, "The QM Troop Problem in Europe from VE to VJ–day," *QMR*, XXVI (January 1947), 27ff.

headquarters was redeployed on 21 May and the Ninth Army followed less than a month later. By 10 July the Fifteenth Army had turned over its occupational duties to British and French zonal agencies. It then became an administrative headquarters charged with conducting the deliberations of the ETO General Board. This body, convened under the presidency of General Gerow, and in October 1945 under General Patton, studied and evaluated the European campaign and prepared over a hundred extremely valuable reports, including several that dealt with Quartermaster activities.

SHAEF and the 6th and 12th Army Groups were inactivated in July, and on the first day of that month U.S. Forces, European Theater (USFET) a new, exclusively American theater headquarters, was activated at Frankfurt under the command of General Eisenhower. At the same time, the American Graves Registration Service was established under the technical control of the Chief Quartermaster. One month later, COMZ became Theater Service Forces, European Theater (TSFET), with headquarters at Versailles. On 1 August the OCQM became the Office of the Theater Chief Quartermaster (OTCQM) and remained with TSFET headquarters. The Office of the Quartermaster, Occupational Forces, became OTCQM (Forward) under General Franks, Deputy Theater Chief Quartermaster. During November the OTCQM moved forward to Frankfurt, but it was temporarily without a head. General Littlejohn had been relieved as theater Chief Quartermaster at his own request. Having accepted an appointment as Commanding General, American Graves Registration Command, he remained behind with that organization at Versailles.[115]

---

[115] (1) GO 279, Hq USFET, 15 Nov 45. (2) Col. Charles C. Odell became theater Chief Quartermaster on 27 November 1945. (3) For subsequent history of the American Graves Registration Command, see Chapter XIX, below.

CHAPTER XIV

Quartermaster Support in the Forward Areas

The sites of the American landing in Normandy have been immortalized under their code names, OMAHA Beach and UTAH Beach. Both sites had the advantages of shelter from westerly storms and a very wide beach at low tide. Deep anchorages were two miles or more offshore, but tides were high enough so that LST's could be beached at high tide and completely dried out— a useful expedient developed during the operation. OMAHA was a five-mile stretch of flat beach, running in an east-west direction near Vierville, St. Laurent, and Colleville-sur-Mer, backed by low sandy hills and flanked by steep rocky cliffs rising from the water's edge. Unfortunately, both the beach and natural exits leading inland from it were commanded from higher ground which had been occupied by a German infantry division during the short interval between the final Allied reconnaissance flights and D-day. OMAHA was therefore the scene of the most dogged enemy resistance and the heaviest casualties.

Some fifteen miles to the west, UTAH Beach stretched in a north-south direction along the southeastern shore of the Cotentin Peninsula. Since it was backed by a lagoon more than a mile wide, with narrow artificial causeways for all exit roads, UTAH did not appear to be a very promising landing site. But the Ger-

man defenders of this beach were too few and scattered for effective mutual support, and were also disorganized by American airborne landings in their rear. Consequently, the initial phases of exploitation proceeded faster at UTAH Beach than at OMAHA.[1]

Maintenance of both beachheads after D-day required that the flow of supplies start as early as possible after the footholds had been assured, a logistical feat to be accomplished in close co-operation with the tactical forces. As already noted, planners had decided that for achieving such co-ordination the supply mission would have to be delegated to the service section of each successive echelon which assumed command of the troops ashore.

The first Quartermaster units in Normandy were organic divisional QM companies and service companies attached to the assault forces. The 29th Quartermaster Company, for instance, arrived off OMAHA Beach on D-day, its men and equipment having left Plymouth and Falmouth in eleven vessels on 1 June. The company's trucks and trailers carried C and K rations, POL, the divi-

---

[1] Harrison, *Cross-Channel Attack*, pages 180–88. and Ruppenthal, *Logistical Support*, Volume I. pages 378–404, describe the terrain and initial supply arrangements within the lodgment areas.

sion's Class II reserve, and miscellaneous supplies. Although the entire company was scheduled to debark with the first and second assault waves, only a reconnaissance detachment of one lieutenant and three enlisted men attached to the 115th Infantry (29th Division) reached shore on D-day. The others landed in the next few days as the opportunity presented itself. By D plus 3 the 29th QM Company was operating from a bivouac area one and a half miles south of Vierville-sur-Mer. Even before the whole company was ashore, one advance detachment came under fire while delivering two truck and trailer loads of gasoline to a tank battalion supporting two of the division's infantry regiments. At noon on D plus 2, the company began to send rations to assault elements, and thereafter it rapidly expanded its activities to include the normal QM functions at division level: operating POL distributing points, distributing rations, clothing, equipage, cleaning materials, and spare parts for stoves and other QM equipment, transporting combat troops, division headquarters sections, and ordnance and signal personnel, shifting division reserve supplies, collecting and evacuating the dead, and gathering and removing salvage. The experience of QM companies assigned to the other assault divisions was generally similar.[2] The veteran 1st

Division quartermaster noted that dispersion, camouflage, and shelter for the troops were more necessary than during the landings in Tunisia and Sicily.[3]

Another type of QM unit participating in the first phase of the assault was a company temporarily attached to one of the assault divisions. Such was the experience of the 3892d Quartermaster Truck Company. Attached to the 1st Infantry Division, this company and its loaded vehicles reached OMAHA Beach early on D plus 1. Only part of the unit could be put ashore because its ferry was grounded and heavily damaged by the enemy. The contingent which had managed to reach shore moved inland and occupied itself in unloading artillery ammunition and delivering gasoline, both of which were badly needed. The remainder of the unit landed, with the loss of several trucks, on D plus 2 only to find that its destination was still in enemy hands. On 9 June the unit was detached from the 1st Division and went to work under the 5th Engineer Spe-

---

[2] For the Normandy assault landings, 6–7 June 1944, the following Quartermaster units received campaign credit with arrowhead (GO 70, 20 Aug 45, as amended):

1st QM Co	97th QM Rhd Co
4th QM Co	Hq and Hq Det, 131st
29th QM Co	QM Bn
90th QM Co	Co A, 203d QM GS Bn
Hq and Hq Det and	Hq and Hq Det and
Med Det, 96th QM	Med Det, 306th QM
Bn	Bn

363d QM Service Co	3168th QM Service Co
503d QM Car Co	3207th QM Service Co
1st and 4th Pltn, 506th	3275th QM Service Co
QM Car Co	3580th QM Truck Co
Hq and Hq Det and	3604th QM Truck Co
Med Det, 533d QM	3712th QM Truck Co
Service Bn	3807th QM Truck Co
556th QM Rhd Co	3820th QM GS Co
559th QM Rhd Co	3891st QM Truck Co
562d QM Rhd Co	3892d QM Truck Co
Hq and Hq Det, 577th	3939th QM GS Co
QM Bn	4042d QM Truck Co
602d QM GR Co	4141st QM Service Co
606th QM GR Co	4142d QM Service Co
2d Pltn, 607th QM GR	4143d QM Service Co
Co	4144th QM Service Co
619th QM Bn	

[3] (1) Memos, QM for CG 29th Div, 21 Jul 44, 3 Aug 44, sub: AAR's for June and July 1944. 329–QM–0.1. (2) See AAR's for June 1944 of the 1st and 4th QM Companies. Hist Br OQMG.

cial Brigade, unloading supplies from grounded barges. The next day part of the company was attached to the 2d Division, whose truck unit had not yet landed. By 15 June the 3892d reassembled under control of V Corps and performed such routine activities as moving 60,000 rations per day from beach dumps to truckheads and shuttling innumerable troops around the beachhead.[4]

As in Mediterranean amphibious assaults, command over supply operations in the initial phase was exercised by Engineer special brigades. By mid-1944 these headquarters had evolved into T/O units of some 5,500 men representing all the technical services, each capable of moving 3,300 ship tons of supplies per day from ships into segregated inland dumps, and supplying the necessary technicians and labor for logistical operations, including evacuation. Three Transportation Corps amphibious truck (Dukw) companies provided most of the cargo capacity; they were administered and maintained by a QM battalion headquarters detachment. A QM service battalion and a QM supply battalion (two railhead companies and a gasoline supply company) were assigned to each brigade. For NEPTUNE, each of the three brigades involved received major reinforcements, including a QM truck company and a graves registration platoon. Moreover the 5th and 6th Brigades, destined for OMAHA Beach, were placed under a provisional brigade group headquarters with still more reinforcements, including the entire 11th Port. By D-

day this group, with all attachments, numbered nearly 30,000 men.[5]

Major portions of these units were included in the assault forces and by the end of D plus 2 ration, POL, ammunition, salvage, and baggage dumps were operating on the beach in each brigade area. This was somewhat behind schedule, owing to enemy artillery fire, vehicle losses, congestion of the beaches by wrecked vehicles and ships, and the need to search the area for mines. Some of the combat units had lost their Class I reserves in the landing, and the ration dumps began issuing immediately. Other supplies were more than adequate.

The next step was development of the so-called beach maintenance areas, where carefully segregated and camouflaged dumps were to be located adjacent to good highways. The sites had been located by photo reconnaissance and were to be fully developed by D plus 3, but actually it was D plus 9 before these inland sites had completely replaced the beach dumps. Meanwhile on 13 June First Army took direct control of all dumps and assumed the command over the Engineer brigades previously exercised by V and VII Corps. The responsibility of the brigades was now limited to unloading ships and passing supplies across the beach to what were now in effect army supply points, although still designated beach maintenance area dumps. These dumps were initially operated by Quartermaster service companies with attached railhead and gasoline supply detachments. As in-

[4] Memo, CO 3892d QM Truck Co for CG V Corps, 4 Aug 44, sub: Unit History, June 1944. V Corps, AG 314.7.

[5] (1) See ch. III, above. (2) *QM Supply in ETO*, VIII, 137–38. (3) *FUSA Rpt of Opns*, 20 Oct 43–1 Aug 44, an. 11. (4) Ruppenthal, *Logistical Support*, I, 331–32, 342–44.

coming tonnage increased, regular railhead and gasoline supply companies operated the larger dumps, with occasional help from service companies. Even the relatively untrained men of the service companies worked well. The only deficiency reported—poor record keeping—was of a nature inevitable in the turmoil of an amphibious operation.[6]

As unloading activities on the beaches hit their stride, masses of supplies began to pour into the dumps. The plan was to center storage, distribution, and services in Cherbourg and a few ot the smaller towns on the Cotentin Peninsula until a large, semipermanent service area could be developed around Rennes and Le Mans. But Cherbourg fell about 10 days later than expected. On 1 July tactical gains were roughly 16 days behind the OVERLORD schedule, and on D plus 49 the southern limit of the beachhead was no farther inland than where the army rear boundary had been expected to be on D plus 20. In short, supplies were concentrated around the beaches in much larger quantities and for a much longer period of time than had been anticipated. Crowding and confusion, and lack of proper inventories and systematic segregation of supplies, previously ignored, began to cause difficulties.[7]

The supply areas behind both UTAH and OMAHA Beaches were of necessity situated in open country, for the small villages in the beachhead offered few

closed storage facilities. Such an area consisted of a number of supply dumps each spread over five to eight typical small Norman fields surrounded by hedgerows, with hastily improvised muddy access roads and poor internal communications. Supplies were moved directly by trucks or Dukws from the beaches to the dumps. In sorting areas, where the vehicles discharged their loads, items were segregated and moved to stacks in the separate storage areas of each service. With organization handicapped by the tactical situation, supply forces had to expand these dumps instead of moving the matériel to depots still farther inland. Allied air superiority made it possible to stack supplies in the middle of the fields, without camouflage. But storage conditions were poor, supplies were roughly handled, there was little dunnage, and few tarpaulin covers.[8] These shortcomings arose from unavoidable haste in the movement of cargo, lack of manpower, and absence of facilities. The means with which to improve the situation—more dunnage and tarpaulins, and more men to stack supplies systematically—became available only gradually.

According to plan, practically all supplies delivered in the first week had been skidloaded. They were transported to the beaches by Dukws, transferred by cranes onto 2½-ton trucks, and carried to sorting areas. Skidloads varied in weight from 1,500 to 3,000 pounds, but their size was carefully limited to permit

[6] (1) 1st Engr Special Brigade AAR, Incl A to an. 4; Opn Rpt NEPTUNE, OMAHA Beach, Prov Engr Special Brigade Group, pp. 221–43. OCMH. (2) Ruppenthal, *Logistical Support*, I, 397, 401.

[7] TWX, CG ADSEC to G–4 ETOUSA, 4 Aug 44, no sub. Littlejohn Collection, sec. II.

[8] (1) Memo, Willkie for Littlejohn, 5 Jul 44, sub: Trip to Far Shore. Littlejohn Reading File, vol. XXVI, item 23. (2) Memo, Chief S&D Div for CQM, 9 Jul 44, sub: Rpt Trip to Continent. Hist Br OQMG.

loading two on a Dukw or truck. If there were no cranes or hoists at the inland dumps, the skids were attached to a sturdy tree and permitted to slide off the back of the truck while the vehicle slowly pulled away. Occasionally the Dukws went all the way to the inland dumps, where they found that no cranes were available. Since the package then had to be opened in the hold of the Dukw itself and the contents removed piecemeal, this use of Dukws failed to expedite deliveries. After the initial flow of skidloads, a larger volume of supplies began to arrive in separate bales, cartons, and crates. Such packages were more difficult to sort than skidloads, so that they were hastily deposited in mixed loads which ultimately had to be segregated and sent to the dumps of the appropriate technical services. This was a time-consuming process, not completed for many months.[9]

With experience, and some easing of pressure due to the development of the Cherbourg area, supply organization and facilities on the beaches improved materially. Segregation and stacking of supplies, as well as stock control, were much better by August than they had been a month earlier.[10] But as beach organization improved, bad weather began to undermine the recent accomplishments. Situated on low land where even the normal water table was high, these beach dumps were often flooded in wet weather. Fortunately, most of the area was pasture land and the turf was strong, but frequently mired trucks had to be unloaded, pulled off the roads by tractors, reloaded, and then helped back onto the road.[11] In late October such unfavorable conditions made it necessary to close the beach supply areas. By this time unloading over the beaches had practically ceased, for better ports and depots closer to the front were then available.

Quartermaster in the Army Group

The 12th Army Group, commanded by General Bradley, was an organization without an exact precedent in American military history. Designed to serve in the field as a senior combat headquarters, it had neither strategic nor logistical responsibilities, but exercised operational control over large-scale military operations involving two or more field armies, in accordance with directives from SHAEF. The 1st Army Group (FUSAG), the predecessor of 12th Army Group, had been given major planning responsibilities in the preinvasion period, being charged with all plans for U.S. ground combat operations in the period from D plus 14 to D plus 41.[12]

[9] (1) Ltr, CO 345th QM Depot Co for QM FUSA, 31 Mar 45, sub: Receiving QM Supplies on the Normandy Beachhead. Hist Br OQMG. (2) "Duck-to-Truck Transfer on the Beach," QMTSJ, VII (13 April 1945), 4–7. (3) Opn Rpt NEPTUNE, OMAHA Beach, Prov Engr Special Brigade Group, pp. 209–19.

[10] (1) IRS, S&D Div to ADSEC QM, 18 Aug 44, sub: Dunnage Situation at OMAHA and UTAH; Memo, Capt Debiase for Chief S&D Div OCQM, 27 Aug 44, sub: Visit to OMAHA Dump. Both in Littlejohn Collection. (2) Memo, Scott to Maj Butler, 19 Aug 44, sub: QM Installations at OMAHA. ADSEC G–2 400.4.

[11] (1) IRS, Field Sv Div to DCQM, 6 Sep 44, sub: Storage Class I on Beach at UTAH; Memo, Chief Veterinary Div OCS [Office of Chief Surgeon] for CQM, 10 Oct 44, no sub. Both in Littlejohn Collection. (2) Ltr, Maj McLean to Doriot, Mil Plng Div OQMG, 30 Oct 44. ETO, 319.25.

[12] (1) OTCQM TSFET Operational Study 10, p. 142. (2) 12th Army Group Rpt of Opns, I, 5.

Planning and implementing the broader aspects of SHAEF plans continued to be major functions after 12th Army Group became operational on 1 August 1944. Thus 12th Army Group decided when additional army headquarters would become operational upon the Continent, determined their missions, and allotted to each the means—supplies and service units as well as combat troops—to achieve its objective. Such functions clearly involved a degree of rivalry with Montgomery's 21 Army Group for cross-Channel cargo and air freight capacity, requiring policy decisions by SHAEF and detailed allocations by BUCO and similar combined agencies.[13]

As the OVERLORD operation progressed, General Devers' 6th Army Group also became a rival for U.S. supplies, combat troops, and service units. In turn, the army groups refereed the rival claims of their component armies. This was a simpler matter for 6th Army Group with two armies to control than for the 12th with its responsibility for three armies and later four. SHAEF assumed responsibility for solving the international complications arising from the fact that 1st French Army was controlled by 6th Army Group, but the latter headquarters had to make special adjustments for differences in organization and in supply requirements. The 12th Army Group had a particularly difficult problem in setting priorities between Hodges' First Army and Patton's Third in August 1944 as they raced across France and both clamored for a larger share of the available gasoline and ammunition. This situation led to the

daily tonnage allocations already described.[14]

From an army group commander's point of view, the correct solution did not require strict equality between armies, but rather that each should be equal to its assigned task. Still, the armies were inclined to argue about their missions as well as the means assigned for fulfilling them, and the decisions recommended to Bradley by his staff were based upon careful computations of capabilities, availabilities, and choices between detailed tactical plans.[15]

As to be expected in a headquarters with such functions and responsibilities, the 12th Army Group quartermaster was almost exclusively a staff adviser to the commanding general on the Quartermaster aspects of large operations. An early decision even deprived the quartermaster of control over army group QM troops, who were placed under the commander of headquarters, special troops. The channel of technical control in the ETO was from the chiefs of technical services within COMZ, via ADSEC, to the armies and their subordinate service units. The requisitioning channel was through the same agencies in the opposite direction, so that the army group was bypassed with regard to both functions. QMC matters coming to army group for decision were primarily determinations of priorities, assignments of QM units, and allocation of controlled items of supply between armies. At army group level these were command decisions, although normally based upon recommendations by the

[13] Pogue, *The Supreme Command*, pp. 253–55, 261–63.

[14] 12th Army Group Rpt of Opns, XII, 194.
[15] (1) 12th Army Group Rpt of Opns, VI, 30, 42, 45. (2) Pogue, *The Supreme Command*, pp. 250–59.

QM Section of the staff. Such recommendations frequently took the form of detailed staff studies.[16] Initially, the 12th Army Group QM Section operated with a personnel allotment of 11 officers and 14 enlisted men. Colonel Younger, former quartermaster of Army Ground Forces and of Second Army, headed an organization that was authorized a brigadier general and 3 colonels.[17] For planning functions in the preinvasion period the section was organized into an Executive Branch, Supply Branch, Troops and Labor Branch, and Field Installations Branch. After planning activities had given way to combat operations, even this modest organization was reduced to Administrative, Supply, and Field Service Branches, and the personnel allotment was pared to 8 officers and 10 enlisted men. In the 6th Army Group there was no Quartermaster Section, and Lt. Col. Richard L. Lewis, the senior QMC officer of the headquarters, maintained a subsection within the office of the G–4 with one officer and two enlisted assistants. In general his functions resembled those of Colonel Younger, but they were even more strictly limited to those of a staff adviser.[18]

The 12th Army Group Quartermaster Section was called upon to make an estimate of service troop requirements for each contemplated tactical operation. This function might at first glance appear superfluous, since theater plans provided for the allocation of definite

numbers of combat troops to the army group, and the correct proportions of service units to be attached to the combat formations could be computed from readily available data. But such allocation scales were based upon averages derived from previous experience, and a specific combat unit is rarely assigned an "average" mission. Moreover, the service units available were almost invariably less than the theoretically desirable number and their theoretical capabilities as listed in staff manuals were also averages that might be radically modified by a wide variety of local conditions. Thus the optimum deployment of Quartermaster troops was an extremely complicated problem, but the army group quartermaster, located within a small compact headquarters where he could watch and even contribute to the formulation of tactical plans, was ideally situated to solve it.

Every change in the tactical dispositions of the armies was reflected in numerous transfers of service units, designed to conserve and utilize them with maximum efficiency. For example, experience at Arnhem (September 1944) and west of Antwerp a month later demonstrated that supplying one or two U.S. combat divisions within the British administrative area involved an extremely uneconomical dispersion of service units. Their presence was essential but their full capabilities were neither required nor utilized. Except for airborne troops, U.S. combat units were not normally committed within the British administrative area thereafter.[19]

Co-ordination of combat operations between 6th and 12th Army Groups

---

[16] 12th Army Group Rpt of Opns, XII, 180, 185.
[17] He was promoted to brigadier general on 13 April 1945.
[18] (1) OTCQM TSFET Operational Study 10, p. 143. (2) Littlejohn seriously questions the necessity of a separate QM staff section at army group level. Interv with Littlejohn, 14 Oct 59.

[19] 12th Army Group Rpt of Opns, VI, 46.

called for major transfers of supporting service units. Such readjustments, which sometimes involved drawing on COMZ and SOLOC service units for duty in the combat zone, were theoretically SHAEF functions, but in practice Littlejohn was given a free hand regarding QM units. A continuing source of difficulty was the consistent SHAEF policy of phasing combat units into the theater ahead of service units, the time lag varying from a week to two months. Shortages of equipment, particularly semimobile trailers for various special purposes, caused still more delays since service units were usually equipped overseas, either in the United Kingdom or at staging areas in Brittany, and could not operate effectively until this process was complete.[20]

In addition to calling for more service units, the armies also tended to demand extra equipment and personnel in excess of authorizations for existing units, especially general purpose vehicles for all types of units, and relief drivers for truck companies. These requests displayed considerable uniformity, and the 12th Army Group quartermaster established a policy of equal authorizations for like units, consistent with the availability of theater reserves. He also recommended theater-wide modifications of T/O&E's, which would give the theater a basis for replenishing its reserves of critical equipment items.[21]

Colonel Younger believed that his function of staff adviser on QM policy required him to maintain a constant and critical scrutiny of Quartermaster operations at all levels. For example,

in October 1944, when the armies were building up supplies for an attack on the Siegfried Line, they still found it hard to obtain the quantities and types of supplies called for by their daily telegrams. This condition was no longer tolerable now that the pursuit was over. Younger sent teams to trace the telegrams through the regulating stations, ADSEC, and the base section shipping points. He found that the cycle from dispatch of the telegram to arrival of supplies varied from ten to fifteen days, and that broken trains, piecemeal deliveries and inadequate documentation made it virtually impossible to reconcile receipts with requisitions. The investigation also revealed that the armies were reacting to unreliable support by accumulating excessive reserves, and that the system whereby the army group allocated tonnage on a daily basis to the armies had outlived its usefulness. Younger recommended that since COMZ controlled transportation it should also allocate tonnages. The recommendation was promptly accepted, but did not measurably improve the situation. Nevertheless, this investigation served a useful purpose by drawing attention to the whole problem of control over tonnage, and possibly speeded up the corrective action already described.[22]

Quartermaster at Army Level

In the ETO the armies represented the highest field supply echelon, and quartermasters at this level were both staff officers and commanders of service troops. They were responsible for main-

[20] *Ibid.*, XII, 215.
[21] *Ibid.*, XII, 180, 185.

[22] (1) *Ibid.*, XII, 200. (2) See ch. XII, above.

taining prescribed army levels of supply, for operating QM depots within army service areas, and for locating, manning, stocking, and operating forward supply points and truckheads. By consolidating and editing requisitions from subordinate units they determined army requirements; and through liaison with corps and division quartermasters they insured the uninterrupted flow of QM supplies and services to the combat elements of the army.

Office of the Army Quartermaster

In late 1944 the Quartermaster Section of an army headquarters was authorized a personnel allotment of 23 officers, 3 warrant officers, and 57 enlisted men, headed by a brigadier general.[23] The organizations of Quartermaster Sections within army headquarters in the ETO were not identical. The desires and working habits of the commanding general and his quartermaster; the mission, composition, and previous experience of the army; and the type and degree of support received from different SOS organizations to the rear—all influenced the type of organization adopted in each case. Nevertheless, the general uniformity of functions to be performed worked against extreme variations. The functions and responsibilities of army quartermasters in the ETO were very similar to those in the Mediterranean theater. The usual organization comprised administrative, transportation, supply, and operations divisions. Most innovations could be ascribed to the fact that COMZ was a co-ordinating

agency supervising supply to several armies and imposed its centralized authority upon their logistical operations. This was in marked contrast to the "favored customer" relationship of a single army to SOS NATOUSA, which was typical of Mediterranean operations. The administrative division normally included a clerical branch, primarily responsible for reports covering activities of more than one division, and a personnel branch, which handled both military and civilian personnel matters. A graves registration branch was sometimes included, but toward the end of hostilities there was a tendency for the army quartermaster to set up a separate graves registration division.[24]

Control over QM operations at army level was exercised along commodity lines. For example, the Class III Branch of the Supply Division supervised the army's QM gasoline supply units and POL depots and dumps. It determined Class III requirements in accordance with supply levels imposed by COMZ, prepared requisitions, and maintained records and inventories. It recommended location of Class III supply points to the Planning and Operations Division, and location of decanting points and bulk storage facilities to the army engineer.

The Supply Division co-ordinated the activities of its branches, monitoring the

---

[23] T/O 200–1, Headquarters, Army, 26 October 1944.

[24] This discussion of the organization and internal functioning of an army quartermaster's office is derived principally from OTCQM TSFET Operational Study 10, pp. 147–54. Additional information came from the McNamara *Memoir*, FUSA and TUSA AAR's (G–4 and QM Sections), and FM 101–10, Organization, Technical, and Logistical Data, August 1949. The last item was already obsolete when issued, but presents a valuable summary of World War II experience.

movement of supplies from COMZ into the army depots, and insuring proper storage and issue to the using troops. It consolidated requisitions and expedited them through the regulating station to the Advance Section, recommended changes in levels and location of supplies as necessary, and advised the army quartermaster on current supply status and supply plans to support future operations. Through its Field Service Branch, it deployed QM service units (Salvage Collection and Repair, Laundry, Bath and Clothing Exchange, and Spare Parts Depots) and insured that they gave effective support to the combat troops. On the basis of ETO experience Littlejohn recommended that the Supply Division include two additional branches, one to handle purchasing and contracting, and the other to handle captured enemy matériel—functions that had previously been concentrated in the army G–4 Section.

The Planning and Operations Division maintained liaison with the G–3 Section and with other headquarters to co-ordinate supply planning with future tactical plans and troop movements. It supervised all army QM units, and prepared movement, attachment, and assignment orders and QM troop lists. It also supervised the training of QM units and operated the army labor pool.

The Transportation Division maintained liaison with rail, highway, and waterways units of the Transportation Corps supporting the army, and advised the army quartermaster on all transportation matters, including air freight. It controlled operations of QM truck units of the army, including planning, assignment, and dispatch. It co-ordinated motor maintenance with the Ordnance

Service, and operated the army motor pool. It arranged for transportation of QM supplies forward from army depots, including co-ordination of rail transport within the combat zone. In the Third Army, transportation was a function of the G–4 rather than the quartermaster. Control of motor transportation was more of a responsibility than an advantage for army quartermasters. During the 4-month period November 1944– February 1945 the Ninth Army quartermaster, Col. William E. Goe, computed that his QM truck units were utilized as follows: Quartermaster, 36 percent; other technical services, 45 percent; personnel transport, 19 percent.[25] These figures may be considered typical for the period covered, which was characterized by heavy fighting and relatively slow advances by all of the American armies. During a pursuit, up to 50 percent of available truck units might be required to transport personnel.

Since the number of truck companies assigned or attached to an army varied from 30 to 45, the above figures imply that, on an average, an army quartermaster had 11 to 16 companies available to haul QM supplies.[26] This was fairly

---

[25] OTCQM TSFET Operational Study 10, p. 149. Complete tabulations of this nature, broken down by services for an entire army, are almost nonexistent. Typical incomplete tabulations, which can only be supplemented by rough estimates, are given in *FUSA Rpt of Opns*, 1 Aug 44–22 Feb 45, IV, 89 (app. 10), and in TUSA AAR II, G–4, 15, 30.

[26] USFET Gen Bd Study 109, p. 34. The theoretical basis of assignment of truck companies to tactical units (never achieved) is given below. Truck companies assigned to corps and extra trucks for armored divisions were attached to corps headquarters. All others were grouped in an army motor pool: per army headquarters, 1 company; per corps headquarters, 2 companies; per division (all types), 3 companies; and per armored division (new type), 1 additional company.

satisfactory under normal conditions, and was definitely preferable to the arrangement in Third Army, where the quartermaster was assigned from 4 to 8 truck companies by G–4, and continually had to borrow additional transportation from the other technical services. In theory, the Transportation Division of G–4 co-ordinated such interservice loans of transportation. In practice, most Third Army truck companies were parceled out to the various technical services and tended to become part of those organizations. Experience showed that it was quicker and more convenient to deal directly with the chiefs of technical services regarding loans of their attached transportation. Since the chiefs were troop commanders as well as staff officers, such dealings could be regarded as being in a command channel. In all the armies, the technical services co-operated readily and promptly, tending to bypass formal staff channels. Nevertheless, command over one's own organic units is more reliable and efficient than the most cordial co-operation.

Reviewing and evaluating his experiences after V–E Day, Colonel Busch, the Third Army quartermaster, recommended that the organization of railhead companies, gasoline supply companies, and depot supply companies, be modified to include a truck "platoon" of 48 trucks—the actual strength of a truck company. This recommendation did not imply any dissatisfaction with the performance of such units, but was designed to insure the army quartermaster's control over organic Quartermaster transportation which could not readily be commandeered for other purposes. Assuming a normal army troop basis, this innovation would have given the

army quartermaster exclusive control over the equivalent of 15 truck companies. The other ETO army quartermasters, who had all benefited by access to an army truck pool, did not favor such a reorganization. They agreed that an increase in the allocation of army transportation, equal to 1 more truck company per assigned armored division, would be desirable. But the salient fact of ETO experience was that the theoretical allocation of truck companies to combat units was never achieved. Even at the end of hostilities, the combat zone was understrength by 19 truck companies.[27]

The shortage of truck companies in the summer of 1944 was further aggravated by insufficient freight handlers. The commanding officer of the 514th QM Group, which administered all Third Army truck companies, called attention to the need for more service company personnel to speed loading and unloading at depots and supply points. This problem persisted even after the supply lines had been shortened, for once the German border had been crossed unit provost marshals at all levels refused to permit the use of local (German) civilians or prisoners as laborers, as had been done in France. Another example of a remedy creating its own problems was presented when the improved rail system brought supplies to the army area, but not directly to the army dumps. Months went by before the engineers could install spur lines to suitable warehouses or hardstands. Meanwhile depots were forced

---

[27] (1) OTCQM TSFET Operational Study 10, pp. 162 a–b. (2) USFET Gen Bd Study 109, p. 34. (3) QM Supply in ETO, VIII, 88.

to handle each shipment twice and naturally demanded more service company personnel.[28]

Army Depots and Combat Zone Distribution

Before the Normandy landings, supply planners had assumed that the average depth of an army area would be about fifty miles, and that it would be uneconomical, and might even be impossible, with the army's facilities alone, to provide support for operations at a depth greater than seventy-five miles.[29] These assumptions were based on current doctrine and reinforced by recent Mediterranean experience. The only major attempt to exceed these limits— the hasty overland advance to capture Tunis in November 1942—had led to failure, and Eisenhower himself commented at the time that such operations were in conflict with accepted methods.[30] There was further support for such assumptions in the OVERLORD Operation Forecast, which predicted heavy fighting, large supply expenditures, a slow rate of advance, and, therefore by inference, a shallow army zone.

All these conditions actually materialized during the first seven weeks of fighting in Normandy, but the situation was not completely conventional, since First Army retained control over the entire supply organization in the lodg-

ment area. On 1 August, 12th Army Group and Third Army became operational on the Continent, and the next day First Army formally established its rear boundary along the Isigny-Carentan highway, and handed over control of the Cotentin Peninsula and the OMAHA area to ADSEC.[31]

With some justification, planners assumed that First Army's logistic operations would hereafter follow the textbook rules, but such was not the case. In general, the experiences of First Army described here apply equally to Third Army.[32] Only eight days had elapsed since the COBRA operation had been launched to force a breakout from the beachhead, but already the campaign had assumed some of the characteristics of a pursuit. Following normal procedure, the order establishing the First Army rear boundary had also designated St. Lô, 16 miles to the south, as the next army service area. Four days later tactical gains had outdistanced this

---

[28] (1) Ltr, CO 514th QM Group to OCQM, 27 Sep 44, sub: Battle Experience of Truck Units. In Hist of 514th QM Group. (2) Ltr, G–1 FUSA to CG 12th Army Group, sub: Additional QM Sv Cos. EUCOM, 322 QM vol. IV. (3) Hist of 471st QM Group, p. 13.

[29] USFET Gen Bd Rpt 27, p. 27.

[30] See ch. III, above.

[31] (1) FUSA Rpt of Opns, 1 Aug 44–22 Feb 45, II, 99–109. (2) 12th Army Group Rpt of Opns, VI, 34–39; XII, 191–98.

[32] The choice of First Army rather than Third Army to illustrate the logistical problems of pursuit was based on the following considerations: (1) *brevity and clarity*—it is believed that a comparable analysis of Third Army's operations would have required an excessive amount of explanation of changing objectives, shifting troop bases, and curving lines of advance that defy accurate computation of road distances; (2) *completeness*—in First Army, truck operations were a QM responsibility and were reported from the QM point of view; in Third Army, truck operations were a G–4 responsibility and were somewhat less completely reported. In all other respects the QM portion of the TUSA AAR, a complete and very valuable document, confirms the experience of First Army. Littlejohn's comment was: "The real reason is McNamara." He felt that FUSA QM operations were especially worthy of careful study. Interv with Littlejohn, 1 Dec 60.

location, and by 12 August QM depots were operational within an army service area at Vire, 42 miles south of Isigny. Three days later the army rear boundary was relocated just north of Vire, and Alençon, 65 miles away, was tentatively selected as the next depot site. But by the 19th Alençon was too far to the rear; that day COMZ and First Army agreed that the new depot was to be at La Loupe, 110 miles from Vire. First Army also stated that it required 62,000 tons of supplies at La Loupe by 29 August, but COMZ indicated that the maximum it could provide was 26,000 tons. Even that figure was only possible with the aid of the Red Ball express, which began to operate on 25 August. Nevertheless QM Class I and III depots were operating at La Loupe by 23 August, having been stocked largely by First Army's own efforts.[33]

On 25 August ADSEC took over QM operations at Vire, and the next day First Army canceled its request for a supply reserve at La Loupe, which was already too far to the rear. Tactical developments during these days were significant, since they represented the first major modification of OVERLORD plans. Both First and Third Armies crossed the Seine on 24 August. They used military bridging, since the Seine bridges had been Allied bombing targets before D-day. On the 25th, the liberation of Paris brought two permanent bridges under American control, but simultaneously increased COMZ requirements of civil affairs supplies by some

2,400 tons per day.[34] The necessity of feeding Paris materially reduced COMZ support for the combat troops. Only 7,000 tons per day could be made available to them, and General Bradley decided that for the time being First Army would receive 5,000 tons, leaving only 2,000 tons per day for Third Army. This momentous decision went into effect on 29 August and within four days had brought Third Army's advance to an abrupt halt.[35]

By the 29th, La Loupe was 200 miles from the front lines and another depot was clearly needed.[36] First Army proposed a site at Senlis, 30 miles beyond the Seine, but at the time this was impossible. The Red Ball was operating no farther east than Chartres. COMZ was pushing forward one rail line behind each army, but the one behind First Army had only reached Arpajon, 62 miles east of La Loupe. The same day the army rear boundary was shifted to a point just west of La Loupe, but no new forward depot was designated. The army would use Arpajon as a temporary dump, and shift its transfer point forward progressively as railroad repairs permitted. Since all supplies were transferred to trucks and sent to the combat troops as soon as they arrived, none of the usual storage problems of an army depot would arise. On this basis, Arpajon was opened on 2 September, and so urgent was the need for POL that issues began the same day. Although the supply situation was becoming critical,

[31] For example, by 29 August POL deliveries totalled 17,259 tons, of which ADSEC had transported only 2,116 tons; but COMZ had loaned to First Army four tank truck companies which would normally have been assigned to ADSEC.

[34] Ruppenthal, *Logistical Support*, I, 577.
[35] The reasons for this decision are given in detail in H. M. Cole, *The Lorraine Campaign*, UNITED STATES ARMY IN WORLD WAR II (Washington, 1950), pp. 20–21.
[36] Rpt cited n. 31 (1).

First Army troops were still pushing forward at great speed. A notable example was the 30th Division, which reached Tournai, Belgium, on 3 September, having advanced 118 miles in 30 hours. Nevertheless, the army zone had very nearly reached the maximum depth. The fact that every army convoy had to cross the Seine was a major handicap to effective operations. On 2 September distances (in miles) from the ADSEC transfer points to the forward Class I and III truckheads, and to the front lines, were as follows: [37]

	La Loupe	Arpajon	Front lines
Truckhead 51, Soissons ..	139	91	50
Truckhead 74, Vervins ..	186	137	15
Truckhead 91, Cambrai .	178	122	35

During the next week, COMZ managed to bring the supply lines forward across the Seine.[38] It proved possible to extend the rail lines faster than the Red Ball express. As planned, trains were unloaded at the end of the railroad, and the temporary dumps were shifted forward as the tracks were repaired. Individual supply trains sometimes conducted their own track reconnaissance, and the situation was so fluid that Colonel McNamara used light aircraft to locate forward-moving trainloads of gasoline. By 5 September the railhead was at Soissons, and the Red Ball reached that town three days later. On 9 September the railhead was shifted forward to Coucy—only twelve miles, but every mile counted for First Army's overworked trucks.

Meanwhile the need for a forward army service area had manifested itself. For the time being it would serve mainly as a traffic control and reconsignment point through which army trucks passed on their way to the forward truckheads. Accordingly, on 6 September First Army established a service area around Hirson–La Capelle, nearly 200 miles northeast of La Loupe. The site was carefully chosen, with excellent rail and highway facilities, but supplies actually accumulated there were negligible. Nevertheless, on 8 September the army rear boundary was moved forward to the Laon-Péronne highway, creating an unusual situation in that for a few days every army convoy to the forward truckheads originated behind the army rear boundary. By 12 September First Army troops, having crossed Belgium and Luxembourg, were partly in Holland and partly on German soil, approaching the Siegfried Line. The supply system had been stretched to the limit, and the pursuit had halted. The distances involved in supplying First Army that day were as follows: [39]

	La Loupe	Soissons	Front lines
Truckhead 53, Signy L'Abbaye	216	77	100
Truckhead 76, Charleroi .	254	115	80
Truckhead 92, Genappe .	276	137	70

Various economies and expedients were employed to provide support in an army zone more than twice as deep as the theoretical maximum. During the pursuit weak enemy resistance and Allied air superiority made it possible to

[37] (1) Robert W. Hewitt, *Workhorse of the Western Front* (Washington, 1946), p. 90. (2) *FUSA Rpt of Opns*, 1 Aug 44–22 Feb 45, II, 108.
[38] (1) Hewitt, *Workhorse of the Western Front*, p. 90. (2) McNamara *Memoir*, p. 142.

[39] (1) Charles B. MacDonald, *The Siegfried Line Campaign*, UNITED STATES ARMY IN WORLD WAR II (Washington, 1963). (2) *FUSA Rpt of Opns*, 1 Aug 44–22 Feb 45, II, 108.

FIRST ARMY RATION DUMP *at Soissons, September 1944.*

leave behind chemical warfare, heavy artillery, and antiaircraft units, and such units contributed more than 1,000 vehicles to the army motor pool for hauling supplies. Moreover, with these units in reserve the supply requirements of the whole army were considerably reduced. The tactical situation permitted a very material reduction in ammunition supplies, and at the height of the emergency requisitions for clothing and signal and medical equipment were arbitrarily canceled. Toward the end of the period deliveries of Class I supplies proved to be insufficient and were supplemented by captured rations. But the need for more and more gasoline to transport combat troops in army vehicles and to operate supply convoys over longer and longer distances nullified most of these savings in other classes of supply. For

the period 6–12 September First Army's gasoline consumption was 571,000 gallons per day, and during this time the forward truckheads were frequently exhausted several hours before a resupply arrived. Vehicles from the combat units frequently traveled far to the rear in search of a load of gasoline.

The excessive hauling distances demanded of army transportation were not the only factors leading to the immobilization of First Army. COMZ was not only unable to move its supply depots forward fast enough; it was also unable to provide sufficient tonnage of supplies to keep two armies moving. The ceiling of 7,000 tons per day to the two armies could not be lifted for several weeks. On 6 September the allocation from COMZ was changed so that First and Third Armies were each to receive 3,500 tons per day. Actual daily receipts by First Army were somewhat less, and included items which had not been requisitioned:

Class of supply	Estimated Requirements (31 August 1944)	COMZ Allocations (6–12 September 1944)	Average Receipts (6–12 September 1944)
Quartermaster:			
Class I	1,150	993	553
Class II and IV	75	0	48
Class III	2,200	2,028	1,954
Ordnance:			
Class II and IV	150	0	49
Class V	1,100	64	413
Signal Corps: Class II and IV	300	129	24
Engineer: Class II and IV	525	286	168
Chemical Warfare: Class II and IV	10	0	0
Medical: Class II and IV	30	0	0
G–5: all classes..	212	0	0
Total (long tons)	5,752	3,500	3,209

The exactness of these receipts as reported is open to doubt, since the situation was extremely confused and not all trips to the rear by army vehicles were reported. Littlejohn later pointed out that this confusion was evidence of faulty advance planning and poor management on the part of COMZ. With more careful selection of supplies to be forwarded, total requirements might have been reduced. But there is no room for doubt that the supplies actually furnished were inadequate for an army in the pursuit. Moreover, the bottleneck was in rail and truck transportation in the Communications Zone; supplies were accumulating at the ports. The real explanation of this inadequacy can be traced to erroneous estimates of transportation requirements, based upon the inaccurate operation forecast used in OVERLORD planning.[40]

Logistically, 12 September may be considered the critical date in First Army operations. Five days later the railhead was brought forward 120 miles in one gigantic stride to Huy, Belgium. At this location it was less than 40 miles from the front lines, permitting a return to textbook methods of army distribution. Moreover, supply deliveries from the rear improved rapidly once the pursuit was over. First Army's tonnage allocation was raised to 5,000 tons per day on 23 September, and 6,585 tons on 15 October. Meanwhile the combat troops had made only small advances against stiffening German resistance, but the service units had acquired the habit of pushing the depot system forward as fast and as far as physically possible. Reconnaissance of the Eupen-Herbesthal area, 50 miles farther east, began even before the first supplies were distributed from Huy on 19 September. The 471st QM Group, which administered First Army depot operations, moved its headquarters to the new location on the 21st, but it was another week before rail repairs had progressed beyond Liège.

On 2 October, officers of the 471st Group conferred at Herbesthal with representatives of the 25th Regulating Station, the army G–4, the ADSEC engineer, and other technical services regarding plans to receive by rail and store all classes of supply in the new area. Colonel McNamara decided that no Class III dump would be set up there for the time being, since the contemplated POL site was less than 10 miles from the front

---
[40] (1) Ruppenthal, *Logistical Support*, I, pp. 491–94. (2) *FUSA Rpt of Opns*, 1 Aug 44–22 Feb 45, II, 107. (3) Interv with Littlejohn, 16 Nov 59.

lines. The depot complex planned at this conference proved far more permanent than anticipated. Except for a brief interruption during the Battle of the Bulge, it served First Army for nearly six months.[41]

QM Group in the Combat Zone

In general, the army quartermasters used QM group headquarters as command agencies to supervise their supply installations and units. The functions of the group headquarters were primarily administrative, but might also include varying degrees of responsibility for supply operations. Three or four groups were normally assigned to an army, and their employment might be based on either a functional or a geographical concept. In the latter case, one group would remain in the rear at the army depot, and each of the others would control QM troops in the area immediately behind a corps, being concerned primarily with forward truckheads. The functional concept, which the ETO quartermaster considered somewhat more efficient, is illustrated by First Army practice of assigning one group to administer transportation of troop units, another for general hauling for all the technical services, and a third to operate the army depot.[42]

Thus on either basis one group headquarters, the most important one from the QMC point of view, was responsible for the main QM depot of each army, and all the units which operated it. The 561st QM Group, which performed this function for Seventh Army, was at one time in command of 10 QM battalions and 68 companies, a force of nearly 11,000 men. But the responsibilities of this headquarters were purely administrative, concerned as they were with unit inspections, personnel discipline and welfare, courier service for subordinate units, and the timely submission and forwarding of routine reports. The group had been formed with personnel from a surplus antiaircraft artillery headquarters late in 1944, and its commander, Col. William F. Watson, reported that as a QM unit its functions had not been basically changed.

The 471st QM Group, which actually operated the First Army QM depot, had very different responsibilities. Under only general supervision from the army quartermaster this unit, which was commanded by Col. Hugh Mackintosh, received, stored, and forwarded all classes of QM supply to First Army truckheads, operated a salvage depot, and provided retail supplies and services to army troops in its locality. But in extreme emergencies Colonel McNamara repeatedly assumed direct control over such vital functions as Class III supply, leaving the group with merely housekeeping duties for gasoline supply and tank truck units.[43] At all times, the army quartermaster maintained close supervision over

[41] (1) *FUSA Rpt of Opns*, 1 Aug 44–22 Feb 45, II, 110–16; IV, 55–62. (2) Hist of 471st QM Group, pp. 20–21. Hist Br OQMG.

[42] *FUSA Rpt of Opns*, 1 Aug 44–22 Feb 45, IV, 79, 91.

[43] (1) Unit History files, Hist Br OQMG. (2) Other depot groups in the ETO were: 519th QM Group, Col. Harold B. Crawell commanding, supporting Third Army; 544th QM Group, Col. Alan L. Fulton commanding, supporting Ninth Army. (3) The relation between McNamara and Mackintosh was a very personal one; the latter was one of the key officers hand-picked to suit his superior. McNamara used Mackintosh's staff as part of his own when required, and methods of co-ordination were always extremely informal. Interv, Franz A. Koehler, Historian, Mil Subs Supply Agency (Chicago) with General Mackintosh, April 1959.

levels of supply in the depot, and since distances were great and telephone service usually unsatisfactory, he provided a radio car to insure that supply status reports reached the army command post several times daily. This practice proved very satisfactory during the pursuit across France, and was used again during the mop-up of central Germany.[44]

The composition of the 471st QM Group as it existed in September 1944 reflects the unit's multiple and varied mission: [45]

471st QM Battalion (M), Hq/Hq Detachment
    3701st QM Truck Co
    3702d QM Truck Co
    3703d QM Truck Co
    3704th QM Truck Co

81st QM Battalion (M), Hq/Hq Detachment
    3705th QM Truck Co
    3706th QM Truck Co
    3707th QM Truck Co
    3708th QM Truck Co

158th QM Battalion (M), Hq/Hq Detachment
    345th QM Depot Supply Co
    348th QM Depot Supply Co
    279th QM Refrigeration Co (M)
    581st QM Sales Co
    200th Gasoline Supply Co
    3814th Gasoline Supply Co
    3192d QM Service Co (Class III)

380th QM Battalion (M)
    134th QM Tank Truck Co (2000 gal.)
    3549th QM Tank Truck Co (750 gal.)
    3584th QM Tank Truck Co (2000 gal.)
    3981st QM Tank Truck Co (750 gal.)

202d QM Battalion (M), Hq/Hq Detachment
    216th QM Salvage Repair Co
    224th QM Salvage Repair Co
    294th QM Salvage Repair Co

    233d QM Salvage Collection Co
    235th QM Salvage Collection Co
    999th QM Salvage Collection Co
    579th QM Laundry Co

532d QM Battalion, Hq/Hq Detachment
    3168th QM Service Co
    3169th QM Service Co
    3170th QM Service Co
    3216th QM Service Co
    3217th QM Service Co
    3218th QM Service Co
    3230th QM Service Co
    3233d QM Service Co

Although some of the constituent battalions of the group were homogeneous and some were not, each represented a logical grouping of functions. Since the group served but did not control the forward truckheads, certain important types of QM units were not included in its organization. The two truck battalions, allocated to move forward all classes of QM supply, were barely able to handle Class I under conditions of pursuit. They represented about 20 percent of the army's normal transport capacity. The tank truck units, on loan from COMZ, were withdrawn after rail tank cars began to reach the army's railheads late in September. The service battalion was simply a labor pool for all QM activities and sometimes for other technical services as well.

Class I operations at a First Army depot were normaly performed by a depot supply company and several service companies. Two depot supply companies had originally been provided to handle Class I and II supplies separately, but they usually worked together so that one depot could receive, sort, and store supplies of all classes while another continued to issue to troops. At the height of the pursuit these units demonstrated that they could operate as many as four

---

[44] Hist of 471st QM Group, p. 19.
[45] (1) Hist of 471st QM Group, p. 12. (2) FUSA Rpt of Opns, 1 Aug 44–22 Feb 45, IV, 79.

sites at once. During the first week in September, issues were made from La Loupe, Arpajon, Soissons, and Coucy, while supplies were accumulated at La Capelle. But such operations were exceptional and inefficient, and were discontinued as quickly as possible.

Another difficulty of the pursuit was the excessive demand for operational rations, which were desired by all troops on the move. These demands, especially for the 10-in-1, exceeded the supply, and an attempt was made to provide B rations irrespective of what the troop units requested. The effort was not very successful since deliveries against the daily telegram lagged as much as seventeen days and aggravated the inherent difficulties of balancing the B ration. From 30 August to 9 September, no B rations whatever were consumed and during the next two days unbalanced B issues were supplemented by various captured food items. As in the Mediterranean, the troops consumed more C rations when 10-in-1's were not obtainable.[46]

Operations at Huy, and especially at Herbesthal, brought new problems for Class I. As at previous locations open storage was the rule, but autumn rains demanded increased emphasis on hardstanding, dunnage, and ballast for roads. Moreover, the units were unfamiliar with large-scale rail deliveries, which required local truck transportation from the unloading points to the depots, and double handling of every package. For all their inadequacies, motor transport deliveries from the rear had been made directly into the depots, and the individual convoys had been of modest proportions when compared to the 500-ton capacity of a single train. Rail service was very irregular at first, so that large numbers of freight handlers and trucks had to be instantly available at unpredictable hours, and sometimes at an unpredictable location within the service area. These conditions, which prevented advance planning and greatly reduced efficiency, led to considerable criticism of the regulating station. Since no attempt was made to provide fixed refrigeration, most of these difficulties did not apply to perishables. The trailers of the QM refrigeration company operated direct from the reefer cars to the truckheads. On the few occasions when more perishables arrived than these trailers could handle, they were loaded on ordinary trucks and speeded to the consuming units. Losses of meat and butter by this practice were negligible, since such surplus perishables only began to arrive in December when cold weather had set in.[47] PX supplies were on a gratuitous basis in First Army, and were distributed with other rations if available. Issues averaged one-third of a PX ration per man per day until 12 September, and two-thirds of a ration thereafter until the German counterattack in December.[48]

Class III supply in First Army comprised several distinct types of operations. Until mid-September 1944, tank trucks on loan from COMZ moved bulk gasoline direct from the end of the pipeline to decanting points at the forward truckheads, bypassing the army depot. Until distances became excessive this operation worked effectively, despite the fact

---

[46] (1) FUSA Rpt of Opns, 1 Aug 44–22 Feb 45, IV, 47, 81. (2) Hist of 471st QM Group, p. 13.

[47] (1) Hist of 471st QM Group, pp. 13, 22. (2) Hist of 514th QM Group, p. 8.

[48] FUSA Rpt of Opns, 1 Aug 44–22 Feb 45, IV, 48, 57.

that the larger tankers were of commercial design and not suitable for cross-country movement. Since truckheads were always located off the roads for security reasons, the trailers developed minor mechanical failures because they were unable to endure any lateral pivoting motion on the trailer hitch. Therefore during August all the 2,000-gallon tankers were deadlined in relays for modification by Ordnance. Thereafter, the trailers gave no more trouble, but as distances to the truckheads lengthened and POL requirements increased, each truck tractor was required to haul an extra 2,000-gallon trailer, which materially shortened the tractor's mechanical life. The turnaround time lengthened to 36, and finally to 48 hours, and all operations, including decanting, went on a 24-hour-a-day basis. Previously, decanting at night had been avoided because of excessive fire hazards, a lesson from Mediterranean experience which had to be ignored during the emergency.[49] These measures were necessary since the pipelines moved forward much more slowly than other means of transportation.[50]

Early in September an intermediate decanting point for the tanker trucks was set up by the 3814th Gasoline Supply Company. Located first at La Loupe, and after 12 September at La Capelle, this terminal provided a shorter and more efficient turnaround cycle for the tankers. Moreover, the 2½-ton military trucks which carried the packaged gasoline forward from this point had a 100-percent

overload capacity. Thus each truck could haul 5 tons of POL to the forward truckheads, greatly speeding up deliveries. The disadvantages of this procedure were the additional labor required for extra handling of the POL and the longer turnaround cycle for 5-gallon cans, which were in critically short supply at the end of the pursuit period.[51]

Another expedient of this period was bulk gasoline supply by air. In late August air freight priorities were assigned to G-5 for relief of Paris, and in early September to Third Army to supplement the very meager allotment of other transportation. First Army began to receive packaged POL at an airstrip near St. Quentin on 14 September, and tanker planes (actually converted bombers) began to land there a few days later, after the runway had been lengthened. Between 20 and 30 September 1,171,825 gallons were delivered by air to St. Quentin and to Florennes, Belgium. A 750-gallon tank truck company was stationed at each airstrip, and carried the gasoline to the nearest decanting point.[52]

Until the end of September, packaged POL dumps in the successive army service areas were all operated by the 200th Gasoline Supply Company. This unit received packaged gasoline by rail as well as by truck, and also handled diesel oil, lubricants, greases, and occasionally small amounts of captured coal. It was subordinate to the same QM battalion, the 158th, which controlled other classes of QM supply in the army depot, and moved with the depot from Vire to La Capelle, and later to Pepinster near

[49] Hist of 471st QM Group, pp. 13-17.

[50] Ruppenthal, *Logistical Support*, I, 510-13, summarizes progress in laying pipelines and reasons for the delay.

[51] Hist of 471st QM Group, p. 16.

[52] (1) *FUSA Rpt of Opns*, 1 Aug 44-22 Feb 45. IV, 60. (2) Hist of 471st QM Group, p. 15.

Liège. Early in October the tank truck companies were turned back to COMZ. The decanting operation at La Capelle was discontinued, and the 3814th Gasoline Supply Company moved to Eupen.

The 308th QM Battalion, which had controlled the tank truck units, was now placed in charge of all Class III operations within the 471st QM Group. By this time tank rail cars were coming into the Liège area, and the army Class III supply level rose rapidly between 1 and 10 October from 0.8 to 4.5 days. An additional gasoline supply company was acquired to decant from the rail cars. Still another decanting point for rail tankers, first at Bastogne and later at Micheroux, was operated by a fourth company beginning in November. Meanwhile demands fell off at the truckheads and additional dumps were set up at Spa and Francorchamps. Thus by mid-November the 308th QM Battalion, controlling four gasoline supply companies and three service companies, was operating two decanting points and four major Class III dumps, in addition to various bulk storage sites and a separate railhead at Theux for receipt and loading of empty cans. Limited facilities and tactical dispersion to avoid flying bombs dictated this scattering of Class III operations over eastern Belgium, but it hindered efficient operations. The 926th Petroleum Products Laboratory, which analyzed all captured gasoline to determine its suitability for U.S. equipment and also attempted to maintain continuous tests of the quality of products received from the rear, could only run periodic spot checks at the various decanting points. Several battalions of Belgian fusiliers were used as security guards and there were no instances of sabotage.

Probably the greatest burden of this dispersion fell on the Engineers, who had to provide fire fighting units at each Class III installation.[53]

Class II and IV items were the stepchildren in the chain of supply during the early months of continental operations, and though space was set aside at the successive army depots it was scarcely used. The First Army's daily maintenance requirement of 75 tons was never met, and in the 6-week period after 16 August, when First Army brought its Class II and IV depot forward from St. Lô, only 1,723 tons were received, a daily average of less than 40 tons.[54] The low priority which COMZ gave to clothing and equipage merely reflected the preferences of the armies and their component units during the advance. Even after Class II and IV installations were opened in the army service areas, they generally received the lowest priority for truck transport or were compelled to use the slower rail facilities. By the time a Class II installation was fully established in the new area, the troops had advanced again beyond ready reach.[55]

Mediterranean experience had demonstrated that distribution of Class II and IV supplies was a complicated process, requiring exact inventory procedures, careful sorting for sizes, and good judgment regarding acceptable substitutes. Since all such supplies were scarce it was definitely undesirable to disperse

---

[53] (1) Hist of 471st QM Group, pp. 5, 10–14, 23–24. (2) FUSA Rpt of Opns, 1 Aug 44–22 Feb 45, IV, 60–64, 72–73.
[54] (1) Hist of 471st QM Group, pp. 16–17. (2) FUSA Rpt of Opns, 1 Aug 44–22 Feb 45, II, 101, 107; IV, 48–49.
[55] (1) USFET Gen Bd Study 109, p. 109. (2) 12th Army Group Rpt of Opns, XII, 199.

more than an essential minimum as a reserve in forward truckheads. Accordingly, the Class II and IV section of the army QM depot normally issued direct to using units, which usually sent back trucks periodically to the depot to claim their allotments. A notable exception to this rule was the QM sales platoon, which sold clothing to officers and kept its two mobile sections on the road to forward units most of the time.

The 345th QM Depot Supply Company, which operated the Class II and IV depot for First Army, found that the units took advantage of available supplies only when the depot was reasonably near their locations. Such a situation was experienced at St. Lô in late July, but was not repeated until the depot was brought forward to Huy in mid-September. During the next two weeks more than 1,400 tons of Class II and IV supplies were issued, replacing some of the items worn out or lost during the pursuit. But cold weather was approaching and a major re-equipment with winter clothing, completely distinct from maintenance, was needed almost immediately. Trainloads of such items began to arrive at Herbesthal, the new depot site, on 5 October, and were supplemented by heavy air freight shipments. Nearly 5,000 long tons were received by 15 October, and thereafter about 1,100 tons per week until the end of the year. Arctic overshoes and sleeping bags remained on the controlled supplies list, and there were a few shortages of specific sizes of winter items, but the end of 1944 generally found First Army well clothed and equipped.[56]

The army's salvage organization, comprising three collecting and three repair companies, was concentrated in the rear depot group under the 202d QM Battalion. Salvage from the combat units was customarily collected at the Class I truckhead and hauled to the rear by returning ration trucks. The salvage collecting companies combed the rear areas for items abandoned during the pursuit, especially jerricans and enemy equipment. The repair companies had originally been organized with two identical platoons to repair only textiles, mess gear, and shoes. During August 1944 they were reorganized with an additional platoon to repair every kind of QM equipment, and received stocks of spare parts for this additional mission. Although the repair companies were normally static, their equipment maintenance platoons were mobile, and toured all forward areas periodically to make necessary repairs.

Numerically, field ranges, gasoline lanterns, and typewriters were the articles most frequently repaired. Probably of equal value in keeping QMC operations rolling were specialized repairs on QM laundry and bath equipment, bakeries, refrigerators, and gasoline dispensers. Shoe repair trailers also visited the forward areas, and in some cases were attached to individual corps for short periods. The general repair platoons operated flexibly, concentrating on tents, shoes, clothing, raincoats, or blankets to alleviate the shortages of the moment at the Class II and IV depot. Low-priority items or those in excess of their repair capabilities were sent to COMZ salvage depots. Frequently, abandoned or salvaged articles were merely dirty and could be returned to

———
[56] (1) Hist of 471st QM Group, pp. 6, 17. (2) Hist of 345th QM Depot Supply Co. Hist Br OQMG.

stock after sterilizing or washing. A laundry company was assigned to the 202d QM battalion from the start of the campaign, and later the fumigation sections of several fumigation and bath companies, which were not needed in the forward areas, were also attached.[57]

As evident from the above, the 471st QM Group gave a very material amount of support to the First Army quartermaster. Colonel Mackintosh, the group commander, reported with considerable pride that his organization, despite its modest size, had performed most of the duties that might be assigned to a QM base depot in the Communications Zone. This was possible because the commanders of the various specialized battalions also served as special staff officers on the group staff. For example, the commander of the 202d Battalion just mentioned was also the salvage officer of the 471st QM Group, and the commanding officer of the 308th Battalion was Class III officer. Mackintosh believed that efficient group operations were fostered by keeping transfers of subordinate headquarters and units to a minimum. Because this policy was observed, well-trained officers were always available to be loaned to newly joined units, which might have extensive experience but were inevitably ignorant of the specialized procedures of the group. Stability also contributed to group morale and *esprit de corps,* as demonstrated in the close co-operation and cordial relations between truck and service companies and the various types of QM supply units which they served. Because of its size (nearly 7,000 men in December), the 471st QM Group was always able to obtain adequate personal services for its men. An Army postal section was attached to the group, and handled mail for all its subordinate units. This was very desirable because of the great mobility and rapid changes of attachment of QM units. During most of 1944 a special services platoon was attached, and the group always had its share of doctors, dentists, and chaplains.[58]

Truckheads

During World War II, truckhead became the current term in the ETO for a forward army distributing point, replacing the term railhead used during and after World War I.[59] This change in terminology had originated in the Mediterranean and reflected the prevailing methods of operation in both theaters, but it did not indicate any change in basic QMC doctrine. Rail transportation to army supply points was employed whenever possible, the ideal method being for ADSEC or CONAD to make up separate trains of balanced supplies to be dispatched to specific combat units. ADSEC provided such service to each corps of Third Army from Verdun for several months. When separate trains could not be forwarded, Third Army considered it worthwhile to break down individual carloads at its army depot and make up trains for individual supply points, which were operated by French civilians or the army's own railroad personnel. At all times there were also

---

[57] (1) Hist of 471st QM Group, pp. 6, 17, 25. (2) OTCQM TSFET Operational Study 10, pp. 41–43.

[58] Hist of 471st QM Group, pp. 28–29.
[59] Even distributing points supplied by rail were frequently referred to as truckheads. See ch. IV, n. 40, above.

supply points inaccessible to rail which had to be served by trucks, and in fact this was the prevailing method during most of the European campaign. None of the other armies attempted to operate railroads, although they used captured trains briefly at every opportunity. ADSEC and CONAD operated trains to forward army supply points whenever physical facilities and the tactical situation permitted.[60]

Forward truckheads were designed to serve each corps and its subordinate combat units, and were normally placed at locations designated by the corps quartermaster. Such locations were often well forward, but never less than ten miles from the front. The various army SOP's all reiterated that these truckheads were army installations, and that their commanders were "personal representatives of the Army Quartermaster, and responsible to him alone." [61] This stipulation referred, of course, to supply operations and policy, and the channels for submission of supply status reports. Truckhead units were usually subordinate to a QM battalion or group for administration and discipline, and to the local corps headquarters for traffic control and tactical security. As the campaign progressed the corps tended to establish corps service areas corresponding to the army service areas already described, so that the truckhead commander's responsibility for reconnaissance was limited to selection of specific buildings, hardstands, and bivouac areas.[62]

Army quartermasters normally assigned 1 or 2 truckheads to serve each corps, depending on such things as width of the corps front, anticipated supply requirements, and availability of service companies or civilian labor. While separate Class I and III truckheads were sometimes used, a typical truckhead consisted of 1 railhead company for Class I, and 1 gasoline supply company. When available, a service company and a bakery company were also attached. During the pursuit, when Class III truckheads had to decant fuel from tanker trucks as well as make issues to combat units, 2 gasoline supply companies per corps were definitely needed. Thus the normal ETO allotment of 7 gasoline supply companies per army provided 2 for each of 3 corps, and 1 for the army Class III dump, but none to distribute POL to the army headquarters and to rear area troops. During the autumn of 1944, COMZ provided First Army with an extra company for this purpose, and later, in evaluating ETO experience, Littlejohn recommended a basis of 8 companies per army. The system of intermediate decanting points already described was manned by taking 1 gasoline supply company from behind each corps. Under this system, forward truckheads handled packaged POL only and their efficiency was greatly increased.[63]

Ration distribution for a corps almost invariably required 2 Class I truckheads, each theoretically manned by a QM rail-

[60] (1) Hist of QM Sec ADSEC, p. 51 and an. E. (2) *CONAD History*, pp. 106–08. (3) TUSA AAR, II, G–4, 20–23, 28–31.

[61] (1) SOP's, Class I and Class III Truckheads, Hq FUSA, Nov 44. File QM–Armies, Hist Br OQMG. (2) FUSA AAR, 1 Aug 44, VI, 160, 170.

[62] Unit histories 1st, 97th, 588th, 692d QM Battalions, 543d, 550th QM Groups. Hist Br OQMG.

[63] (1) OTCQM TSFET Operational Study 10, p. 16; 15, exhibit B. (2) *FUSA Rpt of Opns*, 1 Aug 44–22 Feb 45, IV, 91.

head company. In practice, service companies or other personnel frequently performed this function under the supervision of a small railhead detachment. Such supervision was necessary since ration breakdown was somewhat complicated, and army quartermasters demanded careful documentation of issues to insure that excessive quantities were not drawn. Even with such precautions, overissues often exceeded 10 percent. Railhead companies consisted of well-trained and versatile supply specialists. In addition to Class I, they normally operated salvage collection points, and frequently small Class II and IV depots as well. The T/O&E for these units also provided for Class III distribution, but this function was not performed in the European theater. The ETO troop basis allocated 6 companies to an army, but Littlejohn and most of the army quartermasters recommended that this be increased to 8, and that railhead companies be deployed like gasoline supply companies—2 to each corps, 1 at the army depot, and 1 to operate a supply point for the army headquarters and rear area troops. As utilized in the ETO to distribute Class I, II, and IV supplies, the railhead company could support 60,000 men, or twice its theoretical capacity. In Ninth Army, 2 railhead companies filled the place of a nonavailable depot supply company, and successfully operated a Class I army depot.[64]

During an advance truckheads had to be considerably more mobile than army dumps to keep the troops supplied. In the pursuit across France, First Army's Class I truckheads were displaced on an average of once every four days, in leapfrog fashion by platoons. The average distance moved was 35 miles. From late September until the German counterattack in December, truckheads were relatively static. As the predominant means of transportation changed from truck to rail, supply points were moved to more convenient sites, but space directly alongside a rail line was rarely available. Low-lying sites had to be vacated because of autumn rains. There was a great scarcity of well-drained hardstands, and the period was characterized by emergency open storage along the shoulders of roads, on towpaths along canals, and on airfield runways. In some instances the extreme forward location of the dumps caused difficulties, since routes from combat units to truckheads were parallel to the front. Such lateral routes had low priorities for engineer repairs, and occasionally were subject to enemy artillery fire.[65]

The Ninth Army was unique in the ETO in that it normally assigned a QM group to command the army's QM troops supporting each corps, and to back up the QM battalion commanding the corps' own QM troops. For example, the 543d and 550th QM Groups remained with the VIII and XVI Corps respectively until the German surrender. In addition to the Class I and III truckheads, these groups each controlled two truck companies, a salvage collecting company, and the equipment maintenance platoon of a salvage repair com-

[64] (1) T/O 10–197, 17 February 1945. (2) OTCQM TSFET Operational Study 10, p. 34. (3) "QM Operations in Ninth Army," QMTSJ, VII, No. 26 (29 January 1945) 26. (4) Littlejohn, ed., Passing in Review, ch. 33, exhibit 8.

[65] FUSA Rpt of Opns, 1 Aug 44–22 Feb 45, IV, 47. 51, 56, 60.

pany. The salvage collecting company also sorted salvage, performed minor repairs, and operated a captured enemy matériel depot. Ninth Army's bakeries were not in the truckheads but were grouped to the rear of the corps boundaries under a single battalion headquarters. They were supported by a special bakery materials depot separate from the army Class I depot. The Ninth Army QM office held daily meetings with the group commanders to insure close co-ordination of operations, and used them as a main channel for liaison with the corps quartermasters.[66]

Quartermaster at the Corps Level

As General Bradley aptly put it, the combat head of the corps is larger than its supporting tail. Unlike the army or the division, which were both administrative and tactical units, the corps was essentially a tactical headquarters and, when part of an army, was not a link in the chain of supply. The Quartermaster Section of corps headquarters therefore served primarily as a liaison and co-ordinating agency, with only those operating functions pertaining to the supply of corps troops.[67]

Much of the contact between the corps and army quartermasters was maintained through Quartermaster unit commanders who operated the forward truckheads provided by the army for each corps. Through them, the corps forwarded requisitions and recommended future loca-

tions of army railheads and truckheads. Whenever there was any likelihood that the army supply mission would interfere with the corps tactical mission, the corps prevailed. In October, for example, the Third Army quartermaster was unable to exploit the storage and track facilities at Nancy because the local corps commander wanted supply activity in his area held to a minimum.[68]

A conspicuous exception to the general rule that a corps acted purely as a tactical unit was the VIII Corps move westward into Brittany, while the main body of Third Army turned to the east. Here a separate supply system, based partly on ADSEC and partly on direct shipments from the United Kingdom, was set up for the corps, which in turn established its own supply points for forward distribution. This setup continued until Brittany Base Section assumed control of the Rennes depot on 21 August and became the main source of corps supply. The typical army-corps supply relationship was retained only to the extent that Colonel Busch of Third Army sent the 543d Quartermaster Group to Brest to act as his representative, process VIII Corps requisitions, and act as a provisional regulating station to check on and expedite deliveries.[69] The 543d QM Group remained with VIII Corps when the latter became the nucleus of the new Ninth Army.

Supply arrangements for VIII Corps were extremely informal. In mid-September, as the fight for Brest reached its climax, Lt. William A. Harnist and 10

---

[66] (1)Unit histories, 543d, 550th QM Groups. Hist Br OQMG. (2) "QM Operations in Ninth Army," *QMTSJ*, VII, No. 26 (29 January 1945), 26–29.

[67] (1) Field Service Regulations, Administrative, FM 100–10, 15 November 1945, p. 72. (2) OTCQM TSFET Operational Study 10, p. 163.

[68] (1) TUSA AAR, II, G–4, 28. (2) "QM Operations in Ninth Army," *QMTSJ*, VII, No. 26 (29 January 1945), 25–26.

[69] TUSA AAR, II, G–4, 13; QM, 3.

trucks of the 3909th QM Truck Company set out for a secret rendezvous at Morlaix, a small port deep in the Brittany Peninsula. He carried 26 driver replacements who had just been flown in from England. From Morlaix, these men drove off 26 trucks landed by LST's and loaded with essential supplies for the siege of Brest. Although the area was by no means cleared of the enemy and was without local security of any kind, Lieutenant Harnist's provisional truck unit improvised its own port organization and operated this minor port for nearly a month.[70]

Corps Quartermaster Sections had no organic units but First Army, the earliest army to become operational upon the Continent and a creator of precedents in many fields, attached a QM battalion headquarters and five QM units to each of its corps. These were: a service company, a graves registration company, two truck companies, and a car platoon. Late in September 1944, a laundry company and a fumigation and bath company, previously located in the truckheads, were also attached to each corps. Moreover, two additional truck companies were attached to each corps that controlled an armored division. Subject to availability of units, this pattern was imitated by the other armies on the Continent. The Third Army was an exception with regard to truck units, which it attached to the G–4 Section of each corps headquarters as required. Thus the number of truck units actually present with a corps of Third Army was usually the same, but they were not

commanded by the corps quartermaster.[71]

The office of the corps quartermaster was staffed by four officers and five enlisted men; one or two additional enlisted men were frequently borrowed from the subordinate QM battalion headquarters. This office was both a special staff section of corps headquarters and an agency exercising operational control over subordinate QM units.

The organization of such a unit is illustrated by the OQM, XIX Corps, which was successively under First and Ninth Armies. Its functions were performed by three subsections. The supply subsection made reconnaissance and recommended locations of truckheads and railheads, disseminated information on opening and closing dates of such installations, supervised and conducted inspections to insure that distribution was correct and equitable, and monitored levels of supply and equipment in divisions. The field service subsection supervised operations of all subordinate QM units except the graves registration company. Specifically, it was responsible for allocating services by corps motor and labor pools, laundry, fumigation and bath, and attached salvage units. It also directed the internal salvage collection and repair programs of the corps, and co-ordinated evacuation of surplus items to army salvage points. The graves registration subsection supervised evacuation from divisional graves registration collection points to army cemeteries, and co-ordinated identification procedures with division and corps personnel officers. During periods of forward movement, it established and administered

[70] S. M. Davis, "Patton's Wheels," QMR, XXV, No. 2 (September–October 1945), 23.

[71] (1) FUSA Rpt of Opns, 1 Aug 44–22 Feb 45, IV, 92. (2) TUSA AAR, II, G–4, 14.

cemeteries until they were transferred to army jurisdiction.[72]

The XII Corps Quartermaster Section, which saw continuous duty with Third Army from August 1944 to V–E Day, and may be considered typical for units having no transportation responsibilities, was somewhat differently organized. The field service subsection inspected divisional Quartermaster installations, supervised laundries, bath units, and other supporting quartermaster organizations furnished by Third Army, and made ground and aerial reconnaissance for advanced supply installations. The Class III and evacuation subsection supervised the issue of petroleum products, assumed responsibility for corps level aspects of the graves registration program, and acted as the purchasing and contracting agency for the corps quartermaster. Class I, Class II and IV, and salvage activities, as well as the processing of requisitions for controlled and critical items, fell under the jurisdiction of the supply subsection. In a unit as small as the corps Quartermaster Section all officers and enlisted men had several responsibilities. They were also expected to keep abreast of all QMC activities in the headquarters and be prepared to perform other than assigned duties without loss of organizational efficiency.[73]

While the office of the corps quartermaster defined policies and allocated supplies and services among the combat units, the detailed operations of its subordinate QM units were supervised by the attached Quartermaster battalion,

which was normally located near the rear echelon of corps headquarters. The battalion telephone switchboard was an important link between the corps QM office and the subordinate QM companies. This unit was largely concerned with routine inspections, personnel administration, courts-martial, welfare activities, and the like, but also reported in detail on the supplies and services provided by its subordinate QM companies. Thus, for example, the 1st QM Battalion (Mobile), while supporting XIX Corps all across western Europe, utilized the 970th QM Service Company to operate a Class II and IV depot and a collecting point for captured equipment and fuels. The company's platoons and sections performed miscellaneous services, from digging graves at a corps cemetery in the rear to collecting salvage in the zone of infantry regiments. A major responsibility was loading and unloading the corps truck units as well as the daily train whenever rail service was available. During April 1945 the unit itself operated a train between Hildesheim and Ochersleben, Germany.

The 4045th and 4046th QM Truck Companies transported all classes of supply for XIX Corps units, but their greatest single task was the transportation of combat troops. During August and part of September 1944, they were augmented by a provisional truck company drawn largely from vehicles of attached corps artillery. Allocating truck transportation was a jealously guarded prerogative of the corps QM office. For example, on one occasion the battalion headquarters had to delay a planned displacement until the corps quartermaster released five trucks for the move, although in theory the truck

[72] AAR XIX Corps QM Sec; Hist of 1st QM Bn (Mobile). Both in Hist Br OQMG.

[73] Memo, QM XII Corps for CofS Hq XII Corps, 25 Jun 45, sub: XII Corps QM Sec in Combat. XII Corps, 319.1 (QM).

companies were subordinate to the battalion.[74]

The 3d Platoon, 506th QM Car Company, later redesignated 90th QM Car Platoon, was attached directly to the XIX Corps command post, and was used to transport staff officers and provide courier service. Its vehicles were almost always dispatched singly. With practice, its drivers learned how to read foreign maps and ask directions in foreign languages—special skills needed for this type of duty.

The 852d Fumigation and Bath Company also operated principally in the forward portion of the corps area, providing an exchange of clothing to combat troops and sending soiled clothing to the 599th QM Laundry Company, usually located near the corps command post. Like many similar units in the ETO, the 852d had enough men to operate more than its T/O allowance of two shower trailers, since the fumigation equipment was seldom used. The usual deployment was one platoon near the corps command post for corps troops and one division, and the other platoon in a central location to serve two more divisions. This was not very adequate service, and these "compromise" locations inevitably favored corps and rear area troops at the expense of combat units.

Laundry units were also situated too far to the rear to benefit combat troops, but for somewhat different reasons. The laundry company with its 16 trailers had only four prime movers, which restricted mobility and made it very difficult to split up the company. The 599th usually operated from not more than two locations, both too far to the rear to give

direct service to troops in combat. When the tactical situation permitted, the XIX Corps maintained a rest center supported by one bath and one laundry platoon. General Busch, the Third Army quartermaster, agreed with division quartermasters who believed that laundry and bath units of suitable size and mobility should be attached to divisions to give service to troops actually engaged in combat. At least one AGF observer came to similar conclusions, but given the equipment and troop basis actually available for the European campaign, attachment of such units to corps headquarters was probably the best solution.[75]

Originally, XIX Corps attached one platoon of the 608th Graves Registration Company to each of its subordinate divisions and operated a corps cemetery. Once the Normandy area was left behind, lengthening lines of communication added to the difficulty of evacuation. Nevertheless, casualties were comparatively light during the pursuit, and First Army directed that interments be centralized in cemeteries already established, for which the army took over responsibility. Combat units were directed to evacuate their dead to divisional collecting points, where a detachment of the corps graves registration unit received them and brought them to an army relay point. At the relay point trailer-loads of remains were transferred from corps vehicles to vehicles of the company operating the army cemetery. Under this system, a six-man section from the corps graves registration unit

---

[74] Hist of 1st QM Bn (Mobile). Hist Br OQMG.

[75] (1) OTCQM TSFET Operational Study 10, pp. 162 a–f. (2) Ltr, WD Obsvs Bd ETOUSA to CG AGF, 1 Jul 45, sub: AGF Rpt 1074, Field Laundries; Bath Units. ETO 319.25, AGF Rpts.

was adequate at each division collecting point. This procedure made available teams for a thorough search of areas left behind by the combat troops. As the campaign in the ETO continued, a minimum number of new army cemeteries closer to the front were established, and old cemeteries were transferred to COMZ, but the evacuation system remained basically unchanged. XIX Corps with attached service units was transferred to Ninth Army late in October 1944, and for a short time the 608th had to evacuate remains for no less than seven divisions. During this period, to conserve manpower, Ninth Army dead were interred in the First Army cemetery at Henri-Chappelle.[76]

While corps level QM battalion headquarters had mainly administrative responsibilities for their subordinate operating units, the provost marshal of each corps formulated emergency plans assigning command functions to these headquarters with regard to tactical security in the rear areas. Such plans went into effect at the time of the German counteroffensive in December. For example during the period 17–31 December 1944, Lt. Col. Fred L. Koosa, commanding officer of the 97th QM Battalion, was military commander of the city of Eupen, Belgium, in addition to his normal duties in support of V Corps. The various types of service units under his command had several tactical contacts with enemy units and captured a number of parachutists who had landed in their area.[77]

The Quartermaster in the Combat Division

The smallest combat formation containing all the essential ground arms and services, the division was also the lowest echelon at which the QMC was represented. Tables of Organization provided a Quartermaster company for infantry, cavalry, and airborne divisions. By late 1943 the armored division retained only a divisional quartermaster with his personal staff.[78]

The evolution of organic Quartermaster units within combat divisions through 1943, and their operations in the Mediterranean campaign, have already been described.[79] On 10 June 1944 (D plus 4 in Normandy) the authorized strength of the QM company, infantry division, was officially reduced by seven enlisted men to a total of 186 officers and men, but without significant change in organization. The operating units were three truck platoons and a service platoon. Each of the truck platoons had a strength of 1 officer and 28 enlisted men, operating 16 trucks of 2½ tons capacity. The service platoon consisted of 1 officer and 48 men. The company headquarters was primarily a support and administrative unit; its 30 enlisted men were principally auto mechanics and mess personnel, and its 2 officers were largely concerned with discipline. These functions were subject to little variation, and their performance was virtually the same in all infantry divisions.

---

[76] (1) *FUSA Rpt of Opns*, 1 Aug 44–22 Feb 45, IV, 53–77. (2) QMC Historical Studies, 21, pp. 107–11.

[77] Hist of 97th QM Bn. Hist Br OQMG.

[78] (1) No cavalry divisions were employed in the ETO. (2) The 2d and 3d Armored Divisions retained their supply battalions (actually QM units) all through the European campaign. Cf. Greenfield *et al., The Organization of Ground Combat Troops*, p. 326.

[79] See chs. III and IV, above.

The Office of the Division Quartermaster (ODQM) was a true headquarters, responsible for operations, planning, and co-ordination with other headquarters; its 14 enlisted men were largely clerical. Since the division quartermaster had an assistant or executive officer, a purchasing and contracting officer, and a supply officer to assist him, he was relieved of administrative detail and the more routine aspects of operations. Moreover, under the current T/O, division quartermasters delegated the position of company commander to one of their subordinates, usually a captain.[80]

By formal designation, the division quartermaster was both a special staff officer and a troop commander. His staff functions rarely amounted to more than keeping the G–4 informed of the status of supply, but since his troops were service troops operating in support of combat units, their correct employment involved a great deal of liaison, co-ordination, and planning. The types and quantities of supplies required fluctuated constantly, and during mobile combat the time lag between requisition and delivery become so great that the quartermaster had to do considerably more than merely consolidate the requisitions of subordinate units. Successful and adequate QM support for a division in combat demanded anticipating at least two days in advance the types and quantities of supplies that would probably be required, and the locations where they would be needed at least twelve hours in advance. Supply reserves in the combat units and in the QM company could compensate for occasional errors, but repeated misjudgment of supply needs could lead to exhaustion of both the operating reserves and the physical stamina of the supply personnel.

The necessary forecasting did not require any mystical prophetic power or unusual brilliance, but it did demand an intimate and up-to-date detailed knowledge of the intentions and decisions of subordinate combat unit commanders. Even when available in the forward areas telephone service was not secure enough for a discussion of future operations, so that in practice the division quartermaster or his assistant had to make almost daily visits to the command post of each unit actively engaged. Securing the needed supplies also demanded personal conferences with truckhead commanders, the corps quartermaster, and occasionally with the army quartermaster. The travel involved sometimes exceeded 10,000 miles per month, not including route reconnaissance or selection of new distribution point sites—functions usually delegated to junior QM officers. Despite this time-consuming liaison activity, the division quartermaster was primarily a troop commander. He had to decide personally how and where his men should be employed, and he was responsible for the efficiency of their performance.[81]

In the ETO, infantry divisions were normally supplied by the trucks of the organic QM company, which drew Class I and III supplies daily at an army truckhead and distributed them to the

---

[80] T/O 10–17, QM Company, Infantry Division, 10 June 1944.

[81] (1) "QM Company on the Rhine," *QMTSJ*, VII, No. 23 (8 June 1945), 4-11. (2) AAR's 4th, 28th, 29th, 30th, 80th QM Cos; AAR QM Sec 5th Armd Div. Hist Br OQMG.

vehicles of combat units at a divisional distribution point. The distribution point was manned by the service platoon of the company, which transferred supplies from divisional trucks to those of combat units.[82] Whenever possible, service platoon members also accompanied trucks to the army truckheads to load supplies, as this step resulted in a significant saving of time. Time and not tonnage capacity was the limiting factor in all QM truck operations. Using the ration trucks on their return trips to evacuate salvage and POW's was theoretically desirable and clearly necessary under the conditions of combat. The extra time involved in delivery and unloading at a salvage collecting point or POW inclosure actually imposed a severe strain, since all vehicles were assigned a full schedule of regular duties. Transportation was always at a premium, and was frequently on loan to other technical services and to the combat units. Relief drivers were a constant source of difficulty, since they could seldom be taken from the service platoon, which had to provide the labor to collect salvage, sort laundry, operate unit showers, assist graves registration units, and perform all the miscellaneous services commonly demanded of the quartermaster by other divisional units.

During active combat, when supply lines lengthened and thousands of additional combat troops were attached to each division, the organic QM company proved inadequate for its tasks. Whenever possible, the corps loaned troops from its service company to hard-pressed divisions. Augmentations from

various sources bringing the company strength up to 250 men or more were fairly common, especially during the pursuit across France. Apparently the QM Company, 1st Division, retained the men who had been authorized in 1942 for the old QM battalion, infantry division, until their numbers were reduced by attrition in 1945. The 36th Division QM Company was about 100 men overstrength in the fall of 1944. The 4th Division quartermaster was assigned convalescent combat troops who had been returned to the division but were only fit for limited duty. He also arranged to have battle fatigue cases attached to his unit during their recovery period. In December 1944 the 84th Division quartermaster remarked enviously that "the QM's of the 4th, 29th and 30th Divisions are all operating with about 250 men." [83]

These augmentations were needed particularly for salvage activities. The 84th Division obtained the use of some prisoners (Dutch Nazis), who sorted salvage, scrubbed web equipment, laundered socks, and dried out boots. While not strictly salvage, the last two activities were extremely valuable for morale and health in Holland's wet winter climate. A similar expedient was "Rosey's Repair Shop," organized by a German-speaking enlisted man of the 29th Division QM Company from German civilian construction workers captured at Brest. This unofficial ten-man unit specialized in shoe repair and remained with the division for many months. The division quartermaster remarked that an organic

---

[82] The procedure followed in Italy applied also to the European theater (see page 106).

[83] Unit histories and AAR's, 1st 4th, 36th QM Cos; Personal Ltr, Lt Col Donald S. ("Tim") Himes to Chief Training Div, OQMG, 24 Dec 44, reproduced as an unnumbered OQMG memo. Hist Br OQMG.

unit for this purpose that did not require security guards would have been desirable.[84]

The truck platoons of the QM company likewise required additional men to operate effectively. The T/O allocation of 1 noncommissioned officer and 12 enlisted men for each section of 8 trucks was adequate only for relatively static situations, when the round trip to the army truckhead did not require the services of a relief driver. The overstrength of 26 men per company authorized for army truck units was never extended to divisional QM units, which had to provide relief drivers by unofficial means.[85] On the other hand, the allotment of vehicles to the divisional QM company was adequate even when the round trip to the army truckhead could not be completed in one day.

The 84th Division quartermaster reported in November 1944 that on a typical day he dispatched 14 trucks for Class I, 4 for Class III, 3 for Class II, 3 for salvage and laundry, and the balance for hauling mines, wire, coal, personnel, and so forth. In this instance only 24 trucks were dispatched on purely Quartermaster missions, and of these only the Class II supplies, which had to be brought from an army depot, represented a long haul. Class I and III were drawn at army truckheads at about 0800 each day, and reached the dispatch office (in the bivouac area) by 1100. Under such conditions, trucks were readily available for other duties, and the division QM reported that "about every other night we furnish 40 to 46 trucks to haul an infantry battalion from the line, ordinarily just after dark. We take it to the nearest fumigation and bath unit, where the men bathe, eat a hot meal, and bed down in a quiet area. The next day they are re-equipped as much as possible and return to division reserve or to the line." [86]

The detailed functioning of the office of the division quartermaster varied considerably from one unit to another in the ETO, the main variable being the relative personal importance of the G–4 and the division quartermaster. In the 28th Division, two successive G–4's were former quartermasters of the same division. It was perhaps inevitable that they treated the incumbent division quartermaster as a very junior subordinate, and exercised direct control over all QM functions. The QM company and its dumps were located within a division maintenance area a few miles to the rear of the command post. This area was selected by the G–4 and guarded by a platoon of combat troops who were commanded by the special troops commander. The QM company, with other technical service units in the division maintenance area, was subordinate to Headquarters, Special Troops, in all administrative matters. The transportation section was placed at division headquarters directly under the G–4, and the

[84] AAR 29th QM Co, 1 Dec 44. Hist Br OQMG.

[85] The organization of truck platoons in the QM truck company (T/O 10–57) and in the divisional QM company (T/O 10–17) was almost identical. Authority for overstrength in the former was Rad, Eisenhower to Ground Force Replacement System, EX-62290, 101821A Nov 44.

[86] (1) Donald S. Himes, "Division QM on the Bulge," QMTSJ, VII, No. 8 (23 February 1945), 5. (2) After action reports of other ETO divisions, especially the 2d, 28th, 30th, 35th, and 42d, tend to show that the use of vehicles in the 84th Division as described was typical for nonmobile warfare. QM unit history files, Hist Br OQMG.

division quartermaster had no direct responsibility for this function. Since the transportation officer of the ODQM was also purchasing and contracting officer, purchasing and contracting were also controlled by the G–4. This was of minor importance since in the 28th Division a purchasing and contracting officer in each regiment and in the divisional artillery headquarters did the bulk of emergency local procurement necessary during active operations. The balance of the ODQM, the supply and administrative sections, was physically located with the QM company. The supply section handled all classes of supply including salvage and repair functions. The commander of the service platoon was also designated division Class I officer, and was thus responsible for procurement as well as distribution of rations. The assistant division QM and his small administrative section handled all field service functions and records and kept an up-to-date situation map. This division of responsibilities freed the division QM for the essential task of maintaining constant liaison with division headquarters and with the corps and army QM offices and installations that served the division. Difficulties of communication in a fluid situation and the secret and detailed nature of the information regarding future operations required to co-ordinate QM service for combat units made personal contacts mandatory. Lt. Col. William P. Simmons, Jr., the division quartermaster, was not only constantly on the road himself, but frequently found it necessary to send out all his staff officers and three or four of the six QM company officers in all directions after supplies or information.[87]

The 29th Division probably provided the greatest contrast with the working methods of the 28th. From June until early October 1944, the 29th QM Company maintained two Class III distributing points for the division and delivered Class I, II, and IV supplies direct to using units. Beginning on 5 October, it distributed all classes of supply except solid fuel to the 29th Division and all attached units. This service became a division policy and was only interrupted during periods of extremely mobile warfare. It required transportation from an army dump, unloading and breakdown at a central point within the division area, and reloading and delivery to the ultimate consumer. This was an unusual effort, attempted by other division quartermasters only under exceptionally favorable conditions and regarded by the division staff as the primary responsibility of the division quartermaster, who was able to maintain close control over his own personnel and vehicles for that purpose. This service freed the vehicles of the combat units for other duties, including a variety of chores that in other divisions were often performed by the Quartermaster company. Significantly, the report from this QM company stated that it was "frequently able to assist" other elements of the division by hauling salvage from the forward areas, evacuating POW's and refugees, transporting replacements, moving division forward and rear headquarters installations, and hauling supplies for other technical services.[88] Within most divisions in the ETO, the QM company was utilized as a divisional transportation pool, and the enumerated functions

[87] Hist of 28th QM Co. Hist Br OQMG.

[88] AAR 29th QM Co, 1 Dec 44. Hist Br OQMG.

were regarded as normal Quartermaster responsibilities.

Like the divisions in Normandy and Belgium, those which advanced through southern France found their organic Quartermaster companies an important link in the chain of supply. Whether the front advanced rapidly as in the race up the Rhône valley, or slowly as in the autumn of 1944, a Quartermaster company like Lt. Col. Clifton C. Carter's "Hell drivers" in the 36th Division, closely supported the infantry, setting up ration, clothing, equipment, and petroleum dumps. The rate of advance from the Mediterranean coast was actually faster than the pursuit out of the Normandy beachhead, and the distance division convoys had to travel for supplies was correspondingly longer. Even after the end of the pursuit phase, rail service from the rear developed slowly. In October and November 1944 the 36th QM Company sent three large convoys back to the beaches near Marseille from its location on the upper Moselle—a distance of more than 350 miles. During this period troops and vehicles of other services—for example, Chemical Warfare Service personnel—were attached to the QM company to assist in hauling and handling supplies. The 42d QM Company, 42d Division, had even more need for such assistance, since it lost 10 of its trucks by "permanent dispatch" to other elements of the division—8 were turned into office vans by the advance echelon of division headquarters, 1 was permanently dispatched to the nearest Army post office to deliver division mail, and 1 was assigned to the QM purchasing and contracting officer. This officer was able to purchase such needed items as snow camouflage suits and helmet cam-

ouflage nets for cash, but invariably had to provide transportation himself. Purchasing also involved persistent searching for goods within villages in the division area, which meant that the purchasing officer must have a free hand and adequate transportation.[89]

QM in Armored Divisions

The armored divisions lost their organic supply battalions late in 1943 and the QM element of the division was limited to the quartermaster and his staff of three officers and eleven enlisted men.[90] In the ETO, two QM truck companies were attached to each armored division engaged in combat. In most divisions, one company was used principally for ammunition and the other for all classes of QM supply, including POL. An armored division required about twice as much gasoline as an infantry division, but the entire unit, including infantry elements, was motorized and organic vehicles drew a considerable part of their required POL direct at army Class III truckheads. The attached truck companies were often loaned to move infantry divisions, since the armored infantry did not need such support.[91]

The lack of an organic service platoon was regarded as a major deficiency by all armored division quartermasters. Each of the combat commands normally provided a daily ten-man detail for this duty, but a total of thirty men was about half the number required, especially since the men were rotated in this assignment and never became skillful cargo

[89] AAR's 36th, 42d QM Cos. Hist Br OQMG.
[90] OTCQM TSFET Operational Study 10, p. 125.
[91] AAR's QM Secs 2d, 3d, 4th, 5th, 7th Armd Divs. Hist Br OQMG.

handlers. Service personnel were sometimes available from corps, but not on a dependable daily basis. When armored combat commands operated separately, attachment of a truck platoon to each took care of Class I and III supply without difficulty.

Army depots normally made the division quartermaster draw Class II and IV supplies for the entire division on a consolidated requisition, and experience demonstrated that this was the best method even when the units were scattered. Any other procedure created confusion in the system of rationing critical items and of providing special allowances to armored units. The 5th Armored Division employed a unique system of allowing its subordinate battalions and companies to draw Class I and III supplies directly at truckheads. Noncommissioned officer representatives of the division quartermaster consolidated these individual requisitions at the truckhead. This procedure completely eliminated double handling at a division distribution point and saved about three hours transit time on delivery of supplies to the using units. The burden, of course, fell on the army truckheads, which required about twice as long (one and a half hours versus forty-five minutes) to fill Class I requisitions on this basis. For Class III the difference was considerably less. The 5th Division quartermaster contended that the daily net saving in manpower and vehicles for Class I alone was thirty man-days and fifteen truck-days, a truly impressive figure which tended to confirm the theoretical validity of at least one aspect of General McNair's supply doctrines. The difficulty was that during combat the army truckheads were the critical links

in the whole supply system and operated on very tight schedules. Divisional ration convoys normally visited truckheads "by appointment," and were expected to vacate promptly to make room for the next unit. As long as the division was actively engaged and operating with separate combat commands, First and Third Armies tolerated this unusual procedure. Later in the campaign the division was united under Ninth Army, which insisted that Class I supplies be drawn on a division basis.

The combat operations and logistical procedures of the 5th Armored Division overcame many disadvantages of wide dispersion, and are therefore unusually interesting in view of current tactical concepts. The combat commands were committed in widely separated sectors, frequently behind the enemy lines. QM transportation was attached to the separate commands, and the individual ration convoys usually included armored escort vehicles for security. A 250-mile turnaround was not unusual. The quartermaster's most difficult task was keeping all requisitioning units continuously informed of the location of all army truckheads. Experience also demonstrated that either the division quartermaster or his assistant should have daily personal (not telephonic) contact with the division G–4, each combat command, the corps quartermaster, and those army Class I and III truckheads where his noncommissioned officer representatives were stationed. This involved an enormous amount of travel but was justified by the results. Although the division advanced as much as 70 miles in a single day, and individual combat commands as much as 100 miles, all subordinate units were kept fully supplied within the limits permitted by army level rationing.[92]

The quartermasters of armored divisions, like those of infantry divisions, were unanimously agreed that they could operate more effectively if the more generous allotment of supply personnel authorized to them before the reorganization of 1943 were restored. The best proof of the validity of this contention was the fact that the 2d and 3d Armored Divisions were permitted to retain the older organization, with very minor changes.[93]

QM in Airborne Divisions

Until late in 1944 the Quartermaster company, airborne division, had a strength of 87 officers and men, and comprised a company headquarters, a service platoon, and an airborne truck platoon of jeeps with ¼-ton trailers. For ground combat after a link-up with friendly forces, a standard truck company was normally attached to each division. A new Table of Organization, dated 16 December 1944, increased the size of the airborne QM company to 11 officers and 197 enlisted men. What this reorganization actually amounted to was that the old airborne QM company and the attached truck company were combined and one company headquarters was eliminated. The new T/O was adopted in the European theater in March 1945, although AGF still regarded it as tentative.[94]

Quite apart from the all-important airlift, the supply organization to support airborne operations in the ETO was extremely complicated, comprising no less than five separate echelons: (1) The divisional airborne QM element; (2) the divisional seaborne (or land transported) organic QM element; (3) attached QM troop units; (4) QM depot units at take-off airfields; (5) the organic QM element of division rear.[95]

For Operation NEPTUNE in Normandy, only staff elements represented the QM in the initial parachute jump.[96] Because the troops jumped in darkness and under poor weather conditions, they were so scattered that aerial resupply was extremely difficult. According to plan, a glider landing at dusk on D-day brought in both supplies and reinforcements. The majority of the gliders were wrecked, but most of the supplies were recovered. This was to have been an "on call" resupply, but when it proved impossible to make radio contact, the mission was flown as planned. One parachute resupply was planned—a daylight drop of 480 tons on D plus 1 to be delivered on an "automatic" basis to both divisions. Less than 40 percent of this tonnage was recovered. On 7 June the 440th Group of the 50th Troop Carrier Wing dropped 63 tons of ammunition, 10½ tons of rations, and 21 tons of miscellaneous equipment for the 101st Airborne Division. Three other groups

[92] AAR QM Sec 5th Armd Div. Hist Br OQMG.

[93] (1) AAR 2d Armd Div. Hist Br OQMG. (2) Greenfield et al., The Organization of Ground Combat Troops, pp. 326, 330.

[94] (1) QM Supply in ETO, VIII, 96. (2) OTCQM TSFET Operational Study 10, pp. 123–24. (3) Huston, Airborne Operations, ch. VIII, p. 37.

[95] Huston, Airborne Operations, ch. VII, p. 90.

[96] In the 101st Airborne Division, only the division quartermaster personally made the jump; in the 82d Division, three officers and four enlisted men of the ODQM jumped with the combat troops. AAR's QM-Cos 82d and 101st A/B Divs. Hist Br OQMG.

of the 50th flew missions that day and presumably dropped similar tonnages. The 52d Wing sent off a total of 234 tons to the 82d Division, but many aircraft were forced to turn back. Only 156 tons were actually dropped, and less than 100 tons recovered. The inexperienced unloaders of the 2d QM Depot Supply Company [97] were unable to dump the cargo fast enough, so that in most cases the planes overflew the drop zones before the parachute loads were ejected.[98]

The division quartermasters, using details of combat troops, collected the airdropped supplies that could be located. Some elements of the 101st Division linked up with the amphibious assault on D-day. The 82d Division was joined by the attached 3807th QM Truck Company on D plus 2, even before the entire seaborne QM echelon had reported in. For this operation, it should be noted, the service platoon and the air-transportable truck platoon arrived by sea. With a company of 2½-ton trucks available, the division QM found a force of 23 jeeps somewhat superfluous; clearly, they had arrived too late. The division engaged in conventional ground combat for another 31 days, and the division QM reported that his chief difficulty was replacing the large quantities of Class II supplies lost in the airdrop.[99]

Subsequent operations in the ETO came under the supervision of the First Allied Airborne Army, activated on 2 August 1944 under the command of Lt. Gen. Lewis H. Brereton. The first of these was MARKET, an ambitious project calling for three airborne divisions to secure crossings on 17 September 1944 over three major rivers, the Maas, the Waal, and the Lower Rhine, at Grave, Nijmegen, and Arnhem, respectively. These rivers ran roughly parallel across the southern Netherlands. The airdrops were to be consolidated by Operation GARDEN, a British armored thrust from Eindhoven. For various reasons, MARKET–GARDEN was only partially successful. The British armor, road-bound in the low terrain, took a week instead of three days to reach the south bank of the Rhine, and meanwhile the British 1st Airborne Division, under surprise attack by an unexpected German panzer force, was finally compelled to evacuate its position at Arnhem on the north bank. Poor communications kept higher headquarters in ignorance of the situation at Arnhem for three days, and during this period weather conditions had become so bad that only meager reinforcements could be flown in. The Allies maintained their Maas and Waal bridgeheads, but Arnhem was not recaptured until April 1945.[100]

MARKET demonstrated considerable improvement in airborne techniques. The same airborne units used for the NEPTUNE operation took off from the same airfields in England. The initial airdrops—by daylight, this time—were extremely accurate, and the landing of reinforcements by glider on D plus 1 was entirely successful. On this occasion 3 officers and 48 enlisted men of the

---

[97] No such unit is recorded in the unit files of the Historical Branch of OQMG. Possibly this was a provisional unit, later redesignated an air cargo resupply squadron.

[98] USAF Historical Study 97, pp. 75–76.

[99] (1) AAR's 82d and 101st QM Cos. Hist Br OQMG. (2) Ruppenthal, *Logistical Support*, I, 573.

[100] Pogue, *The Supreme Command*, pp. 281–85.

426th QM Company (101st Airborne Division) landed near Zon, Holland, on D plus 1. Another report states that 146 jeeps and 109 trailers for the 101st Division arrived that day by glider, so that presumably the quartermasters received at least part of their vehicles.[101] Procedures in the QM company, 82d Division, were probably very similar, but have not been recorded in detail. Recalling the failure of the "on call" procedure in Normandy, the G–4, XVIII Airborne Corps, had arranged for all resupply to be automatic, with the division commander reserving the right to cancel specific missions. As in the Normandy operation, resupply cargoes at the take-off airfields in England were packed and loaded on the planes by the 490th QM Depot Company, an ASF unit, and the 1st, 2d, and 3d Air Cargo Resupply Squadrons. These three AAF units had been trained in cargo packing and parachute rigging techniques by the 490th, and all four units were grouped into the 2d Mobile QM Battalion (Provisional), attached to the IX Troop Carrier Command. Resupply requests were channeled from the command posts of the airborne divisions to their own rear echelons in the United Kingdom, and then to the depot units.[102]

Because of the distance from the United Kingdom only one supply mission per day could be flown. On D plus 1, since the skilled pilots of the IX Troop Carrier Command were all occupied with bringing in reinforcements and combat equipment, the parachute resupply missions were flown by 252 bombers of the Eighth Air Force. The ball turrets of the B–24 aircraft had been removed so that loads could be dropped more quickly over the designated drop zones, but quick-release mechanisms were lacking. The pilots were unfamiliar with supply drops, the kick-out crews were completely untrained, and the small drop zones were surrounded by enemy troops. Under such circumstances, it was not surprising that less than 30 percent of the 782 tons of supplies was recovered. Four days of extremely bad weather followed, and resupply missions were limited in scope and poorly executed. By D plus 6 when visibility improved, the tactical situation had deteriorated. In particular the British airhead near Arnhem had been so narrowed down by enemy pressure that even skilled pilots had difficulty dropping supplies into it.

Meanwhile the U.S. airborne units had made contact with friendly ground forces and ceased to rely on air supply. The seaborne echelons joined the 101st Division on D plus 4, and the 82d on D plus 6, respectively. Since the MARKET operation had been located within the British zone, a special U.S. depot organization had been assembled at Brussels under XVIII Airborne Corps. The QM elements involved were four truck companies, a service company, and two graves registration platoons. The 26th, 95th, and 104th U.S. Infantry Divisions were stripped of their vehicles for use in transporting supplies to the Brussels depot, where an average of 627 tons per day was brought in from Normandy. Although the original plans called for immediate relief of the airborne divisions, this proved to be impossible. The 82d

---

[101] (1) AAR 101st A/B QM Co. Hist Br OQMG. (2) Huston, Airborne Operations, ch. VII, p. 63.

[102] Huston, Airborne Operations, ch. VII, pp. 97–98.

and 101st Divisions were engaged in ground combat within the British zone for seven and nine weeks, respectively. Because of the location, quartermasters had even greater difficulties with Class II and IV items than in the case of NEPTUNE, and they required an elaborate organization. As Colonel Younger observed, this commitment of a small U.S. combat force within the British zone resulted in an inefficient employment of QM troops.[103]

Logistically, the most interesting aspect of the MARKET operation was an attempt to set up a forward airhead. On D plus 4 intelligence reported a good German airfield across the Maas River from Grave, not previously identified because it had not been used recently and was unmarked. The British Airborne Corps immediately asked permission to bring in the British Airborne Forward Delivery Airfield Group (AFDAG), an antiaircraft artillery battery, and the U.S. 878th Airborne Engineer Battalion, to be followed by supplies and possibly by the 52 Lowland Infantry Division (Airtransportable). On D plus 9, 209 C-47's landed AFDAG and the antiaircraft unit, the latter without guns because poor weather prevented the use of gliders. In three hours and fifty minutes all planes landed, unloaded, picked up U.S. glider pilots to be evacuated, and took off safely. Although a link-up had been achieved three days earlier, supply by truck was still inadequate and a major aerial resupply at this field was planned for the next day, D plus 10. But that morning a column of 125 trucks of 83 Group (Tactical), Royal Air

Force, arrived without advance notice to organize the field as a fighter base. The resupply mission was canceled and the U.S. Engineer unit was sent elsewhere. Higher headquarters had decided that defense against increased Luftwaffe activity in the area had priority.

This episode typified the perpetual tug-of-war between airborne and air forces. Control over troop carrier aircraft was a particularly sensitive point. Whenever an airborne operation was scheduled, more than 50 percent of "normal" freight airlift of the entire ETO had to be canceled. But the airborne forces contended that they merely "loaned" troop carrier aircraft for freight service when not needed for tactical missions. In this case, the significant feature was the five-day delay before a forward airfield could be occupied. During those five crucial days the British were forced to evacuate Arnhem, the real objective of the whole operation. Bad weather and poor communications were undoubtedly contributing factors, but the enormous number of aircraft already being used for MARKET and the great complexity of all airborne operations were the main deterrents to prompt action. It was most unfortunate that AFDAG, a unique unit without a U.S. counterpart, never had another opportunity to demonstrate its capabilities. Equally unfortunate, and hard to understand in retrospect, is the fact that apparently no advance plans had been made to exploit captured airfields for resupply purposes, although that procedure was a part of U.S. airborne doctrine, and indeed was recognized by airborne experts of all nationalities as a basic requirement for a *strategic* airborne operation. Without its own aerial

[103] (1) Pogue, *The Supreme Command*, p. 284. (2) Ruppenthal, *Logistical Support*, II, 140.

"port of debarkation," even a large airborne operation had only tactical significance.[104]

At Bastogne, the commitment of the 101st Airborne Division may be described as a fortunate accident. At the time of the German Ardennes offensive the division had been in reserve in the Reims area since 27 November, refitting after the MARKET operation. It moved into Bastogne by road on 18 December and received supplies by normal means until it was cut off on the 21st. Then the fact that it was an airborne division contributed a great deal to its survival. Working through its own rear echelon, the 101st maintained very satisfactory liaison with the IX Troop Carrier Command, and arranged for three parachute resupply missions which were 98 percent successful.[105]

Formidable difficulties had to be overcome to achieve these results. The weather was invariably unfavorable. Air cargo personnel, aerial delivery containers, and cargo parachutes were all in very short supply and were concentrated in Great Britain, so that a plan for resupply from French airfields had to be canceled. The British offered to help, but only British containers could be carried in British aircraft, and none were ready-packed with U.S. supplies. Then it developed that the main need was for artillery ammunition, which could not be dropped satisfactorily with parachutes and drop containers of the current design. Gliders were hastily assembled, including many that had been salvaged

after the operations in Normandy and Holland. Supplies successfully landed by glider included 53 tons of ammunition and 2,975 gallons of POL. Largely because of enemy antiaircraft fire, glider operations were only about 61 percent successful. The roads into Bastogne were reopened on 27 December, and further air resupply missions were canceled. As a result of this experience COMZ designed and stockpiled an airtransportable "brick" that could supply an airborne division for one day. It weighed 270.5 tons, and could be readily adapted to an infantry or armored division by addition of suitable artillery ammunition and POL.[106]

VARSITY—the last airborne operation in the ETO—supported the Rhine River crossings of British Second Army and U.S. First Army by an airdrop near Wesel on 24 March 1945. British airborne units were again flown in from the United Kingdom, but the 17th Airborne Division took off from airfields in Belgium and northern France. Since existing airfields in this area were all in use by tactical aircraft, twelve special fields had to be built for the airborne operation, to accommodate some 900 aircraft. The construction effort required 720,000 man-hours and over 13,500 tons of pierced-steel planking, plus large quantities of gravel and asphalt. These statistics explain why the Army Air Forces delayed transferring airborne

---

[104] (1) Huston, Airborne Operations, ch. VII, p. 73. (2) WD Training Cir 113, 9 Oct 43. (3) D/A Pamphlet 20-232, p. 3.

[105] AAR 426th A/B QM Co. Hist Br OQMG.

[106] (1) Huston, Airborne Operations, ch. VII, pp. 104-12. (2) Leonard Rapport and Arthur Northwood, Jr., *Rendezvous with Destiny: A History of the 101st Airborne Division* (Washington: Infantry Journal Press, 1948), pp. 527-32. (3) "Flying QM's Aid Supply of Besieged Bastogne," *QMTSJ* VII, No. 8 (4 May 1945), 9-10. (4) Ruppenthal, *Logistical Support*, II, 163-65.

units to France, although flying weather there was usually more favorable than in Great Britain.[107]

VARSITY itself, although tactically the largest airborne operation in the ETO, was of minor interest logistically.[108] The drop zones were within range of friendly artillery support, only four miles beyond the Rhine, and enemy resistance was slight. The amphibious attack had preceded the airdrop, and the link-up was completed by evening of D-day. In summary, even the most ambitious airborne operations attempted in the ETO were essentially tactical, with limited objectives, and therefore no significant innovations in air supply were required or developed in that theater.

In all the varied methods of operating described above, the divisional QM units were extremely active, and indeed essential. This fact is mentioned only because it was contrary to the basic assumptions and doctrines of the commanding general of Army Ground Forces. As late as October 1943 General McNair personally drafted an AGF directive to the effect that "Division and corps are not in the channel of supply except in emergencies."[109] As an essential corollary he also assumed that the army headquarters could and would push supply points forward so that the using units would not have to haul supplies more than twenty to thirty miles. As in the Mediterranean operations, manpower and vehicular allotments of the Quartermaster company were cut in the confidence that combat battalions and regiments would draw their supplies directly from army truckheads, that vehicles in the Quartermaster company would merely constitute a reserve, that sorting and loading would be done by army service personnel, and that unloading would be handled by the receiving units. In practice, combat conditions in the ETO vindicated the judgments of Mediterranean commanders, who had recommended larger organic QM units, rather than the theories of General McNair. Indeed by his criteria one or another of the American armies was experiencing an "emergency" during at least nine months of the eleven-month European campaign.[110]

The core of the tactical supply problem involved the distance from the division distribution point to the site where supplies were actually available. Divisional QM companies had no difficulty in exceeding the theoretical limitation of about thirty-five miles. But major difficulties arose during mobile warfare, when the army truckheads were sometimes more than 100 miles to the rear; all too often they also failed to have on hand the specific items urgently needed by the combat units, which had to haul from transfer points or even from depots in the Communications Zone. Division

---

[107] Huston, Airborne Operations, ch. VIII, p. 42.

[108] On 24 March 1945, 1,602 aircraft and 1,376 gliders dropped 22,341 troops, 2,390 tons of supplies, 1,096 vehicles, 454 guns, and 390 gallons of POL, in two missions. Over 3,000 Allied fighters sortied that day, and less than 100 German aircraft appeared. Huston, Airborne Operations, ch. VIII, pp. 38–42; ch. IX, p. 14.

[109] Greenfield et al., The Organization of Ground Combat Troops, p. 308.

[110] See "Atlas of the World Battle Fronts in Semimonthly Phases to August 15, 1945," supplement to Biennial Report of Commander Seventh U.S. Army to the Secretary of War, 1 July 1943–30 June 1945.

quartermasters probably considered only the longest hauls experienced worthy of comment, but their reports repeatedly mention trips of 200 miles or more back to the nearest point where necessary supplies were on hand. Divisional QM units frequently reported that their vehicles had averaged 3,000 miles per month, and occasionally even 5,000 miles,[111] and still complained that their divisions were not being adequately supplied. Clearly, these averages represented a volume of supply support that the combat units (regiments and battalions) could never have provided with their own vehicles. On this point, ETO quartermasters and troop commanders were in unanimous agreement.[112]

In fairness to General McNair, it should be pointed out that his doctrine of supply support procedures was entirely consonant with forecasts at SHAEF regarding the nature of operations anticipated on the Continent. The application of his theories was cautious and moderate enough so that the cut-down divisional QM company of mid-1943 was able to function in a quite different manner than originally intended, and under combat conditions that had not been anticipated. Moreover, the variations in operating procedure from one division to the next argue for a hidden margin of support capability, which was not recognized by ETO quartermasters. Nevertheless QM operations were conducted under constant strain and the

continual need to borrow men and vehicles from other organizations—conditions which appeared to justify a larger organization.

Probably the strongest statement in support of an enlarged Quartermaster company at divisional level was that of Colonel Busch, the Third Army quartermaster, who devoted almost half of one major report to a recommendation for the reorganization of this unit.[113] Busch called for the expansion of the divisional Quartermaster company into a battalion composed of a headquarters, two truck companies, and a service company. Third Army, for instance, had always been obliged to dispatch truck companies to enable the divisions to carry on their normal supply functions, while armored divisions had found even these reinforcements inadequate under strained conditions. Busch's conception of an ideal Quartermaster organization at division level also included manpower specializing in ration breakdown, gasoline distribution, and guard duties, and sections providing bath, laundry, salvage and repair services.[114] Coming from a score of battle-hardened division quartermasters, and summarized by Patton's army quartermaster at the close of the victorious European campaign, these recommendations in behalf of a more generously endowed organization were not to be taken lightly. Nor were they.

The sequel is both interesting and instructive. In March 1945 the Army Ground Forces, then headed by Gen.

[111] See, for example, AAR's of 4th, 29th, 30th, 36th, 84th, and 104th Infantry Divisions, and 2d, 5th, and 7th Armored Divisions. Hist Br OQMG.
[112] See, for example, the critical comment by General Busch upon a draft version of this MS, dated 15 November 1954. Hist Br OQMG.

[113] (1) Ltr, QM TUSA to CQM, sub: Some Ideas on QM Orgn, n.d., quoted in OTCQM TSFET Operational Study 10, pp. 162d–162e. (2) TUSA AAR, II, QM, 34–35.
[114] Ltr cited n. 113 (1).

Joseph W. Stilwell, recommended a complete reorganization of the infantry division, including an augmented QM company of 246 officers and men. This was an admission that General McNair's Reduction Board had gone too far in its pruning, and that the organization adopted in 1943 had been found wanting. But shortly thereafter the War Department rejected Stilwell's proposal, remarking that it would have been adopted "if personnel limitations were less critical." [115] In the organization actually adopted by the War Department on 1 June 1945, the infantry division was increased by 1,801 men, so that the burden upon the unchanged QM company was

actually increased.[116] The implication is inescapable that the War Department found McNair's decision, based upon precisely the same considerations, sound at least insofar as the QM company was concerned. At the highest Army level, personnel economy was the overriding factor on both occasions. This is not to say that the QM company authorized for the European campaign was ideal or even efficient, but it represented a practicable minimum organization which had worked in the ETO, and was expected to give adequate performance again in the final campaign against Japan.

---

[115] Greenfield *et al., The Organization of Ground Combat Troops,* p. 476.

[116] (1) *Ibid.,* pp. 472–82. (2) Theater commanders were authorized to request twenty-four additional enlisted men per divisional QM company—thus providing two drivers per vehicle if required.

CHAPTER XV

ETO Supply: Rations

Rations (Class I) were probably the best-handled category of Quartermaster supplies on the European continent, or at least the one causing the fewest crises in the Office of the Chief Quartermaster. The reasons were inherent in Class I operations. A food shortage in any U.S. military unit, no matter how small, was regarded as a major emergency, to be corrected by whatever action necessary within the ascending chain of command. This phraseology is used deliberately, since no matter at what level, a commanding officer is responsible for the proper subsistence of his men. In all wars the technicians of the U.S. Army who have shared the combat commander's responsibility for the subsistence of the troops have had a vivid awareness of the overriding importance of their mission—what one expert has termed a "subsistence philosophy." [1] Emergencies in food supply in the ETO were almost always local, involving transportation or distribution. They were dealt with summarily as they arose, by cutting red tape, juggling transportation priorities,

or arranging for exceptions to command policies, as required. Public opinion would tolerate no other course of action. Even minor expressions of discontent over rations by combat soldiers were echoed in the form of outspoken criticism by the *Stars and Stripes*.[2]

For the U.S. Army, the real problems of subsistence were qualitative rather than quantitative. The objective was to give the combat troops—especially those in contact with the enemy—hot, tasty, varied, and nutritious meals, as soon as possible after the landings. Ideally, such meals should be prepared from fresh bulk foods rather than concentrated preserved items. The nutritional advantages of such a diet are clear, but for combat troops the psychological considerations were actually more important. The disadvantages and even dangers of a monotonous and unpalatable diet under combat conditions were widely underestimated within the Army. The common view was that men working in the open become hungry, and when they finally become hungry enough

---

[1] Littlejohn, ed., Passing in Review, ch. 33, pp. 5, 10-11. Chapter 33 is actually a two-volume monograph. Volume I is a study by Col. Edwin J. Fitzpatrick entitled Subsistence Experience in the ETO in World War II. Volume II is a bulky compendium of reproduced original documents from the Subsistence Division, OCQM, ETO.

[2] (1) See for example, "Paging Littlejohn," an article in *Stars and Stripes* (Paris) of 4 October 1944 criticizing lemon crystals in operational rations, quoted in OCQM ETO Observer Report 1. Hist Br OQMG. (2) Memo, Col Robert T. Willkie for CQM, 5 Sep 44, sub: Food for Combat Troops. Hist Br OQMG.

they will eat whatever is available. So they will, as a general rule, but under the exacting conditions of heavy combat men require a continuous high caloric intake, not only to offset a high expenditure of energy but also to overcome the fatigue and nervous tension that inevitably accompany danger. Under such conditions considerable time may pass before the average soldier becomes hungry enough to eat, for example, an unheated combat ration. In the interim he may become seriously undernourished and weakened, so that his diminished alertness and lowered resistance to disease make him unfit for combat. Then rest and a special remedial diet are required to correct this condition.

A vicious circle appears to operate. Although hungry, men eat only small quantities of monotonous and unpalatable rations. Combat continues, and at the next meal, because of undernourishment, they are more exhausted than before. Exhaustion inhibits appetite, so that at this meal they eat still less. Because of external discipline or unusual conscientiousness, some may eat to keep up their strength despite lack of appetite. As fatigue mounts during prolonged combat, food so taken will lead to nausea among all except the most vigorous. The only effective preventive measure to maintain the efficiency of men in combat for extended periods is to provide varied and appetizing meals prepared from fresh food and served hot.

The OCQM consistently maintained that providing such a diet was a major objective, to be accomplished regardless of the extra work involved in administration, transportation, or storage. The Medical Corps was entirely in accord with this thesis. The common catchall expression "combat exhaustion" was merely another way of saying that most nonbattle casualties were caused by a combination of physical and psychological factors in varying proportions. The condition was very real even though a more exact diagnosis was almost impossible. It would appear to be significant that at "exhaustion centers," which existed solely to treat battle fatigue cases, a special diet was an important part of the treatment. Moreover, attractive meals were considered a major factor in rapid recovery by the wounded.[3]

Early Class I Operations

According to plan, the troops on the beachhead at first subsisted almost entirely on the operational rations they had brought with them. Large-scale issue of food began on 9 June 1944 (D plus 3) and consisted mainly of C and K Rations. But by D plus 6 more than half the rations consumed were 10-in-1's, a proportion that rose to more than 85 percent by the end of the first month on the Continent. In the second week of operations in Normandy, most First Army units drew their rations from truckheads in the Forêt de Cerisy and at Isigny, which was supplied from the ration dump established by the 5th Engineer Special Brigade near OMAHA Beach. By D plus 19, a week after it had been cut off, the Cotentin Peninsula

---

[3] (1) QM Food and Container Institute for the Armed Forces, Operation Studies 1, vol. XII, Ration Development, pp. 4–5, 38, 44, 129. (2) Littlejohn, ed., Passing in Review, ch. 33, p. 163. (3) FUSA Rpt of Opns, 1 Aug 44–22 Feb 45, IV, 184. (4) Personal Ltrs, Hawley to Littlejohn, 20 Dec 44, and Littlejohn to Hawley, 22 Dec 44. Littlejohn Reading File, vol XXXI, item 70.

was crossed by a string of Class I truck-heads.[4]

The earliest effort to supplement the restricted diet of the troops aimed at providing fresh bread and fresh coffee. Though slightly delayed by the decision to bring in additional combat troops, bakery companies with mobile British equipment began to arrive on 30 June. Within two days they were producing fresh bread in quantities that rose rapidly to a rate of 40 pounds per 100 rations. Freshly roasted and ground coffee was somewhat slower in reaching the troops. Initially, the First Army quartermaster had decided not to bring in the large, top-heavy roasters over the beaches, but he changed his mind after seeing the types of heavy equipment landed successfully by other services. The decision to separate them from the bakery companies delayed arrival of the coffee roasters about a month. Although a small amount of soluble coffee was included in the operational rations and was generally acceptable to the troops, all agreed that more coffee should be included. Additional amounts of soluble coffee (1½ pounds per 100 men) were therefore issued with the operational rations until the coffee roasters arrived.[5]

While grateful for the coffee and fresh bread, the troops had used still other means to augment their diet and relieve its monotony. McNamara reported that two or three oranges a week proved very popular. Some of the more enterprising units consumed B rations which they had hoarded on their kitchen trucks before departing from Britain.[6] Irregular though this expedient was, it did not violate sanitary and political directives as did the 9th Infantry Division quartermaster who, when his organization was in bivouac from 1 to 9 July, supplemented the ration by purchasing forty-four beef cattle and six calves from French civilian sources. There was plenty of food in Normandy, but only because it could not be transported to urban centers. Even more than the Allied landing, the preinvasion bombing of railroads and bridges had imposed a hardship upon the inhabitants of French cities, who had fared reasonably well under the German occupation. In Normandy, individual efforts to obtain from civilian sources fruit, eggs, cheese, and other items by purchase or barter were not uncommon during the first month, but ADSEC speedily reminded all supply officers that such unofficial activities were forbidden, and that livestock was among the items specifically not to be purchased according to current ETO directives.[7]

For about six weeks as the combat forces doggedly fought through a maze

---

[4] (1) *FUSA Rpt of Opns*, 20 Oct 43–1 Aug 44, VI, 133, 222–23. (2) See ch. XIII above. (3) For a description of the various rations, bulk and operational, see chapters V and XI, above.

[5] (1) Ltr, CQM to ADSEC QM, 1 Jul 44, no sub; Ltr, ADSEC QM to CQM, 3 Jul 44, sub: Estimate of QM Situation. Both in Littlejohn Reading File, vol. XXVI, items 2 and 6. (2) Memo, Chief Subs Div for CQM, 8 Jul 44, sub: Trailers for Coffee Roasters; Ltr, Fitzpatrick to Willkie, 7 Aug 44. Both in Hist Br OQMG.

[6] (1) G–4 Rpt of Opns, 1st Inf Div, 8 Jul 44. AG 319.1 (1st Inf Div). (2) Ltr, McNamara to Littlejohn, 28 Jul 44. Littlejohn Reading File, vol. XXVI, item 118.

[7] (1) 9th Inf Div Rpt of Opns, 1–31 Jul 44. XII Corps QM Corresp. (2) Ltr, Zwicker to Littlejohn, 11 Jul 44. Littlejohn Reading File, vol. XXVI, item 48.

of hedgerows, rivers, marshes, and canals, operational rations suitable for that type of combat were on hand. But even operational rations were not interchangeable. Each type had its own special purpose and on 14 July, Littlejohn noted with some concern First Army reports that the troops were consuming 140 percent of the anticipated number of 10-in-1 rations, but only 50 and 40 percent respectively of the planned number of K rations and C rations. At this rate, the entire reserve of 10-in-1's would be consumed before 31 October, the earliest date on which an immediate requisition would arrive; moreover NYPE had warned him that production of 10-in-1's was limited, and requisitions already on file would exhaust the supply then available. He suggested to McNamara that units demanding seven 10-in-1 rations per week receive one C ration augmented by one-third of a K ration, and one K ration augmented by one-third of a C ration, thus saving two 10-in-1 rations each week. He also suggested that, if tactically feasible, the B ration be issued immediately to 75 percent of the troops, instead of 50 percent as planned. Meanwhile on 8 July the B ration had been issued for the first time. Even this first issue was received by more than half of the troops in Normandy, and during the next eight days the consumption of 10-in-1's dropped so rapidly that no shortage actually materialized. This experience was merely the first of a series of potentially serious shortages which failed to become critical because of a favorable turn in the tactical situation. The average of issues in Normandy for the month of July—57 percent B rations, 28 percent 10-in-1's, and the balance in

K's and C's—fails to indicate even a potential difficulty.[8]

Levels of Class I Supply

Far more serious than the shortage of 10-in-1's was the fact that it had developed without the OCQM's becoming aware of it. Col. Robert T. Willkie, chief of the Subsistence Division, visiting the far shore on 2 and 3 July, had noted troop preferences and current consumption trends, but had failed to obtain any useful or reliable statistics on inventories or cumulative consumption. McNamara's reports, already mentioned, were no more than rough estimates expressed in round numbers. On 16 July Littlejohn wrote to Colonel Franks, the new acting quartermaster of ADSEC, outlining the statistical reports required, and a limited amount of information began to flow in. Six days later, Littlejohn asked Willkie to prepare a systematic Class I plan which would balance current rates of consumption against supplies on hand and due in through 31 October, and which would also aid in preparing accurate requisitions for the subsequent ninety days—that is, through 31 January 1945.[9]

Writing to the Chief Quartermaster from Cheltenham on 25 July, Willkie

[8] (1) Ltr, Littlejohn to McNamara, 14 Jul 44, sub: Rations for Current and Future Opns; Memo, Willkie for Littlejohn, 21 Jul 44, sub: Comparison of Planned and Actual Use of Opns Rations, 14 Jun–16 Jul 44. Both in Littlejohn Reading File, vol. XXVI, items 26 and 92. (2) *FUSA Rpt of Opns,* 20 Oct 43–1 Aug 44, VI, 199–200, 222–23.
[9] IRS, Willkie to CQM, 5 Jul 44, sub: Trip to Far Shore; Memo, CQM for Franks, 16 Jul 44, sub: Adequacy of Daily QM Rpts; IRS, CQM to Willkie, 22 Jul 44. All in Littlejohn Reading File, vol. XXVI, items 23, 71, 97.

enumerated the steps necessary to achieve Littlejohn's desired objective, a steady and reliable flow of B rations—changing to A rations as soon as possible—for troops on the Continent. First of all, the 60-day level authorized by the War Department would have to be computed "ex-ship"—in other words, ships waiting to discharge their cargoes in European waters were no longer to be considered theater assets. Then the D ration, the 5-in-1, and the 25-in-1 hospital ration, all of which were actually special purpose supplements, were no longer to be computed as part of the level of supply. But these were merely procedural reforms to simplify computation. The real problems were to shift the theater's current assets from the United Kingdom to the Continent at a rate compatible with the transfer of troops, to estimate future requirements by quantity and type of ration for both Britain and France, and to plan for direct receipt of future shipments in the United Kingdom or on the Continent as required. Conforming to Littlejohn's directive, the first portion of this plan was concerned with supply levels. Bearing in mind that troop strength on the Continent would nearly double during the interval, Willkie proposed to shift the days of Class I supply by 31 October as follows:

	23 July 44		31 Oct 44	
Type of Ration	*U.K.*	*Continent*	*U.K.*	*Continent*
Total days all types ..	64	14	59	46
A	45	0	54	0
B	8	4	1	34
C	2	2	1	2
K	2	2	2	2
10-in-1	7	6	1	8

Willkie's plan was submitted the same day to Franks, who promptly approved

it, but with the notation that continental Class I reserves, not including two days rations in the unit kitchens, were as follows on 27 July:

Ration	B	10-in-1	C and K	All types
Days	1.9	3.7	12.5	18.1

In other words, in less than three weeks the critical shortages had shifted from 10-in-1 to B rations. On the other hand, 10,900,000 B rations, roughly 13.5 days supply for the forces on the Continent, were either offshore waiting to be discharged or under way from U.K. ports.[10] Not mentioned by Franks, but a very clear corollary of the continental position as presented, was the fact that Willkie's "ex-ship" formula was no more than a pious wish. Franks merely requested Littlejohn's aid in persuading G–4 to grant a priority to move the supplies ashore, and expressed no alarm about the supply of B rations.

Admittedly, Willkie's calculations were based on limited data. The entire far shore was still a combat zone, so that the pipeline factor (21 days from ship to depot, 16 days for interdepot shipments, and 2 days from depot to truckhead) was based on experience in Britain. Willkie noted that a longer line of communications in France might require a still larger pipeline factor. Four days for losses (at sea, in the pipeline, in battle, or through overissue) and 1 day for consumption were based on current experience. Simple subtraction indicated that on 31 October the safety factor would be 16 days in the United Kingdom and 3 days on the Continent. The chief of the

---

[10] (1) Memo, Willkie for CQM, 25 Jul 44, sub: Problems of Subs Div With the U.S. ETO QM 430. (2) Ltr, QM ADSEC to CQM, 27 Jul 44, sub: Class I Plan Drafted by OCQM, APO 871 [Cheltenham]. ETO QM 430.2.

Subsistence Division considered this level dangerously low, and hoped to improve it by the end of the year.[11]

The most carefully and accurately calculated portion of the plan, based on recent experience data, involved the division of the supply level into the types of rations required. According to long-range calculations, extending into 1945, 82 percent of the troops would subsist on kitchen-prepared (A or B) rations, and 18 percent on operational rations. In actuality, for the entire European campaign the average was 78.9 percent A or B rations and 21.1 percent operational rations, so that the long-term accuracy of this forecast was excellent.[12] But even as the analysis was being prepared, tactical developments on the Continent made all previous experience data obsolete and virtually useless. July 25th will be remembered as the day that Operation COBRA was launched, crushing enemy resistance at St. Lô and leading to a decisive breakthrough. On 30 July Littlejohn wrote to Franks at ADSEC:

My dear Johnnie:

It looks as though the military situation is very much improved and the supply situation is going to be put to a severe test. I am sorry that we did not have Cherbourg stocked according to plans but that is water over the dam.[13]

The breakout from the Normandy beachhead developed into a pursuit with logistical characteristics quite different from those of combat. During the month of August consumption of operational rations averaged not 18 percent as anticipated, but 48 percent.[14] (*Table 14*) Since at this rate, the reserve of operational rations might be exhausted in a matter of days, the OCQM took corrective action. On 7 September 1944, a circular letter informed supply officers at all levels that the following maximum issues of operational rations would be enforced upon the Continent during the next thirty days:

Ration	Percent of Issue to Armies	Percent of Issue to COMZ
10-in-1	32	0
C	20	5
K	10	0

In other words, quartermasters were directed to furnish 38 percent (minimum) of B rations to all requisitioning units in the combat zone, and 95 percent B rations to units in the Communications Zone, irrespective of the desires of the receiving units. Significantly, the circular recognized that units which did not require operational rations for tactical reasons had been demanding them because the B rations did not arrive in the

---

[11] (1) IRS, Willkie to CQM, 5 Jul 44, sub: Trip to Far Shore. Littlejohn Reading File, vol. XXVI, item 23. (2) Staff Study, Subs Div for CQM, 1 Aug 44, sub: Class I Level of Supply, U.K. and Continent. ETO QM 430.

[12] Staff Study, Subs Div for CQM, 1 Aug 44, sub: Class I Level of Supply, U.K. and Continent. ETO QM 430.

[13] (1) Ruppenthal, *Logistical Support*, I, 475–80. (2) Personal Ltr, CQM to Franks, 30 Jul 44. Littlejohn Reading File, vol. XXVIA, item 125.

---

[14] The situation at the end of August was considerably more serious than was indicated by the average for an entire month. FUSA, the only reporting agency on the Continent during July, had transferred about 280,000 troops to TUSA between 29 July and 6 August; therefore, reports that TUSA consumed 90 percent operational rations in August, and FUSA 43 percent, refer to a shifting troop basis. Moreover, FUSA's 43 percent for the month actually consisted of 26 percent until 21 August and 79 percent thereafter, illustrating how Hodges' force shifted from combat to pursuit nearly three weeks after Patton's.

TABLE 14—TYPES OF RATIONS ISSUED ON THE CONTINENT

(Percent)

Month	Types A/B	Type C	Type K	Type 10-in-1
1944				
June (6–30)	—	14	15	71
July.	57	06	09	28
August.	52	14	14	20
September.	58	18	10	14
October.	79	07	05	09
November.	88	03	05	04
December.	87	03	05	05
1945				
January	91	02	03	04
February.	91	02	04	03
March.	88	04	05	03
April[a].	74	08	07	11
May.	[b]87	02	04	07
June.	94	01	03	02
July.	96	01	02	01
August.	95	01	02	02
September.	92	02	04	02

[a] Issues on the southern line of communications are included in the percentages from 1 April 1945 onward. Percentage of type rations issued in the former SOLOC area from 15 August 1944–31 March 1945 are: A/B, 69; C, 08; K, 08; 10-in-1, 07; and D, 08 SOLOC considered type D rations to be a separate category, not a supplement, and reported on that basis.

[b] To May 8 (V–E Day) 81 percent, Average this column, D-day to V–E Day, 78.9 percent.

Source: IRS, Carter to Buel Weare (no date), sub: Percentage of Type Rations Issued on Continent. Reprinted in Littlejohn, ed., Passing in Review, ch. 33, vol. II, app. 4G.

balanced proportions needed to prepare a meal. Detailed instructions for breaking down a 500-ton train or a 60-ton truck convoy into increments of balanced rations were included. The circular also specifically prohibited issuing C or K rations for the noon meal to civilian employees, prisoners of war, and to COMZ units.[15]

The changed tactical situation also called for a revision of the theater's level of supply, and on 11 September Littlejohn requested the following level for the entire theater:

---

[15] OCQM ETO Cir Ltr 43, 7 Sep 44, sub: Program for Consumption of Operational Rations.

ETO LEVEL EX-SHIP

Ration	Days of Supply
B (augmented)	37
B	10
10-in-1	8
C	2
K	3
Total	60

Even if immediately approved, this new level could hardly be expected to change the situation before mid-December. The important aspect of the new plan was the single theater-wide supply level. Despite the optimistic retention of the "ex-ship" formula, this concept reflected cargo discharge difficulties. The number of ships awaiting discharge in European waters was so large that a few returned to the United States without unloading, and many were diverted from Normandy to the United Kingdom. Cross-Channel transportation in shallow-draft vessels to minor French ports made small but fairly adequate supply shipments from Britain available on the Continent. A major consideration in retaining large reserves in Britain was the possibility of emergency airlift to the forward areas. This could be accomplished far more easily from the United Kingdom than from the crowded airfields and disorderly ration dumps in Normandy.[16]

This authorized level of Class I supplies remained unchanged until 3 March 1945, when the War Department directed that it be reduced to 50 days, including cargoes on ships in European waters.[17] During most of the European campaign actual Class I levels on the Continent were far below those authorized. In mid-October the Communications Zone held 18.6 days of supply, and the level was allowed to drop to 10.6 during the following month, when priorities were assigned for unloading ammunition. But by then the principle of supply in depth was finally being implemented, and a week's supply in each army, plus nearly 5 days in ADSEC, were important supplements to the COMZ reserve. By early February 1945, 23 days of rations in the Communications Zone, 15 days in ADSEC, and 5 to 7 days in each army constituted a total of more

than 6 weeks' rations for each combat soldier of the 12th Army Group. Meanwhile, before SOLOC headquarters was disbanded on 12 February 1945, CONAD had accumulated a reserve of 11.1 days' supply for the 734,000 troops of the 6th Army Group, including the 260,000 men of the First French Army, and Seventh Army held another 5.2 days. On 17 February the first consolidated report by the unified Communications Zone estimated 25 days of supply within its own depots for the entire theater, including French and miscellaneous forces and prisoners of war.[18]

For U.S. troops in the theater, problems of Class I supply appeared to be solved. But even as this report was submitted the Allied armies resumed the offensive toward the Rhine and difficulties with food supply promptly reappeared —first as a transportation problem for ADSEC and army level quartermasters, and almost concurrently, as a far greater problem in terms of international aid and population statistics. By definition, a level of ration supply can only be computed in terms of a definite number of people to be fed, and in the spring of 1945 such figures were always uncertain and sometimes entirely lacking. The OCQM had already encountered the problem, and in February had submitted the estimates reproduced in Table 11. But that was only the first of a series of estimates.

The difficulties are well illustrated by the experience of the ADSEC quartermaster, whose responsibility for feeding

[16] (1) Ltr, CQM ETO to TQMG, 11 Sep 44, sub: Class I Levels of Supplies in the ETO. Littlejohn Reading File, vol. XXVIII, item 75. (2) Bykofsky and Larson, *The Transportation Corps: Operations Overseas,* p. 308.

[17] Cable WARX–46911, AGWAR to ETOUSA, 3 Mar 45.

[18] (1) 12th Army Group Pers Rpts with attached 12th Army Group QM Rpts, Oct 44, Feb 45. (2) *CONAD History,* II, 680. (3) Ruppenthal, *Logistical Support,* II, 433. (4) See Chart 4.

POW's increased from 150,000 to 1,500,-000 in less than a week. Under such circumstances, a theater level of supply is only meaningful if the rations for the combat troops are rigidly segregated from those of prisoners and the civilian population, and that was not done. On the contrary, 50 percent of recovered Allied prisoners received the A ration, and after the end of hostilities all U.S. troops accepted a 10 percent reduction in their rations for the benefit of the civilian population of Europe.[19]

Uncertainty over the number of combat troops being fed was another source of difficulty. From the beginning of continental operations, statistical control over ration issues was a complicated process. In theory the daily telegram reflected the actual strength of units, but in practice there was considerable duplication. Individuals were often counted twice, at their own units and also as guests at other units or at leave centers, as students, or as hospital patients. Whole units on temporary detached duty sometimes appeared on two different telegrams, and such duplications were not always spotted by the regulating stations or issuing depots. All these factors were aggravated when troops were on the move, traveling by ship or train, and especially when they were on the march in the combat zone. Troops actually in combat were allowed a 10 percent augmentation of their rations, and the same allowance was made to service troops engaged in unusually heavy labor. Even these authorizations failed to explain the overissue of rations to U.S. troops, which averaged 115 per-cent of actual strength for the entire European campaign.[20] But these statistics should not be regarded solely as evidence of poor control over issues. When the tactical situation was critical there were frequent changes in the type of ration requisitioned, and because of an inevitable time lag in deliveries, the wrong rations often arrived and could not be used. Mobile warfare is an inherently wasteful activity, and it should not be overlooked that it was principally during periods of high overissue that the war was won.

From the point of view of a field army quartermaster, the problem of supply levels often seemed more critical than at higher echelons. The tactical situation of a specific army often shifted more abruptly than that of an entire theater, and the margin of reserves actually available to the troops became progressively smaller as they advanced away from the base depots. Third Army, changing its line of advance repeatedly and moving with great speed, first felt the pinch on 10 August 1944. Over the next two days shipments were short about 350,000 rations, so that army and unit reserves were almost completely exhausted. ADSEC relieved the situation by opening a Class I depot near Laval on 13 August. Meanwhile VIII Corps, operating separately in Brittany, enjoyed a windfall of 150 tons of perishables and 13 carloads of potatoes captured in the St. Malo area.[21]

---

[19] (1) Hist of QM ADSEC, p. 13. (2) Cable EX-21878, ETOUSA to AGWAR, 17 Mar 45. (3) ETOUSA Cir 81, 15 Jun 45.

[20] (1) Littlejohn, ed., Passing in Review, ch 33, vol. I, exhibit 8. The maximum overissue was 132 percent in September 1944, a month when large numbers of troops were being transferred across the Channel, and when much of the combat zone was shifting from operational to Class B rations. (2) See Table 16.
[21] TUSA AAR, II. QM 3, 29.

LOADING A RATION TRAIN *for the Third Army, Verdun, December 1944.*

The second week in September was the most critical period for Class I supplies in both First and Third Armies. Fortunately, Third Army captured 1,300 tons of frozen beef and 250 tons of canned meat at Homécourt near Metz on 9 September, and First Army made a smaller haul (265 tons of fresh beef) at Namur four days later. These were more than merely welcome variations of a monotonous diet. Ration issues to First Army were 260,000 on 11 September, about 100,000 less than the actual strength, and issues in Third Army for the period 8–13 September averaged 153,000 rations for a force of 213,000 men. Nobody actually starved, but First Army reported 1.5 days of supply on hand, and Third Army less than one day.[22]

The second half of September 1944 witnessed an improvement in the ration situation as sudden as the crisis in the first half. Typically, the 1st Infantry Division reported that it had received 12 days of B rations during the month, the first being issued on 18 September.[23] Third Army reported that Class I for the month had included 40 percent B rations, and that 65 percent of its troops were receiving B's at the end of September. First Army consumption was very similar.[24] The months of hard combat that followed were comparatively uneventful for army Class I officers. Dis-

[22] (1) *FUSA Rpt of Opns*, 1 Aug 44–22 Feb 45, IV, 81. (2) TUSA AAR, II, QM 5–8. (3) FUSA and

TUSA G–4 Periodic Rpts for period 10–16 Sep 44. 12th Army Group, 319.1, G–4 Rpts.
[23] 1st Inf Div G–4 Rpt of Activities in September [1944]. Hist Br OQMG.
[24] (1) TUSA AAR, II, QM 6, 29. (2) *FUSA Rpt of Opns*, 1 Aug 44–22 Feb 45, IV, 93.

continuance of the Red Ball express in mid-November was a minor event, as rail service had been improving steadily. COMZ continued to forward Class I supplies direct to the armies until the last week in November. At that time Depot Q–179 at Liège, serving First and Ninth Armies, and Q–178 at Verdun, supporting Third Army, assumed this mission, with an initial level of 4.8 days. Meanwhile reserves had reached 13.4 days in First Army, 5.9 days in the Third, and 9.8 days in Ninth Army. Except in the First Army, where consumption of B rations dropped from 82 percent on 15 December to 49 percent on the 21st, the German Ardennes counteroffensive made little impact on the type of rations consumed. First Army also drew 6 days rations direct from the ADSEC depots around Liège while its own ration reserves were being evacuated. Third Army, feeding 100,000 more men at the end of December than at the beginning, nevertheless managed to issue 76 percent B rations during the entire month.[25]

During the quiet period that followed almost 80 percent of the rations consumed were of the bulk type, and the receipts of fresh meat and vegetables improved so appreciably that the B ration was officially redesignated an A ration. Late in January, Littlejohn attempted to reduce the Class I levels in the army dumps to 5 days. He contended that the armies seldom reported their reserves accurately and tended to leave supplies behind when they moved forward. On a recommendation from 12th Army Group General Lee set a compromise level of 7

days, and on 12 February, when SOLOC was disbanded, the same level was applied to the 6th Army Group. Actually, a small excess of operational rations was accumulated during this period of tactical stability, which proved very useful when the armies crossed the Rhine in March. By mid-April, the conditions of the pursuit across France eight months earlier were almost duplicated. ADSEC moved forward from Namur to Bonn, Germany, on 7 April, but no advance depots were opened, and supplies continued to move directly to the armies from Liège, Verdun, and Metz. By 21 April ration levels were 2.3 days in the First Army, 4.3 in the Third, 4.1 in the Seventh, and 4.4 in the Ninth. ADSEC had not moved any reserves forward, the Rhine bridges were still precarious makeshifts, and the forces east of the Rhine, including prisoners of war and displaced persons, were increasing rapidly. The 12th Army Group considered the Class I situation critical, but no U.S. units actually suffered. A shift to operational rations, comparable to that of the previous August, occurred especially in the First and Third Armies, where they accounted for 70 to 80 percent of all issues. Efforts to supplement these rations with butter and fresh meat, as well as fresh bread, were largely successful.[26]

Balancing the Ration

Related to the problem of attaining a dependable level of bulk rations was the

---

[25] (1) *FUSA Rpt of Opns*, 1 Aug 44–22 Feb 45, IV, 112. (2) TUSA AAR II, QM 13. (3) Ruppenthal, *Logistical Support*, II, 189.

[26] (1) Continental Operating Instrs, OCQM ETO, 19 Feb 45, p. 41. (2) Memo, CQM for G–4, 24 Feb 45, sub: Levels of QM Supply. Littlejohn Reading File, vol. XXXIII, item 133. (3) Progress Rpt, Status of Rations on Continent as of 8 Mar 45, Control Div COMZ, 15 Mar 45. ETO 430.

need to maintain them in a state of balance. On this subject, one of General Littlejohn's subsistence officers observed that "getting a sound Type A or B ration to troops in a theater of operations is far more a matter of intelligent, far-sighted transportation arrangements than a pure subsistence problem."[27] Nowhere was this contention better demonstrated than in the effort to deliver balanced bulk rations to retail consumers of Quartermaster services. The balanced ration was predicated on the availability of all the components necessary for maximum nutritional value and palatability, but the fact that a balanced B ration contained approximately 110 separate components constituted an inherent vulnerability to mishandling. The loss or misplacement of several components had the effect of disrupting the balance, and thereby the menus prescribed by the OCQM. Local corrective action to plan balanced meals further unbalanced reserve supplies.

This problem had been partially anticipated by the prestowing and commodity loading of vessels, with each carrying balanced bricks of Class I supplies.[28] The early bricks consisted principally of operational rations, while later vessels carried an increasing proportion of balanced B rations. This innovation was enormously valuable, especially since months elapsed before the beach dumps in Normandy evolved into base depots capable of sorting supplies effectively. During those months NYPE acted as a Class I base depot for the ETO, and inevitably the normal diffi-

culties between a base and an advance depot were multiplied by the tremendous distance and time lag involved. But the best proof of the value of commodity loading was that far greater difficulties and adjustments were involved in obtaining the few supplies requisitioned by other methods. Tea, cocoa, corned beef, and a few condiments were procured in England and hence omitted from commodity-loaded shipments. Getting these few items across the Channel and distributing them properly among depots on the Continent took much careful planning, co-ordination with other headquarters, and elaborate precautions against loss or pilferage.[29]

Difficulties with commodity loading, while not excessive for a large and complicated operation, were considerable, and centered around the problem of substitution. The practice of substituting items for unavailable ones began at zone of interior depots which shipped rations to NYPE without giving adequate notice of the nature of the substitution. For example, corn that was substituted for beets in the zone of interior was inventoried in the overseas depot as so much more corn. When beets were called for by the consuming organizations in compliance with the theater menu and they were unavailable, the issuing depot was in a position to substitute any one of several canned vegetables rather than maintain the original substitution of corn for beets. This chain reaction of successive substitutions had the effect of aggravating imbalances, with some items becoming excessive while others were in limited supply or

---

[27] Littlejohn, ed. Passing in Review, ch. 33, vol. I, p. 76.
[28] OTCQM TSFET Operational Study 14, exhibit A, app. E.

[29] Littlejohn, ed., Passing in Review, ch. 33, vol. I, p. 83.

exhausted. Indicating how such an un-regulated practice ultimately affected the menu, Littlejohn complained that the substitution of Boston butts for smoked ham without a corresponding reduction in pork loins increased the amount of fresh pork served from four to seven times in fourteen days and the substitution of dessert fruits for pie fruits contributed to a monotonous diet, rejected foods, and excessive waste.[30]

Though Littlejohn's criticisms were valid, the OCQM was ultimately responsible for many of these discrepancies by its failure to submit requisitions to NYPE early enough to allow ninety days for delivery. From the port's viewpoint even this amount of time was insufficient if the local depots supporting NYPE were to make good their shortages from secondary depots, rather than provide free substitutions from available stocks in the hurried effort to meet the ETO's delivery deadlines.[31]

Recognizing the need for closer co-ordination, NYPE sent a succession of observers and liaison officers to the ETO. Once he was aware of the necessity, Littlejohn attempted to maintain an order and shipping time of 120 days. This effort was not very successful because changes in theater policy regarding feeding of non-U.S. personnel demanded repeated revisions of Class I requisitions. On investigation it developed that ship diversions were another major source of difficulty. Even a perfectly balanced brick destined for the United Kingdom was of limited usefulness if landed on the Continent, or vice versa. Usually such diversions were ordered to make available critical supplies of other classes, or even of other technical services, that were aboard.

Gradually, all these difficulties were overcome. The increased order and shipping time operated to decrease substitutions, and the OCQM arranged to be informed by cable whenever such action was unavoidable. Local distribution menus were revised to help use up excesses. Commodity loading of ships, already described, reduced the number of ship diversions. Under Littlejohn's persistent prodding, his Military Planning Division and the Transportation Branch of the Storage and Distribution Division ultimately organized depots in Britain and on the Continent into one coherent system.[32]

Obstacles to the forward delivery of the desired ration components were not confined to difficulties between the OCQM and the zone of interior. Every transfer point and every handling opera-

---

[30] (1) Personal Ltr, Col Evans, NYPE, to CQM, 31 May 44. Littlejohn Reading File, vol. XXIV, item 103. (2) Ltr, CQM to NYPE, 25 Jun 44, sub: Substitution for Requisitioned Components of Subs. Littlejohn Collection, Sec. I. (3) The temporary excess of fresh pork resulted from Littlejohn's objection to salt-packed ham. This item was more than 50 percent salt and packing material by weight, and the packages "wept" brine that ruined other food beneath them. By August 1944 a satisfactory smoked overseas ham was being shipped and the excess of fresh pork in the ration was discontinued.
[31] (1) Ltr, Overseas Supply Off NYPE to CG SOS [ca. 15 Jul 44], sub: Substitution of Subs Items on ETO Requisition. ETO 319.25. (2) Critical comment on preliminary draft MS by Col Hickey, 19 Nov 54. Hist Br OQMG.

[32] Memo, Maj H. M. Jewett for Chief Plng and Control Br NYPE, 12 Aug 44, sub: Rpt of Trip to OCQM ETO; Ltr, CQM to TQMG, 12 Jul 44, sub: ETO Procedure for Requisition of QM Class I Supplies (Exhibit B in Maj Jewett's Rpt). ETO 319.25.

tion along the continental axis of supply constituted a threat to balance. Contributing to what has been described as a "quiet nightmare" were: (1) the tactical necessity of rapid unloading despite the absence of materials-handling equipment on the beaches; (2) the accumulation of scrambled supplies which required sorting before they could be balanced and loaded onto trains; (3) breaking up of balanced trains by an irresponsible shunting of cars en route to the depots; (4) emphasis on tonnage rather than selectivity during the build-up in forward areas; and (5) pilferage all along the line of communications, beginning with the stevedores at the beaches.[33] In retrospect, probably the most serious fault of all was a lack of adequate documentation. Undocumented cargo could be handled with a comfortable anonymity, and it was almost impossible for inspectors to trace the errors, sins of omission, and outright thefts committed along the route.[34]

Farther inland, still other disruptive influences were at work. Late in October, congestion of transportation and receiving facilities at Paris forced the suspension of shipments into that depot. This embargo was imposed abruptly, after portions of four commodity-loaded cargoes had been shipped to Paris from Le Havre, and nearly 8,000 long tons of unbalanced, unsorted cargo had to be segregated, balanced, and shipped to Liège instead. Colonel Franks, the Deputy Chief Quartermaster, personally had to suspend all shipments of B rations from Le Havre for seven days while most of the Quartermaster personnel in Channel Base Section applied themselves to sorting the ration components. When the German "Bulge" counteroffensive caused a similar backlog to pile up at Cherbourg, Col. Chapin Weed, the commander of Q–171, arranged to have several Cherbourg streets blocked off and used them for open storage. Here the cargo of a Class I ship could be stored as a single unit until transportation became available. This expedient required the co-operation of the mayor of Cherbourg, the port quartermaster, and the quartermaster of Normandy Base Section.[35]

But these were isolated and unusual accomplishments brought about by the personal efforts of senior QMC officers. In mid-September Littlejohn noted that there were 63,212,685 pounds of unbalanced supplies, roughly ten million rations, in the theater, and a month later Willkie reported that 35 percent of the food on the Continent was still unbalanced.[36] Steps were taken to set up intermediate collecting and sorting points at Soissons and Sommesous, which, it will be recalled, had recently been termi-

---

[33] (1) Rpt, Problems in Connection with Securing Balanced Rations, n.d.; Memo, Chief Subs Div for CQM, 21 Oct 44, sub: The Distr Factor in the Subs Level. Hist Br OQMG. (2) Littlejohn, ed., Passing in Review, ch. 33, vol. I, pp. 84–85.

[34] Critical comment on preliminary MS by Col Fenton, 19 Feb 54. Hist Br OQMG.

[35] Memo, DCQM for CQM [ca. 1 Nov 44], sub: Class I Offloading at Le Havre; Memo, Chief Subs Div for CQM, 29 Sep 44, sub: Current Class I Problems; IRS, Chief Water Sec Transportation Br to Chief S&D Div, 23 Dec 44, sub: Trip to Normandy Base Sec. All in Hist Br OQMG.

[36] (1) Memo, CQM for QM Div Chiefs, 25 Sep 44, sub: Directive 1—Review of Requisitions. Littlejohn Reading File, vol XXVIIIA, item 192. (2) IRS, Chief Subs Div to CQM, 21 Oct 44, sub: Distr Factor in the Subs Level. Hist Br OQMG.

nals of the Red Ball express. Hopes were that Class I components could be matched up at these sites for balanced delivery to the armies, but Willkie was pessimistic about the effectiveness of this measure. He was particularly incensed by the failure of G–4 to provide a steady, programed flow of transportation to the inland depots. Even the OCQM representative at G–4 headquarters failed to understand that a series of last-minute opportunities to forward one or two freight cars to various destinations was no substitute for continuity.[37] On sending one of his assistants to the field to continue the missionary effort in favor of balanced shipments, Willkie remarked dourly:

The puerile mind immediately thinks that once intermediate depots are established we do not have to worry further about how goods are shipped there. It makes no difference that you are in the midst of unloading a ship at the time, that the ship is loaded (as all ships are loaded) in layers, and that it takes the bottom part to balance the top part. To such a mind it is all right to start shipping in bulk at that particular moment; shipping in bulk—undoing all the work that has been done in the U.S. and destroying possibly two million rations because two million half rations are left at one end and two million half rations moved forward.[38]

Willkie's pessimism was justified. The Soissons and Sommesous locations were quickly left behind by the armies and never developed into important depots. The sites ultimately chosen, Liège and Verdun, were so far forward that as-sembling reserves of food there progressed very slowly. Meanwhile the supply of the troops remained a hand-to-mouth affair, in which the safety factor was very small. If the armies received unbalanced rations they ate unbalanced rations, for there were no local reserves to make good the deficits. Toward the end of 1944, the OCQM was still seriously concerned.[39] Measures had been taken in October to ship 18,000 long tons of selected ration components from the United Kingdom to combine with unbalanced rations on the Continent, but a carefully prepared plan to ship them by small coasters to specific small French ports had to be canceled. Liberty ships were offered as a substitute, but these could not be brought into the same ports. Unloaded at major ports, the supplies would not arrive quickly enough to alleviate the shortages.[40] The unbalanced state of nonoperational rations, plus the allowances which had to be made for the pipeline factor, continued to reduce the levels on hand for distribution. With such a threat to the adequate delivery of nonoperational rations, it was clear that a drain on the supplies of combat rations could be expected. That such a solution could hardly be satisfactory was evident from the fact that this was precisely what the

---

[37] Memo, Chief Subs Div for CQM, 1 Oct 44, sub: Collecting Point for Subs Supplies; IRS, Chief Subs Div to Chief Non-Perishables Br, 8 Oct 44, no sub. Both in Hist Br OQMG.

[38] IRS of 8 Oct 44 cited n. 37, above.

[39] Memo, Chief Subs for CQM, 21 Oct 44, sub: The Distr Factor in the Subs Level; Memo, Chief Subs Div for CQM, 19 Nov 44, sub: Operational Rations; Memo, Chief Subs Div for CQM, 5 Dec 44, sub: Balancing of B Rations. All in Hist Br OQMG.

[40] Memo, Chief Subs Div for Chief Mil Plng Div, 25 Nov 44, sub: Class I ship Reqmts from U.K., and Inds; Memo, Chairman Tonnage Committee OCQM for DCQM, 5 Dec 44, sub: Movement of Supplies ex U.K. Hist Br OQMG.

use of A and B rations was designed to obviate.

The only real cure for the problem of balances would have required a surplus of labor at the ports to inventory the backlog as well as supplies continually being received, and a surplus of rail transportation for interdepot hauls. Neither of these surpluses was available until after the end of hostilities, but various expedients alleviated the situation. *(See Chart 3.)*

One measure that proved helpful, although misunderstood and criticized by the G–4 Division and even by General Somervell, was the accumulation of large reserves in the forward portion of the Communications Zone, a process that began in December. The proportion of unbalanced rations was somewhat reduced merely by assembling them, and the concentration of large, partially balanced tonnages at Liège and Verdun assured that whatever balanced supplies were available were located where they could be utilized. Another advantage of this concentration was that specific balancing components only had to be forwarded to these two locations. For example, on 11 February 1945, coffee was the most critical ration item on the Continent, with only 7.6 days of supply on hand. If coffee was disregarded, sugar, of which there was 19.7 days on hand, became the determining factor. But for the OCQM the significant fact was that discharge and forwarding of an additional 12.1 days' supply of coffee— about 1,650 long tons—would raise the over-all level of balanced rations for the whole theater by 12.1 days, or 28,350,000 rations. The tonnage involved was small enough to be handled as a special shipment and Littlejohn always tried to

have such cargo forwarded from Great Britain or the coastal depots by air, or by LST to a specially designated port. Since these supplies were always critical and the danger of diversion or pilferage was unusually great, an officer normally accompanied each shipment.[41]

The OCQM finally came to the conclusion that, under conditions prevailing in the ETO, attempts to maintain rations in balance while in prolonged transit would never be completely successful. Repeated experience demonstrated that trainloads lost their identity and became unbalanced if they were in transit more than forty-eight hours. Then an additional inventory and balancing process was necessary at the next stop along the line of communications. It followed that such stops should be held to a minimum. The OCQM held that the concept of phased supply in depth should not be applied to rations, but that they should move directly from ports or base depots to forward "filler issue" depots where enough reserves would accumulate to make possible balanced daily issues to armies or other major consumers. This view prevailed even after transportation had improved in the spring of 1945. For example, in March plans were for new advance depots in Germany to be supplied rations direct from Charleroi instead of from Liège and Verdun, which had now become intermediate depots. An additional advantage of this procedure was that it would prevent overcrowding and confusion at the intermediate depots,

---

[41] (1) Daily QM COMZ Situation Rpt, 11 Feb 45. Hist Br OQMG. (2) Computation of coffee tonnage based on Littlejohn, ed., Passing in Review, ch. 33, vol. II, app. 6F. (3) See Chart 4, above.

such as had occurred at Paris the previous October.[42]

Balanced rations were a particular obsession of Colonel Willkie, who possibly attached excessive importance to this aspect of supply. In May 1945 Littlejohn complained to Col. Robert F. Carter, who had replaced Willkie as Chief of Subsistence a month earlier, that excluding unbalanced rations from supply level statistics gave an erroneous impression of the status of subsistence, especially if the shortage was only "a little salt, pepper, cocoa, or some other innocuous article."[43] He directed that all stocks comprising 75 percent or more of balanced rations be so tabulated. Stocks representing less than three-quarters of a balanced ration should be reported simply as tonnage. They could be easily utilized in special menus for non-U.S. personnel. As for the "innocuous articles," the OCQM authorized and sometimes succeeded in distributing a condiment kit, which weighed about 22 pounds and accompanied each 1,000 rations. But breakdown into extremely small quantities was technically difficult, and these kits were always in short supply in the ETO.

Perishable Subsistence

The Cold Storage Depot Plan

In the United Kingdom, the British Government had provided civilian-operated cold storage facilities for the Americans, and prior to D-day U.S. troops had only minor opportunities to gain experience in this field.[44] For the OVERLORD operation, plans were strictly in accordance with official doctrine. As with other subsistence, computation of requirements was a QMC function, but providing the fresh meat and butter required by the troops was a responsibility divided among several technical services. The Transportation Corps, using refrigerated rail cars or mobile refrigerated trailers, moved perishables from reefer vessels to static cold storage plants built or rehabilitated by the Engineers, and maintained by Engineer personnel. Here supplies were received and stored by QM refrigeration companies (fixed). As required, the supplies were issued to QM refrigeration companies (mobile) which transported them either to supply points, or to advance depots where army refrigeration companies exchanged empty trailers for full ones. Maintenance of equipment, spare parts, and such operating supplies as freon or ammonia were the separate responsibility of the service operating the equipment, with two exceptions: the Engineers furnished ice to the Transportation Corps for refrigerated rail cars, and the QMC arranged to maintain the refrigerating units on trailers operated by the Transportation Corps.[45] Since refrig-

[42] (1) IRS, DCQM to G–4 COMZ [ca. 25 Apr 45], sub: Mission of Depots. Hist Br OQMG. (2) Ltr, CQM to QM CBS, 2 Mar 45, sub: Mission of the Charleroi Depot Area. OTCQM TSFET Operational Study 5, exhibit B–10. (3) Littlejohn, ed., Passing in Review, ch. 33, vol. I, pp. 85, 88–90.
[43] (1) Memo, CQM for Carter, 22 May 45, sub: Statistical Rpts, Stock Levels, Balanced Rations, etc. Littlejohn Reading File, vol. XXXVI, item 58. (2) Littlejohn, ed., Passing in Review, ch. 33, vol. I, pp. 41, 164–65.
[44] (1) Littlejohn, ed., Passing in Review, ch. 33, vol. I, p. 95. (2) See ch. X, above.
[45] (1) The Transportation Corps operated 2 mobile refrigeration companies (actually heavy QM truck companies) in the ETO, and the QMC 10 (1 with each army and 5 with COMZ). (2) Littlejohn, ed., Passing in Review, ch. 33, vol. I, p. 94.

erated trailers were components of motor vehicles, their maintenance, apart from refrigeration units, was an Ordnance responsibility.

The above division of responsibility was followed in detail in OVERLORD planning. The OCQM proposed to supply perishables to 40 percent of the troops ashore by July, and to 90 percent by the end of the year. The Engineer construction plan for the necessary cold storage space involved a capacity of 35,-000 long tons by February 1945.[46] The objective of this program—providing ¾ pound of perishables per man to 1,800-000 troops on the Continent by 1 January 1945—sounded modest, but the proposed 60-day level of supply was actually more than was ever achieved before V–E Day. For the first three months, up to 1,000 tons of perishables per week were to be ferried across the Channel in small reefers and issued immediately without being stored. Meanwhile, reserves were to be built up in the Rennes-Laval area along with other U.S. supplies and on D plus 90 issues from continental depots were to begin.

From the first, doubts arose as to the feasibility of this program. As early as November 1943 the Chief Engineer suggested that the OQMG plan to use Quartermaster labor if relocation of prefabricated reefer warehouses became necessary after they had been set up, and on 27 December he informed the Chief Quartermaster that probably only 170 of the 206 standard refrigeration units planned would be available by D plus 240. Meanwhile, Littlejohn had decided that still more refrigerated space was re-

quired, and on 18 April representatives of the Chief Quartermaster, Chief of Transportation, and Chief Engineer met to reconsider the whole question. No change in the division of responsibilities arose from this meeting. But the Engineer representative announced that the whole storage construction program had been phased back 90 days—no newly constructed storage space would be available on D plus 90, and only 6,336 tons on D plus 181.[47] The Chief Quartermaster found this program inadequate. The Chief of Engineers replied that it was not possible to change plans up to D plus 90, but that the total requirement could be met by D plus 240. Littlejohn then appealed to General Ross for reefer ships to be used as temporary storage, a solution that had already been proposed to the Chief of Transportation in Washington. As before, this proposal was turned down for lack of shipping. The QM annex to the OVERLORD Administrative Plan reiterated the scheduled plan of distribution and the division of functions already described, but did not specify the amount of storage to be provided by the Engineers, and the Engineer annex to the plan made no mention of construction of refrigerated warehouses. Equipment to rehabilitate existing cold storage plants was stockpiled in Great Britain, and this portion of the program was expected to proceed on schedule.[48]

---

[46] OTCQM TSFET Operational Study 14, exhibit A, sec. III.

[47] (1) Perishable Subsistence on the Continent, June 1944–June 1945, pp. 2–3. Reprinted in Littlejohn, ed., Passing in Review, ch. 37. (2) QM Supply in ETO, II, 20.

[48] (1) FECOMZ Admin Plan, 15 May 44, QM ann. 8. (2) Perishable Subsistence on the Continent, June 1944–June 1945, p. 4.

Early Operations

In July, when perishables earmarked for the Continent began to arrive, the commodity-loaded refrigerated vessels carried their supplies to England where the cargo was split, reserves being stored in Britain while the balance was transferred onto smaller reefer ships bound for the Continent. But cold storage space in England was quickly filled, so that the transatlantic reefers had to ride at anchor while an insufficient number of smaller shuttle reefers carried their cargo to the Continent a few hundred tons at a time. The resulting delays in unloading occasionally extended to a month, and inevitably created friction between the Transportation and Quartermaster Corps.[49]

Meanwhile an advance detachment of the 283d Refrigeration Company (Fixed) arrived on the Continent on 11 July, and in a matter of hours was at work repairing 280 tons of cold storage space in a shell-damaged dairy at Isigny. After this the 283d, whose prescribed mission was limited to moving cases of frozen meats in and out of cold storage rooms, rehabilitated 80 long tons of cold storage at Les Veys and 375 tons in the naval arsenal at Cherbourg.[50]

Perishable supply operations began on the Continent on 15 July, when the refrigerated British coaster *Empress of Athol* brought in 489 long tons of balanced meats and butter to OMAHA Beach. Its cargo was unloaded by Dukws and distributed to supply points in open trucks. The *Empress of Athol* made two more trips at seven-day intervals, and on 31 July the refrigerator ship *Albangarez* carrying 2,500 long tons of perishables berthed at Cherbourg, where unloading by Dukws was also necessary. Apart from the rehabilitation work just described, no storage space was available on the Continent, and the arrival of the *Albangarez* immediately created a problem. Fortunately, by this time the 3601st and 3612th Transportation Corps Refrigeration Companies and the 279th and 484th QM Refrigeration Companies, all mobile units with motor-drawn trailers, had arrived, and were able to distribute the supplies without spoilage. This was a fundamentally inefficient method of operation, but unfortunately it had to continue for months as successive vessels docked and the storage space in Cherbourg did not materially increase.[51]

The QM Section of ADSEC found that if deliveries of perishable subsistence were not to come to a standstill, it would have to undertake all phases of the operation from shipside to truckheads. It reconnoitered cold storage and ice-manufacturing plants, and directly supervised unloading of reefer boats at ports. It controlled the operation of all mobile refrigeration companies, Transportation Corps as well as Quartermaster, and directed delivery of all perishables to truckheads, distribution points, or cold storage. Meanwhile the fixed refrigeration companies, under ADSEC direction, rehabilitated cold storage and ice-manufacturing plants and also assumed responsibility for their operation and maintenance. After the St. Lô breakthrough, QM personnel

[49] Cable Ex–43642, Hq ETOUSA to AGWAR, 17 Aug 44.

[50] Littlejohn, ed., *Passing in Review*, ch. 33, vol. I, p. 96.

[51] *Ibid.*, p. 97.

found and rehabilitated an additional 1,725 tons of storage space located as follows:[52]

St. Lô	250
Rennes	150
Le Mans	225
Redon	800
Angers	300

This space was less useful than anticipated, since the pre-D-day plan for a supply base in Brittany did not materialize. On 25 August the armies entered Paris, the refrigeration center of France, but the availability and usefulness of its tremendous refrigerated storage space could not be immediately determined. The real problem—storage capacity at the ports—was aggravated by the triumphant eastward advance. Two days later, with the D plus 90 deadline for the beginning of major cold storage operations on the Continent a week away, Littlejohn presented a somewhat alarming analysis of the situation to General Lee. Quartermaster troops had completed rehabilitation of 1,390 tons of space on the Continent, but only 900 tons were at Cherbourg and smaller Normandy ports where they could accept cargo directly from reefer vessels. No new construction had been completed and only one project had been begun by the Engineers. This project would ultimately provide another 2,250 tons of cold storage in ammunition caves near Cherbourg, but only after major technical difficulties were overcome. With this exception all Engineer troops were engaged in repairing railroads and

bridges behind the armies which were pursuing the enemy across France. There was no prospect that any Engineers would become available for cold storage construction, and in any case Littlejohn questioned the advisability of more new construction in the current fluid situation. It was not yet clear where space would be needed. The OCQM had become convinced that for health reasons troops who had been eating operational rations for more than a month would each require a full pound per day of perishables when the pursuit ended. Moreover, ten weeks of practical experience had demonstrated that cold storage space used for retail distribution of mixed supplies was only 66 percent as efficient as anticipated, so that all space requirements had been increased by 50 percent. Even if the original Engineer plan had been carried out in full, the deficit in cold storage space would still be 26,433 long tons at the end of December 1944.[53]

Transportation and Storage Problems

The sole solution, from the viewpoint of the OCQM—and one that had been repeatedly presented to the War Department, The Quartermaster General, the New York Port of Embarkation, and ETO headquarters—called for use of 10,000 tons of small, slow, reefers from the United States as floating storage. If these vessels could be held in Channel waters an average of ten days beyond the normal unloading period they could

[52] (1) *Ibid.*, p. 99. (2) Perishable Subsistence on the Continent, June 1944–June 1945, pp. 4–6.

[53] (1) Ltr, Littlejohn to Lee, 27 Aug 49, sub: Meat and Perishable Reqmts for the Continent. OQMG ETO 430. (2) Perishable Subsistence on the Continent, June 1944–June 1945, pp. 9–11.

be docked at the nearest ports as rapidly as these could be captured and opened. The advantages of such a system were numerous and self-evident. Since small reefers would go to France and most large reefers to the United Kingdom, the OCQM considered that a shorter turnaround time would be insured for the larger reefers. Shortening the distance between the port and the combat forces would relieve the pressure on overland transportation, reduce the number of handlings required, and contribute to the continuity of supply essential to any successful military operation. General Lee agreed with this analysis, and sent a cable to that effect to the War Department on 30 August.[54]

This proposal represented a considerable scaling-down of Littlejohn's original demands, and was in accord with current COMZ recommendations to the War Department regarding all types of shipping, endorsed by General Eisenhower. Nevertheless, NYPE answered that this procedure was not favorably considered. The reefer shortage was as critical in the Pacific as it was in the ETO, and the latter's allocation was limited to five fast reefers with a capacity of 23,000 tons and five slow ones carrying 12,000 tons. A fixed number of vessels meant, therefore, that the monthly shipments from the zone of interior were dependent on the promptness of discharge and return of the

ships from the ETO. Allowing a six week turnaround for fast vessels, and seven weeks for slow, NYPE could deliver 22,500 reefer tons per month. This calculation was based on a maximum of twelve days for discharge—a very optimistic estimate. For a variety of reasons quite apart from the reefer-for-storage concept, cargoes were seldom discharged in less than twenty days.[55]

Since the reefers could not be held for storage purposes and storage facilities ashore were not available, the OCQM decided on 31 August that the only alternative was to request NYPE to curtail the delivery of perishables to Britain for a ten-day period and to reduce deliveries to the Continent by 25 percent. This reduction was followed a week later by a formal request to reduce the October and November shipments of perishables by fifteen thousand and ten thousand tons, respectively.[56] In view of the amount of heat generated by the reefer issue, NYPE was surprisingly cool to this suggestion. Among other considerations, the effect would be to undermine the position of the port in its representations to the Chief of Transportation in Washington and the War Shipping Administration for greater allocations of reefer ships. Col. Ira K. Evans warned Littlejohn that a cutback at this time would be reinstated later only with great difficulty. In particular,

---

[54] (1) Memo, Actg CQM for G–4 COMZ, 11 Aug 44, sub: Refrigeration Reqmts; Ltr, CQM to G–4 COMZ, 22 Aug 44, sub: Supply (of) Fresh Meat . . . ; Cable J13612, ETOUSA to AGWAR, 30 Aug 44. All in OQMG ETO 430. (2) Personal Ltr, Littlejohn to Evans, 3 Sep 44, sub: Reefer Ships. Littlejohn Reading File, vol. XXVIII, item 23.

[55] (1) Rpt, Perishable Subs on the Continent, June 1944–June 1945, p. 12. Hist Br OQMG. (2) Wardlow, *The Transportation Corps: Responsibilities, Organization, and Operations*, pp. 287–91.

[56] (1) Memo, Chief Subs Div for Chief Plans and Training Div, 31 Aug 44, a sub: Review of Reefer Reqmts. Hist Br OQMG. (2) Ltr, CQM to CG NYPE, 8 Sep 44, sub: Re-estimation of Reefer Reqmts. ETO 400.233.

the British needed to rebuild civilian reserves sacrificed to support NEPTUNE.[57]

To conserve reefer space, Littlejohn suggested to General Gregory that larger shipments of such processed meats as smoked ham, *cervelat,* bologna, and salami might be made. Experts at NYPE agreed that this was feasible and might save 33 percent of reefer space. Packed in well-ventilated dry storage, these meats were delivered to the ETO through the winter months with relatively little spoilage. Fresh eggs were also shipped successfully by this method. Serious losses—estimated at 25 percent—were noted among oranges, but investigators found that the selection of thick-skinned varieties overcame this problem.[58]

As with balanced rations, many of the difficulties in the forward shipment of perishables can be traced to deficiencies in handling and transportation. Unloading practices were consistently poor from August through November. The War Department, in fact, claimed that this was the chief reason for the shipping crisis.[59] At Le Havre, which had been opened early in November, the irregular rate of unloading resulted in a decline of 50 percent in the amounts of perishables discharged. The fundamental

causes were poor co-ordination between the port quartermaster and the base section quartermaster and the lowly status of the QM Section within the port organization.

One day unloading activities at Le Havre came to a complete halt with the explanation that no rail cars were available, although at the same time a local cold storage plant contained 1,600 tons of unoccupied cold storage space. The real explanation, of course, was that the dock-to-rail-car transfer was entirely a Transportation Corps operation while the cold storage space was controlled by the QMC. What was required was a QM liaison officer on the job at all times to provide the support of his service as required.

The discharge process was actually a complicated one, requiring careful co-ordination all along the line for efficient performance. The OCQM had to receive advance notice of the arrival of reefers in European waters, select a port, and arrange a berthing priority with G–4. Usually low priority deck cargo had to be cleared off and dispatched to a depot before the hatches could be opened. Then unloading could begin —very often into Dukws, since alongside berths were always scarce. Meanwhile the Military Railway Service had to assemble reefer rail cars at the designated port. They had to arrive in time so that the local QM representative could have them cleaned, iced (with salt added), cooled to a safe temperature, and inspected by a veterinarian. This was a critical operation, for cars not utilized on schedule had to be re-iced and reinspected. Moreover, cars not ready on schedule could not be used in making up the daily train allotted by

[57] (1) Personal Ltr, Evans to CQM, 26 Aug 44. Littlejohn Reading File, vol. XXVII, item 130. (2) The U.S. Army allocation of cold-storage space in the U.K. was nearly doubled for the period April–July 1944. See *QM Supply in ETO,* II, 82.
[58] (1) Ltr, CQM COMZ ETO to TQMG, 14 Sep 44, sub: Ham—Specifications and Method of Shipping; Ltr, TQMG to CQM COMZ ETO, 6 Oct 44, sub: Overseas Ham and Method of Shipment. Both in ETO 431. (2) Ltr, Evans to CQM, 4 Oct 44, no sub; Memo, Chief Subs Div for CQM, 22 Dec 44, no sub. Both in Hist Br OQMGM.
[59] (1) Cable WARX 43793, CofT WD to ETOUSA, 9 Oct 44. (2) Ruppenthal, *Logistical Support,* II, 127–30.

G–4, and cars of nonperishable rations were often substituted. While this practice was economical of scarce tonnage, it meant that trains allotted for perishables frequently included other types of cargo, and thus the position of the OCQM in its efforts to obtain higher priorities for reefer trains was weakened. There was the additional hazard that a few reefer cars attached to a miscellaneous train might suffer spoilage while delayed en route, and a very low probability that the cars would be speedily emptied and returned to the correct port for another load. Such haphazard practices still further reduced the speed with which reefer ships could be returned to NYPE and reduced deliveries to the troops. Early in December, the OCQM was forced to recommend a decrease in the number of fresh meat meals in the COMZ from twelve to seven per week, and to hold the allowance of the armies to ten fresh meat meals per week.[60]

One reason for this decrease was undoubtedly the decision to provide a turkey dinner to the troops for Thanksgiving. It was estimated that a holiday-size portion (one and a half pounds) equaled three normal meat meals, and that the greater bulkiness of poultry, when compared to beef or pork, required refrigerated storage space equal to four and a half normal meat meals. Nevertheless, a commitment to provide turkey to all the troops on the Continent had been made in September, before

the difficulties of an extended line of communications were fully understood. The general opinion was that, irrespective of the morale value of a holiday meal, failure to meet a widely publicized commitment would have a very unfavorable effect. By 18 November apples, oranges, fresh eggs, onions, cabbage, and 1,604 tons of turkey brought in on the *Great Republic* had been distributed by the OCQM, principally in refrigerated vans held at the port awaiting this shipment. The trucks of the mobile bakery companies were also very helpful in this emergency. Some of the combat troops did not receive the special ration until one or two days after Thanksgiving, and a few missed the turkey dinner altogether for tactical reasons, but the OCQM was generally credited with a notable feat of distribution under great difficulties.[61]

Overland movement of perishables has already been mentioned as a limiting factor on clearance of port warehouses, and thus a source of difficulty in unloading ships. Inland deliveries were at first made entirely by the mobile refrigeration companies, since the railroads were not operating. Two QM companies and two Transportation Corps companies were available in July. Three more QM companies arrived from Britain by the end of August, and an additional three during September, although these last were originally scheduled to arrive in November and De-

---

[60] Memo, Chief Subs Div for Chief S&D Div, 20 Nov 44, sub: Priorities—Le Havre; Memo, CQM for G–4 COMZ, 2 Dec 44, sub: Fresh Meat Situation; Memo, Chief Subs Div for Chief S&D Div, 8 Dec 44, sub: Offloading of Fresh Meat From U.K. on Continent. Hist Br OQMG.

[61] (1) IRS, Chief Subs Div to CQM, 22 Nov 44, sub: Effect of Turkey Program on the Supply of Perishables. Hist Br OQMG. (2) Memo, CQM for G–4, 14 Dec 44, sub: Reduction in Issue of Fresh Meat. Littlejohn Reading File, vol. XXXI, item 40. (3) *Stars and Stripes* (Paris) vol. 1, No. 122 (23 November 1944). (3) Perishable Subsistence on the Continent, June 1944–June 1945, p. 29.

cember. The change was a tribute to the value of these units under conditions actually experienced on the Continent. One company was attached to each army and the rest, including the two Transportation Corps companies, were operated as a long-distance truck line by the Quartermaster Corps. This was not their original purpose, but experiment had demonstrated that ordinary open trucks could haul frozen foods for distances up to 100 miles even in summer, if cargoes were covered with tarpaulins and handled promptly on departure and arrival. The mobile units were therefore available for long-distance hauling, and until reefer rail cars began to be available about D plus 90 they hauled all perishables on the Continent.

With its complement of 4 officers and 99 enlisted men, operating 30 ten-ton truck-trailer combinations, the QM refrigeration company (mobile) was an extremely efficient unit. Ten additional administrative vehicles made the company completely self-sufficient, and it was also capable of operating as three separate platoons. Five such companies and two Transportation Corps companies of identical organization were operated in the Communications Zone under the direct supervision of the OCQM. The reason was that their operations from ports to armies crossed several base section boundaries on each trip. For the entire European campaign, these units transported an average of 2,050 long tons per company per week.[62] Five more companies were in the combat zone, each supporting an army, and these units were called on for even more service. For example, on 26 August the Third Army reported that the 485th QM Refrigeration Company had supplied all the army's needs since 10 August by hauling directly from Cherbourg. The turnaround now involved 800 miles per trip, and Colonel Busch asked that an intermediate transfer point be set up. ADSEC and the OCQM arranged for tailboard delivery to Third Army trucks at Le Mans until a cold storage plant there could be put into operation. Meanwhile large cold storage facilities became available at Paris, and the first reefer convoy from Cherbourg reached the French capital on 31 August. Seven days later the first trainload of frozen meats pulled out of Cherbourg for Paris, and by October rail shipments were equal to motor shipments in volume.

Although SHAEF insisted that French and Belgian rail cars should not be requisitioned at a rate that would harm the economies of Allied countries, the Procurement Division instituted an intensive search for unlocated reefer cars, with the understanding that all German cars found, and half of the Allied cars, would be allocated to the U.S. forces. Thus a pool of U.S., German, French, Belgian, and even a few Italian reefer cars was gradually accumulated as follows:[63]

	U.S. cars	Foreign cars	Total
6 September 1944	37	56	93
23 September 1944	37	228	265
30 November 1944	150	320	470
31 December 1944	181	328	509
8 May 1945	181	613	794

[62] (1) Littlejohn, ed., Passing in Review, ch. 33, vol. I, pp. 99–100. (2) T/O 10–247, QM Refrigeration Company (Mobile), 25 February 1944, with Change 1, 3 July 1944.

[63] (1) Perishable Subsistence on the Continent, June 1944–June 1945, pp. 12–13. (2) QM Supply in ETO, II, 34; VII, 150, 240. (3) Littlejohn, ed., Passing in Review, ch. 33, vol. I, pp. 97–99.

TABLE 15—ISSUE OF FRESH MEATS AND DAIRY PRODUCTS ON THE CONTINENT

Month	Long tons off-loaded	Long tons on hand end of month	Long tons issued	Gross pounds issued[a]	Average U.S. military strength	Gross pounds per man per day[a]
July 1944...............	823	0	966	2,163,840	706,269	.0988
August..................	4,949	0	4,949	11,085,760	968,952	.3691
September..............	13,317	0	13,317	29,830,080	1,215,641	.8180
October.................	18,576	4,089	14,487	32,450,880	1,464,258	.7149
November..............	17,232	12,077	9,244	20,706,560	1,579,801	.4369
December..............	19,070	7,229	23,918	53,576,320	1,627,138	1.0622
January 1945...........	26,707	12,240	21,766	48,755,840	1,740,412	.9037
February...............	6,343	6,764	11,819	26,474,560	1,975,120	.4622
March.................	34,629	17,019	24,374	54,597,760	2,039,872	.8634
April[b]..................	40,841	28,686	29,174	65,349,760	2,585,894	.8424
May[b]..................	28,394	27,681	29,399	65,853,760	2,636,250	.8058

[a] Net pounds are 85 percent of gross pounds.   [b] Includes Southern Line of Communications.

Source: Passing in Review, Ch. 33, Exhibit 4.

The number of these rail cars was quite insufficient for the projected program of refrigerated shipments. On 14 September a daily 400-ton train of perishables to Paris was inaugurated, but initial performance—a 15-day turnaround —indicated that daily service could not be maintained. A study on 23 September estimated that with 29 cars per train and a 15-day cycle the requirement would be 435 reefer cars, whereas only 265 were on hand. On the same basis, a daily train with alternating destinations at Homécourt and Namur on a 20-day turnaround would require 580 more cars. Nevertheless, General Lee directed that steps to attain this objective—800 tons moved forward each day— should at least be attempted, and the problem was attacked from all sides at once: more French cars, more U.S. cars, better facilities at both ends to decrease turnaround time, and intensified use of mobile refrigerated vans to support the whole program. Ice was even brought from Paris in trailers to ice rail cars at Cherbourg. The first reefer train left Cherbourg on 22 October for Namur, where, it will be recalled, First Army had captured intact a refrigerated warehouse on 13 September. Largely because of insufficient reefer cars, accomplishments were considerably short of the objective in October and November; tonnages moved forward by rail were 9,700 and 11,000 long tons, respectively, and actual consumption in November was only 9,244 long tons. (*Table 15*)[64]

The increased program of reefer rail shipments was accompanied by renewed controversy between the QMC and the Transportation Corps over their respective responsibilities in this field. The Transportation Corps requested that the OCQM representative at Cherbourg (still the only discharge site in October) assign a specific unloading point for each

[64] (1) Perishable Subsistence on the Continent, June 1944–June 1945, pp. 22–30. (2) QM Supply in ETO, II, 32–34. (3) Littlejohn, ed., Passing in Review, ch. 33, vol. I, p. 104.

car, provide an even flow of reefer cars on loading tracks from storage tracks, maintain a reservoir of perishables at Cherbourg so that reefer trains could be loaded irrespective of unloading rate of reefer ships, and continue shipping from Cherbourg in QMC mobile reefer vans until more reefer cars were provided by the French. The OCQM retorted that cars had been consigned to specific destinations but the Military Railway Service frequently unloaded all the cars at one station, thus causing confusion and delay; that switching operations in a rail yard could not conceivably be considered a QMC function; and that a reserve of perishables would be built up at Cherbourg as soon as the rate of unloading of ships was increased. Rather than wait for more French rail cars, the Transportation Corps should ferry over U.S. reefer cars from Britain as repeatedly requested by the OCQM. Then four of the mobile refrigeration companies could be shifted to their proper function of supporting the armies from Paris, instead of supplying Paris from Cherbourg. This interchange took place as the Communications Zone was under extremely heavy strain to supply the armies recently halted in extended positions along the German frontier. COMZ had just abandoned the concept of a major base in Brittany in favor of Antwerp, and in the interim impossible demands were made upon all agencies at Cherbourg until Antwerp became available.

By early December the situation was much improved and interservice relationships were more cordial. On 22 December Willkie reported to Littlejohn that the experimental shipments of cured, nonfrozen meats were entirely

successful, and that 7,500 long tons of such products were on the way. This should relieve the pressure on railroad reefers as well as reefer ships. Also in transit were 26,000 tons of frozen meat on a regular monthly allotment and 3,000 additional tons gained by shifting shuttle reefers to the transatlantic run. Thus 36,500 tons per month were assured against a requirement of 40,000 for the entire theater. Some 25,000 tons of cold storage space was available in continental locations where it could actually be used. This represented only twenty days of supply, but was about double the food reserves actually on hand. Willkie expected that the current fluid tactical situation (he was referring to the German Ardennes counteroffensive) would reduce demands for fresh meat as the troops shifted to operational rations. These were favorable aspects of the situation. On the other hand the turnaround time for reefers had still not measurably improved, although Brig. Gen. Louis E. Cotulla at NYPE had promised not to deck load reefers thereafter. This should save about two days per vessel. The least favorable circumstance of all was that such reserves as existed had been built up through underconsumption of fresh food by the troops, rather than by efficient transportation.[65]

Despite the unpromising beginning already described, Le Havre developed into a major cold storage port with nearly 5,000 long tons of space. During January 1945 Antwerp, with subsidiary facilities at Brussels, became an even

---

[65] Memo, Chief Subs Div for CQM, 22 Dec 44, sub: Over-all Survey of Perishable and Reefer Situation. Hist Br OQMG.

more important installation, but Cherbourg decreased in importance. With the dissolution of SOLOC in February, Marseille also became an ETO responsibility. At that time the main flow of perishables was as follows:

Antwerp to Namur to First and Ninth Armies
Le Havre to Homécourt to Third Army
Cherbourg to Paris to Fifteenth Army
Marseille to Dijon to Seventh Army

In addition, Paris was the inland distribution center for COMZ, receiving supplies from Le Havre as well as Cherbourg, and also serving Homécourt to a certain extent. As the armies moved forward into Germany they captured and utilized cold storage installations in many places, but only one—at Mannheim—was turned over to a COMZ agency. Depot Q–190 was activated at that location in April to support Seventh Army.[66] The posthostilities pattern of cold storage on the Continent centered on the redeployment ports of Le Havre and Marseille, the new U.S. port at Bremen, and support for the occupation forces in the American Zone of Germany. In September 1945 the following cold storage space in Germany was available: [67]

Location	Capacity (long tons)	Area Served
Berlin	2,500	Berlin District
Bremerhaven	3,000	All U.S.
Bremen	2,000	Zone
Frankfurt	1,500	Western Military
Mannheim	3,380	District
Stuttgart	1,360	
Nuremberg	2,500	Eastern Military
Munich	1,700	District

The QM Refrigeration Company (Fixed)

Almost all cold storage space on the Continent was of prewar origin, and, as anticipated, most of it had to be rehabilitated before it was serviceable. The ten QM refrigeration companies (fixed) available in the ETO maintained and operated these installations, although they had not been organized for that purpose. The unit was originally organized with a headquarters platoon (24 enlisted men), a cold storage platoon (62 enlisted men), and a butchery platoon (45 enlisted men). In the ETO the butchery platoon was not activated, resulting in a unit with a top-heavy organization. Actual operations were conducted at small installations by improvised small detachments, with all the administrative disadvantages that always plague non-T/O units. In the aggregate, the accomplishments of these detachments were more than equal to the theoretical capacity of the T/O unit, which was rated as capable of storing 30 days of perishable supply for 120,000 men. In some instances the detachments supervised civilian or POW labor, and their capacity was then equal to support for 560,000 men per company. A postwar evaluation was that a company with 4 officers, a headquarters of about 15 men, and three 32-man operating platoons would have been ideal for the ETO.[68]

[66] Littlejohn, ed., Passing in Review, ch. 33, vol. II, app. 10E. (2) *OQ Supply in ETO*, II, 34–35.

[67] (1) Littlejohn, ed., Passing in Review, ch. 33, vol. II, app. 10E. (2) Compare with Table 13, last column.

[68] (1) T/O 10–217 QM Refrigeration Company (Fixed) is given in full in *QM Supply in ETO*, VIII, 233–34. (2) USFET Gen Bd Study 109, pp. 90–91.

Local Procurement of Subsistence

Fresh fruits and vegetables were the first French supplies obtained by the U.S. forces after their landing in Normandy. Arriving in this rich agricultural area late in the spring, American quartermasters found not only the fresh fruits and vegetables they had expected, but considerable quantities of eggs, butter, cheese, and fresh meat. Although France as a whole was very short of these products, Allied bombing of railroads to isolate the beachhead had prevented normal movement to urban markets. The original directives had prohibited purchase of such supplies, but it was logical to prevent wasteful spoilage of surpluses and to meet the needs of the troops by procuring these products as quickly as possible. Before the beachhead was a month old, therefore, quartermasters, the general purchasing agent, and civil affairs and local officials made arrangements which permitted the U.S. forces to purchase at official prices, or to requisition through the French Government, whatever food was declared surplus by French regional officials. Meat and dairy products were only included among these surpluses for a very short time.

Agreement on what constituted a just price was not always easily obtained. Farmers, wholesalers, and agents for cooperatives usually cited figures somewhat higher than those listed by the local government, but generally a compromise was reached in the direction of the lowest price. Suppliers were then provided with jute sacks and the military units were given lists of suppliers and pickup points.[69] By the middle of July

ADSEC was receiving such fresh produce as potatoes, carrots, turnips, and cabbages; in the next six weeks, $23,000 worth of fruits and vegetables had been purchased in Normandy and Brittany by that headquarters on a cash basis. Another important development of this period was the arrival of the first boatload of potatoes from Great Britain—a food item that overshadowed continental purchases until V–E Day and even thereafter. Meanwhile, procurement in France developed from an improvised activity to one where supervision and determination of surpluses improved directly with the reorganization of the local governments.[70]

The clearest picture of fruit and vegetable procurement emerges from the history of the 63d QM Base Depot, which served American troops in the Paris-Chartres area and handled an average of 175 long tons of fresh foods weekly. Transport, as everywhere, was the primary problem. With only two trucks per day to pick up these items, the depot encouraged French suppliers to make direct delivery to Class I distributing points. Poor telephone communications in Paris further handicapped the procurement branch in its efforts to coordinate schedules, prepare reports, and make food containers and gasoline available to the farmers. For lack of scales, the depot finally resorted to a railway scale on which deliveries could be measured by weighing delivery trucks both with and without their loads.[71]

---

[69] Maj R. H. Kingston, Rpt on Fresh Vegetables for QM [ca. Jul 44]; Memo, GPA ADSEC for Subs Br OQM ADSEC, 23 Jul 44, sub: Fresh Vegetables. 430 GPA.

[70] Hist of QM Sec ADSEC, pp. 8, 34.

[71] Hist of 63d QMBD, pp. 6–8. Hist Br OQMG

Notwithstanding such inconveniences, by the end of 1944 the base sections were receiving a weekly average of 1,700 tons of French fruits and vegetables. A rough breakdown of receipts for the week ending 23 December reveals the gross quantities delivered within each of the major COMZ sections and an estimate of the most important constituents:[72]

Base section receipts (in tons)		Items received (in tons)	
Total	1,704	Potatoes	919
Normandy	84	Apples	201
Brittany	970	Cabbages	157
ADSEC	401	Onions	143
Seine	205	Carrots	123
Channel	34	Turnips	105
Oise	10	Miscellaneous ...	56

Through the early months of 1945 fresh fruits and vegetables continued to be the major category of Quartermaster supplies procured on the Continent. The amounts obtained rose from 4,850 tons in January to 30,600 tons in April. Table and rock salt, 1,100 and 2,000 tons, respectively, were supplied from the mines at Nancy. The requirement for rock salt, used in icing refrigerator cars, was far greater than this amount, and another 5,000 tons were promised from Marseille. The French also made available a number of food processing plants for coffee roasting and grinding in Paris, Le Havre, and Rouen, converted imported semolina flour into macaroni at Marseille, and made jam at Dijon. The OCQM had to provide coal from its allocation for all these activities, and imported sugar to make jam.[73]

While these subsistence supplies and services were timely and appreciated, the procurement officials were not always confident that they would continue. Stored root vegetables were ruined by unusually cold winter weather. Also, as transportation improved, it gradually became possible to deliver more perishables to civilians in the distressed urban areas. The availability of surpluses for military use had always been at least partly a result of transportation shortages, and decreased in May and June. Britain and France both feared that they would have to default on some of their potato commitments, and Belgian officials notified Allied procurement authorities that in April and May the delivery of perishables would be limited to hospitalized American and British troops. To co-operate fully with the Belgians, 12th Army Group ordered the suspension of all perishable procurement in that country from February to May. Further reflecting the scarcity of these supplies in Belgium, ADSEC, which was vigorously engaged in local procurement at this time, obtained 10 percent less perishables in the entire six-month period from October to April than in the six-week period from 8 September to 25 October 1944. Eager to make use of whatever was procurable, the OCQM accepted from Brittany 30,000 metric tons of potatoes which had been damaged by the cold, and then sped them through the depots before spoilage took its toll.[74]

---

[72] Littlejohn, ed., Passing in Review, ch. 41, pt. 2, p. 21.

[73] QM Procurement on the Continent, January–June 1945. Hist Br OQMG.

[74] (1) Memo, Kingston, OGPA, for GPA, 30 Jan 45, sub: Proc of Fresh Vegetables; Memo, DGPA for GPA, 2 Feb 45, sub: Fresh Fruits and Vegetables. Both in USFET GPA 430. (2) TUSA AAR, II, G-452. (3) Hist of QM Sec ADSEC, p. 34. (4) Memo, Chief Subs Div for Chief S&D Div, 3 Mar 45, sub: Potato Movement ex Brittany Peninsula. Hist Br OQMG.

The combined effects of an unusually cold winter and a severe potato blight had an even more serious effect upon the United Kingdom than upon France. The British Government had been committed to supply 192,000 long tons per month to the U.S. forces during the first half of 1945. Late in January it became apparent that this program would have to be materially reduced. Nevertheless, the British delivered 95,-393 long tons of potatoes, and also 8,191 tons of root vegetables to the U.S. forces on the Continent during the first five months of 1945. In addition, they furnished the French with 30,000 tons of seed potatoes. During the same period, 73,450 tons of fruits and vegetables were procured from the French, all of which required jute sacks supplied by the Procurement Division, and transportation by U.S. agencies.[75]

Anticipating the possible disappearance of procurable perishables in northwestern Europe, Littlejohn began to survey the availability of fresh fruit and vegetables on the Iberian Peninsula. In January negotiations were opened to import 1,000 metric tons of tomatoes from the Canary Islands every ten days for ten weeks. Broadening his plans to include oranges, lemons, onions, potatoes, and pineapples, the Chief Quartermaster received $10,000,000 worth of General Purchasing Board credits for such purchases. By the end of March Spanish and Portuguese items selected for purchase approached 35,000 tons and included, in addition to the above, olives, dried figs, rice, cocoa beans, and coffee.[76]

Although considerable effort had gone into planning the procurement of Iberian perishables, receipts from this source before V–E Day were meager. Roughly four thousand tons of citrus fruits and vegetables left Spanish ports for both Marseille and Rouen in April, but the requirements that Spanish vessels bound for Allied ports obtain British Admiralty clearance led to delays which threatened spoilage. The small receipts of oranges, grapefruits, lemons, and tomatoes were almost exclusively delivered to hospitalized American troops.[77]

In addition to fresh fruits and vegetables, miscellaneous foodstuffs such as spices, vinegar, and yeast were procured in France, Belgium and Luxembourg. Yeast, in particular, was such an essential part of the military bread baking program that negotiations for its continental procurement were begun as early as August 1944. At first the French refused to approve this project, pointing out that they were normally a bread-eating nation, and that their requirements would increase since relief supplies were mainly unmilled wheat. But yeast was essentially a manufactured product, and objections to this program were overcome when the OCQM furnished the producers in Paris and Lille with sugar, coal, and packing materials, and promised also that they would be reimbursed in kind for the use of oils

---

[75] (1) Memos cited n. 74 (1). (2) QM Procurement on the Continent, January–June 1945, pp. 15, 32. Hist Br OQMG.

[76] (1) Ltr, DGPA to Winthrop G. Brown, USCC, 18 Jan 45, sub: Pineapples From Iberian Peninsula;

Ltr, Chief Proc Div to CQM, 26 Mar 45, sub: Subs Proc Program for Spain and Portugal; Ltr, GPA to Foreign Economic Admin Madrid, 2 Apr 45, sub: Proc Program in Iberian Peninsula. All in 091 GPA. (2) Personal Ltr, CQM to GPA, 18 Jan 45, and Incl. 430 GPA.

[77] (1) Personal Ltr, Brown to Col Walter Shorter, DGPA, 30 Jan 45; Rpt, Col Tryon M. Shepherd to CQM, 29 Mar, 19 Apr 45, sub: Weekly Rpts 7 and 10. Both in 091 GPA. (2) Personal Ltr, CQM to TQMG, 31 Jul 45. ETO 321.

and chemicals if local shortages resulted. Belgian production on similar terms began in March 1945, and soon outstripped receipts from France. Yeast from both sources averaged 3.2 tons per day during the first half of 1945, a quantity which contributed notably to the success of baking operations.[78]

Although it does not appear that the French public was seriously antagonized by American food procurement, rumors circulated on the streets of Paris that this program was responsible for civilian food shortages, which were severe in the spring of 1945. Occasional editorials, even some adding that the Allied forces were trying to enter the meat and butter market, gave these stories wider currency and a ring of authenticity. On 30 March 1945 the newspaper *Temps Present* printed an inaccurate and extremely unfriendly editorial, including alleged statements by an official of the French Ministry of Supply, and the general purchasing agent demanded a retraction. As usual in French politics, the incident was more complicated than it first appeared. The French had received about 280,000 tons of relief supplies compared to less than 70,000 tons of food procured by the U.S. forces in France, and, moreover, the general purchasing agent had agreed to offset 37,000 tons of potatoes received with 30,000 tons of British seed potatoes for spring planting. These facts were well known in France but were not mentioned in the offending editorial. The COMZ

public relations officer believed that the Supply Ministry statement had been a "feeler" to provoke further official discussion of increased food supplies for French civilians. Far greater tonnages of relief food had been promised than could be delivered, due to overriding military priorities for transatlantic shipping. If the public relations officer's theory was correct, the maneuver was ill-timed; the current tactical situation did not permit any relaxation of military priorities on shipping.

The final decision was that the known anti-American attitude of the editor of *Temps Present* was the important aspect of the matter, and that contrary to usual U.S. policy, corrective action should be requested through the French liaison mission at COMZ headquarters. The incident was considered closed after a special press release was issued by the Ministry of Supply, and printed in *Temps Present* on April 6th.[79]

Baking and Coffee Roasting Operations

General Littlejohn had recognized the superiority of British-designed baking equipment as early as July 1942. At that time he requested equipment for fifteen companies, but by the end of the year only four sets had been delivered and two of these had been transferred to North Africa. Materials used in manufacturing this equipment were critical, and the OCQM was not completely convinced that it would be wise to convert the bakery organization and equipment of an entire theater in the midst

---

[78] (1) *QM Supply in ETO*, II, 57. (2) Littlejohn, ed., *Passing in Review*, ch. 33, vol. I, p. 70. (3) Ltr, GPA to Chief SAFA, 23 Oct 44, sub: Yeast Reqmts; Memo, Food Br OGPA for G–4, 24 Jan 45, sub: Coal for Yeast Factory. Both in GPA 430.

[79] Memo, GPA for CofS, 5 Apr 45, sub: Misinformation in Connection With Proc of Food, and Inds. USFET GPA 430.

of hostilities. In May 1943 there were still only four sets of bakery equipment on hand, and only two companies actually operating in the United Kingdom.[80]

Meanwhile Maj. John ("Jack") Mac-Manus, a commercial bakery executive of Scottish origin who had recently entered the U.S. Army by direct commission, arrived from the United States in late November 1942. He had been specially selected by The Quartermaster General's Office for the position of bakery officer in the Subsistence Division of the OCQM, but in 1942 that headquarters, after several disillusionments, was not very enthusiastic regarding experts with limited military experience. MacManus was convinced that adoption of the British equipment and development of an entirely new company organization to handle it were the correct procedures, and that action should begin immediately. His forthright manner of self-expression, and possibly also his strong Scottish accent, irritated some of his seniors, and his recommendations were sidetracked for several months. He himself was given other major duties, in addition to continuing as a one-man Bakery Section within the Subsistence Division.[81]

By August 1943 a great deal of progress had been made, largely based on MacManus' convictions of what action was required and on his persuasiveness in obtaining concurrence from the re-

DIESEL ELECTRIC DOUGH MIXER *used in British-type mobile field bakery adopted by the ETO Quartermaster, January 1943.*

sponsible authorities. The British Ministry of War Transport had granted a priority, and Baker Perkins, Ltd., had made a commitment to provide sixty-seven more sets of mobile bakery equipment, including essential spare parts. The Bakery Branch had formulated an entirely new Table of Organization and Equipment for mobile bakery units. They were to be not only completely mobile, but logistically self-sufficient—that is, they were to be able to haul supplies of baking ingredients from army depots, and deliver bread at forward truckheads. The Bakery Branch (still only two officers and one enlisted man) had also organized the 268th Bakery Company to operate as a combined staging area and training center, and had

[80] OTCQM TSFET Operational Study 17, Baking Operations, exhibit A.

[81] (1) Littlejohn, ed., Passing in Review, ch. 36, "Bakeries and Coffee Roasting," by Col. Jack Mac-Manus, pp. 6–8. (2) Deficient technical training of specialists, particularly alleged "experts" with commercial experience, is discussed in Chapter II above.

set up an equipment park and a spare parts depot. Meanwhile the OCQM had taken the plunge in July and informed the War Department that no more U.S.-type bakery equipment was desired in the ETO. Bakery units were to be sent to the theater without equipment.[82]

This decision was not made solely on the recommendations of Major Mac-Manus. Difficulties with U.S.-type equipment used in North Africa, and the superiority of British equipment tested there, had been reported by a succession of OQMG observers, beginning with Captain Pounder. While minor changes in design could increase the reliability of U.S. equipment, the British type was preferable because of other very material advantages for the type of warfare anticipated on the Continent, as indicated by the following tabulation:

Factor	British (T/O&E 10–147S)	U.S. M1942 (T/O&E 10–147)
Personnel requirement	2 Officers	5 Officers
	82 Enlisted men	155 Enlisted men
Equipment	All trailer-mounted:	All portable:
	3 ovens, diesel	32 ovens, gasoline
	1 mixer, electric	16 mixers, gasoline
	1 divider and rounder, electric.	
	2 generators, diesel.	
Daily capacity:		
Normal	25,000 lbs.	24,000 lbs.
Maximum	35,000 lbs.	32,000 lbs.
Fuel consumption:		
Gasoline	None	15 gals. per 1,000 lbs.
Diesel	6 gals. per 1,000 lbs.	None
Flexibility	No divisibility	4 platoons
Trucks required (to move equipment only)	9 (including 4 heavy)	40 (2½-ton)

The economy of the British-type equipment in personnel, transportation, and fuel consumption is very evident. In the revised organization, five additional organic vehicles were provided along with tentage to make the unit independent of permanent housing.[83]

As bakery companies arrived from the United States, they were met at the dock by training center personnel with trucks from the pool of bakery equipment. At Boughton Park near Kettering, each U.S.-type company was split into 2 ETO-type companies, completely fitted out with British equipment, and intensively trained in new procedures. Within 30 days each new unit had moved out to a site where it actually baked bread for American troops. In one instance 8 companies were equipped in 11 days.

---

[82] (1) Littlejohn, ed., Passing in Review, ch. 36, pp. 32–52. (2) Memo, CQM for Cound, 23 Jul 43, sub: Ltr to WD re Bakery Equipment; Ltr, CQM to Maj Gen H. R. Kerr, War Office, 22 Sep 43, sub: Additional Bakery Equip. Littlejohn Reading File vol. XIV, item 67; vol. XVI, item 72.

[83] (1) See Ch. V, above. (2) Littlejohn, ed., Passing in Review, ch. 33, vol. I, p. 123. (3) T/O&E 10–147, QM Bakery Company, and T/O&E 10–

147S, QM Bakery Company Mobile (Special), are given in full in QM Supply in ETO, VIII, 224–25.

This feat is the more remarkable when compared with the difficulties of other QMC units which either had to wait interminably to locate and receive "force-marked" equipment, or else received very incomplete or delayed initial equipment in the theater. By the end of the year 22 companies had been activated, and on 7 January 1944 Littlejohn directed that the Bakery Branch be "moved from a back alley to Main Street and set up as a going concern." MacManus was given a staff of 3 officers and 6 enlisted men, and provision was made for a special bakery inspection and training team in each base section to function under his technical direction. By D-day, the mobile bakeries were producing 55 percent of the bread received by U.S. troops, and 42 companies were available. Ultimately, 55 companies were trained at Boughton Park and saw service on the Continent.[84]

Because green coffee from British Empire sources was available in large quantities in the United Kingdom, coffee was among the commodities approved for reverse lend-lease late in 1942. As the British reserve was exhausted, green coffee was shipped direct from South America for U.S. troops in the British Isles. Initially coffee roasting was performed by British firms, but late in 1942 portable coffee roasting equipment began to arrive in the theater, and tentative plans were made in early 1943 for the activation of a coffee roasting company. But meanwhile the 6-man coffee

roasting detachments were scattered at Class I installations throughout the United Kingdom, and it became clear that a roasting company was no solution to the accompanying problems of decentralized personnel administration and technical supervision.[85] The coffee roaster and the grinder, both of American manufacture, weighed a total of 5,400 pounds. The roaster was fired by anthracite coal, and the grinder was driven by a gasoline engine. Normal capacity was about 1 ton of coffee roasted and ground per 8-hour shift, or 2 tons per day. At 8 pounds per 100 men, this was enough to support 50,000 men. In an emergency 70,000 coffee rations could be produced.[86]

Precisely when and where the suggestion to attach the coffee roasters to the bakery companies originated, is unknown. The idea had merit, since the daily capacities of the two types of equipment synchronized fairly well, but the coffee roasters were portable rather than mobile, and very unwieldy as well. If the whole concept of the deployment of bakery companies was not to be compromised, a mobile trailer mount had to be devised for the coffee roasters. A major difficulty was that the final decision was not made until November 1943, seven months before D-day. Nevertheless, largely through persistent prodding by MacManus, a satisfactory trailer was designed, components secured from the British, and fabrication and assembly

[84] (1) Quotation from IRS, CQM to Franks, 7 Jan 44, sub: T/O for Bakery Br. Littlejohn Reading File, vol. XX, item 15. (2) Littlejohn, ed., Passing in Review, ch. 33, vol. I, pp. 52–59. (3) OTCQM TSFET Operational Study 17, exhibit A.

[85] (1) QM Supply in ETO, II, 59–61. (2) Littlejohn, ed., Passing in Review, ch. 33, vol. I, p. 127. (3) OTCQM TSFET Operational Study 17, p. 7.
[86] (1) Franz A. Koehler, Coffee for the Armed Forces, QMC Historical Studies, Series II, No. 5, p. 19. (2) Littlejohn, ed., Passing in Review, ch. 36, p. 63.

completed by the Ordnance Corps in time for operations on the Continent. Moreover, the coffee grinder was successfully redesigned to operate with a jeep engine instead of the nonstandard and unsatisfactory engine originally supplied. An important feature of the redesigned equipment was inclusion of tentage, so that coffee roasters could operate in the field with the bakeries; sixty-nine roasters were procured, one for each set of bakery equipment.[87]

Since bakery equipment was locally procured in Great Britain and spare parts would have to come from the same source, MacManus decided that his units would require an autonomous spare parts organization. This was to be in addition to a reserve of spare parts issued to each company before embarking, designed to cover six months of operations. Accordingly, special depot trailers were procured from the British and fitted with bins, drawers, and shelves. The need for a completely mobile depot may seem slight, since it moved only four times during the first three months of the European campaign and thereafter was stationary at the Isle St. Germain outside Paris. The important considerations were that spare vehicles in the mobile bakeries were available to move these trailers as needed, and that a unique and very large selection of spare parts was never mislaid in warehouses, but was available for issue even when in transit. With 10,147 different spare parts items involved, all nonstandard and only catalogued by the Bakery Branch itself,

obviously great pains had to be taken to avoid confusion. The fourteen sets of bakery equipment not issued to units and a similar reserve of coffee roasting equipment were also concentrated in the depot on the Isle St. Germain. The installation performed all repairs on its equipment, including motor overhauls normally done by Ordnance. From the beginning this organization edited and filled all requisitions from bakery companies, and in turn placed requisitions upon eight British agencies in order to maintain its stock levels. The depot was operated by one officer and three enlisted men.[88]

These careful and elaborate preparations were vindicated on the Continent, where the bakery companies operated without difficulty from the beginning and usually had a surplus of men and transportation to help other organizations. The 3029th Bakery Company landed on Utah Beach on 30 June and was in operation within twenty-four hours. The 3028th landed a day later and by 2 July the two units were delivering 60,000 pounds of bread daily to First Army truckheads. Meanwhile a French bakery in the Cherbourg Arsenal was rehabilitated and began production on July 9th with twenty-seven French civilians directed by two U.S. enlisted men.

By 20 July, 18 bakeries had arrived. The first 5 of these were formally assigned to First Army, but by informal agreement among quartermasters of First and Third Armies and ADSEC, MacManus supervised and co-ordinated all bakery operations, designating the de-

---

[87] (1) Although sixty-nine sets of bakery equipment were procured, only fifty-five companies were activated. (2) Littlejohn, ed., Passing in Review, ch. 33, vol. I, pp. 128–29; ch. 36, pp. 62–67.

[88] Littlejohn, ed., Passing in Review, ch. 33, vol. I, p. 132; ch. 36, pp. 48, 51, 68–70.

pots where ingredients should be drawn and the truckheads to which bread should be delivered. Fresh bread was issued to practically all troops on the Continent during July, irrespective of whether they were eating operational or B rations. At the end of the month First Army reported that its 7 assigned or attached bakeries had produced 2,-882,655 pounds of bread since the beginning of operations, with an average daily yield of about 25,700 pounds per unit. Even during September, as the armies advanced at top speed across France, production per company was more than 20,000 pounds per day, and some 55,000,-000 bread rations were issued. On 10 October, 38 mobile bakeries were on the Continent including 6 each with First and Third Armies. The others were evenly distributed throughout the rear areas, including 7 companies in Normandy Base Section. The OCQM considered 6 companies per army a normal troop basis, to be slightly modified according to the situation. At the end of hostilities 29 companies were assigned to the 5 field armies in the ETO.

As for COMZ installations, the Delta Base Section was supplied principally by standard U.S.-type bakeries from the Mediterranean theater. The other base sections were adequately supported by mobile-type bakeries. MacManus considered this arrangement of major importance, since U.S.-type units normally requisitioned and utilized civilian bakeries, whereas the mobile type was completely self-sufficient. In a newly liberated area whose civilian population subsisted on bread to a very large degree, it was important to keep civilian bakeries available for civilian relief operations. Thus mobile bakeries in the rear areas

performed a function of almost equal importance to that of units in the combat zone.[89]

In actual operations, coffee roasting was considerably less successful than baking. For this there were two main reasons. First, the plan of operations was not decided upon until late in the build-up period for OVERLORD, and did not leave sufficient time to design and procure equipment and test the proposed procedures. And second, the demand for coffee was far greater than anticipated. Since roasting equipment was not brought to the Continent with the first bakery units, at first the demand for additional coffee was met by issuing the soluble type. Part of this demand resulted from a universal rejection of synthetic lemonade, which was included as a beverage in early versions of the combat rations. Additional factors were serious shortages of tea and cocoa, which were to be supplied by local procurement in Great Britain and therefore were not included in the balanced commodity-loaded ships. The difficulties involved in obtaining special tonnage priorities, transporting supplies across the Channel, and insuring that they were not lost or stolen in the process applied especially to these items, which were shipped in small lots.

At the forward Class I truckheads, these shortages of other beverages resulted in a demand for 50 percent more coffee than anticipated. By 20 July the coffee supply on the Continent was

---

[89] (1) *Ibid.*, ch. 33, pp. 129–33; ch. 36, pp. 70–83. (2) *QM Supply in ETO,* II, 54–55; VIII, pp. 147–48, 158–66. (3) Memo, Chief Subs Div for Chief P&T Div, 10 Oct 44, sub: Presentation of QM Activities. ETO 430.

down to a three-day level. This supply was either canned or soluble coffee, since the roasting and grinding operation was not scheduled to begin until 5 August. As an emergency measure, 100,000 pounds of green coffee were flown in from the United Kingdom, roasted and ground, and issued to the troops by 25 July. The Bakery and Coffee Roasting Branch also discovered 200,000 pounds of roasted unground coffee earmarked for the British Civil Affairs Section, which had been brought into U.S. dumps through some error. This was duly receipted for future replacement and utilized in the emergency. The coffee situation remained critical through August because of low discharge priorities, and the Bakery and Coffee Roasting Branch resorted to various expedients to get coffee ashore, thereupon distributing it in the organic vehicles of the bakery companies. On at least one occasion, when unloading at OMAHA Beach was supposedly impossible because of rough water, the crews of Dukws were induced to discharge coffee by a bribe of cinnamon buns.[90]

An even more serious coffee shortage arose beginning in December, when troops had to remain out of doors in freezing weather for extended periods during the German Ardennes counteroffensive. The coffee roasting equipment had already filled a demand for 50 percent more coffee than originally estimated, but now requisitions suddenly jumped to more than twice the normal amount. The fourteen coffee roasters maintained as a reserve on the Isle St. Germain were put to work, civilian

coffee roasting establishments in Paris were also utilized, and enough coffee to fill all demands was shipped forward to the truckheads. Nevertheless, the significant fact was that requirements increased to an unexpected degree when troops engaged in active operations during cold weather. A good example is provided by Third Army, which consumed 212,000 pounds of coffee in November 1944, and 1,075,000 pounds in January 1945. The lesson appears to be that a very large reserve, either of canned coffee or of coffee roasting equipment and green beans, must be maintained for operational emergencies.[91]

Acceptability of Rations

Troop Views on Rations

In view of the readiness of the American combat soldier at every echelon to be outspokenly critical of the troops and services identified with the rear echelons, it was a high compliment to the quality of the rations that field observers did not encounter more frequent criticism. The packaged rations, which might have borne the brunt of such censure, evidently were very successful in providing a palatable and nourishing diet so long as they were not consumed over too long a period.[92] According to an OQMG observer, unit S–4's found that requisi-

---

[90] Littlejohn, ed., Passing in Review, ch. 33, vol. I, pp. 83, 134–35; ch. 36, pp. 84–87.

[91] Ibid., ch. 33, vol. I, p. 134. (2) TUSA AAR, II, QM 28.

[92] The OVERLORD Class I Plan specified that the type 10-in-1 ration was not to be issued for more than 20 days, and the C and K rations for not more than 6 days. In an emergency, and with substantial supplements, these limits could be extended to 30 and 10 days, respectively. Littlejohn, ed., Passing in Review, ch. 33, vol. II, app. 2A, p. 29.

tioning C and K rations was the easiest way to feed combat troops and tended to continue this practice after the tactical situation no longer justified it. The Third Army quartermaster found it necessary to use his authority to "persuade" troop commanders to discontinue 10-in-1 rations in favor of B rations when tactical conditions permitted. Operational rations were acceptable to the troops largely because they were supplemented by fresh bread, butter, and meat whenever possible. Refrigeration service fluctuated, but fresh bread issues were habitual in the combat zone in the ETO.[93]

Field surveys demonstrated that different categories of troops preferred different rations for different reasons. Undoubtedly the most satisfactory operational ration was the 10-in-1, the development of which had been largely inspired by North African experience. Containing a combination of canned meats, vegetables, spreads, and evaporated milk, a K ration for the noon meal, packages of sugar, soluble coffee, cereal, cigarettes, and candy, it was virtually a portable type B unit which could best be used when the B itself could not be satisfactorily distributed.[94] Because of its size, the 10-in-1 was the particular favorite of artillery, armored, tank-destroyer, and comparable units operating in small groups or crews, and having organic motor transportation in which

they could carry a package of food weighing forty-five pounds, and a small stove for cooking.[95] There were occasional objections to the English type of stew, and many motorized units found the noon K rations included in the 10-in-1 unnecessary, since they were able to cook all their meals. Frequent and outspoken criticism was aimed at the dump personnel, who were accused of retaining the popular II and IV menus for themselves, leaving the other three less popular menus for the combat troops. Late in 1944, a revised 10-in-1 ration began to arrive in the theater which overcame most of the technical disadvantages of the older type. The K ration meal was replaced by a wide variety of meat and vegetable combinations, and the amounts of coffee, cocoa, milk, and sugar were increased. The new pack also included soap, paper towels, halazone tablets, a can opener, and cigarettes.[96]

The popularity of the two most important individually packaged rations—type C and type K—varied from one campaign to another, and also from one type of unit to another. As in the Mediterranean theater, soldiers expressed a dislike for malt-dextrose tablets, but otherwise the K ration, in its three "Cracker-Jack" cardboard boxes, was preferred by the infantryman, especially during periods of activity, because it was more easily carried on his person—

[93] (1) OCQM Field Obsv Rpts File, Sep–Dec 44. Hist Br OQMG. (2) Critical comments on preliminary MS version of this history by Lieutenant Slauta, R&D Div OQMG, dated 8 Oct 54, and by General Busch, QM Third Army, dated 19 Nov 54. Hist Br OQMG.

[94] (1) Littlejohn, ed., Passing in Review, ch. 33, vol. I, p. 31. (2) Risch, The Quartermaster Corps: Organization, Supply, and Services, I, 188–92.

[95] OCQM Field Obsv Rpts 1, 3, 4, 5, 6, 9 10 (covering period September to December 1944); Rpt, What the Soldier Thinks of His Field Rations, Research Br Spec Sv Div, Hq ETOUSA, Oct 44. Both in ETO QM 319.25.

[96] The old and improved menus are tabulated in detail in Littlejohn, ed., Passing in Review, ch. 33, vol. II, app. 4B.

either in boxes or by distributing the packaged contents through the pockets —than the six round metal cans making up the C ration. On the other hand, when the foot soldier was in a stationary position and forced by circumstances to subsist on operational rations, he favored the C ration because it had more meat than the K, was more filling, and could be heated directly in the can. Thus it is understandable that the motorized combat soldier who did not have to stuff cans into pockets or a pack preferred the C ration to the K, and sought to obtain this whenever the 10-in-1 was unavailable. The C ration became even more popular after several new menus, especially beef with noodles and spaghetti with meat balls, arrived late in 1944, though not in sufficient quantities for wide distribution. Rumors of these new menus were widespread long before they became available, and the OCQM got many official inquiries from various tactical headquarters. By the spring of 1945, ten different meat units and six bread and beverage units were available, overcoming practically every objection to earlier versions of this ration.[97]

Because the availability of perishables was unpredictable, dehydrated foods were shipped overseas in quantity. Although shipping these processed foods was easier than handling perishables, their final preparation presented a challenge to the ingenuity of mess personnel throughout the theater. The OQMG had noted the unfavorable reaction of Mediterranean troops to these articles and placed detailed directions on containers in the hope of improving their

acceptability. Nevertheless, dehydrated tomato juice, cabbage flakes, and eggs rarely reached the average ETO soldier in an appetizing form, and he was not impressed by praise of their nutritional value.[98]

Vigorously prosecuted conservation drives occasionally reduced the amounts of dehydrated items found in the garbage but added little to their popularity. Coming from a country where availability alone is not a compelling argument, the American soldier was prepared to reject foods that did not suit his taste. For example, in 1943 all operational rations as well as the B ration included lemon crystals to prepare a noontime beverage. They were readily available, cheap, and provided the vitamins otherwise missing from canned rations in a convenient form which did not readily deteriorate in storage. But lemon crystals were characterized by a biting acidity which could only be counteracted by vast amounts of sugar. Cooks were taught a dozen tricks to disguise them or persuade the troops to consume them, but all in vain. The troops detested the synthetic lemonade and all its variants and offspring. Every observer report from the Mediterranean and European theater alike included complaints on this score, and a good many constructive suggestions were made by the troops. Unfortunately, supplies of vitamin tablets and vitamin-fortified chocolate were very limited, and they had to remain in the critical category controlled by the Medical Corps.

On investigation, none of the other suggestions for a nonperishable source

[97] (1) Sources cited n. 95. (2) Littlejohn, ed., Passing in Review, ch. 33, vol. II, app. 4E.

[98] (1) Littlejohn, ed., Passing in Review, ch. 33, p. 25. (2) See ch. V, above.

of vitamins proved practical. Orange and grape crystals were slightly less acid and less unpopular than lemon crystals, but these products also encountered a good deal of criticism. Since vitamins were considered to be essential and fruit crystals were the only readily available source, they were included in the revised versions of the C, K, and 10-in-1 rations. As a concession to troop preferences, the proportion of orange and grape to lemon crystals was increased, but subsistence specialists in the ETO seriously doubted that these products were effective. The resulting vitamin deficiency was partially counteracted by the vigorous campaign of the OCQM to increase the supply of perishables.[99]

Mess Teams

It became quickly apparent that even the good cooks arriving in the theater were unfamiliar with the preparation of dehydrated foods, while a wider survey concluded that "there were many more messes than there were good cooks, mess sergeants, and mess officers. Unit commanders were too engrossed in the vital problems of training and running their organizations to give their messes as much time as they would have liked."[100] Simply improving the ration would accomplish little if measures were not taken to encourage proper preparation and attractive serving of food, and a

number of steps were taken in that direction.

A Subsistence Laboratory had been part of the OCQM overhead organizations since late 1942. It was responsible for the technical guidance of subsistence activities, which included the preparation of issue menus, the publication of instructional bulletins, and the drafting of specifications for locally procured subsistence. To stimulate constructive thinking by mess personnel and to publicize the creative work performed by cooks in individual installations, the OCQM conducted theater-wide recipe contests. The laboratory was also instrumental in the establishment of the cooks' and bakers' school within the American School Center at Shrivenham, England. This school trained ever-increasing numbers of mess officers, mess sergeants, and cooks and bakers from 1942 through 1944. In April 1945 it was transferred to the QMC and reopened at Chartres, France. At the time of its final transfer to Darmstadt, Germany, in September 1945, it had trained a total of more than 6,000 students. It was a major factor in improving messing in the European theater.[101]

The system of model messes and mess advisers employed in the United Kingdom, already described, proved inadequate under field conditions on the Continent. More training was needed, especially for mess personnel who had arrived direct from the United States. Because distances were greater than in the United Kingdom and travel was very difficult, it was apparent that one

[99] (1) QM School Overseas Obsvrs Rpts, 1944–1945, numbers 2, 5, 6, 9, 21, 29, 39, 48, 52, 54. ETO 319.25. (2) Littlejohn, ed., Passing in Review, ch. 33, p. 26.
[100] Messing in the ETO, a study prepared by Subs Div, OCQM SOS ETOUSA, [ca. 1 Jan 44], p. 4. Hist Br OQMG.

[101] (1) *Ibid.*, pp. 4–7. (2) Littlejohn, ed., Passing in Review, ch. 33, vol. I, pp. 146–48.

model mess in each base section would not be very effective in raising the general level of efficiency. What was needed was a team large enough to take over entire operation of a unit mess if necessary and demonstrate proper procedures on the spot.

Accordingly, in late October 1944 the OCQM set up six mess teams, each consisting of two officers and ten enlisted men. These teams were organized under the QM Service Organization as Composite Company Headquarters, type AC, with attached Mess Detachment, type AF (modified).[102] Each team consisted of a mess officer and a dietitian, and two of each of the following: mess sergeants, first cooks, second cooks, pastry cooks, and meat cutters. The unit was completely mobile, with a jeep and trailer and a 2½-ton truck and trailer. The truck was set up exactly like the mobile kitchen of a combat unit. Littlejohn was insistent that the dietitian of the team should be a woman—either a WAC officer or a Medical Corps technician. He was convinced that a feminine presence would place the regular mess personnel of a unit on their mettle to perform efficiently, and would also make them more amenable to instruction and helpful criticism. With the same psychological factors in mind, one all-WAC and one all-Negro team were organized. All members of a team were not only qualified as mess officers, cooks, pastry cooks, or butchers, but were also skilled in repair of mess equipment, plumbing and lighting, and even in carpentry.

Moreover, they knew what types of QM mess equipment were available in depots, and their recommendations usually meant that a unit's requisition would be honored. These teams were organized under the supervision of Maj. Patrick H. Buckley, former mess adviser of the Western Base Section in England, and were attached to the 537th QM Group located on the Isle St. Germain, outside Paris.[103]

The mess teams received thirty days of special instructions at the American School Center in England, and ten more in France, and were ready to go into the field in late November. They were dispatched from the Office of the Chief Quartermaster only on the request of an army, section, or other major headquarters. Much of their popularity could be attributed to the general understanding that their visits were for instruction rather than inspection, and that they were there actually to perform and demonstrate techniques of improving the operations of kitchen personnel. Working closely with the mess officer and mess sergeant, they checked every phase of a unit's mess activity from head count for strength through receipt of rations, serving of the food, and salvage of the waste. Because the teams could not possibly visit every mess in any given base section or army area, they concentrated on key installations whose visible improvement would most likely influence neighboring messes to raise their standards. Duty with these mess teams was extremely demanding. Experience demonstrated that the best results were

[102] (1) QM Supply in ETO, VIII, 262. (2) Littlejohn, ed., Passing in Review, ch. 47, "Food Service in the ETO During World War II," by Col. Patrick Buckley.

[103] IRS, CQM to DCQM, 17 Oct 44, sub: Ration Menu, Training of Subs Offs, etc. Littlejohn Reading File, vol. XXIX, item 85.

obtained when personnel were rotated between duty in the field and in the QM Subsistence Laboratory every thirty days. This also served to remind field commanders that the teams had been loaned and not assigned to them.

The teams sometimes found that supporting Class I depots were as much in need of instruction and guidance as messes. For example, on 20 December 1944 the theater Chief Surgeon, General Hawley, wrote to the Chief Quartermaster complaining that in Normandy Base Section hospital patients were receiving only C rations. He remarked that good food is the luxury that the battle casualty wants most—even more than good nursing. Littlejohn took prompt official action, but also pointed out to Hawley—a personal friend of long standing—that hospital quartermasters were not firm enough with the depots, and also did not appear to know what they were entitled to. He suggested some "education," and offered to provide it through his mess teams. Thereafter, mess teams included hospitals in their tours and hospital mess officers in their instructional conferences, and there were no further complaints.[104]

The work of the first six teams was so well received that six more were organized in January 1945. In addition to their normal functions, these teams also undertook and successfully accomplished several special projects. They designed pilot models of kitchen cars and prepared troop train menus for feeding reinforcements en route to the front by rail. They set up the first of the famous G.I. Joe diners along the routes of the Red Ball express. They did much of the pioneer work in planning and setting up the messes at Red Horse—the huge complex of staging areas opened around Le Havre early in 1945, and also in the temporary enclosures along the Rhine where almost a million German prisoners had to be fed with virtually no equipment whatsoever. U.S. troops had an unfortunate habit of seizing mess equipment as well as weapons from prisoners of war, who then had to be reequipped by the QMC.[105]

Serving Hot Meals to Front-Line Troops

Techniques employed in serving meals to front-line troops varied with the type of unit, the tactical situation, and the initiative of mess and other personnel. No standard operating procedure was ever formulated. Littlejohn believed that the attitude of the battalion commander was the controlling factor. In most situations, he could modify tactical dispositions enough to make feasible one expedient or another for feeding hot food to his troops. The initiative and effectiveness of mess personnel in the subordinate companies reflected the interest of the battalion commander. It was observed that in aggressive units, mess personnel were also aggressive and provided more cooked meals in the front lines.[106]

[104] Personal Ltrs, Hawley to Littlejohn, 20 Dec 44, and Littlejohn to Hawley, 22 Dec 44. Littlejohn Reading File, vol. XXXI, item 70.

[105] Littlejohn, ed., Passing in Review, ch. 8, p. 4; ch. 33, vol. I, pp. 150–53.

[106] (1) Maj. Gen. R. M. Littlejohn, "Feeding the Infantryman in Combat," QMTSJ (19 October 1945). (2) ETO Combat Obsvr, Immediate Rpt 143 by Col L. A. Webb, XX Corps, 25 May 45. ETO 376.2 (G–3).

Even in the most active situation, troops usually managed to heat a drink from the K or C ration. This was normally done in a canteen cup over a heat unit. The meat component of the C ration could be heated in the can directly over a flame and was superior in this respect to the K ration. Two-burner stoves were normally kept in vehicles, but were sometimes brought forward into foxholes as the situation stabilized. Cooking containers were for the most part large cans obtained from company kitchens. The troops usually heated C rations in boiling water in these cans. Early in 1945, one-burner stoves issued with a nesting pot and frying pan combination became available, and these were more suitable for front-line use. But normally no stoves or pots were carried in an initial advance. They were brought up by supporting or relief troops.[107]

If stoves were not available, improvised heating methods appeared in the front lines as the position stabilized. Gasoline poured over dirt in an empty C ration can provide an adequate but sooty source of heat. It could not be used in positions open to direct enemy observation. The same criticism applied to the expendable heat units issued with the C and 10-in-1 rations; both types were inferior to captured German heat tablets.[108] The 10-in-1 ration was seldom prepared by the infantry in the front lines.

In all but the most exposed positions it was usually possible to provide an A ration, cooked by company mess personnel, to front-line troops. The normal procedure was for all company kitchens to bivouac in the battalion service area. From there, hot food was taken forward in Marmite cans (insulated containers, round). Hot drinks were also transported in such containers if available, but a 5-gallon water can wrapped in blankets was a satisfactory substitute. Food and hot drink containers were transported forward as far as possible by ¼-ton trucks and trailers, which also carried necessary individual mess gear, usually only the cover of the meat can. Front-line troops normally kept their canteen cups and spoons with them at all times, and usually had a knife of some kind. The mess knife and fork and the meat can were not considered essential.

When the troops were advancing, the battalion staff carefully selected routes that could be used for the delivery of food, and it was normal for the battalion S-4 himself to guide the party transporting the first hot meal to a new position. Ideally, the jeep convoy visited each platoon headquarters, but if the tactical situation made such contact impossible, details of runners were waiting at prearranged rendezvous to carry the cans to each unit. Empty cans and meat can covers were retrieved later by the same method. With this arrangement, proximity of the kitchens to the front lines was of secondary importance compared to efficient mess operations uninterrupted by enemy action. If necessary the service area could be as much as five miles to the rear, and meals would still arrive hot in the front lines. On the other hand, company cooks or

---

[107] Ltr, CQM ETO to TQMG, 17 May 45, sub: Serving of Hot Meals to Front-Line Troops (Reference Cable WAR–74126, 28 Apr 45). Littlejohn Reading File, vol. XXXVIA, item 53.

[108] (1) *Ibid.* (2) U.S.-type heat units are described above, page 334, note 43.

other mess personnel were sent forward with the meals as often as possible. Their presence insured efficient and equitable serving of food, and also tended to improve the quality of the ration. By mingling with the men in the line, cooks came to feel that they were an integral part of the fighting team, and duty-bound to deliver attractive, palatable, and nourishing meals. Although this procedure led to casualties among mess personnel, who were not easily replaced, tactical commanders considered it worthwhile.[109]

Special Menus for Allied and Enemy Nationals

ETO quartermasters gained a certain amount of experience in feeding non-U.S. personnel during 1943, when German prisoners were evacuated through England to the United States. As in most other matters involving direct contact with the enemy, the ETO followed procedures established in the Mediterranean. The arrival of the 2d French Armored Division in Great Britain from North Africa in the early months of 1944 provided the OCQM with a real introduction to Allied feeding problems. Here was a unit including Moslems, whose religion forbade them either pork or wine, and Frenchmen who demanded both. Wine was practically unobtainable in the British Isles, but the problem of fresh meat for Moslems was readily solved by trading American pork for British mutton. Providing operational rations for the landing in Normandy was much less simple since all three meals of the K ration con-

tained pork, and of the old type of C rations only meat and vegetable stew was without pork. Under pressure of time, cased assorted C rations had to be issued to the division with the understanding that meat and beans and vegetable hash units would go to Frenchmen, while meat and vegetable stew would be reserved exclusively for Moslem troops.[110]

As the armies advanced into France, and later into Belgium and the Netherlands, natives of these countries were attached to the U.S. forces in various capacities, and the OCQM became responsible for supporting such people to varying degrees. Among civilians, mobile labor units, which received all their meals, were far outnumbered by static labor, which received a midday meal only. Allied military units were engaged in combat, employed as service troops, or given security duties. To establish a workable system for supplying these groups, they were divided into classes of military and paramilitary forces. Type A units, such as elements of General de Lattre's 1st French Army, were regularly constituted forces operating under American field commanders, and drew all their supplies through American supply channels. Italian and Slav service units were also included in this category. Type B units included elements from liberated countries, such as French and Dutch light infantry battalions and Belgian fusiliers and pioneer groups, who received American rations only when operating outside their own countries. Type C and D forces—paramilitary groups which

---

[109] Sources cited n. 106 and n. 107.

[110] Littlejohn, ed., Passing in Review, ch. 33, vol. I, pp. 43–45.

were not part of the regular military forces of liberated countries, such as the French Forces of the Interior, the Gendarmerie, and the Garde Mobile— were supplied from COMZ or army dumps only when under U.S. command. Since U.S. responsibility for these units was constantly fluctuating, obtaining the proper classification and strength figures proved difficult throughout hostilities and, notwithstanding its importance for the replacement of stocks, such information always had to be approximated crudely. Actual issues were almost invariably at odds with even short-term forecasts—a statement admirably illustrated by comparing Table 16 with Table 11.[111]

Toward the end of hostilities reported issues from COMZ depots *(Table 16)* ceased to reflect the number of persons actually being fed with any degree of reliability. During the interval between submission of a daily telegram and receipt of the requested supplies, the numbers needing food often increased tremendously. Class I distributing operations were so far-flung that when it became necessary to add a new category of persons receiving rations—for example, Allied POW's in German hospitals—six weeks were required to revise and distribute new requisition forms and to consolidate statistics on a new basis. The chief of the Subsistence Division, OCQM, therefore believed that the totals for April and May 1945 were too low by several hundred thousand.[112]

The situation was further complicated by a provision in the Yalta agreement of February 1945, giving special status to Soviet nationals liberated in western Europe, and entitling them to the maintenance allowances of recovered Allied military personnel. In effect, this category of personnel was transferred from Civil Affairs jurisdiction and became a direct military responsibility. Not only did this upset existing supply plans—for no such development had been anticipated and the number of liberated Russians rose to about 1,500,-000 by V–E Day—but it aroused the resentment of French, Dutch, Belgian, and Luxembourg displaced persons in Germany who were obliged to accept lower allowances.[113]

No one had foreseen that subsistence requirements for these sundry groups would approach the enormous dimensions and qualitative complexity ultimately reached. At first it did not appear possible, or even desirable, to make a single menu, since dietary preferences and even religious proscriptions had to be honored, and obviously these varied with each nationality. Neither was it possible to follow consistently the menu made out for each group. Colonel Fitzpatrick, a member of General Littlejohn's subsistence staff, who was probably as familiar with ration problems as any officer in the theater, brought out clearly the problems actually involved in the physical distribution of supplies:

Every supply point had the Type A ration and the Type A hospital supplement

---

[111] (1) USFET Gen Bd Study 109, pp. 64–69. (2) *QM Supply in ETO,* IX, 56–57.

[112] (1) Littlejohn, ed., Passing in Review, ch. 33, pp. 140–45. (2) OTCQM TSFET Operational Study 8, exhibit A, gives the total being fed on 15 May 1945 as 7,696,618 persons.

[113] USFET Gen Bd Rpt 35, Displaced Persons, Refugees, and Recovered Allied Military Personnel, pp. 21–22.

TABLE 16—AVERAGE OF DAILY RATION ISSUES

OCTOBER 1944–SEPTEMBER 1945

Week Ending	Type A Ration Categories	Allied Troops	Allied Labor	Enemy POW's	Total
14 October 1944.......	2,433,220	8,997	8,551	161,289	2,612,057
31 October 1944	2,364,899	22,726	8,084	178,993	2,574,702
15 November 1944	2,640,919	37,135	8,634	187,918	2,874,606
30 November 1944	2,620,888	29,954	6,071	190,026	2,846,939
16 December 1944	2,756,037	34,181	8,248	207,796	3,006,262
30 December 1944	2,810,344	37,217	7,432	217,751	3,072,744
13 January 1945.......	2,822,921	48,077	19,970	247,668	3,138,636
27 January 1945.......	2,787,363	54,720	22,565	260,306	3,124,994
10 February 1945......	2,840,045	57,659	30,428	254,700	3,182,832
24 February 1945......	3,017,146	57,663	31,685	250,064	3,356,558
10 March 1945	3,366,334	130,823	54,807	314,685	3,866,649
24 March 1945	3,679,340	393,526	77,206	404,781	4,554,853
7 April 1945	3,974,591	387,382	71,558	622,392	5,055,923
21 April 1945	4,101,077	393,099	91,228	843,131	5,428,535
5 May 1945	3,634,660	381,534	91,181	1,751,513	5,858,888
19 May 1945	3,605,066	634,662	110,325	2,425,532	6,775,585
2 June 1945	3,441,171	603,326	103,077	2,402,940	6,550,514
16 June 1945	3,979,639	336,914	114,088	2,061,167	6,491,808
30 June 1945	3,226,056	314,941	98,147	1,412,099	5,051,743

Source: Littlejohn, ed., Passing in Review, ch. 33, vol. I, Exhibit 7.

to issue. If it had in its neighborhood all of the five Allied categories . . . it would have to issue on six additional scales (two for civilian labor) . . . If it had POW concentrations to supply as well, three additional scales—for working, non-working, and hospitalized prisoners—would figure in its mission. Issuing on eleven different ration scales is a more complicated process than the average supply point can handle. It is quite certain that many of them took short cuts of one kind or another; many issued to all Allied nationals in accordance with the menu authorized for the largest category.[114]

Recognizing the practicality of this field expedient, in March 1945 the OCQM proposed a standard 3,000-calorie continental Allied menu applicable to every category except U.S. and British personnel, invalids, and prisoners of war. National food preferences were recognized by offering food options. With its many substitutions and varying allowances of the same items, this was still a complicated scheme, but considerably less so than five separate menus.[115] All these groups received more grain products, dried peas and beans, and potatoes than did American troops. (*Table 17*) Within the continental category French and Moslem units received the most fresh meat and leafy green and

---

[114] (1) Littlejohn, ed., Passing in Review, ch. 33, vol. I, p. 47. (2) Ltr, CQM for TQMG, 2 Apr 45, sub: Ration Situation in ETO. Littlejohn Reading File, vol. XXXV, item 10.

[115] See *QM Supply in ETO*, II, 97–143 for a breakdown of this composite menu and amounts allotted, and lists of menus for individual meals covering ten-day periods.

yellow vegetables, but less dairy and sugar products than others. Italian service units were given a higher amount of alimentary pastes and other starchy foods such as macaroni and spaghetti, and oils, while liberated Russian displaced persons received more fresh (especially dark) bread and potatoes and were provided with the buckwheat, cabbage, and sauerkraut necessary for such native foods as kasha and borscht. The menu provided 3,000 calories for sedentary personnel, and 3,400 for those engaged in hard labor. It offered the light breakfasts and heavy dinners generally preferred by Europeans, and it was flexible enough to utilize whatever ingredients were actually available at any given time.[116]

Like the separate rations for various nationalities which it superseded, the continental Allied ration was on the borderline of nutritional adequacy, and it was very important that the whole ration be consumed by all to whom it was issued. The preparation of acceptable menus was extremely difficult, since the ingredients available consisted of surplus U.S. Army items, presumably not very popular with the troops; locally procured produce; and a very restricted list of items such as dried eggs that were surplus in the United States despite a severe food shortage in the zone of interior. Moreover, since unbalanced items of the military ration were the primary sources of supply, the foods actually available for issue fluctuated constantly, and included many American ingredients unfamiliar to Europeans. Under the circumstances Capt. Cathryn R. VerMurlen, the chief of the Menu Branch of the Subsistence Division, found that preparing menus for Allied and enemy nationals was by far the most difficult aspect of her assignment. Catering for forces with unfamiliar and widely varying food habits was complicated by the fact that menus were subjected to constant modifications and substitutions, often at very short notice. The Menu Branch found it necessary to institute its own liaison system with the depots, to provide quick notification of changes in availability, and particularly to exploit local sources of fresh foods promptly. Unusual food combinations were frequently necessary, but could only be issued after approval by the Chief Surgeon. Untried menus required extensive checking in the field to assure that they could actually be fed as issued. These activities could only be entrusted to specialists, but the number of qualified dietitians in the theater was very limited. Nevertheless, the officers of the Menu Branch were able to provide a nutritionally adequate and acceptable diet for the various types of personnel for whom the U.S. forces were responsible.[117]

Menus for Prisoners of War

The problem of feeding POW's proved to be not only larger in scope but also more complex than that of feeding Allied nationals. Plans before D–day had anticipated that some 60,000 prisoners

---

[116] (1) *QM Supply in ETO*, II, 137–38; IX, 146–48. (2) Littlejohn, ed., *Passing in Review*, ch. 33, vol. I, p. 46.

[117] Ltr, CQM to CG ETO, 26 May 45, sub: Recommendation for Legion of Merit (Capt VerMurlen); Littlejohn Reading File, vol. XXXVIA, item 76; Memo, CQM for G–4, 7 Mar 45, sub: Menus in Effect in ETO. Littlejohn Reading File, vol. XXXIV, item 26.

would be captured by D plus 90, and that all of them would be evacuated to England as soon as possible. No provision for their support had been made beyond three and a half C rations per prisoner—a suitable type and allowance for men in transit to the United Kingdom. Actually, more than 170,000 men had been captured by early September, and since it was decided to hold most of them on the Continent as laborers, the burden of feeding them fell on COMZ. The policy of feeding C rations to POW's had to be changed as soon as the armies broke out of the beachhead in late July, since C rations were required for the combat troops.

Inevitably, with the improvement of the tactical situation and the increasing influx of prisoners, a shortage of POW rations developed. By the end of November, almost 200,000 POW's had to be fed; by the beginning of March 1945, over 300,000; by the end of March, almost 600,000; a month later, more than 1,500,000; and almost another million surrendered in the next three weeks.[118] (See Table 16.)

With such numbers involved, it became impossible to evacuate them to the rear as fast as they surrendered, and large numbers became responsibilities of ADSEC in the area immediately west of the Rhine. In April that headquarters established large depots solely for POW supplies at Rheinberg (near Duisburg), Sinzig, and Bingen, under control of the 56th QM Base Depot. Sixteen POW camps in those areas had to be supplied largely by collecting captured supplies from the armies and by local procure-

ment, since few U.S. supplies for prisoners arrived during the speedy occupation of Germany. Military bakeries were not available, and local bakers contracted to provide nearly 400,000 pounds of bread per day for 782,000 prisoners in mid-May. At the same time Normandy Base Section was guarding 406,000 prisoners and Oise Section 262,000. The total number in U.S. custody on 20 May was 2,884,762, or about 460,000 more than were receiving U.S. rations. During the months that followed the French and Belgian Governments agreed to accept about 1,600,000 prisoners.

The U.S. forces had begun releasing miners, farmers, and transportation workers as early as March 1945 for labor in occupied areas of Germany. After V–E Day all POW's over fifty years of age were released and in certain areas, especially Austria, enemy soldiers who laid down their arms were not taken into custody unless they were members of the SS or officials of the Nazi party. Supply officers hoped that such persons, classified as Disarmed Enemy Forces, could be fed by the German regional governments responsible for their security. This hope was only partially realized, and in mid-August 732,000 POW's and 588,000 disarmed Germans were still dependent upon the Quartermaster Service. Both received the POW ration.[119]

The terms of the Geneva Convention provided that prisoners would be fed a type A ration equal in quantity and quality to that of custodial troops in base camps, but it soon became apparent that this allowance could not be provided. When reports were received that Ameri-

---

[118] Littlejohn, ed., Passing in Review, ch. 33, vol. I, p. 45.

[119] (1) QM Supply in ETO, IX, 67, 127. (2) Hist of QM ADSEC, pp. 35–37.

TABLE 17—COMPARISON OF CONTINENTAL AND POW RATIONS WITH U.S. RATION

Food group	Continental civilian[a] employee menu 25 April 1945 (lbs/1,000 rations)	Russian repatriates menu 25 April 45 (lbs/1,000 rations)	I.S.U.[b] menu 25 April 1945 (lbs/1,000 rations)	Other[c] liberated manpower menu 25 April 1945 (lbs/1,000 rations)	POW menu #2 nonworking 16 April 45 (lbs/1,000 rations)	POW menu working 16 April 45 (lbs/1,000 rations)	Revised POW hospital supplement Oct 1945 (lbs/1,000 rations)	ETOUSA Cir. 96 12 Sep 1944 (lbs/1,000 rations)	U.S. type May 1945 (lbs/1,000 rations)
Meat (as boneless)	215.63	263.05	246.80	285.50	124.99	124.99	172.00	759.38	738
Eggs (dhy)	60	18	39	22	15	35	30	37.50	36
Milk (as dried)	59.15	20.38	59.89	30.19	39	39	81.51	132.81	145
Cheese	16	49	5	12	13	17	10	(d)	(d)
Total	350.78	350.43	350.69	349.69	191.99	215.99	293.51	929.69	921
Butter, canned-oleomargarine		8		12			30	[e]72.50	[e]65
Other fats	35	15	71	24	19.50	40.50	31.50	46.88	44
Grain products	1,089	1,480	1,085	1,477	933	1,107	60	718.75	714
Sugars & syrups	221	94	202	221	105	202	147	331.25	352
Dried legumes	116	139	142	71	142	142		88.13	80
Potatoes (as fresh)	780	795	415	452	500	750		687.50	567
Tomato & tomato products	115.29	101.92	121.22	103.81	64.33	64.33	57.33	234.30	215
Lemon crystals	2.76	4.14	14.49	6.21	13.80	13.80		[f]156.25	[f]139
Vegetables, leafy, green, and yellow, canned	102.49	113.86	114.93	95.07	73.56	73.56	19.68	406.25	184
Vegetables, leafy, green, and yellow, dhy				10.50	14	14			
Other vegetables, canned	57.57	24.76	75.57	56.64	55.71	55.71		250	159
Other vegetables, dhy	1		2	1	10.50	10.50			
Other fruits, canned	96.75		78.75	101.25	30	68	20.25	312.5	344
Fruits, dried	50	48	43	48			18	43.75	32
Beverages	66	42	38	67	51.50	51.50	10	105	98
Miscellaneous (condiments)	33.35	34.60	40.70	39.85	21.88	21.88	10	143.75	61
Calories	3,000	3,370	3,100	3,185	2,250	2,900	1,112	4,050	4,114

[a] For civilian laborers doing exceptionally hard work, an increase was authorized of 16 lbs. macaroni, 100 lbs. bread and 24 lbs. marmalade per 1,000 rations. This augmentation increased the calories to 3,200.

[b] For Italian service units doing exceptionally hard work, an increase was authorized of 90 lbs. macaroni and 180 lbs. potatoes (fresh) per 1,000 rations. This augmentation increased the calories to 3,300.

[c] A 3,400 calorie diet could be provided by the addition of the following: 14 lbs. [e]eggs, dhy., 150 lbs. bread, and 12 lbs. marmalade per 1,000 rations.

[d] Cheese included with milk products.

[e] Fresh butter with type "A" rations.

[f] Includes citrus fruits & juices.

Source: Passing in Review, Chapter 33, by Col. Edwin J. Fitzpatrick, "Subsistence Experience in the ETO," Pt I, App. 5-A.

can prisoners in German camps were suffering from malnutrition and that the average ration in the German Army approximated 2,700 calories, the OCQM decided that there was no justification for providing the German soldier with a ration increase of 25 percent merely because he had achieved prisoner of war status. General Littlejohn contended, in fact, that it would be wasteful to feed an American ration of 3,700 to 4,000 calories to prisoners who were accustomed to less than American soldiers.[120]

The first continental prisoner of war menu, circulated in August 1944, modified the A ration to eliminate such items as fruit juices, chicken, turkey, ham, and pork loins, and to reduce the quantities of evaporated and powdered milk, fresh butter, condiments, salad oil, coffee, and lard. To offset these reductions, higher allowances were authorized for fresh bread, stewing meats, uncooked cereals, Vienna sausage, chili con carne, and canned meats. These departures from the standard A ration lowered the caloric content of the POW ration and provoked considerable discussion on both sides of the Atlantic. When the issue reached General George C. Marshall, the Chief of Staff, he held that captured troops need not be fed ration components identical to those served American troops, so long as the nutritive value was matched. But it soon proved impossible to meet the latter requirement, in view of the simultaneous occurrence of the world food crisis and the rapid influx of prisoners. Just before V–E Day, in an

effort to feed the thousands of prisoners collected in open enclosures beyond the Rhine, the official POW menu was cut to 2,000 calories for nonworking prisoners and to 2,900 calories for working prisoners. These were lower than the figures agreed upon by Generals Gregory and Littlejohn, but they were still within the recommendations of the National Research Council. General Littlejohn argued that this menu was not likely to lead to malnutrition: "Definitely I do not intend to go along on a ration which will cause prisoners to starve to death, or throw them into our hospitals. Neither do I intend to be a party to a ration which will make the Germans fat." [121]

Reports from field observers confirmed that 2,000 calories were sufficient to maintain the condition of a healthy prisoner whose routine was limited to self-care, but the surveys showed that a majority of prisoners were suffering from various dietary deficiencies when captured. In the months before the final surrender the German army ration was very low in riboflavin and nicotinic acid, and in the last weeks all food supplies had dwindled. It had proved impossible to make good these deficiencies in the temporary enclosures where ADSEC units attempted to feed hundreds of thousands of prisoners, mainly on captured supplies and using rudimentary kitchen equipment. The same surveys showed that in the processes of distribution, breakdown, and food preparation, losses reduced a 2,000 calorie menu to an actual diet of about 1,750 calories. All these factors had led to serious under-

---

[120] (1) *QM Supply in ETO,* IX, 48. (2) Memo, CQM for QM's All Base Secs, 6 Aug 44, sub: Use of POW Clothing and Rations. Littlejohn Reading File, vol. XXVII, item 13.

[121] (1) *QM Supply in ETO,* IX, 66–67. (2) Personal Ltr, Littlejohn to Middleswart, 10 Apr 45. Littlejohn Collection.

nourishment, and the official ration was immediately raised to 2,250 calories for nonworking prisoners and 2,900 for those who were working. Serious cases of malnutrition were hospitalized and placed on the menu for nonworking prisoners plus a 1,100 calorie hospital supplement. Less serious cases received the ration for workers for twenty days before actually being assigned to work details.

Unfortunately, it was not possible to extend these policies to cover the prisoners who had been transferred to other nations. Civil Affairs officials held, with apparent justice, that the rations of prisoners should not exceed those of civilian refugees. This argument ignored the fact that the ration of a captured soldier comprised all the food that he would receive, whereas the ration of a civilian usually meant his official allowance issued against his ration card. It did not include food obtained from relatives in the country, from the black market, or issued as a bonus by his employer. Objections caused by incomplete understanding of this important difference, among both foreign officials and U.S. staff officers, delayed efforts to raise the caloric value of rations for prisoners.[122]

From the first, basic supply doctrine had called for the issue of captured subsistence to prisoners before American foodstuffs were provided; indeed every POW menu bore a clear statement to this effect at the bottom of the page. But throughout hostilities there was a gap between policy and practice. Army and base section quartermasters failed to inventory and report such supplies, thereby making it difficult to transfer excesses

from one area to another. As a result POW's at enclosures in areas lacking captured subsistence continued to be fed C & K rations. Once established, that policy was hard to change, although it was much criticized in light of the need for operational rations among combat troops. In October, Colonel Franks, the Deputy Chief Quartermaster, seeking to alleviate this situation, appointed an officer from the OCQM Subsistence Division to tour the base sections and secure their co-operation. In November Littlejohn complained that he had received exactly one satisfactory inventory of captured enemy supplies to date.[123]

Failure to utilize captured subsistence was less serious than the accompanying misuse of U.S. supplies. Throughout the duration of hostilities violations of menus recurred and drew the attention of subsistence authorities. In fact, outside the QMC there was a tendency to regard menus as suggestions rather than as binding military directives. The excuses offered by the delinquent parties were varied. One unit serving B rations to prisoners contended that it was simpler to consolidate the food drawn for both American and captured troops into a common mess and serve a uniform meal. Even the plea of ignorance was raised to explain the failure to comply with a POW menu. Littlejohn informed the ETO Provost Marshal that officers could be held financially responsible for overissues to POW's but apparently nothing came of this suggestion. Ulti-

---

[122] Littlejohn, ed., Passing in Review, ch. 33, vol. I, pp. 49–50; ch. 32, p. 22.

[123] (1) Ltr, DCQM to QM's All Base Secs, 20 Oct 44, sub: Utilization of Captured German Subs. Hist Br OQMG. (2) OCQM ETO Cir 43, 7 Sep 44, Program for Consumption of Operational Rations. (3) IRS, CQM to DCQM, no sub, 15 Nov 44. Littlejohn Reading File, vol. XXX, item 36.

mately, the OCQM notified the ADSEC quartermaster that every depot, every distribution point, every organization having custody over captured troops was to follow the special POW menu.[124]

Food for Refugees and Displaced Persons

Relief for civilians in the European theater was a Civil Affairs (G–5) responsibility, and the OCQM processed requisitions but did not compute requirements. Civil Affairs supplies were issued in bulk from Quartermaster depots for distribution through Civil Affairs channels. All planners were in agreement that Civil Affairs supplies were to supplement and not to replace local resources. Nevertheless, a minimum relief ration, for planning purposes and to be fed to those without other sources of nourishment, was a basic necessity. After prolonged negotiation in London and Washington, the following basic ration was agreed upon by the Combined Civil Affairs Committee (CCAC) in December 1943: [125]

Item	Ounces	Calories
Cheese	0.50	55
Fats	.50	127
Flour	15.00	1,515
Legumes, dry	1.00	100
Meat and vegetable stew	2.25	65
Salt	.50	...
Soup, dehydrated	2.00	178

Item	Ounces	Calories
Sugar	.50	50
Total	22.25	2,090

Supplemental items:

Item	Ounces	Calories
Milk, evaporated [a]	2.00	74
Coffee (per week) [b]	2.00	0
Vitaminized chocolate [a]	1.00	[c]

[a] Supplement for children and nursing mothers—estimate furnished to 25 percent of total fed.
[b] Furnished to 75 percent of total fed.
[c] Caloric value not given.

Since this allowance was less than the minimum POW ration, the decision received a considerable amount of unfavorable publicity, but Littlejohn pointed out that the official ration was a prisoner's sole source of nourishment, whereas civilians were not without opportunities to supplement that diet, however unreliable or intermittent those opportunities might be.[126]

Total food requirements were likewise a subject of prolonged discussion. One early estimate, submitted to the International Aid Division, ASF, by the OQMG, was based on liberating 25 million people in western Europe in the first three months. These would require 450 million relief rations, or 20 percent of their total subsistence, amounting to 282,000 long tons.[127] Later computations were considerably more conservative. For example, in March 1944 the Supply Subcommittee of the Combined Civil Affairs Committee approved 90-day requirements for the ANVIL operation based on 1,500 calories for 65 percent of a population of 7,600,000, or about 49,000 tons.[128] But once established on

---

[124] (1) Ltr, DCQM to QM's All Base Sections . . ., 20 Oct 44, sub: Utilization of Captured German Subs. Hist Br OQMG. (2) Ltr, Asst AG COMZ to All Sec Comdrs COMZ, 26 Dec 44, sub: Violations of POW Menus. OQM SUSA, 430. (3) Memo, CQM 4 Gen. Reckord, 16 Feb 45, sub: Feeding of POW's. Littlejohn Reading File, vol. XXXIII, item 85.
[125] USFET Gen Bd Study 109, p. 61.

[126] Interv with Littlejohn, 5 Jul 59.
[127] *QM Supply in ETO,* IX, 13.
[128] History of Civil Supply Branch, International Division ASF, p. 169. MS, OCMH.

the Continent, Civil Affairs officials came to the conclusion that the larger figures had been more nearly correct. For the period April–September 1945, for example, the Combined Civil Affairs Committee computed that France alone would require about 500,000 tons of supplies per month, while on a per capita basis the needs of Belgium and the Netherlands were still greater. It was, of course, impossible to meet these requirements for a variety of reasons, including a world-wide food shortage, the rival claims of the Mediterranean theater, shipping shortages, and congestion at ports.

Tactical Civil Affairs planning within the assault forces was on an entirely different basis. SHAEF had allocated cross-Channel transportation for 49,636 long tons of Civil Affairs food in the first 90 days, all except 777 tons being of British origin. The detailed plan for the U.S. forces provided that 725 tons of food would be landed during the first 20 days, and then about 330 tons per day until D plus 90.[129] This plan was followed until it became evident that there was no food shortage in Normandy. On UTAH Beach, the 54th QM Base Depot stored such items as flour, pinto beans, welfare biscuits, and soap, separately from those Quartermaster supplies destined for issue to troops. In the first six weeks of operations, 5,500 tons of Civil Affairs supplies were landed on the beaches, but only 114 tons were distributed, mostly through French civil agencies. When transportation was at a premium during the breakthrough period, these supplies were temporarily left behind with other low priority items with

the result that captured enemy foodstuffs, primarily earmarked for POW's, had to be issued to Allied military units, or released for the use of civilians in urban areas.

German supplies were uncovered in huge quantities. Captured stocks sometimes contained luxury items rather than necessities; the enemy depot at Chartres, for example, turned out to have enormous stocks of chinaware, glassware, silverware, and furniture at a time when Quartermaster inventory teams were hoping to locate badly needed blankets, mess gear, and kitchen utensils.[130]

The discovery of potentially useful captured materials did not in itself assure their availability for either military units or Civil Affairs. Since the rules of land warfare relating to captured equipment did not apply to liberated territories, definitions had to be established for enemy materials uncovered in France which were of uncertain origin or manufacture. The matter came up in connection with supplies discovered in Paris, and was threshed out in protracted correspondence involving Generals Littlejohn, Lee, Lord, and Brig. Gen. Pleas B. Rogers, the commanding general of Seine Section. Littlejohn failed to establish title to the canned vegetables he particularly wanted, but he managed to acquire them on loan, to be replaced later. This was satisfactory in the currently tense tactical situation.

The final decision was that items that had been clearly under French ownership prior to acquisition and were not produced by order of the Germans were available to the Allied forces only by

---

[129] *QM Supply in ETO*, IX, 13, 97, 99.

[130] Ltr, QM Loire Sec to CQM, 15 Sep 44, sub: POW Supplies. Hist Br OQMG.

FOOD ARRIVING IN PARIS *by airlift, August 1944.*

requisition from the French Government. Supplies produced in France by order of the enemy, on the other hand, could be used by Allied forces when needed, but all doubts as to the circumstances of origin were to be resolved in favor of French ownership. Thus, the chief sources of captured food available to the Allied armies had to be those which had been manifestly imported from Germany. Amidst these various categories, confusion inevitably arose from the failure of the French to report captured supplies to the Allies, and failure of the armies to advise G–5 of available surpluses. Even the Germans sought to use their vanishing assets as a weapon to confound Allied unity. On the day before the fall of Paris, the German commander of the city, in a shrewd attempt to prevent local stocks of German food from falling into the hands of the American or French troops, transferred the titles of all such foodstuffs to the International Red Cross.[131] This scheme was thwarted, but the amount of food involved was small in relation to the needs of Paris. By mid-August G–5 set aside 3,000,000 C rations to provide immediate relief, and requested 3,000,000 more as the city fell. The OCQM con-

---

[131] (1) Procedures Followed by Civil Affairs and Military Government in Restoration, Reorganization, and Supervision of Indigenous Civil Administration. USFET Gen Bd Study 33, pp. 114–15. (2) Ltr, CQM to G–4, 23 Sep 44, sub: Captured Food Supplies in SBS. Littlejohn Reading File, vol. XXVIII, item 164.

sidered operational rations unsuitable, as well as critically scarce at the time, and refused the request.

Third Army Civil Affairs shipments, largely canned milk, fats, chocolate, and soap, were the first to reach Paris, and by the end of August a daily allocation of 1,500 tons by 12th Army Group was arriving. Over 100,000 people had fled to rural areas, where they could be fed easily. To alleviate the situation in Paris they were not permitted to return for several weeks. Actually, the city's situation was considerably less serious than anticipated, requiring a restoration of law and order rather more than relief operations. A particularly unfortunate aspect of the situation was that much food had found its way into black-market channels, and that only the wealthier part of the population could afford to purchase it. Black-marketing, regarded as a patriotic enterprise under the German occupation, tended to linger on after the liberation in many parts of France.[132]

Toward the end of September small amounts of Civil Affairs supplies from the beaches began to arrive in northeastern France. The Third Army depot at Verdun received one hundred truck and trailer loads of varied foodstuffs, and in the next two weeks the depot was calling for more food, winter clothing, blankets, and sanitary supplies. After the siege and fall of Metz, Third Army's request

for 1,900 tons of Civil Affairs food was answered with a mere 36 tons, and a stringent situation was relieved only by the capture of 150 tons of frozen beef, 20 tons of frozen pork, and 650 tons of flour.[133] Reliance on captured supplies continued longer than anticipated for a number of reasons. Contrary to expectation, Belgium was in a far more serious state than France, and northeastern France was also suffering and unable to provide aid. These were industrial areas which even in peacetime had a deficit of food. Also, low priorities for transport from the beaches hindered the adequate delivery of G–5 supplies during the first six months.[134]

As the armies moved eastward, and French local and national administrations became fully operative in the rear areas, the responsibility for meeting civilian needs was slowly assumed by French civil agencies, but this applied only to the French zone of the interior, which was extended very gradually. Belgium remained an area of severe shortages, primarily because it continued to be within the combat zone. In February, General Littlejohn was hopeful that the Army's responsibility for all provisioning of French civilians would be speedily terminated, since too many Quartermaster units were involved in this mission at a time when they could have been advantageously used elsewhere. When he recognized that this responsibility was likely to prevail until May, he directed his deputy to employ as much civilian labor as possible for this purpose. "We cannot indefinitely

---

[132] (1) 12th Army Group Rpt of Opns, VII, 15. (2) IRS, G–5 COMZ to G–4, 22 Aug 45, and Inds, sub: Earmarking C Rations. Littlejohn Reading File, vol. XXVII, item 157. (3) Stars and Stripes (London), 1 September 1944, stated that the Paris black market was still flourishing, with eggs selling at 30¢ each and $20.00 demanded for a kilo of butter.

[133] TUSA AAR, II, G–5, 12, 19.
[134] (1) USFET Gen Bd Study 109, p. 63. (2) 12th Army Group Rpt of Opns, VII, 32–33.

tie down military personnel for the handling of civil affairs supplies. Furthermore when a country has large unemployment, and we, in turn, tie up military personnel to feed people either on or off the dole, it does not make good sense to me." [135]

The manpower problem became increasingly irksome as large amounts of Civil Affairs supplies were delivered to Quartermaster depots in broken, damaged, or weakened containers which had not withstood the rigors of handling. Because of insufficient materials and personnel to repack these items properly, Littlejohn suggested prompt local distribution to civilian agencies in the immediate areas where the broken packages were located.[136] Wheat, bulk and bagged, was probably the largest single item of Civil Affairs supplies, reaching amounts which could not be handled in civilian mills or warehouses and which had to be stored under improvised conditions. Furthermore, since the theater lacked individuals qualified to supervise the handling, storage, and milling of bulk wheat, the OCQM was obliged to recruit such technicians from the United States.[137]

At Quartermaster depots, normal procedures were followed in handling Civil Affairs supplies. Extra copies of all receipts and tally-outs were prepared and forwarded to G–5, but otherwise documentation was identical. The initial shipments of Civil Affairs supplies were all British, and many of them were purely military items, not specially marked. This practice caused considerable confusion, since an attempt was made to keep separate records. All G–5 supplies imported from the United States were distinctively marked with six rows of small green dots on a white band. A difficulty of another kind arose because Civil Affairs officers wrongly assumed that Civil Affairs and military stocks were identical and interchangeable, and that they could readily draw on military stocks in forward depots, replacing them with Civil Affairs reserves in rear areas. The OCQM consented to such exchanges only in emergencies, since differences in weights and sizes of containers made for complicated and laborious computations—not just once at a major depot, but every time that Civil Affairs supplies were included in a ration breakdown for a tactical unit. Even more serious was the inferior packing of Civil Affairs supplies, which made it virtually impossible to store these commodities in the open, as was done with military items. This greatly reduced the value of Civil Affairs supplies for use by the troops.[138]

Food in the Final Phases

By the spring of 1945, subsistence for U.S. Forces was only half, and the less complicated half, of the ETO quartermaster's Class I responsibility. On 26

---

[135] Memo, CQM for Franks, 20 Feb 45, sub: Handling of CA Supplies. Littlejohn Reading File, vol. XXXIII, item 114.

[136] (1) Memo, CQM for Chief S&D Div, 5 Mar 45, sub: CA Supplies Received in Damaged Condition. Littlejohn Reading File, vol. XXXIV, item 16. (2) *QM Supply in ETO,* IX, 26–27.

[137] OTCQM TSFET Operational Study 16, Planning for Non-T/O QM Units, p. 13.

[138] (1) Depot Operating Instrs, OCQM, 1 Nov 44, p. 57. (2) OTCQM TSFET Operational Study 12, exhibit A, p. 6. (3) Memo, Chief Subs Div for CQM, 17 Nov 44, sub: Supply Lines. Hist Br OQMG.

April, Littlejohn calculated that he was issuing 6,236,000 rations per day, although his requisitions for the month had presumed a ration strength of only 4.7 million. A very heavy consumption of A rations had resulted from the authorized overissue to combat divisions, air combat crews, and troops engaged in hard labor. At the same time components of this high quality ration were being distributed to clubs, snack bars, and British and French military personnel. SHAEF had ordered that liberated manpower serving under the army groups and in COMZ were to be fed the same scale of ration as the Allied forces with which they were working. The unexpected numbers of enemy prisoners—reaching 1.4 million by 21 April, twice the figure for which POW rations had been requisitioned—constituted another drain.[139] Supply officers had assumed that the enemy prisoners would be fed largely from stocks of captured German food, but these never proved sufficient and there was no alternative but to draw on American rations, usually the operational types. This unanticipated demand for operational rations came at a time when the rapidly advancing armies were drawing heavily on such rations for their own use, and the result was a precipitous drop in the theater reserves of packaged rations.[140]

As if these theater-wide problems were not sufficiently irksome, the War Department notified the various theaters that food reserves in the United States were

being depleted. Fresh and canned meat, canned fruits and vegetables, dehydrated potatoes, rice, dried yeast, and spices were the particularly critical items.[141] While feeding the largest military establishment in its history and seeking to satisfy increasing domestic demands, the United States was obliged to send food supplies to the civilian populations of liberated countries. The theaters were advised that in lieu of solid canned meats and meat cuts they would receive egg products, spaghetti, macaroni, beans, and stews. The ETO managed to surmount these difficulties and the final A ration before V–E Day, although comprising reduced amounts of all the critical items, actually showed a slight increase in nutritional value over the ration authorized in September 1944.[142]

In addition to vigorously supporting General Lee's "no waste" conservation drive, Littlejohn ordered a 10 percent reduction in rations for sedentary military personnel, limitations on guests in military messes, and a cut in the menus of nonworking or moderately working enemy prisoners.[143] The War Depart-

---

[139] (1) Ltr, CQM to CG COMZ, 24 Apr 45, sub: Mil Ration in the ETO. Hist Br OQMG. (2) Hist of QM ADSEC, p. 13.

[140] (1) 12th Army Group Rpt of Opns, XII, 209. (2) FUSA Rpt of Opns, 23 Feb–8 May 45, III, 47, 52. (3) TUSA AAR, II, QM 22, 25, 29. (4) SUSA Rpt of Opns, III, 893.

[141] (1) Cable WARX–46989, AGWAR to SHEAF et al., 3 Mar 45. (2) See Marion Massen, Canned Meats Procurement for the Armed Forces During World War II, Chicago Quartermaster Depot Studies, Report 7, March 1946, pages 95–119, for the best brief statement of canned meat production difficulties at this time.

[142] (1) Ltr, CQM to Hardigg, 21 Mar 45, sub: Subs Requisitions From ETO. Littlejohn Reading File, vol. XXXIV, item 72. (2) See Table 17.

[143] (1) Ltr, CQM to G–4 COMZ, 22 Mar 45, sub. Conservation of Food; Ltr, CQM to TQMG, 27 Mar 45, sub: Supplies for American Red Cross. Littlejohn Reading File, vol. XXXIV, items 73, 96. (2) Cable WARX–16410, AGWAR to ETOUSA, 31 Mar 45. (3) Ltr, CQM to CG COMZ, 24 Apr 45, sub: Mil Ration in the ETO. (4) 12th Army Group Rpt of Opns, XII, 209. (5) Ltr, CG CBS to Units CBS, 3 May 45, sub: Reduction in Issue of A Ration. CBS 430.2.

ment even went so far as to urge a 50 percent reduction in the supplies of lard, evaporated milk, coffee, and sugar issued to the Red Cross for its doughnut and clubmobile program. Littlejohn defended the Red Cross as a major contributor to Army morale and the proposal was dropped.

The termination of hostilities on 8 May did not immediately solve the food shortages. Until the redeployment machinery got into gear, the number of troops in the theater was unchanged and problems of civil affairs and military government continued to increase. Conservation was emphasized and re-emphasized, and the troops for the most part were willing to co-operate. The specter of undernourished displaced persons, emaciated survivors of the concentration camps, and a devastated Europe made most American soldiers accept a reduction in their rations without complaint. Even with this reduction, it was evident that Littlejohn was fully justified in his statement that the ETO A ration was "the best ration that any army has ever had at any time."[144] This was a compliment to his able and hard-working subsistence officers, echoed by General Patton, and even conceded by the hypercritical editors of *Yank*.

The reference was, of course, to the ETO version of the A ration, an outstandingly fine diet for men in combat. This was a careful blend of imported and locally procured foods for which the ingenious dietitians of the Medical Corps deserve special recognition. It appears probable that the ETO A ration

has contributed materially to improved civilian food habits in the United States since World War II. Millions of men returned to their homes after becoming accustomed to a diet containing more fresh meat, more milk products, and more fresh vegetables, fruits, and fruit juices than they had consumed before the war.

But to a subsistence specialist, there was nothing very difficult about formulating an excellent ration if the necessary ingredients, and also the trained cooks to prepare it, were available. Quartermasters in the European theater held that the real difficulties were not in writing the menu but in following it, under any and all conditions of battle, weather, and transportation rationing. They took pride in the fact that they had somehow managed to feed the A ration to 79 percent of all troops during the entire campaign on the Continent. Since the difficulty in distributing a ration was directly proportional to its quality and variety, this consistent success in providing the best possible ration, regardless of the tactical situation, was a major accomplishment. It was done by keeping the whole pipeline from NYPE to the army truckheads filled with balanced rations, a difficult and troublesome process requiring very careful control and painstaking administration. The results materialized as tens of millions of extra hot meals, served to troops who would otherwise have had to eat operational rations. And despite all the technical improvements made during World War II, operational rations were still no satisfactory substitute for kitchen-prepared meals. The subsistence officers of the OCQM and of the base sections, and the Class I officers of the depots and railheads, all being

---

[144] Memo, CQM for Chief Subs Div, 22 May 45, sub: Statistical Rpts, Stock Levels, Balanced Rations. Littlejohn Reading File, vol. XXXVII, item 58.

imbued with the "subsistence philosophy" mentioned at the beginning of

this chapter, felt that the results achieved
had been worth the extra effort.

CHAPTER XVI

Clothing for the ETO Enlisted Man

Clothing and Individual Equipment

Comprising some 50,000 different items, clothing and equipment (Class II and IV) was the most complicated category of Quartermaster supply. The combat troops only needed such supplies intermittently, and in quantities far smaller than their steady requirements for rations and gasoline.[1] But when the need for Class II and IV items arose it was usually immediate and urgent, and required complicated procedures for requisitioning, inventory, distribution, and tariff balancing that were not encountered in dealing with other QM supplies. Except for combat losses, clothing and equipment were regarded as nonexpendable, and troops received a complete new combat-type outfit at the beginning of a campaign. Apart from unexpected tactical developments or drastic changes in the weather, it was assumed that this initial issue would be sufficient for a predictable length of time, during which commanders and senior logistical staff officers expected to ignore the minor shortages that might arise and concentrate on their more essential daily requirements. Consequently the transportation priority assigned to clothing and equipment was kept low until shortages became rather serious, and then was raised to overcome them.

Possibly because of the relatively small tonnages involved, there was a tendency at higher staff levels to minimize the importance of clothing and equipment and an urge to handle this category of supply on the same daily tonnage basis that was successfully applied to rations, gasoline, and ammunition. This was a major error. Needs for clothing and equipment were invariably for specific items and sizes, and not for bulk tonnage. Even at army level there was hardly such a thing as an average daily requirement for Class II and IV supply. The tactical units had understood this from the first, and normally drew such supplies direct from an army depot on a weekly or ten-day basis against a requisition submitted in advance.[2]

Gradually the armies also came to realize that only a large specialized depot, with ample stocks of all Class II and IV supplies to support several armies, could meet these specific de-

---

[1] (1) See Chapter I for definitions of Class II and Class IV supplies. (2) For preinvasion planning, QM Class II and IV items were computed as 4.9 percent of all Quartermaster supplies, a figure roughly confirmed by experience.

[2] Ltr, CG FUSA to CG COMZ, 24 Aug 44, sub: Inadequacy of Present Level of QM Class II and IV Matériel for FUSA. USFET AG 400.34 (QM).

mands. Except for certain standard fast-moving items, an attempt to meet anticipated requirements by building up stocks at army level depots was not successful. After repeated moves by the depots, sizes were no longer properly balanced and inventories were no longer accurate. Stocks tended to become what was surplus to the needs of the particular army being supplied, although the same items might be desperately needed by another army.

The Class II and IV depot at Reims, later designated to serve all the armies in northern France, was formally activated on 23 September 1944 by the 55th QM Base Depot, and played a major role in the initial issue of winter clothing to the troops. Although transportation was very scarce the mechanics of initial issue were simple, and at first Reims operated more as a reconsignment point than as a real depot. Littlejohn had noted the advantages of this site on a major lateral rail line, and it passed to his direct control on 25 October. But another six weeks elapsed before the depot had sufficient balanced stocks to operate efficiently and promptly fill the specific requisitions of the armies. Those stocks were accumulated by mutual agreement of COMZ and 12th Army Group, despite the fact that SHAEF had allocated all tonnages for such supplies directly to the armies.[3]

The QM Class II Plan for OVERLORD

For reasons of mobility, the assault troops landing on the Normandy beaches brought ashore a minimum of clothing and equipment.[4] All troops involved in the initial attack had turned in their winter clothing before leaving the United Kingdom. Moreover, the combat units in the assault also gave up everything not absolutely essential. The only replacement clothing they carried was three pairs of socks per man. Apart from impregnated herringbone twill fatigues, worn primarily as protection against gas warfare but also for warmth and to shed rain, the ETO summer uniform was all wool. For winter, heavier items would be added, but summer items would not be turned in. During the first six weeks of combat, so-called beach maintenance sets were issued to division-sized units every five days. Each set would replace items of the assault outfit lost or destroyed during combat. This system of replacement was most successful, probably because the sets were not intended to augment the meager initial allowances but only to maintain them temporarily. Within those limitations, the sets obviated the usual complicated Class II and IV supply procedures in the forward areas. Replacement was simplified by denying the troops many items normally supplied even during active operations. For tactical units fighting in mild weather the policy was entirely satisfactory.[5]

Clothing Issues in Mild Weather

For the first month on the Continent, units were supplied direct from the beach dumps. The tarpaulin-covered boxes of the original skidloaded beach

---

[3] (1) Ruppenthal, *Logistical Support*, II, 178, 356. (2) See discussion of ADSEC advanced depots in Chapter XIII, above.

[4] See Table 8, above.
[5] See app. A.

ISSUING ITEMS FROM BEACH MAINTENANCE SETS *at the Normandy beachhead near Longueville, July 1944.*

maintenance sets proved useful for open storage of other clothing. Cherbourg, which was destined to become the main depot for the area, absorbing the OMAHA and UTAH dumps, was transferred from First Army to ADSEC control on 16 July. The previous day Littlejohn had assigned the future depot the mission of holding a 60-day level of Class II and IV supply for 385,000 men. By the end of July ADSEC reported that 45,000 long tons of QM Class II and IV supply had arrived on the Continent since D–day, but OCQM observers reported that many useless "filler" items had been included, and that pilferage and careless open storage had diminished the value of the stock.[6]

Littlejohn's depot plan was a first step toward a more orderly system of supply, but before the system could be put into full operation the troops had broken out

---

[6] (1) Hist of QM Sec ADSEC, p. 28. (2) Ltr, CQM to QM ADSEC, 15 Jul 44, sub: QM Depot Plan for Cherbourg; Memo, Littlejohn for Franks, 16 Jul 44, sub: QM and G–4 Rpts. Littlejohn Reading File, vol. XXVIA, items 70, 71.

of the beachhead and the pursuit phase of the campaign had begun. During early August some 600 tons of clothing and equipment were issued to Third Army from a dump at St. Jacques de Nehou, and about 800 tons to First Army from the dump at St. Lô. During the following period of daily tonnage rationing and rigid allocations, gasoline and rations were the important items, and clothing received low priorities. In practice, this meant that when available transportation was less than the allocation, Class II and IV supplies suffered. This applied equally to cross-Channel, rail, and highway tonnage allocations.

By early September the pursuit had ended and army quartermasters had time to take stock of their accumulated shortages, many of them dating back to the period of hedgerow fighting in Normandy. It seemed clear that the troops had lost or abandoned more equipment than had been worn out or used up, but large-scale salvage activities in France were just beginning, and the effectiveness of salvage for replacing inventories was still a matter of conjecture. Prudence demanded that all shortages be covered by requisitions for new items and that the continental depots be permitted to accumulate clothing reserves up to the theater's authorized sixty-day level. On that basis, continental requirements were enormous—about two and a half times the War Department estimate. However, summer was over, and delivery of winter uniforms and equipment to the troops took precedence over replacement of articles lost or worn out since D-day. On 7 September Busch wrote to Littlejohn, "It is getting cold up here. The troops will need heavy clothing very soon. . . ." The fact that

"up here" meant somewhere east of Verdun, nearly 400 miles from the only available ports, certainly complicated the problem. In addition, unit quartermasters were somewhat puzzled as to what the winter combat uniform actually would be.[7]

The Winter Uniform for the European Campaign

Combat operations in winter—a comparatively recent development in warfare—are only possible if troops are properly clothed. As late as World War I, activity diminished in cold weather, and trench-type warfare gave the troops opportunities for shelter that did not exist in the World War II war of movement. Quartermasters in Great Britain reviewed combat experience with winter clothing in North Africa and Italy in 1942 and 1943 and decided that it was not applicable in all respects to the forthcoming ETO campaign. Meanwhile, American troops stationed in the United Kingdom conducted maneuvers in England's very different climate. They were leading a garrison life in a friendly country where troop discipline was of great importance to international relations, and their commanders were convinced that a smart appearance was vital to discipline. The service uniform was worn in most headquarters and by all personnel after duty hours. Limited dry cleaning facilities in Great Britain made it difficult to keep the serge service coat presentable, and light shade olive

---

[7] (1) TUSA AAR, II, QM 6. (2) Personal Ltrs, Littlejohn to Feldman, 4 Sep 44, and Busch to Littlejohn, 7 Sep 44. Littlejohn Reading File, vol. XXVIII, items 29, 49.

drab trousers quickly showed the dirt. Soldiers who had obtained passes were sometimes unable to go on leave because they could not pass inspection, which naturally created a morale problem.

The inadequacy of these garments as a combat uniform had already been demonstrated in North Africa. The solution adopted by officers in both theaters—to wear dark green trousers instead of "pinks"—pointed out the need for a similar darker shade for enlisted men. The olive drab field, or Parsons, jacket, issued since 1941 was also unsatisfactory. It required frequent washing, was hard to iron, and scrubbing soon frayed the collar and cuffs. Quartermasters in North Africa and Great Britain and OQMG observers sent to both theaters all agreed that a new and improved uniform was needed—warmer, more durable, and better looking than the 1941 Parsons jacket, but less constricting and requiring less care than the serge service coat and light shade olive drab trousers. If such a uniform could improve the shabby appearance of combat soldiers, who had the greatest need for recreation and the least opportunity, it would solve many difficult combat zone problems involving the often conflicting demands of discipline and morale. But there were wide differences of opinion as to just how these desirable characteristics were to be achieved. Varying emphasis on comfort, warmth, water repellency, and a smart military appearance could and did result in a wide variety of designs and proposals.[8]

The ETO Concept—The Wool Jacket

Very soon after his arrival in the theater, Littlejohn, whose previous assignment had been as chief of the OQMG Clothing and Equipage Division, became interested in the battle-dress outfit, which constituted the British solution to the twin problems of smart military appearance and combat utility. This consisted of a short bloused jacket, snug-fitting at the waist, and easy-fitting trousers. The trousers were very high-waisted, so that the short jacket provided an adequate overlap but did not constrict body movement. With its belt at the natural waistline the jacket did not "ride up," even during the most vigorous exercise, and presented a trim military appearance. The outfit called to mind the field uniform worn by U.S. troops during the Mexican War[9] and reflected normal British civilian tailoring of trousers and waistcoat, but was contrary to current American civilian styling and military design, which tended toward a tight-fitting, low-cut trouser supported just over the hipbones by a belt. Another typically British feature of the battle dress was the rough, heavy texture of wool fabric, which made it possible to clean the uniform by scrubbing or brushing, and which did not require pressing. The jacket was lined with a heavy shrink-resistant cotton drill,

---

[8] (1) Risch and Pitkin, *Clothing the Soldier of World War II*, pp. 43, 49. (2) Pounder Rpt, p. 29. (3) See ch. VII, above. (4) The OQMG's reaction

to the requirement for a smart appearance well illustrates the lack of effective communication of ideas between that office and the ETO Quartermaster. Agencies in the zone of interior were convinced that Littlejohn and Eisenhower were demanding a dressy uniform. That view is supported by Ruppenthal, *Logistical Support*, II, 223.

[9] *Uniform of the Army of the United States from 1774 to 1889*, Illustrated, authorized by the Secre-

and could be worn with or without undergarments. Such clothing was entirely suitable to the raw but not very cold climate of the British Isles, and could absorb moisture without making the soldier feel damp. Additional advantages were that the battle dress fabric could be impregnated with antigas chemicals for wear in combat, and could be dry cleaned for garrison wear. It could be passed through this cleaning and re-impregnation cycle repeatedly without shrinkage or injury to the cloth. Moreover, the British had available surplus chemicals and impregnating facilities.[10]

Early in 1942 a few battle dress uniforms were issued U.S. troops to make up for clothing shortages of arriving Americans. They were very popular, and the senior commanders in the theater unanimously approved Littlejohn's suggestion that a generally similar uniform, made of the same material but cut to a distinctively American design, would be ideal for U.S. troops in garrison in the British Isles, as well as later in combat. It would replace not only the serge service coat and the current type of field jacket but also the protective impregnated wool shirt and trousers which had been very unpopular with garrison troops in the United Kingdom.[11] The initial ETO request to purchase 5,000 uniforms was not approved by clothing specialists in the OQMG

FIELD MARSHAL MONTGOMERY *wearing the British battle dress uniform on an official visit. June 1945.*

Research and Development Branch. By mid-1942 special uniforms for the Alaska garrison and for armored, parachute, mountain, and amphibious troops had all been developed. Littlejohn's ETO project seemed to the R&D men to be just one more "special development" at a time when OQMG efforts had shifted toward devising a more versatile and generally applicable winter combat uniform. But on 5 October 1942 General Somervell of ASF had personally approved a purchase for test purposes and possible future development.[12] Later in

---

tary of War and prepared by Lt. Col. M. I. Ludington, Quartermaster's Department, U.S. Army, Published by the Quartermaster General [ca. 1890] (commonly referred to as the Ogden Prints), Plate XIX.

[10] Memo, Proc Div OCQM for Under Secretary of State for War (Dir of Ord Sv), 31 Aug 42, sub: Field Jackets. USFET QM 421.

[11] See ch. X, above.

[12] (1) Memo, Styer for Lutes, 18 Sep 42, no sub; Memo, Lutes for Styer, 25 Sep 42, sub: Recommendations of Col MacKeachie; Ltr, Somervell to Lee, 5 Oct 42, sub: Development of a Uniform for Combat Purposes. All in USFET AG 421. (2) Risch, *The Quartermaster Corps: Organization, Supply, and Services*, I, 94.

ETO JACKETS AS WORN BY GENERALS
EISENHOWER AND BRADLEY. *General
Bradley's jacket is an early experimental
version designed and made in England.*

the same month General Lee recommended to the theater commander that 360,000 wool jackets of the new design, enough for all ground and service personnel then in the theater, be purchased locally. On 2 December General Eisenhower authorized a purchase of 300,000, but because of repeated changes in design only 1,000 jackets for test purposes finally became available on 10 May 1943.[13]

Five days earlier a theater circular had settled the matter of protective clothing by directing that impregnated herringbone twills—in other words the fatigue

clothing already in the hands of the troops—would be worn for that purpose. Far from dampening interest in the new type of uniforms, this policy decision actually increased it. In Britain's raw climate, fatigues were normally worn over wool clothing, and impregnation would make them more water-repellent. Members of the 29th Division, the only combat division in England not sent to North Africa for TORCH, had suggested such a combination to an OQMG observer in March 1943, and it was McNamara's final choice for D-day. Scheduled tests of the jacket and matching wool trousers by units of the Eighth Air Force and the 29th Division were completed in July 1943, and both the troops and their commanders were enthusiastic. Even before the tests were completed Littlejohn wrote to Gregory, pointing out the superiority of the ETO wool jacket over the 1941 olive drab field jacket, the mountain and arctic jackets, and even the popular winter combat jacket of the armored forces. He suggested that the ETO jacket be manufactured in substantial quantities. In a separate letter five days later he pointed out the merits of a more loosely fitted wool trouser with larger pockets and a higher waist rise.[14]

As a result of the field tests, the participating troops suggested extensive changes in the jacket. For example, the slash pockets should be replaced by patch pockets higher on the chest, so that they would be accessible above the straps of the field pack. Since this was no longer to be a protective garment,

[13] Ltr, CQM to TQMG, 23 Jun 43, sub: Field Jacket for U.S. Forces; Ltr, CQM to TQMG, 28 Jun 43, sub: Trousers, Sv OD EM. Littlejohn Reading File, vol. XIII, items 50, 66.

[14] (1) SOS ETOUSA Admin Cir 17, 5 May 43. (2) Maj C. M. Burnhome, Rpt 4 to OQMG, 20 Mar 43. OQMG 421.1.

the protective flap at the front and the tight closure at the cuff should be eliminated. Littlejohn described the revised jacket in a letter to Gregory dated 21 July 1943, and sent samples. General Lee was also enthusiastic and in September urged that the new uniform be issued to all ETO troops.[15]

Meanwhile, The Quartermaster General had been requested to develop a similar wool jacket in the United States, first for the Air Transport Command and later for all AAF personnel. In July the ETO commander, General Devers, decided that local production of jackets in the United Kingdom should be stopped until War Department policy had been clarified, and in November all the jackets on hand were turned over to the Eighth and Ninth Air Forces, which were actually in combat and needed them.[16] Shortly after Eisenhower returned to the European theater as Supreme Commander in January 1944, Littlejohn reopened the question, recommending that the ETO type of wool jacket be issued to all ETO troops. Issue of this simple, multipurpose garment would effect a very great saving of money, materials, and labor. Only 300,000 jackets could be produced in the British Isles, and the balance required for 1944—3,115,000—would have to be manufactured in the United States.[17]

On 16 February the OQMG version of the wool jacket was shown to the ETO staff by Capt. William F. Pounder, whose activities as a QM observer in North Africa have already been described. The ETO staff found encouragement in the fact that the OQMG was also interested in developing a wool jacket, but noted wide differences between the OQMG and ETO versions that might lead to complications of supply. Moreover, the current official status of any wool jacket, irrespective of design, in the Army Supply Program was not very encouraging. If approved at all, it would probably replace the pile jacket authorized in December 1943 for wear in cold-temperate climates. Presumably this meant that the wool jacket would not be authorized for the mild-temperate climate of central and western France, where the U.S. forces expected to be fighting during the winter of 1944–45.[18] (Map 3)

One month later, on 14 March, Littlejohn suddenly received a personal letter from Maj. Gen. Russell L. Maxwell, the G–4, War Department, which placed the

---

[15] (1) Ltr, CQM to TQMG, 21 Jul 43, sub: Field Jacket, Wool. Littlejohn Reading File, vol. XV, item 56. (2) Ltr, CG SOS to CG ETO, 14 Sep 43, sub: Jacket, Field, Wool OD. USFET AG 421.
[16] (1) Risch, *The Quartermaster Corps: Organization, Supply, and Services*, I, 94. (2) Ltr, Devers to Littlejohn, 1 Jul 43; Memo, CQM to DCQM, 13 Nov 43, sub: Issue of Field Jackets, with Incls. Littlejohn Reading File, vol. XIV, item 71; vol. XVIII, item 38. (3) The Army Air Forces version was standardized as Jacket, Flying, B–12.

[17] Ltr, CQM to SCAEF, 26 Jan 44, sub: Adoption of Jacket, Field, Wool OD, U.K. Design, for AAF and Continental Combat Forces; Memo, CQM for CG ETOUSA, 4 Feb 44, sub: Development of ETO Type Field Jacket, Wool OD. Both in USFET AG 421.
[18] (1) Ltrs, Pounder to Doriot, 13 and 29 Mar 44. In OQMG Study, Supply of Clothing and Equipment to ETO, 1944, pt. 4, Documentation, 5 Apr 45 (hereafter cited as OQMG Study of 5 Apr 45); ASF OQMG File A45–280, drawer 7. (2) The OVERLORD forecast of operations estimated that it would take the Allies about 330 days to reach the Ardennes-Vosges line, which was approximately where the cold-temperate zone began. (3) The wool jacket and pile jacket were not included in the Anzio test of M1943 items. See ch. VII, above.

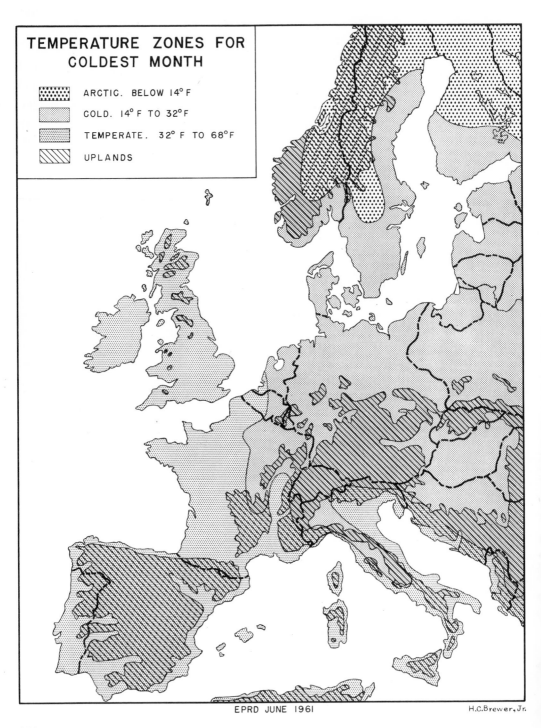

TEMPERATURE ZONES FOR
COLDEST MONTH

ARCTIC. BELOW 14° F

COLD. 14° F TO 32° F

TEMPERATE. 32° F TO 68°F

UPLANDS

EPRD JUNE 1961

H.C.Brewer, Jr.

MAP 3

status of wool jackets in general in a different and far more hopeful light:

The Quartermaster General is studying the issue to your theater alone of the ETO field jacket. The only questions seem to be whether cloth is available in the United States, and whether machines are available. . . . The QMG has estimated your needs to be 4,000,000 for the first year and your production to be zero. The chances for adoption will be improved if you can put into official channels your UK production prospects and your requirements from the United States.

The next day Littlejohn forwarded the above quotation to Col. James H. Stratton, the ETOUSA G–4, with the notation: "This information is somewhat like a bolt out of the blue. It is at variance with all information so far received on this subject." [19] In the light of this development, which seemed to indicate that some kind of a wool jacket was to be authorized in the ETO very shortly, a meeting with OQMG designers to work out a compromise design was clearly necessary. Since Somervell had summoned the chiefs of ETO technical services to a final preinvasion conference in Washington within the next few days, Littlejohn prepared to take care of the jacket matter personally. In accordance with Maxwell's suggestion, Generals Eisenhower and Lee cabled the War Department on 17 March, recommending that the ETO type of field jacket be adopted for all ETO troops. Revised requirements were 4,259,000 jackets, of which 300,000 would be produced by the British.

Littlejohn departed for the United States two days later.[20]

In a series of conferences during April 1944, Littlejohn and his clothing specialist, Maj. Robert L. Cohen, met in Washington with Maj. Gen. Lucius D. Clay of ASF, Colonel Doriot of the Military Planning Division, OQMG, Mr. Meyer Kestnbaum (president of Hart, Schaffner, and Marx), currently OQMG clothing adviser, and several others. Littlejohn obtained a firm commitment from Clay on his desired production program, but had to forego several desirable features of the garment as originally conceived. The rough, heavy, cloth used in the ETO version of the jacket was declared to be unobtainable in the United States. This was a major disappointment. As General Bradley had remarked, it was the British wool material that made it possible for one garment to serve as both a battle and a dress uniform.[21] Nevertheless, it was agreed that the eighteen-ounce serge currently used for the enlisted man's service coat would be substituted. It was likewise agreed that the biswing back and half-belt of the ETO model could be eliminated without decreasing its utility. But the elaborate details of the U.S. model, including pleated pockets, fly front closure and fly pocket flaps, and adjustable sleeve cuffs were all retained. During subsequent conferences attended only by technicians, Major Cohen insisted that the jacket be sized large enough to fit over

[19] IRS, Littlejohn for Stratton, 15 Mar 44, sub: ETO Field Jacket. Littlejohn Reading File, vol. XXII, item 43.

[20] (1) Risch and Pitkin, *Clothing the Soldier of World War II*, p. 57. (2) Ltr, Pounder to Doriot, 29 Mar 44. In OQMG Study of 5 Apr 45, pt. 4. (3) Millet, *Organization and Role of ASF*, p. 81. (4) Ruppenthal, *Logistical Support*, I, 259. (5) Cable W–13166, ETOUSA to AGWAR, 17 Mar 44.

[21] Ltr, Pounder to Doriot, 29 Mar 44. In OQMG Study of 5 Apr 45, pt. 4.

other garments of a winter uniform, but other details of design were decided by civilian consultants of the OQMG. After ASF had accepted the compromise design, Cohen wrote rather dubiously to Littlejohn that ". . . this garment will in all probability serve the purpose and is the best substitute we can get out of the Research and Development Branch." Rather less charitably, the historian of the Philadelphia QM Depot, which had to shoulder the procurement problem, remarked: "In their determination to create a stylish as well as a utilitarian jacket, they brought forth a highly tailored one that proved to be the utter despair of manufacturers." [22]

Later developments demonstrated that this decision regarding design did not arise from ignorance of mass production methods. Apparently the intent of the OQMG to create work for men's dress-clothing manufacturers, a specialized segment of the garment industry that had not received any large government contracts up to this time, was carried out with excessive enthusiasm. Thus a principal reason for emphasis on style was a desire to tap a previously unexploited source of production capacity. Such a policy—if it actually was a deliberate policy—clearly involved increased costs. Its only justification was the possibility of a production bottleneck among the manufacturers already under contract, as hinted at by General Maxwell. [23]

Fear of such difficulties was confirmed when General Clay cabled General Lee on 20 April that only 2,600,000 wool jackets could be shipped to the ETO by the end of 1944, starting with 500,000 in September. He further stated that the wool jacket was officially replacing the serge service coat, which would not be furnished to the ETO thereafter. This was a logical compromise, involving a minimum disruption of the Army Supply Program, since both items were made from an identical wool cloth and overseas experience had demonstrated that the coat was superfluous. But Clay also made it plain that functionally the wool jacket was replacing the 1941 olive drab field jacket. Since the wool jacket allocation was short of requirements by more than a million and would arrive late in the year, he offered 479,000 old style field jackets as substitutes. Little-

---

the OQMG model could not be produced in quantity in the ETO. Ltr, Pounder to Doriot, 29 Mar 44. In OQMG Study of 5 Apr 45. (2) Messrs. Max Udell and Lou Weitz, owners of dress-clothing factories and technical consultants to TQMG, have stated that they deliberately designed the jacket so that it could only be made in their type of shop, which employed more hand tailors than machine operators. Their justification was that over half of the sports jacket manufacturers were already tied up with contracts for M1943 jackets. The dress-clothing manufacturers had a higher wage scale and claimed that they could not bid successfully for inexpensive machine-made garments. Later, some sports jacket manufacturers made the wool jacket successfully. This was done partly by simplifying the garment for machine production and partly by hiring extra hand workers. The Military Planning Division apparently was not fully aware of the industrial implications of the final wool jacket design. It accepted the man-hour computation made for the simpler jacket designed in the ETO (40 percent less labor than a serge coat) and applied it to the final jacket design. This led to a grossly inflated estimate of production capacity. Roberts, Designed for Combat: The Army's Field Jackets, pp. 154, 160, 237.

---

[22] (1) Ltr quoted in *QM Supply in ETO*, III, 61. (2) Norman E. Roberts, Designed for Combat: The Army's Field Jackets (Philadelphia Quartermaster Depot, 1946), p. 134. MS, Hist Br OQMG. (3) Littlejohn, ed., Passing in Review, ch. 42, pt. I, History and Development of the Field Jacket, Wool, OD, by Capt Robert W. Burns, pp. 9–10.

[23] (1) ETO clothing specialists had pointed out in February that the fly front and pleated pockets of

john was disappointed by the curtailed allocation, and somewhat worried by the retarded schedule of deliveries. He considered this reduced ASF commitment barely adequate for the winter needs of combat troops and replacements, with nothing left over for service troops or for maintenance. He nevertheless accepted the substitution of 1941 olive drab field jackets and requisitioned all that were available.[24]

Most of the other clothing items required for winter were familiar garments issued in previous years. They were either on hand in depots, in possession of the troops, or would be brought overseas as individual clothing by additional units arriving in the theater.[25]

The OQMG Winter Uniform

Clothing specialists within the Office of The Quartermaster General were not really interested in any form of wool jacket. They had very different ideas on a suitable winter uniform for combat troops, and the first combat zone test of those ideas, involving the layering principle, had been made in North Africa in March 1943. A more extensive test of the same uniform was being conducted at Anzio as Littlejohn arrived in the United States.[26] He had seen the experimental M1943 assembly in November of the previous year in Washington. Col. Georges F. Doriot of the Military Plan-

ning Division, OQMG,[27] urged that the M1943 was the ideal winter outfit for combat troops anywhere in the projected area of operations, although at the time these garments were not officially accepted, and current plans were to authorize them only for arctic and cold-temperate climates and as replacements for the special winter combat uniform of tank personnel. Littlejohn disagreed. In his opinion Doriot's experimental M1943 outfit, comprising successive layers of separate garments to be put on or taken off as the weather changed, would aggravate Class II distribution problems and was hopelessly complicated and inefficient for dismounted combat troops in a war of movement.[28]

In July 1943, the Quartermaster Board had reported that the M1943 combat outfit was unsatisfactory as an all-purpose universal unit, but recommended that the individual items be considered separately for suitability. In September, ASF approved an experimental procurement of 200,000 sets, to be tested by troops in training in the northern United States. Apparently these tests led to conclusions that the M1943 jacket should replace the old olive drab field jacket, and that the entire M1943 outfit was suitable for cold-temperate climates.

On 15 December 1943, as already described in connection with the outfitting of Mediterranean troops, the War Department issued a new table of clothing

[24] Cable WAR–25862, Clay for Lee, 20 Apr 44; Cable E–25968, Lee to AGWAR, 2 May 44; Cable Ex–36758, Lee to PEMBARK, 7 Jul 44. All in Littlejohn Reading File, vol. XXVIII, item 104.

[25] See app. C.

[26] See discussion of the Anzio test in Chapter VII, above.

[27] Colonel Doriot had become chief of the Military Planning Division in October 1943, following the transfer of Col. David H. Cowles. Doriot continued to serve also as chief of the Research and Development Branch for more than two years. He became a brigadier general in February 1945.

[28] (1) QM Supply in ETO, III, 76, 158. (2) Interv, Ross with Littlejohn, 1 Dec 59.

and individual equipment embodying new concepts and listing a considerable number of new items. The M1943 clothing and a variety of garments previously issued only to mountain divisions, or for duty in arctic regions, might now be authorized by a theater commander on a discretionary basis for all personnel located in cold-temperate, alpine, and low-mountain terrain. He might also authorize additional and still more specialized items for specified percentages of his combat personnel in the same areas. Supply officers were warned that many of the new articles were in process of procurement or distribution, and stocks of substitute items would have to be used up first. In the revised table, the geographic basis of these authorizations within the continental United States was very clearly specified. Overseas, there was no such clear definition. Subject to War Department approval, theater commanders were in effect empowered to authorize the new articles for issue anywhere in the temperate zone. NATOUSA adopted a liberal interpretation of this table after the Anzio tests, generating requirements that the War Department approved only after some hesitation. But at the beginning of 1944 that decision had not yet been made, and interest centered on the reaction of the ETO, numerically the largest overseas theater.[29]

The new table was undoubtedly a disappointment to the OQMG Research and Development Branch since it did not prescribe the M1943 ensemble on a mandatory basis for the entire temperate zone, and plans were made immediately to bring about a change in that direction. A major requisition for the M1943 outfit from the ETO would go far to justify such a modification. It would also require a drastic revision of the Army Supply Program, since procurement up to that time was only for 200,000 men in training in the northern United States.

It was in support of plans to revise the clothing table, sponsored jointly by Colonel Doriot and AGF officials, that Captain Pounder was sent to the ETO in February 1944 with samples of the new items. The timing of this effort in salesmanship was not very propitious. Current plans set D-day in Normandy for 1 May, and preparations for the greatest amphibious assault in history were at fever pitch. Delays in operational planning had forced delays in logistical planning, which was now being completed within ADSEC and COMZ headquarters. Everyone's mental horizon was limited to the crucial assault phase of the operation, and Pounder observed that "there seem to be no plans being made for another winter of war."[30]

This was not quite correct. It would have been more accurate to say that clothing plans for the coming winter had been

---

[29] (1) When authorized by the War Department, the new items might be issued to troops undergoing training in northern New England and New York (specified counties), in the upper peninsula of Michigan, and in the states of North Dakota, Minnesota, and Wisconsin. Issues were also authorized for alpine terrain and mountain areas below the timberline where the average daily minimum temperature during the coldest month was 30°F. or below. Cf. T/E 21, 15 Dec 43. (2) Risch and Pitkin,

Clothing the Soldier of World War II, p. 49. (3) IRS, R&D Div OCQM to Mil Planning Div, 18 Apr 45, sub: Rpt of Maj Paul Siple. Hist Br OQMG. (4) See ch. VII, The Anzio Test, above.

[30] (1) Ltr, Pounder to Doriot, 13 Mar 44. In OQMG Study of 5 Apr 45. (2) Ruppenthal, *Logistical Support*, I, 211–15.

completed and set to one side, and that everyone was too preoccupied with immediate problems even to consider revising them at the moment. Those plans were based on the official SHAEF forecast of post-OVERLORD operations, which was, of course, grossly in error. It indicated that the Allied armies would not reach the Ardennes and Vosges Mountains, where special clothing for wet-cold and low-mountain terrain would be required, until May 1945. For winter combat in western and central France, Littlejohn and his staff considered the type of winter clothing on hand entirely adequate. The fact that it *was* on hand in ample quantities, was extremely important, for as D-day approached the chronic shipping shortages of the ETO mounted to a crisis.[31] Because of its preshipment program in 1943, the OCQM was in the most favorable supply position of any technical service, but for that very reason had

large reserves of clothing, including limited-standard and substitute items, to use up before it could justify new requisitions. Littlejohn considered some of these "obsolescent" items—notably the armored force winter combat jacket and trousers—actually superior to the new designs. He favored some, but by no means all, of the garments now under consideration, and was determined to resist pressure to approve of new items merely because they were new. He had approved the M1943 issues for parachute units, but feared a chaotic situation if all combat units demanded similar garments. Accordingly, Littlejohn told Pounder that he was not to announce his mission or display his wares to anyone but QM clothing experts and military planners. If his samples were given too wide a display, he might oversell his product and create demands that could not be filled. This order was, of course, diametrically opposed to the views of Colonel Doriot, and largely frustrated the latter's objective in sending Pounder to the ETO.[32]

Pounder himself either caught the fever of immediacy, or accepted the frame of reference of the officers, all senior to himself, with whom he was dealing. For example, he suggested to Colonel McNamara that the men in the assault might wear shoepacs. The First Army quartermaster pointed out to him that the wet French spring would soon be over, and then the shoepacs, which wore out quickly and in any case were

---

[31] (1) IRS, R&D Div OCQM (Lt Col Bestor Robinson) to Mil Planning Div, 18 Apr 45, sub: Rpt of Maj Paul Siple. Hist Br OQMG. (2) Representative clothing reserves in the U.K. on 31 May 1944 were:

Item (in thousands)	In Depots	On Ships Offshore
Cap, field, cotton, or substitute.......	1,325	75
Drawers, wool......................	1,875	325
Gloves, wool, leather palm..........	1,300	0
Jacket, field, all types..............	1,380	100
Overcoat, wool....................	365	0
Overshoes, arctic....................	425	100
Raincoat..........................	1,325	50
Shirt, flannel......................	2,420	320
Socks, wool, light and heavy........	5,500	3,900
Trousers, wool OD.................	1,830	320
Undershirt, wool...................	1,450	410

Source: Littlejohn, ed., *Passing in Review*, ch. 28 (Garside Rpt.), app. K.

---

[32] (1) T/E 21, 15 December 1943 stated explicitly that older items were to be issued until exhausted. (2) Special Rpt, Tech Info Br for Gen Gregory, 11 Nov 44, sub: Summation of Action Taken with Reference to Winter Clothing and Equip. In OQMG Study of 5 Apr 45, pt. 4.

unsuitable for marching, would have to be replaced with shoes. This was considered an unwise use of precious cargo space. McNamara was interested in the wool sleeping bag to replace the blanket rolls planned for his assault troops. It would save weight and also make a more secure container for other items of clothing, but he seriously doubted that delivery could be made in time. In general, this was the prevailing reaction to all the samples presented by Captain Pounder. Most of the items he had to offer were currently being produced on a very limited basis. His purpose in coming to the ETO had been to invite requisitions to serve as a basis for future procurement, but his "customers" were interested only in emergency requisitions for stocks actually available. Pounder reported to Doriot that a requisition for ponchos was under consideration, and all available stocks of the new wool field trousers were requested for immediate shipment, but in both cases the quantities involved were small. As he himself expressed it, "plans have been pretty well formulated already and there is a good deal of hesitancy to change them. This is especially true of items of the basic uniform. It is essential that all troops have basically the same uniform. To change would require a huge number of new items to be shipped and cause considerable commotion. . . ." [33] As these words were written, the revised D-day was exactly twelve weeks away.

One major new item, the M1943 jacket, had already been authorized for all theaters, but Pounder brought the first samples seen in the ETO, and the initial reaction to the garment was also in terms of possible emergency requisition. Pounder apparently ascribed to Littlejohn the enthusiasm that some of his staff displayed for this item, stating, "The combination of Jacket Field M-1943 over the ETO Jacket fits into the ETO plans and General Littlejohn is anxious to have it here *in sufficient time* to dress units uniformly." [34] While Littlejohn favored uniformity to avoid further complication of the already intricate Class II supply plans, there is no confirmation in other evidence that he expressed any desire for the M1943 jacket. Pounder had apparently expressed Littlejohn's sentiments far more accurately in an earlier letter to Doriot, writing that the CQM and his staff were "convinced that their jacket ETO is superior [to the Jacket M1943] for this particular theater, and they are presently seeking the permission of General Eisenhower for authorization. Until this jacket ETO is definitely approved or rejected, nothing will be done to change present conditions of the supply of Jackets M-1943." [35] The "present conditions" referred to were the directive in T/E 21 that the M1943 jacket was only to be issued after stocks of the 1941 style jacket were exhausted. As already noted, Eisenhower made his formal decision in favor of the ETO jacket on 17 March. Apparently his choice was based upon the relative desirability of the two jackets, without regard for the

[33] (1) Ltr, Pounder to Doriot, 13 Mar 44. In OQMG Study of 5 Apr 45. (2) For McNamara's clothing plan, see Table 8.

[34] Ltr, Pounder to Doriot, 29 Mar 44. Hist Br OQMG. Italics are Pounder's.
[35] (1) Ltr, Pounder to Doriot, 13 Mar 44. Hist Br OQMG. (2) Interv, Ross with Littlejohn, 1 Dec 59.

possible role of the M1943 as part of an outfit to serve as a substitute for the overcoat. It is likely that the sloppy loose fit of the M1943 had a strong bearing on his final decision. A year earlier, when he wrote to General Marshall regarding the somewhat similar Parsons jacket, he already had positive ideas on what should replace it:

I have no doubt that you have been impressed by the virtual impossibility of appearing neat and snappy in our field uniform. Given a uniform which tends to look a bit tough, and the natural proclivities of the American soldier quickly create a general impression of a disorderly mob. From this standpoint alone, the matter is bad enough; but a worse effect is the inevitable result upon general discipline. This matter of discipline is not only the most important of our internal military problems, it is the most difficult. In support of all other applicable methods for the development of satisfactory discipline, we should have a neater and smarter looking field uniform. I suggest that the Quartermaster begin now serious work to design a better woolen uniform for next winter's wear. In my opinion the material should be very rough wool. . . ." [36]

Littlejohn's opinions were similar. He recalls that the first M1943 jackets he ever saw actually being worn by troops clothed a WAC unit he watched debarking early in 1944. The remarks inspired by their appearance were unprintable, but the Wacs' nickname for these unwieldy garments was sufficiently damning: they called them "maternity jackets." On 17 March, the same day that Eisenhower formally recommended the ETO jacket for all ETO troops,

Littlejohn wrote to General Maxwell:

The ETO field jacket has been through many bloody battles. Definitely all the troops in this theater want it, and personally I think the troops have come to a sound decision regardless of the fact that I am the sponsor of this gem. . . . I have no desire to criticize the model 1943 field jacket as quite likely it fits the problem in some other theater. It is my understanding also that the sweater required to go with the jacket in this theater will not be available for some time to come.[37]

In April 1944, when Littlejohn reached informal agreement with Clay regarding the provision of the ETO wool jacket to the ETO, he also stated that he and his theater commander did not desire the M1943 jacket, except for paratroopers. But the outcome illustrates a fundamental weakness of all special arrangements arrived at outside of channels.[38] The ETO wool jacket would be substituted, in the ETO only, for the serge coat on T/E 21, and thus be brought into the framework of the Army Supply Program, but deletion of the M1943 jacket, an item authorized in all temperate zones, was a far more complicated matter. At the 17 April conference, Col. John P. Baum of the Clothing and Equipage Branch, OQMG Storage and

---

[36] Excerpt from Ltr, Eisenhower to Marshall, date unknown, quoted in OQMG Study of 5 Apr 45, pt. 4, p. 29.

[37] (1) Ltr, Littlejohn to Maxwell, 17 Mar 44. Littlejohn Reading File, vol. XXIV, item 61. (2) Interv, Ross with Littlejohn, 1 Dec 59.

[38] Other efforts by Littlejohn to arrange policy matters by personal contacts with individuals within ASF also went awry. A major instance involved his basic relationship with NYPE, discussed in Chapter XII, above. A minor but embarrassing example was provided by white gloves, belts, and leggings for MP's. Littlejohn arranged this with ASF and G–4 during his April visit to the zone of interior, but the subsequent formal requisition by the ETO Provost Marshal was disapproved. Cf., Ltr, Littlejohn to Feldman, 22 Apr 44. Littlejohn Reading File, vol. XXII, item 6.

Distribution Division, assured Littlejohn and Clay that sufficient 1941 olive drab field jackets were available and could be issued until ETO wool jackets began to arrive in the theater. Possibly neither Clay nor Littlejohn understood the full implications of the procedure whereby ASF planners had inserted the ETO jacket into the Army Supply Program as a substitute for the service coat, leaving the world-wide status of the M1943 jacket undisturbed; or perhaps there was a failure of co-ordination within the bureaucratic mazes of ASF. At any rate, the decision not to accept the M1943 jacket in the ETO was not widely known or clearly understood within ASF.[39]

On 9 May ASF sent a cable to ETO-USA stating that the M1943 field jacket and high-neck wool sweater were intended to replace the olive drab field jacket .and were for issue in all temperate climates. This combination was to be required eventually for all troops in the ETO, and was to be shipped on requisitions from the OCQM. Littlejohn left this message unanswered, apparently assuming that if no requisitions were submitted, no jackets would be shipped. But on 17 May Colonel Baum informed the OCQM that the stock of olive drab field jackets was being depleted faster than expected, and that M1943 jackets were being set up as substitutes for shipment to the ETO on current requisitions for olive drab jackets. The next

day the ETO informed the War Department that it wanted M1943 jackets only for parachutists.[40] Colonel Doriot was convinced that this was an unwise decision, and promptly imparted his views to Clay. Impressed by Doriot's arguments, based on voluminous laboratory experiments and scientific data, Clay cabled two days later:

Tests have indicated that sweater, wool jacket, and field jacket M-1943 give better all weather protection than overcoat, sweater, and short wool jacket, with a 4 pound saving when dry and up to 14 pounds when wet. Jacket M-1943 combination has been approved for issue by War Department and you may have it if you desire. If you still prefer to retain the overcoat and dispense with sweater and M-1943 issue please verify with SHAEF and advise.[41]

The requested verification, signed Eisenhower, was forthcoming on 1 June:

Overcoats necessary to provide warmth and protect troops in this theater. Model 43 field jacket only required for parachutists. Jacket field wool OD ETO type and sweater combination will be required in cold areas. Minimum shipments of model 43 jackets field desired in this Theater. This program has the approval of SHAEF and in addition the approval of Generals Bradley, Hodges and Corlett [XIX Corps Commander].[42]

The above message was only sent after a thorough discussion and concurrences

_____

[39] (1) Memo, Feldman for Clay, 19 Apr 44, sub: Jackets, Field, OD and Jackets, Field, Wool for ETO. SPQXC 421.1 (Jackets, Field). (2) Memo, ASF Reqmts Div for TQMG, 5 May 44, sub: Jacket, Field, Wool for ETO, with Memo for Record attached. SFRMP 421.1 (ASP–QM). (3) Personal Ltr, Littlejohn to Feldman, 14 Sep 44. Littlejohn Reading File, vol. XXVIII, item 90.

[40] (1) Cable WAR–34264, Somervell to Eisenhower, 9 May 44. (2) Littlejohn, ed., Passing in Review, ch. 42, pt. I, pp. 14–15. (3) Cable E–28364, CG U.S. Forces ETO to WD, 18 May 44, sub: Field Jackets. Hist Br OQMG.

[41] (1) Cable WAR–39574, Clay to CG ETO, 20 May 44. (2) The tests are described in detail in Ltr, TQMG to ACofS OPD, 25 May 44, sub: Clothing Efficiency, ETO. Included in OQMG Study of 5 Apr 45.

[42] Cable E–30871, Eisenhower to Somervell, 1 Jun 44.

involving not only the officers named but also Lt. Gen. Walter Bedell Smith, the Chief of Staff, and Maj. Gen. Robert W. Crawford, the SHAEF G–4. Bradley believed that the M1943 jacket was not only unsightly but defective in design; the combat soldier slept in his overcoat, and a short jacket provided no warmth for the legs; the 12th Army Group did not desire the garment. All were in agreement that the M1943 jacket was a superfluous duplicate item. Littlejohn also questioned the validity of laboratory experiments and noncombat field tests, no matter how carefully simulated. Even the Anzio tests, made during combat but in a climate very different from that of the ETO, did not seem to him to be applicable.[43]

On 15 June, Littlejohn wrote to General Feldman asking precisely how many old style field jackets were still available, and the same day submitted a requisition to NYPE for 2,250,000 sweaters. This was his first formal large-scale requisition for any of the new items displayed by Captain Pounder. In accordance with standing instructions, he had already inquired of the port regarding the availability of wool sleeping bags, and on 24 May had received a commitment for 2,580,000 through October, but the formal requisition did not follow until 22 July, when shipping allocations were available and could be cited specifically. This was in accordance with War Department directives and was the normal OCQM method of operating, but it was

not understood by the OQMG, which later accused Littlejohn of excessive tardiness in submitting requisitions.[44]

The New Table of Equipment and the Compromise Decision

On 1 June 1944, a new T/E 21 was published. Contrary to all expectations, it provided neither an increase in the basis of issue for M1943 clothing nor any clarification of the previous basis. Combat boots and ponchos were listed for the first time, but there was still no mention of wool jackets, or of hoods for the M1943 jacket. A new procedure was introduced grouping all issues into either mandatory or discretionary allowances, and combat boots, the M1943 jacket, and the cotton field cap were all made mandatory in temperate overseas areas, subject to availability and after exhaustion of stocks of substitute items. But the allowances for arctic, cold-temperate, and mountain areas remained discretionary. Accordingly, on 20 June Littlejohn cabled the War Department asking for information on clothing and QM equipment that would be used by troops in a winter climate similar to that of Germany and northwestern France.[45] This was really a query regarding production and availability of supplies, subjects on

---

[43] (1) Littlejohn, ed., Passing in Review, ch. 42, pt. I, pp. 17–18. (2) Ltr, Littlejohn to Feldman, 7 Jul 44. Littlejohn Reading File, vol. XXVI, item 27.

[44] (1) WARX–55940, AGWAR to ETOUSA, 20 Jul 44; Cable EX–33226, Lee to CG NYPE, 15 Jun 44; TWX Confs ETOUSA–NYPE, 24 May, 22 Jul 44. All in OQMG Study of 5 Apr 45, pt. 4. (2) WD AGO Ltr, 19 Apr 44, sub: Supply of Newly Standardized Items to Overseas Commands. AG 400 OB–S–SPDDL–M.

[45] (1) Cable E–33902, ETOUSA to AGWAR, 20 Jun 44. In OQMG Study of 5 Apr 45. (2) T/E 21, 1 June 1944, is summarized in Appendix C.

which Littlejohn was never able to obtain satisfactory information. He rightly suspected that the appearance of a new T/E 21 meant that some policy decision or interpretation had been made regarding issue of the new winter garments. Such a decision had been made by the G–4 Division, War Department, but by an almost incredible oversight the OQMG had not been informed. The chain of events leading to this confused situation had begun the previous January.

On 1 January 1944, at a conference attended by representatives of G–1, G–4, AGF, ASF, and the OQMG Military Planning Division, proposals were made to amend the current version of T/E 21, which had been published just two weeks earlier. Specifically, the idea was to expand the special winter clothing allowances for Zone 1 (cold-temperate) and low-mountain terrain to cover the entire temperate zone. A draft amendment to T/E 21, involving eighteen major items, was prepared by the Research and Development Branch, OQMG, approved by AGF, and submitted by the latter to ASF for concurrence on 22 February. ASF in turn requested the views of the OQMG concerning the impact of such a change upon raw materials, labor, production, the civilian economy, and obsolescence of existing stocks.

Maj. Gen. Herman Feldman, replying for The Quartermaster General on 13 March, concurred in the recommendation in principle, but noted the existence of grave limitations upon the productive capacity required to implement it. He recommended that the program be extended over a two-year period, with a limited increase in the basis of issue for 1944, to combat troops in the European

and North African theaters only, and with somewhat more generous allowances in all overseas theaters in 1945. Feldman also recommended that the M1943 jacket, wool jacket, and sweater together should replace the overcoat and old style jacket for combat troops. He disapproved the AGF proposal for issue of shoepacs to all combat troops in winter in the temperate zone, since this would require over five million pairs per year, whereas maximum production from all sources, including the use of mandatory orders, was 880,000 pairs in 1944 and 3,225,000 pairs in 1945. Feldman's recommendations, co-ordinated with a careful appraisal of productive capacity, added up to a disapproval of the proposals of AGF (which had actually originated within the Military Planning Division, OQMG), at least in regard to the calendar year 1944. He also stated that the effectiveness of this modified program was based upon receipt of approval and authorization to begin procurement by 1 April 1944.

ASF ignored the OQMG's deadline and forwarded the correspondence to G–4, War Department, on 15 April, stating its nonconcurrence with most of the original AGF proposals. The ASF recommendations were approved by G–4 on 11 May and forwarded to the OQMG through AGF and ASF. But the correspondence did not reach the OQMG until 29 July, representing a loss of time in transit of seventy-two days and a delay of four months beyond Feldman's suggested deadline. This administrative oversight imposed a severe handicap on the OQMG in procurement planning. Apparently it also contributed to the curious staff decision whereby the entire NATOUSA theater was considered to be an alpine or low-mountain area for clothing issue purposes.[46]

Littlejohn's inquiry of 20 June therefore found the OQMG in a rather poor position to give an accurate and authoritative reply. Colonel Doriot's answer four days later was clearly based upon an assumption that the AGF recommendations would be approved; possibly he believed that they had already been approved. If he was aware of General Feldman's contrary recommendations to ASF, he either misunderstood their tenor or disagreed with the appraisal of U.S. industrial capacity on which they were based.[47] He predicted that mobile operations would soon bring some of the troops into the cold-temperate area of eastern France and western Germany, and recommended that selection of winter clothing to be issued to *all* ETO combat troops should be based upon that premise. He referred specifically to

Captain Pounder's samples and repeated the arguments and recommendations he had made to General Clay a month before, especially regarding the M1943 jacket. He reiterated that this jacket was essential for adequate protection against rain, although he also recommended issue of the poncho. Doriot closed with a suggestion that requisitions be submitted promptly. But Littlejohn felt that he was again being called upon to submit requisitions that might serve as a basis of future procurement, despite the fact that he did not approve of all the items to be procured and despite the fact that General Feldman seriously doubted that such procurement was practicable.

Apparently because Doriot's letter referred specifically to his overseas representative, the latter was asked to make independent recommendations. On 30 June Pounder submitted almost identical recommendations to Littlejohn in the form of a letter he wished to forward, through official channels, to Colonel Doriot.[48] Pounder also forwarded a list of the winter clothing that, he stated, the ETO planned to issue to its troops. This list had been furnished to him by an officer in the Supply Division, OCQM, and was not complete. He pointed out that the ETO uniform was "sadly lacking in water repellent items." He also remarked disparagingly that "they are counting on the poncho synthetic for protection against wet." This was a curious, observation, for both Pounder and Doriot recommended the poncho. Pounder had already reported that the ETO was considering ponchos,

---

[46] (1) Feldman's recommendations are listed in Appendix C, column 2. (2) Ltr, CG AGF to CG ASF, 22 Feb 44, sub: Change to T/E 21, dated 20 Nov 43; 1st Ind, Lutes to TQMG, 28 Feb 44; 2d Ind, Feldman to Dir of Mob Div ASF, 13 Mar 44. ASP–QM 400.34 (T/E 21). (3) Memo, Dir of Plans and Opns ASF for ACofS G–4, 15 Apr 44, sub: Proposed Change to T/E 21, Clothing and Individual Equip; DF, same sub, G–4 to CG ASF, 11 May 44; Memo, CG ASF for TQMG through CG AGF, 18 May 44, same sub. (4) 2d Ind, Feldman to Dir of Mob Div ASF, ATTN: Chief Organization and Allowance Br, 31 Aug 44. SPQRQ 400.34 (18 May 44). All in OQMG Study of 5 Apr 45, pt. 4. (5) See ch. VII, above.

[47] (1) Doriot was aware of production problems, but believed that they could be overcome by the use of mandatory orders, at least to the extent that M1943 uniforms could be issued to all ground combat troops in ETOUSA and NATOUSA. Cf. Memo, Doriot for CG ASF, Reqmts Div, 3 Jun 44, sub: Secret Rad CM–IN 157, 1 Jun 44, Protective Clothing. SPQRD 422.3, Hist Br OQMG. (2) Ltr, Doriot to Littlejohn, 24 Jun 44, sub: Confidential Rad E–39902. In OQMG Study of 5 Apr 45. (3) For Doriot's recommendations in detail, see Appendix C, column 3.

[48] Ltr, Pounder to Doriot, 30 Jun 44. OQMG Study of 5 Apr 45.

and Littlejohn actually requisitioned 250,000 of them on 2 July. This was an experimental requisition to test the reaction of the troops. A week later, Littlejohn wrote to Feldman that all the new items should be handled in the same way:

. . . for example, the poncho, which in my opinion is definitely superior to the raincoat. It is not my policy to force these new items down the throat of troops but to let them see the new items and then to get a cold blooded, disinterested dissertation thereon giving the good qualities and the bad. . . . I am of the opinion that as soon as we can equip a corps or a substantial number of troops with the poncho, we can begin to figure on the raincoat going out of existence.[49]

Littlejohn would have preferred the nylon poncho, which was reserved for tropical areas in the Pacific. Pounder's sample item was a slightly heavier version, made of the same material as the authorized raincoat, and therefore could be produced without difficulty. It was easier to manufacture than a raincoat and could be used as a ground sheet under a sleeping bag or even as a shelter half, but was especially useful for individual protection in cold rainy weather, providing that protection against rain which Pounder had declared to be "sadly lacking." All ponchos had the advantage that one size would fit everyone, and they could be worn over an overcoat, which could hardly be done with a raincoat.

A formal answer to Pounder's letter was made by Colonel Brumbaugh, who was chief of the OCQM Supply Division at the time. Brumbaugh commented in detail on each of the items he recommended rejecting.[50] He agreed that shoepacs were more waterproof than boots or shoes, but they were unsuitable for marching and the soles were not durable. Ski socks were desirable only with shoepacs; use with shoes would require a larger size shoe. Since the overcoat was essential in the ETO climate, the M1943 field jacket was excess; the same applied to cotton field trousers. The bulkiness of leather glove shells with wool inserts hindered use of the trigger finger and made them unsuitable for infantry. Wool gloves with leather palms were preferable. Littlejohn indorsed these views, and within a few days sent Brumbaugh to the United States to expedite a clothing program along the lines indicated. Nevertheless, Brumbaugh was directed to inquire into the availability of the items recommended by Captain Pounder. Colonel Baum informed him that all standard type military shoepacs had been committed to NATOUSA and the arctic reserve, and only 330,000 pairs of shoepacs, all of obsolete types, and 900,000 pairs of ski socks were available. Baum described the trigger finger mitten with wool insert, a new cold-climate combat item, but was of the opinion that the wool glove with leather palm was "more

---

[49] (1) Quotation from Personal Ltr, CQM to Feldman, 9 Jul 44. Hist Br OQMG. (2) Investigation, Supply of Clothing to the ETO, 16 May 1945, prepared for CG ASF by Col. Charles Garside et al; reproduced in full in Littlejohn, ed., Passing in Review, ch. 28, app. K (cited hereafter as Garside Rpt). (3) Memo, Littlejohn for Brumbaugh, 3 Jul 44, sub: Current and Proposed Allowances for Troops in U.K. and on Continent; Memo, Feldman for Brumbaugh, 18 Jul 44, same sub.; Memo, Reqmts Br MP Div OQMG for Lt Col Bellican, 18 Jul 44, same sub. Hist Br OQMG.

[50] (1) IRS, Chief Sup Div for CQM, 2 Jul 44, sub: Comments on Capt Pounder's Rpt of 30 Jun 44. Hist Br OQMG. (2) Brumbaugh's views are summarized in Appendix C, column 4.

presentable and warm enough for most occasions." [51] Brumbaugh had been directed to obtain facts and to seek the advice of General Feldman, but not to make decisions.

Another chore that Brumbaugh was to perform was review and completion of a clothing reserve for a 5,000-man task force to operate in a wet-cold or alpine climate, presumably Norway. Part of the necessary clothing had been forwarded to the ETO from Iceland, and the balance was selected in accordance with Doriot's ideas. But on all major issues the divergence of opinion between Littlejohn and Doriot was so complete that Brumbaugh dealt as much as possible with General Feldman, the Deputy Quartermaster General for Supply Planning, and with officials of the Storage and Distribution Division, even on matters concerning Colonel Doriot's Military Planning Division. [52]

Realizing that an impasse had been reached with Doriot, and that not all of Brumbaugh's questions had been satisfactorily answered, Feldman went to the ETO during the last week in July, just as the armies were breaking out of the Normandy beachhead. None of Littlejohn's experimental requisitions for test purposes had been filled. He still felt that the specific suitability of the OQMG's new items for his theater had not been demonstrated, but the sudden shift to mobile warfare indicated that the troops might reach the German border ahead of schedule and that some greater provision for operations in a colder climate was necessary. Since the quartermasters of the armies were definitely not available to advise on their requirements for these untried garments, [53] the problem had to be approached from the other end—from a survey of what was known to be available. Here Feldman's detailed knowledge of current supply levels, procurement possibilities, and previous commitments, was invaluable. Littlejohn and Feldman jointly outlined a requirement based upon the availability of 446,000 pairs of improved military shoepacs, the most critical item. [54] Supplies of ski socks, ponchos, mufflers, trigger finger mittens, and cotton field trousers were also limited.

Littlejohn found it logical and convenient to frame his requisition as a

---

[51] Pers Ltr, Littlejohn to Feldman, 9 Jul 44; Pers Ltr, Littlejohn to Brumbaugh, 13 Jul 44; Quotation from IRS, Baum for Brumbaugh, 18 Jul 44, sub: Clothing and Footwear. Hist Br OQMG.

[52] (1) Memo, CQM to TQMG, 3 Jul 44, sub: Cold-Climate Clothing; Pers Ltr, Brumbaugh to Littlejohn, 22 Jul 44; IRS, Littlejohn to Col Duncan, 31 Jul 44, sub: Comments on Col Brumbaugh's Letter re Points Covered at OQMG. Littlejohn Reading File, vol. XXVI, items 16, 99, 131. (2) On 25 July Littlejohn wrote to Gregory, suggesting that various key OQMG staff officers including Doriot visit the ETO to clarify current problems. Visits by Brig. Gen. Frank F. Scowden, Maj. Gen. Carl A. Hardigg, and General Owens are recorded in the Littlejohn Papers, but Feldman came instead of Doriot. See Ltr, Littlejohn to Gregory, 25 Jul 44, sub: Visits of Responsible QM Officers to ETO. Littlejohn Reading File, vol. XXVI, item 107.

[53] McNamara and Busch were so immersed in the immediate problems of their armies' headlong advance that they failed to report their large accumulation of Class II shortages until the pursuit ended in September.

[54] (1) IRS, Littlejohn to Feldman, n.d. (ca. 29 Jul 44). sub: Tonnage Figures. ETO QM 421. Hist Br OQMG. (2) Requisition J–48 comprised the following items:

Shoepacs, 12″ with 2 insoles, felt (pair)	446,000
Insoles, block type, replacements (pair)	122,850
Socks, ski (pair)	650,000
Ponchos, nylon type	250,000
Ponchos, raincoat type already requisitioned	250,000
Mitten shell, trigger finger (pair)	569,000
Mitten insert, trigger finger (pair)	1,138,000
Caps, field, cotton with visor	446,000
Trousers, field, cotton	456,600

project for equipping a type field army of 353,000 men, with normal maintenance reserves. During the period of headlong pursuit he referred to it optimistically as the Army of Occupation project. The formal requisition, J–48, was submitted by cable on 15 August for delivery by the end of October. The next day Feldman, who had returned to the United States two weeks before, gave assurance that the supplies were available. Formal approval, except that half the shoepacs would be obsolete types and poncho deliveries would be deferred, was given on 3 September 1944.[55]

On 10 August 1944 this clothing program was submitted to the Preventive Medicine Division, Office of the ETO Chief Surgeon, and received the approval of that office. The OCQM planned to provide one field army with cotton field trousers, ski socks, and "a new type of shoepac, in three widths, with proper orthopedic support." Seventy-five percent of other troops were to receive overshoes.[56] Moreover, every

man in the theater would be issued a wool jacket, a sweater, and a sleeping bag. OCQM referred to these items as "on requisition," and there was no hint that they might not be available at the beginning of cold weather.

It might appear at first glance that General Feldman had succeeded in accomplishing a large part of what Captain Pounder failed to do. Such a view would overemphasize clothing design, while ignoring other aspects of supply. Pounder and Doriot had urged Littlejohn to submit requisitions for enough new type winter clothing to equip all the ground combat troops in the theater, a figure in excess of 1,000,000 men. Although Doriot did not believe that such requisitions were procurable in full he did not concur in the idea that a requisition should be limited to what was known to be obtainable. He believed that the OQMG should be given as its objective the procurement of the absolute maximum quantities of the new items obtainable by the use of mandatory orders and "other extreme procurement methods."[57] The garments so obtained should be distributed on a strict priority basis to those troops in the greatest need of them, a process in which Doriot failed to see any difficulties. But such ill-defined procurement and distribution on a when-as-and-if basis was anathema to Littlejohn, who felt that without firm commitments effective local distribution planning within the theater was virtually impossible. By contrast Feldman, a supply man and not a designer, offered the ETO articles that

[55] (1) Pers Ltrs, Littlejohn to Brumbaugh, 11 Jul 44, and Brumbaugh to Littlejohn, 22 Jul 44. Littlejohn Reading File, vol. XXVI, items 47, 99. (2) Ltrs, Feldman to Littlejohn, 4, 16 Aug 44. Littlejohn Reading File, vol. XXVII, items 7, 134. (3) Cable EX–43895, Lee to Somervell, 15 Aug 44; sub: Winter Clothing for Special Conditions, and Cable WARX–24892, AGWAR to COMZONE ETOUSA, 3 Sep 44, same sub. (4) The procedure for giving advance notice before formal requisition of new items is discussed in connection with the Anzio tests (Chapter VII) and relations with NYPE (Chapter XII), above.

[56] (1) Memo, Office of the Chief Surgeon Preventive Medicine Div for OCQM, 23 Jul 44, sub: Trench Foot; Memo, OCQM for Chief Surgeon Preventive Medicine Division, 10 Aug 44, same sub. Hist Br OQMG. (2) Tom F. Whayne and Michael E. DeBakey, Cold Injury, Ground Type, MEDICAL DEPARTMENT, U.S. ARMY IN WORLD WAR II (Washington, 1958), pp. 144–46, 157.

[57] (1) Memo, Doriot for CG ASF Reqmts Div, 3 Jun 44, sub: Secret Radio CM IN–157, 1 Jun 44, Protective Clothing. Hist Br OQMG. (2) Roberts, op. cit., pp. 58, 65.

appeared to be suitable for the changed tactical situation, in quantities that appeared at the time to be available. As a supply specialist he would not be upset because Littlejohn refused M1943 jackets. By August, the OQMG had ordered over 7,000,000 of them from manufacturers, and presumably any reasonable number could be shipped at short notice if the Chief Quartermaster changed his mind.

To anticipate the final outcome, Littlejohn finally did change his mind and accept the M1943 jacket, but only after it had become clear that nothing else was available. The overcoat worn over the M1943 jacket was a combination that pleased neither Doriot nor Littlejohn, but it was one of the variety of motley outfits still being worn by combat troops in early 1945. Once the ETO had approved the M1943 jacket, the War Department cabled that issues were to be made to all troops as authorized in the current T/E 21, and that olive drab field jackets, winter combat jackets, and similar substitute items were to be withdrawn as soon as possible. This directive merely underlines the lack of effective liaison between the two headquarters, since a shortage of M1943 jackets had already developed, making compliance impossible. Moreover, the troops fortunate enough to have winter combat jackets refused to part with them. The order also did nothing to clarify the status of the overcoat, authorization for which was not withdrawn, either then or later.[58]

Receipt and Forwarding of Winter Clothing

The First Winterization Program 7 September–13 October 1944

On 7 September, the same day that Colonel Busch wrote "It is getting cold up here," Littlejohn sent letters and memos to each army quartermaster and each base section quartermaster in the theater, and also to his deputy back in the United Kingdom.[59] The burden of each message was the same. Supplying winter clothing to the troops was almost entirely a problem of local transportation, and since the OCQM did not control any trains or trucks, quartermasters at all levels must put pressure on their respective G–4's and persuade them that the allocation of tonnage for moving Class II items had to be radically increased. Moreover, the pipeline from Cherbourg to the armies was now over 400 miles long, without any intermediate depots or effective Quartermaster control anywhere along the route. If pilferage, distortion of balanced tariffs, and interminable delays were to be avoided, supplies must be sent direct from the United Kingdom by air or by LST to specific small ports. Two days later, armed with rough estimates of requirements from McNamara and Busch, Littlejohn made a formal request to General Stratton, the G–4 COMZ, for increased cross-Channel transportation and revised priorities. He wanted the Quartermaster tonnage allocation for September raised from 62,000 to 88,750 long tons. He pointed out that for the

---

[58] (1) Cable WARX–60685, AGWAR to ETOUSA, 10 Nov 44. (2) Authorization for the overcoat was also continued in MTOUSA. See Table 3.

[59] Littlejohn Reading File, vol. XXVIII, items 40, 44, 48, 48A, 50, 51, 52, 54, 55.

period June–August 1944, the specific allocation of QM Class II tonnage had been 55,000, but actual receipts had only been 53 percent of that amount. Moreover, reports from the United Kingdom indicated that the 62,000 tons currently allocated for clothing and individual equipment bore such a low priority that they could not be shipped before the end of September. He proposed to reduce his Class I and III tonnages from the United Kingdom by 50 percent, and urgently requested a priority authorization for 50,750 long tons of Class II items, broken down as follows:

Items	Tons
Winter clothing program	10,000
Winter tentage program	10,350
Combat maintenance	29,500
Class B and X clothing for POW's	900

In addition, his Class IV allocation should include 200 long tons of winter clothing to be sold to officers and nurses.

The clothing for enlisted men was intended primarily for 750,000 troops actually in combat—the First and Third Armies on the German frontier, and one corps under Ninth Army besieging Brest. This was normal winter clothing, not special items. It included both initial issues and necessary replacement articles, and the complete issue amounted to 25 pounds per man. (*Table 18*) Littlejohn explained that distribution had to be completed by 1 October if the efficiency of the troops was to be maintained, and requested that 6,000 tons of clothing for troops in the forward areas, and also the clothing for sale to officers, be moved by air.[60] Clothing for Ninth Army and COMZ troops could easily be transported by ship—preferably by LST to small ports where they could be unloaded and expedited by Quartermaster troops. Littlejohn clearly wished to keep these special shipments away from Cherbourg, where more than one hundred ships were waiting to unload and inventory and forwarding procedures were alarmingly inefficient. But Stratton decided that the current overriding priorities for movement of POL and ammunition by air should not be changed. In spite of a personal appeal by Littlejohn, Bradley supported Stratton. Bradley's comment afterwards was:

When the rains first came in November with a blast of wintry cold, our troops were ill-prepared for winter-time campaigning. This was traceable in part to the September crisis in supply for, during our race to the Rhine, I had deliberately by-passed shipments of winter clothing in favor of ammunition and gasoline. As a consequence, we now found ourselves caught short, particularly in bad-weather footgear. We had gambled in our choice and now were paying for the bad guess.[61]

Even in the face of such high level opposition, Littlejohn remained convinced of the necessity of his program and sought alternate means of transportation. At a time when the pursuit was slowing down for want of gasoline this was no simple problem, but the Chief Quartermaster explored every possibility and overcame many obstacles. LST's and coasters were in short supply, and most of the lower priority items had to go to Cherbourg on Liberty ships. Reims had

---

[60] Memo, Littlejohn for Stratton, 9 Sep 44, sub: Transportation for QM Supplies. Littlejohn Reading File, vol. XXVIII, item 60.

[61] (1) Bradley, *A Soldier's Story*, p. 445. (Quotation reprinted by permission of Holt, Rinehart and Winston, Inc.). (2) By contrast SOLOC, with only one U.S. army to support, completed an airlift to the combat troops by 26 September. See discussion of support for the DRAGOON forces in Chapter VII, above.

TABLE 18—SUMMARY OF FIRST WINTER CLOTHING PROGRAM, 7 SEPTEMBER 1944

Item	Basis	Estimated requirements by 1 October	Weight per unit, packed	Total weight, lbs.
Overcoats or mackinaws.........	1 per man not equipped on arrival	750,000	9.00	6,750,000
Gloves, wool (pair).............	1 per man not equipped on arrival	750,000	.36	270,000
Undershirts, wool..............	1 per man to Army troops	750,000	1.06	795,000
Drawers, wool..................	1 per man to Army troops	750,000	.86	645,000
Blankets, wool.................	1 per man	1,500,000	4.65	6,975,000
Cap, wool, knit................	1 per man not equipped on arrival	750,000	.18	135,000
Socks, wool (pair)[a].............	2 per man	2,600,000	.38	988,000
Laces, shoe (pair)[a].............	1 per 2 men in Armies	350,000	.02	7,000
Laces, legging (pair)[a]..........	1 per 2 men in Armies	350,000	.02	7,000
Shoes, service (pair)[a]..........	1 per man in Armies	750,000	4.83	3,622,500
Shirts, wool[a]..................	1 per man in Armies	515,000	1.50	772,500
Trousers, wool[a]................	1 per man in Armies	515,000	2.20	1,133,000
Totals—pounds..............	....	....	25.06	22,100,000
Totals—long tons...........	....	....	....	9,866

[a] Represents estimated necessary replacements to troops now on the Continent. These are *not* considered as initial issues.

been selected as the inland Class II distributing point, and to obtain trains for clothing he arranged to divert ships carrying 800 tons of rations per day (equal to two trains) from Cherbourg to Morlaix, on the northern coast of Brittany. A considerable part of the smaller but more vital portion of the winterization program, involving airlift to the First and Third Armies, was carried out as planned through the personal intervention of General Spaatz. Since transport aircraft were not available, he provided bombers to carry 41 percent of the required clothing to forward airstrips. Perhaps the fact that Littlejohn had personally arranged for Spaatz and his staff to receive 100 sets of the coveted officer type of ETO uniforms a week earlier made this type of informal staff co-ordination easier.[62]

Other expedients outside the tonnage allocations system were employed to move clothing forward. On 16 September three Dukw companies, optimisti-

[62] (1) Memo, Littlejohn for Stratton, 9 Sep 44, sub: Transportation for QM Supplies; Memo, Littlejohn for Smithers, 10 Sep 44, no sub; Ltr, Littlejohn to Franks, 11 Sep 44, sub: Sales Stores. Littlejohn Reading File, vol. XXVIII, items 60, 66, 68. (2) History of QM ADSEC, p. 28. (3) "Bombers Deliver Overcoats to Yanks," *Stars and Stripes*, London, October 4, 1944, p. 1.

cally moving up to support a Rhine crossing, were used to bring more than 300,-000 sets of winter underwear to First Army.[63] Moving 1,000 tons of clothing to the Ninth Army through small Brittany ports was comparatively easy because an LST was available for this shipment. Since Liberty ships could not enter the shallow harbors, these ports were not crowded and service personnel of the army were available to assist in unloading. By contrast, at such deep-water ports as Cherbourg, Le Havre, and Rouen, only 12 Quartermaster ships could be berthed at one time, and at the end of September 61 shiploads of Quartermaster cargo including 12 loaded with clothing and equipment, were waiting to discharge.[64]

A complicated aspect of the winterization program involved the duffel bags that divisions of Third Army had brought to the Continent. These had been stored in various locations within the original beachhead during July. On 9 September the Third Army quartermaster asked ADSEC to send forward over 1,200 tons of the bags for three divisions, and later another shipment for three more divisions was requested. Most of these bags could be located, and had been trucked to the nearest railroad by 25 September, but the sequel was far from satisfactory. Some had been pilfered and no longer contained either blankets or overcoats. The owners of some of the bags had become casualties. Those bags that reached their rightful

owners intact usually duplicated items already issued. Naturally, rail transportation was charged against Third Army's Class II tonnage allocation. The whole procedure was wasteful and inefficient.[65]

The procedure recommended by Littlejohn, and prescribed for First Army troops by Colonel McNamara, also ran into difficulties. The duffel bags of winter clothing that FUSA units turned in before leaving the United Kingdom in June should, in theory, have been salvaged and returned to stock. On 8 September Littlejohn noted with concern that the United Kingdom inventory of overcoats was only 500,000, whereas he believed it should be twice as large.[66] Sorting and returning to stock the overcoats turned in by the combat troops before their departure should have been simple, but salvage operations had been severely hampered by loss of the more experienced salvage units, which were naturally the first to be sent to the Continent.

Nevertheless, bearing in mind the objectives of this first winterization program—to equip combat troops only—it was very successful. At the end of September the First Army chief of staff set up priorities for the currently arriving winter clothing, giving first priority to infantry divisions and last to army troops. Early in October a full issue of regular winter clothing to First Army was completed, with the exception of a 50 percent shortage in arctic overshoes,

[63] *FUSA Rpt to Opns,* 1 Aug 44–22 Feb 45, II, 112.

[64] (1) IRS, Littlejohn to Franks, 13 Sep 44, sub: QM Supply Situation in Brittany Peninsula. Littlejohn Reading File, vol. XXVIII, item 80. (2) See Table 19.

[65] (1) Memo, TUSA QM for Smithers, 9 Sep 44; Ltr, Littlejohn to Busch, 25 Sep 44. Littlejohn Reading File, vol. XXVIII, items 76, 93. (2) Critical comment by General Busch on preliminary draft of this MS, dated 15 Nov 54. Hist Br OQMG.

[66] Memo, Littlejohn for Franks, no sub, 8 Sep 44. Littlejohn Reading File, vol. XXVIII, item 55.

an item not included in the original list. At the same time 6,000 of the new sleeping bags were issued to each division, enough to give each man either four blankets or a sleeping bag and two blankets. Difficulties with the size tariff led to shortages in the medium sizes of field jackets, wool olive drab clothing, and shoes. A similar shortage of wool socks was overcome in military laundries by shrinking size 12 to smaller sizes required in the army depot.[67]

Meanwhile, by 30 September all Third Army troops had a third blanket. Overcoats had been distributed to all except army troops, demonstrating that, like General Bradley, TUSA regarded the overcoat as a combat item. Early in October issues to Third Army similar to those in First Army were completed, and by the end of the month the only shortages were overshoes, raincoats, and leggings. Third Army had received about 4,500 tons of Class II and IV supplies during October—including 1,194 tons delivered by air.[68]

One additional fact might be noted here. Upon his return from the United States in late July, Brumbaugh was appointed Deputy Chief Quartermaster (Rear), replacing Brig. Gen. Allen R. Kimball. There were several reasons for this appointment, despite Brumbaugh's openly expressed preference for a more active assignment. First, there were tremendous quantities of used clothing in the United Kingdom, although progress in salvage and inventory left much to be desired. Brumbaugh, as a clothing specialist, was an ideal man to thaw this frozen asset. Moreover, his ETO experi-

ence fitted him to administer what was becoming essentially a British civilian organization, now that the American units were leaving for the Continent. General Kimball, a senior Quartermaster officer but a recent arrival in the ETO, lacked such specialized experience. An additional problem arose late in August, when the U.K. Base Section was transformed into a semi-autonomous headquarters under the command of Brig. Gen. Harry B. Vaughan, Jr. Littlejohn remembered his rather unsatisfactory relationship with the Forward Echelon, COMZ, when General Vaughan commanded that organization, and decided that the situation demanded an unusually competent and forceful Quartermaster representative in this rearmost echelon of ETO supply. Brumbaugh was therefore given the additional designation of Quartermaster, United Kingdom Base, and remained in London despite the fact that there was no really qualified clothing expert to replace him in the OCQM. Lt. Col. Thomas B. Phillips was confirmed in his temporary position as chief of the Supply Division, and several junior officers of even less experience became branch chiefs.[69]

The Replacement Factor Controversy

At a staff conference in Paris on the morning of 13 October, Littlejohn was able to give a very satisfactory report on progress in winterizing the combat troops. He displayed an impressive chart which showed that, except for blankets and overshoes, quotas for every item of the winterization program had actually been exceeded. But Littlejohn

---

[67] FUSA Rpt of Opns, 1 Aug 44–22 Feb 45, IV, 57–59.

[68] TUSA AAR, QM 6, 28.

[69] (1) Ruppenthal, Logistical Support, I, 211. (2) Littlejohn Reading File, Special Cases Folder, item 5. (3) Interv, Ross with Littlejohn, 11 Jan 60.

referred disparagingly to his achievement as a "so-called winterizing program," explaining that it had merely met preliminary demands brought on by unexpectedly early cold weather. Now he was faced with the real supply problem resulting from accelerated wear and tear of most items of clothing and equipage, and had recently been forced to place heavy emergency demands upon the zone of interior because "regardless of whether this current replacement factor holds true for the whole year, the supplies must be here to meet the known demands." It was therefore imperative that the transatlantic tonnage allocation for QM supplies for November be increased by 172,275 measurement tons. Littlejohn did not need to mention that this would be an increase of 52 percent over his October allocation, and if granted would require sharp cutbacks by the other technical services.[70]

That same afternoon Littlejohn covered much the same ground in an interview with the press, but with somewhat different emphasis. He described the disrupting effects of the unexpected tactical pursuit, which had created local shortages of clothing, and the dramatic airlift, which had overcome them in the forward areas. But AAF and service troops were still seriously short of clothing and blankets. The Chief Quartermaster explained that rates of wear and tear and of loss had been badly underestimated, and that the rate of maintenance shipments from the United States

would have to be increased 250 percent to take care of these revised requirements. Consequently, the productive capacity of the United States must continue unimpaired. Doubtless Littlejohn was referring to increased discussion of the imminence of victory in the American press and wide publicity that had been given to recent contract terminations by the Army. He carefully refrained from referring to delays in current production in the United States, a matter that had been publicized by the War Production Board late in September, but at least one correspondent, David Anderson of the New York *Times,* said that such production was "months behind," and also stated that "the men fighting on the rim of Germany were ill-equipped for winter."[71] This unfortunate statement was only partly true at the time of the press conference; indeed the ostensible reason for calling in the press had been to explain how local distribution problems on the Continent had been overcome.

The *Times* article promptly evoked a demand for explanations from Somervell to Eisenhower and Lee. The head of ASF failed to understand the need to rush clothing by aircraft, and stated that prior to 1 October he had received no reports that War Department replacement factors were inadequate. Littlejohn explained to Lee that he had

---

[70] (1) Command and Staff Conf, 13 Oct 44. EUCOM AG 337, Staff Conferences, vol. II, 1944. (2) Chart is reproduced in *QM Supply in ETO,* III, as app. XXXIII. (3) Computed by author from Monthly Progress Rpts, Statistics Br, Water Div, OCT. Hist Br OQMG.

[71] (1) "U.S. Troops in Reich 'Winterized'; Outfit Change Made in Ten Days," by David Anderson. New York *Times,* October 14, 1944, p. 1. (2) "WPB Charges Delay in Field Jackets" (Special to the New York *Times*) Washington, 29 September 1944. Incl 2 to Pers Ltr, Evans to Littlejohn, 4 Oct 44. Littlejohn Reading File, vol. XXIX, item 16. (3) "Post-War Talk Jumps in U.S." and "Army Steps Up Contract Cuts," both in *Stars and Stripes* (London), 18 September 1944, p. 1.

"stressed the part that air is playing in the supply of the armies." He also stated that he had made repeated informal reports on the inadequacy of the War Department's replacement factors, and that during the last month he had been forced to submit two very large emergency requisitions for additional clothing and equipage.[72]

The above exchange of cables marks the emergence of replacement factors as the major consideration in computing and justifying specific clothing requirements from the ETO. Requirements specialists in the OQMG felt that this was a misuse of replacement factors, which represented long-term trends and were used primarily in computing war production programs at the national level. They recognized that the first stages of any military operation were often marked by unusually heavy demands for Class II supplies, but from their point of view such demands should be met by special projects, such as the PROCO procedure that had been authorized during the build-up for OVER- LORD. Such projects were filled from special reserves and did not disrupt the orderly computation of long-term replacement factors. But Littlejohn had believed even before D-day that the current replacement factors were inadequate, and he had made an unsuccessful attempt to set up a special clothing reserve by the use of PROCO requisitions. When ASF disapproved his special proj-

ects as unjustified, he became convinced that PROCO procedures were ineffective and also that basic requirements statistics in the zone of interior were faulty and would have to be revised. Officials in the OQMG did not agree. That ASF had disapproved Littlejohn's PROCO requisitions was unfortunate, but not germane to their problems. Their current replacement factors should stand until new long-term trends had been confirmed.[73] Littlejohn, on the other hand, felt that the primary objective of the Quartermaster Corps was to fill the needs of the combat soldier, no matter how unpredictable they might be. For that purpose he was ready to follow procedure, distort procedure, or overturn it altogether. His own description of what had occurred on the Continent during the initial period of heavy combat vividly explains the new and unexpected trend in replacement factors:

Normandy is covered with a series of hedges. Each small plot of ground on the farms is completely surrounded by these tall hedges which carry thorns. Furthermore, in the advance across Normandy, the local actions in which small units were engaged frequently consisted of a life-and-death race across a 50-yard space. The American soldier skinned down to the clothes he had on, his rifle, his ammunition belt full of ammunition, and one day's ration. The blankets, the shoulder pack, overshoes, were left in a dugout which he had made for himself. Raincoat and blanket were usually at the bottom. The shelter half was staked down on top of the hole and covered with about two feet of dirt. The items left behind or destroyed by the soldier as indicated above, were scavenged by the natives. Another important thing in the high consumption of

[72] (1) Cable WAR–46609, Somervell to Eisenhower and Lee, 14 Oct 44. (2) Ltr, Littlejohn to Lee, 16 Oct 44, sub: Press Conf, 13 Oct 44. Littlejohn Collection, sec. 1, Conference Reports file. (3) Cable E–54744, Personal to Somervell from Lee, 16 Oct 44. ASF Planning Div, drawer A46–371, ETO– Winter Clothing.

[73] Memo, Doriot for Gregory, no sub, 20 Oct 44. In OQMG Study of 5 Apr 45, pt. 4.

clothing and equipage was the mud. If one dropped his knife, fork, spoon, or mess kit at night it disappeared in the mud and had to be replaced. At the close of the battle of Normandy it was necessary for me to completely re-equip approximately 1,000,-000 American soldiers almost as if they were completely naked.[74]

The real point of contention was whether recent demands from the Continent represented a temporary situation or a new trend. If Littlejohn's view was correct, prudence demanded that the War Department revise its production program immediately instead of waiting until its reserves had been depleted. It was his contention that for at least three months the requisitions from the armies had not reflected their real requirements. Any report of depot issues to date was meaningless unless the unfilled demands of the armies were included, and the same applied to any computation of replacement factors based upon issues alone. Littlejohn's only effective method of assembling a reserve to meet the future needs of the armies was to compute his authorized level of Class II and IV supply (sixty days) in terms of observed, rather than administratively imposed, factors. Gregory, on the other hand, contended that clothing and equipment had been lost during the pursuit rather than expended during heavy combat, and that the existence of a valid new trend had not yet been demonstrated.[75]

The OQMG had sent a factor-computing team to the ETO before the June landings, and it set up reporting procedures and began to collect data in July. Like other theaters, the ETO had been submitting reports of matériel

consumed since mid-1943, but under combat conditions this was a far more complicated process, since the unpredictable element of combat losses was now added to the factors of wear and tear. Capt. Harold A. Naisbitt, who had been specially trained in the Requirements Branch, OQMG, reported that current administrative directives of COMZ and the OCQM were adequate, but that in many cases they were not being followed.[76] The maintenance factor team's first report, covering the period from 6 June to 28 July (D + 52) was so crude that Littlejohn dismissed it as a generalized statement requiring confirmation. On 8 August he wrote to Colonel Franks, the acting quartermaster of ADSEC:

. . . I must have definite information upon which to raise the ante for requisitions. Of course, as you know, if the situation is serious we will issue all the stocks we have and tell Pembark to furnish replacement. Where is my team that was sent to the Continent to do the maintenance factor job? When are they going to give me some new maintenance factors? The other day you gave me an over-all statement that maintenance was running at the rate of 2½ times the current factors. Please expedite this information so that we can use it in the review of requisitions.[77]

Crude and unsatisfactory though they were, the factors submitted on 4 August

[74] Littlejohn, ed., Passing in Review, ch. 6, p. 3.
[75] Memo, TQMG for CQM ETO, 25 Oct 44, sub: ETO Clothing Reqmts. Hist Br OQMG.

[76] Ltr, Naisbitt to CQM, 20 Jul 44, sub: Determination of Rates of Replacement and Consumption. Hist Br OQMG.
[77] (1) Ltr, Naisbitt to CQM, 20 Jul 44, sub: Determination of Rates of Replacement and Consumption; Ltr, Franks to Littlejohn, 4 Aug 44, sub: Continental Maintenance Factors, D Through D + 52. Both in Hist Br OQMG. (2) Memo, Littlejohn for DCQM and Div Chiefs, 28 Jul 44, sub: Tonnage, Quotation from Personal Ltr, Littlejohn to Franks, 8 Aug 44. Littlejohn Reading File, vol. XXVI, item 113; vol. XXVII, item 21.

constituted the last valid report received in over a month. The pursuit across France had already begun, and during that phase of operations improvement in the mechanics of reporting was meaningless, for the clothing issues reported upon were largely confined to COMZ and AAF units. While the armies were engaged in pursuit they were mainly interested in receiving food and gasoline; their requisitions for clothing and personal equipment averaged about 10 percent of normal requirements and actual receipts less than 3 percent.[78]

Under the circumstances, the OCQM was forced to use War Department replacement factors in computing its preliminary combat zone requisitions on the zone of interior. These requisitions, covering the last quarter of 1944, were submitted in late July before the difficulties of the shipping tie-up were fully realized. The computations therefore optimistically listed as assets all clothing held in the United Kingdom. Because of the low replacement factors and the large deductions for current assets, the net requirements upon NYPE were very small, and provoked an inquiry from General Feldman. Meanwhile, Littlejohn was becoming increasingly aware of the true picture. On 4 September he wrote Feldman from Paris, giving revised maintenance factors and remarking that the over-all trend previously reported—two and a half times War Department factors—appeared to be confirmed.

The next day, 5 September, an airmail letter from General Feldman dated 21 August reached the temporary COMZ headquarters at Valognes, demanding an explanation of the very scanty requisitions for regular winter clothing for the fourth quarter of 1944. Feldman stated that all Class II and IV requirements were less than anticipated, and pointed out that requisitions on file from the ETO for a list of sample items of regular winter clothing and equipment amounted to "much less than anticipated in current Army Supply Program." Prominent on the list were overcoats, shirts, socks, and wool trousers, all reported to be on hand in large quantities in the United Kingdom. Nevertheless, if these amounts accurately reflected theater requirements, an immediate cutback in production would be necessary. Littlejohn was in the forward areas investigating precisely this point when the chief of the Clothing Branch replied in a telegram that "requisitions are to stand." [79] This officer was relatively new to his assignment, having been appointed during the reorganization of the Supply Division when Brumbaugh left the OCQM. Fortunately, General Gregory decided to postpone action on the telegram, which was not only contrary to the facts but was also in contradiction to Littlejohn's most recent statements concerning rates of consumption. Clothing specialists in

---

[78] Issues to FUSA in September averaged 39 tons per day, and to TUSA 47 tons per day. FUSA and TUSA AAR's.

[79] (1) Ltr, Feldman to Littlejohn, 21 Aug 44, sub: Requisitions and Current ASP Anticipated Shipments. In OQMG Study of 5 Apr 45. (2) Cable JX–14092, Hq COMZ ETOUSA to WD, 5 Sep 44. (3) Personal Ltr, Littlejohn to Feldman, 4 Sep 44. Littlejohn Reading File, vol. XXVIII, item 29. (4) Memo, TQMG for the Chief of Staff, 3 Nov 44, sub: Requisitions for the ETO. Hist Br OQMG. (5) The episode of 5 September 1944 was discussed in detail in personal letters, Littlejohn to Gregory, 13 January 1945, and Littlejohn to Brumbaugh, 28 January 1945. Littlejohn Reading File, vol. XXXII, items 62, 157.

the OQMG wrongly assumed that Feldman was referring to requirements for *special* winter clothing. They mentioned this telegram whenever any criticism was directed at their handling of winter clothing requisitions. In retrospect it appears probable that Feldman was alarmed at the excessive optimism prevailing in Washington and the tendency to cut back requirements and relax wartime restrictions. He had already mentioned this in a letter to Littlejohn on 11 August. Feldman's letter may also have been an attempt to make a matter of record his informal arrangements with Littlejohn before departing for a new assignment in the Pacific.[80]

Shortages of experienced clothing specialists within the OCQM and repeated changes in the direction of the Supply Division continued to have unfortunate results. The reasons for leaving Colonel Brumbaugh in the United Kingdom have already been explained. His assistance in forwarding clothing from the rear was very valuable, but an experienced Class II expert in the Paris headquarters was sorely lacking. Despite repeated instructions to his entire staff, Littlejohn found it necessary to reprimand the acting chief of his Supply Division for misuse of Class II tonnage. On daily telegrams asking for unspecified Class II tonnage, cots and brooms had been sent to the armies instead of useful clothing and equipage. A month later there was a new chief of the Supply Division, and this admonition had to be repeated.[81] In both cases, the failure was in administrative supervision. Since no Class II forward depot had yet been established, the Supply Division of OCQM was itself processing requisitions from the armies and preparing distribution directives. The problem was to indoctrinate some seventy-five officers and enlisted personnel in a general policy, which had to be applied with discretion. Performance was considerably improved after Colonel Florsheim, former chief of the Storage and Distribution Division, was transferred to the Supply Division in November.[82] This was too late to be helpful in preparing and justifying winter clothing requisitions on the zone of interior. Such requisitions were prepared largely by the Military Planning Division, headed by Col. Albert G. Duncan, and reviewed by Littlejohn personally.

One major reason that the OCQM had no positive and specific clothing requirements from the combat units to transmit to the zone of interior as requisitions was inherent in the supply procedures imposed upon the theater by the G-4, COMZ. The army G-4's allocated tonnage rigidly on a daily basis, and the amount of a requisition could not exceed the allocation for a single day. Consequently, ever since the original landings the army quartermasters had been obliged to record their clothing

---

[80] (1) Ltr, Gregory to Littlejohn, no sub, 28 Sep 44. Littlejohn Reading File, vol. XXVIII, item 202. This letter answered several from Littlejohn to Feldman and explained that the latter had left the OQMG. (2) Personal Ltr, Feldman to Littlejohn, 11 Aug 44, Incl 1 (Clipping from Washington *Post*, August 2, 1944). Littlejohn Reading File, vol. XXVII, item 48. (3) Ruppenthal, *Logistical Support*, II, 23.

[81] (1) Memo, CQM for Chief Supply Div, 18 Sep 44, sub: Misuse of Tonnage. Littlejohn Reading File, vol. XXVIII, item 130. (2) Memo, CQM for Div Chiefs, no sub, 12 Oct 44. Littlejohn Reading File, vol. XXIX, item 51.
[82] OCQM Office Order 4, 6 Nov 44.

needs in the daily telegram, a frustrating procedure since daily estimates were not suited to this class of supply. Requirements were spasmodic and unpredictable. Undoubtedly echoing McNamara, the First Army adjutant general observed, "Combat organizations do not come out of the line on some set schedule—or suffer losses on one." [83] Aggravating this technical difficulty was the fact that clothing received very low priorities, so that a Class II requisition might be arbitrarily canceled day after day. With floods of new requisitions arriving daily, few of which could be filled from current stocks on the Continent, it became virtually impossible to keep track of unfilled requisitions. Littlejohn had hoped that the regulating stations would become centers to tabulate and disseminate such information, and ultimately provided them with a jeep courier service in default of adequate telephone communications. But getting such a complicated administrative organization into operation took time, and meanwhile many unit QM's repeated their requisitions, causing an overlap and increasing the confusion. Early in September Littlejohn asked the armies for rough estimates of their total winter clothing needs, and on the 16th he inaugurated a system of detailed fifteen-day estimates of clothing requirements, to be forwarded by a special courier service. This procedure, while not eliminating the unsatisfactory daily Class II telegrams, supplemented them with a coherent method of programing

foreseeable needs. It began to produce results immediately.

An interesting development that was an integral part of the new requisitioning procedures was the basic maintenance set. This representative group of sixty-eight essential items was a further development of the beach maintenance set already described in connection with the build-up for OVERLORD.[84] The basic maintenance set was not intended for automatic supply, but to simplify the requisitioning procedures of the armies at a time when communication facilities were extremely scanty. By using the provided code references to each item of the set, it was fairly simple to compose a brief and yet specific telegram.[85] It was, however, much easier to establish the needs of the combat troops than it was to fill them. Since stocks had already been depleted by the winterization program, these additional demands could only be met by placing requisitions on the United States.

Requisitions Based on the New Replacement Factors

On 18 September Littlejohn wrote directly to Gregory, requesting that 1,300,-000 blankets, 250,000 overcoats, and various items already on requisition for later delivery be shipped immediately. He requested that the entire list arrive on the Continent by 10 October on one or two commodity-loaded ships, which

---

[83] Ltr, AG FUSA to CG COMZ, 24 Aug 44, sub: Inadequacy of Present Level of Supply of QM Class II and IV Matériel for FUSA. AG FUSA 400.34 (QM).

[84] The beach maintenance set, follow-up maintenance set, and basic maintenance set are compared in Appendix A.

[85] OCQM ETOUSA Cir Ltr 52, 16 Sep 44, sub: Procedure for Supply of QM Items on the Continent. Reprinted in OTCQM TSFET Operational Study 5, app. C–3.

could be given special unloading priorities. He further said: "I am currently
confronted with completely re-equipping
a minimum of 1,000,000 men with all
items of clothing and substantially all
items of equipage. In addition . . .
large numbers of POW's and 100,000
French Territorials." [86] Two days later
in a teletype conference the requisitions
for trousers and arctics were each increased by 500,000 pairs, and on 22 September, having received an authorization for another suit of wool underwear
per man, Littlejohn stated that his requirement was 1,482,000 suits. But all
these were merely stopgap measures to
get the most necessary items onto the
next convoys. On 18 September he
wrote to Evans: "I already have before
me requisitions from the several armies
for complete clothing and equipment.

The only reason my requisitions are no
larger is that I cannot get the shipping." [87]

During late August and early September Littlejohn, like everyone else in the
ETO and many in the United States, had
been caught up in a wave of optimism
about an early German surrender.
This influenced the administrative details of his plans, but did not decrease
their scope. As he remarked in late
August: "Whether the Army fights, rests,
or sleeps, it must eat and must be supplied with clothing. . . . As soon as the
fighting is over, my problem becomes
more difficult rather than less, unlike
certain other Services. . . . For the Quartermaster . . . the only activity that slows
down is burial. . . ." [88]

Nevertheless, the pause in the pursuit
in mid-September was far more than a
breathing space and a chance to take inventory. It carried with it the chill of
disappointment, especially after the
British were forced out of Arnhem, the
only Allied bridgehead over the Rhine,
on September 26th. If the fighting was
to continue all winter, as now seemed
likely, it would not be enough to make
good the current shortages of the armies.
It would also be necessary to plan for
their support during the coming months
on the same tremendous scale, and,
moreover, to give them protection
against the cold weather that was already
beginning. This did not become evi-

[86] Ltr, Littlejohn to Gregory, 18 Sep 44, sub:
Reqmts of Winter Clothing for the ETO. Littlejohn Reading File, vol. XXVIIIA, item 133. The
requirement in detail was as follows:

Prior-ity	Item	Total Required by 10 October	Due in	Addi-tional Being Requisi-tioned
1	Blankets, wool, OD....	1,300,000	(a)	1,300,000
2	Undershirts, wool......	350,000	350,000	....
3	Trousers, wool.........	500,000	232,000	268,000
4	Shirts, flannel.........	200,000	200,000	....
5	Overcoats.............	250,000	....	250,000
6	Jackets, field, OD......	479,000	479,000	....
7	Overshoes, arctic.......	500,000	457,000	43,000
8	Sweaters, high-neck, OD.................	1,000,000	1,000,000	....
9	Gloves, leather palm...	500,000	500,000	....
10	Coats, wool serge......	600,000	....	600,000
11	Handkerchiefs, cotton, OD.................	3,155,000	3,155,000	....

a In a covering letter, Littlejohn explained that an informal
requisition, submitted three days earlier, for 3,140,000 blankets
had been an error. Incomplete information had led the Chief
Quartermaster to believe that no sleeping bags were arriving, so
he had requested two blankets to replace each missing sleeping
bag.

[87] (1) Ltr, Littlejohn to Evans, 18 Sep 44. Little-
john Reading File, vol. XXVIII, item 132. (2) TWX
Conf, 20 Sep 44, sub 1: Revised Reqmts, Winter
Clothing. Hist Br OQMG. (3) Cables WARX–
26068, 6 Sep 44; EX–48901, 22 Sep 44. In OQMG
Study of 5 Apr 45, pt. 4.
[88] Ltr, CQM to G–3 COMZ, 26 Aug 44, sub:
Reorgn of the OCQM and the Base Secs. Littlejohn
Reading File, vol. XXVII, item 128.

dent as quickly in the United States as in Europe. On 27 September Col. Ira K. Evans wrote that Littlejohn's "request for clothing to re-equip one million men has caused a little confusion here as to the exact purpose or necessity. . . . I thought that perhaps it was your intent to re-equip all the combat troops on 'V' Day, so that those going into Germany as well as those returning to the States, will be properly and suitably clothed." Littlejohn replied that "the clothing we are asking for is not for V-Day parades, but to effect supply to the front now." [89]

The piecemeal requisitioning of this period has been criticized as evidence of poor planning, but Littlejohn's correspondence reveals that there was hardly time for any planning at all. Preinvasion plans had to be scrapped when the armies crossed the Seine without stopping, and thereafter every problem had to be met on a day-to-day basis. On 17 September Littlejohn wrote to Evans:

We have been moving around for some days, and it is extremely difficult to get the facts before us. For example, there are no communications between my office and the several depots on the Continent except by cub plane or jeep. The latter never fails but is somewhat slow. Please bear with us if we express our troubles in too vigorous terms but the troops are yelling loudly.

Two days later, on the day his new main office in Paris officially opened, he wrote to Feldman: "I have so many problems today in connection with clothing that it is hard to know just where to start or

stop. . . . The lantern problem is quiet as the troops are moving too fast to light one. . . ." [90] The first order of business was, clearly, to centralize the details of administration previously scattered from Paris via Valognes back to London. He was perturbed to find that "the Divisions have had some junior officer take perfunctory and improper action on matters of considerable importance, the Chiefs of Divisions lacking knowledge thereof." [91] This referred primarily, of course, to the Supply Division and to the famous cable of 5 September to Feldman regarding requisitions.

In addition to the tremendous requirements uncovered in the few previous days, Littlejohn found himself under pressure from another direction— an over-all reduction in the theater's transatlantic tonnage allocation brought on by the tie-up of shipping. *(Table 19)* That situation had already caused delays in the discharge of Quartermaster cargo. The reduced allocation would also, inevitably, slow down deliveries from the United Kingdom.

Beginning on 25 September the whole OCQM staff was put to work reappraising all outstanding requisitions, for if Littlejohn hoped to obtain an increased shipping allocation notwithstanding the theater-wide reduction, he would first have to put his own house in order by ruthlessly weeding out every nonessential item. At the same time he gave his clothing specialists careful and detailed

---

[89] (1) Personal Ltr, Evans to Littlejohn, 27 Sep 44. Hist Br OQMG. (2) Personal Ltr, Littlejohn to Evans, 3 Oct 44. Littlejohn Reading File, vol. XXIX, item 5.

[90] Personal Ltrs, Littlejohn to Evans, 17 Sep 44, and Littlejohn to Feldman, 19 Sep 44. Littlejohn Reading File, vol. XXVIII, items 126, 140.

[91] Memo, CQM for DCQM (Col Franks), 22 Sep 44, sub: Cables, Teleprints, etc. Littlejohn Reading File, vol. XXVIII, item 156.

WINTER CLOTHING *arrives in the front line for a First Army reconnaissance squadron. October 1944.*

instructions regarding new requisitions. The United Kingdom supply level (45 days) was unchanged, but continental levels were to rise from 30 days in October to 60 in December, while the continental troop basis was to rise from 1,601,700 on 20 September to 2,673,600 on 31 December. The initial issues already described *(See Table 18.)* were to be completed for all troops on the Continent and two most important items, sweaters and arctic overshoes, were to be added to the list. One million men were to be completely re-equipped with wool underwear and all outer clothing except sweaters, overcoats, arctics, and combat boots. Inventories in the United Kingdom and cargoes awaiting discharge, insofar as information was available, were to be deducted.[92]

In every aspect except the controversial one of maintenance factors, these were entirely justifiable requirements. Transmitted to NYPE in two teletype conferences on 1 and 3 October, they comprised over 90,000 measurement tons,

[92] OCQM Dir 1, Review of Requisitions, 25 Sep 44. Littlejohn Reading File, vol. XXVIII, item 192.

TABLE 19—CLASS II AND IV TONNAGES DISCHARGED AND MOVED
FORWARD FROM PORTS

JULY 1944–FEBRUARY 1945

	Class II and IV Ships in ETO End of Month	Commodity-loaded QMC Ships (All)	Total Berths Available to QMC	QMC Ships in ETO Not Discharging	Offloading Plus Backlog From Previous Month (Long Tons)	Cleared From Continental Ports (Long Tons)	Backlog at End of the Month (Long Tons)
July...............	5	54	12	42	(a)	(a)	(a)
August.............	8	57	12	45	28,700	12,500	16,200
September..........	12	75	14	61	54,200	15,400	38,800
October............	17	80	18	62	75,900	19,000	56,900
November..........	22	62	17	45	81,100	22,400	58,700
December..........	24	68	17	51	137,800	49,200	88,600
January...........	23	52	23	29	169,500	98,400	71,100
February...........	6	12	23	0	148,800	120,500	28,300

a Information not available.

Source: Study, Incl to Ltr, Littlejohn to Somervell, 3 Mar 45, pt. II.

including 62,400 tons to be delivered before the end of October on an emergency basis. The emergency list included the following major items: [93]

Blankets	1,500,000
Caps, wool, knit	1,000,000
Drawers, wool	2,400,000
Gloves, wool, pairs	1,600,000
Jackets, field, OD	1,500,000
Overcoats	600,000
Overshoes, arctic (pairs) ...	900,000
Shirts, wool	2,000,000
Socks, wool (pairs)	6,000,000
Trousers, wool	3,000,000
Undershirts, wool	2,000,000

Not requested, but prominently listed as due in on previous requisitions, were 2,110,000 wool sweaters and 2,270,000 sleeping bags, also urgently needed before the end of the month. The great size of this requisition, and the number of older requisitions that would have to be canceled to provide shipping space,

threatened to dislocate the convoy schedules from NYPE rather seriously. Nevertheless, crises of this sort were not unknown at the New York port; Littlejohn's trusted associate, Colonel Evans, was very successful in readjusting the flow of Quartermaster supplies.[94]

Although Littlejohn's personal correspondence with Evans and Feldman, and also with Gregory, had anticipated the dimensions of the new requirements, the formal requisition, designated K–94, had a tremendous impact upon the operating levels of the OQMG, the ASF, and NYPE. The chief of the Requirements Branch, OQMG, hastened to

---

[93] Digest of Telecon NYPE–PARIS, 3 Oct 44, sub: Additional Winter Clothing. ETO 337, TWX Confs.

[94] (1) See discussion of relations with NYPE in Chapter XII, above. (2) Ltr, Evans to Littlejohn, 4 Oct 44. Littlejohn Reading File, vol. XXIX, item 16. Evans wrote that similar cancellation and re-scheduling of shipments had been performed for other technical services. (3) The chief of the QM Branch, Overseas Supply Division, NYPE, later remarked that liaison with the OCQM was more satisfactory than with other overseas technical services. Interv, Col T. R. J. Hickey with Dr. Irving Cheslaw, 6 May 52.

point out to Colonel Doriot that the OQMG had received positive assurances from the ETO that no such requisitions would be forthcoming. This was the first of many references to the erroneous telegram of 5 September. The primary reactions seem to have been surprise and indignation that less than thirty days after assuring the OQMG that supplies were sufficient the ETO was making known such tremendous requirements. There was also concern over criticism if they were not filled. But the Requirements Branch reported that the requisition could nevertheless be met. Zone of interior levels for many items would be depleted, but only in a few instances to a serious extent.[95]

The Requirements Branch re-echoed various objections regarding overseas techniques of computing replacement factors which had been made a year before. There was considerable justification for objections to the theater's crude methods of estimating supplies on hand, in default of inventories that had not yet been made. But the suggestion that supplies which appeared to have been consumed had actually disappeared into new supply depots revealed that OQMG operating personnel completely misunderstood the ETO situation. It was precisely because no new Class II depots had been organized, and supply had been hand-to-mouth from the beaches, that the trend in ETO clothing requirements had not been detected earlier. It was especially hard for zone of interior planners to accept the statement that ETO

reports of material consumed over a three-month period, which had been submitted as recently as 6 September, did not constitute a valid basis for estimating the theater's requirements.[96] Littlejohn discussed this apparent discrepancy in detail with Maj. Gen. William M. Goodman, deputy commander of NYPE, who was currently visiting the ETO. Apparently Goodman was convinced of the correctness of the revised requirements as stated, but was not persuaded that like conditions would recur. He believed that most of the supplies had been lost during rapid movement rather than worn out. But Goodman reported that Littlejohn "does not feel justified in reducing these factors inasmuch as he feels that he should be prepared to resupply based on consumption factors as shown." [97]

Meanwhile Littlejohn had been challenged to justify Requisition K–94, and had done so on 10 October in a lengthy cable to General Somervell. It gave specific experience factors about twice as high as War Department maintenance rates for fifteen items, and duly noted that no factors could be reported for sweaters and sleeping bags, since none had arrived in the theater. Despite this defense Colonel Evans reported on 12 October that for eleven of the most important items, shipments would be exactly 50 percent of the quantities requested. Additional supply action was being suspended by the War Depart-

---

[95] IRS, Chief Reqmts Br Mil Plng Div to Dir Mil Plng Div, 4 Oct 44, sub: Winter C&E for the ETO. In OQMG Study of 5 Apr 45, pt. 4.

[96] Ltr, CQM to TQMG, 6 Oct 44, sub: Continental Replacement Factors. Littlejohn Reading File, vol. XXIX, item 41.
[97] Ltr, Goodman to Col H. A. Malin, 8 Oct 44. In OQMG Study of 5 Apr 45, pt. 4.

ment "pending further justification." [98] In that context, it seems clear that Little-john's press conference of 13 October, which has already been described, was part of a deliberate campaign to get his total requirements approved without reservations or delay. A personal letter to Colonel Evans confirms this view:

Some weeks ago it became apparent to me that on clothing and equipage we were walking through the garments like paper and that I was headed for disaster. At that time I started flinging back to Pembark increased requisitions for substantial quantities of practically every item. I personally drew up these requisitions based upon facts and figures obtained from the Armies. Your Headquarters gave me 50% and I believe that you were instrumental in getting me this 50%. You came back at me and asked for a detailed defense, which was immediately forthcoming. . . . Along with the above have been any number of visiting firemen officially sent over by the War Department. . . . Each Chief of Service has had to prepare a set speech for . . . these individuals. On top of this, some weeks ago it became my official duty to conduct a press conference at which time I let the press in on the increased maintenance factors here on the Continent, as it was definitely my intention to see that the soldiers were properly equipped and warm for the winter, and the college professors gotten out of the way. I am very happy to say that—between your office, the A.S.F., and the O.Q.M.G., my new maintenance factors have been approved 90%. The 10% not approved doesn't mean too much. . . .[99]

Littlejohn's personal letters were all on this theme in mid-October. On the 15th he wrote to Gregory: "I know you think that we have gone crazy here in the ETO on clothing and equipage. However, the facts can be substantiated by anyone who desires to investigate them." He added that Goodman and Justice James F. Byrnes had done so during the past week.[100]

Despite the doubts of General Gregory and the openly expressed opposition of his requirements specialists, the whole amount of Requisition K–94 was approved by the War Department on 16 October.[101] This approval was without direct reference to maintenance factors, and incidentally without assurance of prompt delivery—a completely separate and very difficult problem. But the OCQM staff, convinced that their maintenance factors were being accepted at least tentatively, promptly submitted requisitions for clothing for the first three months of 1945. General Owens, the chief of the OQMG Storage and Distribution Division, who had recently visited the ETO and understood Littlejohn's problems, wrote:

We have been reviewing your requisitions for January, February, and March, which arrived here just after my return. As you will probably realize, some of the quantities asked for by you sort of set us back on our heels. On most of the items I am sure that we can meet your requirements. Some will necessitate increased production on which we are now busily engaged. . . .[102]

[98] (1) Ltr, CQM to TQMG, 6 Oct 44, sub: Continental Replacement Factors. Littlejohn Reading File, vol. XXIX, item 41. (2) Cable EX–53583, 10 Oct 44, to Somervell from Lee, signed Eisenhower, sub: Additional Winter Clothing Reqmts. Hist Br OQMG. (3) TWX Conf, sub: Winter Clothing, Col Brown, ETO–Col Evans, NYPE, 12 Oct 44. ETO 337, TWX Conferences.
[99] Personal Ltr, Littlejohn to Evans, 5 Dec 44. Hist Br OQMG.

[100] Ltr, Littlejohn to Gregory, 15 Oct 44. Littlejohn Reading File, vol. XXIX, item 79.
[101] (1) Cable WARX–47278, 16 Oct 44. (2) Memo cited in n. 75. (3) Memo, Doriot for Gregory, no sub, 20 Oct 44. SPQRQ 400. Hist Br OQMG.
[102] Personal Ltr, Owens to Littlejohn, 15 Nov 44. Littlejohn Reading File, vol. XXX, item 113.

In other words, the latest requisitions would require a major revision of the Army Supply Program, which was precisely what Littlejohn had been attempting to bring about. Having won a battle on principles the Chief Quartermaster was now more willing to compromise on some of the specific and technical aspects of the replacement factor problem. He still insisted that priority given to unfilled requisitions from the armies distorted reports of issue for replacement purposes, but conceded that inventories were inaccurate, and that some supplies, although shipped, had never been received.[103]

Probably information received from NATOUSA contributed to Littlejohn's conciliatory attitude. Remembering Sullivan's informal reports of very high replacement factors in Fifth Army during the previous winter, Littlejohn wrote to Middleswart in October, asking for official NATOUSA data on that subject. Middleswart's answer, surprisingly, showed that Mediterranean factors were less than those of the War Department in many cases. To a considerable extent, of course, this reflected the difference of opinion between Middleswart and Sullivan, which has already been described. There were additional reasons for the differences between NATOUSA factors as reported by Middleswart and the earlier Fifth Army reports. Foremost was the trend toward a static tactical situation in Italy, which had a direct and very favorable effect upon both losses and wear and tear. In SOLOC, where Seventh Army's tactical situation could hardly be called static, veteran troops from Italy also reported comparatively low replacement factors. Apparently very generous initial issues contributed to this result. On reviewing the first reports from SOLOC of matériel consumed that passed through his headquarters, Littlejohn decided that neither the basis of computation nor the results could be reconciled with ETO experience, and recommended that SOLOC reports should be submitted separately.[104]

The technicalities of the factor controversy are well illustrated by the example of wool socks. The authorized ETO allowance was three pairs of cushion-sole and two pairs of light or heavy wool socks per man, and the original War Department factors for them were 11.1 and 25 percent, respectively. But cushion-sole socks, the newer and distinctly more desirable item, were in short supply, and the demands of ETO troops, for both initial issue and replacement, were largely filled with heavy or light wool socks—usually the latter. The fragility of light wool socks and the scarcity of cushion-sole were well illustrated in the August 1944 report of matériel consumed, which showed 55.4 percent replacements of the former, and 5.1 percent of the latter. In October

[103] (1) IRS, Littlejohn to Franks, no sub, 3 Oct 44; Ltr, CQM to TQMG, 6 Oct 44, sub: Continental Repl Factors. Littlejohn Reading File, vol. XXIX, items 4, 41. (2) Cable SPQRQ–400, Mil Plng Div OQMG to CQM ETO, 7 Nov 44. sub: Repl Factors. Hist Br OQMG. (3) Ltr, OCQM to TQMG, 1 Dec 44, sub: ETO Developed Repl Factors. OQMG 400.402 ETO.

[104] (1) See discussion of Mediterranean replacement factors in ch. VII, above. (2) Ltr, Middleswart to Littlejohn, 12 Nov 44, sub: NATOUSA QM Issues and Repl Factors, 1 Oct 43–30 Sep 44; IRS, Franks to Mil Plng Div OCQM, 23 Nov 44, same sub. Both in Hist Br OQMG. (3) IRS, Littlejohn to G–4 COMZ, 18 Dec 44, sub: Rpt of Matériel Consumed From SOLOC. Littlejohn Reading File, vol. XXXI, item 56.

Littlejohn requested a 50 percent factor for all socks, but the approved figures were adjusted at 25 percent for cushion-sole, and 33 percent for other wool socks. Meanwhile General Eisenhower, to prevent trench foot, had approved a plan of The Surgeon General to provide a daily pair of clean socks to each combat soldier. Littlejohn did not favor increasing initial issues, but estimated that it would require two or three extra pairs of socks per man to create a revolving reserve in the laundries and bath units. He was granted his desired 50 percent factor for the first quarter of 1945 only. Thereafter, the percentage reverted to 33 percent for both types of socks. This sequence of events illustrates how issue of an inferior substitute article can becloud replacement statistics, and incidentally cause confusion in procurement programing.[105]

In a letter to Gregory dated 1 December, Littlejohn reviewed his own previous recommendations on factors, Colonel Doriot's counterproposals, and cumulative ETO issue experience through October. The Chief Quartermaster admitted, for example, that previous OCQM computations on wool drawers had erroneously included 600,000 initial issues under maintenance. Correction reduced the cumulative issue experience for this item from 19.0 to 14.5 percent, and the OQMG's proposed factor of 12.5 was acceptable. On the other hand, the OQMG accepted the ETO figure of

8.4 percent on arctic overshoes, which doubled the original factor on that item. There was agreement on 70 percent of the articles under consideration, but the exceptions were all items of importance for a winter campaign. Littlejohn pointed out that most of the excepted items were still in short supply, and that requisitions for initial issue would have to be filled before issues for replacement could be made. A conspicuous example was the one-burner stove, a new and very desirable piece of equipment for a squad in combat. The demand was so great that practically all stock was expended for initial issue, and Littlejohn's replacement factor (8.1 percent) was merely an educated guess that rejected experience data entirely, but later proved to be quite accurate.[106]

There was no direct answer to this letter in over a month. During December the Gregory-Littlejohn correspondence, while remaining active, was largely concerned with specific requirements, especially those arising from the German Ardennes offensive. On 5 January Gregory sent a brochure to General Somervell, who was planning to visit the ETO and wanted information on unresolved problems between the OQMG and the Quartermaster organization in Europe. A large number of these problems concerned the Military Planning Division, and presumably the study was prepared by officers of that agency, since it reflected their point of view. Apparently Gregory was unaware of the controversies involved. He wrote to Littlejohn the same day and inclosed a copy of the brochure prepared for the head of ASF. Littlejohn's reply noted that

---

[105] (1) Ltr, CQM to TQMG, 18 Oct 44, sub: NATOUSA Repl Factor for Sock, Wool, and 1st Ind, Doriot to CQM, 25 Oct 44. SPQRQ 420 (Socks, Wool). Hist Br OQMG. (2) OTCQM TSFET Operational Study 6, 1 Nov 45, Combat Replacement Factors. (3) WD Cir 312, 1944. (4) Garside Rpt, tab 13.

[106] Ltr cited n. 103 (3).

Gregory had cleared up several problems, and thanked The Quartermaster General for "the cooperation which I have received during the past ninety days. . . . The inclosure referred to in your letter of January 5th is quite a different matter. I seriously question whether some of the statements made would dignify the Halls of Harvard." In another letter to Gregory dated 14 January Littlejohn again complained that the brochure for General Somervell was "rather loosely written." It gave a very partisan account of the replacement factor controversy, and since all long-range requisitions were based on such factors, it was also an open attack upon Littlejohn's whole requisitioning policy. Specifically, it stated that the interim replacement factors supplied by Captain Naisbitt, for use until continental experience data became available, were actually combat factors derived from NATOUSA, and if the OCQM had followed them, the clothing crisis of September would never have occurred. This was contrary to the facts. For lack of comprehensive experience data from the Continent, Littlejohn had used the replacement factors recommended by Naisbitt, and later found them quite inadequate for combat.

This was essentially a repetition of the Middleswart-Sullivan controversy on the same subject a year earlier. Littlejohn had received Fifth Army statistics direct from Sullivan, and referred to them as "NATO factors." He had no previous knowledge of Middleswart's very different figures covering the entire Mediterranean theater, and referred to them as "War Department factors." But whatever their source, he was just as emphatic as Sullivan in denying that they were suitable for a combat situation. Since Littlejohn referred to his own statistics as "Continental experience factors," and always submitted separate requisitions, based on noncombat factors, for the support of the United Kingdom, there was considerable justification for his view that the ETO should have used Sullivan's rather than Middleswart's statistics until dependable data from the Continent became available. His unsuccessful attempt in January 1944 to justify a PROCO requisition based upon Fifth Army factors has already been described. After that failure to obtain supplies for extraordinary contingencies by the method recommended by the OQMG, he was all the more determined to fill his needs by revising replacement factors.[107]

Littlejohn had basic objections to other statements made in the brochure for General Somervell. In May and June 1944 he had submitted piecemeal requisitions, some of them small and frankly experimental but others of very considerable size, for various items of the new clothing sponsored by the Military Planning Division, OQMG. That agency was either unaware of, or chose to ignore, all such requisitions, and stated that Littlejohn had submitted no such requisitions prior to 15 August. Moreover, the requisition of that date was severely criticized as too small and

---

[107] (1) Memo, TQMG for Somervell, 5 Jan 45, sub: QM Supply Problems, with inclosed brochure; Ltr, CQM to TQMG, no sub, 11 Jan 45. Both in OQMG Study of 5 Apr 45, pt. 4. (2) Personal Ltr, Littlejohn to Gregory, 14 Jan 45. Littlejohn Reading File, vol. XXXIII, item 62. (3) Ltr, Littlejohn to Somervell, 3 Mar 45, no sub, Incl III. Hist Br OQMG. (4) See discussion of replacement factors in Chapter VII, and of clothing and equipment for OVERLORD in Chapter XI, above.

too late to serve as a basis for further procurement. The fact that the requisition of 15 August had been co-ordinated with General Feldman before submission was not mentioned. Also, the OCQM policy of experimental requisitions, to test the reaction of the troops, did not meet the approval of the Military Planning Division. One sentence from a letter Littlejohn had written to Feldman was quoted out of context to convey an impression that the Chief Quartermaster was indiscriminately hostile to all newly developed items.[108] Even more annoying to Littlejohn was a misstatement that 200,000 one-burner stoves, which he had requisitioned for the ETO, were for issue to officers. He suspected that some stoves previously issued had been misappropriated by officers, but explained to both Gregory and Somervell that these were actually required for the combat troops, on a basis of one per rifle squad.[109]

Littlejohn personally discussed this and other such differences between his office and the OQMG with Somervell on 14 and 15 January, and the ASF commander decided a good many matters, including replacement factors, in favor of the ETO Quartermaster. Despite earlier objections from the OQMG, Somervell directed that Littlejohn's requirements for towels, handkerchiefs, and one-burner stoves were to be met. Far more important, the ASF commander decided on the spot that the very heavy responsibilities for clothing and feeding prisoners of war and repatriates, which SHAEF had imposed on Littlejohn, were legitimate calls for American aid. They would be met mainly by local procurement, for which the OCQM needed high-caliber technical personnel. The Chief Quartermaster had warned the OQMG of early requirements for such personnel, but for lack of a policy decision nothing had been done. In this instance General Somervell's correction of an oversight by his own ASF organization was very helpful to Quartermasters on both sides of the Atlantic.[110]

By the end of April 1945, ETO replacement factors, especially for individual clothing items, were coming down to the rates originally set by the OQMG a year before, and Littlejohn now recommended that most of the current ETO factors be reduced. The only conspicuous exception was the M1943 jacket, still noted as being in short supply. With the end of hostilities on 8 May, ETO Quartermaster statisticians began a very ambitious compilation of combat replacement factors, tracing their experience during the entire European campaign, and summarizing trends for each item by ninety-day periods.[111]

In retrospect it may be said that, from a narrowly technical standpoint, the OQMG's requirements specialists were

---

[108] (1) The sentence began with the words: "It is not my policy to force new items. . . ." It has already been quoted in full in correct context on page 564, above. (2) See Ruppenthal, *Logistical Support*, II, 222.

[109] (1) Ltr cited n. 107 (2), above. (2) RAD E–86633, Somervell (from Paris) to Gregory, 15 Jan 45. Hist Br OQMG. (3) McNamara, *Memoir*, p. 158.

[110] (1) Rad E–86633, Somervell (from Paris) to Gregory, 15 Jan 45. (2) Ltrs, CQM to Somervell, 18 Jan 45, sub: Appreciation for Attention Given to QM Problems; ETO Repl Factors for QM Supplies. Littlejohn Reading File, vol. XXXII, items 96 and 97.

[111] (1) Ltr, CQM to TQMG, 30 Apr 45, sub: Repl Factors for ETO. Hist Br OQMG. (2) OTCQM TSFET Operational Study 6, 1 Nov 45.

only doing their duty when they opposed Littlejohn's efforts to increase replacement rates and thereby to influence the Army Supply Program. Their mission was to compute total global requirements over extended periods, so that production could be maintained at a steady rate for maximum efficiency. Such an objective could only be achieved by minimizing extraordinary situations and ignoring short-term trends, which were compensated for by a reserve or safety factor. This was a logical approach to solve major logistical problems at the level of the national war effort, but unfortunately the Requirements Branch was short of personnel, and was forced to use data chosen for ready accessibility rather than for accuracy and timeliness. Requirements specialists were well aware that weeks and sometimes months went by before tactical requirements were reflected in depot issues, but the depot issues were reported at regular intervals in convenient statistical form and the tactical requirements were not. Ironically, these specialists were inclined to blame their inflexible and unsatisfactory statistical procedures upon excessively specific directives from ASF and upon the administrative burden of submitting overly frequent and elaborate reports to that headquarters. Conversely, Littlejohn considered the OQMG to be too much dominated by its own statisticians, and customarily looked to his personal contacts within ASF for policy decisions based upon a broad knowledge of combat operations. The existence of these directly opposing views of the role of ASF in shaping supply policy serve to illustrate the fundamental difference in point of view between the OQMG and

the ETO Quartermaster, a difference by no means limited to replacement factors.[112]

Delays in Receipt of New Items

The difficulties in achieving agreement on design of a wool field jacket have already been indicated. Deliveries presented an even greater problem. In mid-March, before a compromise in design had been settled, the OQMG version of the wool jacket was sent to Philadelphia for a technical analysis. Lt. Col. George Christie, Jr., director of the clothing factory in the Philadelphia QM Depot (PQMD), estimated that a maximum of two million jackets might be produced in the seven months, June–December 1944. Meanwhile the Military Planning Division, OQMG, by taking the monthly production capacity of serge coats (700,000) and arbitrarily adding 40 percent, arrived at a production figure of 6,860,000 jackets for the same period. The estimate that a jacket required 40 percent less labor than a service coat had originally been made regarding the simple ETO version, but as noted above, the OQMG's jacket design was far more elaborate. When General Clay cabled to Lee in April that 2,600,000 wool jackets could be supplied in 1944, he was clearly influenced by the Philadelphia depot's estimate. Nevertheless, the procurement directive that was sent to Philadelphia on 17 May called for delivery of 3,800,000 jackets in the calendar year 1944. Colonel Christie decided

[112] Bradford, *Methods of Forecasting War Requirements for QM Supplies*, QMC Historical Studies, 14, pp. 75–80; 91–93.

that his own factory within the depot, which served as a pilot plant, could produce 30,000 jackets in June.[113]

During early June, bidding by commercial manufacturers was slow. On 5 June the Department of Labor decided that the wool jacket, despite its name, was actually a coat, and approved a 60-cent hourly wage for those making it rather than the 40-cent rate prevailing for jacket manufacturers. This opened the way for new contracts at higher rates, but at the same time several jacket manufacturers withdrew their bids, since they felt that two wage rates in the same factory would inevitably lead to labor dissension. On 17 June the procurement directive was increased by 835,590 jackets to cover a commitment to NATOUSA, and it now became very probable that mandatory orders, a new departure in the clothing industry, would be necessary to procure the required quantity. Since the ETO had stated definitely that M1943 jackets were not required, some contracts for this item might be terminated in favor of wool jackets, but the wage rate considerations already mentioned limited the number of such conversions. Orders for 330,000 M1943 jackets were canceled on 29 June, and the manufacturers concerned contracted for 565,000 wool jackets instead. But the number of jackets on order was still insufficient, and mandatory orders against six contractors, who were capable of manufacturing the wool jacket but had refused to submit bids, were invoked on 20 July. Mandatory orders quickly solved the problem of insufficient bids, but contributed nothing to

the far more serious problem of timely deliveries.[114]

By 6 July Colonel Christie reported that his plant had only completed 11,890 jackets during June, in contrast to his estimate of 30,000. He recommended to the depot procurement officer a whole series of design simplifications that would speed up production, but the Military Planning Division, OQMG, disapproved all changes. On 7 July the PQMD reported contracts for 4,064,500 jackets for 1944 delivery, but the contracts carried no penalties for late delivery, and it was estimated that only 60 percent would be delivered by the end of the year. This was the very day that Littlejohn requisitioned 479,000 old style olive drab field jackets, having established that this was the total number still available. The original plan to provide olive drab jackets until wool jackets became available was no longer feasible, but the full seriousness of the situation was not yet clearly understood either in the OQMG or in ASF headquarters. On 21 July Littlejohn, determined to place his legitimate needs on record, submitted a formal requisition for 3,650,000 wool jackets, and on 4 August Somervell replied that 2,600,000 jackets would probably be the maximum number available in 1944, but possibly the additional 1,050,000 requested could be supplied in January 1945. By contrast, on 15 August the Director of Procurement, ASF, stated that the latest OQMG estimate of jacket production in 1944 was 5,135,000 based

---

[113] Roberts, *op cit.*, pp. 134–35, 153.

[114] (1) Roberts, *op. cit.*, pp. 183–85, 195–201, 210–222, 238. (2) Ironically, the two civilian consultants who had contributed largely to the design of the wool jacket were also contractors who refused to submit bids for it.

on imposition of mandatory orders, authorization of overtime payments to workers, and full mobilization of local Manpower Priority Committees to aid the program. But procurement specialists at PQMD were pessimistic regarding both mandatory orders and the labor situation. Three days later they gave the gloomiest forecast yet: although contracts for 4,738,545 jackets had now been awarded, only 2,327,890 would be forthcoming by the end of the year. Apparently Littlejohn's sources of unofficial information were both speedy and accurate, for on 4 September he wrote to Gregory that he had heard "a series of rumors which have made me somewhat disturbed. These rumors are persistent and consistent. They deal with delayed production on the E.T.O. Uniform."[115] The Chief Quartermaster requested that he be informed weekly regarding deliveries of jackets. The first such report confirmed his worst fears. On 1 September there were 56,400 jackets in QM depots and his share, 47,000, was now being shipped. Deliveries for September were estimated at 300,000, of which he would receive 250,000, or exactly half the number promised to him. Actual production at the year's end was 3,073,581 jackets, or about 89 percent of commitments to the European and Mediterranean theaters, but quantity production started so late that 1944 receipts in

the ETO were only 37 percent of requirements.[116]

Faced with the shortages announced in the cable of 7 September, Littlejohn promptly inquired about possible substitutes, and without even awaiting an answer included 600,000 serge coats on his 18 September requisition. On Requisition K–94 this was increased to 1,050,-000, an amount equal to the reported shortage of wool jackets. The same requisition included a requirement for 1,500,000 olive drab jackets, which was apparently filed to establish a priority demand for all available quantities of this item. On 12 October, Colonel Evans reported that 457,741 arctic field jackets, 245,239 olive drab jackets, and 797,020 serge coats were being shipped against the K–94 requisition.[117] But by late October the armies had reported that the serge coat was not acceptable for combat, even as a substitute, and M1943 jackets were requested instead. Competition with the wool jacket in the restricted labor market had reduced production of M1943 jackets, and the latter were 626,000 behind schedule at the end of October. The shortage was serious, because this was now a mandatory item in all temperate areas throughout the world. It was even being issued to troops on movement orders to the tropics for their comfort en route, so that a radical revision of issue directives

[115] (1) Quotation from Personal Ltr, CQM to TQMG, 4 Sep 44. Littlejohn Reading File, vol. XXVIII, item 30. (2) Roberts, op. cit., pp. 136, 206, 343. (3) Ltr, Littlejohn to Evans, 15 Sep 44, sub: File of Corresp on Wool Jackets for the ETO. Littlejohn Reading File, vol. XXVIII, item 104. (4) IRS, CQM to Feldman, 28 Jul 44, sub: Jackets and Trousers, Wool (New Type). Hist Br OQMG.

[116] (1) Cable WAR–26708, Gregory to CG COMZ, 7 Sep 44. Littlejohn Reading File, vol. XXVIII, item 104. (2) Roberts, op. cit., pp. 373, 417. (3) Garside Rpt, app. K.

[117] (1) Memo, CQM for TQMG, 15 Sep 44, sub: Wool Field Jackets for the ETO. Littlejohn Reading File, vol. XXVIII, item 104. (2) See n. 86, above. (3) TWX Conf, Col Brown, ETO–Col Evans, NYPE, 12 Oct 44. Hist Br OQMG. (4) The arctic field jacket was essentially an olive drab jacket with a heavier wool lining.

was necessary before stocks could be made available to the ETO. The exact number of M1943 jackets sent to the European theater is unknown. Total shipments of this item and various substitutes (not including the wool jacket) were 3,451,000 by 31 December 1944, but only 1,510,000 had actually been received into continental depots.[118]

Littlejohn's unwillingness to accept the M1943 jacket, and his preference for the olive drab jacket, the arctic jacket, the winter combat jacket, and the pile jacket have been severely criticized, more especially since he objected to the M1943 as a complicating factor in supply. Littlejohn's explanation was that these various items were functionally interchangeable—all of them would fit under an overcoat, whereas the M1943 jacket was intended primarily to be an outer garment. It was wind-resistant and fairly water-repellent (though the ETO Quartermaster noted deficiencies in this respect), but of very meager usefulness in adding warmth under an overcoat. And yet, as the situation was developing, the M1943 jacket would have to be worn under an overcoat; the M1943 jacket and sweater combination, without the wool jacket to give extra warmth, was definitely inadequate for the European climate. Unfortunately, many soldiers failed to understand this, and turned in their olive drab field jackets as excess after being issued M1943 jackets.[119]

Actual receipts of the wool field jacket in the ETO were so slow that the prevailing idea in the theater was that this was an item intended primarily for officers. After Littlejohn returned from his April visit to the United States, hardly a day passed when he did not receive a request from some general officer who wanted the new uniform for himself and his staff. On 8 June (D plus 2) he wrote to Feldman:

. . . to occupy Paris properly it will be necessary that we have some of the new field jackets to wear. Frankly, since it was approved I am being bombarded from every angle. I would greatly appreciate getting 5,000 according to tariff sizes . . . at an early date. If I can get the high commanders and their staffs off my neck I will lock the door to the others.[120]

"Locking the door" was notably unsuccessful, and on 8 July Littlejohn requisitioned 100,000 wool jackets and 200,000 pairs of matching trousers specifically for officers, although they were to be of the enlisted design. This request was disapproved, the jackets because the 2,600,000 already promised were the maximum that could be manufactured, and the trousers because they were considered by G-4 to be a nonstandard and unauthorized item. Subsequently, on 26 September, the QMC Technical Committee recommended that the color of enlisted men's trousers be changed from olive drab shade 32 (light) to olive drab shade 33 (dark) after

---

[118] (1) Incl VI to Ltr, Littlejohn to Somervell, 3 Mar 45. Hist Br OQMG. (2) Cable WARX–60685, 10 Nov 44, AGWAR to ETOUSA. (3) Roberts, *op. cit.*, pp. 68, 94. (4) Garside Rpt, tab 7.

[119] (1) Memo, Doriot for Dir Mob Div ASF, 11 Oct 44, sub: Jacket Field. SPQRQ 400.34. (2) Siple Rpt. (3) Pounder challenges the statement that an overcoat would fit over an arctic or pile jacket. Interv with Pounder, 12 Jul 62.

[120] (1) Quote from Personal Ltr, Littlejohn to Feldman, 8 Jun 44. Littlejohn Reading File, vol. XXV, item 14. (2) Memo, CQM for Proc Div OCQM, 30 Apr 44, sub: Special Issue of new Field Jackets; Memo, CQM for Deputy APO 871, 6 May 44, sub: Cloth for Field Jackets. Littlejohn Reading File, vol. XXIII, item 21; vol. XXIV, item 25.

stocks were exhausted. This committee action opened the way for local manufacture of trousers in Europe from dark-colored serge. Littlejohn had already made plans for such production in both the United Kingdom and France, and expediting deliveries of cloth for manufacture of trousers, nontariff uniforms, and officers' clothing was one of the chores that Brumbaugh performed while in the United States. The requirement for cloth was increased to four and a half million yards on Requisition K–94.[121]

The new ETO uniform remained in very short supply all through 1944. At the end of September 12,000 jackets were offshore waiting to be unloaded, but none of American origin had been received at the depots. Littlejohn had found that the locally procured jackets were coveted prestige items. On 14 August he had warned Colonel Duncan, his acting deputy in the United Kingdom, that when these uniforms finally arrived from the United States, they were to be stored under guard at Bristol until required on the Continent. Otherwise, in the current rapidly moving situation "the jackets would get into the distribution channels and we would have a terrible mess on our hands." Ten days later, having heard rumors of delayed deliveries from the zone of interior, he repeated these instructions and added,

"I definitely do not want the new type jackets put into the pipeline of supply until we are ready to equip a substantial portion of the Army with them." [122] By the end of October there were still only 160,000 jackets in stock, though the OCQM was seeking discharge priorities to unload 260,000 more. General Lee directed that the first issues were to be made to the troops in the combat zone. That added another complication, for the wool jacket was a difficult garment to fit correctly, and only a limited number of trained depot personnel was available. Definitely, all combat units could not be fitted out at once, and any system of priorities would lead to invidious comparisons. Littlejohn therefore decided not to issue any jackets to enlisted men until the new year. He estimated that it would be April before he could supply any large number of troops. Early in January 1945 all the army commanders decided to await the end of hostilities before issuing the ETO uniform. By the end of the month, 1,330,-000 jackets had been received in the ETO, but except for equipping enlisted men going to the United States on furlough, and a small number used in tests, no ETO jackets were issued to the troops until after V–E Day.[123] Presumably, if the wool jacket had arrived earlier, it would have been adopted as a winter combat item. Warm winter clothing was at a premium, and the

---

[121] (1) Cable EX–36898, ETOUSA to NYPE, 8 Jul 44. (2) Ltrs, CQM to Brumbaugh, 11 Jul 44, and Brumbaugh to CQM, 22 Jul 44. Littlejohn Reading File, vol. XXVI, items 47, 99. (3) Ltr, CQM to Feldman, 14 Sep 44; Memo, CQM for TQMG, 15 Sep 44, sub: Wool Field Jackets for ETO; Ltrs, CQM to Feldman and Evans, 18 Sep 44; Ltr, CQM to Gregory, 20 Sep 44; Ltr, CQM to Evans, 25 Sep 44; Ltr, Gregory to Littlejohn, 28 Sep 44. Littlejohn Reading File, vol. XXVIII, items 90, 104, 132, 149, 195, 202.

[122] Memos, Littlejohn for Duncan, 14, 24 Aug 44. Littlejohn Reading File, vol. XXVII, items 61, 108.
[123] (1) Garside Rpt, app. K. (2) IRS, CQM to QM UKB, 26 Oct 44; Personal Ltr, Littlejohn to Middleswart, 5 Jan 45; IRS, CQM to Franks, 10 Jan 45. Littlejohn Reading File, vol. XXIX, item 121; vol. XXXII, items 12, 47. (3) TWX Confs QM UKB–OCQM, 24 Dec 44, 1 Feb 45. USFET QM 337.

CONTRASTING JACKETS. *General Eisenhower, wearing the tailored "Ike Jacket" and high-cut tailored trousers, with Generals Marshall and Bradley wearing the standard ETO jacket and trousers.*

variety of garments being worn proves that nothing wearable was rejected by the troops. Whether it would have been as practical and popular as anticipated is another matter. The fact that in the Mediterranean theater this uniform was used only in rest areas and on leave is not conclusive evidence that troops in the ETO would have adopted similar practices. Warfare in Italy was static during the winter of 1944-45, and units had no difficulty in maintaining a reserve of clean clothing to insure that their members could pass inspection and therefore were eligible to visit leave areas. Under conditions of more active combat, such as prevailed in the ETO, a field uniform that could be transformed quickly into a Class A uniform

had real advantages. But, unlike the British jacket, the ETO jacket was a compromise and not a completely dual purpose garment. To be a practical combat item it had to be fitted loose and rather long when worn with old style low-cut trousers. On the other hand, to look well it had to be shortened and tightly fitted, but then it ceased to be a combat item. When ETO jackets were issued in Germany after the end of hostilities, teams of specially trained tailors were sent out to fit them as combat garments, but encountered a good deal of resistance from the troops. The notion that a garrison uniform must be a tight fit seems to be deeply ingrained in the U.S. Army.[124]

Littlejohn's original concept of how to handle special cold-climate clothing was very similar to his ideas on the ETO field uniform—on arrival it should be held at a depot near a port in the United Kingdom to be called forward when needed. At the end of September it had been agreed that the allocation to the separate armies would be made by the Commanding General, 12th Army Group, on advice from his quartermaster, Colonel Younger. This clothing was originally scheduled to arrive in the ETO in September and October, but War Department approval was not immediately forthcoming despite the assurances of General Feldman, and shipment from the west coast, where the arctic reserve was located, also caused

[124] (1) OTCQM TSFET Operational Study 7, Size Tariffs and the Fitting of Clothing. (2) Risch, *The Quartermaster Corps: Organization, Supply, and Services,* I, 95–96. (3) Memo, Littlejohn for Franks, 24 Apr 45, sub: Plan for Fitting and Issue of ETO Field Uniform. Littlejohn Reading File, vol. XXXV, item 48. (4) IRS, Brumbaugh to CQM, 2 Jul 44, sub: Comments on Pounder's Rpt of 30 Jun 44. Hist Br OQMG.

delay. Because the shipping tie-up might cause still further delay within the theater, the OCQM requested on 12 October that all these special items be placed on a single ship so that it would be possible to get them ashore promptly, and control storage and issue. But this was not feasible, since they were already arriving at three different east coast ports. The best that Colonel Evans could offer was shipment on three ships, and even that degree of concentration was not achieved. The OCQM hoped for the best, but inevitably discharge would be slowed up. In directing that stocks were to be accumulated at Reims, a depot that was just beginning to operate, Littlejohn clearly anticipated that deliveries would not be completed for some time. Strict control was very necessary. On 31 October he wrote to Gregory: "Due to advertising in this theater by representatives of the OQMG I am flooded by requisitions from the field for these items. Publicity and good will has sold the idea that stocks in the U.S. are unlimited." [125]

On 12 December COMZ headquarters officially informed the 12th Army Group that over 90 percent of the special clothing was in ETO waters awaiting unloading, and could be distributed by the end of the month if suitable discharge and transportation priorities were provided. It was recommended that issues be confined to divisional troops, and specifi-

QM Issue Point *at Mannheim, Germany. Sign tacked to table reads: "Don't fit your ETO jacket skin tight." January 1946.*

cally to rifle, heavy weapons, combat engineer, and reconnaissance units, since these categories of personnel were most often subjected to prolonged exposure. The total of such personnel in fifty-one divisions (the estimated strength of 12th Army Group on 1 March 1945) was computed as 282,388 men, a number amply provided for by the quantities on requisition.[126]

[125] (1) Quotation from Ltr, CQM to TQMG, 31 Oct 44, sub: QM Supply Situation in the ETO. Littlejohn Reading File, vol. XXIXA, item 145. (2) Memo for Record, QM Sec 12th Army Group, 28 Sep 44, sub: Visit by Younger to OCQM, 26–27 Sep 44. 12th Army Group 200.5. (3) IRS, CQM to Franks, 3 Oct 44, sub: Current Problems. Littlejohn Reading File, vol. XXIX, item 4. (4) TWX Conf, Col Brown, OCQM (Paris)–Col Evans, NYPE, 12 Oct 44. USFET AG 337.

[126] (1) IRS, CQM for Col Odell, 17 Nov 44, sub: Cold-Climate Clothing. Littlejohn Reading File, vol. XXX, item 51. (2) Hist Rpt, G–4 Sec SUSA, 1–30 Nov 44. Seventh Army 319.1 (G–4). (3) Ltr, AG COMZ to CG 12th Army Group, 12 Dec 44, sub: Distribution of Special Winter Clothing. AG 420 OpQM. (4) Seventh Army had requisitioned special winter items for all its personnel from NATOUSA during the planning stage of DRAGOON, but by November its strength exceeded the planned buildup and only 75 percent could be equipped.

In reply, 12th Army Group stated that the above data had been passed on to the armies for their information, but that "It is the policy of this Headquarters to permit Army Commanders to use their own discretion in the matter of equipping troops of their commands in accordance with the tactical situation." [127] This disagreement over the equipment of troops was made irrelevant by the German Ardennes counteroffensive, already under way. Class II and IV supplies were excepted from the embargo placed on outmovements from the ports, but in actual practice Rouen, and especially Antwerp, were soon so clogged that any selective forwarding became almost hopeless. More than a month elapsed before improvement was possible. By 3 January no issues had been made, and the army group had decided that allocations were to be in the proportion of 33 percent to First Army, 35 percent to Third Army, and 18 percent to Ninth Army; the balance was to be held by the army group headquarters for future allocation. It recommended that detailed instructions on the fitting and use of the new items be forwarded to each army direct through technical channels.[128]

Issues of cold climate clothing actually began on 11 January. Six days later, Littlejohn sent identical letters to Colonel Younger and each army quartermaster, warning that no further supplies of these items would be available for about sixty days. He recognized the responsibility of commanders for distribu-

tion of special winter clothing, but submitted again as suggestions, based on the experience of quartermasters in other theaters, the same recommendations regarding priorities that had been forwarded through command channels on 12 December. More important, he transmitted with his letter multiple copies of a mimeographed publication called "Quartermaster Tips #1." This was nine pages of detailed instructions on the purpose, correct fitting, and best methods of wearing, drying, and caring for the new winter clothing. In particular, "Quartermaster Tips" explained the advantages and disadvantages of the shoepac; while warmer, lighter, and dryer than the combat boot, or even an arctic over a combat boot, it induced sweating and required frequent changes of socks and insoles. To prevent "shoepac foot," or maceration, proper fitting of socks, insoles, and shoepacs was particularly important, but also very difficult because two types of shoepacs were being issued—those 12 inches high were on a military last, while the 16-inch model was in varying commercial lasts, most of them smaller than the military type for the same numerical size. Shoepacs were available in only one width.[129]

On 30 January Littlejohn wrote to Colonel Bowden, the distribution specialist whom he had installed—over considerable opposition from the Transportation Corps—as Port Quartermaster, Antwerp: "I got General Ross to issue

---

[127] 1st Ind, Hq 12th Army Group to CG COMZ, 18 Dec 44, to Ltr cited in n. 126 (3), above.

[128] Ltr, AG 12th Army Group to CG COMZ, 3 Jan 45, sub: Special Cold Weather Clothing. Reproduced in *QM Supply in ETO*, III, app. XXXVI.

[129] (1) Ltrs, CQM to each Army QM, 17 Jan 45, sub: Distr of Winter Clothing. Littlejohn Reading File, vol. XXXII, item 81. (2) "Quartermaster Tips #1," 12 Jan 45, distributed by OCQM Hq COMZ ETO. Hist Br OQMG, Improvisations file. (3) An improved military model, in three widths, became available in small quantities in February 1945.

TABLE 20—ISSUES OF SPECIAL WINTER CLOTHING

Issues to the Armies, 17 February 1945
Total Issues and Stock Position, 28 February 1945

Item	First Army	Third Army	Ninth Army	Fifteenth Army	Total Issues to Armies, 17 Feb 45	Total Issues to ETO[a] 1944–28 Feb 45	In Depots 28 Feb 45	On Ships Offshore 28 Feb 45
Cap, field, cotton	125,992	94,261	60,921	5,924	287,098	[e]2,500,000	3,250,000	350,000
Insoles, pair	165,348	151,811	93,365	17,867	428,391	485,000	50,000	550,000
Mitten inserts, pair	336,650	252,363	165,052	60,934	814,999	875,000	295,000	220,000
Mitten shells, pair	189,013	159,200	101,308	47,795	497,316	535,000	158,000	27,000
Muffler, wool	134,372	155,928	73,280	31,844	395,424	850,000	300,000	100,000
Poncho, nylon	59,107	[b]65,005	35,855	11,800	(c)	[c]380,000	100,000	50,000
Poncho, raincoat	106,915	[b]2,400	59,048	23,675	303,805			
Shoepacs, high[d]	69,077	76,008	40,124	14,757	(c)	[d]422,000	75,000	[d]237,000
Shoepacs, low[d]	66,177	76,649	30,047	9,911	382,750			
Socks, arctic	203,163	173,994	118,129	8,549	(c)	[c]970,000	200,000	780,000
Socks, ski	165,858	169,950	99,098	13,553	952,294			
Trousers, field, cotton	132,316	117,626	80,094	13,741	[e]343,777	73,000	355,000	145,000

[a] ETO less SOLOC.
[b] 200,000 British ground sheets issued as substitutes.
[c] Total for both types.
[d] Both were nonstandard types; ETO total includes 23,000 standard military 12″ shoepacs; reserves also include some of this type.
[e] These totals include substitute items.

Source: Issues to Armies from *QM Supply in ETO*, III, 167. Total issues and stock position from Garside Rpt, app. K.

orders to the Port to select out the cold climate clothing. . . . You have most of my critical items lying on your piers. These must be sorted out and delivered direct to the Armies."[130] By mid-February, initial distribution of special winter clothing to the armies was virtually completed. *(Table 20)*

To a large extent, the special cold climate clothing and equipment arrived in the ETO too late to be really useful during the coldest winter months. The OQMG contended that the primary reason for this was the lateness of the major ETO requisition—J–48 dated 15 August 1944. Littlejohn did not agree. The distinction which he made between requirements and requisitions, although it had been approved by General Somervell and was readily comprehended by Feldman and Evans, was never clearly understood within the OQMG. The inquiries that Colonel Brumbaugh had made regarding availabilities in early July were not regarded as official, nor as announcing a firm requirement. Nevertheless, the OQMG cabled assurance on 3 September that the whole of this special requisition, excepting ponchos, could be made available to NYPE by the last day of that month. This proved to be overoptimistic, since some articles had to be drawn from depots as far away as Seattle, and others could only be supplied from current production after being released by the War Department. Most of J–48 was actually shipped during the last half of November.[131]

Littlejohn found that requisitions sub-

mitted much earlier were subjected to the same treatment of optimistic assurances and subsequent delay. A notable example was the wool sweater, one of the few articles requisitioned on the advice of Captain Pounder. Although NYPE made a commitment in June to provide 3,250,000 sweaters by September, that number only became available at the end of January 1945. Even then only 1,775,000 had been issued to the troops; 700,000 more were in transit from the ports, and another 550,000 were aboard ships awaiting discharge. This deficit was especially serious since without a sweater the M1943 jacket did not provide adequate winter protection even in a mild temperate zone.[132]

Littlejohn had inquired of NYPE regarding availability of sleeping bags on 24 May, and was assured that 2,580,000, complete with water-repellent case, would be available by October. He therefore canceled an outstanding requisition for 1,370,000 blankets. On 14 September he commented rather bitterly to Feldman:

I have before me a table showing assets and requirements on blankets. I have an immediate deficit of between 2,000,000 and 3,000,000 blankets, due to the fact that my Equipage Branch was lulled to sleep by Pounder with a promise that sleeping bags would be available in time to supply this Theater. I have just checked my own files and I find that sleeping bags are now promised for delivery here during November and December. The troops want four blankets now. I must have them. Sleeping bags in November and December can be accepted only on a maintenance basis.

---

[130] Ltr, CQM to QM 13th Port, 30 Jan 45. Littlejohn Reading File, vol. XXXIIA, item 166.

[131] (1) See discussion of relations with NYPE in ch. XII, above. (2) Garside Rpt, p. 9.

[132] (1) Cables EX–33226, Lee to CG NYPQ, 15 Jun 44, and WARX–54354, Somervell to CG ETOUSA, 22 Jun 44. (2) Garside Rpt, app. K. (3) Roberts, *op. cit.*, p. 38.

This was a most unfair aspersion upon Captain Pounder, a junior officer who had visited the ETO as a specialist in clothing research and who had no responsibility for production. Moreover, the commitment on deliveries had been made by NYPE, and not by Captain Pounder. But personalities aside, Littlejohn's statement aroused an indignant reaction within the OQMG which reveals how completely that headquarters lacked information on the commitments made by NYPE and on the extent to which they were being met. Actually, only 939,000 sleeping bags had been shipped by the end of September, so that deliveries were 54 percent in arrears. Since one sleeping bag with case was the equivalent of two blankets, Littlejohn's statement was substantially correct.

This episode confirms a lack of coordination between the OQMG and NYPE that can often be inferred from Littlejohn's correspondence with the OQMG. In this case, while production of sleeping bags was slightly in arrears, the main bottleneck was in the Port of New York. Littlejohn confirmed this view by forwarding to Colonel Evans at NYPE a copy of his letter to Feldman. He warned Evans to expect an official cabled request for one or more commodity-loaded ships to carry blankets and sleeping bags direct to the Continent. This was actually a forewarning regarding Requisition K–94. But because of congestion in European ports and the low discharge priorities given to blankets and sleeping bags, another bottleneck developed within the ETO. At the end of October there were 515,000 blankets and 1,740,000 sleeping bags on ships offshore, awaiting discharge, and a month later the number had actually

SLEEPING GEAR, NEW TYPE. *The wool sleeping bag and its cotton sateen cover replaced two blankets. November 1944.*

increased. Littlejohn managed to solve this problem by focusing attention on the current cigarette shortage, an episode that has already been described.[133]

While some of the delays in delivery of new items could be ascribed to unexpected production difficulties, the ETO also experienced delays in the arrival of well-established standard items. In such cases, the difficulty was almost entirely a matter of transatlantic shipping shortages, and the main cause was

---

[133] (1) TWX Conf, NYPE–ETO, 24 May 44. In OQMG Study of 5 Apr 45, pt. 4. (2) Personal Ltrs, Littlejohn to Feldman, 14 Sep 44, and Littlejohn to Evans, 14 Sep 44. Littlejohn Reading File, vol. XXVIII, items 90, 91a. (3) IRS, Asst Chief R&D to Col Bellican, 27 Sep 44, sub: Ltr From Littlejohn. Hist Br OQMG. (4) Garside Rpt, app. K. (5) See p. 391, above.

the tie-up of ships awaiting discharge in the ETO. On 19 October Evans wrote to Littlejohn, with regard to deliveries on Requisition K–94: . . . "there are only so many ships regardless of your requirements, and it appears that those requirements must be cut to fit the ships. . . ." What actually happened with regard to wool undershirts and drawers well illustrates the difficulty: [134]

	Undershirts	Drawers
ETO requested shipment in October	4,355,000	3,967,000
NYPE projected shipping schedule	3,342,000	2,506,000
Actual shipments (October)	1,506,000	1,410,000
Deficit below planned shipment	1,836,000	1,096,000
Deficit below requested shipment	2,849,000	2,557,000

In other words, even after pruning the theater's requests rather severely, NYPE was unable to meet its own schedule.

Footwear and the Trench Foot Problem

As in the Mediterranean theater, the first reaction to the combat boot was very favorable, since the boot would make it possible for the men to discard their hated leggings. ETO troops were delighted with the samples displayed by Captain Pounder, and Littlejohn promptly requested 1,225,000 pairs. But the cuff, which distinguished this item from other footgear, required extra leather, a material in short supply, and it was July 1944 before enough boots

arrived in the theater to issue one pair per man to the field forces. Interim needs were filled by supplying the Type III shoe, which lacked the cuff but was otherwise identical with the combat boot. With their flesh-out leather, soft construction, and rubber soles, both items were considered a great technical advance over previous footgear. Very favorable reports were received after tests were made in North Africa, and although there were occasional references to lack of water-repellent qualities, it was believed that the flesh-out leather would absorb a large amount of dubbing, which would correct this weakness. Even the Anzio test report, while stating that the shoepac was preferable for muddy weather, gave the impression that dubbing would increase the water-repellency of combat boots. Many older officers, including Littlejohn, were also influenced by their recollections of the Pershing boot issued during the First World War, a very satisfactory and comparatively watertight item made of flesh-out leather.[135] Plans were therefore made before the Normandy landing to issue one pair of combat boots and one pair of Type III shoes to each combat soldier. Service and AAF troops would continue, for the time being, to receive two pairs of service shoes per man. Before winter set in, all ETO troops were to receive combat boots as their footgear required replacement. Before D-day Colonel McNamara, after consulting with his G–3, had stated that First Army would not operate in climatic areas

---

[134] (1) Garside Rpt, tabs 3, 4. (2) Ltr, Evans to Littlejohn, 19 Oct 44. Hist Br OQMG. (3) See Table 19.

[135] (1) See ch. VII, above. (2) Ltr, Pounder to Doriot, 13 Mar 44. In OQMG Study of 5 Apr 45. (3) Ltr, Littlejohn to Doriot, 19 Oct 43. Littlejohn Reading File, vol. XVII, item 70. (4) See app. C.

where overshoes would be needed during the winter of 1944–45. This confirmed tactical forecasts made by SHAEF regarding the duration of OVERLORD. Based on the assumption that the combat boot would give adequate cold weather protection, supply plans provided that only 1,200,000 pairs of arctic overshoes would be required. It was expected that most of these overshoes would be issued to troops who did not have combat boots.[136]

The plan to issue overshoes only to those without combat boots was one of the most serious miscalculations of the ETO Quartermaster Service during the continental campaign. As early as 1 October, a QM field observer reported that the Type III shoe and combat boot both absorbed more water than the supposedly obsolescent Type II shoe; dubbing reduced insulation against cold, but did not shed water to any noticeable degree. Two days later, when Littlejohn was making plans to bring over 600,000 pairs of combat boots from the United Kingdom to fill deficiencies in overshoes, Lt. Col. McNally, McNamara's assistant, commented that First Army definitely would not accept combat boots without overshoes. On 5 October, Colonel Muller, the Third Army G–4, urged that COMZ troops be directed to turn in their overshoes for the use of combat divisions. He stated

that every combat soldier needed a pair.[137]

Unfortunately, the need for overshoes did not become evident in time for them to be included in the first winterization program, which was already under way. Lack of overshoes was generally regarded as a major factor contributing to trench foot, and this was particularly true in the early autumn of 1944 before the other contributing factors were clearly understood. Very few cases of trench foot had occurred at the time, but for the week ending 15 October 320 cases were reported in the theater. Incidence increased each week until 17 November, when 5,386 cases were reported. During this period temperatures varied between 40° and 50° F., violent offensive combat was in progress, and rainfall was unseasonably heavy. This was the largest weekly number of cases during the entire European campaign, but two smaller peaks of incidence, in late December and again in mid-January, both coincided with periods of maximum combat activity. In these last two instances, statistics for frostbite and trench foot were combined, since it was often impossible to distinguish between the two forms of injury. Whether the tissues were injured directly by freezing, or indirectly by stoppage of circulation caused by chill above the freezing point, the symptoms were almost identical. In all, 44,728 men

[136] (1) IRS, CQM to Feldman, 28 Jul 44, sub: Shoes. Hist Br OQMG. (2) Ltr, Littlejohn to Smithers, 29 Sep 44. Littlejohn Reading File, vol. XXVIII, item 204. (3) Sec. VII of Incl to Ltr, Littlejohn to Somervell, 3 Mar 45. There were 737,000 pairs of overshoes in the U.K. or due in by mid-July, when the OCQM requisitioned 458,000 more for delivery in October and November 1944. (4) McNamara *Memoir*, p. 148.

[137] (1) OCQM Field Obsv Rpt 1, 1 Oct 44. OQMG 319.25, ETO. (2) Memo, G–4 for CQM, 5 Oct 44, sub: Conf with Gen Patton and TUSA G–4. Hist Br OQMG. (3) Memo, CQM for DCQM, Paris (Col Franks), 3 Oct 44, sub: Sundry Current Problems Littlejohn Reading File, vol. XXIX, item 4.

were hospitalized for either trench foot or frostbite by the end of April 1945.[138]

Trench foot was an injury and not a disease, but it created problems similar to those occurring during a major epidemic, severely taxing medical resources. The feet of the affected soldiers swelled painfully, became discolored, and, if neglected, a considerable proportion became gangrenous and required amputation. Proper treatment required evacuation and prolonged hospitalization, and a large percentage of those stricken were unable to return to combat duty. When it is considered that the overwhelming majority of cases occurred among combat infantrymen, who were also subject to some 83 percent of all combat casualties, the extreme seriousness of cold injuries becomes evident.[139]

Inadequate footgear was only one of many factors contributing to the incidence of trench foot, but it was one the Quartermaster Service might hope to remedy by prompt corrective action. Returning from a visit to the front on 15 November, Littlejohn informed his staff:

Footwear Tariffs: It definitely appears that the footwear tariffs are out of kilter. The troops are requesting overshoes from 9E on up to about 16EEE. This is apparently due to the fact that the overshoe tariff has not been adjusted to the Type III shoe. . . .

Combat Boots and Type III Shoes: Due to the wearing of a number of pairs of socks, there are heavy demands for large sizes in combat boots and type 3 shoes. Here again we run from 9's up to 18's generally in the E, EE and EEE sizes. This necessitates an immediate adjustment of requisitions on

PEMBARK and securing from the UK of all large size shoes. . . .

Defects in the Combat Boot: It was my understanding that combat boots were to be issued in lieu of the overshoe and service shoes. The troops at the front . . . demand overshoes and state that the combat boot leaks, even when heavily dubbed.[140]

Since overshoes had been a last-minute addition to the winterization program for the armies, it had proved impossible to supply all that were needed. On 20 September the OCQM requisitioned 500,000 pairs to meet the additional requirements. But the overshoe, like the combat boot it was now to supplement, had certain faults in addition to the difficulty with sizes already described. Because of rubber shortages, a cloth-top overshoe was the standard military type. It tore easily and leaked readily, and many of the overshoes reissued from salvage after being worn in the United Kingdom had never been repaired. Combat infantrymen often found overshoes too heavy and clumsy for an attack, and discarded them. In some units, this was done at the direction of the officers. Few such overshoes were recovered during the pursuit, and maintenance factors soared. Armored units reported that many overshoes were lost when vehicles, especially personnel carriers, were knocked out in combat. The result was inclusion of 1,300,000 pairs on Requisition K–94 to take care of anticipated losses and wear and tear through the end of the calendar year. Littlejohn was convinced that even this quantity was not enough, and made a determined effort to have additional overshoes issued individually to reinforcements at ports

---

[138] (1) Whayne and DeBakey, *Cold Injury, Ground Type,* pp. 138–401 and Table 23. (2) Note that no overshoes are listed in Table 18.

[139] Whayne and DeBakey, *Cold Injury, Ground Type,* pp. 140–42.

[140] Memo, CQM for Div Chiefs, 15 Nov 44, sub: Comments Following Trip to the Front. Littlejohn Reading File, vol. XXX, item 35.

of embarkation. This proposal was at first turned down as a matter of War Department policy, but Littlejohn appealed to General Maxwell, the War Department G–4, and also enlisted the aid of General Hawley, the theater Chief Surgeon.[141]

Nothing seemed to come of these efforts, and on 2 December he requisitioned another 500,000 pairs of overshoes, a requisition which was promptly approved by ASF. To meet this and other requirements, the OQMG arranged to acquire 700,000 pairs from Navy stocks and to divert another 367,000 pairs from production for the Navy.[142] Also on 2 December, Littlejohn officially recommended that all overshoes be withdrawn from headquarters troops in the Paris area. Four days later, all COMZ section commanders were directed to screen their personnel, and insure that overshoes were retained only by COMZ troops who were doing outdoor work in dumps and depots.[143]

Readjusting the tariff of footwear sizes was no simple matter, since it depended upon accurate inventories. Interim action, to alter the sizes on requisitions already submitted, began as early as 4 November, and by 1 December completely revised winter tariffs for boots and overshoes were sent to NYPE. The OCQM requested that these tariffs be used in filling all requisitions through 15 April 1945, since it was expected that the troops would wear extra socks and require the larger sized shoes and overshoes until that time. On 6 January the OQMG confirmed the correctness of the revisions made in Europe after conducting independent tests of fitting commercial-type overshoes over combat boots and Type III shoes. In theory, an overshoe would fit over a shoe of the same numerical size, but commercial overshoes would not, particularly when fitted over Type III shoes in the broader widths. Each commercial last was slightly different and required a separate fitting table. Apparently no plans had been made to provide for wearing overshoes over combat boots or Type III shoes, and the need for such a procedure had not previously been evident to the Research and Development Branch. New government lasts were being prepared, and production on the revised tariff would begin in February. The new model would be all rubber, a great improvement. Meanwhile, a small number of boots and shoes in the larger sizes were available, but no overshoes in sizes larger than 11, although ETO requisitions demanded sizes as large as 15 on a normal tariff. This situation

---

[141] (1) TWX Conf, Brown, ETO–Evans, NYPE, 12 Oct 44. ETO 337. (2) Cable WARX–48123, Mob Div ASF to Eisenhower, 17 Oct 44. (3) Ltr, Littlejohn to Maxwell, 18 Nov 44. Littlejohn Reading File, vol. XXX, item 62. (4) IRS, CQM to G–4, 20 Nov 44, sub: Overshoes. Hist Br OQMG. (5) Memo for Record, 1 Mar 45, by Lt Col James H. McGuire, QM Sec 12th Army Group. Hist Br OQMG. (6) QM Field Obsv Rpt 7. TSFET QM 319.25.

[142] (1) Cables EX–69078, 30 Nov 44, and EX–70022, 2 Dec 44. (2) Memo, Dir of Supply ASF (Brig Gen Heileman) for TQMG, 8 Dec 44, sub: Additional Overshoes, Arctic, for the ETO, SPDDQ 400 ETO. (3) Memo, TQMG for Dir Distr Div ASF, 15 Dec 44, same sub. SPQXC 421.3 ETO. (4) Incl VII to Ltr, Littlejohn to Somervell, 3 Mar 45. Hist Br OQMG.

[143] (1) Memo, CQM through G–4 for AG, 2 Dec 44, sub: Withdrawal of Overshoes from Hq Troops in Paris Area. Littlejohn Reading File, vol. XXXI, item 4. (2) Ltr, CG COMZ to Sec Comdrs COMZ, 6 Dec 44, sub: Overshoes, Arctic. AG 420 Op GD.

was not completely corrected until March 1945.[144]

Field observers reported that soldiers with large feet, who could not be fitted properly with overshoes, in desperation took smaller sized overshoes and wore them without shoes, but with two pairs of socks and either improvised cardboard innersoles, or felt slippers such as Hollanders wear inside their wooden shoes, or in some cases several thicknesses of blanket. The incidence of trench foot was reduced in all the units that used these and similar improvisations. Medical authorities believed the reason was that all these combinations of footgear made possible free movement of the toes and feet, which improved circulation.[145]

This observation inevitably leads to a discussion of basic ETO dissatisfaction with both the Type III shoe and the combat boot. Both items were constructed on a last of limited flexibility, which made it virtually impossible to wear more than one pair of light wool socks without constricting the feet and reducing circulation. Americans as a nation tend to wear tight-fitting shoes, and most service shoes when issued had been fitted snugly over a single pair of socks, usually the cotton socks issued to recruits in the United States. Such shoes became dangerously tight when even one pair of heavy socks was worn in cold weather, a condition that was aggravated if the shoes had become wet, for the soft leather tended to shrink in drying. But even issuing a larger size shoe was virtually useless. The low toecap and tight instep of the U.S. Army last limited the number of socks that could be worn. And yet, all European footwear specialists considered several pairs of socks to be desirable in cold weather, always providing they did not make the shoe too tight. Unfortunately, this was impracticable with the last being used at that time.[146]

Mr. Lawrence B. Sheppard, a technical adviser to the War Production Board (WPB) on shoes and leather, who visited the theater on Littlejohn's invitation in March 1945, severely criticized the soft-tanning process which caused the leather to shrink when wet, but did not consider the flesh-out construction of the shoe to be significant. He repudiated the theory that a flesh-out construction absorbed dubbing more readily and was therefore superior. For the following winter he recommended a harder tannage and that the leather be reversed to provide a more attractive footgear for reasons of morale. Other experts did not agree with him completely. They argued that, while polished grain-out leather would only shed water for a slightly longer period than dubbed flesh-out leather, wet mud tended to cling longer to the flesh-out surface and continued to soak into the leather even after the wearer had reached dry

[144] (1) Ltr, CQM to TQMG, 1 Dec 44, sub: Footwear Tariffs for the ETO; Ltr, TQMG to CQM ETO, 6 Jan 45, same sub. SPQXC 421.3 ETO; Ltr, OQMG to CG NYPE, 28 Dec 44, sub: Overshoes, Arctic for ETO; SPQXO 400.312. All in Hist Br OQMG. (2) Rpt, Maj Paul Siple for CG ETOUSA, 12 Apr 45, sub: Adequacy of Winter Clothing in ETO.

[145] (1) G-4 Rpt, 1-31 Dec, 1st Inf Div, 1 Jan 45. Hist Br OQMG. (2) OCQM Field Obsv Rpts 3, 5, 7, 8, 9. TSFET QM 319.25. (3) Whayne and DeBakey, Cold Injury, Ground Type, p. 159.

[146] (1) Ltr, CQM to TQMG through Chief Surgeon ETO, CG, COMZ, and CG ASF, 23 Mar 45, sub: Footwear and Socks for Use in ETO. Hist Br OQMG. (2) USFET Gen Bd Rpt 94, Trench Foot. OCMH. (3) Interv with Pounder, 12 Jul 62.

ground. Thus a polished grain-out leather had practical as well as psychological advantages. It was agreed that the welted sole construction of all U.S. footwear was less water resistant than the tap-and-screw construction of the British boot, and incidentally of the Pershing boot worn by U.S. troops in the First World War, but the WPB representative declared that a changeover would mean a complete reorganization of the U.S. shoe industry and was therefore not practicable. Mr. Sheppard's recommendation was for a grain-out combat boot of tightly tanned leather, with a rubber sole. It should have more toe room but no toecap, and the forequarters were to meet over the tongue when properly fitted over a pair of heavy wool socks. One pair of heavy wool socks was considered sufficient.

In winter, all-rubber overshoes were to be worn over this boot. The overshoe tariff should be carefully adjusted to the shoe tariff, and the numerical sizes of overshoes were to be marked so that they would not wear off. This was important, since the tendency of U.S. troops to discard their overshoes in active situations made efficient salvage procedures very necessary. Sheppard believed that troops could wear cushion-sole socks in summer with the same shoes fitted over heavy wool socks in winter, so that seasonal shoe tariffs would be unnecessary. He recommended eliminating both cotton and light wool socks in the ETO to reduce the fitting problem and simplify supply.

All infantry riflemen and troops fighting under similar conditions should wear shoepacs, preferably fitted over two pairs of ski socks, but this was a strictly sea-sonal item, and should be replaced immediately by combat boots at the beginning of warm weather. Such troops would not require overshoes. Sheppard favored an all-rubber shoepac; it would be drier and more comfortable than the rubber and leather type, easier to manufacture, and would not induce more perspiration. He believed that the issue of shoepacs should be carefully restricted to those who clearly needed them, since they presented the difficult supply problem of providing dry ski socks and felt insoles to troops at regular intervals. Ski socks were difficult to launder properly, since the processes for controlling shrinkage in regular wool socks had not been successfully applied to them.

Sheppard also doubted that even the improved shoepac, with built-up heel and firm arch support, was suitable for continued long marches. Since the combat boot and overshoe combination was too heavy for this purpose, the problem of acceptable footgear for continuous marching in cold, wet weather had not been solved even at the end of World War II. Sheppard recognized the problem, and recommended a long-range effort in research and development.[147]

Medical officers agreed with these views, but placed even greater emphasis on the dangers of constriction. They favored the combat boot because it eliminated the legging, which was often too tightly laced. Without leggings it was also easier for the soldier to remove

---

[147] Correspondence between Littlejohn and Gregory regarding Mr. Sheppard's visit, his itinerary in the ETO, a questionnaire presented to him by the OCQM, and his final report to the Chief Quartermaster, dated 18 March 1945, are all reprinted in Littlejohn's Passing in Review, Chapter 31, "Supply of Footwear and Socks in the ETO."

his footwear and give proper care to his feet. Medical officers were of the opinion that ability to maintain circulation, preferably by exercise, but alternatively by massage or even by stamping the feet or wiggling the toes inside roomy footgear, was the all-important factor in preventing trench foot. Water-repellency and insulation against cold were of only secondary importance. These views were officially disseminated in the ETO in a War Department circular and a War Department technical bulletin, and repeated in circulars and memorandums of 12th Army Group and of the individual armies in September and October 1944, but apparently the true importance of preventive measures was not made clear. Even a forceful and characteristic letter from General Patton to his unit commanders apparently had little effect. On 25 November General Hawley wrote to the 12th Army Group surgeon:

I am not sure that the Medical Department has been aggressive enough in this situation. We have published long dissertations on the prevention of trench foot which are too long for anyone to read. Furthermore they lay down so many requirements that, unless the soldier can fulfill all of them, he does nothing. Apparently no one has ever told the small unit commander that the very essence of the prevention of trench foot is the prevention of stagnation of circulation for periods greater than 24 hours.

General Hawley went on to give a personal opinion: if the soldier's shoes were removed once every 24 hours, if the feet were massaged briskly, preferably while they were higher than the hips, and if the water was wrung out of wet socks before they were replaced, cold injury could be prevented in 75 percent of all cases.[148]

Whatever the merits of General Hawley's opinions, combat units were inclined to find a solution to the trench foot problem along less heroic lines. Issues of socks were increased, and many units arranged to have them sent forward daily with the rations. In particular, there was a widespread demand for shoepacs, in addition to those already allocated to rifle, combat engineer, and reconnaissance units. As Littlejohn had remarked to Gregory in October, publicity had sold the idea that stocks in the United States were unlimited. Moreover, the 12th Army Group had virtually rejected the recommendation of COMZ that the shoepac be reserved exclusively for dismounted combat troops. A distinction between combat and service troops for equipment purposes was universally recognized in the theater. Priorities for divisional troops over those attached to corps or armies had proved to be necessary in October when short supplies of normal winter clothing were being distributed. But there was reluctance to accept priorities that cut across the organization of a division, or even of a single regiment. Senior commanders therefore approved the requests from combat support units for a wider distribution of shoepacs, and on 8 December Littlejohn initiated an official

---

[148] (1) Quotation from Whayne and DeBakey, *Cold Injury, Ground Type*, p. 169. (2) Memo, Sheppard for Littlejohn, 18 Mar 45. Reprinted in Littlejohn, ed., *Passing in Review*, ch. 31. (3) Memo, CG TUSA to Corps and Div Comdrs, 21 Nov 44. Reprinted in Whayne and DeBakey, *Cold Injury, Ground Type*, app. F. (4) WD Cir 312, 22 Jul 44, republished in ETO, 2 Sep 44; Tech Medical Bull 81, 4 Aug 44.

cable requesting an additional 500,000 pairs. The reply, citing expert opinion in the OQMG and the Surgeon General's Office, requested that he reconsider this requisition, since a properly fitting service shoe or combat boot and arctic overshoe was regarded as the most satisfactory combination for the ETO. To fill this requisition would require depletion of all reserves and taking over of the entire U.S. shoe industry. It was further stated that Mediterranean experience indicated soldiers were unwilling to wear shoepacs regularly, since they were awkward and subjected the wearer's feet to abrasion at the heel. The cable went on:

It is recognized, however, that the shoepac is the best article for unusual wet and cold conditions where the soldier is required to stand in water continuously. 446,-000 shoe pacs issued to your Theater plus approximately 90,000 issued to units in SOLOC prior to embarkation should provide adequately for any specialized operations for which the shoe pac may be deemed suitable. The Surgeon General stated that trench foot cases can be reduced or eliminated only by rigid compliance with the provisions set forth in WD Cir 312, 1944, and Technical Med Bull No. 81, 4 Aug 44. Issue of the shoe pac will not alleviate this problem.[149]

Littlejohn nevertheless repeated his request on 23 December, pointing out that climatic conditions were extraordinary, that all combat troops were operating continuously ankle-deep in mud, and that the shoepac was the only

mechanical aid that contributed substantially to the prevention of trench foot. It should be noted that this opinion was based entirely upon reports from other theaters—no shoepacs had been issued to troops supported by COMZ at this time. Moreover, SOLOC, where shoepacs had been issued to the infantry of Seventh Army in mid-November, did not officially become part of COMZ until 12 February 1945, and even thereafter co-ordination of technical channels developed gradually. Since compliance with the ETO requisition would deplete the arctic reserve, the matter was referred to the Operations Division, War Department General Staff, which decided that the ETO requisition should be filled.[150]

Although the cable of 23 December had specified that shoepacs should only be sent if they would arrive by 15 February, none had actually been unloaded from ships by that date, and only a very small number from this second requisition was ever issued to ETO troops. Meanwhile on 11 February the G–4, Third Army, had decided to revert back to the overshoe-combat boot combination. The weather had turned rather warm, and men were beginning to suffer from "shoepac foot" due to excessive perspiration. Extra felt soles and ski socks to correct this were in very short supply. Moreover, Third Army complained that shoepacs leaked around the seams where rubber and leather met. Undoubtedly an improvement in the supply of overshoes contributed to this

---

[149] Cable WARX–79550, AGWAR to ETOUSA, 19 Dec 44. This was in answer to Littlejohn's requisition L–79, forwarded by Cable EX–72064, 8 Dec 44. Hist Br OQMG. See also Littlejohn's follow-up inquiry to Gregory on this requisition. Ltr, CQM to TQMG, 4 Jan 45. Littlejohn Reading File, vol. XXXII, item 19.

[150] (1) Cable EX–78065, QM COMZ to AGWAR. 23 Dec 44. (2) Memo, Dir P&O Div ASF for ACofS OPD, 29 Dec 44, sub: Supply of Shoepacs to ETO, and reply, OPD to ASF, 1 Jan 45. SPOPP 420, ETO.

decision. On 21 January Third Army was short 58,000 pairs, but by 13 February this entire requisition, including the scarce large sizes, had been filled. Apparently demands for shoepacs from the other armies were reduced at the same time, for on 16 February Littlejohn was seriously considering storing the shoepacs still on the water awaiting discharge, instead of issuing them. Meanwhile the repeated demands of Littlejohn and Hawley had finally modified policy at NYPE regarding footwear for replacements. Beginning on 13 January, all troops were issued overshoes before embarking for the ETO.[151]

These developments took on added significance when Littlejohn and Hawley began to receive supply and medical reports from Seventh Army, after the ETO logistical reorganization of 12 February. It will be recalled that Seventh Army received shoepacs in mid-November, about sixty days earlier than other ETO troops, but the number of trench foot cases reported from that headquarters, which commanded several veteran divisions transferred from Italy, was not significantly different from the average for the whole theater. The Chief Quartermaster and Chief Surgeon became convinced that their earlier official statements on the necessity for shoepacs should be corrected, and cabled to Somervell that "the character of footwear is by no means the most important factor in trenchfoot. In fact, insofar as

types of footwear yet developed for the Army is concerned, the evidence thus far is that there is little to choose between them." [152] They recommended basic research on the causes of trench foot, pointing out that climate and terrain, tactical situation, troop rotation, combat experience, equipment, and above all foot discipline, had a bearing upon the problem. It should be noted that the U.S. Forces, European Theater, General Board later confirmed these views. In particular, the board agreed that the most important *controllable* factor in trench foot was individual care of the feet—what Littlejohn and Hawley called foot discipline.[153]

This was a lesson that the ETO learned only slowly, and by painful degrees. By early December the trench foot rate was considerably reduced. Higher headquarters had initiated various helpful measures. For example one extra tent with a stove, per company or battery, was authorized to dry clothing and warm men. Some divisions organized regimental showers, and dry socks were made available at most divisional shower points. But then came the German counterattack in the Ardennes, and General Hawley's doubts about the effectiveness of the measures already taken against trench foot were confirmed. In First Army, hardest hit by the German attack, rates were higher than in November. Replacements, who were needed

---

[151] (1) Garside Rpt, app. K. (2) Ltr, Busch to Littlejohn, 11 Feb 45. Quoted in Incl VII to Ltr, Littlejohn to Somervell, 3 Mar 45. (3) Hq ADSEC COMZ, QM Estimates of the Situation, 21 Jan, 13 Feb 45. (4) Memo, Littlejohn for Florsheim, 16 Feb 45, sub: Storage of Shoepacs. Littlejohn Reading File, vol. XXXIII, item 83.

[152] (1) Quotation from unnumbered cable, Littlejohn and Hawley to Somervell, 15 Mar 45. Reprinted in Littlejohn, ed., Passing in Review, ch. 48, app. G. (2) Whayne and DeBakey, *Cold Injury, Ground Type*, Tables 11, 12, 23.

[153] USFET Gen Bd Rpt 94, Trenchfoot, especially ch. 3. This report has been reproduced as Passing in Review, ch. 54.

in mounting numbers as casualties increased, presented a particular problem. They were pushed through the depots at top speed, sometimes arriving in the divisions without proper equipment, and almost invariably without proper indoctrination on cold injuries. Medical observers with all the armies, meeting at Paris in mid-January, decided that proper preventive measures had been formulated, and were even well known in the higher headquarters. What was now required was to disseminate and enforce them, especially at company, platoon, and squad levels. On their recommendation, a theater directive for that purpose was published on 30 January, setting up trench foot control teams in each army, consisting of one line officer and one quartermaster officer. The efforts of these teams were supplemented by a wide use of pamphlets, posters, newspapers, and the radio. By the time this program became fully operational weather conditions were improving, German resistance was deteriorating, and the trench foot rate was dropping rapidly toward zero. Nevertheless, it was believed that the correct approach had been found.[154]

The efficiency of such measures, enforced by discipline and made a command responsibility at all levels, was demonstrated by the British experience in both world wars. Having suffered nearly 100,000 casualties from this source in 1914-15, the British armies in France and Flanders instituted a rigorous program of daily foot inspection and exercise or massage, and only 443 cases were hospitalized for trench foot during 1916–18. In World War II the British record in France was even better—only 206 hospitalized cases of trench foot. It should be noted that the British did not report minor cases treated in quarters, but this was merely one in a long list of differences between British and American practices and experiences in the field that make a direct comparison impossible. About the only definite statement to be made is that the lesser incidence of cold injury in the British armies was not due to any special or unusual type of footwear. The British service shoe (called by the British a boot) had a high toecap and long forequarters, so that it could not be laced too tight over the instep, even when worn with several pairs of socks. Its heavy tap-and-screw sole was watertight but stiff and inflexible, and U.S. troops found it fatiguing to march in. Nevertheless, it was an excellent and very versatile item. The British issued no other footgear to individuals; they used neither shoepacs nor overshoes. For very wet conditions, British units maintained a small reserve of rubber boots as organizational clothing.[155]

Possibly of even greater importance was a consistent British policy of rotating personnel between the front lines and reserve areas, preferably relieving battalions or companies in winter after not more than 48 hours of combat. The

---

[154] (1) Whayne and DeBakey, *Cold Injury, Ground Type,* pp. 177–84, 480–86. (2) Ltr, Hq ETOUSA to CG's, First, Third, Seventh, Ninth, Fifteenth U.S. Armies, 30 Jan 45, sub: Trenchfoot Control Officers. AG 210.453 Op MS. (3) AAR's, 2d, 4th, 8th Divisional QM Co's. Hist Br OQMG. (4) Ltr, Dir Legal Div SGO [Lt Col Mason Ladd, JAGD] to CG COMZ ETO, 25 May 45, sub: Rpt of Investigation Relative to Incidence of Trenchfoot (hereafter cited as Ladd Rpt). Hist Br OQMG.

---

[155] Whayne and DeBakey, *Cold Injury, Ground Type,* pp. 42–47, 198–202.

British termed this "man-management," and taught it to all officers as a matter of basic military doctrine. Naturally, such relief was not always possible, but the First Canadian and Second British Armies both reported increased incidence of trench foot after seventy-two hours or more in the line. No consistent and uniform rotation policy was practiced in the U.S. Army. Lt. Col. Mason Ladd, who investigated the entire trench foot problem for The Surgeon General, commented that the "objective-mindedness" of American commanders was a major cause of the higher American rate for all types of casualties, including trench foot. In this connection, it might be noted that the statement already made, that trench foot casualties tend to be proportionate to the total casualty rate, applies also to the British. During the period of the worst U.S. trench foot casualties, 21 Army Group fought a holding operation in sandy, well-drained terrain on a relatively narrow front, and its total casualty rate was low. The U.S. Ninth Army, engaged in an adjacent area and for a time under British command, had similar low casualty rates.[156]

By contrast, the First, Third, and Seventh U.S. Armies were making an aggressive attack on a wide front, in areas characterized by open terrain with little shelter, muddy river valleys, much snow on high ground, and a harsher climate than the coastal area. Tactical considerations often made rotation or relief of units impossible for weeks on end. When not actually advancing, the troops were often pinned down by enemy fire

in water-filled foxholes. In such fighting, the Germans had a distinct advantage. Enemy statistics are not available but medical observers who examined prisoners were of the opinion that the Germans suffered very little from trench foot in November and early December, when the Americans were advancing, but considerably more during their own Ardennes counteroffensive.[157]

Meanwhile, strained transportation facilities operating over extended supply lines were taxed to the utmost to provide the advancing armies with gasoline, ammunition, and operational rations. The Transportation Corps did not have an opportunity to bring up the kitchen-prepared rations that contributed to good circulation, or to build up adequate stocks of winter clothing in the forward areas. An exhaustive report prepared by The Surgeon General's Office, after enumerating the multiplicity of factors contributing to the trench foot crisis, concluded that "under the type of warfare and the conditions experienced

---

[156] (1) *Ibid.*, pp. 375, 411. (2) Ladd Rpt. (3) Siple Rpt.

[157] German troops were well indoctrinated in the dangers of "frozen feet"—their catchall expression for all cold injuries of the feet. The troops always tried to floor a wet foxhole with planks or logs. Few German units were motorized, and the men were used to long marches and to caring for their feet at all seasons, and not merely in winter. German field boots were the product of decades of development; made of excellent quality, well-oiled cowhide, they were of a design without laces that left ample room for extra socks or footcloths, and did not constrict the feet. The men normally wore heavy wool socks and carried several extra pairs, so special winter issues were not needed. Unlike the British, they were issued a foot salve as a "frostbite" preventive, but German medical doctrine also emphasized the importance of massage. Men suspected of contracting trench foot through negligence were severely punished, but foot discipline was a part of general discipline, and not specially emphasized. Cf. 12th Army Group Rpt of Opns, XIII, 201; Cole, *The Lorraine Campaign*, pp. 593–94.

last winter in the ETO by the American Armies, trenchfoot in substantial amount is believed to have been an unavoidable hazard of war." [158]

Press and Congressional Reaction

The trench foot problem in the ETO and other allied problems regarding adequate winter clothing and equipment were the subject of intense public interest in the United States. COMZ headquarters and all the technical services gave newsmen working in the theater full co-operation and as much information as military security permitted. With some exceptions the material the reporters sent home was accurate, but usually all the factors involved in even an isolated episode were too complex for inclusion in a news story. Their natural interest in the fate of individuals made them ignore, or even contradict, the presentation of the "big picture" as divulged by higher headquarters. Certainly, the public was not reassured about the supply situation in Europe by a headline that declared: "GI's Seen Poorly Clad and Freezing; Eisenhower Admits 'Isolated Cases.'" Similar headlines were rather frequent in the American press in the late winter of 1945. An official inquiry from the War Department to Somervell, who was in Europe at the end of January, brought a reply from Eisenhower with Somervell's con-

currence describing the clothing supply situation in detail. At the time, about 66 percent of the items listed in Table 20 had already been issued, and except for extra-large size overshoes, there were no shortages among line troops. The cable further stated:

Disagreement among individual soldiers as well as Army commanders on relative value of various types of field jackets, socks, and footwear could easily lead to impression that troops are not well clothed. Knit gloves with leather palm are not entirely satisfactory in wet snow, because front line soldiers have no means of drying them. Every effort is being made to substitute wool mittens with removable leather shells. . . . Every soldier had been issued a wool overcoat. However a too prevalent tendency exists on the part of some front line soldiers to discard heavy clothing, particularly overcoats and overshoes, during fast moving action, and this loss reached considerable proportions at times. Salvage of discarded equipment is being energetically pursued, and positive efforts to enforce supply discipline. . . . It is not intended however, to imply that instances do not occur where individuals or units reach the front without the proper clothing and equipment. A case of this kind occurred just recently . . . regarding Engineer Combat Battalions . . . immediate action was taken to fill shortages . . . place responsibility for such supply failure to prevent recurrence, and disciplinary action taken where indicated.[159]

Eisenhower also noted that the trench foot situation was not as severe as in November, and that the few cases of colds and pneumonia reported were

---

[158] (1) Quotation is from Ladd Rpt. (2) Memo, Preventive Medicine Div OCS COMZ for OCQM, 23 Jul 44, sub: Trenchfoot; Cable War–X79550, 19 Dec 44. Hist Br OQMG. (3) Maj Gen Sir Henry L. Tidy and J. M. Browne Kutschbach, *Inter-Allied Conferences on War Medicine, 1942-1945* (London: Staples Press Ltd., 1947), pp. 140–43. (4) Littlejohn, ed., *Passing in Review*, ch. 54, p. 13.

[159] (1) Cables WAR–24746, AGWAR to Somervell, 23 Jan 45, and S–76466, Eisenhower and Somervell to Hull, 24 Jan 45. Hist Br OQMG. (2) Headline appeared in the Chicago *Daily News*, January 26, 1945, over a story by Jack Bell. The same story, under the headline "Doughboy's Clothing Called Inadequate," appeared in Detroit *Free Press*, January 28, 1945.

among headquarters troops, not at the front. The Secretary of War considered this information so important that he personally gave it to the press the same day it was received.[160]

Meanwhile Congress was also taking an interest in the situation. Soldiers with various complaints, notably those who lacked large-size overshoes or heavyweight socks, wrote to the editors of *Stars and Stripes*, to their parents, or to various veterans' organizations. Such letters found their way to Congress, which very naturally demanded explanations from The Quartermaster General's Office. The standard reply, that deliveries from the United States had been adequate and that these were theater problems of transportation and distribution, apparently failed to satisfy either the congressmen's constituents or the press. It should be noted that staff officers in the OQMG and those in the ETO Chief Quartermaster's office both disagreed with this official version. Each group was well aware that deliveries had not been adequate, but each was inclined to place the blame upon the other party. One newsman, who had obtained a rather inaccurate and extremely partisan version of this controversy from individuals in The Quartermaster General's Office, wrote a story that appeared in the Washington *Post* on 18 February, charging General Littlejohn with negligence through failure to requisition winter clothing early enough and in sufficient quantities. The reporter claimed that his information came from "the most qualified sources in Washington."

It should be noted that Generals Gregory and Feldman were on a tour of the Pacific theaters when this article appeared. Capt. Donald Craig, the Technical Information Officer of the OQMG, had recommended against its release for publication, but his advice was ignored.[161]

The Washington *Post* article stated in substance that every item originated by the Research and Development Branch, OQMG, was "vastly superior" or even "ideal," and that sufficient quantities could have been made available to equip a million combat soldiers, if requisitions had not been delayed. Moreover it implied that by February 1945 these articles were available in unlimited quantities and were currently being supplied to every combat soldier and every replacement. In support of this thesis, it gave incorrect requisition dates for several important items, and made no reference whatever to the nonconcurrence of G–4 and Army Service Forces, or to production difficulties, or to the OQMG's repeated failure to fulfill delivery commitments. These omissions left the impression that the ETO did not requisition sleeping bags or Eisenhower jackets until September 1944 and that the theater, rather than the War Department, determined maintenance factors. Littlejohn was of the opinion that the article, and also the brochure pre-

---

[160] "American Troops Properly Equipped," statement by SW in the *Army and Navy Register*, 3 February 1945.

[161] (1) Ltr, Gregory to the Hon. Homer Ferguson, 4 Nov 44; Ltr, Stimson to the Hon. William Lemke, 11 Jan 44; Ltr, Corbin to the Hon. Chan Gurney, 8 Feb 44. SPQEC 420, ETO (2) Ltr, Littlejohn to TQMG, 27 Dec 44, sub: Letters to *Stars and Stripes*. Hist Br OQMG. (3) "U.S. Western Front Clothing: A Factual Report," by George Connery, in the Washington *Post*, February 18, 1945. (4) Memo, Craig for WD Bureau Public Relations, 16 Feb 45. Hist Br OQMG.

pared for Gregory and submitted to General Somervell on 5 January, were part of a malicious campaign to discredit the ETO Communications Zone, and in particular an attack upon himself. Having offered his resignation to General Eisenhower, who emphatically refused to accept it, Littlejohn brought the whole matter officially to the attention of General Somervell on 2 March 1945.[162]

An Official Evaluation

General Somervell directed Brig. Gen. Albert J. Browning, Assistant Director of Matériel, ASF, to investigate Littlejohn's charges, and the actual investigation was conducted by a five-man committee, headed by Col. Charles Garside, General Staff Corps, a New York attorney then on duty with the Purchases Division, ASF. The committee report, submitted on 16 May 1945, dealt solely with the supply of clothing to the ETO. It covered the subject with great thoroughness, but it is unfortunate that a committee invested with sweeping powers to investigate so important a subject did not go further afield and provide constructive criticism of a more useful nature. The report disclosed no evidence of major inadequacies of regular clothing. It exonerated General Littlejohn of any blame regarding tardy requisitions and General Gregory likewise of blame regarding tardy deliveries

of winter clothing. It stated that while ETO requirements increased suddenly in the latter part of 1944, and far beyond the anticipation of either the Chief Quartermaster, ETO, or The Quartermaster General, the reasons were primarily tactical and cast no discredit on anyone. Every effort was made to meet these requirements as speedily as possible, and for such delay as attended those efforts the primary reasons were, again, tactical. Nevertheless TQMG and NYPE succeeded in filling most of these requirements substantially as requested. Items of regular clothing, with the exception of overshoes, were supplied to the troops abundantly and on time. The impact upon zone of interior stocks was tremendous, resulting in depletion of stocks, curtailment of zone of interior issues, and necessity for initiation of new procurement.[163]

The report carefully distinguished between regular clothing and special cold climate clothing. With regard to the latter, it noted differences of opinion with respect to the merits of particular items, but declared such differences to be entirely honest and proper. In support of this statement, it pointed to similar differences of opinion among the using armies. At this point the report itself is open to criticism, since an "honest and proper" but long-standing controversy between two headquarters almost invariably points to a lack of clear policy decisions at the next higher level. That observation can be made even more forcibly regarding another finding of the committee: It stated that a major reason

---

[162] (1) Personal Ltr, Littlejohn to Somervell, 2 Mar 45. Reproduced in Littlejohn, ed., Passing in Review, ch. 28. (2) On 3 March 1945 Littlejohn sent Somervell another brief letter inclosing papers in support of his charges, which were divided into ten section headings. These have already been cited as Inclosures to Ltr, Littlejohn to Somervell, 3 Mar 45.

[163] Investigation, Supply of Clothing to the ETO, 16 May 1945. Reproduced in full in Littlejohn, ed., Passing in Review, ch. 28.

for nonavailability of cold climate items was a policy "which had precluded broader inclusion of indefinite or potential requirements for these items in the Army Supply Program." This appears to be a fairly definite indictment of ASF, which was clearly responsible for that program and failed to make a firm decision. In staff planning even a wrong decision is seldom as bad as no decision, and this is particularly true in controversial cases where, almost inevitably, a minority opinion will declare any decision to be the wrong one.[164]

Apart from the somewhat narrow findings and conclusions already mentioned, the Garside Report included thirty-four detailed studies, each covering an item of regular clothing, cold climate clothing, or sleeping gear, and giving all available data on requisitions, production, shipment to the ETO, depot stocks, and issues to troops for the period January 1944 to February 1945. More important than the Garside Report itself were various subsidiary reports prepared at the direction of the investigating committee, or made available to the committee and used as source material. It might be added that there was at least one voice in disagreement with the findings of the Garside Report. Reviewing the report for General Somervell, Maj. Gen. Clinton F. Robinson, director of

the Control Division, ASF, criticized the administrative procedures of the ETO Quartermaster, noting that requisitions were sometimes improperly forwarded, and shipping schedules in some instances improperly prepared. This apparently referred to teletyped requisitions, which were not always confirmed promptly by formal written requisitions, and occasional incorrect citation of tonnage authorizations. Robinson also found that the ETO had not requisitioned sufficiently far in advance to insure prompt supply, but this observation was considerably weakened by an admission in the same paragraph that "stocks were adequate and *once releases were obtained* shipments moved forward at a rapid rate."[165] It might be inferred that the ASF, which was responsible for such releases, was itself too deeply implicated in what appeared to be a controversy between OQMG and the ETO Quartermaster to render a completely impartial judgment. Certainly if blame for oversights is to be apportioned according to the perfection of staff paperwork, a zone of interior agency will always be able to prove an overseas headquarters at fault. As Colonel Garside observed: "Planning in Washington took on a kind of perfection which could never be attained in the supply of vast armies in the field."[166] But the important facts are that the armies were

[164] (1) *Ibid*. (2) Colonel Garside made an additional informal report to General Browning, dated 12 May 1945 and reproduced with his main report, regarding the controversial personal difference of opinion between OQMG and ETO. In this, while explicitly exculpating General Gregory and his senior assistants, he confirmed that subordinate officials within the OQMG staff had reinforced their convictions regarding proper winter clothing with self-justifying memorandums of a misleading nature, which they communicated to officers in the ETO and to the press.

[165] (1) Memo, Robinson for Somervell, 21 Jun 45, sub: Investigation Supply of Clothing to ETO. DCofS files, 420 ETO. Italics supplied by author. (2) Mr. Sheppard's report on footwear, Major Siple's report on winter clothing, Colonel Ladd's report on trench foot, and the OQMG Study of 5 April 1945, Supply of Clothing to the ETO, 1944, have been cited repeatedly above.

[166] Personal Ltr, Garside to Browning, 12 May 45. Reproduced in Littlejohn, ed., Passing in Review, ch 28.

indeed vast, and that they were supplied, despite all the difficulties. In the final analysis, the occasional misunderstandings and bad-tempered disputes that were carried on across the Atlantic were of very minor importance when compared to the obstacles presented by production bottlenecks, shipping tie-ups, low priorities, and deficits in discharge and forwarding capacity within the theater. These were the real difficulties in supplying clothing to the troops. That they were usually overcome constituted a commendable performance in which the entire Quartermaster Corps could take legitimate pride.

CHAPTER XVII

Other Class II and IV Items

The Winter Clothing Conference and the 1945–46 Winter Uniform

On 29 January 1945, twenty-five of the top ranking quartermasters in the ETO assembled in Littlejohn's office. They were there at the Chief Quartermaster's invitation to pool their opinions and, if possible, to reach agreement on a winter combat uniform for the year 1945–46. Despite all of the thought that had gone into the development of a simple winter uniform during the past three years, both in the theater and in the zone of interior, seventy different basic clothing items were still being worn in the spring of 1945. To explore the possible remedies, a conference had been planned for the previous December, but had to be postponed because of the enemy's counteroffensive in the Ardennes. As Littlejohn stated in his opening remarks, their meeting was to enable each representative

. . . of a major unit [to] express the official opinion of this unit in order that we may determine what is needed, where it is needed and when it is needed. All this is with a view to giving the best possible service during the current winter and for planning the Procurement and Production program for the winter of 1945–1946. I will appreciate it also if the several field representatives will indicate the wishes of their Commands as to clothing to be worn upon the cessation of hostilities for both summer and winter.[1]

In the light of their recent experience in the Vosges Mountains, Seventh Army representatives considered the newly standardized M1943 uniform "basically sound." They liked the jacket, pile liner, cotton field trousers, shoepac, and sleeping bag. On the other hand, they found the overcoat to be of no real use to the infantryman in the field, but they thought it would be suitable as a dress garment in the posthostilities period. Seventh Army had received M1943 clothing through SOLOC from MTOUSA stocks, and there was even enough for several divisions transferred from northern France.[2]

---

[1] (1) Ltrs, CQM to QM Fifth Army, CQM MTOUSA, QM's Each ETO Army and AF, 19 Jan 45, sub: QM Conf on Cold Weather Clothing; Ltrs, CQM to CG's Armies, Army Groups, Air Forces, CQM MTOUSA, and TQMG, 2 Feb 45, sub: Winter Clothing Conf. Littlejohn Reading File, vol. XXXII, pp. 106–09; vol. XXXIII, pp. 14–19. (2) Quotation from Min, First Session Winter Clothing Conf, 29 Jan 45, OCQM. Winter Combat Uniform Def RC 913 FRC. (3) Memo, CQM for TQMG, 9 May 45, sub: Winter Uniform. Hist Br OQMG.

[2] (1) Memo, CQM to Div Chiefs, 15 Nov 44, sub: Comments on Trip. Littlejohn Reading File, vol. XXX, item 35. (2) Memo, Middleswart for Littlejohn, 2 Jan 45, sub: Issue Chart; Comments by General Middleswart upon draft MS this volume (1955). Both in Hist Br OQMG. (3) Fifth Army's generally unsatisfactory experience with the M1943 uniform was not reported at the conference. See ch. VII, above.

Because it had never obtained the complete M1943 uniform in large quantity, the 12th Army Group was unable to take as clear a position on this issue as had the units that had drawn their supplies through southern France. Colonel McNamara of First Army praised the armored force combat suit, but said he would give serious consideration to any substitute jacket on condition that it had sufficient pocket space to eliminate need for special bags or belts. Third Army's quartermaster, Colonel Busch, generally concurred with First Army's position: ". . . there is almost unanimous opinion . . . for the combat trousers and old combat jacket to be given to every soldier, combat or service, as long as he works outside." [3]

Shoes and socks, overcoats and ponchos, as well as other items were discussed at this exploratory conference, but it was apparent that no general agreement could be reached until the 12th Army Group had been given the opportunity to compare more carefully the various uniforms currently available in the theater. It was agreed that such experience could be most quickly obtained by controlled field tests. Meetings were planned for February, when those conducting the tests would be briefed, and a more conclusive conference would be held after the results of these tests were collected and analyzed by the combat units.[4]

At least five hundred sets of uniforms were sent to each of the armies, and Quartermaster technical intelligence personnel brought the equipment to the selected divisions. In Third Army, for example, the 4th Armored and the 26th Infantry Divisions each received three hundred uniforms of each type, along with mimeographed instructions describing the preferred methods for wearing the various clothing assemblies. The purpose of the project was to determine which combination of clothing—the M1943 outer garments over wool field trousers and either a pile jacket or a wool jacket, or the winter combat uniform—would best meet the criteria of simplicity and uniformity. The participating troops were asked to consider such qualities as suitability for combat, water-repellency, wind-resistance, warmth and comfort, adaptability to street wear, adequacy of pockets, and suitability for laundering.[5]

Although no exact procedure was prescribed for the test, 12th Army Group recommended that the uniforms be distributed to small units, preferably to platoons, and rotated among the men throughout the testing period. Also the men were authorized to improvise alternate assemblies at their own discretion. Because it took time to distribute the test garments and the results of the tests were urgently needed, little more than two weeks were given over to the experiment. In mid-March the Chief Quartermaster again called together the quartermasters of the army

---

[3] Quotation from source cited n. 1 (2).

[4] Ltr, CQM to QM 12th Army Group et al., 19 Jan 45, sub: QM Conf; Memo for Record, 12th Army Group, 2 Feb 45, sub: QM Conf. 12th Army Group QM 1, AF Def Sec FRC.

[5] (1) TUSA AAR, II, QM 20, 23. (2) 12th Army Group Rpt of Opns, XII, 204–05. (3) Address by Maj Paul A. Siple, 11 Apr 46, at AWC, sub: Environmental Protection. OQMG Food Conf Rpt, Hist Br OQMG. (4) Ltr, Capt Robert Collett to Lt Col Bestor Robinson, 9 Feb 45, sub: Winter Combat Clothing Experiment—TUSA. Hist Br OQMG. (5) Ltr, CG 12th Army Group to CG FUSA et al., 1 Feb 45, sub: Test of Winter Combat Clothing; Ltr, AG NUSA to CG 12th Army Group, 11 Mar 45, sub: Test of Winter Clothing. NUSA AG 400.112.

ARMORED WINTER COMBAT UNIFORM. *Tankers found it warm and comfortable.*

groups, armies, and air forces in the ETO. To this meeting he also invited representatives from the theater Chief Surgeon's office, the Office of The Quartermaster General, and the War Production Board in Washington, as well as experienced observers from the Mediterranean theater and Fifth Army in Italy. For two days the participants sifted the data from the recent tests and questionnaires that had been circulated by 12th Army Group, particularly as they related to the technical characteristics of the various articles of clothing. On the third and final day of the meeting, the participants attempted to reach agreement on a single combination of clothing that would provide the combat soldier with the most suitable winter uniform.[6]

---

[6] General conclusions of the armies, based on experience in tests, can be found in Ltr, OQM XVIII Corps (A/B) to CQM, 14 Mar 45, sub: Recommended Winter T/O&E for A/B and Corps Units; Ltr, QM 12th Army Group to CQM, 14 Mar 45, sub: Winter Combat Uniform; Ltr, QM FUSA to CQM, 17 Mar 45, sub: Tests for Winter Clothing; Ltr, AG NUSA to CG 12th Army Group, 11 Mar 45, sub: Test of Winter Clothing; AG TUSA to CG 12th Army Group, 11 Mar 45, sub: Winter Combat Uniform. 12th Army Group QM 1, AF Def Sec FRC.

The conclusions of the meeting represented a statement of preferences rather than a meeting of minds. As reported by Colonel Younger, the chairman of a committee appointed to reconcile the diversity of opinions, ". . . the conference was not in total accord on any one item except underwear and shirts. The differences of opinion were not difficult to resolve for most items. The most controversial items of the uniform were caps, jackets, trousers and overcoats." [7]

Agreement was reached on a combination of clothing items generally similar to those worn by Seventh Army and recommended by the representatives from the Mediterranean theater. (See Appendix D.) While rejecting the arctic and Parsons style field jackets, all the representatives spoke highly of the now obsolete armored force combat jacket. Lacking the latter, however, they indicated their willingness to accept the M1943 jacket, the pile jacket or wool field jacket, and high-necked sweater. They stated that the ETO wool jacket would be primarily useful for dress purposes and that the pile jacket required modified tailoring and a water-repellent outer fabric. There was substantial agreement on cotton field trousers, but the standard 18-ounce wool serge trousers normally worn under them were condemned as inadequate. Even the 20-ounce wool field trousers submitted for testing in February were found too light, and a napped 22-ounce fabric was recommended instead. Knowing that production would fall short of full theater requirements, the committee gave as

its second choice winter combat trousers over 18-ounce serge trousers, but observed that the available substitute was cotton field trousers over 18-ounce trousers. A strong preference was expressed for a cotton field overcoat with a liner to replace both the conventional overcoat and the raincoat, but this was not a combat item, and the conferees were willing to accept the wool overcoat in the knowledge that neither time nor materials would be available to produce the desired garment. This decision was undoubtedly affected by adoption of the poncho, which could be worn over an overcoat, while the discarded raincoat could not. The committee also agreed on leather glove shells and wool inserts, on the cotton field cap, and on the hood of the M1943 assembly. [8]

The sentiments of the field forces with regard to footwear were incorporated in the report of Mr. Lawrence B. Sheppard, already described. As has been related, the feeling against the flesh-out boot ran high and the consensus was that the leather should be reversed to provide a russet-colored shoe that could be cleaned and shined. [9] It was agreed that the modified boot would be supplemented in winter by all-rubber overshoes, and that dismounted combat troops were to be issued shoepacs under wet-cold conditions.

In the weeks following the March

[7] Memo, QM 12th Army Group for G–1 et al., 23 Mar 45, sub: Winter Clothing Conf. 12th Army Group QM 1, AF Def Sec FRC.

[8] Ltr, QM 12th Army Group to CQM, 19 Mar 45, sub: Winter Combat Uniform. Hist Br OQMG.
[9] (1) Memo, CQM for TQMG, 23 Mar 45, sub: Footwear and Socks for Use in the ETO. Hist Br OQMG. (2) For similar recommendations by a medical officer, see Memo, Chief Preventive Medicine and Med Intel Br for CQM, 24 Feb 45, sub: Comments on Proposed Items for Winter Uniform. 12th Army Group QM 1, AF Def Sec FRC.

GENERALS AND THEIR JACKETS. *Generals Patch and Devers (first and third from left) are wearing the M1943 jacket popular with troops in the Sixth Army Group; General Brooks (second from left) wears the armored forces jacket favored by many field commanders; General Eisenhower wears an AAF flight jacket, and General Bradley is wearing the ETO wool jacket as designed by OQMG. Paris, November 1944.*

conference, the Chief Quartermaster and his aides analyzed the data collected and evaluated the production problems inherent in the garments recommended by the field forces. In the main these recommendations were accepted and transmitted to the OQMG in the summary report, but on several key items the OCQM had reservations about the compromises reached at the conference. Feeling that the conferees had lacked sufficient experience with all the items considered—the recent tests had only been of two-week duration—and indeed that the number of items under consid-

eration itself had the effect of complicating a clear-cut decision, Littlejohn also felt compelled to modify the recommendations of the committee in line with the production capabilities presented at the meeting.[10]

In a somewhat contradictory fashion, the committee had accepted the M1943 jacket, but had predicated acceptance of the pile jacket upon certain modifications, including substitution of a water-repellent outer fabric. Since the pile

[10] Memo, CQM for TQMG, 9 May 45, sub: Winter Uniform. WDGS 292-420, drawer 641, FRC.

jacket had been designed as a liner for the M1943 jacket, this change cast grave doubts on the utility of the latter item. Moreover, it was doubtful whether the pile jacket could be supplied to the entire theater by mid-September 1945. Littlejohn therefore recommended that the widely popular armored force combat jacket be reinstated in the Army Supply Program and issued as a substitute for the M1943 assembly, including the pile jacket. He held that this would be more desirable than converting the pile jacket into an item that would closely resemble the combat jacket. Also, the combat jacket could be made in 4 standard sizes, while the pile jacket and its companion garment, the M1943 jacket, were manufactured in 13 and 18 sizes, respectively. By eliminating 27 sizes, each of which was a different garment for inventory purposes, the supply problem would be markedly simplified. The same reasoning was applied to the supply of trousers when the OCQM recommended that winter combat trousers be issued in lieu of cotton field trousers over wool field trousers, as advocated at the conference. In this instance, 16 sizes would be eliminated. Simplification along these lines had been specifically recommended by the Third and Ninth Army quartermasters. The armies had also expressed an interest in reducing the number of garments worn by the men at any one time, and adoption of the armored force combat clothing would accomplish that end. This was a repudiation of the layering principle, which provided additional garments to be worn in winter but did not require a complete seasonal change-over of outer clothing. In Littlejohn's view, the issue involved the convenience

of the combat troops versus the convenience of their quartermasters, and the QMC tradition of service permitted only one solution.[11]

These views, it should be noted, were not submitted to The Quartermaster General until the day following V–E Day, and in the weeks during which they were weighed and considered in Washington the ETO quickly sank in importance, becoming an inactive secondary theater. The collapse of the German forces was sudden and complete, and the anticipated Nazi underground resistance movement did not materialize. The occupation of Germany settled into a routine garrison activity which did not keep large forces in the field, and estimates of requirements for combat-type clothing were found to be too high. This proved to be fortunate, since troops located in or ordered to the Far East now received the overriding priorities once accorded to the ETO. Moreover, textile shortages continued and the U.S. economy was strained to equip even troops actively engaged.

Littlejohn's recommendations for revival of the winter combat uniform were rejected by the OQMG, which found that they did not accurately represent the conclusions of the clothing conference. The recommendations of the winter clothing committee were, on the whole, favorably received, but insofar as they deviated from current policy,

───────────
[11] (1) *Ibid*. (2) Ltr, Col Gilbert E. Parker, WD Observer to CG, AGF, 28 Jun 45, sub: AGF Rpt 1067—Field Jackets. OQMG 421 ETO. (3) Ltr, AG NUSA to CG 12th Army Group, 11 Mar 45, sub: Test of Winter Clothing, NUSA AG 400.112. (4) TUSA AAR, II, QM 23. (5) Littlejohn, ed., *Passing in Review*, ch. 30, par. 46.

they could not be put into effect for the winter of 1945–46. In practice, the army of occupation during the first winter in Germany was not even authorized the current winter allowances for combat troops in an active theater. The men were issued neither wool field trousers nor cotton ones, and only one pair of combat boots per man. Even overshoes were a discretionary item, which had to be authorized by the army of occupation commander. The prevailing ETO winter uniform was the M1943 jacket over the ETO jacket, and herringbone twill trousers over 18-ounce serge trousers.[12]

Clothing for Officers

The basic U.S. Army policy of World War II, that officers should purchase all regular uniform items, was extended to the combat zone on the Continent. Mobile sales units served the embarkation areas, and the strict rationing of clothing imposed in Great Britain was relaxed for the departing troops. Also, after D plus 8 improvised sales stores were opened within each Class II and IV dump in Normandy, so that officers might buy enlisted-type field clothing from regular stocks. After D plus 14, a limited number of items for nurses were also available at these stores. On D plus 38 (14 July) the 581st QM Sales Company opened a regular sales store in the town of Isigny, and in the next few days it also began to send mobile units forward to the corps and division service areas. By the end of the month

it had sold nearly $107,000 worth of clothing and insignia, or about $6,300 per day. This was not an unusually large volume of sales for a force of some 850,000 men during combat, but it far exceeded the rate imposed by rationing in the United Kingdom.[13]

Both the large amount of sales and the demand pattern were unexpected. For example, 7,418 cotton drawers were sold, and only 445 woolen drawers, although model stocks planned before D-day provided these items in equal quantities. Confirming the need for field clothing under combat conditions, nurses bought large quantities of herringbone twill shirts and trousers.[14] By early 1945 a revised model stock had been computed to support 10,000 officers for 30 days, with additional items for 1,000 nurses and WAC officers, and 1,000 civilian women with officer status for a like period. This stock weighed approximately 24 long tons.[15]

---

[13] (1) See discussion of clothing in Chapter X, above. (2) *QM Supply in ETO,* V, 17–20. (3) *FUSA Rpt of Opns,* 20 Oct 43–1 Aug 44, VI, 232–34. (4) Officers comprised roughly 18 percent of U.S. forces in the ETO, of these nurses accounted for 0.7 percent, and WAC officers .014 percent. *Cf.* Table 11 and app. B.

[14] *QM Supply in ETO,* V, 17–20.

[15] At the end of the fighting in Europe, QM sales stores were serving approximately the following personnel in the ETO:

Officers (male)	259,000
Nurses	21,100
WAC officers	500
Red Cross	4,000
UNRRA	2,000
Navy	3,900
U.S. civilians	3,500
Total	294,000

Cf. OTCQM TSFET Operational Study 2, pp. 44, 132–51.

---

[12] (1) Memo cited n. 10, with added Comment 3, TQMG for ACofS G–1 WDGS, 11 Jun 45. (2) T/E 21, 1 Sep 45, pt. II, sec. VI.

Officers bought tremendous amounts of clothing in the ETO. In October 1944 Littlejohn estimated that he could sell 500,000 uniforms in a week, whereas he actually had 150 locally made uniforms on hand. Later, in reviewing ETO experience he pointed out that in combat units officers bought a uniform, wore it, slept in it, forded or swam rivers in it, and at the end of two months threw it away. The average consumption for all officers in the theater was some seven uniforms per year, and the Chief Quartermaster observed: "The consumption of clothing by officers, nurses, Wac's and civilians is far beyond the Table of Allowances, or any estimate previously made by me. In the field, the necessity for this increased consumption is evident. In the cities, to me, it is questionable." [16]

Static sales stores had a most unfortunate tendency to favor individual officers of local units at the expense of combat units. Cherbourg and OMAHA sales stores were notable for such discrimination, and on 23 September Littlejohn ordered Colonel Florsheim to investigate all the sales stores in Normandy. They had repeatedly failed to report their inventories, which the Chief Quartermaster proposed to transfer to other sales stores further forward. But apparently the supplies in these stores had been exhausted, and there was nothing to transfer. A month later, Littlejohn wrote to the Quartermaster, Normandy Base Section, pointing out that it was necessary to maintain strict

control over these stories so that officers, including nurses and Wacs, could purchase what they actually needed and no more. He was especially insistent that the practice of buying officers' shoes, to be sold or given away to enlisted men or French civilians, be stopped, but no effective solution of this problem was ever found. Army women, both officer and enlisted, had their own problems. Despite regulations, male officers sometimes managed to buy stockings and girdles, and various other items, for their friends. There was also a good deal of indignation when newspaperwomen, congresswomen, and the casts of United Service Organizations traveling shows were allowed to make inroads into the scanty stocks maintained for women in the Army.[17]

Sales store supplies and sales store units both had very low priorities for cross-Channel transportation. For a short time the 581st Sales Company, already mentioned, was split among the First, Third, and Ninth Armies, each having a single platoon. Because this class of supply was so scarce, pilferage was a serious problem and semiofficial "diversions" by commanders who were determined to provide for their own units were equally troublesome. On 7 September Littlejohn wrote Colonel Busch that his attempts to move such supplies by Red Ball or by ordinary freight had proved disastrous. Thereafter he would move them exclusively

---

[16] (1) Personal Ltr, CQM to Gen Lutes, 15 Oct 44. Hist Br OQMG. (2) Littlejohn, ed., Passing in Review, ch. 6, p. 4. (3) Quotation from Ltr, CQM to G-1 ETO, 4 Dec 44, sub: Women's Uniforms. Littlejohn Reading File, vol. XXXI, item 8.

[17] (1) IRS, Littlejohn to Florsheim, 23 Sep 44, sub: Sales Stores in NBS. Littlejohn Reading File, vol. XXVIII, item 169. (2) Personal Ltrs, CQM to QM NBS (Judd), 28 Oct, 4 Nov 44. Littlejohn Reading File, vol. XXIX, item 132; vol. XXX, item 4. (3) Treadwell, The Women's Army Corp, p. 401.

by air, with an officer accompanying each shipment. Later in September he noted that there was a sales company in Paris that could not function for lack of supplies. He urged the Seine Section quartermaster to open a store even if he had nothing to sell but a few pairs of GI socks. Presumably the spectacle of such a meager stock might be used to apply pressure to the theater G–4, who controlled tonnage priorities.[18]

On 15 October Colonel Brumbaugh finally was able to announce that a substantial shipment of clothing for officers was on the way from Britain. The available vehicles of ten truck companies scheduled for transfer to the Continent had been loaded with sales store items. But meanwhile the largest volume of sales of the entire European campaign was being made to officers in the forward areas. This was part of the winterization program already described. Officers received and paid for items identical with those issued to enlisted men. (*Table 18*). In Third Army, only $10,072 worth of clothing had been sold to 1,118 officers in September, all sales being at a static store. By contrast, 17,818 Third Army customers bought $270,646.46 worth of clothing, almost $9,000 per day, during October, more than half of it from mobile sales units. Sales at the mobile stores averaged nearly $18 per officer compared to about $13.50 per officer at static stores in the rear area. Since it was axiomatic in the ETO that officers would buy all that was author-

ized, an effort was clearly being made to favor the combat units. First Army did not report sales on a monthly basis, but sold $527,617.74 to its officers in the period 13 September–15 December 1944. About 48 percent of this clothing was sold by mobile units. Sales for three months averaged nearly $5,700 per day.[19]

The QM sales company was a very satisfactory and efficient unit, and in the ETO the ideal allocation was considered to be one company per army. Staffed with four officers and 174 enlisted men, and equipped with thirteen 2½-ton trucks and five smaller vehicles, the unit was capable of supplying officers' clothing for a combat force of 600,000 men, and also handled the wholesale distribution of Army Exchange Service items for the same number. The latter function, it should be noted, did not include gratuitous distribution to combat units, which was handled by Class I depots. Unfortunately, there were never enough sales units in the theater, and the normal allocation was two platoons per army in the 12th Army Group. Seventh Army had to get along with only one platoon until late January 1945. The two platoons normally attached to each army operated as mobile stores, visiting corps and division service areas on a regular schedule. The army Class II and IV officer operated a static store at each clothing depot, and sometimes additional stores at large cities within the army area. Such a series of static establishments required considerable numbers of civilian employees, administered by one officer and fifty-one enlisted men, were self-

[18] Ltr, CQM to QM 12th Army Group, 30 Aug 44, sub: QM Sales Co's; Ltr, CQM to QM TUSA, 7 Sep 44, sub: Clothing and Tentage; Ltrs, CQM to QM SBS, 9, 16, and 22 Sep 44, no sub. Littlejohn Reading File, vol. XXVII, item 163; vol. XXVIII, items 48a, 63, 109, 161.

[19] (1) IRS, CQM to Deputy, Paris, 15 Oct 44, sub: Sales Store Clothing. Littlejohn Reading File, vol. XXIX, item 67. (2) TUSA AAR, QM 29. (3) *FUSA Rpt of Opns*, 1 Aug 44–22 Feb 45, IV, 59.

contained units, and operated satisfactorily without supervision.[20]

In the Communications Zone, sales companies operated static sales stores of considerably greater capacity than in the combat zone, but normally had no responsibility for AES supplies. One company could operate three large stores, each of which could make 1,200 sales per day, averaging $10.00 per sale. When augmented by civilian personnel, which was usual in the ETO, the company could administer six such stores. In May 1945 there were fourteen large static stores in the ETO, each located at or near the scene of a significant command, logistical activity, or leave center. In addition, there was a smaller store within the Class II and IV section of each QM base depot. The maximum number of sales units in the theater, six companies plus two platoons, was reached by March 1945. Their distribution was two platoons in each of five armies, three companies in COMZ, and one platoon attached to SHAEF.[21]

Because of the shortages already mentioned, attempts were made to limit purchases in Paris and at some of the other static stores to members of combat units and to flying personnel. Nevertheless, sales stores on the Continent were seldom open more than two days a week because the demand was many times greater than the supply. Moreover, by December 1944 COMZ officers were complaining of discrimination, which had lasted for months. On 4 December Littlejohn recommended to the theater G–1

that a rationing system should be set up, and in January 1945 an ETOUSA circular directed that thereafter clothing and accessories would only be sold on presentation of a ration card. Colonel Busch of Third Army protested that the plan might be necessary in COMZ, but was not worth the trouble in the combat zone, where the armies were already overburdened with paperwork. If army control were exercised through orders limiting the amount an officer could buy, he thought there would be little chiseling. Littlejohn replied that evidently Busch did not have all the facts. Abuses were worst in the rear areas, but were not unknown at the front. This system would protect combat officers, and could be administered by the sales companies so as not to add to the burden of individuals.[22]

Rationing was considerably more complicated in the Communications Zone than among the combat troops, since there were many additional categories of personnel to be served, each of whom required a special ration card. The problem was further complicated because the OCQM had consented to act as distributor of clothing for the American Red Cross, for hostess–librarians, and for Allied Expeditionary Forces Club personnel, all of whom wore distinctive garments. Moreover the OCQM had itself procured a specially designed uniform for female British civilian volunteers with the U.S. forces. Each of these groups was permitted to supplement its

[20] (1) OTCQM TSFET Operational Study 10, pp. 24–25. (2) QM Supply in ETO, V, 17–26; VIII, 77–78. (3) T/O&E 10–157, 18 May 1944, QM Sales Company, Mobile.

[21] OTCQM TSFET Operational Study 2, pp. 44–46.

[22] (1) IRS, CQM to G–1, 4 Dec 44, sub: Women's Uniforms. Littlejohn Reading File, vol. XXXI, item 8. (2) ETOUSA Cir 8, 21 Jan 45. (3) Personal Ltr, Littlejohn to Busch, 15 Feb 45. Littlejohn Reading File, vol. XXXIII, item 78.

own uniform with certain common items of U.S. Army origin.[23]

One reason for uniform shortages in the ETO was that officers arrived in the theater improperly equipped. This problem had been experienced and corrected in the United Kingdom in 1942, but it reappeared on the Continent two years later. Early in January 1945 General Gregory promised to bring the matter to the attention of ASF, but pointed out that many officers went overseas by air, and it was impossible to increase their baggage allowances. Littlejohn took the matter up with General Somervell personally on 12 January, and the latter cabled General Styer the same day that all commissioned personnel should come to the ETO properly equipped for three months. Just what constituted proper equipment was not defined, but Littlejohn wrote to his old friend Colonel Evans at NYPE and arranged that Colonel Barber, currently in the United States to plead for raw materials, should help in preparing an approved list. The CQM suggested that nurses, WAC officers, and civilians should bring enough clothing for four months.[24]

Contrary to expectations, the ETO field uniform was reserved for officers almost exclusively until after V–E Day.

The only exceptions were a few enlisted men of combat units, who wore the uniform on furloughs to the United Kingdom or the zone of interior. The shortage of ETO jackets already described precluded their issue to enlisted men in 1944, but there were more than enough to be sold to officers. The obstacle was ETO insistence that the jacket only be worn with matching dark trousers. Littlejohn's unsuccessful requisition for 200,000 pairs of dark olive drab trousers exclusively for officers in July 1944 has already been mentioned. It was turned down officially because no such item was authorized for officers, but apparently the real reason was that the trousers would, in effect, provide officers with a field uniform distinctively different from that of enlisted men. In practice the ETO uniform was very seldom worn in combat, even by high-ranking officers, but Army Ground Forces considered that identical combat uniforms for officers and enlisted men were of basic importance, and did not concur in even a very modest requisition that would violate this principle.[25]

This War Department decision actually meant that dark shade olive drab trousers would become available from the United States only when there were enough for both officers and enlisted men. Meanwhile they were much in demand, and a limited number could be obtained through local procurement. Both Littlejohn and Lt. Col. Robert L. Cohen, the clothing officer in the Procurement Division, devoted a great deal

---

[23] (1) OTCQM TSFET Operational Study 2, pp. 752–56. (2) In addition to the categories mentioned above, sales privileges were accorded to personnel of the War Shipping Administration, Air Transport Command, and civilians attached to U.S. embassies (male only); and also to male and female U.S. technicians, USO, U.S. correspondents, UNRRA personnel, and Allied officers attached to U.S. forces.

[24] (1) Ltr, Gregory to Littlejohn, 5 Jan 45; Ltr, Littlejohn to Evans, 12 Jan 45; Ltr, Littlejohn to Gregory, 13 Jan 45. Littlejohn Reading File, vol. XXXII, items 30, 59, 62. (2) Cable E–84861 Somervell for Styer, 12 Jan 45.

[25] (1) Memo, Distr Div ASF to Reqmts and Stock Control, 5 Aug 44, with Memo for Record, OQMG Study of 5 Apr 45. (2) IRS, CQM to GPA, 10 Jul 44, sub: Unforeseen Clothing Reqmts for ETO. Littlejohn Reading File, vol. XXVI, item 45.

of time to this activity. Early in October Littlejohn doled out 25 tailor-made uniforms each to the First, Third, and Ninth Armies, and also to General Brereton's new First Allied Airborne Army. SHAEF headquarters wanted 800 uniforms, but the CQM could offer only 100. He explained that 9,000 jackets had arrived, and he was having matching trousers made up in France, Britain, and Eire. By the end of the month a few more were available and Brumbaugh, who had been instrumental in obtaining local procurement, was allowed to retain 40 uniforms for the United Kingdom Base. This was an exceptional concession, since General Lee had directed that, for the time being, the uniform be reserved for combat units at the front. Littlejohn controlled all distribution personally until the end of November. Then, with a prospect that some 15,000 uniforms would be available in December, he asked that Bradley himself settle the delicate matter of priorities for the 12th Army Group. The 6th Army Group had an independent source of supply via SOLOC, and received none. Early in 1945, the strict rule regarding matching trousers was relaxed, and by the end of February 385,000 ETO jackets had been transferred to the sales stores for officers.[26]

[26] (1) IRS, CQM to Deputy, Paris, 4 Oct 44, sub: Uniform Production; Ltrs, CQM to QM's First, Third, and Ninth Armies, to CofS First Allied Airborne Army, and to AG 6th Army Group, 5 Oct 44, sub: Supply of Wool Field Jackets; Ltr, CQM to G–4 SHAEF, 9 Oct 44, sub: Uniforms for Sale to Officers; Ltr, CQM to QM UKB, 26 Oct 44, sub: Issue of Field Uniforms. Littlejohn Reading File, vol. XXIX, items 6, 28, 29, 30, 31, 37, 38, 49, 121. (2) Ltr, CQM to G–4 12th Army Group, 5 Nov 44, no sub. Littlejohn Reading File, vol. XXX, item 14. (3) Garside Rpt, app. K.

The end of the fighting in Europe brought geographical changes in sales store operations, but few changes in procedures or problems. The flow of troops was reversed, and sales activities at all ports were increased to meet the needs of departing officers. Also, on 19 May, Littlejohn directed his deputy for operations to establish a sales store in Frankfurt to replace the one in Paris, which had been by far the most important on the Continent during the months of combat. Littlejohn pointed out that the Paris store had remained fixed, while the locations of the various base section headquarters and other concentration points had shifted continually. Now it seemed that Frankfurt was the only definite point of reference within the emerging U.S. Zone in Germany. It should have as large a stock as possible, especially cloth and findings for made-to-measure uniforms. But in August the Chief Quartermaster made a complaint that sounded very familiar. He said that the movement of sales stocks to the army of occupation had been far too slow. After three months, the supplies on hand in Germany—even in Frankfurt—were negligible, and the situation should be remedied immediately. By the end of the year sales stores were in operation in the Eastern and Western Military Districts, in the Bremen enclave, and in the U.S. Sector of Berlin. By that time the new dark shade olive drab trousers had arrived in sufficient quantities from the United States, and the field uniforms of officers and enlisted men were identical. Being on garrison duty, officers naturally demanded Class A uniforms, but these were still in short supply and available mainly as made-to-measure garments from German tailors.[27]

Uniforms for Nurses and Wacs

Early experience with uniforms for Army women in the ETO has already been described. Later developments generally reflected trends in clothing for enlisted men and officers. The service uniforms originally provided were considered as unsatisfactory as those for male personnel, and for much the same reasons. If anything, the female version of the M1943 field uniform encountered even more disapproval and resistance than its male counterpart. Since pile had proved too bulky, the women's M1943 outfit was provided with heavy wool liners for both jacket and trousers. Prevailing opinion in the ETO was that even with wool liners this uniform was still too bulky for normal field use. When the outer covers were removed, the liners made an unsightly and unnecessarily warm uniform for office wear. For the type of duty required of women in the ETO, where they spent little time out of doors but much in unheated offices and barracks, the feminine version of the ETO uniform, consisting of short jacket, slacks, and skirt, all of matching dark shade 33 olive drab serge, was considered ideal. The theater Chief Nurse and the senior WAC Director were enthusiastic, and the Chief Surgeon agreed with them. But unlike the ETO

uniform for men, which was approved in the zone of interior and shipped to the theater in rather limited quantities, that for women was disapproved *in toto* by the War Department in August 1944. On 7 September Littlejohn wrote to Cohen in the Procurement Division:

Dear Bob,

I just received from Doriot and Feldman about ten pages of baloney which, added up, means that this Theater will not be furnished with a new type field jacket for women.

It is my understanding that you can provide enough of the new type field uniforms for all components of the Army providing cloth is made available to you at an early date.[28]

The above quotation gives an exaggerated estimate of production capabilities in the ETO, but accurately reflects Littlejohn's intention—to fabricate all necessary uniforms for women locally, irrespective of approval or disapproval of the ETO design by zone of interior agencies.

In line with this policy the Chief Quartermaster told Cohen to develop a detailed procurement plan, which was submitted on 4 October. The most desirable material, 18-ounce dark olive drab serge, was in short supply and most of it would be required for male officers' trousers. But enough was on hand to make 1,500 sets (jacket, slacks, and skirt) for nurses and WAC officers, and 300 sets

---

[27] (1) IRS, CQM to Deputy Opns, 19 May 45, sub: Sales Store at U.S. Hq in Germany; Memo for Deputy Admin and QM Occupation Forces, 3 Aug 45, sub: Sales Store Program. Littlejohn Reading File, vol. XXXVI, item 48; vol. XXXIX, item 2. (2) *QM Supply in ETO*, V, 26. (3) Interv, Ross with Littlejohn, 12 Dec 59.

[28] (1) See ch. X, above. (2) Risch, *A Wardrobe for the Women of the Army*, QMC Historical Studies, 12, pp. 132, 134. (3) Quotation from Ltr, CQM to Cohen, 7 Sep 45, sub: Production of Field Uniform. Littlejohn Reading File, vol. XXVIII, item 45. (4) IRS, CQM to Chief Supply Div, 4 Nov 44, sub: Experimental Uniform for Nurses. Littlejohn Reading File, vol. XXX, item 3.

had already been completed in the United Kingdom. Enough 17-ounce material was available to make 6,000 similar women's uniforms, and these would be manufactured in Britain and Eire. The least desirable material was 22-ounce British battle dress cloth. There was enough for 12,000 women's uniforms, to be made up half in Great Britain and half in Eire. Manufacture of women's garrison caps was to be concentrated in France, where 6,000 17-ounce and 8,000 22-ounce caps were to be made. The program was promptly approved, and toward the end of the month, when Cohen was made Chief of the Sales Store Branch, Supply Division, in addition to his duties in the Procurement Division, two WAC officers, Lt. Eileen Dickson and Lt. Jennings, were assigned as assistants to administer the sales stores.[29]

Meanwhile, on 7 October Littlejohn had drafted a formal proposal for a change in the uniform of WAC enlisted women in the ETO. He advocated that the ETO uniform already being supplied to women officers become the service uniform for Wacs, and that issue of the M1943 field uniform for women be discontinued. This was neither the first nor the last such proposal, but was of interest since it was a complete staff study, submitted through channels with the concurrence of the theater WAC staff director, Lt. Col. Anna W. Wilson. The following changes in allowances were involved:[30]

		Proposed	T/E 21
Jacket, WAC, winter		1	2
Jacket, field, M1943, women's ..		0	1
Jacket, pile, women's		0	1
Jacket, field, wool, women's		2	0
Skirt, WAC, winter		1	3
Skirt, field, wool, winter		2	0
Trousers, field, wool, winter ...		2	0
Trousers, outer-cover		0	2
Trousers, wool liner		0	1
Cap, garrison, wool, WAC		0	2
Cap, garrison, wool, WAC (field)		2	0
Total		10	12

The main significance of the above proposal was that it advocated one service uniform for all women in the Army. It was approved and forwarded to the War Department, and Littlejohn wrote several letters to individuals in the OQMG, urging its approval by ASF. But like similar proposals regarding uniforms for women officers, it was turned down mainly because of severe shortages of the required dark shade olive drab serge. In December the War Department stated that a short jacket designed by the OQMG, in a light shade serge to match the WAC winter skirt, would ultimately become available. But meanwhile a few of the battle dress outfits tailored in Eire had been delivered, and Littlejohn directed that they be issued in January from Paris, in accordance with priorities set by the WAC staff director. Enlisted Wacs could be supplied from these sources because they were a minority among Army women in the ETO.[31]

[29] IRS, CQM to Deputy, Paris, 4 Oct 44, sub: Uniform Production; IRS, CQM to Chief Pers, 28 Oct 44, sub: Creation of Sales Store Branch. Littlejohn Reading File, vol. XXIX, items 6, 127.

[30] IRS, CQM to AG ETO through G–1 and G–4, 1 Nov 44, sub: Proposed Changes in Uniform of

Enlisted Women, ETO. Littlejohn Reading File, vol. XXX, item 1.

[31] (1) QM Supply in ETO, III, 93. (2) In February 1945 there were 6,267 enlisted Wacs in the ETO, 378 WAC officers, and about 19,700 nurses. Cf. Treadwell, The Women's Army Corps, p. 772. (3) See Table 11.

But local procurement had begun too late to supply either commissioned or enlisted women with a warm winter uniform. Since a majority had arrived overseas with the M1943 jacket, issue of the wool liner was one solution of the problem, though not a popular one. The OCQM requisitioned 29,000 liners for all women personnel in October, but by mid-December none had arrived. Women in the Army Air Forces suffered particularly, since many were assigned to night shifts in unheated buildings and underground operations centers. The situation was declared an emergency, and the issue of men's winter underwear was authorized until women's winter underwear and various other authorized winter garments for women, including the wool jacket liners, finally arrived. But the ETO uniform was much preferred to any of these items, and the OCQM managed to issue at least one to each WAC member before the end of the winter.[32]

The uniform of 22-ounce British cloth, which Colonel Cohen had considered the least desirable of the locally procured garments for women, found favor with the Army Nurse Corps. On 31 October the Chief Surgeon's Office requested from 5,000 to 8,000 British battle dress uniforms for women on an experimental basis, commenting that "The Medical Corps is not satisfied with the Field uniform presently provided for nurses."[33] Littlejohn promptly approved, stipulating that Wacs also be included in the experiment, that priority be given to individuals serving with combat ele-

ments, and that geographical priority be from front to rear. Two days later he wrote to Lt. Col. Ida W. Danielson, director of ETO Nursing Service, that every nurse on field duty would shortly receive a British Auxiliary Territorial Service (ATS) uniform. Since it was experimental, this would be a gratis issue. He also referred to Colonel Danielson's recent letter, which praised the comfort and smartness of the new ETO uniform, and the helpfulness shown by Colonel Cohen and Lieutenant Dickson in distributing it. The WAC officer had personally brought truckloads of uniforms, with tailors, into the First and Third Army areas, and had sold and fitted ETO uniforms to 300 nurses in the most advanced units. Littlejohn replied that he hoped to have an adequate number of the new field uniforms for all nurses and Wacs in the forward areas within the next sixty days. He further observed: "My personal view is that a good-looking woman in a bad-looking uniform results in a bad combination. I feel certain that you and I and the Director of the W. A. C. can do a lot to correct this . . . ."[34] Apparently there was a good deal of truth in the last sentence, for as nurses and Wacs returning from Europe began to bring ETO uniforms to the United States, it proved impossible to stem the tide of their popularity, and they were formally authorized for optional wear in the zone of interior, but not for issue, on 9 January 1945.[35]

---

[32] (1) *QM Supply in ETO*, III, 92. (2) Treadwell, *The Women's Army Corps*, p. 397.

[33] IRS, ExO OCS to CQM, 31 Oct 44, sub: Field Jackets, Wool, for ANC in Field. Littlejohn Reading File, vol. XXX, item 3.

[34] (1) *Ibid.*, Comment 2, CQM to Chief Supply Div, 4 Nov 44. (2) Ltr, Dir Nursing Sv to CQM, 25 Oct 44; Ltr, CQM to Dir Nursing Sv, 6 Nov 44. Littlejohn Reading File, vol. XXX, item 16.

[35] (1) Treadwell, *The Women's Army Corps*, p. 533. (2) Risch, *A Wardrobe for the Women of the Army*, p. 134.

Quantitatively, women's clothing was always a minor item in the ETO, and it was normally stored at a single depot. In the United Kingdom this was at Thatcham (G–45) and the first concentration point for women's items on the Continent was at Cherbourg. Experience in Normandy confirmed the wisdom of a single depot for women's clothing, for the stocks brought ashore at various points as part of the follow-up maintenance sets were quickly reduced to broken sizes that made stock control very difficult. Moreover, several different items were packed in one container, so every package had to be opened, exposing clothing to weather and to theft. This could only be corrected after all supplies had been brought into guarded storage under cover at Cherbourg. Shortly after this was accomplished, the entire stock was moved to Paris, where the initial prescribed mission was a sixty-day level for 3,500 women. Inadequate as it was, even this level was not quickly achieved. The distribution of women's items to all units in the theater, including those in the combat zone, was made directly from Depot Q–177 (Paris) by a mobile sales unit. This unit replenished stocks in the static sales store within each army Class II depot, and also sold clothing directly to women in the forward areas. This system was so successful that the CQM proposed a similar procedure to handle male officers' clothing in each army. The armies would each retain only one sales platoon, to run a static sales store, and COMZ would operate two more in each army area to distribute directly to the combat units and also to move clothing from the ports by organic transportation. But the 12th Army Group rejected the proposal, and only women's clothing was handled in this manner.[36]

Local procurement was still the main source of women's clothing in the spring of 1945. By March, the 6,000 uniforms of 22-ounce cloth ordered in Eire were completed, and since nurses were most in need of a heavy uniform, the entire quantity was turned over to them with the concurrence of the theater WAC staff director. Such agreement was possible because Colonel Cohen's local procurement program was finally beginning to deliver adequate quantities of uniforms in standard dark serge, and a monthly allocation could be made to both Wacs and nurses. But one result of this increased production had a most unfortunate effect upon the morale of Army women, especially enlisted Wacs. Since ample quantities of the ETO uniform were now in sight, it was decided that it would be made available to U.S. civilian women employees, who were now beginning to arrive in the theater. Although the civilians were to wear the uniform with distinctive insignia, Wacs still felt that this policy accorded to civilians an unearned distinction that should have been reserved for those who had gained it through military service.[37]

---

[36] (1) *QM Supply in ETO*, III, 95–96. (2) Memo, Chief Pers for CQM, 28 Dec 44, sub: Over-all Allocation of QM Units to Maj Comds. Littlejohn Reading File, vol. XXXI, item 102.

[37] (1) Memos, CQM for Chief Supply Div, 18 Mar 45, sub: Garments for Wacs and ANC; 19 Mar sub: Distr of Garments Now in Production; 19 Mar sub: Field Uniforms for Nurses and Wacs; 19 Mar, sub: Monthly Allotment of Field Uniforms to ANC and WAC. Littlejohn Reading File, vol. XXXIV, items 46, 55, 56, 57. (2) Treadwell, *The Women's Army Corps*, p. 401.

Clothing for Allies and Dependent Groups

The QMC was less responsible to Allies and dependent groups for clothing and equipment than for food. In theory, its Class II and IV obligation to displaced persons was confined to the equipping of assembly centers and the warehousing of civil affairs clothing to be distributed by G–5. In practice, G–5 reserves were far from adequate, and the OCQM had to provide very considerable quantities of military supplies, including Class X and Class B clothing, and even some serge service coats. In crowded refugee camps such uniforms quickly developed an unsightly appearance, which had a most unfortunate effect upon the morale of U.S. troops wearing the same uniform. On 15 April 1945 a theater directive placed such issues under the direct control of General Lee, who was required to approve each issue and maintain accurate records of such supplies.[38] In the period immediately after V–E Day, the ETO wool jacket was the only distinctive garment issued solely to U.S. troops, a fact that goes far to explain the extraordinary efforts made to distribute it to American units.

Initial issues for French regular military forces were provided by the British Commonwealth—principally by the Canadians. As long as these forces were under U.S. command, subsequent replacement issues were made—or at least attempted—by the Americans. Support for French paramilitary units, which were not officially recognized by SHAEF, was a different and nearly insoluble problem. In October 1944, for example, when everyone on the Western Front was seeking winter clothing, calls were also placed on American supply sources to equip the troops of the French Forces of the Interior (FFI) fighting with the 94th Infantry Division in the south of Brittany. These bands of irregulars were occasionally integrated with American troops on the front line, and were particularly useful for reconnaissance and patrol missions. Maj. Gen. Harry J. Malony, commanding the 94th Division, strongly urged the theater commander to approve the issue of winter clothing to these French units lest the cold weather force them back to their homes, leaving gaps in the line that he could not fill effectively. Realizing that American clothing was scarce, and that captured German supplies were not sufficiently available, Malony was even willing to take impregnated protective clothing so long as it was suitable to provide body warmth.[39]

Clothing and Equipment for Prisoners of War

Plans made before D-day were based on capturing 120,000 prisoners during

---

[38] (1) See discussion of QM support for G–5 in ch. XII, above. (2) *QM Supply in ETO*, IX, 20–25, 107. (3) Ltr, CG ETOUSA to CG's USSTAF, Each Army Group, Each Army, COMZ, etc., 15 Apr 45, sub: Responsibility and Procedures for Supply of QM Items to Agencies and Pers Other Than U.S. Army. AG 400/1 OpGD. Reprinted in OTCOM TSFET Operational Study 8. (4) OTCOM TSFET Operational Study 12, pp. 3–5. (5) USFET Gen Bd Study 109, p. 68.

[39] (1) Vigneras, *Rearming the French*, p. 356. (2) *QM Supply in ETO*, IX, 55. (3) Ltr, CG 94th Div to CG ETO, 2 Oct 44, sub: Issue of Protective Clothing to FFI. Hist Br OQMG. (4) See ch. VII, above.

the first three months of combat on the Continent. All were to be evacuated to the United Kingdom, and eventually a considerable number to the United States. The maximum responsibility of U.S. forces at any one time was estimated at 30,000 prisoners, a number that could easily be supplied with captured or salvaged items. The first month of combat appeared to confirm these estimates, and, moreover, apart from underwear and toilet articles, the first prisoners captured were adequately equipped. But late in August, SHAEF directed that all POW's who were physically fit and appeared to be co-operative be retained on the Continent as laborers. At that time there were already 170,000 in POW enclosures on the Continent. Their number was increasing daily, while the expected flow of captured equipment from the combat troops into COMZ depots did not materialize. It was understandable that the armies should retain captured matériel to meet their own needs, but the necessity of guarding and rationing such supplies was only gradually realized, and, meanwhile, looting and poor controls made for the dissipation of captured stocks. The gradual correction of this situation is narrated in a subsequent chapter.[40]

With the increasing numbers of captured troops and the early onset of winter, prisoner of war enclosures needed blankets, mess gear, and tentage. Salvage depots in the United Kingdom held ample quantities of such items, but they had not yet been sorted. Moreover, cross-Channel transportation was scarce, and stringently rationed. Since winter clothing for the American troops was also scarce at the time, continental salvage inventories were low because of the soldiers' reluctance to turn in items that could not be replaced. Loire Section enclosures were able to obtain small quantities of equipment from Seine Section, but never enough to escape the charge of "unsanitary conditions . . . on account of the lack of proper equipment." [41]

By October, Littlejohn was reluctantly calling on the zone of interior for help. A sudden call from SHAEF to supply 400,000 prisoners and some 200,000 displaced persons had come as "a blow between the eyes," and he was prepared to procure comforters, underwear, nonstandard mess gear, and overcoats wherever he could find them. By late December the basis of requirements had increased to 1,100,000 persons, and the Chief Quartermaster reported that ETO stocks hardly met 50 percent of his needs, with specific shortages existing in drawers, towels, shoes, socks, and mess gear. The OQMG canvassed depots in the zone of interior for usable salvaged clothing, but only 10 percent of the amounts requisitioned could be located. The inadequacy of these quantities was pain-

---

[40] (1) QM Supply in ETO, IX, 65. (2) DA Pamphlet 20–213, Lt. Col. George G. Lewis and Capt. John Mewha, History of Prisoner of War Utilization by the United States Army, 1776–1945 (Washington, 1955), p. 219. (3) Memo, Chief Supply Div for DCQM, 21 Aug 44, sub: Outline of Plan of Supply POW Labor Groups; Memo, Chief Supply Div for DCQM, 21 Aug 44, sub: Drain on Stocks; Memo, Chief Supply Div for DCQM, 23 Aug 44, sub: Proposed Plan for Control of Captured Class II and IV Supplies. All in Hist Br OQMG. (4) See discussion of captured enemy matériel in ch. XX, below.

[41] Ltr, QM Loire Sec to CQM, 15 Sep 44, sub: POW Supplies. Hist Br OQMG.

fully evident by V–E Day, when U.S. responsibility for German POW's alone had swelled to a total of 2,835,000.[42]

In the interests of economy, action was taken to make prisoners somewhat self-sustaining by equipping at least one camp per base section with captured sewing machines, findings, shoe lasts, salvaged rubber, and tent repair kits, all of which would enable them to make their own repairs to clothing, shoes, and tentage. Although the OQMG was unable to provide clothing for prisoners, there was a possibility during February 1945 that cloth surplus to the needs of the Foreign Economic Administration could be made available. Accordingly the OCQM instructed Q–256, the great salvage depot with headquarters at Reims, to open a prisoner of war clothing factory. Personnel of Q–256 and of the POW and Captured Enemy Materiel Branch, Installations Division, OCQM, jointly surveyed possible sites, and decided to locate the factory at Aachen. Plans were made for a very large installation, to be supervised by a composite battalion headquarters, two composite company headquarters, and a service company. More than 5,000 prisoners were to be assigned, including interpreters, foremen, tailors, garment inspec-

GERMAN PRISONERS *at Rheims repairing captured clothing. January 1945.*

tors, cutters, cobblers, and sewing machine mechanics.[43] Before the project actually went into production in an old umbrella factory, numerous obstacles arose to plague the participants. Satisfactory rehabilitation of the plant required recruiting of electricians and plumbers, importing of cutting machines and cutting tables from Belgium, reconstruction of the center section of the plant, deactivation of numerous booby traps, and removal of rubble, which

---

[42] (1) Ltr, CQM to TQMG, 15 Oct 44, no sub. Littlejohn Reading File, vol. XXIX, item 79. (2) *QM Supply in ETO,* IX, 141. (3) Memo, Chief Opns Br Mil Plng Div for Chiefs S&D Div, Proc Div, Mil Plng Div, 17 Jan 45, sub: Reqmts for Repatriates and POW's in the ETO; Memo S&D Div for Mil Plng Div, 13 Feb 45, sub: Clothing for Hostile and Allied POW's. Both in OQMG 400.354 ETO. (4) Ltr, DCQM ETO to TQMG, 23 Jan 45, sub: Clothing for Hostile and Allied POW's. Reprinted in OTCQM TSFET Operational Study 8, exhibits A, D.

[43] (1) Ltr, Asst CQM to QM CBS, 29 Nov 44, sub: Plan for Handling POW Repairs. Hist Br OQMG. (2) Ltr, Hq Q–256 to CG Oise Sec, 22 Feb 45, sub: Pers for POW Clothing Factory at Aachen. USFET QM 323.3 WBS.

reached second story windows. Unfortunately the promised cloth from the United States was required by UNRRA and could not be made available, but plans were made to use locally procured cloth, and to operate the factory on a reduced scale.[44] The clothing factory was in production by 31 March, and early in April a thousand garments were coming off the line daily. During the next two months, almost 100,000 garments were made of a German material known as *feldgrau,* but with the end of the war and the drawing of occupation zone boundaries, Aachen found itself in the British area, and the factory had to be moved to Bamberg.[45]

As the only COMZ echelons permitted to follow the armies into Germany, ADSEC and CONAD became the chief custodians of the flood of prisoners collected in enclosures along the Rhine. In April, particularly after the collapse of the Ruhr pocket, First Army alone bagged half a million prisoners, more than 50 percent of its total for the entire continental campaign. Their evacuation to enclosures west of the Rhine put a heavy strain on Quartermaster truck units, and their supply similarly taxed the ingenuity of Quartermaster personnel.[46] ADSEC by this time was fully aware that normal requisitioning methods would not promptly bring the re-

quired matériel and that captured stocks could not be expected from army sources without special pleading, and then only in token quantities. Therefore, the initiative was taken by diverting three salvage collecting companies from their regular tasks and assigning them to pursue every clue to the whereabouts of captured equipment. A high priority was given to the truck transportation needed to bring these stocks to three central prisoner of war supply points at Rheinberg, Sinzig, and Bingen.

The sudden importance of this responsibility in the spring of 1945 was reflected by the establishment of a prisoner of war division within the office of the ADSEC quartermaster that acted as the agency for the requisitioning and distribution of supplies for captured troops in the area. By V–E Day, ADSEC's quartermaster was preparing to relinquish these supply points to the British, who were assuming control of the Rhine provinces. The prisoner population in ADSEC alone now approached 800,000, crowded into a dozen enclosures which were little more than densely inhabited open fields guarded by personnel from the 106th Infantry Division and operated by Quartermaster battalions under the supervision of the 56th QM Base Depot. Barely 20 percent of the prisoners were under shelter and there were no hospital tents for the sick. Summarizing his situation to Littlejohn, Colonel Smithers of ADSEC wrote:

Aside from the 750 tons received from Fifteenth Army, no subsistence has been received nor do I expect any. What desirable Class II and IV we have received has been entirely at the sufferance of the Armies, upon personal appeal and has been insignificant in relation to the demands which are being put upon us by the influx of prisoners of

---

[44] (1) *QM Supply in ETO,* IX, 71. (2) OTCQM TSFET Operational Study 8, exhibit C–5.

[45] *QM Supply in ETO,* IX, 70–71. *Feldgrau* (field gray) was actually the color designation of the German uniform. By early 1945 this meant a blended cloth composed of varying proportions of fine wool, crossbred wool, waste sweepings, shoddy, and wood pulp fiber.

[46] *FUSA Rpt of Opns,* 22 Feb 45–8 May 45, III, 159–162. See also TUSA AAR, II, PM 28; and *CONAD History* I, 266–71.

war. We have taken every means at our command to increase these amounts, but with negligible results.[47]

CONAD's responsibility, some 230,000 prisoners concentrated in the Heilbronn-Ludwigshafen area, was more modest but also more permanent, since those cities were in the American zone of occupation. The termination of hostilities of course did not spell the solution of this problem, nor did it even cause an immediate drop in the numbers to be cared for. A partial solution lay in the release of prisoners who could be transferred to fill the demands for labor by other governments, or cleared to return to their homes. Such action was accelerated after ADSEC and CONAD were deactivated in July, and the armies had to assume all occupation functions.

Strength Forecasts

The greatest difficulty for the QMC in supplying prisoners of war, displaced persons, and repatriates was caused by uncertainty as to the numbers who would have to be supplied. While no long-range forecast subject to the fortunes of war could be more than an approximation, the OCQM was convinced that this important subject deserved more care and forethought than it was receiving in higher headquarters. As already described, the OCQM submitted its own personnel forecast *(See Table 11.)*, which was finally accepted by COMZ for lack of better information, but meanwhile delays had severely impaired the effectiveness of requisitions. Specific Quar-

termaster responsibilities for Class II and IV supply to foreign nationals were determined by higher headquarters, and were only indirectly influenced by the number of persons in each category actually present in the ETO. For example, only those French troops actually under U.S. command at any given time were a Quartermaster responsibility. The classification of recovered Russian personnel as Allied prisoners rather than displaced persons, an unexpected result of the Yalta Conference, added considerably to demands for QM supplies. On 15 May 1945, the OCQM was responsible for supplying 7,341,381 persons with Class II and IV items that ranged from clothing and mess gear to soap, toothpaste, and tobacco. The number of persons in each category, and their daily allowances of Class II and IV supplies, were as follows:[48]

Category	Strength	Class II and IV (lbs. per day)
U.S. military and others in Category 1	3,181,588	1.69
Hospital patients (all)	169,277	.6864
French military including Moslems	355,551	1.7842
Recovered Allied military personnel (including (Russians)	725,716	.6157
POW's (excluding hospital patients)	2,835,425	.488
Mobile civilian employees	31,837	.2224
Italian and Slav units	41,987	1.0569

Tentage

The Quartermaster Class II and IV supply plan for OVERLORD made no pro-

[47] (1) Personal Ltr, Smithers to Littlejohn, 27 Apr 45. Hist Br OQMG. (2) Hist of QM Sec ADSEC, pp. 36–37.

[48] (1) OTCQM TSFET Operational Study 8, exhibits A and C–8. (2) QM Supply in ETO, IX, 46, 63. (3) USFET Gen Bd Study 109, p. 67.

TABLE 21—ETO TENTAGE REQUIREMENTS, ALLOCATIONS, AND RECEIPTS

Description	21 May 44 Requirement D Day– D+240	14 Jun 44 Requirement 1 Sep 44– 31 Dec 44	6 Aug 44 Requirement 1 Aug 44– 31 Jan 45	Shipped 1 Jan 44– 30 Jun 44	Allocation 1 Jul 44– 31 Dec 44	Shipped in Convoys Jan 1945
Fly, tent, wall, large.............	......	......	....	......	6,738	......
Fly, tent, wall, small............	......	......	bc(114,908)	......	......	......
Paulin, large...................	20,962	37,458	d169,412	48,228	71,811	25,388
Paulin, small...................	28,350	......	c(30,351)	......	11,435	......
Screen, latrinea................	......	16,607	3,567	20,027	9,398	3,567
Tent assemblya.................	1,770	1,448	1,250	529	0	......
Tent, command posta...........	......	6,029	(2,024)	8,675	2,262	......
Tent, hospital, warda..........	8,694	......	24,042	14,857	9,520	6,965
Tent, maintenance, sheltera.....	......	......	788	796	805	......
Tent, pyramidala...............	123,648	......	(e)	154,557	(e)	......
Tent, squada...................	......	112,449	f271,468	34,226	73,737	28,480
Tent, storagea..................	27,421	......	(e)	1,726	(e)	......
Tent, surgical-operating, truck..	......	......	....	......	86	......
Tent, wall, largea..............	6,692	......	(e)	886	20	......
Tent, wall, smalla.............	5,116	9,607	g(77,545)	......	107,393	72,720

a Complete with poles and pins.
b ( ) represent excess items.
c These excesses applied against (d).
d Net requirement after subtracting (c) excesses.

e Squad tents substituted for these items.
f These excesses applied against (g).
g Net requirement after subtracting (f) excesses.

Sources: QM Supply in ETO, V, pp. 67–69, 125–28; Memo, TQMG to CQM, 12 Oct 44. Hist Br, OQMG; Cbl SPTAA–40412, 3 Jan 45 NYPE to COMZ ETO; Memo Opns Br, Mil Plan Div OQMG to Rqmts Br, 4 Nov 44, sub: Status of CY 1944 Tentage for ETO. OQMG 421.4 ETO.

vision for tentage in excess of T/E allowances prior to D plus 45. By D plus 240, a phased transition of all camps and depots from canvas-covered structures to huts and buildings made of wood and metals was to be completed. An OCQM estimate dated 21 May 1944 stated that by 1 February 1945, tentage would be required for 1,686,000 of the 2,500,000 men expected on the Continent, but assets were thought to be more than sufficient. About 500,000 would be housed in buildings constructed or rehabilitated by the Engineers, tentage for 1,225,000 would be brought over from the United Kingdom as that vast staging area was closed down, while tentage for another 200,000 men was on requisition. Tarpaulins for 14,000,000 square feet of open storage were either on hand or had

been requisitioned.[49] (Table 21)

Very shortly thereafter information was received that squad tents were becoming available as a standard replacement of pyramidal, storage, hospital ward, and large wall tents. Taking advantage of this very desirable simplification, the OCQM also made minor adjustments in its requirements, and submitted Requisition H–7, for the last four months of 1944, on 14 June. But this requisition was submitted too late to affect deliveries. By the end of June the theater's current requirements had been very nearly filled in terms of older models of tentage. This proved to be fortunate, since production of the new

---

[49] (1) ETOUSA COMZ SOP No. 5, April 1944. (2) QM Supply in ETO, V, 64–65.

squad tents did not materialize according to schedule.[50]

By late July, when the troops were securely lodged on the Continent, there were strong indications that these earlier estimates had been too optimistic, and that tentage and tarpaulins for both personnel and storage would be needed in much larger quantities. Tentage was being retained in the United Kingdom because storage activities were not phased out on schedule, and because combat troops were held there longer than expected. Moreover, the British found that they were unable to meet their commitments to provide additional permanent housing after D-day because civilians could not return to locations retained as training and embarkation areas. Meanwhile, delays in the rehabilitation of Cherbourg prevented the importation of materials needed by the engineers to construct housing and storage. July was also the month of some of the heaviest Allied aerial bombardments of the war, which concentrated on logistical as well as tactical targets and caused even more damage than the attacks designed to isolate the lodgment area. The purpose of these attacks was to assist a breakout by the field forces, which would lead to mobile warfare and still greater demands for tentage as permanent billets were left behind. Littlejohn summarized all these facts for The Quartermaster General and warned him that "the QMC must be prepared to house substantial numbers, if not all, of the American troops on the European Continent," and to supply tarpaulin for more than 61,000,000 square feet of open storage. He promised to submit revised tentage requirements as soon as he had consulted with General Feldman, who was then in the ETO. The formal requisition, J–69, was forwarded on 6 August.[51]

But Feldman brought rather alarming news. Canvas and cotton duck production was just being resumed after the sharp cutbacks of 1943. He estimated that the whole of U.S. current production was only adequate to produce 47 percent of ETO tentage requirements. Littlejohn wrote to the ETO Chief Engineer on 31 July, hoping that substitute storage space could be provided. Maj. Gen. Cecil R. Moore's reply four days later brought little comfort: "I am most concerned over the question of tentage and feel that our requirements are a minimum. . . . Hutting is in short supply and . . . does not afford a satisfactory answer for our mobile armies on the Continent." Littlejohn forwarded this reply to Feldman, by then returned to Washington, and received back the comment: "I wish to point out that the duck situation is still very serious. Therefore the Engineers must be *required to produce*." [52]

---

[50] (1) Memo, Chief Opns Br Mil Plng Div OQMG for Chief Reqmts Br, 4 Nov 44, sub: Status of Calendar Year 1944 Tentage for ETO. OQMG 424.1 ETO. (2) Risch, *The Quartermaster Corps: Organization, Supply, and Services*, I, 168–69. (3) Ltr, CQM ETO to CG NYPE, 14 Jun 44, sub: Requisition 3400–QM–II–H7. ASF File, Tentage.

[51] (1) Ltr, CQM to TQMG, 12 Jul 44, sub: Heavy Tentage for ETO. Littlejohn Reading File, vol. XXVI, item 54. (2) Memo, CQM for Feldman, 28 Jul 44, sub: Tentage. OQMG 400 ETO. (3) *QM Supply in ETO*, V, 128. (4) Table 51, Column 4.

[52] (1) Memo, CQM for CE ETO, 31 Jul 44, sub: Tentage for Housing and Storage; Memo, CE for CQM, 4 Aug 44, same sub; Personal Ltr, Feldman to Littlejohn, 16 Aug 44 [underlining as in original]. Littlejohn Reading File, vol. XXVIA, item 127; vol. XXVII, items 28, 134. (2) Col R. T. Stevens and R. A. Butland, The QMC Duck and Webbing Pool (OQMG, 1950), p. 39, and Supplement, pp. 2–3. Hist Br OQMG.

This was clearly wishful thinking in the early stages of a mobile campaign, when Engineer Corps responsibilities and difficulties were even greater than the Quartermaster's. At Gregory's suggestion, General Somervell inquired whether the tentage requisition was absolutely essential. Littlejohn's answer dated 26 August was emphatic: "Only a cessation of hostilities or building of hutments will reduce these requirements," and two days later, in a personal letter to Feldman, the CQM brought up for the first time the possibility of local procurement of duck on the Continent. This was a momentous proposal, which if adopted would require taking over most of the French cotton textile industry. No doubt it was a response to Feldman's discouraging report from the zone of interior. On 11 August the DQMG had written: "No change in the situation as I outlined it. . . . Upon my return, a meeting was held with WPB, the producers of duck and webbing yarn, and ASF . . . to emphasize that the war was far from over, and that requisitions for tentage would be increased rather than decreased." Littlejohn wrote to Feldman on 28 August: "Every paulin I have is being yelled for from three or four places," and on 14 September he warned Brumbaugh in England: "We cannot afford to scrap a blanket or a tent of any kind."[53]

No formal answer to Requisition J–69 was received until 13 October, when the OCQM was informed that its allocation would be about 25 percent of the amount required. Littlejohn prepared an official letter to General Somervell requesting substitute nonstandard or salvaged tents, since requirements for housing prisoners of war and repatriated Allied prisoners were running far beyond any original estimate. The armies were still planning to house all combat troops under canvas for the winter, and also to use paulins rather than warehouses in their service areas. In view of the serious shortage of tents, billeting appeared to be the only solution. Billeting of troops in Germany was definitely contrary to current antifraternization policies. Moreover, destruction of German cities appeared to be so great that displaced persons would occupy most of the available housing. The G–5 sections of the armies expected that billeting troops with families in Allied territory might create problems and therefore approached the matter with hesitation. Civil Affairs policy guidelines were generally interpreted as forbidding such a procedure. Third Army, operating entirely on French soil, came to an agreement with the *SAFA* organization late in October 1944. First Army, with its front line largely in Germany, had an entirely different problem, but nevertheless began to make similar arrangements with Belgium, the Netherlands, and Luxembourg during November.[54] In practice it was

---

[53] Personal Ltr, Feldman to Littlejohn, 11 Aug 44; Memo, CQM to Somervell, 26 Aug 44, sub: Answers to Questions Submitted by TQMG; Personal Ltr, Littlejohn to Feldman, 28 Aug 44. Littlejohn Reading File, vol. XXVII, items 48, 129, 150. Personal Ltr, Littlejohn to Brumbaugh, 14 Sep 44. Littlejohn Reading File, vol. XXVIII, item 92.

[54] (1) Ltr, AG COMZ to CG ASF, 24 Oct 44, sub: Tentage. ETO 424 Q–S. (2) 12th Army Group Rpt of Opns, XII, 97. (3) Memo for Record, OQM 12th Army Group, 28 Sep 44; TWX Conf, OCQM and NYPE, 12 Oct 44. Littlejohn Collection. (4) Ltr, Maj W. H. McLean to Doriot, 27 Oct 44, no sub. OQMG 319.25 ETO. (5) Ltr, DCQM to TQMG, 12 Dec 44, sub: Substitute Paulin Material. OOMG 424.1, ETO. (6) TUSA AAR, II G–5, 14. (7) *FUSA Rpt of Opns*, 1 Aug 44–22 Feb 45, an. 3, p. 185.

found that Europeans do not share the traditional American repugnance toward billeting, and that whatever civilian housing was needed by the troops would be made available without difficulty.

Partially resigned to the improbability of obtaining tentage in the amounts requisitioned, the CQM in early December called upon G–4 for a revised policy statement on the billeting of troops in Germany. Even with prospects of obtaining knock-down hutments from Switzerland and the zone of interior, he estimated that 90 percent of the troops would require tentage, that available and prospective supplies would at best serve 1,500,000 troops by March, and that 750,000 troops would still lack adequate housing. Shortly after the elimination of the Bulge, shipments of tentage from the zone of interior were resumed, although still in quantities less than even those of the October allocation. Front line troops, at the same time, also used existing buildings and the basements of demolished structures, and found them preferable to living under canvas. Such use of existing facilities became the typical procedure and by V–E Day it was noted that tentage was required for only 50 percent of the continental troops, and that supplies were ample.[55]

Materials-Handling Equipment

Except for the heavy-duty equipment used at ports, materials-handling equip-ment in the ETO was a Quartermaster Class IV category of supply. The various technical services computed their own requirements, and after review by G–4 submitted them to the OCQM for requisitioning, either locally or in the United States. This was largely a mechanical function since the OCQM did not edit such requisitions, and materials-handling equipment was not a prominent subject in Quartermaster correspondence. On the other hand, the General Purchasing Agent was actively interested, especially in roller conveyors, since large numbers were purchased both in the United Kingdom and later on the Continent. Small ball or roller bearings were the most critical component of such conveyors, and since the British bearing industry was overloaded with orders for armament, some 54,000,000 bearings to meet combined requirements were imported from the United States in 1943. Nevertheless, conveyors were always in short supply in the ETO. In March 1945 Colonel Smithers reported that his two QM base depots in ADSEC had only 1,714 ten-foot sections. Since they were now operating railheads and transfer points within Germany, where the use of POW's was forbidden by theater policy, conveyors were especially desired as a labor-saving device. The G–4, COMZ, was unable to fill requisitions. ADSEC could use another 5,000 sections if they were made available from other QM installations.[56]

---

[55] (1) Memo, CQM for G–4, COMZ, 5 Dec 44, sub: Proposed Housing Plan for . . . Troops on Continent; Memo for Record, OQM Hq 12th Army Group, 28 Sep 44. Both in Hist Br OQMG. (2) Memo for Record, OQM and Opns ASF for Actg Dir Plans and Opns ASF, 25 Dec 44, sub: Tentage. OQMG 424.1 ETO. (3) Memo, Dir Plng Div ASF for Dir Plans and Opns ASF, 16 Jan 45. OQMG 421 ETO. (4) 12th Army Group Rpt of Opns, XII, 205. (5) *FUSA Rpt of Opns*, 1 Aug 44–22 Feb 45, IV, 70.

[56] (1) Littlejohn, ed., Passing in Review, ch. 41, pt. I, pp. 61–64. (2) Ltr, QM ADSEC to CQM, 22 Mar 45, sub: Roller Conveyors. Littlejohn Reading File, vol. XXXIV, item 74.

The requirements of the ETO Quartermaster Service as a whole for such equipment varied widely from depot to depot, according to the type of supplies in which that particular depot specialized, the general layout of the installation, and the amount of daily traffic. Receipts and issues by barge, by rail, and by truck each demanded somewhat different types of equipment. Nevertheless, a rough average was ascertained by surveying the performance and the requirements of the following five major QM depots: Q–177, Paris; Q–178, Verdun; Q–180, Reims; Q–181, Le Havre; and Q–183, Charleroi. On 30 April 1945 these depots each had an average storage capacity of 180,000 long tons of supplies, about two-thirds being open storage. The average of closed storage was 580,000 square feet, and the average tonnage handled per day, in and out included, was 5,500 long tons. All classes of QM supply and every type of COMZ depot operation were represented. Average requirements for equipment were as follows:

Item	Per Daily Movement (long tons)
1 section, gravity conveyor, straight ..	5
1 section, curved	314
1 crane, mobile, 5-ton or under	5,000
1 forklift, truck, 3-ton or under	353
1 tractor, warehouse	184
1 trailer, warehouse	24
1 truck, hand, 4-wheel	45
1 truck, hand, 2-wheel	24

In submitting these figures, the Chief Quartermaster emphasized that they were only suitable for the roughest kind of preliminary calculations. There were no standard methods of calculating requirements for such equipment, and the recommended method was to determine the needs of each depot individually, after deciding on its mission and location.[57]

Local Procurement

Procurement in the United Kingdom

Contrary to expectations, British production in 1944 was almost as high as in previous years, and the local procurement program already described was successfully continued after D-day. Although some commitments, notably for officers' uniforms and wool socks, had not been completed by the end of the year, the amounts delivered were very large and included winter items badly needed by American troops.[58]

Detailed information on procurement in 1945 is not available. Class II supplies delivered during the period January–June 1945 were 5,438 long tons compared to 11,127 tons for the whole of 1944. Shortly after V–E Day, procurement in Britain was removed from the control of the OCQM and became an autonomous activity of the United Kingdom Base. As a further result of the end of hostilities, contracts for a total of 1,529

---

[57] OTCQM TSFET Operational Study 2, p. 47.

[58] (1) See discussion of local procurement in ch. X, above. (2) Littlejohn, ed., Passing in Review, ch. 41, pt. I, p. 121. (3) The following are representative deliveries from the U.K. during 1944:

Blankets	323,045
Caps, wool knit	450,000
Drawers, wool	1,900,000
Gloves, wool knit (pairs)	743,960
Jackets, field, wool OD	309,479
Socks, wool, heavy (pairs)	4,203,800
Trousers, field, wool OD	418,236
Trousers, officers', dark OD	49,562

long tons of Class II supplies had been canceled by 30 June 1945.[59]

Field Procurement on the Continent

From D-day to the end of 1944, most of the supplies actually delivered to the U.S. Army from continental sources resulted from field procurement, either purchased "off the shelf" or manufactured from raw materials locally available. Needless to say, only very limited quantities were available, but under the emergency of combat requirements and the additional handicap of a bottleneck in port capacity, whatever could be obtained from such sources was tremendously valuable. Examples were 17,900 stoves suitable for heating tents, purchased in France in October, and 26,400 knives and 60,000 spoons, located in Belgium a month later.[60]

A major instance of spot procurement was provided by the emergency need for snow camouflage garments, beginning in November 1944. French stocks of white cloth were meager, but practically all of them were made available on operational priorities, either through high-level agencies such as the general purchasing agent, or by direct purchases of QM procurement officers in the base sections or attached to armies. Some 60,000 square yards were also imported from the United Kingdom, but Belgium was the chief source of white cloth. ADSEC purchased nearly 520,000 square yards, paying the equivalent of $250,000 in Belgian

currency. The cloth was transferred direct to the armies.[61]

First Army concentrated its production in the hands of the 602d Engineer Camouflage Battalion, which maintained a factory system in Belgium and provided 88,000 white garments of various types. Third Army purchased 800,000 square meters of cloth in Belgium, and made contracts with three French firms to manufacture camouflage clothing. Moreover, two of its subordinate corps made similar contracts, and in addition military units, notably the 13th Chemical Maintenance Company and the 300th QM Salvage Repair Company, made quantities of such garments. In Ninth Army, Military Government personnel mounted public-address systems on trucks, and then drove through German towns in their area, demanding white cloth from civilians. This direct-requisition procedure gathered in 41,500 bed sheets, and Ninth Army also purchased 32,000 linear feet of cotton cloth in Belgium. Five factories, two in the Netherlands and three in Germany, produced 70,000 snow suits for Ninth Army. The 255th QM Battalion obtained 250,000 meters of cloth for Seventh Army at Épinal, but in general such functions were performed for SOLOC by the higher level agencies in the Communications Zone. The total number of snow camouflage garments manufactured was reported by the general purchasing agent as 131,125, but the operations of individual units and agencies enumerated above seem to indicate that this figure was far too low.[62]

---

[59] QM Procurement on the Continent, January–June 1945, p. 32. MS Hist in QM ETO Lend-Lease Records.

[60] (1) Littlejohn, ed., Passing in Review, ch. 41, pt. II, pp. 32–35. (2) Field procurement as defined in the ETO is described in ch. XII, above.

---

[61] (1) *QM Supply in ETO*, III, 31. (2) Hist. QM ADSEC, p. 35.

[62] Royce Thompson, Local Procurement in the ETO, D-day to V-E Day. MS in OCMH.

Long-Range Procurement on the Continent

The organization for long-range headquarters procurement, the broad policies involved in such a program, and the raw materials import project have already been described. The armies liberated the industrial regions of northern France and Belgium, where such operations might be undertaken, in August 1944, just as Littlejohn was becoming aware of production difficulties in the United States. During the next month, French and Belgian textile trade associations, working with Colonel Barber, conducted a survey of continental productive capacity, and on 3 October Littlejohn included 3,000,000 yards of olive drab serge on Requisition K–94, his emergency request for winter clothing. This was in addition to 1,500,000 yards already requisitioned. It was primarily needed to manufacture locally 800,000 ETO-type wool jackets and an equal number of wool trousers which, it now appeared, would not be produced on time in the zone of interior.

The cloth requisition was viewed with disapproval by the OQMG for several reasons. Littlejohn realized that it would be many months before any deliveries were realized from newly initiated procurement in recently liberated areas, and accordingly refused to cancel any requisitions on the United States for finished items until locally manufactured goods actually began to appear. But this meant that for many months he would be receiving both cloth and finished garments, which the OQMG considered wasteful and unnecessary. Indeed the whole ETO procurement program was considered unnecessary, and a

reflection upon the abilities of the OQMG. The first reaction was that this latest requisition for cloth could not be filled until June 1945, and that deliveries on earlier requests would carry over into the new year. This was one of the problems discussed in General Gregory's brochure of 5 January 1945 for General Somervell. In general, Somervell overruled Gregory, directing that cloth be provided insofar as available, and that the necessary procurement experts be sent to the ETO.[63]

After considerable delay, on 6 December 1944 an agreement was reached with the French Government regarding procurement of clothing. The French agreed to manufacture 2,500,000 sets of wool uniforms comprising trousers, jacket, and garrison cap, and 100,000 sets of women's garments consisting of slacks, skirt, jacket, and cap. This was an agreement in principle only, involving governments and not manufacturers, and subject to deliveries of cloth from the United States. It would have required over nine million yards of cloth, but on 9 December the War Department cabled that 1,525,250 yards had already been either approved or shipped, and that the ETO would not receive any more cloth during 1945. Early in January 1945 The Quartermaster General was able to offer the ETO an additional 250,000 yards per

---

[63] (1) See discussion of procurement organization in ch. XII, above. (2) Personal Ltr, Littlejohn to Feldman, 28 Aug 44. Littlejohn Reading File, vol. XXVII, item 150. (3) Personal Ltrs, CQM to TQMG, 20 Sep 44, and TQMG to CQM, 28 Sep 44. Littlejohn Reading File, vol. XXVIII, items 149, 202. (4) Personal Ltrs, CQM to TQMG, 18, 25 Dec 44, 13 Jan 45; Personal Ltrs, TQMG to CQM, 13, 26 Dec 44, 5, 19 Jan 45. Hist Br OQMG. (5) Rad E–86633, Somervell (from Paris) to Gregory, 15 Jan 45.

month beginning in February, but he acknowledged that most of the yardage previously promised was still in depots awaiting shipment, and only a small quantity had left the zone of interior. Meanwhile, French estimates of their ability to manufacture clothing had proved as inflated as American estimates regarding available cloth. Early in June the Procurement Division, OCQM, reported that 505,000 pairs of trousers were actually on requisition, in both France and Belgium, and that deliveries to date had been 131,000. For garrison caps, the figures were 234,000 on requisition and 25,000 delivered. Of 200,000 garments for women on requisition, 11,000 jackets, 50,000 skirts, and 30,000 slacks had been completed. Production was only beginning, and nearly $35 million worth of clothing was scheduled for delivery in 1945 from France, Belgium, the Netherlands, and Luxembourg. However, the advisability of cutting back these contracts was already being discussed, and on 13 July War Department orders directed that all long-term production programs in the ETO be terminated by 30 September. The cloth remaining in the theater at that time was transferred to Germany, where it was used to make individually tailored uniforms.[64]

Since the textile shortage in the United States was a result of insufficient spinning, knitting, and weaving capacity, while stocks of raw materials were ample,

General Somervell and various WPB officials encouraged Littlejohn to undertake a complete textile program. Gregory, and Littlejohn himself, were somewhat dubious, but such a program had great possibilities for the economic rehabilitation of Europe, and might possibly relieve pressure on the United States during a protracted war against Japan. A letter from the Chief Quartermaster to General Goodman at NYPE reveals that the difficulties of the project were not underestimated.

Some of the boys from Washington have been over here and have suggested that I go into production on tentage to meet my requirements. Maybe this is the final answer to this problem. However, I had this job in the OQMG from 1940 to 1942, and then—to my chagrin—I found that in the States, where cotton, labor, and machinery were all available, that it took 9/12 months to produce a substantial quantity of tentage. Over here we have the additional problems of no raw materials, no coal, no transportation, and displaced labor. Regardless of all these obstacles I intend to go for production of textiles in a serious way.

Another letter, written to Barber while that officer was in Washington, was equally revealing: ". . . discuss with General Gregory personally, key personnel for the duck program. Get [Col. Robert T.] Stevens if possible. . . . The Procurement Division in OQMG must not become too optimistic because we agree to do the best we can. . . ."[65]

The cotton production program on the Continent fared no better than did

---

[64] (1) Littlejohn, ed., Passing in Review, ch. 41, pt. II, p. 37. (2) Cable X–74953, AGWAR to ETOUSA, 9 Dec 44. (3) Ltr, TQMG to CQM, 5 Jan 45. In Study of 5 Apr 45, pt. 4. (4) Procurement on the Continent, January-June 1945, MS Hist in QM ETO Lend-Lease Records. (5) Cable WAR–30829, Minton for Allen, 13 Jul 45. (6) Interv, Ross with Littlejohn, 1 Dec 59.

[65] Quotations from Ltr, CQM to Goodman (CG NYPE), 23 Nov 44, and Ltr, CQM to Col T. V. Barber, Chief/Proc Div OCQM, 26 Dec 44. Littlejohn Reading File, vol. XXX, item 83; vol. XXXI, item 85.

the wool clothing project, primarily because it also depended upon receipts of raw materials from the United States. The Chief Quartermaster had hoped to produce fine cotton items such as handkerchiefs, bath towels, and bedding, as well as tentage. While the receipt of 37,000 bales of raw cotton and patterns for tents was mildly encouraging, the amount fell far short of the 193,000 bales required for the cotton production project through 1945.[66]

By the end of March, contracts for the partial fulfillment of cotton requirements had been accepted in France and Belgium. Among these were tentative commitments for 1,100,000 pillowcases, 2,300,000 bed sheets, 13,000,000 handkerchiefs, 7,000,000 bath towels, and 23,000,000 yards of cotton duck. The largest part of these deliveries was forecast for the last quarter of 1945. But a shortage of raw cotton, and the absence of cotton findings and finishing compounds, together with urgent civilian needs and coal shortages, made the French unwilling to undertake more than half the fine-cotton projects assigned to them. The Belgians were anxious to co-operate, but awaited the arrival of raw materials, including coal. All these factors, plus the fact that a resurvey of light cotton goods on hand and forthcoming showed that the theater would be able to meet its requirements, led to cancellation of the

cotton production program in June 1945.[67]

Meanwhile a very large knit goods project, involving 7,000,000 sets of wool underwear, 6,000,000 pairs of gloves, and 2,500,000 sweaters, was also under consideration in France. Scoured wool was not available in the United States, and it was estimated that 30,000 tons of greasy wool would be required. But the French Government decided that it could not spare the 31,000 long tons of coal needed to complete this program, and rejected it on 2 June 1945. The Belgian Government accepted a program for roughly 40 percent of the above items for delivery in March 1946, provided the raw materials arrived in September of the current year. But on 8 June 1945 the War Department canceled all shipments of wool for the manufacture of knit goods.[68]

Insignia were items important to Army morale, and large numbers were locally procured. Contrary to expectation, hand embroidery was not available in large quantities in France, and only 140,000 handmade sets of 810,000 required were produced by June 1945. By September, 2,886,067 machine-embroidered insignia, 2,712,257 metal insignia, and over 82,800 meters of ribbon for decorations had been delivered. This production was very modest compared with estimated requirements, which totaled

[66] (1) Ltr, TQMG to CQM, 13 Nov 44, sub: Towels, Bath, and Handkerchiefs. Hist Br OQMG. (2) Memo, Actg Chief Materiel Br ASF for Chief Mil Plng Div, 18 Nov 44, sub: Cotton Duck Production. GPA 423 RAC. (3) Memo, Mil Plng Div OQMG for Proc Div OQMG, 1 Feb 45, sub: Shipment of Cotton for Use in Cotton Duck Prod; Ltr, CQM for OQMG, 30 Apr 45, Raw Cotton Reqmts. Both in OQMG 423 ETO.

[67] (1) GPA Rpt, Continental Production, 26 Sep 44 to 31 Mar 45, 15 Apr 45. OQMG 400.12 ETO. (2) Ltr, CQM to TQMG, 1 Jun 45, sub: Prod of Cotton Textiles in Europe. Hist Br OQMG.
[68] (1) QM Supply in ETO, III, 33–35. (2) QM Procurement on the Continent, January–June 1945, p. 21. (3) Cable WAR–14108, 8 Jun 45. (4) Ltr, Corbin (Actg TQMG) to CQM, 23 Jun 45, sub: Manufacturing Program in ETO. OQMG 423 ETO.

nearly 24,000,000 emblems, insignia, and decorations of various kinds.[69]

A rather large project for procurement of paper was concentrated entirely in Belgium. Some 6,000 tons of wood pulp from the United States were to be combined with 17,000 tons of pulp and waste paper from Germany. The Belgian contribution was 4,000 tons of straw and 40,000 tons of coal, and the desired total was 27,000 tons of finished paper. More than half was to be used as office stationery and blank forms, but the requirement also included kraft cartons, wrapping paper, and toilet paper. By September 1945 deliveries included nearly 8,000,000 sheets of sulphite paper and 18,100 cartons. Moreover, paper was one of the few categories of supply considered essential for the occupation forces and therefore the contracts were not canceled.[70]

In general, procurement in Belgium was considerably more satisfactory than in France, the chief reason being a fundamental difference in the national economies of the two countries. In time of peace Belgium had been a heavily industrialized nation with a food deficit and large exports, and after liberation unemployment and lack of raw materials were major problems. By contrast French industry was mainly geared to produce for home consumption, and many essential raw materials, especially food, were locally available within the country. The most pressing problem in France after liberation was transporting raw materials to urban centers. Once this was solved local demands saturated French industry, and there was little labor available for Allied procurement programs. An additional complicating factor was France's ambitious rearmament program, which naturally had prior claims on the nation's productive capacity. Disagreement over the need for such a program, and over France's future role as an occupation power in Germany, culminated during the last week in April 1945 when de Gaulle ordered the 1st French Army to remain in Stuttgart in defiance of orders from General Devers. General Eisenhower promptly directed that all issues of equipment to French Metropolitan Program units, then being activated, be suspended. The political issues were soon resolved, and maintenance issues to General de Lattre's forces were never interrupted, though except for those units destined for the Far East, no French units received initial issues of U.S. equipment thereafter. Needless to say, after this episode French deliveries of equipment similar to that needed for their own forces were extremely meager.[71]

Viewing U.S. procurement on the Continent in perspective nearly two decades later, it appears that raw material deliveries from the United States were slow and conclusion of agreements for overseas production was still slower. Most of the major contracts were signed in the period April–June 1945, and most

[69] (1) QM Procurement on the Continent, January–June 1945, p. 20. (2) *QM Supply in ETO,* I, 162–63; III, 128–29.

[70] (1) Exhibit A with Ltr, CQM to TQMG, 18 Dec 44, sub: Proc Program for Continent. Hist Br OQMG. (2) *QM Supply in ETO,* I, 166–67. (3) IRS, GPA to CQM, 25 Aug 45, sub: Paper Proc in Belgium. USFET GPA 462.

[71] (1) Littlejohn, ed., *Passing in Review,* ch. 41, pt. II, pp. 1–3. (2) Ltr, Deputy GPA to Dir Proc Div ASF, 13 Mar 45, sub: Production in France (3) Vigneras, *Rearming the French,* p. 361.

of them had been canceled by the end of August. With the benefit of hindsight, it seems clear that the whole program was too late to be worthwhile, but it should be borne in mind that the atomic bomb was one of the best-kept secrets in history, and without the bomb the military situation had a radically different appearance. Japan was expected to resist invasion even more desperately than Germany. For example, as late as 24 July 1945 the Combined Chiefs of Staff still accepted 15 November 1946 as a "conservative logistical planning date" for the end of Japanese resistance. Viewed in that light, the continental procurement program was merely an effort to make a noncombatant overseas theater self-sufficient, during an expected additional year of hostilities, in those categories of supply that were causing difficulties in the United States.[72]

[72] Kline, *Washington Command Post*, p. 346.

CHAPTER XVIII

Supply of Fuels and Lubricants in the ETO

In the ETO, as in the Mediterranean theater, the Quartermaster Service was responsible for computing POL and solid fuel requirements of the U.S. Army, of Allied ground forces other than British, and of Civil Affairs (G–5) authorities. These requirements were co-ordinated with those of the Army Air Forces and the U.S. Navy in European waters by the Area Petroleum Office, an overseas agency of the Army-Navy Petroleum Board, which also represented the U.S. military forces in POL matters concerning the British Government. Strictly military matters concerning the Allied forces were co-ordinated through the POL Division of SHAEF. Total U.S. requirements in Europe for all purposes were formulated by a local U.S. Petroleum Board under the chairmanship of Averell Harriman, the President's special lend-lease representative in London. Other members of this board included Littlejohn, Wayne Allen (the general purchasing agent), and representatives of the Navy and Army Air Forces. Harriman's successors in 1944–45 were field representatives of the Federal Economic Administration (FEA). The Area Petroleum Office and the British War Office presented co-ordinated military requirements to FEA for pro-

graming on a quarterly basis. Inevitably, there was considerable duplication and functional overlapping among all these agencies. Actual requisitioning by the Petroleum and Fuels Division of the OCQM was limited to oils and greases called forward from NYPE, packaged liquid fuels requisitioned from the United Kingdom, and solid fuels locally procured both in Great Britain and on the Continent.[1]

Liquid Fuels

Although POL was a Quartermaster item of supply, actual storage and distribution operations demanded a great deal of co-operation among the technical services, and co-ordination at this level was performed by a POL section of G–4, COMZ. The Transportation Corps directed ocean tankers to specific berths where they were discharged by the Engineers into their own storage tanks or pipelines, operated by the Engineer Military Pipeline Service, or into rail tank

---

[1] (1) USFET Gen Bd Study 109, Quartermaster Operations, p. 144. (2) IRS, Area Petroleum Off (Col Barnes) to P&F Div OCQM, 26 Oct 44, with Inds, sub: Supply of MT80 and Derivatives to Far Shore. USFET Petroleum Office, 400.42. (3) Risch, *Fuels for Global Conflict,* pp. 37–41.

cars of the Military Railway Service, a Transportation Corps agency. In either case, the next link in the chain of forward movement was usually provided by Transportation Corps tank trucks, most of them operated by the Transportation Section of ADSEC. The Quartermaster Corps re-entered the picture wherever its gasoline supply companies decanted liquid fuels into 5-gallon cans or 55-gallon drums, normally for storage in a QM depot. These were forwarded as required to Class III truckheads, either in the organic trucks of the gasoline supply company or in general purpose trucks of the local base section, which were regarded as Transportation Corps vehicles. Alternatively, the packaged POL might be picked up by Transportation Corps truck companies attached to armored divisions, or by the organic QM companies of infantry divisions, which were actually truck units.

If the administrative details of Class III supply were complicated, the commodities themselves were not. POL supplies for both the British and the U.S. forces were rigidly standardized to specifications of the War Department Committee on Liquid Fuels and Lubricants. The agreement whereby both nations used 80-octane leaded gasoline (MT80) for all normal purposes in the United Kingdom has already been described. This arrangement was extended to continental operations, and the benefits from such standardization far outweighed any minor technical difficulties. Later, small quantities of unleaded gasoline (white petroleum) were procured to run special equipment, but Class III supply still consisted of only 16 items—5 kinds of grease, 3 weights of motor oil and one of gear oil, kerosene, diesel fuel, white pe-

troleum, MT80, aviation gasoline (100-octane), coal, and wood.[2]

Initial Distribution Procedures

For the invasion, drawing on Mediterranean experience, the First Army quartermaster ordered that each vehicle should arrive in the beachhead with full tanks and also carry extra gasoline in 5-gallon cans. Jeeps were to carry 2 jerricans; weapons carriers and small trucks, 5; 2½-ton trucks, 10; and Dukws 20. Tanks and half-tracks were to bring enough fuel for 150 operational miles, and this fuel was expected to last six days. Distances were short in the restricted beachhead, and these supplies were ample.[3]

According to plan, small coasters from British Channel ports began arriving off OMAHA and UTAH Beaches on D plus 1, and their cargoes of 5-gallon cans were discharged into the Dukws of the engineer special brigades. The first gasoline dumps ashore were simply small piles of these cans, hastily unloaded in the fields behind the beaches by the gasoline supply companies attached to the engineer brigades. This simplified procedure was completely satisfactory as long as the narrow beachhead limited the need for gasoline. Moreover in a circumscribed area, small POL dumps were less vulnerable to enemy artillery fire.

By D plus 6 the OMAHA Beach POL stocks had been moved inland to beach maintenance areas astride the Tour-en-

---

[2] (1) See above, ch. X. (2) Risch, *The Quartermaster Corps: Organization, Supply, and Services,* I, 43. (3) Littlejohn, ed., *Passing in Review,* ch. 18.
[3] *FUSA Rpt of Opns,* 20 Oct 43–1 Aug 44, VI. 131, 136.

SHIP-TO-SHORE PETROLEUM LINE.   *Tankers at Cherbourg after the Allied occupation were at first unable to tie up at the dock.*

Bessin–Formigny–La Cambe road. Except for the period 20–22 June, when violent Channel storms prevented unloading on the beaches, receipts of gasoline at these dumps were always greater than issues. By D plus 7 over a million gallons of gasoline were on hand, and by D plus 21 the reserve was 27,000 gross tons, or more than 7,500,000 gallons. For two months the delivery of packaged POL was maintained largely in accordance with the plans of the OCQM, which G–4 had considered superfluous. By mid-July an average of 2,600 gross long tons of packaged fuel came ashore

each day, and a total of 142,702 tons had been forwarded from the United Kingdom. This was fortunate, since plans to deliver bulk POL via pipeline were delayed about six weeks.[4]

The main change from the planned POL supply procedure in the beachhead was in the handling of 5-gallon cans. To keep these containers in circulation,

[4] (1) Opn Rpt NEPTUNE, OMAHA Beach, Prov Engr Special Brig Gp, pp. 221–43. OCMH. (2) *FUSA Rpt of Opns*, 20 Oct 43–1 Aug 44, VI, 135. (3) Ruppenthal, *Logistical Support*, I, 501–04. (4) See above, ch. XI.

First Army had established the principle of "no can, no gas," which required using units to return one empty can for each full can drawn. Crowding and heavy traffic at the POL dumps forced a modification of the published First Army SOP, consumers being directed to deliver their empty cans to collection points outside the dump area where bulk gasoline would be made available later for refilling the cans.[5] Once loosened, the system of control deteriorated. Troops discarded empty cans wherever convenient, ignoring the collecting points. When the armies streamed out across France this habit became a major problem, but even in the beachhead the disappearance of cans from distribution channels presented difficulties. McNamara was forced to assign two company-sized units the mission of collecting cans.

To supplement packaged POL, the Minor Pipeline System was begun in the UTAH Beach area on D plus 7, and was completed by the end of June. By mid-July the port of Cherbourg had finally been cleared, and measures had been taken to start the Major Pipeline System, which was to become the backbone of the gasoline distribution system on the Continent. Two additional large pipelines were built later: the Southern System extending northward from Marseille, and the Northern System stretching eastward from Antwerp. By the end of hostilities all three systems had crossed the Rhine. Construction and operation of these pipelines, which were intended to be the main connecting links between the deep-water ports and the ultimate consumer, was an Engineer responsibility, but one in which the Quartermaster Service was vitally interested. In addition to providing a transportation capacity which other methods could not match, pipelines had several very desirable technical characteristics. They permitted the transmission of gasoline over the roughest terrain; they reduced congestion on roads where traffic was already heavy and limited; and they carried gasoline over long distances by day or night, regardless of weather conditions, and without the costly expenditure of gasoline in transit.[6]

The Role of the ADSEC Quartermaster

These techniques required administrative control as well as technical proficiency. For maximum efficiency, pipelines had to be in continuous use at full capacity. If the spigots at a pipehead had to be turned off because no containers were available, the stoppage represented a loss that could not be made good later. Holding such stoppages to a minimum was no simple matter, since the capacity of a 6-inch pipeline was nearly 500,000 gallons per day. This might be decanted into rail tank cars or tank trucks of the Transportation Corps, into drums or 5-gallon cans of the Quartermaster Corps, or into stationary tanks constructed or requisitioned by the Engineers. A normal day's operations at a pipehead included all these operations, and initially it seemed logical for control to be exercised by a G–4 representative of the commander within whose area the pipehead was located. In practice, something far more dynamic than

---

[5] *FUSA Rpt of Opns*, 20 Oct 43–1 Aug 44, VI, 136.

[6] USFET Gen Bd Study 109, p. 140.

staff control over the activities of several technical services was needed. On 20 August the ADSEC G–4 agreed that the Quartermaster Service should take over responsibility for all POL activities forward of the pipehead.[7]

Colonel Smithers, the ADSEC quartermaster, welcomed this decision, and immediately requested several highly qualified POL technicians from Littlejohn to implement it. The CQM was entirely in accord with this suggestion. He appointed Col. Lyman R. Talbot, the chief of his Petroleum and Fuel Division, as a special POL liaison officer of the OCQM, and sent him to ADSEC with several assistants. Talbot was informed that he now had a "roving commission," and that his team would operate through the regulating stations, which Littlejohn concurrently strengthened by providing jeeps to run a courier service and expedite requisitions. Talbot's main mission was to assume control over the tank truck companies and organize an effective, continuous operation from the end of the pipeline to the forward areas. COMZ had loaned four of these companies to First Army and two to Third Army, and was itself operating fourteen more. Empty jerricans also presented a major problem. Over 2,000,000 had been left behind in Normandy, and Talbot was made responsible for filling and forwarding them. Littlejohn arranged with the Chief of Engineers for Talbot and Smithers to select convenient sites along the pipeline where it could be tapped to fill the cans.[8]

On 16 July First Army began turning over its POL installations to ADSEC, which it still regarded as one of its own subordinate units. On 25 July it finally became possible to bring a tanker ship into Cherbourg, where ADSEC began decanting operations the next day. The first stretch of the Major Pipeline, twenty-nine miles south to La Haye-du-Puits, had already been laid, and on 1 August the first large inland decanting point was opened there. It was manned by three gasoline supply companies and a service company, and was soon decanting 250,000 gallons per day.[9]

On 1 August Third Army became operational and began to requisition POL from ADSEC. First Army continued to control dumps near the beaches and to draw POL from them for several days, but by 15 August both armies were being supplied through daily "telegrams," which were actually brought to ADSEC headquarters by couriers. When ADSEC moved out of the beachhead area on 19 August, it turned over to Normandy Base Section ter POL pack-

---

Transportation Corps: Operations Overseas, p. 331. (3) Ltr, CQM to Franks, 2 Sep 44, sub: Tankers; Personal Ltr, Littlejohn to Smithers, 3 Sep 44; Ltr, CQM to CofEngrs, 2 Sep 44, sub: Supply of Gasoline Forward. Littlejohn Reading File, vol. XXVIII, items 12, 16, 28. (4) Colonel Talbot was replaced as chief of the Petroleum and Fuel Division by Col. Richard T. Bennison, but by mid-November the latter was POL field representative, OCQM, at Verdun, and Talbot had a similar function at Liège; Colonel Franks was chief of Petroleum and Fuel Division from November 1944 until January 1945, when he was replaced by Col. Robert T. Hollis. Same file, vol. XXX, items 37, 60; vol. XXXII, item 33.

[9] Ltr, CO 210th QM Bn (M), (Maj R. E. Boulter), to Brig Gen Howard L. Peckham, 24 Aug 44, sub: Facts re Decanting and Depot Opns of QM Depot Q–6 at La Haye-du-Puits. Hist Br OQMG.

---

[7] Personal Ltr, Smithers to Littlejohn, 20 Aug 44; Ltr, CQM to QM ADSEC, no sub, 29 Aug 44. Both in Littlejohn Reading File, vol. XXVII, item 158.

[8] (1) Ltrs cited n. 7. (2) Bykofsky and Larson, *The*

GASOLINE CANS FOR THE THIRD ARMY *being transferred to trucks at Le Mans, August 1944.*

age dumps and five decanting points with the following reserves:

	Gallons
MT80 gasoline	15,257,453
Diesel and kerosene	6,783,631
Aviation POL	939,355
Total	22,980,439

The actual situation was not as favorable as these statistics appeared to imply. POL consumption in the restricted beachhead had been very low. Vehicles had averaged thirteen miles per day in contrast to the predicted fifty, which offset the delay in clearing Cherbourg harbor, and these reserves were approximately at the planned levels. But their location was most unfavorable. Many officers were confident that the pipelines could be extended promptly, but Littlejohn was not among them. On 7 August he wrote to General Ross that the pipeline program was not keeping up with the armies, and suggested that 200 tank rail cars be shipped across the Channel to bridge the gap. But rail reconstruction was too slow to justify such a move, and trucks had to carry most of the load. A month later, when the pipelines reached Chartres, the armies were on the German frontier, nearly 300 miles farther east.[10]

POL in the Pursuit

The pursuit across France was carried on at a pace that depleted the reserves of the armies in a matter of days. Third Army's sweep westward into Brittany and south to Le Mans in early August consumed more fuel than First Army's heavy fighting around Vire. Although Patton's troops drew about 380,000 gallons a day compared to FUSA's 280,000, the meager Third Army reserve was gone by 7 August, while First Army still controlled tremendous dumps in the ADSEC area. The troops detached to capture Brest were supplied from shallow-draft tankers sent into Morlaix and other Brittany ports, but the main Third Army force, though it relied partly on rail cars of packaged gasoline, depended principally on trucks, most of them coming to the various army POL supply points from La Haye-du-Puits.[11] A large number of these trucks were organic vehicles of Third Army or its subordinate combat units. Under the system prevailing in that army, they were not under the control of the army quartermaster, but simply returned to their units with gasoline that was not reported as having been received. TUSA requisi-

tions, based as they were on incomplete records of gasoline consumed, provided inadequate quantities for future consumption, and the combat units were encouraged to continue these informal procedures. Operating under such a loose system, TUSA did not appear to be alarmed when its stocks fell from 1.3 days of supply on 5 August to 0.28 days on the 19th. Meanwhile First Army stocks dropped from 10.5 to 3.9 days. Although consumption by FUSA units had exceeded receipts, a large part of this drop represented reserves that could not be brought forward and that had been transferred to ADSEC. But daily needs were being met, the tactical situation was extremely encouraging, and the 12th Army Group reported that there were no critical shortages that would affect operations. Similarly, when General Lee asked his chief petroleum officer if the decline in POL stocks was serious, the latter replied on 26 August:

This apparent drop in POL reserves is based on issues from stocks at the bases, and not consumption, hence represents the "filling" of the delivery system to the rapidly expanding occupied area. The import rate to the Continent is commensurate with vehicle population, scale of activity, and the reasonable buildup of stocks. Personal investigation shows that no shortage or failure of supply has existed to date.[12]

That opinion reflected both faulty reporting procedures and a reporting time lag caused by inadequate signal communications. Consumption had already increased, and was about to increase a great deal more. During the last week

---

[10] (1) Hist QM ADSEC, pp. 14–15. (2) Ruppenthal, *Logistical Support*, I, 508–11. (3) TUSA AAR II, QM, 4. (4) Littlejohn, ed., *Passing in Review*, ch. 18, p. 16. (5) Ltr, CQM to CofT, 7 Aug 44, sub: Supply of POL to the Far Shore. Littlejohn Reading File, vol. XVII, item 15. (6) Bykofsky and Larson, *The Transportation Corps: Operations Overseas*, pp. 341–42.

[11] (1) 12th Army Group G–4 Periodic Rpt 3, 21 Aug 44. 12th Army Group 319.1. (2) TUSA AAR, QM, 4.

[12] (1) Memo, CG COMZ for Chief Petroleum Off, 26 Aug 44, sub: POL Reserves on the Continent. USFET 400.42 Petroleum Off. (2) 12th Army Group Periodic Rpt 3, 21 Aug 44. (3) Royce Thompson, ETO Field Commands Gasoline Status, August–September 1944. MS in OCMH.

in August and the first week in September Third Army's requisitions suddenly began to reflect actual needs more closely, and thereafter gasoline receipts which averaged 260,000 gallons per day were reported as less than 40 percent of the required amounts. Even 500,000 gallons captured in the Reims-Chalons area provided little relief. Patton's troops were virtually immobilized between the 1st and 4th of September, and Third Army reported that for the first time its enterprising Class III supply officers "could not find sufficient gasoline one way or another. The Army, at this time, was so far from the source of supply that *entire dependence* had to be placed on receipts against daily telegram requests." [13]

By contrast, First Army relied increasingly on transportation under its own control, including 500 trucks provided by artillery and chemical warfare units, and four tank truck companies loaned by ADSEC. Between 19 and 29 August, FUSA sent its own trucks back to the Communications Zone for 90 percent of the 15,000 tons (5,500,000 gallons) of POL received. For five consecutive days —in the period when it was supposed to be enjoying top priority for fuel—First Army received no POL whatever via ADSEC transportation. [14]

Meanwhile, between the first week of August and the 19th, while reserves of the armies were dropping, continental stocks actually increased from 25.8 to 27 million gallons. They dropped during the rest of the month, but on 3 September, when the shortage at the front was

at its worst, the chief petroleum officer informed a Staff and Command Conference that over-all stocks were again increasing. [15] The supply crisis was entirely a local one in the forward areas, brought on by the rapid increase in the depth—and also the breadth—of the combat zone. The number of combat divisions operating had decreased from 21 in mid-August to 16 in early September, but the armies fanned out after they crossed the Seine, more than doubling the 12th Army Group front as they swept up to the German frontier. Meanwhile the pipeline had reached Chartres on 8 September, and Dourdan on the 15th. This meant that the minimum distance the organic and provisional truck companies had to travel for a load of gasoline was 250 miles, always assuming that the pipeline was working at full capacity and able to supply them. ADSEC did not open its first POL installations east of the Seine—Soissons and Sommeous—until after the pursuit had ended on 12 September. Tremendous quantities of fuel were consumed by the supporting echelons. Red Ball alone, for example, was consuming 300,000 gallons daily, and reducing by that amount the supplies that it could deliver to the forward elements. [16]

Civil Affairs operations for the relief of Paris were supported mainly by Red Ball and rail shipments, but also required direct allocations of gasoline. Over 5,000 French volunteers in the Normandy area were organized into a provisional transportation force by G-5.

[13] (1) TUSA AAR, II, QM, 4, 6. (Italics were supplied by author.) (2) Cole, *The Lorraine Campaign*, p. 52.

[14] *FUSA Rpt of Opns*, 1 Aug 44–22 Feb 45, II, 104; IV, 51.

[15] Ruppenthal, *Logistical Support*, I, 509.

[16] (1) *Ibid*, 509ff. (2) AAR's, XIX Corps, 31 Aug 44, 30 Sep 44. FUSA Opn Rpts, FRC. (3) QM Notes for G-4 Rpt of Opns, XII Corps, 12–31 Aug 44. XII Corps 319.1, FRC.

Normandy Base Section assigned them vehicles (later replaced from 1,500 Civil Affairs trucks held in England) and used the volunteer units to transport supplies to Paris. COMZ and ADSEC each authorized issuance to them of 5,000 gallons of gasoline daily. After the crisis at Paris had passed, these units were moved forward and continued to give valuable assistance to COMZ in transporting Civil Affairs supplies. All through the European campaign the issue of POL from Civil Affairs allocations for Allied vehicles contributed materially to relief operations.[17]

ADSEC at this time had only fragmentary records of how much gasoline was passing through, and thus was unable to effect any co-ordination between supplying agencies and the front. Although diesel fuel proved to be far less important than had been anticipated, each army required about 10,000 gallons per day, principally for its tank destroyer units. These requirements were frequently unfilled, and oils and greases seldom arrived in the proportions requested, causing the armies to suspect that their requisitions were being ignored, and that POL supply was, for all practical purposes, an automatic procedure. Emergency airlift relieved these small specific shortages.

Commandeering of gasoline further complicated the situation. For example, on one occasion a truck convoy of seventy-six 2,000-gallon tankers consigned to ADSEC was diverted into Patton's forward areas. This was a normal consequence of the methods of self-help in POL supply that had been allowed to develop within Third Army. Even

more serious was the practice of seizing the reserve fuel trucks carried for the return trip. Such seizures caused several convoys to be stranded and seriously hampered transport operations. By the time official action could be taken to correct this situation, POL supply was much improved, and in any case Red Ball trucks had received instructions not to make delivery forward of the TUSA rear boundary.[18]

The armies were not the only offenders. It took time for the newly established base sections to organize their procedures. On 24 September Littlejohn reprimanded the Loire Base Section quartermaster for failing to submit a requisition:

I judge from your conversation that you have been getting along by setting up a temporary truck train and going out and stealing from dumps. . . . Naturally if you do not submit a daily telegram and let your requirements be known, a daily train cannot be shipped to you.[19]

In September every available method was being used to deliver MT80 to the armies except railway tank cars, which were employed mainly in moving aviation gasoline to Ninth Air Force and diesel fuel for civilian relief in the Paris area. But the 12th Army Group quartermaster declared that current tonnages did not meet maintenance requirements,

---

[17] QM Supply in ETO, IX, 22–23.

[18] (1) Memo for Record, Col Caryl R. Hazeltine, DQM 12th Army Group, 1 Sep 44; AAR, QM Sec 5th Armd Div, Sep 44. Both in Hist Br OQMG. (2) Memo, QM BBS for G–4 BBS, 3 Sep 44, no sub. Lorraine Dist 463. (3) Ltr, AG Hq ETOUSA to CG TUSA, 15 Sep 44, sub: Commandeering of Gasoline Supplies, with Inds. AG 463.7 OpGD. (4) QM Supply in ETO, IV, 42.
[19] Ltr, CQM to QM Loire Sec, no sub, 24 Sep 44. Littlejohn Reading File, vol. XXVIIIA, item 180.

and Colonel Smithers of ADSEC requested that tank cars be assigned to supply the armies. This was attempted during October, but rail traffic was still very irregular, aggravating the problem of quick turnaround for tank cars. Storage tanks were rarely available in the forward areas. The armies could and did decant their daily needs, but they were not equipped to cope with a feast-or-famine cycle of bulk deliveries. Despite the shortage of jerricans—a problem that will be discussed presently—these containers remained the chief method of delivery to the armies.[20]

POL Airlift

Notwithstanding the urgent need for POL, deliveries to the armies by airlift were negligible in August. Third Army received about 100,000 gallons at Bricy airstrip near Orleans from 27 to 29 August, but the C–47 aircraft of IX Troop Carrier Command were then withdrawn for tactical airborne operations. Converted bombers were available but could not use the small forward airstrips. During the week beginning 5 September, Third Army received over 3,900 long tons of POL by air at Reims, Renneville, and Étain, or about 12 percent of all TUSA receipts for the month. All this was packaged POL, the method preferred by the AAF, but the supply of jerricans in Britain was nearly exhausted.[21]

On 14 September a meeting of the in-terested parties in London decided the details of a bulk POL airlift to the Continent. The thirteen persons present represented the COMZ G–4, the Area Petroleum Office, U.S. Strategic Air Forces, Eighth Air Force, U.K. Base, the British Petroleum Board, and CATOR (Combined Air Transport Operations Room), an agency of the Allied Expeditionary Air Forces. The Ninth Air Force, which had agreed to surrender four airfields in France and Belgium for this operation, and the ETO Engineer and Quartermaster Services, which would have to receive and store the gasoline, were not represented. Despite the cumbersome staff machinery involved, B–24 aircraft began discharging bulk POL on 18 September, and by the end of the month over 2.5 million gallons, about 7,000 long tons, had been delivered. First Army received more than half of this tonnage at Clastres, France, and Florennes, Belgium.[22] Bulk delivery by U.K.-based bombers was continued for a fortnight and then was discontinued, partly because of increased emphasis on forwarding of winter clothing. It provided only 10 percent of gasoline needs for this period.[23]

Intermediate POL Depots and New Ports

A very stringent POL shortage continued through October. Stubborn Ger-

---

[20] (1) Note, QM 12th Army Group to CQM, 9 Sep 44, no sub; Personal Ltr, QM ADSEC to CQM, 16 Sep. 44, no sub. Both in Hist Br OQMG. (2) See above, ch. XII.

[21] (1) TUSA AAR, QM, 4, 6. (2) Pogue, *Supreme Command*, pp. 258, 280.

[22] Min of Mtg to Discuss Airlift of MT80 in Bulk, 14 Sep 44; Rpt of Action Taken After 14 Sep Mtg, 18 Sep 44; Cable U68052, USSTAF to ETOUSA, 14 Sep 44, sub: Airlift of Bulk Gas. All in USFET Petroleum Off Airlift, USFET 463.72.

[23] (1) Ltr, Chief Petroleum Off to ANPB, 3 Oct 44, sub: Bulk Distr on Continent to Forward Areas. USFET 400.42 Petroleum Off. (2) QM Supply in ETO, IV, 44–45. (3) Hist of QM Sec ADSEC, p. 17. (4) See above, ch. XIV.

man resistance at Aachen and along the Moselle increased the demand for ammunition, and considerable Class II tonnage was also required to winterize the troops. The decision to bring another army, the Ninth, into the line further reduced the rail capacity available for POL, and meanwhile construction of the pipeline had been temporarily halted at Coubert, southeast of Paris. At the beginning of the month Cherbourg was still the only major discharge port for POL, with but a single exposed berth for tankers. Bad weather conditions and increased consumption had reduced continental reserves to five days of supply. There was clearly a need for reorganization in every aspect of POL supply— new ports nearer to the front, improved land transportation, new depots immediately behind the combat zone, and rigid economy by the armies while these improvements were being made.[24]

First Army's efforts in support of the British operations to clear Antwerp received first priority, so that the full weight of the POL shortage fell on the Third Army. Sheer necessity forced TUSA to mend its informal ways and to give its quartermaster authority to ration gasoline. A preliminary computation in September allowed 5,000 gallons per day for each infantry division and 25,000 gallons per armored division. By early October accumulated experience in a more stable situation led to a drastic revision of these allocations. The daily allowance for an infantry division was

raised to 6,500 gallons, while that of an armored division was cut 50 percent to 12,500 gallons. The total daily allocation for the 304,870 men of Third Army was 266,690 gallons of MT80 gasoline, or 0.8747 gallons per man per day, broken down as follows: [25]

Army troops	105,030
Corps troops (XX Corps)	17,500
Corps troops (XII Corps)	15,475
Infantry divisions (six)	39,000
Armored divisions (three)	37,500
Attached USAAF units	33,930
Attached COMZ troops	11,000
Miscellaneous (attached)	7,255

This allocation approximated average daily receipts in October and was almost exactly 67 percent of the current daily requisition—400,000 gallons. Experience confirmed that such quantities were barely sufficient to meet minimum requirements in a static situation. A significant detail was that corps troops needed more gasoline than an armored division in strictly defensive operations.

In November, the POL situation took a sharp turn for the better. The beneficial effects of discharge through new ports at Le Havre, Petite Couronne (near Rouen), and Ostend were beginning to be felt. ADSEC Engineers made plans to build a 5,000-barrel (210,000 gallon) storage tank at each army decanting site, which would give these installations a very desirable degree of flexibility. But far more important, the OCQM now gave serious attention to the development of major POL depots immediately to the rear of the combat zone. These would take over most of

[24] (1) *FUSA Rpt of Opns*, 1 Aug 44–22 Feb 45, II, 112. (2) TUSA AAR, II, G–4, 33. (3) Memo, CQM for Col Franks, 5 Oct 44, sub: Supply of POL and Solid Fuel. Littlejohn Reading File, vol. XXIX, item 19. (4) Personal Ltr, Younger to Littlejohn, 1 Oct 44 Hist Br OQMG.

[25] (1) TUSA AAR, QM, 8. (2) QM XII Corps, Rpt of Opns Oct 44 (dated 4 Nov 44). Hist Br OQMG.

the bulk decanting from the armies and also exploit all available commercial storage space.[26]

This plan was put into effect by bringing forward gasoline supply companies from the rear. At the end of October there were ten such companies in Seine Section, principally at the Dourdan and Coubert pipeheads, whereas ADSEC controlled but one. Since the companies at the pipeheads were only decanting 500,000 gallons a day, several of them were surplus. On 11 December ADSEC reported that it controlled nine gasoline supply companies, five at Liège and four at Verdun, but estimated that it needed six more. The development of POL facilities and operations at these two locations was slow and accompanied by growing pains similar to those experienced in the expansion of the Class I mission at the same locations. ADSEC was by training and experience a mobile organization, and its quartermasters had operated more as expediters than as depot administrators. They were not fitted for the static mission that was now thrust upon them. Littlejohn's solution was to send forward qualified specialists. On 16 November he informed Smithers that the two young majors he was sending to the 58th and 62d QM Base Depots were "among the most competent not only in Europe, but in the world." [27] He

requested that any POL officers senior to these two majors be released for reassignment. Not unnaturally, this request was ignored, and to insure compliance with his wishes the Chief Quartermaster had to maintain Talbot and Bennison—full colonels—as his POL representatives at Liège and Verdun. Further demonstrating the seriousness of the POL situation, Littlejohn relieved Colonel Franks as DCQM so that Franks could give his full attention to his duties as chief of the Petroleum and Fuel Division.[28]

Packaged POL was normally stored in the open, but suitable locations were scarce. In western Europe's wet autumn climate, paved access roads were absolutely essential, and cans could only be stacked on dunnage or well-drained hardstands. Verdun itself had only limited storage facilities, especially for POL, which demanded elaborate fire precautions and considerable dispersion. The 62d QM Base Depot, which was to be responsible for support of Third Army from that area, established eight Class III subdepots at various rail sidings, mostly north and east of the city. For U.S. supply purposes, Uckange became "Oklahoma City," Chattancourt became "Titusville," and the other depots received similar American names. In this area, more than thirty miles in diameter, over 47,000 long tons of POL were stored, and daily shipments to Third Army ran as high as 1,500,000 gallons daily. Gasoline products were peculiarly susceptible to sabotage, and POW labor could only be used in these depots under strict

---

[26] (1) Memo, Talbot for Bennison, 4 Nov 44, sub: Rpt of Trip to Armies; Memo, Col Ettele for QM ADSEC, 29 Oct 44, sub: Plan of Supply–Gasoline. Both in Hist Br OQMG. (2) TUSA AAR II, QM, 11. (3) IRS, CQM for O'Dell, 15 Nov 44, sub: POL and Solid Fuel. Littlejohn Reading File, vol. XXX, item 37.

[27] (1) Ltr, CQM to Smithers, 16 Nov 44, sub: Commissioned Pers in the 58th and 62d QMBD's. Littlejohn Reading File, vol. XXX, item 42. (2) See above, ch. XIII.

[28] (1) See above, n. 8(4). (2) Ltr, Col Ettele to QM ADSEC, 29 Oct 44, sub: Plan of Supply–Gasoline, with Ind. Hist Br OQMG. (3) Hq ADSEC, QM Estimate of Situation, 11 Dec 44. USFET QM 319.1, ADSEC.

PRISONERS OF WAR *filling gasoline cans at Liège, Belgium.   March 1945.*

supervision. Five to seven gasoline supply companies were assigned to the 62d QM Base Depot from December 1944 to the end of hostilities.[29]

At Liège, the 58th QM Base Depot was able to solve its POL storage problems in an entirely different way. A divided four-lane boulevard, stretching for more than two miles along the River Meuse, could be closed off because it led to a demolished bridge. This provided both an access road and hardstands for storage, with a capacity of 41,000 long tons. Nearby rail yards could accommodate 350 cars simultaneously, and on the average 190 trucks were used each day between the dump and the freight yard. But even this was not enough to support

both First and Ninth Armies, and in February 1945 an even larger POL subdepot was opened at Lutterade in the Netherlands, about thirty miles to the north. The 58th QM Base Depot operated these installations with only four gasoline supply companies, but utilized large numbers of POW laborers; 750 were employed daily at the main Liège POL depot alone. Although it successfully supported two armies, Liège only gradually accumulated reserves in excess of those held in the Verdun area. The explanation is that Liège was itself closely supported by nearby intermediate depots at Namur and Charleroi, a pipehead at Ghent, and the great port depots of Antwerp and Ostend. Logistically, this was far more efficient than the long line of communications from Verdun back to Le Havre and Cherbourg. The only

---

[29] Hist 62d QM Base Depot (n.d.). Hist Br OQMG.

major disadvantage of the Liège site was that it was somewhat concentrated, particularly since the area was continually under attack by flying bombs. Only once, on 17 December, did these robot missiles cause a major fire in the Liège POL installation, and this was quickly brought under control by Engineer fire fighting units.[30]

Although Liège was in the path of the German Ardennes counteroffensive, it was far to the rear of the First Army dumps, which were more immediately threatened and rightly received transportation priorities for evacuation. Apart from filling and sending back to Charleroi all available empty cans, AD-SEC moved little POL out of Liège. Incoming trains were unloaded farther to the rear, and requisitions by the combat units drew down reserves in First Army dumps from 6.4 days of supply on 15 December to 0.8 days on 1 January 1945.[31] First Army had deliberately adopted a hand-to-mouth system of supply. During January most of its POL was forwarded direct from intermediate or port depots in Channel Base Section. Meanwhile Third Army's POL reserves had increased slightly, but not as fast as its supply responsibilities were enlarged in the changed tactical situation. Total reserves to support 12th Army Group were reduced by 6,000,000 gallons during the German attack, but still exceeded 13,000,000 gallons at the beginning of 1945. In contrast to these American statistics, Field Marshal von Rundstedt's planners estimated that the German Ardennes operation would require 35,000 metric tons of fuel, for three armies or twenty-two divisions. What was actually made available to them was 18,000 metric tons, or about 4,750,000 gallons.[32]

COMZ Operations of Gasoline Supply Companies

The gasoline supply company had a strength of three officers and 125 enlisted men. It was one of the few truly mobile QM units, being provided with twenty-one 2½-ton trucks and eight other vehicles. Its organization was flexible, permitting each of its two platoons to operate separately. In the COMZ it was primarily a depot unit concerned with receiving, storing, and distributing balanced quantities of all Class III supplies, including coal or wood, and not merely with forwarding gasoline. It usually stocked can-marking tags, extra nozzles for jerricans, and spare parts for gasoline dispensers if available. It normally issued gasoline on a can-for-can exchange basis and was responsible for cleaning, refilling, and tagging the empty cans. A gasoline supply company was authorized four power-driven gasoline dispensers of 100 gallons per minute capacity, each mounted on a ¾-ton truck. This equipment had superseded an 80-gallon per minute dispenser in the spring of 1944, and both models were in extremely short supply. Several companies came ashore in Normandy without their dispensers

---

[30] Hist 58th QM Base Depot. Hist Br OQMG.
[31] (1) Hist of QM Sec ADSEC, pp. 19–20. (2) Hq ADSEC, QM Estimate of Situation, 20 Dec 44, 11 Jan 45. USFET QM 319.1, ADSEC.

[32] (1) Littlejohn, ed., Passing in Review, ch. 21. (2) In *Command Decisions* (New York: Harcourt, Brace and Company, Inc., 1959), Number 17, Charles V. P. von Luttichau gives a figure of 4,000,000 gallons of POL as the amount set aside to carry the German forces to the Meuse River.

and functioned mainly as truck companies to haul POL. The shortage persisted; moreover, experience demonstrated that dispensers wore out rapidly under the hard usage they received. At first spare parts were entirely lacking, and they remained critically short until the end of hostilities. It was necessary to mass-produce oversized rotors locally and rebore the housings to fit them. The companies were also equipped with 30-gallon per minute dispensers, which proved inadequate. The standard allotment of 3,200 jerricans to each company also proved inadequate. This was a capacity load (16,000 gallons) for the company's twenty-one trucks, but operations at COMZ pipeline terminals required eight to fourteen jerricans daily for each can issued to the using units. In practice, the rotation of cans was arranged between army and depot quartermasters, and their status as organizational equipment in the gasoline supply companies was ignored.[33]

Although the company included fifty-six laborers, normal rear area operations were carried on by local civilians or POW's. Under such conditions the main duties of U.S. personnel were truck driving, labor supervision, security, and supply accounting. The unit's capabilities varied widely according to local operating conditions. If all supplies arrived in bulk and had to be decanted and no outside labor was available, the company could receive and move to storage 70,000 gallons per day. With one QM service company or other equivalent labor attached and all receipts in 5-gallon cans, daily capacity was raised to 300,000 gallons. Even this was not the maximum. In a static situation, when there was time to train U.S. service company troops in the specialized technical aspects of POL distribution, Class III personnel could be spread very thin. Examples of extreme dilution were POL dumps at Jambes Secours and Flawinne, both in the vicinity of Namur, where the 58th QM Base Depot held a total of over 1.5 million gallons of aviation gasoline in reserve for the Ninth Air Force. Each of these dumps was operated by one enlisted man and 100 POW's.[34]

In Great Britain before the Normandy landings, the gasoline supply companies assembled reserves of canned POL at depots for cross-Channel operations. In the Communications Zone on the Continent, several gasoline supply companies normally operated together at a single installation. The usual complement at a pipehead was three gasoline supply companies and one service company, under the command of a mobile QM battalion headquarters. Other Class III installations might be manned by from two to seven gasoline supply companies, supplemented by service companies, POW's, or both. As already described, the normal complement of an army was seven gasoline supply companies. The ETO was authorized eighty-seven gasoline supply companies, but only eighty-three were actually in the theater by the end of hostilities, and not

---

[33] (1) USFET Gen Bd Study 109, pp. 157–61. (2) OTCQM TSFET Operational Study 10, pp. 14–16. (3) Littlejohn, ed., Passing in Review, ch. 18, p. 13. (4) T/O&E 10–77, 1 April 1942. (5) See discussion of POL functions of the QM group in the combat zone in Chapter XIV above.

[34] (1) See n. 33 (1) and (2). (2) Hist of 58th and Hist of 62d QMBD's. Unit hist files, Hist Br OQMG.

all of these were fully equipped. The Chief Quartermaster held that this number was inadequate, and without their equipment such units were of very limited usefulness. At least two companies that arrived without dispensers were equipped with extra trucks and 750-gallon skid tanks borrowed from the Air Forces, and operated as additional tank truck companies with ADSEC. After V–E Day POL specialists suggested that the gasoline supply company be re-equipped with tank trucks instead of cargo trucks, but this was not done when the T/O&E was changed on 21 June 1945. The main change at that time was the addition of four 3,000-gallon collapsible tanks for bulk storage.[35]

Two Italian gasoline supply companies served in southern France with the 6th Army Group, and as early as February 1945 the ETO Military Labor Service proposed to activate twenty-five similar units using German POW's. Shortages of equipment, and also of qualified U.S. officers, slowed down this program, but all of these units had been organized by 10 May 1945. They were rated as extremely efficient, and their presence made it possible to redeploy or deactivate similar U.S. units; only nine American companies were retained for occupation duties in Germany for a force of 400,000 men.[36]

Petroleum Products Laboratories

The assembling of packaged POL reserves for OVERLORD began in the summer of 1943 at the POL depots. Since U.S. units in Britain used bulk gasoline except during maneuvers, there was little turnover in these canned reserves. The cans therefore had to be checked for gum formation, a service that was at first performed by commercial laboratories. As the workload increased in the fall, the OCQM ordered a mobile testing laboratory from Baird & Tatlock, Ltd., a London firm which had already made similar equipment for the U.S. units in the TORCH operation. Initially, this laboratory was manned by casual QM personnel.[37]

Meanwhile American equipment for the same purpose was under development, and a T/O&E for a regular QM unit was authorized on 25 May 1943. Two such units, minus equipment, arrived in the theater in January and February 1944 and received training in the British-procured laboratory. In March 1944 these units were reorganized, each being split into a base and a mobile detachment under composite T/O&E 10–500. Before D-day the U.S. equipment had arrived, and in mid-June the 926th and 927th QM Petroleum Products Laboratories (Mobile) were attached to the First and Third Armies respectively. These mobile detachments, designated FB teams on the

[35] (1) See above, ch. XIV. (2) Littlejohn, ed., Passing in Review, ch. 18, pp. 13, 23. (3) OTCQM TSFET Operational Study 15, p. 15 and exhibit A. (4) T/O&E 10-77, 21 June 1945 and Special List of Equipment.

[36] (1) Chart, Reallocation of All ETO QM Units, Troops Br, Pers Div OCQM, 3 Dec 44. Hist Br OQMG. (2) Dr. William H. Maehl, Labor Services and Industrial Police in EUCOM, 1945–50, apps. C, D. MS in OCMH. (3) DA Pamphlet No. 20–213, p. 245. (4) Ltr, CQM to TQMG, 25 Feb 45, sub: Availability of QM Lieutenants. Littlejohn Read-

ing File, vol. XXXVIII, item 137. (5) *QM Supply in ETO,* VIII, 173.

[37] See above, ch. IX. (2) Littlejohn, ed., Passing in Review, ch. 18, pp. 11, 13, 35. (3) Ltr, CQM to TQMG, 17 Jul 44, sub: QM Petroleum Testing Lab. Littlejohn Reading File, vol XXVIA, item 75.

composite T/O, were used in armies and advance sections of COMZ to test POL products for accidental contamination or sabotage, and to test captured POL for type and serviceability. The FB detachments, each with a strength of one officer and five enlisted men, were both operationally and administratively subordinate to their respective base detachments, sending POL samples to the latter for detailed analysis. Base detachments, designated FA's, were used in ports and base sections to check the quality and water content of POL arriving by ship or pipeline, inspect bulk storage facilities, make detailed analyses of any POL product, and provide inspection service for all POL activities. Each FA detachment had a strength of two officers and ten enlisted men. Since the two detachments were often separated by distances of several hundred miles, the arrangement whereby FA detachments controlled FB teams had both administrative and technical disadvantages. In July 1944 Littlejohn pointed out to The Quartermaster General the advantages of the British-type laboratory. It was a completely mobile, self-contained, nine-man unit, yet capable of performing all the tests made by the standard U.S.-type base detachment. Unfortunately, the British were able to produce only a very limited number of these laboratories. The final U.S. troop basis included six FA and six FB units. After V–E Day, Colonel Talbot recommended that future POL laboratory equipment consist of augmented mobile detachments, able to move anywhere and to serve any headquarters.[38]

Experience in the theater indicated that water contamination was a major problem for POL laboratories. Surprisingly little water was in the gasoline pumped ashore from tankers. Investigation showed that the water used as a seal to combat evaporation in commercial-type storage tanks often entered the pipelines, partly because of the inexperience of the operating personnel, and partly because such storage was not standardized, and even skilled operators needed special instructions on the characteristics of each installation. Rapid distribution of POL made it very difficult to trace such contamination even after it was detected. Rail tank cars and tank trucks were not drained off frequently enough, and spread the contamination. The problem was eventually solved by strict control at the source, including careful instruction of the gaugers at the tank farms.[39]

The Jerrican

In the British Isles, gasoline was distributed to U.S. units by civilian agencies of the British Government, much of it being issued at commercial-type filling stations. Combat-type distribution involving jerricans was only practiced to a limited extent during maneuvers, and few of the difficulties that materialized in actual combat operations were experienced. There was no indication that in combat the fighting units

---

[38] (1) TO&E 10–547, 25 May 1943. (2) OTCQM TSFET Operational Study 10, p. 83; Study 15, exhibit A. (3) *QM Supply in ETO*, IV, 22. (4) See above, n. 24 (2) and (3).

[39] (1) Capt. Howard G. Sholl, "QM Petroleum Products Laboratory," *QMTSJ*, VIII, No. 6, pp. 9–10. (2) Ltr, 926th QM Petroleum Products Lab to CG FUSA, 15 Jul 44, sub: Rpt of QM Activities 15 Jun–15 Jul 44, and Incl. USFET Petroleum Office, 400.14.

would find it difficult, or even impossible, to return 5-gallon cans for refilling. Early in the campaign Littlejohn noted that a base depot company, several salvage companies, and several gasoline supply companies in the Le Mans area ignored the thousands of jerricans abandoned along the roads by combat troops, and took no action to collect them until specifically directed to do so.[40] Clearly, the elaborate training given to these units in the United Kingdom had not prepared them for what actually came to be one of their major duties. An even greater problem arose when army dumps displacing forward were forced to abandon large stocks of empty cans. Such cans were too bulky to form an efficient pay load for a vehicle, and whenever large quantities were assembled, it was usually more desirable to move bulk POL to fill the cans, rather than transport the empty cans to a source of bulk POL. Littlejohn and Talbot repeatedly set up temporary decanting points solely to fill and forward such cans, especially for Third Army. First Army initially controlled more tanker trucks, and was seldom in this predicament.[41]

By the end of August the supply of jerricans had become a critical factor limiting the forward supply of POL. Littlejohn directed that Talbot make the solution of this problem the first order of business in his new assignment.

He also informed the quartermasters of the newly organized base sections that jerricans left behind during pursuit phases should be collected, filled, and sent forward. Littlejohn pointed out to the Normandy Base Section quartermaster on 2 September that such action was vital and that there were over a million empty cans scattered across the Normandy area. When three weeks had gone by and the only visible reaction had been a request from Normandy Base Section for still more cans, he expressed his irritation as follows:

From what I can gather, since you have no super-duper staff on POL, your office assumes that all responsibility in operations are to be assumed by me here in Paris . . . complaints have been coming in from your end about no cans. We will take the appropriate action here. However, it is up to you in your office to see that cans in your base section are filled and ready for return to the front. . . . You have got three Base Section Depots, each with a very substantial staff, any one of which is more than ample to do the job.[42]

Toward the front, the situation was somewhat different. Since there were not enough jerricans, part of the requirements of the armies was sent forward in bulk, and naturally a considerable reserve of cans was kept on hand for local decanting at every location where bulk deliveries were expected. There was an inevitable conflict of interests, and Littlejohn was at first inclined to believe that it should be settled in favor of the pipehead decanting points. On

[40] Personal Ltr, CQM to Smithers, 24 Sep 44. Littlejohn Reading File, vol. XXVIIIA, item 178.
[41] (1) Ltr, QM TUSA to CQM, no sub, 18 Sep 44. Hist Br OQMG. (2) Ltr, CQM to QM TUSA, 24 Sep 44, no sub. Littlejohn Reading File, vol. XXVIIIA, item 184b. (3) Hist of QM ADSEC, p. 16. Hist Br OQMG. (4) Ltrs cited n. 8 (3), above.

[42] Ltrs, CQM to QM NBS, no sub, 2, 24 Sep 44. Littlejohn Reading File, vol. XXVIII, items 17, 182.

or recovered from abandoned POL dumps.[49]

Meanwhile, in view of limited jerrican production in the United States, the British agreed to make extraordinary efforts to increase their production. By early December they were able to assure the U.S. forces that 546,000 cans per month would be available to them during 1945. This number seemed sufficient at the time, when added to the 5,400,000 due from the United States, and to the number of cans expected from continental production. But manufacture of jerricans in France and Belgium was considerably delayed, and it was fortunate that the British were able to exceed their commitments. During the period 1 January–30 May 1945 they supplied the U.S. forces with 4,124,810 jerricans and 194,949 fifty-five-gallon drums.[50]

In December 1944, the French assured the Chief Quartermaster that they could produce 12,000,000 jerricans during the coming year if sheet steel was supplied from the United States. The OCQM placed a requisition on NYPE for 64,000 long tons of sheet steel, enough for 9,420,000 cans. By the end of March, 10,500 cans had been produced in France, and the amount on demand had been reduced to 7,500,000. Littlejohn estimated that only 15 percent of this amount could be completed by 1 July, but felt that the contract should not be canceled even if the war in Europe ended very quickly. The cans could be used to equip troops deploying to the Pacific, and cancellation would have a bad effect upon Franco-American relations. But by 11 May, three days after V–E Day, the Chief Quartermaster had received word from OQMG that, apart from basic T/E allowances, jerricans for the redeployed troops were to be supplied from the United States. Production contracts were to be canceled immediately, and local requirements were to be met by rehabilitating worn-out cans, principally in Germany. About 10,000,000 cans were involved, to be repaired at the rate of one million per month. When the contract with the French Government was canceled on 30 May, 287,450 new jerricans had been delivered. About 15,000 tons of sheet steel became surplus and was transferred to the Army-Navy Liquidation Commission. A contract with Belgium for 795,000 new cans was not canceled, but deliveries were not completed until the following year.[51]

Early in April 1945 Littlejohn reported that, if the Germans did not surrender until 1 July and the Allied troop build-

[49] (1) QM Supply in ETO, IV, 33. (2) "Kids Lend a Hand in ETO Jerrican Drive," QMTSJ, VII (4 May 1945), 22–23. (3) Ltr, Co-ordinator of Allied Info Svs to CQM, 13 Dec 44; Ltr, CQM to CofS COMZ, 27 Dec 44, sub: Jerrican Campaign; Ltrs, CQM to Minister of National Education and Minister of the Interior, 4 Jan 45, sub: Thanks for Aid in Jerrican Campaign. Littlejohn Reading File, vol. XXXI, items 52, 91; vol. XXXII, items 20A, 20B.

[50] (1) Ltr, Chief Petroleum Off to The War Office, 21 Oct 44, sub: Supply of Returnable Cans from the U. S.; Ltr, Chief Petroleum Off to GPA, 2 Dec 44, sub: Availability of 5-Gallon Returnable Cans. Both in USFET Petroleum Office 458.11, Containers. (2) Hist of QM Proc on the Continent, Jan-Jun 45, n.d. Hist Br OQMG.

[51] (1) Ltr, CQM to TQMG, 2 Apr 45, sub: Jerrican Reqmts; Ltr, CQM to TQMG, 11 May 45, sub: Jerrican Reqmts, 1945; Ltr, Littlejohn to Smithers, no sub, 15 May 45; IRS, CQM to Franks, 26 May 45, sub: 5-Gallon Cans. Littlejohn Reading File, vol. XXXV, item 11; vol. XXXVI, items 31, 37, 74. (2) Hist of QM Proc on the Continent, Jan–Jun 45 n.d. Hist Br OQMG.

up continued as planned, his maximum requirement for jerricans would be 19,186,000, based on the needs of five American armies and one French army at full strength. These figures were based on a seventeen-day reserve for an average army of 346,000 men, supported by 204,000 COMZ troops. Such a force would require 3,197,666 jerricans.[52]

No actual need for 19 million jerricans ever developed, but the above requirements per army were based upon ten months' experience and remained valid until the end of hostilities. The exact number of jerricans used by the U.S. forces during the European campaign is unknown. Littlejohn estimated that there were 15,500,000 cans on hand at the time of the landings, that one-third of these had been lost or worn out in ten months of combat, and that the number on hand at the end of March was still 15,500,000. This would imply that about 21,000,000 cans were in use in the ETO before V–E Day. Colonel Talbot estimated the number as 19,000,000.[53]

In the combat zone, the U.S. forces computed the maintenance factor for jerricans at 10 percent per month. The British estimate, 5 percent per round trip in an average of 13 days, was very slightly higher. Littlejohn was in agreement with these figures. In his letter of 2 April, he stated that all the older jerricans still on hand were near the end of their useful life; in fact if the fighting

continued, he expected 10,000,000 cans to become unserviceable during the next 90 days. For posthostilities conditions, he recommended a factor of 3.3 percent per month.[54]

Consumption Rates

The logistical factors used in forecasting POL requirements for OVERLORD have already been described. *(See Table 9.)* They called for 1.9081 gallons or 15.4788 gross pounds per man per day. Gross figures were used because initial POL supply was to be in jerricans. These statistics were equivalent to 10.756 net pounds per man, or 214 net long tons of POL per day of combat for a division slice of 40,000 men. Late in May 1944 radically different experience factors, amounting to 150 net tons per division slice of 45,000 men, were received from the Mediterranean theater. Requisitions for three months of combat had already been submitted, but new logistical factors, strongly influenced by the AFHQ reports, were prepared by the OCQM in June and were the basis for forward requisitioning on the British War Office by the Area Petroleum Office.[55]

The new figures, amounting to 153 tons daily per division slice of 40,000 men, also included certain changes in the proportions of various POL products. These changes were based on the specific troop and organic vehicle population of the ETO. In August, the first

---

[52] Ltr. Littlejohn to Gregory, 2 Apr 45, sub: Jerrican Reqmts. Littlejohn Reading File, vol. XXXV, item 11.

[53] (1) *Ibid.* (2) Ltr, Littlejohn to GPA, 27 Mar 45, sub: Jerrican Reqmts. Littlejohn Reading File, vol. XXXIV, item 94. (3) Littlejohn, ed., Passing in Review, ch. 18, p. 33.

[54] (1) See sources cited n. 53. (2) *QM Supply in ETO*, IV, 34.

[55] Ltr, Chief Petroleum Off to ANPB, 24 Nov 44, sub: Evolution of POL Logistics in the ETO. ETO 463.

month in which comprehensive figures for continental consumption were compiled, the new over-all estimate appeared to be very accurate, but it was already apparent that the allowance for diesel fuel was too large. In September, when the pursuit across France had to be supported almost entirely by truck transport, daily consumption figures increased abruptly to 248.3 tons per division slice. October consumption was considerably lower (197.2 tons), but the Area Petroleum Office was convinced that a new trend had been confirmed and requested a revised logistical factor at the end of that month. On 27 November Colonel Franks submitted a new factor of 1.9535 gallons per man per day, more than the original OCQM estimate of the preceding January, but suggested that this be used with a division slice of 35,000 men (190.6 tons). Apparently the suggestion was ignored, for the Area Petroleum Office reported the new factor to Washington as 217.6 tons per normal division slice. But December consumption was only 164.2 tons, and another revision was necessary.[56]

The OCQM accepted the standard 40,000-man basis and submitted a figure that was an average of all continental consumption experience to date. This amounted to 192.1 long tons per division slice or 14.088 gross pounds per man per day. The OCQM used the latter figure for the first time to compute levels of Class III supply on hand in its mid-January situation report, and apparently the Area Petroleum Office began to estimate future requirements for POL on the same basis very shortly thereafter. Late in April that office reported an average factor for combat conditions, derived from ten months' experience, of 1.5968 gallons per man per day, or 177 tons per division slice. This was stated to be the equivalent of 11.7 pounds per man, a mixed figure neither gross nor net, which presumably represented actual tonnage unloaded in ETO ports, where both bulk POL and filled jerricans were discharged. There is no evidence that the OCQM ever accepted this computation. At the end of hostilities it was using a factor of 12.993 gross pounds per man per day, exclusive of Civil Affairs requirements. This amounted to 182.1 long tons per division slice. No breakdown of components is available.[57]

Summarizing the experience of the European campaign in November 1945, the OCQM recommended an over-all planning figure for future combat operations of 13.48 gross pounds per man per day, broken down into 12 pounds of gasoline, one pound of other liquid fuels, and 0.48 pounds of lubricants. For more detailed planning, the OCQM recommended use of the same figures that had been developed in January 1945.[58]

---

[56] (1) Ltr, Area Petroleum Office to P&F Div OCQM, 26 Oct 44, sub: Supply of MT80 and Derivatives to Far Shore, with Ind, Franks to Area Petroleum Office, 27 Nov 44. USFET Petroleum Office 400.42. (2) USFET Gen Bd Study 109, p. 152. (3) Min, Mtg American Petroleum Products Comm London, 30 Jan 45. EUCOM 337, Confs Gen III, 44.

[57] (1) See Table 9. (2) USFET Gen Bd Study 109, pp. 154–55. (3) Hq COMZ ETOUSA: Semimonthly QM Supply Situation Rpt (15 Jan 45) dated 28 Jan 45; Hq COMZ ETOUSA, Weekly QM Situation Rpt (12 May 45) dated 17 May 45. USFET QM 319.1.
[58] OTCQM TSFET Operational Study 2, pages 16 and 38, gives gross and net POL factors in detail, including proportions of the various types of fuels and lubricants required.

Meanwhile, the field forces were having somewhat similar difficulties in establishing a basis for their short-term requisitions for specific tactical units. In theory, a combat zone division slice was 30,000 men, and its rate of consumption was assumed to be somewhat greater than 75 percent of the theater's 40,000-man slice. Initially, the First Army rejected the OCQM figure of 15.4788 gross pounds per man, and insisted on a factor of 24 pounds. The 12th Army Group at first concurred in this figure but in August decided to conform to the original OCQM estimate. This proved quite satisfactory in a rapid pursuit, provided that only organic and officially attached combat units controlled by an army headquarters were counted. In other words, an arbitrary and very low strength figure had been balanced by an equally arbitrary and excessive consumption figure. There was something to be said for this method of calculating. The official field strength of an army was a fairly stable statistic and easily obtained, while its actual strength fluctuated and was often inaccurately reported. Franks had attempted to apply such a procedure to the theater as a whole, but was unable to oppose the concept that a theater level division slice must add up to 40,000 men. When the tactical situation stabilized and gasoline consumption decreased, it became necessary to revise field forces factors, and there was inevitably an urge to use the more complete personnel statistics which had recently become available. Going to the opposite extreme from Franks, 12th Army Group statisticians based their computations on the ration strength of the armies plus 20 percent for miscellaneous units attached to the army

group, and in March 1945 proposed a factor of 1.0831 gallons (6.7584 net pounds) per man per day. Neither the OCQM nor the Area Petroleum Office favored this figure. The difficulty in all such computations was not the total POL consumption in the combat zone, which was known with considerable accuracy by early 1945, but the adoption of procedures that would give meaningful and useful forecasts.[59]

A report prepared by the Statistics Section, G–4 SHAEF, cast some light on this problem. Total POL consumption by four U.S. armies and one French army was shown for a twenty-eight-day period (24 February–23 March 1945), and pounds per man per day were reported in terms of both field strength and ration strength. This report demonstrated conclusively that field strength was inferior to ration strength as a basis for reporting POL consumption. The latter method gave results more compatible with the theater level statistics of the OCQM and the Area Petroleum Office. Moreover, since the strength of attached units varied from about 4 percent in the 1st French Army to more than 30 percent in Third Army, a statistical approach which ignored these units gave distorted results and exaggerated the variations among the individual armies. Even figures based on ration strength varied so greatly from one army to another that averages for the whole combat zone seemed to be of doubtful validity. The extremes reported were 7.222 pounds per man in 1st French Army and 10.445 pounds in Third Army, the average being 9.294

---

[59] USFET Gen Bd Study 109, pp. 152–53.

Since coal was extremely scarce, the highest priorities went to those railroads supplying the armies, even to the extent of diverting fuel earmarked for hospitals. It appeared that little coal would be available for heating troop billets during the coming winter, and the OCQM began an extensive wood procurement program in August 1944. The French allocated 372,500 cords of cut wood to the U.S. forces, but this was not enough, and a separate U.S.-administered woodcutting project was quickly organized. Consideration was also given to cutting and drying peat in Normandy, but this idea was quickly abandoned when the cost in money and manpower was weighed against the low thermal value of the fuel.[67] With regard to woodcutting, the Procurement Division of the OCQM made detailed arrangements with the governments of France, Belgium, and Luxembourg, and the base sections organized and administered the POW logging camps. By early September, the first two camps were cutting wood in the Cerisy Forest of Normandy with conspicuous success. Although twelve more camps had been opened in the Brittany, Loire, and Oise Base Sections by mid-December, they could not boast similar achievements, and in January 1945 total firewood production had only reached 36,000 cords of the one million required. Thereafter, performance improved somewhat. By 1 June 138,000 cords had been procured,

and nearly 100,000 cords had been issued. Of even greater importance, despite the small quantities involved, was the supply of wooden pit props for the coal mines. By the end of 1945, 63,400 cords of pit props had been produced.[68]

The disappointing results of the woodcutting program could be attributed to lack of co-operation between military and civilian officials, inadequacy of tools, equipment, and transportation, and shortages of supervisory personnel. In remote areas it was also very difficult to provide the POW woodcutters with housing that complied with the terms of the Geneva Convention.[69] Wood, like peat, was expensive in terms of time and manpower as compared with coal. Producing one cord of wood required three man-days while one ton of coal required one man-day, and in terms of fuel value wood required twice the transportation facilities needed for coal. Finally, whereas coal was ready for use when received, wood required six to eight months of seasoning to give maximum fuel value. Despite all these disadvantages, the wood procurement program was considered worthwhile because of the extreme shortage of coal.[70]

Some of the reasons for the shortage of solid fuels have already been mentioned. The mining program on the Continent, dominated by the civilian governments of the liberated countries,

[67] (1) Ltr, Asst Petroleum Off BBS to QM BBS, 21 Aug. 44, sub: Class III Supply for BBS; Ltr, Chief P&F Div to CO 53d QM Base Depot, 7 Sep 44, sub: Solid Fuel for Troops. Both in 463 Lorraine District. (2) QM Supply in ETO, IV, 73. (3) Littlejohn, ed., Passing in Review, ch. 41, pt. II, p. 15.

[68] (1) QM Supply in ETO, IV, 87–88. (2) Littlejohn, ed., Passing in Review, ch. 18, p. 21. (3) QM Procurement on the Continent, Jan–Jun 45. Hist Br OQMG.

[69] (1) Memo, Chief P&F Div BBS for QM BBS, 12 Sep 44, sub: Problems Confronting P&F Div. London Areas Office 1943–44. (2) Memo, Chief P&F Div for DCQM, 18 Feb 45, sub: Rpt of Trip. Hist Br OQMG.

[70] USFET Gen Bd Study 109, p. 162.

was inadequate to meet combined military and civilian requirements, and was further handicapped by labor shortages and inefficient management. Meanwhile imports actually declined during the campaign, partly because of a worldwide coal shortage. Since first priority was given to military uses and second to local industry, private civilian consumers suffered extreme privation, and inevitably a large black market flourished. The civilian authorities were not very zealous in stamping out this traffic, and were sometimes inclined to divert coal earmarked for the U.S. forces to their own nationals. The OCQM was obliged to send units into the mining areas to supervise deliveries. Even this was not the final difficulty. The prewar coal trade of western Europe had been based on inland waterways. Since these were the last transportation facilities to be restored to operation, most of the coal for the U.S. forces during the winter of 1944–45 had to be carried on the already overburdened railroads.[71]

POL in the Final Offensives

Early in January 1945, as the German salient in Belgium was being reduced, measures were taken to increase POL supplies and improve procedures to support the projected campaigns into Germany. All gasoline supply companies were directed to organize "alert units" of twelve 2½-ton trucks and trailers which could be hastily dispatched to fill spot demands within a radius of 150 miles. The depots at Liège and Verdun assumed the major responsibility for delivery of packaged gasoline to 12th Army Group, and their decanting activity rose sharply from 5,700,000 and 4,200,000 gallons, respectively, in January, to 25,300,000 and 10,200,000 gallons in March.[72]

This was part of the plan for a system of supply in depth. Of the 53,000,000 gallons of packaged fuel to be set up as a reserve for the northern armies, only 4,000,000 gallons were to be situated in the rearward base depots; 13,000,000 gallons were to be located in the army areas, 24,000,000 in the advanced areas, and 12,000,000 gallons in the intermediate area. The stores of bulk gasoline, on the other hand, showed an opposite pattern, with supplies increasing from front to rear: the advance depots (Maastricht, Liège, Trooz, Nancy, and Thionville) were to hold 4,000,000 gallons, intermediate depots (Charleroi, Reims, Soissons, Cambrai, Epernay, and Paris) 8,000,000 gallons, and port storage (Antwerp, Le Havre, Petit Couronne, and Cherbourg) 57,000,000 gallons. These reserves amounted to some 440,000 gross long tons, or over sixty days of supply for the 12th Army Group. Meanwhile, at the end of February CONAD imposed an embargo on POL shipments to Seventh Army and 1st French Army, since both were holding more than their authorized eight days of supply.[73] In a

[71] (1) *Ibid.*, pp. 165–66. (2) Littlejohn, ed., Passing in Review, ch. 18, pp. 28–30.

[72] (1) Memo, CG COMZ for All COMZ Sec Comdrs, 31 Dec 44, sub: Organization of Gas Supply Cos; Memo, DCQM for AG COMZ, 2 Jan 45, sub: Publication of Proposed Gas Supply Co Plan, and Inds. Both in EUCOM 322, FRC. (2) Ltr, CO 52d QM Base Depot to CQM, 11 Jan 45, sub: Storage of POL Products; Memo, Talbot for Franks, 13 Jan 45, sub: Rpt on Trip to 52d QM Base Depot. Both in Hist Br OQMG. (3) Hist of QM Sec ADSEC, p. 22.
[73] (1) Ltr, DCQM to G–4 COMZ, 27 Feb 45, sub: Emergency Plan for Support of Rapid Advance. Hist Br OQMG. (2) *CONAD History,* II, 704.

HEAVY DUTY DISPENSERS *and large tank trucks here speed up the decanting of gasoline into jerricans at the Ninth Army dump in Wegberg, Germany.   March 1945.*

further attempt to expedite the forward delivery of gasoline, in March the Communications Zone gave ADSEC the privilege of withdrawing bulk gasoline from the pipeline and shipping it forward without prior COMZ clearance.[74] This measure came at a time when combat elements were crossing the Rhine and gasoline expenditures were rising with a rapidity reminiscent of the preceding summer.

With the unexpected capture of a

Rhine bridge at Remagen, First Army reported that the "crust of enemy resistance" was broken, and in its subsequent rush eastward switched the supply priority from ammunition to gasoline. To bring fuel to the advancing forces demanded the utilization of every resource. First Army promptly called for delivery of 200 tank cars per day to the west bank of the Rhine and a large-scale airlift of gasoline. The Third Army, speeding toward Frankfurt, received bulk gasoline at the forward supply points both by air and by tank truck. On 30–31 March alone, Third Army obtained more than a half million gallons

[74] Cir, Hq ADSEC, 24 Mar 45, sub: POL Withdrawals From ADSEC Area Pipelines, and Inds. ADSEC 463, RAC.

of MT80 at forward airstrips. Seventh Army, with three armored divisions spearheading the attack via Mannheim on Nuremberg, was consuming similar quantities of gasoline. On 12 May the OCQM reported that a one-day requirement on the Continent of gasoline alone amounted to 4,466,000 gallons, other POL products being required in the usual proportions.[75]

POL requirements on such a scale could only be moved by pipeline, and plans for the final offensive had included extending the pipeline systems already mentioned into Germany itself. In mid-March the pipehead of the Northern System was at Maastricht, where it served both First and Ninth Armies. An extension northward, to serve Ninth Army only, had reached Roermond but was not yet in operation. The Major System from Cherbourg had been extended via Coubert (near Paris) to Thionville, where it supplied Third Army. The Southern System supporting the 6th Army Group up the Rhône valley had reached Saaralbe. As the armies crossed the Rhine all these pipeheads were still some distance to the rear, and as quickly as possible four short independent pipelines, one to serve each army, were laid across the river itself. These might be termed tactical pipelines, since they were built by army engineers primarily to reduce truck traffic over the Rhine bridges. The pipeline crossing for the Ninth Army at Wesel was linked to the Northern System immediately on completion on 28 March, and never operated

independently. A line serving the First Army, laid on an infantry footbridge at Mehlem near Remagen, was completed the same day. It was filled with gasoline brought partly by tank truck from Maastricht, and partly by rail from Antwerp. A similar pipeline crossing for Third Army at Mainz was in operation by 8 April, and was linked to the Major System extending from Thionville two weeks later. By 20 April the Southern System had a terminal east of the Rhine at Sandhofen, north of Mannheim. None of these systems were extended farther toward the east. The fuel that was not carried in tank cars to support the armies was stored in tanks that had been captured or erected on the east bank of the Rhine, and later at Giessen and Alsfeld. As the advance into Germany progressed, tank cars brought bulk fuel to forward decanting points at such eastward locations as Gutersloh, Hannover, Wuerzburg, and Nuremberg.[76]

Pipehead and decanting point operations in this period ran into a variety of difficulties. Supplies were ample but transportation was not. The sporadic arrival of tank cars, the inability of the armies to return sufficient empty jerricans, and the loss of time because of frequent forward displacement of decanting operations all worked against effective use of the pipelines' entire capacities. Even in the final week of the campaign, when the tactical situation was becoming static and cause for optimism was increasingly evident, these factors were contributing to a threatening

[75] (1) *FUSA Rpt of Opns*, 22 Feb 45–8 May 45, II, 63; III, 40, 44. (2) TUSA AAR II, QM, 23. (3) SUSA Rpt of Opns, III, 890. (3) Weekly QM Situation Rpt as of 12 May 45, dated 17 May 45. USFET QM 319.1.

[76] (1) Ruppenthal, *Logistical Support*, II, 436. (2) Hist of QM Sec ADSEC, pp. 22–23. (3) *CONAD History*, I, 237. (4) Hist of 53d QM Base Depot, p. 8. (5) Littlejohn, ed., Passing in Review, ch. 18.

situation which was on the verge of becoming critical.[77]

The XYZ mission of the 518th Quartermaster Group was a good example of the role of motor transport in this supporting operation. On 15 April the 518th, with two battalion headquarters and fourteen truck companies, or about 700 trucks, launched its mission of delivering a half-million gallons of bulk gasoline daily from Mainz to Third Army decanting points at Hanau and Alsfeld. Hanau was a sixty-mile round trip from the pipehead, while Alsfeld involved a one-hundred-and-fifty-mile turnaround. Col. Donald C. Foote, commanding officer of the group, established a statistical section in his headquarters to schedule the loading and dispatching of vehicles, and to formulate hauling plans. Proper scheduling was the key to successful movement of MT80 by truck. Its basic requirements were the maintenance of an even rate of loading and unloading, familiarity with turnabout times of different types of vehicles, and knowledge of the hours during which gasoline was available at railheads and pipeheads. The group fell slightly short of its objective in the first week of operations, but by the second week of May, the average daily load had increased to 686,000 gallons. On its best single day, 6 May, the group delivered 1,098,000 gallons—enough gasoline to move six armored divisions and six infantry divisions one hundred miles.[78]

The April airlift of gasoline amounted to almost 10,500,000 of the 58,000,000 gallons delivered by ADSEC to 12th Army Group.[79] In response to the requests submitted by the armies, the 73d Quartermaster Base Depot at Metz, whose activities may be considered as illustrative, hauled packaged gasoline to several airstrips on the outskirts of the town. Twenty-four hours after being alerted, the depot made available for loading six hundred tons of MT80. Italian service companies handled loading promptly and efficiently by locating the containers in 590-can piles (roughly five plane loads each), and little more than a plane's length apart on the perimeter track of the airfields. The average daily shipment to the Third and Seventh Armies from this source alone approximated 75,000 gallons. In one instance at least, gasoline was lifted to a unit which had encountered unexpected enemy resistance. When the 10th Armored Division broke through in the Crailsheim area, the enemy blew the Neckar and Jagst River bridges, interdicted the temporary bridges, and stranded the division. The local airfield at Crailsheim was under steady enemy fire, but this did not deter the delivery of 20,000 gallons (plus rations and ammunition) by C-47's with only the loss of a single plane.[80]

Situation After V–E Day

In the period immediately after the German surrender, redeployment movements actually increased the demands

---

[77] (1) *FUSA Rpt of Opns*, 22 Feb–8 May 45, III, 49. (2) Memo, Deputy QM ADSEC for ADSEC, 3 May 45, no sub. Hist Br OQMG.
[78] "Support Third Army . . .," *QMTSJ*, VIII (3 August 1945), 16.

[79] Hist of QM Sec ADSEC, p. 23.
[80] (1) Hist of 73d QM Base Depot, pp. 94–95. (2) SUSA Rpt of Opns, III, 892–93.

for POL. Meanwhile imports decreased rapidly as the ETO became a low priority theater, and the liberated countries clamored for return of their tank cars and commercial storage tanks. It became clear that whatever POL was stored in these facilities, which had a total capacity of some 570,000 tons, would have to be moved forward promptly into Germany or surrendered to the local civilian governments. Because the advance sections of COMZ had been disbanded in mid-June, supplies had to be transferred directly to the Third and Seventh Armies, the senior occupation headquarters in Germany. These units were not prepared to undertake major logistical POL operations representing many times their authorized levels of supply. Nevertheless, they finally agreed to do so, and very large reserves were concentrated at Giessen and Mannheim for Seventh Army, and at Nuremberg for Third Army. Thereafter, the Marseille-Sarrebourg pipeline was transferred to the French Government, and the other pipelines were dismantled. It was originally intended to ship them to the Far East but after V–J Day they were disposed of locally as surplus property.[81]

Meanwhile a permanent base POL depot for the occupation forces was established at Farge—a port between Bremen and Bremerhaven—where the German Navy had built about 230,000 tons of underground storage. The first tanker arrived at Farge on 15 June 1945, and distribution from that point began a month later.[82]

Summary

By V–E Day, the dispersion of American military forces throughout western Europe clearly demonstrated the significant role of petroleum in successful ground war. A war of mobility had been waged, and the heavily motorized armies which landed in Normandy and Provence had figuratively floated to Germany on a sea of tetraethyl-leaded gasoline. By and large, the Quartermaster Corps had operated effectively as a retailer of this product. While responsibility for many of the POL difficulties experienced in the ETO was shared with other technical services, the Quartermaster Corps had to shoulder the major responsibility for occasional shortages arising from an inadequate jerrican supply. Reviewing Quartermaster operations during the European campaign, the USFET General Board emphasized the advantages of the 5-gallon container for the distribution of packaged gasoline, and warned of the detrimental effects of jerrican shortages on combat operations.[83]

That evaluation, of course, applies only to the European campaign. Procedures in the Pacific theaters, where combat troops rejected 5-gallon cans in favor of drums, demonstrated that the jerrican was not indispensable. But ETO experience confirmed the flexibility and convenience of the smaller container in a deep continental combat zone where trucks were the primary

---

[81] (1) Supply and Distribution of Petroleum Products in the ETO (historical data from files, P&F Div OCQM). Hist Br OQMG. (2) Littlejohn, ed., Passing in Review, ch. 18, pp. 27–28.

[81] Littlejohn, ed., Passing in Review, ch. 18, pp. 27–28.

[83] USFET Gen Bd Study 109, pp. 139–40, 146–47.

means of transportation. Jerricans made it possible to transport POL in any motor vehicle, without special handling equipment of any kind, and to establish forward dumps without shelter and with a minimum of camouflage. But these containers also had inherent disadvantages. They reduced the net pay load by 25 percent, and empty 5-gallon cans made an extremely bulky, inefficient load for standard vehicles.[84]

Rapid filling of jerricans presented a particularly difficult problem. It could only be done quickly with heavy-duty power dispensers which were bulky, noisy, and required continual repair. The nature of this equipment, which was completely unsuited for use in the forward areas, goes far to explain the slow tempo of the refilling cycle, and the excessive number of jerricans that were required to maintain a steady flow of POL to the combat troops from decanting sites far to the rear. It seems clear that, in the future, every improvement in dispensers will reduce the requirement for jerricans. Improvements in pipeline techniques and in the design of bulk transporters, including airborne tankers, will have the same effect. The ultimate result, if this trend continues, is that jerricans, along with other manually operated equipment, will disappear entirely in a completely mechanized combat zone.

---

[84] In April 1945, the QM Company, 3d Infantry Division, reported that specially designed side racks made it possible for one truck to haul 600 empty jerricans, three times the normal load. This was particularly important at a time when almost all rearward-moving trucks were being used to transport POW's. Of special interest is the fact that this was described as a new improvisation during the last month of the European campaign. AAR 3d QM Co, Hist Br OQMG.

CHAPTER XIX

Graves Registration Service

The graves registration activities of the Quartermaster Corps in the ETO go back to 9 December 1941, when Americans first approached the British War Office regarding burial and mortuary facilities for American military personnel expected in Northern Ireland early in 1942.[1] Throughout the rest of the war, the ETO Graves Registration Service worked in close co-operation with the Imperial War Graves Commission, which was instrumental in providing grave sites in Great Britain and Northern Ireland. By May 1943, thirteen burial sites, with a capacity of 230,000 graves, had been reserved exclusively for American use. This number proved to be far in excess of requirements, since plans to evacuate casualties from France never materialized. Only two locations —Cambridge, near Eighth Air Force bases, and Brookwood, a U.S. cemetery of World War I southwest of London, were retained as permanent sites after the end of hostilities. The United Kingdom was an important base for U.S. naval and air operations, and over 9,000 Americans were interred there by April 1945. But this was essentially a static cemeterial program, closely resembling activities of national cemeteries in the zone of interior. Bodies were embalmed by British civilian concerns and buried in locally procured wooden caskets. Nevertheless, the Graves Registration Division, OCQM, acquired a certain amount of useful experience in the administration of cemeteries and in documentation, which could be applied under active combat conditions.

Ground combat operations on the scale of OVERLORD inevitably meant a far greater number of casualties than those experienced before the Normandy landings. Personnel were needed in the field during hostilities to locate, collect, identify, evacuate, and bury the bodies. In the interests of morale, both on the battlefield and at home, these measures had to be taken speedily, accurately, and with proper respect. A succession of studies outlining the organization and methods for a successful graves registration program on the Continent began to appear in October 1943. During the following spring these studies were absorbed into the Mounting Plan of SOS and the NEPTUNE Plan of First Army.

With regard to both the location of cemeteries and the assignment of trained graves registration units in the forward areas, every effort was made to benefit by the experience of American troops

---

[1] Except where footnotes indicate otherwise, this discussion of graves registration activities is heavily indebted to Chapter VI of the monograph by Edward Steere, *The Graves Registration Service in World War II*, pages 93–131, which represents the most recent research and analysis of available data.

in World War I and more recently in the Mediterranean theater. There was no desire to emulate the employment of 2,240 temporary burial sites in 1917–18 nor to repeat the technical and administrative difficulties that had arisen later when the time came to concentrate or repatriate the dead. First Army's Burial and Graves Registration Plan, therefore, foresaw the possibilities and advantages of operating corps or even army cemeteries in preference to divisional or task force burial sites. Drawing on his experience in North Africa, Colonel McNamara emphasized also that the effective collection of battlefield dead depended on the presence of trained graves registration companies in the field rather than reliance on makeshift teams detailed from among the combat troops. He felt very strongly that administration of this program and supervision of burial records were army level responsibilities.[2]

The Graves Registration Division, OCQM, was responsible for the training of graves registration units in the United Kingdom in preparation for the cross-Channel assault. Maj. (later Lt. Col.) Maurice L. Whitney, who had been division chief since July 1943, supervised the training and allocation of these units, and drafted most of the theater level regulations governing their burial procedures in the field. In May 1944 he became graves registration officer of the Forward Echelon, COMZ, and was succeeded as Chief, Graves Registration and

Effects Division, OCQM, by Lt. Col. Arthur C. Ramsey. This officer remained in the United Kingdom, and on 13 August Lt. Col. Earl F. Sechrest became the new chief.[3]

Personnel for Graves Registration Activities

The OVERLORD troop basis for First Army included three assigned graves registration companies and two more on loan from SOS. This provided one company for each of four corps (including one to be transferred later to Third Army) and one company to remain directly under army headquarters. For the initial lodgment phase, one platoon was attached to each of the amphibious assault divisions and each engineer special brigade. The NEPTUNE build-up schedule called for eighteen graves registration platoons to be ashore by D plus 12 to support a force of eleven divisions. On D plus 6, there were fourteen platoons in the two lodgment areas, attached to units as follows:[4]

Platoon	Unit
OMAHA *Beach*	
Hq 606th GR Company	
with 2 platoons	V Corps
1st Platoon	1st Infantry Division
2d Platoon	29th Infantry Division
2d Platoon, 607th GR Company	5th Engr Special Brigade
3d Platoon, 607th GR Company	6th Engr Special Brigade
2d Platoon, 608th GR Company	XIX Corps

---

[2] (1) War Dept Summary Sheet, 8 Sep 45, sub: Current Plan for Return of American Dead and Establishment of Overseas and U.S. Cemeteries, pp. 5–7. Hist Br OQMG. (2) Operations of QMC During the World War, Monograph 2: Extracts From Historical Report of CQM, A.E.F., France (Schuylkill Arsenal, U.S. QMC School, 1929), pp. 91, 96. (3) McNamara *Memoir*, p. 98.

[3] (1) *QM Supply in ETO*, VII, 3. (2) Littlejohn, ed., Passing in Review, ch. 26, pp. 2, 3; ch. 29, app. C. (3) The graves registration and effects functions had been combined in a single division on 15 March 1944.
[4] (1) *FUSA Rpt of Opns*, 20 Oct 43–1 Aug 44, VI, 145, 194–98. (2) Unit Histories, 603d, 607th GR Cos. Hist Br OQMG.

Platoon	*Unit*
	UTAH *Beach*

Hq 603d GR Company
with 2 platoons ......VII Corps
  1st Platoon ....4th Infantry Division
  2d Platoon ....9th Infantry Division
4th Platoon, 607th GR
Company ....1st Engr Special Brigade
1st Platoon, 3041st GR
Company ....VII Corps (for 82d AB
                   Division)
2d Platoon, 3041st GR
Company ....VII Corps (for 101st AB
                   Division)

On the following day, D plus 7, the graves registration platoons attached to the engineer special brigades reverted to the First Army quartermaster, who thereupon assigned one company each to the V, VII, VIII, and XIX Corps, and retained the 607th Graves Registration Company under his own control to operate an army cemetery. That basis of allocation was maintained in the First and Third Armies all through the fighting in Europe, and was also regarded as ideal by the Seventh and Ninth Army quartermasters, who had to get along with three companies each during most of the campaign. Behind the combat zone, graves registration units were concentrated at the forward cemeteries, where activity was greatest. ADSEC and CONAD attempted to keep at least two platoons at each cemetery where interments were still being made, but even in the late spring of 1945 only ten graves registration companies and three separate graves registration platoons were available in the entire Communications Zone. Thus the total ETO allocation was twenty-four and three-fourths graves registration companies.

It was often necessary to operate a cemetery with service company personnel, directed by a few enlisted graves registration technicians. Large numbers of laborers were needed at every cemetery, since graves registration units themselves did not normally dig graves, build roads, or dig drainage ditches, but the exact number utilized is not known. Such laborers were usually POW's, but since skilled technicians were not required they were supplied from base section labor pools, which did not report separately on labor used for various purposes. The number of local civilians employed was negligible. During the pursuit across France, First Army used about 250 U.S. service personnel and an equal number of POW's in its cemeteries. Later, in the fighting along the German frontier, these numbers dropped to 150 service troops and 50 POW's. Third Army did not report on POW's used for graves registration purposes, but utilized an average of two and a half QM service companies at its cemeteries throughout the European campaign, with the heaviest utilization (four companies) falling in the period December 1944–March 1945, when the tactical situation made the use of POW's inadvisable. Ninth Army normally allotted one service company per corps for this purpose. In the Communications Zone, once burials had been completed, the function of supervising routine custodial activities was usually transferred to a QM composite company headquarters, type AC.[5]

---

[5] (1) *FUSA Rpt of Opns*, 1 Aug 44–22 Feb. 45. VI, 54, 65. (2) TUSA AAR, QM, 30–33. (3) Ltr, CQM to QM ADSEC, 29 Jul 44, sub: Additional GR Cos; Ltr, Littlejohn to Franks, no sub, 30 Jul 44. Littlejohn Reading File, vol. XXVIA, items 122, 125. (4) *QM Supply in ETO*, VIII, 158–67. (5) Biweekly AAR's, OQM, NUSA. Hist Br OQMG. (6) Hq NBS, Forecast of QM Activities, 10 Jan–10 Feb 45, n.d. Hist Br OQMG.

Graves Registration Supplies

In the ETO, graves registration supplies were considered to be Class II expendable items, and were stocked at Class II and IV depots. Since sheets and blankets were both in short supply, cotton mattress covers were normally used as shrouds. The beach maintenance sets for Operation NEPTUNE included one mattress cover for 375 man-days, and follow-up sets decreased this allowance to one for 450 man-days. At the end of July 1944, the supply in Normandy had been depleted, and Littlejohn instructed his rear headquarters in London to ship 50,000 mattress covers immediately—by air if necessary. During the next several months, graves registration supplies were requisitioned by daily telegram as were other Class II supplies, with the same unfortunate results. After this procedure was amended in December 1944, Littlejohn prescribed that 20-day credits of graves registration supplies should be established for each army and base section. These credits were primarily to define depot missions, and not to control issues. Emergency requisitions of supplies actually used in processing the dead, such as mattress covers, crosses, and effects bags, were always honored regardless of credits, but it was sometimes necessary to edit requisitions for the distinctive equipment of graves registration units, such as rubber gloves and stripping knives. In the base sections, quartermasters were called upon to supply such items as flagpoles, fencing materials, garden tools, grass seed, and shrubs for use at cemeteries. Only articles locally procurable in the ETO were supplied for this purpose.[6]

Land to be used as cemetery sites was, legally, no different from land requisitioned for other military purposes. NEPTUNE plans specified that the designation of cemetery locations was a function of corps commanders, to be delegated to division commanders if necessary. The actual selection was usually made by a graves registration staff officer or the commander of a graves registration unit. From the first, these officers realized that many of the sites selected would probably become permanent cemeteries, and attempted to exercise foresight in choosing desirable locations. Nevertheless, at the end of hostilities all cemeteries still had the official status of temporary burial sites, a situation that continued until 5 August 1947, when the President approved Public Law 368. That act empowered the Secretary of War to acquire foreign land for U.S. military cemeteries, and thereafter formalities were speedily concluded for the permanent acquisition of five sites in France, two in Belgium, and one each in the United Kingdom, the Netherlands, and Luxembourg. More than forty other sites were evacuated, rehabilitated, and returned to their rightful owners.[7]

Burials in the Lodgment Area

As with other QM activities, work planned for the first two days on the beaches was delayed by unexpected difficulties. Sites that had been earmarked

---

[6] (1) Ltr, CQM to DCQM (Rear), 31 Jul 44, sub: Supply on Far Shore. Littlejohn Reading File, vol. XXVIA, item 130. (2) See above, ch. XI. (3) USFET Gen Bd Study 107.

[7] (1) *FUSA Rpt of Opns*, 20 Oct 43–1 Aug 44, III, 100–107. (2) Littlejohn, ed., Passing in Review, ch. 26, pt. I, pp. 26–34.

for burial purposes were still in enemy hands. The 3d Platoon, 607th Graves Registration Company, landed on OMAHA Beach on D-day and immediately set up a collecting point on the beach, within the sector of the 6th Engineer Special Brigade. A site for a cemetery, later designated St. Laurent No. 1, had been selected on a hill just inland from the beach, and the 309th QM Railhead Company and the 3168th QM Service Company were detailed to dig graves and assist in evacuation. The dead on and behind the beach were numerous, however, and enemy snipers discouraged the digging of graves. Since prompt disposal of the bodies had become imperative for sanitary reasons, temporary burials at a site known as St. Laurent No. 2 were made by digging trenches in the sand with a bulldozer. Colonel McNamara had given express instructions that no burials were to be made on the beaches, and this emergency site was never regarded as a cemetery; it was closed at midnight on 10 June, after 457 interments had been made. During the next week all these bodies were moved to St. Laurent No. 1, but even so the temporary burials had not been a waste of time. The original lodgment area was so constricted that the presence of the dead had actually hampered tactical and close support operations, and also had a demoralizing effect upon reinforcements coming ashore. A very similar situation prevailed on UTAH Beach, where the 4th Platoon, 607th Graves Registration Company, made 356 emergency burials at Pouppeville for the 1st Engineer Special Brigade. The two airborne divisions which dropped in the area behind UTAH Beach before dawn of D-day established

their own emergency cemeteries, using organic personnel. Sgt. Elbert E. Flagg of the 603d Graves Registration Company landed with the glider force of the 82d Airborne Division late on D-day, and on D plus 1 selected a site near Blosville, where 530 bodies were interred in the next few days, partly by men of the 407th Airborne QM Company and partly by French labor. The Quartermaster Section, 101st Airborne Division, directed similar emergency burials at a site near Heisville, which were also performed by organic teams. These were hasty battlefield burials, in graves not more than three feet deep. They were never meant to be permanent.

Meanwhile, the 1st Platoon, 603d Graves Registration Company, opened a cemetery for the 4th Infantry Division at St. Martin-de-Varreville on D plus 3, and simultaneously the 2d Platoon of the same company established another cemetery for the 9th Infantry Division at Ste. Mère-Eglise. The next day, the 2d Platoon, 606th Graves Registration Company, opened a cemetery for the 29th Division at La Cambe. Thus by June 10th there were eight cemeteries in the two beachheads, or one per division. But during the next week, when graves registration platoons were pulled back from the brigades and divisions and one graves registration company was assigned to each corps, there was a very natural trend to reduce the number of cemeteries. Although First Army had taken over operation of St. Laurent on 13 June, V Corps did not open another cemetery until after the St. Lô breakthrough, preferring to evacuate back to that location. The VII Corps began to operate Ste. Mère-Eglise on 16 June, but finding the site too small, opened a separate cemetery for enemy dead at Orglandes three days later. Since the original cemetery was filled very rapidly by transferring bodies from Heisville, Pouppeville, and St. Martin, another site, Ste. Mère-Eglise No. 2, was opened on 25 June. La Cambe had been taken over by XIX Corps on 15 June, and on 24 June a new cemetery was opened at Blosville for VIII Corps, near the emergency burial ground of the 82d Airborne Division. First Army began to operate Orglandes for both VII and VIII Corps on 17 July. It should be noted that all the sites retained in operation were on good roads; Ste. Mère-Eglise, Blosville, and La Cambe were on N 13, the main Cherbourg-Paris highway. By 8 August all these cemeteries, containing more than 30,000 dead, had been transferred to ADSEC.[8]

Collection and Identification

The collection, evacuation, and identification procedures which necessarily began on the battlefield were varied and to some extent improvised. Because the precombat training of the field soldier did not include instruction in graves registration procedures, the green corps and divisions in Normandy learned only by experience the most efficient way to employ both trained graves registration personnel and collection teams detailed from organic combat units. Each corps used a different system in Normandy, but that of the VII Corps, in its drive to Cherbourg, was judged by the First Army quartermaster to be the model for future operations, and the testimony of observers indicates that it was employed by other units and armies in subsequent campaigns. The company headquarters and all four platoons of the 603d Graves Registration Company were concentrated at the VII Corps cemetery, first at Ste. Mère-Eglise and later at Marigny. Details were dispatched from the company to operate collecting points as required for each division. Such a team normally consisted of four men, and from one to three teams were sent to each division as required by the tactical situation. The unit collection teams carried the bodies to a battalion collecting point in the vicinity of the battalion aid station, from which they were evacuated to the division collecting point by regimental service troops. Here bodies were identified and transferred to graves registration company vehicles for delivery to the corps cemetery. Organic company transportation was supplemented by eight 2½-ton trucks from VII Corps. This system made it possible for one company to evacuate and bury the dead from as many as seven divisions without requiring additional personnel. The identification of as many bodies as possible at the collecting point before they were removed from the vicinity of the divisions also resulted in a reduction in the percentage of unknown bodies delivered to the cemeteries.[9]

---

[8] ADSEC reported taking over seven cemeteries in which First and Third Armies had interred 30,302 bodies. The FUSA report states that ten cemeteries were transferred, including three empty sites with no bodies. Both reports agree that St. Martin was turned over before disinterments from that site had been completed. Orglandes, containing over 6,000 enemy dead, was the largest American cemetery in Normandy. Cf. Hist of QM Sec ADSEC, app. L; FUSA Rpt of Opns, 1 Aug 44–22 Feb 45, IV, 90.

[9] FUSA Rpt of Opns, 20 Oct 43–1 Aug 44, VI, 145–47.

This method of operating became the normal one in the ETO, despite the very considerable burden it placed upon the combat units. The current organization of the graves registration company, which has already been described in connection with Mediterranean operations, made it impossible for that unit to assume greater responsibilities. An augmented graves registration company, capable of locating the dead on the battlefield and handling the entire evacuation procedure, was authorized by the War Department in September 1944. But the revised T/O called for 265 officers and men, an increase of more than 100 percent, and since no corresponding increase in personnel was made available, such units were never used in the European theater. Inexperienced tactical units were inclined to complain that these duties tied up men and vehicles needed for combat, but actual practice in the field demonstrated that prompt evacuation and identification of the dead by their own units brought the best results. Whenever circumstances made such action impossible, the proportion of unidentified dead promptly increased. Notable examples were the airborne operations in Holland and rear-guard actions during the German Ardennes offensive; in both instances tactical considerations forced a delay in evacuation. With combat experience, the troops came to place increased emphasis upon correct identification of the dead, and showed greater willingness to co-operate toward that end. For example, by the end of October 1944 it was the consensus of division quartermasters within the battle-hardened XIX Corps that additional graves registration personnel were not

needed. The troops themselves actually preferred to evacuate and assist in the identification of their own comrades rather than leave them lying unattended in the fields to be picked up later.[10]

After the breakthrough at the end of July 1944, the lengthening lines of communication complicated evacuation. In an attempt to hold the number of cemeteries to a minimum, First Army set up a system of relay points where trailer-loads of remains were transferred from corps vehicles to army graves registration vehicles and removed to the rear for burial. Furthermore, with the combat elements rushing across France and inevitably overlooking isolated bodies, collecting teams from the graves registration company at army level were dispatched to sweep the areas and check on reports, often fragmentary or inaccurate, of bodies located by civilians, military police, and civil affairs units.

While no single factor can conceivably explain the strengths and weaknesses of graves registration procedures in the combat zone, the records of the summer offensive in both northern and southern France indicate that pursuit warfare and lengthened lines of communications adversely affected the evacuation system. In a fluid battle situation, characterized by the disengagement of the enemy and decreased enemy artillery fire, the number of casualties naturally decreased, but simultaneously the organic collection teams had less time to locate and evacuate the dead, and supporting graves registration units were

[10] (1) See above, ch. VIII. (2) T/O 10-298, 26 Sep 44. (3) OCQM Field Obsv Rpt 3, 30 Oct 44; OCQM Field Obsv Rpt 7, 4 Dec 44. Both in QM ETO 319.25. (4) Ltrs cited n. 5 (3). (5) 12th Army Group Rpt of Opns, XII, 219.

dispersed over wider areas. Thus, amidst fewer casualties, the summer offensive saw the proportion of unknowns increase in all the armies.

The percentage of unidentified bodies interred became the accepted yardstick of efficiency in graves registration operations in the ETO. The wartime record of First Army was 1.6 percent, including 1.2 percent in Normandy, 2.2 percent in the pursuit across France, and 1.4 percent in the fighting along the German frontier. This compared favorably with the 1.1 percent achieved by Fifth Army under more favorable conditions in Italy. Third Army, beginning with 3.8 percent in August 1944, speedily improved its performance and at the end of the war had succeeded in identifying all but 0.58 percent of the dead interred in its cemeteries.[11]

The most significant improvement in the identification performance of Third Army undoubtedly resulted from insistence that all identifications be checked at the corps collecting points. This

---

[11] The corresponding figure for World War I was 2.2 percent. Probably a more accurate impression would be given by stating that First Army succeeded in identifying 98.4 percent of the dead buried under its administration, whereas Third Army identified 99.42 percent, and the AEF 97.8 percent. These figures reflect the fortunes of war, as exemplified by fairly favorable conditions of weather, tactics, and transportation. For example at Margraten in the Netherlands, the only cemetery for American dead administered by Ninth Army, the total identified was only 92.04 percent. This unfavorable ratio can in large part be accounted for by the great number of unidentified dead transferred to that cemetery from emergency burial sites of the 82d and 101st Airborne Divisions, established during the MARKET operation. But since Ninth Army decided not to establish even temporary cemeteries on German soil, it seems likely that excessively long evacuation distances also contributed to the high percentage of unknowns at Margraten.

meant that trailers had to be unloaded and reloaded, greatly increasing the labor involved, but experience proved that the great majority of unidentified bodies could be identified by simply inquiring of the combat units, if the inquiry was made promptly enough. What this amounted to was placing the identification process forward with the evacuation phase of graves registration, instead of with the burial phase at the cemetery. The system was very similar to that of VII Corps already described.

In its campaign through the Brittany Peninsula, the 6th Armored Division found that record keeping on deceased personnel was much improved if, in addition to identifying the bodies at the collecting point, the teams also presented to the divisional adjutant general a list of bodies delivered to the cemetery. The subsequent experience of the 6th Armored serves as a valuable example of refinement in evacuation and identification procedures as Third Army troops moved eastward across France. Graves registration teams were organized by each combat command, which operated local collecting points in its own forward service area. From these points, the bodies were removed to the division collection point situated advantageously along the axis of supply between the division rear and the army cemetery. Operating under the assumption that the possibility of identification diminishes as the bodies change hands, registration personnel held remains at the collecting points until a certification of identity was obtained. If identification tags were missing from the body, or if effects in a burnt-out tank did not reveal laundry marks, pay books, identification cards, or personal jewelry, such circumstantial evidence as the name, number, and type of vehicle, names and known fate of other crew members, and location and date of action, was sent to the division graves registration officer for further analysis.

In December, Third Army made another major contribution to the techniques of battlefield identification by having the Signal Section photograph facial remains which had been artfully reconstructed by the use of cosmetic wax. This procedure frequently aided recognition by friends and former comrades, and proved particularly useful in distinguishing American from German dead after the Ardennes fighting, in which a whole enemy unit infiltrated the American sector wearing U.S. uniforms and identification tags. But Third Army's most significant contributions to the graves registration service were, first, emphatic and explicit recognition that a positive identification was the last great service a combat unit could perform for its fallen comrades; and second, the elimination of the platoon as a working unit within the graves registration company. The organizational change was simply an improved means of achieving the recognized objective. The small collecting teams sent to corps service areas were specialists in identification, trained to co-operate with the combat units. The rest of the graves registration company was composed of specialists in cemetery maintenance. This functional separation of duties made four platoon headquarters unnecessary. Third Army burial directives enumerating these principles, while very similar to those of other armies in general content, spelled them out more definitely and were pervaded by a distinctive tone of command.

In the immediate postwar period the USFET General Board indorsed Third Army views on the need for specialists, for a reorganization of the graves registration company, and for a clearer delineation of responsibilities.[12]

Cemeteries in the Combat Zone

By the middle of September, First Army was on the German frontier. During the pursuit across France 4,000 Americans had been interred in five FUSA cemeteries—Le Chene Guerin, Gorron, St. André, Solers, and Fosse—which had been opened between 8 August and 8 September. Almost immediately upon becoming operational on 1 August, Third Army departed from its plan to employ corps cemeteries and instituted an army cemetery system. The VIII Corps cemetery at Blosville, at the neck of the Cotentin Peninsula, was transferred to Patton's forces on 1 August along with the corps itself, but was operated as an army cemetery thereafter. In successive weeks Third Army cemeteries were opened at St. James, St. Corneille, Villeneuve-sur-Auvers, Champigneul, and Andilly, in the path of Patton's summer sweep along the right flank of the Allied advance.

As the American front line stabilized along the fortified German border, each army took steps to establish a single cemetery that was as close as possible to the front lines and still equally accessible to its component corps and divisions. First Army selected a site at the Belgian village of Henri-Chapelle near Limbourg, and on 25 September opened the cemetery that ultimately became one of the two largest U.S. burial grounds

---

[12] USFET Gen Bd Study 107, pp. 5–6, 12.

on the Continent. Ninth Army, which had recently arrived from Brittany to take position on the left flank of the American line, lacked sufficient graves registration personnel to maintain a separate cemetery and for seven weeks evacuated its own dead to Henri-Chapelle. On 10 November, General Simpson's forces opened their own cemetery near Margraten, in the southeast corner of the Netherlands, and evacuated their dead to this point for the duration of the war. Meanwhile Third Army, which had opened a cemetery at Andilly near Verdun on 12 September, moved it to Limey, south of Metz, a month later, when heavy rains prevented further operations at the older site. When Patton's forces turned north to help reduce the Bulge, it was necessary to open new cemeteries at Grand Failly, north of Verdun, on 23 December, and at Hamm, in the suburbs of Luxembourg City, on 29 December.

These multiple locations in the same general area were required by a complicated tactical and logistical situation. Reviewing his experience after the end of the fighting in Europe, the TUSA quartermaster believed that normally an army cemetery could be utilized until evacuation distances to it exceeded 100 miles. Presumably that opinion was based upon performance in Germany, where Third Army opened cemeteries at Stromberg near Bingen, at Butzbach south of Giessen, at Eisenach, and finally at Nuremberg. First Army operated over even greater distances, evacuating its dead to Ittenbach, in the original Remagen bridgehead, until April 1945, when a new site was selected at Breuna near Warburg. None of the U.S. cemeteries in Germany were large, and im-

mediately after V–E Day all of them were evacuated, most of the dead being transferred to Henri-Chapelle, Hamm, and St. Avold, a Seventh Army cemetery in eastern France.[13]

Seventh Army's experience illustrates the special problems of mountain warfare. Épinal cemetery, as already pointed out, was easily accessible to the VI Corps, but not to the XV Corps, operating to the north. The farther the troops advanced to the east, the more rigidly their movements were channelized by the steep mountain roads through the Vosges. On 4 December the 46th Graves Registration Company opened a new cemetery at Hochfelden, fifteen miles northwest of Strasbourg, which was in effect a XV Corps site. The VI Corps continued to evacuate to Épinal. But within a few days both corps were redeployed to attack northward into the Siegfried Line. Because of the limited road net neither existing cemetery was adequate for the northward attack, and on 18 December a cemetery was opened at Niederbronn. The new site was less than twenty miles north of Hochfelden in a straight line, but the distance on roads passable in the wintertime was nearly five times as great. Niederbronn was overrun by the Germans early in January, and although quickly recovered was never reopened. Épinal and Hochfelden continued in use until St. Avold, the largest Seventh Army cemetery, was opened on 15 March.[14]

In general, Third Army buried German dead in separate cemeteries, while

---

[13] (1) TUSA AAR, QM, 31, (2) *FUSA Rpt of Opns*, 22 Feb–8 May 45, III, 94. (3) Littlejohn, ed., *Passing in Review*, ch. 26, pt. I, p. 3.
[14] (1) See above, ch. VIII. (2) *QM Supply in ETO* VII, 49–53.

First, Seventh, and Ninth Armies used the same cemeteries for both U.S. and enemy dead, but segregated them by plots. Both systems implied that the number of U.S. and German burial sites would be approximately equal, and this was actually the case. The armies attempted to provide equal care for all war dead, a policy Littlejohn heartily endorsed. On 17 February he wrote to Col. Henry W. Bobrink, recently appointed chief of the Graves Registration and Effects Division:

1. Yesterday I discussed at length with Lt Gen Patton, the CG Third Army, the burial of American Dead, Allied Dead, and enemy Dead.

2. General Patton advised me that the enemy does one thing exceptionally well— and that is giving proper and adequate burial to his own Dead, and that he extends the same courtesy to our Dead, and to the Dead of our Allies.

3. General Patton further stated that it is his policy to apply the German policy in burying the Dead in the Third Army area. . . .

4. I would like you to follow the general policy which is set forth above.

5. Personal opinions shall in no way have a bearing on this problem.[15]

General Patton's policy prevailed in COMZ. It might also be noted that the wisdom of Third Army policy, regarding separate cemeteries for German dead, was later vindicated. When the time came to concentrate American dead at large permanent cemeteries, the German plots at Margraten, Henri-Chapelle, and Épinal had to be evacuated. Such

action was not necessary at any Third Army cemetery.[16]

Cemeterial Improvements

ADSEC's graves registration activities began on the Continent at the end of June when, as a subordinate unit of First Army, ADSEC was assigned the mission of evacuating both American and enemy dead from the hospitals, pillboxes, and streets of Cherbourg. For the first two weeks, this task was executed by a four-man detail from the 99th Infantry Battalion, but with the arrival of the 610th Graves Registration Company a more orderly system was instituted. By late July ADSEC was moving forward, and the 56th QM Base Depot organized the 1st QM Group, under the command of Colonel Whitney, to assume graves registration responsibilities. By the time Normandy Base Section came into existence in mid-August, this unit of trained specialists had taken over direction of all the cemeteries in the Cotentin Peninsula, and its responsibilities continued to expand over the next seven months as the base section increased in size. By early 1945 the group was supervising sixteen cemeteries in Normandy and Brittany Base Sections, operated by three graves registration companies. This supervision was mainly concerned with the technicalities of identification, concentration of remains

---

[15] Memo, CQM for Chief GR&E Div OCQM, 17 Feb 45, sub: Burial of the Dead. Littlejohn Reading File, Vol. XXXIIIA, item 89.

[16] (1) General Patton himself lies buried in Hamm Cemetery, Luxembourg. (2) Littlejohn, ed., Passing in Review, ch. 26, pt. I, p. 27. (3) On 8 May 1945 the total of enemy dead in ETO cemeteries was 71,423. Cf. COMZ Weekly Estimate of QM Situation, 17 May 45. Hist Br OQMG.

in cemeteries expected to be permanent, and statistical reporting, but the group also directed routine custodial, maintenance, and beautification activities, including the employment of a local landscape architect.[17]

Colonel Whitney considered his main function to be a systematic sweeping of old battlefields to insure that all American dead were located, identified, and interred in official cemeteries. Apparently he felt that in this mission he was acting as a direct field representative of the Chief Quartermaster, and his SOP for the group so stated. But Littlejohn's concept was that the group was a team of specialists, to be loaned to base sections as needed. Significantly, he directed that Whitney's first operation plan should be submitted through channels. Friction continued for months, and in March 1945 Col. John H. Judd, the Normandy Base Section quartermaster, requested that Whitney be relieved. Instead, Littlejohn, who considered Whitney his ablest graves registration technician, moved the group headquarters into Oise Section. Quite apart from the conflict of personalities, this forward displacement was urgently necessary for tactical reasons. The armies were already crossing the Rhine, and ADSEC and CONAD were preparing to follow them. Oise Section was destined to inherit most of the evacuated territory up to the German frontier, including eight large cemeteries, during the next few weeks. Shortly thereafter, the Chief Quartermaster also called forward the

three veteran graves registration companies that had operated under the 1st QM Group in Normandy.

Controversy over control of these units had undoubtedly been one source of friction between Whitney and Judd, but the real issue was more basic. Judd felt that his base section graves registration officer had been shunted aside by Whitney, and had had no opportunity to prepare himself for the very considerable responsibility now suddenly thrust upon him. Whitney found Judd lacking in understanding of the basic graves registration mission, and was particularly incensed that the group's very detailed records of operations in Normandy were retained by the Normandy Base Section instead of being forwarded to the OCQM in Paris. On the other hand, it was only natural that an officer who considered himself ill-prepared for his duties should insist on retaining all available records that might be helpful. The problem appears to have been one more instance of conflict between technical and territorial channels of control, resembling several narrated earlier. Littlejohn admitted that, since the chiefs of his graves registration field crews were normally senior to base section graves registration officers, it was proper to make special arrangements regarding command in each case. In this instance repeated changes in base section commanders and in chiefs of the Graves Registration Division at OCQM had contributed to the misunderstanding. Undoubtedly this episode reinforced Littlejohn's conviction that, in the post-hostilities period, successful completion of the graves registration mission would require an autonomous theater level

<hr>

[17] (1) Hq NBS, Forecast of QM Activities, 10 Jan–10 Feb 45, n.d. Hist Br OQMG. (2) Littlejohn, ed., Passing in Review, ch. 26, pt. II, pp. 5–6.

graves registration command, independent of the base section commanders.[18]

In the routine of taking over army cemeteries, ADSEC's graves registration personnel established a regular procedure for maintenance. The graves registration platoon attached to a burial site first undertook an inventory of the graves, checked it against the cemetery's records, and sent a copy of the inventory to the OCQM. Since the armies had no time to begin a beautification program, ADSEC initiated measures in this direction. OCQM directives provided that roads had to be laid out, fences were to be constructed around the grounds, and temporary peg-type grave markers were to be replaced by crosses or Stars of David as soon as possible. Then, if there was time, individual plots were to be mounded to allow for sinkage, and plans were to be made for landscaping.[19]

Proper cemetery maintenance was always difficult, and hampered as much by the weather as by the combat situation. At Marigny, where most of the casualties of the battle for St. Lô had been hastily buried, the identification of exhumed bodies was handicapped by decomposition. Heavy rains filled open graves, and the 1st QM Group had to improvise a drainpipe system by joining together open-ended fifty-gallon drums. During an inspection trip through Normandy in mid-October, Littlejohn learned that

crosses should stick into the ground at least two feet so they would remain upright even in mud. He directed that the specifications for wooden crosses be amended and that all local procurement contracts be changed to provide extra length.[20] At Margraten, rains transformed the site into a mire that trapped road-building equipment and swallowed the gravel and rocks that had been deposited to form a roadbed. Finally, a corduroy road of logs had to be constructed to permit the resumption of cemeterial activities in this area of "water-filled graves, dirty crosses, and mud-soaked men." [21]

Late in 1944, ADSEC's graves registration activities encountered two special situations which illustrated the continual need for adaptability among military units. When ADSEC divided its installations between ADSEC North at Liège and ADSEC South at Verdun, support for a large number of military hospitals was similarly divided. Initially, each hospital in the northern area had to evacuate its own dead to Fosse Cemetery, some sixty miles to the rear. This put an intolerable strain on Medical Corps transportation, and General Hawley appealed personally to Littlejohn. The Chief Quartermaster pointed out that medical installations, like combat units, were entitled to graves registration evacuation service from a central collecting point. Before the end of January, ADSEC had established one collecting point for Liège and another for Verdun, and a daily delivery to the

[18] (1) Personal Ltrs, Littlejohn to Judd, 5, 19 Mar 45. Littlejohn Reading File, vol. XXXIV, items 21, 58. (2) IRS, CQM to Deputies, 13 Mar 45, sub: Notes Made of Record on Recent Trip. Same file, vol. XXXIV, item 32. (3) Littlejohn, ed., Passing in Review, ch. 26, pt. II, pp. 5–6 and app. B. (4) Hist QM Sec Oise Sec, 1–30 Apr 45. Hist Br OQMG.
[19] (1) Littlejohn, ed., Passing in Review, ch. 26, pt. II, app. A. (2) Hist of QM Sec ADSEC, p, 38.

[20] IRS, CQM to Franks, 22 Oct 44, sub: Amended Specification of Grave Crosses. Littlejohn Reading File, vol. XXIXA, item 102.
[21] QM Supply in ETO, VII, 55.

cemeteries was made from each. A few weeks later, the sudden German counterattack aimed at Liège converted ADSEC's graves registration units into combat area collecting teams, just as ADSEC's supply depots suddenly were called upon to serve as forward distribution points to the defending divisions. The northern nose of the salient was divided into subsections with collecting points at Liège, Fosse, and Marche. Contrary to the usual procedure of collecting points evacuating to the cemeteries, these collecting teams devoted all their efforts to a sweeping operation, while the cemeteries sent vehicles forward to gather the bodies and return them for burial. This activity continued after the German attack was repulsed, and to support it ADSEC opened a cemetery of its own on 8 February at Neuville-en-Condroz near Liège. Thereafter, remains from the hospitals in the northern ADSEC area were also evacuated to that site.[22]

The resumption of the eastward advance dictated that ADSEC cemeteries be relinquished, and they fell directly under quartermaster base depots, which frequently complained that ADSEC had accomplished little and that a great deal of work still had to be done. For example, Andilly and Limey were taken over in February by the 73d QM Base Depot, after being under ADSEC's jurisdiction for two months, but they were still in poor condition. Local civilians were fully employed on the farms, and while prisoner labor was available at several neighboring depots, the graves registration units had neither transportation to bring POW's daily to the cemeteries nor guards to maintain their own prison camps. The base depot called for engineers to install an extensive drainage system, and for service troops to supervise prisoners of war and Italian service personnel who would be employed to align and paint crosses, improve roads and paths, seed plots to grass, and plant shrubbery. These needs were met by moving forward graves registration units from Normandy, as noted above. Wartime beautification activities culminated on Memorial Day, 1945. Special attention was given to making the burial sites as presentable as possible for the military ceremonies which took place at each cemetery that day. The OCQM provided a printed paper flag for each grave, and was able to supply cloth flags at several large cemeteries on 27 May.[23]

Meanwhile, investigation teams, usually composed of several Americans and an interpreter, extended the search for isolated burials and unburied remains. To assure that none of these was moved until all possible evidence necessary for identification had been obtained, it became the established policy that no isolated body could be removed until the case was reviewed and permission to disinter was granted by the OCQM.[24] The *Service des Sepultures Militaires*, a French organization corresponding to the American Battle Monuments Commission, provided a great deal of useful information for identification purposes. The graves registration program was

---

[22] (1) Hist of QM Sec ADSEC, p. 39. (2) DF, Chief Surgeon ETO to CQM, 4 Jan 45, sub: Graves Registration, and reply, 24 Jan 45. Littlejohn Reading File, vol. XXXIIA, item 116.

[23] Hist QM Sec Oise Sec, 1–31 May 45. Hist Br OQMG.

[24] Hist of 73d QMBD, pp. 40–41; Hist of 62d QMBD, p. 54. Hist Br OQMG.

also considerably aided in identifying isolated burials by local residents, especially farmers and members of the organized underground movement. Such unofficial assistance frequently shed light on the date and circumstances of the death, and corroborative evidence was occasionally found in the records of the local town hall or police station.[25]

For all of the improvisation in the interim, the cemeterial program by the end of hostilities bore a reasonable resemblance to the one conceived before D-day. Not the least of these goals, it will be recalled, was to concentrate burials in as few cemeteries as possible. That this plan was successfully realized is illustrated by the fact that in World War I, 75,000 casualties were interred in more than 2,000 scattered burial areas, while in World War II, amidst highly mobile and widespread tactical operations, only 54 cemeteries were used for more than 117,000 U.S. casualties.[26]

Personal Effects

Return of effects to the relatives of men who die in battle has been a responsibility of U.S. commanders since 1776. In an overseas theater such return involves collecting, processing, and temporary storage of personal belongings, all of which have long been Quartermaster functions. The QM Lost Baggage and Effects Depot, established at St. Nazaire, France, in March 1918, was an earlier example of this logical combination of closely allied functions. On 23 September 1942 the QM depot in London, Q–110, was designated to fulfill precisely the same purposes. The depot commander was appointed a summary court-martial, and was thereby authorized to open sealed packages and to perform various other fiduciary duties. Officials of the United Kingdom gave prompt assurance that effects of American personnel would be exempt from taxation, but estates had to be settled in accordance with British law. This provided that articles of primarily sentimental value could be released immediately, but monetary assets had to be held in the country for six months to satisfy possible claims. Soldiers missing in action, mostly aviators, were considered alive for a six-months period, and thereafter their assets were held for another six months, as those of other deceased persons. On 19 January 1943, Maj. Abraham Meisel was appointed theater effects quartermaster and assumed functions previously fulfilled by the commanding officer of Depot Q–110. In November 1943 the waiting period for persons missing in action was reduced to two months before presumption of death, and the period to satisfy local claims after death was likewise shortened to two months. This change represented a British concession to policies considered desirable by the OCQM. The same policies, with very minor adjustments, were followed on the Continent.[27]

---

[25] (1) Hist of 63d QMBD, p. 31. Hist Br OQMG. (2) USFET Gen Bd Study 107.

[26] (1) See above, n. 16(2). (2) War Dept Summary Sheet, 8 Sep 45, sub: Current Plan for Return of American Dead and Establishment of Overseas and U.S. Cemeteries, pp. 5–7. (3) Opns of QMC During the World War, Monograph 2, pp. 91, 96.

[27] (1) Schuyler D. Hoslett, The Army Effects Bureau of the Kansas City QM Depot, MS Hist, Jul 44. Hist Br OQMG. (2) QM Supply in ETO, VII, 64–71.

Meanwhile personal belongings other than cash assets were creating problems of an entirely different kind. Small items that might be sent to the Army effects quartermaster in Kansas City by parcel post caused no difficulty, but bulky articles that could not be shipped in accordance with current transportation policy created a dilemma. Article of War 112, designed to protect the heirs of the deceased, permitted sale of effects only if no heirs could be found. The effects depot, at Liverpool since May 1943, was already overcrowded, but neither the theater effects quartermaster nor the theater adjutant general was willing to assume responsibility for action contrary to the Articles of War, despite the pressing problems involved. The Adjutant General in Washington was equally cautious, suggesting that permission of the heirs should be secured before any sale. When no action had been taken by midsummer of 1944, the assistant adjutant general of the 2d Bombardment Division, Eighth Air Force, registered a complaint. His unit was being almost overrun by a multitude of automobiles, motorcycles, bicycles, carts, and even horses and dogs. Surely authority could be given to sell these effects. The commanding generals of the Eighth Air Force and United States Strategic Air Forces were in agreement, and the effects quartermaster was willing to comply, but only if authorized by a theater directive. Meanwhile Littlejohn, having received informal assurance of moral support from Lt. Col. John R. Murphy, the Army effects quartermaster in Kansas City, decided to adopt a more practical interpretation of existing regulations. He directed that Colonel Whitney, who had become chief of a combined Graves Registration and Effects Division in March 1944, arrange for sale of the bulky items and transmit the proceeds to Colonel Murphy. The new procedure was regularized by War Department Circular 85 of 16 March 1945, which restricted the authority to sell effects to duly authorized representatives of the theater commander.[28]

One expedient in First Army's efforts to reduce the load carried by soldiers in the Normandy landings was to require that all individuals, when alerted for the attack, send their personal effects to the Liverpool depot, packed in regulation boxes provided for that purpose. In January 1944 the Plans and Training Division, OCQM, recommended requisitioning 500,000 boxes, size 4x8x12 inches, for this purpose. In April, Boughton and Sudbury, two general depots in the Midlands, were designated as temporary effects depots to supplement Liverpool, since the assault troops were expected to turn in from 400 to 500 carloads of effects and baggage per week. The effects quartermaster estimated that he would require over 442,000 square feet of covered storage space by D plus 60.[29]

During the initial phase on the Continent, effects collecting points were operated as branches of Class II and IV QM depots, and evacuated all effects to Liverpool. The Effects Quartermaster, Continent, began to operate on 13 July as a branch of the 64th QM Base Depot at Isigny. This unit immediately began processing effects for direct transmission to the United States, but collections

---

[28] (1) *QM Supply in ETO*, VII, 81–83. (2) Littlejohn, ed., Passing in Review, ch. 26.

[29] (1) See above, ch. XI. (2) *QM Supply in ETO*, VII, 74–75.

speedily outran evacuation. By late August 7,000 square feet at Isigny and 56,000 square feet at Cherbourg were in use, and plans were made to acquire 25,000 more at Le Mans. On 25 September the Personal Effects and Baggage Depot in Paris was opened at Depot Q–177A, and thereafter all effects and lost baggage on the Continent were forwarded to that point. Collecting points in the combat zone evacuated to dumps designated by ADSEC; the latter and the base sections sent effects to Paris by mail if possible, otherwise under armed guard. Despite repeated prodding by Littlejohn, effects operations were not moved forward to Reims until mid-December, although the depot had officially moved there on 20 November. Colonel Ramsey, former chief of the Graves Registration and Effects Division in the United Kingdom, became effects quartermaster in December. Littlejohn had expressed his dissatisfaction with Ramsey's predecessor in the following terms:

It looks as though my whole Graves Registration and Effects Division is entrenched behind the ramparts of Paris, sitting on its fanny smoking big cigars and dreaming about something which may or may not happen. . . . Last week we had the Inspector General in on this project. I found the Effects Depot still in Paris, after I had ordered it to move weeks ago.[30]

Although Ramsey did an able job of reorganizing the effects depot, apparently the armies had grown accustomed in the interim to operating without such an installation. On 11 December, having examined the procedures current in the forward areas, the Chief Quartermaster demanded of his personnel officer: "Why do we need an effects depot at all if everything is shipped direct from the battlefield to Kansas City?"[31] Actually only the positively identified effects of personnel definitely known to be deceased could be handled in that fashion. A depot close behind the front was absolutely essential to hold the personal belongings of those missing in action, of those in hospitals, and an ever-increasing backlog of unclaimed and unidentified baggage. Since Q-256, the salvage depot at Reims, was overcrowded, an independent QM effects depot, Q–290, was opened at Folembray on 29 January 1945. Here in a former glass factory were 150,000 square feet of covered storage and billets for 20 officers and 185 enlisted men, the entire military complement of the installation.[32]

A major cause of difficulty in processing effects was the fact that all of an enlisted man's clothing was government property, and because of clothing shortages in the theater extra clothing not on his person had to be salvaged for reuse. An officer's clothing, apart from certain special-purpose articles, was assumed to be his personal property. The baggage of both officers and men often contained miscellaneous items of organizational equipment urgently needed in the theater, especially mess gear, shelter halves, intrenching tools, and webbing articles. The duffel bags of equipment left behind in Normandy by many units have already been mentioned as a problem

---

[30] IRS, Littlejohn to Lt Col M. K. Goodwin (Actg DCQM), 27 Nov 44, sub: Personal Effects Policies. Littlejohn Reading File, vol. XXX, item 98.

[31] IRS, CQM to Col Odell, 11 Dec 44, sub: Handling of GR Supplies. Littlejohn Reading File, vol XXXI, item 19.

[32] QM Supply in ETO, VII, 77–78.

with regard to delivery of winter clothing to the combat troops. They posed an almost equal problem to effects quartermasters, since in some units nearly half of the original owners had become casualties—either dead or hospitalized. This was realized only after several large shipments of such bags had arrived in the combat zone, where many could not be delivered to their owners. On 5 December the Chief Quartermaster informed the quartermasters of the First, Third, and Ninth Armies that the OCQM would provide transportation to take all such bags to the recently opened effects depot at Reims for processing, classification, and salvage.[33]

A great variety of personal articles had been found in the pockets, duffel bags, and footlockers of American casualties. While unit graves registration officers usually removed food, candy, toilet supplies, and any items that might cause embarrassment to the next of kin, the application of this policy was carefully checked along the line of evacuation. Such items as money, fountain pens, cameras, watches, jewelry, books, paintings, photos, wine, and medals, among others, were sent rearward by the combat units to army Class II and IV depots, and in turn passed back to ADSEC effects collecting points. The 62d Quartermaster Base Depot at Verdun, for example, handled 155 truckloads of such items from 1 November to 30 June, principally from Third Army, but also from adjacent hospitals. Here the effects were received and recorded before they were delivered to the

effects quartermaster at Reims, and later at Folembray. Personal property that belonged with a body already identified—and this was the more typical case—was evacuated with the minimum possible delay to the zone of interior. That belonging to persons whose death was not definitely established, on the other hand, was held in the communications zone for sixty days before shipment to the United States. Effects that might aid in identifying bodies were usually held at cemeteries. In executing this responsibility, as in the care of cemeteries, special effort was taken to assure proper handling. For example, after experience had proved that watches and fountain pens were often broken when cloth effects pouches were shipped to the United States in mail sacks, boxes were provided to protect fragile articles. Extra precaution was taken to prevent pilferage from the warehouses, packages were always transferred under special guard, and the backgrounds of civilians employed in this activity were carefully checked for honesty.[34]

The American Graves Registration Command

At the end of hostilities in Europe, plans had already been made to wind up most Quartermaster activities in the Allied countries. Many combat and service troops and a large part of the theater supplies had already been moved

---

[33] Ltrs, CQM to QM's First, Third, Ninth Armies, 5 Dec 44, sub: Personal Effects. Littlejohn Reading File, vol. XXXI, items 12a, 12b, 12c.

[34] (1) Hist of QM Sec ADSEC, p. 40; Hist of 62d QMBD, pp. 52, 54; Continental Operating Instrs, OCQM ETO, 19 Feb 45, pp. 56–57. All in Hist Br OQMG. (2) QM Supply in ETO, VII, 74–78. (3) IRS, CQM to Odell, 11 Dec 44, sub: Handling of GR Supplies. Littlejohn Reading File, vol. XXXI, item 19.

forward into Germany and Austria. Plans to dispose of remaining supplies and close down service installations were well advanced. Graves registration was by far the largest item of unfinished Quartermaster business within the liberated countries. No formal policy decisions had yet been made, but a strong popular sentiment dictated that this activity could not be transferred to enemy territory. It would have to be brought to completion where it had begun, either by repatriation of war dead or by the establishment of permanent cemeteries in Allied countries. It was therefore clear that whatever organization inherited these responsibilities would have to become largely self-sufficient when the base sections were inactivated and the various U.S. headquarters were moved into Germany.[35]

Littlejohn had foreseen many of these problems, and it could be said that the organization of the 1st QM Group, to operate in the quiescent rear areas of COMZ, had been a modest step toward their solution. On 7 June 1945 Littlejohn discussed the matter in detail with General Eisenhower, who stated he was willing to release control of graves registration operations in the theater to The Quartermaster General, provided the personnel appointed to direct this function met with his approval. The Supreme Commander confirmed that no permanent cemeteries were to be established on enemy soil, and directed that

first priority be given to evacuating U.S. dead from those areas in Germany and Austria which were shortly to come under French, British, or Russian control. He further suggested that all bodies be concentrated at Henri-Chapelle and one cemetery in Normandy, but Littlejohn questioned the advisability of this. The Chief Quartermaster prophesied that Congress would soon act to authorize return of the dead to the United States, which would involve moving bodies twice.[36]

Eisenhower and Bradley concurred in the appointment of Brig. Gen. James W. Younger, the former QM, 12th Army Group, and on 18 June, as an interim measure, the latter was made chief of the Graves Registration and Effects Division, OCQM. On 2 August, Younger became Director General, U.S. Theater Graves Registration Service, Theater Service Forces, European Theater, while remaining a member of Littlejohn's staff. The mission, authority, and troop basis of this new headquarters were rather ill-defined, and likely to remain so, since the high level command structure of the theater was undergoing evolution and all personnel planning was nullified again and again by sweeping demobilization directives from Washington. For example, late in August Gregory warned Littlejohn that the new headquarters would be expanded to administer graves registration activities in the Mediterranean and Middle East theaters, and plans were made calling for a strength of nearly 7,000 men, organized into 267 QM units. By contrast, the units ac-

---

[35] This brief summary of the origin, mission, and initial organization of the American Graves Registration Command is derived from Edward Steere and Thayer M. Boardman, *Final Disposition of World War II Dead, 1945–51,* QMC Historical Studies, Series II, No. 4 (Washington, 1957), especially Chapter V.

[36] IRS, CQM to Col Bobrink, Chief GR&E Div, 8 Jun 45, sub: GRS in Europe. Littlejohn Reading File, vol. XXXVII, item 11.

tually assigned at the time—three group headquarters, four battalion headquarters, and fifteen graves registration companies—had an authorized strength of about 2,000. But they actually mustered less than half that number, and most of those remaining were eligible for redeployment under the point system. Even more serious was the fact that few of the officers and men remaining with the units were experienced and technically qualified. Striving to overcome these handicaps in the ETO, Younger largely ignored his potential responsibilities in the Mediterranean and concentrated on setting up a five-zone territorial organization, mainly to care for the cemeteries on the Continent and in the United Kingdom. Littlejohn became Commanding General, American Graves Registration Command, on 1 October, and attempted with little success to organize five field commands which would undertake a systematic combing of battle terrain in Europe, the Mediterranean, North Africa, and the Middle East. General Younger assumed command of one such field unit at Fulda, Germany, in October to conduct a sweep of Germany, Poland, and Czechoslovakia, but none of the others were activated. Doubtless it was a relief when on 11 December General Lee decided that the scheme conceived in Washington was impracticable, and that graves registration activities in the three theaters were not to be combined.

Littlejohn retained Younger's organization of five cemeterial zones, redesignating them as sectors and placing them under the supervision of Colonel Talbot, chief of the Cemetery Plant Division, American Graves Registration Command. They were geographically identical with existing base sections, so their logistical support presented few problems. But efforts to organize mobile units to locate and concentrate the dead ran into endless difficulties. On paper, a second field command was established at Brussels on 15 November, but for many weeks it was simply an office with a few officers and civilians and no subordinate units whatever. At this juncture Littlejohn decided that his dual role was prejudicial to efficient performance in either sphere of action, and asked that he be relieved as theater Chief Quartermaster.[37] Colonel Odell was appointed to that post on 24 November 1945, and Littlejohn was able to give undivided attention to the organizational structure and manpower problems of the American Graves Registration Command. No permanent and satisfactory solution to the problem of lack of trained manpower was ever found, but by early January 1946 the Graves Registration Command was assured that 7,244 officers and men, about evenly divided between green recruits and transfers from the antiaircraft artillery, would be available until 1 July 1946. Thereafter its strength was to be reduced to 2,500. To provide for the long-range requirements of this force, depots were taken over by the command at Isle St. Germain and Fontainebleau, and requisitions were made upon surplus theater

_____

[37] When Littlejohn was relieved as Chief Quartermaster, he brought the OCQM historical files with him to the American Graves Registration Command, where they were extremely useful. He later observed that, in retrospect, an active Historical Branch of the command, to collect on-the-job information on a current basis during combat, would have been of inestimable value to the Quartermaster Corps and to the U.S. Army. Cf. Littlejohn, ed., Passing in Review, ch. 26.

stocks of clothing, accommodation stores, office supplies, equipment, and motor vehicles. Under pressure from Congress, which reflected the impatience of the American people, the OQMG had conceived a hasty plan to comb all battle areas during the first half of 1946, and to complete the entire project in two years. But Littlejohn insisted that requisitions should be based upon requirements for a five-year period and shaped his storage policy accordingly. He doubted that even a very large labor force could operate effectively without intensive training, for which no facilities had been prepared. Even his estimate of the time required proved to be somewhat overoptimistic.

By March 1946, when Littlejohn turned over command to Colonel Odell and departed for the United States, the dimensions of the task facing the American Graves Registration Command were fairly clear, although decisions on how it was to be performed were still lacking. On V–E Day approximately 117,000 Americans were buried in fifty-four temporary cemeteries. Eleven months later the number of cemeteries had been reduced to thirty-six, and it was estimated that recoveries would bring the total number of burials to over 148,000. A decision had been made in principle that next of kin might decide whether their dead were to be repatriated or were to remain overseas, but the information upon which to base a poll of relatives was not yet available. There were sharp differences of opinion as to what the results

of such a poll might be, which in turn influenced opinions on the number of burial sites that should be retained as permanent cemeteries. The final result was that some 41 percent of the 146,000 bodies ultimately recovered remained in the ETO, and the ten sites proposed by the Graves Registration Command in April 1946 became the cemeteries approved by Congress in August 1947.[38]

In the postwar Graves Registration Command, it was generally agreed that some of the mistakes, omissions, and oversights committed in graves registration activities during combat were clearly unavoidable, but others were not. Whether avoidable or not, an exhaustive effort was made later to resolve every discrepancy that arose, and a large postwar organization devoted nearly six years to that activity. Repatriation of the dead and establishment of permanent overseas cemeteries were not wartime activities, but they offer valuable lessons to combat graves registration officers. It is most important to remember that no action regarding graves registration matters taken in wartime is final, and that every wartime decision, no matter how trivial, will be subject to later scrutiny.

---

[38] It was only in the final stages of selecting permanent cemeteries that the American Battle Monuments Commission entered the picture. This organization was responsible for World War I cemeteries, and Littlejohn had been giving informal assistance to its representatives in the ETO since the fall of 1944. Apparently by mutual agreement, the commission took no part in current wartime graves registration activities.

CHAPTER XX

Miscellaneous Quartermaster Services

In the European theater, Quartermasters provided all the services that had been made available in the Mediterranean and a few extra as well.[1] Probably the most varied of all Quartermaster activities came under the general heading of "service," or labor. This commonly implied the stevedore and porterage duties in which QM service companies had been trained, but also came to include the wide variety of functions that these companies were actually called upon to perform. Such units comprised about 45 percent of Quartermaster strength in the theater, and served as a reservoir of semiskilled labor to meet all contingencies. They provided most of the security guards at depots, supervised civilian labor, and guarded prisoners of war. With special training or technical supervision they could and did, on occasion, perform the whole gamut of Quartermaster functions.

A considerable number of service companies, and a few other QM units, were attached or permanently assigned to the other technical services. In February 1945 the OCQM reported that in COMZ alone there were 9½ service companies being used by Ordnance, 4½ by the Engineers, 6 by the Signal Corps, and 1 by the Transportation Corps, which also utilized 3 QM railhead companies. By the end of hostilities, the Transportation Corps was also using 2 QM service battalion headquarters, and Ordnance had borrowed 2 QM composite company headquarters. In the armies, only headquarters and service companies were involved, but in addition to assignments similar to those in COMZ the distribution of QM service companies to other technical services normally included 2 companies at medical depots, and occasional loan of a company to Civil Affairs and to the Provost Marshal.[2]

Bath and Laundry Services

Experience in North Africa and Italy had confirmed the desirability of baths and clean clothing for combat troops, but had also demonstrated the extreme difficulty of providing such services in the forward areas. Even at the end of the fighting in Italy the Fifth Army quartermaster concentrated his bath and laundry units at rest areas, where they

---

[1] For example gardening service, already described in the U.K. (chapter X), was also made available on the Continent in early 1945 by the Subsistence Division, OCQM. But the armies were on the move into Germany, and gardening activity before V–E Day was largely confined to convalescent hospitals. Cf. *QM Supply in ETO*, VI 99–100.

[2] (1) Hq COMZ ETO, Wkly QM Activities Rpts, 25 Feb, 8 May 45. ETO QM 319.1. (2) TUSA AAR, QM, 33. (3) *FUSA Rpt Opns*, 23 Feb–8 May 45, III, 77, 87–88.

were only available to combat troops on rotation. The obsolete and immobile equipment of the QM sterilization companies, the only bath units available until the summer of 1944, was not suitable for employment farther forward.[3] Laundry trailers were somewhat less clumsy, but were usually placed near the bath units.

For the European campaign, Quartermaster planners in the United Kingdom were determined to give better service. This was a matter of necessity, since conditions in the ETO brought on urgent problems not encountered in the Mediterranean theater. In a colder climate troops wore more and heavier clothing, which increased the danger of insect infestation. Moreover, plans provided for a steady advance by armored and motorized forces. There would be little opportunity for the rotation into rest areas that was often possible during the Italian campaigns. Under the conditions expected in France, mobile equipment was needed. The OCQM was especially hopeful regarding the improved trailers of the QM fumigation and bath companies. Only five of these new units had reached the ETO by March 1944, but it was hoped that equipment to reorganize the twelve sterilization companies in the theater in conformity with the new T/O&E would arrive before D-day. The equipment never arrived, and the Engineers, who were responsible for baths for comfort and cleanliness, suffered a similar disappointment. The ETO Chief

Engineer had requisitioned 600 mobile shower units in the spring of 1944, but by July only 32 units, all earmarked for the USAAF, had arrived, and there was no prospect that any more would be available before the end of the year. In theory, delousing was the primary mission of the QM fumigation and bath company and the sterilization company, but the OCQM had also made plans to provide as many baths as possible for the troops. By July only two more fumigation and bath companies had arrived, making a total of seven available for service in the combat zone. The twelve sterilization companies already mentioned could provide 30,000 baths per day, but only in rear areas.[4]

Production and delivery of the large bath and laundry trailers constituted a major bottleneck, retarding the build-up. From October 1944 to February 1945, the coldest, wettest, and muddiest months that northern Europe had experienced in decades, the 12th Army Group deployed only an average of 12 fumigation and bath companies and 15 semimobile laundry companies in its combat zone, at evacuation hospitals, salvage repair sites, and bath points. Meanwhile the even less well-serviced 6th Army Group had to get along with 3 fumigation and bath companies and 8 laundry companies.[5]

Besides additional companies of these types, less mobile and more specialized

---

[3] (1) See above, ch. VIII. (2) *QM Supply in Fifth Army*, pp. 29, 68. (3) The QM Fumigation and Bath (F&B) Company, T/O&E 10–257, was authorized on 1 June 1943, but none were reported in MTOUSA until July 1944.

[4] (1) *QM Supply in ETO*, VI, 81. (2) Eight Chemical Corps decontamination companies served in the ETO, and in the absence of chemical warfare contributed to bath and laundry service for combat troops. Cf. Leo P. Brophy and George J. B. Fisher, *The Chemical Warfare Service: Organizing for War* UNITED STATES ARMY IN WORLD WAR II (Washington, 1959), pp. 458–59.

[5] 12th Army Group Rpt of Opns, XII, 255.

units were also available to provide the same services in the Communications Zone. For example, in December 1944 there were 16 sterilization companies as well as 7 fumigation and bath companies to give showers to COMZ troops, and 78 fixed laundry sections, each capable of serving a 1,000-bed hospital, to supplement 11½ semimobile laundry companies.[6]

It might appear that deployment of the units discriminated against combat troops, the more so since service troops had access to civilian laundry and bathing facilities seldom available to those in the front lines. That sentiment was emphatically expressed by the troops themselves at the time, and concurred in by a majority of division quartermasters. On the other hand, the armies did not use their assets very efficiently. They operated the service units actually assigned to them at an average rate of less than half their capacity. Combat quartermasters demanded additional units of the types then available, but they also unanimously recommended the development of smaller, lighter, less vulnerable, and more easily camouflaged equipment, suitable for employment nearer the front. All the various vehicular and mechanical improvisations developed by the combat units were smaller than standard equipment, and the same trend was noticeable in the experimental models under development in the United States at the end of hostilities. It appears that the type of equipment then

available could not be operated far enough forward to serve front-line troops effectively, and deployment of more bath and laundry units in the combat zone would not have improved service to combat units.[7]

Showers in the Field

Four fumigation and bath companies were available to each army during the winter months of the European campaign, but quartermasters later agreed that seven would not have been excessive. The two platoons in the company each had a supply section which maintained a clothing exchange at the shower point and an operating section which took care of a trailer containing 24 shower heads, later increased to 36. Whenever possible, one platoon was attached to each division on the line, thereby enabling the division quartermaster, with his knowledge of the location and mission of the units, to place the platoon closer to the troops to be served. More often one platoon served two divisions, while the other provided baths for corps troops plus another division. A location equally accessible to two headquarters was rather far from both of them, so that service was rarely satisfactory. At maximum capacity, the company could process 3,600 men in a 16-hour day, or an infantry division in slightly more than four days. Such service was only possible under ideal conditions, when a division was withdrawn from combat, when an entire fumigation and bath company was available to serve

---

[6] Chart, Reallocation of All ETO QM Units, prepared by Troops Br OCQM, 12 Dec 44. Hist Br OQMG. Three of the laundry companies with 6th Army Group and two with COMZ were Italian units; one sterilization company was also Italian. See also, app. B.

[7] (1) Risch, *The Quartermaster Corps: Organization, Supply, and Services,* I, pp. 155–66. (2) USFET Gen Bd Study 108, Service Opns of the QMC, pp. 27, 31. (3) 12th Army Group Rpt of Opns, XII, 255.

it, and when all the necessary supplies were at hand, including 20,000 gallons of clear water daily.[8]

During the first weeks in Normandy, the critical need for troops and supplies delayed the landing of bath units. Two companies, the 857th and 863d, were scheduled to arrive on OMAHA by D plus 21, but reports indicate that they did not begin operations until eleven days later. When Colonel McNamara detailed one platoon of the 863d Fumigation and Bath Company to XIX Corps on 9 July, he also outlined the principles to be followed in making the most efficient use of the unit. Because of the scarcity of units and the size of the beachhead, he emphasized the importance of marching troops to the bath point, rather than taking the bath point to the troops. Because of the vulnerability and conspicuous silhouette of the bathing equipment, he requested that it be located out of range of enemy artillery and carefully concealed from enemy air observation.[9]

Soon after the bath units began to operate and when divisional quartermasters were able to think about providing some of the less essential services, several combat divisions displayed their own improvisations. The battle-wise 1st Division Quartermaster Company converted a captured German sterilization unit, some pipe, and a latrine screen into a six-head portable shower. About the same time, the 4th Division built its own ten-head unit, which was mounted and carried on the bed of a 2½-ton truck. Before the European campaign was over,

many other divisional quartermaster companies confirmed the need for such services by constructing comparable field expedients out of salvaged and captured equipment. In March 1945, the QM company of the 28th Division was finally able to draw one of the mobile Engineer shower units already mentioned from a First Army supply point. It was operated by an 11-man crew and had a maximum daily capacity of 894 men. The entire outfit could be packed on a one-ton trailer.[10]

The pursuit across France upset the bath program much as it had affected all other Quartermaster activities. Combat troops were moving too quickly to utilize rearward bath points, and frequent displacement of the bath companies made them inoperative over long periods of time. In the fall of 1944 and through the winter, the more stabilized tactical situation encouraged greater use of bath facilities. Troops took advantage of showers and tubs wherever they found them, procedures varying from area to area. On the northern flank of the American line, the 29th and 30th Infantry Divisions and the 2d Armored, as well as corps and army troops north of Aachen, forsook the tented quartermaster bath units in favor of indoor shower facilities that were available at coal mines in and around Heerlen, Holland.[11] On the other hand, First Army units in other areas used the bathing facilities at rest camps operated by corps, and more than 300,000 men were accommodated in

---

[8] (1) T/O&E 10–257, 3 July 1944, authorized a unit of 3 officers and 85 enlisted men. (2) OTCQM TSFET Operational Study 10, p. 47.

[9] FUSA Rpt of Opns, 20 Oct 43–1 Aug 44, VI, 196, 230–31.

[10] (1) 4th QM Co, AAR for July, 4 Aug 44; 28th QM Co, AAR, Mar 45. Hist Br OQMG. (2) OCQM Field Obsv Rpt 1. ETO 319.25, QM.

[11] OCQM Field Obsv Rpt 3 [ca. 30 Oct 44]. ETO 319.25, QM.

three months from September through November.[12]

The onset of cold and wet weather in 1944 made the clothing exchange feature of the bath operation as attractive as the hot shower itself. Imitating Fifth Army practices in Italy, First Army started this two-in-one service in July. Third Army was more conservative and waited until the end of November before introducing the clothing exchange.[13] Wherever such an exchange was part of the shower service—the practice was found at divisional as well as at corps shower points—the procedures were very similar to those, discussed earlier, in the Mediterranean area. But one significant difference was that whenever possible bath and laundry units were brought farther forward in the ETO. For example at Homburg Haut, France, one platoon of the 859th Fumigation and Bath Company served 1,500 men of the 80th Division daily within eight miles of the front lines. To maintain a 2,000-set stock of clean clothes for exchange, a platoon of the 899th Semimobile Laundry Company located itself near Homburg Haut and devoted its efforts to laundering all soiled garments that were found serviceable.[14]

Several divisions in First Army, in an effort to assure an ample stock of clothing for an exchange system, reduced the soldier's allowance to one complete uniform and held the rest of the issued clothing in a revolving reserve. Garments left behind by casualties, and other miscellaneous salvage, were utilized in the same way. Where this was the practice, it was often possible to obtain a fresh woolen outer uniform as well as clean undergarments at the shower point. Inevitably, the clothing exchange program involved a problem of sorting clothing and measuring it for size. As in Italy, the solution reached was to maintain three sizes only—large, medium, and small. While such a procedure by Class II and IV depots in the rear invariably brought protests, the troops found it acceptable in the forward areas.[15]

Fumigation and Delousing Activities

In contrast to the trench warfare of World War I, the war of movement in the ETO, plus the shower system and the two-ounce can of insecticide issued to every man, spared the troops the discomfort of body lice known by the veteran of the American Expeditionary Force as "cooties." Early in continental operations, it became evident that this was not a real threat and that the six methyl bromide fumigation chambers in each fumigation and bath company were superfluous. While still in Normandy, McNamara removed the six chambers from each bath company and assigned them to First Army's salvage dump, where they remained for most of the continental campaign. Salvaged articles that were not obviously dirty were normally fumigated, rather than washed, before reissue. This applied particularly to woolen articles. Fumigation chambers were often turned over to sterilization

---

[12] *FUSA Rpt of Opns*, 1 Aug 44–22 Feb 45, IV, 59, 96.
[13] *FUSA Rpt of Opns*, 20 Oct 43–1 Aug 44, VI, 141. (2) TUSA AAR, II, QM, 12.
[14] (1) OCQM Field Obsv Rpt 9 [ca. 20 Dec 44], and Photographic Annex. ETO 319.25, QM. (2) TUSA AAR, II, QM, 16, 18. (3) See above, ch. VIII.

---

[15] Personal Ltr, Sgt Don Robinson to Brig Gen G. F. Doriot, 17 Jul 45. Hist Br OQMG.

FUMIGATING WOOL CLOTHING *at a salvage dump in Normandy, July 1944.*

companies for use in the base sections, since the steam sterilizers authorized for these units shrank woolens excessively.[16]

Even if American troops did not need delousing, it was quickly evident that prisoners of war did. The armies were moving too quickly to deal with this problem during the summer, and the responsibility fell to ADSEC. To cope with the situation, the ADSEC quartermaster used several QM sterilization companies. These were less mobile than fumigation and bath companies because of their large van-type steam sterilization and bath trailers, but their large personnel complements made them better equipped to bathe and dust such con-

centrations of prisoners as the 75,000 collected at Le Mans and Alençon, 15,000 at Suippes, and 50,000 at Compiègne.[17]

The armies felt no need for fumigation materials or bulk DDT until they entered Germany and exposed the squalor of the Allied prisoner of war camps. In addition to an appalling incidence of malnutrition and pulmonary tuberculosis, the occupants were infested with lice, and outbreaks of typhus occurred in Cologne and Aachen early in March. The persons and possessions of recovered Allied military personnel, displaced persons, and liberated political prisoners had to be fumigated or dusted

[16] USFET Gen Bd Study 108, Sv Opns of the QMC, p. 30.

[17] (1) *Ibid.*, p. 29. (2) Hist of QM ADSEC, pp. 47, 48. (3) OTCQM TSFET Operational Study 10, p. 30.

with DDT before the people could be permitted freedom of movement, particularly in a westerly direction across the Rhine.[18]

Laundries

Semimobile laundry companies attempted to operate across Europe in the same way as the bath units, but there were basic defects in the organization and equipment of the laundry units. The supposedly self-sufficient organizational structure of the laundry sections and platoons was hampered by the fact that only four organic truck tractors were provided in each company. These were only able to move the sixteen laundry trailers assigned to the unit by a slow shuttling system, or occasionally by borrowing prime movers from higher echelons. In a war of rapid movement these were awkward improvisations and, judging by the frequency of complaint from the armies, quite inadequate. Moreover, in the ETO laundry priorities went to evacuation hospitals, medical depots, salvage installations, and troop units, in that order. The planned War Department troop basis, five companies per army, was theoretically able to handle the higher priorities plus 37 percent of troop requirements. That allotment did not actually materialize until March 1945, when the cold weather was nearly over, and even then the laundry units handled only 5 to 10 percent of troop laundry. Colonel Busch of Third Army, who was the strongest advocate

of additional QM services for the combat troops, recommended ten laundry companies per army. The five companies per army actually assigned in the spring of 1945 were normally distributed as follows: one in support of each of three corps; one split into eight sections serving medical installations; one processing salvage and also serving army troops.[19]

Attaching a semimobile laundry section to each evacuation hospital proved eminently successful since the vital medical services could have their laundry done without loss of time due to backlogs or transportation difficulties. But such deployment also involved a certain risk of damage by enemy fire as indicated by the repeated instances of Third Army laundry units having been bombed and disabled. Like the shower units, laundry trailers were too large, conspicuous, and vulnerable for satisfactory service in the forward areas.[20]

The laundries attached to corps operated primarily to serve the clothing exchanges at the bath points. In the fall of 1944, as part of the campaign against trench foot, these laundries assumed the additional responsibility of providing dry socks to the field troops. The program was separate from that of clothing exchange, and one which generally worked through the ration distribution system. Salvage collecting squads were placed at the ration dumps, where they issued clean socks to units on the

[18] (1) Hist of QM Sec ADSEC, p. 48. (2) *FUSA Rpt of Opns*, 23 Feb–8 May 45, II, 81.

[19] (1) USFET Gen Bd Study 108, pp. 22–25. (2) Ltr, Col Gilbert E. Parker, WD Obsv, to CG AGF, 1 Jul 45, sub: AGF Rpt 1074, Field Laundries: Bath Units. ETO 319.25. (3) See ch. VIII, above.
[20] (1) *FUSA Rpt of Opns*, 20 Oct 43–1 Aug 44, VI, 135. (2) TUSA AAR, II, QM, 12, 19.

basis of morning report strengths, and collected the dirty socks. Occasionally, laundries delivered socks direct to division supply points.[21]

The theoretical capacity of the laundry companies was service to 48,000 men per week, based upon 6 pieces or 4½ pounds per man laundered in seven 16-hour days. This was frequently achieved when units turned in their laundry in bulk and assumed the responsibility for sorting and distribution to individuals. Operating on the individual bundle system, maximum capacity was 30,000 bundles per week. These were maximum figures, based upon optimum working conditions. Over a period of eleven months, the laundries of the 12th Army Group operated at about 42 percent of capacity. The relative immobility of laundry units meant that they were seldom far enough forward to be readily accessible to combat units. It was found that the laundries supporting corps could rarely establish anything resembling a regular schedule. Combat forces were subject to movement on short notice, there was no uniformity in the amounts of laundry brought in by the units, and high priority orders appeared without warning. The Ninth Army concluded that it was preferable simply to make arrangements with the laundry companies on a catch-as-catch-can basis, and Third and Seventh Army records provide supporting evidence.[22] An illuminating day-by-day account of the frustrations endured by a field unit in seeking laundry service was presented by the 404th Field Artillery Group in a detailed chronology intended to prove that "laundry facilities have been both inadequate and unsatisfactory:"

8 Dec 44, the 899th Laundry Company located in the vicinity of Fremery was preparing to move and therefore refused to accept laundry from this unit.

13 Dec 44, the 899th Laundry Company located in the vicinity of Remering refused acceptance of laundry of this unit as they had more laundry than they could handle at this time.

16 Dec 44, the 899th Laundry Company . . . stated that since they were handling laundry for two divisions, it would be impossible to handle laundry from this unit for the time being.

18 Dec 44, the 899th Laundry Company . . . accepted the laundry of this unit but only after considerable persuasion.

24 Dec 44, when an attempt was made to recover laundered items it was found that the 899th Laundry Company had moved. After investigation . . . it was found that the laundry had been left in an adjacent field. Investigation revealed that among 47 bundles laundered, there were many items missing as well as a complete bundle. Further inspection of laundered items revealed that a majority . . . were very soiled.[23]

It should be noted that the poor performance recorded above was that of a unit operating under the inefficient bundle system. Laundries that operated in the forward areas in support of clothing exchanges usually did much better—one reason being that the revolving stock system reduced sorting operations. In December 1944 and January 1945 the

---

[21] (1) TUSA AAR, II, QM, 12. (2) *FUSA Rpt of Opns,* 1 Aug 44–22 Feb 45, IV, 59. (3) Maj J. E. McCormick, Jr., "QM Operations in NUSA," *QMTSJ,* VII, No. 28 (29 June 1945), 29.

[22] (1) Source cited n. 21 (3). (2) 3d Ind, QM XV Corps for G–4 XV Corps. Hist Br OQMG. (3) OTCQM TSFET Operational Study 10, p. 28.

[23] Ltr, CO 404th FA Group to CG XII Corps, 3 Jan 45, sub: QM Laundry Sv, and Ind. Hist Br OQMG.

laundries of Third Army, operating mainly in direct support of bath points, produced 97 percent and 103 percent respectively of their theoretical capacity. Laundry units in First Army showed wide variations in performance, from the 38 percent showing of one green unit to an astonishing 121 percent of capacity, maintained for 68 consecutive days by the 595th QM Laundry Company supporting V Corps.[24]

Immediately behind the combat zone ADSEC operated a modest number of semimobile laundry companies, primarily to provide service for salvage installations. Here again troop clothing had the lowest priorities and could only be laundered when military or civilian facilities developed capacity in excess of primary requirements.[25] When ADSEC's seventeen general hospitals began to arrive on the Continent in the middle of July 1944, each was assigned a fixed hospital-type laundry platoon which, for all practical purposes, was an organic part of the medical installation. Because of this affiliation, hospitals obtained dependable laundry service during the breakthrough period; they were the only ADSEC units to do so.

ADSEC laundry units in Normandy experienced various technical and organizational difficulties. Swift moving currents provided adequate quantities of water, but many streams were so shallow that the pumps sucked in dirt and loose materials, and became clogged. To prevent this, the laundry units deepened the stream beds and submerged box frames to form a still pool from which clear water could be drawn. Meanwhile, the main administrative problem of the laundry units attached to hospitals could be traced to a lack of enough Quartermaster officers to permit the assignment of an officer to each platoon. The units were headed by QM noncommissioned officers and commanded by the senior officer of the medical unit to which they were attached. The laundry officer of ADSEC's Quartermaster Section attempted to supervise their technical operations, but this was an impossible task for one man, and a satisfactory remedy to the problem was never found.[26]

Since ADSEC's quartermaster base depots were somewhat more static than the depots and dumps in the combat zone, it was easier for that echelon to supplement its laundry shortages by exploiting commercial facilities in the cities and towns along the axis of advance. In fact, ADSEC's initial operations on the Continent began in the second week of July—about the same time that First Army provided such service to the combat troops—when four commercial laundries in Cherbourg and their civilian workers went to work for the Americans. As was usual in the case of any procurement of local services, extensive repairs had to be made to the plants and operating supplies had to be furnished. In Belgium, ADSEC again surveyed commercial facilities and began negotiations for their use. In Namur and Liège, static Belgian military laundries were available, again after making repairs and

[24] (1) TUSA AAR, QM, 16, 18. (2) *FUSA Rpt of Opns,* 1 Aug 44–22 Feb 45, IV, 116. The 595th produced 2,306,872 lbs. of troop, organizational, and salvage laundry between 16 Dec 44 and 22 Feb 45, or an average of 35,248 lbs. per day.

[25] Hist of QM Sec ADSEC, p. 44, an. D, pp. 3, 5.

[26] (1) *Ibid.,* pp. 44–45. (2) In November 1944 each Laundry Platoon, Hospital, Type B, was reorganized into two Laundry Sections, Type EJ, each commanded by a technical sergeant. This was part of the QM cellular organization, T/O 10–500.

installing equipment, but the services of the Liège plant were periodically interrupted by enemy V–1 bombs.[27]

Meanwhile, COMZ service troops throughout France, especially in the urban areas, looked to commercial facilities. Where troops were billeted in hotels, where the American Red Cross maintained overnight accommodations for troops on leave or furlough, and where transient billets were situated along arterial military highways, it was necessary to obtain laundry services from local plants. These were generally available, but not before repairing or replacing equipment and furnishing coal, soap, and bleach. In addition to these and other delays inherent in the local procurement program, prices, bundle sizes, and transportation also had to be agreed upon.[28] Ultimately working arrangements were reached, but it is safe to conclude that "locally procured" laundry service negotiated by the individual soldier who reimbursed a laundress with cigarettes, candy, soap, or rations was in many respects the single most satisfactory system for keeping troops in clean clothing.

Salvage Collection and Repair

For two years in the United Kingdom, each base section had been largely responsible for its own salvage. Depots within each section specialized in the

various salvage categories—clothing, equipment, general supplies, and footwear. Unit supply officers sorted salvage carefully and insured that it was forwarded to the correct depot, since new items could only be obtained in exchange for old ones. In the last few weeks before D-day, a combination of factors overloaded the salvage organization and caused complete breakdown of this procedure. The normal seasonal turn-in of winter clothing coincided with preparations for an amphibious attack, and combat troops discarded many slightly worn articles which would have been considered entirely adequate for garrison duty. Meanwhile, Colonel McNamara had issued specific orders that the assault troops were to turn in a whole list of individual clothing and equipment items considered nonessential in the initial operation of seizing a beachhead. Carrying the same idea one step further, combat commanders made similar reductions in the organizational equipment of their units. Having experienced somewhat similar conditions during the TORCH operation, the OCQM designated most of the QM depots in the British Isles and all of the assembly areas near the south coast of England as salvage collection points. Lydney (Q–140) on the lower Severn was set up as a central salvage repair depot.[29]

The departing combat units turned in a veritable avalanche of unwanted items, averaging ten pieces per man and considerably exceeding the amounts anticipated by the OCQM. Salvage was a new additional assignment for most of the depots, earlier concerned with storage alone. Receipts ran as high as 6,000,000

---

[27] (1) Same as n. 25. (2) Hist of 58th QMBD. Hist Br OQMG.

[28] (1) QM Supply in ETO, VI, 93–94. (2) Allowances of coal for static laundries are described in Ch. XV. (3) The allowances for laundry soap, originally 2,160 lbs. per 1,000 men for 30 days, were increased to 2,800 lbs. as a result of ETO experience. Similarly, the allowance of bleach was increased from 12 to 42 pounds. Cf. OTCQM TSFET Operational Study 2, p. 93.

[29] (1) QM Supply in ETO, VI, 39–41. (2) Hist of Q–140. Hist Br OQMG. (3) See Table 8.

pieces per week, and arrived as an unsorted mixture of old and new articles, wet and dry, clean and dirty—Quartermaster items indiscriminately mixed with those of the other technical services and of British accommodation stores. Inexperienced junior officers, assigned to what depot commanders regarded as a low-priority activity, had to tackle their problems mainly with newly hired British civilian labor. Worst of all, the OCQM had not yet formulated any policy on decentralized sorting, processing, return to stock, or reissue of salvaged QM articles. On 14 June Littlejohn began a memorandum on the subject to his deputy with the statement "We are definitely behind the eight ball on our salvage activities." [30] The Chief Quartermaster directed that an SOP for salvage operations be published immediately, that the departure of certain laundry and fumigation and bath units to the Continent be delayed, that laundry and dry cleaning service for garrison troops in the United Kingdom be temporarily suspended, and that fumigation, rather than laundry or dry cleaning, be performed on all clothing and blankets not visibly dirty. Colonel Bennison of the Installations Division was to have ready a co-ordinated salvage plan, concurred in by all concerned, within the week, and Colonel Rosaler of Field Service was to monitor its execution. But an unmanageably large backlog had been built up before these positive measures were taken, and the U.K. salvage organization took seven months to work its way through the accumulation.

The commitment of U.S. troops on the Continent immediately presented a salvage problem almost as great and of a different kind. Much equipment had been damaged and abandoned, but still more was lost or thrown away by men who seemed to have forgotten even the rudiments of supply discipline. The American soldier—frequently confident to the point of arrogance about the limitless production facilities of the United States—was all too inclined to be careless and extravagant with his equipment. Also, practically every battle casualty, whether a litter case, walking wounded, or only a victim of battle fatigue, was sure to lose or discard much of his equipment, and probably some clothing as well. Salvage was therefore primarily a matter of collection and segregation. It was possible to return to stock a surprisingly high proportion of all salvaged clothing and equipment, either without any processing at all, or at most after scrubbing, laundering, or fumigation. Specific percentages of the various categories of salvage collected in the ETO that could be returned to use, either as Class B for U.S. troops or as Class X for other personnel, are given below:[31]

	Cloth-ing	Equip-age	Regu-lar Sup-plies	Foot-wear
Class B	32	73	77	46
Repaired	(4)	(16)	(37)	(14)
Returned without repair	(28)	(57)	(40)	(32)
Class X	53	20	8	43
Repaired	(9)	(4)	(1)	(26)
Returned without repair	(44)	(16)	(7)	(17)
Scrap (unrepair-able)	15	7	15	11

[30] (1) Quotation from IRS, CQM to DCQM, 14 Jun 44, sub: Salvage. Littlejohn Reading File, vol. XXV, item 28. (2) OTCQM TSFET Operational Study 15, p. 5.

[31] Information for General Board—Salvage, prepared by Capt Flax, Installations Div OTCQM TSFET, 16 Nov 45. Hist Br OQMG.

SALVAGE COLLECTION *at dump in Normandy, July 1944.*

Salvage collecting companies had a theoretical capacity to support 75,000 men, and salvage repair companies (semimobile), a capacity for 50,000 men. For an army of 3,000,000 men, the requirement was therefore 40 and 60 companies, respectively, but actual numbers on hand by the end of 1944 were 16 collecting and 19 repair units, increased to 21 of each by the end of hostilities. The actual capacity of these units was considerably greater than expected, but there was nevertheless a serious shortage of salvage capacity, especially in the combat zone. Analyzing the ETO experience in retrospect, Littlejohn recommended a troop basis of four companies of each type per army, instead of three as used during the European campaign, and even this allotment was based on the assumption that semimobile repair companies were to do minor repairs only, evacuating all other salvage material to fixed repair companies in the Communications Zone.[32]

As in the Mediterranean theater, the fixed salvage repair company was located exclusively in the Communications Zone, and did not operate. Rather, it was a supervisory headquarters controlling very large numbers of civilian employees, POW's, and commercial concerns under contract. Used in this way, a fixed salvage repair company had a capacity far in excess of its rated ability to support 100,000 men. The three companies available in the ETO gave fairly adequate support to the entire theater, either by repairs in their own

[32] (1) OTCQM TSFET Operational Study 10, QM Units, Organizations, and Personnel, pp. 31–33, 41–43. (2) OTCQM TSFET Operational Study 15, Planning for T/O QM Units, pp. 11–12, 15, and exhibit B. (3) See App. B.

shops or by arranging commercial contracts.[33]

While salvaged articles arrived at depots in better condition than had been anticipated and required a minimum of processing, the wartime volume of salvage received on the Continent was far greater than expected. After hostilities came to an end it increased still more, although receipts never again reached the tremendous volume of salvage turned in as the troops were leaving the British Isles in June 1944. Expressed in terms of pieces turned in per thousand men per month, ETO salvage experience before, during, and after combat operations was as follows:[34]

Situation Category	Static U.K. Experience	Operational		Post-Operational Continent
		Expected Continent	Actual Continent	
Clothing	860	960	2,434	3,754
Equipage	325	320	603	1,426
Regular supplies	25	10	84	189
Footwear	85	100	169	288
Total	1,295	1,390	3,290	5,657

Salvage in the Combat Zone

Service companies attached to the Engineer brigades began to collect salvage on both OMAHA and UTAH Beach a few days after the initial landings. Two QM salvage collecting companies were in Normandy by D plus 30, and thereafter dispatched patrols daily to recover what had not been carried to the

Class I truckheads on returning ration trucks. Shortly after the liberation of Cherbourg, the 229th QM Salvage Collecting Company opened a collecting point there, designated warehouses that would be used for storage and processing when facilities permitted, and began hiring civilian labor. On 25 July salvage activities in Cherbourg came under the command of the 56th QM Base Depot, and thereafter base depots were the normal administrative link between each base section and its salvage units. Three Quartermaster salvage repair companies were operating under First Army by 22 July, and by 1 August, notwithstanding their frequent movement, they had processed and repaired more than 100,000 pieces of equipment.[35]

During the period of pursuit, salvage repair companies, like other units with heavy equipment, were unable to keep up with the combat troops; the gap between them and the front lines hampered efficient handling of salvage. Also, the scarcity of Class II and IV supplies in this period discouraged the troops from turning in anything not completely unserviceable. Littlejohn wrote to Feldman on 19 September: "The lantern problem is quiet as the troops are moving too fast to light one."[36] But the Chief Quartermaster was well aware that the gasoline lantern was a fragile and temperamental piece of equipment, which required careful servicing. It had already given trouble, and would become the subject of loud complaints as

---

[33] OTCQM TSFET Operational Study 10, pp. 56–59.

[34] (1) QM Service Reference Data, vol. II (rev.), 1 Jan 44, p. 42. (2) Information for General Board —Salvage, prepared by Capt Flax, 16 Nov 45. Hist Br OQMG.

[35] (1) Hist of Depot Q–140. Hist Br OQMG. (2) Hist of QM Sec ADSEC, p. 41. (3) FUSA Rpt of Opns, 20 Oct 43–1 Aug 44, VI, 135, 228, 229. (4) Hist of 56th QMBD. Hist Br OQMG.

[36] Personal Ltr, Littlejohn to Feldman, 19 Sep 44. Littlejohn Reading File, vol. XXVIII, item 140.

soon as the pursuit ended. Other equipment was also far from satisfactory. Normal QMC policy in previous campaigns had been to repair lanterns, field ranges, immersion heaters, and similar items in base shops, or to turn over such duties to Ordnance if possible.[37] Littlejohn was convinced that in large-scale operations, where a communications zone had to support several armies, such a procedure would give very slow service and leave the troops without their equipment for extended periods of time. The conventional QM salvage repair company (semimobile) was only equipped to repair shoes, clothing, and tentage. As early as May 1944, he was considering the inclusion of a six-man mechanical repair section in these companies to provide combat zone service to general-purpose QM equipment such as field ranges and lanterns, which were used throughout the Army. On D-day General Lee made the Chief Quartermaster solely responsible for maintaining special-purpose QM equipment as well— that is, the distinctive equipment of QM units, such as sewing machines, gasoline dispensers, and the trailer-mounted equipment of bakery, laundry, bath, and mobile refrigeration units. These had previously been the maintenance responsibility of Ordnance, but earlier in the year the ETO Chief Ordnance Officer had declared that other duties having higher priority would make it impossible to provide this service on the Continent.

One such duty was battlefield salvage

of heavy Ordnance items, theoretically a QM responsibility, but performed by the Ordnance Service in the ETO. The seven-man Ordnance detachments with the QM collecting companies were kept very busy at the truckheads, sorting out small arms, ammunition, and other Ordnance items. In January 1945 the 237th Salvage Collecting Company (XII Corps) was receiving about 30,000 rounds of ammunition per week, much of it in damaged belts and in the pockets of salvaged clothing. Signal and Chemical Warfare Service detachments with the company were similarly employed to process salvaged articles for their respective services.[38]

Salvage collection procedures in the combat areas were fully developed by November 1944. OCQM directives emphasized the use of organic personnel for salvage collection all across the Continent, but compliance varied from unit to unit. The 5th Infantry Division, for example, dispatched a daily salvage patrol of four infantrymen and one 2½-ton QM company truck to scour its area for abandoned clothing and equipage.[39] By contrast, the 80th Division, supporting the 6th Armored Division during the November campaign around Metz, exhibited a disregard for property that ultimately provoked an investigation by the inspector general of XII Corps.

[37] (1) See above, ch. VIII. (2) Ltr, McNally (FUSA) to QM ADSEC, 24 Jul 44, sub: Repair Parts for QM Equip; Ltr, CQM to Feldman, 29 Aug 44. Littlejohn Reading File, vol. XXVI, item 118; XXVII, item 159.

[38] (1) Littlejohn, ed., Passing in Review, ch. 10, pt. II, p. 2. (2) Hq ETOUSA SOP 30, 6 Jun 44; Hq COMZ ETOUSA SOP: QM Maint and Spare Parts Supply, 6 Jun 44. ETO AG 400.402. (3) Ltr, CQM to Feldman, 29 May 44, sub: Handling of Spare Parts and Repair of QM Equip in the Field. Littlejohn Reading File, vol. XXIV, item 84. (4) Memo, Capt R. L. Moore for G–4, XII Corps, 7 Jan 45, sub: Rpt of Visits. Hist Br OQMG.
[39] OCQM Field Observation Report 7. ETO 319.25 QM.

Along a two-mile stretch of road in the 80th Division area, an inspector general officer picked up almost 200 items, ranging from wool overcoats to full boxes of caliber .30 ammunition, and still left much scattered about the area. Believing that infantry usually remained in an area longer than armor, the inspector recommended that wherever an infantry division supported an armored unit the infantry be made responsible for salvage collection.[40]

Role of the Reorganized Salvage Repair Company (Semimobile)

Special-purpose QM equipment, even more emphatically than the general-purpose items, was too scarce and precious to remain deadlined in rear area repair shops. To fulfill his new maintenance responsibilities, Littlejohn organized a twelve-man equipment maintenance platoon in each semimobile salvage repair company. This platoon was completely mobile and able to repair any Quartermaster item of a mechanical nature. Its major piece of organic equipment was a machine shop, improvised by converting one of the company's textile repair trailers. Its personnel were taken partly from a pool of cellular-type mechanical maintenance teams available in the United Kingdom, and partly from existing unit organizations, and retrained in specialized mechanical skills at Lydney Depot (Q–140). Since the modified company was unchanged in personnel strength and the necessary extra equipment was available locally, the Chief

Quartermaster authorized the new company organization by QM circular letter on 28 August 1944. Thereafter, companies in the Communications Zone were modified as retrained personnel became available and exchanged for the conventional companies already attached to the armies.[41]

The specialists in the equipment platoon were expected to give instruction on preventive maintenance and the proper way to make repairs. An important feature of these platoons was the supply of spare parts they carried for their own use and for issue to the combat units they served. Apparently there was some difficulty in introducing this new concept in the middle of a campaign, for in November Littlejohn wrote to Franks: "I don't want any more statements that the troops do not need the parts. What they need are spare parts plus some help in fixing their equipment."[42]

Reports from the combat units indicate that whenever parts were available, the units themselves completed a very considerable volume of repairs. Repair sections within the QM companies of the 4th, 8th, and 84th Divisions averaged repairs to three field-range fire units and two typewriters per day. Parts for lanterns and one-burner stoves arrived sporadically, and repairs to these items

---

[40] Ltr, Asst IG XII Corps to CG XII Corp, 17 Nov 44, sub: Abandonment and Waste of Government Property. AG 312, XII Corps G–4.

[41] (1) OTCQM TSFET Operational Study 10, p. 43. (2) *QM Supply in ETO*, VIII, apps XLI and XLII. (3) IRS, CQM to DCQM, 2 Sep 44, sub: Mobile Repair Co's, etc; IRS, CQM to Chief R&D Div, sub: Article on Salvaged Items. Littlejohn Reading File, vol. XXVIII, items 22, 95.

[42] IRS, CQM to Heywood, 23 Sep 44, sub: Problems Confronting Installations Div; Quotation from IRS, CQM to Franks, 9 Nov 44, sub: Sundry Problems Encountered During Trip Around the Armies. Littlejohn Reading File, vol. XXVIIIA, item 166; vol. XXX, item 26.

MOBILE SHOE REPAIR TRAILER *designed to serve combat units in the field.*

ran as high as twenty per day for brief periods. The quartermaster of the 28th Division decided not to organize a repair section within his QM company, since not enough spare parts were available to make such a step worthwhile. Conversely, the 83d Division quartermaster did not engage in repair activities because his division was so well served by the 202d QM Battalion. This First Army unit controlled all the army's salvage collection and salvage repair companies, usually three of each, and several laundries. It was normally located at the First Army Class II and IV depot, and was apparently able to give prompt

service to combat units despite being separated from them by considerable distances—in January 1945, for example, the 83d Division was 75 miles forward from Wavre, Belgium, where the 202d was currently located. The fact that shoe repair trailers and the mobile equipment repair platoons already mentioned were sent forward to serve individual combat units as required undoubtedly contributed to this satisfactory service.[43]

Nevertheless, Littlejohn and the

---

[43] AAR's, 4th, 8th, 28th, 83d, and 84th QM Companies (Divisional); AAR, 471st QM Group. Unit History Files. OQMG.

USFET General Board later agreed that a less centralized employment of salvage units, as practiced in Third Army, was preferable. Its method involved a separate salvage center supporting each corps, consisting of a salvage collecting company, a salvage repair company, one or more fumigation chambers, and three or more laundry sections. Details from the salvage collecting company not only collected salvage at Class I truckheads but also sorted it and, using their own transportation, routed material to the army Class II and IV depot, to laundries, or to the adjacent salvage repair company. The only Third Army salvage activity operating centrally for the whole army was a special field range repair unit, formed from one platoon of the 3234th QM Service Company. The Seventh and Ninth Armies conducted salvage operations under an even less centralized system. Collecting companies attached to each corps evacuated salvage back to specific repair companies, usually located deep in the army zone. Mobile equipment-maintenance platoons operated forward with the collecting companies, but otherwise there was little liaison between the two types of salvage units.[44]

Regardless of the method employed to handle the flow of salvage, statistics of the 12th Army Group clearly show that salvage repair capacity was inadequate in the combat zone. In particular, the poor showing of the repair companies during mobile operations casts doubt on the correctness of their designation as semimobile. They did their best work when the situation was relatively static, confirming the opinion that their equipment, like that of laundry and bath units, was too heavy and slow moving for mobile modern warfare. Relative performance during the month ending 15 February 1945, when the situation was fairly static, and during the month ending 15 April, when the armies were advancing across Germany, well illustrates the difference:[45]

	Month Ending	
	15 Feb 45	*15 Apr 45*
Salvage collecting companies available	8	11
Total salvage collected (pieces)	3,747,324	4,433,560
Salvage collected per company per day	15,110	13,001
Total shipped to COMZ ..	2,355,863	2,977,363
Salvage repair companies available	9	10
Total salvage repaired (pieces)	525,718	233,999
Salvage repaired per company per day	1,884	755
Reissued or returned to stock, unrepaired	421,880	1,269,794

As the above tabulation shows, the salvage collecting companies, which were also responsible for a good deal of sorting, reissue, and return to stock, made a far greater contribution to ETO supply during both static and mobile situations. The USFET General Board concluded that the solution was a larger number of smaller and more mobile repair units, preferably incorporated into the combat divisions. In particular, the board felt that to evacuate large quantities of unprocessed material to COMZ for repair and then return it to the forward areas

---

[44] (1) OTCQM TSFET Operational Study 10, pp. 31–33, 41–43. (2) TUSA AAR, QM, 3, 7, 12, 16. (3) NUSA Monthly QM Rpts. Hist Br OQMG.

693–028 O—65——47

was "an obvious waste of transportation and in-transit stocks." [46]

Problems of Classification,
Repair Priority, and Reissue

The repair companies were aware of the advantages of performing repairs on the spot. Whenever the tactical situation made it possible they sent forward tent repair teams, typewriter repair teams, and the shoe repair trailers already mentioned. Besides saving transportation, such on-the-spot repairs had the additional psychological value of keeping articles entirely out of the much maligned salvage cycle. A unit working directly for its "customers" could provide personal service to the original owner. Such service went far to overcome the prejudice of the troops against used articles, which were regarded as "repaired" if returned to their owners, but as "salvage," and by inference junk, if reissued. Littlejohn gave a good deal of personal attention to the problem of persuading the troops, and more important their commanders, to accept Class B—used but serviceable—clothing and equipment. Army Regulations and theater circulars directed that Class B items be issued before Class A, but were often ignored. Early in the campaign units were inclined to shop around until they found a depot which had no Class B stocks, and therefore issued new (Class A) items on all requisitions. With increasing shortages, the troops found used but serviceable articles, particularly winter clothing, to be acceptable, and issuing Class B ahead of Class A became the

normal procedure in the ETO. The one exception made was the issue of Class A clothing for reasons of morale to convalescents discharged from hospitals. But the troops retained strong views on accepting reclaimed shoes, and in general their commanders supported them. Irrespective of condition, repaired shoes that could not be returned to the original owner were usually evacuated to COMZ for use by civilians or prisoners of war.[47]

The decision as to what was suitable for reissue in the combat zone, either with or without repairs, and what was only suited for issue to prisoners of war or civilian refugees, presented a difficult problem. In general, separate standards had to be set up for each item, based upon relative scarcity or abundance as well as physical condition, and such standards were modified to correspond to changing supply levels. Top priorities for the repair units were usually identical with the controlled items lists of Class II and IV depots, but there were some exceptions. For example, a major consideration in deciding that most repaired shoes were to be considered Class X was the need for more POW laborers, who required the shoes to perform effective outdoor work. Such revisions of general policy aggravated an already confused situation. Items processed in the United Kingdom shortly after D-day for shipment to the Continent were in particularly chaotic condition. During the second half of November 1944 the

---

[46] USFET Gen Bd Study 108, pp. 8–14. (Quotation on page 12.)

[47] (1) IRS, Littlejohn to Gen Kimball, DCQM, 15 Jun 44, sub: Class B Clothing. Littlejohn Reading File, vol. XXV, item 37. (2) IRS, CQM to ACofS G–4. 21 Jun 44, sub: Utilization of Used Clothing; AAR, 2d QM Co, Dec 44. Hist Br OQMG. (3) TUSA AAR, QM, 12.

OCQM received complaints from combat units of First Army that items arriving in the forward areas marked Class B were not suitable for issue, and also reports from its own field liaison officers that 80 percent of the clothing located at UTAH marked Class X was actually combat serviceable and included such scarce items as field jackets. Col. Beny Rosaler, chief of the Field Service Division, had ready solutions for both problems: he recommended that combat units be educated to accept garments of less than parade-ground elegance, and he also urged that the field jackets be shipped to the 64th QMBD, recently moved to Reims, for sorting. But on the central problem of classification he could only comment that it required highly qualified personnel with good judgment.[48]

Salvage in the Rear Areas

For all the emphasis on pushing salvage services into the forward areas, the steady accumulation of salvage created a mountainous backlog in the rear areas for processing and storage. Salvage installations at Marseille, Dijon, and Vesoul supporting the 6th Army Group were operated largely by Italian service units. By the end of the year base depots at Cherbourg, Rennes, Le Mans, Paris, Reims, and Liège were all conducting salvage operations for the 12th Army Group. For labor they used non-

military personnel almost exclusively. At first the depots depended mainly on civilians, including some displaced Russian women who were very willing workers. Administrative difficulties in moving such personnel forward, however, and the increasing availability of POW's encouraged the depots to use larger numbers of prisoners. The base sections also made maximum use of commercial repair facilities, but these ventures were often delayed by such difficulties as disrupted public utilities and the absence of proper equipment. Reminiscent of Quartermaster experiences in North Africa and Italy, Brittany Base Section reported that repairs by a French shoe factory would be possible only if the Americans could provide a power generator, bench jacks, diesel oil, and sewing and stitching machines.[49]

The largest single salvage installation in the ETO was Q–256, established at Reims on 29 September 1944. It was administered by the 64th QM Base Depot and operated by the 696th QM Salvage Repair Company (Fixed). These two units had been trained together at Lydney. Tables of Organization provided that such a combined salvage headquarters would operate with 586 attached service troops or civilian employees. Under the command of Col. Albert Barden, this unit ultimately supervised some twenty times that number, largely prisoners of war, and undertook fifth echelon

[48] (1) Ltr, QM ADSEC to CO 62d QMBD, 13 Jan 45, sub: Processing of Critical Items of Salvage. ETO Q-SI 400.93. (2) IRS, Mil Plng Div OCQM to Field Sv Div, 14 Nov 44, sub: Condition of Individual C&E Arriving in Army Areas; Ltr, DCQM to QM ADSEC, 26 Jan 45, sub: Change in Classification of Salvage Items as Class X. Both in Hist Br OQMG.

[49] (1) See above, ch. VIII. (2) IRS, AG Opns to QM and G–1 (in turn), 14 Oct 44, sub: Employment of Russian Women as Civilian Laborers. ETO AG 230. (3) Ltr, CQM to QM ADSEC, 22 Oct 44, sub: Outfit of Russian Women in ADSEC. Littlejohn Reading File, vol. XXIX, item 106. (4) 1st Ind, BBS to OCQM, 9 Oct 44, sub: Civilian Shoe Repair Facilities in BBS. Hst Br OQMG.

maintenance and manufacturing projects never contemplated by the War Department. Patterning the organization after the one Colonel Hutchins had initiated at Depot Q–180—also at Reims—Barden set up an elaborate German officer staff, which handled practically all details of POW administration, both in the prison compound and in the shops. Colonel Bennison, who as Oise Section quartermaster was generally responsible for all QM operations at Reims, made the following observations on the use of German personnel: [50]

Without recourse to a scheme of this sort, a salvage depot will never do its job as the organic troops assigned are sufficient only to form a skeleton organization. After V–E Day when the now notorious point system disrupted the American Army, this depot as well as most of the other QM depots were operated 90% by Germans. Incidentally, one couldn't ask for better personnel. We made the barest pretense of guarding and even the Germans had many a laugh at the futility of our efforts. To paraphrase Mr. Churchill, "Never were so many guarded by so few."

Depot Q–256, with its facilities scattered throughout the city of Reims, received overflow salvage directly from the armies. In addition to routine processing and packaging, the depot conducted a program of manufacturing, remodeling, and improvisation. Scrap materials were used to reinforce paratroop trousers, fabricate BAR belts and rocket ammunition pouches, and patch tentage. Materials ostensibly destined for scrap were converted into other types of end items: old tires were used to make soles for prisoners' shoes, badly torn shirts and raincoats were transformed into wiping rags, aprons, and typewriter covers, and old wool was converted into "shoddy" blankets.[51]

Besides the fixed repair activities at Reims salvage depot, twelve mobile repair teams and two technical crews worked out of this installation in answer to calls from the field. Whenever the teams found damaged equipment that could not be readily repaired in the field, they exchanged a repaired item for the disabled one and thus reduced to a minimum the time units had to spend without the use of their equipment. Captured articles provided the revolving fund for this extra service. The depot also sent individual technicians to various other depots to train prisoners and civilian employees in specialized repairs.[52]

Ultimately, Q–256 also had to operate a complete machine shop where motors and other heavy equipment, including QM equipment trailers, were rebuilt, although this was originally a responsibility of Ordnance. Such activities were performed in rented French shops with captured German lathes, presses, and other heavy duty machinery. Sufficient machine tools were available to permit the occasional manufacture of badly needed spare parts such as flame cups for one-burner stoves and rotors for gasoline

---

[50] (1) Quotation from Littlejohn, ed., Passing in Review, ch. 38, p. 21. (2) QM Supply in ETO, VI, 31. (3) OTCQM TSFET Operational Study 10, p. 58. (4) Hist of Depot Q–140. Hist Br OQMG.

[51] (1) Ltr, CO 64th QMBD to Chief Installations Div OCQM, 16 Dec 44, sub: Machinery and Equip. Hist Br OQMG. (2) Anon., "The 64th QMBD," QMTSJ, vol. VII, No, 21 (27 April 1945), 11–13.
[52] (1) Memo, ASF-QM Spare Parts Team for TQMG, 5 Mar 45, sub: 64th QMBD Opns. ETO QM 400.4. (2) Hist of 63d QMBD, p. 33. Hist Br OQMG.

dispensers.[53] By the end of March 1945 the Reims salvage depot occupied 500,000 square feet of closed space and 350,000 feet of open space; this was more than double the total space set aside for Quartermaster salvage and reclamation in all the U.K. depots as of January 1944. At the close of 1944, the depot had processed nine million items, and in March 1945 it was handling 160,000 pieces per day.[54]

Meanwhile the 223d QM Salvage Company (Fixed) had been handling a considerably smaller central salvage operation for the 6th Army Group at Vesoul, nominally under the control of the 71st QMBD at Dijon. In December, the equipment for a full-sized base salvage installation arrived at Marseille, and preliminary plans were made to establish it at Strasbourg. The German counteroffensive in the Ardennes made it necessary to revise the plan, and by late January it had been decided to install the new plant at Nancy, where Salvage Depot Q-599 was already operating. At this location the installation would come under the direct supervision of the 73d QM Base Depot, then en route from England. Repaired clothing would go to Depot Q-186, which opened at Nancy at about the same time. As a first step, the 7176th Semimobile Salvage Repair Company (Italian) was sent forward and began operating in trailers on 24 February. During March two more Italian units, the 7134th and 7177th, moved up from Vesoul to Nancy, and by the end of the month the 9026th and 9032d PW Labor Companies (German) (Salvage Repair) had also arrived. Progress in installing the fixed plant for the use of the 223d Salvage Repair Company was slow, but on 15 March the new salvage depot was formally activated and given the designation Q-257, in conformity with the COMZ depot numbering system. Colonel Rosaler, who had recently replaced Colonel Bennison as chief of the Installations Division, inspected the new depot on 27 March. He recommended that Q-257 give salvage support to Third Army as well as to Seventh Army. Salvage receipts from the 1st French Army had been negligible since the formal separation of French Base 901 from CONAD on 19 February.[55]

Warm weather ensued in April soon after a resumption of the offensive east of the Rhine. Under mobile tactical conditions, there was little prospect that the turn-in of winter clothing and equipment would be more orderly than it had been in Great Britain a year earlier. To prevent normal salvage channels from being swamped, the OCQM instructed ADSEC and CONAD to establish special installations to receive the clothing. The main requirements were good transportation and unloading facilities and ample covered storage space where unsorted clothing could be dried and protected from the weather until processed. Sites with these characteristics were at a premium and not available at all in the most desirable forward locations. Accordingly, ADSEC set up a temporary

[53] Progress Rpt, Sub-Team 1, QM Mobile Equipment Spare Parts Team to TQMG, 19 Mar 45. SPQOM 451.9.

[54] (1) QM Supply in ETO, VI, 105. (2) Rpt of Opns, 64th QMBD, 21 Apr 44. 64th QMBD RAC. (3) Rpt, 64th QMBD, sub: Class B Salvage Shipped and Scrapped 1–28 Feb 45. Littlejohn Collection.

[55] (1) Littlejohn, ed., Passing in Review, ch. 43, p. 16. (2) Hist 73d QMBD, p. 105. Hist Br OQMG unit files. (3) CONAD History, II, 849–89. (4) Ruppenthal, Logistical Support, II, 379.

depot at Seilles near Huy, Belgium, and CONAD selected a site at Thaon near Épinal. By 7 April both these installations had been transferred to Oise Intermediate Section. At Seilles, Depot Q–179–B was operated by a detachment from the 58th QM Base Depot, assisted by the 176th QM Laundry Company and over 500 civilian employees. This force segregated Class A and B clothing, performed minor repairs and laundering, and shipped serviceable clothing to Q–185 at Lille, the new Class II depot for the First and Ninth Armies. Depot Q–256 at Reims received Class C items for major repairs and Class X items for issue to POW's. Similarly, Q–257–B at Thaon sent serviceable items to Q–186 at Metz, the new Third and Seventh Army clothing depot, and articles needing repairs to Q–257 at Nancy. Everything intended for combat troops was sorted for size and baled before shipment. The labor force at Thaon consisted of a QM battalion headquarters, a laundry company, 300 civilians, 2,350 prisoners, and a service company for guard duty. Inevitably, some winter clothing strayed into normal salvage channels, but when Seilles and Thaon suspended operations in early July, over 10,000 tons of winter clothing, footwear, gloves, headgear, and sleeping bags were packed and ready to follow the troops leaving the European theater on redeployment.[56]

Redeployment led to a major increase in QM salvage activities, and was largely responsible for the fact that the rate of salvage receipts jumped from 3,290 pieces per thousand men per month during combat to 5,657 pieces after V–E Day. Redeployment salvage operations were concentrated in the Oise Intermediate Section, in direct support of the Assembly Area Command. This organization operated seventeen tent cities in the general vicinity of Reims. With a capacity of 270,000 men at a time, the camps were in use for nearly a year. Units being redeployed were instructed to bring all clothing and equipment with them to the AAC camps, where those going directly to the Far East would replenish their T/E allowances of combat serviceable clothing and equipment by replacement, repair, laundry, dry cleaning, or initial issue as required. Troops returning to the United States retained only minimum essential equipment, but were more concerned with the condition of their uniforms than were troops headed for the Pacific.[57]

Quartermaster difficulties in providing these services were aggravated by the large number of QM units that were also being redeployed and therefore not available to service other troops. During May 1945 the number of nonmilitary personnel employed by the Oise Section quartermaster increased from 58,000 to 71,000, while alert notices decreased the working force of QM troops from 17,000 to about 14,000. The AAC operated somewhat like a field army, and the AAC quartermaster, Col. Richard B.

[56] (1) Ltr, QM Oise Intermediate Sec to QM Lorraine District, 26 Apr 45, sub: Mission of Q–257. Hist Br OQMG. (2) Memo, Chief Sv Installations Br for QM ADSEC, 8 Mar 45, sub: Liège Depot Plan for Winter Clothing; Ltr, Chief Field Sv OQM ADSEC to CO 56th QMBD, 3 May 45, sub: Salvage to be Taken Over From Third Army. ETO 400.9 ADSEC. (3) Anon., "It Happened Last Spring," QMTSJ, VIII, No. 10 (7 September 1945), 11–13.

[57] QM Problems in the Supply of the AAC, n.d., prepared by Hist Rec Sec OTCQM. Hist Br OQMG.

Thornton, had corresponding duties. The 75th Infantry Division was pressed into QM duty to give direct support in the camps themselves. Rear area support was provided largely by non-American units. On 31 May 1945, a total of 155 such units were operating in Oise Section alone, and 86 more had been authorized for activation as follows:

	POW (German)	Italian	Mobile Civilian	
Bakery companies	6	(3)	2	....
Depot supply companies	10		4	....
Fumigation and bath companies	1		1	....
Gasoline supply companies	3	(1)	1	....
Laundry companies ..	5	(5)	2	....
Railhead companies ..	7	(4)	1	....
Salvage collecting companies	1		1	....
Salvage repair companies	8	(1)	5	....
Service companies	59	(64)	15	23 (8)

With the above labor force, Oise Intermediate Section calculated that it could process 2,627,231 QM articles of all types through its salvage facilities each week and also provide 444,800 pounds of laundry and 227,000 pounds of dry cleaning weekly.[58]

Spare Parts

The Mediterranean theater had introduced Americans to the problems of spare parts supply, including exasperating difficulties with extra parts for British-manufactured equipment, which had to be forwarded by Littlejohn's organization. Spare parts was an enormously complicated technical subject, involving tens of thousands of distinct and separate items of supply, each with its own specific purpose and distinctive maintenance factor. The storage and distribution difficulties experienced in supplying balanced rations and correctly computed clothing tariffs were multiplied a thousandfold in regard to spare parts. Information on the subject, even after two years of war, was fragmentary, self-contradictory, and at once too detailed and too inaccurate to form a basis for intelligent generalizations. Any effort at improved reporting was hampered by lack of standardization, of parts catalogues, and of interchangeable parts lists. Many major Quartermaster items of equipment were of prewar commercial design, and the OQMG tended to follow the manufacturer's own recommendations on parts requirements, based on peacetime commercial operation. Manufacturers were under pressure to increase production of end items and reluctant to make more spare parts. Overseas quartermasters thought this attitude arbitrary and unreasonable, but ASF investigators found that faulty overseas distribution practices apparently caused as many spare parts shortages as did the actual wear and tear of continuous operation under combat conditions.[59]

While U.S. units were training in Great Britain before D-day, they found no serious fault with the scale of spare parts supply provided from the zone of interior. They did find that spare parts packages tended to be small and incon-

[58] Hq AAC, Hist of Activities of the QM Sec, 1–31 May 45. Hist Br OQMG.

[59] (1) Alvin P. Stauffer, Supply of Spare Parts for Materials-Handling Equipment, passim. Hist Br OQMG. (2) Extract of Rpt, ASF–QM Spare Parts Team 1 to OCQM, 24 Mar 45. ETO QM 400.41.

spicuous, bore markings that were only intelligible to a specialist, and were all too easily mislaid. By early 1944 spare parts culled from all depots in the United Kingdom had been concentrated at Lydney. This became the sole parts depot for special-purpose QM equipment (used only by QM units) and the reserve parts depot for general-purpose QM equipment, used throughout the Army. In theory, NYPE sent a one-year supply of parts with each special-purpose item of equipment and a six months' supply with each general-purpose item, but, like the force-marked reserves of expendable supplies that were to accompany U.S. units overseas in 1943, some of the spare parts failed to arrive. Also, there was confusion as to precisely when and how many major items of equipment had arrived overseas, and therefore as to when requisitioning of additional spare parts should begin and for what quantities. Col. Ira Evans visited the ETO in May 1944 and provided considerable clarification, but as late as 5 June Littlejohn expressed some uneasiness about adequacy of requisitions already submitted and about the accuracy of requirements forecasts.[60]

Plans for the initial assault provided that units were to carry with them a 60-day supply of spare parts for office machines and a 30-day supply for other general-purpose QM items. Additional spare parts for field ranges, considered to be the one really vital item of equipment, would also be included in beach maintenance sets and follow-up mainte-

nance sets, which together were designed to maintain supply through D plus 41 (16 July). For the period from D plus 41 through D plus 90, ADSEC had requisitioned enough spare parts to maintain a 30-day level in each using unit and an additional 30-day supply in the army Class II depot. QM units were to carry a 90-day supply of special-purpose spare parts, which would last until the 64th QM Base Depot could establish a central parts depot on the Continent. In each case the level of supply was in terms of maintenance factors provided by NYPE.[61]

On learning of this plan, General Gregory pronounced it to be eminently sound and practical, but Littlejohn was still dubious, and on 25 July asked Gregory to send his parts specialist to the ETO to provide still further clarification. The doubt was amply justified, for three days later McNamara forwarded to Littlejohn a letter written by his deputy, Colonel McNally. It said in part:

1. The following items are proving short-lived and are being turned in for salvage with no hope of doing anything about them: lanterns, gasoline; cookers, 1-burner; cookers, 2-burner; heaters, immersion type. This is because there has been no supply of a few simple replacement parts, although all have been asked for. As a result, there is a critical shortage of cookers, and stocks of lanterns and heaters are being depleted.

2. Parts for typewriters, adding machines, and duplicating machines are sorely needed. There are none. Machines which could easily be fixed are now being cannibalized to provide spare parts. Typewriter parts have also been asked for.

McNally further reported that enough

[60] (1) QM Supply in ETO, VI, 52. (2) Ltr, Littlejohn to Feldman, 14 May 44, sub: Spare Parts Problems; Ltr, CQM to DCQM, 5 Jun 44, sub: Salvage and Spare Parts Plan. Littlejohn Reading File, vol. XXIV, item 50; vol. XXV, item 8.

[61] (1) QM Supply in ETO, VI, 52–53. (2) FUSA Rpt of Opns, 20 Oct 43–1 Aug 44, VI, 240–45.

field range parts were on hand or due in by D plus 90 to service 13,400 ranges for a month, but this supply was entirely insufficient. He requested a further 30-day supply for another 18,750 field ranges, to arrive by D plus 90. Even more significantly, he suggested using NATOUSA maintenance factors until revised rates for combat in the ETO could be determined.[62]

Littlejohn was aware that while McNally's report was undoubtedly correct as far as the combat zone was concerned it by no means told the whole story. Few of the prescribed reserve spare parts for combat units had actually come ashore with the equipment. Much of this reserve was still on the water awaiting discharge, and more had been mislaid in the huge dumps at the beaches. Moreover, no plans had been made by mid-July for distinctive markings of packages containing such items, nor for their concentration at any one continental port or dump. Yet the Installations Division in the United Kingdom had already shipped over substantial quantities. The Chief Quartermaster remarked: ". . . unquestionably these stocks will be scattered all over creation and you may or may not get them back together in the next 30/60 days . . . Definitely shipments of this kind should go under guard, especially when we are so short . . . have every man at the beach,

at the dumps etc. watch for these supplies."[63]

Littlejohn several times reiterated the instructions about shipping spare parts under guard, adding that they should preferably travel by air and never be surrendered to anyone except authorized QM officers.[64] But he also became convinced that quantities on requisition from the United States were insufficient and submitted additional requests by cable. Transportation between Britain and the Continent was so unreliable that he sent in separate requisitions for each destination. Once these requisitions were on file the Chief Quartermaster, with characteristic impatience, started pulling personal wires to have at least part of the shipment moved by air. On 9 August he wrote to the Deputy Quartermaster General:

My Dear Herman,

The spare parts problem has definitely gotten me into the doghouse. My Cheltenham office went to sleep on the assumption that spare parts covered field ranges only and not many of them, hence the necessity of bringing over here all the spare parts that should have been requisitioned a long time ago. . . . Will you please put your shoulder to the wheel, get one of the field officers who is currently on orders to come over here by air. Have him catch up these spare parts for lanterns and immersion water heaters, put them in his hip pocket . . . find me and make delivery.[65]

---

[62] (1) Ltr, CQM to OQMG, 1 Jul 44, sub: Maint and Spare Parts Plan for ETO. ETO Q—Installations 300.8. (2) Ltr, CQM to TQMG, 25 Jul 44, sub: Visits of Responsible QM Officers to the ETO. Littlejohn Reading File, vol. XXVI, item 107. (3) Personal Ltr, McNamara to Littlejohn, 28 Jul 44, with Incl, McNally to QM ADSEC, 26 Jul 44, sub: Repair Parts for QM Equip. Littlejohn Reading File, vol. XXVIA, item 118.

[63] Ltr, Littlejohn to Franks, no sub, 20 Jul 44. Littlejohn Reading File, vol. XXVI, item 89A.
[64] (1) Personal Ltrs, Littlejohn to Franks, 4, 8 Aug 44; to Brumbaugh, 8 Aug; to Rosaler, 23 Aug, Littlejohn Reading File, vol. XXVII, items 6, 11, 19, 103. (2) Ltr, Bennison to QM, BS #1, 27 Aug 44, sub: Operating Supplies for Salvage Repair Co's. Lorraine District 400.403.
[65] Ltr, Littlejohn to Feldman, 9 Aug 44, sub: Spare Parts. Littlejohn Reading File, vol. XXVII, item 39.

Feldman replied two days later that the "field officer" would be Brig. Gen. Carl A. Hardigg, who was flying to the ETO to confer on subsistence problems. It is unlikely that any field officer would have been allowed a "hip pocket" large enough to carry the cargo Hardigg brought with him:

1,200 gasoline valves for immersion-type water heaters
400 burner assemblies for immersion-type water heaters
3,000 conversion sets for Coleman gasoline lanterns
3,000 conversion sets for American gasoline lanterns

The weight of this shipment was not recorded, but it amounted to about 10 percent of the entire July requisition of spare parts for the Continent.[66]

The above episode provided the only bright spot in the spare parts picture during 1944. The marking and packaging for shipment of spare parts was a particular source of grief. Ship manifests recording automatic deliveries of spare parts from the United States only listed so many crates of parts for a major machine. Thus, it was impossible to know what specific parts were in transit until the boxes were received, opened, and tallied. One might expect that shipments from Britain against specific requisitions would arrive in more orderly condition, but this was not the case. Through November, every shipment of parts to Reims from the United Kingdom included several packages that were erroneously marked, and again a time-consuming task of inventorying was re-

quired. Some examples of such careless warehousing procedures were markings that read "50 Refractory Bricks," when the actual contents were twelve GI overcoats, and "Women's Rayon Hose," when the contents were radiator hose. Improper markings on the initial stocks of parts for immersion-type water heaters resulted in their loss for months at a time when they were in critical demand. Precisely the same unfortunate situation prevailed at the Marseille depot, which received all its supplies directly from the United States.[67]

In addition to these problems, spare parts suffered the same pipeline hazards and low priorities as other Class II and IV supplies. The time lag in shipments from New York extended from four to eight months. Since every shipment was deficient in a number of expected items, the spare parts team sent by the ASF to investigate at Q-256 suggested that the Reims depot send an officer to NYPE to accompany the parts shipments through the overseas supply pipeline. The same suggestion was made by the team which inspected Q-572 at Marseille, the only other central parts depot in the ETO.[68]

Meanwhile the reorganization of the salvage repair companies proceeded very slowly. Even after the reshaping had been completed the new equipment

---

[66] Personal Ltr, Feldman to Littlejohn, 11 Aug 44, with Incl. Littlejohn Reading File, vol. XXVII, item 48.

[67] (1) Memo, Warehouse Off 64th QMBD to Chief Spare Parts Br 64th QMBD, 13 Nov 44, no sub; Memo for Record, Maj J. H. McGuire, Field Sv Div 12th Army Group, 9 Dec 44. Both in Hist Br OQMG. (2) Rpt, ASF Spare Parts Team to OQMG, 28 Feb 45. ETO QM 400.4.

[68] Ltr, OIC ASF–QM Spare Parts Team to OQMG, 28 Feb 45, sub: Progress Rpt, Sub-Team 1; Ibid., 19 Mar 45; Rpt, ASF Spare Parts Team 5 to TQMG, 25 Mar 45, sub: Spare Parts Procedures. All in ETO 400.4 (QM).

maintenance platoons did not prove altogether satisfactory as mobile parts depots for the armies. The original plan provided for the following:

Parts Distribution	Days
With the using unit	30
With the supporting mobile repair unit .	30
With the 64th QM Base Depot	60
ETO total	120

One difficulty was that, for the majority of items, the size of a thirty-day supply— in other words, the specific maintenance factor—had not been accurately determined. There was even QM-procured equipment for which no stock numbers or specific nomenclature had ever been disseminated overseas. Determination of just what parts should be carried, and in what quantities, was a slow matter of trial and error, and meanwhile excess stocks of some items were built up while others remained so scarce that no reliable data ever became available on how many were needed. In late September Littlejohn instructed his Installations Division to take a middle-of-the-road attitude, neither forcing unwanted parts on the units nor refusing them a small stock of the scarcer items. By this time the OCQM has acquired at least a rough idea of true requirements, but the mobile platoons had proved themselves to be more adept at repairing equipment than at administering stocks of spare parts, and in mid-October Littlejohn suggested that they be removed from the supply chain. Instead, he proposed to issue 30-day credits to each army, to be held in the army's own Class II dump or in the 64th QM Base Depot, as each army quartermaster preferred.[69]

Adoption of this procedure somewhat improved the situation, but in December stocks at Q–256 were still seriously short. Transportation was strictly rationed, and it was only occasionally possible to forward a few tons of spare parts from the ports to Reims. Any improvement was anticipated more from local procurement, especially in Belgium, than through shipments from the United States or from England. Although no parts for gasoline dispensers had been received, the depot managed to repair every dispenser turned in. Like the semimobile repair companies, the 64th QMBD was more efficient at repairing equipment than at administering a depot, and in January 1945 Colonel Duncan, chief of the Military Planning Division, OCQM, was very dubious about the accuracy of the spare parts inventories submitted. This was rather serious since the OCQM maintained no stock record cards on spare parts, and all requisitions on the United States were based on these inventories. He proposed that preparation of requisitions be turned over to the Spare Parts Branch, Installations Division, and recommended that ten more clerks and five more typists be assigned to that unit. In March 1945, officers of an ASF–QM spare parts team reported that inventory and stock accounting procedures at Q–256, Reims, were admirable, but the records were so new that they

---

[69] (1) Ltr, CQM to Franks, 4 Aug 44, sub: Supply of Spare Parts and Maint of Equip; IRS, CQM to Rosaler, 23 Aug 44, sub: Spart Parts, Salvage and Laundry Problems; Ltr, CQM to Heywood, 23 Sep 44, sub: Problems Confronting Installations Div. Littlejohn Reading File, vol. XXVII, items 6, 103; vol. XXVIII, item 166. (2) Ltr, DCQM to QM 12th Army Group, 14 Oct 44, sub: Distr of Spare Parts, Hist Br OQMG. (3) OCQM ETO Cir Ltr 69, 15 Oct 44.

provided little useful information. The main reason was that stock levels had only recently improved, and many items never previously available had been added to the inventories. Significantly, parts depots in the ETO did not maintain back-order files, a typical practice of depots which have been plagued by non-availability of supplies.[70]

One autonomous spare parts operation deserves special notice. Colonel Mac-Manus ran his bakery units entirely with British military equipment, which had been field-tested, and for which spare parts maintenance factors were known. But, illustrating the extreme complexity of every spare parts problem, MacManus was unable to adopt British maintenance factors since they were based on interchangeability of parts between bakery units and other diesel-electric powered British machinery, notably the equipment of searchlight and radar units. With some difficulty, MacManus was able to get approval for increased maintenance factors, since his spare parts depot would be serving only fifty-five mobile bakeries, in contrast to the hundreds of units of various types supported by corresponding British parts depots. The same unfavorable distribution factor applied to the American equipment used by the mobile refrigeration companies. Copying the procedures of the bakery units, subsistence officers set up a mobile refrigeration spare parts depot at the same location, on the Isle St. Germain.

These were the only categories of QM equipment not served by the 64th QM Base Depot.[71]

Captured Enemy Matériel

Before the Normandy landings, First Army ordered that enemy matériel captured in the campaign be safeguarded in precisely the same way as U.S. Government property, but no important quantities of the matériel were in the hands of First Army units before the breakout from the beachhead at the end of July. Thereafter both First and Third Armies captured considerable amounts of food and POL, which were issued directly to the troops since Allied supplies were short. On 8 September 1944 the 12th Army Group gave each army authority to use any captured matériel found within the army sector, either for military or civil affairs purposes, and shortly thereafter the First Army quartermaster transferred 7,600 tons of captured food to civil affairs, for civilian needs in urban areas.[72]

With transition to a more static tactical situation, reports of captured quartermaster-type enemy matériel became frequent. The QM, Third Army, organized a captured enemy matériel guard and inventory detail within his Field Service Section on 20 September, and on 1 October the First Army quartermaster created a Captured Materiel Section

---

[70] (1) Memo for Record, Maj McGuire, Field Sv Br 12th Army Group, 9 Dec 44; Memo, Chief Mil Plng Div for CQM, 12 Jan 45, sub: Status of Spare Parts Levels. Both in Hist Br OQMG. (2) Memo, ASF–QM Spare Parts Team ETOUSA for TQMG, 24 Mar 45, sub: Theater QM Spare Parts Opns. ETO QM 451.9.

[71] (1) See description of mobile bakery spare parts depot in ch. XV, above. (2) Littlejohn, ed., Passing in Review, ch. 36, p. 69. (3) QM Supply in ETO, VI, 59. (4) Rpt of Spare Parts Sub-Team 1 to TQMG, 24 Mar 45. SPQOM 451.9 ETO.

[72] (1) FUSA Rpt of Opns, 20 Oct 43–1 Aug 44, VI, 218; ibid, 1 Aug 44–22 Feb 45, IV, 48, 108. (2) 12th Army Group Admin Instr 23, 8 Sep 44.

within the Supply Division. This staff unit of two officers and five enlisted men operated as an information center on captured supplies. It conducted field investigations through six QM intelligence teams, each composed of one officer and sixteen enlisted men. The enlisted men came from the 235th and 999th Salvage Collecting Companies. The officers were technical service replacements borrowed from the First Army replacement depot, which had a surplus of technical service officers. Their duties consisted of following up leads on possible locations of enemy supplies, making inventories of whatever was found, guarding the property, and evacuating previously unreported types of enemy equipment through intelligence channels. The Captured Materiel Section circulated the inventories to the appropriate QM sections and to other technical services, including G–5. Army agencies desiring captured supplies were responsible for transportation thereof, since the Captured Materiel Section was not a supply section and never became involved in storage or physical transfers of equipment. Whatever could not be used within First Army was released through the G–4 Section to COMZ. Apparently the G–4 consolidated Quartermaster surpluses with those of the other technical services, and no information through this channel ever became available to Littlejohn. Fortunately, McNamara also sent information copies of his surplus releases to the 58th QM Base Depot, which received most of these supplies. On 15 November, having seen an inventory of captured matériel stocks on hand at Huy, Belgium, under control of the 58th QMBD, Littlejohn commented: "This is the first specific information I have been able to obtain as to what is happening to captured enemy supplies." [73] He directed that a 30-day supply be set aside for ADSEC and First Army, and that the balance of the stocks be shipped to the rear, where they were badly needed to supply prisoner labor at work in the COMZ depots. On 1 December, he formally designated Q–175 at Le Mans as the key depot for captured supplies for the entire Continent.

In the Third and Seventh Armies, captured supplies were handled somewhat differently. Third Army designated a captured matériel warehouse in Nancy, to be used by all technical services, and during December organized a Quartermaster Captured Enemy Matériel Detachment, which operated in forward areas somewhat similar to the QM intelligence teams of First Army. This unit concentrated enemy matériel at warehouses under its own control, notably at Metz, and was both a staff and an operating unit. In Seventh Army, captured supplies were handled simply as a separate category of salvage and reported by tons every fifteen days as part of the salvage backlog. During April 1945, apparently to conform to the practices of the northern group of armies, the CONAD quartermaster established a section to locate, report on, consolidate, and warehouse captured enemy matériel. This was an entirely new function in CONAD and was performed

---

[73] (1) IRS, CQM to DCQM, 15 Nov 44, sub: Captured Enemy Supplies and Local Proc Forward. Littlejohn Reading File, vol. XXX, item 46. (2) TUSA AAR, QM, 7. (3) *FUSA Rpt of Opns*, 1 Aug 44–22 Feb 45, IV, 104–05, 107. (4) Over-all QM Supply and Storage Plan, OCQM ETO, 1 Dec 44. ETO QM 400.302.

by personnel of the QM remount depot assigned to that headquarters.[74]

The postwar evaluation by the US-FET General Board was that policy directives, procedures, and responsibilities regarding captured enemy matériel had not been spelled out in enough detail before operations began. In effect, enemy matériel constituted a separate source of supply for the troops units, not subject to the veto of G–4 or the technical services. The 12th Army Group quartermaster reported that he was obliged to disapprove a great many requests for items in excess of T/E allowances, especially tentage, kitchen equipment, and one-burner stoves. It was natural under the circumstances for the combat units to retain whatever they captured in these categories, and equally natural for the Chief Quartermaster to complain that he never received such items.

Apart from their real needs, combat troops apparently kept a good many items merely as souvenirs. In particular, the practice of stripping POW's of all equipment to insure that they had no concealed weapons went much too far. On 17 October Littlejohn wrote to Smithers: "I have no defense for [requisitions to support] POW's turned over to me practically naked. What happens to their mess gear? And their blankets? They must have had something, somewhere. It looks to me as though we are not being sufficiently energetic forward in taking inventories and putting guards over enemy property. By the time that we arrive, the local inhabitants have taken whatever was available. . . . My office is also at fault in not having followed this captured enemy property

problem sufficiently. I am taking action. . . ." The next day he ordered that the Captured Materiel Branch of the Storage and Distribution Division intervene energetically in the current operations in ADSEC and the armies. He concluded: "We cannot continue to bring supplies for POW's from the States when there are supplies here. I cannot defend getting supplies when same are being dissipated as they are at the present time." [75]

Unfortunately, these statements were all too true. In March, when SHAEF directed that a study be made of clothing and equipment requirements for non-U.S. personnel, the Chief Quartermaster listed his assets from all sources. Two requisitions on the United States had been disapproved, and he pointed out that everything that was available was needed for POW's alone and nothing would be available for other categories unless favorable action was taken on new requisitions he had submitted recently. In justification of those requisitions, he had submitted the same statistics forwarded to SHAEF. The clothing and equipment available through June 1945 to support 842,000 prisoners and 305,000 miscellaneous Allied personnel—a very conservative strength estimate—included the major items listed below. The small proportion derived from captured enemy sources is particularly striking: [76]

---

[74] (1) TUSA AAR, QM, 9, 12. (2) *CONAD History*, II, 617, 631, 646. (3) Littlejohn, ed., *Passing in Review*, ch. 43, p. 37.

[75] (1) Quotations are from Ltr, CQM to QM ADSEC, no sub, 17 Oct 44, and IRS, CQM to DCQM, 18 Oct 44, sub: Sundry Problems. Littlejohn Reading File, vol. XXIXA, items 90, 92. (2) USFET Gen Bd Study 108, pp. 19–20. (3) 12th Army Group Rpt of Opns, XII, 197.

[76] IRS, G–4 COMZ to OCQM, 4 Mar 45, sub: Clothing for French Liberated Manpower, and Comment 1, 7 Mar 45 with Incl, same sub. Reprinted in OTCQM TSFET Operational Study 8, exhibit C–4 and C–5.

Item	On hand captured	On hand Class X	Salvage expectancy	Total assets
Drawers, wool and cotton	32,746	519,957	961,259	1,513,962
Shirts, wool and cotton	2,598	81,950	135,553	220,101
Shoes, pair	3,055	731,950	0	735,005
Trousers, wool and cotton	7,770	238,136	312,810	558,716
Work gloves (all types)	800	257,671	84,808	343,279
Raincoats (all types)	0	0	181,598	181,598
Blankets	456	60	27,627	28,143
Mess gear	47,312	1,215	10,328	58,855
Shelter halves	8	0	701	709
Towel	0	3,386	0	3,386

During the closing phase of the Ardennes battle, the Chief Quartermaster enjoyed one minor success in the generally unsatisfactory sphere of captured matériel. He was at dinner with General Bradley when an aide brought in a radiogram from a German corps commander who wanted to surrender his whole corps. Bradley passed the message to his guest with the remark: "More trouble for the Quartermaster." Littlejohn recommended that Bradley decline to accept the surrender unless the Germans brought in all of their unit mess equipment, and also all individual mess gear, blankets, and bedding. The surrender was arranged on those terms.[77]

---

[77] Littlejohn, ed., Passing in Review, ch. 8, p. 4.

CHAPTER XXI

Concluding Observations

Quartermaster operations during any conflict necessarily reflect the character of the combat operations they support. One of the salient new developments of World War II was the establishment of unified overseas theater commands as executive agencies of the President and the Joint Chiefs of Staff. This delegation of command authority made it possible to exploit the recently increased mobility of combat units by a more flexible deployment of forces. Inevitably, this innovation demanded a corresponding increase in the flexibility of logistical support by all the technical services. In the war against Germany, quartermasters were called upon again and again to adjust to unexpected situations and to meet unanticipated requirements. On the whole, however, their own command confronted them with more surprises than did the enemy, and QMC staff officers rapidly acquired the ability to turn out Quartermaster plans to support any and every type of operation—often on very short notice. The basic mission of the Quartermaster Corps was a very simple one, which has been defined as "taking care of people." But soldiers engaged in different types of operations required different types of support, and it was seldom possible to learn accurately in advance when and where specialized supplies would be required, or for how many men.

The time element was especially critical in Quartermaster planning, the more so because, while everyone paid lip service to the principle that service troops should prepare the way for combat troops, somehow the combat troops always arrived first, and in greater numbers than expected. TORCH was an excellent example of such difficulties. In theory, a headquarters which was preparing to launch an attack on the Continent with 1,000,000 men should have been able to mount a side expedition of 60,000 men to another theater with little difficulty. But for the Quartermaster, this call in mid-September 1942 came at the worst possible time, when QMC military personnel amounted to less than 2.7 percent of U.S. troops in the United Kingdom, or about half the planned ratio. In round numbers, the OCQM was operating with less than 5,000 troops and rather more than 12,000 newly hired British civilians. In five short weeks this labor force had to select several million man-days of specific Quartermaster supplies from seventeen depots, none of them established more than sixty days, and ready all cargo for a long sea voyage. This was no more than a small-scale prologue to later difficulties, but TORCH included many of the problems quartermasters were to meet again and again during the next three years—including misinformation regarding the climate of the proposed area of combat.

The war in North Africa and later in southern and western Europe was characterized by a steadily increasing scale of U.S. operations, from a single corps to three army groups fighting in two different theaters. Later phases of combat were not merely magnified repetitions of earlier operations. There were tactical and logistical innovations in each campaign, and a corresponding evolution in QM administrative organization, both in the combat zone and behind it. The quartermaster of an American corps within a British or Allied army had independent functions that largely disappeared when his corps became one of several within an American army. Yet it would not be entirely accurate to state that those functions had merely been transferred to an army level quartermaster. Similarly, a single army quartermaster dealing directly with a base section commander (and sometimes appealing over the latter's head to theater headquarters) was in a very different position from one such army quartermaster among several who had to place their co-ordinated requirements upon a COMZ organization through an army group G–4.

Littlejohn was a firm believer in personal contacts with quartermasters both above and below his own position in the chain of command, especially with the army quartermasters. During the fighting in western Europe he attempted to maintain intimate relationships similar to those that had developed among the smaller headquarters involved in earlier Mediterranean campaigns. His memorandums to his personal staff following his frequent visits to the front are among the most valuable and interesting of his

records. But this policy of intimate liaison broke down precisely when it was most urgently needed—during the period of "frantic supply" to the troops speeding across France. Littlejohn's proposed solution—the organization of a private QM courier service—had to await the availability of jeep transportation, which did not materialize in time. But this was not a wasted effort; QM couriers were very helpful in easing the adjustment to static warfare as the pursuit slowed to a halt. A similar situation arose during the final phase of fighting in Germany, but by that time combat quartermasters were able to take the initiative. Issuing radio-equipped vehicles to mobile QM headquarters was merely the first step. The real vindication of close liaison came when supply commanders decided that prompt reports to the rear were essential, even if they had to be laboriously encoded by hand before transmission.

Tactical considerations also led to unexpected demands upon the OCQM itself, and action by the enemy contributed directly to many surprises with regard to the types and quantities of Quartermaster supplies required during specific phases of military operations. A headlong pursuit required different types of rations than for an advance against obstinate opposition, and no logistician foresaw the interaction of tactics and geography that generated a need for 19,-000,000 jerricans. The hasty German retreat across France in the fall of 1944 involved the Allies in supply difficulties that had an especially hard impact on the Quartermaster. Inadequate ports and increasingly long and disorganized lines of communication were not conducive to the forwarding of balanced assortments of articles. The soldier who had eaten the same meal three times in twenty-four hours was likely to be highly critical of Quartermaster supply. The German retreat inland, away from the warmth of the Gulf Stream, had the effect of moving the troops into a much colder climatic zone and complicated the problem of clothing supply. Generally, none of the supply problems were so serious as to be crippling, but none were solved promptly. A truly efficient supply procedure for major Quartermaster items, prompt and sensitive enough to provide precisely the required selection of articles without undue delay, had still not evolved by the end of hostilities in Europe.

Various experiments and expedients were initiated to improve supply procedures. Within his own theater, General Littlejohn was something of an innovator. Many of his ideas won the approval of G–4 and the other technical services, but senior headquarters in the zone of interior were somewhat less receptive toward new ideas from overseas theaters. His efforts to modify his methods of placing requisitions upon NYPE were at least partially successful, but both ASF and OQMG were slow to give official recognition to those methods. His simultaneous efforts to keep the OQMG informed on the status of requisitions upon NYPE were largely dependent upon personal correspondence with one man, General Feldman, and suffered a serious breakdown when that officer was transferred to the Pacific. Littlejohn's attempts to rectify specific difficulties by informal contacts within ASF headquarters met with but varying degrees of success and often encountered much opposition and resentment. Nev-

ertheless, he believed this to be the most effective means available to an overseas logistical commander who wished to influence policy, or to arrange for departures from established policy, in higher headquarters at home. Such methods were only possible for an officer whose judgment was respected. Littlejohn realized that his professional reputation was at stake every time he made such a personal appeal, but this was often the only way to obtain urgently needed supplies in time. Naturally, such out-of-channels action added to the administrative workload of lower echelons, which preferred to continue with their familiar procedures, but there is no evidence that senior commanders resented it. All through the war in Europe, Littlejohn maintained very cordial relationships with such men as General Maxwell in G–4 and Generals Somervell, Lutes, and Styer in the ASF, and also with The Quartermaster General, despite Littlejohn's controversies with some of General Gregory's subordinates.

Many of the problems and surprises thrust upon quartermasters during the war against Germany stemmed from subsidiary Quartermaster responsibilities for such services as salvage for all the technical services, laundries, baths, and graves registration. The provision of clean clothing and baths was an essential service that for the individual combat soldier often loomed larger than the Quartermaster's primary supply functions. But providing such services for American combat troops was only one of the Corps' responsibilities in an overseas theater. Far greater in size, and possibly even in ultimate importance, was responsibility for administering and safeguarding the supply operations of G–5 (civil affairs). Since that agency dealt primarily with foreign governments and with official relief organizations, and only to a limited extent with individuals, estimates of the number of people dependent upon G–5 operations have been influenced more by considerations of national interest than by standards acceptable to statisticians. In the smaller Mediterranean theater quartermasters believed that the number exceeded five million.

Direct Quartermaster responsibilities, while smaller, were large enough. At the end of hostilities in Europe, the OCQM was feeding and otherwise supporting 7,629,600 persons, of whom only 3,059,942, or 40.1 percent, were U.S. military personnel. At the same time, the ETO Quartermaster Service was employing 195,000 non-Americans, while its military strength was 133,600, or 40.6 percent of the total QM labor force. These figures include Quartermaster troops in the combat zone, who utilized very limited numbers of non-American employees, usually on an unofficial basis since few combat commanders authorized such employment. In the Communications Zone, where the quartermaster might be called master in his own house, the proportion of non-Army labor was far greater. Here the OCQM had direct control over QM installations which employed a working force consisting of 46 percent prisoners of war, 33 percent Allied personnel of various kinds, and only 21 percent U.S. troops.[1]

These statistics serve to illustrate that the Quartermaster Service in the ETO was a large organization with unexpectedly large responsibilities, staffed partly

by U.S. troops but employing a majority of foreigners with no previous knowledge of the language, organization, or working methods of their employers. What such an enterprise required beyond all else was expert supervision, but precisely here lay one of the most serious deficiencies of the Quartermaster Service. The number of Regular officers in the QMC had never been large, and the calls upon this small group for logistical staff duties outside the Quartermaster Service were heavy and persistent. Many of those remaining were middle-aged, and because of the strenuous efforts demanded of them on the Continent, there was an alarming attrition for reasons of health. Of the officers transferred from the combat arms to the QMC, many lacked competence commensurate with their rank; others might be used as commanders of QM units after some indoctrination, but few were useful in the complex operation of major installations, where OCQM policies were interpreted and applied. The result was that the OCQM was forced to train overseas its own specialists, supervisors, and staff officers, a very successful expedient, but one that required time.[2]

The rapid increase in the numbers of nonmilitary personnel whom the Quartermaster was called upon to support was the greatest of the unexpected problems encountered during the war against Germany. Because of the unavoidable time

---

[1] OTCQM TSFET Operational Studies 8, 11, 15.

[2] (1) Of 333 newly commissioned second lieutenants, QMC, sent to the ETO late in 1943, Littlejohn estimated that 50 percent were lieutenant colonels two years later. Also, their presence in the theater had made it possible to transfer more experienced officers from troop units to staff duty. Cf. Littlejohn, ed., Passing in Review, ch. 10, p. 5. (2) Risch, The Quartermaster Corps: Organization, Supply, and Services, II, pp. 177–84.

lag in supply, actual Quartermaster responsibilities in May 1945 had to be met with the supplies requisitioned in January, when estimates of future requirements had been much more modest. The estimate for prisoners of war, for example, had been a maximum of 842,000 by June 1945, whereas the actual peak of nearly 3,000,000, was reached in May. The miscalculation was not in the numbers that would require support; the OCQM had underestimated the speed of military operations in the occupation of Germany and had overestimated the ability of Allied nations to feed and support their own nationals and the prisoners captured by their armies. The real mistake, in the Chief Quartermasters' opinion, was the failure to reach policy decisions on supply responsibility early enough at the highest command levels. Littlejohn's attempt to force such a decision at the COMZ level in February 1945 failed. But whoever was at fault, the actual result was that on 8 May the theater ration level had dropped to an ominous 17.3 days of supply.[3]

The examples cited demonstrate that the Quartermaster Service received something less than perfect co-operation from higher staff levels in its attempts to anticipate and meet requirements during the war against Germany. Nevertheless a technical service exists to serve the combat forces, and if those forces are slow in making tactical decisions and

policy determinations vital to supply planning, the technical service itself must at least attempt to remedy these deficiencies, and then meet the estimated requirements. The extent to which requirements upon the Quartermaster were normal and predictable, and the extent to which the OCQM was successful in meeting all requirements, including the abnormal and unpredictable ones, is something that each reader must decide for himself. The process includes an evaluation of the performance of G-4 and some of the other technical services, and involves a critical appraisal of both planning and operations in the separate and sometimes conflicting fields of tactics and logistics.

In the planning phases of World War II, logisticians tended to talk about and think in terms of "limiting factors" and "the iron laws of logistics." Equally, tactical planners tended to ignore those laws and factors, or even regard them as meaningless professional shop talk. In large operations the workings of cause and effect are usually obscured by a considerable time lag, during which extraneous factors can enter the equation and becloud the final result. Moreover, a good tactician is an optimistic pragmatist who will argue that no factor is extraneous if it contributes to victory. According to this argument every newly conceived expedient, and every happy windfall of local procurement or captured supplies is a legitimate part of the final equation and tends to prove that the "limiting factors" are somewhat elastic, and the "iron laws" can sometimes be bent. But this line of thought influences the tactician to demand the impossible—or what the logistics expert considers impossible—as a matter of habit,

---

[3] (1) OTCQM TSFET Operational Study 8. (2) OCQM Weekly Situation Report, 17 May 1945, gave a ration level of 8 May of 21.3 days, but this was based on an erroneous personnel strength of 6,197,319. (Recalculated by the author using strength cited on p. 735, above.) (3) The authorized ration level of the theater was 50 days.

and sooner or later those demands run counter to real limitations, as distinguished from the theoretical ones used in logistical planning. Thus ETO quartermasters could claim with complete sincerity that they had accomplished far more than they themselves had believed possible, although they failed, in some minor respects, to meet the requirements of the combat troops. Moreover, it sometimes happened that after performing miracles, seemingly in stride, the Quartermaster Service failed to meet comparatively modest demands. The explanation, of course, is that miracle working only looks easy. It is actually an expensive process that uses up assets which, in a large theater, will only be missed after a period of time.

The record of European experience during World War II demonstrates the reality of limiting factors in Quartermaster operations, even though they proved to be somewhat less constricting than originally believed. Ignoring matters outside the quartermaster's sphere of activity, the main limiting factors that became evident were time and manpower, the two being intimately related. Every Quartermaster activity was somehow related to a corresponding activity of the combat troops, and in every case the quartermaster's share of the job took longer: to plan, to organize, and to execute. And since Quartermaster planning could not begin until tactical planning was well advanced, Quartermaster staffs often had to plan and operate at the same time. This, of course, applied also to G–4 and all the technical services, and suggested a separation of functions under separate headquarters, an expedient that never received a fair trial in the ETO.

The Forward Echelon, Communications Zone, originated as a planning staff in the United Kingdom, and was actually operational on the Continent only for a short time in July 1944. The reasons for its demise were complex, but one cause was the fact that operations appeared to be progressing according to plan and further planning was expected to be a matter of minor adjustments. The shortage of logistical staff officers in the theater was so pressing that a stand-by headquarters was an intolerable extravagance. Even before Forward Echelon was absorbed by Headquarters, Communications Zone, early in August, Littlejohn had been forced to transfer the Quartermaster element of the former staff to bolster ADSEC. Within a matter of days thereafter, the armies decided to pursue across the Seine without pausing, and existing logistical plans had to be scrapped.

The new tactical situation demanded stopgap support measures, and insofar as Quartermaster activities were concerned, there was no staff agency and no available personnel to formulate new long-range plans. Even the reinforced Quartermaster element of ADSEC was barely able to give direct support to the armies rushing across France, and the division chiefs of the OCQM were personally processing ADSEC requisitions and controlling the flow of supplies. Hand-to-mouth supply from the beaches to the armies continued for over three months after D-day. Meanwhile intermediate QM depots developed haphazardly, and did not prepare themselves adequately to assume the expanded responsibilities that were ultimately assigned to them. Apparently the other technical service staffs became equally immersed in day-to-day operations, and also neglected their wider responsibilities.

While FECZ was probably too extravagant a solution of the planning problem, some solution was urgently needed for many months before General Somervell finally installed his own ASF planning specialist, General Robinson, in COMZ as Deputy Chief of Staff for Planning. Unfortunately, by that time a false economy in the use of staff officers by COMZ had resulted in a most unfortunate reaction by various headquarters in the combat zone. The practice of sending field-grade officers to hand-carry requisitions to the rear and insure prompt deliveries was a glaring example of the manpower wasted when combat units lost confidence in the organization that supported them. Such confidence was more easily lost than rekindled, and even the outspoken disapproval of General Somervell failed to put an end to the practice.

Similar shortages of time and trained manpower became evident when Quartermaster units were sent straight to France and required to begin operating immediately without a period of orientation and on-the-job training in the United Kingdom. The few units that had the benefit of such training were too busy to disseminate what they had learned, and the newcomers had to learn by making mistakes. One reason for the inadequate training of the newly arrived units was that they were recently activated, and activations had been delayed because of lack of training facilities in the United States. Meanwhile the Quartermaster Service in the United Kingdom was severely hampered by a shortage of manpower. It had accepted inadequately trained units from the zone

of interior and trained them while they performed essential duties, but only on a small scale. Any enlargement of this program would, of course, have required a critical evaluation of what had already been accomplished, but such an evaluation was almost an impossibility.

Quite apart from methods of training, the proper functions and practical capabilities of QM units under field conditions were not firmly established. Mediterranean experience had confirmed that many older types of units required modification, but had not provided time for testing the revised versions. Some types of QM units had been authorized so recently that information on their organization, purpose, and functions was seriously inadequate even among the officers assigned to the new units, and entirely lacking among logistical planners. The OCQM was forced to assemble information on this subject and publish manuals in the United Kingdom. The situation might have been corrected by staff officers who understood the significance of time and manpower, and who were also expert in Quartermaster unit training. But still left unanswered was the question of where such staff officers were to be developed.

The training of QM units in the zone of interior was a bone of contention among the AGF, AAF, and ASF, with the OQMG playing a minor role in the controversy. The notion that every major element of the Army could train its own QM units satisfactorily with a minimum of specialized technical guidance implied a very limited recognition of the specialized techniques and acquired skills of the Quartermaster Service. None of these senior headquarters appeared to be promising training grounds for the type of QM staff officer required. Probably in this, as in so many other essential matters, there was no substitute for combat experience.

Whatever the reasons, the fact remains that many of the Quartermaster troop units actually sent to the Continent were inadequately trained, and the natural reaction of their commanders was to demand more and better trained service troops. As long as the First Army quartermaster could meet each QM unit commander personally every few days and state precisely what supplies he wanted and when, where, and how many, he received reasonably satisfactory service. After the original beachhead area was expanded and two armies required support, lack of training and above all lack of trained leadership became painfully evident. And yet, by the end of 1944 those same Quartermaster units had overcome their lack of training in the hard school of combat experience and were giving very satisfactory support indeed. They had even overcome their early inadequacy in numbers, and only to a small extent by reinforcements from the zone of interior. They accomplished this primarily by employing a foreign labor force that exceeded their own numbers in the Communications Zone by a ratio of nearly four to one. That feat should dispel any doubts about the adequacy of their training, for the efficient use of foreign labor is a difficult technique, by no means easily acquired. Moreover, the program derived very lit-

tle benefit from advance planning, for the intention had been to hire French civilians, whereas nearly half of the labor actually in use consisted of prisoners of war.

Delay in formulating a realistic policy on the utilization of POW's, and still further delay in the organization of the Military Labor Service were serious oversights in staff planning. Earlier decisions on these matters would have solved many problems for all the technical services. For the Quartermaster, the introduction of regularly organized prisoner of war units under the Military Labor Service was a somewhat mixed blessing. It could certainly use 400 units trained in specific Quartermaster skills, but was hard pressed to find the 3,600 American officers and enlisted men required for supervision.

While a general evaluation of Quartermaster operations in the war against Germany must be a matter for individual judgment, it does appear that manpower and time are among the most important factors in determining success or failure. As in all military operations, every major Quartermaster problem involved manpower, solving manpower problems involved training, and training took time. Training efficient logistical staff officers took the most time of all, clearly indicating that their proper training was the most important peacetime responsibility of the Quartermaster Corps.

Appendix A

COMPARISON OF QUANTITIES LISTED IN BEACH MAINTENANCE SETS,
FOLLOW-UP MAINTENANCE SETS, AND BASIC MAINTENANCE SETS

(450,000 Man-days of Supply)

Code*	Item	Unit	Quantity			Weight (L/T)
			Beach Maintenance§	Follow-up	Basic	Basic
	Clothing					
AA	Belt, web, waist....................	each	———	1,200	1,725	0.03
AB	Drawers, cotton, shorts.............	each	———	4,000	5,190	.48
AC	Drawers, wool.....................	each	3,000	3,800	2,295	.88
AD	Gloves, wool, OD (leather palm)......	pair	ª3,600	ᵇ1,800	1,725	.03
AE	Handkerchiefs, cotton...............	each	———	16,800	6,885	.12
AF	Headbands, liner, adjustable.........	each	4,800	1,600	2,505	.11
AG	Helmets, steel.....................	each	1,200	630	630	.63
AH	Jackets, field, OD..................	each	2,700	2,115	1,944	2.71
AI	Jackets, HBT......................	each	1,680	2,100	4,875	3.56
AJ	Laces, legging.....................	pair	———	4,320	4,605	.04
AK	Laces, shoe.......................	pair	———	3,000	4,605	.04
AL	Leggings, canvas, dismounted........	pair	3,600	3,000	2,760	1.29
AM	Liner, helmet, steel................	each	2,700	1,260	1,235	.005
AN	Neckbands, liner, helmet...........	each	4,800	1,800	2,505	.11
AO	Raincoats, dismounted..............	each	———	1,865	1,383	1.92
AP	Shirts, flannel, OD.................	each	3,000	3,800	3,075	2.05
AQ	Shoes, service, type III.............	pair	9,000	6,000	3,900	8.41
AR	Socks, wool.......................	pair	47,520	30,240	10,370	.87
AS	Suits, 1-piece, HBT................	each	1,620	1,680	621	.80
AT	Trousers, HBT.....................	each	1,680	3,500	4,860	3.18
AU	Trousers, wool, OD.................	each	2,880	3,780	2,295	2.25
AV	Undershirt, cotton, sleeveless........	each	———	3,780	5,190	.95
AW	Undershirts, wool..................	each	3,000	3,800	2,290	1.04
	Individual Equipment					
AX	Bag, canvas, field, OD M1936........	each	1,200	650	528	.48
AY	Belt, cartridge, cal. .30.............	each	960	440	342	.25
AZ	Belts, mag. BAR...................	each	360	180	7	.009
BA	Belt, pistol, or revolver.............	each	1,200	400	540	.18
BB	Blankets, wool, OD.................	each	6,000	4,020	4,020	8.34
BC	Cans, meat, M1932.................	each	1,440	1,260	630	.39
BD	Canteens, M1910...................	each	1,800	900	1,245	.59
BE	Carrier, pack, M1928...............	each	1,200	600	593	.17
BF	Cover, canteen, dismounted..........	each	2,160	1,980	1,673	.44
BG	Cups, M1910......................	each	1,260	945	630	.94

COMPARISON OF QUANTITIES LISTED IN BEACH MAINTENANCE SETS, FOLLOW-UP
MAINTENANCE SETS AND BASIC MAINTENANCE SETS—Continued

| Code* | Item | Unit | Quantity | | | Weight (L/T) |
			Beach Maintenance §	Follow-up	Basic	Basic
	Individual Equipment—Continued					
BH	Forks, M1926......................	each	6,000	2,000	1,665	.07
BI	Haversacks, M.1928................	each	1,200	600	591	.89
BJ	Knives, M1926....................	each	6,000	2,000	1,665	.08
BK	Pins, tent, shelter, wood.............	each	——	10,800	9,930	.71
BL	Pockets, mag., D.W. M1923.........	each	900	100	60	.006
BM	Pockets, mag., D.W., carbine........	each	900	400	519	.04
BN	Poles, tent, shelter..................	each	——	1,100	1,319	1.00
BO	Pouches, 1st aid, M1924.............	each	3,000	1,500	1,245	.11
BP	Spoons, M1926........	each	6,000	2,250	1,245	.10
BQ	Tent, shelter half..................	each	——	2,250	1,319	1.76
	Organizational Equipment					
BR	Axe, Intrenching...................	each	600	100	115	.112
BS	Bag, canvas, water, **sterilizing**	each	——	18	20	.17
BT	Bag, carrying, ammunition..........	each	240	160	209	.12
BU	Bag, carrying, rocket...............	each	——	120	61	.04
BV	Carrier, axe, intrenching.............	each	600	60	115	.01
BW	Carrier, cutter wire.................	each	600	60	76	.007
BX	Carrier, pickmattock, intrenching.....	each	600	150	239	.04
BY	Carrier, shovel, intrenching..........	each	1,200	300	881	.16
'BZ	Cutters, wire, heavy...............	each	600	50	51	.02
CA	Pickmattock, intrenching.............	each	600	250	239	.32
CB	Shovel, intrenching.................	each	1,200	480	881	1.00
	Regular Supplies					
CC	Calcium, hypochlorite....,..........	tube	6,912	4,000	13,500	.14
CD	Candles, type II..................'....	pound	5,400	600	6,000	3.35
CE	Compound, germicidal rinse..........	pack	——	5,472	5,400	.65
CF	Dubbin, (4-oz. cans)...............	each	——	7,632	2,750	.11
CG	Lime, chlorinated (bleach pwd).......	pound	——	——	7,500	4.19
CH	Paper, toilet, rolls (1,000 sheets).......	roll	14,400	10,000	16,200	5.36
CI	Soap, laundry, ord. issue.............	pound	6,120	15,000	32,401	14.90
CJ	Can, water, 5-gallon................	each	——	——	360	1.77
CK	Container rd. insulated, w/inserts.....	each	——	35	17	47
CL	Heater, water, immersion type........	each	——	15	8	.25
CM	Lantern, gasoline...................	each	144	24	24	.03
CN	Picks, handled, R.R.................	each	——	24	9	.04
CO	Ranges, field, pack "B"..............	each	6	5	11	1.96
CP	Shovels, D-handled, R.P. #2..........	each	——	54	35	.08
	Total weight, long tons........	—	77.52§	c97.4	——	82.659
	Weight per man per day (pounds).	—	.3859	.485	——	.4115

* Code refers to Basic Maintenance Set only.
a Gloves, leather, heavy.
b Also 1,600 pairs gloves, leather, heavy, and 600 pairs gloves, riding,.unlined.
c Weight for all items including many not listed in this Table.
§ Since the Beach Maintenance Set was for 75,000 man-days, all quantities have been multiplied by 6 to give an accurate comparison with the other sets.

Appendix B

QUARTERMASTER TROOP BASIS IN THE ETO

Type of Unit and T/O	T/O	Authorized Strength	Planning Basis 1,118,000 men	Actual Strength 8 Mar 44	Planning Basis 2,400,000 men	Actual Strength 10 Nov 44	Planning Basis 2,818,000 men	Actual Strength 31 Jan 45	Planning Basis[a] 3,161,000 men	Actual Strength 9 May 45
Hq & Hq Co QM Base Depot	10–520–1	154			15	15	17	17	17	17
Hq & Hq Det, QM Battalion	10–536	28	45	54	107	85	120	97	106	105
Hq & Hq Det, QM Bn (Mobile)	10–56	31	6	4	25	22	25	23	23	23
Hq & Hq Det, QM Group	10–22	30			20	29	32	32	34	34
Bakery Co, Mobile, Special	10–147S	82	32	36	32	52	32	53	57	55
Bakery Co, Standard	10–147	168			23	1	37	2	3	3
Depot Co, Supply	10–227	188	26	27	41	40	49	43	47	45
Base Depot Co	10–367	75							9	7
Gasoline Supply Co	10–77	128	52	21	100	75	96	79	87	83
Graves Registration Co	10–297	128	14	3	28	20	23	21	24¾	22¾
Laundry Co (Semi-mobile)	10–167	273	20	15	35	30	43	36	40½	39½
Laundry Platoon Hospital Type B	10–287	33	56		96		96			
Laundry Section Type EJ	10–500	16				87		97	97	97
Petroleum Products Laboratory (F)	10–547	18	4	3	5	5	5			
Petroleum Products Laboratory (F) Type FA	10–500	12						6	6	6
Petroleum Products Laboratory (M) Type FB	10–500	6				4		6	6	6
Railhead Company	10–197	177	26	13	60	48	69	54	60	60
Refrigeration Co (M)	10–247	103	6	5	10	8	10	10	10	10
Refrigeration Co (F) (–)[b]	10–217	98	4		10	10	11	11	11	11
Sales Company (M)	10–157	178	4	3	6	6+⅔	8	6+⅔	6+⅔	6+⅔
Salvage Collecting Co	10–187	204	12	5	24	16	24	19	24	21
Salvage Repair Co (SM)	10–237	211	16	2	22	17	24	18	22	21½
Salvage Repair Co (F)	10–317	206	1	10	2	2	4	3	3	3
Service Company	10–67	227	138	92	283	218	300	250	274	268
Sterilization Company	10–177	153		12	14	12	26	13	15	15
Fumigation & Bath Company	10–257	88	17	5	23	21	23	24	24	24

Unit	T/O						
Composite Group Hq, Type AE	10–500	24	—	—	7	7	7
Composite Bn Hq, Type AD	10–500	17	—	—	34	38	38
Composite Co Hq, Type AC	10–500	12	—	—	28	52	66
Composite Supply Platoon AB, AE, BA	10–500	30	—	—	3	3	3
Composite Supply Section Type BA	10–500	21	—	—	1	1	1
Composite Supply Section Type BC	10–500	38	—	—	3	3	3
Office Machine Rep Team DI	10–500	2	—	—	15	15	15
Auto Mechanic Team AE	10–500	2	—	—	8	8	8
C&E Repair Team DA	10–500	9	—	—	7	7	7
Base Depot Supply & Sales Co	10–387	130	—	—	—	1	1
Pack Company	10–18	77	—	—	—	1	1
Composite Service Co[c]	10–500	144	—	—	—	1	1
War Dog Platoon	10–500	21	—	—	—	—	1
Total (Actual Strength)[d]		45,846	—	—	109,895	126,210	133,613

[a] Final approved ETO Troop Basis.
[b] Minus butchery platoon.
[c] Consists of 1 AC, 1 AF, 5 AK, 3 CC and 3 CE teams.
[d] Includes COMZ and Field Forces; excludes subunits organic to combat units, and units transferred to TC or USAAF. Both attrition and local modifications of T/O's caused units to vary from authorized strength.

Source: Operational Study 15, Planning for T/O Quartermaster Units, OTCQM TSFET, 1 Nov 45.

Appendix C

Comparison of Winter Clothing and Equipment Recommendations, Summer 1944

Clothing	T/E 21, 1 June 1944 (1)	Feldman 13 March 1944 [a] (2)	Doriot 24 June 44 (3)	Brumbaugh 2 July 1944 (4)	Substitute Items (5)
Boots, service, combat (pair)	1-EM T/Opns (M)	2-EM (except 1-EM issued shoepac).	1-EM	1-EM, A, B, C Units.	Shoes, service
Cap, field, cotton, OD	1-EM (M)	....	1-EM	1-EM	Cap, wool, knit
Cap, field, pile	1-EM Ar, Z-1, Mtn.	....	10 percent A units	....	Toque, wool, knit
Coat, mackinaw	1-EM SigC, Mech (M).	1-SigC, Mech (unless issued jacket ETO).	....	1-EM not issued overcoat	Overcoat, wool
Gloves, shell, leather (pair) and inserts, wool (pair).	1-Mtd EM, Veh Opr, Para.	....	....	....	Gloves, riding unlined w/wristlet, knit
Gloves, wool, leather palm (pair)	1-EM (M)	....	1-EM, A, B, C Units	1-EM	Gloves, wool, OD
Hood, field, OD, M1943	....	1-EM T/Opns in T/O Units.	1-EM	....	Muffler, wool
Jacket, field, M1943	1-EM (M)	1-EM no change	1-EM	....	Jacket, field, OD
Jacket, field, pile	1-EM Ar, Z-1, Mtn, Tk Crew.	....	....	....	Jacket, combat, winter
Jacket, wool, ETO	....	1-EM T/Opns in T/O units.	1-EM	1-EM	Coat, wool, serge
Mitten shells, trigger-finger (pr) w/2 pairs inserts, wool.	1-EM Ar, Z-1, Mtn.	1-EM T/Opns A, C units.	....	80% Spec Task Force.	Glove, wool, leather palm
Muffler, wool, OD	1-EM Ar, Z-1, Mtn.	None; see hood, field, OD.	....	....	....
Overcoat, wool, roll collar	1-except EM issued mackinaw (M).	1-EM not issued Jkt ETO or Mackinaw.	....	1-EM	....

Item					
Overcoat, parka type, w/pile liner..	1-EM ArW, 50% Z-1, 25 percent Mtn		10% A units	1-EM Spec Task Force.	Overcoat, parka type, reversible
Overshoes, arctic, cloth top (pr)....	1-EM T/Opns when authorized.		1-EM not issued shoepac.	1-EM requiring same.	Overshoes, arctic, rubber top
Parka and trousers, wet weather....	1-EM ArW only		5% A units	80% Spec Task Force.	Hat, Jacket, & trousers, rain Raincoat
Poncho, lightweight or synthetic resin.	1-EM when authorized.		1-EM, A, B, C units.	1-EM, A, B, C units.	
Raincoat, rubberized.	1-EM (M)		1-EM, D, E units.	1-EM, D, E units.	
Shoepacs, 12" (pr) w/2 pr insoles....	1-EM Ar, Z-1, Mtn.	1-EM, A, C units, ETO&NATO only.	1-EM, A, B, C units	1-EM, Spec Task Force	Shoepacs, 16" or 10" (issue w/out insoles)
Shirt, flannel, OD....	2-EM (M)		2-EM	2-EM	
Shoes, service (pr) and leggings (pr).	1-EM T/Opns (2 in ZI).			1-A, B, C units, 2-D E units.	
Socks, wool, cushion-sole (pr)....	3-EM T/Opns when available.		3-EM	3-EM	Socks, wool, light or heavy
Socks, wool, light or heavy (pr)....	2-EM (M)			2-EM	Socks, wool, arctic
Socks, wool, ski (pr)....	4-EM Ar, Z-1, Mtn.	3-EM issued shoepacs	3-EM, A, B, C units.	5-EM Spec Task Force.	
Suit, working, HBT or jacket & trousers, HBT.	2-EM (M)			2-EM	
Sweater, high neck....	1-EM Ar, Z-1, Mtn.	1-EM T/Opns in T/O units.	1-EM	1-EM	
Trousers, fld, cotton, OD w/Suspenders.	2- EM,Ar, Z-1, Mtn, 1-EM Tk Crew.	1-EM T/Opns in T/O units.	2-EM		Trousers, kersey-lined
Trousers, field, wool, 20 oz....	1-EM, Ar, Z-1, Mtn, Tk Crew.			2-EM when available.	Trousers, combat, winter or Trousers, kersey-lined
Trousers, wool, OD....	2-EM (M)	2-EM	2-EM	2-EM	
Undershirt and drawers, wool....	2-EM (4-Arctic) (M).	3-EM	2-EM	2-EM	

COMPARISON OF WINTER CLOTHING AND EQUIPMENT RECOMMENDATIONS, SUMMER 1944—Continued

Equipment	T/E 21, 1 June 1944 (1)	Feldman 13 March 1944[a] (2)	Doriot 24 June 44 (3)	Brumbaugh 2 July 1944 (4)	Substitute Items (5)
		(a)			
Bag, clothing, waterproof	1–EM, jungle Opns.		1–EM	2–EM Spec Task Force.	
Bag, duffel	1–EM (M)		1–EM	1–EM Spec Task Force.	Bag, barracks
Bag, sleeping, mountain	1–EM Ar, Z–1, Mtn.		1–EM not in billets.	1–EM Spec Task Force.	Bag, sleeping, kapok
Bag, sleeping, wool	1–EM T/Opns	1–EM, T/Opns in T/O unit.	1–EM, A. B, C units.	1–EM	2 Blankets, wool
Blanket, wool, OD	2–EM (4-Arctic)		2–A, B, C units 4–D, E units.	2–EM	
Brush, mountain	1–EM, Ar, Z–1, Mtn.		10% A units	1–EM Spec Task Force.	
Case, water-repellent, bag, sleeping	1–EM, T/Opns (M)	1–EM, T/Opns in T/O unit.	1–EM, A, B, C units.	1–EM.	
Pack, field	1–EM Ar, Z–1, Mtn.		1–EM		Haversack
Pad, insulating, bag sleeping	1–EM Ar, Z–1, Mtn.		10% A units	1–EM Spec Task Force.	Comforter, cotton (in billets)
Tent, mountain, 2-man, complete	10% Ar, 50% Z–1, 50% Mtn		5% A units	½–EM, Spec Task Force.	Tent, shelter-half
Tent, shelter-half, complete	1–EM (M)		1–EM	1–EM	

(M) = Mandatory Allowances.
Ar, Z–1, Mtn = Arctic, Zone I (cold-temperate), mountainous areas.
ArW = Arctic wet-cold areas.
Para = paratrooper.
exc = except
Veh Opr = vehicle operator.
Mech = issued to mechanics.
SigC = issued to Sig Corps personnel.
[a] General Feldman's recommendations are given for the year 1944 only. They refer to changes in T/E 21, and not to a complete uniform.

Unit Categories: A—AGF Combat.
B—AGF Service.
C—ASF Combat.
D—AAF Combat.
E—Balance of overseas personnel.

Appendix D

Winter Clothing Recommendations for 1945–1946

	WC Committee, Recommendations 19 March 1945	CQM, ETO Recommendations 9 May 1945	OQMG Recommendations 11 June 1945
Underwear and Shirts:			
Drawers, wool	2	[a]2	2
Undershirts, wool	2	[a]2	2
Shirts, flannel, OD	2	2	2
Headgear:			
Cap, field, cotton, OD	1	[c]1	1
Cap, field, pile	1 (L)	....	....
Cap, garrison, shade #33	....	[b]2	1
Hood, M1943	1	[c]1	....
Handwear (pairs):			
Gloves, leather, heavy	[d]1 (L)	1 (L)	1 (L)
Glove, shell, leather	[e]1	1	1
Glove, insert, wool	[e]2	2	1
Mitten, shell, trigger finger	1 (L)	1 (L)	1 (L)
Mitten insert, trigger finger	2 (L)	2 (L)	2 (L)
Footwear (pairs):			
Boots, service combat	[f]2	[f]2	2
Shoepacs M1944, 12″ w/insoles *or* Overshoes, arctic, all rubber	[g]1	1	1
Boots, rubber, hip or knee	1 (L)	....	....
Waders, over the shoe	1 (L)	....	....
Socks, wool, heavy	3	3	2
Socks, wool, ski	[h]3	[h]3	[h]3
Socks, wool, cushion sole	[i]3	3	3
Jackets, Coats, Sweater:			
Jacket, combat, winter	[m]0	[c]1	0
Jacket, field, OD or arctic	0	0	....
Jacket, field M1943	1	0	1
Jacket, field, pile	[k]1	0	0
Jacket, field, wool, ETO	[b]1	[b]1	[n]1
Sweater, high neck	1	1	1
Trousers:			
Trousers, combat, winter	[q]0	[c]1	0
Trousers, wool, 18 oz	[b]2	2	[n]2
Trousers, field, wool 20 oz	[o]0	[o]0	....
Trousers, field, wool 22 oz napped	[p]1	1	[p]1
Trousers, field, cotton	1	0	1
Overcoats:			
Overcoat, field cotton, w/liner	[r]1	[s]1	[t]0
Overcoat, parka type, pile lined	1 (L)	....	....

WINTER CLOTHING RECOMMENDATIONS FOR 1945–1946—Continued

	WC Committee, Recommendations 19 March 1945	CQM, ETO Recommendations 9 May 1945	OQMG Recommendations 11 June 1945
Rainwear:			
Parka and trousers, wet weather	1 (L)	. . . .	. . . .
Poncho, light weight.	u1	v1	u1
Snow Camouflage:			
Mittens, over, white.	1 (L)	1 (L)	1 (L)
Parka and trousers, over, white.	1 (L)	1 (L)	1 (L)
Miscellaneous:			
Muffler, wool.	1	0	. . . .
Necktie, cotton, mohair.	w2	. . . .	b2
Suspenders, trousers.	1 (L)	0	. . . .
Bag, sleeping, wool w/case.	1	1	1
Bag, sleeping, mountain.	1 (L)	1 (L)	. . . .
Blanket, wool, OD.	2	2	2

. . . . No comment.

O Recommend elimination.

(L) Limited issue: Same limits as specified by T/E 21 unless otherwise noted.

a Wool content to be increased to 50%; to be treated for shrinkage resistance; to be issued in 3 sizes only.

b For non-combat wear only.

c To be dyed Shade #33.

d For drivers and manual laborers. Should be modified to fit over glove, wool, insert.

e Possible production difficulties, but glove, wool, leather palm is not a satisfactory substitute.

f Modified last, grain-out leather.

g Production capacity does not permit issue of both items to same personnel.

h Issued only with shoepacs.

i Production limited, but socks, wool, light, are not a satisfactory substitute.

k Production capacity does not permit complete issue to entire theater strength by 15 September 1945. Requires modified lining, water-repellent outer cover, pockets.

m This is committee choice of substitute for Jkt pile, but availability is limited. Available substitute is Jkt wool ETO, considered suitable mainly for dress.

n OQMG considers this item satisfactory for field use.

o This item tested before conference and judged inadequate.

p Napped construction considered essential. Production inadequate to meet full ETO requirements. OQMG will recommend to ASF as soon as production becomes feasible.

q This item over 18 oz. trousers is preferred committee substitute for cotton field trousers over 22 oz. trousers. Cotton field trousers over 18 oz. trousers considered inadequate.

r Materials and time not available to supply in desired quantities. Substitute is Melton wool overcoat, 32 oz.

s Not required for combat, but desirable for sentries, drivers, and personnel on furlough who need rain protection as well as warmth. Particularly desirable for mechanics, who cannot wear ponchos.

t Superior to current overcoat but unnecessary for combat troops and unjustifiable during current textile shortages.

u Nylon production limited. Poncho, medium weight or of raincoat material acceptable, and OQMG agrees to furnish it.

v Not recommended for mechanics. Cotton field overcoat gives satisfactory rain protection for mechanics, furlough personnel, etc. Raincoat, either resin or rubber, is not a satisfactory substitute.

w To be issued after V–E Day.

Sources: Ltr. Col James W. Younger (chairman) et al. to CQM, 19 Mar 45, sub: Winter Combat Uniform. Hist Br, OQMG. Memo, CQM, ETO for TQMG, 9 May 45, sub: Winter Uniform; Comment No. 3, 11 June 45, sub: same. TQMG for AC/S G-1, WDGS. WDGS 292–420 Dr. 641 DRB AGO.

Bibliographical Note

Quartermaster activities in the war against Germany are reflected in at least five general categories of source material —U.S. Army Official records, semiofficial and unofficial collections of U.S. Army records, manuscript histories, reproduced reports and unit histories, and published works. Although no contemporary historical interviews with Quartermaster officers were undertaken, the successive authors of this volume have sought the testimony of a few senior QMC commanders and staff officers who were able to clarify obscure points by reason of their firsthand knowledge of events. Moreover a preliminary manuscript version of this volume was submitted to a wide selection of QMC commanders and staff officers who participated in operations in both the Mediterranean and European theaters. Their comments, both critical and helpful, have been acknowledged in the Introduction.

Among the official records of combat headquarters overseas, the main sources used in the preparation of this volume were those reflecting the activities of G–4 divisions and Quartermaster sections of the various staffs. After each of the relatively short initial campaigns, armies, corps, and divisions prepared AAR's which included relatively complete coverage of G–4 and QM activities, including some information on the performance of QM units. During the longer campaigns which followed, those same headquarters submitted periodic reports of their activities, usually on a

monthly basis. During this phase of operations, reports by QM units in the combat zone also became more common, and those maintained from earlier phases on a periodic basis became more complete. Coverage of the combat activities of organic QM companies of divisions, especially infantry divisions, is notably good, and a file of photostat copies which is believed to be complete is maintained in the Unit History Files in the Office, Quartermaster Historian.

Material from nearly all the official records of administrative and logistical headquarters in the overseas theaters concerned have been used in the preparation of this volume. As in the case of combat headquarters, those pertaining to G–4 and QM activities are the most important, but the records of G–5 (Civil Affairs), of the other technical services, especially the Engineers and the Transportation Corps, and those of the General Purchasing Agent contained much material reflecting QM activities. Correspondence with military and civilian agencies of foreign governments, conducted variously by quartermasters direct, by logistical commanders, or through U.S. embassies in the countries concerned, also provide important information used in this volume. Senior administrative headquarters in the theaters gave guidance to subordinates through cables and radio messages, bulletins, circular letters, and the like. These were normally routed through AG channels, and the significant ones for Quartermaster history, principally in the fields of organization, personnel, and supply policy, bore appropriate numbers according to the AGO decimal-subject system. Monthly reports of the activities of base sections and of QM units within base sections were usually more complete than corresponding reports from the combat zone. After the end of hostilities some of the base sections also retired considerable bodies of their own records and those of predecessor commands. The periodic reports of QM base depots and QM Groups, which included considerable information on their subordinate QM units, were particularly useful. Copies are maintained in the QM Unit History Files, already mentioned. With a few exceptions, some of which are noted below, retained original records of overseas headquarters were located in the Army's Kansas City Records Center, later (1960) absorbed by the General Services Administration Federal Records Center, Kansas City, Mo.

Of official materials originating in the zone of interior, those most important for this volume were records of the Office of The Quartermaster General comprising correspondence with the overseas theaters concerned, and intra-office memoranda regarding dealings with those theaters. Correspondence between the OQMG and various persons and subagencies of the Army Service Forces, especially the Director of Materiel, and with various depots and ports, especially with the Overseas Supply Division, New York Port of Embarkation, also reflect QM activities in the overseas theaters concerned. Direct correspondence between the ASF and overseas theaters, and between the NYPE and overseas theaters, also contain extremely

important information for the purposes of this volume. Retained zone of interior records of Army commands and installations (including depots and ports) are in Kansas City. Permanent records of headquarters agencies of the War Department (including OQMG and ASF) are in World War II Records Division of the National Archives located at GSA, FRC, Alexandria, Va.

Observer reports constitute a special category of primary documents. The report by Capt. W. F. Pounder, Jr., on QM Operations in the North African theater 5 March–2 June 1943, is in the Quartermaster Historian's Office, OQMG. A file of reports by OCQM ETO observers is in the same location. Reports prepared by observers sent out by the OQMG are among OQMG records regarding the overseas theater concerned, usually filed under number 319.25. Army Ground Forces records have not been consulted, but reports of AGF observers are filed among OQMG records, sometimes under 319, sometimes under numbers referring to troop units or to specific items of food, clothing, or equipment.

Most of the material actually used in the preparation of this volume consists of photostatic copies of documents which have been collected gradually over the last fifteen years successively by Dr. Alvin P. Stauffer, former chief, Historical Branch, OQMG, by Dr. William Chaikin, Dr. Irving Cheslaw, Mr. Charles Romanus, and by Mr. William Ross. Since many documents are duplicated, with copies filed in various places and collections, and since the various holdings have repeatedly been physically moved and administratively transferred, it is often extremely difficult to cite the location of the original document. In the many doubtful cases, the location given is simply that of the photocopy.

The Littlejohn Collection is by far the most important of the unofficial collections of documents reflecting QMC activities in the war against Germany. This material was collected from 1942 by the Historical Records Branch, Military Planning Division, Office of the Chief Quartermaster, ETO. From early 1944 on, this collection virtually duplicated the records emanating from the OCQM. For many important documents there are multiple duplications, filed by subject, by addressee, and by originating suboffice. The collection also included other primary source material on QMC operations received by that headquarters as well as secondary sources. The strictly documentary portion of this collection has been dispersed. The "Summary of Documents in the General Littlejohn Collection," a finding aid prepared by the OQMG Records Administrator in January 1956, lists four main bodies of documents at four locations, which are designated as follows:

Section I, at the QM Technical Library, Fort Lee, Va., includes approximately nine boxes of key documents of historical value; three boxes of QM unit histories; a copy of a microfilm (Job #600–93) which comprises 44 reels and reproduces the documents cited in *Quartermaster Supply in the ETO in World War II* by Richardson and Allan; and sundry other documents, especially the QM portions of various operational plans.

Section II, at the Federal Records Center, Kansas City, Mo., comprises approximately twenty-one boxes of factual records and photographs of QM service

operations in the European theater.

Section III, at the Army War College Library, Carlisle Barracks, Pa., consists principally of the Littlejohn Reading Files (June 1942–November 1945, inclusive)—a record of General Littlejohn's personal outgoing correspondence, including many signed originals of letters received, and copies of most of his intraoffice written directives to his immediate personal staff. All these constitute a complete and very useful chronological summary of most of the problems encountered and solutions proposed at the OCQM level. Some of this intraoffice material and much of the more personal correspondence is not recorded elsewhere.

Section IV, in the personal possession of General Littlejohn and to be bequeathed by him to the QM Library at Fort Lee, is a body of correspondence that is of personal or patriotic significance but of minor value for QM historical purposes.

The Sullivan Papers were also consulted in the preparation of this volume. They are a semiofficial collection of materials, assembled by Brig. Gen. Joseph P. Sullivan, the Fifth Army Quartermaster, that consist of fifteen boxes of documents reflecting QM activities in Fifth Army, and include certain personal items. They are maintained as a separate collection at the QM Library, Fort Lee, Va. Other unofficial collections of documents used include the Middleswart Papers, personal papers and copies of various documents in the possession of Maj. Gen. William H. Middleswart and the Poore Papers, personal papers that include the Poore Journal and copies of various documents collected by the late Lt. Col. James E. Poore, Jr., now in the possession of General Middleswart.

Manuscript histories and studies utilized in the preparation of this volume include the following:

Robert W. Komer, "Civil Affairs and Military Government in the Mediterranean Theater." Copies on file in the Quartermaster Historian's Office, OQMG and in OCMH. "Fifth Army Quartermaster History," a manuscript prepared by Col. (later Brig. Gen.) Joseph P. Sullivan in 1948, has been cited as the "Sullivan MS." A photostat copy is available at the Quartermaster Historian's Office, OQMG; the original is at the QM Library, Fort Lee, Va. "History of the QM Section, Hqrs Advance Section, COMZ, ETO, 28 December 1943–25 June 1945," n.d.; copy in Quartermaster Historian's Office, OQMG. Norman E. Roberts, "Designed for Combat–The Army's Field Jackets," Philadelphia QM Depot, 1946. This is an unpublished field historical study on file in the Office, Quartermaster Historian, OQMG. "The Administrative and Logistical History of the ETO," a manuscript history in 11 volumes prepared under the direction of Dr. Roland G. Ruppenthal, and on file in OCMH.

Extensive use has been made of the following miscellaneous publications:

Reports of the General Board, U.S. Forces, European Theater, especially No. 108, "Service Operations of the QMC," and No. 109, "QM Supply Operations." These are also on file in OCMH.

TSFET OTCQM "Operational Studies," 17 in number, were prepared by the Office of the Theater Chief Quartermaster, Theater Service Forces, European Theater, late in 1945 primarily for the use of the General Board mentioned above. They are critical evaluations of contemporary QM units and established procedures, and are on file in the Army War College Library, The Army Library, and elsewhere. They have also been incorporated as exhibits into the series "Passing in Review."

"Passing in Review" is a miscellaneous collection of studies, reports, and personal reminiscences by General Littlejohn and former members of the staff of the OCQM, ETO. The first seventeen are brief personal comments and evaluations of the "Operational Studies" mentioned above, to each of which one of the seventeen studies has been appended as an exhibit. The rest of this series, 54 chapters in all, was prepared in the United States in the period 1945–55. These chapters bear some similarity to the Foreign Military Studies prepared for the Office, Chief of Military History, by German generals. Like those studies their value and accuracy varies, and is directly proportionate to the amount of documentary material which the author had available for use in refreshing his memory. Nevertheless, even those containing obvious errors in dates, statistics, and the like, have proved valuable to understanding and interpreting official documents. Chapter 46 of the "Passing in Review" series has been singled out for special attention, since it covers operations in the Mediterranean as well as the European theater, and has been rather widely circulated as an independent publication under the title, "QM Activities of II Corps Thru Algeria, Tunisia, and Sicily, and First Army Thru Europe," by Brig. Gen. Andrew T. McNamara and compiled by Col. Raymond F. McNally; this was multilithed at Fort Lee, Va., 1955. This has been cited as the McNamara *Memoir*.

Complete sets of the entire "Passing in Review" series are available at OCMH, and at the Army War College Library. Nearly complete sets are on file at the Quartermaster Historian's Office, OQMG, and at the Quartermaster Library, Fort Lee, Va.

"QM Service Reference Data," (7 vols.) were repeatedly revised and re-issued by the OCQM, SOS, ETOUSA. Printed versions of September 1942, July 1943, December 1943, January 1944, and many mimeographed addenda are on file in the Office, Quartermaster Historian, OQMG. Complete files are also to be found in the QM Library, Fort Lee, Va. The final postwar revisions appear as OTCQM TSFET "Operational Studies" Nos. 1–4, 6, 7. and 10, and as exhibits attached to corresponding chapters of the "Passing in Review" series. They are of especial value in analyzing and interpreting statistics.

All of the following unit histories were printed or lithographed overseas by the headquarters concerned. They were derived primarily from formal periodic reports, and provide valuable contemporary information on the actual conditions of combat or direct support. Most of them include specific portions dealing with Quartermaster operations, and all provide valuable data on the utilization of QM supplies and services.

First U.S. Army Report of Operations, 20 October 1943–8 May 1945 (14 vols., n.d.)

Third Army After Action Report, 1 August 1944–9 May 1945 (2 vols.)

Fifth Army History (9 vols., n.d.)

Seventh U.S. Army Report of Operations, 1944–45 (3 vols., Aloys Graef, Heidelberg, 1946)

Report of Operations 12th Army Group (14 vols., n.d.)

CONAD History (3 vols., Aloys Graef, Heidelberg, 1945)

Logistical History of NATOUSA–MTOUSA (G. Montanino, Naples, 1946)

History of the Quartermaster Section, Peninsular Base Section, MTO, in the Italian Campaign, ed. by Lt. Col. James P. Littlejohn, n.d.

Final Report of the Chief Engineer, ETO, 1942–45 (2 vols. Hervé et Fils, Paris, n.d.)

Certain publications originating at The Quartermaster School, Camp Lee, Va., (now Fort Lee), have been distributed widely through the Quartermaster Corps, and to a lesser extent throughout the Army, but have never been formally published. The *Quartermaster Training Service Journal* (called the *Bulletin* until December 1943) appeared weekly from October 1942 to October 1945, when issue was apparently suspended. It has been cited in footnotes as *QMTSJ*. Originally produced in mimeograph form for the faculty of the QM School, it was expanded into a training aid to assist in the technical instruction of QM personnel throughout the world. It contained many announcements of newly developed QM items. It printed letters and formal reports regarding activities of QM units overseas, and occasional critiques of QM organization and procedures. An incomplete file is in the Office of the QM Historian, OQMG, and complete files are available at The Army Library and at the library of The Quartermaster School.

Quartermaster Supply in the European Theater of Operations in World War II by Eudora R. Richardson and Sherman Allan (10 vols., Camp Lee, Va., 1947–48) is a very complete first narrative based on official sources, including Sections I and II of the Littlejohn Collection cited above. It has been cited in footnotes as *QM Supply in ETO*. It is particularly valuable for its elaborate appendices, which reproduce tables, charts, and documents of historical significance. Copies are available at serv-ice schools and in many military libraries, but at few other institutions.

Quartermaster Supply in the Fifth Army in World War II, by Eudora R. Richardson and Sherman Allan (Camp Lee, Va., 1950) is based primarily on the Sullivan Papers, including General Sullivan's manuscript narrative already cited. It is an excellent account of army-level QM operations supported by many reproductions of original documents . Distribution was similar to that of *QM Supply in ETO*.

Published secondary sources are listed only in the footnote citations.

Glossary

AAA	Antiaircraft Artillery
AAC	Assembly Area Command
AAF	Army Air Forces
AAR	After action report
AB	Airborne
ABS	Atlantic Base Section
AC	Air Corps
ACofS	Assistant Chief of Staff
Actg	Acting
Admin	Administrative
ADSEC	Advance Section, Communications Zone
AEF	American Expeditionary Forces, World War 1
AES	U.S. Army Exchange Service
AF	Air Force
AFDAG	Airborne Forward Delivery Airfield Group
AFHQ	Allied Forces Headquarters
AFLRS	Allied Forces Local Resources Section
AGCT	Army General Classification Test
AGF	Army Ground Forces
AGO	Adjutant General's Office
AGRC	American Graves Registration Command
AGWAR	Adjutant General, War Department
Amph	Amphibious
ANC	Army Nurse Corps
ANCFX	Allied Naval Commander, Expeditionary Force
ANPB	Army-Navy Petroleum Board
Anvil	The planned 1944 Allied invasion of southern France in the Toulon-Marseille area (later Dragoon)
Arcadia	U.S.-British staff conference at Washington, December 1941–January 1942
Armd	Armored
Arty	Artillery
ASF	Army Service Forces
Asgmt	Assignment
Asst	Assistant
Atchd	Attached
ATS	Auxiliary Territorial Service (British)

AVALANCHE	Invasion of Italy at Salerno
BANG	Zone III, Northern Ireland
BBS	Brittany Base Section
Bd	Board
BEF	Brazilian Expeditionary Force
BID	Brazilian infantry division
BIGOT	Special security procedure for OVERLORD
BOLERO	Build-up of troops and supplies in the United Kingdom in preparation for a cross-Channel attack
Br	Branch, British
Brig	Brigade, Brigadier
BRIMSTONE	Plan for the capture of Sardinia. Canceled.
BRUSHWOOD	Subtask force of Western Task Force for the attack on Fedala
BUCO	Build-up Control Organization
Bull	Bulletin
CA	Civil Affairs
CA	Coast Artillery
CATOR	Combined Air Transport Operations Room
CBS	Channel Base Section
CCAC	Combined Civil Affairs Committee
C&E	Clothing and equipment
CEM	Captured enemy matériel
CENT	Task force in Sicily assault landing
CFLN	French Committee of National Liberation
CG	Commanding general
Cir	Circular
COBRA	The operation launched by First Army on 25 July 1944 designed to break out of the Normandy lodgment
CofS	Chief of Staff
Comdr	Commander
COMZ	Communications Zone
CONAD	Continental Advance Section, Communications Zone
CONBASE	Continental Base Section
Conf	Conference
Corresp	Correspondence
COSSAC	Chief of Staff to the Supreme Allied Commander (Designate)
CP	Command post
CTF	Center Task Force
DCofS	Deputy Chief of Staff

DCQM	Deputy Chief Quartermaster
DGPA	Deputy general purchasing agent
DIME	Task force for Sicily assault landing
Dir	Directive
Distr	Distribution
Div	Division
DQM	Division quartermaster
DRAGOON	Final code for the invasion of southern France
DP	Distribution point
Dukw	A six-wheel 2½-ton amphibian truck
EBS	Eastern Base Section
Ech	Echelon
Engr	Engineer
Equip	Equipment
ETO	European Theater of Operations
ETOUSA	European Theater of Operations, United States Army
Evac	evacuation
ExO	Executive officer
F&B	Fumigation and Bath
FBO	Field bake oven
FEA	Foreign Economic Administration
FEC	French Expeditionary Corps
FECZ	Forward Echelon, Communications Zone
FFI	Forces Françaises de l'Intérieur (French Forces of the Interior)
FM	Field manual
FRC	Federal Records Center
FUSA	First U.S. Army
FUSAG	1st U.S. Army Group
G–1	Personnel division of a headquarters
G–2	Military intelligence division
G–3	Operations and/or training division
G–4	Supply division
G–5	Civil affairs and/or military government division
GFRS	Ground Force Replacement System
GLUE	Zone II, South Britain
GO	General Order
GOALPOST	Task force for assault landing in Mehdia–Port–Lyautey area, North Africa
Gp	group
GPA	General purchasing agent
GPB	General Purchasing Board

GR	Graves registration
GR&E Div	Graves Registration and Effects Division
GRO	Graves registration officer
GRS	Graves Registration Service
GS	Gasoline Supply
HBT	Herringbone twill
Husky	Code for Allied invasion of Sicily in July 1943
IBS	Island Base Section (Sicily)
IG	Inspector General
Ind	Indorsement
Info	Information
Instl	Installation
Instr	Instruction
Intel	Intelligence
Interv	Interview
IRS	Informal Routing Slip
ISU	Italian service unit
JAGD	Judge Advocate General's Department
Jnl	Journal
Joss	Task force for Sicily assault landing
LBS	Loire Base Section
LCI	Landing craft, infantry
Ln	Liaison
Log	Logistical
LST	Landing ship, tank
L/T	Long ton
Magnet	Plan for the shipment of American forces to Northern Ireland
Maint	Maintenance
Market-Garden	Operation to secure bridgehead over the Rhine
MBS	Mediterranean Base Section
Med	Mediterranean
Memo	Memorandum
MG	Military Government
Mil	Military
MLS	Military Labor Service
Mob (Div ASF)	Mobilization
MP	Military Police
MT80	Motor transport gasoline, 80-octane
MTO	Mediterranean Theater of Operations
MTOUSA	Mediterranean Theater of Operations, U.S. Army
NA	North Africa
NAAFI	Navy-Army-Air Force Institute (British)
NATOUSA	North African Theater of Operations, U.S. Army

NBS	Normandy Base Section
NCO	Noncommissioned officer
NEPTUNE	Operations within OVERLORD, 1944
NIBC	Northern Ireland Base Command
NIGHTLIGHT	An operation against Norway (never carried out)
NUSA	Ninth U.S. Army
NYPE	New York Port of Embarkation
Obsv	Observer
OCE	Office, Chief of Engineers
OCMH	Office, Chief of Military History
OCOT	Office, Chief of Transportation
OCQM	Office of the Chief Quartermaster (ETOUSA)
OCS	Office of the Chief Surgeon
OCSigO	Office of the Chief Signal Officer
OCT	Office of the Chief of Transportation
OD	Olive drab
ODQM	Office of the Division Quartermaster
Off	Officer
OGPA	Office of the general purchasing agent
OIC	Officer in charge
OKW	Oberkommando der Wehrmacht (German Armed Forces High Command)
OMAHA	Landing beach in Normandy
OPD WDGS	Operations Division, War Department General Staff
Opns	Operations
OQM	Office of the Quartermaster
OQMG	Office of The Quartermaster General
ORB	Organizational Records Branch
Ord	Ordnance
Orgn	Organization
OSD	Overseas Supply Division, New York Port of Embarkation
OTCQM	Office of the Theater Chief Quartermaster
OVERLORD	Plan for the invasion of northwest Europe, June 1944
P&C	Purchasing and contracting
P&F	Petroleum and Fuel
P&O Div	Planning and Operations Division
P&T Div	Plans and Training Division
PBS	Peninsular Base Section
PEMBARK	Code name for the commander of a port of embarkation
PENBASE	Peninsular Base Section

Pers	Personnel
Plng	Planning
Plat	Platoon
POL	Petrol, oil, and lubricants
POW	Prisoner of War
PQMD	Philadelphia Quartermaster Depot
Proc	Procurement
PROCO	Projects for Continental Operations, a system of requisitioning supplies and equipment for special operations
Prov	Provisional
Purch	Purchasing
PX	Post exchange
QMBD	Quartermaster Base Depot
QMC	Quartermaster Corps
QMR	Quartermaster Review
QMSO	Quartermaster supply officer
QMTSJ	Quartermaster Training Service Journal
QUADRANT	The first Quebec Conference, August 1943
R&D	Research and Development
RAC	Ration Accessory Convenience
Rad	Radiogram
RAF	Royal Air Force
RANKIN A, B, C	Plans for return to the Continent in the event of deterioration of the German position
RASC	Royal Army Service Corps
RED VAULT	An operation of II Corps in Tunisia
Repl	Replacement
Reqmts	Requirements
Rhd	Railhead
RHUMBA	Plan for reversing BOLERO and transferring U.S. forces, supplies, and logistic structure from the United Kingdom to the Continent
ROUNDUP	Various 1941–43 plans for a cross-Channel attack in the final phases of the war
SAFA	Service d'Aide aux Forces Alliées
S&D	Storage and Distribution
SATIN	Plan for U.S. II Corps operation against Sfax, Tunisia. Canceled.
SBS	Southern Base Section
Sec	Section
SEXTANT	International conference at Cairo, November and December 1943.

SGO	Surgeon General's Office
SHAEF	Supreme Headquarters Allied Expeditionary Force
SHARK	Task Force (II Corps), HUSKY plan
SHINGLE	Amphibious operation at Anzio, Italy
Ship ton	40 cubic feet of cargo space
SLEDGEHAMMER	Plan for a limited-objective attack across the Channel in 1942
SLOE	Special list of equipment
SOLOC	Southern Line of Communications
SOP	Standing operating procedure
SOS	Services of Supply
SOXO	Zone I, North Britain
SPOBS	Special Army Observer Group in London
SS	*Schutzstaffel* (Elite Guard)
Subcom	Subcommittee
Subs	Subsistence
SUSA	Seventh U.S. Army
Sv	Service
SvC	Service Command
SW	Secretary of War
T/A	Table of Allowances
TAG	The Adjutant General
T/BA	Table of Basic Allowances
TC	Transportation Corps
TCQM	The Chief Quartermaster
T/E	Table of equipment
Telecon	Telephone conversation, conference
TFA	Task Force A
TIGER	Rehearsal for OVERLORD
TLOS	Troop List for Operations and Supply
T/O	Table of Organization
T/O&E	Table of Organization and Equipment
TORCH	Allied invasion of North and Northwest Africa, 1942
TQMG	The Quartermaster General
TRIDENT	International conference in Washington, May 1943
TSFET	Theater Service Forces, European Theater
TUSA	Third U.S. Army
UGLY	Shipping address code name for United Kingdom
U.K.	United Kingdom
UKB	United Kingdom Base
UNRRA	United Nations Relief and Rehabilitation Administration

USAAF	U.S. Army Air Forces
USAFBI	U.S. Army Forces, British Isles
USAFIME	U.S. Army Forces, Middle East
USANIF	U.S. Army Northern Ireland Forces
USCC	United States Commercial Corporation
USFET	U.S. Forces, European Theater
USFOR	U.S. Forces
USO	United Service Organizations
USSAFE	U.S. Strategic Air Forces, Europe
USSTAF	United States Strategic Air Forces
Utah	Landing beach in Normandy
Varsity	Airdrop east of the Rhine
WAC	Women's Army Corps
Wac	Member of Women's Army Corps
WAAC	Women's Army Auxiliary Corps
Waac	A member of the WAAC
WBS	Western Base Section
WD	War Department
WPB	War Production Board
WSA	War Shipping Administration
WTF	Western Task Force
ZI	Zone of interior

UNITED STATES ARMY IN WORLD WAR II

The multivolume series, UNITED STATES ARMY IN WORLD WAR II, consists of a number of subseries which are planned as follows: The War Department, The Army Air Forces, The Army Ground Forces, The Army Service Forces, The Western Hemisphere, The War in the Pacific, The Mediterranean Theater of Operations, The European Theater of Operations, The Middle East Theater, The China–Burma–India Theater, The Technical Services, Special Studies, and Pictorial Record.

The following volumes have been published or are in press:*

The War Department
Chief of Staff: Prewar Plans and Preparations
Washington Command Post: The Operations Division
Strategic Planning for Coalition Warfare: 1941–1942
Strategic Planning for Coalition Warfare: 1943–1944
Global Logistics and Strategy: 1940–1943
The Army and Economic Mobilization
The Army and Industrial Manpower

The Army Ground Forces
The Organization of Ground Combat Troops
The Procurement and Training of Ground Combat Troops

The Army Service Forces
The Organization and Role of the Army Service Forces

The Western Hemisphere
The Framework of Hemisphere Defense
Guarding the United States and Its Outposts

The War in the Pacific
The Fall of the Philippines
Guadalcanal: The First Offensive
Victory in Papua
CARTWHEEL: The Reduction of Rabaul
Seizure of the Gilberts and Marshalls
Campaign in the Marianas
The Approach to the Philippines
Leyte: The Return to the Philippines
Triumph in the Philippines
Okinawa: The Last Battle
Strategy and Command: The First Two Years

---

* The volumes on the Army Air Forces, published by the University of Chicago Press. are not included in this list.

The Mediterranean Theater of Operations
Northwest Africa: Seizing the Initiative in the West
Sicily and the Surrender of Italy

The European Theater of Operations
Cross-Channel Attack
Breakout and Pursuit
The Lorraine Campaign
The Siegfried Line Campaign
The Supreme Command
Logistical Support of the Armies, Volume I
Logistical Support of the Armies, Volume II

The Middle East Theater
The Persian Corridor and Aid to Russia

The China–Burma–India Theater
Stilwell's Mission to China
Stilwell's Command Problems
Time Runs Out in CBI

The Technical Services
The Chemical Warfare Service: Organizing for War
The Chemical Warfare Service: From Laboratory to Field
The Corps of Engineers: Troops and Equipment
The Medical Department: Hospitalization and Evacuation, Zone of Interior
The Ordnance Department: Planning Munitions for War
The Ordnance Department: Procurement and Supply
The Quartermaster Corps: Organization, Supply, and Services, Volume I
The Quartermaster Corps: Organization, Supply, and Services, Volume II
The Quartermaster Corps: Operations in the War Against Japan
The Quartermaster Corps: Operations in the War Against Germany
The Signal Corps: The Emergency
The Signal Corps: The Test
The Signal Corps: The Outcome
The Transportation Corps: Responsibilities, Organization, and Operations
The Transportation Corps: Movements, Training, and Supply
The Transportation Corps: Operations Overseas

Special Studies
Chronology: 1941–1945
Military Relations Between the United States and Canada: 1939–1945
Rearming the French
Three Battles: Arnaville, Altuzzo, and Schmidt
The Women's Army Corps
Civil Affairs: Soldiers Become Governors
Buying Aircraft: Matériel Procurement for the Army Air Force

Pictorial Record
The War Against Germany and Italy: Mediterranean and Adjacent Areas
The War Against Germany: Europe and Adjacent Areas
The War Against Japan

Index

U.S. GOVERNMENT PRINTING OFFICE : 1965   O—693–028